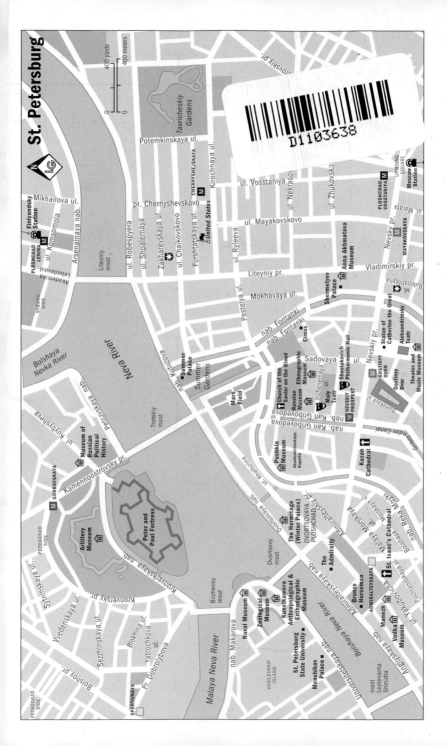

St. Petersburg

400 yards
400 meters

Tavricheskiy
Gardens

Potemkinskaya ul.

D1103638

Mikhailova ul.
Finlyandsky
Station

Arsenalnaya nab.

Liteyniy
most

PLOSHCHAD
LENINA

Akademika
Lebedeva

Bolshaya
Nevka River

VYBORG
SIDE

pr. Chernyshevskovo

ul. Robespyera
ul. Shpalernaya
Zakharevskaya ul.
ul. Chaikovskovo
Furshtatskaya ul.
ul. Ryleeva

CHERNYSHE/SKAYA

Kirochnaya ul.

ul. Vosstaniya
United States
ul. Mayakovskovo

ul. Nekrasov

ul. Zhukovsko

PLOSHCHAD
VOSSTANIYA

UPRISING
SQUARE
Moscow
Station

ul. Mara

Nevskiy pr.

MAYAKOVSKAYA

Anna Akhmatova
Museum

Vladimirskiy pr.

ul.
Rubinshteyna

Neva River

Liteyniy pr.

Mokhovaya ul.

Pestelya ul.

nab. Fontanki
nab. Fontanki

Shermetyev
Palace

Circus

Statue of
Catherine the Great
Aleksandrinsky
Teatr

Theater and
Music Museum

Summer
Palace

Summer
Gardens

Mars
Field

Church of the
Savior on the Blood

Russian
Museum

Ethnographic
Museum

Sadovaya

Maly
Teatr

Inzhenernaya

Shostakovich
Philharmonic Hall

Nevskiy pr.

GOSTINY
DVOR

Dumskaya ul.

Gostiny
Dvor

NEVSKIY
PROSPEKT

Trotskiy
most

Kamennoostrovskiy pr.

Museum of
Russian
Political
History

GORKOVSKAYA

PETROGRAD
SIDE

Petrovskaya nab.

nab. Kan Griboyedova
nab. Kan Griboyedova

Pushkin
Museum

Akademicheskaya
Kapella

ul. khalturin

Kazan
Cathedral

Embedor Canal

Peter and
Paul Fortress

Artillery
Museum

Kronverskaya nab.

Kronverskiy pr.

Sytninskaya ul.

Blokhina
ul.

Sezzhinskaya ul.

Wedenskaya ul.

Bolshoy pr.

PETROGRAD
SIDE

Birzhevoy
most

Dvortsovy
most

The Hermitage
(Winter Palace)

DVORTSOVAYA
PLOSHCHAD,

Admiralteyskiy pr.

The
Admiralty

Bolshaya Neva River

nab. reki Moyki

Malaya Moskaya ul.

Bolshaya Moskaya ul.

St. Isaac's Cathedral

Bronze
Horseman

ADMIRALTEYSKAYA

Manezh

Vodka
Museum

Angliyskaya nab.

most
Leytenanta
Shmidta

Admiralteyskaya nab.

Naval Museum

Zoological
Museum

Kunstkamera
Anthropological &
Enthographic
Museum

St. Petersburg
State University

Menshikov
Palace

Universitetskaya nab.

nab. Makarova

Malaya Neva River

Blokhina
ul.

Yablochkova
ul.

Pr. Dobrolyubova

SPORTIVNAYA

VASILYEVSKY
ISLAND

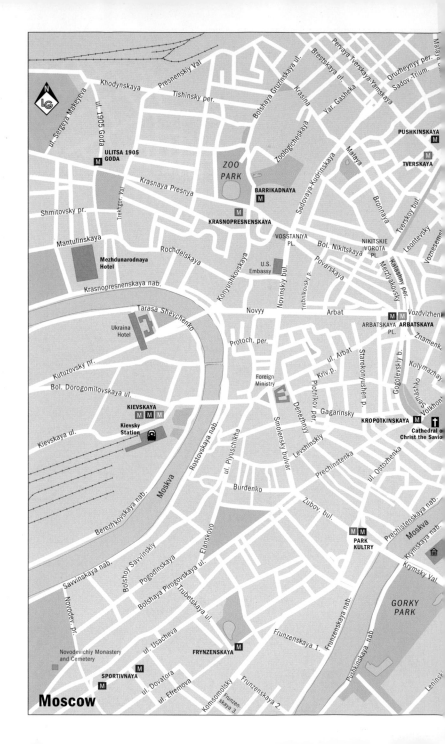

Moscow

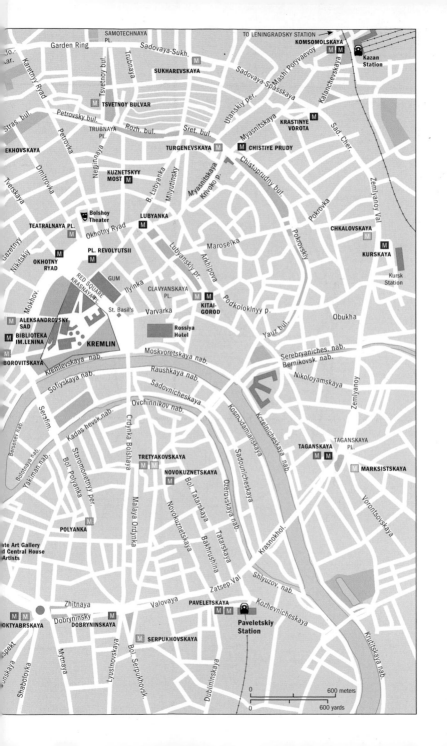

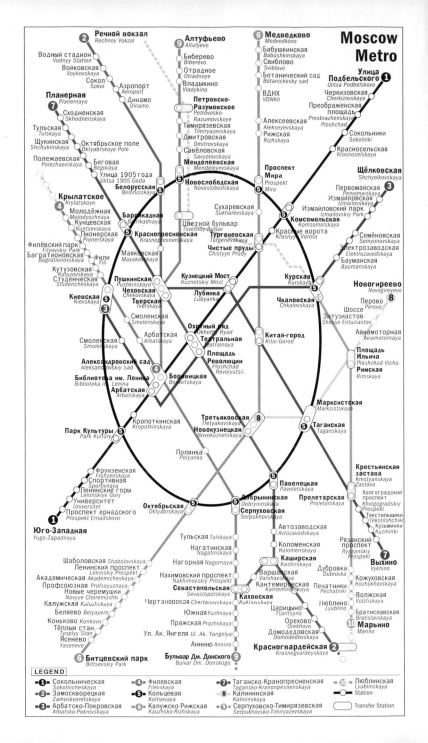

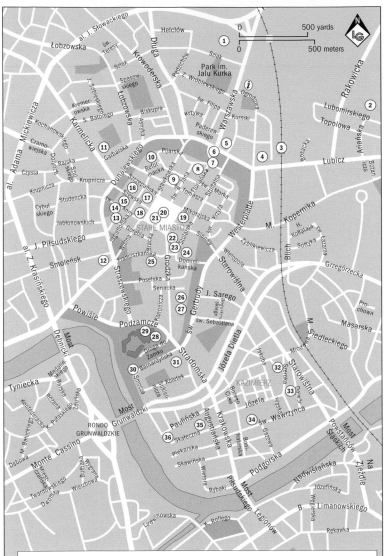

Central Kraków

Akademia Ekonomiczna, **2**
Almatur Office, **22**
Barbican, **6**
Bernardine Church, **31**
Bus Station, **4**
Carmelite Church, **11**
Cartoon Gallery, **9**
Collegium Maius, **14**
Corpus Christi Church, **34**
Czartoryski Art Museum, **8**
Dominican Church, **24**

Dragon Statue, **30**
Filharmonia, **12**
Franciscan Church, **25**
Grunwald Memorial, **5**
History Museum of Kraków, **17**
Jewish Cemetery, **32**
Jewish Museum, **33**
Kraków Glowny Station, **3**
Monastery of the
  Reformed Franciscans, **10**
Pauline Church, **36**
Police Station, **18**
Politechnika Krakowska, **1**

St. Andrew's Church, **27**
St. Anne's Church, **15**
St. Catherine's Church, **35**
St. Florian's Gate, **7**
St. Mary's Church, **19**
St. Peter and Paul Church, **26**
Stary Teatr (Old Theater), **16**
Sukiennice (Cloth Hall), **20**
Town Hall, **21**
United States Embassy, **23**
University Museum, **13**
Wawel Castle, **28**
Wawel Cathedral, **29**

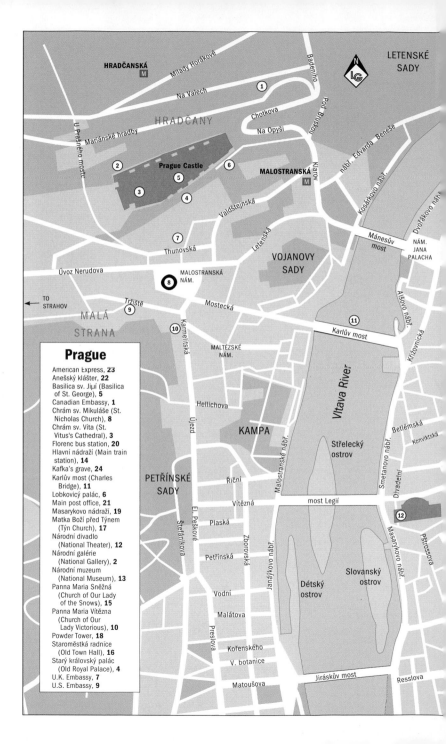

Prague

American Express, **23**
Anežský klášter, **22**
Basilica sv. Jiří (Basilica of St. George), **5**
Canadian Embassy, **1**
Chrám sv. Mikuláše (St. Nicholas Church), **8**
Chrám sv. Víta (St. Vitus's Cathedral), **3**
Florenc bus station, **20**
Hlavní nádraží (Main train station), **14**
Kafka's grave, **24**
Karlův most (Charles Bridge), **11**
Lobkovicý palác, **6**
Main post office, **21**
Masarykovo nádraží, **19**
Matka Boží před Týnem (Týn Church), **17**
Národní divadlo (National Theater), **12**
Národní galérie (National Gallery), **2**
Národní muzeum (National Museum), **13**
Panna Maria Sněžná (Church of Our Lady of the Snows), **15**
Panna Maria Vítězna (Church of Our Lady Victorious), **10**
Powder Tower, **18**
Staroměstská radnice (Old Town Hall), **16**
Starý královský palác (Old Royal Palace), **4**
U.K. Embassy, **7**
U.S. Embassy, **9**

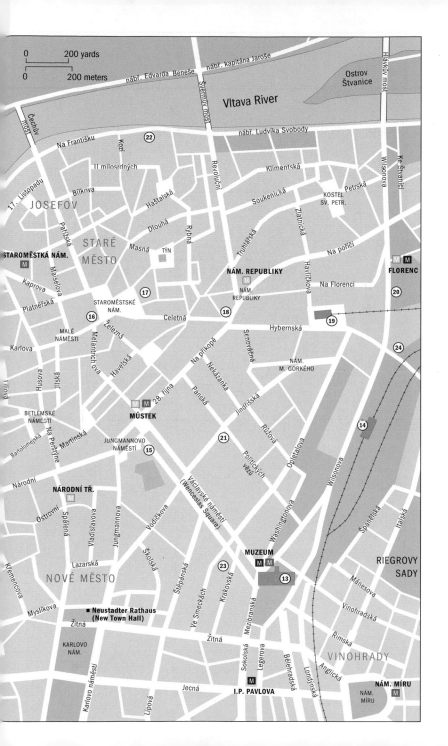

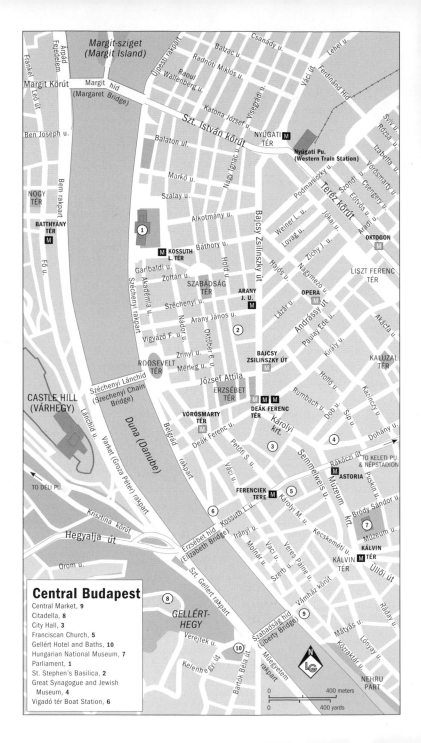

Central Budapest

Central Market, **9**
Citadella, **8**
City Hall, **3**
Franciscan Church, **5**
Gellért Hotel and Baths, **10**
Hungarian National Museum, **7**
Parliament, **1**
St. Stephen's Basilica, **2**
Great Synagogue and Jewish
  Museum, **4**
Vigadó tér Boat Station, **6**

LET'S GO

■ PAGES PACKED WITH ESSENTIAL INFORMATION

"Value-packed, unbeatable, accurate, and comprehensive."

—The Los Angeles Times

"The guides are aimed not only at young budget travelers but at the independent traveler; a sort of streetwise cookbook for traveling alone."

—The New York Times

"Unbeatable; good sight-seeing advice; up-to-date info on restaurants, hotels, and inns; a commitment to money-saving travel; and a wry style that brightens nearly every page."

—The Washington Post

■ THE BEST TRAVEL BARGAINS IN YOUR BUDGET

"All the dirt, dirt cheap."

—People

"Let's Go follows the creed that you don't have to toss your life's savings to the wind to travel—unless you want to."

—The Salt Lake Tribune

■ REAL ADVICE FOR REAL EXPERIENCES

"The writers seem to have experienced every rooster-packed bus and lunar-surfaced mattress about which they write."

—The New York Times

"[Let's Go's] devoted updaters really walk the walk (and thumb the ride, and trek the trail). Learn how to fish, haggle, find work—anywhere."

—Food & Wine

"A world-wise traveling companion—always ready with friendly advice and helpful hints, all sprinkled with a bit of wit."

—The Philadelphia Inquirer

■ A GUIDE WITH A SPIRIT AND A SOCIAL CONSCIENCE

"Lighthearted and sophisticated, informative and fun to read. [Let's Go] helps the novice traveler navigate like a knowledgeable old hand."

—Atlanta Journal-Constitution

"The serious mission at the book's core reveals itself in exhortations to respect the culture and the environment—and, if possible, to visit as a volunteer, a student, or a teacher rather than a tourist."

—San Francisco Chronicle

LET'S GO PUBLICATIONS

TRAVEL GUIDES
Australia 8th edition
Austria & Switzerland 12th edition
Brazil 1st edition
Britain 2006
California 10th edition
Central America 9th edition
Chile 2nd edition
China 5th edition
Costa Rica 2nd edition
Eastern Europe 12th edition
Ecuador 1st edition
Egypt 2nd edition
Europe 2006
France 2006
Germany 12th edition
Greece 8th edition
Hawaii 3rd edition
India & Nepal 8th edition
Ireland 12th edition
Israel 4th edition
Italy 2006
Japan 1st edition
Mexico 21st edition
Middle East 4th edition
New Zealand 7th edition
Peru 1st edition
Puerto Rico 2nd edition
South Africa 5th edition
Southeast Asia 9th edition
Spain & Portugal 2006
Thailand 2nd edition
Turkey 5th edition
USA 23rd edition
Vietnam 1st edition
Western Europe 2006

ROADTRIP GUIDE
Roadtripping USA

ADVENTURE GUIDES
Alaska 1st edition
Pacific Northwest 1st edition
Southwest USA 3rd edition

CITY GUIDES
Amsterdam 4th edition
Barcelona 3rd edition
Boston 4th edition
London 15th edition
New York City 15th edition
Paris 13th edition
Rome 12th edition
San Francisco 4th edition
Washington, D.C. 13th editio

POCKET CITY GUIDES
Amsterdam
Berlin
Boston
Chicago
London
New York City
Paris
San Francisco
Venice
Washington, D.C.

LET'S GO EASTERN EUROPE

JANE YAGER EDITOR
ALEX PASTERNACK ASSOCIATE EDITOR
ALEXANDER ROTHMAN ASSOCIATE EDITOR

RESEARCHER-WRITERS

AMELIA "MOLLY" ATLAS
PIOTR BRZEZINSKI
JASON CAMPBELL
NEASA COLL

ALEXIE HARPER
JORDAN HYLDEN
JUSTIN JENNINGS
JENNIFER KAN

STEPHANIE O'ROURKE

DAVID I. PALTIEL MAP EDITOR
RACHEL M. BURKE MANAGING EDITOR

ST. MARTIN'S PRESS ⁂ NEW YORK

HELPING LET'S GO. If you want to share your discoveries, suggestions, or corrections, please drop us a line. We read every piece of correspondence, whether a postcard, a 10-page email, or a coconut. **Address mail to:**

> **Let's Go: Eastern Europe**
> **67 Mount Auburn St.**
> **Cambridge, MA 02138**
> **USA**

Visit Let's Go at **http://www.letsgo.com,** or send email to:

> **feedback@letsgo.com**
> **Subject: "Let's Go: Eastern Europe"**

In addition to the invaluable travel advice our readers share with us, many are kind enough to offer their services as researchers or editors. Unfortunately, our charter enables us to employ only currently enrolled Harvard students.

Maps by David Lindroth copyright © 2006 by St. Martin's Press.

Distributed outside the USA and Canada by Macmillan.

ISBN: 0-312-34891-6
EAN: 978-0-312-34891-5
First edition
10 9 8 7 6 5 4 3 2 1

Let's Go: Eastern Europe is written by Let's Go Publications, 67 Mount Auburn St., Cambridge, MA 02138, USA.

Let's Go® and the LG logo are trademarks of Let's Go, Inc. Printed in the USA.

HOW TO USE THIS BOOK

Dobrý den, adventurous reader. Call me ◪**Let's Go: Eastern Europe.** This year, a dedicated, perhaps obsessed team of researchers and editors went to new lengths to bring you the best that this sprawling, culturally rich, and rapidly changing region has to offer. While working tirelessly to expand our coverage of the up-and-coming and ever-enchanting Baltic coast and strengthen our chapters on the amazing indoor and outdoor gems of Bulgaria, Slovakia, and Ukraine, we focused on adding unbeatable budget listings along the vibrant Croatian coast. There's also more to be found in Slovenia than before, and the powerhouses of Poland, the Czech Republic, Hungary, Moscow, and St. Petersburg have never had stronger coverage. It's a good thing too, because there's hardly been a better time to go.

GREETINGS. Inside the first pages of this book you'll find a comprehensive introduction to planning your trip. The first chapter, **Discover Eastern Europe,** provides a rundown on the highlights in Eastern Europe and—for those who appreciate a bit of structure in their lives—proposes some **suggested itineraries. Life and Times** gives a brief synopsis of the history and culture of the region, while the **Essentials** section outlines the practical information you'll need to prepare and execute your journey. **Beyond Tourism** offers a refreshing perspective on travel, and suggests diverse ways to deeply immerse yourself in the culture of your destination.

CHAPTER BY CHAPTER. Our chapters are divided by country, listed alphabetically from Bulgaria to Ukraine. Each chapter begins with a detailed introduction to the country's history, culture, and practical travel information. Major cities are listed thereafter, and then smaller cities and hubs. Newly introduced ◪**tipboxes** are peppered throughout the chapters, pointing out insider information that every travel-savvy explorer should know. Keeping with *Let's Go* tradition, each of our chapters is jam-packed with hidden deals, detailed maps, and **sidebars,** which provide in-depth looks at the traditions, politics, and gems that would keep even locals on the edge of their seats. Our final chapter, **Gateway Cities,** is meant to ease a traveler's voyage into the region through Berlin, Vienna, Venice, and Munich.

PRICE DIVERSITY. We list establishments in order from best to worst. Our absolute favorites are denoted by the *Let's Go* ◪**thumbpick.** Since the best value doesn't always come at the cheapest price, we've also incorporated a scale from ❶ to ❺ for ranking food and accommodations (❶ being the cheapest), where each icon corresponds to a specific range. Tables at the beginning of each chapter list country-specific price ranges, but be sure to check out the **master table** (p. xviii).

LANGUAGES. From Estonian to Hungarian, languages can present a unique challenge to visitors of the region. If gesticulating wildly and speaking slowly and loudly isn't working, we've listed some key words and useful phrases in the major tongues of each of our countries, which you'll find in the **Glossary** at the back of the book (and sometimes in the **Language** section at the start of each chapter).

A NOTE TO OUR READERS. The information for this book was gathered by *Let's Go* researchers from May through August of 2005. Each listing is based on one researcher's opinion, formed during his or her visit at a particular time. Those traveling at other times may have different experiences since prices, dates, hours, and conditions are always subject to change. You are urged to check the facts presented in this book beforehand to avoid inconvenience and surprises.

CONTENTS

Eastern Europe:
Chapter Divisions

FINLAND

SWEDEN

Lake Ladoga

Vyborg

St. Petersburg

Narva

Novgorod

Petrozavodsk

Tallinn

Estonia
pp. 230-266

Russia
pp. 563-619

Pskov

Gulf of Riga

Moscow

Riga

Latvia
pp. 353-377

Baltic Sea

Klaipėda

Smolensk

Lithuania
pp. 378-416

Kaunas

Vilnius

Gdańsk

BELARUS

Poland
pp. 417-514

Poznań

Warsaw

Chernbyi

Łódź

Wrocław

Lublin

Kyiv

Prague

Kraków

Lviv

Ukraine
pp. 688-738

Czech Republic
pp. 158-229

Ivano-Frankivsk

Český Krumlov

Kirovohrad

Slovak Republic
pp. 620-660

Bratislava

Moldova
pp. 560-562

AUSTRIA

Budapest

Cluj-Napoca

Odessa

Szombathely

Hungary
pp. 267-352

Slovenia
pp. 661-687

Romania
pp. 515-560

Pécs

Tulcea

Zagreb

Timișoara

Croatia
pp. 101-157

Bucharest

Constanţa

BOSNIA AND HERZEGOVINA

SERBIA AND MONTENEGRO

Mangalia

Black Sea

Split

Pleven

Adriatic Sea

Bulgaria
pp. 72-100

ITALY

Sofia

Plovdiv

MACEDONIA

ALBANIA

GREECE

Aegean Sea

TURKEY

RESEARCHER-WRITERS

Amelia "Molly" Atlas
Hungary, Slovenia

Late nights at the *Let's Go* office reading all about the gorgeous nature, friendly locals, and enchanting locales of Hungary convinced Molly that she had to hang up her editor's hat, load up the iPod, and try the hearty fare for herself. After beefing up our coverage of the pleasant southern plains, documenting her love affair with Budapest in the form of new listings, and even covering some of eastern Slovenia with ease, Molly had time left to take a much-deserved tour around the rest of the region. Molly, you fared more than heartily— we lift our jugs of Bull's Blood wine to you!

Piotr Brzezinski
Slovak Republic and Poland

Efficient, direct, and with an eye for organization, Piotr improved our coverage throughout his route. Sure, he may have overslept a connection and gotten thrown off a train in Middle-of-Nowhere, Slovakia, but this seasoned traveler knew how to get right back on track. In fact, he got far enough ahead that he managed to pop over to a rave at a Serbian castle without adversely affecting his route. He also un-muddled directions, vivified prose, and imbued his crystal-clear Kraków copy with just the right spunky, independent spirit.

Jason Campbell
Ukraine

Jason was no stranger to Ukraine, having spent two years working as a Peace Corps Volunteer near Kyiv. His return to the Borderland was certainly a triumphant one: it may have taken him hours upon hours to get information about train prices from surly, unwilling tellers, but get them he did. He also successfully navigated a rental car through mountain hamlets, clued us in to local secrets, and learned a thing or two from *babushki* on his way—all in a mere five weeks, and still our Ukrainian coverage has never been better. Jason is now applying his talents to a job at the Government Accountability Office.

Neasa Coll
Estonia, Latvia, and Lithuania

Subsisting on ice cream, Neasa bicycled tirelessly across a land of meteorite craters, drifting sand dunes, and Soviet relics, all the while sending us copy that was just as enchanting as the Baltic countryside. Gifts came too: mafia-chic Russian chocolates, Latvian concert posters, pins from the 1980 Olympics. Even while befriending Estonian paper boys, elderly Lithuanians, and Calvin Johnson, Neasa still found time to write lovely features and to expand our coverage of the bewitching Baltic Coast. Neasa, we'll see you at the Depeche Mode Baar in Tallinn.

Alexie Harper
Moscow and St. Petersburg

Emerging from *Let's Go* retirement for one last travel tour de force, polyglot powerhouse and long-time Italophile Alexie tackled the mean streets (and unbelievable sights) of St. Petersburg and Moscow. The (relatively new) language was the easy part. Wallet-thieves, bitter hostel managers, surly bouncers, and finger-itching police convinced her she really was in Russia. And her cool, plucky performance and local know-how convinced us that she's got a bit of Russian in her. *Brava! Nyet—zamechatelnaya!*

RESEARCHER-WRITERS

Jordan Hylden
Romania and Bulgaria

Eastern Europe was no match for this North Dakota farm boy, who weathered train strikes, pickpockets, and Bucharest, all without missing a beat. An unflinching reporter, Jordan braved Transylvanian cemeteries by night, saw Judgment Day played out in gruesome detail on the frescoed walls of remote monasteries, and found time to send back thoughtful, acute copy and overhaul our Bulgaria coverage. Have we mentioned that he also read *The Brothers Karamazov* during his route? Jordan, do you ever sleep?

Justin Jennings
Czech Republic

Show us one disheveled, philosophical grad student and we'll show you reams of pensive, cigarette-fueled copy; twenty pounds of shipped-home receipts; and an unceasing stream of travel curiosity. Justin braved piles of tourists, sleepless days and nights, and at least one travel companion who may or may not have been a fatigue-induced hallucination. He also got to cavort with Czech bikers and turned his talent as a writer towards improving our Czech Republic coverage.

Jennifer Kan
Croatia and Slovenia

A tough and seasoned budget traveler with Hollywood credentials, Jen's as comfortable trekking near former minefields as she is chatting up locals in hammock-strewn Dalmatian clubs. Communication hitches, a temperamental ferry system, and a ghost didn't stop this travel dynamo from winding her way through Croatia and Slovenia with the verve of a globe-hopping crocodile hunter (budget travel crocodiles!), collecting valuable tips and colorful stories along the way.

Stephanie O'Rourke
Poland

Steph was the best Let's Go researcher the Poland route has ever seen. Whether eating seriously old-school meats or extremely delicious cream cakes, tracking down make-out spots or pilgrimage sites, enduring vaguely comic minor ailments or youth hostels that smelled like socks, our woman in Warsaw charmed everyone in her path. Tourist bureau officals, hipsters, and re-enacters of medieval battles all swooned, and so did we. The only thing we awaited more eagerly than her weekly phone calls was her brilliant, brilliant copy.

CONTRIBUTING WRITERS

Candace Bertotti — *Berlin*

Shelly Jiang — *Munich, Vienna*

Morgan Kruger — *Venice*

Inna Livitz — *Editor, Let's Go: Italy*

Anna Mattson-Dicecca — *Associate Editor, Let's Go: Italy*

Jeremy Todd — *Editor, Let's Go: Europe*

Meghan Sherlock — *Associate Editor, Let's Go: Europe*

Stefan Zebrowski-Rubin — *Associate Editor, Let's Go: Europe*

Hannah Brooks-Motl is a writer and teacher who lives and works in Prague, where she has not yet found herself. She is a graduate of Macalester College. Her favorite Czech beer is Staropramen; her favorite Czech food is the dumpling.

Ian Hancock is the UN representative to the International Romani Union and a professor of linguistics and English at the University of Texas, Austin, where he directs the Romani Archives and Documentation Center. His books include *We Are the Romani People* and *A Handbook of Vlax Romani*.

ACKNOWLEDGMENTS

TEAM EASTERN EUROPE THANKS: The unflappable Rachel Burke, our hero; our tough and tireless RWs, for letting us live vicariously through them; Rachel Burke; David, for undertaking superhuman feats of perfectionism and sleep deprivation in the interest of our maps; Rachel Burke; Virginia, our irrepressible double agent; Seth, who is as wise as Dumbledore; Rachel Burke; Stuart, an incomparable 11th hour AE; the Starbucks-swilling croquet mavens of WEUR; Molly Atlas, Andrea Halpern, Jenn Ortegren, Mallory Hellmann, Lucy Lindsey, Emily Gee, Hannah Brooks-Motl, Adrienne Gerken, Ella Steim, Laura Martin, Clay Kaminsky, and war journalist Kevin Feeney. Also: Rachel Burke.

JANE THANKS: AlexAlex, my brave comrades, for tracksuits, the Berlin Wall, and the hitting stick; Rachel, for kindness and patience that were as tireless as your edits; Seth, for daytime drinking and other moral support; Rachel Nolan, for being so obsessively in love with me; the trivia team; Jenn, Sara, Alex K., Gabby&Adam, and Jess; and my family. Jordan Johnson, look: your name is in the book.

ALEX P. THANKS: Liz, Ronen, Neil, Tim, and my Winthrop droogs. Anna for taking me to EEUR, sort of. Eastern Europe, just for being there really. Mom and Dad and my grandparents for bailing me out that time, after I was arrested. Greg, of course, Present!, Ross, Turtleface, William, Sanford, McLean, our fearless leader Jane, and many people called Alex for doing so much good for our name. Etc.

ALEXANDER THANKS: Alex and Jane for making scores of sleepless nights actually seem like fun; our co-workers for all their help and goodwill; Virginia and Simon for the good times at 124 Oxford Street; the Snoot for saving my life; Andrew James Kane, the wind beneath my wings.

DAVID THANKS: Jane, our fearless leader, for catching everything; Alex P. for teaching me to love Cyrillic; Alex R. for Ukraine; Katherine for her wisdom under pressure; and Mapland.

Editor
Jane Yager
Associate Editors
Alex Pasternack, Alexander Rothman
Managing Editor
Rachel M. Burke
Map Editor
David I. Paltiel
Typesetter
Christine Yokoyama

LET'S GO

Publishing Director
Seth Robinson
Editor-in-Chief
Stuart J. Robinson
Production Manager
Alexandra Hoffer
Cartography Manager
Katherine J. Thompson
Editorial Managers
Rachel M. Burke, Ashley Eva Isaacson, Laura E. Martin
Financial Manager
Adrienne Taylor Gerken
Publicity Manager
Alexandra C. Stanek
Personnel Manager
Ella M. Steim
Production Associate
Ansel S. Witthaus
IT Director
Jeffrey Hoffman Yip
Director of E-Commerce
Michael Reckhow
Office Coordinator
Matthew Gibson

Director of Advertising Sales
Jillian N. London
Senior Advertising Associates
Jessica C.L. Chiu, Katya M. Golovchenko, Mohammed J. Herzallah
Advertising Graphic Designer
Emily E. Maston

President
Caleb J. Merkl
General Manager
Robert B. Rombauer
Assistant General Manager
Anne E. Chisholm

Railways of
Eastern Europe

1 2 3 4 5

PRICE RANGES>>EASTERN EUROPE

Our researchers list establishments in order of value from best to worst; our favorites are denoted by the Let's Go thumbs-up (🖒). Since the best value is not always the cheapest price, however, we have also incorporated a system of price ranges, based on a rough expectation of what you will spend. For **accommodations,** we base our range on the cheapest price for which a single traveler can stay for one night. For **restaurants** and other dining establishments, we estimate the average amount a traveler will spend. The table below tells you what you will *typically* find in Eastern Europe at the corresponding price range; keep in mind that no system can allow for every individual establishment's quirks.

ACCOMMODATIONS	WHAT YOU'RE *LIKELY* TO FIND
❶	Camping; most dorm rooms, such as HI or university dorm rooms. Expect bunk beds, concrete, and a communal bath; you may have to provide or rent towels and sheets. Some basic highwayside hotels in rural areas.
❷	Most backpacker and party hostels in major cities: you may find Internet, English-speaking staff, and included breakfast. Outside major cities, some more-or-less spartan pensions and B&Bs. You may have a private bathroom.
❸	A small room with a private bath. Hotels with 70s decor in provincial cities; decked-out pensions in small towns. Should have decent amenities, such as phone and TV. Breakfast may be included in the price of the room.
❹	In major cities, similar to 3, but with more amenities and more tasteful decor, or in a more touristed area. In small towns, may be downright luxurious.
❺	Large hotels and upscale chains. Some more modest hotels in amazing locations. If it's a 5 and it doesn't have the perks you want, you've paid too much.
FOOD	WHAT YOU'RE *LIKELY* TO FIND
❶	Street-corner stands, kebab and *shawarma* huts, and milk bars. Some *bliny* and *pierogi*. Ice cream and some cafe snacks. Cafeteria-style offerings.
❷	Pizza, unpretentious piles of meat, and deep-fried regional cuisine. Most dishes in which the main ingredient is potatoes. Pancakes, *naleśniki*, and breakfast items. Likely a sit-down meal.
❸	Seafood, wild game, meaty entrees. Many medieval-themed and hunting-lodge-decor establishments. A wine list. A cheeseburger in Moscow. Tip'll bump you up a couple dollars, since you will have a waiter.
❹	A somewhat fancy restaurant. Upscale vegetarian entrees. Attentive service. Decent Indian or Thai food in major cities. Few restaurants in this range have a dress code, but some may look down on t-shirt and jeans.
❺	The all-out version of the local food: duckling, venison medallions, wildfowl with foie gras. French words on the menu and a decent wine list. Slacks and dress shirts may be expected.

DISCOVER EASTERN EUROPE

It is hard to say how unified the region we call Eastern Europe ever truly was. One thing is for sure: in this era of reborn nationalism and cultural pride, countries that once lived on the same Bloc now have little in common and, in some cases, little to do with each other. In the past two decades, many Eastern European states have made concerted efforts to integrate themselves with the global (or at least Western) community. Behemoth Russia, on the other hand, remains somewhat unpredictable and isolated from her neighbors. Perhaps all that can be said of the region as a whole is that the countries here are changing—and that the resulting aura of uncertainty, potential, and adventure makes the area a haven for budget travelers. Untouristed cities, pristine national parks, empty hostel beds, and cheap beer abound. Budapest, Kraków, Prague, and St. Petersburg will charm even the most jaded backpacker, while the jagged peaks of the Tatras and dazzling beaches of the Dalmatian Coast are sure to stagger any nature lover.

Eastern European bureaucracies can be infuriating, most locals may be unfamiliar with the English language (or indeed the Roman alphabet), and, in some cases, amenities Westerners take for granted may be hard to find—but the road here is always rewarding. Your senses will be bombarded and, more likely than not, your conceptions of rationality challenged; after all, you can't use a bottle of vodka as a visa anywhere else in the world. Should the absurdity of the post-Soviet world ever get you down, take comfort in knowing that for every stoic border guard and badgering *babushka*, there are countless locals willing to give you a bed, a shot of homemade liquor, and a ride to the next town. If you bring along flexibility, patience, and resilience, you'll have an incredible journey through one of the most geographically varied, historically rich, and culturally dynamic areas of the world.

WHEN TO GO

Summer is Eastern Europe's high season. What this means, however, varies for each country and region. Budapest, Kraków, and Prague swarm with backpackers, while "high season" in the countryside simply means that hotels might actually have guests staying in them. Along the Adriatic, Baltic, and Black Sea coasts, tourists flock while it is warm enough to lounge on the beach, usually from June to September. In the Tatras, Julian Alps, and Transylvanian Alps, there is both a summer high season for hiking (July-Aug.) and a winter high season for skiing (Nov.-Mar.). In low season, you'll often be the only tourist in town. Although securing accommodations will be easier in low season, high season brings with it, for better or worse, an entire subculture of young backpackers. Major national holidays are listed in the introduction to each country. Festivals are detailed in city listings where appropriate; major festivals in each country are summarized on p. 5.

DISCOVER

WHAT TO DO

Like a tracksuit-clad mafioso on a Moscow street corner, Eastern Europe has got what you need, encompassing both heavily backpacked cities and sleepy hamlets.

🚩 IN HIGH SPIRITS

Let's be frank: a lot of people come to Eastern Europe to party, and for good reason. The alcohol is potent and cheap, and the nightlife famously vibrant. But you'd be doing yourself a disservice to sleep off that hangover all day; Eastern Europe offers a spectacular range of religious (architectural) experiences. From Romans to Roma and Muslims to Magyars, the many people who have inhabited Eastern Europe have left some extraordinary relics and ruins, and you don't have to be religious to marvel at them. Still, the cathedrals, synagogues, mosques, cemeteries, and monasteries of the region may easily inspire some serious devotion.

GOD IS GOOD	GOOD GOD, I'M DRUNK
WAWEL CASTLE (KRAKÓW, POL). Since the 10th century, monarchs have been coronated and buried on the grounds of this remarkable complex, which houses masterly tapestries and treasures. (p. 452)	**ŁÓDŹ KALISKA (ŁÓDŹ, POL).** "Bar" hardly describes this rambling, eclectic funhouse, which shares its name with the influential Łódź art collective that designed it. (p. 488)
BONE CHAPEL OF KUTNÀ HORA (CZR). After the Plague left the village's graveyard with a surplus of corpses, a monk, and later an artist, decided to do a little decorating. (p. 196)	**MAAILM (TARTU, EST).** Its decor fueled by old magazines, pillows, and swings, this pub is just like your wacky best friend's attic—except it serves amazing milkshakes. (p. 265)
WOODEN ARTICULATED CHURCH (KEŽMAROK, SLK). Swedish sailors helped build the porthole windows of this Reformation church, constructed in the shape of a Greek cross. (p. 641)	**PROPAGANDA (MOSCOW, RUS).** New and old and white Russians get mixed up in this hip expat-friendly hot spot, where tasty dinners give way to a thumping dance party come midnight. (p. 593)
CATHEDRAL OF CHRIST THE SAVIOR (MOSCOW, RUS). This reconstruction of St. Basil's—originally commissioned by Alexander I and torn down by Stalin—is unforgettable. (p. 586)	**ROMANIAN AND HUNGARIAN PALINČA.** Clear your evening schedule, and your physical vicinity, before downing the tasty and powerful moonshine, which often exceeds 120 proof. (p. 530)
ST. NICHOLAS ORTHODOX CATHEDRAL, KAROSTA (LIEPAJA, LAT). Set amid a sea of Soviet housing complexes, this gold-gilded church has survived the test of time, despite its lack of supporting columns. (p. 373)	**EASTWEST COCKTAIL AND DANCE BAR (DUBROVNIK, CRO).** With its private Dalmatian beach location and spectacular views, EastWest's motto, "Welcome to Heaven" is not unreasonable, especially after a few drinks. (p. 156)
CHURCH OF THE ASSUMPTION (BLED, SLO). The chapel itself ain't much to write home about, but its setting—on a tiny island in the center of Lake Bled—is otherworldly. (p. 677)	**METELKOVA MESTO (LJUBLJANA, SLO).** Get lost among the art-punks and graffitti at the best club/hostel/art collective complex ever to be housed inside a former Soviet miitary barracks. (p. 674)
WIELICZKA SALT MINES (KRAKÓW, POL). Undertake a journey to the center of Blessed Kinga, a church buried 200m underground—and carved entirely out of salt. (p. 460)	**PUB 13 (ALBA IULIA, ROM).** Built into the medieval citadel wall, this hot number packs in an international crowd that lines the incredibly long bar and lounges on an outdoor terrace. (p. 542)
METROPOLITAN CATHEDRAL (TIMIŞOARA, ROM). Thirteen green-and-gold spires cap this regal orthodox church, whose real eerie beauty comes out during nightly vespers. (p. 547)	**NOVOWIEJSKIEGO STREET (POZNAŃ, POL).** Come nighttime, students transform this thoroughfare of cafes into a raging bar and club scene; check out club W Starym Kinie. (p. 492)
ST. ISAAC'S CATHEDRAL (ST. PETERSBURG, RUS). The 100kg of pure gold that coats its Italian dome (which housed a museum of atheism under the Soviets) is visible for miles. (p. 609)	**SOPOT, POL.** This beach town near Gdańsk plays home to Eastern Europe's own slice of Ibiza, a Baltic club paradise where nights are as long as the wooden pier. (p. 508)
PANNONHALMA ABBEY (GYŐR, HUN). This 1000-year-old monastery contains one of the largest libraries in the country. (p. 312)	**ZÖLD PARDON AND RIO (BUDAPEST, HUN).** Sweaty summer crowds gyrate to fresh rock and house at these Danube-side hot spots. (p. 296)

〽 OUTDOORS

Ditch the crowds of Prague and head for the wonders of the Eastern European wilderness. From the rolling hills of Poland and the Czech Republic to the sand dunes of Lithuania and the jagged peaks of Slovenia, the region's rough edges are a thrillseeker's Eden. The Tatras, Julian Alps, and Carpathians offer Olympic-quality skiing, heart-stopping hang-gliding, and spectacular views from their endless—and lightly traveled—hiking trails. The beaches of Eastern Europe come in every variety: sandy, wide and windswept beside the Baltic in Estonia, Latvia, Lithuania, and Poland; rocky, colorful, and cafe-dotted along the sun-drenched Adriatic in Croatia and Slovenia; and wild and spectacular on the intensely blue (not black!) Black Sea Coast. Bicyclists can traverse the Estonian islands, the shores of Hungary's Lake Balaton, and the glassy Mazury Lakes of Poland.

BY LAND	BY SEA
MT. HOVERLA (YAREMCHE, UKR). The tallest peak in Ukraine offers great skiing, hiking, mushroom hunting, and a bevy of wooden huts to satisfy any aspiring Slavic woodsperson. (p. 737)	**MIĘDZYZDROJE (WOLIN ISLAND, POL).** This Baltic island has more glacial lakes, sweeping sea bluffs, old forts, hiking, cycling, and bison than you've ever seen in one place. (p. 498)
FĂGĂRAŞ MOUNTAINS (SIBIU, ROM). Wildflower meadows, cloud-shrouded summits, and superb views of Wallachian plains and Transylvanian hills have earned the Făgăraş renown among Romanian hikers. (p. 538)	**BRAĆ AND HVAR (DALMATIAN COAST, CRO).** These islands delight both chic beachgoers and ocean-adventurers with their breathtaking scenery, white pebble beaches, and nightlife as thrilling as their water sports. (p. 144, p. 146)
DOBŠINSKÁ ICE CAVES (SLOVENSKY RAJ, SLK). An awe-inspiring 110,000 cubic meters of beautifully frozen water got its start during the last Ice Age. (p. 645)	**BLED, SLO.** Slovenia's only island, in the middle of Lake Bled and ringed by the Julian Alps, is achingly beautiful—for a challenge, swim there from the lakeshore. (p. 675)
OPEN-AIR MUSEUM OF FOLK ARCHITECTURE AND RURAL LIFE (LVIV, UKR). In this wooden "town," detailed houses, barns, and 18th-century churches simulate cooperative farm life. You'll find similar museums around the region. (p. 732)	**DRIFTING DUNES OF PARNIDIS (NIDA, LIT).** Settlers have lived in this section of the Curonian Spit since the late 14th century, but their villages have been buried by shifting dunes on several occasions. (p. 415)
MARIBORSKO POHORJE, SLO. A hiker's and skier's paradise, these hills have trails with lovely views from the top of the cable car. (p. 686)	**YALTA, UKR.** Take a walk on the wild side of post-Soviet life in this lavish seaside city, where day-trips lead to spectacular caves. (p. 718)
MALÁ FATRAS AND SLOVENSKÝ RAJ. Avoid the overcrowded High Tatras and head to Slovakia's best hiking options, replete with alpine meadows, steep ravines, and limestone peaks. (p. 639, p. 645)	**PLITVICE LAKES NATIONAL PARK (CRO).** Endless forested hills, 16 lakes, and hundreds of waterfalls make this heavenly refuge one of Croatia's most spectacular places to wander. (p. 119)
SKOCJANSKE AND POSTOJNA CAVES (LJUBLJANA, SLO). Mind-blowing tours of these incredibly stunning caverns offer visitors a unique window into the country's *other* underground scene. (p. 674)	**ESTONIAN ISLANDS.** Sail to Hiumaa, where Soviet neglect has encouraged a wealth of wildlife, or cross to the small island of Kassari: walk the Saaretip peninsula, and you'll get the feeling you're walking to the end of the world. (p. 251)
ČESKÝ KRUMLOV (CZR). Biking, hiking, and kayaking have drawn tourists back to this medieval town, but the crowds are easily escapable. (p. 208)	**LAKE BALATON (BALATONFÜRED, HUN).** The best of Hungary's natural bounty, and a strong resort culture, surround Hungary's largest lake. (p. 325)
BADACSONY (HUN). Among the four resort towns at the base of the nearby volcanic mountain near Balatonfüred, this offers the best views, the best treks, and the best wine cellars. (p. 327)	**DANUBE RIVER.** Lifeline of Central Europe, the mighty Danube glides through Bratislava and Budapest before making a dramatic finish in the ripe-for-exploration Danube Delta, ROM. (p. 559)

DISCOVER

⚑ LITERARY GLORY

Eastern Europeans love their poets and novelists—and, for that matter, their playwrights, song writers, and essayists—so much that they sometimes elect them as presidents and prime ministers. The veneration of literary heroes is so intense that the graves and homes of many national poets have become pilgrimage sites. The literary glories of Eastern Europe do not captivate only Eastern Europeans: throngs of Anglophone aspiring Kafkas flooded east across the fallen Berlin Wall to create the expat Prague and Budapest cafe culture of the 1990s. Whether you're looking to trace the journey of Dostoevsky's Raskalnikov across St. Petersburg or write the next *Crime & Punishment*, Eastern Europe has enough fog-draped bridges, white nights, and haunted landscapes to inspire any writer, reader, or literary character.

WRITER'S BLOC

ANTON CHECKHOV'S HOUSE (YALTA, UKR). See the desk where Checkhov wrote the Cherry Orchard; witness first-hand the regional habit of making pilgrimage sites of the homes of great writers. (p. 721)

ELIE WIESEL. Visit the Nobel Laureate's childhood residence in Sighetu Marmatiei, ROM, the cultural center of Romania's most traditional region. (p. 548)

MOSCOW LITERARY MUSEUMS. Get to know Moscow's literary legacy at the city's museums devoted to renowned writers like Anton Chekhov, Fyodor Dostoevsky, Alexander Pushkin, and Leo Tolstoy. (p. 591)

ADAM MICKIEWICZ. Follow the path of the great Romantic poet from the Vilnius, LIT, Mickiewicz Museum all the way to the Warsaw, POL, Mickiewicz Museum. (p. 395, p. 442)

SZOMBATHELY'S LEOPOLD BLOOM. Celebrate Bloomsday in Szombathely, HUN, where the Hungarian origins of James Joyce's character are grounds for a festival every June 16. (p. 316)

LESYA UKRAINKA MUSEUM. Learn about Ukraine's foremost female writer at the collection housed in her longtime home at Yalta. (p. 721)

FRANZ KAFKA'S TOMB. Everyone's favorite angst-meister takes his final (probably troubled) sleep in the **New Jewish Cemetery** in the city of Prague, CZR. (p. 190)

VACLEV HAVEL'S CELL. Stay in his cell in Prague's Pension Unitis Art Prison Hostel and get inside the mind of the region's most famous living playwright, political dissident, and Velvet revolutionary. (p. 175)

GRASS'S GENIUS. Stop by Gdańsk, POL, to see the landscape that once inspired Gunter Grass's beautifully crafted, Nobel Prize-winning epic *The Tin Drum*. (p. 500)

PUSHKIN THE ENVELOPE. See the statue in St. Petersburg, RUS, that inspired the poem, "The Bronze Horseman." Check out Dostoevsky's grave while you're in town. (p. 608)

SO YOU WANT TO BE AN EXPAT

KRAKÓW, POL. Take a seat in a Rynek-side cafe with all the tourists—or score a cheap apartment in Kazimierz, the 600-year-old Jewish quarter of Kraków, now home to a colorful scene of artists, expats, and assorted local eccentrics. (p. 445)

MOSCOW, RUS. Brood on historic streets to your heart's content. If you need some comfort food, there's always the burgers and shakes at Starlite Diner. (p. 574)

BRAŞOV, ROM. Play the ski bum in Braşov, or go all Goth and hang out around Bran Castle, the inspiration for modern takes on the vampire myth. If you go the latter route, *Let's Go* recommends stocking up on garlic and turtlenecks. (p. 533)

WARSAW, POL. So concrete, so imposing, so mid-90s Berlin: what fodder for your novel! Not to mention the opportunities to drink your money away in Warsaw's awesome nightlife. (p. 426)

KAFE KOHVICUM (TALLINN, EST). A beautiful but unintimidating staff serves cheap and delicious coffee to a mostly local crowd in this cozy, candle-lit basement cafe. (p. 242)

PRAGUE, CZR. The obvious choice, for many good reasons. You can teach a little English while you pen that novel, right? (p. 165)

CAFE ZOOM (ST. PETERSBURG, RUS). The sleek decor and old-library motif draw the city's artists and literati, who enjoy good food and frequent readings and performances. (p. 606)

VILNIUS, LIT. This city boasts a small-but-thriving expat scene entirely worthy of the quirky, oddball sensibilities of Lithuania. Just brace yourself for winter. (p. 385)

KYIV, UKR. Settle in Kyiv to see first-hand the struggle to improve a democracy. Get a job at the English-language *Kyiv Post*, and chat with your coworkers over pints at The Drum. (p. 697)

DUBROVNIK, CRO. If walled cities are your thing, you should definitely consider setting up shop in lovely Dubrovnik. We hear it's the new Prague. (p. 150)

✻ FÊTES! FIESTAS! FESTIVALS!

COUNTRIES	APRIL - JUNE	JULY - AUGUST	SEPTEMBER - MARCH
BULGARIA	**Festival of the Roses** June, Kazanluk	**Int'l Jazz Festival** Aug., Varna (p. 94) **Sofia Music Week** June, Sofia (p. 80)	**Love is Folly Film Festival** Aug.-Sept., Varna (p. 94) **International Jazz Festival** Oct., Sofia (p. 80)
CROATIA	**Eurokaz Theater Festival** June, Zagreb (p. 109) **Cest is d'Best** June, Zagreb (p. 109) **Int'l Children's Festival** June-July, Šibenik	**Int'l Folklore Festival** July, Zagreb (p. 109) **Biker Days Festival** July, Pula (p. 120) **Split Summer Festival** July-Aug., Split (p. 138)	**Int'l Puppet Festival** Sept., Zagreb (p. 109) **Marco Polo Festival** Aug-Sept., Korčula (p. 148) **International Jazz Days** Oct., Zagreb (p. 109)
CZECH REPUBLIC	**Prague Spring Festival** May-June (p. 165) **Prague Fringe Festival** June (p. 165)	**Int'l Film Festival** July, Karlovy Vary (p. 202) **Int'l Music Fest** July-Aug., Český Krumlov (p. 208)	**Int'l Organ Festival** Sept., Olomouc (p. 224) **Jazz Goes to Town** Oct., Hradec Králové (p. 215)
ESTONIA	**Country Dance Festival** June, Pärnu (p. 247) **Jaanipaev** June, Tallinn (p. 237) **Grillfest** June, Tallinn (p. 237)	**Beersummer** July, Tallinn (p. 237) **Watergate** July, Pärnu (p. 247)	**White Lady Days** Aug., Haapsalu (p. 250) **Dark Nights Film Festival** Dec., Tallinn (p. 237) **Student Jazz Festival** Feb., Tallinn (p. 237)
HUNGARY	**Bloomsday Festival** June, Szombathely (p. 316) **Danube Festival** June, Budapest (p. 276) **Sopron Festival Weeks** June-July (p. 313)	**Golden Shell Folklore** July, Siófok (p. 321) **Szeged Open Air Festival** July-Aug. (p. 343) **Sziget Rock Festival** Aug., Budapest (p. 276)	**Jazz Days** Sept., Debrecen (p. 340) **Éger Vintage Days** Sept. (p. 299) **Festival of Wine Songs** Sept., Pécs (p. 334)
LATVIA	**Midsummer's Eve** June (p. 359) **Opera Music Festival** July, Sigulda (p. 375)	**Rīgas Ritmi Music Festival** July, Rīga (p. 359)	**Chamber Choir Festival** Sept., Rīga (p. 359)
LITHUANIA	**Vilniaus Festivalis** May, Vilnius (p. 385) **Pažaislis Music Festival** May-Sept., Kaunas (p. 398)	**Thomas Mann Festival** July, Nida (p. 415) **Night Serenades** Aug., Palanga (p. 411)	**Vilnius Jazz Festival** Sept.-Oct., Vilnius (p. 385) **SIRENOS Theater Festival** Sept.-Oct., Vilnius (p. 385)
POLAND	**Int'l Short Film Festival** May, Kraków (p. 445) **Wianki** June, Kraków (p. 445)	**Street Theater Festival** July, Kraków (p. 445) **Highlander Folklore** Aug., Zakopane (p. 467)	**Jazz Festival** Mar., Poznań (p. 488)
ROMANIA	**Int'l Theater Festival** June, Sibiu (p. 538)	**Medieval Festival** July, Sighişoara (p. 536)	**Int'l Chamber Music** Sept., Braşov (p. 533)
RUSSIA	**Music Spring** Apr., St. Petersburg (p. 595)	**White Nights Festival** June-July, St. Petersburg	**Russian Winter Festival** Dec.-Jan., Moscow (p. 574) **Maslyanitsa** Feb. (p. 573)
SLOVAK REPUBLIC	**Int'l Festival of Ghosts and Spirits** May, Bojnice	**Festival of Marian Devotion** July, Levoča (p. 642)	**Bratislava Music Festival** Sept.-Oct. (p. 626) **Jazz Days** Oct., Bratislava (p. 626)
SLOVENIA	**Int'l Wine Fair** Apr., Ljubljana (p. 667) **Break 22 Festival** June, Ljubljana (p. 667)	**Bled Days** July (p. 675)	**Int'l Film Festival** Nov., Ljubljana (p. 667) **Kurent Carnival** Feb., Ptuj (p. 686)
UKRAINE	**Lviv City Days** May (p. 726)	**Local Sheep Cheese Festival** Sept., Uzhhorod (p. 734)	**Golden Lion Theater Festival** Sept., Lviv (even numbered years; p. 726)

DISCOVER

SUGGESTED INTINERARIES

THE NEW PRAGUE (3 WEEKS)

Tartu, EST (2 days)
Leave the stag parties back in the Irish Pubs of Old Town Tallinn, and head off the beaten path to explore the cathedral ruins, quirky public art, and vibrant street life of this university town, where free concerts abound in summer (p. 260).

START

Liepāja, LAT (2 days)
On the spectacular Latvian coast, the sea breezes are as refreshing as the lack of tourists. Eat plenty of fresh local fish and stroll the 2km pier on the beach at neighboring Karosta (p. 372).

Klaipėda and Nida, LIT (2 days)
Scramble across the drifting sand dunes, meet folk sculptures in the seaside forest, and sample the eight excellent varieties of local brew švyturys (p. 406).

Český Krumlov, CZR (1 day)
If you tire of the maze-like city's medieval buildings and perplexing Revolving Theater, hit up Mama Nature for some sweet hiking or rafting down the Vltava (p. 208).

Gdańsk, POL (2 days)
This cosmopolitan city on the Baltic finds the perfect complement to its graceful historical district in the sandy beach and seaside glamor of neighboring Sopot (p. 500).

Wrocław, POL (2 days)
With all the bridges and spires of Prague—and none of the crowds—Wrocław is both debaucherous and dreamy: the bars and clubs are every bit as superlative as the sights (p. 476).

END

Budapest, HUN (2 days)
Hipper than its old nickname might suggest, "the Paris of Eastern Europe" bubbles with hot springs underneath and a hotter east-meets-west pizzazz that lasts from dawn til dawn (p. 276).

Kyiv, UKR (2 days)
Stroll through verdant parks, hang out with dead monks in the Kyiv-Cave Monastery, and plug into the still-buzzing energy of the recent Orange Revolution (p. 697).

Lviv, UKR (2 days)
The cultural center of Ukraine, replete with cafes, winding streets, and national pride. Make sure to save a day for the Open-Air Museum of Folk Architecture and Rural Life (p. 726).

Zagreb, CRO (2 days)
The cobblestoned capital has grown into a worthy east-west checkpoint, replete with a breathtaking old town, world-class museums, and a boisterous club scene (p. 109).

Ljubljana, SLO (2 days)
The beat of the underground art scene centered at festive Metelkova Mesto emanates day and night, mingling with the old world culture of this refreshingly petite capital (p. 667).

DISCOVER

BEEN THERE, DONE THAT (4 WEEKS)

START

St. Petersburg, RUS (3 days)
Simply spectacular and utterly paradoxical, this lavish city-on-a-marsh, like its must-see Hermitage museum, survived an assault of Soviet style to remain fit for a tsar—or the adventurous traveler (p. 595).

Tallinn, EST (2 days)
The area around the historic Gothic square of Raekoja Plats offers beer gardens, steeples and towers to climb, and the powerful Museum of Occupation; gorgeous Kadriorg Palace is a nice walk away (p. 237).

Rīga, LAT (2 days)
A day wandering through its renowned Art Nouveau architecture and rowing a boat down river comes to a grand finale with a night at the opera and a morning in the clubs (p. 359).

Vilnius, LIT (2 days)
Cycle through the relaxed, lovely old town—a Unesco World Heritage site—before enjoying the hills, cafes and Frank Zappa statue of this electic, influential capital (p. 385).

Warsaw, POL (2 days)
Don't judge the Polish capital by its looks—this forward-looking city is one of the region's most compelling. Exuberant nightlife and a cutting-edge arts scene contrast the painful past evident in the city's historical sights (p. 426).

Kraków, POL (4 days)
Do judge Poland's darling by its looks. From mighty Wawel Castle to the spectacular Old Town Square and the stylish students who pack the city's cellar clubs, the beauty of Kraków will overload your senses (p. 445).

Prague, CZR (4 days)
Club until dawn, take a nap, and then head back out to explore the city's cobblestone streets, hearty fare, and cubist architecture. Repeat (p. 165).

Vienna, AUT (2 days)
This sultry, svelte city showcases Central Europe's riches like no other: world-class museums, unforgettable cafés, and the breeding ground of the world's finest music (p. 748).

Budapest, HUN (3 days)
Go for the goulash and prehistoric labyrinths, and just try to pull yourself away from the show-stopping art and cafe culture, the underground club life, and the soothing baths (p. 276).

Dalmatian Coast, CRO (2 days)
Hit up the hot rocks on Hvar or Brac islands, make an extended ferry stop in tree-lined Zadar, then bus inland to the cosmopolitan comforts of Zagreb (p. 134).

Dubrovnik, CRO (2 days)
Marvel at how the war wounds of Eastern Europe's coastal jewel have healed as you recline like royalty on the Adriatic before a night out at the clubs (p. 150).

END

THE UGLY: SOVIET RELICS (3 WEEKS)

Rīga, LAT (3 days)
Social Realist statuary dots the city; the Soviet past is documented in a memorable video at the Museum of Barricades (p. 359).

Hiumaa, EST (2 days)
As you bicycle through Estonia's best-preserved forest, thank the USSR for the pristine state of this remote island: by restricting access to it, the Soviets unwittingly preserved many rare plants and animals (p. 256).

Soviet Missile Base, LIT (2 days)
Tour the corridors and decaying underground bunkers, then climb through a hatch and stare down the barrel of a missile silo (p. 414).

Moscow, RUS (3 days)
Hyper-capitalism has only slightly tarnished the greatest Soviet relic, with its imposing concrete facades and concrete-like bureaucrats (p. 574).

END

Vilnius, LIT (2 days)
The sinister former KGB headquarters is now a museum where isolation cells and torture chambers are chillingly preserved (p. 385).

Warsaw, POL (3 days)
The Stalinist Palace of Culture that towers over gargantuan Plac Defilad is a powerful reminder of the days of the Warsaw Pact (p. 426).

Lódz, POL (3 days)
Glimpse the Poland of 20 years ago in this sooty city where the bars are as good as the economy is bad (p. 483).

Berlin, GER (2 days)
The east side is an electric neighborhood where massive urban renewal meets lingering Soviet style (p. 739).

START

Nowa Huta, POL (2 days)
These massive steelworks outside Kraków, one of the largest-scale urban planning projects in the Eastern Bloc, backfired wildly when Nowa Huta became a hotbed of dissent (p. 457).

THE BEAUTIFUL: OUTDOORS (2 WEEKS)

Tatras Mts., SLK/POL (2 days)
Towns like Slovenský Raj lie among underground waterfalls, rugged trails, and breathtaking vistas (p. 471).

Mt. Hoverla, UKR (1 day)
Lounge in saunas, go mushroom picking, and absorb folk culture around Ukraine's highest peak (p. 737).

Eger, HUN (1 day)
Eger's bitter Turkish occupation couldn't touch its wonderful ranges of deep green hills and a warm atmosphere without the hustle of Budapest (p. 299).

Translyvania, ROM (1 day)
The Carpathian mountains boast some of Europe's best skiing and hiking and cradle charming, untouristed hillside towns (p. 533).

Lake Balaton, HUN (2 days)
Relax on the waterfront of Central Europe's largest lake, hike the nature preserve of Tihany peninsula, and take the thermal waters in lakeside spa towns (p. 321).

Bled, SLO (1 day)
The crags of the Julian Alps rise above a subalpine lake that cradles Slovenia's only island, home to an exquisite 13th century castle (p. 675).

Black Sea Coast, ROM/BUL (2 days)
Soak up the sun and party on the beaches of multicultural Varna and Constanta, then head north to the wild Danube Delta (p. 557).

START

END

Dalmatian Coast, CRO (2 days)
Nature lovers flock to the pebbly wilds of Cres Island for birdwatching, and swanky stars come to relax on the leafy shores of Hvar and Brac (p. 134).

Veliko Tarnovo, BUL (2 days)
In Bulgaria's most beautiful city, scramble over the ruins of a Roman citadel and explore surrounding hill towns and monasteries (p. 97).

ESSENTIALS

PLANNING YOUR TRIP

ENTRANCE REQUIREMENTS
Passport (p. 9). Required for citizens of Australia, Canada, Ireland, New Zealand, the UK, and the US to enter all countries in Eastern Europe.
Visa (p. 10). Required of all foreign citizens entering Russia, for US citizens entering Ukraine after an absence of more than 6 months, and of some foreigners entering other countries in Eastern Europe. Consult your destination's **Entrance Requirements** section for more information.
Letter of Invitation (p. 10). Required of all foreign citizens entering Russia.
Inoculations (p. 20). Recommended up-to-date on DTaP (diphtheria, tetanus, and pertussis), Hepatitis A, Hepatitis B, MMR (measles, mumps, and rubella), Polio booster, and Typhoid.
Work Permit (p. 10). Required of foreigners planning to work in Eastern Europe.

EMBASSIES AND CONSULATES

Eastern European embassies and consulates abroad are listed in the **Documents and Formalities: Embassies and Consulates** section at the beginning of each country chapter. American, Australian, British, Canadian, Irish, and New Zealand embassies and consulates in Eastern European countries are listed in the **Practical Information** sections for the capitals of each country.

DOCUMENTS AND FORMALITIES

PASSPORTS

REQUIREMENTS
Citizens of Australia, Canada, Ireland, New Zealand, the UK, and the US need valid passports to enter any country in Eastern Europe and to re-enter their home countries. Many European countries will not allow entrance if the holder's passport expires within six months; returning home with an expired passport is illegal and may result in a fine.

NEW PASSPORTS
Citizens of Australia, Canada, Ireland, New Zealand, the UK, and the US can apply for a passport at any passport office or at selected post offices and courts of law. Citizens of these countries may also download passport applications from the official website of their country's government or passport office. Any new passport or renewal applications must be filed well in advance of the departure date, though most passport offices offer rush services for a very steep fee. Note, however, that "rushed" passports still take up to two weeks to arrive.

PASSPORT MAINTENANCE
Photocopy the page of your passport with your photo, as well as your visas, traveler's check serial numbers and any other important documents. Carry one set of copies in a safe place, apart from the originals, and leave another set at home. Con-

EASTERN EUROPE AND THE EUROPEAN UNION. Eight Eastern European nations joined the EU on May 1, 2004: the Czech Republic, Estonia, Hungary, Latvia, Lithuania, Poland, the Slovak Republic, and Slovenia. What implications does this have for the traveler to Eastern Europe? Estimates vary as to the date these countries will adopt the euro; Estonia, Slovenia, and Lithuania are currently aiming to fulfill the criteria set forth as early as 2007, while the Czech Republic has set its target date for 2010. Hungary has taken an even more cautious approach, vowing to adopt the euro in 2010 only if the economy can handle it. Unstable economic conditions in Latvia have caused leaders to second-guess the initial 2007 goal, while the Slovak Republic predicts 2008-10. Poland has chosen to remain entirely mysterious on the topic, refusing to announce a specific date for euro adoption. Similarly, borders may not open to citizens of other EU member states for several years. For now, bring your passport and be prepared to exchange your currency. Much is changing quickly, so check before you go to see what progress has been made in your destination country regarding integration into the EU.

sulates also recommend that you carry an expired passport or an official copy of your birth certificate. **If you lose your passport,** immediately notify the local police and the nearest embassy or consulate of your native country. To expedite its replacement, you will need ID and proof of citizenship. A replacement may take weeks and may be valid only for a limited time. Any visas stamped in your old passport will be irretrievably lost. In an emergency, ask for temporary traveling papers that will permit you to re-enter your home country.

VISAS, INVITATIONS, AND WORK PERMITS

VISAS
Visas can be purchased from your destination country's consulate or embassy. In most cases, you will have to send a completed visa application (obtainable from the consulate), the required fee, and your passport. Private organizations within your own country may offer visa services as well. For more information on each country's visa requirements, see the **Documents and Formalities** section at the beginning of each country chapter. US citizens can take advantage of the **Center for International Business and Travel** (CIBT; ☎ 800-925-2428), which secures visas for travel to almost all countries for a variable service charge. Double-check on entrance requirements at the nearest embassy or consulate of your destination country for up-to-date info before departure. US citizens can also consult http://travel.state.gov/foreignentryreqs.html.

INVITATIONS
In its visa application, Russia requires an invitation from a sponsoring individual or organization. Specialized travel agencies can arrange for those without private sponsors, as well as hotels at which you plan to stay. Many travel agencies will take care of visa processing (including letters of invitation). Two such establishments are **www.waytorussia.net** and Boston's **Info Travel** (☎ 617-566-2197; www.infortravel.com). For more agencies that specialize in countries of the former USSR, see **Russia Essentials: Visa and Entry Information,** p. 563. Requirements change rapidly, so always double-check with the relevant embassy.

WORK PERMITS
Admission as a visitor does not include the right to work, which is authorized only by a work permit. Entering to study requires a special visa. For more information, see **Beyond Tourism** (p. 61).

IDENTIFICATION

When you travel, always have at least two forms of identification on you, including at least one photo ID. A passport combined with a driver's license or birth certificate is usually an adequate combination. Never carry all your IDs together; split them up in case of theft or loss, and keep copies in your luggage and at home.

STUDENT, TEACHER, AND YOUTH IDENTIFICATION

The **International Student Identity Card (ISIC)**, the most widely accepted form of student ID, provides discounts on some sights, accommodations, food, and transportation; access to a 24hr. emergency helpline; and insurance benefits for US cardholders (p. 21). Applicants must be full-time secondary or post-secondary school students at least 12 years of age. Because of the proliferation of fake ISICs, some services (particularly airlines) require additional proof of student identity.

The **International Teacher Identity Card (ITIC)** offers teachers the same insurance coverage as the ISIC and similar but limited discounts. For travelers who are under 26 years old but are not students, the **International Youth Travel Card (IYTC)** also offers many of the same benefits as the ISIC.

Each of these identity cards costs US$22 or equivalent. ISICs and ITICs are valid until the new year unless purchased between September and December, in which case they are valid until the beginning of the following new year. Thus, a card purchased in March 2006 will be valid until December 31, 2006, while a card purchased in November 2006 will be valid until December 31, 2007. IYTCs are valid for one year from the date of issue. To learn more about ISICs, ITICs, and IYTCs, try www.myisic.com. Many student travel agencies (p. 25) issue the cards; for a list of issuing agencies or more information, see the **International Student Travel Confederation (ISTC)** website (www.istc.org).

ESSENTIALS

The **International Student Exchange Card (ISE Card)** is a similar identification card available to students, faculty, and youths aged 12 to 26. The card provides discounts, medical benefits, access to a 24hr. emergency helpline, and the ability to purchase student airfares. An ISE Card costs US$25; call ☎800-255-8000 for more info, or visit www.isecard.com.

CUSTOMS

Upon entering any country, you must declare certain items from abroad and pay a duty on the value of those articles if they exceed the allowance established by that country's customs service. Note that goods and gifts purchased at **duty-free** shops abroad are not exempt from duty or sales tax; "duty-free" merely means that you need not pay a tax in the country of purchase. Duty-free allowances were abolished for travel between EU member states but still exist for those arriving from outside the EU. Upon returning home, you must likewise declare all articles acquired abroad and pay a duty on the value of the articles in excess of your home country's allowance. In order to expedite your return, make a list of any valuables brought from home and register them with customs before traveling abroad, and keep receipts for all goods acquired abroad.

MONEY

CURRENCY AND EXCHANGE

A chart at the beginning of each country chapter lists the August 2005 exchange rates between local currency and Australian dollars (AUS$), Canadian dollars (CDN$), New Zealand dollars (NZ$), British pounds (UK£), US dollars (US$), and EU euros (EUR€). Check the currency converter on financial websites such as www.bloomberg.com and www.xe.com, or with a large newspaper for the latest exchange rates. As a general rule, it's cheaper to convert money abroad than at home. While currency exchange will probably be available in your arrival airport, it's wise to bring enough foreign currency to last the first 24 to 72 hours of a trip.

When changing money, go only to banks or exchange offices that have at most a 5% margin between their buy and sell prices. **Convert large sums** (unless the currency is depreciating rapidly), **but no more than you'll need** within that one country, since it may be difficult or impossible to change it back. Some countries, such as the Czech Republic, Russia, and the Slovak Republic, may require transaction receipts to reconvert local currency. Of foreign currencies, US$ or EUR€ are the most widely—and at times the only—foreign currencies accepted for exchange.

If you use **traveler's checks** or bills, carry some in small denominations (the equivalent of US$50 or less) for times when you are forced to exchange money at disadvantageous rates, but bring a range of denominations since charges may be levied per check cashed.

In some countries of Eastern Europe, US$ or EUR€ will be preferred to local currency. Although some establishments post prices in US$ or EUR€ due to high inflation and will insist that they don't accept anything else, avoid using Western money. Not only are such prices generally more expensive than those in the local currency, but Western currency may also attract thieves.

TRAVELER'S CHECKS

Traveler's checks are one of the safest and least troublesome means of carrying funds. American Express and Visa are the most recognized brands. Many banks and agencies sell them for a small commission. Check issuers provide refunds if the checks are lost or stolen, and many provide additional services, such as toll-free refund hotlines abroad, emergency message services, and stolen credit card assistance. It is best to get checks in either US$ or EUR€. They are readily accepted in Prague and similar urban centers, but unfortunately it is difficult—if not impossible—to cash these checks in rural areas and anywhere in Russia. Ask about toll-free refund hotlines and the location of refund centers when purchasing checks. Always carry emergency cash.

American Express: Checks available with commission at select banks, at all AmEx offices, and online (www.americanexpress.com; US residents only). American Express cardholders can also purchase checks by phone (☎800-721-9768). Checks available in Australian, British, Canadian, European, Japanese, and US currencies, among others. American Express also offers the Travelers Cheque Card, a prepaid reloadable card. Cheques for Two can be signed by either of two people traveling together. For purchase locations or more information, contact AmEx's service centers: in Australia ☎800 688 022, in New Zealand 423 74 409, in the UK 0800 587 6023, in the US and Canada 800-221-7282; elsewhere, call the US collect at 1-801-964-6665.

Travelex: Thomas Cook MasterCard and Interpayment Visa traveler's checks available. Travelex/Thomas Cook offices cash checks commission-free but are less common in Eastern Europe than American Express. For information about Thomas Cook MasterCard in the UK call ☎0800 622 101, in the US and Canada ☎800-223-7373; elsewhere call the UK collect at +44 1733 318 950. For information about Interpayment Visa in the in the UK call ☎0800 515 884, in the US and Canada ☎800-732-1322; elsewhere call the UK collect at +44 1733 318 949. For more information, visit www.travelex.com.

Visa: Checks available (generally with commission) at banks worldwide. For the location of the nearest office, call the Visa Travelers Cheque Global Refund and Assistance Center: in the UK ☎0800 515 884, in the US 800-227-6811, elsewhere, call the UK collect at +44 2079 378 091. Checks available in British, Canadian, European, Japanese, and US currencies, among others. Visa also offers TravelMoney, a prepaid debit card that can be reloaded online or by phone. For more information on Visa travel services, see http://usa.visa.com/personal/using_visa/travel_with_visa.html.

CREDIT, DEBIT, AND ATM CARDS

Where they are accepted, **credit cards** often offer superior exchange rates—up to 5% better than the retail rate used by banks and other currency exchange establishments. Credit cards may also offer services such as insurance or emergency help and are sometimes required to reserve hotel rooms or rental cars. **Master-Card** (a.k.a. EuroCard in Europe; **MC**) and **Visa** (a.k.a. Carte Bleue; **V**) are the most welcomed; **American Express (AmEx)** cards work at some ATMs and at AmEx offices and major airports.

The use of **ATM cards** is relatively widespread in Eastern Europe, particularly in urban locations. Depending on the system that your home bank uses, you can most likely access your personal bank account from abroad. ATMs get the same wholesale exchange rate as credit cards, but there is often a limit on the amount of money you can withdraw per day (usually around US$500). There is typically also a surcharge of US$1-5 per withdrawal. While ATMs are generally easy to come by, particularly in cities, it can't hurt to carry a bit of extra cash if traveling in rural regions.

Debit cards are as convenient as credit cards but have a more immediate impact on your funds. A debit card can be used wherever its associated credit card company (usually MC or V) is accepted, yet the money is withdrawn directly from the holder's checking account. Debit cards often also function as ATM cards and can be used to withdraw cash from associated banks and ATMs throughout Eastern Europe. Ask your local bank about obtaining one.

The two major international money networks are **MasterCard/Maestro/Cirrus** (for ATM locations ☎800-424-7787 or www.mastercard.com) and **Visa/PLUS** (for ATM locations ☎800-843-7587 or www.visa.com). Most ATMs charge a transaction fee that is paid to the bank that owns the ATM.

GETTING MONEY FROM HOME

If you run out of money while traveling, the easiest and cheapest solution is to have someone back home make a deposit to your bank account. Failing that, consider one of the following options.

WIRING MONEY

It is possible to arrange a **bank transfer,** which means asking a bank back home to **wire money** to a bank abroad. This is the cheapest way to transfer cash, but it's also the slowest, usually taking several days or more. Note that some banks may only release your funds in local currency, potentially sticking you with a poor exchange rate; inquire about this in advance. Money transfer services like **Western Union** are faster and more convenient than bank transfers—but also much pricier. Western Union has many locations worldwide. To find one, visit www.westernunion.com, or call in Australia ☎800 173 833, in Canada 800-235-6000, in the UK 0800 83 38 33, or in the US 800-225-5227. Money transfer services are also available to **American Express** cardholders and at select **Thomas Cook** offices.

US STATE DEPARTMENT (US CITIZENS ONLY)

In serious emergencies only, the US State Department will forward money within hours to the nearest consular office, which will then disburse it according to instructions for a US$15 fee. To use this service, you must contact the Overseas Citizens Service division of the US State Department (☎317-472-2328; nights, Su, and holidays 202-647-4000).

10 4 2 6 1
7 8 9 5 3

TOP TEN LIST

TOP 10 WAYS TO SAVE MONEY IN EASTERN EUROPE

1 The **open-air market:** definitely the place to buy your breakfast. Possibly the place to buy your tracksuits and DVDs.

2 **Internet is free** at many tourist bureaus and libraries—plus you won't have to stand in line while chain-smoking teens play CounterStrike.

3 Avoid any establishment with **English words** in its name or on a sign or menu outside.

4 Most **museums** have free days; at many of them, **permanent exhibits** are always free.

5 Look for **private microbuses** that run between cities—often they're cheaper and more comfortable than train or buses.

6 High-quality **beer** and **vodka** is dirt-cheap at the grocery store; do most of your drinking *before* you hit the clubs.

7 **Talk to the locals.** They know where the good deals are; the kid in the bunk beside you at the hostel doesn't.

8 If you take a **cab,** always have someone who speaks the local language call ahead for you so you won't be ripped off.

9 But don't take a cab; **rent a bike** instead—it's a cheap, fast, fun way to tour a city.

10 If you're bound for a major tourist city, go in winter—prices will be much lower, and Prague looks great in the snow.

COSTS

The cost of your trip will vary considerably, depending on where you go, how you travel, and where you stay. The most significant expense will probably be your round-trip **airfare,** which can be much more expensive than a ticket to Western Europe (see **Getting to Eastern Europe: By Plane,** p. 24). Before you go, it's helpful to spend some time calculating a per-day **budget** that will meet your needs.

STAYING ON A BUDGET

Generally, a bare-bones day in Eastern Europe (camping or sleeping in hostels/guesthouses, buying food at supermarkets) will cost about US$20; a slightly more comfortable day (sleeping in hostels/guesthouses and the occasional budget hotel, eating one meal a day at a restaurant, going out at night) will run about US$30-45. If you spend more than that you'll be living like royalty. But even these ranges vary throughout the region: expect to spend US$10-15 more per day in Croatia, Slovenia, and Estonia, and US$5 less in Lithuania, Ukraine, and the Slovak Republic. Also, don't forget to factor in emergency reserve funds (at least US$200) when planning how much money you'll need. Eastern Europe is the budget traveler's paradise. The price of a hostel in London equals that of a quality hotel in most of Eastern Europe, while local restaurants and transportation services charge a fraction of their Western counterparts. Often the difference of a couple US$ or EUR€ in price means an improvement by leaps and bounds in quality.

TIPS FOR SAVING MONEY

Some simpler ways include searching out opportunities for free entertainment, splitting accommodation and food costs with trustworthy fellow travelers, and buying food in supermarkets rather than eating out. Do your laundry in the sink (unless you're explicitly prohibited from doing so). Museums sometimes have certain days once a month or once a week when admission is free; plan accordingly. If you are eligible, consider getting an ISIC or an IYTC; sights and museums may offer reduced admission to students and youths. For getting around quickly, bikes are the most economical option. Renting a bike is cheaper than renting a moped or scooter. Don't forget about walking, though; you can learn a lot about a city by seeing it on foot. Drinking at bars and clubs quickly becomes expensive. It's cheaper to buy alcohol at a supermarket and imbibe before going out. That said, don't go overboard. Though staying within your budget is important, don't do so at the expense of your health or a great travel experience.

TIPPING, BARGAINING, AND TAXES

For information on tipping, bargaining, and taxes, refer to the **Essentials: Tourist Services** and **Money** sections of each country.

PACKING

Pack lightly: Lay out only what you absolutely need, then take half the clothes and twice the money. The Travelite FAQ (www.travelite.org) is a good resource for tips on traveling light. The online **Universal Packing List** (http://upl.codeq.info) will generate a customized list of suggested items based on your trip length, the expected climate, your planned activities, and other factors. If you plan to do a lot of hiking, also consult **The Great Outdoors**, p. 41. Some frequent travelers keep a bag packed with all the essentials: passport, money belt, hat, socks, etc. Then, when they decide to leave, they know they haven't forgotten anything.

Luggage: If you plan to cover most of your itinerary by foot, a sturdy **frame backpack** is unbeatable. (For the basics on buying a pack, see p. 42.) Toting a **suitcase** or **trunk** is fine if you plan to live in one or two cities and explore from there, but not a great idea if you plan to move around frequently. In addition to your main piece of luggage, a **daypack** (a small backpack or courier bag) is useful.

Clothing: Eastern European climate is highly variable from region to region, so be prepared for all kinds of weather. No matter when you're traveling, it's a good idea to bring a warm jacket or wool sweater, a rain jacket (Gore-Tex® is both waterproof and breathable), sturdy shoes or hiking boots, and thick socks. Flip-flops or waterproof sandals are must-haves for grubby hostel showers, and extra socks are always a good idea. You may also want one outfit for going out, and maybe a nicer pair of shoes. Women should bring a **head covering** for mosque and monastery visits.

Sleepsack: Some hostels require that you either provide your own linen or rent sheets from them. Save cash by making your own sleepsack: fold a full-size sheet in half the long way, then sew it closed along the long side and one of the short sides.

Converters and adapters: Throughout Eastern Europe, electricity is 220 or 230V AC, enough to fry any 110V appliance. **Americans** and **Canadians** should buy an adapter (which changes the shape of the plug) and a converter (which changes the voltage; US$20). Don't make the mistake of using only an adapter (unless appliance instructions explicitly state otherwise). **Australians**, **Brits**, **Irish**, and **New Zealanders** (who use 230V at home) won't need a converter, but they will need a set of adapters to use anything electrical. Check out **http://kropla.com/electric.htm** for more info.

Toiletries: Condoms, deodorant, razors, tampons, and toothbrushes are often available, but it may be difficult to find your preferred brand; bring extras. Contact lenses are likely to be expensive and difficult to find, so bring enough extra pairs and solution for your entire trip. Also bring your glasses and a copy of your prescription in case you need emergency replacements. If you use heat-disinfection, either switch temporarily to a chemical disinfection system (check first to make sure it's safe with your brand of lenses), or buy a converter to 220/240V.

First-Aid Kit: For a basic first-aid kit, pack bandages, a pain reliever, antibiotic cream, a thermometer, a multifunction pocketknife, tweezers, moleskin, decongestant, motion-sickness remedy, diarrhea or upset-stomach medication (Pepto Bismol® or Imodium®), an antihistamine, sunscreen, insect repellent, burn ointment, and a syringe for emergencies (get an explanatory letter from your doctor).

Other useful items: For safety purposes, you should bring a money belt and small padlock. Basic **outdoors equipment** (plastic water bottle, compass, waterproof matches, sunglasses, hat) may also prove useful. A needle and thread can come in handy. Also consider bringing electrical tape for patching tears. If you're looking to cut costs and want to do laundry by hand, bring detergent, a small rubber ball to stop up the sink, and string for a make-shift clothes line. **Other things** you're liable to forget: an umbrella, an **alarm clock,** safety pins, rubber bands, a flashlight, earplugs, garbage bags, and a small calculator.

Important Documents: Don't forget your passport, traveler's checks, ATM and/or credit cards, adequate ID, and photocopies of all of the aforementioned in case these documents are lost or stolen (p. 9).

SAFETY AND HEALTH

GENERAL ADVICE

While many parts of Eastern Europe are considered safe for travel, safety considerations vary from country to country. The new EU members, in particular, have been working to improve tourist infrastructure in recent years, making parts of the region increasingly stable for travelers. The Czech Republic and Poland, for instance, are as safe as—if not safer than—Western Europe and are far removed from the situation in the Balkans. In most countries, you will find that crime is restricted primarily to pickpocketing on busy streets and public transportation. Travelers should exercise caution when taking night trains due to recent robberies. For more information, see **Night Trains,** p. 27. For concerns specific to individual regions, see the **Essentials: Health and Safety** section of each country chapter.

In any type of crisis situation, the most important thing to do is **stay calm.** Your country's embassy abroad (p. 9) is usually your best resource when things go wrong; registering with that embassy upon arrival in the country is often a good idea. The government offices listed in the **Travel Advisories** box (p. 19) can provide information on the services they offer their citizens in case of emergencies abroad.

LOCAL LAWS AND POLICE

Laws in Russia tend to be stricter than elsewhere in the region, especially for foreigners. For more details, see Russia's **Essentials** section, p. 563.

DRUGS AND ALCOHOL

Remember that you are subject to the laws of the country in which you travel, not to those of your home country. Throughout Eastern Europe, recreational drugs—including marijuana—are illegal, and often carry a much heavier jail sentence than in the West. For more specific information on the drug laws of Eastern European countries, consult the website at the US State Department's Bureau for International Narcotics and Law Enforcement Affairs (www.state.gov/g/inl/). If you carry **prescription drugs** while you travel, bring a copy of the prescriptions themselves and a note from a doctor. Alcohol laws vary throughout the region; be familiar with local laws if this issue may affect you. The legal drinking age in most Eastern European countries is 18.

SPECIFIC CONCERNS

TERRORISM

As a result of the Sept. 11, 2001 attacks on the US, airports throughout the world have heightened security. Terrorist acts are rare in Eastern Europe, and potentially violent situations are confined to the volatile regions of Russia. Terrorism in Russia has been blamed on **Chechen separatists,** a largely Muslim ethnic group in the Russian Caucasus region.

TRAVEL ADVISORIES. The following government offices provide travel information and advisories by telephone, by fax, or via the web:

Australian Department of Foreign Affairs and Trade: ☎ 1300 555 135; www.dfat.gov.au.

Canadian Department of Foreign Affairs and International Trade (DFAIT): ☎ 800-267-8376; www.dfait-maeci.gc.ca. Call for their free booklet, *Bon Voyage...But.*

New Zealand Ministry of Foreign Affairs: ☎ 044 398 000; www.mft.govt.nz/travel/index.html.

United Kingdom Foreign and Commonwealth Office: ☎ 020 7008 1500; www.fco.gov.uk.

US Department of State: ☎ 202-647-5225; http://travel.state.gov. Visit the website for the booklet *A Safe Trip Abroad.*

ESSENTIALS

PERSONAL SAFETY

EXPLORING AND TRAVELING

To avoid unwanted attention, try to blend in as much as possible. Consider adopting the dress prevalent in the country where you are traveling. For women, skirts may be more appropriate than shorts and, for both men and women, it may be best to avoid baggy jeans, sneakers, and sandals, as well as flashy, brightly colored clothing. Backpacks also make one stand out as a tourist; courier or **shoulder bags** are less likely to draw attention, though in countries such as the Czech Republic, they are considered too effeminate for men. Familiarize yourself with your surroundings before setting out, and carry yourself with confidence. Check maps in shops and restaurants rather than on the street. If you are traveling alone, be sure someone at home knows your itinerary, and never admit that you're by yourself. When walking at night, stick to busy, well-lit streets and avoid dark alleyways. If you ever feel uncomfortable, leave the area as quickly and directly as you can.

As much as you may be tempted, do not "explore" in eastern Croatia: the countryside is littered with **landmines** and **unexploded ordnance (UXO).** While de-mining is underway, it will be years before all the mines are removed. UXOs are not a danger on paved roads or in major cities. Road shoulders and abandoned buildings are particularly likely to harbor UXOs.

There is no sure-fire way to avoid every threatening situation you might encounter while traveling, but a good self-defense course will give you concrete ways to react to unwanted advances. **Impact, Prepare, and Model Mugging** (☎ 614-221-2811) can refer you to local self-defense courses in the US. Visit www.impactsafety.org for a list of nearby chapters. Workshops (2-3hr.) start at US$50; full courses (20hr.) cost US$350-500.

If you are using a car, learn local driving signals and wear a seatbelt. Children under 40 lb. should ride only in specially designed carseats, available for a small fee from most car rental agencies. Study route maps before you hit the road, and, if you plan on spending a lot of time driving, consider bringing spare parts. Be sure to learn the local roadside assistance number. Park your vehicle in a garage or well-traveled area, and use a steering wheel locking device in larger cities. **Sleeping in your car** is one of the most dangerous (and often illegal) ways to get your rest. For info on the perils of **hitchhiking,** see p. 32. Most countries in Eastern Europe require an International Driving Permit for foreigners intending to travel by car.

POSSESSIONS AND VALUABLES

Never leave your belongings unattended; crime occurs in even the most demure-looking hostel or hotel. Bring your own padlock for hostel lockers, and don't ever store valuables in any locker. Be particularly careful on **buses** and **trains;** horror stories abound about determined thieves who strike while travelers are sleeping. Carry your backpack in front of you where you can see it. When traveling with others, sleep in shifts. When alone, use good judgment in selecting a train compartment: never stay in an empty one, and use a lock to secure your pack to the luggage rack. Try to sleep on top bunks with your luggage stored above you (if not in bed with you), and keep important documents and valuables on your person.

There are a few steps you can take to minimize the financial risk associated with traveling. First, **bring as little with you as possible.** Second, buy a few combination **padlocks** to secure your belongings either in your pack or in a hostel or train station locker. Third, **carry as little cash as possible.** Keep your traveler's checks and ATM/credit cards in a **money belt**—not a "fanny pack"—along with your passport and ID cards. Fourth, **keep a small cash reserve separate from your primary stash.** This should be about US$50 (US$ or EUR€ are best) sewn into or stored in the depths of your pack, along with traveler's check numbers and important photocopies.

In large cities like Prague, Budapest, and Bucharest, **con artists** often work in groups and may involve children. Beware of certain classics: sob stories that require money, rolls of bills "found" on the street, mustard spilled (or saliva spit) onto your shoulder to distract you while they snatch your bag. **Never let your passport or your bags out of your sight.** Beware of **pickpockets** in city crowds, especially on public transportation. Also, be alert in public telephone booths. If you must say your calling card number, do so very quietly; if you punch it in, make sure no one can look over your shoulder.

If you will be traveling with electronic devices, such as a laptop computer or a PDA, check whether your homeowner's insurance covers loss, theft, or damage when you travel. If not, you might consider purchasing a low-cost separate insurance policy. **Safeware** (☎ 800-800-1492; www.safeware.com) specializes in covering computers and charges US$90 for 90-day comprehensive international travel coverage up to US$4000.

PRE-DEPARTURE HEALTH

In your **passport,** write the names of those you wish to be contacted in case of a medical emergency; also list any allergies or medical conditions you want doctors to be aware of. Matching a **prescription** to a foreign equivalent may not be safe or possible. Carry up-to-date, legible prescriptions or a statement from your doctor with the medication's trade name, manufacturer, chemical name, and dosage.

IMMUNIZATIONS AND PRECAUTIONS

For travel to Eastern Europe, the Center for Disease Control (CDC) recommends up-to-date vaccinations for **MMR** (measles, mumps, and rubella), **DTaP** or **Td** (diphtheria, tetanus, and pertussis), **OPV** (polio), **HbCV** (haemophilus influenza B), and **HBV** (Hepatitis B), **Hepatitis A,** and **Typhoid.** Adults traveling to Russia or Ukraine should consider getting an additional dose of **polio** vaccine if they have not already had one during their adult years. The viral infection tickborne encephalitis occurs principally in Central Europe, so avoid wildlife areas where possible. Bulgaria requires documentation verifying that you are **HIV negative** in order to issue visas for periods longer than one month to study or work in the country. Russia and Ukraine both require documentation of HIV-negative to issue visas longer than 90 days. The Slovak Republic and Hungary require documentation for persons staying longer than one year. Latvia and Lithuania require documentation for those seeking a residency permit. A **rabies** vaccine is recommended due to stray dogs in Eastern Europe, especially in Latvia. For recommendations on immunizations, consult the CDC (p. 21) in the US or the equivalent in your home country.

INSURANCE

Travel insurance covers four basic areas: medical/health problems, property loss, trip cancellation/interruption, and emergency evacuation. Though regular insurance policies may well extend to travel-related accidents, you may consider purchasing separate travel insurance if the cost of potential trip cancellation, interruption, or emergency medical evacuation is greater than you can absorb. Prices for travel insurance purchased separately generally run about US$50 per week for full coverage, while trip cancellation/interruption may be purchased separately at a rate of US$3-5 per day depending on length of stay.

Medical insurance (especially university policies) often covers costs incurred abroad; check with your provider. **US Medicare** generally does not cover foreign travel; **Canadian** provincial health insurance plans increasingly do not either. Check with the provincial Ministry of Health or Health Plan Headquarters for details. **Homeowners' insurance** (or your family's coverage) often covers theft during travel and loss of travel documents (passport, plane ticket, etc.) up to US$500.

ISIC and **ITIC** (p. 11) provide basic insurance benefits to US cardholders, including US$100 per day of in-hospital sickness for up to 60 days and US$5000 of accident-related medical reimbursement (see www.isicus.com for details). Cardholders have access to a toll-free 24hr. helpline for medical, legal, and financial emergencies overseas. **American Express** (☎800-528-4800) grants most cardholders automatic collision and theft car rental insurance, and ground travel accident coverage of US$100,000 on flight purchases made with the card.

. **STA** (p. 25) offers a range of **insurance plans** that can supplement your basic coverage. Other private insurance providers in the US and Canada include: Access America (☎800-284-8300; www.acessamerica.com), Berkely Group (☎800-797-4514; www.berkely.com), CSA Travel Protection (☎800-873-9855; www.csatravelprotection.com/comfort), Travel Assistance International (☎800-821-2828; www.europ-assistance.com), and Travel Guard (☎800-826-4919; www.travelguard.com). Columbus Direct (☎020 7375 0011; www.columbusdirect.co.uk) operates in the UK, and AFTA (☎02 9264 3299; www.afta.com.au) in Australia.

USEFUL ORGANIZATIONS AND PUBLICATIONS

The US **Centers for Disease Control and Prevention** (**CDC**; ☎877-FYI-TRIP; www.cdc.gov/travel) maintains an international travelers' hotline and an informative website. The CDC's comprehensive booklet, *Health Information for International Travel* (The Yellow Book), an annual rundown of disease, immunization, and general health advice, is free online or US$40 from the Public Health Foundation (☎877-252-1200; http://bookstore.phf.org). Consult the appropriate government agency of your home country for consular information sheets on health, entry requirements, and other issues abroad. For quick information on health and other travel warnings, call the **Overseas Citizens Services** (M-F 8am-8pm; ☎888-407-4747, after hours 202-647-4000, from overseas 317-472-2328), or contact a passport agency, embassy, or consulate abroad. For information on medical evacuation services and travel insurance firms, see the **British Foreign and Commonwealth Office** (www.fco.gov.uk). For general health info, contact the **American Red Cross** (☎800-564-1234; www.redcross.org).

STAYING HEALTHY

Common sense is the simplest prescription for good health while you travel. Drink lots of fluids to prevent dehydration and constipation, and wear sturdy, broken-in shoes and clean socks.

ONCE IN EASTERN EUROPE

ENVIRONMENTAL HAZARDS

Dehydration: Common sense is the simplest prescription for good health while traveling. Drink water to prevent dehydration. Since tap water quality in Eastern Europe is highly variable, in some countries you will need to buy bottled water or boil your own. It is particularly important to avoid tap water in Russia and Ukraine, but a good general principle to drink bottled water throughout the region.

Hypothermia and frostbite: A rapid drop in body temperature is the clearest sign of overexposure to cold. Victims may also shiver, feel exhausted, have poor coordination or slurred speech, hallucinate, or suffer amnesia. *Do not let hypothermia victims fall asleep.* To avoid hypothermia, keep dry, wear layers, and stay out of the wind. When the temperature is below freezing, watch out for frostbite. If skin turns white or blue, waxy, and cold, do not rub the area. Drink warm beverages, stay dry, and slowly warm the area with dry fabric or steady body contact until a doctor can be found.

High Altitude: Allow your body a couple of days to adjust to less oxygen before exerting yourself. Note that alcohol is more potent and UV rays are stronger at high elevations.

INSECT-BORNE DISEASES

Many diseases are transmitted by insects—mainly mosquitoes, fleas, ticks, and lice. Be aware of insects in wet or forested areas; wear long pants and long sleeves, tuck your pants into your socks, and buy a mosquito net. Use insect repellents such as DEET and spray your gear with permethrin.

Tickborne Encephalitis: A viral infection of the central nervous system transmitted by tick bites or by unpasteurized dairy products. Occurs in wooded areas of Croatia, the Czech Republic, Estonia, Latvia, the Slovak Republic, Slovenia, and less frequently in Bulgaria and Romania. Vaccination recommended for those traveling in these areas for more than 3 weeks during warm weather months. Risk of contraction low when precautions are taken.

Lyme Disease: A bacterial infection carried by ticks and marked by a circular bull's-eye rash of 2cm or more. Later symptoms include fever, headache, fatigue, and aches. Antibiotics are effective if administered early. Left untreated, Lyme disease can cause problems in the joints, heart, and nervous system. Travelers spending time in wooded areas in Eastern Europe are more likely to be exposed to ticks. If you find a tick, grasp the head with tweezers as close to your skin as possible and apply slow, steady traction. Removing a tick within 36hr. reduces the risk of infection. Do not remove ticks by burning them or by coating them with nail polish remover or petroleum jelly.

FOOD- AND WATER-BORNE DISEASES

Prevention is the best cure: be sure that your food is properly cooked and the water you drink is clean. Peel fruits and vegetables and avoid tap water (including ice cubes and anything washed in tap water, like salad). Other culprits are raw shellfish, unpasteurized milk, and sauces containing raw eggs. Buy imported bottled water, or purify your own water by bringing it to a rolling boil or treating it with **iodine tablets.** Food- and water-borne diseases are the primary illnesses that affect travelers to Eastern Europe.

Hepatitis A: A viral infection of the liver caused by contaminated water, ice, shellfish, and unwashed produce. Symptoms include fatigue, fever, loss of appetite, nausea, dark urine, jaundice, vomiting, aches and pains, and light stools. The illness can range from mild symptoms over 1-2 weeks to a more severe illness lasting several months. Travelers are at risk of contracting the infection; the risk is highest in the countryside, but it may also be present in urban areas. Ask your doctor about the vaccine (Havrix or Vaqta) or an injection of immune globulin (IG; formerly called gamma globulin).

Typhoid Fever: Caused by the salmonella bacteria. Common in villages and rural areas in the developing regions of Eastern Europe. Though mostly transmitted through contaminated food and water, it may also be acquired by direct contact with another person. Early symptoms include fever, headaches, fatigue, loss of appetite, constipation, and a rash on the abdomen or chest. Antibiotics can treat typhoid, but a vaccination (70-90% effective) is recommended for all travelers to affected regions.

OTHER INFECTIOUS DISEASES

Diphtheria: The 1990s saw a massive diphtheria outbreak in the former Soviet Union, and travelers to this area are still at risk for this highly infectious disease. Early symptoms, including severe sore throat, swollen lymph nodes, and fever, can lead to paralysis, heart failure, and death. Be up-to-date on diphtheria vaccinations before traveling.

Hepatitis B: A viral infection of the liver transmitted via bodily fluids (i.e., sexual contact or needle sharing). Symptoms may not surface until years after initial infection; they include jaundice, loss of appetite, fever, and joint pain. A 3-shot vaccination sequence is recommended for health-care workers, sexually active travelers, and those planning to seek medical treatment abroad; it must begin 6 months before traveling. Chronic HBV is not particularly common in Eastern Europe, with the exception of Russia, where rates are slightly higher.

Rabies: Transmitted through the saliva of infected animals. Fatal if untreated. By the time symptoms (thirst and muscle spasms) appear, the disease is in its terminal stage. If you are bitten, wash the wound thoroughly, and seek immediate medical care. Try to have the animal located. Exposure is treated by a 28-day regimen of rabies vaccine and immune globin injections in a 5-shot series. A rabies vaccine (3 shots given over a 21-day period) is available but only semi-effective. Those who will be exposed to or handling wild animals should consider getting the vaccine.

Tuberculosis: Tuberculosis (TB) is on the rise throughout Eastern Europe. Symptoms include fever, persistent cough, and bloody phlegm. TB is usually transmitted by breathing air in an enclosed area with an infected person. If untreated, the disease is fatal. It usually responds to antibiotics. If you think you are infected, tell your doctor you have been to Eastern Europe recently, as the recent return of TB indicates a drug-resistant strain that requires special treatment.

AIDS and HIV: For detailed information on **Acquired Immune Deficiency Syndrome (AIDS)** in Eastern Europe, call the **US Centers for Disease Control's** 24hr. traveler's hotline (☎877-394-8747), or contact the **Joint United Nations Programme on HIV/AIDS (UNAIDS),** 20 ave. Appia, CH-1211 Geneva 27, Switzerland (☎41 22 791 3666; fax 22 791 4187). Note that several countries in Eastern Europe, including Bulgaria, Hungary, Russia, the Slovak Republic, and Ukraine, require documentation that you are HIV-negative if you are those planning an extended visit for work or study; some of these countries deny entrance to those who test HIV-positive.

OTHER HEALTH CONCERNS

MEDICAL CARE ON THE ROAD

The quality and availability of medical assistance varies greatly throughout Eastern Europe. In Westernized cities, like Prague and Budapest, there are generally English-speaking medical centers or hospitals for foreigners; the care there tends to be better than elsewhere in the region. In rural areas and the more impoverished regions of countries such as Russia and Romania, adequate and English-speaking health facilities may be impossible to find. In the event of an emergency, go to your embassy for aid and recommendations. Tourist offices sometimes have the names of local doctors who speak English. The quality of medical service varies from region to region, although few hospitals are maintained at Western standards. Private hospitals will generally have better facilities than the state-operated hospitals. For more specific information about healthcare, see the **Safety and Health** section of the chapter for the country to which you are traveling.

Special support services are available for those concerned about access to medical support while traveling. The *MedPass* from **GlobalCare, Inc.,** 6875 Shiloh Rd. E., Alpharetta, GA 30005, USA (☎800-860-1111; www.globalcare.net), provides 24hr. international medical assistance, support, and medical evacuation resources. The **International Association for Medical Assistance to Travelers (IAMAT;** US ☎716-754-4883, Canada 416-652-0137; www.iamat.org) has free membership and lists English-speaking doctors worldwide. If your **insurance** policy does not cover travel abroad, you may wish to purchase additional coverage.

Those with medical conditions (diabetes, allergies to antibiotics, epilepsy, heart conditions) may want to obtain a stainless-steel **MedicAlert ID tag** (1st year US$35, annually thereafter US$20), which identifies the condition and gives a 24hr. collect-call number. Contact the **MedicAlert Foundation,** 2323 Colorado Ave., Turlock, CA 95382, USA (☎888-633-4298, outside US 209-668-3333; www.medicalert.org).

WOMEN'S HEALTH

Women traveling in unsanitary conditions are vulnerable to **urinary tract** and **bladder infections,** common and very uncomfortable bacterial conditions that cause a burning sensation and painful urination. If symptoms persist, see a doctor.

Tampons and **pads** are hard to find in some areas of Eastern Europe. It's advisable to take supplies along. **Reliable contraceptive devices** may also be difficult to find. Women on birth control pills should bring enough to allow for possible loss or extended stays. Condoms are increasingly available but usually expensive and variable in quality.

GETTING TO EASTERN EUROPE

BY PLANE

When it comes to airfare, a little effort can save you a bundle. If your plans are flexible enough to deal with the restrictions, courier flights are the cheapest. Tickets bought from consolidators and standby seating are also good deals, but last-minute specials, airfare wars, and charter flights often beat these fares. Students, seniors, and those under 26 should never pay full price for a ticket.

AIRFARES

Airfares to Eastern Europe peak roughly between mid-June and early September (high season); holidays are also expensive. The cheapest times to travel are November through mid-December and mid-January through March. Midweek (M-Th mornings) round-trip flights run US$40-100 cheaper than weekend flights, but they are generally more crowded and less likely to permit frequent-flier upgrades. Not fixing a return date ("open return") or arriving in and departing from different cities ("open jaw") can be pricier than round-trip flights. Patching one-way flights together is the most expensive way to travel. For those willing to make the extra effort, the least expensive route is often to fly into London and connect to one of the many discounted flights that carriers such as EasyJet (www.easyjet.com) and RyanAir (www.ryanair.com) make to Eastern Europe. Another cheap option is to fly into London, Paris, Munich, or Milan and reach your destination by train or bus.

If your destination is only one stop on a more extensive globe-hop, consider a round-the-world (RTW) ticket. Tickets usually include at least five stops and are valid for about a year; prices range US$1200-5000. Try **Northwest Airlines/KLM** (☎800-447-4747; www.nwa.com) or **Star Alliance,** a consortium of 16 airlines including United Airlines (☎800-538-2929; www.staralliance.com). Round-trip commercial **fares** to the larger, more touristed cities (Budapest, Prague, Warsaw) from the US or Canadian east coast can usually be found, with some work, for US$600-800 in high season; from the UK, UK£100-180; from Australia, AUS$3000-4000; from New Zealand, NZ$3000-3500. Tickets to mid-range cities, including Bucharest, Moscow, Sofia, and Zagreb, generally cost about US$200 more, while Bratislava, Kyiv, and the Baltic capitals can cost US$1000-1400/UK£400-600/AUS$4000-5000/NZ$5000-7000. Prices drop US$200-500 the rest of the year. For Eastern European-based flights, there are a number of new discount airlines, including SkyEurope (www.skyeurope.com), which have cheap fares to the major cities and some hubs in Western Europe.

BUDGET AND STUDENT TRAVEL AGENCIES

While knowledgeable agents specializing in flights to Eastern Europe can make your life easy and help you save, they may not spend the time to find you the lowest possible fare—they get paid on commission. Travelers holding **ISICs** and **IYTCs** qualify for big discounts from student travel agencies. Most flights from budget agencies are on major airlines, but in peak season some may sell seats on less reliable chartered aircraft.

STA Travel, 5900 Wilshire Blvd., Ste. 900, Los Angeles, CA 90036, USA (24hr. reservations and info ☎800-781-4040; www.sta-travel.com). A student and youth travel organization with over 150 offices worldwide (check their website for a listing of all their offices), including US offices in Boston, Chicago, L.A., New York, San Francisco, Seattle, and Washington, D.C. Ticket booking, travel insurance, railpasses, and more. Walk-in offices are located throughout Australia (☎1300 733 035), New Zealand (☎0508 782 872), and the UK (☎0870 1 600 599).

Travel CUTS (Canadian Universities Travel Services Limited), 187 College St., Toronto, ON M5T 1P7, CAN (☎1-866-246-9762; www.travelcuts.com). Offices across Canada and the US including Los Angeles, New York, Seattle, and San Francisco.

USIT, 19/21 Aston Quay, Dublin 2, IRE (☎01 602 1904; www.usitworld.ie). Ireland's leading student/budget travel agency has 22 offices throughout Northern Ireland and the Republic of Ireland.

Wasteels, Skoubogade 6, 1158 Copenhagen K., DEN (☎3314 4633; www.wasteels.com). A huge chain with 180 locations across Europe. Sells Wasteels BIJ tickets discounted 30-45% off regular fare, 2nd-class international point-to-point train tickets with unlimited stopovers for those under 26 (sold only in Europe).

COMMERCIAL AIRLINES

The commercial airlines' lowest regular offer is the **APEX** (Advance Purchase Excursion) fare, which provides confirmed reservations and allows "open-jaw" tickets. Generally, reservations must be made one to three weeks ahead of departure. Book peak-season APEX fares early. Use **Expedia** (www.expedia.com) or **Travelocity** (www.travelocity.com) to get an idea of the lowest published fares, then use the resources outlined here to try and beat those fares. Low-season fares should be appreciably cheaper than **high-season** counterparts.

TRAVELING FROM NORTH AMERICA

Air France: France ☎33 820 820 820, US and Canada 800-237-2747; www.airfrance.com. Covers much of Eastern Europe via Western Europe.

FLIGHT PLANNING ON THE INTERNET. The Internet may be the budget traveler's dream when it comes to finding and booking bargain fares, but the array of options can be overwhelming. Many airline sites offer special last-minute deals on the Web: **STA** (www.sta-travel.com) and **StudentUniverse** (www.studentuniverse.com) provide quotes on student tickets, while **Orbitz** (www.orbitz.com), **Expedia** (www.expedia.com), and **Travelocity** (www.travelocity.com) offer full travel services. **Priceline** (www.priceline.com) lets you specify a price and obligates you to buy any ticket that meets or beats it; **Hotwire** (www.hotwire.com) offers bargain fares but won't reveal the airline or flight times until you buy. Other sites that compile deals for you include www.bestfares.com, www.flights.com, www.lowestfare.com, www.onetravel.com, and www.travelzoo.com. For those flying from within Europe, **EasyJet** (www.easyjet.com) offers inexpensive flights from London to Prague and Budapest, and **SkyEurope** (www.skyeurope.com) has cheap flights between the major Eastern European cities and to London. Increasingly, there are online tools available to help sift through multiple offers; **SideStep** (www.sidestep.com/air) and **Booking Buddy** (www.bookingbuddy.com) let you enter your trip information once and search multiple sites. An indispensable resource on the Internet is the **Air Traveler's Handbook** (www.faqs.org/faqs/travel/air/handbook), a comprehensive listing of links to everything you need to know before you board a plane.

Austrian Airways: UK ☎87 0124 2625, US and Canada 800-843-0002; www.aua.com. Connects to many Eastern European cities via Vienna.

Delta Air Lines: US and Canada ☎800-221-1212, UK 800 41 4767; www.delta.com. A reliable US carrier serving Eastern Europe.

Finnair: ☎800-950-4768; www.us.finnair.com. Cheap round-trips from San Francisco, New York, and Toronto to Helsinki; connections throughout Europe.

KLM: ☎870 507 40 74; www.klm.com. Connects to a number of cities in Eastern Europe via Amsterdam.

Lufthansa: Canada ☎800-563-5954, US 800-645-3880; www.lufthansa.com. Has a wide variety of routes covering most of Eastern Europe.

TRAVELING FROM THE UK AND IRELAND

The **Air Travel Advisory Bureau** in London (☎0870 737 0021; www.atab.co.uk) gives referrals to agencies and consolidators that offer discounted airfares from the UK.

Aer Lingus: Ireland ☎1 886 8844; www.aerlingus.ie. Return tickets from Dublin, Cork, and Shannon to Amsterdam, Bologna, Brussels, Copenhagen, Düsseldorf, Frankfurt, Lisbon, Madrid, Málaga, Milan, Munich, Nice, Paris, Rome, Vienna, and Zürich.

British Airways: UK ☎87 0850 9850, Canada and US 800-247-9297; www.britishairways.com. Flies into most large cities in Eastern Europe.

SAS: UK ☎20 8990 7159, US and Canada 800-221-2350; www.scandinavian.net. Reliably connects to Baltic cities.

FROM AUSTRALIA AND NEW ZEALAND

Air New Zealand: ☎800 737 000; www.airnewzealand.com. Reasonable fares from Auckland to London and special sales at much lower prices.

Lufthansa: Australia ☎13 0065 5727, New Zealand 800 94 5220; www.lufthansa.com. Offers reliable flights that connect to a number of cities throughout Eastern Europe.

Qantas: Australia ☎13 13 13, New Zealand 9 357 8900; www.qantas.com. Flies from cities in Australia and New Zealand to London, where connecting flights are easy to find.

TICKET CONSOLIDATORS

Ticket consolidators buy unsold tickets in bulk from commercial airlines and sell them at discounted rates. Not all of them are reliable, so insist on a receipt that gives full details of restrictions, refunds, and tickets, and pay by credit card (in spite of the 2-5% fee) so you can stop payment if you never receive your tickets. For more info, see www.travel-library.com/air-travel/consolidators.html.
NOW Voyager, 45 W. 21st St., Ste. 5A, New York, NY 10010 (☎212-459-1616; www.nowvoyagertravel.com) arranges discounted flights, mostly from New York, to Barcelona, London, Madrid, Milan, Paris, and Rome. Other consolidators worth trying are **Rebel** (☎800-732-3588; www.rebeltours.com), **Cheap Tickets** (☎888-922-8849; www.cheaptickets.com). Yet more consolidators on the web include **Flights.com** (www.flights.com) and **TravelHUB** (www.travelhub.com). *Let's Go* does not endorse any of these agencies. As always, be cautious, and research companies before you hand over your credit card number. In London, the **Air Travel Advisory Bureau** (☎87 0737 0021; www.atab.co.uk) provides names of consolidators and discount flight specialists. From Australia and New Zealand, look for consolidator ads in the *Sydney Morning Herald* and other papers.

BY TRAIN

Flying into a Western European city and then taking a train to Eastern Europe often proves to be the cheapest option. Many travelers fly into Milan to connect by train to the Balkans; Munich or Berlin to reach Poland, the Baltics, and Ukraine; and Vienna for the short train ride to the Czech and Slovak Republics and Hungary. Check out **transit visa** requirements if you plan on passing through other Eastern European countries en route to your final destination. Those touring the EU on their way to or from Eastern Europe might consider a **Eurailpass**—keep in mind that it is **not valid in Eastern Europe,** with the exception of Hungary. Trains in Eastern Europe are generally a reliable means of travel, as trains run both within countries and across national borders. Rail infrastructure is slightly weaker, however, in areas of the Balkans. Dubrovnik, Croatia is not connected by rail.

 NIGHT TRAINS. Try to avoid night trains, especially on lines that connect Warsaw or Kraków with Prague, Budapest, or Berlin. Theft is rampant on these trains, and staying awake or traveling with a friend sometimes is no help: many travelers have reported a scam in which groups of thieves board the night train and pass cannisters of sleeping gas beneath the doors of train compartments. Travelers pass out, then wake to discover that they have been robbed.

BY BOAT

Ferries in the **North** and **Baltic Seas** are reliable and comfortable. Those in the **Black Sea** are less predictable, and traveling between the coasts of Romania, Bulgaria, Ukraine, and Russia is no easy task. Those content with deck passage rarely need to book ahead but should check in a few hours early and allow extra time to get to the port. **Polferries** (☎91 32 26 140; www.polferries.pl), in Poland, go from Świnoujście, Poland to **Ronne, DEN** (6hr.) and **Ystad, SWE** (7hr.) and from Gdańsk, Poland to **Oxelösund-Stockholm** (17hr.) and **Nynäshamn** (7hr.), both in Sweden. **Silja Line** (US ☎800-533-3755; www.silja.com) leaves Helsinki, FIN to **Rīga, LAT** (17hr., mid-June to Dec.), **St. Petersburg, RUS** (15hr., May 1-Sept. 27), and **Tallinn, EST** (3hr., June to mid-Sept.). Also Turku, EST to **Stockholm, SWE** (12hr., Jan. -Sept.).

GETTING AROUND EASTERN EUROPE

Fares are either **single** (one-way) or **return** (round-trip). "Period returns" require you to return within a specific time frame; "day return" means you must return on the same day. Unless stated otherwise, *Let's Go* always lists single fares. Round-trip fares in Eastern Europe are usually less than double the one-way fare.

BY PLANE

 AIRLINE SAFETY. The airlines of the former Soviet Republics do not always meet safety standards, especially for internal flights. When flying within Eastern Europe, it's often safest to spend the few extra rubles and book a seat on a Western airline rather than a domestic carrier. When a foreign carrier is not an option, the *Official Airline Guide* (www.oag.com) and many travel agencies can tell you the type and age of aircraft on a particular route. The **International Airline Passengers Association** (US ☎800-821-4272, UK 020 8681 6555; www.iapa.com) provides region-specific safety information. The American **Federal Aviation Administration** (☎866-835-5322; www.faa.gov) reviews the airline authorities for countries whose airlines enter the US.

Flying across Eastern Europe on regularly scheduled flights can devour your budget, but if you're short on time (or flush with cash) you might consider it. Student travel agencies sell cheap tickets, and budget fares are often available in the spring and summer on popular routes. Consult budget travel agents and local newspapers for more info. A number of European airlines offer discount coupon packets. Most are available only as tack-ons for transatlantic passengers, but some are stand-alone offers. Most must be purchased before departure. **SkyEurope** is a new discount airline specifically serving Eastern Europe, with cheap fares between most major cities (☎2 4850 4850; www.skyeurope.com). **Europe by Air** (☎888-387-2479; www.europebyair.com) offers a *FlightPass* (US$99 per flight) that allows you to country-hop between over 150 European cities. **SAS** (☎800-221-2350; www.scandinavian.net) sells one-way coupons for travel within the Baltics and greater Europe. Most are available only to transatlantic SAS passengers, but some **United** and **Lufthansa** passengers also qualify (US$65-225).

BY BUS OR TRAIN

Second-class seating on Eastern European trains is pleasant, and compartments, which fit two to six, are great places to meet fellow travelers. Trains, however, are not always safe in terms of personal safety, especially at night. For safety tips, see **Safety and Health,** p. 18. For long trips make sure you are on the correct car, as trains sometimes split at crossroads. Destinations listed in parentheses on Eastern European train schedules require a train switch, usually at the town listed immediately before the parenthesis. When traveling through Eastern Europe by train, you can either buy a **railpass**, which allows you unlimited travel within a particular region for a given period of time, or rely on buying individual **point-to-point tickets** as you go, which is generally a much better value. Almost all countries give students or youths (under 26) discounts on domestic rail tickets, and many sell a student or youth card that provides 20-50% off all fares.

Some Eastern European countries require **transit visas** for all travelers just passing through the country by train; for example, trains from Central Europe must pass through Belarus to reach the Baltics or Russia. Be aware that some domestic

trains in Ukraine pass through Moldova, which requires a transit visa. To avoid getting detained in Minsk, Chişinău, or elsewhere, have your paperwork in order or ensure that your route works around countries with transit visas. For more information, consult the **Visa and Entry Information** section of each country.

Many train stations have different counters for domestic and international tickets, seat reservations, and information—check before lining up. Seat reservations (usually US$3-10) are only required on select trains (usually major international lines), but you are not guaranteed a seat without one. Reservations are available on major trains as much as two months in advance, and Europeans often reserve far ahead of time. The Moscow-St. Petersburg train is famous for selling out weeks in advance during the summer.

All over Eastern Europe, buses reach rural areas inaccessible by train. In addition, long-distance bus networks may be more extensive, efficient, and sometimes more comfortable than train services. In the Balkans, air-conditioned buses run by private companies are a godsend. **Contiki Holidays,** 801 E. Katella Ave., 3rd fl., Anaheim, CA 92805, USA (☎866-266-8454; www.contiki.com) offers a variety of European vacation packages designed exclusively for 18- to 35-year-olds. For an average cost of US$65 per day, tours include accommodations, transportation, guided sightseeing, and some meals. **Eurolines,** 4 Cardiff Rd., Luton, Bedfordshire, L41 1PP, UK (☎990 14 32 19; www.eurolines.com), is Europe's largest coach operator, offering passes (UK£113-299) for unlimited 15-, 30-, or 60-day travel between 500 destinations in 25 countries, including many spots in Eastern Europe and Russia. It has offices in most countries in Eastern Europe; see website for details.

READING AND RESOURCES ON TRAIN TRAVEL.
Info on rail travel and railpasses: www.raileurope.com.
Point-to-point fares and schedules: www.raileurope.com/us/rail/
fares_schedules/index.htm. Allows you to calculate whether buying a railpass will save you money.
European Railway Server: www.railfaneurope.net. Links to rail servers throughout Europe.

BY CAR

Public transportation is generally the best way to get around in Eastern Europe, and travelers unfamiliar with the region and its roads will likely find catching a bus or train more efficient than driving. Because car rental prices in Eastern Europe can be among the highest on the continent and gas (petrol) is not always readily available (particularly unleaded), travel by bus, train, and sometimes even by plane, can be a cheaper alternative to hitting the road. Roads are often poorly maintained, and roadside assistance rarely exists, contributing to some of the highest driving fatality rates in the world. In recent years, a network of limited access highways has been expanding in Eastern Europe, such as an expressway linking Budapest to Vienna. On the whole, conditions worsen the farther east you travel. As driving gains popularity in Central Europe, however, support services for drivers have been on the rise in countries like the Czech Republic, Hungary, and Poland. If you do choose to strike off on your own, know the laws of the countries in which you'll be driving and read up on local road conditions. For an informal primer on European road signs and conventions, check out www.travlang.com/signs. The **Association for Safe International Road Travel (ASIRT),** 11769 Gainsborough Rd., Potomac, MD 20854, USA (☎301-983-5252; www.asirt.org), can provide more specific information about road conditions.

DRIVING PRECAUTIONS. When traveling in the summer or in the desert, bring substantial amounts of water (a suggested 5L of **water** per person per day) for drinking and for the radiator. For long drives to unpopulated areas, register with police before beginning the trek, and again upon arrival at the destination. Check with the local automobile club for details. When traveling for long distances, make sure tires are in good repair and have enough air, and get good maps. A **compass** and a **car manual** can also be very useful. You should always carry a **spare tire** and **jack, jumper cables, extra oil, flares,** a **flashlight,** and **heavy blankets** (in case your car breaks down at night or in the winter). If you don't know how to **change a tire,** learn before heading out, especially if you are planning on traveling in deserted areas. Blowouts on dirt roads are exceedingly common. If you do have a breakdown, **stay in your car;** if you wander off, there's less likelihood trackers will find you.

DRIVING PERMITS AND CAR INSURANCE

INTERNATIONAL DRIVING PERMIT (IDP)

If you plan to drive a car while in Eastern Europe, you should have an International Driving Permit (IDP), though certain countries allow travelers to drive with a valid American, British, or Canadian license for a limited number of months. It is useful to have one anyway, in case you're in an accident or stranded in a small town where the police do not speak English. Information on the IDP is printed in 10 languages, including German and Russian. An IDP, valid for one year, must be issued in your home country. The application requires one or two photos, a current local license, an additional form of identification, and a fee. To apply, contact your home country's automobile association or visit the **International Automobile Driver's Club** (www.driverlicense.net).

CAR INSURANCE

Most credit cards cover standard insurance. If you rent, lease, or borrow a car, you need an **International Insurance Certificate (green card)** to certify that you have liability insurance that applies abroad. You can get a green card at car dealers (for those leasing cars) or rental agencies, some travel agents, and some border crossings. Rental agencies in some countries may require you to purchase theft insurance.

BY BICYCLE

Although bringing your own bike is not worthwhile in most of Eastern Europe, cycling is one of the best ways to explore the region and get off the beaten path, literally. In many countries, especially the Baltic countries, Poland, and Slovenia, **renting** a bike will allow you to see much more of the natural scenery. For more information, consult the **Practical Information** section of the city or town in which you will be traveling.

BY THUMB

Let's Go never recommends hitchhiking as a safe means of transportation, and none of the information presented here is intended to do so.

Hitchhiking involves serious risks, including theft, assault, sexual harassment, and unsafe driving. If you do decide to hitch, consider where you are. Hitching remains relatively common in Eastern Europe, though Westerners are a definite target for theft. In Russia, the Baltics, Poland, and some other Eastern European countries, hitchhiking can be akin to hailing a taxi, and drivers will likely expect to be paid a sum at least equivalent to a bus ticket to your destination.

KEEPING IN TOUCH

The ease of communication varies widely from country to country. In Central European countries, such as Hungary, Poland, and the Czech Republic, postal and telephone systems are as reliable and efficient as in the US and Western Europe. Even the Russian mail system now offers relatively speedy delivery to the West. However, in Bulgaria and Ukraine—particularly outside the capital cities—postal services are less predictable and should not be depended upon. Phone cards can also be problematic throughout the region: double-check with your phone card carrier before departure in order to ensure that their service will allow you to call home. Keeping in touch can be troublesome, inefficient, and downright mind-boggling. For country-specific information, read **Essentials: Keeping in Touch** in each country chapter.

BY EMAIL AND INTERNET

The World Wide Web has made its way into Eastern Europe. Every major city now has some sort of Internet access, usually cybercafes. While it may be more difficult to find in smaller towns and the rural countryside, Internet access is often available in public libraries, hostels, and tourist offices. Rates are reasonable; 1hr. costs US$1-3 on average, though rates fluctuate from country to country.

Though in some places it's possible to forge a remote link with your home server, in most cases this is a much slower (and thus more expensive) option than taking advantage of free web-based email accounts (e.g., www.hotmail.com; www.yahoo.com; and www.gmail.com, which requires an invitation). Travelers with laptops can call an Internet service provider via a modem. Long-distance phone cards specifically intended for such calls can defray normally high phone charges; check with your long-distance phone provider to see if it offers this option. Bringing a laptop is generally a liability, however, and in some countries it may be considered offensive to use one in public. Internet cafes and free Internet terminals at public libraries or universities are listed in the **Practical Information** sections of major cities. For lists of additional cybercafes in Eastern Europe, check out www.cybercafes.com or www.netcafeguide.com.

BY TELEPHONE

CALLING HOME FROM EASTERN EUROPE

A **calling card** is probably cheapest and your best bet. Calls are either billed collect or to your account. You can often call collect without possessing a company's calling card, just by dialing their access number and following the instructions. **To obtain a calling card** from your national telecommunications service before leaving home, contact the appropriate company listed below. Be forewarned that not all calling card companies offer service in every Eastern European country. Before settling on a calling card plan, be sure to research your options in order to pick the one that best fits both your needs and your destination.

To call home with a calling card, contact the local operator for your service provider by dialing the access numbers listed in the **Essentials: Keeping in Touch** section at the beginning of each country chapter and on the inside of the back cover. Not all of these numbers are toll-free; in many countries, phones will require a coin or card deposit to call the operator. Wherever possible, use a calling card for international calls—the long-distance rates for national phone services are often exorbitant. Where available, locally purchased **prepaid phone cards** can be used for direct international calls, but they are still less cost-efficient than calling cards purchased through the service providers listed above. **In-room hotel calls** invariably include an arbitrary and sky-

PLACING INTERNATIONAL CALLS. The international dialing prefixes and country codes of Eastern European nations are listed at the beginning of each country chapter and on the inside of the back cover. To call Eastern Europe from home or to call home from Eastern Europe, dial:

1. The **international dialing prefix.** To dial out of Eastern Europe, use the international dialing prefixes listed at the beginning of each chapter and on the inside of the back cover; **Australia,** 0011; **Canada** or the **US,** 011; the **Republic of Ireland, New Zealand,** or the **UK,** 00. The international dialing prefix for each country in Eastern Europe can be found in the Facts and Figures table of every Essentials chapter.

2. The **country code** of the country you want to call. To call **Australia,** dial 61; **Canada** or the **US,** 1; the **Republic of Ireland,** 353; **New Zealand,** 64; the **UK,** 44; for Eastern European nations, codes are listed at the beginning of each country chapter and on the inside of the back cover.

3. The **city/area code.** *Let's Go* lists the city/area codes for cities and towns in Eastern Europe opposite the city or town name, next to a ☎. Omit initial digits in parentheses (e.g., (0)12 for Kraków) when calling from abroad.

4. The **local number.**

high surcharge and will sometimes charge you for the call even if you use a calling card. You can usually make **direct international calls** from pay phones, but if you aren't using a calling card you may need to drop your coins as quickly as your words.

Placing a **collect call** through an international operator is even more expensive but may be necessary in case of emergency. You can place collect calls through the service providers listed above even if you don't have one of their phone cards. To reach an English-speaking operator, you must dial the phone company access number for the country you're in.

COMPANY	TO OBTAIN A CARD:
AT&T (US)	☎ 800-364-9292 or www.att.com
Canada Direct	☎ 800-561-8868 or www.infocanadadirect.com
MCI (US)	☎ 800-40-00-00 or http://consumer.mci.com
New Zealand Direct	☎ 0800 000 000 or www.telecom.co.nz
Telstra Australia	☎ 13 22 00 or www.telstra.com

CALLING WITHIN EASTERN EUROPE

The simplest way to call within the region is to use a coin-operated phone or to use **prepaid phone cards,** which are slowly phasing out coins in most Eastern European countries. Rates tend to be highest in the morning, lower in the evening, and lowest on Sunday and late at night.

CELLULAR PHONES

The international standard for cell phones is **Global System for Mobile Communication (GSM).** To make and receive calls in Eastern Europe you will need a **GSM-compatible phone** and a **SIM (Subscriber Identity Module) card,** a country-specific, thumbnail-sized chip that gives you a local phone number and plugs you into the local network. Many SIM cards are **prepaid,** meaning that they come with calling time included and you don't need to sign up for a monthly service plan. Incoming calls are frequently free. When you use up the prepaid time, you can buy additional cards or vouchers (usually available at convenience stores) to get more. For more information on GSM phones, check out www.telestial.com, www.orange.co.uk, www.roadpost.com, or www.planetomni.com. Companies like **Cellular Abroad** (www.cellularabroad.com) rent cell phones that work in a variety of destinations around the world, providing a simpler option than picking up a phone in-country.

> **GSM PHONES.** Just having a GSM phone doesn't mean you're necessarily good to go when you travel abroad. The majority of GSM phones sold in the United States operate on a different **frequency** (1900) than international phones (900/1800) and will not work abroad. Tri-band phones work on all three frequencies (900/1800/1900) and will operate through most of the world. As well, some GSM phones are **SIM-locked** and will only accept SIM cards from a single carrier. You'll need a **SIM-unlocked** phone to use a SIM card from a local carrier when you travel.

TIME DIFFERENCES

A map with Eastern European time zones is on the inside back cover of this book—Vancouver, CAN and San Francisco, USA are GMT -8; New York, USA is GMT -5; Sydney, AUS is GMT +10; and Auckland, NZ is GMT +12. All Eastern European countries observe Daylight Saving Time.

GMT + 1				GMT + 2		GMT + 3
Hungary	Croatia	Czech Republic	Latvia	Romania	Bulgaria	Moscow and St. Petersburg
Slovakia	Slovenia	Poland	Estonia	Lithuania	Ukraine	

BY MAIL

SENDING MAIL FROM EASTERN EUROPE

Airmail is the best way to send mail home from Eastern Europe. **Aerogrammes,** printed sheets that fold into envelopes and travel via airmail, are generally available at post offices. Write *"par avion"* or "airmail" in the language of the country you are visiting (in Cyrillic if applicable) on the front. Most post offices will charge exorbitant fees or simply refuse to send aerogrammes with enclosures. Surface mail is by far the cheapest and slowest way to send mail. It takes one to three months to cross the Atlantic and two to four to cross the Pacific—good for items you won't need to see for a while, such as souvenirs or other articles you've acquired along the way that are weighing down your pack.

SENDING MAIL TO EASTERN EUROPE

Mark envelopes "airmail," *"par avion,"* or airmail in the language of the country that you are visiting, otherwise your letter or postcard will never arrive. If regular airmail is too slow, **Federal Express** (Australia ☎13 26 10, Canada and US 800-463-3339, New Zealand 0800 73 33 39, UK 0800 12 38 00; www.fedex.com) offers three-day service to most of Eastern Europe, though international rates are expensive. **Surface mail** is by far the cheapest way to send mail, though it is also the slowest. It takes one to three months to cross the Atlantic and two to four to cross the Pacific. **General delivery** *(Poste Restante)* averages seven days to Eastern Europe.

For a country-by-country guide to what can and can't be sent to each country, consult the US Postal Service at http://pe.usps.gov/text/Imm/Immctry.html, which also tells you how mail is likely to be treated upon arrival in each country. There are several ways to arrange pick-up of letters sent to you by friends and relatives while you are in Eastern Europe.

ESSENTIALS

Mail can be sent to Eastern Europe through **Poste Restante** (the international phrase for General Delivery) to almost any city or town with a post office. While *Poste Restante* is reliable in most countries, it is far less likely to reach its intended recipient in less developed nations. Addressing conventions for *Poste Restante* vary by country; *Let's Go* gives instructions in the **Essentials: Keeping in Touch** section at the beginning of each country's chapter. Be sure to include the street address of the post office on the third line lest mail never reach the recipient. As a rule, it is best to use the **largest post office** in the area, as mail may be sent there regardless of what is written on the envelope. When possible, it is usually safer and quicker to send mail express or registered—this also ensures that mail will arrive in postally problematic countries. When picking up your mail, bring a passport for identification. There is often no surcharge; if there is, it usually does not exceed the cost of domestic postage. If the clerks insist that there is nothing for you, have them check under your first name as well.

AmEx's travel offices will act as a mail service for cardholders if contacted in advance. Under this free **Client Letter Service,** they will hold mail for up to 30 days and forward upon request. Some offices will offer these services to non-cardholders (especially those who have purchased AmEx Travelers Cheques), but you must call ahead. *Let's Go* lists AmEx office locations in the **Practical Information** section of many large cities.

ACCOMMODATIONS

HOSTELS, HOTELS, AND PENSIONS

Hostels are generally laid out dorm-style, often with large single-sex rooms and bunk beds, though a small number do offer private rooms for families and couples. They sometimes have kitchens and utensils for your use, bike rentals, storage areas, transportation to airports, breakfast, and laundry facilities. There can be drawbacks: some hostels close during certain daytime "lockout" hours, have a curfew, don't accept reservations, impose a maximum stay, require a minimum stay, or, less frequently, require that you do chores. In Eastern Europe, a bed in any sort of hostel will usually cost you US$10-15.

For inexpensive **hotels,** singles in Eastern Europe cost US$20-35 per night, and doubles US$30-60. You'll typically share a hall bathroom; a private bathroom will cost extra, as may hot showers. Smaller **guesthouses** and **pensions** are often cheaper than hotels. Not all hotels take **reservations,** and few accept checks in foreign currency. After hostels, pensions are the most common budget accommodation in Eastern Europe. A cross between a hostel and a hotel, a pension is generally clean, safe, and family-run, similar to a bed and breakfast. Pensions usually rent by the room but occasionally offer dorm-style accommodations. In Eastern Europe, a single room in a pension runs US$15-20.

 A HOSTELER'S BILL OF RIGHTS. There are certain standard features that we do not include in our hostel listings. Unless we state otherwise, you can expect that every hostel has no lockout, no curfew, a kitchen, free hot showers, some system of secure luggage storage, and no key deposit.

HOSTELLING INTERNATIONAL

Joining the youth hostel association in your own country automatically grants you membership privileges in **Hostelling International (HI),** a federation of national hosteling associations. HI hostels are scattered irregularly throughout Eastern Europe, but, if you will be spending time in the more touristed areas of Croatia, Hungary, and Poland, an HI card is a worthwhile investment. Hostels in Bulgaria,

Get into the Mood in Budapest!

Croatia, the Czech Republic, Estonia, Hungary, Lithuania, Poland, Romania, Russia, the Slovak Republic, and Slovenia accept reservations via the **International Booking Network** (☎202-783-6161; www.hihostels.com). HI's umbrella organization's web page (www.iyhf.org) lists the web addresses and phone numbers of all national associations, and is a great place to begin researching hostels in a specific region. Other comprehensive hosteling websites include www.hostels.com and www.hostelplanet.com. **Guest memberships** are not valid in much of Eastern Europe, but it is a good idea to ask anyway. Most student travel agencies (p. 25) sell HI cards, as do all of the national hosteling organizations listed below. All prices listed below are valid for **one-year memberships** unless otherwise noted.

Australian Youth Hostels Association (AYHA), 422 Kent St., Sydney, NSW 200 (☎02 9261 1111; www.yha.com.au). AUS$52, under 18 AUS$19.

Hostelling International-Canada (HI-C), 205 Catherine St. #400, Ottawa, ON K2P 1C3 (☎613-237-7884; www.hihostels.ca). CDN$35, under 18 free.

An Óige (Irish Youth Hostel Association), 61 Mountjoy St., Dublin 7 (☎830 4555; www.irelandyha.org). EUR€20, under 18 EUR€10.

Hostelling International Northern Ireland (HINI), 22-32 Donegall Rd., Belfast BT12 5JN (☎02890 32 47 33; www.hini.org.uk). UK£13, under 18 UK£6.

Youth Hostels Association of New Zealand (YHANZ), Level 1, Moorhouse City, 166 Moorhouse Ave., P.O. Box 436, Christchurch (☎0800 278 2990 (NZ only) or 03 379 9970; www.yha.org.nz). NZ$40, under 18 free.

Scottish Youth Hostels Association (SYHA), 7 Glebe Cres., Stirling FK8 2JA (☎01786 89 14 00; www.syha.org.uk). UK£6, under 17 £2.50.

Youth Hostels Association (England and Wales), Trevelyan House, Dimple Rd., Matlock, Derbyshire DE4 3YH (☎08707 708 868; www.yha.org.uk). UK£15.50, under 26 UK£10.

Hostelling International-USA, 8401 Colesville Rd., Ste. 600, Silver Spring, MD 20910 (☎301-495-1240; www.hiayh.org). US$28, under 18 free.

BOOKING HOSTELS ONLINE. One of the easiest ways to ensure you've got a bed for the night is by reserving online. Click to the **Hostelworld** booking engine through **www.letsgo.com,** and you'll have access to bargain accommodations from Argentina to Zimbabwe with no added commission.

OTHER TYPES OF ACCOMMODATIONS

UNIVERSITY DORMS

Many **colleges** and **universities** open their residence halls to travelers when school is not in session; some do so even during term-time. Usually situated amid student centers, these dorms often prove to be invaluable sources on things to do in the city. Finding a room may take a couple of phone calls and much planning in advance, but the hassle can be worth it. Rates tend to be low, and many offer free local calls. Tourist offices can often provide more information about this option.

PRIVATE ROOMS

An increasingly popular option in rural locations is to rent a room in a private home. Although it may seem dangerous, going home with an old woman from the train station or knocking on doors advertising private rooms (often marked by *zimmer frei, sobe,* etc.) is legitimate, generally reliable, and often preferable to staying in a hostel. Prices tend to be competitive with hostel and pension prices.

Home exchanges offer the traveler various types of homes (houses, apartments, condominiums, villas, and even castles), as well as the opportunity to experience local life from within and to cut down on accommodations fees. For more infor-

Where's your bed at?
Choose from 10,000 hostels online

eenie
mo
meenie
minee

Free Gold Card!

Pay no booking fees for six months with
a free hostelworld gold card! Sign up at
www.hostelworld.com/LGgold and
start saving money on bookings today!

beds from*

Prague	$9
Riga	$10
Krakow	$8
Budapest	$9
Dubrovnik	$14

Book online at:
www.hostelworld.com

hostelworld.com
book your bed before you go

*Prices correct at the time of publication. Prices in $US are based on persons sharing and may vary.

mation, contact the following numbers: **HomeExchange Inc.**, P.O. Box 787, Hermosa Beach, CA 90254, USA (☎800-877-8723; www.homeexchange.com), includes listings from Bulgaria, Croatia, the Czech Republic, Hungary, Poland, Romania, and Russia. **Intervac International Home Exchange** (www.intervac.com) has two offices in Eastern Europe: **Intervac Czech Republic,** Antonin and Lena Machackovi, Pod Stanici 25/603, 10/CSFR 10 200 Praha, CZR (☎2 71 96 16 47; antonin.machacek@iol.cz); and **Intervac Poland,** Ewa and Stanisław Krupscy, Mackiewicza 12, 31-213 Kraków, POL (☎12 415 18 18; intervac@york.edu.pl).

CAMPING

Eastern Europe offers many opportunities for hiking, biking, mountain climbing, camping, trekking, and spelunking. Camping is one of the most authentic ways to experience the vacation culture of the region: Eastern Europeans tend to spend their vacations exploring the outdoors. There is very little English-language literature on outdoor opportunities and adventures available in the region. Untrampled as the Eastern European wilderness is, however, it's surprisingly difficult to truly rough it. In most countries, camping within the boundaries of national parks is either illegal or heavily restricted; many areas require a camping permit. Check with the local tourist office or locals before setting up camp in an area that's not explicitly designated for camping. Regulations vary: in Russia, for example, camping is extremely restricted, whereas Bulgaria allows campers almost anywhere. Alternatively, you can often stay in a **chata** located within a park; these huts offer dorm-style rooms for US$5-10, running water (not always hot), and some sort of mess hall. **Organized campgrounds** that offer tent space and bungalows are often situated around the borders of parks. All campgrounds have running water; some offer restaurants and other facilities. Tent sites range from US$3-10 per person with a flat tent fee of US$5-10. Bungalow fees are usually US$5-10.

THE GREAT OUTDOORS

The **Great Outdoor Recreation Pages** (www.gorp.com) provides excellent general information for travelers planning on camping or spending time in the outdoors.

LEAVE NO TRACE. *Let's Go* encourages travelers to embrace the "Leave No Trace" ethic, minimizing their impact on natural environments and protecting them for future generations. Trekkers and wilderness enthusiasts should set up camp on durable surfaces, use cookstoves instead of campfires, bury human waste away from water supplies, bag trash and carry it out with them, and respect wildlife and natural objects. For more detailed information, contact the **Leave No Trace Center for Outdoor Ethics,** P.O. Box 997, Boulder, CO 80306 (☎800-332-4100 or 303-442-8222; www.lnt.org).

USEFUL RESOURCES

For information about camping, hiking, and biking, write or call the publishers listed below to receive a free catalog. Travelers planning to camp extensively in Eastern Europe might consider buying an **International Camping Carnet.** Similar to a hostel membership card, it's required at some campgrounds and provides discounts at many others. It's available in North America from the **Family Campers and RVers Association** (www.fcrv.org); in the UK from **the Caravan Club;** Australians, Irish, and New Zealanders can obtain one from their national automobile associations. An excellent general resource for travelers planning on camping or spending time in the outdoors is the **Great Outdoor Recreation Pages** (www.gorp.com).

Automobile Association, Contact Centre, Lambert House, Stockport Rd., Cheadle, SK8 2DY, UK (☎0870 600 0371; www.theaa.co.uk). Publishes *Caravan and Camping: Europe* (UK£9). They also offer European road atlases.

The Mountaineers Books, 1001 SW Klickitat Way, #201, Seattle, WA 98134, USA (☎800-553-4453; www.mountaineersbooks.org). Over 600 titles on hiking, biking, mountaineering, natural history, and conservation.

WILDERNESS SAFETY

Stay warm, dry, and hydrated. Prepare yourself for an emergency by always packing raingear, a hat and mittens, a first-aid kit, high energy food, and extra water for any hike. Be sure to check all equipment before setting out. Wool or warm layers of synthetic materials designed for the outdoors make the best hiking apparel; never rely on cotton for warmth, as it is useless when wet. Check **weather forecasts** and pay attention to the skies when hiking. In Croatia there is a risk of **landmines** still buried in parks and the wilderness. To minimize the danger, stay on the beaten path and consider purchasing a local **landmine map.**

CAMPING AND HIKING EQUIPMENT

WHAT TO BUY

Good camping equipment is both sturdy and light. North American suppliers tend to offer the most competitive prices.

Sleeping Bags: Most sleeping bags are rated by season; "summer" means 30-40°F (around 0°C) at night; "four-season" or "winter" often means below 0°F (-17°C). Bags are made of **down** (warm and light, but expensive, and miserable when wet) or of **synthetic** material (heavy, durable, and warm when wet). Prices range US$50-250 for a summer synthetic to US$200-300 for a good down winter bag. **Sleeping bag pads** include foam pads (US$10-30), air mattresses (US$15-50), and self-inflating mats (US$30-120). Bring a **stuff sack** to store your bag and keep it dry.

Tents: The best tents are free-standing (with their own frames and suspension systems), set up quickly, and only require staking in high winds. Low-profile dome tents are the best all-around. Worthy 2-person tents start at US$100, 4-person US$160. Make sure your tent has a rain fly and seal its seams with waterproofer. Other useful accessories include a **battery-operated lantern,** a plastic **groundcloth,** and a nylon **tarp.**

Backpacks: Internal-frame packs mold well to your back, keep a lower center of gravity, and flex adequately to allow you to hike difficult trails, while **external-frame packs** are more comfortable for long hikes over even terrain, as they carry weight higher and distribute it more evenly. Make sure your pack has a strong, padded hip-belt to transfer weight to your legs. There are models designed specifically for women. Any serious backpacking requires a pack of at least 4000 in^3 (16,000cc), plus 500 in^3 for sleeping bags in internal-frame packs. Sturdy backpacks cost anywhere from US$125 to US$420—your pack is an area where it doesn't pay to economize. On your hunt for the perfect pack, fill up a prospective model with something heavy, strap it on correctly, and walk around the store to get a sense of how the model distributes weight. Either buy a **rain cover** (US$10-20) or store all of your belongings in plastic bags inside your pack.

Boots: Be sure to wear hiking boots with good **ankle support.** They should fit snugly and comfortably over 1-2 pairs of **wool socks** and a pair of thin **liner socks.** Break in boots over several weeks before you go to spare yourself blisters.

Other Necessities: Synthetic layers, like those made of polypropylene or polyester, and a pile jacket will keep you warm even when wet. A **space blanket** (US$5-15) will help you to retain body heat and doubles as a groundcloth. Plastic **water bottles** are vital;

look for shatter- and leak-resistant models. Carry **water-purification tablets** for when you can't boil water. Although most campgrounds provide campfire sites, you may want to bring a small **metal grate** or **grill**. For those places (including virtually every organized campground in Europe) that forbid fires or the gathering of firewood, you'll need a **camp stove** (the classic Coleman starts at US$50) and a propane-filled **fuel bottle** to operate it. Also bring a **first-aid kit, pocketknife, insect repellent,** and **waterproof matches** or a **lighter**.

WHERE TO BUY IT

The mail-order and online companies listed below offer lower prices than many retail stores, but a visit to a local camping or outdoors store will give you a good sense of the look and weight of certain items and allow you to check the fit of backpacks or boots.

Campmor, 28 Parkway, P.O. Box 700, Upper Saddle River, NJ 07458, USA (☎888-226-7667; www.campmor.com).

Discount Camping, 880 Main North Rd., Pooraka, South Australia 5095, AUS (☎8 8262 3399; www.discountcamping.com.au).

Eastern Mountain Sports (EMS), 1 Vose Farm Rd., Peterborough, NH 03458, USA (☎888-463-6367; www.ems.com).

L.L. Bean, Freeport, ME 04033, USA (US and Canada ☎800-441-5713, UK 0800 891 297, elsewhere 207-552-3028; www.llbean.com).

Recreational Equipment, Inc. (REI), Sumner, WA 98352, USA (US and Canada ☎800-426-4840, elsewhere 253-891-2500; www.rei.com).

ESSENTIALS

SPECIFIC CONCERNS

SUSTAINABLE TRAVEL

As the number of travelers on the road continues to rise, the detrimental effect they can have on natural environments becomes an increasing concern. With this in mind, *Let's Go* promotes the philosophy of **sustainable travel**. Through a sensitivity to issues of ecology and sustainability, today's travelers can be a powerful force in preserving and restoring the places they visit.

Ecotourism, a rising trend in sustainable travel, focuses on the conservation of natural habitats and using them to build up the economy without exploitation or overdevelopment. Travelers can make a difference by doing advance research and by supporting organizations and establishments that pay attention to their impact on their natural surroundings and strive to be environmentally friendly.

ECOTOURISM RESOURCES. For more information on environmentally responsible tourism, contact one of the organizations below:
Conservation International (www.conservation.org).
Green Globe 21 (☎ 61 2 6257 9102; www.greenglobe21.com/Travellers.aspx)
International Ecotourism Society, 733 15th St. NW, Washington, D.C. 20005, USA (☎ 202-347-9203; www.ecotourism.org).
United Nations Environment Program (UNEP; ☎ 33 1 44 37 14 41; www.uneptie.org/pc/tourism).

RESPONSIBLE TRAVEL

The impact of tourist money on the destinations you visit should not be underestimated. The choices you make during your trip can have potent effects on local communities—for better or for worse. Travelers who care about the destinations and environments they explore should become aware of the social and cultural implications of the choices they make when they travel. Simple decisions such as buying local products instead of globally available products, paying a fair price for the product or service, and attempting to say a few words in the local language can have a strong, positive effect on the community.

Community-based tourism aims to channel tourist money into the local economy by emphasizing tours and cultural programs that are run by members of the host community and that often benefit disadvantaged groups. This type of tourism also benefits the tourists themselves, as these tours often take them beyond the traditional tours of the region. An excellent resource for general information on community-based travel is *The Good Alternative Travel Guide* (UK£10), a project of **Tourism Concern** (☎ +44 020 7133 3330; www.tourismconcern.org.uk).

TRAVELING ALONE

There are many benefits to traveling alone, including independence and greater interaction with locals. On the other hand, any solo traveler is a more vulnerable target of harassment and street theft. As a lone traveler, try not to stand out as a tourist, look confident, and be especially careful in deserted or very crowded areas. Stay away from areas that are not well lit. If questioned, never admit that you are traveling alone. Maintain regular contact with someone at home who knows your itinerary, and always research your destination before traveling. For more tips, pick up *Traveling Solo* by Eleanor Berman (Globe Pequot Press,

US$18), visit www.travelaloneandloveit.com, or subscribe to **Connecting: Solo Travel Network,** 689 Park Rd., Unit 6, Gibsons, BC V0N 1V7, Canada (☎ 800-557-1757; www.cstn.org; membership US$30-55).

WOMEN TRAVELERS

Solo female travelers are still a relatively new phenomenon in much of Eastern Europe, particularly in public places like bars and restaurants. Women traveling alone may encounter quizzical stares, although less so in Central Europe than in the countries to the east. The attitudes that contribute to these surprised looks, when coupled with crime in urban areas, can make for dangerous situations. Hostels which offer single rooms that lock from the inside or religious organizations that provide rooms for only women offer female travelers the most security. Some communal showers in some hostels are safer than others; check before settling in. Hitchhiking is never safe for lone women, or even for two women traveling together. Choose train compartments occupied by women or couples; ask the conductor to put together a women-only compartment if there isn't one.

Generally, the less you look like a tourist, the better off you'll be. Dress conservatively, especially in rural areas. Wearing the clothes that are fashionable among local women will cut down on stares, and a *babushka*-style kerchief discourages even the most tenacious of catcallers. Some travelers report that wearing a wedding band or carrying pictures of a "husband" or "children" is extremely useful to help document marital status. In cities, you may be harassed no matter how you're dressed. Your best answer is no answer at all. Staring straight ahead will do a world of good that reactions usually don't achieve. The extremely persistent can sometimes be dissuaded by a firm, loud, and very public "Go away!" in the appropriate language. If need be, turn to an older woman for help; her stern rebukes should usually embarrass the most persistent harassers into silence.

Let's Go lists emergency numbers (including rape crisis lines) in the **Practical Information** of most major cities. Memorize the emergency numbers in places you visit, and consider carrying a whistle on your keychain. A self-defense course will not only prepare you for a potential attack but also heighten your awareness and boost your confidence (see **Personal Safety,** p. 19). Make sure you are aware of the health concerns that women face when traveling (see **Women's Health,** p. 24, and the **Health and Safety** section at the beginning of each country's chapter).

GLBT TRAVELERS

The legality of homosexuality is an issue in much of Eastern Europe, and homosexuality is strongly stigmatized in the Balkans, much of the former Soviet Union, and many rural areas. Regardless of the legality, homophobic views persist, and public displays of homosexuality give local authorities an excuse to be troublesome. Even within major cities, gay nightclubs and social centers are often hidden and frequently change location, though in such cities as Prague and Budapest, gay nightlife is gradually becoming more common. Be aware that GLBT rights are a particularly charged issue in devoutly Catholic Poland. For coverage of the current legal and social climate in each country, consult the website of the **International Lesbian and Gay Association** (www.ilga.org). *Let's Go* lists local gay establishments. Word of mouth is often a great source for finding the latest hot spots. Listed below are contact organizations, mail-order bookstores, and publishers that offer materials addressing some specific concerns. **Out and About** (www.planetout.com) offers a biweekly

newsletter addressing travel concerns and a comprehensive site addressing gay travel concerns. The online newspaper **365gay.com** also has a travel section (www.365gay.com/travel/travelchannel.htm).

Gay's the Word, 66 Marchmont St., London WC1N 1AB, UK (☎20 7278 7654; www.gaystheword.co.uk). The largest gay and lesbian bookshop in the UK, with both fiction and non-fiction titles. Mail-order service available.

Giovanni's Room, 1145 Pine St., Philadelphia, PA 19107, USA (☎215-923-2960; www.queerbooks.com). An international lesbian/feminist and gay bookstore with mail-order service (carries many of the publications listed below).

International Lesbian and Gay Association (ILGA), Ave. des Villas 34 1060, Brussels, Belgium (☎32 2 502 2471; www.ilga.org). Provides political information, such as homosexuality laws of individual countries.

> **FURTHER READING: GLBT TRAVEL.**
> *Spartacus 2003-2004: International Gay Guide.* Bruno Gmunder Verlag (US$33).
> *Damron Accommodations Guide, Damron City Guide,* and *Damron Women's Traveller.* Damron Travel Guides (US$11-19). For info, call ☎800-462-6654 or visit www.damron.com.
> *Ferrari Guides' Gay Travel A to Z, Ferrari Guides' Men's Travel in Your Pocket, Ferrari Guides' Women's Travel in Your Pocket,* and *Ferrari Guides' Inn Places.* Ferrari Publications (US$16-25).
> *The Gay Vacation Guide: The Best Trips and How to Plan Them,* by Mark Chesnut. Kensington Books (US$15).

TRAVELERS WITH DISABILITIES

Unfortunately, Eastern Europe is largely inaccessible to disabled travelers. Ramps and other amenities are all but nonexistent in most countries. Contact your destination's consulate or tourist office for information, arrange transportation early, and inform airlines and hotels ahead of time of any special accommodations required. Guide-dog owners should inquire as to the specific quarantine policies of each destination. **Rail** is probably the most convenient form of travel for disabled travelers in Eastern Europe: some stations have ramps, and some trains have wheelchair lifts, special seating areas, and specially equipped toilets. The railways of Bulgaria, the Czech Republic, Hungary, Poland, and the Slovak Republic all offer limited resources for wheelchair accessibility.

USEFUL ORGANIZATIONS

Accessible Journeys, 35 West Sellers Ave., Ridley Park, PA 19078, USA (☎800-846-4537; www.disabilitytravel.com). Designs tours for wheelchair-users and slow walkers.

Directions Unlimited, 123 Green Ln., Bedford Hills, NY 10507, USA (☎800-533-5343). Books individual vacations for the physically disabled; not an info service.

Flying Wheels, 143 W. Bridge St., P.O. Box 382, Owatonna, MN 55060, USA (☎507-451-5005; www.flyingwheelstravel.com). Escorted trips to Europe.

Mobility International USA (MIUSA), P.O. Box 10767, Eugene, OR 97440, USA (☎541-343-1284; www.miusa.org). Books and other publications.

Society for Accessible Travel and Hospitality (SATH), 347 Fifth Ave., #610, New York, NY 10016, USA (☎212-447-7284; www.sath.org). An advocacy group that publishes free online travel information and the travel magazine *OPEN WORLD*.

MINORITY TRAVELERS

Minority travelers, especially those of African or Asian descent, will usually meet with more curiosity than hostility, especially outside big cities. Travelers with darker skin of any nationality may experience some prejudice, particularly in the Balkan region, where ethnic tensions run high, and in Moscow and St. Petersburg, where they may experience police harassment. Anti-Muslim sentiment lingers in the Balkans from the conflicts that plagued the region throughout the 1990s. **Roma** (gypsies) also encounter substantial hostility in Eastern Europe. The ranks of **skinheads** are on the rise in Eastern Europe, and minority travelers, especially Jews and blacks, should regard them with caution. **Anti-Semitism** is still a problem in many countries, including Lithuania, Poland, Romania, and the former Soviet Union; it is generally best to be discreet about your religion.

DIETARY CONCERNS

Vegetarian and **kosher** dining is often a challenge in Eastern Europe, although vegetarian restaurants are on the rise in Central Europe. Most of the national cuisines tend to be meat- (particularly pork-) heavy. **Markets** are often a good bet for fresh vegetables, fruit, cheese, and bread. The **North American Vegetarian Society,** P.O. Box 72, Dolgeville, NY 13329, USA (☎518-568-7970; www.navs-online.org), offers information and publications for vegetarian travelers. There are many resources on the web; try **www.happycow.net** for starters.

Travelers who keep kosher may find a few options in large cities but should beware of restaurants labeled "Jewish," many of which are not actually kosher. For information on kosher restaurants, contact synagogues in larger cities. A good resource is the *Jewish Travel Guide*, by Michael Zaidner (Vallentine Mitchell; US$17), which lists synagogues, kosher restaurants, and Jewish institutions in over 110 countries.

ADDITIONAL RESOURCES

Let's Go tries to cover all aspects of budget travel, but we can't put *everything* in our guides. Listed below are books and websites that can serve as jumping-off points for your own research.

USEFUL PUBLICATIONS

Central Europe Profiled, Barry Turner ed. St. Martin's Press, 2000 (US$18). A breakdown of the culture, politics, and economy of each country in Eastern Europe.

On Foot to the Golden Horn, by Jason Goodwin. Picador, 2000 (US$11). Join this fellow backpacker on a journey from Poland to Turkey.

TRAVEL PUBLISHERS AND BOOKSTORES

Adventurous Traveler Bookstore, P.O. Box 2221, Williston, VT 05495, USA (☎800-282-3963; www.adventuroustraveler.com).

Globe Corner Bookstore (☎800-358-6013; www.globecorner.com). A wide variety of travel guides and background reading.

Hunter Publishing, 470 W. Broadway, 2nd fl., South Boston, MA 02127, USA (☎617-269-0700; www.hunterpublishing.com). Extensive catalog of travel guides and adventure travel books.

Rand McNally, P.O. Box 7600, Chicago, IL 60680, USA (☎847-329-8100; www.randm-cnally.com). Publishes road atlases.

WORLD WIDE WEB

Many countries' embassies maintain websites where you can check visa requirements and news related to your destination (see **Embassies and Consulates,** p. 9). For general information about travel check out the listings below.

 WWW.LETSGO.COM. *Let's Go's* website features a wealth of information and valuable advice at your fingertips. It offers excerpts from all our guides as well as monthly features on new hot spots in the most popular destinations. In addition to our online bookstore, we have great deals on everything from airfares to cell phones. Our resources section is full of information you'll need before you hit the road, and our forums are buzzing with advice from other travelers. Check back often to see constant updates, exciting new tips, and prize giveaways. See you soon!

THE ART OF BUDGET TRAVEL

▨ **How to See the World:** www.artoftravel.com. Great travel tips, from cheap flights to self defense to local culture.

Robert Young Pelton's Dangerous Places: www.comebackalive.com/df. Helpful hints and amusing anecdotes for those going off (way off) the beaten path.

INFORMATION ON EASTERN EUROPE

▨ **In Your Pocket:** www.inyourpocket.com. The online version of an excellent series of city and regional guides. The coverage of the Baltic states is particularly thorough.

CIA World Factbook: www.odci.gov/cia/publications/factbook/index.html. Tons of vital statistics on Eastern Europe's geography, government, economy, and people.

Foreign Language for Travelers: www.travlang.com. Provides free online translating dictionaries and lists of phrases in various European languages, including Czech, Hungarian, and Polish.

Geographia: www.geographia.com. Highlights, culture, and people of Eastern European countries.

PlanetRider: www.planetrider.com. A subjective list of links to the "best" websites covering the culture and tourist attractions of several countries, including the Czech Republic, Hungary, and Russia.

LIFE AND TIMES

During the Cold War, Westerners imposed the name "Eastern Europe" on the Soviet satellites east of the Berlin Wall. The title has always been a geographic misnomer: Vienna lies farther east than Prague; the geometric center of Europe is in Lithuania; and most of Russia is in Asia. To understand the remarkable complexity of Eastern Europe, picture a map of the region from little more than a decade ago: in 1989, there were seven countries behind the Iron Curtain; today, 19 independent states occupy that same area. In the past decade and a half, the region has undergone astounding political and cultural transformation. Soviet Communism has fallen from power, but history still casts a heavy shadow across Eastern Europe. The region is united by what it longs to leave behind—political upheaval and foreign domination—and by what it now confronts—a more optimistic but similarly unpredictable future. To overcome its troubled past, Eastern Europe must face lingering political and economic problems. The European Union and NATO have welcomed some states of the former Eastern Bloc, but others must tackle domestic poverty, ethnic strife, and corruption if they hope to curry the favor of the West. Amid such uncertainty, Eastern Europe has become a prime holiday destination. While spirited travelers once ventured to Paris, London and Rome, today Prague, Budapest, and Dubrovnik entice a new generation of backpackers, aspiring expats, and even luxury travelers. This influx of tourist money is a major force for economic and cultural transformation, as many Eastern European countries shift to service-driven economies and angle to join their western neighbors in the economic zone of the European Union. Exactly what will emerge when all the smoke clears is anyone's guess, but the sun will certainly continue to rise in the east.

PEOPLE AND CULTURE

THE PEOPLES OF EASTERN EUROPE

The fall of the Iron Curtain has increased diversity in Eastern Europe, but the region's population remains fairly homogeneous. Most Eastern European countries are inhabited by Slavic peoples. After the Great Migration (p. 54), the Slavs split into **West Slavs** (Czechs, Poles, and Slovaks), **South Slavs** (including Croats and Slovenes) and East Slavs (including Russians and Ukrainians). **Bulgarians,** originally of Turkic origin, have been ethnically integrated into Slavic culture.

The non-Slavic peoples inhabiting Central and Eastern Europe include Estonians, Hungarians, Latvians, Lithuanians, and Romanians. **Latvians** and **Lithuanians** belong to the Baltic branch of the Indo-European family. **Estonians,** who also occupy the Baltic Coast, form a branch of the Baltic Finns, descendants of the Finno-Ugric family who have been strongly Germanized. **Hungarians** constitute the "Ugric" part of the Finno-Ugric family. They separated from other Finno-Ugric tribes in the Urals and, at the end of the 9th century, migrated southwest to the Carpathian Basin. Hungarian minorities still live in Transylvania and the southern region of the Slovak Republic. **Romanians** are descendants of Dacians.

For centuries, Eastern Europe was home to the world's largest **Jewish** population; today, a sizeable Jewish community remains only in **Russia,** and this population is decreasing. The state-sponsored Nazi genocide of WWII obliterated much of the Jewish presence in the region, and most Jews who remained in Eastern European countries at the war's end have since emigrated. **Roma,** known as gypsies, came from northern India during the Middle Ages. They now live in small, tight-knit communities across Eastern Europe, particularly in Bulgaria, the Czech and Slovak Republics, Hungary, and Romania. After the fall of the Berlin Wall, Anglophone **expats** flooded Eastern Europe and created distinct cultures in Prague, Budapest, St. Petersburg, and elsewhere.

RELIGION

Christianity had spread to most of Eastern Europe by the 10th century—though Lithuania remained pagan well into the fourteenth century—and it remains the principal religion in the region today. The monks **Cyril** and **Methodius** brought Christianity to the Slavs, and today most Bulgarians, Romanians, Russians,-and Ukrainians subscribe to the **Eastern Orthodox** faith. With the exception of the Baltic states, which have been influenced by German **Protestantism,** all other nations of Eastern Europe are predominantly **Roman Catholic.** The same fault line that splits countries using the Cyrillic alphabet from those using the Roman alphabet divides Eastern Orthodox from Roman Catholic countries. Religiosity across the region is anything but consistent: Poland is one of the most devoutly Catholic countries in the world, while its nominally Catholic next-door neighbor, the Czech Republic, is one of the world's most atheistic countries. Czech iconoclasm dates at least to the 14th century, when **Jan Hus** called for church reform, preceding Martin Luther's **Protestant Reformation** by a full century. With Soviet rule came officially atheist governments and the repression of churches. Yet most Eastern European countries saw a Christian revival after the fall of communism in the early 1990s, and today religious faith in Eastern Europe is much more visible than it was just a few decades ago. Christianity plays a larger public role in most Eastern European countries than it does in much of Western Europe. **Islam** has a significant presence in Bulgaria and in parts of Russia. **Judaism** constitutes another important minority religion, practiced mainly in Russia.

LANGUAGE

With the exception of Estonian and Hungarian, which are **Finno-Ugric** (though not mutually intelligible), all nations in Eastern Europe speak languages of **Indo-European** origin. Romanian, like French and Italian, belongs to the **Romance** branch, and Latvian and Lithuanian to the **Baltic** branch. **Romani,** the language of the Roma (gypsies), is an Indian language related to Hindi. Bulgarian, Croatian, Czech, Polish, Slovak, Slovenian, Russian, and Ukrainian are all **Slavic** languages. Bulgarian, Russian, and Ukrainian use the Cyrillic alphabet, while all other regional languages are written in the Roman alphabet. For phrasebooks and glossaries of key Eastern European languages, see p. 767.

 IT'S ALL GREEK TO ME. When the Greek priest Cyril and his brother Methodius set off on a Christian mission to convert the Slavs in AD 863, they brought more than their religion. To succeed where others had failed, the brothers translated liturgical text into a dialect known as **Old Church Slavonic,** and in doing so created the first Slavic literary language. Their followers would later adapt the alphabet they used to create modern **Cyrillic.** The new language proved wildly popular, but Rome disapproved of spreading God's word in any tongue less dignified than Latin. The brothers were summoned to explain themselves before Pope Nicholas I, who died before they arrived in 868. While his successor Adrian II gave their mission his full blessing, Cyril fell ill and died before he could return to preach. Cyril and Methodius's work facilitated Slavic unions in the name of religion and language, and made possible the great empires of Bulgaria and Kyivan Rus.

FOOD

Travelers will find much of the best food in Eastern Europe not at restaurants, but at **open-air markets**. The region boasts excellent local fruits, vegetables, breads, and dairy products. Although food specialties vary from region to region, Eastern Europe stands united in its love of **sausage**. There are endless varieties of packed meat products; the spiciest are from Hungary. The ubiquitous meat, cabbage, potatoes, and beetroot of Central European cuisine are best described as hearty, whereas seafood and lighter cuisine are more plentiful on the coasts. Local **cheeses** are not to be missed: highlights include Romania's distinctive tree cheese, *brânză de copac;* the intricately decorated *oscypek* of the Tatras mountains; and *monouri*, a spicy Russian feta. **Vegetarian** restaurants remain rare in much of Eastern Europe, but vegetarian options abound in most major cities. Cosmopolitan restaurants and fast food chains are also popping up across the region. Generally, Eastern European renditions of Italian and other European cuisines are a lot better than the region's takes on Chinese, Thai, and other Asian cuisines. See the **Food and Drink** section of each chapter introduction for country-specific information.

ALCOHOLIC DELIGHTS

Eastern Europe can drink you under the table, and with high-quality, locally produced libations to boot. **Beer, vodka, absinthe, brandy,** and even **wine** abound in the region. The world's best beers—and highest rate of beer consumption—are in the Czech Republic: world famous *Pilsner Urquell* is produced in Plzeň (p. 198) while České Budějovice (p. 205) brews the delectable *Budvar* (called Budweiser in the Czech Republic; *not* to be confused with the American brand). The best **beer** in the Czech Republic, *Krušovice*, is produced in Prague (p. 165); enjoy it after an eerily green glass of the most romanticized of the region's liquors, absinthe. Lithuania (p. 378) and Latvia (p. 353) also brew excellent locals beers. Poland (p. 417) is the birthplace of **vodka**, and regional wisdom holds that Polish vodka and Czech beer are as good as Polish beer and Czech vodka are bad. Top-notch Polish *wódki* include Chopin, Wyborowa, and Żubrówka. Drinking good vodka is also a popular pastime, to say the least, in Russia and Ukraine. Eastern Europe excels at **homemade liquors**. The plum liquor *palincă* is ubiquitous in Hungary (p. 267) and Romania (p. 515). Not-quite-alcoholic Ukrainian *kvas*, is sold from fermented beets or fruits, is sold from barrels on the streets of Kyiv (p. 697). In Karlovy Vary, CZR (p. 202), you can imbibe *becherovka*, an herb liquor said to have curative powers. Hungary currently holds the crown for Eastern Europe's finest **wines**—don't miss famous Bull's Blood in Eger (p. 299), Aszú in Tokaj (p. 306), and the wines of Badacsony (p. 327). Croatia (p. 101) is also up-and-coming in the world of wines. The wines of Melnik, BUL are so good, Winston Churchill had them shipped to England, even during WWII. See the **Food and Drink** section of each chapter introduction for country-specific information. And stand forewarned: there's a reason many Slavic languages have a specific word for "to drink one's money away."

GEOGRAPHY

LAND AND WATER

The vast majority of Eastern Europe consists of several low-altitude **plains,** which cover much of the Baltic states, Hungary, Poland, southern Romania, European Russia, the southern Slovak Republic, and Ukraine. Most of the Czech Republic sits on a plateau, the Bohemian Massif. The largest mountains in Eastern Europe are the **Carpathians,** which include the **Tatras,** running along the Polish-Slovak border. The easternmost **Alps,** the Julian range, stretch into Slovenia, and the **Balkan Mountains** span from eastern Serbia to the Bulgarian Black Sea coast.

Russia's **Volga** is the longest river in Europe. The **Danube,** which flows through nine countries and creates natural borders between Hungary and the Slovak Republic and between Bulgaria and Romania, is integral to the region's economy and ecosystem. Other rivers include the **Dnipr** in Ukraine, the **Vltava** in the Czech Republic, and the **Odra** and **Wisła** in Poland. These rivers empty into three seas: the **Adriatic,** the **Baltic,** and the **Black.** Whereas the Baltic coast is composed entirely of lowlands, that of the Adriatic is characterized by dramatic mountains, jagged peninsulas and miniature islands. **Lake Balaton,** in Hungary, is Central Europe's largest lake; **Lake Ladoga,** in northwestern Russia, is the largest in Europe.

CLIMATE

The sun shines on the Eastern Bloc, despite what anti-communist propaganda—television images of rainy Warsaw and ice-cold Moscow—used to suggest. In fact, Eastern Europe is so expansive that the climate is extremely varied. In the **central regions,** such as Poland and the Czech and Slovak Republics, summers (May-Sept.) are warm and winters (Dec.-Feb.) can be bitingly cold. The **Baltic states** have a climate similar to that of southern Scandinavia. **South** toward the Mediterranean Sea, in Croatia and Slovenia, summers become hot and winters mild. It is similarly warm along the Bulgarian, Romanian, Russian, and Ukrainian **Black Sea Coast.**

Avg Temp (high/low)	January		April		July		October	
	°C	°F	°C	°F	°C	°F	°C	°F
Bratislava, SLK	2/-3	36/26	16/4	60/40	26/14	79/58	15/6	59/42
Bucharest, ROM	1/-6	34/22	16/4	64/42	28/16	83/60	18/6	64/42
Budapest, HUN	1/-4	34/24	16/6	61/43	26/15	79/59	16/7	61/44
Kyiv, UKR	-4/-10	25/-14	14/5	57/41	25/15	77/59	13/6	55/43
Ljubljana, SLN	2/-4	35/25	15/4	59/40	26/14	79/59	16/6	61/43
Moscow, RUS	-6/-12	21/11	9/1	49/34	22/13	71/55	7/1	45/33
Prague, CZR	1/-4	34/24	12/2	54/36	22/12	72/54	12/4	54/39
Rīga, LAT	-2/-5	29/22	9/2	48/35	21/13	69/56	10/5	50/41
Sofia, BUL	2/-5	36/23	15/4	59/40	26/13	78/56	16/6	61/42
Tallinn, EST	-2/-6	28/21	7/1	45/33	20/13	68/55	8/3	47/38
Vilnius, LIT	-4/-9	25/16	6/2	51/34	22/12	71/54	10/3	50/38
Warsaw, POL	-1/-6	30/21	13/3	55/37	22/11	72/52	12/4	54/40
Zagreb, CRO	3/-2	37/28	16/8	61/46	26/16	79/61	15/8	59/47

WAR AND PEACE, ABRIDGED

SLAVS (BEFORE AD 800)

**3000-2000 BC
Slavs** arrive in Europe.

With the exception of Hungary, Romania, and the Baltic countries, the countries in this book are populated primarily by **Slavic** peoples, who constitute the largest ethnic and linguistic group in Europe. Believed to have originated in Asia, the Slavs migrated to Eastern Europe during the 3rd or 2nd millennium BC. The movement of ancient tribes westward in the 5th and 6th centuries AD sparked the **Great Migration,** during which

Slavs penetrated deeply into Europe. Over time, the Slavs tended to mix with other peoples who came to their lands. In Bulgaria, for instance, the Slavic majority assimilated the Turkic Bulgar ruling class around the 8th century. The Slavs of present-day Ukraine similarly assimilated the Varangians (Vikings) and in the mid-9th century established Eastern Europe's first major civilization, **Kyivan Rus.**

Despite shared roots, the Slavic peoples have never enjoyed any natural unity. The division of Christendom in 395 into the Roman Empire and the Byzantine Empire split the Slavs into two culturally distinct groups. The fault line between the two religious groups cuts directly through the Balkans: the Croats and Slovenes were tied to Rome, while the Bulgarians, Romanians, and Serbs were loyal to Constantinople. Since the split, the political and social history of western Slavs, like the Czechs and Poles, has been linked to Western Europe, while the southern and eastern Slavs have been influenced far more by their eastern neighbors, especially the **Ottoman Turks.**

OTTOMANS AND HAPSBURGS (800-1914)

Beginning in the 9th century, several short-lived kingdoms rose and fell in Eastern Europe, such as the **Empire of Great Moravia,** which included Bohemia, Hungary, Moravia, and Slovakia at its peak in 830. The **Hungarian Kingdom,** one of the few Eastern European empires to achieve longevity, first came to power in the early 11th century. With the exception of a year-long Tatar occupation in 1241, the kingdom grew for more than 500 years and eventually reached north to Polish Silesia, south to Croatian Pannonia, and east to Romanian Wallachia. The kingdom met its end at the 1526 **Battle of Mohács** at the hands of the Ottomans, while the remaining Hungarian territories not claimed by the Ottomans fell into Austria's rising Hapsburg dynasty.

The **Russians** came into their own by the end of the fifteenth century, when Ivan III finally threw off the Mongol yoke. Meanwhile, the **Ottoman Empire** firmly established itself in southeastern Europe when it crushed the **Serbs** in 1389 at the **Battle of Kosovo.** The empire expanded to control vast tracts of southeastern Europe and became one of the most powerful regimes in the world. Polish king **Jan III Sobieski** turned back the tide of Ottoman advance into the heart of Europe when he defeated the Ottoman Turks at the **Siege of Vienna** in 1683. A series of losses to Russia from the seventeenth to the nineteenth century compounded the Ottoman imperial decline that set in after the failed Siege of Vienna.

As the Ottoman Empire was floundering, the **Russian Empire** was rapidly expanding east to the Pacific and west into Poland and Ukraine. The **Polish-Lithuanian Commonwealth** (1569-1795) had been one of the largest realms in Europe and the first modern democratic state. In a series of three **partitions of Poland** (1772-1795), the commonwealth was dissolved as Polish territory was divided among Austria, Prussia, and Russia. The Rus-

AD 284-305
Emperor **Diocletian** ruled the Roman Empire from Salona, near Split, Croatia.

7th century
Slavs establish the first **Kyiv** settlement.

9th century
The **Cyrillic** alphabet is codified.

882
The **Kyivan Rus** dynasty begins.

1222
The **Golden Bull** charter establishes political rights in Hungary.

1223
Genghis Khan invades Central Europe.

1386
Lithuania becomes the last country in Europe to accept **Christianity.**

1462-1505
Duke of Muscovy **Ivan III** begins to unify all East Slavic lands.

1569
The **Union of Lublin** forms the **Polish-Lithuanian Commonwealth.**

1682-1725
Peter the Great modernizes Russia.

LIFE AND TIMES

1825
Russian soldiers attempt the **Decembrist coup.**

1854-1856
The **Crimean War** erupts.

1867
The **Austro-Hungarian Empire** forms.

1905
The **1905 Revolution** fails.

1912-1913
First and Second **Balkan Wars.**

1917
Vladimir Lenin completes the **Russian Revolution,** becoming the first dictator to test Karl Marx's ideas.

1918
Czar **Nicholas II** and his family are executed; Yugoslavia and Czechoslovakia are formed, while Estonia, Latvia, Lithuania, and Poland gain independence.

1924
Lenin dies; ruthless **Josef Stalin** becomes Russian dictator for almost 30 years.

1925
Brilliant Russian filmmaker Sergei Eisenstein directs the monumental **Battleship Potemkin.**

sians also wrested Baltic territory from Sweden. In 1794, the Russian-Ottoman **Treaty of Küçük Kaynarca** granted the Russian tsar authority over all Orthodox Christian subjects of the Ottoman Empire. By 1801, the Russians controlled Estonia, Latvia, Lithuania, eastern Poland, and Ukraine, but further expansion was halted by the mid-nineteenth century. The **1878 Congress of Berlin** marked the end of the **Russo-Turkish Wars** and severely curtailed the Ottoman sphere of influence.

During this period, the colossal **Austrian Empire,** under the control of the **Hapsburg** family, swallowed most of Central and Eastern Europe. The Hapsburgs came to dominate Central Europe after the Battle of Mohács and gained control of all of Hungary by 1699. The Hungarians remained restless subjects, however, and in 1867 the Austrians entered into a **dual monarchy** with the Hungarians, creating the **Austro-Hungarian Empire,** in which Hungary was granted autonomy. Until 1918, Austria-Hungary controlled what are now the Czech and Slovak Republics, Croatia, Slovenia, and parts of Poland, Romania, and Ukraine. By the 19th century, nearly all of Eastern Europe was controlled by the Ottoman, Russian, or Austro-Hungarian Empires. Following **Napoleon's** brief dominion over Europe, a surge of **Pan-Slavism,** a movement for the unity of Slavic peoples, swept through the subordinated nations.

DEATH OF THE GREAT EMPIRES (1914-1938)

World War I began with an attempt by the Serbs to free the South Slavs from the clutches of the Austro-Hungarian Empire. Serb nationalists of the illegal **Black Hand** movement believed that their cause would best be served by the death of **Archduke Franz Ferdinand d'Este,** the likely heir to the Austro-Hungarian throne. On June 28, 1914, Bosnian Serb nationalist **Gavrilo Princip** assassinated Ferdinand and his wife Sophia in Sarajevo. Exactly one month later, Austria-Hungary declared war on Serbia, and soon full-scale war broke out as France, Germany, Russia, Great Britain, Montenegro, Serbia, and the Ottoman Empire came to the aid of allies. As they were under the control of Austro-Hungary and the Ottoman Empire, most Eastern Europeans fought alongside the **Central Powers.** The Baltic nations were controlled by both Germans and Russians and remained divided in their alliances between the **Allies** and the Central Powers. Ukraine became a hotly contested battleground and eventually fell to German wartime occupation.

As the war dragged on and catastrophic losses caused the death toll to skyrocket, the Russian people became increasingly frustrated with their inefficient government. Coupled with a crippled wartime economy, the tension finally erupted in the **Russian Revolution.** Riots over food shortages began in March 1917 and led to the Tsar's abdication. In November, the **Bolsheviks,** led by **Vladimir Ilyich Lenin,** took power and established the world's first communist government. Nationalist independence movements emerged throughout the Russian Empire on the heels of the March 1917 revolution, and the empire crumbled. With support from the West, Estonia, Latvia, and Ukraine won brief independence from Russia, and Lithuania likewise freed itself from German rule. Poland became an independent state for the first time since 1792.

While the Russian Empire disintegrated, victorious powers dismantled the defeated Austria-Hungary. The Czechs and Slovaks united to create Czechoslovakia. Romania's size doubled with the acquisition of Bessarabia, Bucovina, and Transylvania. Finally, in keeping with the vision of South Slav nationalism that had sparked the war, 1918 saw the creation of the Kingdom of Serbs, Croats and Slovenes, later known as Yugoslavia. In 1922, the Bolsheviks declared the **Union of Soviet Socialist Republics (USSR)**, which included Belarussian, Russian, Transcaucasian, and Ukrainian territories. The **interwar period** was a turbulent time, as many states, independent for the first time in centuries, struggled to establish their own governments, economies, and societies in a period made even more unstable by the global **depression** of the 1930s.

"PEACE IN OUR TIME" (1938-1945)

Just two decades after WWI ravaged the continent, **World War II** rose out of its many lingering conflicts. **Adolf Hitler** was determined to reclaim the "Germanic" parts of Poland and Czechoslovakia that Germany had lost in the Treaty of Versailles. He claimed that the 3 million Germans living in the Czechoslovak Sudetenland were being discriminated against by their government. Hoping to avoid another war, France and Britain ignored Hitler's glaring aggression against a sovereign country and adopted their infamous policy of appeasement. France and Britain sealed Czechoslovakia's fate on September 30, 1938, by signing the Munich Agreement with Germany, which ordered all non-German inhabitants of the Sudetenland to vacate their homes within 24 hours and permitted the German army to invade. Upon his return from Munich, British Prime Minister **Neville Chamberlain** mistakenly believed he had secured "peace in our time." Hitler, however, ignored the stipulations of the agreement and proceeded to annex the remainder of Czechoslovakia, which he turned into the Bohemian-Moravian Protectorate in March 1939. Hitler and Stalin shocked the world in August, 1939, by signing the **Molotov-Ribbentrop Nonaggression Pact,** forging an uneasy alliance between the two historical enemies. Secret clauses detailed a dual invasion of Poland—Germany would control the western two-thirds, while the USSR would keep the eastern third. In September 1939, Hitler annexed Poland, sparking WWII.

The Nonaggression Pact lasted only until June 1941, when Hitler launched Operation Barbarossa, a surprise invasion of the Soviet Union. The German army advanced as far as the gates of Moscow before being turned back, as much by the harsh winter as by Stalin's army. Following the 1941 **Anglo-**

1938
The Munich Agreement places Czechoslovakia under German control.

1939
Slovakia declares independence as a nationalist Christian state; under the terms of the **Nazi-Soviet NonAgression Pact,** Josef Stalin occupies the Baltic countries while Adolf Hitler invades most of Poland.

1941
Anglo-Soviet agreement turns the tide of war.

1943-1944
The **Warsaw Ghetto Uprising** and the the larger **Warsaw Uprising** a year later attempt to save the city from the Nazis. Both attempts ultimately fail.

1944
Bulgaria becomes a communist republic.

1945
Anti-Nazi resistance leader **Josip Brož Tito** declares an independent socialist **Yugoslavia;** rejecting the **Yalta Conference,** Josef Stalin unconditionally refuses to allow free elections in the nations of Eastern Europe.

LIFE AND TIMES

1949
Hungary becomes a communist republic under **Mátyás Rákosi;** the USSR denonates an **atomic bomb.**

1955
The Soviets' **Warsaw Pact** draws Eastern Europe into a military alliance to rival the **North Atlantic Treaty Organization (NATO).**

1956
Khrushchev denounces the terrors of the Stalinist period in his "Secret Speech"; the **Hungarian Revolution** is crushed by Soviets.

1961
Berlin Wall rises.

1961
The USSR begins the **space race.**

1968
The **Prague Spring** of political and economic reform is quelled by the Soviets, who usher in 20 years of repression.

1978
Karol Wojtyla becomes the first Polish Pope, taking the name **John Paul II.**

Soviet Agreement, the USSR joined the Allied forces. This was a major turning point in the war, as were the Allies' decisive victories in 1942. The people of Eastern Europe suffered greatly in WWII. Of approximately 60 million total war casualties, Soviet troops and civilians accounted for 20 million, the largest loss of life that any country suffered. Poland, however, lost the largest percent of its population; the 6 million Poles who died in the war accounted for a staggering 20% of the country's pre-war population. More than half of the estimated 6 million Jews murdered in **Nazi concentration camps** were Polish. Before World War II, Eastern Europe had been the geographical center of the world's Jewish population, but Hitler's "final solution" succeeded in almost entirely eliminating the Jewish communities of Czechoslovakia, Hungary, Lithuania, Poland, and Ukraine through both genocide and forced emigration.

THE RUSSIANS ARE COMING! (1945-1989)

The wartime alliance between the Soviet Union and the West had been an uneasy one. Plans for postwar division of power in Europe were sketched out as early as 1944 and were sealed at the **Yalta Conference** in February 1945. Germany was divided into four zones, administered by Britain, France, the USSR, and the United States. The Soviets also oversaw newly liberated Bulgaria, Czechoslovakia, Hungary, Poland, and Romania, a plan that the Allies accepted with the expectation that these countries would be allowed to hold free elections—a detail that Stalin's government ignored. Between 1945 and 1949, the USSR established a ring of satellite People's Democracies in Eastern Europe. The American, British, and French zones of Germany coalesced into capitalist West Germany, and the Soviet zone became the satellite state of East Germany. With the consolidation of a capitalist West and a communist East, the **Iron Curtain** descended and the **Cold War** began.

To counter the American **Marshall Plan,** which funneled aid to European countries in an attempt to preserve democratic capitalism, communist nations created the **Council for Mutual Economic Assistance (COMECON),** an organization meant to facilitate and coordinate the economic growth of the Soviet Bloc, in 1949. Later that year, the West established the **North Atlantic Treaty Organization (NATO),** a military alliance meant to "keep the Americans in, the Russians out, and the Germans down." In 1955, the Eastern Bloc retaliated with a similar alliance, the **Warsaw Pact,** which maintained Soviet military bases throughout Eastern Europe and tightened the USSR's grip on its satellite countries. The only communist European country never to join the Warsaw Pact was **Yugoslavia,** where former partisan **Josip Brož Tito** broke from Moscow as early as 1948 and followed his own vision of combining communism with a market economy.

After Stalin's death in 1953, and **Nikita Khrushchev's** denunciation of him in the so-called **Secret Speech** of 1956, the Soviet Bloc was plagued by chaos. In Hungary and Poland, **National Commu-**

nism, or the belief that the attainment of ultimate communist goals should be dictated internally rather than by orders from Moscow, gained popularity, threatening Soviet domination. The presence of Russian troops throughout Eastern Europe, however, enabled Moscow to respond to rising nationalist movements with military force. The Soviets violently suppressed the 1956 **Hungarian Revolution** and workers' strikes in Poland, and executed renegade Hungarian leader **Imre Nagy** in 1958. The **Berlin Wall** was erected in 1961, creating a physical symbol of the economic, political, and ideological divide between East and West. The **Prague Spring** of 1968 witnessed another wave of violent suppression as the Czechoslovakian dissident movement demanded freedom and attention to human rights and was instead met with Soviet tanks. Political repression coupled with the economic stagnancy of the **Leonid Brezhnev** years (1964-82) increased unrest and resentment toward Moscow among the satellites. The 1978 selection of Polish-born Karol Wojtyła as **Pope John Paul II** further undermined Soviet control in Eastern Europe: the Polish Solidarity movement, the first Eastern Bloc dissident movement in which elite intellectuals and industrial workers joined together to oppose Soviet rule, was ignited by the new pope's 1979 visit to Poland and provided a model for dissident movement across the region for the next decade.

THE WALL FALLS (1989 ONWARD)

When **Mikhail Gorbachev** became Secretary General of the Communist Party of the USSR in 1985, he began to dismantle the totalitarian aspects of the Soviet regime through his policies of **glasnost** (openness) and **perestroika** (restructuring). The new freedom of political expression gave rise to increasing displays of dissidence, which finally erupted in 1989 with a series of peaceful revolutions throughout Eastern Europe. In June, Poland voted the Communists out of office, electing **Lech Wałęsa** and the **Solidarity Party** to create a new government. This Polish victory was swiftly followed by a new democratic constitution in **Hungary** in October, the crumbling of the Berlin Wall on November 9, the resignation of the **Bulgarian** communists on November 10, the **Velvet Revolution** in Czechoslovakia on November 17, and the televised execution of Romania's communist dictator, **Nicolae Ceaușescu,** on December 25. Almost all the Warsaw Pact nations had successfully—and almost bloodlessly—broken away from the Soviet Union.

The **USSR** crumbled shortly after its empire. By June 1990, **Estonia, Latvia,** and **Lithuania** all declared independence from Moscow. **Ukraine** followed suit at the end of 1991. In an attempt to keep the USSR together, Gorbachev condoned military force against the rebellious Baltic republics. A conflict erupted in Vilnius, Lithuania, in January 1991, killing 14. By September, the USSR had dissolved and all of its constituent republics and satellite nations had achieved full independence.

Following Tito's death in 1980, Yugoslavia slowly disintegrated. Economic inequality among its different republics brought suppressed nationalist sentiments to the surface.

1980
The first independent workers' union in Eastern Europe, **the Polish Solidarność** (Solidarity), is born, but repressed a year later under Soviet martial law.

1985
Russian President **Mikhail Gorbachev** begins an age of political and economic reform under *perestroika*.

1986
The worst nuclear accident in history strikes **Chernobyl,** Ukraine.

1989
Czechoslovakia, Hungary, and Poland **sever all ties** to the USSR; revolution breaks out in Romania; Berlin Wall falls.

1990
Slovenia holds the **first democratic elections in Yugoslavia** since before WWII.

1991
The USSR violently supresses revolt in Vilnius before collapsing; the **Commonwealth of Independent States (CIS)** is formed.

LIFE AND TIMES

2004
The Czech Republic, Estonia, Latvia, Lithuania, Hungary, Poland, Slovakia, and Slovenia join the **EU.** Viktor Yushchenko wins the Ukrainian presidency in the nonviolent **Orange Revolution.**

Inspired by the developments in the rest of Eastern Europe, both **Croatia** and **Slovenia** declared independence on June 25, 1991; the Serb-controlled government responded with military force. The conflict in Slovenia lasted only 10 days, but Croatia's attempts to secede resulted in a protracted, genocidal war that continued until the signing of the US-negotiated **Dayton Peace Agreement** in November 1995.

Today, the former Soviet satellites are moving, with varying degrees of success, toward democracy and market economies. In March 1999, the Czech Republic, Hungary, and Poland joined NATO. May 2002 saw the formation of the **NATO-Russia Council,** a strategic alliance between Russia and the organization originally established as a military alliance against it. Bulgaria, Estonia, Latvia, Lithuania, Romania, the Slovak Republic, and Slovenia were welcomed as new members of NATO in April 2004. The following month, the Czech Republic, Estonia, Hungary, Latvia, Lithuania, Poland, the Slovak Republic, and Slovenia became part of the **European Union (EU).** Bulgaria and Romania are expected to join in 2007.

BEYOND TOURISM

A PHILOSOPHY FOR TRAVELERS

BEYOND TOURISM HIGHLIGHTS

LEARN TO DIRECT a film in Prague or St. Petersburg (p. 67).

PLANT fruit on an organic farm in Slovenia (p. 66).

PLAY with Bosnian refugee children in Croatia (p. 63).

LIVE with a family in Poland while teaching high school students (p. 64).

Let's Go believes that the connection between travelers and their destinations is important. We've watched the growth of the "ignorant tourist" stereotype with dismay, knowing that many travelers care passionately about the communities and environments they explore—but also knowing that even conscientious tourists can inadvertently damage natural wonders and harm cultural environments. With this "Beyond Tourism" chapter, Let's Go hopes to promote a better understanding of the countries of Eastern Europe and enhance your experience there.

In the developing world of Eastern Europe, there are many different options for those who seek to go beyond tourism. Opportunities for **volunteerism,** with both local and international organizations, abound. You can also **study,** either by enrolling directly in a local university or by doing independent research. While *Let's Go* discourages **working** in the developing world, as it may take employment from locals who need it most, there are many opportunities for anglophones to serve a genuine local need by **teaching English.**

As a volunteer, you can participate in projects ranging from aid assistance with the struggling Roma population at a Bulgarian work camp to counseling those coping with the stress of the Balkan conflict, either on a short-term or long-term basis. Studying at a college or language program is another way to immerse yourself in the culture of this dynamic region. From filmmaking to language-learning, these programs enable you to peek beneath the touristed veneer of cities such as Prague and St. Petersburg and discover the inner life of ambitious post-Soviet countries.

 Start your search at **www.beyondtourism.com,** Let's Go's searchable database of alternatives to tourism, where you can find exciting feature articles and helpful programs listed by country, continent, and program type.

VOLUNTEERING

Volunteering can be a fulfilling way to experience another culture, and is very common in Central and Eastern Europe. Both local and international programs offer exciting alternatives to travel, from building playgrounds to monitoring wolf populations to teaching English. While many volunteer services charge a participation fee, which can be surprisingly hefty, they frequently cover airfare and living expenses. Some other programs ask only that volunteers pay for travel and incidental expenses, and some programs even pay volunteers a daily stipend. Researching a program before committing is wise: talk to people who have participated in the program and find out what you're getting into, as living and working conditions vary greatly. Different programs are geared toward different ages and experience levels, so make sure you are not taking on too much or too little.

The more informed you are and the more realistic your expectations are, the more enjoyable your volunteer experience will be. The best way to find opportunities that match your interests may be to explore the General Resources below, as well as the literature listed at the end of the chapter. For short-term volunteers, the most common option is a work camp, which for a few hundred dollars will offer a place to live and work on projects including agriculture, environmental protection, childcare, or construction.

WHY PAY MONEY TO VOLUNTEER?

Many volunteers are surprised to learn that some organizations require large fees or "donations." While this may seem ridiculous at first glance, such fees often keep the organization afloat, in addition to covering airfare, room, board, and administrative expenses for the volunteers. (Other organizations must rely on private donations and government subsidies.) If you're concerned about how a program spends its fees, request an annual report or finance account. A reputable organization won't refuse to inform you of how volunteer money is spent. Pay-to-volunteer programs might be a good idea for young travelers who have the money and are looking for more support and structure (such as pre-arranged transportation and housing), or anyone who would rather not deal with the uncertainty inherent in creating a volunteer experience from scratch.

GENERAL RESOURCES

Action Without Borders (www.idealist.org). An extensive Internet bulletin board listing over 46,000 volunteer organizations, with a versatile search engine.

Coordinating Committee for International Voluntary Service, UNESCO House, 31 r. François Bonvin, 75732 Paris Cedex 15, France (☎33 1 4568 4936; www.unesco.org/ccivs/). This umbrella organization links over 140 NGOs worldwide. The "Members" section on the website includes a list of volunteer branches throughout Central and Eastern Europe with contact information.

Transitions Abroad, P.O. Box 745, Bennington, VT, 05201 USA (☎1-802-442-4827; www.transitionsabroad.com). The preeminent "beyond tourism" magazine also publishes a number of books and hosts an extensive online resource on opportunities to volunteer, work, or study abroad.

Working Abroad (www.workingabroad.com). An online network of voluntary and professional work organizations. For a US$52 fee, they provide a personalized listing of overseas opportunities based on one's capabilities and interests.

BALKAN REBUILDING

Armed conflict in the Balkans—from the devastating war in Croatia and Bosnia in the early 90s to the 1999 war in Kosovo—has left deep scars and open wounds throughout the region. Genocide and subsequent intervention by the international community left 300,000 dead and millions more displaced, and did massive damage to the region's infrastructure and economy. While most of the ethnic tensions that spawned the conflicts have died down, disagreements between ethnic Albanians and Serbs still threaten to destabilize Kosovo, which is presently a province of Serbia but is governed by the United Nations. A variety of organizations continues to pick up the pieces by assisting refugees, helping children, and repairing the landscape. Volunteering for these organizations is a particularly good opportunity for foreigners whose primary objective is peace and stability, not the promotion of one group over another.

Balkan Sunflowers, Bregu i Diellit 2, Bl. 13 Apt. 32, Priština, Kosovo, Serbia and Montenegro (☎381 38 246 299; www.balkansunflower.org). Throughout the Balkan region. Programs generally last 6 weeks. Volunteers often work with children.

Coalition for Psychotrauma and Peace, Gunduliceva 18, 32000 Vukovar, Croatia (☎385 32 444 662; www.cwwpp.org). Work for 1½-2yr. in education and health care related to long-term conflict stress in **Croatia.**

Firefly UK/Bosnia, 3 Bristo Pl., Edinburgh, Midlothian, EH1 1 EY, UK (☎44 79 56 98 38 85; www.fireflybosnia.org). Scottish organization that arranges summer camps in **Croatia** for refugees from Bosnian youth centers.

United Nations High Commission for Refugees (UNHCR), Case Postale 2500, CH-1211 Genève 2 Dépôt, Switzerland (☎22 739 8111; www.unhcr.ch), will gladly provide advice on how and where to help.

YOUTH AND HEALTH OUTREACH

Aid to Russia and the Republics (ARRC), P.O. Box 200, Bromley, Kent, BR1 1QF, UK (☎44 20 8460 6046). Christian-based humanitarian organization with projects focused on helping children in **Russia** and **Ukraine.**

Cadip, 111-1271 Howe Street, Vancouver, British Columbia, V6Z 1R3, Canada (☎1-604-628-7400; www.cadip.org/). Runs work camps of young volunteers who assist with orphan childcare in **Bulgaria.** Housing fee $235. Travel costs separate.

Camp Counselors USA (CCUSA), 2330 Marinship Way, Ste. 250, Sausalito, CA 94965 USA (☎1-415-339-2728; www.ccusa.com). Places young volunteers at summer camps in **Croatia, Hungary,** and **Russia** for durations ranging 1-12 weeks.

Cross-Cultural Solutions, 2 Clinton Pl., New Rochelle, NY 10801 USA (☎1-800-380-4777; http://crossculturalsolutions.org). 2- to 12-week education and social service placements in **Russia** and many other countries. 17+. From US$2175.

Doctors Without Borders, 333 7th Ave., 2nd fl., New York, NY 10001 USA (☎1-212-679-6800; www.doctorswithoutborders.org/volunteer). Medical and non-medical volunteer assignments wherever there is need.

Downside Up, 15 Ozerkovsky per., Moscow 115184, RUS (☎/fax 011 7 951 00 79; www.downsideup.org). Bike 250km through the **Moscow** region in late Aug. to raise money for this organization that benefits Russian children with Down's syndrome.

Global Volunteer Network (www.volunteer.org.nz). Volunteer opportunities helping children in **Romania** and **Russia.** From US$600.

Peacework, 209 Otey St., Blacksburg, VA 24060, USA (☎1-800-272-5519; www.peacework.org). Volunteer with orphans in **Russia** and help refugee children in the **Czech Republic** for 1- to 3-week stints.

Russian Orphan Opportunity Fund (ROOF), Voznesenskiy per. 8, 103 009, Moscow, RUS (☎/fax 7 095 229 5100; www.roofnet.org). Provides Russian orphans with vocational training, English-language proficiency, and computer literacy.

UNICEF (United Nations Children's Fund), 5-7 avenue de la Paix, CH-1211 Geneva 10, Switzerland (☎41 22 909 5433; www.unicef.org/ceecis). UN organization, with offices throughout Eastern Europe. Accepts volunteers for teaching and healthcare projects. By application. Undergraduate degree and work experience required.

COMMUNITY DEVELOPMENT

European Roma Rights Center, H-1386 Budapest 62, P.O. Box 906/93, Hungary (fax 36 1 413 22 01; www.errc.org). Those of Romani origin can apply for a human rights advocacy internship in **Hungary** lasting 6 weeks to 6 months. 18+.

Habitat for Humanity International, 121 Habitat St., Americus, GA 31709, USA (☎1-229-924-6935, ext. 2551; www.habitat.org). Volunteers build houses in over 83 countries, including **Bulgaria, Hungary, Poland, Romania,** and the **Slovak Republic.** From 2 weeks to 3 years. Short-term program about US$1350; airfare not included.

MAR-Bulgarian Youth Alliance for Development, P.O. Box 201, 1000 Sofia, Bulgaria (☎359 29 80 20 37; www.mar.bg). Places volunteers in Bulgarian work camps for 2-3 weeks. Aid Roma population or foster environmental awareness.

Peace Corps, Office of Volunteer Recruitment and Selection, 1111 20th St. NW, Washington, D.C. 20526, USA (☎1-800-424-8580; www.peacecorps.gov). Sends volunteers to developing nations, including **Bulgaria, Romania, and Ukraine.** Typical assignments in Eastern Europe focus on business, education, or environmental issues. Must be a US citizen age 18+ willing to make a 2-year commitment. By application. Bachelor's degree usually required.

Service Civil International Voluntary Service (SCI-IVS), SCI USA, 5474 Walnut Level Rd., Crozet, VA 22932, USA (☎1-206-350-6585; www.sci-ivs.org). Placement in work camps throughout Eastern and Central Europe. 18+. US$175 for 2 weeks.

Volunteers for Peace, 1034 Tiffany Rd., Belmont., VT 05730, USA (☎1-802-259-2759; www.vfp.org). Arranges placement in work camps throughout Eastern Europe. Membership required for registration. Annual *International Workcamp Directory* US$20. 2- to 3-week programs average US$200-400.

LITERACY AND CULTURAL EXCHANGE

Bridges for Education, 94 Lamarck Dr., Buffalo, NY 14226 USA (☎1-716-839-0180; www.bridges4edu.org). Runs 4-week summer "peace camps" in **Bulgaria, Estonia,** and **Romania.** Fee $930 plus travel and other expenses. Scholarships available.

Global Volunteers, 375 E. Little Canada Rd., St. Paul, MN 55117, USA (☎1-800-487-1074; www.globalvolunteers.org). Short-term volunteer opportunities (1-3 weeks) in **Hungary, Poland, Romania,** and **Ukraine.** Programs focus on teaching and aiding children. From US$2000; airfare not included.

Jewish Volunteer Corps, American Jewish World Service, 45 W. 36th St., New York, NY 10018 USA (☎1-800-889-7146). Places volunteers at summer camps and Jewish community centers in **Russia** and **Ukraine.**

Kitezh Children's Community (http://atschool.eduweb.co.uk/ecoliza/files/kitezh.html). Teach English to **Russian** orphans in a rural setting. Young people taking a "gap year" between high school and college are especially welcome as volunteers.

Learning Enterprises, 2227 20th St. NW #304, Washington, DC 20009 USA (☎001 202 309 3453; www.learningenterprises.org). 6-week summer programs place first-time English teachers in rural **Croatia, Hungary, Romania,** and **Slovakia,** with the option to switch countries half-way. No-fee program includes orientation and room and board with a host family, but volunteers must pay for airfare and expenses.

WorldTeach, 79 JFK St., Cambridge, MA 02138 USA (☎1-800-483-2240; www.worldteach.org). Live with a family in **Poland** and teach English to high-school students. US$3990.

EXPAT FUN
Teaching English as a Foreign Language in Prague

In the 1990s, people began comparing Prague to Paris in the 1920s. Both were allegedly fueled by the same sort of boozy, poetic energy that expats find so irresistable. Prague was cheap, glamorous, full of cobblestone streets. By the time I graduated college, I knew that life held something more than it was currently offering—something grander, more like the image of Prague.

Don't want to go to grad school? Tired of the service industry? The burgeoning Teaching English as a Foreign Language (TEFL) field may be for you. English teachers in Prague are a scruffy lot. We are tourists with permanent addresses. If you want to immerse yourself in a culture, to learn the language and meet locals, Prague is probably not the best place to do it.

The good news is that jobs are plentiful, and getting started at TEFL is a simple, if costly, affair. First you need to get certified. These days TEFL has become a colossal business, and dozens of schools offer the four week, 120hr. training course. Such schools mushroom and disappear overnight, so research is recommended. The training experience is a bit like summer camp: often isolated on the outskirts of Prague, students participate in mock-lessons meant to teach methodology, but which more often resemble elementary school with their emphases on maps and games. Training also provides a mini social scene. The people I did my TEFL course with became my roommates and my first few friends here.

Once the strange initiation rites of TEFL are done, the apartment found and paid for through the nose, then the job hunt begins. Language schools are rampant in Prague, though "school" is a bit of a misnomer since they are actually more like agencies in the business of hooking up clients with teachers. The schools develop reputations: one hires good-looking American girls for their male clients, another buries its teachers in paperwork and pays poorly. There are distinct benefits to working for these schools, which provide textbooks and other teaching materials. But they also act as middlemen, and teachers see only a fraction of what students pay for their services. Do-it-yourself teaching—which depends on posting fliers and holding classes in coffeeshops—is popular but harder to do. Most students come from companies that prefer to work with professional schools.

I was so broke that I took the first job I could find. I had come to Prague with the misconception that life here was dirt cheap. Essential items like food, beer, and cigarettes are still inexpensive, but rent, clothing, books, and movies cost about what they would in, say, Phoenix, Arizona.

The expat scene, though large, quickly grows claustrophobic. You yearn to meet some Czechs. Basically, the Czechs I've met are my students, who are accountants, marketing directors, and human resources personnel. They are older and better dressed than I am, and they have an unrefreshing fixation on grammar. We hold classes around their work schedules: early morning, lunchtime, evenings.

It took about four months to build up a full schedule of three- to four classes a day, and by then I was already exhausted from constantly having to offer peppy praise and soft correction. I have become a stunning conversationalist, however, and can engage you for hours on the topic of your weekend plans. If nothing else, teaching English has forced me out of the narcissistic shell I developed in college. I'll return to the states broke, but also well armed and ready for small talk.

Hannah Brooks-Motl is a graduate of Macalester College. Though she has yet to "find" herself there, she lives and works in Prague. Her favorite Czech beer is Staropramen; her favorite Czech food is the dumpling.

CONSERVATION AND PRESERVATION

Auschwitz Jewish Center, 36 West 44th Street, Suite 310, New York, NY 10036 USA (☎1-212-575-1050; www.acjf.org). Offers fully-paid two-week or eight-week programs for college students and recent graduates in Oswiecim, Poland, focusing on cultural exchange and the study of pre-war Jewish life in Poland, with visits to the Auschwitz-Birkenau State Museum and other sites.

Archaeological Institute of America, 656 Beacon St., Boston, MA 02215 USA (☎1-617-353-9361; www.archaeological.org). The *Archaeological Fieldwork Opportunities Bulletin,* available on the website, lists field sites throughout Europe including **Bulgaria, Poland, Romania, Russia,** and **Ukraine.** Print edition, with additional info, US$20.

Brethren Volunteer Service, 1451 Dundee Ave., Elgin, IL 60120 USA (☎1-800-323-8039, ext. 410; www.brethrenvolunteerservice.org). Places volunteers with environmental and civic groups in the **Slovak Republic.**

BTVC, 163 Balby Rd., Balby, Doncaster DN4 0RH, UK (☎44 01302 572 224). Week-long wildlife and wilderness preservation projects throughout Central and Eastern Europe. Book early for the trip to the **Slovak Republic,** which monitors bear and wolf predator populations in the Tatras Mountains. Fee and accommodation €450-700.

Earthwatch, 3 Clocktower Pl., Ste. 100, P.O. Box 75, Maynard, MA 01754 USA (☎001 800 776 0188 or 001 978 461 0081; www.earthwatch.org). Arranges 1- to 3-week programs in the **Czech Republic, Estonia, Poland, Romania,** and **Russia** to promote conservation of natural resources. Programs average US$2000.

Eco-Centre Caput Insulae-Beli, Beli 4, 51559 Beli, Cres Island, Croatia (☎/fax 385 51 840 525; www.caput-insulae.com). Volunteers protect the natural, cultural, and historical heritage of Cres Island, **Croatia.** 2 weeks 122-271.

EcoVolunteer, Attn: Mr. Roel Cosijn, Meyersweg 29, 7553 AX Hengelo, Netherlands (☎31 74 250 8250; www.ecovolunteer.org). Offers wildlife conservation programs with animals ranging from Croatian vultures to Polish beavers. Programs in **Bulgaria, Croatia, Poland,** and **Russia.**

INEX—Association of Voluntary Service, Senovážné nám. 24, 116 47 Praha 1, Czech Republic (☎420 234 621 527; www.inexsda.cz/en/index.php). Ecological and historical preservation efforts, as well as construction projects, in the **Czech Republic.**

Tahoe-Baikal Institute, P.O. Box 13587, South Lake Tahoe, CA 96151 USA (☎1-530-542-5599; www.tahoebaikal.org). Environmental exchange (typically 10 weeks). College students and young professionals spend 5 weeks at Lake Tahoe, CA and 5 weeks at Lake Baikal, **Russia.** AmeriCorps workers can receive a stipend with this program.

World Wide Opportunities on Organic Farms (WWOOF), Main Office, P.O. Box 2675, Lewes BN7 1RB, England, UK (www.wwoof.org). Arranges volunteer work on organic and eco-conscious farms around the world. Branches in **Czech Republic** and **Slovenia.**

STUDYING

VISA INFORMATION
In most Eastern European countries, studying requires a special **student visa.** Applying for such a visa usually requires proof of admission to a university or program in your country of destination. Contact your local consulate or embassy. For additional visa information, see **Essentials** (p. 9) or consult the **Consulates and Embassies** section at the beginning of each country chapter.

Study-abroad programs range from language lessons to university-level courses. To choose a program that best fits your needs, do as much research as you can before making your decision—determine costs and duration, as well as what kind of students participate in the program and whether accommodations are provided. Keep in mind that while programs in which many students speak your language may allow you to feel comfortable in the community, they will limit your opportunities to practice the language or befriend other international students.

Foreign-study programs have multiplied rapidly in Eastern Europe. Most undergraduates enroll in programs sponsored by universities in their home countries, and many university study-abroad offices can provide advice and information. Libraries and bookstores are helpful sources of current information on study abroad programs, as are easy-to-use websites like **www.iiepassport.org, www.languagesabroad.com, www.petersons.com/stdyabrd, www.studyabroad.com,** and **www.worldwide.edu.** If you are fluent in an Eastern European language, you may want to consider enrolling directly in a **foreign university.** This route is usually less expensive and more immersive than programs run by **American universities,** though it may be harder to get domestic university credit for your scholarly adventures abroad. Contact the nearest consulate for a list of educational institutions in your country of choice. There are also several international and national fellowships available (e.g., Fulbright or Rotary) that fund stays abroad. Below are several organizations that run programs in Eastern European countries.

AMERICAN PROGRAMS

American Field Service (AFS), 71 W. 23rd St., 17th fl., New York, NY 10010 USA (☎ 1-212-807-8686; www.afs.org), with branches in over 50 countries. Offers summer-, semester-, and year-long homestay exchange programs for high school students and graduating seniors in the **Czech Republic, Hungary, Latvia, Russia,** and the **Slovak Republic.** Community service programs also offered for young adults 18+. Teaching programs available for current and retired teachers. Financial aid available.

American Institute for Foreign Study (AIFS), River Plaza, 9 West Broad St., Stamford, CT 06902 USA (☎ 1-800-727-2437; www.aifsabroad.com). Organizes programs for study in universities in the **Czech Republic, Poland,** and **Russia.** Financial aid and scholarships available. US$75 application fee.

Association for International Practical Training (AIPT), 10400 Little Patuxent Pkwy., Ste. 250, Columbia, MD 21044 USA (☎ 1-410-997-2200; www.aipt.org). Runs 8- to 12-week and year-long programs in Eastern Europe for college students aged 18-30 who have completed 2 years of technical study as well as year-long programs for qualified professionals under 35. Scholarships available. US$75 application fee.

Council on International Educational Exchange (CIEE), 7 Custom House St., 3rd fl., Portland, ME 04101 USA (☎ 1-800-407-8839; www.ciee.org). Work, volunteer, and academic programs in the **Czech Republic, Hungary, Poland,** and **Russia.**

NYU Study Abroad, 7 East 12th Street, 6th fl., New York, NY 10003 USA (☎ 001 212 998 4433; www.nyu.edu/studyabroad). Offers a semester or year of liberal arts undergraduate study at the NYU Center in Prague, near Charles University.

NYU, Tisch School of the Arts, 721 Broadway, 12th fl., New York, NY 10003 USA (☎ 1-212-998-1500; www.specialprograms.tisch.nyu.edu). Spend time in **Prague** studying filmmaking and directing a film, or take film and acting classes in **St. Petersburg.**

School for International Training, College Semester Abroad, Admissions, Kipling Rd., P.O. Box 676, Brattleboro, VT 05302 USA (☎ 1-800-257-7751; www.sit.edu). Semester- and year-long programs in the **Balkans,** the **Czech Republic, Poland,** and **Russia.** Must have completed at least 1yr. of college with a minimum 2.5 cumulative GPA. US$12,000-13,050. Financial aid available. Also runs the **Experiment in International Living** (☎ 001 800 345 2929; www.usexperiment.org), 5-week summer programs (US$5000) that offer high-school students cross-cultural homestays, community service, ecological adventure, and language training in **Poland.**

The School of Russian and Asian Studies, 175 E. 74th, Suite 21B, New York, NY 10021 (☎ 1-800-557-8774; www.sras.org). Provides study abroad opportunities at language schools and in degree programs at Russian universities. Also arranges work, internship and volunteer programs throughout Russia.

University Study Abroad Consortium, USAC/323, Reno, NV 89557 USA (☎ 1-775-784-6569; www.usac.unr.edu). Offers a program of studying Czech language and culture in **Prague** for the duration of a summer, semester, or year. From US$2780.

Youth for Understanding USA (YFU), 6400 Goldsboro Rd., Ste. 100, Bethesda, MD 20817 USA (☎ 1-866-493-8872 or 1-240-235-2100; www.yfu.org). Places US high school students for a year, semester, or summer in **Estonia, Hungary, Latvia, Poland, Russia,** or **Ukraine.** US$75 application fee plus $500 enrollment deposit.

EASTERN EUROPEAN PROGRAMS

American University in Bulgaria, Blagoevgrad 2700, Bulgaria (☎ 359 73 888 218; www.aubg.bg). University in **Bulgaria** based on the American liberal arts model. Accepts international students.

Central European University, Nador u. 9, Budapest 1051, Hungary (☎ 361 327 30 00; www.bard.edu/ceu). University affiliated with the Open Society Institute-Budapest offers English-language program for international students in conjunction with Bard College. Tuition US$14,500 per semester. Financial aid available.

Charles University, Vratislavova 10/29, 128 00 Praha 2, Czech Republic (www.ujop.cuni.cz). Central Europe's oldest university offers courses in Czech language, culture, and history for durations ranging from 6 weeks to 10 months.

Hungarian Dance Academy, Columbus u. 87-89, Budapest H-1145, Hungary (☎ 361 273 34 34; www.mtf.hu). Summer dance programs for international students.

Jagiellonian University, Centre for European Studies, ul. Garbarska 7a, 31-131 Kraków, Poland (☎ 48 12 431 1575; www.ces.uj.edu.pl). University founded in 1364 offers undergraduates summer and semester programs in Central European studies and Polish language. Semester tuition €3500. Scholarships available.

Liden & Denz Language Centre, Transportny per. 11 5th fl., 191119 St. Petersburg, Russia (☎ 7 812 325 22 41; www.lidenz.ch). **Branch** at Grusinski per. 3-181, ground fl., 123056 Moscow, Russia. Russian language classes and cultural excursions into **Moscow** and **St. Petersburg.**

Lithuanian Academy of Music, Gedimino pr. 42, 2600 Vilnius, Lithuania (☎ 370 5 261 26 91; www.lma.lt, rektoratas@lma.lt). Classes in music, art, and theater in **Lithuania.** Offers music classes in English.

Lomonosov Moscow State University, A-812a, Main Building, Moscow State University, Leninskie Gory, Moscow 119992-GSP-2, Russia (☎ 7 035 939 3510; www.ied.msu.ru). **Russia**'s oldest university welcomes international students.

Odessa Language Center, (☎ 380 482 345 058; www.studyrus.com). Spend a year or a summer in **Ukraine** learning Russian and taking courses on history and culture.

The Prague Center for Further Education and Professional Development, Pštrossova 19, Nové Město, 110 00 Praha 1, Czech Republic (☎ 420 257 534 013; www.prague-center.cz/etlbar.html). Teaches courses on art, filmmaking, and design in **Prague.**

University of Bucharest, 36-46, M. Kogălniceanu Bd., Sector 5, 70709 Bucharest, Romania (☎ 40 21 307 7300; www.unibuc.ro, info@unibuc.ro). Accepts international students for study in **Romania.**

University of West Bohemia, Univerzitní 8, 306 14 Plzeň, Czech Republic (☎ 420 377 631 111; www.zcu.cz). An international university centrally located in a student-friendly **Czech** brewery city.

LANGUAGE SCHOOLS

Language schools are often independently run organizations or divisions of foreign universities; they rarely offer college credit. Language schools are a good alternative to university study if you desire a deeper focus on the language or a slightly less rigorous course load. **American Councils for International Education,** 1776 Massachusetts Ave. NW, Ste. 700, Washington, D.C. 20036 USA (☎1-202-833-7522; www.actr.org), offers summer-, semester-, and year-long college-level Russian-language programs throughout the former USSR. Programs in **Russia** range US$6000-16,000. Prices for programs in Central Europe vary depending on location and specifics, but are generally lower. **Languages Abroad,** 413 Ontario St., Toronto, ON Canada M5A 2V9 (☎1-800-219-9924 or 1-416-925-2112; www.languagesabroad.com), has two- to eight-week language programs (US$1200-3000) in **Croatia,** the **Czech Republic, Hungary, Poland,** and **Russia.** Participants live in homes or university dorms. The organization also offers volunteer and internship opportunities (18+), and language programs for corporate executives (26+) and young multilinguals (10+).

WORKING

Traveling for long periods can get expensive; many travelers try their hand at odd jobs for a few weeks at a time to help finance another month or two of travel. In Eastern Europe, teaching English is often the easiest way to make extra cash. Still, many countries in the region make it hard for foreigners to get jobs, as locals often have a hard time finding employment themselves; when it is possible, legal employment pays little. When considering work, travelers should be mindful of their effect on developing economies where locals are in need of employment.

LOCAL CLASSIFIEDS

Most Eastern European capitals produce a weekly English-language publication, which often includes solicitations from local agencies, organizations, and companies seeking short- and long-term English-speaking workers.

Bulgaria: The Sofia Echo (www.sofiaecho.com).

Czech Republic: The Prague Post (www.praguepost.com).

Estonia, Latvia, and Lithuania: The Baltic Times (www.baltictimes.com).

Hungary: The Budapest Sun (www.budapestsun.com).

Poland: The Warsaw Voice (www.warsawvoice.pl).

Romania: Nine O'Clock (www.nineoclock.ro).

Russia: The Russia Journal (www.russiajournal.com).

Slovak Republic: The Slovak Spectator (www.slovakspectator.sk).

Ukraine: The Kyiv Post (www.kyivpost.com).

LONG-TERM WORK

Teaching jobs abroad rarely pay well, although some elite American and international schools offer competitive salaries. **Volunteering as a teacher** is a popular option. Volunteer teachers often get some sort of a daily stipend to help cover living expenses. In almost all cases, you must have at least a bachelor's degree to be a full-fledged teacher, though students can sometimes obtain summer positions as tutors. The demand for English instructors in Eastern Europe remains high, though the market has been saturated in heavily touristed cities, like Budapest and Prague. Many schools require teachers to have a **Teaching English as a Foreign Language (TEFL)** certificate. Those without the certificate are not necessarily excluded from teaching, but certified teachers tend to find higher-paying jobs. Placement agencies or university fellowship programs are the best resources for finding teaching jobs in Eastern Europe. **Transitions Abroad** (www.transitionsabroad.com, offers an updated online listing of teaching and other work opportunities. You can also contact schools directly or try your luck once you get there. If you are going to do the latter, the best time of year is several weeks before the school year starts in September. Taking on individual students as a **private English tutor** is a popular alternative to traditional teaching positions in Eastern Europe; contact schools about potential pupils to help you get started. The following organizations are helpful in placing teachers:

Central Bureau for Educational Visits and Exchanges, 10 Spring Gardens, London SW1A 2BN, UK (www.britishcouncil.org/education/students). Places qualified British undergraduates and teachers in teaching positions in **Hungary, Russia,** and **Slovenia.**

Central European Teaching Program, 3800 NE 72nd Ave, Portland, OR 97213 USA (☎ 1-503-287-4977; www.ticon.net/~cetp/). Places English teachers in state schools in **Hungary** and **Romania** for one semester ($1500) or 10 months ($2000).

Czech Academic Information Agency, Dům Zahraničních Služeb, Senovážné nám. 26, PO Box 8, 111 06 Prague, Czech Republic (☎420 2 24 22 9698; www.dzs.cz/scripts/detail.asp?id=599). Helps prospective English teachers find posts in state primary and secondary schools in small **Czech** towns.

International Schools Services (ISS), 15 Roszel Rd., P.O. Box 5910, Princeton, NJ 08543 USA (☎1-609-452-0990; www.iss.edu). Hires teachers for more than 200 overseas schools, many in Eastern Europe. Candidates should have experience with teaching or international affairs. Bachelor's degree and 2-yr. commitment required.

Office of Overseas Schools, US Department of State, Room H328, SA-1, Washington, D.C. 20522 USA (☎1-202-261-8200; www.state.gov/m/a/os/). Keeps comprehensive lists of schools abroad and agencies that place Americans to teach abroad.

Petro-Teach, Westpost, P.O. Box 109, Lappeenranta 53101, Finland (www.petroteach.com). Places teachers from abroad in schools in St. Petersburg, **Russia,** for a semester or a full academic year. US$3000-5000.

THROUGH THE RED TAPE: VISAS AND PERMITS

Though working in Eastern Europe is rewarding, it entails jumping through an exhausting set of bureaucratic hoops. Already dealing with rampant unemployment, most countries make it very difficult for foreigners to work, requiring a work permit as well as a visa or a permit for temporary residency. In some countries, to make it all the more confusing, a particular type of visa, often called a "visa with work permit," is required in addition to (not as a replacement for) a work permit. These visas are issued from the nearest consulate or embassy (see the Embassies and Consulates section of each country chapter). Applying for one will require you to present your work permit, which must be issued directly from the Labor Bureau of the country in question. Given these complications, making contact with prospective employers within the country is a good way to expedite permits or arrange work-for-accommodations swaps. For US students and young adults, the simplest way to get legal permission to work abroad is through Council Exchanges Work Abroad Programs, which can help you obtain a 3- to 6-month work permit and/or visa and provide assistance finding jobs and housing (US$300-425).

AU PAIR WORK

Most au pairs are women aged 18-27, who work as live-in nannies, caring for children and doing light housework in exchange for room, board, and a small spending allowance or stipend. In many countries, au pairs are required to be enrolled in college during their stay. While the au pair experience allows foreigners to get to know a country without the high expenses of traveling, the job often involves long hours for mediocre pay. Payment varies widely with placement, and much of the au pair experience really does depend on the family for which you'll be working.

AuPairConnect, Max Global, Inc., 8370 W. Cheyenne Ave. #76, Las Vegas, NV 89129, USA (www.aupairconnect.com).

Svezhy Veter, 426000 Izhevsk P.O. Box 2040, Russia (☎7 341 24 50 037; www.svagency.udm.ru/sv/aupair.htm).

SHORT-TERM WORK

Working in a hostel or restaurant and teaching English are the most common forms of employment among travelers to Eastern Europe. Opportunities tend to be more abundant in larger cities, but so do prospective workers, creating increased competition. Word-of-mouth is often the best resource when seeking a job; ask other backpackers and friendly hostel owners for tips on an appropriate opportunity. Consult the exhaustive resources and opportunities at **www.transitionsabroad.com.** Another popular option is to work several hours a day at a hostel or on a farm in exchange for free or discounted room or board.

INTERNSHIPS

Internships, usually for college students, are a good way to segue into working abroad, although they are often unpaid or poorly paid (many say the experience, however, is well worth it). **Internships International,** 1612 Oberlin Rd., Raleigh, NC 27608, USA, offers unpaid internships and connections to language schools in cities around the world, including Budapest, **Hungary.** A fee of US$1100 guarantees placement in an internship. (June-Nov. ☎1-207-443-3019; Dec.-May 1-919-832-1575; www.internshipsinternational.org.)

FURTHER READING

Alternatives to the Peace Corps: A Directory of Third World and U.S. Volunteer Opportunities, by Joan Powell. Food First Books, 2000 (US$10).

Alternative Travel Directory: The Complete Guide to Traveling, Studying & Living Overseas, by Mader and Nolting. Transitions Abroad, 2002.

How to Live Your Dream of Volunteering Overseas, by Collins, DeZerega, and Heckscher. Penguin Books, 2002 (US$17).

International Dictionary of Volunteer Work, by Whetter and Pybus. Peterson's Guides and Vacation Work, 2000 (US$16).

Peterson's Study Abroad. Peterson's, 1999 (US$30).

Summer Jobs Abroad 2003, by James and Woodworth. Peterson's Guides and Vacation Work, 2003 (US$18).

Work Abroad: The Complete Guide to Finding a Job Overseas (Work Abroad) (Paperback) by Hubbs. Transitions Abroad, 2002.

Work Worldwide: International Career Strategies for the Adventurous Job Seeker, by Mueller. Avalon, 2000.

BULGARIA
(БЪЛГАРИЯ)

From the pine-covered slopes of the Rila, Pirin, and Rodopi mountains to the beaches of the Black Sea, Bulgaria is blessed with a countryside rich in natural resources and steeped in ancient traditions. The history of the Bulgarian people, however, is not as serene as the landscape: crumbling Greco-Thracian ruins and Soviet-style high-rises attest to centuries of turmoil and political struggle. Though Bulgaria's flagging economy and dual-pricing system for foreigners can dampen the mood, there's plenty of natural beauty, folksy quaintness, and good nature to go around. Rewarding experiences await on the beautiful Black Sea Coast, in cosmopolitan Sofia, and in picturesque villages. And until the country adopts a more western bent, you can bet that Bulgaria will be happily free of crowds.

DISCOVER BULGARIA: SUGGESTED ITINERARIES

THREE DAYS Two days are probably enough to take in **Sofia's** (p. 80) museums, cathedrals, and cafes. Going to the **Rila Monastery** (1 day; p. 88) is often easier said than done, but its gorgeous atmosphere and environs are worth it.

ONE WEEK If two days among the stunning ruins of **Veliko Tarnovo** (p. 97) isn't enough, bus down to **Plovdiv** (2 days; p. 89) for more Roman remains before heading to the **Rila Monastery** (1 day). End in bustling **Sofia** (2 days).

ESSENTIALS

WHEN TO GO

Bulgaria's temperate climate makes it easy to catch good weather. Spring (April-May) is pleasant and has a bevy of festivals and events. Summer (June-Sept.) isn't too hot, making it perfect for hiking and beachgoing. Just expect crowds on the Black Sea Coast and at campgrounds. Skiing is good from December until April.

FACTS AND FIGURES

Official Name: Republic of Bulgaria.	**Land Area:** 110,550 sq. km.
Capital: Sofia.	**Time Zone:** GMT +2.
Major Cities: Burgas, Plodiv, Varna.	**Language:** Bulgarian.
Population: 7,451,000.	**Religions:** Bulgarian Orthodox (83%).

DOCUMENTS AND FORMALITIES

EMBASSIES AND CONSULATES. Foreign embassies for Bulgaria are in Sofia. For embassies and high commissions at home, contact: **Australia,** 4 Carlotta Rd., Double Bay, NSW 2028, (☎2 327 7592; www.users.bigpond.com/bulcgsyd); **Canada,** 325 Stewart St., Ottawa, ON N1K 6K5 (☎613 789 3215; www.ncf.ca/bg-ottawa/Embassy.html); **Ireland,** 22 Bulington Rd., Dublin 4 (☎1 660 3293; bgemb@eircom.net); **UK,** 186-188 Queensgate, London SW7 5HL (☎20 7584 9400; www.bulgaianembassy.org.uk); **US,** 1621 22nd St., NW, Washington, D.C. 20008 (☎202 387 0174; www.bulgaria-embassy.org).

ENTRANCE REQUIREMENTS

Passport: Required for all travelers; must be valid for 3 months beyond stay.

Visa: Not required of citizens of Australia, Canada, New Zealand, Ireland, the UK, and US for up to 30 days.

Letter of Invitation: Not required for those who do not need a visa.

Inoculations: Recommended up-to-date on DTaP (diphtheria, tetanus, and pertussis), Hepatitis A, Hepatitis B, MMR (measles, mumps, and rubella), Polio booster, and Typhoid.

Work Permit: Required of all foreigners planning to work in Bulgaria.

International Driving Permit: Required of all those planning to drive.

VISA AND ENTRY INFORMATION. Citizens of Australia, Canada, Ireland, New Zealand, the UK, and the US do not need a **visa** for stays of up to 30 days. Citizens of other EU countries and those planning to stay more than 30 days must obtain a 90-day visa from their local embassy or consulate. Generally, the easiest way to extend your visa is to temporarily leave and return. If staying in a private residence, **register your visa** with police within 48 hours of entering Bulgaria; hotels and hostels will do this for you. Keep the registration with your passport, and make sure you are re-registered every time you change accommodations. A Bulgarian **border crossing** can take several hours, as there are three different checkpoints: passport control, customs, and police. The border crossing into Turkey is particularly difficult. Try to enter from Romania at Ruse or Durankulac.

TOURIST SERVICES AND MONEY

TOURIST OFFICES. Tourist offices and local travel agencies are generally knowledgeable and good at reserving private rooms; some mostly plan itineraries. Staffs are helpful and sometimes speak English, German, or Russian. Big hotels often have an English-speaking receptionist and **maps** and make good resources.

MONEY. The **lev** (**lv**; plural **leva**) is the standard monetary unit (1 lev = 100 stotinki), though sometimes US dollars or euros are accepted. **Inflation** is around 6%. Private banks and exchange bureaus change money, but bank rates are more reli-

BULGARIA

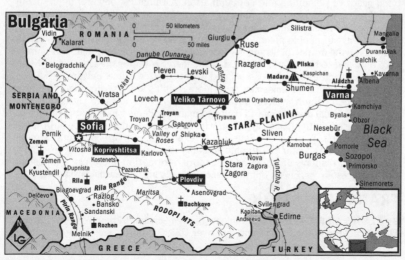

able. The four largest **banks** are Bulbank, Biochim, Hebros, and DSK. It is illegal to exchange currency on the street. **Traveler's checks** can only be cashed at banks. Many banks also give Visa **cash advances. Credit cards** are rarely accepted. **ATMs** give the best exchange rates; are common throughout Bulgaria; usually accept MasterCard, Visa, Plus, and Cirrus; and give the best rates. Beware of officially sanctioned **tourist overcharging;** museums and theaters will charge foreigners double or more, a practice that many locals frown upon.

LEVA (LV)		
	AUS$1 = 1.20LV	1LV = AUS$0.83
	CDN$1 = 1.32LV	1LV = CDN$0.76
	EUR€1 = 1.96LV	1IV = EUR€0.51
	NZ$1 = 1.12LV	1LV = NZ$0.90
	UK£1 = 2.88LV	1LV = UK£0.35
	US$1 = 1.61LV	1LV = US$0.62

HEALTH AND SAFETY

EMERGENCY   **Police: ☎ 166. Ambulance: ☎ 150. Fire: ☎ 160.**

While basic **medical supplies** are available in Bulgarian hospitals, specialized treatment is not. Emergency care is better in Sofia than in the rest of the country, but it's best to avoid hospitals entirely. Travelers are required to carry proof of insurance. Air evacuation, for extreme emergencies, runs about US$50,000.

The sign "Apteka" denotes a **pharmacy.** There is always a night-duty pharmacy in larger towns. *Analgin* is headache medicine; *analgin chinin* is for colds and flu; *sitoplasty* are bandages. Foreign brands of *prezervatifs* (condoms) are safer. Prescription drugs are difficult to obtain—bring your own supply. Fiber tablets are a must, as it's easy to get constipated on a Bulgarian diet. Public **bathrooms** ("Ж" for women, "M" for men) are often holes in the ground; pack toilet paper and hand sanitizer; expect to pay 0.05-0.20lv. **Tampons** are widely available. Don't buy bottles of **alcohol** from street vendors, and be careful with homemade liquor—there have been cases of poisoning and contamination. Asthmatics, beware: most of Bulgaria's restaurants, bars, and public transportation are heavily smoke-filled.

Be aware of petty **street crime,** especially pickpocketing and purse snatching. Also be wary of people posing as government officials; ask them to show ID. Be wary of buying drinks for strangers—the price may prove astronomical. Be sure to take only marked taxis and ensure that the meter is on for the entire ride. Nightclubs in large cities are often associated with organized crime; beware of fights.

It's generally fine for **women** to travel alone, but it's always safer to have at least one travel companion. Wear skirts and blouses to avoid unwanted attention. Visitors with physical **disabilities** will confront many challenges in Bulgaria. **Discrimination** is focused on the **Roma** (gypsies), who are considered a nuisance at best and thieves at worst. While hate crimes are rare, persons of a foreign ethnicity might receive stares. Acceptance of homosexuality is slow in coming; it is prudent to avoid public displays of affection. For more information about gay and lesbian clubs and resources, check out **www.queer_bulgaria.org** or **www.bulgayria.com.**

TRANSPORTATION

BY PLANE. All flights to Sofia connect through **London, BRI,** or Western Europe. Though tickets to the capital may run over US$2500 during the summer months, budget airline WizzAir offers cheap flights from London, **Paris, FRA,** and **Frankfurt,**

GER, through **Budapest, HUN.** Budget travelers might also consider flying into a nearby capital—Athens, Istanbul, or Bucharest—and taking a bus to Sofia. Bulgarian airports are on par with international standards.

BY TRAIN. Bulgarian trains run to **Greece, Hungary, Romania,** and **Turkey** and are better for transportation in the north; **Rila** is the main international train company. Find international timetables at www.bdz-rila.com/index_en.htm. The train system is comprehensive but trains are slow, crowded, and smoke-filled. Purse-slashing, pickpocketing, and pinching (yes, pinching) have been reported on more crowded lines. Buy tickets at the Ticket Center (Bileti Tsentur) stations. There are three types of trains: express (*ekspres*), fast (*burz*), and slow (*putnicheski*). Avoid *putnicheski* at all costs—they stop at anything that looks inhabited, even if only by goats. Arrive well in advance if you want a seat. Stations are poorly marked and often only in Cyrillic; know when you're reaching your destination, bring a map, and ask for help. First class (*purva klasa*) is identical to second (*vtora klasa*), and not worth the extra money. Store luggage at the *garderob*.

BY BUS. Buses are better for travel in eastern and western Bulgaria and are often faster than trains, but less frequent and comfortable. Buses head north from Ruse, to Istanbul from anywhere on the Black Sea Coast, and to Greece from Blagoevgrad. For long distances, **Group Travel** and **Etap** have modern buses with A/C and bathrooms for 50% higher than trains. Some buses have set departure times; others leave when full. Grueling local buses stop everywhere for a bumpy, sweaty ride.

BY TAXI AND BY CAR. Yellow taxis are everywhere in cities. Refuse to pay in dollars and insist on a ride *sus apparata* (with meter); ask the distance and price per kilometer. Don't try to bargain. Some taxi drivers rig the meters to charge more. Tipping **taxi drivers** usually means rounding up to the nearest lev or half-lev. Some Black Sea towns can only be reached by car. Renting is cheapest from a local agency, which will charge less than the €15-30 that larger companies charge. While urban roads are in fair condition, rural roads are in poor repair.

BY BIKE AND BY THUMB. Motoroads (www.motoroads.com) and travel agencies offer bike tours; when bicycling in urban areas, stay alert as drivers disregard traffic signals. Hitchhiking is rare in Bulgaria—drives are not likely to stop. While those who hitchhike say it is generally safe, *Let's Go* does not recommend it.

KEEPING IN TOUCH

PHONE CODES	**Country code: 359. International dialing prefix:** 00. From outside Bulgaria, dial int'l dialing prefix (see inside back cover) + 359 + city code + local number. Within Bulgaria, dial city code + local number for intercity calls and simply the local number for calls within a city.

Internet cafes can be found throughout urban centers, cost approx. 0.60-1lv per hr., and are often open 24hr. Making international **telephone** calls from Bulgaria can be a challenge. Pay phones are ludicrously expensive; opt for the phone offices. If you must make an **international call** from a pay phone with a card, purchase the 400 unit, 22lv card. Units run out quickly on international calls, so talk fast or have multiple cards ready. There are two brands: **BulFon** (orange) and **Mobika** (blue), which work only at telephones of the same brand; BulFon is better and more prevalent. To **call collect,** dial ☎01 23 for an international operator. The Bulgarian phrase for collect call is *za tyahna smetka*. For **local calls,** pay phones seldom accept coins, so it's best to buy a phone card (see above).

You can also call from the post office, where a clerk assigns you a booth, a meter records your bill, and you pay when finished. "Свъздушна поща" on letters indicates **airmail**. It is far more reliable than ground transport, but sometimes it is difficult to convince postal workers to let you pay extra to have letters sent airmail. Sending a letter abroad costs 0.60lv to Europe, 0.90lv to the US, and 0.80-1.00lv to Australia or New Zealand; a Bulgarian return address is required. Packages must be unwrapped for inspection. Register important packages and allow two weeks for them to arrive. Mail can be received general delivery through Poste Restante, though it is unreliable. Address envelope as follows: Jordan (First name), HYLDEN (LAST NAME), POSTE RESTANTE, писма до поискване централна поща, Гурко 6 (post office address, optional), София (city) 1000 (postal code), Ъългария (Bulgaria).

ACCOMMODATIONS AND CAMPING

BULGARIA	❶	❷	❸	❹	❺
ACCOMMODATIONS	under 20lv under €10 under $12	20-35lv €10-18 $12-22	36-50lv €18-26 $23-31	50-70lv €27-36 $32-44	over 70lv over €36 over $44

Bulgarian **hotels** are classed on a star system and licensed by the Government Committee on Tourism; rooms in one-star hotels are nearly identical to rooms in two- and three-star hotels, but have no private baths. All accommodations provide sheets and towels. Expect to pay US$9-50, with most hotels running US$25-35. Beware that foreigners are often charged double or more what locals pay. **Hostels** can be found in most major cities and run US$10-18 per bed. Almost all include free breakfast and many offer Internet and laundry services. For a complete list of hostels in Bulgaria, see www.hostels.com/en/bg.ot.html. **Private rooms** are cheap and usually have all the amenities of a good hotel (US$6-12); with the right language skills and persistence, they can be found in any small town. Outside major towns, most **campgrounds** provide spartan bungalows and tent space.

FOOD AND DRINK

BULGARIA	❶	❷	❸	❹	❺
FOOD	under 4lv under €2 under $3	4-8lv €2-4 $3-5	9-14lv €4-7 $5-9	15-18lv €7-9 $9-11	over 18lv over €9 over $11

Food from **kiosks** is cheap (0.60-2.50lv); **restaurants** average 6lv per meal. Kiosks sell *kebabcheta* (sausage burgers), sandwiches, pizzas, and *banitsa sus sirene* (feta cheese filled pastries). Try *shopska salata*, a mix of tomatoes, peppers, and cucumbers with feta cheese. *Tarator*, a cold soup made with yogurt, cucumber, garlic, and sometimes walnuts, is also tasty. Bulgaria enjoys meat. *Kavarma*, meat with onions, spices, and egg is slightly more expensive than *skara* (grills). **Vegetarians** should request *iastia bez meso* (iahs-tea-ah bez meh-so) for meals without meat. **Kosher** diners would be wise to order vegetarian meals, as pork often works itself into main dishes. Bulgarians are known for cheese and yogurt—the bacteria that makes yogurt from milk bears the scientific name *bacillus bulgaricus*. *Ayran* (yogurt with water and ice) and *boza* (similar to beer, but sweet and thicker) are popular drinks that complement breakfast. Breads and meats are often plain-tasting; soups and main dishes offer more flavor. Bulgaria exports mineral water and locals swear by its healing qualities. **Tap water** is generally safe to drink, though home-brewed beers and other alcohols produced on hand should be approached with caution. Melnik produces famous red **wine**, while the northeast is known for its excellent white wines. On the Black Sea Coast, *Albenu* is a good sparkling wine. Bulgarians begin meals with *rakiya* (grape or plum brandy). Good Bulgarian **beers** include Kamenitza and Zagorka. The drinking age is 18.

LIFE AND TIMES

HISTORY

BATTLES OF THE BULG. Though Bulgaria was officially founded in the 7th century AD, making it the the third oldest country in Europe, the earliest settlers came to the Bulgarian region sometime during the Middle Paleolithic Period, between BC 100,000 and 40,000. Between 852 and 927, emperor **Boris I** and his son **Simeon I** integrated the Bulgars and Slavs under a common language (Old Church Slavonic) and religion (Christianity). Around this time the Slavic majority was also assimilating the Bulgars. **The First Bulgarian Empire** did not last long, however, and was conquered by Byzantium in 1018. A revolt led by the brothers Ivan and Peter Asen of Tarnovo established the **Second Bulgarian Empire** in 1185. This eventually extended from the Black Sea to the Adriatic, but was also fairly short-lived. In 1396 the Turks conquered what was left of a Bulgaria weakened by internal upheaval, wars with the Serbian and Hungarian kingdoms, and Mongol attacks.

REVOLUTIONARY RUMBLINGS. For the next 500 years, Bulgaria suffered under the **"Turkish yoke."** During this period of repression, bandits known as **heiducs** kept the spirit of resistance alive. At last the **National Revival,** a period of Bulgarian cultural and educational awakening, was triggered when a monk from Athon named **Paisiy Hilendarski** wrote a history of Bulgaria in the 1760s. The movement grew decidedly political when leaders **Lyuben Karavelov** and **Vasil Levski** created the Bulgarian Secret Central Committee. The revolutionaries planned the **April Uprising,** which was so brutally suppressed that it became known throughout Europe as the **Bulgarian Horrors.** A conference of European leaders convened after the uprising and proposed reforms, which Turkey rejected. Russia declared war in response.

PUSHING BOUNDARIES. The **Russo-Turkish War** (1877-78) ended with the **Treaty of San Stefano** and the expansion of Bulgaria's boundaries from the Danube to the Aegean and to the Black Sea. Austria-Hungary and Britain, however, were unhappy with such a large Slavic state in the Russian sphere of influence. Another pan-European conference in 1878, the **Congress of Berlin,** overturned San Stefano to create a smaller state. Although the new state began on an egalitarian note, resentment over its borders lingered and in-fighting kept tensions high. Eventually border disputes erupted in the **First** and **Second Balkan Wars** in 1912 and 1913.

THE WORLD WARS. The brief wars resulted in a further loss of territory for Bulgaria, which abandoned its initial neutrality in WWI and sided with the Central Powers in the hope of recovering its losses. Though Bulgaria was neutral at the start of WWII, a lust for Greek and Yugoslav territories caused Boris III (1894-1943) to join the Axis Powers in 1941, and in 1944 the Soviet Union declared war on Bulgaria. Elections in 1945 left Bulgaria a Communist republic.

GROWING PAINS. Bulgaria saw nationalization under **Georgi Dimitrov** in the late 1940s, isolationism under **Vulko Chervenkov** in the 1950s, and rapid industrialization and alignment with the Soviet Union under **Todor Zhivkov** from 1962-89. With sociologist **Zhelyu Zhelev** as president and poet **Blaga Dimitrova** as vice-president in the post-Soviet 90s, a new government embraced openness and ended repression of ethnic Turks. The decade, however, was not kind to Bulgaria. Economic troubles led to soaring inflation, and the situation stabilized only when Prime Minister **Ivan Kostov's** Union of Democratic Forces party rose to power in 1997.

TODAY

Kostov's government fell out of favor for its slow pace of reforms and amid increasing accusations of corruption. A surprising candidate won the prime ministry in 2001: **Simeon II**, the former child-king who had been deposed in 1946. Economic progress has continued, and Bulgaria was accepted into NATO in 2004. While the country is slated to join the EU in 2007, the actual date of membership is contingent upon the pace of reforms, especially anti-corruption measures.

PEOPLE AND CULTURE

Around 7.5 million people live in Bulgaria. Population growth is currently negative, with a birthrate of 9.66 per 1000 people, and a much higher death rate of 14.26 per 1000. The country is overwhelmingly **Bulgarian**, with **Turks** and **Roma** together representing 14.1% of the population. An additional 2% consists mostly of Tatars, Macedonians, and Circassians. Bulgarians are 83% **Bulgarian Orthodox**, with a **Muslim** minority of 12%, and various groups making up the remainder. The Communist government forcibly assumed supervision of the Bulgarian church in 1949. The state tolerated religion but promoted atheism, and continued to do so with diminishing effort after the new government was established in 1989. **Bulgarian** is a South Slavic language written in the Cyrillic alphabet. A few words are borrowed from Turkish and Greek, but most vocabulary is Slavic. **English** is spoken by young people in cities and tourist areas. **German** and **Russian** are often understood. The Bulgarian alphabet is much the same as Russian (see **It's All Greek to Me,** p. 52) except that "щ" is pronounced "sht" and "ъ" is "ŭ" (like the "u" in bug). For a phrasebook and glossary, see **Glossary: Bulgarian,** p. 767.

YES AND NO. Bulgarians shake their heads from side to side to indicate "yes" and up and down to indicate "no," the exact opposite of Brits and Yanks. For the uncoordinated, it's easier to just hold your head still and say *da* or *neh*.

CUSTOMS AND ETIQUETTE. Making the **"V" sign** signifies showing support for the opposition party; don't do it. Do not address new acquaintances by their first name. Always shake someone's hand when introduced. If invited to someone's home, it is a good idea to bring a **gift** of flowers, candy, or wine. Don't bring calla lilies or gladioli, as they arc only used for weddings or funerals. To thank someone or to say hello, give them postcards of your home town. Ask permission before taking someone's photograph. Avoid wearing baggy shorts or backpacks–you will stick out as a tourist. Button-down shirts and long pants are a safe bet.

Seat yourself at **restaurants** and ask for the *smetka* (сметка; bill) when you're done. It is customary to share tables in restaurants. *Nazdrave!* (Наздзаве!) means "Cheers!"—you're sure to hear this in bars. When clinking glasses (or beer mugs), make sure to look the person in the eye and call *Nazdrave!* loudly. While dining, rest your wrists on the table; do not put one hand in your lap. **Tipping** is not obligatory, but 10% doesn't hurt, especially in Sofia where waitstaff expect it. Restaurants and *mekhani* (механи; taverns) usually charge a fee to use the restrooms.

THE ARTS

Following the arrival of Church Slavonic, Bulgarian literature entered a **Golden Age** and was on pace to compete with that of **Constantinople** when conquest by the Byzantines stalled progress. Following a resurgence in the 13th and 14th centuries, literary culture went into hibernation during the 500 years of Ottoman rule. In 1762 **Paisiy Hilendarski's** romanticized *Istoria slavyanobulgarska* (Slavo-Bulgarian History) sowed the seeds of the National Revival. Using their works as a tool for liberation, realists **L. Karavelov** and **V. Drumev** depicted small-town life, **Khristo Botev** wrote passionate revolutionary poetry, and journalists **Petko Slaveykov** and **Georgi Rakovski** drew on folklore to whip the populace into a revolutionary fervor.

The early 20th century saw Bulgarian poetry experimenting with the avantgarde and maturing as a form in the work of **Peyo Yavorov.** Arguably Bulgaria's most important 20th-century poet, **Elisaveta Bagryana** skillfully fused the experimental and the traditional in her love poems.

Bulgarian **folk music** belongs to the Balkan tradition. Music differs according to region but is usually played on local variants of Turkish instruments, and accompanied by distinctive chain dances. Bulgarian **womens' choirs** are one of the region's unique features; singers produce polyphonic, drone-like tones.

Like Bulgarian literature, the **visual arts** were hampered by Ottoman rule, but rebounded during the National Revival. Through the 20th century, most artists depicted Bulgarian life from a realist perspective. Particularly notable are the paintings of **Vladimir Dimitrov** and the graphic art of **Tsanko Lavrenov.**

HOLIDAYS AND FESTIVALS

Holidays: New Year's Day (Jan. 1); Baba Marta Spring Festival (Mar. 1); Liberation Day (Mar. 3); Orthodox Easter (Apr. 23, 2006; Apr. 8, 2007); Labor Day (May 1); St. George's Day (May 6); Education and Culture Day/Day of Slavic Heritage (St. Cyril and Methodius Day) (May 24); Festival of the Roses (Kazanlŭk) (June 5); Day of Union (Sept. 6); Independence Day (Sept. 22); Christmas Holiday (Dec. 24-26).

Festivals: Christmas and **New Year's** are marked by the two related Bulgarian customs of *koledouvane* and *souvakari.* On Christmas, groups of people go from house to house and perform *koledouvane,* or caroling, while holding beautiful oak sticks called *koledarkas.* On New Year's, a group of *sourvakari* whish their neighbors well while holding decorated cornel rods called *sourvachka.* **Baba marta** (Spring Festival) celebrates the beginning of spring. Bulgarians tradicitionally give each other *martenitzas,* small red and white tassels formed to look like a boy and a girl. These fertility charms are meant to be worn around the neck or pinned on until pregnancy is achieved. The **Festival of Roses** is celebrated in Kazanlŭk and Karlovo on the first Sunday in June.

ADDITIONAL RESOURCES

Balkan Ghosts: A Journey Through History, by Robert Kaplan (1994). Both an engaging travelogue and an accessible regional history.

Beyond Hitler's Grasp: The Heroic Rescue of Bulgaria's Jews, by Michael Bar Zohar (2001). An in-depth study of the resistance to anti-Semitism in Bulgaria during the country's alliance with Nazi Germany.

Voices of Sibyls: Three Bulgarian Poets, by Elisaveta Bagryana (1996). Selections of contemporary Bulgarian poetry.

SOFIA (СОФИЯ) ☎(0)2

Far from the Soviet grayscape you might expect, Sofia (pop. 1,100,000) is a city of magnificent domed cathedrals and grand old buildings, all set against the backdrop of nearby Mt. Vitosha. Although the city lacks the old-world feel of Prague or Vienna—when Sofia was made Bulgaria's capital in 1879, it was a muddy village of 12,000 residents—it is remarkably diverse. Skateboarders listen to American rock music in front of the Soviet Army monument, while worshippers pass each other near the central square on their way to a synagogue, mosque, or cathedral. A history of oppression has left Bulgaria unsure of its identity, but Sofia remains lively.

⌐ TRANSPORTATION

Flights: Airport Sofia (International info ☎937 22 11). Bus #84 is to the right as you exit international arrivals. Buy tickets (0.50lv) at kiosks with "Билети" (bileti) sign. Runs from the airport to Eagle Bridge (Орлов Мост; Orlov Most), near Sofia University, 10min. walk from the city center. Minibus #30 (in front of international arrivals exit; 1lv) runs between the airport and pl. Sv. Nedelya (Св. Неделя) along bul. Tsar Osvoboditel (Цар Освободител). Minibus has no specific stops; to ride, flag it down and request a stop. If you take a taxi, make sure to go with **OK Supertrans;** others will overcharge you. They have a desk inside the terminal and a stand outside; fare should run about 5lv.

Trains: Tsentralna Gara (Централна Гара; Central Train Station), Knyaginya Mariya Luiza (Княгиня Мария Луиза; www.centralnaavtogara.bg), a 1.6km walk north from pl. Sveta Nedelya past the department store TSUM (ЦУМ) and the mosque. Trams #1 and 7 run between pl. Sveta Nedelya and the station; #9 and 12 head down Hristo Botev (Христо Ботев) and bul. Vitosha (Витоша). See website for timetables. Info booth and ticket counter are on the 1st fl. To: **Burgas** (7 per day, 13.30lv); **Plovdiv** (7 per day, 6lv); **Ruse** (4 per day, 12.30lv); **Varna** (5 per day, 16lv). Trip lengths and prices depend on type of train (Пътнически, *putnicheski,* slow; Бърз, *bure,* fast; Експрес, *ekspres,* express). Train schedules change with the season, so call ahead. International tickets available at the **Rila Travel Bureau** (☎932 33 46) desk on the 1st fl., to the left of the main entrance. Open daily 7am-11pm. Destinations include: **Athens, GCE** via **Thessaloniki, GCE** (3 per day, 30lv; to Thessaloniki, where you must purchase a separate ticket for Athens); **Bucharest, ROM** (2 per day, 36lv); **Budapest, HUN** via Bucharest (1 per day, 120lv), and **Istanbul, TUR** (1 per day, 36lv).

Buses: Private buses, which leave from the parking lot across from the train station, are a bit pricier than trains—and often speedier and more comfortable. Several international bus companies are across from the entrance to the train station. **Group Travel** ticket office open daily 7am-7pm. Sends buses to: **Burgas** (18 per day, 18lv); **Varna** (9 per day, 22lv); **Veliko Tarnovo** (9 per day, 12lv), and other domestic and international destinations. Book in advance, and arrive 30-45min. early, to guarantee seat.

Public Transportation: Trams, trolleys, and **buses** cost 0.50lv per ride, 2lv for 5 rides, day pass 2.20lv. Buy tickets from the driver or at kiosks with "билети" (bileti) signs in the window; exact change only. Punch the tickets in the machines on board to avoid a 5lv fine. If you put your backpack on a seat, you may be required to buy a 2nd ticket, or pay a 5lv fine for an "unticketed passenger." All transportation runs daily 5:30am-11pm; after 9pm service becomes less frequent.

Taxis: Some travelers relate horror stories about many local taxi companies, but **OK Supertrans** (ОК Съпертранс, ☎973 21 21) remains a reliable option. Always make sure the company's name and phone number are on the side of the car, and insist that the driver turn on the meter. Many drivers don't speak English, so learn to pronounce Bulgarian names for destinations. 0.40-0.45lv per km; slightly more expensive 10pm-6am.

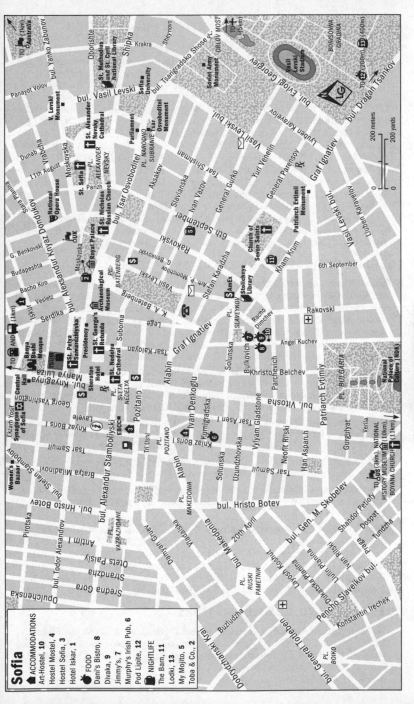

BULGARIA

Sofia

▲ ACCOMMODATIONS
Art-Hostel, **10**
Hostel Mostel, **4**
Hostel Sofia, **3**
Hotel Iskar, **1**

● FOOD
Dani's Bistro, **8**
Divaka, **9**
Jimmy's, **7**
Murphy's Irish Pub, **6**
Pod Lipite, **12**

▮ NIGHTLIFE
The Barn, **11**
Lodki, **13**
My Mojito, **5**
Toba & Co., **2**

◄✦ 🛈 ORIENTATION AND PRACTICAL INFORMATION

Sv. Nedelya Church is the locus of the city center, **pl. Sveta Nedelya** (Света Неделя), which is flanked by the Sheraton Hotel and the Presidency building. **Bul. Knyaginya Mariya Luiza** (Княгиня Мария Луиза) connects pl. Sveta Nedelya to the train station. Trams #1 and 7 run from the train station through pl. Sveta Nedelya to **bul. Vitosha** (Витоша), one of the main shopping and nightlife thoroughfares. Bul. Vitosha links pl. Sveta Nedelya to **pl. Bŭlgaria** and the huge, concrete **Natsionalen Dvorets na Kulturata** (Национален Дворец на Културата; **NDK, National Palace of Culture**). Historic **bul. Tsar Osvoboditel** (Цар Освободител; Tsar the Liberator) runs by the Presidency building on the north, starting at **pl. Nezavisimost** (Независимост). Follow the yellow brick road (bul. Mariya Luiza) to the former **Royal Palace**, the **Parliament** building, and **Sofia University**; along it are some of the city's hottest spots for dancing and drinking. The free *Insider's Guide* (available at the Sheraton Hotel and at tourist centers) is indispensible to English speakers. *The Program* (Програмата, Programata; www.programata.bg) is a weekly city guide. The print version is in Bulgarian; look online for English. **Maps** are available in the lobby of the Sheraton Hotel (open 24hr.) and the open-air book market at Slaveykov Sq. (Славейков) on Graf Ignatiev (Граф Игнатиев).

TOURIST, FINANCIAL, AND LOCAL SERVICES

▨ Tourist Office: Odysseia-In/Zig Zag Holidays, bul. Stamboliyski 20-B (Стамболийски; ☎980 51 02; www.zigzagbg.com). From pl. Sv. Nedelya, go down Stamboliyski and take the 2nd right on Lavele; Odysseia is on the left. Knowledgeable, friendly staff answer questions and arrange tour packages, including homestays in Bulgarian villages, tours of Sofia, trips to Rila Monastery, and outdoor excursions such as rock climbing, spelunking, biking, skiing, and snowshoeing. Consultation 5lv per session. Open in high season daily 8:30am-7:30pm; in low season closed weekends. MC/V.

Embassies: Australia, Trakiya 37 (☎946 13 34). Consulate only. **Canada,** Moskovska 9 (Московска; ☎946 13 34). **UK,** Moskovska 9 (☎933 92 90). Open M-Th 9am-noon and 2-4pm, F 9am-noon. Citizens of **Ireland** or **New Zealand** should contact the UK embassy. **US,** Kozyak 16 (☎937 51 00). Open M-F 9am-noon, 2-4pm.

Currency Exchange: Bulbank (Булбанк; ☎923 21 11), pl. Sv. Nedelya 7, cashes **traveler's checks** for 0.2% to 2% commission in lv or US dollars, issues traveler's checks for 0.5% commission, and exchanges currency. 24hr **ATM** outside. Open M-F 8am-6pm.

Luggage Storage: Downstairs at the central train station. 0.80lv per piece. Claim bags 30min. before departure. Open daily 6am-midnight.

Library: Stolichnya Biblioteka (Столичня Библиотека), Slaveykov 4 (☎980 66 88, ext. 530) has an English section. Library cards 6lv. Open M-Tu and Th-F 8:30am-noon and 12:30-5pm, W noon-5pm.

Cultural Center: Euro-Bulgarian Cultural Centre (EBCC; Евро-Български Културен Център; Evro-Bulgarski Kulturen Tsentr), bul. Stamboliyski 17 (☎988 00 84; www.eubcc.bg). Knowledgeable, English-speaking staff provides info about cultural activities in Sofia. Check out the Arts Cinema, the bookstore Khelikon (Хеликон), and the art gallery. Provides **Internet** (1.20lv per hr.; open M-F 9am-9pm, Sa-Su 11am-7pm), scanning, and photocopies. Open M-F 9am-7pm, Sa 12:30-5:30pm.

EMERGENCY AND COMMUNICATIONS

24hr. Pharmacies: Apteka Sv. Nedelya (Аптека Св. Неделя), pl. Sv. Nedelya 5 (☎950 50 26), on bul. Stamboliyski. **Apteka Vasil Levski** (Аптека Васил Левски), bul. Vasil Levski 70 (☎986 17 55), around the corner from Popa (the statue at the east end of Patriarkh Evtimiy; Патриарх Евтимий).

Medical Services: State-owned hospitals offer foreigners free 24hr. emergency aid, but the staff may not speak English, and many facilities are not up to Western standards. **Pirogov Emergency Hospital** (Пирогов), bul. Gen. Totleben 21 (Ген. Тотлебен; ☎51 531), across from Hotel Rodina. Take trolley #5 or 19 from the center. **Okruzhna Bolnitsa Hospital** (Окръжна Болница), Mladost 1, Dimitar Mollov 1. (☎91 965, emergencies 720 039) Has a ward for foreigners but is far from the city center. For dog bites or emergency tetanus shots (10lv), go to **First City Hospital** (Първа Градска Болница; Lurva Lradska Bointsa), bul. Patriarkh Evtimiy 37 (☎988 36 31).

Telephones: Telephone Center, General Gurko 4 (Гурко; ☎980 10 10). Go right out of the post office on Vasil Levski and then left on Gurko; it's a large white building 1 block down. Offers telephone, fax, and photocopy service. To make a call, go to windows 2 or 3; staff will assign you a booth. Local calls 0.09lv, international calls 0.36lv per min. **Internet** 0.80lv per hr., 1.40lv per 2hr., 2lv per 3hr. Fastest connections in town.

Internet: Stargate, Pozitano 20 (Позитано), near Hostel Sofia. 1lv per hr. Open 24hr.

Post Office: General Gurko 6 (Гурко; ☎949 64 46). From bul. Vitosha (Витоша), turn onto Alabin (Алабин) and walk east. The street becomes Gen. Gurko; post office is the large white building past the telephone office. International mailing at windows #6-8 in the 2nd hall. **Poste Restante** at window #12, 2nd hall; international money transfers at window #4 in the 1st hall. Open M-Sa 7am-8:30pm, Su 8am-1pm. **Postal Code:** 1000.

ACCOMMODATIONS

Big hotels are rarely worth the exorbitant prices—smaller, privately owned hotels or hostels are better alternatives. If the hostels are full, private rooms are often the best options (available through Odysseia-In, see **Tourist Office,** p. 82).

Hostel Sofia, Pozitano 16 (Позитано; ☎989 85 82; www.hostelsofia.com). From pl. Sv. Nedelya, walk down Vitosha. Turn right on Pozitano. Walk 1 block; the hostel is on the right. Look no further for a warm atmosphere, home-cooked Bulgarian breakfasts, and the most comfortable, fluffy feather pillows this side of the Danube. The friendly couple who own the place are eager to make you feel at home. Shared kitchen, a balcony, and a living room with cable TV. Shared bath. Laundry 5lv. Reception 24hr. Flexible checkout. Dorms €10 for 1st and 2nd nights, €9 thereafter. Cash only. ❶

Art-Hostel, Angel Kŭnchev 21A (Ангел Кънчев; ☎987 05 45; www.art-hostel.com). From pl. Sv. Nedelya, walk down Vitosha and turn left on William Gladstone. Walk 2 blocks and turn right on Angel Kŭnchev. Both a hostel and a bohemian artists' gathering place. Draws a lively, international crowd that tends to stay up late at the bar and in the outdoor garden. Kitchen, bar, free Internet, tea room, and garden. 2 shared showers and bathrooms. Large breakfast included. Linen included. Laundry 5lv. Reception 24hr. Dorms in summer €10 for 1st to 3rd nights, €9 thereafter; in winter €8/7. Cash only. ❶

Hostel Mostel, Ivan Denkoglu 2 (Иван Денкоглу; ☎922 32 96. www.hostelmostel.com). From bul. Vitosha, turn west onto Denkoglu. Bright, clean, and new, with a large common room, cable TV, and helpful, English-speaking staff. Tons of free amenities: breakfast, 1 beer per day, Internet, kitchen, luggage storage, pasta, and Sofia map. Free pickup from train and bus stations. Daytrips €30 per person for groups of 3 or more. Laundry €2. Check-out noon. Reserve ahead. Dorms in summer €10 for 1st to 2nd nights, €9 thereafter; in winter €9/8. Cash only. ❶

Hotel Iskar, Iskar 11b (Искър; ☎986 67 50; www.hoteliskar.com). Walk up bul. Mariya Luiza and turn on Ekzarh Iosif. Head right for 2 blocks, turn right on Bacho Kiro and go left on Iskar. Newly furnished, well-appointed rooms in refurbished old building. Restaurant/bar downstairs. Rooms fill quickly, so call ahead. English spoken. Breakfast €2. Check-out noon. Doubles with detached private bath,€25, with private bath in room €37. 3-bed apartment €49. Cash only. ❸

📷 FOOD

From fast food to Bulgarian classics, low-priced meals are easy to find. Over 100 shops and a fast-food court fill **Central Hall** (Хали; Khali), a modern, three-floor cross between a shopping mall and an open-air market, selling everything from caviar to cucumbers, and watches to rugs. It's across from the mosque on bul. Mariya Luiza 25. (☎917 61 06. Open daily 7am-midnight.) The **Women's Bazaar,** just down Ekzarh Yosif (Екзарх Йосиф) past the synagogue, is a more traditional **open-air market.** (Open daily dawn-dusk.) **Raffy's** fantastic ice cream stands dot the city. (two scoops 1.30lv.) **TSUM** (ЦУМ), on bul. Mariya Luiza, is a modern shopping mall with boutiques and cafes. (Open M-Sa 10am-9pm, Su 11am-8pm.)

📷 **Dani's Bistro,** Angel Kunchev 18A (☎987 45 48). This quiet streetside cafe is known for its friendly staff and savory dishes. Everything on the menu is delicious, including the chicken fettuccine (8.40lv) and the New Orleans chicken salad, which comes with a giant loaf of bread (8.90lv). Ask about the superb-but-unlisted apple cobbler (3.70lv). Wine from 4.20lv. Delivery M-Sa. Open daily 10am-10pm. Cash only. ❸

Divaka (Дивака), William Gladstone 54 (Уилям Гладстон; ☎989 95 43). Turn east from bul. Vitosha. So popular you might have to share a table with strangers. The dining room calls to mind a greenhouse. Tasty options include huge salads (1.70-3.50lv) and *sacheta* (сачета), enormous heaps of veggies and meat served sizzling on an iron plate (6.50lv). English menu. Vegetarian options. Beer from 0.90lv. Open 24hr. Cash only. ❷

Murphy's Irish Pub, Kŭrnigradska 6 (Кърниградска; ☎980 28 70). An international crowd frequents this small Irish outpost. Try the 8oz. steak (14.90lv), steak-and-kidney pie (7.90lv), or the gigundous Irish breakfast (9.90lv), served until 6pm. The requisite pint of Murphy's is 4.50lv. Live music F. Open daily noon-12:30am. Cash only. ❷

Pod Lipite (Подъ Липите), Elin Pelin 1 (Елин Пелин; ☎866 50 53). Walk down Graf Ignatiev, which becomes bul. Dragan Cankov when it hits the park; keep going for a long time. Pod Lipite serves authentic Bulgarian cuisine in a rustic atmosphere. The daring might try the *koilyovski hotch-potch,* a tasty jumble of pork ribs, tongue, ears, and vegetables (7.90lv). English menu. Beer from 0.90lv. Wine from 21lv per bottle. Entrees 5.80lv-13lv. Vegetarian options. Outdoor terrace. Call ahead. Cash only. ❷

Jimmy's, Angel Kŭnchev 11 (☎980 30 39), with branches all over the central city. Sofia's celebrated Jimmy's dishes out 30 flavors of gourmet ice cream (0.70lv per scoop) on crowded outdoor tables. Try alcoholic ice-cream drinks (2.29-4.19lv) like the "Chocolate Kiss." Open M-Sa 7:30am-midnight, Su 10am-midnight. Cash only. ❶

📷 SIGHTS

📷**BOYANA CHURCH (БОЯНСКА ЦЪРКВА; BOYANSKA TSURKVA).** In the woods of the Boyana suburb, this UNESCO World Heritage site boasts some of the most striking religious artwork in the country. The church houses murals dating back to 1259 painted by an unknown medieval master; the church is considered to be one of the best-preserved and finest examples of artwork from its time. Ask the curator to show you where pastors scribbled on the murals in the 17th and 18th centuries. (☎959 09 39. Take bus #64 from Hladilnika, or a taxi from the center, 4-5lv. Open daily 9:30am-6pm. 10lv, students 5lv. Tour in English 5lv. English pamphlet 5lv.)

ST. ALEXANDER NEVSKY CATHEDRAL. The gold-domed Byzantine-style St. Alexander Nevsky Cathedral (Св. Александър Невски; Sv. Aleksandur Nevski), erected from 1904 to 1912 in memory of the 200,000 Russians who died in the 1877-78 Russo-Turkish War, was named after the patron saint of the tsar-liberator. Housing over 400 frescoes by Russian and Bulgarian artists, it is the grandest edifice in all of Sofia. In a separate entrance to the left of the church, the **crypt** contains a spectacular array of painted icons and religious artifacts from the past 1500 years. The adjacent square has become a marketplace for religious, WWII, and Soviet souvenirs. *(In the center of pl. Alexander Nevsky. English captions. Open daily 7am-7pm; crypt open Tu-Su 10am-5:30pm. Cathedral free. Crypt 4lv, students 2lv. Guided tours of the crypt for 5 or more people 25lv, for fewer than 5 20lv.)*

CATHEDRAL OF ST. NEDELYA. The focal point of pl. Sveta Nedelya, the domed cathedral (Катедрален Храм Св. Неделя; Katedralen Khram Sv. Nedelya) is a reconstruction of the 14th-century original, which was destroyed by a bomb in an attempted assassination of Boris III in 1925. The current frescoes date from 1975. The church remains full of life; you're likely to happen upon a baptism or wedding. *(At center of pl. Sveta Nedelya. Open daily 7am-6:30pm. Liturgy 9am, also Sa 6pm.)*

ST. NICHOLAS RUSSIAN CHURCH (СВ. НИКОЛАЙ; SV. NIKOLAI). Named for the patron saint of marriage, fish, and sailors, this 1913 church was built to appease a Russian diplomat unwilling to worship in Bulgarian churches. Richly hued patterns, elegant domes, icons from the Novgorod school, and exquisite ornamentation make the church a sight to behold. *(On bul. Tsar Osvoboditel near pl. Sveta Nedelya. Open daily 8am-6:30pm. Liturgy W-Su 9am, W also 5pm, Sa also 5:30pm. Free.)*

SYNAGOGUE OF SOFIA (СОФИЙСКА СИНАГОГА; SOFIYSKA SINAGOGA). Built upon a foundation of Jewish gravestones, Sofia's only synagogue opened for services in 1909. The synagogue boasts a vast interior and was modeled after the Sephardic synagogue in Vienna. Recent renovations repaired damage done by a stray Allied bomb from WWII, which miraculously didn't explode. A museum upstairs outlines the history of Jews in Bulgaria. *(On the corner of Ekzarh Yosif (Екзарх Йосиф) and George Washington (Георг Вашингтон). Walk to the gate on Ekzarh Yosif and ring the bell. Open daily 8am-4pm. Services daily 8am, also Sa 10am. Museum open M-F 8am-12:30pm, 1-3:30pm. Museum 2lv, students 1lv. Synagogue free, donation requested for repairs.)*

BANYA BOSHI MOSQUE. Constructed in 1576 during the Ottoman occupation, this mosque escaped the fate suffered by the 26 others that once existed in Sofia. During the communist era, all mosques in Sofia except Banya Boshi were shut down or destroyed. The mosque's name derives from the old Turkish bath upon which it is built. *(Across from Central Hall, on Mariya Luiza. Open daily 3:30am-11:30pm.)*

ST. GEORGE'S ROTUNDA (СВ. ГЕОРГИ; SV. GEORGI). Near a former Roman bath and the ruins of the ancient town of Serdica, the 4th-century rotunda is Sofia's oldest preserved building. St. George's itself is covered in 11th- to 14th-century murals. After it was converted from a bath to a church in the 5th century, it served as a house of worship under Bulgarians, Byzantines, and Turks. The beautiful original murals, which were covered by the Ottomans, have been restored and now adorn the functioning church and a small art museum. *(In the courtyard enclosed by the Sheraton Hotel and the Presidency. Enter from bul. Tsar Osvoboditel or Suborna. Some English captions. Open in summer daily 8am-6pm. Services daily 9am.)*

CHURCH OF SEVEN SAINTS. Erected in 1528 at the request of Sultan Süleyman the Great, this former mosque earned the name "Black Mosque" for its dark granite composition. The Turks later used it as an arms depot; in 1903 it was turned into a church honoring saints involved in the creation of the Cyrillic alphabet. Frescoes detail the creation of the alphabet and the conversion of the Slavs. *(On Graf Ignatiev. Some English captions. Open daily 8am-6:30pm.)*

ST. SOFIA CHURCH (СВ. СОФИЯ; SV. SOFIYA). The oldest Eastern Orthodox church in Sofia, this church lent its name to the city in the 14th century. During the 19th century, when the church was being used as Sofia's main mosque, a series of earthquakes repeatedly destroyed the minarets. Amazingly, the 5th-century floor **mosaic** survived. The **crypt**, under restoration, contains tombs that date from the 2nd century. *(On pl. Alexander Nevsky. Some English captions. Open daily 7am-7pm.)*

THEATERS. **Rakovski** (Раковски) is Bulgaria's theater hub, with six venues along a 1km stretch. A left on Rakovski leads to the columns of the 1950 **National Opera House.** Walking down Rakovski, a right on Slavyanska (Славянска) leads to the **Ivan Vazov National Theater** (Народен Театър Иван Вазов; Naroden Teatur Ivan Vazov), an ornate early 20th-century edifice with a peaceful park. The park, with its graceful fountain and statues, is a favorite place to sip coffee or play chess.

NATIONAL PALACE OF CULTURE. This monolith was erected by the Communist government in 1981 to celebrate the country's 1300th birthday. The Palace of Culture (Национален Дворец на Културата; Natsionalen Dvorets na Kulturata) houses a number of restaurants, cinemas (screening both local and recent American movies), and concert halls. Its 12 halls host everything from conferences to chamber music to rock concerts. *(From pl. Sv. Nedelya, take bul. Vitosha to bul. Patriarkh Evtimiy and enter the park. The Palace is at the far end. ☎ 166 23 68; www.ndk.bg. Ticket office open daily 8:30am-7pm. Cinema downstairs; tickets 4-10lv.)*

NATIONAL HISTORY MUSEUM. Once the opulent residence of former Bulgarian dictator Todor Yivkov, the fortress-like Natural History Museum (Национален Исторически Музей; Natsionalen Istoricheski Muzey) now traces the evolution of Bulgarian culture since prehistoric times and houses some of the country's most precious archaeological treasures, including Greek and Thracian gold artifacts and a large amount of medieval church art. The 30min. ride is worth the trip. *(Residence Boyana, Palace 1. Take minibus #21, trolley #2, or bus #63 or 111 to Boyana. Even then it's a walk; hiring a taxi, 5lv, is highly recommended. ☎ 955 42 80. Some English captions. Open daily 9:30am-5:30pm. 10lv, students 5lv. Tours in English 10lv.)*

NATIONAL ART GALLERY. Displaying Bulgaria's most prized traditional and contemporary art, the National Gallery (Национална Художествена Галерия; Natsionalna Khudozhestvena Galeriya) showcases an array of exhibits, predominantly paintings from the 19th and 20th centuries, beginning with the National Revival movement. *(In the Royal Palace on bul. Tsar Osvoboditel. English captions. Open Tu-W and F-Su 10:30am-6:30pm, Th 10am-9pm. 4lv, students 2lv; Tu free. Guided tours in English for groups of 5 or more 25lv, for fewer than 5 20lv.)*

♫ 🎭 ENTERTAINMENT AND NIGHTLIFE

To get the latest events and nightlife listings, buy the English-language newspaper, the *Sofia Echo* (2.40lv), from a kiosk. For more info, consult the Cyrillic guide called the **"Program"** (Програмата; www.programata.bg). Sofia's weeklong **Beer Fest** takes place in late summer. Each night, different bands light up the crowd with traditional Bulgarian music, as well as pop and jazz. Fish and chips (1.50lv) complement beer (0.80lv). The event takes place in Alexander Batemberg Square, which also houses the three-week stint of open-air performances called **Opera in the Square.** Concerts are regularly staged outside the **National Palace of Culture.** The **International Jazz Festival** comes to Sofia the 2nd week of October. Catch the traditional **Sofia Music Week** festival during the first week of June in Bulgaria Hall.

Nightlife centers on **bul. Vitosha** and Sofia University at the intersection of **Vasil Levski** and **Tsar Osvoboditel.** Young people often meet at **Popa**, the irreverent nickname for Patriarkh Evtimiy's monument, where bul. Patriarkh Evtimiy intersects with Vasil Levski and **Graf Ignatiev.**

▓ **My Mojito,** Ivan Vazov 12 (Иван Вазов; ☎088 770 94 32). Walk down Rakovski from Slaveykov Sq. toward the National Assembly. Turn right on Ivan Vazov. Mojito is on the corner with 6 Septemvri. A young crowd flocks to My Mojito, where students party until sunrise to deafeningly loud music. Most crowded for the Th Retro Party. Cover F-Sa men 5lv. Beer from 3.30lv. Mixed drinks from 5.50lv. Open daily 9:30pm-late.

Lodki, in the park beyond Vasil Levski Stadium. Follow Graf Ignatiev over the bridge; it becomes bul. Dragan Cankov. Turn left at the fenced-in car lot. After a short walk, turn right into the park. Follow the music, students, and lights. "Lodki" is the unofficial name for an outdoor bar in the park; in good weather, young Sofians flock here for the cheap beer and the chill atmosphere. Beer from 1.20lv. Open in summer daily 8pm-late.

Toba & Co, 6 Moskovska (Московска; ☎989 4696.) Behind the Royal Palace, in the courtyard. You can't do this at Buckingham. Party like a tsar in the garden and back room of the former Bulgarian monarch's residence. Complete the experience with a White Russian (4.60lv). Beer from 1.60lv. Open daily 10pm-late.

The Barn, 22 6 Septemvri. From Graf Ignatiev, turn right at 6 Septemvri; #22 is on the right. Turn into the alley behind the diner and walk through the unmarked wooden door. If the door is closed, knock hard. Once touted as the most exclusive club in Sofia, the Barn has opened its doors to the public but retains a haughty ubercool attitude. Inside, savor the candlelit, cave-like ambience. Beer from 2lv. Open daily 8pm-late.

▶ DAYTRIP FROM SOFIA

VITOSHA NATIONAL PARK (ПРИРОДЕН ПАРК ВИТОША)

Take tram #9 from the intersection of Hristo Botev and Makedonya to Hladilnika Station, the last stop. From there, take bus #122 to the Simeonovo lift, which goes to Khizha Aleko (Хижа Алеко), or bus #93 to the Dragalevtsi lift, which goes to Bai Krustjo and Goli Vrkh stations. Visit Sa-Su, the only time most of the park, including the lifts, is open. Bus schedules are unreliable; taxis are a better choice (7-10lv). Bring bug spray.

Although it lies just next to Sofia, Vitosha National Park mutes the din of the neighboring metropolis. The park shelters a monastery, a river, and a waterfall, but **Mount Vitosha,** rising 2290m to its peak, Cherni Vruh (Черни Връх), dominates this natural sanctuary. Conquering the mountain by trekking the marked trails from Aleko hut (Хижа Алеко; Khizha Aleko) is the most popular activity, followed by winter-time skiing and snowboarding on Vitosha's scenic slopes. Pick up English maps and brochures from the **Information Center,** 400m. uphill from Restaurant Vodenitsata. (Природозащитен Информационен Центер "Витоша." ☎967 31 40; www.vitoshacentre.org. Open daily 8:30am-5:30pm.) The info center is a good first stop for any trip to the mountain; trails and points of interest are poorly marked, and those unfamiliar with the area will likely need help. Paths at the top of the mountain are marked on the map, but there are few trail markers; even the most experienced hikers need a guide. The most direct, difficult path starts at the lift station by the bus station. Ride the **Dragalevtsi chairlift** (0.80lv) to either the Bai Krustjo station or the higher Goli Vrkh station. Other exploration opportunities include **hikes** to the **peak,** the **Dragalevtsi Monastery** (20min. walk uphill past the chairlift), and **Boyanna Waterfall** (farther east; not accessible by foot from info center). Paths are dotted with well-marked **campsites** and shelters; several sites are at the immediate top of the chairlift, including the Aleko hut. For a taste of Bulgarian folk culture and the traditional *nestinari* dance, try **Restaurant Vodenitsata ❸** (Ъоденицата), by the chairlift, set next to a picturesque, rushing mountain stream. (☎967 10 58. Entrees 8-18lv. Open daily noon-midnight.)

RILA MONASTERY (РИЛСКИ МАНАСТИР) ☎(0)7054

Rila Monastery (Rilski Manastir) was built in the 10th century as a refuge from the outside world. It sheltered the arts of icon-painting and manuscript-copying during the Byzantine and Ottoman occupations, remaining an oasis of Bulgarian culture during five centuries of foreign rule. Today, its spectacularly colorful murals make it the most artistically significant monastery in Bulgaria. The sanctuary is surrounded by tree-covered mountains and fast-moving streams.

TRANSPORTATION AND PRACTICAL INFORMATION. Take **tram** #5 from pl. Sveta Nedelya to Ovcha Kupel Station (Овча Къпел) to make the daily bus to **Rila Town** (2hr., 10:20am, 5lv). From there, you can hop on a **bus** to the monastery (30min., 3 per day, 1.50lv). The last bus back to Sofia leaves in mid-afternoon; staying the night is recommended. There is an **ATM** on the storefront opposite the bus station in Rila Town. Blue Mobika **telephones** are by the shops behind the monastery; phone cards are available in the souvenir shop.

ACCOMMODATIONS AND FOOD. Hotel Rilets ❸ (Хотел Рилец), down the road from the monastery, is aging but retains some of its past glory. Low prices, a beautiful dining room, and private baths make up for small beds and old furnishings. From the rear of the monastery, follow the leftmost road to the intersection; turn right and follow the signs. (☎0887 84 98 80. Reception daily 8am-midnight. Singles €22; doubles €36. Cash only.) Inquire at room #170 in the monastery about staying in a heated **monastic cell ❷**, but be prepared for bare rooms and no shower. (☎22 08. Monastery doors close at 9pm during summer and 7pm during winter; ring the bell if you're out later than that. Cells 25lv.) **Camping Bor ❶** is tucked away at the base of the mountains with clean but bare campsites and bungalows. Walk down the leftmost road behind the monastery and take a right across the bridge at the triangular intersection, then take a left and follow the signs. (2-bed bugalows €5 per person. €5 per tent. €1 per car.) Behind the monastery are several cafes and a mini-mart. Try the monks' homemade bread (0.50lv) or slice into a chicken steak (5lv) at **Restaurant Rila ❶**, a *mekhani* (механи; Bulgarian folk restaurant) with a beautiful view of the mountains. (☎048 89 04 18. Entrees 2.50-12lv. Open daily 8am-midnight.)

SIGHTS. The original 10th-century monastery was destroyed. Today's monastery was built between 1834 and 1837, save for a brick tower which dates from the 14th century. The monastery's vibrant murals were painted by brothers Dimitar and Zahari Zograf—"Zograf" actually means "mural painter"—who were famous for their work at the Troyan and Bachkovo monasteries. The 1200 frescoes on the central chapel form a brilliantly colored outdoor art display. The iconostasis is also one of the largest and most ornate in Bulgaria. Inside lies the heart of Bulgaria's last tsar, Boris III. (Open daily in high season 6am-6pm; in low season 8am-6pm. Backpacks, cameras, shorts, and sleeveless shirts not permitted. Free.) The **museum** in the far right corner of the monastery displays centuries-old weapons, embroidery, illuminated texts, and icons. The exhibit includes a ▨**wooden cross** that took 12 years to carve and left its creator, the monk Rafail, blind. The cross is carved with fantastically detailed miniature figures that depict scenes from the Bible and the lives of the saints. (Open daily 8:30am-4:30pm. 5lv, students 3lv.)

HIKING. Maps and hiking routes through **Rila National Park** are posted on signs at the monastery. Alternatively, look in the **Manastirski Padarŭtsi** (Манастирски Падаръци) shop, just outside the monastery's back entry, for a Cyrillic map of the paths (6lv). Incredible views—particularly at **Seventh Lake**

(Седемте Езера; Sedemte Ezera) and **Malovitsa** (Мальовица)—and welcoming huts *(hizhi)* await in the park. Expect to pay around US$2 for a spot to sleep. Follow the **yellow markings** to the **Khizha Sedemte Ezera** (Хижа Седемте Езера; Seventh Lake Hut; 6½hr.). The **blue** trail leads to **Khizha Malovitsa** (Мальовица; 7hr.). The **red trail** leads to the highest hut in the Balkans (6hr.).

Don't miss the short hike (1hr.) to the **cave** where Holy Ivan, the builder of Rila Monastery, lived and prayed for years. To reach it, walk down the road behind the monastery. After the triangular intersection, head left up the path through the field. Follow the "гроб" signs *(grob;* grave), which point the way to the church where Ivan was originally buried. Behind the church is the entrance to the cave. It's believed that passing through will purify your soul. Enter at the bottom and crawl through the dark winding passages. A flashlight or lighter is helpful. According to legend, this part of the journey represents the journey out of the womb. Emerge at the top for a symbolic rebirth—unless you have sinned too much, in which case, the story goes, rocks will fall on you. Next, continue uphill 40m to the spring and cleanse yourself in the cold mountain spring near the shrine to St. Ivan. You're now ready to enter the chapel guilt-free.

SOUTHERN MOUNTAINS

The thickly forested mountains of Rila, Pirin, and Rodopi sheltered Bulgaria's cultural and political dissidents during 500 years of Turkish rule. Local monks preserved their culture in secret by copying manuscripts in remote monasteries. Other dissidents, like the *haiduc* outlaws, took an activist approach, using mountain hideouts to launch attacks against unwanted visitors. Today, the mountains still cradle traditional Bulgarian culture both in monasteries and in rural villages.

PLOVDIV (ПЛОВДИВ) ☎(0)32

Plovdiv (pop. 376,000) is a city that spans the ages. Long ago, it was an important city in the Roman empire. Traces of this former glory remain, and visitors will be treated to ruins of theaters, temples, and palaces, including a remarkably intact amphitheater, one of the best-preserved in the world. Additionally, the Old Town is graced with charming National Revival houses and churches.

TRANSPORTATION. The main **train station** is on bul. Khristo Botev (Христо Ботев; ☎63 27 20). Ticket counters open daily 7:30am-7:30pm. Trains run to: **Burgas** (5hr., 4 per day, 9.50lv); **Sofia** (2½hr., 8 per day, 6lv); **Varna** (5½hr., 3 per day, 11.80lv). Most trains from Sofia to Burgas or Istanbul, TUR stop in Plovdiv. **Rila station,** bul. Khristo Botev 31a (☎64 31 20), sells international train tickets. Open M-F 8am-7:30pm, Sa 8am-2pm. There are 3 main **bus stations** in Plovdiv; each serves different destinations. The Yug (south) and Rodolpi stations are within walking distance from the center. Take a city bus or taxi (2lv) to the Sever (north) station. **Yug** (Юг; South; ☎62 69 37), bul. Khristo Botev 47, across from the train station, is the main station. Buses service South Bulgaria and go to: **Asenovgrad** (30min., every 30min., 1lv); **Blagoevgrad** (4hr., 3 per day, 10lv); **Sofia** (2hr., every 30min., 9lv); **Burgas** (4hr., 4 per day, 12lv); and **Varna** (4hr., 2 per day, 16lv). Private firms send buses to various international destinations, including Istanbul, TUR (5 per day; 30lv, students 27lv). **Sever** (Север; North; ☎95 37 05) is at the intersection of Dimitr Stambolov (Димитър Стамболов) and Pobeda (Победа). Bul. Ruski becomes Pobeda across the river. Take bus #12 from the intersection of Ruski and Gladston (Гладстон). Ticket counter open 6am-8pm. Buses to **Koprivshtitsa** (2hr., 1 per day,

BULGARIA

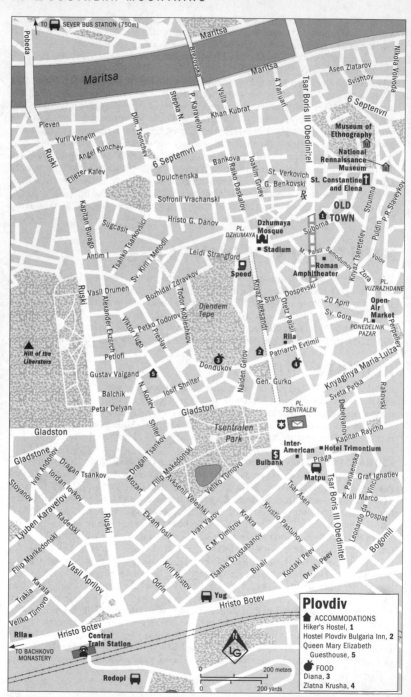

Plovdiv

🏠 ACCOMMODATIONS
Hiker's Hostel, 1
Hostel Plovdiv Bulgaria Inn, 2
Queen Mary Elizabeth
   Guesthouse, 5
🍎 FOOD
Diana, 3
Zlatna Krusha, 4

5.50lv), **Pleven** (4hr., 2 per day, 12lv), and **Ruse** (5hr., 8am, 14lv). **Rodopi** (Родопи; ☎697 607), behind the train station through the underpass, services the **Rodopi Mountains.** Buses run to **Smolyan** (1hr., 5 per day, 7.50lv), via **Bachovo.**

◨◨ ORIENTATION AND PRACTICAL INFORMATION. Although the center is clearly defined, Plodiv's streets are poorly marked; an up-to-date **map** is essential. Street vendors sell good Cyrillic maps (3lv). Running past the train station, the east-west thoroughfare **bul. Khristo Botev** (Христо Ђотев) marks the town's southern edge. With your back to the train station, turn left on Khristo Botev to get to **bul. Ruski** (Руски); a right turn on Ruski takes you across the river and to bus station Sever. Khristo Botev also intersects with **bul. Tsar Boris III Obedinitel** (Цар Ђорис III Обединител), which runs to the **Maritsa River** (Марица), at the northern end of **Stariya Grad** (Стария Град; Old Town). The pedestrian way **Knyaz Alexander** connects to the central square. In the middle of town, bul. Tsar Boris III Obedinitel runs along the eastern side of **pl. Tsentralen** (Централен). To get to the center from the train station, take bus #2, 20, or 26 (0.40lv) or cross under bul. Khristo Botev and take **Ivan Vazov** (Иван Вазов). **Exchange currency** at **Bulbank** (Ђулбанк), Ivan Vazov 4, on the right when facing Hotel Trimontium, which also cashes **traveler's checks** for 0.2% commission. (☎60 16 01. Open M-F 8am-6pm.) **Luggage storage** is in the train station. (0.80lv per bag. Open 24hr.) The **pharmacy** is **Apteka 47 Tunela** (Аптека Тунела), at bul. Tsar Boris III Obedinitel 62. From pl. Tsentralen, follow bul. Tsar Boris III Obedinitel through the tunnel. (☎62 60 17. Open M-F 7am-midnight, Sa-Su 9am-midnight.) **Telephones** for international calls are in the **post office** building on pl. Tsentralen (☎65 73 20. Open daily 6am-11pm.) The **Internet** cafe, **Speed,** Knyaz Alexander 12, on the left before the mosque, has new computers and a clean, smoke-free atmosphere. (1lv per hr., 2lv per 3hr.; 30min. min. Open 24hr.) The **post office** is on pl. Tsentralen, and has **Poste Restante** in the room to the left of the entrance across from the park. (Open M-Sa 7am-7pm, Su 7-11am.) **Postal Code:** 4000.

◨◨ ACCOMMODATIONS AND FOOD. In Plovdiv, higher prices don't always mean higher quality. Prices triple during trade fairs (the first weeks of May and the end of September). Reserve ahead in July and August, as budget hotels are often full. The clean and friendly ▨**Queen Mary Elizabeth Guesthouse ❶,** Gustav Vaigand 7, rolls out the red carpet for weary guests. The English-speaking owner is eager to help. From Ruski, turn left on Gustav Vaigand. It's on the right side, 100m down; ring the bell. (☎62 93 06. Laundry €1 per kg. Reception 24hr. Rooms 15lv. Cash only.) **Hiker's Hostel ❶,** Suborna 59 (Съборна), has a great location in Plovdiv's historic Old Town. Perks include free Internet, pickup service, and large breakfasts. Walking north on Alexander, turn right at Dzhimaya onto Suborna. It's a 5min. walk uphill, on the left. (☎899 89 82 66; www.hikers-hostel.org. Laundry. Dorms €10. Cash only.) **Hostel Plovdiv Bulgaria Inn ❶,** Naiden Gerov 13 (Найден Геров), offers bare-bones accommodations that are cheap, clean, and decently located. (☎63 84 67. Reception 24hr. Dorms €10. Cash only.)

Plovdiv has an array of Bulgarian restaurants with pleasant outdoor seating. The **open-air market,** in pl. Ponedelnik Pazar just north of pl. Tsentralen, sells all sorts of fruits and veggies. (2-3lv per kg. Open daily dawn-dusk.) Popular cafes line the pedestrian street Knyaz Alexander. Walking toward Old Town on Knyaz Alexander, take a right at Hotel Bulgaria, then another right, to get to **Zlatna Krusha** (Златна Круша) ❶, Otetz Paisii 30, where you can fuel up on deep-dish pizza (3.50-5.50lv) or tortellini bolognese (5lv) on the shaded balcony. (☎67 05 05. English menu. Open daily 11am-midnight.) **Diana** (Даяна) ❷, Dondukov 3, at the base of Plovdiv's central hill, specializes in large portions of skewered meat. Try

BULGARIA

the excellent mushroom appetizer (5lv), or go all-out with the giant "Sword of the Tsar" (13.80lv), served tableside straight off the sword. (☎ 62 30 27. English menu. Vegetarian options. Entrees 2.10-14.50lv. Open daily 9am-midnight. Cash only.)

◼ **SIGHTS.** Most of Plovdiv's treasures are on Stariya Grad's **Trimontium** (three hills). End a long day of sightseeing with an evening stroll up the Hill of the Liberators to see a wonderful view of the city. A 2nd-century ▨**Roman Amphitheater** (Античен Театър; Antichen Teatŭr), one of the best preserved in the world, looms over the city. It serves as a popular performing arts venue, hosting the **Festival of the Arts** and the **Opera Festival** in June. Most festival tickets are available at the opera box office on the ground floor of the Inter-American building on pl. Tsentralen. Movies are often screened here; keep an eye out for schedules. To reach the amphitheater, turn right off Knyaz Alexander on Suborna and then right up the steps along Mitropolit Paisii. Continue uphill to another small set of steps next to the music academy. At the top, walk past the cafes to the theater. (Open daily 9am-7pm. 3lv.) An **ancient stadium** (Античен Стадион; Antichen Ctadion), which once seated 30,000 spectators, now consists of just the poorly preserved bottom 10-15 rows. The public may view, but not enter, the ruins. An unfortunate bit of city planning has allowed a garish glass-and-metal cafe/bar (now closed) to be built literally on top of the stadium. Follow Knyaz Alexander to the end; the stadium is underneath pl. Dzhumaya. Built in the 4th century, the **Church of St. Constantine and Elena** is embellished with murals and icons dating from an artful 1832 renovation. It's on Suborna near the Museum of Ethnography. (☎ 62 45 78. Open daily 9am-6pm. Free.)

◪ **DAYTRIP FROM PLOVDIV: BACHKOVO MONASTERY** (БАЧКОВСКИ МАНАСТИР). Bulgaria's 2nd-largest monastery is in the Rodopi Mountains, 28km south of Plovdiv. Bachkovo Monastery (Bachkovski Manastir; ☎ 332 72 77) was built in 1083 by Georgian brothers Grigory and Abazy Bakuriani, and is known for its original architecture and fine murals. A refuge for repressed Bulgarian culture and literature during the 500 years of Turkish rule, Bachkovo today draws crowds for its rich history and artistic treasures. The main church is home to the **Icon of the Virgin Mary and Child** (икона Света Ѓогородица; ikona Sveta Bogoroditsa), which is said to have miraculous healing powers. When the Turks plundered the monastery, the monks hid the icon in the mountains. It was rediscovered by an unsuspecting shepherd centuries later. Next door, the brightly colored paintings of famed National Revival artist Zahari Zograf decorate the 12th-century **Church of Archangels.** Ask to be let into the **Trapezaria** (old dining room; 4lv) across the courtyard, which is covered floor-to-ceiling with well-preserved, centuries-old murals. A short walk uphill leads to the **ossuary chapel,** the only 11th-century structure left standing by the Turks. Farther down the road, small shrines line hiking paths that are labeled with yellow-and-white markings. Take to the hills for a pleasant, unchallenging hike with frequent picnic areas and mountain vistas.

Buses (30min., every 30min., round-trip 3lv) leave from platform #1 at Rodolpi station. It's the Smolyan bus; ask for Bachkovo. Once there, follow the cobblestones uphill. (Open daily 8am-8pm. Free. Tour in English 6lv, but call ahead.)

KOPRIVSHTITSA (КОПРИВЩИЦА) ☎(0)7184

Tucked away in the forested hills of the Valley of Roses, Koprivshtitsa is a charming little village of stone cottages and winding streets, where you're just as likely to pass a horse-drawn cart as a car. It was here in 1876 that Todor Kableshkov's "letter of blood" urged rebellion against Turkish rule, starting a war that eventually led to the liberation of Bulgaria. Today, visitors stroll the cobblestone streets, eat in traditional restaurants, and soak up centuries' worth of folk culture.

☎️ TRANSPORTATION AND PRACTICAL INFORMATION. A bus timed to meet the train runs from the train station to town (15min., 6 per day, 1lv). **Trains** go to **Plovdiv** (3½hr., 3 per day, 4.90lv) via **Karlovo**, and **Sofia** (2hr., 5 per day, 5.20lv). **Private buses** also go to **Plovdiv** (2½hr., 1 per day, 5lv) and **Sofia** (2hr., 4 per day, 5.50lv). The **bus station** posts bus and train schedules in Bulgarian; the tourist office (see below) has the schedules in English.

To reach the **main square** from the bus station, walk left 200m on the road that runs next to the river. It's next to the park; look for the large stone monument. The English-speaking staff at the **tourist office**, 20 April, in the main square, provides **maps** (2lv), rents mountain bikes (2lv per hr.), arranges accommodations, and explains **bus** and **train schedules.** (☎21 91; tourist_center@yahoo.com. Open daily 9am-7pm.) **Currency exchange** and 24hr. **ATM** service are available at **DSK Bank** (Банка ДСК), next to the bus stop on Hadzhi Nencho 68. (☎21 42. Open M-F 8am-4pm.) **Pharmacy Apteka Lyusi** (Аптека Люси), Lyuben Karavelov 2 (Любен Каравелов), is on the other side of the park from the main square. (☎20 06 or 21 82. Open M-Sa 9am-noon and 3-6pm.) Across the street is the town's **medical clinic** (Амбулатория; Ambulatoriya), Lyuben Karavelov 3. (☎28 84 or 20 56. Open M-Tu and Th-F 8am-1pm and 3-5pm, W 8am-5pm.) The **post office**, in the main square next to city hall at Lyuben Karavelov 14, has card-operated **telephones** outside. (Open M-F 7:30am-noon and 1-4:30pm.) **Postal Code:** 2077.

☎️☐ ACCOMMODATIONS AND FOOD. There are many hotels and **private rooms** in Koprivshtitsa. Check with the tourist office. Prices vary, but expect to pay about 30lv for a room in the center. **Hotel Trayanova Kŭshta** (Траянова Къща) ❶, Gerenilogo 5 (Гeрeнилого), has spacious rooms near the center. Make a sharp right from the tourist office, then walk uphill past the souvenir shop and White Horse tavern; it's the first left at the top. Large rooms are decorated in a traditional style, with TVs, private baths, and a shared balcony. (☎30 57. BulFon telephones available. Reception 24hr. Check-out noon. Rooms 30-36lv.) A great budget option is **Yudostoverenye Kŭshta** (Юдостоверение) ❶, on Purva Pushka 23 (Първа Пушка). From the tourist office, walk towards the park and take the road that skirts around to the right. Continue to the arched stone bridge, then turn right; it's on your left. Rooms have comfortable beds, TVs, and minibars; some have private balconies. (☎22 87. Breakfast 3lv. Shared bath. Check-out noon. Rooms 20lv. Cash only.) **Hotel Kalina** (Калина) ❸, Palaveev 35 (Палавеев), offers luxurious rooms with hardwood floors, private baths, thick rugs, TVs, and minibars. With your back to the main square, cross the bridge and take a left; Kalina is on the right. (Breakfast included. Reception 24hr. Check-out noon. Singles 36lv; doubles 50lv.)

It's easy to find great Bulgarian food at any *mekhana* (механа; tavern). **Mekhana "20 April"** ("20 Април") ❶ is in the main square. The attentive staff serves scrumptious *sirene po trakiyski* (сирене по тракийски; Thracian stewed cheese) for a mere 3.30lv. (☎048 91 64 30. Entrees 3-5lv. Open daily 8am-midnight.) **Strannopriemnitsa "Dedo Liben"** (Странноприемница "Дедо Либен") ❷, across the square and just over the bridge, offers traditional Bulgarian cuisine and a rich selection of wines. (☎071 84. Entrees 3-30lv. Open daily 11am-midnight.)

☐ SIGHTS. The wonderfully preserved **National Revival houses**, the homes of the town's first settlers, are an important part of Bulgaria's heritage. Many have enclosed verandas and delicate woodwork, and six have been turned into **museums.** The 1831 **Georgi Benkovski Museum-House** (Георги Бенковски) immortalizes the life of the leader of the "Flying Troop," a cavalry unit that fought in the revolution. From the post office, walk across the bridge and up the cobblestone road; take a right at the top on Petko Kŭlev (Петко Кълев) and go straight for 5min. The museum is downstairs on the right. (Open M and W-Su 9:30am-5:30pm.)

BULGARIA

The **Dimcho Debelyanov Museum-House** (Димчо Дебелянов) is the birthplace of Debelyanov, one of Bulgaria's best-loved poets, who was killed in WWI. There are originals of his works on the first floor and photographs on the second. (Open Tu-Su 9:30am-5:30pm.) The house of the merchant **Lyutovata** (Лютовата) boasts spectacular decorations and a collection of fine Bulgarian carpets. (Open M and W-Su 9:30am-5:30pm.) Tickets are available at the houses and at the shop (Купчийница; Kupchiynitsa) next to the tourist office. (Open W-Su 9:30am-5:30pm. Admission to all houses 5lv, students 3lv. English tours 15lv.)

BLACK SEA (ЧЕРНО МОРЕ)

Bulgaria's most popular destination for foreigners and natives alike, the Black Sea Coast is covered with centuries-old fishing villages, secluded bays, energetic seaside towns, and plastic resorts. In Varna, the folk traditions of the past often clash with luxury resorts and bronzed German tourists, but more secluded beaches and tiny villages lie only slightly off the beaten track.

VARNA (ВАРНА) ☎(0)52

By 600 BC, Varna (pop. 400,000) was already the thriving Greek town of Odessos, and it later gained in importance when the Romans conquered it. Both cultures left indelible marks, none more evident than the immense Roman thermal baths and the Old Town, still known as the "Greek quarter," which contains a large Greek population. Today, Varna remains a cosmopolitan hub, the fastest-growing city in Bulgaria, and tourists come from across the region to soak up rays on its beach.

Black Sea Coast of Bulgaria

TRANSPORTATION. The **train station,** near the commercial harbor, sends trains to: **Veliko Tarnovo** (4hr., 5 per day, 9lv); **Plovdiv** (7hr., 3 per day, 9-12lv); **Ruse** (4hr., 2 per day, 7.50lv); **Shumen** (1½hr., 7 per day, 4.25lv); **Sofia** (8hr., 6 per day, 15lv). **Rila**, Preslav 13 (☎63 23 47), sells tickets to **Budapest, HUN** (27hr.; Tu, F, Su 5:30pm; 136lv) and **Istanbul, TUR** (12hr.; 1 per day; 43lv, with bed 64lv) via **Stara Zagora.** Open M-F 8am-6:30pm, Sa 8am-3pm. To reach the **bus station,** Vladislav Varenchik (Владислав Варенчик), take city bus #1, 22, 40, or 41 from either the train station or the side of the cathedral opposite the post office, or walk 30min. on Preslav from pl. Nezavisimost to Varenchik. **Buses** are the best way to and from **Burgas** (2½hr., 5 per day, 8.25lv). **Private buses** leave for **Sofia** from the bus station (6hr., 17 per day, 23lv). **Minibuses** depart from the private

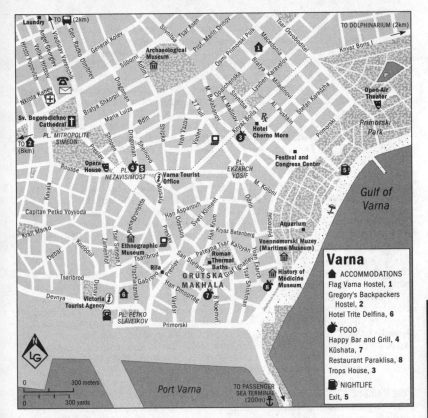

Varna

🏠 ACCOMMODATIONS
Flag Varna Hostel, **1**
Gregory's Backpackers
    Hostel, **2**
Hotel Trite Delfina, **6**

🍴 FOOD
Happy Bar and Grill, **4**
Kŭshata, **7**
Restaurant Paraklisa, **8**
Trops House, **3**

🌙 NIGHTLIFE
Exit, **5**

BULGARIA

station **Mladost** (Младост). Cross the busy street in front of the station; it's to the left and down the street. Look for signs and minibuses parked out front. To: **Balchik** (40min., 1 per hr. 6:30am-7pm, 3lv) and **Burgas** (2hr.; 7:30am, 1 per hr. 9am-5pm, 5:30pm; 6lv). City **buses** cost 0.60lv; pay on board. Bus stops are marked with small black signs displaying the bus number, some of which are knocked over.

🔳🗺 **ORIENTATION AND PRACTICAL INFORMATION.** All major sights are within a 30min. walk of one another. To get to the central **pl. Nezavisimost** (плю Независимост) from the train station, take **Tsar Simeon I** (Цар Симеон Ш). Varna's main pedestrian artery, **bul. Knyaz Boris I** (Княз Ђорис Ш), starts at pl. Nezavisimost, and **Slivnitsa** connects it to the sea garden's main entrance. **Preslav** (Преслав) heads from pl. Nezavisimost to the **Sv. Bogorodichno Cathedral.** To reach the beach from the train station, go right on **Primorski** (Приморски).

The newly opened **tourist office** is on the pedestrian walkway, Knyaz Boris I, near the Moussala Palace Hotel. Alternatively, **Sea Shadow Travel** boasts Patrick, one of the most helpful and knowledgeble guides in Varna, who offers individualized tours for affordable prices. (☎0887 36 47 11;. www.guide-bg.com. Prices vary; around €20 per daytrip.) **Bulgarian Post Bank,** Knyaz Boris I 3, in pl. Nezavisimost, cashes AmEx **traveler's checks** for 1.2% commission and exchanges currency. (☎686 903. Open M-F 8:30am-5pm.) Several **ATMs** are in pl. Nesavisimost; others line Knyaz Boris I and Slivitsa. Store **luggage** at the train station, by the end of track #8. (3lv per bag. Open daily 6am-10:50pm. The **laundromat**, Byalata Pantera (Бялата Пантера), zh. Kyuri 28 (Кюри), is north of the post office on Vladislav Varenchik. (Wash 2lv, dry 1.50lv. Open daily 8am-9pm.) The **pharmacy** is at Slivenitsa 22, just across from Hotel Cherno More. (☎610 226. Open M-F 8:30am-11pm, Sa-Su 9am-9pm.) For **medical services**, go to **Polyclinic Sv. Klementina** (Ллумунтинф), bul. Suborni 40 (Съборни; ☎60 38 02.) Enter the **telephone office**, bul. Suborni 42, from the right of the main post office entrance. (Open daily 7am-11pm.) **Internet**, scanning, and printing are at **Bulstar 2000**, Preslov 35. (☎633 449. 8am-10pm 1lv per hr., 10pm-8am 0.80lv per hr. Open 24hr.) The **post office**, bul. Suborni 42, is behind the cathedral. **Poste Restante** is in the central room at window #12. (☎614 666. Open M-F 8am-noon and 1-5pm.) **Postal Code:** 9000.

⌐⌐ ACCOMMODATIONS AND FOOD. Victorina Tourist Agency, Tsar Simeon I 36, offers **private rooms.** (☎60 35 41. Open daily Apr.-May 10am-6pm; June-Sept. 7am-9pm. Singles from 24lv.) **Astra Tour,** near track #6 at the train station, finds private rooms. (☎60 58 61; astratur@yahoo.com. Open in summer daily 7am-9pm. Singles from €10.) Locals approach backpackers at the train station to offer lodging for 10-15lv. Perhaps the best hostel in the Balkans, ▨ **Gregory's Backpackers Hostel ❶** is in Zvezditsa (Звездица) village, 82 Fenix (Феникс), about 8km from Varna. Call ahead to arrange free pickup, or take the #36 bus. Run by a cheery young English couple, Gregory's features home-cooked breakfasts, a small swimming pool, a big TV with plenty of DVDs, leather couches, and an amazing bar. They also arrange daytrips. (☎379 909; www.hostelvarna.com. Laundry. Internet 1.40lv per hr. Call or e-mail ahead. Dorms €10. Cash only.) Closer to the action, **Flag Varna Hostel ❶** is in a central Varna apartment at 25 Opalchenska. The amenities don't hold a candle to Gregory's, but Flag does organize daytrips and offer free laundry, clean beds, and lockers. (☎648 877; flagvarna@yahoo.com. Dorms €10. Cash only.) **Hotel Trite Delfina** (Трите Делфина) ❸ (Three Dolphins), Gabrovo 27, boasts well-kept, spacious rooms with cable TV and private baths. (☎60 09 11. Breakfast included. Reception 24hr. Check-out noon. Call 3-4 days ahead. Singles 55lv; doubles 65lv.)

Bul. Knyaz Boris I and **Slivnitsa** swarm with cafes and kiosks. Many beachside restaurants serve fresh seafood. For an elegant dining experience, head to ▨**Restaurant Paraklisa** (Параклиса) ❸, Primorski 47, a traditional Bulgarian restaurant with a convent-like atmosphere ("Paraklisa" means "in the chapel") and terrific food. The lamb-drop *sarma* (diced liver, rice, and herbs) is very good and very Bulgarian. The chef permits half and even quarter orders. (☎611 830. English menu. Beer from 1lv. Entrees 6-25lv. Open daily 11am-midnight.) **Trops House** (Тропс Къща) ❶, at bul. Knyaz Boris I 48, dishes up the cheapest cafeteria grub in town. (Entrees 1-4lv. Open daily 8:30am-10:30pm.) **Kúshata** (Къщата) ❷, 8 Noemvri 7, is also a good traditional Bulgarian place, with items like *pletena nadenitsa*, a giant braided sausage for 4.80lv. (☎60 28 79. Beer from 1.10lv. Entrees 4.80-16lv. Open daily 10am-midnight. Cash only.) A quintessential Varna experience, **Happy Bar and Grill ❷**, in pl. Nezavisimost, got its start as a hamburger stand here in 1994, and today is the flagship of one of the country's most popular chains, as locals will proudly let you know. Although the decor is American through-and-through, the menu has a Bulgarian twist, with salads and skewered meats. (☎606 338. Beer from 1.10lv. Entrees 4.86-11.10lv. Open daily 9am-2am. MC/V.)

◪ SIGHTS. The well-preserved ▨**Roman Thermal Baths** (Римски Терми; Rimski Termi), the largest ancient complex in Bulgaria, stand on 13 San Stefano in the old quarter, **Grütska Makhala.** (Гръцка Махала. ☎600 059. Open Tu-Su 10am-5pm. 3lv, students 2lv.) In pl. Metropolite Simeon, the **Sv. Bogorodichno Cathedral** is one of the most impressive in Bulgaria, with a breathtaking painted interior that took 50 years to complete. The colorful murals, which depict Biblical scenes, are a fascinating blend of ancient Orthodox style and modern technique, incorporating perspective and realism to a degree unusual for an Orthodox church. (Open daily 7am-7pm. Free.) The **Ethnographic Museum** (Етнографски Музей; Etnografski Muzey), Panagyurishte 22, features displays depicting Varna's seafaring past. (☎ 63 05 88. Some English captions. Open in high season Tu-Su 10am-5pm; in low season Tu-F only. 4lv, students 2lv.) The ⚑**Archaeological Museum** (Археологически Музей; Arkheologicheski Muzey), in the park on Maria Luiza 41, traces the region's history from the Stone Age, with a dazzling array of artifacts from the first recorded civilization in Europe and the world's oldest discovered golden treasures. (☎ 681 030. English captions. Open in high season Tu-Su 10am-5pm; in low season Tu-Sa only. English tours 20lv, booklet 6lv. 5lv, students 2lv.)

📷🎭 **ENTERTAINMENT AND NIGHTLIFE.** Hidden among the fountains and trees in the seaside gardens, at the corner of bul. Tsar Osvobotidel and bul. Primorski, is a vine-covered **open-air theater** (☎ 61 28 03; open M-F 11am-8pm; tickets 5-8lv), home of the biannual **International Ballet Festival** (May-Oct.). Buy tickets at the gate or at the Festival and Congress Center (see below). The pink **Opera House**, on pl. Nezavisimost, has weekly performances and sells theater tickets. (Opera ☎ 22 33 88; www.operavarna.bg. Open M-F 10:30am-2pm and 2-7pm. Tickets 10-20lv. Theater ☎ 60 07 99. Open M-F 10am-1pm and 2-8pm, Sa 10am-1pm and 4-6pm; closed July-Aug. Tickets 6lv.) In late August, Varna holds an **International Jazz Festival.** The international music festival **Varna Summer** (Варненско Лято; Varnensko Lyato; www.varnasummerfest.org) runs from June 21 to July 28; tickets are available at the Opera House. The **Festival and Congress Center**, on 2 Slivnitsa, with cafes, Internet, and a cinema, draws a younger crowd. (Center box office open daily 11am-8pm.) From late August to early September, the international **Love is Folly** film festival takes place at the complex.

Beaches are cramped in summer but make for an enjoyable afternoon. The sands stretch north from the train station and are separated from bul. Primorski by the seaside gardens. Dedicated beachgoers should consider purchasing an umbrella (7lv) rather than renting one (3lv). In summer, a long strip of discos and bars rocks the beach. Crowds pack the outdoor disco **Exit**, a two-level, three-bar, raucous beach party. Take Slivnitsa to its end at the sea garden, proceed down the steps, and head left. Hip-hop reigns, but don't expect any bumping and grinding. (Drinks 3-6lv. Cover F-Sa 3lv. Open daily 10pm-5am.)

VELIKO TARNOVO (ВЕЛИКО ТЪРНОВО) ☎(062)

Perched on the slopes above the Yantra River, 5000-year-old Veliko Tarnovo (Veh-LEEK-oh TURN-oh-voh) was Bulgaria's capital from 1185 to 1393, and was home to the nation's greatest kings—Petur, Asen I, Kaloyan, and Asen II. Tapping into its glorious legacy, Bulgarian revolutionaries wrote Bulgaria's first constitution here in 1879. Today, Tarnovo is filled with testaments to its noble past, none more breathtaking than the enormous hilltop fortress Tsarevets, former home to tsars, which still keeps watch over the town's sparkling river and winding streets.

🚆 **TRANSPORTATION.** The **train station** is south of town and across the river; it's a hike from the center, so your best bet is a taxi (3lv) or city bus #4, 5, or 13 (0.50lv). For some destinations, you'll have to switch trains in nearby **Gorna Oryakhovitsa** (Горна Оряховица). Bus #10 runs to Gorna from the main square;

it's timed to meet trains (1.40lv). Trains run to: **Burgas** (6hr., 6 per day, 11lv); **Pleven** (1½hr., 16 per day, 3.30lv); **Ruse** (2½hr., 6 per day, 5.20lv); **Sofia** (5hr., 9 per day, 12lv); **Tryavna** (1hr., 8 per day, 2.90lv); **Varna** (4hr., 5 per day, 11lv). International destinations include: **Istanbul, TUR** (10hr., 1 per day, 36lv); **Thessaloniki, GCE** (12hr., 2 per day, 64lv); **Bucharest, ROM** (6hr., 3 per day, 23lv); and **Budapest, HUN** (22hr.; 1 per day; 128lv, students 98lv; sleeping car only). Train tickets are sold at the station and at the **Rila** agency, Kaloyan 2a (Калоян), directly behind the tourist bureau, off the main square. (☎62 20 42. Open M-F 8am-4:30pm, Sa 9am-3pm.)

The west **bus station, Avtogara Zapad** (Автогара Запад), on Nikola Gabrovsky (Рикцла Гфбзцвски), is 5 stops from the center on bus #10 (0.50lv), heading right when facing the post office. Buses run to: **Gabrovo** (40min., 13 per day, 3lv) and **Stara Zagora** (3hr., 7 per day, 6lv). **Minibuses** and buses connect V. Tǔrnovo with Gorna. **Minibuses** run from the intersection of Nikola Gabrovsky and Bǔlgaria in V. Tǔrnovo to Gorna's train station (20min., every 30min., 1lv). **Etap,** a private daily bus service to most major cities, is located in Hotel Etur, on Aleksandur Stamboliyski. (☎63 05 64. Open 24hr.) Rent a **bike** at Gorgona Rent-a-Bike, Zelenka 2 (Зеленка). Walk upstairs to the right of the municipal building on the main square and veer to the right at the top. (☎601 400. Open M-F 10am-1pm, 2-7pm; Sa 10am-2pm. High-quality mountain bikes 10lv per day.)

■✚⚫ ORIENTATION AND PRACTICAL INFORMATION. Veliko Tarnovo is

spread along a loop of the Yantra River, with its central square, **pl. Mayka Bulgaria** (Майка Ъългария), located on the outside bank. Through the center, the main drag follows the river east, changing its name as it goes: it begins as **bul. Vasil Levski,** becomes **Nezavisimost** (Независимост), and turns into **Stefan Stambolov** (Стефан Стамболов), **V. Dzhandzhiyata** (В. Джанджията), **Nikola Pikolo** (Никола Пиколо), and **Mitropolska** (Митрополска) as it reaches the ruins of **Tsarevets Krepost** (Царевец Крепост). The other key street, **Khristo Botev** (Хзисто Ъотев), intersects Nezavisimost at pl. Mayka Bulgaria. With your back to the **train station,** go uphill along the river to the left for 10min. and then cross the bridge, which leads to **Aleksandǔr Stamboliyski** (Александър Стамболийски). Turn right on Khristo Botev (Христо Ъотев). You can also take almost any bus (0.50lv, timed to meet trains) from the station; ask the driver *"za tsentura?"* ("to the center?")

The **tourist office,** Khristo Botev 5, is in the main square, pl. Mayka Bulgaria. The helpful staff offer information about transportation, accommodations, tour guides, car rental, excursions into the surrounding area, and more. (☎62 21 48. English spoken. Open M-F 9am-noon and 1-6pm. Maps 3lv.) **Exchange currency** at **Hebros Bank,** Vasil Levski 13 (Васил Левски), just off the main square, which cashes AmEx **Traveler's Cheques** for 0.1% commission. A 24hr. **ATM** is outside. (☎61 10 05. Open M-F 8am-5pm.) **Luggage storage** is at the train station. Luggage must be claimed at least 30min. prior to the departure of your train. (2lv per day. Open 24hr.) The **24hr. pharmacy,** (Денонощна Аптека), Vasil Levski 29, a 5min. walk from the main square, past Hebros Bank. (☎60 04 33. Cash only.) Find **medical services** at **Policlinica** (Поликлиника), Marno Pole 21 (Марно Поле), across the square from the municipal building and post office. (☎62 19 60. Open M-Sa 8am-7pm.) **Matrix Internet Club,** Nezavisimost 32 (Независимост), along the main street, is open 24hr. (☎60 59 59. 0.68-0.98lv per hr.) The **post office,** Khristo Botev 1, on the main square, shares a building with the **telephone office.** Use the main entrance on the corner. (☎61 22 85. Open M-F 7am-7pm, Sa 8am-noon and 1-4pm. **Poste Restante** is out the door and to the right, down the stairs between the main building and the next. Open M-F 7am-6pm, Sa 7am-3pm. **Postal Code:** 5000.

⚑⚐ ACCOMMODATIONS AND FOOD. Rooms in Veliko Tarnovo are plentiful, and if you wear a backpack for more than five seconds in public, you'll be approached by locals offering **private rooms** (10-20lv), which can also be arranged through the tourist bureau. **⚑Hiker's Hostel,** Rezervoarska 91 (Резервоарска) ❶, is the only hostel in town. Hiker's serves enormous free breakfasts and has free Internet. The top-floor balcony has perfect view of Tsarevets. The staff offers free pickup and daytrips to various locations. With your back to the post office, head right on Nezavisimost, which becomes Stambolov. Veer left on Rakovski (Раковски), the uphill cobblestone street that splits from the main road. Go straight at the small square on Rakovski, and take the smaller uphill street to the left. (☎969 16 61; www.hikers-hostel.org. Dorms 20lv. Cash only.) **Hotel Comfort,** Panayot Tipografov 5 (Панайот Типографов) ❸, has brand-new furnishings, private baths, amazing views, and comfortable beds that justify the prices. Follow directions for Hiker's Hostel, but go left at the small square and continue straight; the hotel is on the left. (☎62 87 28. Breakfast 5lv. Laundry. Reception 24hr. Check-out noon. Singles €25; doubles €30; apartments with private balconies €40. Cash only.) **Hotel Trapezitsa** (Трапезица) ❶, Stambolov 79, offers spartan, inexpensive lodgings with clean sheets and private baths. Request a room with a view. From the main square, follow Nezavisimost until it becomes Stambolov; it's right next to Shtastlivetsa Pasta and Pizza. (☎62 20 61. Reception 24hr. Check-out 11am. 2-to 4-bed dorms 19-23lv; singles 31lv; doubles 46lv. ISIC discount 2lv. Cash only.)

A large **open-air market** sells fresh fruit and veggies (0.60-2.50lv per kg) daily from dawn to dusk at the corner of Bulgaria and Nikola Gabrovsky, and there's a *mekhana* (механа; tavern) on just about every balcony overlooking the river. **⚑Shtastlivetsa Pasta and Pizza** (Щфстливуцф) ❷, Stambolov 79, is next door to the Trapezitsa Hotel. Calling this a pizza parlor is an understatement—you could spend an hour reading the 2 separate menus of seemingly infinite Bulgarian, Italian, Turkish, Roma and other dishes. Portions as big as the menu, a streetside terrace, and a beautiful view in back earn this place a local reputation as the best in town. There's a streetside terrace in front and a beautiful view in back. (☎60 06 56. Medium pizza 2.80-7.50lv. Pasta 1.90-3.80lv. Entrees 3.90-16.90lv. Open daily 11am-1am. MC.) The small pub **Starata Mekhana** (Стфзфтф Мучфнф) ❷, Stambolov, has an amazing view overlooking a river and Tsarevets fortress. Try the chicken soup. (☎63 88 78. Beer from 0.90lv. Open daily noon-midnight. Cash only.) Take your pick from a large assortment of sizzling hand-tossed pizzas, cooked to crispy perfection in the flames of the open-fire oven, at **La Scalla Pizzaria** ❶, Khristo Botev 14. (☎63 58 11. Pizzas 3.50-7lv, calzones 3.90-6lv. Open daily 9:30am-midnight.)

◙ SIGHTS. The ruins of ancient **⚑Tsarevets** (Царевец) still dominate the skyline of Veliko Tarnovo. Much of the citadel was destroyed by Turks in 1393, but long stretches of the outer wall and several inner towers still stand. Nikola Pikolo leads to the gates and *kasa* (каса; ticket counter. Open 8am-7pm. 4lv. Tours in English 10lv.) At the pinnacle of the hill stands the beautiful and aptly named **Church of the Ascension** (Църква Възнесениегосподне; Tsŭrkva Vŭzneseniegospodne), restored in 1981 for Bulgaria's 1300th anniversary. Back in town, the **National Revival Museum** (Музей на Възраждането и Учредително Събрание; Muzey na Vŭzrazhdaneto i Uchreditelno Cubraine) exhibits items from the National Revival movement, including the first Bulgarian Parliament chamber and the first Bulgarian constitution. From the center, follow Nezavisimost until it becomes Nikola Pikolo, then veer right on Ivan Vazov. It's a light blue building, set off from the street. (☎62 98 21. No English captions. Open M and W-Su 9am-6pm. 4lv.) Two

BULGARIA

other museums flank the main building; downstairs to the left is the **Archaeological Museum** (Археологически Музей), in the same building as the library. Ring the bell if the door is locked. Medieval and ancient items from Tŭrnovo, religious frescoes, and the skeleton of a man who may have been a Bulgarian king serve to trace the region's history. (Open Tu-Su 8am-6pm. 4lv.)

♫ 🎭 ENTERTAINMENT AND NIGHTLIFE. On summer evenings there's often a ▨**sound-and-light show** above Tsarevets Hill—huge projectors light the ruins for an unforgettable sight. (Show starts between 9:45 and 10pm.) There is no set schedule for the show; it goes off whenever enough tourists scrape together 400lv. Ask at the tourist bureau for details. If a hard day of medieval tourism has left you in want of more modern pleasures, try the clubs that line the main street. It's Halloween every night at **Scream Club,** on Nezavisimost (Независимост), a bar done up in blood-red pleather sofas. The fun starts, of course, at the witching hour. (Beer from €1. Cover €1. Open daily midnight-5am.)

CROATIA
(HRVATSKA)

One of Eastern Europe's most fought-over treasures, Croatia has once again attracted the attention of luxury-seekers, naturalists, and backpackers alike, who came in droves before the 1991 breakup of Yugoslavia. From the sun-kissed beaches and breathtaking cliffs around the lovely coastal city of Dubrovnik up to the picturesque shores of Istria, from the dense forests around Plitvice and the cosmopolitan offerings of capital Zagreb, Croatia's wonders never cease. Despite its idyllic location along the Adriatic Sea, Croatia has long been situated in the middle of dangerous political divides and has played home to deadly ethnic tensions in the past decade; it was only after the devastating 1991-95 ethnic war that Croatia achieved full independence for the first time in 800 years. While some marked-off areas still contain land mines, the biggest threats to the traveler tend to be the hordes of other tourists who clog the ferryways come summer, and the ever-rising prices, high by Eastern European standards. Still, this friendly, fun-loving, and up-beat country demands to be seen, at any cost.

 DISCOVER CROATIA: SUGGESTED ITINERARIES

THREE DAYS Spend a day poking around the bizarre architecture of **Split** (p. 138) before ferrying down the coast to the beach paradise of either **Hvar** or **Brac** islands (1 day; p. 144). Then make your way to former war-zone—and what some consider Eastern Europe's most beautiful city—**Dubrovnik** (1 day; p. 150).

BEST OF CROATIA, ONE WEEK Enjoy the East-meets-West feel of **Zagreb** (1 day; p. 109) and head to **Zadar** (1 day; p. 134) with a few hours' stop in gorgeous **Plitvice National Park** (p. 119). Next, ferry to tree-lined **Korčula** (1 day; p. 148) before **Hvar** and **Brac** (2 days). End your journey in **Dubrovnik** (2 days).

FACTS AND FIGURES

Official Name: Republic of Croatia.

Capital: Zagreb.

Major Cities: Dubrovnik, Ploce, Split.

Population: 4,496,000.

Land Area: 56,414 sq. km.

Time Zone: GMT + 1.

Language: Croatian.

Religions: Roman Catholic (88%).

ESSENTIALS

WHEN TO GO

Croatia's best weather lasts from May to September, and crowds typically show up along the Adriatic coast in July and August. If you go in late August or September, you'll find fewer crowds, lower prices, and an abundance of fruits like figs and grapes. Later autumn is wine season. While April and October may be too cool for camping, the weather is usually nice along the coast, and private rooms are plentiful and inexpensive. You can swim in the sea from mid-June to late September.

Croatia

DOCUMENTS AND FORMALITIES

ENTRANCE REQUIREMENTS
Passport: Required for all travelers.
Visa: Not required for stays of under 90 days for citizens of Australia, Canada, Ireland, New Zealand, the UK, and the US.
Letter of Invitation: Not required for citizens of Australia, Canada, Ireland, New Zealand, the UK, and the US.
Inoculations: Recommended up-to-date on DTaP (diphtheria, tetanus, and pertussis), Hepatitis A, Hepatitis B, MMR (measles, mumps, and rubella), Polio booster, and Typhoid.
Work Permit: Required of all foreigners planning to work in Croatia.
Driving Permit: Required for all those planning to drive in Croatia.

EMBASSIES AND CONSULATES. Embassies of other countries to Croatia are all in Zagreb (p. 109). Croatia's embassies and consulates abroad include: **Australia,** 14 Jindalee Crescent, O'Malley ACT 2606, Canberra (☎2 6286 6988; croemb@dynamite.com.au); **Canada,** 229 Chapel Street, Ottawa, ON K1N 7Y6

(☎613-562-7820; www.croatiaemb.net); **New Zealand,** 291 Lincoln Rd., Henderson (☎9 836 5581; cro-consulate@xtra.co.nz), mail to: P.O. Box 83-200, Edmonton, Auckland; **UK,** 21 Conway St., London W1P 5HL (☎020 7387 2022; ambof-fice@croatianembassy.co.uk); **US,** 2343 Massachusetts Ave. NW, Washington, D.C. 20008 (☎202-588-5899; www.croatiaemb.org).

VISA AND ENTRY INFORMATION. Citizens of Australia, Canada, Ireland, New Zealand, the UK, and the US do not need a visa for stays of up to 90 days. All visitors must register with the police within 48hr. of arrival—hotels, campsites, and accommodation agencies should automatically register you, but those staying with friends or in private rooms must do so themselves to avoid fines or expulsion. To register, go to room 103 on the 2nd floor of the central police station at Petrinjska 30. (☎456 36 23, after hours 456 31 11. Bring your passport and use form #14. Open M-F 8am-4pm.) Police may check foreigners' passports anywhere and at any time. There is no entry fee. The most direct way of entering or exiting Croatia is by a bus or train between Zagreb and a neighboring capital.

TOURIST SERVICES AND MONEY

Even the smallest towns have a branch of the excellent and resourceful **state-run tourist board** *(turistička zajednica).* Their staff speak English and give out **free maps** and booklets. Private agencies *(turistička/putnička agencija),* such as the ubiquitous **Atlas,** handle private accommodations. Local outfits are cheaper.

Most tourist offices, hotels, and transportation stations **exchange currency** and traveler's checks; banks have the best rates. Croatia's monetary unit, the **kuna** (kn), which is divided into 100 lipa, is extremely difficult to exchange abroad, except in Bosnia, Hungary, and Slovenia. Inflation hovers around 2.5%, so prices should stay relatively constant in the near future. Most banks give MasterCard and Visa cash advances, and credit cards are widely accepted. ATMs are everywhere.

Expect to spend anywhere from 300 to 470 kuna per day. Travel in Croatia is becoming more costly, with the bare minimum for accommodations, food, and transport costing 240kn. **Tipping** is not expected, although it is appropriate to round up when paying; in some cases, the establishment will do it for you—check your change. Fancy restaurants often add a hefty service charge. **Bargaining** is reserved for informal transactions, such as hiring a boat for a day or renting a private room directly from an owner. Posted prices should usually be followed.

KUNA (KN)			
	AUS$1 = 4.57KN	1KN = AUS$0.22	
	CDN$1 = 4.98KN	1KN = CDN$0.20	
	EUR€1 = 7.41KN	1KN = EUR€0.14	
	NZ$1 = 4.22KN	1KN = NZ$0.24	
	UK£1 = 10.87KN	1KN = UK£0.09	
	US$1 = 6.06KN	1KN = US$0.17	

HEALTH AND SAFETY

EMERGENCY	**Police:** ☎112. **Ambulance:** ☎112. **Fire:** ☎112.

Travel to the former conflict area of the **Slavonia** and **Krajina regions** remains dangerous due to **unexploded landmines,** which are not expected to be cleared until at least 2010. In 2005, a tourist was injured by a mine on the island of Vis, which inspectors had previously declared safe. If you choose to visit these or other regions, do not stray from known safe areas, and consult the Croatian Mine Action

CROATIA

Center website at www.hcr.hr. **Pharmacies** sell Western products, including tampons, sanitary napkins (*sanitami ulosci*), and condoms (*prezervativ*). UK citizens receive free medical care with a valid passport. Tap water is chlorinated, and while relatively safe, may cause mild abdominal upsets. **Bottled water** is readily available. **Women** should go out in public with a companion to ward off unwanted displays of machismo. **Disabled travelers** should contact **Savez Organizacija Invalida Hrvatske** (☎ 1 369 4502), in Zagreb, as cobblestones and a lack of ramps render it a more difficult area. **Homosexuality** is slowly becoming accepted; discretion is best.

TRANSPORTATION

Croatia Airlines flies to and from many cities, including **Frankfurt, London, Paris,** Zagreb, Dubrovnik, and Split. Rijeka, Zadar, and Pula also have tiny international airports. Book in advance for a cheap seat or consider buying a flight pass from Europe by Air (www.europebyair.com), which will let you fly anywhere on Croatia Airlines for US$99 per leg. **Trains** (www.hznet.hr) run to Zagreb from **Budapest, HUN; Ljubljana, SLN; Venice, ITA;** and **Vienna, AUT,** and continue on to other Croatian destinations. Due to the 1991-95 war, trains are very slow and nonexistent south of Split. *Odlazak* means departures, *dolazak* arrivals. **Buses** (www.akz.hr) run faster and farther than trains at comparable prices. Tickets are cheaper if you buy them on board, bypassing the 2kn service charge at station kiosks. Mandatory luggage storage (3kn) is enforced only on crowded lines.

If you're on the coast, take a **Jadrolinija ferry** (www.jadrolinija.hr). Boats sail the Rijeka-Split-Dubrovnik route, stopping at islands on the way. Ferries also go to **Ancona, ITA** from Split and Zadar and to **Bari, ITA** from Split and Dubrovnik. Though slower than buses and trains, ferries are more comfortable. A basic ticket provides only a place on the deck. Cheap beds sell out fast, so buy tickets in advance.

Anyone over 18 can rent a **car** in larger cities (350-400kn per day), but parking and gas are expensive. Rural roads are in bad condition, and those traveling through the Krajina region and other conflict areas should be cautious of off-road **landmines.** Decking a car on a ferry can be quite expensive. **Hitchhiking** is relatively uncommon and not recommended by *Let's Go.* **Moped** and **bike rentals** (50-80kn per day) are an option in resort or urban areas.

KEEPING IN TOUCH

PHONE CODES	**Country code: 385. International dialing prefix: 00.** From outside Croatia, dial int'l dialing prefix (see inside back cover) + 385 + city code + local number. Within Croatia, dial city code + number, or simply the number for local calls.

Most towns, no matter how small, have at least one **Internet** cafe. Connections on the islands are slower and less reliable than those on the mainland. Post offices usually have **public phones;** pay after you talk. All phones on the street require a *telekarta* (phone card), sold at newsstands and post offices. Fifty "impulses" cost 23kn (1 impulse equals 3min. domestic, 36s international; 50% discount 10pm-7am, Su, and holidays). Calls to the US and Europe can be expensive (20kn per min.); Voicecom and Telnet cards offer the best rates. International access numbers can be found on the inside back cover. For the **international operator,** dial ☎ 901. Croatia, which has two **cell phone** networks, T-Mobile and VIP. If you bring or buy a phone compatible with the GSM 900/1800 network, SIM cards are widely available and cost around 400kn. The **Croatian Post** is reliable. Mail from the US arrives within a week. *Avionski* and *zrakoplovom* both mean "airmail." Mail addressed to **Poste Restante** will be held for 30 days at the main post office. Address envelopes: Jennifer (First name) KAN (LAST NAME), POSTE RESTANTE, Pt. Republike 28 (post office address), 20000 (postal code), Dubrovnik (city), CROATIA.

ACCOMMODATIONS AND OUTDOORS

CROATIA	❶	❷	❸	❹	❺
ACCOMMODATIONS	under 100kn under €14 under US$17	100-150kn €14-20 US17-25	150-210kn €20-29 US$25-35	210-360kn €21-49 US$35-60	over 360kn over €49 over US$60

For info on Croatia's youth hostels (in Zagreb, Pula, Zadar, Dubrovnik, Šibenik, Krk, Veli Losinj, and Punat), contact the **Croatian Youth Hostel Association**, Savska 5, 10000 Zagreb (☎ 1 482 92 94; www.hfhs.hr/front/index.php?jezik=en). **Hotels** in Croatia can be expensive—an overnight stay in Zagreb will be at least US$80. If you opt for a hotel, call a few days ahead, especially in summer along the coast.

Apart from hostels, **private rooms** are the only budget accommodations options. Look for *sobe* signs, especially near transportation stations. English is rarely spoken by room owners. Agencies generally charge 30-50% more if you stay fewer than three nights. All accommodations are subject to a tourist tax of 5-10kn (one reason the police require foreigners to register). Croatia is one of the top **camping** destinations in Europe—33% of travelers stay in campgrounds. Facilities are usually comfortable, and prices are among the cheapest along the Mediterranean. Camping outside of designated areas is illegal. For more info, contact the **Croatian Camping Union**, HR-52440 Poreč, Pionirska 1 (☎ 52 451 324; www.camping.hr).

FOOD AND DRINK

CROATIA	❶	❷	❸	❹	❺
FOOD	under 40kn under €5 under US$7	40-70kn €5-10 US$7-12	71-110kn €10-15 US$12-18	111-190kn €15-26 US$18-31	over 190kn over €26 over US$31

Croatian cuisine is defined by the country's varied geography. In continental Croatia around and east of Zagreb, heavy meals featuring meat and creamy sauces dominate. *Purica s mlincima* (turkey with pasta) is the regional dish near Zagreb. Also popular are *burek*, a layered pie made with meat or cheese, and the spicy Slavonian *kulen*, which is considered one of the world's best **sausages** by a panel of German men who decide such things. *Pašticada* (slow-cooked meat) is also excellent. On the coast, textures and flavors change with the presence of **seafood** and Italian influence. Don't miss out on *lignje* (squid) or *Dalmatinski pršut* (Dalmatian smoked ham). The **oysters** from Ston Bay have received a number of awards at international competitions. If your budget does not allow for such treats, *slane sardele* (salted sardines) are a tasty substitute. **Vegetarian** and **kosher** eating are difficult in Croatia, but not impossible. In both cases, pizza and bakeries are safe and ubiquitous options. Price is usually the best indicator of quality for **wines.** Mix red wine with tap water to get the popular *bevanda*, and white with carbonated water to get *gemišt*. *Šljivovica* is a hard-hitting plum brandy found in many small towns. *Karlovačko* and *Ožujsko* are the two most popular beers.

LIFE AND TIMES

HISTORY

DALMATIANS 101. Today's Croatia has its roots in the Roman province of **Dalmatia**, with its capital at **Salona**, near what is now Split (p. 138). The Slavic ancestors of Croatia's present inhabitants settled the region in the 6th and 7th centuries, partly expelling and partly assimilating the indigenous Illyrian population. Over the next two centuries, the Croats slowly accepted **Catholicism.** In the 9th century, an independent Croatian state was consolidated by **King Tomislav** (910-928), who earned papal recognition for his country. Pope Gregory crowned **King Zvonimir** in 1076, solidifying Croatia's orientation toward Catholic Europe.

UNDER THE HUNGARIAN YOKE. In 1102, the Croatian Kingdom entered into a dynastic union with Hungary. Croatia was soon stripped of all independence and effectively disappeared for 800 years. Following Hungary's defeat by the Ottomans in 1526, the **Austrian Hapsburgs** took over what remained of Croatia and turned it into a buffer zone against Ottoman aggression. Orthodox Christians from the Ottoman-controlled area migrated to the region, laying a foundation for the Serbian minority in Croatia. The Croats, led by **Josip Jelačić,** attempted to please their Austrian rulers by remaining loyal to the empire when Hungary revolted in 1848, but their later demands for self-government fell on deaf ears.

BITTERSWEET UNION. After Croat troops fought alongside the Germans and Austro-Hungarians during WWI, Croatia declared **independence** from a defeated Austria-Hungary on December 1, 1918, and announced its incorporation into the **Kingdom of the Serbs, Croats, and Slovenes** under Serbian **King Alexander.** To the dismay of the Croats, Alexander eventually declared a dictatorship and renamed the kingdom **Yugoslavia.** In 1934, Alexander was killed by Croat nationalists from the **Ustaše** (Insurgents), a terrorist organization demanding Croatian independence.

TITO'S REIGN. The Ustaše finally achieved Croatia's "independence" in 1941 in the form of a fascist puppet state. Seeking to eliminate the country's Jewish and Serbian populations, the ruthless regime killed more than 350,000 people in massacres and concentration camps. Though the government supported the Axis powers during **WWII,** the majority of Croats joined the communist-led **Partisan** resistance early in the war. The Partisans, led by **Josip Broz Tito,** demanded the creation of a federal Yugoslav state. In 1945, as communist regimes took power across Eastern Europe, the **Socialist Federal Republic of Yugoslavia** declared its independence. Though Yugoslavia broke from Moscow in 1948, it retained communism and suppressed civil rights and the ambitions of Croat nationalists. Many of the student leaders of a 1971 independence movement were imprisoned, but their struggle eventually led to the ratification of a new Constitution in 1974.

A COSTLY FREEDOM. The rotating presidency established upon Tito's death was unable to curb the tide of nationalism. In April 1990, Croat nationalist **Franjo Tudjman** was elected President of Croatia, and on June 25, 1991, Croatia declared **independence.** Tensions between Croats and the Serbian minority escalated rapidly. Claiming to protect Serbian nationals, the Serb-controlled **Yugoslav National Army** invaded Croatia, driving out hundreds of thousands of Croats from **Eastern Slavonia** and shelling Vukovar, Zadar, and Dubrovnik. Meanwhile, the Serbian minority declared its own independent republic, **Serbian Krajina,** around Knin in central Croatia. Not until the destruction of Dubrovnik did international political leadership realize that Croatia was occupied. In January 1992, the European Community recognized Croatia's independence, and a UN military force arrived to quell further fighting and ethnic cleansing. In May 1995, Croatia seized Krajina, expelling over 150,000 Serbs. Croatia's experience at the hands of the Serbian military did not stop the Croatian leadership from making claims on Bosnia and Herzegovina, sending troops, and massacring Bosnian Serbs and Muslims. The 1995 **Dayton Peace Accords,** negotiated by American Richard Holbrooke, established a cease-fire in Bosnia and Herzegovina and stabilized the disputed areas of Croatia.

TODAY

HOW CROATIA IS RULED. Croatia is a **parliamentary democracy** with extensive executive powers invested in the president, who is elected by popular vote for a five-year term. The **Sabor** is a parliament representing 21 administrative districts; deputies are elected for four years. Amid repeated allegations of unfair elections, **Franjo Tudjman** served as President from 1991 until his death in December 1999. During his tenure, Tudjman and his nationalist **Croatian Democratic Union** (Hrvatska Demokraticka Zajednica; HDZ) established Croatia as a sovereign state, but HDZ's corruption, abuse of power, and censorship of the media also isolated the country from the West. The 2000 elections transferred power to the democratically inclined left. In 2000, a pro-Western liberal, **Stipe Mesić** of the Croatian People's Party (HNS), became President and immediately began accession talks with the EU and NATO. The 2003 elections installed new HDZ leader **Ivo Sanader** as Prime Minister, but Mesić was narrowly re-elected to the presidency in 2005.

CURRENT EVENTS. With an economy dependent upon tourism, Croatia suffered severely from war in the Balkans. In the aftermath, **unemployment** rates skyrocketed to over 20%. The country's hopes for recovery were halted by the 1999 Kosovo crisis, which once again discouraged Western tourists from travel to the Balkans. Economic reforms have met with strong resistance from both parliament and the public, further hindering growth and reconstruction. As the political situation continues to calm, and with encouragement from the EU, Croatia has now focused on improving the legal system and rebuilding the nation's infrastructure to support its booming tourism industry. Though the country is expected to join the EU by the end of the decade, accession will remain elusive until Zagreb captures Gen. **Ante Gotovina,** who is wanted for alleged war crimes against ethnic Serbs.

PEOPLE AND CULTURE

DEMOGRAPHICS. An overwhelming 90% of Croatia's inhabitants are ethnic **Croats.** The country retains a significant **Serbian** minority (4.5%) despite an exodus at the end of the war in 1995. Tensions between Serbs and Croats still run high, but outbreaks of violence are now rare. Each community remains relatively closed to the other, and the Serbian population suffers from stigmatization and unemployment. Croatia's **Bosniak** minority (0.5%) also suffers discrimination, but to a much milder extent than the Serbian population. Nearly all of the ethnically Croat population is **Roman Catholic.** Serbs remaining in the country belong to the **Serbian Orthodox** Church, while the Bosniak minority practices **Islam.**

LANGUAGE. Croats speak **Croatian,** a South Slavic language written in the Latin alphabet. The language fairly recently became distinguished from Serbo-Croatian. Only a few expressions differ from Serbian, but be careful not to use the Serbian ones in Croatia—you'll make few friends. **German** and **Italian** are common second languages among adults. Most Croatians under 30 speak some **English.** For a phrasebook and glossary, see **Glossary: Croatian,** p. 769.

CUSTOMS AND ETIQUETTE. If you wear **shorts** and **sandals,** you'll stick out as a tourist in the cities, but will blend in along the coast. Though southern Croatia tends to be of a beach-oriented mentality, remember that this land of skin and shorts is also devoutly Catholic. Avoid jumping from the beach to the cathedral without a change of clothes (long pants or skirts and close-toed shoes). Croats have few qualms about **drinking** and **smoking,** but abstain in buses, trains, and other marked areas. Maintain eye contact when clinking glasses before you drink. If you don't, local superstition holds you will have seven years of bad luck.

CROATIA

UNTYING THE CRAVAT

While many might suspect the necktie to have originated in Italy or France, the word *cravat* (from *hrvat*, or *croat* in Serbo-Croatian) clues us into its real roots. According to legend, a Croatian woman once tied a scarf around her true love's neck as a token of her devotion; the historical record shows that the tie was first worn by Croatian soldiers fighting in the service of Austria during the Thirty Years' War.

Recently, Croatia has launched a campaign to use its *cravat* heritage to establish ties with the rest of the world. In 1990, the non-profit organization Academia Cravatica was born, solely responsible for promoting what the group's founder Marijan Busic calls "Croatia's contribution to the global culture." In 2003, the Pula Arena served as the neck for the largest cravat in the world, an 808m long red "mega-tie." Recently, the organization opened a traveling art exhibit, The Challenge of the Tie, which addresses the neckwear's ambiguous purpose through the work of Croatian and international artists. After visiting the Baltics, the exhibit toured to acclaim in early 2005, bringing "tie art" and Croatian culture to audiences in Egypt and South Africa.

As British historian Norman Davies observes, "Of course, those who deny the influence of Europe's smaller nations should remember that Croats hold us all by our necks."

THE ARTS

LITERATURE. Croatian texts first emerged during the 9th century, but for the next 600 years literature consisted almost entirely of translations from other European languages. Dubrovnik was the only independent part of Croatia after 1102 and produced literature that had a lasting impact on Croatian culture. After the city's devastation by an earthquake in 1667, the nexus of Croatian literature shifted north. The 16th-century dramatist **Martin Držić** and the 17th-century poet **Ivan Gundullé** raided Italy for literary models, combining them with traditions from back home. During Austrian and Hungarian repressions of the Croatian language in the 19th century, **Ljudevit Gaj** led the movement to reform and codify Croatian vernacular. **August Šenoa,** Croatia's dominant 19th-century literary figure, played a key part in the formation of a literary public and in completing the work that Gaj had begun. Croatian prose sparkled in the late 20th century. **Dubravka Ugrešić's** personal, reflective novels, which discuss nostalgia and the revision of history, have become instant best-sellers. The novelist **Slavenka Drakulić** is popular abroad.

THE VISUAL ARTS. Characterized by the rejection of conventional and "civilized" depictions, **native art** presides as the most popular painting style. This movement, begun by **Krsto Hegedušlć** (1901-71), is highly influenced by folk traditions. It eliminates perspective and uses only vivid colors. Croatia's most famous modern sculptor and architect, **Ivan Meštrović,** has achieved fame outside Croatia. His wooden religious sculptures can be seen in London's Tate Gallery and New York City's Metropolitan Museum of Art, as well as in squares throughout his homeland. **Vinko Bresan** is Croatia's most prominent contemporary filmmaker. His 1996 comedy, *How the War Started on My Island (Kako je poceo rat na mom otoku)*, won multiple awards and is enormously popular both at home and abroad.

HOLIDAYS AND FESTIVALS

Holidays: New Year's Day (Jan. 1); Epiphany (Jan. 6); Easter Sunday and Monday (Apr. 16 and 17); May Day (May 1); Anti-Fascist Struggle Day (June 22); National Thanksgiving Day (Aug. 5); Assumption of the Blessed Virgin Mary (Aug. 15); Independence Day (Oct. 8); All Saints' Day (Nov. 5); Christmas (Dec. 25-26).

Festivals: In June, Zagreb holds its own version of Woodstock, the catch-all festival Cest Is D'Best. An easygoing philosophy keeps revelers on city streets out all night (p. 117). Open-air concerts and theatrical performances make the Dubrovnik Summer Festival (*Dubrovački Ljetni;* from early July to late Aug.) the event of the summer in that city (p. 155). During the same period, a similar festival showcasing music and theater takes over Split. From July to August, Korčula (p. 148) unsheathes the Festival of Sword Dances *(Festival Viteških Igara)* with performances of the *Moreška, Moštra,* and *Kumpanija* sword dances swashbuckling all over the island. Zagreb's International Puppet Festival (late Aug. to early Sept.) draws children and adults alike.

ADDITIONAL RESOURCES

GENERAL HISTORY

The Balkans, by Misha Glenny (2000). An engaging survey of the history of the Balkans over the past century, with a special emphasis on the recent fall of Yugoslavia.

Croatia: A Nation Forged in War, by Marcus Tanner (1998). A British journalist's powerful, if somewhat pro-Croat, take on the nation's troubled history.

FICTION, NONFICTION, AND FILM

Balkan Ghosts: A Journey Through History, by Robert Kaplan (1994). A travel narrative guiding the reader through the political complexities of Croatia and its neighbors.

Black Lamb and Grey Falcon, by Rebecca West (1941). Written just before WWII, this classic weaves history and personal experience into a captivating narrative.

The Bone Lady, by Clea Koff (2004). An anthropologist's haunting account of studying mass graves illuminates the tragedy of violent ethnic cleansing in parts of Croatia.

How the War Started on My Island, directed by Vinko Bresan (1996). This unusually comedic film about recent Balkan violence was hugely successful.

How We Survived Communism and Even Laughed, by Slavenka Drakulić (1993). A series of perceptive essays on everyday life before and after the Balkan conflict.

ZAGREB   ☎(0)1

Though many visitors treat Zagreb as little more than a stop-over en route to the Croatian coast, exploring Croatia's largest city is a perfect introduction to the country as a whole. Combining youthful dynamism with Old World charm, Croatia's capital seems more like a low-key, cleaner, and smaller Paris than a stronghold of the former Communist bloc. In the old city center, a refuge from the outskirts' more industrial areas, smartly-dressed *Zagrebčani* outnumber visitors, enjoying the sights and smells of outdoor cafes, flower markets, and fresh fruit stands. One downside is the city's shortage of hostels, which can be remedied by taking an affordable private room *(sobe)*. With its welcoming (and English-speaking) inhabitants, a growing economy, impressive cultural offerings, and beautiful unspoiled surroundings, Zagreb is an attractive blend of East and West.

◪ INTERCITY TRANSPORTATION

Flights: Pleso (☎626 52 22; www.zagreb-airport.hr), about 30min. from the city center. **Airport lost and found** ☎456 22 29. Croatia Airlines provides **buses** (☎615 79 92; www.plesoprijevoz.hr) between the main bus station and the airport (daily every 30min. 5:30am-7:30pm, 25kn). **Taxis** to the city, which can be found behind the Croatia Airlines office, start their meters at a hefty 25kn and cost 150-250kn. **Croatia Airlines,** Zrinjevac 17 (toll-free ☎080 07 777, 481 96 33, reservations 481 96 33 or 487 27 27; www.croatiaairlines.hr) offers flights to and from most cities in Europe. Flying to

GETTING IN. When you first arrive in Zagreb, your best bet is to take cash out at the ATM in the airport (better rates than exchanging currency and no commission, which is usually 1.5%), and if you need to make international phone calls to let loved ones know you've arrived, call from the post office in the airport (better rates than with a phone card and very user-friendly—just call from their telephone booth and pay at the counter when you're done).

Zagreb from overseas might prove cheaper if connecting in London (coming eastbound) or Vienna (coming westbound) to a European budget airline, train, or bus. Domestic destinations include **Dubrovnik** (1hr., 3-7 per day), **Split** (45min., 4-7 per day), and **Zadar** (40min., M-F and Su 2-3 per day). Sometimes, the plane is cheaper than the bus. International flights to the Balkan region include **Sarajevo, BOS** and **Skopje, MAC.** There are no flights from Zagreb to Belgrade, SMN. Also inquire here to book flights on other airlines. Open M-F 8am-8pm, Sa 8am-2pm.

Trains: Glavni Kolodvor (Main Station), Trg Kralja Tomislava 12 (☎060 333 444, international info 378 25 32; www.hznet.hr.) From the bus station, take tram #2, 6, or 8 to the 3rd stop ("Glavni Kolodvor"). If you aren't using a railpass, buses are generally considered better for Croatian travel, except for the following destinations: **Ljubljana** (2 hr.; 7 per day; one-way 100kn, round-trip 130kn), **Split** (new day trains 6hr., 3 per day, 166kn; night train 8½hr., 2 per evening, 166kn), **Sarajevo** (9hr., 1 per day, 168kn). To: **Rijeka** (4-6hr., 3 per day, 102kn); **Split** (6-9hr., 5 per day, 152kn); **Belgrade, SMN** (6½hr., 5 per day, 130kn); **Budapest, HUN** (7½hr., 1 per day, 224kn); **Sarajevo, BOS** (9¼hr., 1 per day); **Skopje, MAC** (15½hr., 1 per day, 264kn); **Venice, ITA** (6hr., 1 per day, 320kn); **Vienna, AUT** (6½hr., 2 per day, 355kn); **Zurich, SWI** (14hr., 1 per day, 647kn). There are no trains to **Dubrovnik.** AmEx/MC/V.

Buses: For travel within Croatia, buses are often more efficient than trains. **Autobusni Kolodvor** (Bus Station), Držićeva bb (☎060 313 333; www.akz.hr, click on "Vozni red"). Buy tickets on either side of the ticket area. Luggage storage downstairs next to *peron* (platform) 106 (1.20kn per hr). Restrooms (2kn) next to luggage storage. To: **Dubrovnik** (11hr., 8 per day, 180 kn); **Pula** (4½hr., 14 per day, 107-146kn); **Rijeka** (3½hr., 27 per day, 115kn); **Split** (7-9hr., 27 per day, 120kn); **Belgrade, SMN** (6½hr., 4 per day, 188kn); **Frankfurt, GER** (15hr., 2 per day, 630kn); **Ljubljana, SLN** (2½hr., 2 per day, 150kn); **Sarajevo, BOS** (8½hr., 3 per day, 220kn); **Skopje, MAC** (13hr., 1 per day, 325kn); **Vienna, AUT** (8hr., 2 per day, 250kn). **Plitvice** (2½hr., 19 per day, 72kn), **Varaždin** (1¾hr., 20 per day, 50kn). Large backpacks 6kn extra.

Ferries: Jadrolinija, in the Marko Polo Travel Agency, Masarykova 24 (☎481 52 16; www.jadrolinija.hr). Reserves tickets for travel along the Dalmatian coast to **Dubrovnik, Rijeka, Split, Zadar,** and the islands, and to **Ancona** and **Bari, ITA.** Pick up one of their helpful schedules if you plan on taking ferries, the best way to move along the coast. To ensure a good seat, check in 30-45min. before departure. Open M-F 8am-5pm.

■ ORIENTATION

Unlike the city's sprawling outskirts, the center of Zagreb is easily walkable. To the north, historic **Gornji Grad** (Upper Town) is composed of the **Kaptol** and **Gradec** hills. Gradec, where most of the historic sites are located, is referred to simply as **Gornji Grad.** The central **Donji Grad** (Lower Town) is home to most of the museums, squares and parks. The **Sava River** separates these neighborhoods from the modern residential area **Novi Zagreb** (New Zagreb). Both Gornji and Donji Grad are bustling centers of activity, but the winding streets of Gornji Grad tend to be more peaceful. Most shopping is located around the city's central square, **Trg bana Josipa Jelačića,** and on **Ilica,** the commercial artery that runs through the square.

CROATIA

CROATIA

Zagreb

♦ ACCOMMODATIONS
Evistas, 24
Mirna Noć, 2
Omladinski Turistički
Centar (HI), 23
Ravnice Youth Hostel, 1

● FOOD
Kobasice, 11
Millennium, 13
Pingvin, 15
Pivnica Vallis Aurea, 10
Restaurant Boban, 14
Taverna, 5
VIP, 12
Zdravljak Nova, 9

NIGHTLIFE
Aquarius, 26
BP Club, 16
Gallery, 27
Indy's, 7
Khala, 3
Pivnica Medvedgrad, 25
Tolkien's House, 6

🏛 MUSEUMS
Arts Pavilion, 22
Museum of Arts and
Crafts, 17
Ethnographic Museum, 20
Mimara Museum, 21
Klovićevi Dvori
Gallery, 8
Gallery of Modern Art, 19
Strossmayer Gallery, 18
Studio Meštrović, 4

TO MAKSIMIR PARK,
ZAGREB ZOO (1.5km),
🏠 (2km), 🏠 (5km)

Domjanićeva
Guljufova
Gotočeva
Kamaufova
Pekkova
Derenčinova
Pavla Šubića
Crvenog Križa
Ljudevita
KVATERNIKOV TRG
Voćarska
Jurkovićeva
TRG PETRETRI CEV
Vojnovićeva
Stančićeva
Višeslavova
KRESIMIROV TRG
Držićeva
■ Tram
Autobusni
Kolodvor
Antuna
Laginjna
Bauera
Zvonimirova
Hrvojeva
Kraljice Jelene
Križanićeva
Branimirova
TO US (600m)

KAPTOL
Vončinina
SRC Salata
Vlaška
ČUK
Rubetićeva
Smičiklasova
Martićeva
Rakloga
TRG ŽRTAVA FAŠIZMA
Janka
Draškovićeva
Državljavova
Laundry
Misljavova
Trpimirova
Domagojeva

Šalata
Novakova
Ribnjak
Ribnjak Park
Cathedral of the Assumption
Čegraževa
Bakačeva
TRG HRVATSKIH VELIKANA
Jurišićeva
Palmotićeva
Đordićeva
Boškovićeva
Amruševa
Petrinjska
Hatzova
Šenoe
Movie Theater Cinestar ■
Vatroslav Lisinski
Concert Hall

Nova Ves
Australia
Tkalčićeva
Mikovlićeva
Vinodoka
Beroslav
Kaptol
Opatovina
Opatička
Radićeva
Parliament
Kamenita
St. Mark's
Lotrščak Tower
Strossmayerovo
Demetrova
Ilica
Mesnička
Tuskanac
GORNJI GRAD
Skalinska
Dolac Market
Stone Gate
St. Catherine's
Funicular
PREFADOVICEVA
TRG BANA JEL AČIĆA
TRG Bogovićeva
Berislavićeva
Jadrolinija
Preradovićeva
Gunduličeva
Kozum Supermarket
Vačšavska
Frankopanska
Dalmatinska
Medulićeva

TRG BRA CE MA ŽURANI ĆA
Croatian National Theater
MAR SALA TITA
ROOSEVELTOV TRG
Canada
DONJI GRAD
Konzum
Hebrangova
Žerjavićeva
Kumičićeva
Haulikova
TRG KRALJA TOMISLAVA
Gajeva
Trenkova
STROSSMAYEROV TRG
KNEZA AC
Croatia Airlines
AmEx Airlines
TIC
Tesla
Po Zrinu
Trg

Croatian
TRG KRALJA PETRA SVAI ĆA
Miramarska
Mihanovićeva
BOTANI ČKI VRT
MARULI ĆEV TRG
Vodnikova
Crnatkova
Kumičićeva
Savska
Kršnjavoga
Jukićeva
Brozova
Klaićeva
Prilaz Gjure Deželića
Kačićeva
BRITANSKI TRG
Dezmanova
Zamenhofova
Radnički dol
Pantovčak ul.
Primorska
Kranjčevićeva

TO SAVA RIVER (1.6km),
NOVI ZAGREB (3km)

🏠 TO MIROGOJ CEMETERY (3km)

TO US (600m)
Glavni Kolodvor ■ Tram

🏠 25 🏠 26 🏠 27
TO 🏠 LAKE JARUN

300 meters
300 yards
0

THE STREETS... Finding your way around Zagreb can be tricky. Many street names appear differently on street signs than on maps and in addresses because of grammatical declensions. The root of the name remains the same, but the ending changes. For instance, a street sign may say Trg Petra Preradovica (the square of Petra Preradovica), but it will be more commonly known as Preradoviceva trg (Preradovica's square). In general, the case declension from proper street name to an address or map changes the ending from -a to -ova or -eva (Gaja to Gajeva) and from -e to -ina (Tesle to Teslina). In addition, "bb" (bez broja) after a street name means buildings on the street are not numbered. Furthermore, street names sometimes change from block to block. When exploring the city, try to rely on landmarks, and count streets when necessary.

⌐ LOCAL TRANSPORTATION

Trams: The **Zagreb Electric Tram** is the main way you'll cruise around town (☎36 51 555; www.zet.hr). Organized by number (1-17), trams are often sweltering in the summer and packed year-round but do cover the entire city. Buy tickets at any newsstand (6.50kn) or from the driver (8kn). Day pass 18kn. Punch them in boxes near the doors—an unpunched ticket is as good as no ticket. Fine for riding ticketless is 150kn. Night trams run every 30min. midnight-4am; tickets cost 20% more. Pick up a tram route map at the TIC (see **Tourist and Financial Services**, p. 112).

Buses: (☎660 04 46). Beyond the city center, buses pick up where the trams stop. All the same rules and fares apply as for trams.

Taxis: On Gajeva south of Teslina, at the corner of Trg Jelačića and Bakačeva, and in front of major hotels and the bus and train stations; cabs tend to be plentiful at night. 25kn base, 7kn per km, luggage 5kn; prices rise 20% 10pm-5am, Su, and holidays.

◪ PRACTICAL INFORMATION

TOURIST AND FINANCIAL SERVICES

Tourist Office: Tourist Information Center (TIC), Trg Jelačića 11 (☎481 40 51; www.zagreb-touristinfo.hr). The friendly, resourceful staff will supply you with **free maps** and pamphlets. Ask for the invaluable and free *Zagreb Info A-Z* and *Zagreb in Your Pocket* pamphlets for updated listings. Also request the free *Events and Performances,* a monthly list of cultural offerings. You can also buy a **Zagreb Card** (valid 3 days; 90kn), which covers all bus and tram rides and provides discounts in restaurants and museums. Open M-F 9am-9pm, Sa 9am-5pm, Su 9am-2pm.

Embassies and Consulates: Australia, Centar Kaptol, Nova Ves 11, 3rd fl. (☎489 12 00, emergencies 098 41 47 29). Open M-F 8:30am-4:30pm. **Canada,** Prilaz Gjure Deželića 4 (☎488 12 00; fax 488 12 30). Open M-F 10am-4pm. **New Zealand,** Trg S. Radića 3 (☎615 13 82). Open M-F 8:30am-4pm. **UK,** Lučića 4 (☎600 91 00; www.britishembassy.gov.uk/croatia). Open M-Th 8:30am-5pm, F 8:30am-2pm. **US,** Thomas Jefferson 2 (☎661 22 00; www.usembassy.hr). Open M-F 8am-4:30pm.

Currency Exchange: You'll get better rates by going directly to ATMs, and you won't have to pay the standard 1.5% commission fee. You'll see *Mjenjačnica* (money exchange places) and **Zagrebačka Banka** everywhere. The main branch is at Trg Jelačića 10 (☎610 40 00). Cashes **traveler's checks** (1.5% commission). Open M-F 7am-8:30pm, Sa 7:30am-noon. **Splitska Banka,** Trg N. Š. Zrinkog 16 (☎487 33 02). **Western Union** available. Open M-F 8am-7pm, Sa 8am-noon. **ATMs** *(bankomat)* are at the bus and train stations and all over the city center. Locals usually pay cash for everything.

LOCAL SERVICES

Luggage Storage: At the train station. 10kn per piece per day. At the bus station, 2nd fl. 1.20kn per bag per hr., 2.30kn for bags over 15kg. Both open 24hr.

English-Language Bookstore: Algoritam, Gajeva 1 (☎481 86 72; fax 481 74 97), next to Hotel Dubrovnik. Carries international newspapers, magazines, and music on the ground fl. The basement holds Croatian phrase books, English fiction and classics, and travel guides. Books 50-400kn. Open M-F 8:30am-9pm, Sa 8:30am-3pm. AmEx/MC/V.

Photo Services: Foto Plus, Praška 2 (☎481 84 20), right off the main square. Print photos from a digital camera for 2kn per picture. Copy your memory card to a CD for only 10kn. Friendly staff. Open M-F 8am-7pm, Sa-Su 8am-4pm. AmEx/DC/MC/V.

Laundromat: Predom, Draškovićeva 31 (☎461 29 90). No English spoken. 2-day service 2-30kn per item; next-day 50% more. Open M-F 6am-9pm, Sa 8am-4pm.

EMERGENCY AND COMMUNICATIONS

Police: Department for Foreign Visitors, Petrinjska 30 (☎456 36 23, after hours 456 31 11). Room 103 on the 2nd fl. of the central police station. If you are not staying in a hotel or hostel, you will need to **officially register** your arrival with the police. Bring your passport and use form #14. Open M-F 8am-4pm.

Pharmacy: You'll find a *ljekarnas* (pharmacy) on just about every other block. 2 centrally located *ljekarnas* are on the corners of Petrinjska and Boškovićeva, and Teslina and Masarykova. **Gradska Ljekarna Zagreb,** Zrinjevac 20 (☎487 38 73). Most open M-F 7am-8pm, Sa 7am-2:30pm. **24hr. service** at Ilica 43 (☎484 84 50). AmEx/D/MC.

Medical Services: Hospital REBRO, Kišpatićeva 12 (☎238 88 88). Open 24hr.

Telephones: Be aware that pay phones take only prepaid cards, not coins. Buy a **phone card** (*telekarta,* 40-100kn; Voicecom has good rates on international calls) from any news kiosk, or call from a phone at the **post office** and pay afterward (6kn per min.).

 WHERE IT'S @ . Can't find that all-important @ key on any keyboard in Croatia? Never fear—it's Ctrl-Alt-V.

Internet: The *Zagreb Info A-Z* pamphlet lists several Internet cafes. **Charlie Net,** Gajeva 4a (☎488 02 33), through the courtyard and on the right. Friendly, English-speaking staff. Great connections. Printing and scanning. 16kn per hr. Open M-Sa 8am-10pm. **Sublink Cyber Cafe,** Teslina 12 (☎481 13 29), through the courtyard, upstairs, and to the left. 15kn per hr. Open M-Sa 9am-10pm, Su 3-10pm.

Post Office: Post offices are plentiful: look for the yellow "Poste" sign. Next to the train station is Branimirova 4 (☎484 03 45). From Branimirova, turn left up the stairs. **Poste Restante** on 2nd fl. (desk #3). Desk #1 **exchanges currency** and cashes **traveler's checks** for 1.5% commission. Open 24hr. Central Post Office, Jurišićeva 4 (☎481 10 90). Open M-F 7am-9pm, Sa 8am-6pm, Su 8am-2pm. **Postal Code:** 10000.

▐ ACCOMMODATIONS

Cheap accommodations are scarce in Zagreb, and budget travelers are quickly becoming more common. When hostels are full, try a **private room** through **Evistas.** From the train station, take a right on Branimirova, a quick left onto Petrinjska, and then a right onto Augusta Šenoe (it's #28; buzz to go in). This friendly travel agency can register you and reserve beds in private rooms or hotels, even at the height of festival season. (☎483 95 46; evistas@zg.hinet.hr. Open M-F 9am-1:45pm and 3-8pm, Sa 9:30am-5pm. Singles 185-200kn; doubles 264kn; triples 345kn; apartments 390-750kn. Min. 2-day stay for apartments. 20% more for 1 night only; 30%

more during festivals; under 26 10% off. Tax 7kn.) Foreigners entering Croatia must **register** with the police (see **Emergency and Communications,** p. 113) within 48hr. of arrival (hostels and hotels will register you automatically).

▓ **Ravnice Youth Hostel,** 1. Ravnice 38d (☎233 23 25; www.ravnice-youth-hostel.hr). Tram #11 or 12 from Trg Jelačića, #4 from the train station, or #7 from the bus station to Dubrava or Dubec. The unmarked Ravnice stop is 2 stops past football stadium "Dinamo." You'll see Maksimir Park and the zoo on the left. When you get to the 2nd light past Dinamo, you'll see a white sign marked "hostel." Rooms in this friendly, family-run hostel are clean, with brightly colored tie-dye curtains and hardwood floors. English spoken. Laundry 40kn. Internet 16kn per hr. Bike rental 8kn per hr., 60kn per day. Reception daily 9am-10pm. Check-out noon. Dorms 112kn. Cash only. ❶

Mirna Noć, Miroševečina 35 (☎298 34 44; www.mirnanoc.com). Take the #7 or 12 tram to Dubrava, then the 205 bus to Miroševečina (past the peach church and green factory-looking hospital), and walk across the field (15m). This homey, dependable hostel offers clean rooms. Free Internet. *Sobe* (rooms): singles 180kn; doubles 250kn. Apartments: singles 200kn; doubles 300kn; triples 400kn; quads 500kn. Cash only. ❷

Omladinski Turistički Centar (HI), Petrinjska 77 (☎484 12 61; www.hfhs.hr). With your back to the train station, walk right on Branimirova; Petrinjska will be on your left. Omladinski isn't the Four Seasons, but it's the cheapest option in Zagreb. A fantastic location helps sweeten the deal, and when you walk out, you have a great view of the Cathedral of the Assumption. Free luggage storage. Reception 24hr. Check-in 2pm-1am. Checkout 9am. 6-bed dorms 80kn; singles 158kn, with bath 218kn; doubles 211/286kn. ❶

◖ FOOD

Zagrebčani adore meat, and restaurant menus reflect their carnivorous tastes, offering local specialities like *truca*, grilled veal scallop stuffed with Dalmatian ham, mushrooms, and cheese. If you're hungry, skip the many Italian offerings and try a *zagrebački*, a native dish with meat wrapped in ham and cheese, served with potatoes and bread. *Štrukli*, Croatia's national food, is like boiled cheesecake. For cheap eats, try a *pekarna* (bakery, every block or two) for fresh rolls and pastries or a fresh fruit market (strawberry season in June is heavenly). The largest open-air market, **Dolac,** is behind Trg Jelačića in Gornji Grad, along Pod Zidom. Here you can find great deals—go upstairs for picture-perfect vegetables and fruit, or head downstairs for cheese, meat, pasta, and fish. (Open M-Sa 6am-3pm, Su 6am-1pm.) There are grocery stores throughout the city. **Konzum** is at the corner of Preradovićeva and Hebrangova. (Open M-F 7am-8pm, Sa 7am-3pm. AmEx/MC/V.)

▓ **VIP,** Preradovicev trg 5 (☎152 86 96), right on the western side of the square. Look for the "KinoZagreb" sign and the red umbrellas. This restaurant offers tasty and inexpensive Italian fare and great people-watching in the middle of the flower market. Sandwiches 15kn. Pizza 25-32kn. Pasta and lasagna 25-40kn. Internet 15kn per hr. ❶

▓ **Millennium,** Bogovićeva 7 (☎481 08 50), between Trg. b Jelaića and Trg. Preradovicev. This stylish ice-cream place offers *sladoled* (ice cream) whipped into artful clouds of sugary bliss that taste as good as they look. Despite a fancy, white-leather interior and gourmet flavors, a scoop is only 5kn. Open daily 9am to 11pm. Cash only. ❶

Pingvin (Penguin), Teslina 7. Right next to BP Club, this sandwich shop is a local favorite. Grilled sandwiches 12-20kn. Open M-Sa 24hr., Su 5am-noon. Cash only. ❶

Kobasice, Cesarceva bb. Right off of the main square on your way to the Cathedral, this wooden hot dog stand sticks a tasty *kobasice* (sausage) into a fresh half-baguette. Try the spicy *kobsice u pecivu* for 12kn. Open M-Sa 9am-11pm. Cash only. ❶

Restaurant Boban, Gajeva 9 (☎481 15 49). Frequented by locals, this subterranean restaurant offers delicious Italian fare. Dine on pastas (28-55kn) and salads (29-35kn) under high ceilings with brick arches, or relax over a cappuccino (9kn) in the upstairs cafe or the outdoor garden. Open daily 10am-11pm; cafe 7am-11pm. ❷

Pivnica Vallis Aurea (Golden Valley), Tomičeva 4 (☎483 13 05). From the bottom of the funicular, walk down the hill toward Ilica; the restaurant is on the left. This local favorite offers large portions of traditional Croatian meaty offerings with a slight Hungarian twist. English menu. Entrees 28-50kn. Open M-Sa 9am-11pm. AmEx/MC/V. ❷

Zdravljak Nova, Ilica 72/1 (☎481 00 59), at Meduličeva. A world of peace, love, and tofu. One of Zagreb's few macrobiotic offerings, Zdravljak serves up healthy and tasty Asian-influenced vegan cuisine. Entrees 39-75kn. Open M-Sa noon-10pm. The matching health store downstairs, **bio&bio** (☎484 80 85), offers everything from tofu, tempeh, and soymilk to Brita water filters, makeup, and *The Tao of Pooh (Tao mede Pooha)*. Open M-F 8am-10pm, Sa 8am-3pm. AmEx/DC/MC/V. ❸

Taverna, Čirilometodska 2 (☎485 17 75). They serve drinks only, but sitting under one of their umbrellas on a warm day with a fresh *slatka limunada* (lemonade the way it should be: made with real lemons, tart and lightly sweetened) is well worth 13kn. Coffee 4kn. Tea 8kn. Beer 10kn. Open M-F 7:30am-11pm, Sa-Su 7:30am-1am. Cash only.

◐ SIGHTS

Zagreb is divided into two parts: medieval **Gornji Grad** (Upper Town), where most of Zagreb's churches reside, perched on the neighboring hills of Kaptol and Gradec; and Viennese-influenced **Donji Grad** (Lower Town), home to most museums, squares, cafes, and parks. The Lower Town is also known as "Lenuzzi's green horseshoe," named after the Viennese architect who designed its string of eight parks in the late 19th century. The best way to explore Zagreb is by foot. A short ramble up any of the streets behind Trg Jelačića, the main city square, leads to the Upper Town, where you can wander through winding cobblestone streets and visit most sights in one day. To explore the more commercial Lower Town, start at Trg Jelačića and head south along Gajeva, west along Masarykova, south through the parks to the Botanic Gardens, east again along Mihanoviceva, and north again through three other parks until you return to the main square. To give your weary feet a rest, hop on the **funicular,** an entertaining but peculiarly inefficient way of getting up the short hill. (Open 6:30am-9pm. 3kn, with Zagreb Card free.) Walk down Ilica from Trg Jelačića; the funicular is on the right. The free and informative *Zagreb: City Walks*, available at the TIC, has additional sightseeing routes.

CATHEDRAL OF THE ASSUMPTION (KATEDRALA MARIJINA UZNESENJA). Known simply as "the Cathedral," this originally medieval church has graced Zagreb since the late 11th century. There seems no end in sight for the additions and renovations that began centuries ago following sieges by the Tatars; the neo-Gothic bell towers (actually a meter different in height), visible from nearly anywhere in the city, were added in 1902. The dazzling gilded interior is decked out in a range of deep colors with ornate mosaic-trimmed pillars and gold candelabras. *(Kaptol 1. Open daily 10am-5pm. Services M-Sa 7, 8, 9am; Su 7, 8, 9, 10, 11:30am. Free.)*

ST. MARK'S CHURCH (CRKVA SV. MARKA). The red-and-white checkered tiles on St. Mark's roof, which might help orient you if lost in Gornji Grad, surround the colorful coat of arms of Croatia, Dalmatia, and Slavonia on the left side and that of Zagreb on the right. The entrance to the church is on the left (west) side, which leads you to an interior with gold ceilings and dark, newly restored frescoes. *(From the top of the funicular, turn right and then left onto Cirilometodska; the church is straight ahead. Entrance to the left. Open daily 7am-1:30pm and 5:30-7pm. Free.)*

LOTRŠČAK TOWER (KULA LOTRŠČAK). Part of the original city wall, this 13th-century white tower with an observatory on top offers a great panoramic view of Zagreb. Originally built for fortification purposes, the tower transformed when the danger of Turk attacks subsided, becoming a fireman's surveillance lookout, a city alarm tower, a warehouse, and a wine cellar. The cannon near the top of the tower has been fired at noon every day since 1877. *(At the corner of Strossmayerovo and Dverce, right at the top of the funicular. Open May-Sept. Tu-Su 11am-8pm. 10kn, students 5kn.)*

ST. CATHERINE'S CHURCH (CRKVA SV. KATRINSKI). Built by Jesuits between 1620 and 1632, St. Catherine's simple white exterior does nothing to prepare you for the elaborate inside. Decorated with gifts from Croatian nobles and designed by Italian master Anton Joseph Quadrio, the pink interior, covered in intricate white swirls and curlicues, contrasts starkly with the six black-and-gold shrines lining the sides. *(Katarinin trg bb. From the top of the funicular, the 1st church on your right. Open M-F and Su 7am-11pm, Sa 7am-6:30pm. Services M-F 6pm, Sa 6:30pm, Su 11am. Free.)*

MIROGOJ CEMETERY. When you see the 12 cream-colored and green towers framing the majestic main entrance, just north of the Cathedral, you'll think Mirogoj looks more like a palace. Cypress trees, wide avenues, and endless rows of elaborate gravestones comprise the serene park. This beautiful cemetery is the resting ground for an array of notable Croatians: mafiosos, writers, the first president of Croatia Franjo Tudjman, and even one of the stars of Croatia's soccer team Dinamo, buried in 2004. *(Take the 106 "Mirogoj" bus from Kaptol in front of the Cathedral; 8min., every 15min. Open M-F 6am-8pm, Su 7:30am-6pm. Free. No cameras.)*

RIBNJAK PARK. Spacious and tree-covered Ribnjak Park offers the chance for a peaceful walk without leaving the city. *(Behind the Cathedral. From Trg Jelačića, turn down Jurišićeva, then right on Palmotićeva. The entrance is on the left.)*

MAKSIMIR PARK AND THE ZAGREB ZOO. Covered in gentle meadows, lakes, and tall oaks, Maksimir Park is one of the largest parks in southeast Europe—so big, in fact, that hundreds of animals reside comfortably in the **Zagreb Zoo** within the park's borders. If the seal or piranha shows, rhinos, elephants, hippos, birds, and pumas aren't your bag, take a stroll or a bike ride on the shaded paths between the huge trees, and pass by the white swans in the willow-lined lake. *(From Trg Jelačića, take tram #11 or 12 to Dubrava or Dubec. Get off across the street from the stadium. Continue walking down the road; the park entrance is on the left. Park open daily sunrise to sunset. Free. Zoo open daily 9am-8pm; ticket office closes 7pm. 20kn, under 7 10kn.)*

🏛 MUSEUMS

While you may not find many famous masterpieces in Zagreb, there are enough interesting collections and exhibits to occupy the art-lover for a few days. For a complete list, consult the monthly *Zagreb: Events and Performances*, free at the TIC (see **Tourist and Financial Services**, p. 112). Trams #12, 13, 14, and 17 reach the Museum of Arts and Crafts, the Mimara, and the Ethnographic Museum.

■ **ETHNOGRAPHIC MUSEUM (ETHNOGRAFSKI MUZEJ).** Displaying artifacts from Croatian voyages to Africa, Asia, and South America in the 19th and 20th centuries, this museum also offers a look at Croatia's traditional culture, with rotating exhibits focusing on diverse regions of the country. It includes an eclectic mix of traditional costumes and etchings of local architecture. *(Mažuranićev trg 14, across the street from the Mimara. ☎482 62 20; www.etnografski-musej.hr. English captions. Open Tu-Th 10am-6pm, F-Su 10am-1pm. 15kn, students and over 60 10kn; Th free. Cash only.)*

STUDIO MEŠTROVIČ. This was the former home and studio of the most celebrated Croatian sculptor, Ivan Meštrovič, responsible for many of the buildings and statues in Zagreb, including the reliefs in St. Mark's, the statue in front of the Art Pavilion, the statue in Strossmayer trg and the statue in front of the National Theater. His work has been recognized worldwide, and he was the first Croatian artist given a one-man exhibition at the Metropolitan in New York City. A nice sculpture garden features an ivy-covered brick wall. *(Mletačka 8, just behind St. Mark's Church.* ☎ *485 11 23. Open Tu-F 10am-6pm, Sa-Su 10am-2pm. 20 kn, students 10kn. Cash only.)*

KLOVIČEVI DVORI GALLERY (GALERIJA KLOVIĆEVI DVORI). The old wooden front doors of the former 17th-century monastery open to glass doors and a stark white and glass interior. The modern and contemporary selection favors found art and political statements. Exhibits rotate frequently; check the listings. After visiting the gallery, enjoy a coffee (7kn) in the elegant courtyard. *(Jesuitski trg 4, to the left of St. Catherine's.* ☎ *485 19 26. Open Tu-Su 11am-7pm. 20kn, students 10kn. Cash only.)*

MUSEUM OF ARTS AND CRAFTS (MUZEJ ZA UMJETNOST I OBRT). While the name may recall summer camp, there is little childish about this showcase of Croatian craftsmanship, which features delicate porcelain teacups and saucers, intricate woodwork, tapestries, wrought-iron pieces, and graphic art. *(Trg Maršala Tita 10.* ☎ *488 21 11. Open Tu-F 10am-7pm, Sa-Su 10am-2pm. 20kn, students 10kn. Cash only.)*

GALLERY OF MODERN ART (MODERNA GALERIJA). This attractive gallery features rotating exhibitions of Croatia's best artists. With a collection of 9500 paintings, sculptures, watercolors, drawings, and prints, this gallery is a great way to explore the budding modern art scene. *(Hebrangova 1, across from the Strossmayer Gallery.* ☎ *492 23 68. Open Tu-Sa 10am-6pm, Su 10am-1pm. Prices vary by exhibition. Cash only.)*

MIMARA MUSEUM (MUZEJ MIMARA). A former grammar school, this museum features a vast and varied collection from prehistoric Egyptian art to a handful of lesser-known works by famed European masters including Raphael, Velasquez, Renoir, Manet, Rubens, and Rembrandt. *(Rooseveltov trg 5.* ☎ *482 81 00. Open Tu-W and F-Sa 10am-5pm, Th 10am-7pm, Su 10am-2pm. 20kn, students 15kn. Cash only.)*

STROSSMAYER GALLERY (STROSSMAYER GALERIJA STARIH MAJSTORA). Go up two flights in the beautiful Croatian Academy of Arts and Sciences. Founded by Bishop Josip Juraj Strossmayer in 1884, the permanent collection includes paintings from Flemish, Dutch, French, and Italian schools from the Renaissance through Baroque periods. *(Zrinjskog trg 11.* ☎ *489 51 11 or 489 51 15. Open Tu 10am-1pm and 5-7pm, W-Su 10am-1pm. 10kn, students 5kn. Cash only.)*

🎵 🌿 ENTERTAINMENT AND FESTIVALS

If visual arts aren't your cup of tea, fear not—performance is Zagreb's middle name. As always, the latest schedules and contact info can be found in the monthly *Zagreb: Events and Performances*, available for free at the TIC. Classical-music-lovers should seek out **Vatroslav Lisinski Concert Hall,** Trg Stjepana Radića 4, about two blocks behind the train station, home to the Zagreb Philharmonic and visiting orchestras and artists from abroad. (☎ 612 11 66. Office open M-F 9am-8pm, Sa 9am-2pm. Tickets 50-100kn for local performers, 100-300 for foreign performers. Student discounts available.) The **Croatian National Theater** (Hrvatsko Narodno Kazalište), Trg Maršala Tita 15 (☎ 482 85 32), puts on dramas, ballets, and operas. At **Jarun Lake** you can find "Theater on the Water" during the summer months, while the nearby **Sports and Recreation Center** hosts **Jarunfest,** a series of musical theater, ensemble, and operetta performances in late June and early July. From April to October, the **Arts Pavilion** in Zrinjevac Park holds weekly Promenade

Concerts, varied performances from tango to jazz. Jazz fans should head for **BP Club** (see **Nightlife**, p. 118) and remember International Jazz Days in October. If you're in the mood for a recent American movie, tickets are cheap (15-29kn). The largest and most popular cinemas are **Cinestar,** Branimirova 29 (☎468 66 00; www.blitz-cinestar.hr), in the Branimirova Shopping Center, and **Broadway 5,** Nova Ves 11 (☎466 76 86; www.broadway-kina.com), in the Centar Kaptol.

In mid- to late July, Zagreb holds the **International Folklore Festival,** the premier gathering of European folk dancers and singing groups. Each year kicks off with a **blues festival** in January. In the beginning of June, streets burst with performances for the annual Zagreb street festival **Cest is d'Best** ("The Streets are the Best"), and the **Eurokaz Avant-Garde Theaters Festival.** The huge **International Puppet Festival** occurs in early September, and late October sees Zagreb's **International Jazz Days.** Every year, mid-December is filled with the colorful **Christmas Fair.** For up-to-date, detailed info and schedules, check out www.zagreb-touristinfo.hr.

🅽 NIGHTLIFE

The colorful and lively outdoor **cafes** lining the street **Tkalčićeva,** in Gornji Grad, attract young people from all over the city. Most of the cafes in Donji Grad are indistinguishable but pleasant. Many **discos** are open all week, except in the beginning of August, when the entire city goes on holiday. The best nightlife is at **Lake Jarun,** which is a pain to get to but worth the trip. There are many options, so it's ideal for barhopping or splitting up, if you have a large group with divergent musical tastes. When you arrive at the lake, laid-back **Lake City,** Županići 3, will be the first bar on the left. As you continue, you'll pass **Piranha Bar,** with a 12 ft. long fish tank and house music, and **Macao,** with sofas for people-watching.

▧ **Aquarius,** Aleja Mira bb (☎364 02 31), on Lake Jarun. Tram #17 from the center; get off on Srednjaci, the 3rd stop after Studenski dom "S. Radić." At the church, cross the street. It's the last building on the boardwalk (15min.). This popular lakeside cafe and nightclub is worth the trek. Boogie in- or outside, or take a late-night dip in the lake. Drinks 15-45kn. Cover 30kn. Cafe open daily 9am-9pm; club Tu-Su 10pm-4am. Cash only.

▧ **Khala,** Nova Ves 17 (☎486 06 47), just up the street from the Cathedral in the Kaptol Center/Broadway 5 movie complex. Or, go up Tkaliceva, past the outdoor bars and cafes. White arches, handmade paper menus, and low tables give Khala a cooler-than-thou vibe, with a mix of Arabic flavor. The interior, with suspended pillars and low-lying plants and chandeliers, matches the trendsters who come decked out to look nonchalant and fabulous. Drinks from 14kn. Open M-Th 8am-1am, F-Su 8am-4am. Cash only.

▧ **Pivnica Medvedgrad,** Savska 56 (☎617 71 19). Tram #13, 14, or 17 from Trg Jelačića to the corner of Avenija Vukovar and Savska. A local favorite, with the cheapest beer in town. This microbrewery's homemade beer (18kn per 1L) attracts all types. Try the whole-grain bread and čevapčići (small sausages served with raw onion; 22kn), or nibble on some perec (soft pretzels; 2kn). Open M-Sa 10am-midnight, Su noon-midnight.

Gallery, Mate Ljubaka bb on Lake Jarun (☎091 113 32 21), on the way to Aquarius on the lakefront. Surrounded by oversized white plant pots. A drapery of white threads covers the entrance of this upscale bar, while egg-shaped bubbles overhead filled with fairy lights add to the hip flair. DJs spin house, R&B, retro, with digressions into 80s and 90s on Tu and "underground kinky" on F. Dress nicely. Open daily 10am-4am. Cash only.

BP Club, Teslina 7 (☎481 44 44), on the right side of the courtyard, down the yellow stairs. The classic venue for jazz in Zagreb, as well as blues, trance, and a lot of U2, BP keeps it cool year-round. Live music Sept.-Apr. Open daily 5pm-2am.

Tolkien's House, Vsanicanijeva 8, next door to Indy's. Indulge your questionable hobbit fetish at this quirky Irish pub, festooned with memorabilia from J.R.R. Tolkien's books. Even if you don't consider yourself part of the Fellowship of the Ring, you'll still enjoy the Irish music and Guinness (27kn). Drinks 13-32kn. Open M-Sa 9am-11pm, Su 10am-11pm. Sister bar **Fantasy Club in Tolkien's Pub,** Katarinin trg 3, is down the street. Budweiser special: the more you drink, the cheaper it gets. Open M-Sa 8am-midnight.

Indy's, Vranicanijeva 6 (☎485 20 53). From St. Mark's, go down Cirilometodska and right on Vranicanijeva. Enjoy a creatively named Martian Sex Monster (30kn) or a Test Tube Baby (20kn) in the private salmon-colored interior. Open daily 9am-11pm.

🔅 DAYTRIPS FROM ZAGREB

Defining the crests of Zagreb's surrounding hilltops are the 56 mysterious **castles** of Hrvatsko Zagorje (the region north of Zagreb), formerly owned and constructed by warring Croatian nobles. They now lie in various states of disrepair, waiting to be conquered with cameras instead of cannons. Trakošćan is in the best shape and is one of the most popular. Consult *Zagreb and Surroundings*, available at the TIC in Zagreb (see **Tourist and Financial Services,** p. 112) to explore the others.

TRAKOŠČAN

From the Zagreb bus station, take a bus to Varaždin (1¾hr., 20 per day, 50kn), and change to a local bus (1¾hr.; M-F 11 per day, Sa-Su 7 per day; 35kn). Leave early in order to make the connection. You might want to time it so you don't collide with all the kids getting out for lunch or after school: try to avoid the noon-2pm buses. The last bus back from Trakošćan to Varaždin leaves M-F around 9pm, Sa-Su around 5pm. ☎42 79 62 81. Open daily Apr.-Oct. 9am-6pm; Nov.-Mar. 9am-4pm. 20kn, students 10kn. English booklet 20kn.

The white walls of ◼Trakošćan rise high above the surrounding forests and rolling hills. Built as a defense tower in the 13th century, it passed in 1584 to the Drašković nobility, who enlarged and refurbished it, retaining the castle until WWII. Today, stately family portraits, elaborate tapestries, mounted antlers, and collections of firearms and armor from the 15th to 19th century are on display in the castle's preserved interior. Aside from its detailed woodwork and different-colored rooms, the castle evokes a fairy-tale world, with knight's armor mixed in with the surreal paintings of Julijana Erdödy, the first woman in Croatia to achieve the title of an academic painter. Take pictures in her bedroom and you might catch the painter's ghost on film. Leave time to wander around the quiet lake and to hike through the hills, if only to escape the crowds of Croatian schoolchildren. The restaurant at the bottom of the hill is expensive, so bring a sandwich.

On the way to the castle, stop off in **Varaždin.** Nicknamed Little Vienna, this charming former capital of Croatia (1756-76) makes a perfect interlude between bus rides on the way to and from the Trakošćan castle. Its narrow streets, lined with outdoor cafes and streetlamps with hanging flowers, make this the perfect place to take a leisurely stroll. Across the street from the bus station is a Konzum where you can stock up on snacks before going to the castle. To get to the town center, continue past Konzum away from the bus station and veer left. You'll know you've arrived when you're surrounded by pastel-hued Baroque buildings.

PLITVICE LAKES NATIONAL PARK

Buses run from Zagreb (2½hr., every 30min., 70kn) and Zadar (2½hr., 6-7 per day, 72kn). Ask the bus driver to let you off at one of the park entrances. Tourist office ☎75 20 15 or 75 10 13; www.np-plitvicka-jezera.hr. Park open daily 7am-7pm. July-Aug. 95kn, students 55kn; May-June and July-Oct. 75/45kn; Nov.-Apr. 45/22kn. MC/V. Tour-

CROATIA

ist centers at each of the 3 park entrances sell tickets and offer maps and a guide. Most buses stop near tourist center #2. To get to the center, walk toward the pedestrian overpass. Head up the stairs and follow the path on the left downhill.

 Plitvice Lakes National Park lies in the Krajina region, where Croatia's bloody war for independence began. Throughout the conflict (1991-95), the Serbians holding the area planted **landmines** in the ground. There are still landmines in the surrounding area. Under no circumstances should you leave the road or the marked paths. It's worth visiting the natural wonder of the Plitvice lakes; just be cautious about where you walk.

Though it's a bit of a trip from either Zagreb or Zadar, █**Plitvice Lakes National Park** (Nacionalni Park Plitcicka Jezera) is definitely worth the transportation hassle. Some 30,000 hectares of forested hills, dappled with 16 lakes and hundreds of waterfalls, make this pocket of paradise one of Croatia's most spectacular sights. Declared a national park in 1949, Plitvice was added to the UNESCO World Heritage list in 1979 for the unique evolution of its lakes and waterfalls, which formed through the interaction of water and petrified vegetation. A system of wooden pathways hovering just above the iridescent blue surface of the lakes winds around the many waterfalls. Two bus routes (every 20min.) help you get around the park, while a boat runs on the largest of the lakes (every 30min.). Though most tourists circulate around the four lower lakes (Donja Jezera) to snap pictures of Plitvice's famous 78m waterfall, **Veliki Slap** (trail F, 2-3hr.), the true adventurer explores the hidden falls of the 12 upper lakes, **Gornja Jezera** (4hr.). If you find yourself awestruck by the heavenly beauty and can't bring yourself to leave, the private accommodation service across from tourist center #2 will find you a room. (Open daily noon-9pm. Singles 150kn; doubles 220-300kn.)

ISTRIA

The Istrian Peninsula lies on the northern part of the Adriatic Coast, where the Mediterranean kisses the foot of the Alps. Influenced throughout history by its rather pushy neighbor, the region seems almost more Italian than Croatian. Today, the mosaics of Poreč, ruins of Roman Pula, unspoiled 19th-century Rovinj, and the clear waters of the Adriatic lend this area a touch of paradise.

PULA   ☎(0)52

At the threshold of Pula's old center, a billboard welcomes visitors to the "3000-year-old town." Pula's Roman amphitheater, an entertainment stage since ancient times, has featured everything from gladiatorial combat to rock concerts. Despite the tourist crowds, Pula (pop. 65,000) maintains its laid-back character. Relax on the rocky coast, mingle in outdoor cafes, and soak in the vibrant culture.

▊ TRANSPORTATION

Trains: Kolodvorska 5 (☎54 17 83). Ticket window open daily 8am-4pm. To: **Rijeka** (2½hr., 3 per day, 47kn); **Zagreb** (7hr., 3 per day, 112-125kn); **Ljubljana, SLN** (7½hr., 2 per day, 127kn).

Buses: Trg Istarske Brigade bb (☎50 29 97), off Ulica 43 Istarske Divizije. Ticket office open M-Sa 4:30am-8:30pm; tickets can also be purchased on board. To: **Dubrovnik** (15hr., 1 per day, 441kn); **Poreč** (1½hr., 8-14 per day, 43kn); **Rijeka** (2½hr., 14-21

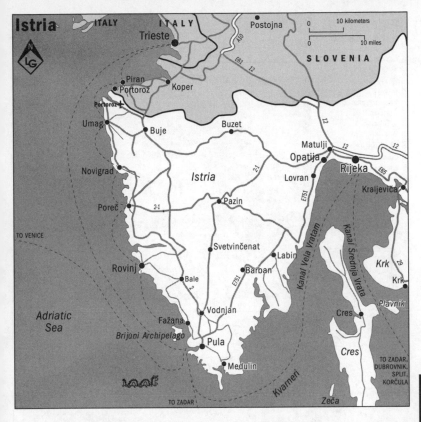

Istria

ITALY · Trieste · ITALY · Postojna · SLOVENIA

Piran · Portorož · Koper

Umag · Buje · Buzet · Matulji · Opatija · Rijeka · Kraljevica

Novigrad · Istria · Lovran

Poreč · Pazin

TO VENICE

Svetvinčenat · Labin

Rovinj · Bale · Barban · Krk · Krk

Adriatic Sea · Vodnjan · Cres · Plavnik

Fažana · Pula · Cres

Brijuni Archipelago · Medulin · Kanal Vela Vratam · Kanal Srednja Vrata

TO ZADAR · Kvarneri · Zeča · TO ZADAR, DUBROVNIK, SPLIT, KORČULA

per day, 71kn); **Rovinj** (1hr., 12-23 per day, 27kn); **Šibenik** (9hr., 3 per day, 257kn); **Split** (10hr., 3 per day, 309kn); **Zagreb** (5-6hr., 15 per day, 155kn); **Koper, SLN** (3¼hr., 2 per day, 93kn); **Trieste, ITA** (3hr., 5 per day, 88-112kn); **Milan, ITA** (8½hr., in summer 1 per day, €100); **Venice, ITA** (6hr., 1 per day, 170kn).

Ferries: Jadrolinija Jadroagent, Riva 14 (☎21 04 31; fax 21 17 99). Open M-F 8am-4pm, Sa-Su 11am-4pm. To: **Zadar** (8hr., 5 per wk., 123kn); **Venice, ITA** (6hr., 2 per wk., 365kn).

Public Transportation: Local **buses** depart from the bus station, and most stop on Giardini (M-Sa every 20min., Su 1 per hr.; until 10:30pm). Purchase tickets on board (10kn) or at newsstands (8kn).

Taxis: (☎22 32 28). Opposite the bus station. 23kn base, 7kn per km; 3kn per bag. A cheaper option is **Citycab** (☎091 111 10 52). 30-50kn anywhere within greater Pula.

▓ ▓ ORIENTATION AND PRACTICAL INFORMATION

Sergijevaca, Pula's main street, circles around the central hill in **Stari Grad** (Old Town) and turns into **Kandlerova** after the **Forum. Castropola,** a parallel street higher up, also circles the hilltop. To get to Sergijevaca from the **train station,** walk on Kolodvorska for 5min., keeping the sea to your right. Turn right onto **Istarska** at the **amphitheater.** Follow Istarska through its name change to **Giardini.** After the park, a right through the tall **Arch of the Sergians** (Slavoluk Sergijevaca) leads to Sergije-

Pula

ACCOMMODATIONS
Hotel Riviera, **1**
Omladinski Hostel (HI), **2**
Stoja Camping, **5**

FOOD
Biska, **9**
Pizzeria Jupiter, **6**
Restoran Markat
 Splendid, **4**
Valsabbion, **11**

NIGHTLIFE
Corso, **8**
Cvajner Cafe, **7**
Lungo Mare, **10**
Rock Caffe, **3**

TO ZADAR, VENICE

Adriatic Sea

TO FAŽANA
AND BRIJUNI
NATIONAL
PARK (7km)

Monteghiro

TO (50m),
(5km)

Kolodvorska
Tišćanska
Splitska
Arenaturist
Atlas
TRG NA MOSTU
43 Istarske
Divizije
Trinajstićeva
Starih Statua
Flavijevska
Faverijska
ACI Pula Marina
Amphi-
theater
Scalierova
Croazia
Teslina
Rakovičeva
Riva

Uljanik

SEE STARI GRAD INSET

Kandlerova
STARI
GRAD
Castropola
Sergijevaca
Flaciusova
Carrarina
Istarska
Giardini
Sv. Martina
Zadarska
Zagrebačka
Flanatička
Metlačka
Cyber Cafe

Anticova ul. Smareglina

Dobrilina
NARODNI
TRG Open-Air
Market
TRG
REPUBLIKE
Preradovićeva
M. Ronigova
Mutilska

Park - Vergerijeva
Montezaro
Cara Emina
Gajeva
Tartinijeva
Radučeva
Kačića Miošića
Marsovog polja
Vinzuza

Sv. Polikarpa
Bečka

Katalinića Jeretova

TO AND
(1.2km)

Kochova
Brijunska
Brijuni
Agency
Ljudevita Posavskog
Velog Jože
Galijotska
Verudela
Sisplac
Zaljev Valsaline
Lungomare
Verudela
Monte Paradiso
Facchinettjeva
Cesta Prekomorskih brigada
De Franceschijeva
Geravaisova

Adriatic Sea

Stari Grad

TRG SV.
TOME
Cathedral of the Assumption
of the Blessed Virgin Mary

Riva
Enigma
Twin Gate
Dubrovačke B.
Carrarina
Istarska

Kandlerova
Archaeological
Museum of Istria

Historical
Museum of Istria
(Venetian Fortress)
Roman
Theater
Zadarksa
TAXI

Temple of
Augustus
Tourism Office
Pula
TRG
FORUM
Sv. Franje
Castropola
Sergijevaca
De Villiev uspon
Cvečićev
Glavinićev

STARI
GRAD
Algoritam
DANTEOV
TRG
Anticova
Držićeva
Arch of
the Sergians
Laginjina
Flanatička
Kino
Zagreb
Smareglina
Dalmatinova

Dobrilina

TO (2km)

N

0   400 meters
0   400 yards

vaca, which runs down to the Forum and the waterfront. To get there from the **bus station,** turn left onto Ulica 43 Istarske Divizije, veer left at the roundabout onto Flavijevska, and left at the amphitheater onto Istarska.

Tourist Office: Tourism Office Pula, Forum 3 (☎21 29 87; www.pulainfo.hr). Friendly English-speaking staff provides useful city **maps;** info on accommodations, events, and entertainment. Ferry and bus schedules. Open M-Sa 8am-midnight, Su 10am-6pm.

Currency Exchange: Zagrebačka Banka (☎38 54 57), at the corner of Giardini and Flanatička. Exchanges cash for no commission and cashes **traveler's checks** for 1.5% commission. Open M-F 7:30am-7pm, Sa 8am-noon. A currency exchange machine is outside **Raiffeisen Bank,** 43 Istarske Divizije, next to the bus station. **Banka Sonic,** Sergijevaca 16, exchanges cash for no commission and has **Western Union** services. Open M-F 8am-6pm, Sa 8am-noon. **ATMs** are common in the city center.

Luggage Storage: At the bus station. 1.20kn per hr., over 15kg 2.20kn per hr. Open M-F 4:30-9:30am, 10am-6pm, and 6:30pm-midnight. Su 5am-midnight.

English-Language Bookstore: Algoritam, off Sergijevaca toward the post office, stocks recent fiction and travel guides. Books 50-140kn. Open M-F 9am-9pm, Sa 9am-2pm.

Police: Trg Republike 2 (☎53 21 11).

24hr. Pharmacy: Ljekarna Centar, Giardini 15 (☎22 25 44). From 9pm until 7am, use the side window on Giardini instead of the main entrance. AmEx/MC/V.

Hospital: Clinical Hospital Center, Zagrebačka 34 (☎21 44 33). Open 24hr.

Internet: mmc luka, Istarska 30, a block from the amphitheater. Fast connections in a hip bar. 20kn per 30min. Open M-Sa 8am-midnight. **Enigma,** Kandlerova 19 (☎38 26 15). Open daily June-Sept. 10am-midnight; Oct.-May 10am-2pm and 5-8pm.

Post Office: Danteov trg 4 (☎21 59 55; fax 21 89 11). Go left for mail and right for **Poste Restante** (open M-F 7am-10pm, Sa 7am-2pm, Su 8am-noon) and **telephones.** Open M-F 7am-8pm, Sa 7am-2pm, Su 8am-noon. **Postal Code:** 52100.

▐▎ ACCOMMODATIONS

Private accommodations will be your most convenient choice when you come to Pula. Several agencies help visitors locate private rooms, but the tourist office can help find the best deals. **Arenaturist,** Splitska 1, inside Hotel Riviera, arranges **private rooms** throughout Pula. (☎52 94 00; www.arenaturist.hr. Open M-Sa 8am-8pm, Su 8am-1pm. 50% more for 1 night, 25% for 2-3 nights. Registration 10kn.)

▨ **Omladinski Hostel (HI),** Zaljev Valsaline 4 (☎39 11 33; www.hfhs.hr). From the bus station, catch bus #2 toward "Veruda" at the far end of the station. After 10min., the bus turns onto Verudela. Get off at the 1st stop on Verudela. Follow the HI signs and go downhill. Though a trek from the center, this beachside getaway attracts a mix of families, teenage tour groups, and backpackers. Feels like summer camp. Private cove, diving school, bar, trampolines, shared showers. Internet access. Simple breakfast included. Reception daily 8am-10pm. Call ahead. Dorms July-Aug. 100kn; Sept. and June 84kn; Oct. and May 79kn; Nov. and Apr. 74kn. Camping July-Aug. 65kn; Sept.-June 40kn. Nonmembers 10kn extra per night. Registration fee 10kn. Tax 4.50-7kn. ❶

Hotel Riviera, Splitska 1 (☎21 11 66), across the park from the amphitheater by the waterfront. This old, elegant hotel has kind staff and views of the waterfront. Breakfast included. Sept-July singles €46; doubles €72. Aug. singles €51; doubles €82. ❹

Stoja Camping (☎38 71 44). From Giardini, take bus #1 to Stoja to the end. Within walking distance of town (20min.), surrounded by beaches. Showers, bathroom, sports facilities, restaurant, and grocery. €3-14 per person. Electricity €2.50. ❶

🞆 FOOD

Fresh fish, meat, and cheese are available in the **market** building. (Fish market open M-Sa 7am-1:30pm, Su 7am-noon; meat and cheese markets open M-Sa 7-noon, Su 7am-2pm.) **Puljanka** grocery store has several branches throughout the town, including one at Sergijevaca 4. (Open M-F 6am-8pm, Sa 8am-1:30pm, Su 7am-noon.) Buffets and fast-food restaurants line **Sergijevaca.** There is an open-air fruit and vegetable **market** at Trg Narodni, off Flanatička. (Open daily 6am-2pm.)

▨ **Biska,** Sisplac 15 (☎38 73 33). From the center, take bus #2 to the 1st stop on Veruda. Backtrack on Veruda, past Tomasinjeva, and turn left on Sisplac. This small cafe in residential Veruda serves large portions of seafood and pasta. Entrees 25-75kn. Open June-Sept. M-Sa 9am-11pm, Su 2-11pm; Oct.-May M-Sa 9am-10pm, Su 2-10pm. ❶

Valsabbion, Pješčana uvala IX/26 (☎21 80 33). Take bus #2 from Giardini, toward the hostel. After getting off, turn left down the hill and walk along Prekomorskih Brigada (5min.), then go right on the 1st unnamed road leading to Veruda Marina. Walk until you round the tip of the peninsula (20min.); Valsabbion is on the right, 100m past the marina. A "slow food" restaurant in a sea of fast food establishments, Valsabbion tenderly prepares every dish (entrees 95-150kn) from scratch, which makes for long waits and excellent food. ❹

Pizzeria Jupiter, Castropola 42 (☎21 43 33). Walk behind the bus station along Carrarina, past the Archaeological Museum. Curve to the left up the ramp; it's on the left. Lauded by Pulians young and old, this is the perfect spot for a bite before amphitheater concerts. Pizza 20-39kn. Open M-F 9am-11pm, Sa-Su 1-11pm. AmEx/DC. ❶

Restoran Markat Splendid, Trg Privoga Svibvija 5 (☎22 32 84), across from the far side of the market building at Narodni trg. A Croatian version of the school-lunch lady fills trays with inexpensive delights in this cafeteria-style eatery. Soups, salads, and entrees 6-30kn. Open M-F 9:30am-9pm, Sa-Su 9:30am-4pm. Cash only. ❶

🞈 SIGHTS

▨**AMPHITHEATER.** Completed in the AD first century during the reign of Roman Emperor Vespasian, the arena was used for gladiatorial combat until sport killing was outlawed in the 4th century. Today, it houses entertainment of a different sort: concerts, from opera to heavy metal. An underground system of passages, constructed as a drainage system, now houses a **museum** of Istrian history. *(From the bus station, take a left on 43 Istarske Divizije and another on Flavijevska, which becomes Istarska. Open daily 8am-9pm; in low season 8am-4pm. 20kn, students 10kn. English booklet 30kn.)*

 THE AMPHITHEATER FOR FREE. The highlight of your visit to Pula needn't set you back by US$40. Climb the hill to the left of the amphitheater, situate yourself in sight of the stage, and you may be able to see the entire show for free, at a distance not much farther away than some of the best seats in the house. Since the sound quality surpasses the view, the arrangement's better for concerts than for ballet or dance performances. Go early to get good seats, as the locals have known this trick for years—or maybe even centuries.

ARCH OF THE SERGIANS (SLAVOLUK OBITELJI SERGII). The sturdy stone arch was built in 29 BC for three local members of the Sergii family, one of whom commanded a Roman battalion at the battle of Actium between Mark Antony and Octavian. It is now a gateway to Sergijevaca, Pula's main street. *(From the amphitheater, follow Istarska left as it turns into Giardini. The arch is on the right.)*

THE FORUM. The Forum, at the end of Sergijevaca, was the central gathering place for political, religious, and economic debates in Roman days. Today, the original cobblestones lie buried safely 1.2m beneath the ground and the square is used primarily for cafe lounging and gazing at the nearby Temple of Augustus.

TEMPLE OF AUGUSTUS (AUGUSTOV HRAM). This remarkably preserved temple, constructed between 2 BC and AD 14, was dedicated to Roman Emperor Octavian Augustus. Until the early Middle Ages, two similar temples stood nearby; the larger was destroyed, but the rear wall of the smaller Temple of Diana now serves as the facade of the City Hall from which Pula has been governed since 1296. The Temple of Augustus houses a small **museum** with pieces of Roman statues and stone sculptures from the AD first and 2nd centuries. *(At the Forum.* ☎*21 86 89. Open M-F 9:30am-1:30pm and 4-9pm, Sa-Su 9:30am-1:30pm. 4kn, students 2kn.)*

OTHER SIGHTS. Up the hill from Castropola, the **Venetian Fortress** *(Kaštel)* has guarded Pula since Roman times, but in 2002 it became the **Historical Museum of Istria** (Povjesni Musej Istre), a small maritime and military history exhibit. *(Open daily in summer 8am-8pm; in winter 9am-5pm. 10kn.)* On the nearby hilltop stand the remains of a **Roman Theater** (Malo Rimsko Kazaliste). Farther down is the **Twin Gate** (Dvojna vrata). The **Archaeological Museum of Istria** (Arheološki Muzej Istre), up the hill from the Twin Gate, offers an overview of Istria's history, with an emphasis on Roman stone artifacts from the 2nd century BC to the AD 6th century. *(Carrarina 3.* ☎*21 86 09. Open May-Sept. M-F 9am-8pm, Su 10am-3pm; Oct.-Apr. M-F 9am-2pm. 12kn, students 6kn. English guidebook 30kn.)* Near the waterfront, off Trg Sv. Tome, the **Cathedral of the Assumption of the Blessed Virgin Mary** (just Katedrala to the locals), constructed in the AD 4th century, is in remarkably good shape.

🌿 🎵 FESTIVALS AND BEACHES

Amphitheater shows are the impressive highlight of a trip to Pula. Open seating allows you to sit or stand wherever you can climb. Tickets (150-800kn) are available at the theater from the booking agency, **Lira Intersound** (☎21 78 01; open M-F 8am-3pm), or from tourist agencies. The popular **Biker Days Festival** takes place during the first week of August. (Tickets 150kn.) Exhibitions at this chrome-and-leather celebration have included female mud wrestling. Movie buffs can enjoy the **Pula Film Festival** (www.pulafilmfestival.com), which occurs in mid-July. The **International Accordion School** hits town in the 2nd half of July, offering a series of concerts and classes. The annual **Festival "Monte Paradiso,"** turns an old army barracks into a stage and mosh pit in the first weekend in August. **Kino Zagreb,** Giardini 1, shows Hollywood movies with Croatian subtitles. (Nightly 7, 9pm. 15-20kn, midnight special 12kn.) You wouldn't guess it when looking at the shipyards, but Pula is lined with private coves and **beaches.** To scope out the perfect spot, start by taking bus #1 to Stoja Campground. Facing the sea, walk left down the coastline. Rock shelves line the sea from the campground to a hostel. A pleasant pebble beach curves in front of a hostel, which offers **paddleboats** (40kn per hr.). For quieter, less crowded beaches, head to the neighboring town of **Fazana.**

📻 NIGHTLIFE

Lungo Mare, Gortanova Uvala bb (☎39 10 84). Take bus #2 or 7 from Giardini, get off at Verud, go right on Verudela to Hotel Pula, and go down to the sea. Cafe by day, raging club by night, this outdoor chameleon blasts music in its own cove. *Favorit* 25kn per 1L. On the beach and along the road, young Pulians gather for raucous Croatian **tailgates** most Th-Sa summer nights. Open daily 10am-4am.

CROATIA

HOUSING WITH A TOUCH OF HOME

Budget hotel rooms are hard to find in Croatia. As a result of the 1991 war and the subsequent refugee situation, many of the country's hotels and hostels were severely damaged, leaving a huge vacuum in the accommodation market. Only now are tourist hotels starting to re-emerge, but they tend to be catered toward luxury-seekers rather than to budget travelers. So, how can you sleep on the cheap in Croatia without resorting to the local park bench? The answer is that ubiquitous blue word: *sobe*. Literally meaning "room," *sobe* signifies that a private room is for rent in a person's house or apartment. This is the best, and in some towns the only, option for budget travelers in Croatia.

At first glance, the idea of staying in a stranger's house overnight can be intimidating, to say the least. On most occasions, I wouldn't stop to chat with a random person shouting "room" at me in seven different languages, let alone trust them with myself and my belongings. In addition to saving a significant amount of cash, however, staying in a *sobe* can be extremely rewarding. It can provide a unique glimpse into Croatian life and culture that you would never know existed if you had shelled out 400kn for a night in the local hotel.

With your nightly rate, you get to see how people live their daily

Corso, Giardini 3 (☎53 51 47). Occupying a prime people-watching spot in Stari Grad, this chic cafe/bar is often filled with trendy young Pulians sipping *bijela kava* (latte; 9kn) by day and mixed drinks (40kn) by night. Open daily 8am-midnight.

Rock Caffe, Scalierova 8 (☎21 09 75). Not to be confused with the "harder" worldwide chain, this oak bar with pool tables has a terrace. *Pivo Točeno* (draft) 12kn per 0.5L. Open M-Sa noon-3pm and 6pm-midnight, Su 6pm-midnight. Cash only.

Cvajner Cafe, Forum 2 (☎21 65 02). Inside, modern art jives with Roman-style frescoes on the walls and a bank vault next to the bar. Outside, tables provide views of the Temple of Augustus. *Dupli* cappuccino 10kn. Mixed drinks 40kn. Open daily 8am-11pm.

POREČ ☎(0)52

A stone's throw from Slovenia and Italy, Poreč sits on a tiny peninsula jutting into the azure Adriatic. The town is brimming with gorgeous Gothic and Romanesque houses, unique 6th-century Byzantine mosaics, Roman ruins, and, unfortunately, throngs of tourists. Nevertheless, this foreign influx gives the town an internationally festive flair, and Poreč proves a fun stop as you island-hop down the coast.

⌷ TRANSPORTATION. There is no train station for Poreč. The **bus station,** K. Hoguesa 2 (☎43 21 53; MC), sends buses to **Pula** (1hr., 8 per day, 39kn); **Rijeka** (2hr., 5 per day, 64kn); **Rovinj** (1hr., 6 per day, 29kn); **Zagreb** (6hr., 4 per day, 171kn); **Koper, SLN** (30min., 3 per day, 56kn); **Ljubljana, SLN** (5hr.; Aug. 3 per day, June-July and Sept. 2 per day, Oct.-May 1 per day; 121kn); **Portoroz, SLO** (1½hr., 2-3 per day, 45kn); **Trieste, ITA** (2hr., 3 per day, 65kn). MC or cash only.

⬛ 🔧 ORIENTATION AND PRACTICAL INFORMATION. Poreč is easy to navigate. The marina is situated behind, or downhill from, the bus station, while the town center is just behind and to the right of the station, through the park. Facing the bus station, go around the right side of the building and head through the park. You'll see a sign for the tourist office (an "i," with an arrow pointing left). Follow the sign and go up pedestrian **Milanovića,** which will curve left and then right to reach the main square, **Trg Slobode** (a 5min. walk). The main pedestrian walkway, **Decumanus,** begins at **Trg Slobode** and runs through **Stari Grad** (Old Town), which is lined with shops, cafes, and restaurants. The **tourist office,** Zagrebačka 9, is up the road and to the right from Trg Slobode and should be your first stop for **free maps,**

accommodation info, bus schedules, and pamphlets galore. (☎45 12 93; www.istra.com/porec. Open May-Oct. M-Sa 8am-10pm, Su 9am-1pm and 4-10pm; Nov.-Apr. daily 8am-4:30pm.) **Zagrebačka Banka,** Obala M. Tita bb, by the sea, **exchanges cash** for no commission, cashes **traveler's checks** for 1.5% commission, and provides **Western Union** services. (☎45 11 66. Open M-F 7:30am-7pm, Sa 8am-2pm.) There is a MC **ATM** and a **currency exchange** machine outside. Other MC/V ATMs are available throughout Stari Grad. **Luggage storage** is available at the bus station. (10kn. Open daily 5-9am, 9:30am-5:30pm, and 6-9pm.) The **pharmacy** is at Trg Slobode 13. (☎43 23 62. Open daily July-Aug. 7:30am-10pm; Sept.-June M-Sa 7:30am-8pm.) The tourist office has one computer with free **Internet** (15min. limit), but be prepared to wait. Connections at **Cybermac,** M. Grahalića 1, are slow and expensive. From Trg Svobode, head up Zagrebačka and turn left before the tourist office, then right. (☎42 70 75. 30kn per 30min., 42kn per hr. Open M-Sa 8am-midnight, Su 10am-midnight). The **post office,** Trg Svobode 1, is opposite the pink church with the yellow facade. (☎43 18 08. Open Sept.-June M-F 8am-3pm, Sa 8am-1pm, July-Aug. M-F 8am-noon and 6-9pm, Sa 8am-1pm.) **Postal Code:** 52440.

⌐⌐ ACCOMMODATIONS AND FOOD. Accommodations in Poreč are abundant but expensive, particularly if you're staying fewer than three nights. There are many travel agencies that book private rooms. The tourist office can also recommend or book rooms. **Eurotours,** Nikole Tesle 12, has decent rates and a huge stock of rooms in locations ranging from the city center to the hinterlands of Poreč. (☎45 15 11; eurotours@pu.hinet.hr. Open daily June-Aug. 7:30am-10pm; Sept.-May 8am-2pm and 5-9pm. Doubles 270-443kn; apartments 194-280kn. 30% more for stays under 3 nights. Registration fee 15kn.) **Hotel Poreč ❺,** R. Končara 1, has clean, modern rooms with TV, fridges, and phones. (☎45 18 11; www.hotelporec.com. July 30-Aug. 27 singles €59; doubles €90. Jan. 2-Mar. 19, Apr. 2-30, and Sept. 24-Dec. 30 €36/52. Mar. 19-Apr. 2, Apr. 30-July 2, and Sept. 10-24 €39/58. AmEx/MC/V.) Both of the following **campgrounds** offer a range of services (grocery stores, restaurants, laundromats) and are accessible by the same bus from the station (25min.; 5 per day 6:15am-9:20pm to Lanterna, 7:30am-10:30pm back to Poreč; 20kn). **Lanterna Camp ❶** is 13km to the north and has a beach. (☎40 45 00. Open Mar.-Oct. 20-40kn per person, 42kn per tent. Electricity 9.50kn.) Save on your laundry bill at the nudist camp and apartment village **Solaris ❶.** (☎40 40 00. Open Mar.-Oct. Camping 42kn per person, 59-78kn per tent or car. Apartments 353-405kn.)

lives among the marble alleyways and postcard-perfect islands of Dalmatia. You get to experience the smells of *real* Croatian cooking (no, people don't really eat pizza and risotto for every meal); the religious undercurrent of the country as shown through the icons that adorn the walls of its homes; and how everybody, even grandmas, watches soccer when a Slavic team is playing. If you share a language with your host, you might hear stories of what it is like to live though three empires, Communism, Fascism, and a bloody civil war. On a lighter note, you get restaurant tips and laundry access.

Throughout my time here, I was consistently impressed by the hospitality with which my hosts received me. That said, there are a few **tips** for making your experience as safe and comfortable as possible: the safest rooms are those which are listed with a certified travel agency, like Atlas, and those which are registered with the local tourist authorities. Often, these are identified by a shiny blue placard with the word "SOBE" in capital letters (beware of counterfeits). When in a city, ask to see where the room is on a map before negotiating: the lower the price, the more remote the location. Be sure to check out the room before making any kind of deal and to set a price before settling in. If the first option doesn't work out, there are always more rooms in the land of *sobe*.

—Lauren Rivera

Ulixes ❷, Decumanus 2, peaceful and away from the main tourist strip, offers a daily replenished selection of fresh meat and seafood. The beautiful terrace overlooks the stone walls of Stari Grad. (☎45 11 32. Entrees 60-110kn. Open daily noon-3pm and 6pm-midnight.) **Gostionica Istra ❸,** Milanovića 30, by the bus station, sells delicious fish, meat, and pasta dishes. (☎43 46 36. Entrees 25-80kn. Open daily noon-10pm.) **Nono ❶,** Zagrebačka 4, across the street from the tourist office, serves a variety of huge pizzas. (☎45 30 88. Pizza 25-45kn. Open daily noon-midnight.) Perched atop the tower, **Caffe Torne Rotunda,** Narodni trg 3, provides a postcard-perfect view of Poreč's tiled rooftops and bright ocean. (Macchiato 16kn. Open daily 10am-1am.) **Konzum** supermarket is at Zagrebačka 2, next to the church at Trg Slobode. (☎45 24 29. Open daily 7am-10pm.)

⑥ SIGHTS. From Trg Slobode, walk down to the **Pentagonal Tower** (Peterokunta Kula), built in 1447 as a city gate. Continuing down Decumanus, turn right on Sv. Eleuterija to find the 6th-century ▧**St. Euphrasius's Basilica** (Eufrazijeva Bazilika), which was placed on UNESCO's World Heritage list in 1997 for its preserved **mosaics.** Across from the basilica entrance stands the octagonal baptistry and **bell tower,** which you can climb for a view of the tiled roofs of Poreč. (Open daily 9am-7pm. Services M-Sa 7:30am, 7pm; Su 7:30, 11am, 7pm. Basilica free. Bell tower 10kn.) To the right of the basilica entrance, the **museum,** housed in the ancient bishop's palace, displays fragments of the intricate floor mosaics from the original chapel floor. (☎091 521 78 62. Open daily 10am-3pm and 4-7pm. 10kn.) Returning to Decumanus, head down through Trg Marator and toward the right to the pile of stones and columns on the left side that was once the Roman **Temple of Neptune,** constructed around the AD first century. A stroll left along Obala m. Tita, next to the ocean, brings you to the **Round Tower,** a 15th-century defensive structure.

◪◩ BEACHES AND ENTERTAINMENT. Beaches in Poreč, as along most of the Istrian coast, are steep and rocky but offer convenient tanning shelves cut into the shoreline. The best sites near town are south of the marina. Hop on the passing **mini-train** (9am-11pm every 35min., 15kn), or face the sea on Obala m. Tita, turn left, and head along the coast for about 10min. to reach the **Brulo** resort, which offers **waterslides** (10kn per hr.), **tennis** (50kn), and **minigolf** (10kn) to non-guests. Another 5min. walk takes you to the outdoor playground of the **Blue Lagoon** (Plava Laguna) resort, and 10min. more gets you to the **Green Lagoon** (Zelena Laguna). Or, take a bus straight to the latter (10min., 7 per day, 9kn). To escape the crowds, continue past the Green Lagoon toward the marina (30min.). A ferry leaves from the marina for the less-popular, quieter **Saint Nicholas Island** (Sveti Nikola), just across the harbor. (Every 30min. 6:45am-midnight, round-trip 15kn.) The trip is worth it if you're looking for a secluded rock shelf. However, if it's a scenic beach you crave, stick to the mainland. To see more of the coast, rent a **bike** from **Ivona,** Prvomajska 2, a block up from the tourist office and across Trg J. Rakovca. Ask for a **free bike map.** Its two trails take you through more than 50km of olive groves, forests, vineyards, and medieval villages. (☎43 40 46. 15kn per hr., 30kn per 3hr., 60kn per day. ID or passport required. Open M-Sa 8am-1pm and 4-7pm, Su 8am-1pm.)

Any beach that has a name also has a hotel complex and a disco, invariably frequented by (mostly German) tourists of all ages. To dance with a young and more local crowd, walk 10min. south down the beach past the marina to the open-air, Roman-columned **Colonia Iulia Parentium.** (☎51 89 41. Open daily June 4-Sept. 4 9pm-4am.) **Mango Mambo,** Trg Marafor 10, the coolest of a cluster of bars and cafes at the end of Decumanus, stays lively throughout the week with wild cocktails (32kn) like the "rubber duck" and the "slippery surprise." (Open daily 6pm-4am.)

ROVINJ ☎(0)52

An Istrian treasure, Rovinj (ro-VEEN; pop. 14,000) was once the favorite summer resort of Austro-Hungarian emperors for its natural, spa-like atmosphere. Vacationers still bask in the town's unspoiled beauty. Once Istria's central fishing settlement and a fortress for the Venetian Navy, Rovinj's crystal-clear waves, elegant, cobblestoned marina, and laid-back attitude offer a quiet, picturesque escape.

▐ TRANSPORTATION. Rovinj sends **buses** to **Poreč** (1hr., 7-10 per day, 29kn); **Pula** (1hr.; 20 per day 4:40am-7pm, M-Sa also 11:30pm; 27kn); **Rijeka** (3½hr., 7 per day, 93kn); **Zagreb** (5-6hr., 9 per day, 150kn); **Belgrade, SMN** (13hr., 2 per day, 325kn); **Ljubljana, SLN** (5hr., in high season 1 per day, 146kn); **Trieste, ITA** (2½hr., 2-3 per day, 92kn). The tourist office (see below) has **free maps** for suggested bike routes 22-60km long. Rent bikes at **Bike Planet**, Trg na Lokvi 3, across the street from the bus station. (☎81 11 61. 20kn per hr., 70kn per day. Open M-Sa 8:30am-12:30pm and 5-8pm.) **Globtours**, Rismondo 2, off the main square on the waterfront, also rents bikes. (15kn per hr., 40kn per ½-day, 60kn per day.)

▄▐ ORIENTATION AND PRACTICAL INFORMATION. Turn left out of the bus station and walk down **Nazora** toward the marina or up on **Karera** to **Stari Grad** (Old Town). Or turn right out of the bus station, onto **Carera**, a little, shop-lined street to get to the main square. The main tourist info office is just past the main square, away from the marina. Street signs and numbers are often difficult to find or nonexistent, but the town is small enough that you won't stay lost for long. The **tourist office** nearest to the bus station is just around the corner; it's the yellow-orange building on the corner at Nello Quarantotto bb. The friendly, English-speaking staff will cash **traveler's checks** and **exchange money** with no commission. (☎81 16 59. **Internet** 5kn per 10min. Bike rental 20kn per hr., 20kn per ½-day, 70kn per day. Open 9am-1pm and 5-10pm.) **Zagrebačka Banka**, Carera 21, right next to the main square (Trg m. Tita), will cash traveler's checks for a 1.5% fee (20kn min.) and exchange money for no commission. (☎81 11 88. Open M-F 7:30am-8pm, Sa 8am-2pm.) There are several **ATMs** in the town center near Stari Grad. For **luggage storage**, ask for *garderoba* at the ticket counter of the bus station on M. Benussi. (☎81 14 53. 10kn, over 30kg 15kn. Open 6:30am-8:30pm.) With your back to the bus station, turn right on M. Benussi to get to **Gradska Ljekarna**, M. Benussi bb, a **pharmacy**. (☎81 35 89. Open M-F 7:30am-9pm, Sa 8am-4pm, Su 9am-noon. AmEx/MC/V.) **A-Mar**, Carera 26, down the street from the bus station, has 10 computers with fast connections. (☎841 211. 18kn per 30min. MC/V.) **Poste Restante** and **telephones** are available at the **post office**, M. Benussi 2, 30m uphill and to the right of the bus station. (☎81 33 11. Open M-F 7am-8pm, Sa 8am-noon and 6-9pm.) **Postal Code:** 52210.

▐▐ ACCOMMODATIONS AND FOOD. As usual, your best bet for a budget room is to search for a **private room.** Across the street from the bus station, **Natale,** Carducci 4, arranges rooms in and around the center. Call ahead in the summer. (☎81 33 65; www.rovinj.com. Open July-Aug. M-Sa 7:30am-9:30pm, Su 8am-9:30pm; Sept.-June M-Sa 7:30am-8pm, Su 8am-noon Singles €14-18; doubles €20-26; apartments €32-57. Price includes registration and tax.) For solo travelers, **Globtours ❷**, Rismondo 2, is a good option. (Open daily Sept.-June 9am-9pm, July-Aug. 9am-11pm. Doubles 180-260kn.) The **Hotel Monte Mulini ❸**, A. Smareglia bb, offers clean rooms, all with bath and some with balconies. Facing the sea at the end of Nazora, walk to the left past the marina and go up the stone steps on your left. (☎81 15 12; mulini@jadran.tdr.hr. Breakfast and dinner included. Singles €22-

40; doubles €34-70. **Camping Polari ❶,** 2.5km east of town, also has a supermarket and several bars. Take one of the frequent buses (6min., 9kn) from the bus station. (☎80 15 01; fax 81 13 95. July-Aug. 100kn per person; June 85kn per person.)

Hotspot **Veli Jože ❸,** Svetog Križa 3, at the end of the marina past the tourist office, serves great seafood amid funky maritime artifacts, including a primitive deep-sea diving suit. Prices vary by season, but you can usually get first-rate fish for 250kn per kilo. (☎81 63 37. Open daily noon-2am. AmEx/MC/V.) For a great deal and a filling meal in the perfect waterfront location, head across the street to **Stella di Mare ❷,** S. Croche 4, whose terrace overlooks the ocean. (Huge pizzas and pastas 30-45. Seafood 45-120kn. Open daily 10am-11pm. AmEx/MC/V.) If you'd like a change from the waterfront, head to **Neptun ❷,** J. Rakovca 10. This cute sidewalk restaurant serves tasty Italian fare at decent prices. (☎816 086. Entrees 34-150kn. Open 8am-midnight. AmEx/DC/MC/V.) Buy groceries at **Trg na Lokvi bb,** between the bus station and the sea. (Open M-Sa 6:30am-8pm, Su 7am-noon. AmEx/DC/MC/V.) There is an **open-air market** on Trg Valdibora with fruit, vegetables, cheese, and homemade liquor, which you can sample for free. (Open daily 7am-9pm.)

🖪 SIGHTS. Although Rovinj has been surrounded by walls since the 7th century, only three of the original seven gates—**St. Benedict's, Holy Cross,** and the **Portico**—survive today. When entering Stari Grad, you'll probably walk through the **Balbijer Arch** (Balbijer luk), a Baroque structure built on the site of the 17th-century outer gate, just off Trg Maršala Tita. Narrow streets lead uphill to the 18th-century **St. Euphemia's Church** (Crkva Sv. Eufemije), built when Rovinj was a fortress under the Venetian Navy. During Roman Emperor Diocletian's reign, Euphemia and other Christians were imprisoned and tortured for refusing to deny their faith. The 15-year-old martyr survived the torture wheel, but not the pack of lions. Amazingly, the beasts left her body intact, and her fellow Christians encapsulated it in a **sarcophagus.** The vessel made its way to Constantinople but disappeared in 800—only to float mysteriously back to Rovinj later that year. Today, Euphemia is the patron saint of Rovinj, and her sarcophagus, behind the right altar, is often visited by locals, particularly on St. Euphemia's Day (Sept. 16). The stairs up to the **bell tower** (61m) lead visitors to a majestic view of the city and sea (10kn). In summer, the lawn outside hosts classical music performances. (Church free. Open M-Sa 10am-2pm and 4-6pm, Su 4-6pm. Services Su 10:30am, 7pm.)

The **City Museum of Rovinj,** Trg Maršala Tita 11, has changing displays, including local modern art, and archaeological exhibits. (Open Tu-Sa in high season 9am-noon and 7-10pm; in low season 10am-1pm. 15kn.) Boats anchored in the harbor are eager to take off on trips to the 22 nearby **islands** (90kn) or to the serene **Lim Fjord** (100kn), a flooded canyon that separates Rovinj from Poreč. Buy tickets at the tourist office or from boat owners. Prices and departure times vary by boat.

🎵🖪 ENTERTAINMENT AND NIGHTLIFE. For the best beaches in the area, take a ferry to **🖪Red Island** (Crveni Otok; 15min., 17 per day, 20kn), where nude sunbathing is permitted. On the mainland, reach natural rock shelves by walking left past the marina for 30min. and cutting through **Golden Cape** (Zlatni Rt). Alternatively, join locals on the patios cut into the peninsula. Ferries from the marina also go to beaches on **Katarina Island** (Sv. Katarina; 7min., 1 per hr. 5:45am-midnight, 10kn). At night, Rovinj's cafe culture springs to life. Most of the action takes place along the marina or in **🖪Valentino Bar,** via Santa Croce 28 (☎83 06 83). Recline in the neo-colonial decadence of **Zanzi Bar's** palmetto bushes and garden torches, next to the tourist office on the marina. This bar attracts international trendsters with its array of cocktails (20-50kn) and swanky decor. (Open daily

8am-1am.) **Bar Sax Cafe,** Ribarski Prolaz 4, in an alley off the marina, hosts lively patrons inside and out. There's a bar but no sax. (*Favorit* 14kn per 0.5L Mixed drinks 25-35kn. Open daily 8am-3am.)

For three days in the last week of August, Rovinj looks to the sky for **Rovinjska noć** (Rovinj Night), its famous annual night of fireworks. On the 2nd Sunday of August, international artists come to display their work at the traditional open-air art festival, **Grisia,** held on the street of the same name. **Kanfanar** (July 25th), a folk festival dedicated to St. Jacob, features traditional Istrian music played on *mih* (bagpipes) and the *roženice* (flute), and a healthy spread of regional cuisine— wine, cheese, and the famous Istrian olive oil.

GULF OF KVARNER

Blessed with long summers and gentle sea breezes, the islands just off the coast of mainland Croatia are natural tourist attractions.

RIJEKA   ☎(0)51

A typical sprawling Croatian port town, Rijeka (ree-YEH-kah) is a functional trans-portation hub but not exactly the prettiest stop in Croatia. It earns its keep by pro-viding access to the islands in the Gulf of Kvarner and the Dalmatian coast.

If you need to stay in Rijeka, try **Prenoćište Rijeka ❸,** 1. Maja 34/1, which is close to the train and bus stations and offers reasonable rates. With your back to the train station, turn right on Krešimirova and left on Alessandra Manzonia. As you continue up the hill for 5min., the road becomes 1. Maja. Look for a small white sign on the right. (☎55 12 46; www.zug.hr. Reception 24hr. Singles 200kn, with bath 280kn; doubles 270/550kn. AmEx/MC.) **Viktorija ❶,** Manzoni 1a, on the left as you head to the hotel, serves a good selection of grilled specialties (29-85kn) and pizza. (☎33 74 16. Open M-Sa 7am-11pm, Su noon-11pm.) A large **supermarket** is in the building next door, to the right of the train station. (Open daily 6am-10pm.)

There is a **train station** located at Kralja Tomislava 1. (☎21 33 33. Info desk open daily 8:30am-3:30pm.) Trains run to: **Split** (7hr., 2 per day, 157kn) via **Ogu-lin; Zagreb** (3½hr., 7 per day, 102-117kn); **Berlin, GER** (11¾hr., 3 per day, 1001kn); **Budapest, HUN** (9hr., 2 per day, 326kn); **Ljubljana, SLN** (2½hr., 4 per day, 83kn); **Vienna, AUT** (9hr., 1 per day, 450kn). The **bus station,** Žabica 1, is down Krešimi-rova, to the right of the train station. (☎21 38 21. Open daily 5:30am-9pm.) Buses run to: **Dubrovnik** (12hr., 3 per day, 375kn); **Krk Town** (1½hr., 13 per day, 44kn); **Pula** (2½hr., 1 per hr., 70kn); **Split** (8hr., 12 per day, 236kn); **Zagreb** (2½hr., 1 per hr., 119kn); **Ljubljana, SLN** (3hr., 2 per day, 116kn); **Sarajevo, BOS** (13hr., 6 per wk., 231kn); **Trieste, ITA** (2hr., 6 per day, 58kn). For ferry tickets, Riva 16, face the sea from the bus station and go left to Jadrolinija. (☎21 14 44. Open M and W-F 7am-8pm, Tu and Sa 7am-6pm.) **Ferries** run to: **Dubrovnik** (18-24hr., June-Sept. F and Su 8pm, 233kn); **Hvar** (12½hr.; M, W, F, and Su 8pm; 187kn); **Korčula** (15-18hr., 4 per wk., 210kn); **Sobra** (21hr., 2 per wk., 233kn); **Split** (12hr., 4 per wk., 169kn). Prices drop September-June.

Free maps are available at the **tourist office,** Korzo 33. From the stations, turn right onto Trpimirova, cross the street, and continue right down the pedestrian street Korzo. (☎33 58 82; www.tz-rijeka.hr. Open June 15-Sept. 15 M-Sa 8am-8pm, Su 8am-2pm; Sept.16-June 14 closed Su.) The train station has a bank, which **exchanges currency** and cashes **traveler's checks** for no commission, and it also has an AmEx/MC/V **ATM.** (☎21 33 18. Open M-Sa 8am-8pm, Su 8am-12:30pm.) **Luggage storage** is in the train station (10kn per day; open 9am-11am, 11:30am-6:30pm, and 7-9pm) and in the bus station (9kn, backpacks 10kn; open daily 5:30am-10:30pm).

CROATIA

GIVING BACK

FOR THE BIRDS

Yes, the Eurasian griffon really exists—and it's every bit as extraordinary as the mythological creature whose name it shares. With a wingspan of 2.8m and weighing up to 15kg, it's one of the largest flying birds on the planet, as well as one of the longest-living species (some live up to 60 years).

But size and lifespan can't beat the threat of extinction that the endangered griffon now faces. Enter Goran Susic, who founded the Eko-centar Caput Insulae in 1993, just outside the town of Beli (pop. 80) on the island of Cres. To protect the griffons his primary goal, Susic realized a much larger project was in order. Now, the nonprofit NGO strives to safeguard not only the birds, but also their environment and the cultural heritage of the local people of Cres.

Much of the center's work focuses on rescuing baby griffons from accidental dives into the water and nursing poisoned or injured birds back to health. Other projects educate people about the griffons, the natural life and history of Cres's Tramuntana peninsula, and eco-consciousness in general.

Paying volunteers are encouraged to help out at Caput Insulae for at least a week, but are welcome to stay for as little as a day—or indefinitely. Those who are at least 16 years of age and have an interest in ecological or historical preservation are wel-

KRK ISLAND ☎(0)51

Croatia's largest island, Krk is only a short ride across the Krk Bridge. The white stone mountains that rise right out of the clear, blue water are stunning toward its southern end, in the town of Baška. While Baška reels in a large catch of tourists, Krk Town remains more peaceful.

KRK TOWN

Krk Town is the perfect place to stop for a day and night as you begin island-hopping down the coast. Its picturesque little cobblestoned alleys are fun to explore, and cool, mellow bars are in abundance.

▉▉ TRANSPORTATION AND PRACTICAL INFORMATION. Buses run from Rijeka to **Krk Town** (1½hr., 10-16 per day, 37kn), and most continue to **Baška** (40min., 5-9 per day, 19kn). **Jadrolinija** operates a **ferry** between Baška and Lopar on the northern tip of Rab Island. (June-Aug. only. 1hr.; 4 per day; 31kn, car 140kn, bike 30kn.) The **bus station** (☎22 11 11) is at Šetalište Sv. Bernardina 1. **ATMs** are outside. To get to Stari Grad and its main square, **Vela placa**, from the bus station, walk to your right (keeping the sea on your right). The tourist and travel agency **Autotrans**, Šetalište Sv. Bernardina 3, on the right side of the bus station, if you're facing it, **exchanges currency** and cashes **traveler's checks** for no commission. (☎22 26 61; fax 22 21 10. Open M-Sa 8am-9pm, Su 9am-1:30pm.) **Erste Bank**, on Trg b. Josipa Jelačića, up and left of Vela pl., offers **Western Union** services and has a MC/V **ATM.** (Open M-F 8am-8pm, Sa 8am-noon.) There's a **pharmacy** at Vela pl. 3. (☎22 11 33. Open M-F 7:30am-8pm, Sa 7am-noon and 6-8pm, Su 9-11am. AmEx/DC/MC/V.) **Enigma Internet Cafe**, Šetalište Sv. Bernardina bb, is on the 2nd floor of the building across the street from the bus station. (☎222 300. 10kn per hr. Open M-F 8am-1:30pm and 5:30-9pm. Cash only.) The **post office**, Trg b. Josipa Jelačića bb, offers **Western Union** services, gives MC **cash advances,** and has **phones** inside and outside. (☎22 11 25. Open M-F 7am-8pm, Sa 7am-2pm.) **Postal Code:** 51500.

▉▉ ACCOMMODATIONS AND FOOD. Autotrans (see above) books private rooms. (July-Aug. singles 100-150kn; doubles 180-240kn. In low season 70-110/140-200kn. Tourist tax 4.50-7.50kn. Stays under 4 days 30-50% more. Registration 10kn.) *Sobe* signs line **Slavka Nikoliča** and **Plavnička,** but before you climb the hill, be forewarned that many owners deal only through agencies. The tree-covered **Autocamp**

Ježevac ❶, Plavnička bb, is a 5min. walk from the bus station away from Stari Grad with the sea to the left. The reception is not the white shack you see on the right before the gates; it's through the gates, past all the campers, at the end of the road. Follow the street slightly uphill and then downhill (7min.) to get to the end. (☎22 10 81; jezevac@zlatni-otok.hr. Mar. 23-May 31 and Sept. 1-Oct. 15 25.50kn per person, 17kn per tent. July 1-Aug. 31 36/24kn. June 33/22.50kn.) Although touristy at first glance, **Galeb ❷,** Obala hrvatske mornarice bb, serves delicious Adriatic standards, including the fabulous *pureći odrezak* (turkey with rice, curry, and pineapple; 70kn), on a terrace overlooking the marina. (Meat entrees 35-80kn. Vegetarian dishes 30-40kn. Open daily 9am-midnight.) There's also a **supermarket** across the street from the bus station, Šetalište Sv. Bernardina bb (☎85 82 02. Open daily 7am-9pm. AmEx/DC/MC/V.)

◙ 🄻 SIGHTS AND ENTERTAINMENT. The town's main attraction is its 14th-century fortification, **Kamplin,** which is visible at the **South Town Gate** (Mala Vrata), the entrance to Stari Grad on the marina. The waters around Krk Town offer more excitement than the town itself. **Fun Diving Krk,** Brace Juras 3, leads underwater expeditions throughout the year. (☎/fax 22 25 63; www.fun-diving.com. Beginners: 1 dive €45, 2 dives €79; everything included. Experienced divers: full day with 2 dives €39, with full equipment €59. Snorkeling €13. All are 9am-4pm at Island of Plavnik, 45min. away by boat. They sell juice and lunch on the boat, but you can also just bring your own. Cash only.) Less-populated, cleaner beaches are farther away, in **Autocamp Ježevac** (see above). ▨**Šoto Baterije,** a self-dubbed "chill out lounge," is a laid-back, self-service bar right on the rocks, just above the water. It's near the church at the top of Stari Grad, past the smooth white stone square. There should be a sandwich sign saying "cool drinks and music"—otherwise, go around the round tower to find the door. (Open daily 8pm-1am. Cash only.) **Casa di Padrone,** Šetalište Sv. Bernardina bb, is right on the waterfront as you head away from the bus station, past the stands, before the row of restaurants. (☎222 128. Cash only.) **Volsonis,** Vela Placa 8, is on the right side. (☎221 951. Heineken 15kn. Open daily 8am-2am. Cash only.) If you're craving late-night munchies, head past Volsonis; before you reach Erste Bank, you'll see **Ane,** a fast-food stand on the right side. (Hot dog 10kn. Hamburger 15kn. Open 9am-2pm and 5pm-4am. Cash only.)

come to assist the small permanent staff in everything from showing tourists around and monitoring forest activity to picking olives and managing sheep. Volunteers also get a chance to repair old buildings, clean the beaches and trails, and cook for fellow volunteers.

Work is done primarily in the morning, from around 9am to 1pm, with afternoons free for hiking or going on an excursion—maybe a boat ride along the coast to see if any griffons have fallen into the water, or a ride in one of the Eko-centar's Jeeps to a nearby village.

Volunteers stay in the main building, a former primary school built in 1929 during the fascist occupation of Cres. Each room's door is emblazoned with an artistic rendering of a local myth, and just inside a painted elf keeps guard over guests. There's a communal space where volunteers can hang out together—when they're not spending time with the griffons, a donkey, two sheep, a dog, two cats, two turtles, and assorted other resident creatures.

Buses go to Beli from Cres Town twice per day (30min.; M-Sa 7am, 3:50pm; returns 8am, 4:50pm; 21kn). Once you reach Beli, backtrack from the bus stop about 150m to find the entrance for the Eko-centar. €149 per week, €271 per 2 weeks, €331 per 3 weeks, €391 per 4 weeks, plus €6 per day for food. Contact the Eko-centar directly for best rates. ☎/fax 385 51 840 525; www.caput-insulae.com.

DALMATIAN COAST

After his last visit to Dalmatia, George Bernard Shaw wrote: "The gods wanted to crown their creation and on the last day they turned tears, stars, and the sea breeze into the isles of Kornati." Shaw's words speak to the entire Dalmatian Coast—a stunning seascape of unfathomable beauty set against a backdrop of dramatic, sun-drenched mountains. Azure blue waters delicately wash onto endless stretches of rocky beach, and even during the busiest travel seasons, many parts of the coast remain the perfect refuge from the bustle of urban Europe. With more than 1100 islands (only 66 are inhabited), Dalmatia contains Croatia's largest archipelago, and boasts the cleanest and clearest waters in the Mediterranean.

ZADAR   ☎(0)23

Zadar (pop. 77,000), the administrative center of northern Dalmatia, hides its many scars well. Allied attacks destroyed Zadar during WWII and the recent war (1991-1995) shattered much of what had been rebuilt. Residents have restored their homes yet again and the city now stands beautifully rejuvenated. With the extraordinary Kornati Islands just a boat ride away and a history so well preserved that Roman ruins serve as city benches, Zadar is the quintessential Dalmatian city.

▐▀ TRANSPORTATION

Trains: Ante Starčevića 4 (☎21 25 55). Info office open M-F 7:30am-3:30pm and 6:30-9:30pm. To **Zagreb** via **Knin** (5-7hr., 3 per day, 185kn; 1 direct, 148kn).

Buses: Ante Starčevića 1 (☎21 10 35, info 21 15 55). More reliable than trains. To: **Dubrovnik** (8hr., 9 per day, 155-207kn); **Rijeka** (4½hr., 13 per day, 129kn); **Split** (3hr., 2 per hr., 77-91kn); **Zagreb** (5hr., 1 per hr., 103-107kn); **Ljubljana, SLN** (8hr., 1 per day, 207kn); **Sarajevo, BOS** (6hr., 1 per day, 197kn); **Trieste, ITA** (7hr., 2 per day, 150kn).

Ferries: Ferries run May 25-June 26 and Sept. 16-Oct. 2 and depart from Liburnska Obala, 5min. up from the pedestrian bridge. **Jadrolinija** (☎25 48 00) has ferry info and sells tickets. Open M-F 6am-9pm, Sa 5:30am-midnight, Su 7am-9pm. To: **Dubrovnik** (16hr., 2 per wk., 157kn); **Korčula** (12hr., 2 per wk., 119kn); **Rijeka** (7hr., 2 per wk., 97kn); **Split** (6hr., 2 per wk., 97kn); **Ancona, ITA** (6hr., 4-7 per wk., 306kn).

Public Transportation: Schedules for buses (M-Sa every 15-20min., Su and holidays 1 per hr. 5:30am-11pm) are posted at the main bus station and at most stops. Station names are rarely posted at each stop; ask for help. Buy tickets from the driver (6kn) or any kiosk (round-trip 10kn) and validate on board.

✦▐ ORIENTATION AND PRACTICAL INFORMATION

Most of the city's businesses and sights are scattered along **Široka,** the main street in **Stari Grad** (Old Town). The **bus** and **train stations** are at Ante Starčevića 1. To get to Široka, with your back to the main entrance, go through the pedestrian underpass and continue straight until you hit **Zrinsko-Frankopanska.** Follow this street (and the signs to the "Centar") all the way to the water, then walk along the left side of the harbor to the first gate of Stari Grad. Široka branches off **Narodni trg** to the right after you pass through the gate. Alternatively, hop on bus #2 or #4 to Poluotok. Facing the water, head right to the main gate opposite the footbridge.

Tourist Office: Tourist Board Zadar, M. Klaića bb (☎31 61 66; tzg-zadar@zd.tel.hr). Go straight on the road from the main gate to the far corner of Narodni trg. **Free maps** and an info booklet on Zadar. Open daily 8am-8pm; in summer 8am-midnight.

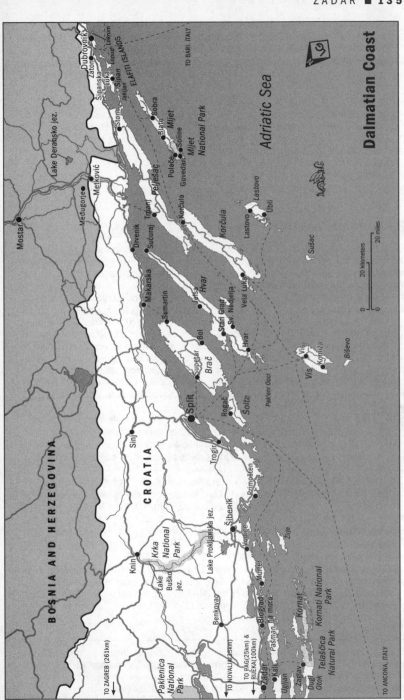

Dalmatian Coast

Currency Exchange: Hypo Alpe-Adria-Bank, Barakovića 4 (☎20 09 00), on the left side as you enter the main gate of Stari Grad. Exchanges currency for no commission and cashes **travelers checks** for 1.5% commission. Open M-F 8am-8pm, Sa 8am-noon.

Luggage Storage: At the bus station; follow the *garderoba* signs. 1.20kn per hr.; over 15kg 2.20kn per hr. Open daily 6am-10pm. **Bagul Garderoba,** opposite the Jadrolinija office on the waterfront. 5kn per hr., 15kn per day. Open M-Sa 7am-9pm, Su 5-9pm.

Pharmacy: Barakovića 2 (☎21 33 74). Open M-F 7am-9pm, Sa 8am-noon.

Internet: Gradska Knjižnica Zadar (Zadar City Library), Stjepana Radića 116 (☎31 57 72). Cross over the pedestrian bridge and continue 2 blocks; the library is on your left. 10kn per hr.; 10kn min. Open M-F 8am-7pm, Sa 8am-1pm. **Acme,** Matafara 2a, next to the Forum and St. Donat's church. Look for signs off Siroka. They have 7 computers and a decent connection. 10kn per 30min. Open 9am-9pm. Cash only.

Post Office: Nikole Matafara 1 (☎25 05 06), off Široka. Has **telephones** inside and gives MC **cash advances. Poste Restante** at the main post office, Kralja Držislava 1 (☎31 60 23). Open M-Sa 7am-9pm. **Postal Code:** 23000.

ACCOMMODATIONS

Zadar has a youth hostel, but it's far from Stari Grad, not too impressive, and you may ultimately end up spending a good deal on bus tickets. The best option is to find a **private room** in the center of town. You can try to find *sobe* (room) signs, but a more reliable option is the **Aquarius Travel Agency,** inside the main gate at Nova Vrata bb. From the bus station, take bus #2 or 4 to Poluotok. Facing the water, go right and head to the the 2nd city entrance on your right across from the footbridge. (☎/fax 21 29 19; www.jureskoaaquarius.com. Open daily 7am-10pm. Singles 100-150kn; 2-person apartments 250-300kn. Tax 5.50-7kn.) **Miatours,** Vrata Sv. Krševana, is another good option, closer to the bus station. You'll see a Jadrolinija booth to the right and a *garderoba* to the left of the entrance. They book private accommodations, provide maps and the Zadar city guide (with a map of the town on the last page), and offer transportation to nearby islands. (☎25 44 00 or 25 43 00; www.miatours.hr. Open July-Aug. 8am-8pm, Sept.-June 8am-2:30pm. Singles and doubles 100-150kn per person. AmEx/DC/MC/V.)

> **TIP** **MAKING CONNECTIONS.** If you're staying in a private room while island hopping, make sure to ask your host whether he or she knows anyone at your future destinations. It's likely there will be a cousin or friend they can call for you—saving you from having to haggle with people at the stations and docks.

Omladinski Hostel Zadar (HI), Obala Kneza Trpimira 76 (☎33 11 45; www.hfhs.hr), on the waterfront at the outskirts of town. From the station, take bus #5 heading to Puntamika (15min., 6kn) or bus #8 to Diklo (20min., 6kn), ask the driver to let you off at the 1st stop after Autocamp Borik. Walk left. This huge harborside complex has plenty of dorm rooms, a bar, and sports facilities. Breakfast included. Reception daily 8am-10pm. Check-out 10am. Call ahead. July 1-Aug. 29 102kn. Prices drop in low season. Tourist tax 5.5-7.5kn. Nonmembers 11.50kn extra per night. ❶

Autocamp Borik, Gustavo Matoša bb (☎33 20 74; fax 33 20 65), on the beach. Follow directions to Hostel Zadar and look for large signs on the right. Ample, clean sites, but the trees don't quite block the road noise. July-Aug. 52.50kn per person, 60kn per tent, 75kn per car. Tax 7.50kn. May-June and Sept. 37.50/45/52/50/5.50kn. ❶

FOOD

The **Konzum** supermarket has several branches, including Široka 10 and J. Štrossmayerova 6. (Both open M-Sa 7am-9pm, Su 7am-8pm.) A **market** on Zlatarska, below Narodni trg and past the cinema, sells produce, meat, cheese, and bread; it also doubles as a densely packed flea market. (Open daily 6am-2pm.)

▓ **Trattoria Canzona,** Stomorica 8 (☎21 20 81). Right in the middle of the young hangout spot and always packed. Try the Warm-Cold Salad, (lettuce and tomatoes covered in sauteed mushrooms, baby shrimp, and onions; 45kn). Tasty entrees 30-70kn. Open 10am-11pm. Cash only. ❷

Restaurant Dva Ribara (Two Fishermen), Blaža Jurjeva 3 (☎21 34 45), off Plemića Borelli. A local favorite. In addition to the ubiquitous Croatian standards, this mythical duo offers leafy salads, vegetarian plates (30-38kn), and a colorful array of pizzas (30-50kn). Open daily 10:30am-midnight. ❶

Foša, Kralja Dmitra Zvonimira 2 (☎31 44 21),. Named after the inlet upon which it sits outside the city walls, Foša grills up sizable portions of fresh fish (45-160kn) and meat (55-75kn) on a wide patio overlooking the bay. The atmosphere is romantic after sundown. Open M-Sa 11am-midnight, Su 5pm-midnight. ❷

🗗 SIGHTS

▓ **SEA ORGAN.** The coolest sight in Zadar is its Sea Organ, claimed to be the first of its kind in the world. Designed by architect Nikola Bašić, with the help of other Croatian experts in hydraulics, organ-pipe-making, and tuning. Rushing seawater causes pipes beneath this 70m long stairway to play notes at random. The resulting music sounds something like a whale choir might.

FORUM. The most storied area in Zadar is the ancient Forum, a wide-open square ornamented with heaped stone relics, located on Široka in the center of the peninsula. In the evenings, watch out for kids driving around a section of the ruins in rented mini play-cars. Built in Byzantine style in the early 9th century, **St. Donat's Church** (Crkva Sv. Donata) sits atop the ruins of an ancient Roman temple; the ruins are still visible from inside. Today, the building is one of only three circular Catholic churches in the world. Though no longer a place of worship, it is still used for the occasional high school graduation. *(Open daily 9am-2pm and 4-8pm. 5kn.)*

ST. MARY'S CHURCH (CRKVA SV. MARIJA). Across the square and toward the water from St. Donat's, St. Mary's is a more traditional place of worship. It houses the fabulous **Permanent Exhibition of Religious Art** (Stalna Izložba Crkvene Umjetnosti). Its gold and silver busts, reliquaries, and crosses are regarded as some of Croatia's most precious artifacts—shrewd nuns keep a close watch over visitors. *(Trg Opatice Čike 1. ☎21 15 45. Buy tickets to the left of the church. Open M-Sa 10am-1pm and 6-8pm, Su 10am-1pm. 20kn, students 10kn.)*

ARCHEOLOGICAL MUSEUM (ARHEOŠLOKI MUZEJ). Next to St. Mary's stands this museum, which documents the epochal history of Zadar with aerial photographs of towns and archaeological sites, beautiful medieval stonework, and innumerable shards of prehistoric pottery. *(☎25 05 16. Open M-F 9am-1pm and 6-9:30pm, Sa 9am-1pm. 10kn, students 5kn.)*

NATIONAL MUSEUM (NARODNI MUZEJ ZADAR). The National Museum offers a more accessible and entertaining view of the city's history. Scale models of Zadar chronicle its development through the centuries. *(From St. Mary's, follow the same street to the other side of peninsula away from the water; the museum is on the right. ☎25 18 51. Open M-Tu and Th-F 9am-2pm, W 9am-2pm and 5-7pm. 10kn, students 5kn.)*

🎵 📷 ENTERTAINMENT AND NIGHTLIFE

To find the local youth, check out the sidewalk cafes along **Varoška** and **Stomorica,** just off of Špire Brusine. **The Garden,** Bedemi zadarskih pobuna bb, at the end of the peninsula, tucked away on the right side, is a bar owned by a former UB40 drummer. Lounge on white sofas or mattresses on the wooden deck overlooking

CROATIA

the marina. The music ranges from reggae to ambient to funk. (☎36 47 39. Beer 11-20kn per 0.33L. Mixed drinks 28-45. Open 11am-1am. Cash only.) Perfect for a casual sunset drink, **Caffe Bar Forum,** on Široka at the Forum, has comfortable chairs and outdoor seating overlooking the ruins. (*Karlovačko* 13kn per 0.33L. Open daily 7:30am-midnight.) **Kino Pobjeda,** on Jurja Dalmatinca just off Narodni trg, shows mainstream English-language movies with Croatian subtitles in an enormous theater. (Daily 6:30-11pm. 15-25kn. Later screenings are more expensive.) Zadar also hosts classical and medieval music concerts in beautiful St. Donat's Cathedral from early July to mid-August. Ask the tourist office for details.

SPLIT   ☎(0)21

Metropolitan and bustling Split (pop. 300,000) is by no means a typical Dalmatian town. Croatia's 2nd-largest city, it is more a cultural center than a beach resort, boasting a wider variety of activities and nightlife than any of its neighbors. Stari

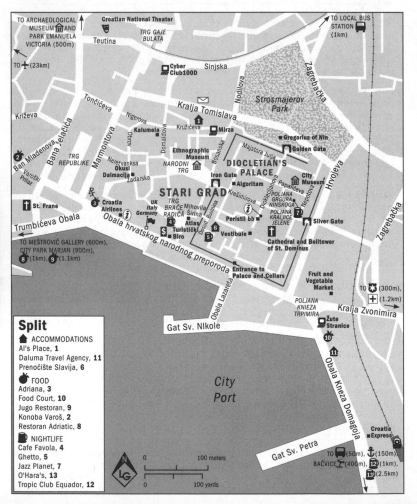

Split

🔺 ACCOMMODATIONS
Al's Place, **1**
Daluma Travel Agency, **11**
Prenoćište Slavija, **6**

🍎 FOOD
Adriana, **3**
Food Court, **10**
Jugo Restoran, **9**
Konoba Varoš, **2**
Restoran Adriatic, **8**

🍷 NIGHTLIFE
Cafe Favola, **4**
Ghetto, **5**
Jazz Planet, **7**
O'Hara's, **13**
Tropic Club Equador, **12**

Grad, wedged between a high mountain range and a palm-lined waterfront, is framed by a luxurious palace where Roman emperor Diocletian spent his summers. In the 7th century, the local Illyrian population fled to the palace to escape the attacks of marauding Slavs, and built a town, incorporating the walls and arches of the palace into their houses and public squares. The result is a city with some of Europe's most puzzling, and surely most interesting, architecture.

☞ TRANSPORTATION

Flights: Split Airport (☎20 35 06; fax 20 35 07) sends planes to domestic and international destinations. A bus (30kn, 25min.) runs between the airport and the waterfront near the catamaran dock, Gat. Sv. Nikole, 1½hr. before each departure. **Croatia Airlines,** Obala hrvatskog narodnog preporoda 9 (☎36 29 97), flies through Split Airport. Airport open M-F 8am-8pm, Sa 9am-noon.

Trains: Obala Kneza Domagoja bb (☎33 85 25, info 33 34 44). Due to the destruction of railways during the recent war, trains are very inefficient; use buses. Trains do not run south of Split. Ticket office open daily 6am-10pm. To: **Rijeka** (12hr., 2 per day, 147kn) via **Oguli; Zadar** (6½hr., 1 per day, 68kn) via **Knin; Zagreb** (5-8hr.; 5 per day; one-way 158kn, round-trip 248kn); **Budapest, HUN** (16hr., 1 per day, 375kn) and **Ljubljana, SLN** (12hr., 2 per wk., 213kn).

Buses: Obala Kneza Domagoja 12 (☎33 84 83, schedule info 060 32 73 27). Domestic tickets sold inside at main counter, international tickets *(međunarodni karte)* in the small office to the right. Open daily 5am-11pm. To: **Dubrovnik** (4½hr.; 19 per day; 89-122kn, round-trip 156-193kn); **Rijeka** (7hr., 13 per day, 220kn); **Zadar** (3½hr., 2 per hr., 97kn); **Zagreb** (5½hr., 2 per hr., 140kn); **Ljubljana, SLN** (11hr., 1 per day, 260kn); **Sarajevo, BOS** (7½hr., 6 per day, 142kn). Buses to **Trogir** (30min.; 3 per hr.; 19kn, round-trip 25kn) leave from the **local bus station** on Domovinskog rata.

Ferries: Obala Kneza Domagoja bb (☎33 83 33; fax 33 82 22). To: **Dubrovnik** (8hr., 5 per wk., 115kn); **Korčula** (6hr., 6 per wk., 32-97 kn); **Rijeka** (10½hr., 5 per wk., 140kn); **Ancona, ITA** (10hr., 4 per wk., 274kn); **Bari, ITA** (25hr., 3 per wk., 274kn).

Public Transportation: Buses run all night but are few and far between after midnight. Buy tickets (8kn) from the driver and punch them on board.

Taxis: Many wait in front of Diocletian's Palace on Obala hrvatskog narodnog preporoda and at the bus station/ferry terminal. Base 18kn, 9kn per km. **Radio Taxi** (☎970).

◄✦ 7 ORIENTATION AND PRACTICAL INFORMATION

The **train** and **bus stations** lie on **Obala Kneza Domagoja** across from Gat Sv. Petra, where the ferries arrive. With your back to the stations, follow Obala Kneza Domagoja, often referred to as **Riva,** to the right along the water until it runs into **Obala hrvatskog narodnog preporoda,** which runs roughly east to west. Behind this boulevard, opposite the water, lies **Stari Grad** (Old Town), centered on the main square, **Narodni trg,** and packed inside the walls of **Diocletian's Palace** (Dioklecijanova Palača). To reach Stari Grad from the local bus station, go right on **Domovinskog Rata,** which becomes **Livanjska** and then **Zagrebačka.** Go right on **Kralja Zvonimira** at the end of Zagrebačka and follow it to the harbor.

Tourist Offices: Turistički Biro, Obala hrvatskog narodnog preporoda 12 (☎/fax 34 71 00), sells **maps** of Split (15-30kn). Open M-F 8am-9pm, Sa 8am-10pm. **Tourist Information Center (TIC),** Peristil bb (☎34 56 06), beside the cathedral, hands out free, detailed maps of Stari Grad and brochures. Both sell the **Splitcard** (35kn, valid 72hr., free if you stay in a city-registered hotel for 3 nights or more), which is good for freebies and discounts at museums, theaters, hotels, restaurants, and shops.

CROATIA

Consulates: UK (☎34 60 07, emergencies 091 455 53 26; open M-F 9am-1pm), **Italy**, and **Germany** all share a building, Obala hrvatskog narodnog preporoda 10, above Zagrebačka Bank. UK consulate is on the 3rd fl.

Currency Exchange: Splitska Banka, Obala hrvatskog narodnog preporoda 10 (☎34 74 23). Exchanges currency for no commission and cashes **traveler's checks** for 2% commission. **Western Union** available. Open M-F 8am-8pm, Sa 8am-noon.

American Express: Atlas Travel Agency, Trg Braće Radić 6 (☎34 30 55). Open M-Sa 8am-8pm, Su 8am-noon and 6-9pm.

Luggage Storage: At the bus station kiosk marked *Garderoba*. 20kn per day. Also at the train station, Obala Kneza Domagoja 6. 20kn per day. Both open daily 6am-10pm.

English-Language Bookstore: Algoritam, Bajamotijeva 2. Decent selection of novels and nonfiction in English. Books 50-150kn. Open M-F 8am-8:30pm, Sa 8am-1pm. AmEx/DC/MC/V. **Žute Stranice** (see below) offers a broader array of options.

Police: Trg Hrvatske Bratske Zajednice 9 (☎30 71 11). From Stari Grad, take Kralja Zvonimira and bear right onto Pojišanka; the station is on the right.

Pharmacy: Marmontova 2 (☎34 57 38). Open M-F 7am-8pm, Sa 7am-1pm. MC/V.

Hospital: Klinička Bolnica Split, Spinčiceva 1 (☎55 61 11). From Stari Grad, follow Kralja Zvonimira until it runs into Poljička. Turn right onto Pt. Iza Nove Bolnice; the hospital is on the right. Cash only.

Internet: Žute Stranice, Obala Kneza Domagoja 1 (☎33 85 48). Aussie proprietor Steve hooks you up for 30kn per hr., sells used English-language paperbacks, and gives advice on getting around. Open daily 7am-9pm. **Cyber Club 100D,** Sinjska 2/4 (☎34 81 10), around the corner from the main post office, near the McDonald's on Marmontova. The cheapest option in Split. 9 computers with fast connections. Cold and hot drinks 2-8kn. 18kn per hr.; 15min. minimum. Memory card reader and CD-burning 15kn. Open M-Sa 9am-10pm, Su 4-10pm. Cash only.

Post Office: The main branch is at Kralja Tomislava 9 (☎36 14 21). Mail through the main doors; **Telephones** and **fax** through the doors to the left. Also **exchanges currency** for 1.5% commission. Open M-F 7:30am-9pm, Sa 7am-1pm. **Poste Restante** at Hercegovačka 1 (☎38 33 65). Take Zagrebačka from Stari Grad to Domovinskog Rata and go left onto Pt. Stinica (20min.). Take a right onto Hercegovačka. Open M-Sa 7am-8pm. Buses #5, 9, 10, and 13 run here from the market; ask the driver where to get off. More convenient is the location on the waterfront near the bus and train stations at Obala Domagoja 3 (☎38 34 74). **Telephones** on the left, **Western Union** services, and **currency exchange** for 1.5% commission. Open daily 7:30am-9pm. **Postal Code:** 21000.

▛ ACCOMMODATIONS

For a city its size, Split has a paltry selection of accommodations, a lingering effect of the war. **Daluma Travel Agency,** Obala Kneza Domagoja 1, near the bus and train stations, can help find **private rooms.** (☎33 84 84; www.tel.hr/daluma-travel. Open M-F 7am-9pm, Sa 8am-2pm. Singles 230kn, with bath 255kn; doubles 380kn.) If affordability is a priority, consider staying with people who advertise at the bus station and ferry landing, offering rooms at substantially lower rates than agencies. It is advisable to take a look at any room before striking a deal—rooms are of varying quality. Moreover, Split is a sprawling city, and particularly low prices may indicate long bus rides into town. The lone hostel in Split, **Al's Place ❷**, Kruziceva 10, located right in Stari Grad, feels like a cozy pension. British Al is an expert on Split, the surrounding areas and Croatia in general, and organizes group dinners, nights out on the town, and excursions to go horseback riding. Book early, as the 12 beds fill up fast, though Al will help you find a place if he's booked. (☎098 918 29 23; www.hostelsplit.com. Dorms June-Aug. 120kn; Sept.-May 100kn. Cash only.)

Recently renovated **Prenoćište Slavija** ❹, Buvinina 2, in the middle of Stari Grad, has 54 beds in clean, high-ceilinged rooms, all with bath. It's right next to some of the hippest cafes in town. Follow Obala hrvatskog narodnog preporoda to Trg Braće Radića and head right, then right again on Mihovilova Širina. Signs lead up the stairs. (☎ 32 38 40; www.hotelslavija.com. Breakfast included. Reception 24hr. Check-out 11am. Singles 500kn; doubles 650kn; triples 780kn; quads 890kn.)

🍴 FOOD

There are small **supermarkets** inside the Jadrolinija complex across from the bus station (open M-Sa 6am-9pm, Su 7am-9pm) and at Svačićeva 4 (open daily 7am-10pm). If you're in Stari Grad and don't feel like shelling out for a restaurant meal, go to **Okusi Dalmaciju,** Dobrić 14, the market just off of Trg Brače Radić. With your back toward the water, head left through the square and down the street parallel to the waterfront—it will be on your right. (☎ 34 31 85. Open M-Sa 6:30am-9pm, Su 7am-1pm. AmEx/DC/MC/V.) There's also an organic market and bakery, **Kalumela,** Domaldova 7, near the northern edge of Stari Grad, between the northwest corner of Narodni Trg and Kralja Tomislava. It offers soy, tofu, and rice products as well as baked goods. (☎ 34 81 32. Open 8am-9pm. AmEx/DC/MC/V.) The **food court** ❶, Obala Kneza Domagoja 1, between Stari Grad and the stations, has fast food and custom-made sandwiches. (8-15kn. Open daily 8am-midnight.)

▨ **Jugo Restoran,** Uvala Baluni bb (☎ 37 89 00). Facing the water on Obala hrvatskog narodnog preporoda, walk right along the waterfront (10min.) to Branimirova Obala. Veer right at the fork near the marina; go left on the 1st street after the fork and head through the park; it's on the left. This modern restaurant, boasting one of the best views in Split, seduces the beautiful people with excellent seafood, brick-oven pizza, and homemade Slavonian sausage. Entrees 30-200kn. Open daily 11am-midnight. AmEx/MC/V. ❷

▨ **Restoran Adriatic,** Uvala baluni bb (☎ 39 85 60). Just before the crop of trees at the end of the marina. Only slightly more expensive than the average tourist eatery, elegant Adriatic offers a stellar seaside view and an impressive, pizza-less cuisine. Try the *piletina okko* (grilled chicken with ham, eggs and cheese; 60kn) or pasta with shrimp in bean soup, an old fisherman's recipe (55kn). Don't skip dessert, especially their elaborate fruit, ice cream and chocolate Unfinished Strudel *(Nedovršeni Štrudel),* which looks like a pile of hay but tastes nothing like one. With the changing wind, it's best to sit inside during lunch and outside during dinner. Cover 12kn. AmEx/DC/MC/V. ❷

Konoba Varoš, Ban Mladenova 7 (☎ 39 61 38). Facing the water on Obala hrvatskog narodnog preporoda, head right on Varoški Prilaz and then left on Ban Mladenova. A true Dalmatian feast, prepared and served in a den adorned with fishing nets and wine racks. Try the spaghetti with mushrooms (35kn), or prepare your taste buds for something different—steamed octopus (75kn), ostrich steak (80kn), or bread-crumbed frogs (260kn per kg). Open M-F 9am-midnight, Sa-Su noon-midnight. AmEx/DC/MC/V. ❷

Adriana, Obala Hrvatskog narodnog preporoda 8 (☎ 34 00 00). Always packed, this sprawling terrace restaurant stands out among the plethora of waterfront cafes for its ambience and quality. Serves a wide array of hearty Croatian fare ranging from fish dishes (45-320kn) and grilled meats (50-75kn) to enormous pizzas (30-40kn). Try the black cuttlefish risotto (55kn). Cover 5kn. Open daily 8am-midnight. AmEx/MC/V. ❷

👁 SIGHTS

DIOCLETIAN'S PALACE (DIOKLECIJANOVA PALAČA). The eastern half of Split's Stari Grad occupies the one-time fortress and summer residence of the Roman Emperor Diocletian. The colossal stone palace, built between AD 395 and 410, has seen its fair share of empires—and refugees. Having first protected Roman royalty, it later served as sanctuary for Galla Placidia, daughter of Byzantine Emperor Theodosius, and her son Valentinius III, who were dodging the blades of usurpers. In the 7th century, local residents used the fortress to protect themselves from Slavic raids, and they later built their city within its walls. Today, it's a museum of classical and medieval architecture. *(Across from the taxis on Obala hrvatskog narodnog preporoda. Go the right and down into the cool, dark corridor.)*

CELLARS. The city's haunting cellars are located near the entrance to the palace. Nearly two millennia ago, the dark stone passages served as the floor for the emperor's apartments. The central hall runs from Obala hrvatskog narodnog preporoda to the Peristyle and holds booths that sell local crafts. The hall on the left houses an interactive station that gives a wealth of history about the palace and city while entertaining visitors with Renaissance music. Some archaeological finds are displayed in hallways to the left of the entrance. The airier right side is used as a gallery that houses rotating exhibits by local artists, authors, and filmmakers. Every year the palace becomes more complete as more rooms (some right under local residences) are excavated. *(Cellars open M-F 9am-9pm, Sa-Su 10am-6pm. 8kn.)*

CATHEDRAL. The cathedral on the right side of the Peristyle is one of architecture's great ironies: it's one of the oldest Catholic cathedrals in the world but was originally the mausoleum of Diocletian, who was known for his violent persecution of Christians. The cathedral **treasury,** upstairs and to the right, displays 15th-century ecclesiastical garments, delicate 13th-century books, and many silver busts and goblets. Construction began on the adjoining **Bell tower of St. Domnius** (Zvonik Sv. Duje), in the 13th century and took 300 years to complete. The view is incredible, but take a buddy—the climb up the 186 steps can be a bit unnerving. *(Cathedral and tower open daily 8:30am-8pm. Cathedral 5kn. Tower and treasury 5kn.)*

OTHER SIGHTS IN STARI GRAD. Stari Grad is framed on its eastern side by the **Silver Gate** (Srebrna Vrata), which leads to the main open-air market. Outside the north **Golden Gate** (Zlatna Vrata) stands Ivan Meštrović's portrayal of **Gregorius of Nin** (Grgur Ninski), the 10th-century Slavic champion of commoners. The western **Iron Gate** (Željezna Vrata) leads to Narodni trg. Medieval architecture dominates this side of town, where many of the houses are crumbling with age and occasionally drop their stones. **Park Emanuela Victoria,** off Zrinsko-Frankopanska en route to the Archaeological Museum, is a great locale for a daytime stroll. Another nice park with a great view of the ocean and surrounding islands is **Sustipan,** located right at the end of the marina—just look for the trees at the end of the peninsula facing the bus and train stations. A cemetery until WWII, this quiet and peaceful park is perfect for a picnic or a nap while waiting for your ferry, bus, or train out of Split. (Open daily 6am-11pm.)

🏛 MUSEUMS

🏛 MEŠTROVIĆ GALLERY (GALERIJA IVANA MEŠTROVIĆA). The gallery has a comprehensive collection of works by famed Croatian sculptor **Ivan Meštrović** (see **The Visual Arts,** p. 108), and tremendous views of the ocean. The entrance fee includes the **gallery,** housed in a stately villa that the artist built for himself, and the 17th-century **Kaštelet,** decorated with wood carvings depicting New Testament scenes. While all of Meštrović's works are dazzlingly intricate, his marble Roman Pietà (ground floor) and agonized Job (first floor) are particularly impressive. *(Šetaliste Ivana Meštrovica 46. A 25min. walk along the waterfront, or take bus #12 from the stop across from Trg Franje Tudjmana. ☎34 08 00 or 34 08 01. Open June-Aug. Tu-Sa 9am-9pm, Su noon-9pm; Sept.-May Tu-Sa 10am-3pm, Su 9am-4pm. 20kn, students 10kn. English booklet 20kn.)*

ARCHAEOLOGICAL MUSEUM (ARHEOLOŠKI MUZEJ). One of the oldest museums in Croatia, this venerable institution makes fascinating shards of pottery. The beautiful garden is filled with an impressive hodgepodge of Roman statuary and finds from Solana, a nearby ancient town. *(Zrinsko-Frankopanska 25. From the waterfront, follow Marmontova to Trg Gaje Bulata, turn left on Teutina, and take the 1st right. ☎31 87 21. English captions. Open Tu-F 9am-noon and 5-8pm, Sa-Su 9am-1pm. 10kn, students 5kn.)*

CITY MUSEUM (MUZEJ GRADA SPLITA). Houses a minimal selection of artifacts but tells the history of Split in detail. Set beside a scenic stone courtyard, the 15th-century building was designed by **Dalmatinac,** architect of Šibenik's Cathedral. *(Papalićeva 1. From the Golden Gate, enter Stari Grad and turn left on Papalićeva. ☎36 01 71; www.mgst.net. English placards. Open Tu-F 9am-9pm, Sa-Su 10am-4pm. 10kn, students 5kn.)*

ETHNOGRAPHIC MUSEUM (ETNOGRAFSKI MUZEJ). This museum displays artifacts of Croatia's domestic and ceremonial life in times past and is quite interesting if you enjoy intricate old clothing. *(Narodni trg 1. ☎34 41 64; www.et-mu-st.com. Open M-F 9am-2pm and 5-8pm, Sa 10am-1pm. 10kn, students 5kn.)*

🏖 🎵 BEACHES AND ENTERTAINMENT

The rocky cliffs, wide green hills, and pebbly beaches on the western end of Split's peninsula make up 100-year-old **City Park Marjan,** a great expanse for walking or jogging. From Obala hrvatskog narodnog preporoda, face the water and head right (15min.). Paths are indicated on the map; you can find your own way, but watch for signs marking trails that lead to private lands. The closest beach to downtown Split is crowded **Bačvice,** a favorite among nocturnal skinny-dippers. Bačvice is the starting point of a strip of popular bars along the waterfront. In early May, Split honors its patron saint, St. Domnius, with festivities in Stari Grad, which include Dalmatian *klapa* singers, folk dancing, and a lot of bingo. From mid-July to mid-August, Split hosts an annual **Summer Festival.** The region's best artists and international guests perform ballets, operas, plays, and classical concerts in the town's churches and ruins. (Info and ticket reservations ☎36 30 14. Tickets 754-215kn.)

🎵 NIGHTLIFE

Bačvice is where all the clubs are—tons of bars and clubs sit side by side, with all kinds of music, in a two-story complex. Head away from Stari Grad, past the bus and train stations, and continue left along the water (after crossing the bridge over the train tracks) and down the hill; just follow the crowds and the noise. In Stari Grad, the popular bars for young people are just off **Trg Brače Radić.** Head toward the Slavija Hotel and continue up the stairs to find bar after bar of local hipsters.

▨ Ghetto, Dosud 10 (☎36 00 50), at the top of stairs, off Brače Radić. This colorful club features an eccentric decor of neon, shaggy carpet, and beanbags. Cool, open courtyard. DJs spin funk and lounge. Open M-Sa 10am-2am; in winter 10am-midnight. Cash only.

Tropic Club Equador, Kupalište Bačvice bb (☎32 35 71). Just past Bačvice beach. 2nd fl. of the club complex. Dancing the rumba under the stars on the Latin-themed terrace bar might be easier after a few tropical cocktails (27-47kn). Open daily 9am-3am.

O'Hara's, Uvala Zenja 3 (☎51 94 92). Follow the waterfront past Tropic Club Equador for another 20min. 2 floors of raging techno. Cover 30kn. Open Th-Su 11pm-late.

Cafe Favola, Trg Brače Radić 1. (☎34 48 48). A chic, laid-back bar that lures both locals and tourists with views of one of the city's quieter but most beautiful squares. *Prošek* 10kn. Open daily 7am-midnight.

Jazz Planet, Grgura Ninskoga 3 (☎34 76 99). Hidden on a tiny but lively square opposite the City Museum, Jazz Planet has comfy chairs outside and a mellow yellow color scheme inside that mixes well with jazz and beer. Occasional live music. Guinness 25kn per 0.5L, *Bavaria* 14kn per 0.25L. Open M-Th and Su 1pm-midnight, F-Sa 8am-2am.

BRAČ ISLAND: BOL   ☎(0)21

Central Dalmatia's largest island, Brač (brach) is an ocean-lover's paradise. But it has more to offer than just its location: the churches, galleries, nightlife, and water sports in its town, Bol (pop. 1500), will keep loungers and adventures occupied for days. Most visitors come here for Zlatni rat (golden horn), a sleepy picturesque peninsula of smooth white pebble beach just a short walk from the town center.

⟅ TRANSPORTATION. The **ferry** from **Split** docks at **Supetar** (1hr.; July-Aug. 13-20 per day, Sept.-June 7 per day; 25kn). From there, take a **bus** to **Bol** (1hr., 9 per day, 15kn). The last bus back to the ferry leaves at 7pm; the last ferry to Split leaves at 10:15pm (June-Aug.) or 8:30pm (Sept.-May). A bus also departs to and from **Zagreb** (8¾hr., 1 per day, 185kn). The bus station is a 7min. walk away from the ferry dock at Supetar. Alternatively, a **catamaran** runs to Bol from **Split.** (☎63 56 38. 40min. M-Sa leaves Bol 6:30am, Split 4pm; Su 7:30am/4pm. 22kn. Buy tickets on board.)

⬛⛏ ORIENTATION AND PRACTICAL INFORMATION. Bol is organized around a waterfront of many names. At the bus stop and marina, the waterfront is called **Obala Vladimira Nazora.** Left of the bus station (facing the water) it becomes **Riva,** then **Frane Radića,** then **Porat bolskih pomorca.** To the right it's **Put Zlatnog Rata.** Facing the sea on the far side of the small marina, walk 5min. to the left of the bus station to reach the **tourist office,** Porat bolskih pomorca bb. It dispenses a free Bol guide and a large selection of **free maps.** (☎63 56 38; www.bol.hr. Open M-Sa 8:30am-2pm and 5-9pm, Su 9am-1pm.) Facing the water, walk right from the bus station to reach the walkway, Put Zlatnog Rata, which leads to the larger hotels, Zlatni rat, and other small beaches along the way. **Splitska Banka,** Radića 16 (☎63 51 55) **exchanges currency** at no commission. A 24hr. **ATM** sits outside. **Adria Tours,** Obala Vladimira Nazora 28, to the right of the bus station facing the water, **rents scooters** (200kn per day) and **cars** (500kn per day, unlimited km). The Adria office also books rooms and organizes excursions (70-190kn) to nearby islands. There's a **pharmacy** and **medical clinic** at Porat bolskih pomorca bb. (☎63 59 87. Open M-Sa 7:30am-9pm, Su 8am-noon.) **M@3X,** on Rudina a few doors down from Aqvarius, has fast and cheap **Internet.** (www.orca-sport.com/caffe. 25kn for 1st hr., 20kn per hr. thereafter. Open daily 9:30am-11:30pm.) The **post office,** Uz Pjacu 5, has **telephones** outside. (☎63 56 78. Open M-Sa 7:30am-9pm.) **Postal Code:** 21420.

⌐⊡ ACCOMMODATIONS AND FOOD. If the locals are all at the beach, leaving no one at the ferry dock or bus station to offer you a room, **Adria Tours** (see above) can help. (☎63 59 66; www.adria-bol.hr. Open daily 8am-9pm. July-Aug. 60-115kn per person; singles 105-170kn. Tax 10kn. 20% surcharge for stays under 4 nights.) Note that finding a single room can be very difficult in Brač; call ahead or you may have to splurge on a double. Adria Tours offers special deals on local hotel rooms from €75. The extravagant **Hotel Kaštil ❺,** Frane Radica 1, is housed in a baroque manor that once served as a silk and silver trading post, and has small but spotless rooms with striking views of Hvar Island. All rooms have TVs, A/C, phones, and bathrooms. (☎63 59 95; www.kastil.hr. Breakfast buffet included. Singles 287-620kn; doubles 402-899kn. Rates vary by season.) There are five **campgrounds** around Bol; the largest is **Kito ❶,** Bračka bb, on the main road into town. (☎63 55 51. Open May-Sept. 60kn per person, tent and tax included.)

Konoba Gušt ❷, Frane Radića 14, offers shaded respite among hanging fishing gear, quirky photos, and local diners, and serves an array of fresh seafood. (☎ 63 59 11. Entrees 40-150kn. Open daily noon-2am.) Drawing flocks of locals and tourists to its hearty portions and picture perfect terrace view, **Taverna Riva ❸**, Trg Brace Radica 5, serves savory fish and meat, such as grilled tuna (75kn), alongside traditional Croatian pastas and risottos. (☎ 63 52 36; www.riva-bol.com. Entrees 42-160kn. Cover 10kn. Open daily 11am-3pm and 6-11pm. AmEx/MC/V.) If you're tired of bringing picnic lunches to the beach, the cafeteria **Plaža Zlatni Rat ❶**, under the pines off the famous pebble beach, is the answer to paper bags and pâté. (☎ 63 52 22. Salads and grilled specialties 20-50kn. Open daily 8am-6pm.) **Pizzeria Topolino ❶**, Riva 2, on the waterfront in the town center, has tasty pizza and pasta (25-50kn), traditional Croatian meat dishes (55-75kn), and an impressive selection of salads. (☎ 63 57 67. Salads 20-40kn. Open daily 8am-2am.) For a quick and tasty grilled sandwich, try **Mancini ❶**, Rudina 26, located right across (and slightly to the left) from the bus station on the waterfront. Try the spiced salami for 20kn. (Drinks 12-20kn. Sandwiches 15-25kn. Burgers 25kn. Open 11am-4am. Cash only.) **Supermarket KERUM,** on Uz Pjacu up the hill from the post office, has 10-12kn sandwiches. (☎ 71 83 00. Open M-Sa 6am-10pm, Su 6:30am-10pm.) **Konzum,** Riva bb (☎ 71 83 00), located right on the waterfront, tucked in on the corner of Uz Pjacu, the street that leads to the post office, has a good selection and reasonable prices.

⑥ 🔊 SIGHTS AND ENTERTAINMENT. The **free map** distributed by the tourist office shows all the town's sights, the most important of which is the 1475 **Dominican Monastery,** located on the eastern tip of Bol. Facing the water, walk left for 15min. beyond the tourist office. The highlight of the monastery is Tintoretto's altar painting of the **Madonna with Child.** Apparently concerned they'd need a refund, the monks kept the masterpiece's invoice, which is on display in the **museum,** among other artifacts of local history. (☎ 77 80 02. Museum and monastery open daily 10am-noon and 5-7pm. 10kn. Dress appropriately.) The **Dešković Gallery,** on Porat bolskih pomorca, behind the pharmacy, exhibits contemporary Croatian art in a small, 17th-century Baroque mansion. (Open daily 6-10pm. 5kn.) More art comes to town during **Bol Cultural Summer** (Bolsko Kulturno Ljeto), which runs throughout July and August and features a variety of classical and folk music concerts. (Tickets free-20kn, depending on event.) The English-speaking staff at **Big Blue Sport,** Podan Glavice 2, on the way to Zlatni rat, organizes an array of watersports. Back on land, they also offer beach volleyball and rent **bikes.** (☎ 098 21 24 19; www.big-blue-sport.hr. Beach volleyball 50kn per hr. Bikes 15kn per hr., 70kn per day. Open daily 9am-7pm.) If you crave velocity, **waterskiing** (200kn, with lesson 300kn), **windsurfing** (8hr. course 800kn; rentals 360kn per day, 280kn per ½-day) and **banana boat rides** (50kn per person, 3-person min.) are available through **Nautic Center Bol.** (☎ 63 53 67; www.nautic-center-bol.com. Walk-ins welcome. Open 9am-6pm.) **Diving Center Dolphin,** 50m down the waterfront from Big Blue Sport, offers a one-day dive with equipment rental (€30), "discovery" intro dives (€35), and a five-day PADI certification course (€260). Book at least one day early. (☎ 091 250 80 33; www.diving-dolphin.com. Open 9am-7pm. Cash only.) **Boat rentals** are available through Adria Tours (see above) and along the waterfront past the bus station. The **outdoor cinema,** opposite the bus station, has nightly showings, weather permitting. (Shows 8:30-11pm. Tickets 15-18kn.)

🔊 NIGHTLIFE. Bol's awe-inspiring natural beauty shines even brighter once the sun goes down. Soak in the calm sea under the clear starry sky near one of the small piers along **Put Zlatnog Rata,** or head to the center of town for a surprisingly lively night scene. **Varadero,** at the base of Hotel Kaštil, has the hippest terrace in town, complete with wicker couches, tiki torches, and ambient house. It's the per-

CROATIA

fect place to start the morning with a frothy cappuccino (9kn) or cap off the night with a delicious cocktail. (Mixed drinks 35-50kn. Open daily 9am-1am.) To get out of Stari Grad, go to ▨**Bolero,** Put Zlatnog Rata bb or Promenada bb, located just past Big Blue Sports if you're heading away from Stari Grad. (Open 8am-2am. Cash only.) Join a friendly crowd of vacationing Croatian youths and a live DJ at **Aquarius,** which starts at Rudina 26 and spills over across the street to an outdoor terrace on Radića 8, overlooking the beach. (☎63 58 03. Open May-Sept. daily 9am-1am; Oct.-Apr. M-Th and Su 9am-11pm, F-Sa 9am-midnight. Cash only.)

HVAR ISLAND   ☎(0)21

This narrow, 88km long island affords breathtaking views of the mainland mountains from its high, rugged hills. A favorite summer getaway for chic urbanites and yacht-bound high rollers, the town plays host to sun-worshippers from mid-July through August. Fortunately, the nearby Pakleni Otoci (Hellish Islands) provide enough beach for everyone. Many resort hotels actually guarantee the weather—if the temperature dips too low or it rains long enough, rooms are on the house.

☞ TRANSPORTATION. Ferries make the trip from **Split** to Hvar's **Stari Grad** (Old Town; 2hr.; June 21-Sept. 9 M-Th 3 per day, F-Su 5 per day; 32kn, with car 216kn). From there, **buses** scheduled around the ferry take passengers to **Hvar Town** (25min., 7 per day, 15kn). Alternatively, head straight from Split to Hvar Town: there's a fast **catamaran** in the morning (1 hr., 1 per day, 32kn) in addition to a regular ferry (2hr., 2 per day, 32kn). A bus runs to Hvar Town from **Jelsa** (40min.; M-Sa 6 per day, Su 5 per day; 19kn), from which **taxi boats** run every morning at 9am to Bol on Brač Island (40-50kn). To reach the **bus station,** walk through Trg Sv. Stjepana from the marina and then left of the church; the station is on your left. **Jadrolinija,** Riva bb, on the left tip of the waterfront, sells ferry tickets. (☎74 11 32. Open M-Sa 5:30am-1pm and 3-8pm; Su 8-9am, noon-1pm, and 3-4pm. Opening hours vary according to ferry schedule.) **Pelegrini Tours,** Riva bb, located next to the post office, runs a catamaran between Hvar and **Komiža** for daytrips during the summer (1½hr., 1 per wk., round-trip 160kn). Pelegrini also **rents cars** (513kn per day) in the summer. (☎74 27 43; pelegrini@inet.hr. Open daily 7am-1pm and 5-9pm.)

◧ ⑦ ORIENTATION AND PRACTICAL INFORMATION. Hvar Town has virtually no street names and even fewer signs. The main square, **Trg Sv. Stjepana,** directly below the bus station by the waterfront, is the one place graced with a name. Facing the sea from the main square, take a left along the waterfront to reach the **tourist office, bank,** and **ferry terminal;** a right leads to the major hotels and beaches. The tourist office, **Turistička Zajednica,** Trg Sv. Stjepana 16, is on the corner of the main square closest to the water. The smiling staff has detailed **maps** of the island (20kn) and bus schedules. (☎74 10 59; www.tzhvar.hr. Open daily 8am-10pm; in low season 8:30am-noon.) **Splitska Banka,** Riva 4, offers **Western Union** services, **exchanges currency** for no commission, and cashes **traveler's checks** for 1% commission. (Open M-F 8am-2:30pm and 6-8pm, Sa 8-noon.) There's an **ATM** outside the bank and an AmEx/MC **ATM** across the harbor in front of **Privredna Banka Zagreb,** Riva bb. **Store luggage** at the bus station (*garderoba;* 10kn per hr., 60kn per 12-24hr.), which also has **restrooms** (3kn), **showers** (20kn), and a **laundromat** (wash 50kn per 30min., dry 15kn; detergent 5kn). A well-stocked **pharmacy** is at Trg Sv. Stjepana. (☎74 10 02. Open M-F 8am-9pm, Sa 8am-1pm and 6-9pm, Su 9am-noon. AmEx/DC/MC/V.) **Internet Club Luka Rent,** at Riva bb, has Internet access and offers a variety of rentals. (☎74 29 46; www.lukarent.com. Internet 30kn per hr. Bikes 20kn per hr., 70kn per day. Scooters 70-80/250-300kn. Boats 300-1700kn per day, 6-person max. AmEx/DC/MC/V.) Alternatively, there's **Cima,** Dolac bb. From the bus station, veer left away from Trg Sv. Stjepana, cross the street, and look for a blue sign with dolphins. (☎71 87 52. 30kn per hr. Open daily 9am-2pm and 5-11pm.) The **post office** is on Riva just past Splitska Banka, and has **phones, Western Union** services and **Poste Restante.** (☎74 24 13. Open M-Sa 7:30 am-9pm.) **Postal Code:** 21450.

⚏❑ ACCOMMODATIONS AND FOOD. As in other Croatian resort towns, the only budget accommodations are **private rooms,** and even these are expensive. **Pelegrini Tours,** located next to the post office, can make arrangements. (July 31-Aug. 28 doubles 269-360kn; July 3-31 and Aug. 28-Sept. 11 277kn; May 1-July 3 and Sept. 12-Oct. 2 219kn; in low season 146kn. Tax and registration 4.50-7kn. 30% surcharge for stays under 3 nights.) Kind **Luka Visković,** Lućica bb, has a three-story house with doubles, some with private baths, and a shared kitchen, located just minutes from Hvar Town. If you call ahead of time, he may even come pick you up at Stari Grad from the ferry dock; if he's booked, he might help you find somewhere else to stay. (☎74 21 18, mobile 091 734 72 30. July 100-120kn per person; Aug. 150-200kn per person. Cash only.) If the agencies can't help, check with the tourist office. Settle the price with your host upon arrival. Ask the tourist office about the going rate, then bargain around that. Many locals hang around the bus station offering rooms for less, and some even make the trip to Stari Grad to meet ferries and offer you a ride. If all else fails, look for *sobe* (room) signs down the waterfront from the main square. However, if resort-style luxury is more your taste, head to the newly renovated **Hotel Adriatic ❺,** whose spacious rooms have views of the marina. From the ferry stop, facing the water, turn right and follow the bay as it curves. (☎74 10 24. All meals included. Rooms €33-42. Taxes 4.50-7kn. 30% more for stays under 3 days. AmEx/MC/V.)

Overpriced pizza and pasta restaurants line the waterfront and the square. For a cheaper and better meal, head one block up the steps leading from the main square to the fortress to visit ▨**Luna ❷.** On the gorgeous rooftop terrace, you'll dine on excellent fish, poultry, and meat standards. Try the fettucine with salmon (59kn) for a flavorful treat. (☎74 86 95. Entrees 50-120kn. Cover 8kn. Open daily noon-3pm and 6pm-midnight). For a splurge, **Macondo ❹,** one street above Luna, transforms a marble alleyway into a seafood connoisseur's dream. Elegant ambience and gourmet fish dishes (70-240kn), such as lobster risotto (140kn) keep this upscale bistro consistently packed. (☎74 28 50. Open daily noon-2pm and 6pm-midnight). For a more casual meal, dine with a spirited local crowd under hanging lanterns and grapevines at **Alviz ❷,** opposite the bus station. Hearty grilled meats (50-85kn) alongside vegetable lasagna (40kn) and delicious salads (20-35kn) satisfy carnivores and vegetarians alike. (☎74 27 97. Open daily 6pm-midnight.) A small **open-air market** between the bus station and the main square sells primarily fruits and vegetables. (Open daily 7am-8pm.) There's also a large **Konzum** at Dolac bb, next to the open-air market and bus station, which stocks anything you'll need. (☎77 82 30. Open daily 7am-10pm. AmEx/DC/MC/V.) The **Studenac supermarket,** on Trg Sv. Stjepana is small but well stocked. (Open M-Sa 7am-10pm, Su 7am- 9pm.)

◪ SIGHTS. The stairs to the right of the square (as you face the sea) lead to a 13th-century **Venetian fortress,** with amazing views of the town and surrounding islands. Although Turkish attacks weakened the fortress, the lightning bolt that struck the gunpowder room proved even more devastating. (Open daily 8am-midnight. 10kn.) Inside, you'll find a tiny **marine archaeological collection** (hidroarheološka zbirka) displaying Greek and Byzantine relics from shipwrecked boats. (Open daily 10am-4pm. Admission included in fortress ticket.) The **Gallery Arsenal,** up the stairs next to the tourist office, is worth a look. It features rotating exhibits by local artists. (☎74 10 09. Open daily 10am-noon and 8-11pm. 10kn.) Stop by the **Last Supper Collection** in the **Franciscan monastery,** down Riva past the ferry terminal, which includes another famous *Last Supper*, an oil-painting by Matteo Ignoli. (☎74 11 23. Open M-Sa 10am-noon and 5-6pm. 15kn, students 10kn.)

NIGHTLIFE AND FESTIVALS. The most crowded bars line the waterfront. For something smaller and more intimate, head to **Caffe Bar Jazz**, Burak bb, on a side street uphill from Splitska Banka. The bar's funky footstools, Technicolor interior, inexpensive drinks, and local flavor help revive the sun-weary psyche for a nocturnal second wind. (Vodka and juice 15kn. Open daily 8pm-2am.) For an authentic taste of Dalmatia, **Konoba Katarina**, Groda bb, on the steps to the fortress, offers delicious homemade sweet and dry wines in a wood-paneled cellar. Samples abound, and the decadent dessert wine *prosek* is so good you might be tempted to take a bottle home. (Wine 35-70kn. Open daily 10am-1pm and 6pm-midnight.) At the end of Riva past the Jadrolinija office, **Carpe Diem** has loud live DJs and the best outdoor terrace on the waterfront, always busy with hip and hot 20-somethings. Jumpstart a vigorous day of sunbathing with a delicious cappuccino (25kn) or fruit smoothie. (Beer 25-30kn. Mixed drinks 55-75kn. Open daily 9am-2am.) Walk all the way around to the opposite side of the marina and up the garden path on your right to get to the local disco **Veneranda,** which has dancing indoors and outside around a big fountain that invites wading. (Open daily 10pm-5am.) Earlier in the evenings, this same space functions as an **open-air cinema.** Look for posters advertising what's playing. (Tickets 15-20kn.)

During the **Days of Theater** in the last two weeks of May, Hvar celebrates the stage above the Arsenal in one of Europe's oldest **community theaters,** dating from 1612. The Franciscan monastery and the theater host outdoor drama performances during the **Hvar Summer Festival.** (Mid-June to early Oct. Performances 30-50kn.) For 10 days each September, the monastery hosts the **Shakespeare Days Festival,** which includes performances and workshops dedicated to the Bard. Inquire at the tourist office (see above) for more info.

BEACHES AND ISLANDS. To enjoy some of the Adriatic's clearest waters, you'll have to brave the loud, crowded **beaches.** Quieter beaches as well as terraced rock sunbathing and swimming areas are a 20min. walk to the left down the waterfront. Or, head to **Jevolim, Ždrilca,** and **Palmižana,** known collectively as the **Hellish Islands** (Pakleni Otoci). The last is home to **Palmižana beach,** which has waterside restaurants, rocks for tanning, sparse sand, and an area frequented by nude bathers at the far tip of the cove. **Taxi boats** run between the islands. (Every 30min. 10am-6:30pm, round-trip 20-40kn.)

KORČULA ISLAND ☎(0)20

Korčula (KOHR-choo-lah) got its name from the Greek words *kerkyra melaina* (black woods) because of the dark macchia thickets and woods that cover the island. Korčula Town (pop. 4000) faces the stunning mountains of the Croatian mainland, just a short ferry trip away. A healthy crop of tourists has made it significantly more developed than its neighbors Vis and Mljet, while weekly sword dances in the summer, a superb music scene, and friendly locals combine to create one of the most exciting atmospheres along the coast.

TRANSPORTATION. Korčula is one of the few islands served by buses (which board a ferry to the island). The **bus station** is at Porat bb. (☎71 12 16. Ticket window open M-Sa 6:30-9am, 9:30am-4pm, and 4:30-7pm; Su 2-7pm.) **Buses** run to: **Dubrovnik** (3½hr., 2 per day, 77kn); **Split** (5hr., 1 per day, 90kn); **Zagreb** (11-13hr., 1 per day, 209kn) via **Knin** or **Zadar; Sarajevo, BOS** (6½hr., 4 per wk., 145kn). For **ferry info** and tickets, check the **Jadrolinija** office, 20m toward Stari Grad (Old Town) from the ferry landing. (☎71 54 10. Open M-F 5:30am-7pm, Sa-Su 7:30am-7:30pm.) **Ferries** run from Korčula Town to **Dubrovnik** (3½hr., 5 per wk., 79kn), **Hvar** (3hr., 1-2 per day, 79kn), and **Split** (5hr., 1 per day, 97kn). Ferries arrive in **Korčula Town** or in

Vela Luka on the opposite side of the island. A bus meets ferries for the latter and transports you to Korčula Town (1hr.; 5 per day; 30kn, plus 10kn for each bag stored). The most convenient option is to go directly to Korčula Town, either from Split or Dubrovnik, as the buses from Vela Luka are often overcrowded. **Marko Polo** also runs a **catamaran** that goes directly from Korčula Town to Hvar and Split (2 or 3hr., respectively; 6am; 55kn.) For a **taxi**, call ☎71 54 52.

■**ĭ ORIENTATION AND PRACTICAL INFORMATION.** The town is situated beside the sea on the end of the island. **Stari Grad** (Old Town) was built on a small oval peninsula, and its streets are arranged in a herringbone pattern. Outside the city walls, medieval, Baroque, and modern houses blend together, tapering off into hotels farther down the coastline. Street addresses are rare, but the town is small and easily navigable. The **tourist office, Turistička Zajednica,** Obala Dr. Franje Tudjmana 6, is on the opposite side of the peninsula from the bus and ferry terminals. To get there, face the water and walk left, following the main street as it curves away from the marina and passing the Jadrolinija office along the way. When you reach the water on the other side, head right along the water toward the peninsula to Hotel Korčula; the office is just before the hotel in a glass building. (Open M-Sa 8am-3pm and 4-8pm, Su 9am-1pm.) **Splitska Banka,** in front of the stairs to Stari Grad, **exchanges currency** for no commission, cashes **traveler's checks** for 2% commission, gives **cash advances,** and offers **Western Union** services. (☎71 10 52. Open M-F 8am-4pm, Sa 8am-noon.) There is a 24hr. MC/V **ATM** outside Splitska Banka and another around the corner toward Stari Grad. The **pharmacy,** Trg Kralja Tomislava bb, is at the foot of the Stari Grad stairs. (☎71 10 57. Open M-F 7am-8pm, Sa 7am-noon and 6-8pm, Su 9-11am. AmEx/MC/V.) For fast Internet access, a good choice is **Tino Computers,** Pr. Tri Sulara 9, before Stari Grad, on a little street heading away from the marina. (☎71 60 93. 25kn per hr.; 10kn min. Open daily 9am-midnight.) **Rent-a-Dir,** next door to Marko Polo, rents **cars** (296kn per day; €100 deposit), **scooters** (185-250kn per day; 50kn deposit), and **boats.** (☎71 19

MARKO! POLO! Wondering why Marko Polo's name is dropped so much here? While evidence is sketchy at best, locals believe the explorer was born in Korčula, pointing to records showing that the shipbuilding Polo family settled in the area in the 13th century. Whatever you believe, you can visit the remains of what is alleged to be Marko Polo's house, near the Town Museum (see **Sights**), and appreciate the festival Korčula throws in his honor in early July.

08. 10-person boat 520-1850kn per day; boat license required. Open daily 9am-8pm.) The **post office** is just to the right of the pharmacy (facing the stairs) at Trg Kralja Tomislava. It has **Poste Restante, telephones,** and **currency exchange** for 1.5% commission. (☎71 11 32. Open M-Sa 7:30am-9pm.) **Postal Code:** 20260.

∫∟ ACCOMMODATIONS AND FOOD. Korčula Town's only hostel, ■**The Korčula Backpacker,** Hrvatske Bratske Zajednice 6, provides a great seaside location and a very social atmosphere. Manager Zlatko, a young South-African-born Croatian, provides a wealth of info on the area. Book ahead or look out for someone in a cowboy hat and holding a sign at the bus station. (☎098 997 63 53; www.thekorculabackpacker.blogspot.com. 4-, 6-, or 10-bed dorms 90kn.) If you're seeking peace and quiet, **Marko Polo ❶,** Biline 5, on the waterfront where the ferries dock, will arrange private accommodation for you. (☎71 54 00; www.korcula.com. Open daily 8am-9pm. July 12-Aug. 23 singles 188kn; doubles 263kn; triples 330kn. May 17-July 11 and Aug. 24-Sept. 30 150/210/285kn. Oct.-May 16 105/150/210kn. 30% more for stays under 3 nights.) Or, look for *sobe* (room) signs uphill from the bus station away from Stari Grad or on the road to Hotel Park (see below). While not exactly budget, **Hotel Park ❸,** Šetalište, F. Kršinića 102, offers simple, functional rooms near the beach, some with balconies and marina views. From the bus station, walk away from Stari Grad along the waterfront and follow the signs. (☎72 62 86; marketing@htp-korcula.hr. Breakfast included. July and Aug. singles 532-628kn; doubles 760-912kn. Sept. and June 319-395/608-760kn. Jan. and May 319-395/456-608kn.) Camping is available farther out at **Autocamp Kalac ❶**, with a sandy beach and nice views of the mainland across the water. A bus (10min., 1 per hr., 13kn) runs to the camp from the station. (☎71 11 82. Reception daily 7am-10pm. 40kn per person, 35kn per tent. Tourist tax 7.5kn.)

Tired of Croatian seafood and Italian pastas and pizzas? Try ▧**Fresh ❶**, the wrap and smoothie stand right next to the bus station. (☎091 896 75 09. Smoothies 20kn. Sangria 25kn per bucket. Wraps 20-25kn. Open daily 8am-2am. Cash only.) At ▧**Adio Mare ❷**, Marko Polo bb, next to Marko Polo's house, local specialties like *korčulanska pasticada* (beef stewed in vegetables and plum sauce with dumplings; 70kn) or *Ražnjic Adio Mare* (mixed meats skewered with apples, onions, and bacon; 60kn) draw crowds. (☎71 12 53. Entrees 40-80kn. Open M-Sa 5:30pm-midnight, Su 6pm-midnight.) Up the double staircase to the right of the tourist office, **Pizzeria Agava ❶**, Cvit. Bokšic 6, offers tasty Italian fare with huge, share-worthy portions. (Pizzas 34-74kn. Pasta 29-36kn. Open daily 9am-2pm and 6pm-2am.) Restaurants in Korčula are expensive and tourist-driven. There is a string of nearly identical *konoba* overlooking the bay down the road from Gaudi (see **Entertainment and Nightlife**). They serve the usual assortment of seafood and pasta, but you'll pay for the view. The frugal should try **Konzum** supermarket (open M-Sa 6:30am-9pm, Su 7am-9pm), by the bus station and next to Marko Polo; and the open-air **produce market** to the right of the Stari Grad stairs (open daily 6am-9pm).

◪ **SIGHTS.** Korčula's grandest tribute to its patron, **St. Mark's Cathedral** (Katedrala Sv. Marka), sits at the highest point of the Stari Grad peninsula. Planning began in the 14th century, inspired by the founding of the Korčula Bishopric, but construction wasn't completed until 1525. The Gothic-Renaissance cathedral is complemented by the older **bell tower.** (Open daily 9am-9pm. Services M-Sa 6:30pm; Su 7, 9:30am, 6:30pm. Dress appropriately.) The **Abbey Treasury of St. Mark** (Opatska Riznica Sv. Marka), next to the cathedral, houses a large collection of 12th-century manuscripts, Renaissance and Baroque drawings, religious robes, and coins. (Open M-Sa 9am-10pm. 15kn.) The **Town Museum** (Gradski Muzej) is opposite the treasury in the Renaissance Gabrielis Palace and displays nearly five millennia of Korčula's culture, including everything from 5000-year-old knives to a 19th-century wedding dress. (Open M-Sa 10am-9pm. 10kn, students 5kn.)

▨▧ **NIGHTLIFE AND FESTIVALS.** The most popular bar these days is thatched-roof **Dos Locos**, Šet. F. Kršinića 14, located right next to the bus station. For a club-like vibe, try **Gaudi**. The cafe outside has gorgeous views, but the real action happens inside the stone cocoon of sound and colored lights behind it. Go up the ramp to the right of the steps that lead to Stari Grad (toward the cannon) and it will be on your left. (Beer 12-18kn. Nightclub open daily 11pm-4am.)

Carnival celebrations, including weekly masked balls *(maškare)*, are held from Epiphany to Ash Wednesday. (Free.) The beginning of July is dedicated to the **Marco Polo Festival.** Events include folk entertainment and a grand reconstruction of the famous 1298 naval battle in the Pelješac channel between Korčula and the mainland in which Signore Polo and the forces of Venetian Korčula clashed with Genoa's navy.

DUBROVNIK ☎(0)20

Lord Byron considered Dubrovnik (du-BROV-nik; pop. 43,770) "the pearl of the Adriatic," and George Bernard Shaw knew it as "Paradise on Earth." Although it would be hard for any locale to live up to such adulation, a stroll along the sun-kissed white marble of the vibrant Old Town soon reveals why this Venetian city merits such praise. Although ravaged by war in 1991 and 1992, Dubrovnik appears miraculously scarless; only close inspection reveals the occasional bullet hole. For centuries, the azure waters, golden sunsets, and Italian marble of this Adriatic gem have enchanted visitors, who are beginning to return. You'd be smart to join them.

⌐ TRANSPORTATION

Flights: Dubrovnik Airport Ćilipi (DBV; ☎ 77 33 77) serves national and European destinations. 30kn bus to airport from main station leaves 1½hr. before each flight. **Croatia Airlines,** Brsalje 9 (☎41 37 76 or 41 37 77), just outside the Stari Grad (Old Town) gate (Pile). Open M-F 8am-4pm, Sa 9am-noon.

Buses: Pt. Republike 19 (☎35 70 88). To get to Stari Grad, keep your back to the bus station and turn left onto Ante Starčevića. Follow this road uphill to the Pile Gate (25min.). Local buses running to Stari Grad make several stops along Ante Starčevića before reaching Pile. To: **Rijeka** (12hr., 4 per day, 345kn); **Split** (4½hr., 16 per day, 125kn); **Zadar** (8hr., 8 per day, 220kn); **Zagreb** (11hr., 8 per day, 180kn); **Frankfurt, GER** (27hr., 2 per wk., 800kn); **Ljubljana, SLN** (14hr., 1 per day, 380kn); **Medugorje, BOS** (2½hr., 1 per day, 77kn); **Mostar, BOS** (3hr., 2 per day, 77kn); **Sarajevo, BOS** (6hr., 1 per day, 157kn); **Trieste, ITA** (15hr., 1 per day, 340kn).

Dubrovnik

▲ ACCOMMODATIONS
Apartmani Burum, 3
Autocamp Solitudo, 9
Begović Boarding House, 7
Hotel Zagreb, 6
Youth Hostel (HI), 1

🍴 FOOD
Buffet Kamenice, 11
Konoba Atlantic, 5
Lokarda Peskarija, 12
Mea Culpa, 9

🍸 NIGHTLIFE
Buža, 13
Club Roxy, 2
EastWest Cocktail and
Dance Bar, 4
Hemingway's, 13
Latino Club Fuego, 8
Jazz Cafe Troubador, 13

CROATIA

Ferries: Jadrolinija, Obala S. Radića 40 (☎41 80 00; www.jadrolinija.tel.hr/jadrolinija). Open M-Tu and Th 8am-8pm, W and F 8am-8pm and 9-11pm, Sa 8am-2pm and 7-8pm, Su 8-10am and 7-8:30pm. The ferry terminal is opposite the Jadrolinija office. Face away from the bus station and go left; when the road forks, bear right (5min.). To get to Stari Grad, with your back to the ferry dock, walk left 50m along Gruška obala to the bus stop and take bus #1a, 1b, or 3 to the last stop. To: **Korčula** (4hr., 4 per wk., 79kn); **Rijeka** (22hr., 2 per wk., 233kn); **Sobra** (2hr., 2 per day, 35kn); **Split** (8hr., 4 per day, 115 kn); **Zadar** (16hr., 1 per wk., 157kn); **Bari, ITA** (9hr., 5 per wk., 329kn).

Public Transportation: (☎35 70 20). All **buses** except #5, 7, and 8 go to Stari Grad's Pile Gate. Tickets 8kn at kiosks, 10kn from the driver. Exact change required except on buses #1a and 1b. The driver checks everyone's ticket upon boarding.

Taxis: Radio Taxi Dubrovnik (from bus station ☎35 70 44, from Pile Gate 42 43 43). 25kn base, 8kn per km. 50kn from the bus station to Stari Grad. 200kn to the airport.

■✳🛈 ORIENTATION AND PRACTICAL INFORMATION

The walled **Stari Grad** (Old Town) is the city's cultural, historical, and commercial center. Its main street, called both **Placa** and **Stradun**, runs from the **Pile Gate,** the official entrance to Stari Grad, to the **Old Port** at the opposite tip of the peninsula. Outside the city walls, the main traffic arteries, **Pt. Republike** and **Ante Starčevića,** sandwich the **bus station** from the front and rear, respectively, merge into Ante Starčevića, and end at the Pile Gate. The new **ferry terminal** in Gruž is a 15min. bus ride from Stari Grad. To the west of Stari Grad, two hilly peninsulas—**Babin Kuk** and **Lapad**—are home to modern settlements, sand beaches, and hotels.

 Do not explore the beautiful bare mountains rising above Dubrovnik—these peaks may still harbor concealed **landmines.**

Tourist Offices:

Tourist Board, Ante Starčevića 7 (☎42 75 91; ured.pile@tzdubrovnik.hr). From the bus stop at Pile Gate, take Ante Starčevića away from Stari Grad; the office is on your left. Distributes **free maps** and offers inexpensive **Internet** (5kn per 15min). Ask for the free *Dubrovnik City Guide.* Open M-Sa June-Sept. 8am-8pm; Oct.-May 8am-3pm.

Turistička Zajednica Grada Dubrovnika, Cvijete Zuzorić 1/2, 2nd fl. (☎32 38 87; www.tzdubrovnik.hr). From the end of Placa, turn right between St. Blasius's Church and Cafe Gradska Kavana, and take the 1st right. The English-speaking staff hands out the invaluable *City Guide* (free). Open June-Aug. M-F 8am-4pm, Sa 9am-3pm, Su 9am-noon; Sept.-May M-F 8am-4pm.

Turistički Informativni Centar (TIC), Placa bb (☎42 63 54; fax 42 63 55), next to the fountain at the head of Placa. Arranges private rooms, **exchanges currency** for 2% commission, and gives out **free maps** of the city. Open daily June-Aug. 9am-8pm; Sept.-May 9am-7pm.

Budget Travel: Atlas, Cira Carica 3 (☎0800 44 22 22; www.atlas-croatia.com). The friendly, English-speaking staff arranges accommodations, sells plane and ferry tickets (ask about student and under-26 discounts), **exchanges currency** for 1% commission, and sells AmEx **traveler's checks.** Organizes expensive but convenient tours to: **Elafiti Islands** (2 per wk., 295kn); **Mljet National Park** (3 per wk., 400kn); **Neretva River Delta** (2 per wk., 395kn with lunch); **Mostar, BOS** (2 per wk., 320kn). Branches at Sv. Đurđa 1 (☎44 25 74), near the Pile Gate, and at Gruška Obala (☎41 80 01), near the ferry terminal. All open June-Aug. M-Sa 8am-9pm, Su 8am-1pm; Sept.-May M-Sa 8am-8pm, Su 8am-1pm. AmEx/DC/MC/V.

Currency Exchange: Nova Banka, Placa 16 (☎32 10 19). This centrally located bank exchanges currency for no commission, cashes **traveler's checks** (for 1.5% commission), and offers **Western Union** services. **ATM** located outside. Open M-F 8am-10pm, Sa 8am-noon. Branch at Pt. Republike 9 (☎35 63 33), next to the bus station. Open M-F 8am-10pm, Sa 8am-noon.

Luggage Storage: At the bus station kiosk marked *Garderoba*. 15kn per day. Open daily 4:50am-9pm.

English-Language Bookstore: Algoritam, Placa 8, on the main walkway in Stari Grad. Open M-Sa 9am-11pm, Su 10am-1pm. AmEx/DC/MC/V.

Internet: Dubrovnik is full of Internet cafes. There are 3 outside the main gate of Stari Grad. Inside the gate are others, and Lapad also has several. Most charge 5-10kn per 15min. **Internet Park** in Lapad, Šetalište Kralja Zvonimira bb (☎35 68 94), located outdoors in the middle of a park. Right off the main pedestrian walkway that leads to the beach, next to Hotel Park. 10 computers with good connections. 5kn per 15 min.

Post Office: Široka 8 (☎32 34 27), in Stari Grad. Has a number of public **telephones** and **Western Union**. Open M-F 7:30am-9pm, Sa 10am-5pm. **Postal Code:** 20108.

ACCOMMODATIONS

Dubrovnik offers accommodations in the city center, by the beach in Lapad, and near the ferry terminal. Due to lingering damage from the war and the subsequent refugee situation, however, the city's hotel scene leaves something to be desired—establishments tend to be either exorbitantly expensive or somewhat run-down. Consequently, a **private room** or **apartment** tends to be the most comfortable and least expensive option. Arrange one through the TIC, or through **Atlas** (singles 100-150kn; doubles 120-375kn). For potentially cheaper rooms, try your luck with the locals holding *sobe* signs who hover around the bus and ferry terminals. They may start by asking absurd prices but tend to drop to reasonable rates with some bargaining (doubles should go for 100-150kn per person). Be sure to agree on a price and ask to see the room before settling down anywhere.

■ **Apartmani Burum,** Dubravkina 16 (☎435 467), in Babin Kuk on the hill above Lapad. Take bus #6 to Babin Kuk and get off 2 stops past the Lapad post office. Cross the street and head up Mostarska, follow the street as it winds uphill, and turn left at Dubravkina. Kind owner Brigita offers 25 beds and a common kitchen. Some rooms have balconies and private baths at no added cost. Social atmosphere, with beaches nearby. The owner's brother-in-law, Nikola, will gladly drive you to Burum if you make arrangements ahead of time, and may even drive you around town; call ☎091 564 3929. Linens included. Dorms 100-125kn; doubles and triples 200-300kn. ❷

Begović Boarding House, Primorska 17 (☎43 51 91). From the bus station, take bus #6 toward Dubrava; ask the driver to let you off at Post Office Lapad. Facing the pedestrian walkway, turn right at the intersection, go left at the fork, and take the 1st right on Primorska. Go uphill and turn left at the fork; it will be on the left side at the very end. Call ahead and the hospitable owner, Sado, will pick you up at the bus or ferry terminal. A cozy villa with 10 spacious doubles, kitchens, TVs, and a terrace shaded by fig trees. Social atmosphere. If the house is full, Sado will arrange a place with one of his neighbors down the road. Doubles 110-120kn per person; triples 80-100kn per person. ❶

Youth Hostel (HI), B. Josipa Jelačića 15/17 (☎42 32 41; www.hfhs.hr). With your back to the bus station, turn left onto Ante Starčevića. Walk along the road for 10min., turn right at Pera Rudenjaka and left at the end of the street onto b. Josipa Jelačića. Look for a concealed HI sign on the left immediately after #17. The hostel is at the top of the stairs, on the right. From the ferries, take bus #12 toward Pile to the stop after the bus station. Small but clean doubles, quads, and 6-person dorms. Breakfast 5kn. Check-out 10am. Curfew 2am. Dorms July-Aug. 26 120kn; Aug. 27-Sept. 20 and June 105kn; Sept. 21-Oct. and May 95kn; Nov.-Apr. 85kn. 10kn discount for HI members. ❶

Hotel Zagreb, Šetalište Kralja Zvonimira 27 (☎43 61 46; fax 43 60 06). Follow directions to Post Office Lapad (see above). Walk through the 1st intersection and turn left onto the pedestrian walkway Šetalište Kralja Zvonimira; it's on the left, near the beach and an array of cafes. This hotel offers a wonderful veranda and clean rooms with hardwood floors, bath, TV, A/C, and phone. Breakfast included. Reception 24hr. Singles 400-660kn; doubles 1400-2120kn. Tourist tax 5.50-7kn. AmEx/DC/MC/V. ❸

Autocamp Solitudo, Iva Dulčića 39, Babin Kuk (☎44 86 86; sales.department@babinkuk.com), 5km from Stari Grad. From the bus station, take bus #6 toward Dubrava and ask the driver to let you off at Autocamp. Follow the signs downhill. Campground equipped with clean bathrooms, small grocery store, cafe, laundry facilities, and access to a long and uncrowded beach. Reception daily 7am-10pm. 31kn per person, 70kn per tent or car. AmEx/MC/V. ❶

🖸 FOOD

Most restaurants in Stari Grad offer decent pizzas and pastas at similar prices (40-70kn), which are generally lower than in other Croatian towns. Though food is reasonably priced, drinks can be costly. **Prijeko,** the first street parallel to Placa on the left when coming from Pile Gate, is lined with *konobi* (taverns), which cater almost exclusively to tourists. The **open-air market,** on Gundulićeva Poljana, sits behind St. Blasius's Church. (Open daily 7am-8pm.) **Konzum,** facing the market, offers groceries at very low prices by Stari Grad standards. (Open daily 7am-8pm. AmEx/MC/V.) Another location, with the same hours, is outside the Stari Grad gate, Marijana Čavića 1a. If you're staying in Lapad, check out **Kerum** supermarket, Kralja Tomislava 7, which has a wider selection and fresh produce. With your back to Post Office Lapad, turn left toward the white shopping center; Kerum is on the ground floor of the mall, at the back. (Open M-Sa 7am-10pm, Su 8am-9pm.)

🍴 **Lokarda Peskarija,** Na Ponti bb (☎32 47 50). From the bell tower at the end of Placa, turn right on Pred Dvorom and take the 1st left out of the city walls. This charming outdoor cafe is one of Dubrovnik's best. Tucked behind the Old Port, it offers the freshest and, surprisingly, least expensive seafood in Stari Grad. Large, steaming pots of mouthwatering risotto, filled to the brim with shellfish, are sure to delight even the pickiest of palettes. Seafood 35-50kn. Open daily 8am-midnight. ❷

Konoba Atlantic, Kardinala Stopinga 42 (☎098 185 96 25). Take bus #6 to Post Office Lapad and go straight on the walkway; take a right on the staircase before Hotel Kompas, which takes you to Kardinala Stopinga. This tiny, family-run restaurant above the beach is worth the walk. Homemade bread, some of the best pasta in Croatia (49-260kn), and a wide range of seafood (48-120kn). Open daily noon-11pm. ❷

Mea Culpa, Za Rokum 3 (☎32 34 30). This lively pizzeria, tucked in to the back alleys of the Stari Grad, serves Dubrovnik's freshest Italian fare. Mea Culpa ("I'm guilty") lives up to its name in indulgence. Portions are massive: a pizza or calzone feeds 2. Don't fret if the prospect of finishing your meal is daunting; the staff will happily wrap it up in a take-home box. Pizza 20-35kn. Pasta 35kn. Open daily 8am-midnight. ❶

Buffet Kamenice, Gundulićeva poljana 8 (☎32 36 82). Stari Grad's best greasy spoon, Kamenice specializes in shellfish (38kn) and other edible aquatic delicacies under a large umbrella beside the market. For breakfast, try a fluffy omelette (20-30kn). Open M-Sa 7am-10pm, Su 10am-10pm. ❶

🖸 SIGHTS

Stari Grad is packed with churches, museums, palaces, and fortresses—every turn yields an eyeful. The most popular sights are those along the broad Placa, but much of Dubrovnik's history is off the beaten path.

🏛 **CITY WALLS.** Providing stunning views of orange tiled roofs set against the sapphire blue backdrop of the Adriatic, a climb atop the city walls (Gradske zidine) is the highlight of any trip to Dubrovnik. Originally constructed in the 8th century, the thick limestone connects more fanciful towers, fortresses, and gates than you'll be able to count. The fortifications took their present form in the 13th century when the newly independent city needed stronger defenses against potential Turkish attacks. Once you've seen the sunset from the top of the walls, you may never leave the city. *(Entrances to walls are through the Pile Gate on the left and at the Old Port. Open daily May-Oct. 9am-7pm; Nov.-Apr. 10am-3pm. 30kn.)*

FRANCISCAN MONASTERY AND PHARMACEUTICAL MUSEUM. Masterly stonework encases this 14th-century monastery (Franjevački Samostan). The southern portal that opens on the Placa includes a Pietà relief by the Petrović brothers, the only relic from the original church. The cloister was built in 1360 by Mihoje Brajkov. No two capitals of the colonnade are the same. Take a stroll into the gardens and check out the glass-encased shell holes, one of the few reminders of the city's war-torn past. The monastery also houses the oldest working pharmacy in Europe, established in 1317. The small museum displays elegant medicinal containers, historical tools, icons, and gold and silver jewelry. *(Placa 2, on the left side of Placa, just inside Pile Gate next to the entrance to the city walls. ☎42 63 45. Open daily 9am-6pm. 10kn, children 5kn. Appropriate dress recommended for those visiting the chapel.)*

CATHEDRAL OF THE ASSUMPTION OF THE VIRGIN MARY. This Baroque cathedral (Riznica Katedrale) was built after the previous Romanesque cathedral was destroyed in the 1667 earthquake. In 1981, the foundations of a 7th-century Byzantine cathedral were found beneath the cathedral floor, necessitating considerable revision of Dubrovnik's history. The cathedral **treasury** houses religious relics collected by Richard the Lionheart, Roman refugees, and a few centuries of fishermen. Crusaders in the 12th century brought back a silver casket from Jerusalem that contains an ancient garment allegedly worn by Jesus. *(Kneza Damjana Jude 1. From Pile Gate, follow Placa to the Bell Tower and turn right on Poljana Marina Držića. Cathedral open daily 6:30am-8pm. Treasury open M-Sa 8am-5:30pm, Su 11am-5:30pm. 7kn.)*

ORTHODOX CHURCH AND MUSEUM OF ICONS. Around 2000 Serbs live in Dubrovnik—only a third of the prewar population. The museum (Pravoslavna Crkva i Muzej Ikona) houses a variety of 15th- to 19th-century icons gathered by local families. According to Serbian tradition, each household is protected by a specific saint, and any member of the family traveling abroad collects icons depicting that saint. *(Od Puča 8. From Pile Gate, walk 100m down Placa and turn right onto Široka, the widest side street. Turn left down Od Puča. Church open daily 8am-noon and 5-7pm. Museum open M-Sa 9am-2pm.)*

MOSQUE. This former apartment serves Dubrovnik's 5000 Bosnian Muslims. The beautifully carpeted room upstairs is divided in two: one half contains an Islamic school for children, and the other is used for prayer. A small anteroom serves as a social center for the Bosnian community. Tourists are welcome in the mosque (Džamija) if they take off their shoes and dress appropriately. *(Miha Pracata 3. From Pile Gate, walk down Placa and take the 8th street on the right, M. Pracata. The mosque is marked by a small sign on the left side of the street. Open daily 10am-1pm and 8-9pm.)*

SEPHARDIC SYNAGOGUE. Round off your tour with a visit to the 2nd-oldest Sephardic synagogue (Sinagoga) in Europe (the oldest is in Prague), which is home to a Jewish community that now numbers fewer than 50. Most of Dubrovnik's Jewish archives were lost during the Nazi occupation, but a number of families (Jewish, Catholic, and others) risked their lives to hide many of the synagogue's possessions in their own homes. *(Žudioska 5. From the Bell Tower, walk toward Pile Gate and take the 3rd right onto Žudioska. Open May-Oct. M-F 9am-8pm. Museum 10kn.)*

◖ ✾ BEACHES AND FESTIVALS

One of the most beautiful beaches in Dubrovnik lies just beyond the city walls. From the **bell tower,** turn left onto Svetog Dominika, bear right after the footbridge, and continue along Frana Supila. Descend the stairs next to the post office to discover a pristine **pebble beach** with spectacular views of Lokrum Island. Although privately owned, the *bajne* is free and open to the public. The best beach in the area is on the nearby island Lopud, and has sand, not stones. (See **Daytrips,** p. 157). Alternatively, for sand, palms, and crowds, hop on bus #6 toward Dubrava and ask to get off at Post Office Lapad. Go through the intersection to the pedestrian boulevard and follow the bikinis. You can also continue on the path to the beach below Hotel Bellevue. Walk along Starčevića (10min.), then take a left after the hotel. For a surreal seaside experience, take a swim in the cove at the foot of the wreckage of the old **Hotel Libertas,** still marked on most maps. The hotel was damaged during the recent war and then abandoned. Another option is the nearby island of **Lokrum,** which features a **nude beach.** Ferries run daily from the Old Port (20min.; 9am and every 30min. 10am-6pm; round-trip 35kn). To get to the nude beach, follow the main path from the ferry stop that traces the perimeter of the island; veer left at the restaurant and follow the "FKK" signs. For those who prefer to stay clothed, there is a smaller beach adjacent to the boat dock, as well as a gorgeous **nature preserve** worth exploring. The **Dubrovnik Summer Festival** (Dubrovački Ljetni Festival; mid-July to mid-Aug.) transforms the city into a cultural mecca and lively party scene. (☎32 34 00; www.dubrovnik-festival.hr.)

■ NIGHTLIFE

Young hipsters and cafe loungers flock to **Stari Grad.** An older crowd congregates in **Šetalište Kralja Zvonimira,** near Begović Boarding House (see **Accommodations,** p. 153), a hotspot for cafes, bars, and evening strolls by the nearby sea.

EastWest Cocktail and Dance Bar, Frana Supila bb (☎41 22 20). EastWest lives up to its motto, "Welcome to Heaven." Situated on a private beach with spectacular ocean views, this lounge epitomizes luxury. The dressed-to-impress clientele relaxes on the bar's plush white couches, while the beautiful people congregate in the sand "living room," complete with leather sofas on the beach. Those craving complete relaxation after a long day or night out can recline on one of the decadent beachside canopy beds. Beer 12-30kn. Mixed drinks 33-78kn. Open daily 8am-3am.

Buža, Crijevićeva 9. From the open air market, walk up stairs toward the monastery. Veer left and follow the signs along Od Margarite for "Cool Drinks and the Most Beautiful View." Hidden on a bed of boulders beneath the city walls, this laid-back terrace perched on the Adriatic is a perfect spot for conversing under spectacular sunsets or the constellations. Beer 17-22kn. Open 9am-late.

Jazz Cafe Troubador, Buničeva 2 (☎41 21 54), around the corner from Hemingway's. Even if you're not huddling over a *pivo* on this lively cafe's patio, hang out at the nearby square at night to catch the town's hottest jazz, as combos often play outside. Soda 20kn. Beer 18-40kn. Wine 40kn. Open daily 10am-1am; in summer later. Cash only.

Hemingway's, Pred Dvorum bb. This small yet swanky bar, facing Poljana M. Držića, has the longest cocktail menu in Stari Grad. With gorgeous views of the Rector's Palace and the bell tower and comfy chairs, Hemingway's is the perfect place to sit back and enjoy Dubrovnik's beauty. Mixed drinks 40-50kn. Open daily 9am-1am; in summer 9am-3am.

Club Roxy, B. Josipa Jelačića 11. Only a short stumble from the HI hostel, the Roxy's hanging motorcycles and hot-rod paraphernalia beckon a relaxed local crowd looking to avoid the downtown crunch. Coffee 6kn. Domestic draft 15kn per 0.5L. Guinness 18kn per 0.33L. Open daily 8am-late.

Latino Club Fuego, Pile Brsalje 11, right outside Pile Gate. Because this is the only place open until 4am, many party-goers end up here. Cover 30kn; 1 drink included.

🔌 DAYTRIPS FROM DUBROVNIK

LOPUD ISLAND

A ferry (50min.; in summer M-Sa 4 per day, Su 1 per day; round-trip 26kn) runs to Lopud and the Elafiti Islands. The beach is on the opposite side of the island from the village. Facing the water at the dock, turn left and walk 8min. Take a left on the concrete walkway between the palm tree park and the wall, where you'll see a sign for Konoba Barbara. Head uphill and bear right at the fork. After about 15min. you'll see steps that lead down through a dirt trail to the beach.

Less than an hour from Dubrovnik, Lopud is an enchanting island, with one of the best beaches on the Adriatic. The tiny village, dotted with white buildings, chapels, and parks, stretches along the island's waterfront *(obala)*. Currently under renovation, **Dordič Mayneri** remains among the most beautiful parks in Croatia. Signs from Kavana Dubrava on the waterfront point to the **museum**, the meeting place for **tours** (Th 9am) of the church, museum, and monastery. A 15min. stroll along the waterfront leads to a gazebo with a breathtaking view of the white cliffs and the dark-blue sea. A short walk in the other direction brings you to the abandoned **monastery.** Though it is slated for reconstruction and development, its current semi-ruined state makes for wonderful exploration. Be careful: many of the floors have collapsed. The Plaža Šunj **beach,** treasured by locals, has that special quality that most of the Dalmatian Coast lacks: sand.

MLJET NATIONAL PARK

Take a ferry, run by Atlantagent, Obala S. Radića 26 (☎41 90 44), behind the Jadrolinija office. The ferry (1½hr., June-Sept. 1 per day, round-trip 120kn) leaves in the morning, stops in Pomena, and returns in the evening. In winter, the Jadrolinija ferry drops passengers on the eastern side of the island in Sobra (2hr., 2 per day, 32kn). The bus meets the ferry in Sobra and travels to its western end, Pomena (1hr., 12kn). Park entrances are in Polače and Pomena. ☎74 40 58; www.np-mljet.hr. 90kn admission ticket for all, including the boat and minivan rides in the park. Atlas and other travel agencies offer 1-day excursions to the park. Private rooms (75-100kn) available in Sobra or Pomena; inquire at the cafe or look for signs.

Mljet's relative isolation and small population make it an ideal location for a national park. The saltwater **Large** and **Small Lakes** (Veliko and Malo Jezero), created by the rising sea level 10,000 years ago, are the most unique formations on the island. Every 6hr., the direction of flow between the lakes changes with the tides, so the water is constantly cleansed. In the center of Veliko Jezero sits the **Island of St. Maria** (Sv. Marija), home to a beautiful, white-stone **Benedictine monastery,** built in the 12th century and abandoned 700 years later when Napoleon conquered the area. Today, it houses a restaurant and a church. Skip this restaurant and the other one on the island; bring your own lunch and enjoy a picnic virtually anywhere.

If you have time, **Polače** is worth a stop for its **Roman ruins** and **Christian basilica,** once part of the 2nd-largest Roman city in Croatia. Unfortunately, most of the city is now underwater. Get off at Polače (which also has a tourist office), walk 2km to Pristanište, to the park's info center, and jump on the boat to St. Maria (5min., 1 per hr.). To return, take the boat to Mali Most (2min.) and walk another 3km to Pomena. If you get tired, a minivan run by park management may give you a ride, or you can catch one of the Atlas-operated buses.

CROATIA

CZECH REPUBLIC
(ČESKÁ REPUBLIKA)

From the Holy Roman Empire through the USSR, the Czechs have long stood at a crossroads of international affairs. Unlike many of their neighbors, the citizens of this small, landlocked country have rarely resisted as armies marched across their borders, often choosing to fight with words instead of weapons. As a result, Czech towns and cities are among the best-preserved and most beautiful in Europe. Today, the Czechs face a different kind of invasion, as enamored tourists sweep in to savor the magnificent capital, the welcoming locals, and the world's best beers.

 DISCOVER CZECH REPUBLIC: SUGGESTED ITINERARIES

THREE DAYS You know where to go. Stroll across the **Charles Bridge** (p. 182) to see **Prague Castle** (p. 187), leave the beaten-tourist-path to explore areas like **Josefov** (p. 185), and have some beer.

ONE WEEK Keep exploring Prague (5 days; p. 165); there's plenty more to see. Relax at the **Petřín Hill Gardens** (p. 186) and visit the **Troja** chateau (p. 189). Once you need a break from the big city, head to **Český Krumlov** (2 days; p. 208) for hiking, biking, and another ancient castle.

BEST OF CZECH REPUBLIC, THREE WEEKS Begin with 2 weeks in **Prague,** including a daytrip to the **Terezín** concentration camp (p. 196). Then spend 4 days in UNESCO-protected **Český Krumlov** getting to know the bike trails and floating down the **Vltava River** in an inner tube. Check out the weird **Revolving Theater** while you're at it (p. 212). Wrap things up with 3 days in Olomouc, making sure to leave time for a daytrip to the gorgeous, Renaissance **Kroměříž** chateau (p. 227).

FACTS AND FIGURES

Official Name: Czech Republic.
Capital: Prague.
Major Cities: Brno, České Budějovice.
Population: 10,250,000.

Time Zone: GMT + 1.
Language: Czech.
Religions: Roman Catholic (27%), Protestant (2%), other (3%), unspecified (9%), unaffiliated (59%).

ESSENTIALS

WHEN TO GO

The Czech Republic is the most touristed country in Eastern Europe. It may be wise to avoid the high season (July-Aug.), though the weather is most pleasant during summer. Book in advance for travel to any area during a festival or Christian holidays like Christmas and Easter. The best compromise between weather and crowding will probably be found in late spring or early fall.

DOCUMENTS AND FORMALITIES

ENTRANCE REQUIREMENTS
Passport: Required for all travelers.

Visa: Not required for stays of under 90 days for citizens of Australia, Canada, Ireland, New Zealand, and the US. Citizens of the UK may remain in the country for up to 180 days without a visa.

Letter of Invitation: Not required for citizens of Australia, Canada, Ireland, New Zealand, the UK, and the US.

Inoculations: Recommended up-to-date on DTaP (diphtheria, tetanus, and pertussis), Hepatitis A, Hepatitis B, MMR (measles, mumps, and rubella), Polio booster, and Typhoid.

Work Permit: Required for all foreigners planning to work in the Czech Republic.

Driving Permit: Required for all those planning to drive in the Czech Republic.

EMBASSIES AND CONSULATES. Foreign embassies to the Czech Republic are in Prague (p. 165). For Czech embassies and consulates abroad include: **Australia,** 8 Culgoa Circuit, O'Malley, Canberra, ACT 2606 (☎02 6290 1386; canberra@embassy.mzv.cz); **Canada,** 251 Cooper St., Ottawa, ON K2P OG2 (☎613-562-3875; ottawa@embassy.mzv.cz); **Ireland,** 57 Northumberland Rd., Ballsbridge, Dublin 4 (☎01 668 1135; dublin@embassy.mzv.cz); **New Zealand,** see Australia; **UK,** 26-30 Kensington Palace Gardens, London W8 4QY (☎020 7243 1115; www.mzv.cz/london); **US,** 3900 Spring of Freedom St. NW, Washington, D.C. 20008 (☎202-274-9100; www.mzv.cz/washington).

VISA AND ENTRY INFORMATION. Citizens of Australia, Canada, New Zealand, and the US do not need a visa for stays of up to 90 days, UK citizens for up to 180 days. Visas are available at those countries' embassies or consulates. You cannot obtain a Czech visa at the border. Processing takes seven to 10 days when submitted by mail, five days when submitted in person. With the application, you must submit your passport; one photograph (two if applying to the Czech consulate in Los Angeles) glued—not stapled—to the application; a self-addressed, stamped envelope (certified or overnight mail); and a cashier's check or money order.

TOURIST SERVICES AND MONEY

KORUNY (Kč)	
AUS$1 = 18.15Kč	10Kč = AUS$0.55
CDN$1 = 19.76Kč	10Kč = CDN$0.51
EUR€1 = 29.33Kč	10Kč = EUR€0.34
NZ$1 = 16.75Kč	10Kč = NZ$0.60
UK£1 = 43.29Kč	10Kč = UK£0.23
US$1 = 24.15Kč	10Kč = US$0.41

Municipal **tourist offices** in major cities provide info on sights and events, distribute lists of hostels and hotels, and often book rooms. Be aware, however, that in Prague these offices are often crowded and may be staffed by disgruntled employees. **CKM**, a national student tourist agency, books hostel beds and issues ISICs and HI cards. Most bookstores sell a national hiking map collection, *Soubor turistických map*, with an English key. The Czech unit of currency is the **koruna** (crown; **Kč**), plural koruny. **Inflation** is around 3.2%. **Banks** offer good exchange rates. **Komerční banka** is a common bank chain. ATMs are everywhere—look for the abundant *Bankomat* signs—and offer the best exchange rates. **Traveler's checks** can be exchanged almost everywhere, though rarely without commission. MasterCard and Visa are accepted at most establishments, but many hostels and lower-priced places remain wary of plastic.

HEALTH AND SAFETY

EMERGENCY	Police: ☎ 158. Ambulance: ☎ 112. Fire: ☎ 150.

Medical facilities in the Czech Republic are of high quality, especially in Prague, and major foreign insurance policies are accepted. **Pharmacies** are *Lékárna*, with the most common chain being Droxies; they and supermarkets carry international brands of *náplast* (bandages), *tampóny* (tampons), and *kondomy* (condoms). For prescription drugs and aspirin, look for pharmacies marked with a green cross. Petty **crime** has increased in recent years, especially on public transportation; beware of pickpockets prowling among the crowds in Prague's main squares and tourist attractions. **Women** traveling alone should experience few problems in the Czech Republic. However, caution should be exercised while riding public transportation, especially after dark. **Minorities** should not encounter too much trouble, though travelers with darker skin might be discriminated against. Gay nightlife is taking off in the Czech Republic, but open displays of **homosexuality** may not be accepted; GLBT travelers should expect to encounter stares and are advised to remain cautious in public situations, especially outside Prague.

TRANSPORTATION

Most major European carriers, including **Air Canada, Air France, American Airlines, British Airways, ČSA, Delta, KLM, Lufthansa**, and **SAS** fly into Prague. The easiest and cheapest way to travel between cities in the Czech Republic is by **train. Eastrail** is accepted in the Czech Republic, but **Eurail** is not. The fastest international trains are *EuroCity* and *InterCity* (*expresní;* marked in blue on schedules). *Rychlík* trains are fast domestic trains (*zrychlený vlak;* marked in red on schedules). Avoid slow *osobní* trains, marked in white. *Odjezdy* (departures) are printed on yellow posters, *příjezdy* (arrivals) on white. Seat reservations (*místenka;* 10Kč) are recommended on express and international trains and for first-class seating. Czech **buses** are quicker and cheaper than trains for travel in the countryside. **ČSAD** runs national and international bus lines, and many European companies operate international service. Consult the timetables or buy a bus schedule (25Kč) from kiosks. Roads are well kept, and **road-side assistance** is usually available. US citizens must have an International Driving Permit as well as a **US driver's license. Taxis** are a safe way to travel, though many overcharge you. Negotiate the fare beforehand and make sure the meter is running during the ride. Phoning a taxi service is generally more affordable than flagging a cab on the street. Although the practice is common in the Czech Republic, *Let's Go* does not recommend **hitchhiking.**

KEEPING IN TOUCH

PHONE CODES	**Country code:** 420. **International dialing prefix:** 00. From outside the Czech Republic, dial int'l dialing prefix (see inside back cover) + 420 + city code + local number. Within the Czech Republic, simply dial the local number.

Internet access is readily available throughout the Czech Republic. Internet cafes offer fast connections for 1-2Kč per minute. Card-operated **phones** (175Kč per 50 units; 320Kč per 100 units) are simpler to use and easier to find than coin phones. You can purchase **phone cards** *(telefonní karta)* at most *Tábaks* and *Trafika* (convenience stores). To make domestic calls, dial the entire number. City codes no longer exist in the Czech Republic, and dialing zero is not necessary. To make an international call to the Czech Republic, dial the country code followed by the entire phone number. Calls run 8Kč per minute to Australia, Canada, the UK, or the US; and 12Kč per minute to New Zealand. Dial ☎ 1181 for English info, 0800 12 34 56 for the international operator. International access codes include: **AT&T** (☎ 00 800 222 55288); **British Telecom** (☎ 00 420); **Canada Direct** (☎ 800 001 115); **MCI** (☎ 800 001 112); **Sprint** (☎ 00 420 87 187); and **Telstra Australia** (☎ 00 420 061 01). The **postal system** is reliable and efficient, though finding English-speaking postal employees can be a challenge. A postcard to the US costs 12Kč, to Europe 9Kč. To send **airmail**, stress that you want your package to go on a plane *(letecky)*. Go to the customs office to send packages heavier than 2kg abroad. **Poste Restante** is generally available. Address envelopes as follows: Justin (First name) JENNINGS (LAST NAME), POSTE RESTANTE, Jindřišská 14 (post office street address), 110 00 (postal code) Praha (city), CZECH REPUBLIC.

ACCOMMODATIONS AND CAMPING

CZECH REPUBLIC	❶	❷	❸	❹	❺
ACCOMMODATIONS	under 320Kč under €11 under US$13	320-500Kč €11-17 US$13-21	501-800Kč €17-27 US$21-33	801-1200Kč €27-41 US$33-50	over 1200Kč over €41 over US$50

Hostels and **university dorms** are the cheapest options in July and August; two- to four-bed dorms cost 250-400Kč. Hostels are clean and safe throughout the country, though they become scarce in areas with few students. **Pensions** are the next most affordable option at 600-800Kč. **Hotels** (from 1000Kč), tend to be more luxurious and more expensive than hostels or pensions. From June to September, reserve at least a week ahead in Prague, Český Krumlov, and Brno. If you can't keep a reservation, call to cancel so that some weary backpacker doesn't have to sleep on the street. **Private homes** are not nearly as popular (or as cheap) as in the rest of Eastern Europe. Scan train stations for *Zimmer frei* signs. As quality varies, do not pay in advance. There are many **campgrounds** strewn about the country; however, most are open only from mid-May to September.

CZECH REPUBLIC

FOOD AND DRINK

CZECH REPUBLIC	❶	❷	❸	❹	❺
FOOD	under 80Kč under €3 under US$3	80-110Kč €3-4 US$3-5	111-150Kč €4-5 US$5-6	151-200Kč €5-7 US$6-8	over 200Kč over €7 over US8

Loving Czech cuisine starts with learning to pronounce *knedlíky* (KNED-lee-kee). These thick loaves of dough, feebly known in English as dumplings, are a staple. Meat, however, lies at the heart of almost all main dishes; the **national meal** (known as *vepřo-knedlo-zelo*) is *vepřové* (roast pork), *knedlíky*, and *zelí* (sauerkraut). If you're in a hurry, grab *párky* (frankfurters) or *sýr* (cheese) at a food stand. **Vegetarian** restaurants serving *bez masa* (meatless) specialties are uncommon outside Prague; traditional restaurants serve few options beyond *smažený sýr* (fried cheese) and *saláty* (salads), and even these may contain meat products. Eating **kosher** is feasible, but beware—pork may sneak unnoticed into many dishes. Ask for *káva espresso* rather than *káva:* the Czech brew may be unappealing to Westerners. *Jablkový závin* (apple strudel) and *ovocné knedlíky* (fruit dumplings) are favorite sweets, but the most beloved is *koláč*—a tart filled with poppy seeds or sweet cheese. Moravian **wines** are of high quality. They're typically drunk at a *vinárna* (wine bar) that also serves a variety of spirits, including *slivovice* (plum brandy) and *becherovka* (herbal bitter), the **national drink.** World-class local brews like *Plzeňský Prazdroj* (Pilsner Urquell), *Budvar,* and *Krušovice* dominate the drinking scene.

LIFE AND TIMES

HISTORY

BEGINNINGS. According to legend, Father Čech climbed Říp Mountain near present-day Prague, and, seeing how good it was, ordered the land settled. Textbooks, however, trace the civilization back to the first-century arrival of the Celtic Boii. By the 6th century, Slavs had settled in the region, and by the 10th century, the Czechs were united under the **Přemyslid Dynasty.** Wenceslas (Václav), legendary patron saint and king of Bohemia, was one of the dynasty's earliest rulers. In 1114, the Holy Roman Empire invited the Czech kings to join.

PEACE THROWN OUT THE WINDOW. The reign of Holy Roman Emperor **Charles (Karel) IV** (1346-1378) was a golden era. His feats included the promotion of Prague to an Archbishopric and the founding of Charles University, the first university in Central Europe, in 1348. Unfortunately, Charles's eldest legitimate son, Václav, was unable to attain the golden heights of his father. During his reign, proto-Protestant **Jan Hus** was burned at the stake for his protests against the corruption of the ruling Catholic church. In response to the execution, the **Hussite movement** organized the **First Defenestration of Prague** in 1419—protestors threw members of the city council out the window of the Council House. Years of fighting followed. Two centuries later, the **Second Defenestration of Prague** set off the **Thirty Years' War** (1618-48). This time the victims survived, saved by a pile of manure. The Protestants' eventual defeat was sealed when they suffered an early, harsh blow in the Battle of White Mountain in November 1620. Their loss led to the absorption of Czech territory into the Austrian Empire and three centuries of oppression.

CHECKMATE. The nationalism that engulfed Europe during the 19th century invigorated the Bohemian peoples. The sentiment was crushed, however, in the imperial backlash that followed the 1848 revolutions. While WWI did little to increase harmony among the nationalities of the Hapsburg Empire, mutual malcontent united the Czechs and Slovaks. In the postwar confusion, **Edvard Beneš** and **Tomáš G. Masaryk** convinced the victorious Allies to legitimize a new state joining Bohemia, Moravia, and Slovakia into Czechoslovakia. This First Republic enjoyed remarkable economic prosperity but was torn apart when Hitler exploited the Allies' appeasement policy. The infamous **Munich Agreement** (1938) handed the Sudetenland to Germany. The following year, Hitler annexed the entire country.

UN-CRUSHED VELVET. Following the Allied liberation, the Communists won the 1946 elections, seizing permanent power in 1948. In 1968, Communist Party Secretary **Alexander Dubček** sought to reform the country's nationalized economy and ease political oppression during the **Prague Spring.** The Soviets invaded immediately. **Gustáv Husák** became Communist Party Secretary in 1969, ushering in 20-years of repression: he denounced the Prague Spring, consolidated power, and bestowed the title of President upon himself in 1975. Czech intellectuals protested his human rights violations with the nonviolent **Charter 77** movement. Its leaders were persecuted and imprisoned, but still fostered increasing dissidence. Communism's demise in Hungary and Poland, and the fall of the Berlin Wall in 1989 opened the way for Czechoslovakia's **Velvet Revolution,** named for the nearly bloodless transition to a multi-party state system. The Communist regime's violent suppression of a peaceful demonstration outraged the nation, which retaliated with a strike. Within days the Communists resigned, and **Václav Havel,** long-imprisoned playwright and leader of both Charter 77 and the Velvet Revolution, became president in December 1989. Slovak pleas for independence grew stronger and, after much debate, the Czech and Slovak Republics parted ways on January 1, 1993.

TODAY

The country enjoyed a rapid revival after Communism but has recently experienced economic stagnation and rising unemployment. In 1997, the economic policies of Prime Minister **Václav Klaus** resulted in a tremendous depreciation of the koruna's value, and the 1998 elections allowed **Miloš Zeman,** leader of the **Social Democrats,** to form the first left-wing government since 1989. **Vladimir Spidla** replaced Zeman as head of the Social Democrats and, in June 2002, the party topped the polls, making Spidla prime minister. Having won only 70 of 200 seats in Parliament, the Social Democrats were forced to ally with a number of centrist parties in order to form a tiny 101-seat majority. Playwright and former dissident **Václav Havel,** re-elected to the presidency in 1998 by a single vote in Parliament, remained the country's official head of state until the 2003 presidential election. The constitution barred Havel from seeking a 3rd term. In 2004, the young and relatively unknown Social Democrat **Stanislav Gross** succeeded Spidla as prime minister. Allegations of misconduct led to his resignation less than a year later, however, and **Jírí Paroubek** soon replaced him as the leader of the troubled party.

The Czech Republic joined **NATO** in March 1999 and was admitted to the **EU** in May 2004. Lingering economic problems mean that the country may not enter the Euro zone until as late as 2010. Czech policies toward the **Roma** (gypsies), who suffer high poverty and unemployment, have drawn international criticism. In 2000, the Czech Republic and Austria disagreed over a Czech nuclear power plant near the countries' shared border, and in 2002 Germany objected to the Czech refusal to revoke the **Benes Decree,** which legalized the expulsion of millions of ethnic Germans and Hungarians from Czechoslovakia after WWII. In August 2002, the Czech Republic suffered **severe flooding.** Much of the western half of the country was affected, causing damage to roads, railway lines, and landmarks.

CZECH REPUBLIC

PEOPLE AND CULTURE

Czech is a West Slavic language, closely related to Slovak and Polish. **English** is widely understood among young people, and **German** can be useful, especially in South Bohemia because of its proximity to the German and Austrian borders. In eastern regions, you're more likely to encounter **Polish**. **Russian** was taught to all school children under communism, but use your *"privet"* carefully as the language is not always welcome. Firmly established customs govern wining and dining. When beer is served, wait until all raise the common *"na zdraví"* (to your health) toast before drinking, and always look into the eyes of the person with whom you are toasting. Similarly, before biting into a saucy *knedlík*, wish everyone *"dobrou chut"* (to your health). The **tipping** rate is around 10%.

THE ARTS

LITERATURE. The Czech Republic is a highly literate country where writers hold a privileged position as important social and political commentators. From the first Czechoslovak president, **T.G. Masaryk,** to the recently retired **Václav Havel,** literary figures have proven to be the nation's most powerful citizens. The Hapsburgs repressed Czech literature in the 18th century, but the 19th century saw a literary renaissance. In 1836, **Karel Hynek Mácha** penned his celebrated epic *May (Máj)*. The 1858 founding of the literary journal *Máj*, named after Mácha's poem, marked the beginning of the **National Revival,** when nationalist literary output exploded. One of its brightest stars, **Bozena Němcová,** introduced the novel to modern Czech literature with *Granny (Babička;* 1855). **Jaroslav Hašek's** satire, *The Good Soldier Švejk (Osudy dobrého vojáka Švejka za svetové války;* 1920-23), became a classic commentary on life under Hapsburg rule. **Franz Kafka's** work is pervaded by the circumstances of his position as a German-speaking Jew in his native Prague. **Jaroslav Seifert** and **Vítězslav Nezval** produced lasting, image-rich works of poetry. In 1984, Seifert became the first Czech writer to receive a Nobel Prize.

The Czech literary tradition remains strong today. The country's best known contemporary writer is **Milan Kundera,** whose philosophical novel *The Unbearable Lightness of Being,* set against the backdrop of Communist Prague, met with international acclaim. His novels, as well as those of writer **Josef Škvorecký,** continue to be popular both at home and abroad. Former president **Havel** is a well-known playwright with several revered dramas to his name.

MUSIC. The 19th-century National Revival brought out the best in Czech music. The nation's most celebrated composers, **Antonín Dvořák, Leoš Janáček,** and **Bedřich Smetana,** are renowned for transforming Czech folk tunes into symphonies and operas. Dvořák's *Symphony No. 9, From the New World,* combining Czech folk tradition with melodies gathered during the composer's trip to America, is probably the most famous Czech masterpiece. Among Czechs, however, Smetana's symphonic poem *My Country (Má vlast)* remains more popular.

THE VISUAL ARTS. Marie Čerminová Toyen, a Surrealist born in Prague, immigrated to Paris in the 1920s to work with André Breton. One of the most important Czech artists of the 20th century, **Alfons Mucha** also worked in Paris and helped develop art nouveau. **Josef Čapek** was a Cubist and cartoonist best known for his satirical depiction of Hitler's ascent to power. While few Czech architects have become household names, the country itself is rife with architectural treasures. Both **Český Krumlov** and **Kutná Hora** have been declared protected cultural monuments by UNESCO for their medieval buildings and winding streets. In **Prague,** architectural styles intermingle, juxtaposing the 1000-year-old **Prague Castle** with daring examples of art nouveau and the world's only realized Cubist buildings.

FILM. The Czech Republic has been successful in the film world. In 1967, director Jiří Menzel's *Closely Watched Trains (Ostře sledované vlaky)* won the Academy Award for Best Foreign Film. Director **Miloš Forman** immigrated to the US in 1968 and exploded into the film industry with the acclaimed *One Flew Over the Cuckoo's Nest* (1975). His 1984 film *Amadeus* won eight Oscars. Film has become increasingly popular in the Czech Republic, and **Karlovy Vary** hosts a major film festival. In 1997, **Jan Svěrák's** *Kolya* brought the Oscar back to the Czech Republic.

HOLIDAYS AND FESTIVALS

Holidays: New Year's Day (Jan. 1); Easter Holiday (Apr. 16-17); May Day/Labor Day (May 1); Liberation Day (May 8); Sts. Cyril and Methodius Day (July 5); Jan Hus Day (July 6); Czech Statehood Day (Sept. 28); Independence Day (Oct. 28); Struggle for Freedom and Democracy Day (Nov. 17); Christmas (Dec. 24-26).

Festivals: The Czech Republic hosts a number of internationally renowned festivals. If you are planning to attend, reserve a room and your tickets well in advance. Classical musicians and world-class orchestras descend on Prague (p. 165) for the Spring Festival held from mid-May to early June. Held each June, the Five-Petaled Rose Festival, a boisterous medieval festival in Český Krumlov (p. 208) features music, dance, and a jousting tournament. *Masopust*, the Moravian version of Mardi Gras, is celebrated in villages across the Czech Republic from Epiphany to Ash Wednesday (Jan.-Mar.). Revelers dressed in animal masks feast, dance, and sing until Lent begins.

ADDITIONAL RESOURCES

GENERAL HISTORY

The Coasts of Bohemia, by Derek Sayer (2000). Weaving together politics and culture, Sayer's lively narrative is scholarly but accessible.

Prague in Black and Gold, by Paul Dementz (1998). A comprehensive yet engaging account of the complicated past of Central Europe.

FICTION AND TRAVEL BOOKS

The Garden Party, by Václav Havel (1993). A collection of the former Czech president's acclaimed dramas.

Prague: A Traveler's Literary Companion, by Paul Wilson, ed. (1995) A series of essays and short stories by various Czech authors illuminating the historical and literary significance of Prague's monuments and cityscapes.

The Unbearable Lightness of Being, by Milan Kundera (1984). This lyrical novel about two couples has become a classic of high Modernism, and is one of the most famous works to emerge from the Czech Republic.

FILM

Kolya, directed by Jan Svěrák (1996). The Academy Award-winning story of a Czech musician who finds himself in charge of his stepson after his wife leaves the country.

Closely Watched Trains, directed by Jiří Menzel (1966). Another Oscar-winner, this film recounts the lives and loves of Czech railway employees during WWII.

CZECH REPUBLIC

PRAGUE (PRAHA)

From the nobility of Prague Castle to the pastel facades of the Old Town Square, Prague (pop. 1,200,000) is a city on the cusp of the divine. King of Bohemia and Holy Roman Emperor, Charles IV foresaw a royal seat worthy of his rank and refashioned Prague into a city of soaring cathedrals and lavish palaces. A maze of shady alleys lends the city a dark and dreamy atmosphere. Even today, an ethereal magic hangs over Prague, captivating writers, artists, and tourists alike. The magic has been well tested in recent years. Since the lifting of the Iron Curtain, hordes of outsiders have flooded the venerable capital. In summer, most locals leave for the countryside and the foreigner-to-resident ratio soars above nine-to-one. Beer runs cheaper than water in these tourist-filled streets, but look elsewhere to find the city's true spirit. Walk a few blocks from any of the major sights and you'll be lost in the labyrinthine cobblestone alleys. But even in the hyper-touristed Staré Město (Old Town), Prague's majesty gleams: the Charles Bridge, packed so tightly in summer that the only way off is to jump, is still breathtaking at sunrise, eerie in a fog, and stunning after a fresh snowfall.

✈ INTERCITY TRANSPORTATION

Flights: Ruzyně Airport (☎220 111 111), 20km northwest of the city. Bus #119 runs between the airport and Metro A: Dejvická (5am-midnight; 12Kč, 6Kč per bag). Buy tickets in kiosks or machines but not on board. An **airport bus** run by **Cedaz** (☎220 114 296; 20-45min., every 30min. 5:30am-9:30pm) stops outside Metro stations at nám. Republiky (90Kč) and Dejvická (60Kč). **Taxis** to and from **Ruzyně** can be expensive but may be the only option at night. Try to settle on a price before starting (400-600Kč). Airlines include: **Air France,** Václavské nám. 57 (☎221 662 662); **British Airways,** Ruzyně Airport (☎222 114 444); **Czech Airlines (ČSA),** V Celnici 5 (☎239 007 007); **Delta,** Národní třída 32 (☎224 946 733); **KLM,** Na Příkopě 21 (☎233 090 933); **Lufthansa,** Ruzyně Airport (☎220 114 456); **Swissair,** Pařížská 11 (☎221 990 444).

Trains: (☎221 111 122, international info 224 615 249; www.vlak.cz). English spoken on international info line and attempted at station info offices. Prague has 4 main terminals. **Hlavní nádraží** (☎224 615 786; Metro C: Hlavní nádraží) and **Nádraží Holešovice** (☎224 624 632; Metro C: Nádraží Holešovice) are the largest and cover most international service. Domestic trains leave from **Masarykovo nádraží** (☎840 112 113, 221 111 122; Metro B: nám. Republiky), and from **Smíchovské nádraží** (☎972 226 150; Metro B: Smíchovské nádraží). International trains run to: **Berlin, GER** (5hr., 5 per day, 1400Kč); **Bratislava, SLK** (4½-5½hr., 6 per day, 576Kč); **Budapest, HUN** (7-9hr., 4 per day, 1400Kč); **Kraków, POL** (7-8hr., 4 per day, 874Kč); **Moscow, RUS** (31hr., 1 per day, 3000Kč); **Munich, GER** (7hr., 5 per day, 1650Kč); **Vienna, AUT** (4½hr., 6 per day, 925Kč); **Warsaw, POL** (9½hr., 3 per day, 1290Kč).

Buses: (☎900 149 044; www.vlak-bus.cz). The state-run **ČSAD** (☎257 319 016) has several bus terminals. The biggest is **Florenc,** Křižíkova 4 (☎900 149 044). Metro B or C: Florenc. Info office open daily 6am-9pm. Buy tickets in advance. To: **Berlin, GER** (7hr., 1 per day, 850Kč); **Budapest, HUN** (8hr., 1 per day, 1550Kč); **Paris, FRA** (14hr., 3 per day, 2200Kč); **Sofia, BUL** (24hr., 5 per day, 1600Kč); **Vienna, AUT** (5hr., 1 per day, 600Kč). 10% ISIC discount. The **Tourbus** office (☎224 218 680; www.eurolines.cz), on the main fl. of the terminal, sells tickets for **Eurolines** and airport buses. Open M-F 7am-7pm, Sa 8am-7pm, Su 9am-7pm.

✦ ORIENTATION

Shouldering the river **Vltava,** greater Prague is a mess of suburbs and maze-like streets. Fortunately, nearly everything of interest to travelers lies within the compact downtown. The Vltava runs south-northeast through central Prague, separating **Staré Město** (Old Town) and **Nové Město** (New Town) from **Malá Strana** (Lesser Side). On the right bank of the river, Staré Město's **Staroměstské náměstí** (Old Town Square) is Prague's focal point. From the square, the elegant **Pařížská ulice** (Paris

Street) leads north into **Josefov**, the old Jewish quarter. Just south of Staré Město, the more modern **Nové Město** houses **Václavské náměstí** (Wenceslas Square), the administrative and commercial core of the city. To the west of Staroměstské nám., the picturesque **Karlův most** (Charles Bridge) spans the Vltava, connecting Staré Město with **Malostranské náměstí** (Lesser Town Square). **Pražský Hrad** (Prague Castle) overlooks Malostranské nám. from **Hradčany** hill. Prague's **train station, Hlavní nádraží**, and **Florenc bus station** are northeast of Václavské nám. All train and bus terminals are on or near the **Metro** system. To get to Staroměstské nám., take Metro A line to Staroměstská and follow Kaprova away from the river. Kiosks and bookstores sell an indexed *plán města* (map), essential for newcomers to the city.

⊏ LOCAL TRANSPORTATION

Public Transportation: Prague's **Metro, tram,** and **bus** services are excellent and all share the same ticket system. 8Kč tickets are good for 1 15min. ride or 4 stops on the Metro. 12Kč ticket valid for 1hr. of bus, tram, and Metro travel, with unlimited connections in the same direction. Large bags, bikes, and baby carriages 6Kč. Validate tickets in machines above the escalators to avoid 400Kč fines issued by plainclothes inspectors who roam the transport lines. Buy tickets at newsstands, *tabák* kiosks, machines in stations, or DP (*Dopravní podnik;* transport authority) kiosks. DP offices (☎222 646 350; open daily 7am-6pm), near the Jungmannovo nám. exit of the Můstek Metro stop, sell **multi-day passes** valid for the entire network (1-day 70Kč, 3-day 200Kč, 1-week 250Kč, 15-day 280Kč). The 3 **Metro** lines run daily 5am-midnight: A is green on maps, B is yellow, and C is red. **Night trams** #51-58 and **buses** #502-514 and 601 run after the last Metro and cover the same areas as day trams and buses (every 30min. 12:30-4:30am); look for dark blue signs with white letters at bus stops. For the most up-to-date information, contact DP (☎296 191 817; www.dpp.cz).

Taxis: Radiotaxi (☎272 731 848) or **AAA** (☎140 14). 30Kč base, 22Kč per km, 4Kč per min. waiting. You can hail a cab anywhere on the street, but call ahead to avoid getting ripped off. To sidestep the taxi scams that run rampant, always ask for a receipt (*"Prosím, dejte mi paragon"*) with distance traveled and price paid. If the driver doesn't comply, you aren't obligated to pay. Many drivers speak some English.

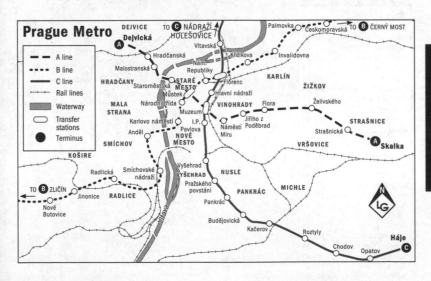

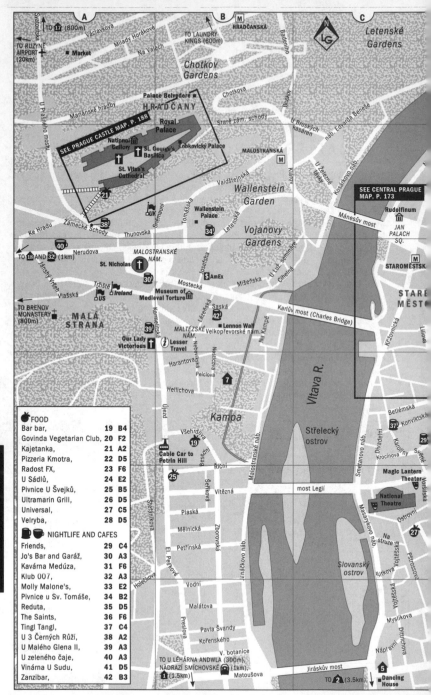

FOOD

Bar bar,	19	B4
Govinda Vegetarian Club,	20	F2
Kajetanka,	21	A2
Pizzeria Kmotra,	22	D5
Radost FX,	23	F6
U Sádlů,	24	E2
Pivnice U Švejků,	25	B5
Ultramarin Grill,	26	D5
Universal,	27	C5
Velryba,	28	D5

NIGHTLIFE AND CAFES

Friends,	29	C4
Jo's Bar and Garáž,	30	A3
Kavárna Medúza,	31	F6
Klub 007,	32	A3
Molly Malone's,	33	E2
Pivnice u Sv. Tomáše,	34	B2
Reduta,	35	D5
The Saints,	36	F6
Tingl Tangl,	37	C4
U 3 Černých Růží,	38	A2
U Malého Glena II,	39	A3
U zeleného čaje,	40	A3
Vinárna U Sudu,	41	D5
Zanzibar,	42	B3

CZECH REPUBLIC

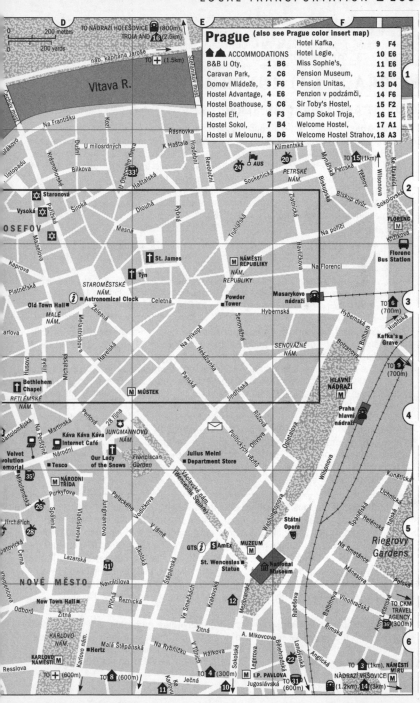

Prague (also see Prague color insert map)

▲▲ ACCOMMODATIONS

B&B U Oty,	**1**	**B6**
Caravan Park,	**2**	**C6**
Domov Mládeže,	**3**	**F6**
Hostel Advantage,	**4**	**E6**
Hostel Boathouse,	**5**	**C6**
Hostel Elf,	**6**	**F3**
Hostel Sokol,	**7**	**B4**
Hostel u Melounu,	**8**	**D6**
Hotel Kafka,	**9**	**F4**
Hotel Legie,	**10**	**E6**
Miss Sophie's,	**11**	**E6**
Pension Museum,	**12**	**E6**
Pension Unitas,	**13**	**D4**
Penzion v podzámčí,	**14**	**F6**
Sir Toby's Hostel,	**15**	**F2**
Camp Sokol Troja,	**16**	**E1**
Welcome Hostel,	**17**	**A1**
Welcome Hostel Strahov,	**18**	**A3**

CZECH REPUBLIC

Car Rental: Hertz, at the airport (☎233 326 714; www.hertz.cz/en). Cars from 1880Kč per day for the 1st 5 days with unlimited mileage. Must have a 1-year-old driver's license and major credit card. 21+. Open daily 8am-10pm. Branch at Karlovo nám. 28 (☎222 231 010). Open daily 8am-10pm.

⁊ PRACTICAL INFORMATION

TOURIST AND FINANCIAL SERVICES

Tourist Office: The green "i"s around Prague mark the myriad tourist agencies that book rooms and sell **maps,** bus tickets, and guidebooks. The main **Pražská Informační Služba** in the Old Town Hall (PIS; Prague Information Service; ☎12 444; www.pis.cz), sells maps (25-199Kč) and tickets for shows and public transport. Open Apr.-Oct. M 11am-6pm, Tu-Su 9am-6pm; Nov.-Mar. M 11am-5pm, Tu-Su 9am-5pm. Branches at Na příkopě 20 and Hlavní nádraží (in summer M-F 9am-7pm, Sa-Su 9am-5pm; in low season M-F 9am-6pm, Sa 9am-3pm), and in the tower by the Malá Strana side of the Charles Bridge (open Apr.-Oct. daily 10am-6pm).

Budget Travel:

CKM, Mánesova 77 (☎222 721 595; www.ckm-praha.cz). Metro A: Jiřího z Poděbrad. Sells budget air tickets to those under 26. Also books accommodations in Prague from 250Kč. Open M-Th 10am-6pm, F 10am-4pm.

GTS, Ve smečkách 27 (☎222 211 204; www.gtsint.cz). Metro A or C: Muzeum. Offers student discounts on airline tickets (225-2500Kč within Europe). Open M-F 8am-10pm, Sa 10am-4pm.

Lesser Travel, Karmelitská 24 (☎257 534 130; www.airtickets.cz). Offers student airfares. Open M-F 10am-5pm.

Embassies and Consulates: Australia, Klimentská 10, 6th fl. (☎296 578 350; www.embassy.gov.au/cz.html) and **New Zealand,** Dykova 19 (☎222 514 672) have consulates, but citizens should contact the UK embassy in an emergency. Australian consulate open M-Th 8:30am-5pm, F 8:30am-2pm. **Canada,** Muchova 6 (☎272 101 800; www.canada.cz). Open M-F 8:30am-12:30pm and 1:30-4:30pm. Consular section is open only in the morning. In emergencies, call the embassy number and remain on the line to be transferred to the Watch Office in Ottawa. **Ireland,** Tržiště 13 (☎257 530 061; fax 257 531 387; irishembassy@iol.cz). Metro A: Malostranská. Open M-F 9:30am-12:30pm and 2:30-4:30pm. **UK,** Thunovská 14 (☎257 402 111; consular and visa info prague@fco.gov.uk; other info info@britain.cz). Metro A: Malostranská. Open M-Th 9am-noon. **US,** Tržiště 15 (☎257 530 663, after-hours emergency ☎253 12 00; www.usembassy.cz). Metro A: Malostranská. Open M-F 8am-4:30pm. Consular section open M-F 9am-noon.

The different lengths of telephone numbers, ranging from 4 to 9 digits, can be confusing. Prague updates its phone system incessantly. The city modified all numbers in 2002, adding a 2 before most land lines and removing the 0 for mobile numbers. Updated numbers have 9 digits; if a number has fewer than 9, it either is an information or emergency line or is missing a city area code. The city area code is the first three digits of a number, usually a 2 followed by a number between 10 and 35. The numbers listed here reflect the most recent changes, but call the city's telephone info line for any updates (☎141 11).

Currency Exchange: Exchange counters are everywhere and rates vary wildly. Don't bother with the expensive hotels, and never change money on the streets. **Cheque-points** are plentiful and stay open until about 11pm, but sometimes charge suspicious commissions, so know your math. Try bargaining. **Komerční banka,** Na příkopě 33

(☎222 432 111; fax 224 243 018), buys notes and checks for 2% commission. Open M-W 9am-6pm, Th-F 9am-5pm. Branch at Staroměstské nám. 24. Open M-F 9am-5pm. **E Banka,** Václavské nám. 43 (☎222 115 222; www.ebanka.cz). Open M-F 8am-7pm.

ATMs: Though you can't throw a rock without hitting a currency exchange, ATMs are surprisingly scarce, and are most often found attached to banks.

American Express: Václavské nám. 56 (☎222 800 224). Metro A or C: Muzeum. AmEx **ATM** outside. **Western Union** services available. MC/V **cash advances** (3% commission). Open daily 9am-7pm. Branches at Mostecká 12 (☎257 313 638; open daily 9:30am-7:30pm), Celetná 17 (☎222 481 205; open daily 8:30am-7:15pm), and Staroměstské nám. 5 (☎224 818 388; open daily 9am-7:30pm).

LOCAL SERVICES

Luggage Storage: Lockers in train and bus stations take 2 5Kč coins. Fine for forgotten lock code 30Kč. For storage over 24hr., use the luggage offices to the left in the basement of Hlavní nádraží. 15Kč per day, bags over 15kg 30Kč. Fine for forgotten lock code 30Kč. Open 24hr. with breaks 5:30-6am, 11-11:30am, and 5:30-6pm.

English-Language Bookstores:

☒**The Globe Bookstore,** Pštrossova 6 (☎224 934 203; www.globebookstore.cz). Metro B: Národní třída. Exit Metro left on Spálená, make the 1st right on Ostrovní, then the 3rd left on Pštrossova. A haven for English speakers, this bookstore and coffeehouse sells a wide variety of new and used books and periodicals, and offers **Internet** (1.50Kč per min.). Doubles as a cafe serving up fruit smoothies (55-70Kč) and brunch late into the afternoon—perfect after a day of sleeping off an alcohol-induced fog. Open daily 10am-midnight.

Anagram Bookshop, Týn 4 (☎248 957 37; www.anagram.cz). Metro A: Staroměstská. Behind Týn Church, a short way down Týn. Anagram stocks a wide selection of literary fiction, philosophy, political theory, art books, and literary guides to Prague. The proprietor is a wealth of knowledge of the literary and political history of Prague. Trade-ins are available for store credit. Open M-Sa 10am-10pm, Su 10am-6pm. MC/V.

Big Ben Bookshop, Malá Štupartská 5 (☎224 826 565; www.bigbenbookshop.com). Metro A: Staroměstská. Open M-F 9am-6:30pm, Sa 10am-5pm, Su noon-5pm. MC/V.

Laundromat: Laundry Kings, Dejvická 16 (☎233 343 743; www.laundry.czweb.org). Metro A: Hradčanská. Trams #1, 8, 18, 25, 26. Exit Metro to Dejvická, cross the street, and turn left. Travelers flock here at night to watch CNN and pick each other up. Bulletin board for apartment-seekers, English teachers, and "friends." Internet 55Kč per 30min. Wash 80Kč per 6kg, dry 90Kč, more for heavier materials; detergent 10-20Kč.

FROM THE ROAD

CZECH THE SCHEDULE

Catching intercity transport in the Czech Republic is a tricky endeavor. Czech bus and train stations are littered with posted schedules, each a maze of numbers, hammers, sickles, and circles that bear a closer resemblance to target practice than an intelligible course from point A to point B.

The clearest Czech train and bus schedules are on the Internet, at www.vlak.cz, which has recently been translated into English. But in case you arrive at the station without having done any online research, here's a rough guide to deciphering the hieroglyphics you'll encounter on the schedule: crossed mallets indicate services that operate only on weekdays. The number 6 indicates Saturday service. A "K" or an "L" accompanied by a number corresponds to notes at the bottom of the schedule which detail periods of time during which the bus does not run as scheduled. Also, check the arrival time at your destination: if you see a vertical or zig-zagged line running through it, this means that the service is express and passes through but does not stop at that destination. With this code cracked, you can breathe a sigh of relief, knowing you really will get to Litomyšl, even though you're on a bus labeled "Libec."

—Lauren Rivera

Open M-F 6am-10pm, Sa-Su 8am-10pm. Last wash 9:30pm. **Laundromat/Internet Cafe,** Korunní 14 (☎222 510 180; www.volny.cz/laundromat). Metro A: nám. Míru. Trams #10, 16, 22, 23. English spoken. Internet 30Kč per 15min. Wash and dry 70Kč each; detergent 75Kč. Open daily 8am-8pm.

Bike Rental: Praha Bike, Dlouhá 24 (☎732 388 880; www.prahabike.cz). Bikes delivered to your hotel. Bike rental includes helmet, lock, luggage storage, and map. Bike rentals 200Kč per 2hr., 500Kč per 8hr., 550Kč per 10hr.; 2hr. minimum. 10% ISIC discount. 2hr. city bike tours daily May 1-Sept. 15 11:30am, 2:30, 5:30pm; Sept. 15-Oct. 31

Central Prague (also see Prague color map)	
🏠 **ACCOMMODATIONS**	🌙**NIGHTLIFE**
Apple Hostel, **9**	Cafe Marquis de Sade, **16**
Hostel Týn, **10**	Karlovy Lázně, **18**
Hotel King George, **23**	Kozička, **6**
Ritchie's Hostel, **17**	Le Chateau, **15**
Traveller's Hostel Dlouha, **1**	Roxy, **2**
Traveller's Hostel Husova 3, **24**	U staré paní, **25**
U Lilie, **19**	Ungelt, **14**
🍴 **FOOD**	☕**CAFES**
Cafe Bambus, **3**	Bakeshop Praha, **7**
Country Life, **21**	Bohemia Bagel, **8**
Jáchymka, **11**	Cafe Ebel, **13, 22**
Klub architektů, **27**	Paneria, **12**
Pizza Express, **25**	
Pizzeria Roma, **20**	
U Řozvarilů, **5**	

2:30pm; Mar. 14-Apr. 30 2:30pm. Prague parks tours daily May-Sept. 5:30pm. All tours €13. Trips outside Prague can also be arranged. Open daily 9am-7pm.

EMERGENCY AND COMMUNICATIONS

Emergency: ☎112.

24hr. Pharmacy: U Lékárna Anděla, Štefánikova 6 (☎257 320 918 or 257 324 686; after-hours 257 320 194; lekandela@volny.cz). Metro B: Anděl. With your back to the Anděl Metro station, turn left and follow Nádražní, which becomes Štefánikova. Open M-F 7am-9pm, Sa-Su 8am-9pm. After-hours service M-F 9pm-7am and from Sa 1pm to M 7am. For after-hours service, press button marked *Pohotovost* to left of the main door.

Medical Services: Na Homolce (Hospital for Foreigners), Roentgenova 2 (☎257 271 111, reception for foreigners 257 272 146; www.homolka.cz). Bus #167 runs to the hospital from Na Knížecí (Metro B: Anděl). Open 24hr. **Canadian Medical Center,** Veleslavínská 1 (☎235 360 133, after hours 724 300 301; www.cmc.praha.cz). Most major payment plans accepted. Open M, W, F 8am-6pm; Tu and Th 8am-8pm.

Telephones: Virtually everywhere. Card phones are the most common and convenient. Phone cards are sold at kiosks, post offices, and some exchange establishments for 175Kč per 50 units and 350Kč per 100 units; don't let kiosks rip you off. Coins also accepted (local calls from 4Kč per min.).

Internet: Internet access is everywhere in Prague; however, it is also more expensive than in the rest of the Czech Republic. Access is available in libraries, hostels, cafes, bars, and even laundromats. **Národní třída** is home to several lab-like cyber cafes.

■**Bohemia Bagel,** Masná 2 (☎224 812 560; www.bohemiabagel.cz). Metro A: Staroměstská. The Internet kiosks to either side, beneath ceilings painted with stars, are one of the better deals in Prague at 1.80Kč per min. Open daily 9am-midnight.

Káva Káva Káva, Národní třída 37 (☎253 142 68; www.kava-coffee.cz). Metro B: Národní třída. Across the street from Tesco, to the right and through the arch on the left. Classic European coffeehouse: patrons sit out front around marbletop tables, or people-watch through giant glass windows. Espresso from 45Kč. Milkshakes 40Kč. Internet downstairs 2.50Kč per min. until 6pm, 2Kč per min. thereafter; 20Kč minimum. Open M-F 7am-10pm, Sa-Su 9am-10pm. AmEx/MC/V.

Professional PC Arena G8, Národní třída 25 (☎777 571 537 or 605 732 966). Metro B: Národní třída. Across from Tesco, inside the Pasáž paláce Metro. Past KFC, follow the sign that says "Laser Game" downstairs, through the arcade. Check your email next to the tweens pounding back Dr. Pepper while pounding each other at CounterStrike. Internet 1Kč per min. Open 24hr.

Post Office: Jindřišská 14 (☎221 131 445). Metro A or B: Můstek. **Poste Restante** available. Take number from kiosk in main hallway and wait to be called. Internet 1Kč per min. Tellers close 7pm. Open daily 2am-midnight. **Postal Code:** 110 00.

Central Prague

200 meters

200 yards

Havlíčkova

Masarykovo nádraží

Zlatnická

Na Poříčí

V Celnici

NetCafe

Truhlářská

Albert Grocery

Revoluční

Benediktská

Rybná

Králodvorská

NÁM. REPUBLIKY

NÁMĚSTÍ REPUBLIKY

Hybernská

Senovážná

SENOVÁŽNÉ NÁM.

Diažděná

Jubilee (Jubilejní)

Jeruzalémská

TO HLAVNÍ NÁDRAŽÍ (700m)

U půjčovny

Růžová

Jindřišská

St. Henry (sv. Jindřich)

Nekázanka

Mucha Museum

Panská

V Cípu

U Obecního Domu

Rybná

Municipal House (Obecní dům)

Powder Tower (Prašná brána)

Templová

House of Cadlim

OVOCNÝ

TRH Theatre Ticket Office

Estates Theatre (Stavovské divadlo)

Na příkopě

Museum of Communism

MŮSTEK

WENCESLAS SQUARE

Masná

Rámová

Dlouhá

Big Ben Bookshop

St. James (sv. Jakub)

Jakubská

Malá Štupartská

Anagram

Celetná

Stupartská

Ungelt

House of the Golden Ring

Tynská

Týn Church (Panna Marie před Týnem)

Kamziková

Karolinum (Charles University)

Havelská

St. Gall (sv. Havel)

Havelská Ulička

Provaznická

Na můstku

Rytířská

28. října

TO (50m)

Kozí

Praha Bike

V Kolkovně

Dušní

Týnská

Goltz-Kinský Palace

Kožná

Železná

STAROMĚSTSKÉ NÁM.

UHELNÝ TRH

V. kotcích

Havelská

Skořepka

Spanish (Španělská)

Věženská

Dušní

St. Salvator (sv. Salvátor)

Image Theater

AmEx

Jan Hus Statue

Melantrichova

Michalská

Jilská

St. Giles (sv. Jiljí)

Zlatá

Husova

Zatecká

Michalská

El. Krásnohorské

Old-New (Staronová)

Jewish Town Hall (Židovská radnice)

Maiselova

Maisel (Maislova)

Church of St. Nicholas (sv. Mikuláš)

Kafka Museum

Pařížská

Široká

Pařížská

Astronomical Clock

MALÉ NÁM.

Old Town Hall (Staroměstská radnice)

STARÉ MĚSTO

Platnéřská

Linhartská

MARIÁNSKÉ NÁM.

Husova

Jilská

Karlova

Czech Museum of Fine Arts

Veleslavova

JOSEFOV

Dvořákovo nábř.

Na rejdišti

Rudolfinum (Dům umělců)

Decorative Arts Museum (Umělecko-prům/slové)

JAN PALACH SQ.

Brehová

Klaus (Klausová)

Jewish Cemetery

Ceremonial Hall

Pinkas (Pinkasova)

Červená

Maiselova

Kaprova

17 listopadu

STAROMĚSTSKÁ

Valentinská

Maiselova

Žatecká

Řásek loustek Theater

City Library of Prague

Semináriská

Husova

Betlemské NÁM.

Bethlehem Chapel (Betlémská kaple)

Řetězová

Liliová

Náprstkova

Náprstek Museum

Smetana Museum

Theater at the Balustrade (Divadlo na zábradlí)

Anenská

ANENSKÉ NÁM.

Stříbrná

Na zábradlí

Karlova

Karoliny Světlé

Klementinum and sv Klimenti (St. Clement Church)

Thomas Cook

St. Francis (sv. František)

TO CHARLES BRIDGE (50m)

Aišovo nábř.

Mánesův most

Alšovo nábř.

Veleslavínova

Křižovnická

Platnéřská

Kozí

CZECH REPUBLIC

ᴳ ACCOMMODATIONS

While hotel prices have risen exponentially, hostel prices have stabilized around 300-600Kč. Small, family-run hostels are cheaper than the large hostels in the center of town. Reserve rooms in advance, and at least a month ahead in June, July, and August. Many hostels have 24hr. reception and require check-in after 2pm and check-out by 10am. Though less common than in other parts of Eastern Europe, affordable rooms are being rented out by a growing number of Prague residents.

ACCOMMODATION AGENCIES

Hawkers, most of whom are mere hired agents, besiege visitors at the train station. Many offer legitimate deals, but some just want to rip you off. The going rates for **apartments** hover around 600-1200Kč per day, depending on proximity to the center; haggling is possible. If you're wary of bargaining on the street, try a private agency. Staying outside the center is convenient if you're near public transport, so ask where the nearest stop is. If in doubt, ask for details in writing. You can often pay in US dollars, but prices are lower in koruny. Some travel agencies will book accommodations (see **Tourist and Financial Services,** p. 170).

HOSTELS

If you're schlepping a backpack in Hlavní nádraží or Holešovice, you will likely encounter hostel runners offering cheap beds. Many hostels are university dorms that take in travelers from June to August. These rooms are easy options for those without reservations. For more than a mere bed, there are plenty of smaller, friendlier alternatives, most of which have an English-speaking staff.

STARÉ MĚSTO

Apple Hostel, Krádlodvorská 16 (☎224 231 050; www.applehostel.cz), at the corner of Revoluční and nám. Republiky. Metro B: nám. Republiky. Prague hostels don't get much more social than Apple Hostel: guests cram into the common room, shouting to one another in various languages about which club to hit next. The staff is friendly, but may not be able to keep ahead of plumbing trouble. Breakfast included. Safe deposit 200Kč. Laundry 120Kč. Internet 1Kč per min. Check-out 10am. Key deposit 200Kč. See website for rather complicated price system. Mar. 11-Nov. dorms 470-540Kč; singles 1150Kč, with bath 1350Kč; doubles 1300/1600Kč. Jan. 2-Mar. 10 and Nov.-Dec. 27 dorms 270-440Kč; singles 950/1150Kč; doubles 1100/1400Kč. ❷

Travellers' Hostels (☎224 826 6623; www.travellers.cz). Travellers' has 5 locations around Prague. That Travellers' is a franchise means they have all the facilities backpackers want. It also means you're being heavily target-marketed as a "backpacker."

Dlouhá 33 (☎224 826 662; fax 224 826 665). Metro B: nám. Republiky. Exit the Metro and walk toward Hotel City Center, following Revoluční toward the river. Go left on Dlouhá; the hostel is on the right. Large rooms, unbeatable location, and a terrace bar make up for the peeling paint. The only Travellers' Hostel open year-round, it has social dorms and more private renovated apartments. Laundry 150Kč. Internet 1Kč per min. Book 2-3 weeks ahead in summer. 10-bed dorm 370Kč 6-bed dorms 430Kč; singles 1120Kč, with bath 1300Kč; doubles 620/720Kč. Apartments 2100-3000Kč. 40Kč ISIC discount. AmEx/D/MC/V. ❷

Husova 3 (☎222 220 078). Metro B: Národní třída. Turn right on Spálená (which turns into Na Perštýně), then right on Husova. Smaller, quieter, and in the middle of Staré Město, with bright rooms, gingham sheets, and heavenly pillows. Outdoor picnic area. Kind staff. Satellite TV. English spoken. Breakfast included. Open July-Aug. 4- to 5-bed dorms 450Kč; doubles 620Kč. ❷

Hostel Týn, Týnská 19 (☎224 828 519; www.hostel-tyn.web2001.cz). Metro A: Staroměstská. From Staroměstské nám., head down Dlouhá, bear right on Masná, and turn right again on Týnská. Hostel is through the gate to the right. Located in the heart of Staré Město, Hostel Týn skillfully avoids the extremes of overcrowding and boredom: dorms are small, but the crowd is young and social. Soft beds. Clean, orderly facilities. No common room. 5-bed dorms 400Kč; doubles 1100Kč. 200Kč deposit. ❷

Ritchie's Hostel, Karlova 9 (☎222 221 229; www.praguehostel.net). Metro A: Staroměstská, down Karlova from the Charles Bridge, past the small square. Ritchie's is right in the thick of the tourist district, but the professional staff make sure that no tackiness enters the premises. The several ancient buildings that make up the hostel are spare, but always clean and functional. Safes €1 per day, lockers €2 per day. Internet €1 per 20min. 6-bed dorm 450Kč; doubles 1890/2000Kč. MC/V. ❷

NOVÉ MĚSTO

▨ **Hostel u Melounu** (At the Watermelon), Ke Karlovu 7/457 (☎224 918 322; www.hostelumelounu.cz). Metro C: IP Pavlova. With your back to the Metro, turn left on Sokolská, make an immediate right on Na Bojišti, and turn left at the street's end on Ke Karlovu. Hostel u Melounu provides a welcome respite from the often impersonal hostels of downtown Prague. Located in a former hospital, it has soft beds, clean bathrooms, welcoming and helpful English-speaking staff, and a large garden. Breakfast included. Check-out 10am. Internet 2Kč per min. Dorms 400Kč; singles 550Kč; doubles 450Kč. 30Kč ISIC discount. AmEx/MC/V. ❷

▨ **Pension Unitas Art Prison Hostel/Cloister Inn,** Bartolomějská 9 (☎224 221 802; www.unitas.cz). Metro B: Národní třída. With Tesco on your right, cross Národní and continue down Na Perštýně. Turn left on Bartolomějská. Once home to a Communist jail, the "pink prison" today offers clean and pleasant dorms. The bright decor makes it hard to imagine what Václav Havel's cell looked like when he was incarcerated here. A small plaque marks Havel's cell, #6. The more spacious Cloister Inn is upstairs in former offices of the secret police. Reception 24hr. Reserve ahead. Dorms 270Kč. Apr.-Oct. singles 1100Kč; doubles 1400Kč; triples 1800Kč; quads 2100Kč. Nov.-Mar. 1000/1200/1500/1800Kč. MC/V. Hostel ❶/hotel ❹

Miss Sophle's, Melounová 3 (☎296 303 532; www.missophies.com). Metro C: IP Pavlova. Take 1st left from subway platform, then follow Katerinská to 1st right onto Melounová. For the stylish budget traveler, a brick cellar lounge and artistically spare dorm decor make up for the absence of a kitchen. Free Internet. Reception 24hr. In high season dorms 400Kč; singles 1500Kč; doubles 1800Kč; triples 2000Kč; apartments 1800-2500Kč. In low season 300/1200/1500/1700/1400-1900Kč. Cash only. ❷

Hostel Advantage, Sokolská 11-13 (☎224 914 062; www.advantagehostel.cz). Metro C: IP Pavlova. From the Metro, take the stairs on the left leading to Ječná, cross the street, make a left onto Sokolska, and the hostel will be 100m down on your right. Amid brightly colored, animal-stenciled rooms, Hostel Advantage gives you a good night's sleep in the middle of Nové Město for reasonable prices. It also sometimes gives you watery bathroom floors. Breakfast included. Free luggage storage. Free Internet. 4- to 8-bed dorm 400Kč; double 500Kč. 10% ISIC discount. ❷

MALÁ STRANA AND VINOHRADY

Hostel Sokol, Nosticova 2 (☎257 007 397). Metro A: Malostranská. From the Metro, take tram #12 or 22 to Hellichova; or, walk from Malostranské nám. down Karmelitská about 300m. Take a left on Hellichova, then last left on Nosticova, and watch for signs. Hostel is at the far end of a small park, past the restaurant on your left. Reception on 3rd fl. There is nothing flashy about Hostel Sokol. You will not find hip murals and crazy fonts on the walls, but rather reliable functionality at excellent prices. Sheets are bright white. Facilities are clean. Roof terrace and kitchens upstairs. Reserve ahead. A special rate is offered at neighboring Bohemia Bagel. Reception 24hr. Check-out 10am. June-Sept. 16-bed dorms 350Kč; doubles 900Kč. Oct.-May 300/700Kč. ❶

Hostel Elf, Husitská 11 (☎222 540 963; www.hostelelf.com). Metro B: Florenc. Take Bus #207 to U Památníku. Hostel is upstairs through the wooden gate next to the orange wall surrounded by swooshy paint. Elf has a highly social atmosphere, bright colors, and a multitude of services. Comfy leather couches in the living room and gardened terrace out front. Transport to airport 450Kč. No alcohol in dorms. Breakfast included. 100Kč deposit for sheets in dorms. Laundry 200Kč. Free Internet. 9-bed dorms 290Kč; singles 700Kč, with baths 1000Kč; doubles 840/1200Kč. ❶

Domov Mládeže, Dykova 20 (☎222 511 777; www.dhotels.cz). Metro A: Jiřího z Poděbrad. Exit the Metro at Vinohradská. Walking toward the huge clock, cross the street and take your 1st right on Nitranská, which dead-ends into a park. Turn left on Dykova, which isn't signposted. Walk about 100m. Located in an up-and-coming neighborhood, surrounded with new bars and aging mansions, Domov Mládeže offers a wide range of accommodations with an equally wide range of sizes and prices. Gleaming bathrooms. Breakfast included. Reserve ahead. 2- to 7-person dorms 370-480Kč; singles 500-1700Kč; doubles 940-1360Kč. 10% ISIC discount. ❷

OUTSIDE THE CENTER

⛵ **Hostel Boathouse**, Lodnická 1 (☎241 770 051; www.aa.cz/boathouse). Take tram #21 from Národní třída south toward Sídliště. Get off at Černý Kůň (20min.), go down the ramp from the tram, turn left toward the Vltava, and follow the yellow hostel signs. Věra has one of the most highly praised staffs in all of Europe, and she remembers almost every guest's name. Walls are covered in letters of thanks from former guests. Beds and pillows are the softest in Prague. The Boathouse serves meals (hot dinner 120Kč) and offers board games, Internet, satellite TV, and laundry (150Kč). Breakfast included. Call ahead; if they're full, Věra might let you sleep in the hall. Email reservations preferred. 3- to 5-bed dorms above a working boathouse 340Kč; 8-bed dorm 360Kč. ❶

Penzion v podzámčí, V podzámčí 27 (☎241 444 609; www.sleepinprague.com). From Metro C: Budějovická, take bus #192. Request that the driver stop at Nad Rybníky. The hostel is up the hill behind the bus stop. The friendly staff provides homey service, including laundry (100Kč). Communal kitchen, satellite TV, comfy beds, and amazing hot chocolate. Highway-side rooms can be noisy. Breakfast 40Kč. Internet 100Kč per hr. Reserve in advance. July-Aug. dorms 330Kč; doubles 790Kč; triples 1080Kč. Sept.-June 310/690/960Kč. 30Kč student discount. ❶

Welcome Hostel, Zíkova 13 (☎224 320 202; www.bed.cz). Metro A: Dejvická. Exit Metro on Šolinova and go left on Zíkova. A true bargain: an entire room in a spacious university dorm for the cost of a Staré Město dorm bed. Close to airport shuttle. If full, they can book you at their sister hostel (see below). Check-in 2pm. Check-out 9:30am. Singles 400Kč; doubles 500Kč; triples 600Kč. 10% ISIC discount. ❷

Welcome Hostel at Strahov Complex, Vaníčkova 7 (☎224 320 202; www.bed.cz). Take bus #149 or 217 from Metro A: Dejvická to Koleje Strahov (15min.) and cross the street to reach the hostel reception, located in Block 3. Right by an enormous stadium, Strahov is 10 concrete blocks of bright blue high-rise dormitories. Rooms are basic but clean and only 10min. by foot from Prague Castle. Not convenient but sufficient. Open July-Sept. Singles 300Kč; doubles 440Kč. 10% ISIC discount. ❶

Sir Toby's Hostel, Dělnická 24 (☎283 870 635; www.sirtobys.com). Metro A: Vltavická. From station, take any of the trams headed to your left. Get off at Dělnická. Tram deposits you on Komunardů. Keep walking in direction of the tram and turn left on Dělnická. Sir Toby's occupies a renovated art nouveau building in a neighborhood of shops and pubs. Neither the most nor the least social hostel. Windows overlook garden and street. Breakfast 80Kč. Laundry 150Kč. Internet 50Kč per hr. Dorms 340-390Kč. ❷

HOTELS AND PENSIONS

As tourists colonize Prague, hotels are upgrading their services and their prices; budget hotels are now scarce. Call several months ahead to book a room for the summer and confirm by fax with a credit card. For something out of the ordinary, try the admirably renovated prison cells at the Cloister Inn (see above).

STARÉ MĚSTO

■ **Hotel King George** (Dům U Krále Jiřího), Liliová 10 (☎222 220 925; www.kinggeorge.cz). Metro A: Staroměstská. Exit at nám. Jana Palacha. Facing the river, turn left and walk down Křižovnická until you reach a tunnel, then turn left onto Karlova. Liliová, the 1st right, is easily missed. Enter through restaurant. Expensive but worth a splurge. Rooms have televisions, minibars, couches, private baths, and even full-sized desks. Buffet breakfast included, as well as a 10% discount on anything bought at the restaurant downstairs. Safes 60Kč per night. Reception daily 7am-11pm. Mar.-Oct. singles 2250Kč; doubles 3100Kč; triples 4300Kč; apartments 3100Kč-6550Kč. Prices fall by 300Kč Jan.-Feb. and Nov.-Dec. ❺

U Lilie, Liliová 15 (☎222 220 432; www.pensionulilie.cz). Metro A: Staroměstská. Follow the directions to Dům U Krále Jiřího. U Lilie boasts a lovely courtyard; satellite TV, telephone, and minibar in every room. Breakfast included. Singles 1850Kč; doubles 2150Kč, with bath 2800Kč. Cash only. ❺

NOVÉ MĚSTO

■ **Pension Museum**, Mezlbranská 15 (☎296 325 186; www.pension-museum.cz). Metro C: Muzeum. From the Metro, go right on Mezibranská and walk uphill. It's on the right. Ultra-modern B&B near Wenceslas Sq. Beautiful courtyard leads to elegant rooms with TVs and spacious baths. Welcoming staff. Decadent breakfast buffet included. Reserve at least a month in advance. Apr.-Dec. singles 2240Kč; doubles 2650Kč; apartments 2750-4450Kč. Jan.-Mar. 1450/1800/1790-3180Kč. AmEx/MC/V. ❺

Hotel Legie, Sokolská 33 (☎224 266 231, reservations 224 266 240; www.legie.cz). Metro C: IP Pavlova. From the Metro, turn left on Ječná; hotel is across the street. The unattractive Soviet facade of this high-rise hotel hides sparkling rooms with private showers, phone, and cable TV; some afford great views of Prague Castle. Breakfast included. Apr.-Oct. and Jan. singles 2500Kč; doubles 3000Kč; triples 3900Kč. Feb. and Nov.-Dec. 1800/2100/2800Kč. AmEx/MC/V. ❺

OUTSIDE THE CENTER

Hotel Kafka, Cimburkova 24 (☎222 781 333, reservations 224 225 769), in Žižkov near the TV tower. From Metro C: Hlavní nádraží, take tram #5 toward Harfa, #9 toward Spojovací, or #26 toward Nádraží Hostivař; get off at Husinecká. Head uphill on Seifertova 3 blocks and go left on Cimburkova. Spotless, comfortable hotel located in a residential neighborhood. Phone and TV in every room. Breakfast included. Apr.-Oct. singles 1700Kč; doubles 2300Kč; triples 3200Kč; quads 3500Kč. Nov.-Mar. 1000/1300/1700/2200Kč. MC/V with 5% commission. ❺

B&B U Oty (Ota's House), Radlická 188 (☎257 215 323; www.bbuoty.cz). Metro B: Radlická. Exit the Metro up the stairs to the left, go right past Bistro Kavos on Radlická, and walk 400m. Although it's far from the city center, U Oty offers spacious, well-furnished, clean rooms at an affordable price. Best for groups of 2 or more due to the walk to and from the Metro station along a poorly lit highway. Kitchen. Breakfast included. Laundry free after 3 nights. Reserve ahead. Singles 700Kč; doubles 770Kč; triples 990Kč; quads 1300Kč. 100Kč extra if staying only 1 night. ❸

⚐ CAMPING

Campsites have taken over both the outskirts and the centrally located Vltava Islands. Reserve bungalows in advance. Tents are generally available without prior notice. Tourist offices sell a guide (15Kč) to campsites near the city.

Camp Sokol Troja, Trojská 171 (☎/fax 233 542 908). From Metro C: Nádraží Holešovice, take bus #112 to Kazanka, the 4th stop. Prague's largest campground, north of the center in the Troja district. A unique camping experience—pitch a tent and admire the beautiful houses of one of Prague's wealthiest neighborhoods. Sparkling bathing facilities. At least 4 similar establishments line the same road. July-Aug. 130Kč per person, 90-180Kč per tent. Oct.-June 70-150Kč per tent. Private rooms available. July-Aug. singles 320Kč; doubles 640Kč. Oct.-June 290/580Kč. ❶

Caravan Park, Císařská louka 599 (☎025 40 925), on the Císařská louka peninsula. Metro B: Smíchovské nádraží, then any of the 300-numbered buses to Lihovar. Go left on the shaded path as you head to the river (1km). Or, take a ferry: every hr. until about 10pm from the landing, 1 block from Smíchovské nádraží (10Kč). Small, tranquil campground on the banks of the Vltava. Clean facilities, friendly staff, and convenient cafe. Currency exchange on premises. 95Kč per person, 90-140Kč per tent. Local tax 15Kč per person; national tax 5%. Students exempt from local tax. ❶

◖ FOOD

The nearer you are to the center, the more you'll pay. In less-touristed areas, you can have pork, cabbage, dumplings, and a beer for 75Kč. Always bring cash and check the bill, as you'll pay for everything, including ketchup and bread; some restaurants try to massage bills higher. For lunch, *hotová jídla* (prepared meals) are cheapest. Though vegetarian establishments are plentiful, veggie options at traditional Czech restaurants often remain limited to fried cheese, Balkan cheese salad (similar to Greek salad), and cabbage. For fresher alternatives, head to the **daily market** at the intersection of Havelská and Melantrichova in Staré Město.

STARÉ MĚSTO RESTAURANTS

▩ **Jáchymka,** Jáchymova 4 (☎224 819 621). Walk up Pařížská and take a right on Jáchymova. A favorite among locals, Jáchymka serves heaping portions of traditional cuisine in a lively, casual atmosphere. Try the goulash with dumplings (95Kč) or a massive meat *escalope* (98-195Kč). For those who prefer lighter fare, salmon with pasta and vegetables (128Kč) will also satisfy. Open daily 11am-11pm. MC/V. ❷

▩ **Klub architektů,** Betlémské nám. 52A (☎224 401 214; www.klubarchitektu.com). Metro B: Národní třída. Take Spálená until it becomes Na Perštýně, then turn left on Betlémské nám. Walk through the gate immediately on your right and descend underground. Klub architektů is a magnificent hybrid of first class and budget. Enjoy intimate lighting and an ancient cellar setting. Vegetarian options include imitation sausage (150Kč); enormous-bird options include ostrich filet (320Kč). Non-smoking section. English spoken. Beer from 39Kč. Entrees 90-320Kč. Open daily 11:30am-midnight. Kitchen closes at 11pm. Reservations recommended. AmEx/MC/V. ❸

Country Life, Melantrichova 15 (☎224 213 366; www.countrylife.cz). Metro A: Staroměstská. Follow directions to U Špirků (see below). After days of dumplings and fried cheese, Country Life's salad bar is the perfect answer to any fresh-veggie cravings. Pick up a plate and head to Country Life's 3 buffets (hot, cold, salad); you'll pay 22.90Kč per 100g for whatever fits on your plate. Juice from 20Kč for beet root. Soups 20Kč. Open M-Th 9am-10:30pm, F 9am-5pm and Su 11am-8:30pm. ❷

Cafe Bambus, Benediktská 12 (☎224 828 110; www.bambus.cz). Metro B: nám. Republiky. Follow directions to Hostel Dlouhá 33 (see **Accommodations,** p. 174) and take a left on Benediktská. Step out of the tourist jungle into this African oasis where masks, statuettes, and crocodiles adorn the walls. Sweet and savory Czech pancakes 55-75Kč. Asian and international cuisine with Czech flavors 55-228Kč. Open M-Th 10am-1am, F 10am-2am, Sa 11am-2am, Su 11am-11pm. ❷

NOVÉ MĚSTO RESTAURANTS

▩ **Radost FX,** Bělehradská 120 (☎224 254 776; www.radostfx.cz). Metro C: IP Pavlova. Locals and expats agree that Radost has the best vegetarian food in town. A range of healthy yet hearty entrees, including pizzas, salads, sandwiches, pastas, and stir-fries (105-195Kč) satisfies even the staunchest of carnivores. A cafe, lounge, art gallery, and nightclub in one, Radost boasts one of the hippest atmospheres in the city. Brunch Sa-Su 95-140Kč. Italian night Su 5pm-2am. Open daily 11am-late (at least 3am on weekdays and 5am on weekends). ❸

▩ **Universal,** V jirchářích 6 (☎224 934 416). Metro B: Národní třída. Follow directions to Velryba (below), but head right around the church to V jirchářích. A fusion of Mediterranean, French, and Asian flavors, Universal offers huge, fresh salads (119-170Kč) in a bright dining room. Imaginative entrees (115-329Kč) go brilliantly with a glass or two of Moravian wine (small carafe 50Kč, large carafe 100Kč). Scrumptious Su brunch buffet (135Kč). Open M-Sa 11:30am-1am, Su 11am-midnight. ❸

U Sádlů, Klimentská 2 (☎224 813 874; www.usadlu.cz). Metro B: nám. Republiky. From the square, take Revoluční toward the river and go right on Klimentská. A descent into the candlelit entry reveals a medieval dining dungeon. The armor by the bar suggests that portions are bountiful enough to sustain a full day of knight-errantry—or sightseeing. The staff can help you order traditional meals (105-235Kč) from the Czech-only menu. Reserve ahead. Open M-Sa 11am-1am, Su noon-midnight. AmEx/MC/V. ❸

Ultramarin Grill, Ostrovní 32 (☎224 932 249; www.ultramarin.cz). Metro B: Národní třída. With your back to the Metro, turn left and immediately right; Ultramarin will be on the left. This classy copper- and wood-filled bar and restaurant provides a chic alternative to the more touristed options in Staré Město. An open grill, woven mat chairs, and occasional live music explain why this place is a favorite with locals. The chef specializes in steak, duck, and lamb (100-165Kč), making the menu a meat dream come true. Krušovice on tap. Open daily 10am-11pm. AmEx/MC/V. ❸

Velryba (The Whale), Opatovická 24 (☎224 932 391; www.kavarnavelryba.cz). Metro B: Národní třída. Cross the tram tracks and follow narrow Ostrovní, then take a left on Opatovická. Enjoy a cheap Czech or Italian pasta dish (62-145Kč) among a diverse crowd of locals, expats, suits, and tourists, or slip back to the plush cafe for coffee (espresso 22Kč) or wine. Open daily 11am-midnight. Cafe and gallery open daily 11am-9pm. ❷

Pizzeria Kmotra, V jirchářích 12 (☎224 945 809). Metro B: Národní třída. Follow the directions to Universal. It may look quiet from the outside, but descend into the cellar of this lively pizzeria and you'll find droves of diners devouring huge salads, pizzas, and pastas (85-140Kč). Open daily 11am-midnight. AmEx/MC/V. ❷

Govinda Vegetarian Club, Soukenická 27 (☎224 816 631). Metro B: nám. Republiky. Walk down Revoluční, away from the Obecní Dum, and turn right on Soukenická. Hindu gods gaze upon customers eating delicious vegetarian stews. Set menu includes stew, rice, salad, and chutney. Small portions 80Kč, large 90Kč. Open M-F 11am-5pm. ❶

U Řozvarilů, Na Poříči 26. Metro B: nám. Republiky. Exit the station on Na Poříči and take a sharp right around the church. Quality dining doesn't come cheaper—Czech regulars gorge themselves on traditional meals like meat with cream sauce (42Kč) and potato dumplings (13-15Kč). The stainless steel decor of this cafeteria-style establishment may feel sterile, but the jovial company and hearty food make perfect antidotes. Open M-F 7:30am-8:30pm, Sa 8am-6pm, Su 10am-6pm. AmEx/MC/V. ❶

MALÁ STRANA RESTAURANTS

Bar bar, Všehrdova 17 (☎257 313 246). Metro A: Malostranská. Follow the tram tracks from the Metro station down Letenská, through Malostranské nám., and down Karmelitská. Take the left on Všehrdova after the museum. The diverse selection of meats, cheeses, and veggie dishes (45-125Kč), as well as delicious sweet and savory Czech-style filled pancakes (48-89Kč), will please every palate. Funky atmosphere for whisky (from 65Kč) and jazz. Open M-Th and Su noon-midnight, F-Sa noon-2am. MC/V. ❶

Pivnice U Švejků, Újezd 22 (☎257 313 244; www.usvejku.cz). Metro A: Malostranská. From the Metro, head down Klárov and right on Letenská. Bear left through Malostranské nám. and follow Karmelitská until it becomes Újezd. Converted to a restaurant in 1993, this former inn dates back to 1618. After a few beers (or a massive 1L brew), try to dance with the accordionist (plays after 7pm). The restaurant was named for Švejk, of Hašek's novel *The Good Soldier Švejk;* murals of the hero cover the walls. Few vegetarian options. Entrees 118-148Kč. Open daily 11am-midnight. AmEx/MC/V. ❸

Kajetanka, Hradčanské nám. (☎257 533 735). Metro A: Malostranská. Exit the Metro and walk down Letenská, through Malostranské nám. Climb Nerudova until it curves around to Ke Hradu. Kajetanka is at the foot of the castle about 100m uphill. This cafe survives because its outdoor terrace offers a spectacular view over the red-tiled roofs of Prague. Salads and meat dishes (119-369Kč) aren't special, but the hordes of tourists don't seem to mind. Open daily Apr.-Sept. 10am-8pm; Oct.-Mar. 10am-6pm. ❹

LATE-NIGHT EATING

4:45am. Charles Bridge. Discos are still pumping ferociously, but all you can hear is your stomach. Grab a *párek v rohlíku* (hot dog) or a *smažený sýr* (cheese sandwich) on **Václavské nám.**, or a gyro on **Spálená.** Make a morning of it with Prague's late-night cuisine. Hungry hipsters can head to **Radost FX** (p. 179).

Pizzeria Roma, Liliová 15 (☎777 268 145). Metro A: Staroměstská or Night Tram #51: Staroměstská. From the Charles Bridge, take the 2nd right off Karlova on Liliová. At 3am, there's no reason Pizzeria Roma has to make a good pizza: most of the clientele won't know the difference. Nevertheless, Roma's tomato sauce and mozzarella are still fresh and the crust still crispy and chewy. Even for the humorously inebriated, hay rides in the wagon above the bar are not permitted. Margherita pizza 99Kč. Bolognese pizza 119Kč. Open 24hr. Pizza served until 7am. ❸

Picante, Revoluční 4 (☎222 322 022). Metro B: nám. Republiky or Night Tram #52: nám. Republiky. At the corner of Revoluční and nám. Republiky. Inside Picante is a giant display of the various "Menus," or combo deals. These range 99-129Kč and tend to be small. In order to get enough food, you'll shell out about what you would at the average US taqueria. Worth it if you absolutely insist on Mexican. Open 24hr. ❶

Pizza Express, Na Můstku 1 (☎224 229 500). Metro A or B: Můstek or Night Tram #51: Můstek. 100m from Můstek, across from the Prague Tourist Center. Completely serviceable pizza and gyros. Pastries from 30Kč. Entrees 39-79Kč. Open Tu-Su 24hr. ❶

SUPERMARKETS

The basements of most Czech department stores have food halls and supermarkets. *Potraviny* (delis) and vegetable stands can be found on most street corners.

Tesco, Národní třída 26 (☎222 003 111; www.tesco-shop.cz). Next to Metro B: Národní třída. Open M-F 7am-10pm, Sa 8am-8pm, Su 9am-8pm. AmEx/MC/V.

Albert (☎221 229 311), at the corner of Revoluční and nám. Republiky, out in front of the Kotva department store. Metro B: nám. Republiky. 2-floor supermarket with fresh cheese and deli counters. Open M-Sa 7am-9pm, Su 8am-9pm.

◪ CAFES

When Prague journalists are bored, they churn out yet another "Whatever happened to cafe life?" feature. The answer: it turned into *čajovna* (tea house) culture. Tea is all the rage, and many tea houses double as bars or clubs by night. Java junkies shouldn't fret: quality coffeehouses still abound. If you desire email and fiction, rather than just sugar, with your coffee, see the **Globe Bookstore** (p. 171).

◪ Bohemia Bagel, Masna 2 (☎224 812 560; www.bohemiabagel.cz). Metro A: Staroměstská. An expatriate favorite, Bohemia Bagel dishes up a giant, American-style breakfast of pancakes, eggs, bacon, and hashbrowns (The Charles IV; 160Kč), as well as a bottomless cup of coffee for 45Kč. Background music runs the gamut: James Brown, Europop, DJ Optik. Terrace out back. English spoken. Entrees 125-185Kč. Open M-F 7am-midnight, Sa-Su 8am-midnight. Branch at Újezd 16. Open daily 9am-midnight.

Cafe Ebel, Řetězová 9. (☎603 441 434). Metro A or B: Staroměstská. 2 things are hard to find in Prague cafes: freshly ground beans and cups to go. Ebel has both. In addition to excellent coffee, Ebel offers a great continental breakfast (165Kč), panini (100Kč), and quiches (60-100Kč). English menu. Espresso 40Kč single, 50Kč double. Open M-F 8am-8pm, Sa-Su 8:30am-8pm. AmEx/MC/V. Branches: Týn 2 (open daily 9am-10pm); Kaprova 11 (open M-F 8am-8pm, Sa-Su 8:30am-8pm).

Kavárna Medúza, Belgická 17 (☎222 515 107). Metro A: nám. Míru. Head down Rumunska, and turn left at Belgická. Nearly everything here is well worn: the tables bear the marks of long use, and the light fixtures have grown a patina. During the day, locals read or chat quietly, but at night the space fills with impeccably dressed hepcats. Good luck finding a seat. Excellent espresso and "Czech traditional pancakes" (*staročeská pelačincky sladké;* thin pancakes with plum jam, cinnamon, whipped cream and dollops of ice cream; 48Kč). Entrees 44-200Kč. Open M-F 11am-1am, Sa-Su noon-1am.

Bakeshop Praha, Kozí 1 (☎602 682 477; info@bakeshop.cz). From Old Town Square, follow Dlouhá to the intersection of Kozí. International in the best way, Bakeshop Praha would be at home in any major city. An excellent, lemony version of the blueberry muffin costs 25Kč. Pastries cost less to-go. Bakery also serves salads, sandwiches, quiche and breads. Branch at Lázenska 19, off Mostécka in Malá Strana. Open daily 7am-7pm.

Paneria, Kaprova 7 (☎224 827 401; www.paneria.cz), on the corner of Kaprova and Valentinska. Paneria is a budget jewel: it's almost impossible to find pastries of this quality for these prices. Rolls for 3Kč? Eclairs for 8Kč? What? The friendly staff laugh good-naturedly as you point at things you can't pronounce. Espresso from 32Kč. Open daily 7am-8pm. Branch at Dlouhá 25 (☎224 827 401). Open M-F 7am-10pm.

U zeleného čaje, Nerudova 19 (☎225 730 027). Metro A: Malostranská. Follow Letenská to Malostranské nám. Stay right of the church and head down Nerudova. This adorable shop at the foot of Prague Castle takes tea to new heights. Choose from over 60 varieties of fragrant tea. To add a little kick, try an alcoholic tea mixed drink like the Boiling Communist (35Kč). Sandwiches 25-59Kč. Open daily 11am-10pm.

◎ SIGHTS

One of the only major Central European cities unscathed by WWII, Prague is a well-preserved combination of labyrinthine alleys and Baroque buildings. You can find respite from the throngs of tourists by heading beyond Staroměstské nám., the Charles Bridge, and Václavské nám to nám. Miru, Vinohrady, and the southern part of Nové Město. While there are few places in the center left untouched by tourists, the crowds have overlooked many of the city's most beautiful areas. To see a Prague not entirely made of crystal and souvenir shops, visit a suburban sight, head north of Staré Město, or explore any of the city's beautiful gardens.

CZECH REPUBLIC

Best traveled by foot, central Prague—Staré Město, Nové Město, Malá Strana, and Hradčany—is compact enough to be traversed in one day, but deserves more. Don't leave the city without strolling through the synagogues of Josefov, exploring the heights of Vyšehrad, or meandering through the streets of Malá Strana.

STARÉ MĚSTO

LITTLE GREEN MEN. Crossing Prague's streets provides an interesting puzzle for foreigners. There are stoplights with designated crossing areas for pedestrians, but the lights seem eternally stuck on the "don't walk" signal, a red man standing still. Indeed, one can easily wait five minutes for the walking green man to light up, only to have to race across the street before the red man reappears. Prague's crossings seem intended for sprinters instead of ordinary folk, but you won't see any jaywalkers. Drivers are unlikely to stop, and jaywalking is generally not acceptable. So instead, join the Czech crowd on the street corner and begin your wait for that elusive little green man.

Settled in the 10th century, Staré Město (Old Town) is a maze of narrow streets and alleys. Eight magnificent towers enclose **Old Town Square** (Staroměstské nám.) in the heart of Staré Město. The vast stone plaza fills with blacksmiths, painters, carriages, and ice-cream vendors in summer. As soon as the sun sets, the labyrinth of narrow roads and alleys fills with a younger crowd seeking midnight revelry at Staré Město's jazz clubs and bars.

CHARLES BRIDGE (KARLŮV MOST). This Baroque footbridge has become one of Prague's most treasured landmarks. Charles IV built the 520m bridge to replace the wooden Judith, the only bridge crossing the Vltava, which washed away in a 1342 flood. Defense towers border the bridge on each side; the shorter *Malostranská mostecká věž* (Malá Strana Bridge Tower) dates from the 12th century, while the taller *Staroměstská mostecká věž* (Old Town Bridge Tower) was erected in the 15th century. Both towers offer splendid views of the river and of Prague's most precious sites. Over the years, the bridge has been decorated with 16 Baroque statues, but don't be fooled—they are replicas. The originals are locked away in local museums, safe from tourists and pigeons. According to local legend, on this bridge the hapless St. Jan Nepomuk was tied in goatskin and thrown into the river for concealing the extramarital secrets of his queen from a suspicious King Wenceslas IV. A halo of five gold stars appeared as Jan plunged into the icy water. The right-hand rail, from which Jan was supposedly tossed, is now marked with a cross and five stars between the 5th and 6th statues. Place one finger on each star and make a wish. *(The best way to reach Charles Bridge is on foot. Nearest Metro stops A: Malostranská on the Malá Strana side and A: Staroměstská on the Staré Město side.)*

OLD TOWN HALL (STAROMĚSTSKÉ RADNICE). Next to the grassy knoll in Old Town Square, Old Town Hall is the multi-faceted building with the trim blown off the front. The Hall was partially demolished in WWII, and the original pink facade now juts out from the tower. Old Town Hall has long been a witness to violence— crosses in front mark the spot where 27 Protestant leaders were executed on June 21, 1621 for staging a rebellion against the Catholic Hapsburgs. Now the main office of Prague Information Services occupies the first floor. On the 2nd floor, one of the locations of the **City Gallery of Prague** hosts short-term exhibits of contemporary Czech art. The 3rd holds the entrance to the tower, where you can take in an aerial view of Staroměstké nám. Walk up or take the elevator. Outside, crowds throng on the hour to watch the **astronomical clock** chime as skeletal Death empties his hourglass and a procession of apostles marches by. The clock's operation stops for the night at 9pm. *(Metro A: Staroměstská; Metro A or B: Můstek. In*

Staroměstské nám. Open in summer M 10am-7pm, Tu-F 9am-7pm, Sa-Su 9am-6pm. Exhibition hall 20Kč, students 10Kč. Clock tower open daily 10am-6pm; enter through 3rd fl. of Old Town Hall. 50Kč, students 40Kč. Tours of the interior available on the hr.; 50Kč, students 40Kč.)

JAN HUS STATUE. Burned at the stake in 1415 for his diatribes against the Catholic Church's quest for greater earthly power and its practice of selling indulgences, Jan Hus now stands as a symbol of Czech nationalism. In this massive Expressionistic tableau, impassioned figures writhe in the background while Jan stands stoically apart. *(In the center of Staroměstské nám.)*

TÝN CHURCH (CHRÁM MATKY BOŽÍ PŘED TÝNEM). Across from Old Town Hall, the spires of the Gothic Týn Church rise above a mass of medieval homes. The Týn only recently opened its sanctuary to tourists, who are still restricted to the very back of the church. However, you can see enough of the high Gothic interior to be impressed. Topped by statues of saints, the giant white columns supporting the nave lead forward through the church to the gold-encrusted altar. The famous astronomer Tycho Brahe is buried in the church's hallowed halls. *(In Staroměstské nám.; enter through the tunnel to the left of Cafe Italia. Sightseeing M-F 9am-noon and 1-2pm. Mass W-F 6pm; Sa 8am; Su 11am, 9pm. July-Aug. also 12:30pm. Free.)*

ST. JAMES'S CHURCH (KOSTEL SV. JAKUBA). Barely a surface in the Baroque St. James's Church remains un-figured, un-marbleized, or unpainted. Keep your hands to yourself, though: legend has it that 500 years ago a thief tried to pilfer a gem from the Virgin Mary of Suffering, whereupon the figure sprang to life and yanked off his arm. Taking pity on the man, the monks invited him to join their order. He accepted and remained pious. Note the sculpture of Jesus with his head in his hands. *(Metro B: Staroměstská. On Malá Štupartská, off Staroměstské nám. behind Týn Church. Open M-Sa 10am-noon and 2–3:45pm. Mass Su 8, 9, 10:30am.)*

MUNICIPAL HOUSE AND POWDER TOWER (PRAŠNÁ BRÁNA, OBECNÍ DÚM). The juxtaposition of styles represented by the Gothic Powder Tower and the Municipal House provides a fitting entrance to Staré Město. Built on the former site of the royal court, the Municipal House was designed and built entirely by Czech representatives of the art nouveau movement. Inside, Neoclassical figures support archways and light fixtures while worked metals imitate trees and flowers. Ceilings and domes painted by Alfons Mucha fit perfectly the daily orchestral performances of classics from the repertoire. *(Nám. Republiky 5. Metro B: nám. Republiky. www.obecni-dum.cz. Open only by tour, available at various times 10am-6pm. 150Kč.)*

Next door, the Gothic **Powder Tower** is a staid reminder that city design is not all sweetness and light. One of the last remnants of the city walls that once protected Staré Město, the Powder Tower was rendered obsolete by the construction of Nové Město beyond its borders. Today, you can still climb the winding tower to appreciate the expansive views from its topmost lookout. *(Metro B: nám. Republiky. Open daily July-Aug. 10am-10pm; Sept.-Oct.and Apr.-June 10am-6pm. 50Kč, students 40Kč.)*

JAN PALACH SQUARE (NÁMĚSTÍ JANA PALACHA). Downriver from the Charles Bridge, Jan Palach Square offers a peaceful view of the Vltava and the castle. Originally called Red Army Square, the square was renamed in 1990. It now honors one of the Red Army's great opponents, the student Jan Palach, who set himself on fire on Václavské nám. to protest the 1968 Soviet invasion. On the river banks, stone lions guard the Rudolfinum, a concert hall that hosts the annual classical music *Pražské jaro* (Prague Spring). Across the tram tracks from the Rudolfinum, the main building of the Faculty of Arts of **Charles University** (Filozofická fakulta Univerzity Karlovy) shelters a statue of Palach. A path from Jan Palach Square hugs the Vltava. You can cruise the river in paddleboats, for rent just under the Mánesů for 100Kč per hour. *(Metro A: Staroměstská. Just off the Metro exit on Křížovnická.)*

NOVÉ MĚSTO

Nové Město (New Town) has become the commercial core of Prague of late. There's little else new in Nové Město, which Charles IV established in 1348 as a separate municipality. Today, the monumental facade of the National Museum and the solemn serenity of Mary of the Snows and the Franciscan Gardens contrast the consumer chaos that is Wenceslas Square.

WENCESLAS SQUARE (VÁCLAVSKÉ NÁMĚSTÍ). More a boulevard than a square, Wenceslas Square owes its name to the equestrian statue of 10th-century Czech ruler and patron St. Wenceslas (Václav) that stands in front of the National Museum. At his feet in solemn prayer kneel smaller statues of the country's other patron saints: St. Ludmila, St. Agnes, St. Prokop, and St. Adalbert (Vojtěch). The perfectionist sculptor Josef Václav Myslbek completed the statue after 25 years of work. The inscription under St. Wenceslas reads, "Do not let us and our descendants perish." Today, the square sweeps down from the statue past department stores, posh hotels, trashy casinos, and art nouveau architecture. The boulevard has become more commercial in recent years, but the view of the statue from the Můstek stop remains hypnotic at full moon. *(Metro A or B: Můstek serves the bottom of the square; Metro A or C: Muzeum serves the top of the square.)*

FRANCISCAN GARDEN (FRANTIŠKÁNSKÁ ZAHRADA). Amazingly, the Franciscans have maintained this bastion of serenity in the heart of Prague's commercial district. An ideal escape from Wenceslas Sq., the rose garden provides a perfect spot to relax or relax. Enjoy the statue of the boy eternally trying—and failing—to drink water from a seashell. *(Metro A or B: Můstek. Enter through the arch to the left of the intersection of Jungmannova and Národní, behind the Jungmannova statue. Open daily Apr. 15-Sept. 14 7am-10pm; Sept. 15-Oct. 14 7am-8pm; Oct. 15-Apr. 14 8am-7pm. Free.)*

CHURCH OF OUR LADY OF THE SNOWS (KOSTEL PANNY MARIE SNĚŽNÉ). Founded by Charles IV in 1347, Our Lady of the Snows was meant to surpass St Vitus's as the largest church in Prague. The Gothic walls are, indeed, higher than those of any other house of worship, but there wasn't enough in the coffers to complete the building. The result: extraordinarily high ceilings in a church of strikingly short length. *(Metro A or B: Můstek. From the bottom of Wenceslas Sq., turn left on Jungmannovo nám.; the entrance is behind the statue.)*

THE DANCING HOUSE (TANČÍCÍ DŮM). Built by American architect Frank Gehry, of Guggenheim-Bilbao fame, in cooperation with Slovenian architect Vladimir Milunic, the building—known as "Fred and Ginger" to Western visitors and as the "Dancing House" to Czechs—is one of Prague's most controversial landmarks. Its nicknames derive from the building's undulating glass wall and paired cone and cube, which evoke a dancing couple. It opened in 1996 amid a stretch of art nouveau buildings. *(Metro B: Karlovo nám. Exit to Karlovo nám. and head down Resslova toward the river. It's at the corner of Resslova and Rašínovo nábřeží.)*

VELVET REVOLUTION MEMORIAL. Under Národní's arcades stands a memorial to the hundreds of Czech citizens beaten on November 17, 1989. Police attacked a march organized by students to mourn the Nazi execution of nine Czech students some 50 years earlier. The simple yet moving plaque depicts a wall of hands. The inscription—*Máme holé ruce* (Our hands are empty)—was the protesters' cry as they were beaten by the police. Visitors place flowers in the fingers of the memorial in remembrance. At the nearby **Magic Lantern Theater** (Laterna magika divadlo), Národní 4, Revolutionary leader Havel once plotted to overthrow the old regime. *(Metro B: Národní třída. Exit the Metro and head down Spálená; go left on Národní. The memorial is in the arcade across from the Black Theater.)*

JOSEFOV

Prague's historic Jewish neighborhood and the oldest Jewish settlement in Central Europe, Josefov is north of Staroměstské nám., along Maiselova and several side streets. Its cultural wealth lies in five well-preserved synagogues. In reaction to the Pope's 1179 decree that all good Christians avoid contact with Jews, Prague's citizens constructed a 4m wall surrounding the area. The gates were opened in 1784, but the walls didn't come down until 1848, when the city's Jews were first granted limited civil rights. The closed neighborhood bred fantastical legends, many of which surrounded the famed **Rabbi Loew ben Bezalel** (1512-1609), who, according to legend, created the golem—a creature made from mud that came to life to protect Prague's Jews. Rabbi Loew lived at Široká 90, now a private residence. In an ill-conceived attempt to turn Prague into a small Paris (evident in today's Pařížská), devoid of all less desirable neighborhoods, the whole quarter, save the synagogues, was demolished in the late 19th century. When the Nazis rose to power, most of Prague's Jews were deported to Terezín (see **Terezín,** p. 196) and the death camps. Ironically, Hitler's decision to create a "museum of an extinct race" led to the preservation of Josefov's old Jewish cemetery and synagogues. *(Metro A: Staroměstská. From the Metro, walk down Maiselova, which is parallel to Kaprova. ☎ 222 325 172; www.jewishmuseum.cz. Synagogues and museum open M-F and Su Apr.-Oct. 9am-6pm, Nov.-Mar. 9am-4:30pm; box office closes 30min. earlier. Closed Jewish holidays. Admission to all synagogues except Staronová Synagogue 300Kč, students 200Kč. Staronová Synagogue 200/140Kč. Admission to all sites 500/400Kč. Buy tickets at any of the synagogues. A head covering is required for men at most sites; kippahs 5Kč.)*

PINKAS SYNAGOGUE (PINKASOVA SYNAGOGA). At the time of the Nazi takeover, 118,310 Jews lived in the Prague ghetto, many of them refugees from the conquered provinces. A few fled before further Nazi persecution, but about 92,000 remained. Of these, 80,000 were deported to meet their deaths in Terezín or other concentration camps. Today, their names cover the walls of Pinkas Synagogue, otherwise bare but for the simple wooden timbers that hold the building up. Upstairs, drawings made by children imprisoned at Terezín, as well as various relics from daily life there, give faces to a few of the names. In a cast photo from the children's theater, no one smiles. *(On Široká, between Žatecká and Listopadu 17.)*

OLD JEWISH CEMETERY (STARÝ ŽIDOVSKÝ HŘBITOV). The Old Jewish Cemetery stretches between the Pinkas Synagogue and the Ceremonial Hall, its small expanse filled entirely with the aged, cracked and broken stone markers of thousands of graves. Between the 14th and 18th centuries, the graves were dug in layers. Over time, the earth settled and those from the bottom fought to the surface, pushing other stones aside like new teeth. Now, the gravestones of rich and poor, young and old lean together and against one another. Rabbi Loew is buried by the wall opposite the entrance. His grave can be recognized by the pebbles and coins placed atop it. *(At the corner of Široká and Žatecká.)*

SPANISH SYNAGOGUE (ŠPANĚLSKÁ SYNAGOGA). The Spanish Synagogue gets its name entirely from the Byzantine-Moorish, or "Spanish Moorish," style in which it is built. The interior is a complex of domes, covered in golden stars and lattice, amid complex patterns of dark blue, green, and brownish red. This was the first synagogue to adopt the Reform movements of the 1830s. On display is a history of Czech Jews in the post-Enlightenment era. *(On the corner of Široká and Dušní.)*

MAISEL SYNAGOGUE (MAISELOVA SYNAGOGA). This synagogue displays treasures from the extensive collections of the Jewish Museum, which were only returned to the city's Jewish community in 1994. Its exhibits render an excellent history of the Jews in Bohemia and Moravia, including Prague's ghetto and the events that took place within it. *(Maiselova, between Široká and Jáchymova.)*

OLD-NEW SYNAGOGUE (STARONOVÁ SYNAGOGA). The oldest operating synagogue in Europe and the earliest Gothic structure in Prague, the tiny Old-New Synagogue is still the religious center of Prague's Jewish community. Behind the iron gates fly the tattered remnants of the Star of David flag flown by the congregation in 1357, when Charles IV first allowed them to display their own municipal emblem. Prague's Jews were the first to adopt the Star of David as their official symbol. *(On the corner of Maiselova and Pařížská. Entrance fee not included in price of museum ticket. Open in summer M-Th and Su 9:30am-6pm, F 9:30am-5pm. Services F and Sa at 8pm reserved for practicing members of the Jewish community. 200Kč, students 140Kč.)*

JEWISH TOWN HALL (ŽIDOVSKÁ RADNICE). Once the administrative center of Josefov, the Jewish Town Hall was one of the few Jewish administrative centers in Europe to survive WWII. The small Hebrew clock at the top of the Rococo town hall runs counter-clockwise. On the other side of the building, a statue of Moses by František Bílek was hidden from the Nazis during the war. *(Next to the Old-New Synagogue, on the corner of Maiselova and Červená. The building is permanently closed to the public.)*

MALÁ STRANA

The hangout of criminals and counter-revolutionaries for nearly a century, the cobblestone streets of Malá Strana have become the most prized real estate on the Vltava. Urbanites dream of flats overlooking St. Nicholas's Cathedral, while affluent foreigners sip beer in the former hangout of Jaroslav Hašek and his bumbling soldier Švejk. Malá Strana seems to have realized the vision of its 13th-century designer, King Přemysl Otakar II. In the 15th century, the Austrian nobility built great churches and palaces here. Now carefully restored, Malá Strana is home to some of Prague's most impressive architecture.

■ **PETŘÍN HILL AND GARDENS (PETŘÍNSKÉ SADY).** Petřín Gardens, on the hill beside Malá Strana, provide a tranquil retreat from Prague's urban bustle and offer spectacular views of the city. Although the climb to the garden's peak is steep, the beauty of its forested footpaths is worth the trek. For a more relaxed ascent, take the funicular to the top from just above the intersection of Vítězná and Újezd. *(Look for Lanovka Dráha signs. Daily every 10-15min. 9am-11pm; 20Kč.)* A plethora of delights awaits you at the summit: lush rose gardens, a small Eiffel-esque Tower *(open daily 10am-10pm; 50Kč, students 40Kč)*, the city's observatory, and the Church of St. Lawrence. *(☎257 315 272. Open daily 10am-9:30pm. 50Kč, students 40Kč.)* Just east of the park, Strahov Stadium, the world's largest, covers the space of 10 soccer fields.

■ **WALLENSTEIN GARDEN (VALDŠTEJNSKÁ ZAHRADA).** This tranquil, 17th-century Baroque garden is enclosed by old buildings that glow on sunny afternoons. General Albrecht Wallenstein, owner of the famous Prague palace of the same name and hero of Schiller's grim plays (the *Wallenstein* cycle), held parties here among classical bronze statues. When the works were plundered by Swedish troops in the waning hours of the Thirty Years' War, Wallenstein replaced the original casts with duplicates. Frescoes inside the arcaded patio depict episodes from Virgil's *Aeneid*. *(Letenská 10. Metro A: Malostranská. Exit the Metro and turn right on Letenská. The garden will be on the right. Open Apr.-Oct. daily 10am-6pm. Free.)*

ST. NICHOLAS'S CATHEDRAL (CHRÁM SV. MIKULÁŠE). St. Nicholas's Cathedral's towering dome is one of Prague's most discernible landmarks. This is also the only church in Prague that might out-Baroque St. James's: St. Nicholas's is claustrophobically full of paintings and statuary. Climb the stairs to the left of the Altar of the Virgin Mary (itself left of the main altar), and the lofty perspective will reveal that much of the Cathedral's marble is actually painted. On the other hand, you can also see how hard the muralists worked to paint details that people on the ground would never, ever see. Concerts are held each night in the early evening.

(Metro A: Malostranská. Follow Letenská from the Metro to Malostranské nám. ☎ 257 534 215. Open daily 8:30am-4:45pm; last entrance 4:45pm. 50Kč, students 25Kč. Entrance to pray 8:30am-9am, free. Concerts 390Kč, students 290Kč.)

CHURCH OF OUR LADY VICTORIOUS (KOSTEL PANNY MARIE VÍTĚZNÉ). The Church of Our Lady Victorious is an odd mix of tourist destination and pilgrimage site. The church itself is plain in comparison to the nearby St. Nicholas. Inside, however, the church contains the famous polished-wax statue of the **Infant Jesus of Prague,** which many believe can perform miracles for the faithful. According to legend, the statue arrived in Prague in the arms of a 16th-century Spanish noblewoman who married into Bohemian royalty; the plague bypassed the city shortly thereafter. In 1628, the Carmelite abbey gained custody of the statue and allowed pilgrims to pray to it; the public has been enamored ever since. In the back of church, a small museum displays some of the vestments given to the Infant Jesus over the centuries. *(Metro A: Malostranská. Follow Letecká through Malostranské nám. and continue on Karmelitská. ☎ 257 533 646. Open daily 8:30am-7pm. Mass in 5 languages. Museum open M-Sa 9:30am-5:30pm, Su 1-6pm. No admittance during mass. No talking. Free.)*

PRAGUE CASTLE (PRAŽSKÝ HRAD)

Take tram #22 or 23 from the center, get off at "Pražský Hrad," and go down U Prašného Mostu past the Royal Gardens and into the Second Courtyard. Or, hike up picturesque Nerudova street. ☎ 224 373 368; www.hrad.cz. Open daily Apr.-Oct. 9am-5pm; Nov.-Mar. 9am-4pm. Ticket office opposite St. Vitus's Cathedral, inside the castle walls. Tickets provide you with access to 5 different routes. Route A gets you into everything; 350Kč, students 175Kč. Tickets are valid for 2 successive days.

Prague Castle has been the seat of the Bohemian government since it was built over 1000 years ago. Over the last century, liberal presidents, Nazi despots, and Communist officials have all held court here. After the declaration of independent Czechoslovakia in 1918, first President Tomáš Masaryk invited Slovenian architect Josip Plečnik to rebuild his new residence, which had suffered from centuries of Hapsburg neglect. Plečnik not only restored all the castle's buildings and redesigned its gardens, but added fountains, columns, and embellishments. Arrive on the hour to catch the changing of the guard, which takes place daily 5am-midnight.

HRADČANY SQUARE AND FIRST CASTLE COURTYARD. Outside the Castle gates at Hradčany Sq. lies the **Šternberg Palace,** home to the National Gallery's collection of European Old Masters, including works by Rembrandt, El Greco, Goya, and Rubens. *(☎ 230 090 570. Open Tu-Su 10am-6pm. 150Kč, students 70Kč.)* The Baroque **Matthias Gate** (Matyášská brána), inside the First Castle Courtyard, is the castle's official entrance. Plečnik designed the two spear-like wooden flagpoles next to it.

SECOND CASTLE COURTYARD AND ROYAL GARDEN (KRÁLOVSKÁ ZAHRADA). After passing through Matthias Gate, turn left in the Second Castle Courtyard for access to the lush Royal Garden. Recently opened to the public after years as a private paradise for only the highest Communist officials, the serene Royal Garden offers a respite in the midst of one of the city's most popular tourist attractions. Past the tulip beds, the trickling **Singing Fountain** spouts its watery, harp-like tune before the **Royal Summer Palace.** Place your head under the fountain to hear the chiming water. *(Royal Garden open Apr.-Oct. 24hr.)*

THIRD CASTLE COURTYARD. In the Third Castle Courtyard stands Prague Castle's centerpiece, the colossal **St. Vitus's Cathedral** (Katedrála sv. Víta), which was completed in 1929, some 600 years after construction began. Right of the high altar stands the silver **tomb** of **St. Jan Nepomuk** (Náhrobek sv. Jana Nepomuckého). A statue of an angel holds a silvered tongue believed to have belonged to Jan, whose tongue was reputedly silvered after he was thrown into the Vltava by King Charles

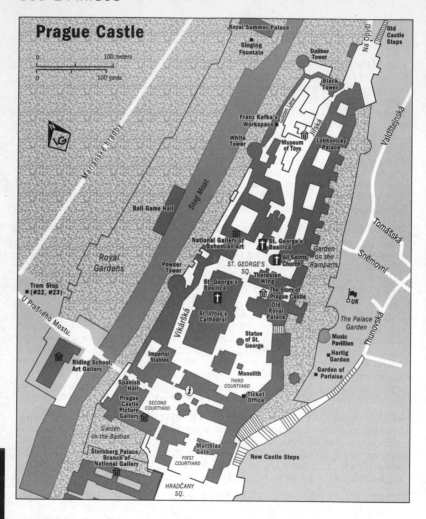

Prague Castle

0 ———— 100 meters
0 ———— 100 yards

Royal Summer Palace

Singing Fountain

Dalibor Tower

Na Opyši

Old Castle Steps

Black Tower

Franz Kafka's Workspace

Golden Lane

Jiřská

White Tower

Museum of Toys

Lobkovický Palace

Valdštejnská

Marianské hradby

Stag Moat

Ball Game Hall

National Gallery of Bohemian Art

St. George's Basilica

All Saints Church

Garden on the Ramparts

Tomášská

Sněmovní

Royal Gardens

Powder Tower

ST. GEORGE'S SQ.

Theresian Wing

Tram Stop ■ (#22, #23)

St. George's Basilica

The Story of Prague Castle

Old Royal Palace

UK

Ú Prašného Mostu.

Vikářská

St. Vitus's Cathedral

Statue of St. George

The Palace Garden

Thunovská

Music Pavillion

Hartig Garden

Imperial Stables

Monolith

Garden of Pariaise

THIRD COURTYARD

Riding School; Art Gallery

Spanish Hall

Prague Castle Picture Gallery

SECOND COURTYARD

i

Ticket Office

Garden on the Bastion

Sternberg Palace Branch of National Gallery

Matthias Gate

FIRST COURTYARD

New Castle Steps

HRADČANY SQ.

IV (see **Charles Bridge,** p. 182). It remains on display, though the story was officially proven false in 1961. The walls of **St. Wenceslas's Chapel** (Kaple sv. Václava) are lined with precious stones and paintings telling the saint's story. In an adjoining but inaccessible room, the real crown jewels of the Bohemian kings are sealed behind a door with seven locks, the keys to which are kept in the hands of seven different religious and secular Czech leaders. Attack the 287 steps that spiral up to the roof of the **Great South Tower** for one of the city's best views. Alternatively, head underground to the **Royal Crypt** (Královská hrobka) to visit Emperor Charles IV's tomb. All four of Charles's wives are buried together in the grave to his left, along with a handful of other Czech kings. To the right of St. Vitus's, the **Old Royal Palace** (Starý královský palác) is one of few castles in the Czech Republic that allows visitors to wander largely unattended. This may be because its rooms are almost completely bare. Listen to your feet thump across the giant, smooth floorboards of **Vladislav Hall**, where jousting competitions were once held. Directly across from the entrance, in the audience hall, long red benches surround a single red throne. In back of the hall, a door leads onto the balcony of the castle chapel, and a view that for centuries was enjoyed only by the castle's rulers. Across the courtyard from the Old Royal Palace stands the Romanesque **St. George's Basilica** (Bazilika sv. Jiří) and its adjacent convent. Built in AD 921, the simple yet elegant basilica enshrines the tomb of St. Ludmila, complete with skeleton on display. A mason who stole Ludmila's thighbone supposedly activated a vicious curse that killed three people before the mason's son restored the bone to the grave. The convent next door houses the **National Gallery of Bohemian Art,** which displays art ranging from the Gothic to the Baroque. In the medieval galleries, Master Theodorik's ecclesiastical portraits, the relief from *Matka Boží před Týnem* stands out; upstairs, Michael Leopold Willmann's paintings warrant a visit. *(Open Tu-Su 10am-6pm. 100Kč, students 50Kč.)*

JIŘSKÁ STREET. Jiřská begins to the right of the basilica. Halfway down, the tiny, colorful, and extremely crowded **Golden Lane** (Zlatá ulička) heads off to the right. The alchemists who once worked here, attempting to create gold, inspired the street's name. **Franz Kafka** had his workspace at #22. A welcome respite from the souvenir-peddling that occupies every other house on the street, the house is now a small bookstore selling his and other Prague writers' work. Upstairs, a hallway displays replicas of the Bohemian court's armory; shoot the crossbow for 50Kč. Back on Jiřská, the **Lobkovický Palace** has a replica of Bohemia's coronation jewels and a history of the Czech lands. *(Open Tu-Su 9am-4:30pm. 40Kč, students 20Kč.)* Across the street from the Palace is the **Museum of Toys** (Muzeum hraček), the personal toy collection owned by cartoonist and filmmaker Ivan Steiger. *(☎224 372 294. Open daily 9:30am-5:30pm. 50Kč, students 30Kč.)* The **Old Castle Steps** (Staré zámecké schody) at the end of the street descend to Malostranská.

OUTER PRAGUE

If you have more than two days in Prague, you may have a chance to explore the green fields, majestic churches, and panoramic vistas of the city's outskirts, all hidden from the touring hordes.

▨ TROJA. Located in a beautiful neighborhood, Troja is the site of French architect J. B. Mathey's masterly **chateau,** one of the city's best-kept secrets. The colossal palace, overlooking the Vltava, includes a terraced garden, oval staircase, and magnificent collection of 19th-century Czech artwork. Strap on a pair of leather slippers provided at the door. It's hard to tell what's more beautiful—the famous landscapes and moving portraits that line the palace walls, or the intricate frescoes featuring royal, mythical, and religious figures that adorn the ceilings. Don't miss the **Main Hall,** Prague's answer to the Sistine Chapel, covered from floor to ceiling in magnificent frescoes. *(Metro C: Nádraží Holešovice, take bus #112 to Zoologická Zahrada. Open Apr.-Oct. Tu-Su 10am-6pm; Nov.-Mar. Sa-Su 10am-5pm. 140Kč, students 70Kč.)* If you fancy wilder pursuits, venture next door to the **Prague Zoo.** *(Open daily 9am-7pm. Apr.-Sept. 80Kč, students 50Kč; Oct.-Mar. 50/30Kč.)*

PRAGUE MARKET (PRAŽSKCTRZNICE). This old-school Eastern European market remains Prague's best place to haggle over clothing, fresh produce, jewelry, and everything else. Rows of stalls and Czechs of all ages make this a truly authentic shopping experience. *(Take tram #3 or 14 from nám. Republiky to Vozovna Kobylisy; get off at Pražskátrznice. Open M-F 8am-6pm, Sa 8am-1pm.)*

BŘEVNOV MONASTERY. The oldest monastery in Bohemia was founded in AD 993 by King Boleslav II and St. Adalbert, who were both guided by a divine dream to build a monastery atop a bubbling stream. **St. Margaret's Church** (Bazilika sv. Markéty), a Benedictine chapel, awaits you inside the complex. Beneath the altar rests the tomb of the vegetarian St. Vintíř. Czechs claim that on one particular diplomatic excursion, St. Vintíř dined with a German king who, being a fanatical hunter, served up a main course of pheasant slain by his own hand. The saint prayed for deliverance from the embarrassment of having to decline the king's offering, whereupon the main course sprang to life and flew out the window. The monastery's green bell tower and red roof were the only parts of the original Romanesque structure that were spared when the Dientzenhofers, Prague's leading father-and-son architects, redesigned the complex in a High Baroque style. Pack a lunch and take a stroll along the stream leading to the small pond to the right of the church. Guided tours (in Czech only) are essential, as they allow you to access the monks' quarters and the crypt. *(Metro A: Malostranská. Take a 15min. ride uphill on tram #22 to Břevnovský klášter. Facing uphill, cross the road to the right. Entrance is on the left, under the statue of the monk. Church open only for mass: M-Sa 7am, 6pm; Su 7:30, 9am, 6pm. Tours Sa-Su 10am, 2, 4pm. 50Kč, students 30Kč.)*

NEW JEWISH CEMETERY. Although less visited than the more central Old Jewish Cemetery, the New Jewish Cemetery is one of Central Europe's largest burial grounds. Enigmatic writer Franz Kafka is interred here. Obtain a map and, if you're male, a mandatory head covering from the attendant before entering the cemetery. *(Metro A: Želivského. Open Apr.-Sept. M-Th and Su 9am-5pm, F 9am-2pm; Oct.-Mar. M-Th and Su 9am-4pm, F 9am-1pm. Closed Jewish holidays. Free.)*

▥ MUSEUMS

Visiting Prague's art museums is like finding the music venue that hosts bands you've never heard of, and introduces you to new favorites. There are new treasures to discover, variations on old themes, and styles you won't find elsewhere.

▨ MUCHA MUSEUM. This is the only collection devoted entirely to the work of Alfons Mucha, the Czech Republic's most celebrated artist, who gained his fame in Paris for his poster series of "la divine Sarah," Sarah Bernhardt, Paris's most famous actress. It was through this series that Mucha pioneered the art nouveau movement. Be sure to see the collection of Czech and Parisian posters, including the famous *Gismonda* which revolutionized poster design, as well as Mucha's panel paintings. *(Panská 7. Metro A or B: Můstek. Head up Václavské nám. toward the St. Wenceslas statue. Hang a left on Jindřišská and turn left again on Panská. ☎221 451 333; www.mucha.cz. Open daily 10am-6pm. 120Kč, students 60Kč.)*

CITY GALLERY PRAGUE (GALERIE HLAVNÍHO MĚSTA PRAHY). The City Gallery of Prague has seven locations throughout the city and its suburbs. Four of these are permanent collections, while three are venues for temporary exhibitions. The **House of the Golden Ring** is one of only two permanent collections in Prague proper. Its massive collection of 19th- and 20th-century Czech art will provide guests with more than enough to occupy an afternoon. The four floors of winding corridors lead through Czech contributions to all the major art movements of the past two centuries. *(Týnská 6. Metro A: Staroměstská. Behind and to the left of Týn Church in Old Town Sq., through a small door. ☎222 327 677; www.citygalleryprague.cz. Open Tu-Su 10am-6pm. Top 3 floors 60Kč, students 30Kč; entire museum 70Kč; 1st Tu of each month free.)*

MUSEUM OF MEDIEVAL TORTURE INSTRUMENTS. Brace yourself for a steady barrage of inhumanity. The thorough historical background given for each gruesome device is more than you might expect from a museum that also runs an exhibit of spiders and scorpions—"The biggest and most exciting!" *(Mostécka 21. Metro A: Malostranská. Follow Letenská from the Metro and turn left on Mostécka. ☎608 889 361; torture@post.cz. Open daily 10am-10pm. 120Kč.)*

MUSEUM OF COMMUNISM. Nowhere on earth will you find more propaganda posters, busts of Stalin, and pitchforks than at this museum, dedicated to showing how Communism affected Czech life. A Soviet-era punchcard time-clock advises you that "Timely arrival to work deals the decisive strike against the American aggressors!" The museum terminates with a powerful documentary about the Czech struggle for independence that led up to the Velvet Revolution. *(Na Příkopě 10. Metro A: Můstek. Exit the Metro and turn right on Na Příkopě; enter through Casino. ☎224 212 966; www.museumofcommunism.com. Open daily 9am-9pm. 180Kč, students 140Kč.)*

CZECH MUSEUM OF FINE ARTS (ČESKÉ MUZEUM VÝTVARNÝCH UMĚNÍ). The Czech Museum of Fine Arts takes up three buildings along Husova in Prague's Staré Město. In these three buildings, the Museum puts on exhibitions derived from its extensive collections of works by Czech artists throughout the ages. The first two floors are devoted to a history of Czech Cubism, while the downstairs gallery exhibits works of Western European Modernists. *(Husova 19-21. Metro A: Staroměstská. Follow Karlova down from Charles Bridge. Turn right on Husova. ☎222 220 218. Open Tu-Su 10am-6pm. 50Kč, students 20Kč.)*

MONUMENT TO NATIONAL LITERATURE (PAMÁTNÍK NÁRODNÍHO PÍSEMNICTVÍ). Part of the Strahov Monastery, the star attraction here is the **Strahov Library,** with its magnificent **Theological and Philosophical Halls.** *(Strahovské nádvoří 1. From Metro A: Hradčanská, take tram #25 toward Bílá Hora to Malovanka. Turn around, follow the tram tracks, then turn right on Strahovská through an arch, into the park. The museum is inside the monastery on the left. ☎220 516 671. Open daily 9am-noon and 1-5pm. 70Kč, students 50Kč.)*

NATIONAL MUSEUM (NÁRODNÍ MUZEUM). With a commanding view over all of Wenceslas Square, the National Museum provides a wonderful starting place for a tour of Nové Město. While the paleontological and anthropological exhibitions inside the museum are less than thrilling, the impressive exterior is worth a stop. *(At the head of Wenceslas Square. Metro A or C: Muzeum. Open daily May-Sept. 10am-6pm; Oct.-Apr. 9am-5pm; closed 1st Tu of month.)*

🔊 ENTERTAINMENT

THEATER

It is hard to overstate the role of theater in Czech culture. Prague remains a center for the artform: on any given night, a world-class performances are staged in town, from classics to the avant-garde. For a list of current concerts and performances, consult *The Prague Post, The Pill, Threshold,* or *Do města-Downtown* (the latter three are free and are distributed at many cafes and restaurants). Most performances begin at 7pm; unsold tickets are sometimes available 30min. before show time. The majority of Prague's theaters close in July and August, but the selection is extensive during the rest of the year. June brings all things avant-garde with the **Prague Fringe Festival,** which features dancers, comedians, performance artists, and everyone's favorite, mimes. (š224 935 183; www.prague-fringe.cz.)

> **National Theatre** (Národní divadlo), Národní třída 2/4. Metro B: Národní třída. The National Theatre opened in 1883. It was Prague's 1st venue for performances in the Czech language, and an important symbol of national pride; fittingly, the building fuses classical architecture with images from Czech mythology. Also oversees the **Estates Theatre** and the **Kolowrat Theatre.** Tickets for all 3 theaters are available at the box

office in Kolowrat Palace at Ovocný trh 6, beside the Estates Theatre, or at Národní třída 2-4 (☎224 901 448, reservations 224 901 487. www.narodni-divadlo.cz). Open daily Sept.-June 10am-6pm, and 45min. before each show. Formal dress required. Tickets 30-1000Kč. Discounted tickets announced as they become available.

State Opera (Státní opera), Wilsonova 4. (Info ☎296 117 111, box office 224 227 266; www.opera.cz/en). Metro A or C: Muzeum. This gorgeous neo-Rococo building is now home to the Prague State Opera, as part of the National Theatre. Box office open M-F 10am-5:30pm, Sa-Su 10am-noon, 1-5:30pm, and 1hr. before each show.

Theatre Image Black Light Theatre, Pařížská 4 (☎222 314 448; www.imagetheatre.cz). Every performance at Theatre Image is silent, conveying its message through dance techniques and black light. Shows daily 8pm. Box office open daily 9am-8pm.

Laterna Magika, Národní třída 4 (☎224 931 482; www.laterna.cz). Also delivering silent performances, the acclaimed Laterna Magika began in 1958 at the world exposition in Brussels. Box office open M-Sa 10am-8pm. Tickets 680Kč, students 540Kč.

Marionette Theater (Říše loutek), Žatecká 1 (☎224 819 322; www.mozart.cz). Metro A: Staroměstská, trams #17 and 18, or bus #207. On the corner of Žatecká and Mariánské nám. The world's oldest marionette theater is a cultural staple of the Czech Republic. The current show, a version of Mozart's *Don Giovanni* performed entirely by puppets, has been running since 1991. The humorous, amazingly lifelike marionettes include a drunken Mozart who interacts with the audience during interludes. Performances M-Tu and Th-Su 8pm. Tickets available at the box office on Žatecká 1, the secondary box office at Celetná 13, and the tourist office in the Old Town Hall. Box office open June-Oct. daily 10am-8pm. 490Kč, students 390Kč.

MUSIC

The **Prague Spring Festival** (www.festival.cz) is a world-class showcase of talent from across the globe. Even the army and police bands of the Czech Republic get a chance to perform. Prague Spring opens with Smetana's "Má Vlast" (My Country) and closes with Beethoven's 9th symphony. Tickets are available at the Prague Spring box office in the Rudolfinum, Hellichova 18. (☎257 31 25 47; www.ticketpro.cz. Open M-F 10am-6pm.) It's hard to walk down Staroměstké nám. without having thrust into your hand a flyer—or 20—advertising orchestral concerts in nearby churches and halls. These tend to cost about US$15. The beautiful rooms in which they are held, such as Municipal Hall's art nouveau Smetana Hall, are as much of a draw as the music itself. Shows are usually around 8pm.

FILM

Prague has its share of theaters showing big-budget American blockbusters. Even more common, however, are small cinemas showing art-house and independent films from all around the world. The **Kino Perštýn**, Na Perštýné 6 (☎221 668 432), shows one or two recent films daily. International films are shown with Czech subtitles and Czech films with English subtitles. Call ahead for reservations. **KinoSvětozor Arthouse**, Vodičkova 41 (☎224 946 824; www.kinosvetozor.cz), has two screens, the *velký* (big) and the *malý* (small), with a total of eight screenings per day. Recent American hits are on the menu, but so are all sorts of international classics. (1st show 11am, last 9:15pm. Bar and box office open daily at 10:30am. Tickets 100Kč unless otherwise noted.)

◪ NIGHTLIFE

The best way to experience Prague at night is through an alcoholic haze. With some of the finest beers in the world on tap, pubs and beer halls are among the city's favorite places for nighttime pleasures. These days, however, authentic pub experiences are often restricted to the suburbs and outlying Metro stops; in central Prague, Irish pubs and American sports bars are cropping up all over, charging high prices for foreign beers. You may have to look a bit harder for them, but a few trusty Czech pubs remain scattered throughout Staré Město and Malá Strana.

Prague is not a clubbing city, although there are enough dance clubs pumping out techno to satisfy those craving the Euro-club scene. More popular among Czechs are the city's many jazz and rock clubs, which host excellent local and international acts. Otherwise, you can always retreat to the Charles Bridge to sing along with aspiring Brit-pop guitarists. Whichever way you indulge in Prague nightlife, swig a few pints of *pivo*, grab some 4am snacks (see **Late-Night Eating**, p. 180), and forgo the night bus for the morning Metro.

 THE REAL DEAL. Many bars in Prague now display prominent NO STAG PARTIES signs in their windows. Why, you ask? Well, stag parties tend to: sing so loud it chases away business; tear up bars; perpetrate most of Prague's few violent crimes; and get all naked and fat out on terraces. The stag party is not a wide-ranging creature, however, and it lumbers about almost entirely within the area between Staroměstské nám. and the Charles Bridge. Intrigued? Horrified? To join in—or avoid—the raucous destruction, here are some places to go, or to stay the hell away from: **George and Dragon,** Staroměstské nám. Named after England, mothership of most stags. **O'Caffrey's,** next to George and Dragon. For when you want that Irish Pub atmosphere, in order to destroy it with your mates. **U Fleků,** the saddest casualty: the oldest beer hall in Prague is often full of stag parties. In general, any establishment that prints its name in English somewhere on its facade is likely to be a den of stag. You stand warned. —Justin Jennings

BEER HALLS AND WINE CELLARS

Vinárna U Sudu, Vodičkova 10 (☎222 232 207). Metro A: Můstek. Cross Václavské nám. to Vodičkova and follow it as it curves left. Undiscovered by tourists, this Moravian wine bar looks plain from its 1st fl. entrance, but beneath the facade sprawls a labyrinth of catacombs and cavernous cellars, where the carafes of smooth red wine (125Kč) go down frighteningly fast. Whether you choose to isolate yourself in one of the many cellars or challenge locals to a match of foosball, the wine and atmosphere are sure to leave you smiling. Open M-Th 1pm-2am, F-Sa 1pm-3am, Su 3pm-1am.

Pivnice u Sv. Tomáše, Letenská 12 (☎257 531 835; www.pivnice-sv-tomas.cz). Metro A: Malostranská. Go downhill on Letenská. The mighty dungeons echo with boisterous revelry. Sing drunken ballads with beer in one hand and meat from the roasting spit in the other. (Roasting spit meats must be ordered a day in advance; 350-400Kč.) Beer 40Kč. Live band 7-11pm. Open daily 11:30am-midnight. Kitchen closes 10pm. MC/V.

BARS

Kozička, Kozí 1 (☎224 818 308; www.kozicka.cz). Metro A: Staroměstská. Take Dlouhá from the square's northeast corner, then bear left on Kozí. The giant cellar bar is always packed—you'll know why after your first *Krušovice* (30Kč). Great if you're looking for a Czechmate. Open M-F noon-4am, Sa 6pm-4am, Su 6pm-3am. MC/V.

Cafe Marquis de Sade, Melnicka 5. From Metro B: nám. Republiky, go down U Obecního Domu to the right of the Obecního Dum. Take a right on Rybna, a left on Jakubská, and a left on Melnicka. This spacious bar soothes the senses with rich red velvet walls. Ascend the wrought-iron staircase to the loft, knock back a "shot de fuck up" (80Kč), and scope out the crowd below. Open daily 2pm-2am.

Le Chateau, Jakubská 2 (☎222 316 328). From Metro B: nám. Republiky, walk through the Powder Tower to Celetná, then take a right on Templová. On the corner of Templová and Jakubská. Nonstop techno-rock keeps the place pumping until the wee hours. Open M-Th noon-3am, F noon-4am, Sa 4pm-4am, Su 4pm-2am.

Zanzibar, Saská 6 (☎312 246 876). Metro A: Malostranská. From the square, head down Mostecká toward the Charles Bridge, turn right on Lázeňská, and left on Saská. The tastiest, priciest, and most exotic mixed drinks this side of the Vltava (80-190č). Cuban cigars 29-169Kč. Open daily 5pm-3am.

U 3 Černých Ruží, Zámecká 5. Metro A: Malostranská. Take tram #12, 22, or 23 to Malostranské nám and turn right, then left on Zámecká. At the foot of the New Castle Steps. A small, quirky bar that pours endless pints at low prices (Budvar 18Kč) for a thirsty local crowd. If you can still stand after sitting in one of the not-so-comfy armchairs, end the night with a moonlit walk to the castle. Open daily 11am-midnight.

Molly Malone's, U obecního dvora 4 (☎224 818 851; www.mollymalones.cz). Metro A: Staroměstská. Turn right on Křižonvická, away from the Charles Bridge. After nám. Jana Palacha, turn right on Široká, which becomes Vězeňská; turn left at its end. Grab 3 friends, 4 pints of Guinness (80Kč), and head for the loft. Irish and British newspapers Su. Live music Th 9pm-midnight. Open M-Th and Su 11am-1am, F-Sa 11am-2am.

Jo's Bar and Garáž, Malostranské nám. 7. Metro A: Malostranská. If you can't bear the idea that the people at the next table might not speak English, Jo's Bar is the perfect spot for you. Foosball, darts, card games, and a dance floor downstairs. Some of Prague's best DJs spin acid jazz, techno, house, and dance. Beer 40Kč. Long Island Iced Tea 115Kč. Open daily 11am-2am. AmEx/MC/V.

CLUBS AND DISCOS

▨ **Radost FX,** Bělehradská 120 (☎224 254 776; www.radostfx.cz). Metro C: IP Pavlova. Although heavily touristed, Radost remains the gem of Prague nightlife, playing only the hippest techno, jungle, and house music from internationally renowned DJs. The spacious, ventilated chill-out room is perfect for taking a break from the dance floor and watching the throngs of trendy clubbers strut their stuff. Creative drinks (Frozen Sex with an Alien 140Kč) will expand your clubbing horizons. Also serves brunch (see **Nové Město Restaurants,** p. 179). Cover 100-200Kč. Open M-Sa 10pm-5am.

Roxy, Dlouhá 33 (☎224 826 296; www.roxy.cz). Metro B: nám. Republiky. Walk up Revoluční to the river; go left on Dlouhá. Hip locals and informed tourists come to this converted theater for experimental DJs and theme nights. Watch out for swooping butterflies from the balcony above. Beer 30Kč. Cover Tu and Th-Sa 100-350Kč. Open M-Tu and Th-Sa 9pm-late.

Karlovy Lázně, Novotného Lávka 1 (☎222 220 502). An irresistible location beneath the Charles Bridge. The teenagers and early 20-somethings in line at the door stare eagerly at televisions broadcasting from inside this pulsing 4-story complex. Different rooms play R&B, techno, oldies, and pop music every night. Cover 120Kč, 50Kč before 10pm and after 4am. Open daily 9pm-5am.

Klub 007, Chaloupeckého 7 (☎257 211 439; www.klub007strahov.cz). Metro A: Dejvicka. From Dejvicka take bus #217 to Stadion Strahov and walk uphill on Chaloupeckého for 450m. For a truly local experience, make the hike out to 007. A favorite with local university students, this club is better for music-appreciation than dancing. Hard core, punk, and reggae alternate nights. Open M-Sa 7pm-2am.

JAZZ CLUBS

U staré paní (The Old Lady's Place), Michalská 9 (☎603 551 680; www.jazzlounge.cz). Metro A or B: Můstek. Walk down Na můstku at the end of Václavské nám. through its name change to Melantrichova. Turn left on Havelská and right on Michalská. High, plush orange stools, small black tables and a black metal bar face the stage, where on any given night you can take in the products of the Czechs' real love for jazz. Pilsner Urquell 45Kč. Performances every night at 9pm. Cover M-Th and Su 150Kč, F-Sa 200Kč. Open daily 7pm-2am. AmEx/MC/V.

Ungelt, Týn 2 (☎224 895 748; www.jazzblues.cz). Metro A or B: Staroměstská. From Old Town Square, follow Týnska and take a right on Týn. A passage in the unassuming bar upstairs leads down into the vaults of this UNESCO-protected building. There waits a small, low-lit room with stone walls and polished wood tables where people chat in many languages. Musicians provide background with lots of soloing and lots of electric bass. Menu of absinthe mixed drinks includes the Hemingway (absinthe, sparkling wine, ice; 90Kč). They've also got commemorative t-shirts (200Kč) in case you want to be that guy. Beer 38Kč. Live concerts daily 9pm-midnight; cover 200Kč, students 150Kč, or listen from the pub for free. Open daily 8pm-midnight.

Reduta, Národní 20. (☎224 933 487; www.redutajazzclub.cz). Metro A: Národní třída. Exit on Spálená, take a left on Národní, and go through the facade of the Louvre cafe. This classic jazz venue is an old haunt of Presidents Clinton and Havel, as photos attest. Cover 200Kč. Open daily 9pm-midnight.

U Malého Glena II, Karmelitská 23 (☎257 531 717; www.malyglen.cz). In the basement of U Malého Glena, there's a bar and a small stage with a handful of tables. And on M nights, Stan the Man and his Bohemian Blues Band play English songs under low lights. Other nights there's salsa, other nights jazz. Bernard Beer 35Kč per 0.5L. Cover 100-150Kč. Shows start at 9:30pm, except F and Sa, when they start at 10pm. Open daily 8pm-2am. Call ahead for weekend tables. AmEx/MC/V.

GLBT PRAGUE

Prague's gay and lesbian scene is developing fast and in many directions: transvestite shows, stripteases, discos, bars, cafes, restaurants, and hotels aimed at gay and lesbian travelers can be easily found. At any of the places listed below, you can pick up a copy of *Gayčko* (60Kč), a glossy magazine mostly in Czech. Check out www.praguegayguide.net or www.praguesaints.cz.

The Saints, Polská 32 (☎ 222 250 041; www.praguesaints.cz; www.saintsbar.cz). Metro A: Jiřího z Poděbrad. On Vinohradská, head away from the giant clock. Take a right on Slavikova and then the 2nd left on Polská. The Saints is an advocacy group that introduces GLBT visitors to Prague and organizes the local community; they also run a small, comfortable club. With plush couches, small tables, and free Wi-Fi, the welcoming club draws a mixed crowd of men and women, queer and straight, Czech and foreign. Beer from 22Kč. Open M-Th 1pm-2am, F and Sa 5pm-4am, Su 1pm-1am.

Friends, Bartolomejská 11 (☎224 236 272; www.friends-prague.cz). Metro B: Národní třída. Exit on Spálená, turn right, and cross Narodní třída, heading down Na Perštýně. Turn left on Bartolomejská. The only GLBT dance club in Staré Město, Friends has a rotating schedule of parties and theme nights. The tapestried interior attracts a young local crowd early in the week, with the tourist ratio creeping up on weekends. Women and straight customers are welcome. Beer from 20Kč. Open daily 6pm-5am. No cover.

Tingl Tangl, Karolíny Světlé 12 (☎777 322 121; www.tingl-tangl.cz). From Metro B: Národní třída, turn right on Spálená, left on Národní, and right on Karolíny Světlé; under the arch to the left. Draws crowds to cabarets where magnificent drag queens lip-sync on stage. Women welcome. Cover 120Kč. Open W and F-Sa 10pm-5am.

⚡ DAYTRIPS FROM PRAGUE

When you're in the city, it's easy to forget that there are places worth visiting outside Prague. Even if you're only spending a few days in the capital, take the time to explore the towns and sights in the surrounding Bohemian hills. A day spent wan-

BONE-CHILLING CHAPEL

In and around Prague, you will find churches of stone, brick, iron, glass—and one of bones. Kutná Hora, a small, picturesque village 1hr. from Prague, is both famous and infamous for its ossuary, a chapel filled with artistic and religious creations made entirely from parts of human skeletons. The village was originally formed around silver mines; its morbid side only came out when the plague and a superstition about the holiness of the village's graveyard combined to leave the cemetery overflowing with corpses. The Cistercian Order built a chapel in order to house the extra remains, and in a fit of whim (or possibly insanity), one monk began designing flowers from pelvises and crania. He never finished the ossuary, but the artist František Rint eventually completed the project in 1870, decorating the chapel from floor to ceiling with the bones of over 40,000 people.

Trains run from Hlavní Nádraží (1hr., 1 per hr., round-trip 112Kč). A 1km. walk from the train station. From the train station, turn right, then left, and left again on the highway. After 500m, turn right at the church. The ossuary is at the end of the road. Open daily Apr.-Sept. 8am-6pm; Oct. 9am-noon and 1-5pm; Nov.-Mar. 9am-noon and 1-4pm. 35Kč, students 20Kč. Camera 30Kč, video 60Kč.

dering through the resplendent castles of Karlštejn or exploring the former concentration camp of Terezín will give you a richer experience and a more complete understanding of the Czech Republic's history.

TEREZÍN (THERESIENSTADT)

Buses from Florenc (1hr., 15 per day, 61Kč). Exit at the Terezín stop by the tourist office. You can also catch a train from Hlavní Masarykovo to the station 2km from town. Ask for directions, as there are no street signs or signposts. Trains are more reliable on weekends. The museum 500m right of the bus stop sells tickets to Terezín's sights. ☎416 782 576; www.pamatnik-terezin.cz. Open daily Apr.-Sept. 9am-6pm; Oct.-Mar. 9am-5:30pm. Museum, barracks, and fortress 180Kč; students 160Kč. Crematorium and graveyard open M-F and Su Apr.-Oct. 10am-5pm; Nov.-Mar. 10am-4pm. Free.

The fortress town of Terezín (Theresienstadt) was built in the 1780s by Austrian Emperor Josef II to safeguard his empire's northern frontier. In 1940, Hitler's Gestapo set up a prison in the Small Fortress, and in 1941 the town became a concentration camp. By 1942, the entire prewar civilian population had been evacuated, and the town became a way-station for over 140,000 Jews awaiting transfer farther east. Terezín was one of Hitler's most successful propaganda ploys: the camp was intended to paint a false portrait of ghetto life for Red Cross delegations. Sparkling clean bathrooms and sleeping facilities were created purely for show. The large park that dominates the town square was built to create an illusion of aesthetic and athletic opportunities for residents, yet, except for publicity stunts, Jews were not allowed to enter it. Nazi films described the area as a "self-governed" settlement, where Jews were allowed to educate their children, partake of arts and recreation, and live a "fulfilling" life. In reality, overcrowding, malnourishment, and death chambers killed over 30,000 people in the camp. Since the war, Terezín has been repopulated, and life goes on in the former concentration camp. Supermarkets occupy former Nazi offices and families now live in the barracks.

TOWN AND CEMETERY. To walk the eerily quiet streets of Terezín is to confront its ghosts. Every building here was used to house and monitor Jews during the war. The former school has been converted into a **museum** of life in the camp, displaying documents that place Terezín in the wider context of WWII. The museum's most moving exhibits are dedicated to the rich artistic life that emerged among the Jews in response to the horrors of persecution—the 2nd floor features original paintings, music, theater, and poetry by children and adults imprisoned in Terezín. East of the marketplace, the **Magdeburg Barracks** document the lives of Jews within their prison walls. Outside the walls lie Terezín's **Cemetery and Crematorium,** where Nazis disposed of the remains of the executed.

SMALL FORTRESS. The Small Fortress sits across the river, much of it left bare and untouched for visitors to explore freely. Permanent exhibitions chart the town's development from 1780 to 1939 and the story of the fortress during WWII. Above the entrance hangs the ironic epitaph of the Nazi concentration camps: *"Arbeit macht frei"* (Work shall set you free). The true horror of this phrase comes alive in the dim underground passage to the excavation site, where those imprisoned here were buried after being literally worked to death. Liberators uncovered mass graves after the war and transferred many of the bodies to the memorial cemetery. *(Open daily Apr.-Oct. 8am-6pm; Nov.-Mar. 8am-4:30pm. Closed Dec. 24-26 and Jan. 1. 160Kč, students 130Kč.)*

KARLŠTEJN

Trains from Hlavní nádraží (55min., 4 per day, 46Kč). Head right from the station and take the 1st left over the Berounka River. Turn right after the bridge, take a left onto the sidewalk that splits off from the road, and walk through the village (25min., steeply uphill). ☎311 681 617; www.hradkarlstejn.cz. Open Tu-Su July and Aug. 9am-6pm; Sept. and May-June 9am-5pm; Oct. and Apr. 9am-4pm; Jan.-Mar. 9am-3pm. Closed daily noon-1pm. Mandatory tours in English: 7-8 per day, hours vary; 200Kč, students 100Kč; groups must reserve in advance. Chapel tours July-Oct. by reservation only; adults 300Kč, students and children 100Kč. ☎274 008 154 or email rezervace@stc.npu.cz. No pictures; no cell phones; "translating prohibited." MC/V.

Karlštejn is a Bohemian gem, a walled and turreted fortress built by Emperor Charles IV in the 14th century. The castle rambles over the peak of a mountain, looking out magisterially over the surrounding countryside, while the tiny, eponymous one-street town clings to the side, selling souvenirs. The basic and rather short tour of the castle takes you through the vassals' hall, Charles's bedchamber, his banquet hall, and the audience chamber where he met with ambassadors. Though the **Chapel of the Holy Cross** houses the castle's most precious jewels and holy relics, it is excluded from the tour. Some items from Charles's treasure chest, however, appear on the main tour, including the skull of the dragon killed by St. George (looking suspiciously like a crocodile skull), and a replica of Charles's crown, the original of which supposedly contains a fragment of Jesus's crown of thorns. The chapel is covered with portraits of saints painted by the Gothic artist **Master Theodorik.** Self-guided tours of the bell tower and the clock tower are free.

Back in Karlštejn, you can take a coach ride through town by standing anywhere and paying 99Kč when the coach shows up, or by calling ☎0380 158. The surrounding countryside is part of the Bohemian karst region, the only place in the world where the karst ash tree can be found. It is also home to over 1380 butterfly species. Enjoy the splendor, but be careful: trails are not always clearly marked.

WEST BOHEMIA

Bursting at the seams with healing waters of all sorts, West Bohemia is an oasis. Over the centuries, emperors and intellectuals alike soaked in the waters of Karlovy Vary (*Carlsbad* in German). Today, tourists still flock to the town's bubbling springs and wander through its colonnades, but they come seeking beer, including one of the world's finest brews, Pilsner Urquell.

CZECH REPUBLIC

PLZEŇ ☎377

Tell Czechs you're going to Plzeň (PUHL-zen-yeh; pop. 175,000), and they may advise you to spend your time elsewhere, thinking back to the days when this city was notorious for its pollution. Efforts to clean up the city, however, have left its beautiful architecture and gardens looking fresh and new. But it is world-famous beer, not architecture, that lures so many to Plzeň. Among the Pilsner Brewery, the Brewery Museum, and the countless beer halls, Plzeň is a beer-lover's utopia.

◪ TRANSPORTATION

Trains: ☎322 079. On Širková between Americká and Koterovská. Domestic tickets on the 1st level; international tickets on the 2nd. Open M-F 3:15am-2am, Sa 2:45am-2am, Su 3:30am-12:30am. To **Prague** (1¾hr., 12 per day, 140Kč) and **Český Krumlov** (3hr., 3 per day, 140-200Kč) via **České Budějovice.**

Buses: Husova 58 (☎237 237). Open M-F and Su 5am-10:30pm, Sa 5am-8pm. Many Euroline buses pass through en route to **Prague** (2hr., 16 per day, 70-80Kč) from **France, Germany, the Netherlands,** and **Switzerland.** To **Karlovy Vary** (45min., 16 per day, 65-80Kč).

Public Transportation: Trams run until 11:45pm; **night trams,** labeled with an N followed by the number of the tram, take over after 11:45pm, with service every hr. Get tickets (12Kč, backpacks 4Kč) from any *tabák* or from machines at the tram stops, and punch them on board by pressing hard on the orange box. Machines require exact change. Fine for riding ticketless 200-1000Kč. Tram #1 goes to the train and bus stations, nám. Republiky. Tram #4 runs north-south along Sady Pětatřicátníků.

Taxis: Radio Taxi (☎377 377). Taxis stalk the stations and nám. Republiky.

◪◪ ORIENTATION AND PRACTICAL INFORMATION

Nám. Republiky, the main square, from which the city's sights branch out, lies at the center of a grid of parks and streets. Restaurants and cafes cluster outside the square. Nightlife is concentrated around the square and along **Smetanovy sady.** From the **train station,** turn right on **Širková** and enter the pedestrian underpass. When you emerge from the **Americká** exit, continue down Širková (300m). Turn left on **Pražská,** then right at the fork to reach nám. Republiky. From the **bus station,** turn left on **Husova.** After it becomes Smetanovy sady, turn left on **Bedřicha Smetany** and follow it to the square (15min.).

Tourist Office: Městské Informační Středisko (MIS), nám. Republiky 41 (☎035 330; www.icpilsen.cz). Offers **free maps,** books rooms, and sells OSKAR phone cards. Little English spoken. **Internet** 5Kč up to 5min., 20Kč for 6-15min., 40Kč for 16-30min., 2Kč per min. thereafter. Open daily 9am-7pm.

Budget Travel: GTS Int, Pražská 12 (☎328 621; www.gtsint.cz). Arranges plane and train tickets. Open M-F 8am-5pm.

Currency Exchange: Plzeňská Banka, nám. Republiky 16 (☎235 354), cashes **traveler's checks** for 2.5% commission. Open M-F 8:30am-4:30pm. A **24hr. currency exchange** machine sits in **ČSOB,** Americká 60, near the train station. MC/V **ATMs** are scattered throughout nám. Republiky.

Luggage Storage: On the 1st fl. of the train station. 12Kč per day, bags over 15kg 23Kč per day. Lost ticket charge 30Kč. Open daily 7-11:15am and 11:35am-7pm. Lockers 30Kč per day (24hr. limit).

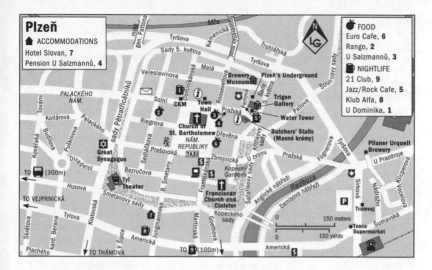

Plzeň

↑ ACCOMMODATIONS
Hotel Slovan, **7**
Pension U Salzmannů, **4**

🍴 FOOD
Euro Cafe, **6**
Rango, **2**
U Salzmannů, **3**
🍺 NIGHTLIFE
21 Club, **9**
Jazz/Rock Cafe, **5**
Klub Alfa, **8**
U Dominika, **1**

Emergency: ☎ 155.

Pharmacy: Lékárna U Bílého Jenorožce, nám. Republiky (☎ 240 288 or 533 259), near the corner of Prešovská and Bedřicha Smetany. Open M and W-Th 7am-6pm, Tu and F 7am-8pm, Sa 8am-noon.

Internet: Internet Café IG, Kopeckého sady 15. 1st 30min. 0.80Kč per min., 0.70Kč per min thereafter. Open M-F 9am-10pm, Sa 10am-8pm, Su 2-9pm. **Internet Kavárna Aréna,** Františkánská 10 (☎ 220 402). Ring bell to enter. 0.90Kč per min. Open M-F 9am-10pm, Sa-Su 10am-10pm.

Post Office: Solní 20 (☎ 211 543). **Poste Restante** available at the windows. Open M-F 9am-7pm, Sa 8am-1pm, Su 8am-noon. **Postal Code:** 30101.

🏠 ACCOMMODATIONS

There aren't many budget accommodations in Plzeň, as the tourist industry caters mainly to older German travelers. **MIS** (p. 198) books **private rooms** (from 179Kč; 10-15min. walk from main square). **Pensions** range from 300 to 900Kč.

Hotel Slovan, Smetanovy sady 1 (☎ 227 256; http://hotelslovan.pilsen.cz), at the corner of Jungmannova and Smetanovy sady. The Slovan has the kind of decaying grandeur that you might associate with the scene of clandestine Soviet doings. Nonetheless, the rooms are appointed with functional, if not pretty, furnishings and appliances. Decent English and excellent German spoken. Reception 24hr. Budget rooms with shared bathrooms: singles 530Kč; doubles 810Kč. Luxury rooms with private bathrooms and breakfast: singles 1450Kč; doubles 2100Kč. AmEx/D/MC/V. ❸

Pension U Salzmannů, Pražská 8 (☎ 235 855; www.usalzmannu.cz.) Attached to the well-known restaurant of the same name, this pension has an unbeatable location and reasonable prices. Rooms and bathrooms are spotless and well equipped. They are, however, very few in number, especially at the lower end of the price range. No English, but excellent German spoken. Budget singles with shared baths from 550Kč; doubles from 700Kč. Nicer rooms with private bath 1500Kč. Luxury suites 1900Kč. ❸

FOOD

Every meal in Plzeň should include a glass of Pilsner Urquell, a smooth, golden beer, or its dark, stronger brother, Purkmistr. If you can't decide, have a Řezané, a Czech black-and-tan, which mixes the two varieties. For groceries, try **Potraviny Nuen,** at nám. Republiky 30 (open M-F 7am-7pm, Sa 7am-noon), or **Tesco,** Sirková 47 (open M-W 7am-7pm, Th-F 7am-8pm, Sa-Su 8am-6pm; AmEx/MC/V).

U Salzmannů Restaurace, Pražská 8 (☎235 855). Just when you think you've had enough of beer halls, U Salzmannů re-justifies their existence. Established in 1637, the restaurant specializes in the old Czech standbys, though some are modified in ways you don't find elsewhere. The "fried cheese in the potato dough" is huge and perfectly crispy (74Kč). Giant Pilsner Urquell 25Kč. Side of fries 24Kč. Open M-Th and Sa-Su 11am-11pm, F 11am-midnight. MC/V. ❸

Euro Cafe (Kavárna Europa), nám. Republiky 12 (☎329 999). The colorful interior is accented by murals of various European capitals. The Euro Cafe's menu is composed almost entirely of salads (from 40Kč; tuna and other toppings 10-20Kč extra). Breakfast—including bagels, cereal, and yogurt—is served 8-10:30am. Have an espresso, read one of the fashion magazines provided, and try to forget about period dress for a while. Open M-F 8am-10pm, Sa 8am-6pm, Su 10am-6pm. Cash only. ❶

Rango, Pražská 10 (☎329 969; www.rango.cz). Rango is one of the few restaurants in Plzeň that does not pledge allegiance to a particular brand of beer. Stucco walls, stained glass, and candlelit tables create an urbane mood. Entrees hover around 100-150Kč. *Risotto con di frutti del mar* is recommended (much shellfish; 150Kč). Open M-F 11am-11pm, Sa-Su noon-11pm. MC/V. ❹

SIGHTS

■GREAT SYNAGOGUE (VELKÁ SYNAGOGA V PLZŇI). From outside, it might be hard to tell just what kind of building the Great Synagogue of Plzeň is. The construction looks vaguely church-like, flanked with Moorish-style, onion-domed towers. Indeed, town leaders long ago determined that the plans for the synagogue too closely resembled a church, and ordered that the spires be lowered and that "Oriental" elements be introduced. Inside, the high, arched ceilings recall the best of high neo-Renaissance architecture, and the magnificent acoustics are employed for a series of classical concerts each year. Though it is the 3rd-largest synagogue in the world, the building was out of use for many years: most of Plzeň's Jews fled during the Nazi occupation, and the postwar Jewish population continued to dwindle. Regular services resumed in 1998, in the "Winter Synagogue" at the rear of the building. *(From the southern end of nám. Republiky, go down Prešovská to Sady Pětatřicátníků and turn left; the synagogue is on the right. Concert info at www.synagogaconcerts.cz. Open Apr.-Sept. M-F and Su 10am-6pm; Oct. M-F and Su 10am-5pm; Nov. M-F and Su 10am-4pm. 40Kč, students 30Kč.)*

PILSNER URQUELL BREWERY. By 1842, over 30 independent brewers plied their trade in Plzeň's beer cellars. These brewers formed a union called the Pilsner Urquell Burghers' Brewery (Městsanský Pivovar Plzenský Prazdroj), hoping to create the best beer in the world. Many would agree that they succeeded with the legendary **Pilsner Urquell.** As you walk through the huge gate and spot the famous Prazdroj sign behind the billowing smoke, it's hard not to feel like you've entered beer heaven. Knowledgeable guides explain what makes the beers so tasty and lead thirsty visitors to the fermentation cellars for samples straight from the barrel. The cellars can get chilly; bring a sweater. *(From nám. Republiky, follow Pražská east over the Radbuza River, where it becomes U Prazdroje; cross the street and take the pedestrian overpass. ☎062 888; www.beerworld.cz. 1¼hr. tours daily 12:30, 2pm. 120Kč, students 60Kč.)*

In large groups, every 21st person is free. Reservations available: call or email visits@pilsner.sab-miller.com in advance.) Don't miss Na Spilce, the on-site beer house, where Pilsner pours forth at 20Kč per pint. *(☎062 755; 062 901; na.spilce@pilsner.sabmiller.com. Open M-Th and Sa 11am-10pm, F 11am-11pm, Su 11am-9pm.)*

REPUBLIC SQUARE (NÁMĚSTÍ REPUBLIKY). Imperial dwellings loom over this marketplace, but none overshadow the country's tallest belfry, that of the **Cathedral of St. Bartholomew** (Katedrále sv. Bartoloměje). Inside, Gothic statues and altars bow to the stunning 14th-century statue Plzeňská Madona. Tourists can climb 60m to the tower's observation deck for a dazzling—if dizzying—view of town. *(Tours Apr.-Dec. W-Su 10am-4pm. Tower open daily 10am-6pm. 20Kč, students 10Kč.)* The square's other architectural attraction is Plzeň's Renaissance town hall, topped by a golden clock. *(Nám. Republiky 39.)*

WATER TOWER COMPLEX. Head down Pražská from the square to reach the **water tower** (vodárenská věž), which once stored the crystal-clear water needed for fine beer. *(Pražská 19.)* A 40min. tour of the tower and **Plzeň's underground** (Plzeňské podzemí) winds through the cellars where the town's burghers used to brew their beers. *(Perlová 4. ☎225 214. Open June-Sept. Tu-Su 9am-5pm; Oct.-Nov. and Apr.-May W-Su 9am-5pm. Tours 30-40min.; last tour leaves 4:20pm. 45Kč, students 30Kč.)* Next door, the **Trigon Gallery** features artworks by recent and contemporary artists. *(Pražská 19. ☎325 471. Open M-F 10am-5pm, Sa 10am-noon. 10Kč, students 5Kč.)*

OTHER SIGHTS. The sprawling **Brewery Museum** (Pivovanské Muzeum) displays all things beer, from medieval taps to a coaster collection. Learn about the history of brewing through miniature brewing plants, reconstructed malt houses, chemical laboratories, and simulated pub environments. Fun fact: Hammurabi's Code included regulations concerning beer. *(Veleslavínova 6. From the square, go down Pražská and turn left on Perlová, which ends at Veleslavínova. ☎377 235 574; fax 377 224 955. Open daily Apr.-Sept. 10am-6pm; Jan.-Mar. 10am-4pm. Free English brochure. 60Kč, students with ISIC 30Kč.)* The black iron gate of the **Franciscan Church and Cloister** (Františkánský kostel a klášter) leads to a quiet garden with statues and several ice-cream vendors. Inside, the highlight is the 15th-century **Chapel of St. Barbara,** which is covered with brilliant frescoes. *(Enter at Františkánská 11, south of nám. Republiky. Open M and W 9-11:45am and 2-5pm, Tu and Th-F 9-11:45am. 30Kč, students 15Kč.)* At the edge of Staré Město, you can stroll and relax in the **Kopecký gardens** (Kopeckého sady) while brass bands perform. *(Františkánská runs into the park south of nám. Republiky.)*

⬛ NIGHTLIFE

Thanks to students from the University of West Bohemia, Plzeň abounds with bars and late-night clubs. Things heat up around 9:30pm.

▨ 21 Club, Prokopova 21 *(☎220 860)*. Going south from nám. Republiky, turn left on Americká. At the McDonald's on the corner, turn right on Prokopova. The club is on the left. Downstairs, in a darkened cellar, actual Czechs actually dance—with abandon—to rock-and-roll cut together with techno beats. In the 1st of 2 bars upstairs, purple lights swirl over the figured wood of the bar. In the 2nd, Renaissance- and Rococo-style paintings and figurines surround the bartender. In the very back, foosball and gambling. Open M-F 11am-3am, Sa 1pm-3am, Su 3-11pm. Cash only.

Jazz/Rock Cafe, Sedláčkova 18 (www.jazzrockcafe.cz). From the square, go down Solní and take the first left on Sedláčkova. Staying true to the Czech fascination with all things rock-and-roll, the walls are decorated with images of Aerosmith, Led Zeppelin, and Lou Reed. And Billy Idol. Stucco walls, low lighting, and beer from 35Kč. Check website for shows. Open M-F 10am-4am, Sa 6pm-4am, Su 4pm-2am. Cash only.

Klub Alfa (☎606 842 526), at intersection of Americká and Jungmannova. In the basement, the rock club "Deep Purple" keeps you infused with speed metal, death metal, and liquor (Jim Beam 47Kč). Stained-glass saints look on, their faces contorted with the effort of rocking. Upstairs, the local kids dance in a truly gigantic ballroom, where a statue of a knight on horseback rides to eternal party victory. Open M-Th and Su 7:30pm-5am, F-Sa 7:30pm-6am. Cash only.

U Dominika, Dominikánská 3 (☎223 226), off nám. Republiky. Even during the middle of the day, hordes of people congregate in Dominika's large, open space just to sit and drink. Leafy decor evokes a constant garden party. Stage in the back for rock and jazz shows. Open M-Th 10:30am-12:30am, F 10:30am-1am, Sa 11:30am-1am, Su 11:30am-midnight. Cash only.

KARLOVY VARY ☎353

From the bus station, Karlovy Vary (pop. 60,000) doesn't look like much, but a stroll into the spa district reveals why Johann Sebastian Bach, Peter the Great, Sigmund Freud, and even Karl Marx frequented salons here. Along the serene, willow-lined Teplá is a row of ornate pastel buildings. The town now hosts mostly older Germans and Russians seeking the springs' therapeutic powers.

⌷ TRANSPORTATION. The **train station** (☎913 145) is northwest of the center and has few connections. Trains run to **Prague** via **Chomutov** (4hr. plus 1-2hr. layover in Chomutov, 4-5 per day, 280Kč) and **Berlin, GER** (6-8hr., 1 per day, 1300Kč). **Buses** are more convenient. The **bus station** (☎504 516), on Západní, is closer to town and sends buses to: **Plzeň** (1¾hr., 10 per day, 80Kč) and **Prague** (2½hr., 10 per day, 120Kč). Buy tickets on board. **Local buses** pass through the main city stop on **Varšavská** (10Kč) and run 4am-10pm. **Night buses** are infrequent. **Taxis** line the main bus stop (Varšavská) and the street in front of the train station. **Centrum Taxi,** Zeyerova 9 (☎223 000), has 24hr. service.

◪🖪 ORIENTATION AND PRACTICAL INFORMATION. Karlovy Vary sits at the confluence of two rivers. The commercial district lies below the **Ohře River,** and **T.G. Masaryka** leads to the **Teplá River.** The spa district, called **Kolonáda** (Colonnade), begins at **Hotel Thermal,** from which **Mlýnská nábřeží** winds through the town's hot springs, changing its name to **Lázeňská, Tržiště,** and **Stará Louka** before ending at the **Grandhotel Pupp.** To reach the spa district from the **train station,** take bus #11 or 13 to the last stop. It's 15min. downhill on foot. Cross the street and go right on **Nákladní.** Take the first left and cross **Ostrovský most** at the highway. Follow the Teplá to T.G. Masaryka, which leads to Hotel Thermal. To get to the center from the **bus station,** turn left and take the left fork of the pedestrian underpass, toward Lázně. Turn right at the next fork, following the sign for the supermarket, and go straight up the stairs to reach T.G. Masaryka, which runs parallel to **Dr. Davida Bechera,** the other main street.

Pick up **maps** (free-40Kč), theater tickets (150-600Kč), and *Promenada* (15Kč), a monthly booklet with event schedules, at the **Infocentrum tourist office,** Lázeňská 1, which also **exchanges currency** for no commission. (§353 224 097; www.karlovyvary.cz. Open Jan.-Oct. M-F 8am-6pm, Sa-Su 10am-4pm; Nov.-Dec. M-F 7am-5pm.) **Komerční banka,** Tržiště 11, exchanges currency for 2% commission and has a MC/V **ATM** outside. (☎222 205. Open M-F 9am-noon and 1-5pm.) **Luggage storage** is at the train station. (10Kč per day, bags over 15kg 20Kč. Lockers 5Kč.) **Centralni Lékárna,** Dr. D. Bechera 3 is a **pharmacy.** (☎230 886. Open M-F 8am-6pm, Sa 8am-noon.) The **hospital,** Bezrucová 19 (☎115 111), is northwest of the spa district. Surf the **Internet** at **W.D. Group Computers and Internet,** IP Pavlova 19/641-3, at the farthest northeast corner of the

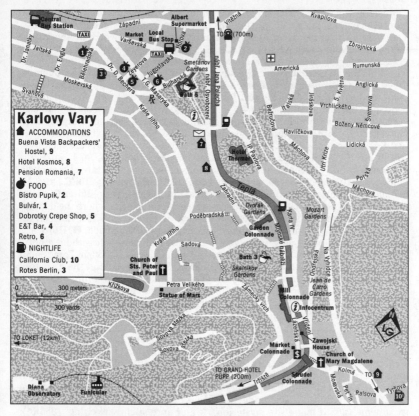

Karlovy Vary

🏠 ACCOMMODATIONS

Buena Vista Backpackers'
  Hostel, 9
Hotel Kosmos, 8
Pension Romania, 7

🍴 FOOD

Bistro Pupik, 2
Bulvár, 1
Dobrotky Crepe Shop, 5
E&T Bar, 4
Retro, 6

🍸 NIGHTLIFE

California Club, 10
Rotes Berlin, 3

Hotel Thermal complex. (☎227 42. 1Kč per min. Open M-F 9am-6pm, Sa 8:30am-noon.) The **post office,** T.G. Masaryka 1, offers **Western Union** and **Poste Restante** services. (☎161 107. Open M-F 7:30am-7pm, Sa 8am-1pm, Su 8am-noon.) **Postal Code:** 360 01.

⌨🖫 ACCOMMODATIONS AND FOOD. Budget accommodations are hard to come by in Karlovy Vary. For festival time in July, most rooms are booked four to five months in advance. **Infocentrum** books rooms (from 400Kč). Private agencies can also help you out. **City Info** is at the kiosk at T.G. Masaryka 9. (☎223 351. Open daily 10am-6pm. Singles in pensions from 630Kč; hotel doubles from 950Kč.) A quick bus ride out of the spa district will save you quite a few crowns.

　📷Buena Vista Backpackers' Hostel ❶, Moravská 42, offers a world of comfort. (☎239 071. Dorms 370Kč.) For luxurious, modern rooms and exceptional service, head to **Pension Romania ❹,** Zahradní 49, next to the post office on the corner of Zahradní and T.G. Masaryka. All rooms come with baths, TVs, telephones, and fridges. (☎222 822; www.romania.cz. Breakfast included. Singles 950Kč, student singles 715Kč; doubles 1580Kč, with view of river 1680Kč; triples 1900Kč. Oct.-Mar. 15-30% discount.) Nearby, **Hotel Kosmos ❹,** Zahradní 39, offers clean, simple rooms overlooking the Teplá with private baths, TVs, and fridges. (☎225 476; www.hotel-kosmos.cz. Breakfast included. May-Oct. 15 singles 950-1180Kč; doubles 1450-1750Kč; apartments 1950Kč. Prices drop Oct.-Apr.)

Meals in the spa district are expensive, but the ambience and food may be worth the extra money; cheaper options hide in the commercial district. Karlovy Vary is known for its sweet *oplatky* (wafers; around 6Kč), which are almost as enjoyable as the soothing spa waters. You can watch them being made at the kiosk next to City Info, on T.G. Masaryka, or get them from any of the vendors who line the streets. If you crave something sweeter, check out the **Dobrotky Crepe Shop ❶** on Zeyerova between Dr. D. Bechera and T.G. Masaryka, where you can design your own dessert for 14-25Kč. (Omelettes 14-30Kč. Open M-F 9am-7pm, Sa 10am-noon.) **Retro ❸**, T.G. Masaryka 18 (entrance on Bulharská), surrounds you with old musical memorabilia and serves dishes ranging from chicken *consomme* with homemade noodles (25Kč) to the "maxi steak on beer" (279Kč). Vegetarian dishes are few, but some of the many salads are meatless. (☎100 710. Open M-Th 10am-1am, F 10am-3am, Sa 11am-3am, Su 11am-1am.) Faithful regulars dine on scrumptious portions of hearty Czech fare at the lovely outdoor terrace at **E&T Bar ❸**, Zeyerova 3. (☎226 022. Entrees 40-210Kč. Open M-Sa 9am-2am, Su 10am-2am.) The funkiest cafe in Karlovy Vary, **Bulvár ❹**, Bélehradská 9, offers international dishes amid an eclectic interior where the decorations range from birdcages to coat hangers and oxcarts. (☎585 199. Entrees 40-299Kč. Open daily 11am-2am.) Cafeteria-style dining at **Bistro Pupik ❶**, Horova 2, across from the local bus stop on Varšavská, fills your stomach without emptying your wallet. (☎173 223 450. Entrees 50-75Kč. Open M-F 7:30am-7pm, Sa-Su 8am-5pm.) There is also an **Albert** supermarket, Horova 1, behind the bus stop. Look for the *Městská tržnice* (city market) sign, and be sure to bring a 5Kč coin for a shopping cart. (Open M-F 6am-7pm, Sa 7am-5pm, Su 9am-5pm. MC/V.) For fresh fruit and vegetables, the row of stalls on **Varšavská** provides a good selection of produce fresh off the farm.

🖸 **SIGHTS.** As Karlovy Vary is a spa town, sightseeing here involves mainly self-indulgence in all its various forms. Just strolling along Mlýnské nábř. is a sight in itself. The **spa district** begins with the manicured gardens of the Victorian **Bath 5** (Lázně 5), Smetanovy sady 1, across from the post office. Bath 5 offers the widest selection and most affordable treatments in town. Among these delights are thermal baths (355Kč), underwater massages (360-600Kč), paraffin hand treatments (255Kč), and the mysterious "water cure slightly exciting" (355Kč). More arcane procedures include "traction" (18Kč) and "lymph drainage by hand" (600Kč); however, these are available only with a doctor's prescription or a solemn declaration of sickliness. (☎222 536; www.spa5.cz. Pool and sauna open M-F 8am-9pm, Sa 8am-6pm, Su 10am-6pm. 90Kč. Treatments M-F 7am-3pm; select treatments Sa 7am-noon. Reserve 1-2 days in advance. MC/V.) Cross the bridge on T.G. Masaryka, turn right, and continue along the river. The path crosses back over the Teplá and leads through the **Dvořák Gardens** to the Victorian **Garden Colonnade** (Sadová kolonáda). Here, you can sip the supposedly curative waters of the **Snake Spring** (Hadí pramen) from a serpent's mouth and the **Garden Spring** (Sadový pramen; 105-300Kč) from a vase held by a marble peasant woman. Bring your own cup, or buy a porcelain one from the kiosks. During the summer months, the Colonnade also hosts free outdoor **concerts** (daily 2-3:30pm). **Bath 3**, at Mlýnské nábř. 5, offers massages. (☎225 641; www.lazneIII.cz. Neck and shoulder massage 455Kč, full body 735Kč. Treatments daily 7-11:30am and noon-3pm. Pool and sauna open M-F 3-7pm, Sa 1-6pm. 90Kč.) Next door, the Greek-inspired **Mill Colonnade** (Mlýnská kolonáda) shelters five separate springs with water that tastes less pungent than that of its neighbors. Farther along, the former **market** *(tržiště)* appears by the white **Market Colonnade** (Tržní kolonáda), where two springs bubble to the surface. Across the street, the **Zawojski House,** now the Živnostenská Banka, displays art nouveau architecture.

The best view of the building's ornate gilding is from across the river. The modernist **Strudel Colonnade** (Vřídelní kolonáda), a massive iron-and-glass building, looms next door. Inside, springs flow like faucets next to clothing stores and souvenir shops; the impressive **Strudel Spring** (Vřídlo pramen) spouts 30L of water per second at 72°C. (Open daily 6am-7pm.)

At the end of Stará Louka sits **Grandhotel Pupp.** Founded in 1774 by Johann Georg Pupp, the impressive Grandhotel was the largest in 19th-century Bohemia. From the right side of the hotel, follow the narrow walkway Mariánská to the funicular, which leads to the **Diana Observatory** and a breathtaking view of the city and surrounding forest. (Funicular runs every 15min. June-Sept. 9:15am-6:45pm; Oct. and Apr.-May 9:15am-5:45pm; Nov.-Dec. and Feb.-Mar. 9:15am-4:15pm. 40Kč, round-trip 60Kč. Tower open daily 9am-7pm. Free.) To return to town, you can either take the funicular back down or wind your way through the wooded paths of Petra Velikého, which ends at a statue of **Karl Marx.** The stern likeness commemorates Marx's visits to the bourgeois spa between 1874 and 1876. The statue stands at the border of one of the most expensive parts of town. Coincidence? Who knows. Around the corner on Krále Jiřího, the onion domes of the 19th-century, Russian Orthodox **Church of Saints Peter and Paul** stick out over the treetops. Six-winged seraphs look out from each of the blue-and-gold structure's gables.

◨ ▣ ENTERTAINMENT AND NIGHTLIFE. Cultural activities abound in Karlovy Vary. *Promenáda* (15Kč), a brochure available at the tourist office, lists the month's concerts and performances; it also includes info for Karlovy Vary's **International Film Festival,** held in July, which screens independent films from all over the globe. If you plan to attend, buy a pass to see five films per day inside **Hotel Thermal,** the festival's center. Tickets go quickly, so get to the box office early. You can also buy tickets from the kiosks lining Mlýnské nábř. Otherwise, try your luck at purchasing remainders 1hr. before each showing. The town's hotels and pensions fill up months in advance, so reserve early or camp at a site outside of town.

Like its restaurants, Karlovy Vary's nightlife is geared toward older tourists. Though clubs are sparse, expensive cafes abound. **Rotes Berlin,** Jaltská 7, off D. Bechera, seems to attract every young person in Karlovy Vary to its seductive red interior. (☎ 233 792. Beer from 15Kč. Mixed drinks 35-70Kč. Live DJs mix things up most nights. Open M-F noon-2am, Sa-Su 3pm-2am.) It's a steep hike up Kolmá from behind the Church of Mary Magdalene to **California Club,** Tyrsova 2, but the club's late hours and hot dancing make it worth the trek. (☎ 173 222 087. Beer from 15Kč. Open daily 1pm-5am.)

SOUTH BOHEMIA

Truly a rustic Eden, South Bohemia's hills make the region a favorite among Czech cyclists and hikers, who flock to the countryside to traipse through castles, observe wildlife in virgin forests, and guzzle Budvar from the source.

ČESKÉ BUDĚJOVICE   ☎ 38

České Budějovice (CHES-kay BOO-dyeh-yoh-vee-tseh; pop. 97,000), deep in the heart of the Bohemian countryside, is a great base for exploring the surrounding region. It lacks the small-town charm of Český Krumlov but boasts a beautiful town square and plenty of beer. The city is home to the great Budvar brewery, and it seems like every other building houses a pub where beer flows freely—quite helpful, since it may take a stein before you can pronounce the town's name.

⊏ TRANSPORTATION. The **train station** is at Nádražní 12. (☎7 854 490. Info office open daily 6:30am-6:30pm. Ticket booths open daily 3:45am-midnight.) **Trains** run to: **Brno** (4½hr., 3 per day, 274Kč); **Český Krumlov** (50min., 8 per day, 46Kč); **Plzeň** (2hr., 10 per day, 162Kč); **Prague** (2½hr., 12 per day, 204Kč); **Milan, ITA** (2330Kč); **Munich, GER** (1494Kč); **Rome, ITA** (3201Kč). **Buses** run from Žižkova, around the bend from the train station. (☎6 354 444. Info office open M-F 5:30-10:15am and 10:45am-6:30pm, Sa 8am-noon, Su 8-11:30am.) Destinations include: **Brno** (4½hr., 6 per day, 200Kč); **Český Krumlov** (50min., 25 per day, 25Kč); **Plzeň** (2¾hr., 1 per day, 110-140Kč); **Prague** (2½hr., 10 per day, 120-144Kč); **Milan, ITA** (14hr., 2 per wk., 2030Kč); **Munich, GER** (4½hr., 3 per wk., 1000Kč). Explore České Budějovice by **bus** and **trolley** (info ☎6 358 116). Buy tickets (10Kč for 1 bus, 12Kč for transfer) at the tourist office, kiosks, *tabáky,* or machines by bus stands. Punch them on board. Buses run only on the major roads that encircle the city center (Na Sadech, Lidická tř., Rudolfovská tř., Husova tř.) You get 20min. per ticket. How do they know? They just know. For a **taxi,** call **Taxi-Budějovice** (☎800 141 516).

⬛🛈 ORIENTATION AND PRACTICAL INFORMATION. Staré Město (Old Town) centers on the gigantic **nám. Přemysla Otakara II.** From the train station, turn right on **Nádražní** and hang a left at the first crosswalk on the pedestrian **Lannova třída.** This stretch of road, which becomes **Kanovnická** after the canal, meets the northeast corner of nám. Otakara II. The **bus station** is on **Žižkova.** To get to the center from the bus station, turn left on Žižkova and then right on **Jeronýmova.** Go left on Lannova třída, which leads to the center. Friendly, English-speaking staff at **Turistické Informační Centrum (TIC),** nám. Otakara II 2, provide **free maps** and have listings of available accommodations, including a giant book of private rooms. (☎6 801 413; www.c-budejovice.cz. Open M-F 8:30am-6pm, Sa 8:30am-5pm, Su 10am-noon and 12:30-4pm.) **Komerční Banka,** Krajinská 15, off nám. Otakara II, cashes **traveler's checks** for a 2% commission. (☎7 741 147. Open M-F 8am-5pm.) MC/V **ATMs** line nám. Otakara II. **Luggage storage** is along the right wall of the train station. (12Kč per day, bags over 15kg 45Kč per day. Open daily 5:15am-8:30pm. Lockers 12Kč per day. Be sure to set the combination on the inside of the locker door before you shut it.) **Omikron,** nám. Otakara II 25, has a small selection of English-language books, maps, and newspapers. (☎077 46 68 34 57. Open M-F 8am-6pm, Sa 8am-noon.) Other services include: **emergency** ☎7 878 90; a **pharmacy** at nám. Otakara II 26 (☎6 353 063; open M-F 8am-6pm); and a **hospital,** B. Nemcove 54 (☎7 871 111). At **Babylon Cafe and Cocktail Bar,** nám. Otakara II 30, 5th fl., young people drink, smoke, and use the Internet, all to the latest radio hits. (☎728 190 461. 1Kč per min. Open M-F 10am-8pm, Sa 1-9pm, Su 1-10pm.) **Na Půdě Internetovy Klub,** Krajinská 28, has flat-screen computers with the fastest connections in town. (☎7 313 529; www.napude.cz. 15Kč per 15min. Open daily 9am-10pm. MC/V.) The **post office,** nám. Senovážné 1, is the large pink-and-pink building south of Lannova as it enters Staré Město. (☎7 734 122. **Poste Restante** at windows #12 and 13. Take a number from the machine to the right of the entrance; wait to be called. Open M-F 7am-7pm, Sa-Su 8am-noon.) **Postal Code:** 37001.

🛏 ACCOMMODATIONS. Hostels are scarce in České Budějovice, but **private rooms** come in abundance, and the **TIC** has a big book of listings. To get to the **AT Penzion ❸,** Dukelská 15, head right on Dr. Stejskala from nám. Otakara II. Turn left at the first intersection and follow Široká, veering right on Dukelská. Go straight, well beyond the big yellow museum on your left. Private baths, well-furnished rooms, and friendly family management make this residential pension well worth the extra crowns. (☎387 312 529; fax 387 651 598. Breakfast 50Kč. Book in advance for summer months. Singles 500Kč; doubles 800Kč.) This pension is apt to be full, but the same family has recently opened an equally attractive 2nd location, the **Alton Hotýlek ❸** (formerly **AT Penzion 2**), Na Nábřeží 14. (☎608 421 004 or 608 860 353; www.altonhotylek.cz. Breakfast 100Kč. Singles 650Kč.)

🚹 **FOOD.** The main streets of nám. Otakara II and their offshoots house numerous restaurants. It's very easy to find a table on a terrace, a giant glass of world-renowned beer, and a plate heaped with always-substantial Czech cuisine. Vegetarianism and non-native cuisines have begun to catch on; most such food can be found in the streets and alleyways off the main square. The grocery store **Ovoce a Zelenina Nedorost,** Dr. Stejskala 8 (☎6 356 048) off nám. Otakara II, has a remarkably wide selection of fresh fruits and vegetables, as well as a bakery. **Zeleninovy Bar ❶** (Vegetable Bar), nám. Otakara II 2, is through the tunnel next to the pharmacy, at the back of a verdant courtyard. This tiny, cafeteria-style restaurant is a great budget option and a haven for vegetarians. After several beery days, nothing feels quite as good as real vitamins coursing through your fat-clogged veins. (☎ 721 61 183. Open M-F 8am-6pm. Cash only.) At **Restaurace Kněžská ❷,** Kněžská 1, locals chat with the bartender at unadorned tables. Those with deep pockets might enjoy "Jagersteak" (sirloin, cream, champignons; 249Kč). Excellent margherita pizza (50Kč) and garlic soup (25Kč) are cheaper options. (☎6 358 829. Entrees 25-249Kč. Open M-Th 10am-11pm, F 10am-midnight, Sa 11am-midnight. Cash only.) **Česká Rychta ❸,** nám. Otakara II 30, under Grand Hotel Zvon, has a large menu of steaks, as well as a list of "Small Things for Beer Drinkers," which includes treats like "piquant meat paste on toast" (68Kč). Pilsner Urquell (29Kč per 0.5L) makes a great complement to any "Small Thing." (English menu. Open M-Th 10am-11pm, F-Sa 10am-midnight, Su 11am-10pm. Cash only.) **Restaurace u Královské at the Hotel Malý Pivovar ❸,** Karla IV 8-10, is just off nám. Otakara II, behind and to the left of the Hotel Malý Pivovar's lobby. When you're sick of eating like a backpacker, head here for classy cuisine that won't break the bank. The thick menu contains a huge wine list and is organized mostly by meat, including the category "wild." (☎6 360 471; budvar.hotel@cbu.pvtnet.cz. Entrees 35-550Kč. Wear your nice shirt. Open daily 7-10am, 11am-2pm, and 6-11pm. Cash only.) Despite the Brazilian name, the menu at **Restaurant Rio ❶,** Hradební 14, is pure Czechia with a few American bar-food items thrown in. Head north on Černé věže; Rio is tucked in a small alleyway to the right. (☎6 350 572. English menu. Entrees 25-100Kč. Open M-Th 10am-11pm, F 10am-11pm, Sa 4-11pm, Su 4-10pm. Cash only.)

🎦 **SIGHTS.** For beer mavens, **Budvar Brewery,** Karoliny Světlé 4, is a mecca— but even dabblers are sure to find it fascinating. Waiting for your tour in the cool, glassy lobby of the last state-run brewery in the Czech Republic, take a minute to marvel at the giant display, "Our Beer Around the World," which shows how many nations Budvar has conquered to date. Africa and South America are presently safe; Mexico should watch its back. Multilingual guides are remarkably knowledgeable about Budvar's brewing process. And yes, there is free beer on the tour. (Take bus #2 toward Borek from anywhere on Na Sadech. Get off at the Budvar stop. ☎7 705 341. www.budvar.cz. Tours start every hr., on the hr., daily 9am-4pm. Tasting tours in Czech 60Kč, students 30Kč; in English 100/50Kč. AmEx/V.)

Surrounded by colorful Renaissance and Baroque architecture, and encompassing over one hectare of cobblestone, **nám. Otakara II** is a big square. The early 18th-century Baroque **town hall** (radnice) rises a full story above the square's other buildings. The ornate 1726 **Samson's Fountain** (Samsonova kašna) stands in the center of the square, making it a great orientation point. Samson's right eye looks across the square to the 72m **Black Tower** (Černá věž), at the inter-

CZECH REPUBLIC

section of Hroznová and Černé véze. The balcony offers panoramic views of České Budějovice and environs, including Brno, nám. Otakara II, and those ubiquitous scars of communism. Four maps on the parapet describe the view. Tall visitors should exercise caution, as they will encounter at least seven opportunities to test their skulls' resilience. (☎6 352 508. Open daily 10am-6pm; last climb 5:45pm. The climb up is free, but the balcony is 20Kč.) The tower once served as a belfry for the neighboring 17th-century Baroque **Cathedral of St. Nicholas** (Chrám sv. Mikuláše). Choral and orchestral concerts now make use of the cathedral's acoustics; check the posted schedules. (Open daily 7am-6pm.) České Budějovice's other famous place of worship is the **Cloister Church of the Sacrifice of the Virgin Mary** (Klášterní Kostel Obětování Panny Marie), located in historic nám. Piaristické. The cobbled square and small courtyard garden offer a respite from the more touristed main square. (☎7 311 263. Visits M-Th 2-4pm, Su 9:30-11:30am.) **The Museum of Motorcycles (Jihočeské Motocyklové Muzeum)** stands next door to the Panny Marie complex. The more than 100 bikes on display provide a thorough history of motorcycle production, from the early 20th century to the present. The collection of WWII-era bikes is particularly impressive. Harley-Davidson seems to hold a place of special reverence. (☎723 247 104. Open Tu-Su 10am-6pm. 40Kč, students 20Kč.)

◪ **NIGHTLIFE.** České Budějovice is more of a pubbing than clubbing town. Bars line the cobblestone streets of the town center, but the hidden pubs on the upper floors of the buildings overlooking **nám. Otakara II** are the best way to taste the local scene. Watch for signs on the street or sidewalk that point to the action. Posters around town also advertise summertime open-air **concerts** around the lakes, including the **Emmy Destinn International Music Festival** in late August. **MotorCycles Legend Pub,** Radniční 9, is no theme bar: the pictures on the wall are of real, local bikers who patronize the bar. Metallica rules the jukebox, aided and abetted by Rammstein and Poison. Shots of rum start at 2025Kč, and regulars are surprisingly friendly once you get beyond the initial stare-off. Nonetheless, it's a good idea to visit in a group—but not one big enough to be mistaken for a gang. (☎6 354 945. Open M-Sa 5pm-3am, Su 5pm-midnight. Cash only.)From MotorCycles Legend Pub, go down the small covered alley on the left of the fork. Cross the river and turn right through the small park. **K2,** Sokolský ostrov 1, is to the right, next to Plavecký Stadion. If it weren't for the Soviet-era car inexplicably parked in the back of the room, this could be a local dance/rock club anywhere in the world. Couples cavort in dark corners and posters cover every inch of the walls. (☎706 54 891. Tu Tequila Party, Th Oldies, F Rock Night, Sa concerts and DJs. Cover 30-60Kč. Free with ISIC before 10pm. Open M-Tu and Th-Sa 9pm-3am. Cash only.) With windows open to the náměstí, **Zeppelin Heaven Club,** nám. Otakara II 38, 3rd fl., serves drinks to a chill, conversational crowd over native and international alterna-rock. A view of Samson Fountain, lit in a deserted square below the window, goes well with beer. (☎6 352 681; www.zeppelin.cz. Budvar 25Kč. Open M-Th 11am-1am, F 11am-late, Sa 6pm-late. Cash only.)

ČESKÝ KRUMLOV ☎38

This once-hidden gem of the Czech Republic has been discovered—some might say besieged—by tourists seeking refuge from Prague's hectic pace and overcrowded streets. Český Krumlov (CHES-kee KRUM-loff) won't disappoint those who wander its medieval streets, raft down the meandering Vltava, and explore the enormous 13th-century castle. This UNESCO-protected town, with its country-

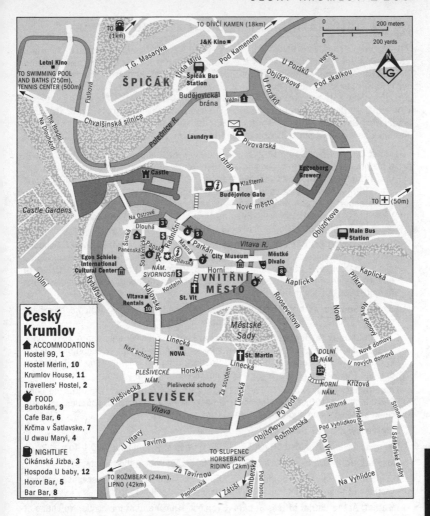

Český Krumlov

⌂ ACCOMMODATIONS
Hostel 99, **1**
Hostel Merlin, **10**
Krumlov House, **11**
Travellers' Hostel, **2**

🍴 FOOD
Barbakán, **9**
Cafe Bar, **6**
Krčma v Šatlavske, **7**
U dwau Maryi, **4**

🍸 NIGHTLIFE
Cikánská Jizba, **3**
Hospoda U baby, **12**
Horor Bar, **5**
Bar Bar, **8**

side charm and beautiful surrounding hills, can be explored for days. Apart from hiking, horseback riding, and kayaking, the town lures visitors with affordable accommodations and burgeoning nightlife.

TRANSPORTATION

Trains run from Nádražní 31 (☎7 551 111), 2km uphill from the center, to **České Budějovice** (1hr., 8 per day, 46Kč) and **Prague** (2½hr., 8 per day, 224Kč). A bus runs from the station to the center of town (5Kč). **Buses** run from Kaplická 439 (☎380 715 415) to **České Budějovice** (30min.; M-F 33 per day, Sa-Su 14 per day; 26Kč) and **Prague** (3hr.; M-F 9 per day, Sa-Su 6 per day; 130-145Kč). For **taxis,** call **Krumlov Taxi** (☎380 712 712) or catch one in nám. Svornosti.

■✴ 🛈 ORIENTATION AND PRACTICAL INFORMATION

The curves of the **Vltava River** cradle the central square, **náměstí Svornosti.** The main **bus station** is on **Kaplická,** east of the square. From the bus station, take the path behind the terminal to the right of stops #20-25. Go downhill from the intersection with Kaplická. At the light, cross the highway and go straight on **Horní,** which leads into the square. If you get off the bus at the **Špičák** stop north of town, it's an easy downhill walk to the center. From Špičák, take the overpass, walk through **Budějovice Gate,** and follow **Latrán** past the castle and over the Vltava. It becomes **Radniční** as it enters Staré Město and leads to nám. Svornosti.

Tourist Office: Nám. Svornosti 2 (☎0 704 622; www.ckrumlov.cz/infocentrum). Among a plethora of services, the Tourist Information Center books accommodations, sells trail maps (50-90Kč), and rents audioguides (1hr. 100Kč, students 80Kč; 2hr. 150/100Kč; 3hr. 180/120Kč; each additional hr. 30/20Kč; 500Kč deposit). Also arranges passenger transport (car and minibus) to Budapest, Linz, Munich, Prague, Salzburg, and Vienna. Ask about DHL services. Bus and train listings are on the placards on the wall across from the front desk. Open M-Sa 9am-1pm and 2-7pm.

Currency Exchange: Bank SMW, Panská 22 (☎0 712 221), cashes **traveler's checks** for 0.75% commission (100Kč min.). Exchanges cash for 1.5% commission (30Kč min.). Open M, W, F 8:30am-5pm; Tu and Th 8:30am-4pm. There is a 24hr. MC/V **ATM** on the left side of Horní, just before nám. Svornosti. Another on the right side of Latrán/ Radniční just outside the square.

Luggage Storage: At the train station, across from the ticket booths. 15Kč per day, bags over 15kg 20Kč per day. Open daily 6:15am-7:15pm.

English-Language Bookstore: Shakespeare and Sons (Shakespeare á Synové), Soukenická 44 (☎271 740 839; www.shakes.cz). An excellent selection of books in English, as well as German, French, and Spanish. Both the *Tractatus Logico-Philosophicus* and *The Da Vinci Code.* English spoken. Open daily 11am-7pm.

Laundromat: Lobo, Latrán 73 (☎0 713 153; www.pensionlobo.cz), part of the Lobo Pension. Wash 100Kč, dry 10Kč per 10min.; detergent and fabric softener included. Open M-F 9am-noon and 1-4pm, Sa 9-11am.

Emergency: ☎0 717 646.

Pharmacy: Nám. Svornosti 16 (☎0 711 787). Open M-F 8am-noon and 1-4pm.

Hospital: Horní Braná, Hřbitovní 424 (☎0 761 911), behind the bus station.

Telephones: Card-operated phones are around the corner from the post office on Pivovarská and near Krumlov House. Buy cards inside or at local *tábaky.*

Internet: At the **tourist offices** at nám. Svornosti (DIAC) and at the castle. No chairs at nám. Svornosti location. 5Kč per 5min.; 10Kč min. **Internet Café,** Zámek 57 (☎0 712 219), in the same building as the castle tourist office. 1Kč per min. Open daily 9am-8pm. **VLTAVA,** Kájovská 62. Enter at the left side, toward Café Retro. 1Kč per min. Open M-F 9am-5pm.

Post Office: Latrán 193 (☎0 716 610). **Poste Restante** at window #2 on the right. Open M-F 7am-6pm, Sa 8am-noon. **Postal Code:** 38101.

🛏 ACCOMMODATIONS

Krumlov's stellar hostels offer the best beds in town. They fill up fast in summer, so make reservations at least four days in advance. **Private rooms** abound; look for *Zimmer frei* signs on Parkán, or contact the **tourist office.**

▨ **Krumlov House,** Rooseveltova 68 (☎0 711 935, mobile 728 287 19; www.krumlovhostel.com). From nám. Svornosti, turn left on Rooseveltova and follow the signs. Founded, owned, and operated by backpackers, this hostel is highly communal and cost-effective. Well-used instruments and books fill the living room. Spacious dorms. Clean bathrooms. English-speaking staff arranges everything from massages to horseback riding. Free innertubes in summer and skates in winter. Laundry in summer; 150Kč per 5kg. 6-bed dorms 250Kč; doubles 600Kč; suites 750Kč. 7th night free. MC/V. ❶

Hostel Merlin, Kájovská 59 (☎602 432 747; www.hostelmerlin.com). From nám. Svornosti, go left on Kájovská. Merlin is on the right just before the bridge. Privacy and ease are the orders of the day at Merlin. Free Internet 8am-8pm (30min. limit). Free coffee and tea 24hr. Balcony and back yard are open to guests. Free innertubes in summer and free skates in winter. 10% off raft, canoe and kayak rentals at VLTAVA. Reception daily 11am-8pm. Check-out 10am. Beds in singles or doubles 250Kč. Cash only. ❶

Hostel 99, Vežni 99 (☎0 712 812; www.hostel99.com). From nám. Svornosti, take Radniční—which becomes Latrán—toward castle, across the river, to the city gate. Turn right on Vežni just before the gate. A gypsy band, jazz nights, free beer W...this seeming caricature of a party hostel is saved by welcoming, knowledgeable staff. Clean bathrooms, kitchens, and dorms. English spoken. Free safes in rooms. Laundry service 200Kč per load. Internet 30Kč per 30min., 50Kč per hr. Check-out 11am. Attic beds 250Kč; 4- to 10-bed dorms 300-390Kč; doubles 700Kč. 7th night free. Cash only. ❶

Travellers' Hostel, Soukenická 43 (☎0 711 345; www.travellers.cz). Take Panská from nám. Svornosti and go right on Soukenická. Part of a chain, this social hostel has an unbeatable location just off nám. Svornosti. Comfy beds. Excellent, free continental breakfast includes coffee, tea, and all you can eat Czech pastries. Satellite TV, pool table and foosball available. Lively bar on first fl. is a backpacker hub. Laundry 150Kč per load. Internet 1.50Kč per min. In high season 4- to 11-bed dorms 300Kč; doubles 380Kč. In low season 270/340Kč. 10% off with ISIC. 7th night free. MC/V. ❶

🄵 FOOD

While many restaurants pander to tourists, a few manage quality and distinction. Český Krumlov is home to the oldest cuisine in Bohemia, so medieval-style food abounds. There are at least two grocery stores in Krumlov proper, at opposite ends of the town: **Jednota Potraviny,** Latrán 55 (☎0 472 830; open M-F 7am-6pm, Sa 7am-noon, Su 9am-3pm), and **NOVA Potraviny,** Linecká 49. (☎607 915 911; open M-Sa 7am-7pm, Su 7am-5pm.)

▨ **U dwau Maryi** (Two Marys), Parkán 104 (☎0 717 228). From nám. Svornosti, turn right on Radniční and take the 2nd right on Parkán. Outside is a poster explaining that U dwau Maryi labors to be as faithful as possible to Old Bohemian cooking, with its flavor palette based on cabbage, eggs, fruits, honey, legumes, milk, millet, milk, mushrooms, and fruits. Waitstaff in period dress speak excellent English, laugh among themselves, and shout orders to the kitchen through a hole in the wall. Vegetarian options. Delicious "rolled cookies" made with raisins, brown sugar, and nuts 20Kč. Open daily 11am-11pm. ❶

Cafe Bar, Pánska 17 (☎0 712 785). A few days in Krumlov can leave you weary of waiters in a poofy shirts and flagon after flagon of mead. Despair not, for there is quiet, modern Cafe Bar. The couple who run it maintains an atmosphere that is at once familial and hip. Early jazz on the hi-fi; terrace in the back. Excellent espresso from 30Kč. 39Kč gets you the "Big Sandwich," which is what it says it is; not the most sophisticated delicacy, but that's not really the point. Open daily 10am-10pm. Cash only. ❶

Laibon, Parkán 105. Vegetarians wandering the Czech lands can rejoice: Laibon has the customary fried cheese, to be sure, but also more complex delights, ranging up to the 149Kč Labyrint Chuti (Labyrinth of Tastes), a sampler platter of most of the restaurant's

CZECH REPUBLIC

specialties, including lentil-, hummus-, and carrot-based dishes. The terrace out back goes all the way down to the river and sits right next to the bridge that connects the castle to the town. Open daily 11am-11pm. Cash only. ❶

Krčma v Šatlavske, Horní 157 (☎0 713 344), actually more on Masná, just left off the intersection with Horní. Perhaps you have tried Laibon and are now ready for more meat. Rejoice again. A giant fire in the middle of the dark dining room is the stage for preparing massive quantities of tasty flesh. The "Mix Gril" gets you chicken, beef, and sausages with traditional white sauce and a small salad (189Kč). If it gets too hot, head outside to the wood tables that snake around the corner of Horní and Masná. Open daily noon-midnight. Reservations recommended. Cash only. ❷

Barbakán, Kaplická 26, halfway down the stairs heading to the river, on your right. Long, multi-party tables look out from the stone patio to a gorgeous scene of foliage high over the river. English menu. Entrees run 85-195Kč, including a menu of juicy steaks in the low- to mid-100s. Open daily 11am-midnight. AmEx/MC/V. ❷

🄶 SIGHTS

Towering above Krumlov since the 1200s, the **Castle** (Zamek) has been home to a succession of Bohemian and Bavarian noble families. Follow Radniční across the river to the castle's main entrance on Latrán. From the center, follow the crowds climbing the hill, note the gigantic bears in the moat as you cross the bridge, and enter the stone courtyards. The courtyard, off Latrán, includes the TIC, an Internet cafe, bathrooms, the Lapidarium, the dungeon, and an art gallery *(sloupova sín)*. The 2nd courtyard, off a ramp after the moat, includes the castle's box office, the information center, the **Castle Tower** (Zámecká Vež) and a 2nd art gallery (Máselnice). **Route of the Castle** tours **I** and **II** begin in the 3rd courtyard, which is smaller and surrounded by benches. The 4th courtyard houses the Baroque **Castle Theater** (Zámecké Divadlo), a registered UNESCO World Heritage site. Fifth and last are the also-Baroque **Castle Gardens** (Zámecká Zahrada), followed by Krumlov's **Revolving Theater** (Otáčivé Hlediště; Garden open daily June-Aug. 8am-7pm; Sept. and May 8am-6pm; Oct. and Apr. 8am-5pm. Free.)

Routes of the Castle I and **II** each last an hour. **Route I** covers the castle chapel, its older Baroque rooms, and Eggenberg Hall, in which a giant gilded coach squats, having been used exactly once to deliver gifts to the pope. The tour concludes amid the festive excess of the frescoed **Masquerade Hall,** where concerts are still held. **Route II** moves through the Schwarzenbergs' portrait gallery and showcases their 19th-century suites. Both tours depart from the 3rd stone courtyard. Tickets are sold at the **box office** in the 2nd courtyard. (☎0 704 721. Open Tu-Su June-Aug. 9am-noon and 1-6pm; Sept.-Oct. and Apr.-May 9am-noon and 1-5pm; last tour 1hr. before closing. Tour in Czech 100Kč, students 50Kč; in English 160/80Kč. MC/V.) Tours of the **Castle Theater** are approximately 40min. The majority of the tour is narrative, so English-language tours are recommended. (Open daily May-Oct. 10-11am and 1-4pm. Tour in Czech 100Kč, students 50Kč; in English 180/90Kč. All tours incur a 10% service fee for reservations, and a 100% service fee for tours scheduled outside of regular hours.) Make your way up the **Castle Tower** for an eyeful of medieval and Renaissance architecture, cradled among the hills and dales surrounding Krumlov. (Open daily June-Aug. 9am-5:30pm; Sept.-Oct. and Apr.-May 9am-4:30pm. 35Kč, students and children 20Kč.) Down from the heights and into the depths, the **Labyrinth of Castle Cellars** has been transformed into a gallery of ceramic art. The current display features stylized human and animal forms. For instance, Miroslav Páral's "Depozit" features humanoid figures with dog heads in various pained poses, straddling luggage. Most pieces are for sale. Ambient music wafts through the chilly rooms. (Open daily 10am-5pm. 45Kč.)

Across the bridge from the castle, the ⬛Egon Schiele Art Center (Egon Schiele Art Centrum), Široká 70-72, highlights the work of the Austrian painter Egon Schiele (1890-1918), who set up shop in Krumlov in 1911. The citizens ran him out of town, however, when he started painting burghers' daughters and local prostitutes in the nude. Although the Schiele exhibit only takes up about half of one of the three floors of the Art Center, biographical information and artifacts—including furniture Schiele designed for his studio—make this a stellar monument to the artist. The rest of the museum is devoted to his Expressionist contemporaries. (☎0 704 011; www.schieleartcentrum.cz. Open daily 10am-6pm. 180Kč, students 105Kč.)

🎵 🌺 ENTERTAINMENT AND FESTIVALS

The **Revolving Theater** (Otáčivé Hlediště), in the castle garden, hosts opera, ballet, Shakespeare, and classic comedies for the summer season of the South Bohemian Theater Company. Watching the bleachers as they rotate to face different sets is as entertaining as the Czech-only shows. (Reservations ☎6 356 643; www.otacivehlediste.cz. The tourist office lists showings and sells tickets. Performances June-Sept. Tu-Su 8:30-9:30pm. Box office open Tu-Su 1-7pm. Tickets 224-390Kč. For a 30% discount, purchase remainders 1hr. before showtime outside the main entrance to the castle gardens.) **Kino J&K,** Highway 159 next to the Špičák bus stop, shows the latest Hollywood blockbusters. (☎0 711 892. Tickets 40-70Kč.) The same company runs the town's summer **open-air cinema,** the **Letni Kino.** Heading north on Latrán, take a left on Chvalšínská. Continue to a sign for Na Ziméku on the right, with a parking lot behind. The Letni Kino is back and to the left in the parking lot. (☎0 711 892. Open July-Aug. Shows 9:30pm. 74Kč.)

For **The Celebrations of the Five-Petalled Rose,** the 3rd weekend of every June, the citizens of Český Krumlov don tights and doublets to party like it's 1588. The festival commemorates the reconciliation between brothers who were kings of two of the five city-states controlled by their family in the late 16th century. Throughout the event, the streets overflow with people, food, theater, music, dancing, and beer. Specific festivities include a medieval feast, a fireworks show, and the Tournament of the Roses, during which contestants prove their mettle in feats of strength that include jousting. On the final day, the champion of the Tournament enters the Revolving Theater to play chess against an actor depicting the king, using human "pieces"; of course, the king always wins. Reserve accommodations early. Admission is free for those wearing tights, armor, or poofy dresses. (Book tickets through the TIC or Unios Tourist Service, Zámek 57, ☎380 725 110 or 380 725 119; tourist.service@unios.cz. Info available at www.ckrumlov.cz/slavnosti. 3 days 200Kč; F 100Kč, Sa 150Kč, Su free; disabled guests free.)

Krumlov hosts several world-class music festivals. The **Chamber Music Festival** in the Castle (☎721 470 558; hpelzova@wo.cz) runs for 10 days starting in late June. The **Early Music Festival** (☎0 711 681 or 724 045 727; www.earlymusic.cz) occurs in early July and lasts a week and a half, overlapping with the six-week-long **International Music Festival Český Krumlov** (☎241 445 404 www.czechmusicfestival.com).

🍺 NIGHTLIFE

Party animals enjoy the city's full array of bars and cafes, many of which line Rybářská. You'll find most of the city in a slumber on weekdays, though the fun picks up early Friday evening and lasts all weekend long.

Cikánská Jizba (Gypsy Bar), Dlouhá 31 (☎0 717 585), left off Radniční. Sketches of ordinary people line one wall, with gypsy *objets d'art* framing a crucifix on another. On weekends, locals and tourists jam the place to listen to gypsy bands and drink beer that starts at 18Kč. On weeknights, the bartender sits and drinks with the locals. Cikánská Jizba is always welcoming to a traveler whose throat is dry. Jack Daniels 45Kč. Open M-Th 11am-10pm, F-Sa 11am-midnight. Cash only.

Hospoda U baby ("oo BAH-bee"; "Granny's Pub"), Rooseveltova 66 (☎721 983 577), next to Krumlov House. Don't be thrown when Rooseveltova curves off but the sidewalk keeps going straight, or when the street numbers suddenly start to get smaller instead of larger. Soldier on. Families lean over wood tables worn smooth by countless elbows. Open M-Th 3-10pm, F 3-11pm, Sa 6-11pm. Cash only.

Horor Bar, Masná 129 (☎728 682 724). With a giant metal cross hanging over the bar, red-draped tables, candelabras, and a broken grand piano, Horor Bar is perhaps the goth-est place on earth. Paintings of famous horror movie scenes line the walls. Despite all this, the bar, built in the bottom of an old Protestant church, is low-key and perfect for quiet conversation. Pilsner Urquell 40Kč. Open daily 6pm-late. Cash only.

Bar Bar, Kaplická 3 (☎777 100 432). The word "bar" occurs twice in the name, presumably because that's what it is: a bar. A stone patio winds behind the building; inside, tropical murals zest up the walls. Alterna-rock on the jukebox. Bernard is on tap, and liquors are well stocked. Foosball in the corner. Open daily 8pm-late. Cash only.

⚠ OUTDOOR ACTIVITIES

Český Krumlov is truly a paradise for the outdoorsy. The town lies at the southern border of the 212 sq. km **Chko Blanský Les Protected Landscape Area,** within which are a monastery, **Zlatá Koruna,** as well as the ruins of the Schwarzenbergs' summer mansion, **Dívčí Kámeru.** South of town lie the Šumava foothills, which run along the Austrian border; the **Cistercian monastery** at **Vyšši Brod;** and the **castle** at **Rožmberk.**

BIKING. At least four major biking trails run through Český Krumlov, forming wandering and often mountainous routes to all the above-mentioned sites, as well as to numerous small towns and villages. Biking maps of the region are available at the **Tourist Information Center** shop for around 70Kč. **Bikes** can be rented at **VLTAVA,** Kajovská 62. Some hostels, including Hostel Merlin (see p. 211), have special discounts with the agency. Bicyclists are advised to keep their bikes locked in even the smallest towns. (☎0 711 978; www.ckvltava.cz. Bike rental 320Kč for 1st day, 300Kč for 2nd day. Open daily 9am-5pm.)

KAYAKING/CANOEING/RAFTING/INNERTUBING. Throughout the summer, a steady stream of canoes and innertubes fills Krumlov's river. Many hostels provide free innertubes; for kayaks, canoes and rafts, VLTAVA provides numerous package trips that range in distance (5-35km) and in time (1-8hr.). The route from Vetrni to Krumlov is the shortest (kayaks 330Kč, canoes 500Kč, rafts 700Kč). From Vyšši Brod back to Krumlov is the longest (kayaks 650Kč, canoes 930Kč, rafts 1500Kč). Contact VLTAVA for the full list of trips. Boats, paddles, waterproof bag, life jackets, maps, and transport to and from Český Krumlov are all available.

HORSEBACK RIDING. To reach **Slupenec Horseback Riding Club** (Jezdecký klub Slupenec), located at Slupenec 1 (☎/fax 0 711 052; www.jk-slupenec.cz), go to the end of Rooseveltova, where it intersects the highway. Another intersection with Křížová is on the right. A sign indicates the distance (2km) to Slupenec. Turn left onto Křížová, then take an immediate right onto Rozmberska. Continue on Rozmberska to Slupenec. Trips last from an hour (250Kč) to several days (from 2500Kč, depending on size of group and duration). Longer trips include refreshments and take you high into the hills above Český Krumlov. (English and German spoken. Horses available Tu-Su 9am-6pm. Call ahead.)

SWIMMING. An indoor swimming pool *(plavecký bazén)*, Fialková 225, is north of town, near the Letni Kino. Follow Latrán north and turn left onto Chvalšinská. Turn right on Fialková. (☎0 711 702. Adult 1½hr. swim 30Kč, any longer swim 40Kč; students 30Kč. Open Tu 7-10:30am, 2:30-4pm, and 6-11pm; W 7-8am, 10am-5pm, and 6-10pm; Th 7-8am and 1:30-4pm; F 7-10:30am, 12:30-5pm and 6-10pm; Sa 1-9:30pm; Su 1-9pm.)

TENNIS. The **Tenis Centrum Český Krumlov**, Chvalšinská 247, across from the swimming pool, offers three indoor grass courts and three outdoor clay courts for rental by the hour. Rackets and lessons also available. (☎/fax 0 711 418; tenis@tenis-centrum.cz. Open daily 8am-midnight. In high season, courts 8am-3pm 370Kč, 3-9pm 450Kč, 9pm-midnight 290Kč. In low season, courts 300Kč. Racket rentals 80Kč.)

EAST BOHEMIA

From the fertile lowlands of the Elbe to the mountain ranges that create a natural border with Poland, oft-overlooked East Bohemia has skiing, sightseeing, and swimming opportunities to spare. Under Hapsburg rule, the Czech language was kept alive among the people of East Bohemia. Consequently, within these villages many 19th-century Czech intellectuals and nationalists were born. Today, Hradec Králové, the region's administrative and cultural center, combines marvelously preserved medieval buildings with a lively urban pace.

HRADEC KRÁLOVÉ   ☎49

At the confluence of the Elbe and the Orlice Rivers, Hradec Králové (HRA-dets KRAH-lo-veh), literally "Queens' Castle," once served as a depository for royal widows. Now it's a youthful university town full of art nouveau buildings. Cyclists rule the boulevards of the city, which has built many bike paths to accommodate them. Hradec Králové prides itself on its entertaining skills, and schedules many cultural events, festivals, and outdoor activities each year.

█ TRANSPORTATION. The **train station** is at Riegrovo nám. 914. (☎553 75 55. Open daily 3am-11:30pm; info center open daily 6am-7pm.) Trains go to **Prague** (2hr., every hr. 5am-8pm, 222Kč). **Buses** run from the train station to **Prague** (2hr., every hr., 72-80Kč). Buy tickets on board. **Public bus** tickets (9-11Kč) are sold at kiosks and at the station. Validate your ticket in the red boxes by pulling the black lever toward you. **Sprint Taxis** (☎551 51 51) are in front of the train station.

█ █ ORIENTATION AND PRACTICAL INFORMATION. Hradec Králové feels like two separate towns separated by the **Labe** (Elbe) River. On the west side, the pedestrian-only **Čelakovského** is a favorite local drag along the shop-infested **Nové Město** (New Town). The east side is home to the churches and cafes of **Staré Město** (Old Town). The **train** and **bus stations** are next to each other, on the edge of Nové Město away from the river. To get to **Velké náměstí** (Great Square) from the stations, take a right on Puskinova and then a left on **Gočárova třída.** Follow Gočárova through Nové Město to the river, cross the bridge, and continue a block. When you hit **Čs. armády,** head left and turn right on **V kopečku,** which leads to Velké nám. Buses #1, 5, 6, 11 and 16 go from Hlavní Nadraží to the Adalbertinum stop, just outside the city center. The English-speaking staff at **Information Center,** Gočárova třída 1225, arranges accommodations and sells tickets to events in town. They also provide **maps** (free-69Kč) and info on town festivals, which run throughout the year; the most famous are in June and October. (☎553 44 85; www.ic-hk.cz. Open

June-Aug. M-F 8am-6pm, Sa 10am-4pm; Sept.-May M-F 8am-6pm.) **Komerční Banka,** Čelakovského 642, at Masarykovo nám., charges 2% commission on **currency exchange** and has an **ATM** inside. (☎581 55 50. Open M-F 8:30am-5pm.) The train station has **luggage storage.** (10Kč, bags 15kg and up 20Kč. Lockers 10Kč. Open 24hr.; breaks 10:45-11:15am, 1:25-1:40pm, and 6:30-7pm.) Other services include: **emergency** ☎158 (24hr.); **police,** Dlouhá 211/10 (☎551 52 84); a **pharmacy, Centrální lékárna,** across from Komerční Banka (☎551 16 14; open M-F 7am-6pm, Sa 8am-noon); and the **hospital,** Sokolská 534, south of Staré Město (☎583 11 11). **Internet and Games Klub No Way,** Kotěrova 847, has powerful computers with fast connections. (9am-9:30am free, 9:30am-1pm 20Kč per hr., 1pm-5pm 30Kč per hr., 5pm-midnight 20Kč per hr.) **Gamesbar,** Ak. Heyrovského 1178, down the street from Hotelový Dům, has similiarly powerful computers with 1Mbps connections. (☎608 979 088; www.gamesbar.cz. 20Kč per hr. Open M-F noon-midnight, Sa-Su 5pm-midnight.) The **post office,** Riegrovo nám. 915, is next to the train station. Get a ticket from the machine in the waiting area. Send packages at window #6. (☎554 07 33. **Western Union.** Card **telephones** in front; buy cards inside. Open M-F 7am-7pm, Sa 7am-1pm, Su 8am-noon.) **Postal Code:** 500 02.

ⓕⒺ ACCOMMODATIONS AND FOOD. You won't find budget accommodations in the center of Staré Město. Inexpensive options are plentiful around the university, just a short walk south of the center. The best rooms for your buck are at **Hotelový Dům ❶,** Ak. Heyrovského 1177, a 10min. walk from Staré Město. From the train station, take bus # 1, 9, 21, or 28 to Heyrovského, cross Sokolská, and take the first right on Heyrovského. Clean, cheap rooms have fridges and desks. (☎551 11 75; www.hotelovydum.cz. Reception 24hr. Check-out 9am. Dorms 200Kč; doubles 560Kč.) Farther outside the center is **Hotel Garni ❷,** Na Kotli 1147. All its rooms have bath. It also offers more basic hostel-style accommodations in the summer. Take bus #1, 9, or 28 from the station to Hotel Garni; it's to the right of the bus stop. (☎576 36 00. Breakfast included. Reception 24hr. Dorm singles 500Kč. Apartments with TV, fridges, and telephones singles 690Kč; doubles 1260Kč. Hostel beds July 15-Sept. 15 250Kč. 80-200Kč discount for HI members.) In a great location, **Penzion Pod Věží ❸,** Velké nám. 165 offers massive, luxurious rooms equipped with TV, phones, private baths, and minibars. Rooms facing the front have views of Velké nám. (☎551 49 32; www.pod-vezi.cz. Breakfast included. Singles 1100Kč; doubles 1575Kč. 10% discount on cash payments. AmEx/MC/V.)

Staré Město boasts many pubs and restaurants offering traditional Czech cuisine. In Nové Město, **Pivnice Gobi ❶,** Karla IV 522, is an underground student hangout with inexpensive meals but a menu limited to sausages, frankfurters, and fried cheese. It also features pool, darts, foosball, and a big-screen TV. (☎551 10 03. Entrees 21-135Kč. Open M-Th 2:30pm-1am, F 2:30pm-3am, Sa 5pm-3am, Su 5pm-1am.) The best lunch option is **Jídelna Praha ❶,** Gočárova 1229, a cafeteria-style local favorite serving large, scrumptious portions. (☎556 18 97. Entrees 30-80Kč. Open M-F 8am-4pm, Sa 8am-noon.) For lighter fare, **Atlanta ❸,** Švehlova 504, offers an excellent selection of salads, both meaty and meatless (80-130Kč). Its sprawling outdoor patio dominates Masarykovo nám. (☎551 54 31. Entrees 90-300Kč. Open M-Th 8am-midnight, F 8am-1am, Sa 9am-1am, Su 10am-11pm. MC/V.) The giant supermarket **Tesco,** nám. 28. října 1610, sells groceries. (Buses #1, 3, 7, 10, 12, 13. ☎507 21 11. Open M-F 7am-8pm, Sa 7am-7pm, Su 8am-6pm.)

ⒼⒹ SIGHTS AND ENTERTAINMENT. Most sights in Hradec Králové are on **Velké nám.,** the center of Staré Město. Here, the 1307 **Church of the Holy Spirit** (Kostel Svatého Ducha) attests to the town's royal past with priceless items, like a 1406 tin baptismal font (one of the oldest in Bohemia) and tower bells affectionately named Eagle and Beggar. (Open M-Sa 10-11am and 2:30-3:30pm,

Su 2-3:30pm. Free.) Climb up the 71m **White Tower** (Bílá věž) beside the church to see a giant bell and a view of the town. You may feel your inner clappermeister stirring, but the bell-ringing is reserved for eight burly men who have been assigned to perform the honor on special occasions only. (Open daily 9am-noon and 1-5pm. 20Kč, students 10Kč.) In the middle of the square, the excellent **Gallery of Modern Art** (Galerie moderního umění), #139, showcases 20th-century Czech painting and sculpture. The floors lead you chronologically through Czech takes on Impressionism, Cubism, Expressionism, and more recent trends, showcasing artists like Emil Filla and Josef Váchal. One highlight is the first-floor gallery's collection of František Bílek's wood sculptures. (☎551 48 93. Open Tu-Su 9am-noon and 1-6pm. Permanent collection 25Kč, students 10Kč; exhibitions 15/5Kč.) Walk across the square from the museum to the Baroque **Church of the Assumption of the Virgin Mary** (Kostel Nanebevzetí Panny Marie), constructed by Jesuits (1654-66). Prussian soldiers destroyed its interior in 1792, but 19th- and 20th-century renovations have revived the building. (Open daily 10am-5pm. 20Kč, students 10Kč.)

In late October, Hradec Králové's largest festival, **Jazz Goes to Town** (www.jazzgoestotown.com), features musicians from all over the world. The action takes place at the **Aldis Center**, Eliščino náb. 357 (☎505 21 11), and at pubs all over town. You can buy tickets at the tourist office. For more information, call ☎541 11 40. The **Theater Festival of European Regions** (www.klicperovodivadlo.cz) is held in late June. Classic and modern plays are performed daily all over town by professional groups from the Czech Republic and nearby regions. Schedules and tickets are available at the tourist office (call ☎551 48 76. **Hogo Fogo Bar,** 19 Eliščino náb., is a relaxing pub where the students flock when night falls. (☎551 55 92. Beer 18Kč. Open M-Th 3pm-1am, F 3pm-3am, Sa 4pm-3am, Su 4pm-1am.)

LITOMYŠL ☎461

Litomyšl (LIT-ohm-ee-shil) is home to a magnificent chateau and enchanting architecture. While you can easily cover the town in a day, the relaxed village atmosphere and lack of tourists may seduce you into staying longer.

▐▌ TRANSPORTATION AND PRACTICAL INFORMATION. The train station Nádražni 510 (☎612 203), is inconvenient, and most trains require a connection. **Trains** go to **Hradec Králové** (2hr., several per day, 88Kč). **Buses** run from Mařákova 1078 (☎613 352) to **Hrádec Kralové** (1hr., 12 per day, 52Kč). There aren't many taxis in town, so call ahead for **Taxi Dańsa** (☎602 411 844).

Litomyšl's tiny center is dominated by the banana-shaped **Smetanovo náměstí** (Smetana Square). A series of small, uphill paths leads to the chateau and gardens that make up the town's cultural core. Almost everything of interest is either on the main square or on one of its side streets. To reach the center from the **bus station**, turn left on Mařákova and follow it over the river to Tyršova. Turn left and then bear left again at Braunerovo nám. to get to Smetanovo nám. The **tourist Office,** Smetanovo nám. 72, provides **free maps** of the town center, has accommodations listings, and sells phonecards. (☎612 161; www.litomysl.cz. English spoken. Open M-F 9am-7pm, Sa-Su 9am-3pm.) **Komerční banka,** Smetanovo nám. 31, cashes **traveler's checks** for 2% commission and has an **ATM.** (Open M-F 8:30am-4:30pm.) Other services include: a **pharmacy, Lékárna U anděla Strážce,** Smetanovo nám. (open M-F 7:30am-5:30pm, Sa 8am-noon); a **hospital,** J.E. Purkyně 652 (☎655 111), south of the center, off Mařákova; **Internet** at the **tourist office** (see above; speedy connections for 1Kč per min.); and the **post office,** Smetanovo nám. 15 (☎654 372; open M-F 8am-6pm, Sa 8am-noon). **Postal Code:** 570 01.

⌐☐ ACCOMMODATIONS AND FOOD. While Litomyšl does not have much to offer in terms of budget accommodations, it is too small and untouristed a location to have sky-high prices. If saving crowns is your priority, you will have to venture about 10min. outside the center. Camping is the cheapest option (from 50Kč). Inquire at the tourist office for details. If you prefer something more central, █**Pension Kraus ❷**, Havlíčkova 444, although relatively more expensive, is still the best deal around. From the main square, walk to the northernmost end and continue down Havlíčkova; it's on the right. This beautiful pension provides bright, spacious rooms in a peaceful atmosphere, complete with a summer garden. Soft beds, satellite TV, and sparkling, private bathrooms complement the well-furnished settings. (☎614 823; www.pension-kraus.cz. Breakfast buffet 100Kč. Singles 500Kč; doubles 800Kč. AmEx/MC/V.) Outside the center, the **Pedagogical School ❷**, Strakovská 1071, provides basic rooms in a university boarding house. It has clean, comfortable beds, shared baths, and communal kitchenettes. From the bus station, turn left on Mařákova and then make a right on Strakovská, which is the local highway. Continue for 600m; the school is on the right. (☎654 612; novotna@vospspgs.lit.cz. Open June-Sept. Doubles 400Kč; triples 600Kč.)

Litomyšl's restaurant selection is not huge, but its portions are large and its prices low. Most menus are limited to Czech cuisine, so vegetarians may be stuck with fried cheese. The majority of the town's restaurants are scattered along the main square and the uphill paths to the chateau. Overlooking a serene cobbled square, **Restaurace Pod Klásterem ❷**, B. Nemcove 158, is always packed with locals enjoying massive platters of grilled meats and lighter pastas. The lovely, geranium-filled outdoor terrace is the perfect place to indulge in a delicious ice cream sundae. (☎602 712 703. Entrees 90-120Kč. Open M-Th 11am-11pm, F-Sa 11am-1am, Su 11am-10pm.) **Supermarket Kubik ❶**, at Smetanovo nám. 72, carries groceries. (Open daily 7am-8pm. MC/V.)

◻◻ SIGHTS AND ENTERTAINMENT. The town's highlight is the magnificent UNESCO-protected █**chateau,** which overlooks the center from its hilltop perch. Built between 1568 and 1581 by Vratislav of Perštejn, the chateau was intended to relieve the homesickness of the supreme chancellor's wife, Marie Manrique de Lara of the Spanish Mendoza family, who desperately missed the Renaissance architecture of her home country. The elegant arcades are adorned with thousands of *grafitti*, all of which, like snowflakes, have unique geometrical shapes. Tours wind through the chateau's salons and parlors, but the main attraction is the 1797 wooden **theater.** To get here from the square, ascend Váchalova, take a right, and hang a quick left up the covered stairs. (☎611 066. Open May-Aug. Tu-Su 9am-noon and 1-5pm; Sept. Tu-Su 9am-noon and 1-4pm; Oct. and Apr. Sa-Su 9am-noon and 1-5pm. Tour 1 covers the theater and state rooms. Tour 2 starts in the chapel and travels through the many banquet rooms. Both tours last 50min. Tours in Czech 60Kč, students 30Kč; in English 120Kč. Free English info available on tours in Czech.)

Visitors can also stroll through the birthplace of "Bartered Bride" composer **Bedřich Smetana,** situated in the castle brewery. While the exhibit is tiny, seeing Smetana's cradle while his compositions play in the background is a must for any music-lover. (See chateau opening hours. 20Kč, students 10Kč.) The surrounding **castle gardens** make a lovely break after a tour. (Open M-Sa 5am-10pm, Su 8am-8pm. Free.) Opposite the chateau, locals lounge among the garden statues of **Klášterní Zahrady.** (Open daily 8am-11pm. Free.) Two blocks away, on Terezy Novákové 75, lies the **Portmoneum House.** Its interior was vibrantly decorated by experimental painter **Josef Váchal** in the 1920s. (☎612 020. Open May-Sept. Tu-Su 9am-noon and 1-5pm. 40Kč, students 20Kč. Ring the bell to enter.) During the last weeks of June, the chateau courtyard houses the **Smetana Opera Festival**. (Check www.litomysl.cz for dates, as well as info on other local festivities. ☎616 070. Tickets 80-1200Kč.)

MORAVIA

Winemaking Moravia forms the easternmost third of the Czech Republic. Home of the country's finest folk music and two leading universities, it is also the birthplace of a number of Eastern European notables, including Czechoslovakia's first president, Tomáš G. Masaryk; psychoanalyst Sigmund Freud; and chemist Johann Gregor Mendel, avatar of modern genetics. Tourists have yet to weaken Brno's cosmopolitan vigor or disrupt Olomouc's cobblestoned charm. Outside the city, the low hills of the South Moravian countryside harbor the remarkable chateau of Kroměříž and the architectural pearls of Telč.

BRNO   ☎(0)5

The Czech Republic's 2nd-largest city, Brno (berh-NO; pop. 388,900) has been an international marketplace since the 13th century. Today, emissaries of global corporations compete for space and sales among local produce stands. The result is a dynamic and spirited city where historic churches soften the bustle of the streets.

▐▀ TRANSPORTATION

Trains: Nádražní (☎541 171 111). To: **Prague** (3-4hr., 12 per day, 130-160Kč); **Bratislava, SLK** (2hr., 5 per day, 250Kč); **Budapest, HUN** (4hr., 3 per day, 945Kč); **Vienna, AUT** (1½hr., 5 per day, 536Kč).

Buses: ☎543 217 733. On the corner of Zvonařka and Plotní. To **Prague** (2½hr., several per day, 140Kč) and **Vienna, AUT** (2½hr., 2 per day, 400Kč).

Public Transportation: Tram, trolley, and **bus** tickets at a *tábak* or any kiosk. 10min. 8Kč, 40min. 13Kč; 24hr. pass 50Kč. Luggage requires an extra ticket; 10min. 4Kč, 40min. 6Kč. Fine for riding ticketless 400-800Kč; ticket checks are common. Bus routes #90 and above run all night; trams and all other buses run daily 5am-11pm.

Taxis: Impulse Taxi (☎542 216 666). Taxis line Starobrněnská and Husova.

◼✦ ￼ ORIENTATION AND PRACTICAL INFORMATION

Everything in central Brno is accessible by foot. Its main streets radiate from **nám. Svobody** (Freedom Square). From the **train station** entrance, cross the tram lines on **Nádražní,** turn left, walk 15m, and then turn right on **Masarykova,** which leads to nám. Svobody. From the **bus station,** facing the main schedule board, ascend the stairs at the leftmost corner of the station. Go straight on the pedestrian overpass and follow the foot path, which runs aside **Plotní.** Pass **Tesco** and take the pedestrian underpass to the train station. When you resurface, with your back to the train station, go left on Nádražní; Masarykova is on the right.

Tourist Office: Kulturní a informační centrum města Brna, Radnická 8 (☎542 211 090), inside the town hall. From nám. Svobody, go down Masarykova, turn right on Průchodní, and then right on Radnická. **Free maps** of the city center. Sells maps of the entire city (29-79Kč). Open M-F 8am-6pm, Sa-Su 9am-5pm.

Budget Travel: GTS International, Vachova 4 (☎844 140 140 or 257 187 100). English spoken. ISIC 250Kč. Open M-F 9am-6pm, Sa 9am-noon.

Brno

⌂ ACCOMMODATIONS
Hostel Astorka, 7
Pension U Leopolda, 3
Travellers' Hostel
   Jánska, 6

☕ FOOD AND CAFES
Caffetteria Top Shop, 4
Dávné Časy, 9
Cafe and Cocktail Bar, 10

★ ENTERTAINMENT
Lucerna, 1
Palace Cinema, 8

▮ NIGHTLIFE
Divadelní hospoda
   Veselá husa, 11
Mersey, 2
Pivnice Minipivovar
   Pegas, 5

Lužánsky Gardens

Kotlářská
Sušilova
Tučkova
Burešova
Lidická
Drobného

TO AND (1km)

Botanická
Cihlářská
Lužánecká

Antonína Slavíka
Vlhnického sady
Drobného
Heřtotova
Čertopolní
Durdíkova

třída kapitána Jaroše
Jeřábkova

Sokolská
Kounicova
Smetanova
Antonínská

NÁM. 28. ŘÍJNA
Bartošova
Kudelova

Traubova
Kumova
Merhavitova
Francouzská

Závodní
Pekárenská
Veveří
Slovákova
Mezírka
Mášova
Lidická

JANÁČKOVO NÁM.

Milady Horákové
Příční
Stará
Příkop

Anna Nováka
Jaselská
ŽEROTÍNOVO NÁM.

MORAVSKÉ NÁM.

Rooseveltova
Koliště
Bratislavská
Köttrova

MOBILNÍ TRH

Marešova
Brandlova
Jošová

Red Church
Church of St. Thomas

Ponávka
Cejl
Vlhká

Údolní

KOMENSKÉHO NÁM.
JAKUBSKÉ NÁM.

SEE INSET

Koliště

Gorazdova
Trýbova
Úvoz
Pellicova

Špilberk Castle
Špilberk Park
Špilberk
Hlídka

NÁM. SVOBODY

DOMINIKÁNSKÉ NÁM.

TO TELČ

Basilica of the Assumption of the Virgin Mary
Mendelianum

Sladová
Pellicova
Pekařská
Kopečná
Anenská

ZELNÝ TRH

Skořepka
Křenova

Pirovarská
Veletržní
Křížová
Václavská
Ypsilantiho

Pekařská
MENDLOVO NÁMĚSTÍ

Hybešova

Vodní

Nádražní
Spálená
Ponávka
Rumiště
Mlýnská

Soukenická
Úzká

Dornych
Plotní
Dornych

Bělidla
Zahradnická
Nádražní
Bezručova

Nové sady

Trnitá

Poříčí
Bakalovo nábřeží
Náplavka
Křídlovická

Uhelná

Zvonařka
Koštálová

TO (3km)
Bus Station

Rosická
Plotní

Inset

KOMENSKÉHO NÁM.
Opletalova
Solniční
JAKUBSKÉ NÁM.
Church of St. James
Jezuitská
Jaštova
Mozartova
Vachova
Dvořákova

Opera and Theater Tickets
Rooseveltova
Sukova
Za divadlem
Koliště

Úvoz
Beseta
Bookstore
Jakubská
Rašínova
Běhounská
Bezručova

GTS Int'l
Koblížná
Divadelní
Mahen Theater

Skrytá
Středova
Panenská
Plague Column

NÁM. SVOBODY

Postovská
MALINOVSKÉHO NÁM.

Za divadlem
Orlí

Hlídka
Pellicova
Pekařská

DOMINIKÁNSKÉ NÁM.
Husova
Dominikánská
Mečová
Panská
Jánská
Minoritská
Orlí
Měňínská
Masarykova
Novobranská
Benešova

Grand Bus Station

Kopečná
Studánka
Leitnerova
Anenská

TAXI
Starobrněnská
Peroutkova
Biskupská
Pekluá
Petrská
Zámečnická

Old Town Hall
ZELNÝ TRH
Market
Františkánská

Novobranská
Josefská

Jircháře

Peter and Paul Cathedral
Františkova Monument
Denisovy Gardens

KAPUCÍNSKÉ NÁM.
Capuchin Monastery
Bašty
Nádražní

Tesco

N
LG

0   300 meters
0   300 yards

Currency Exchange: Komerční banka, Kobližná 3 (☎521 271 11), just off nám. Svobody. Gives V **cash advances,** cashes **traveler's checks** for 2% commission (50Kč min.), on the 2nd fl., and has an AmEx/MC/V **ATM.** Open M-F 8am-5pm.

Luggage Storage: At the train station. 17Kč per 15kg bag per day, 26Kč per 15-20kg bag, 25Kč per 25kg bag, 35Kč plus 9Kč per 5kg thereafter. Lockers 10Kč per day. Open 24hr.

English-Language Bookstore: Barvič á Novotný, Česká 13 (☎542 215 040; www.barvic-novotny.cz). Wide fiction selection. Open M-Sa 8am-7pm, Su 10am-1pm. MC/V.

Laundromat: Kavarna Pradelna, Hybešova 45. Take tram #1 or 2 from the train station to "Hybešova"; it's 25m ahead on the left. Wash 60Kč, dry 40Kč; detergent 35Kč. Offers the best **Internet** rates in town. M-F 30Kč per hr., Sa-Su 20Kč per hr. Open M-F 10am-1am, Sa 2pm-1am, Su 2-11pm.

Pharmacy: Kobližná 7 (☎542 212 110). Open M-F 7am-10pm, Sa 8am-1pm. AmEx/ MC/V. **Lékárna Koliště,** Koliště 49 (☎545 424 811). Open 24hr. MC/V.

Hospital: Urazova Nemocnice, Ponávka 6 (☎532 260 111). From nám. Svobody, take Kobližná to Malinovského nám. Continue on Malinovského nám. to Celi (300m) and take a left on Ponávka. There are 10 hospitals in the Brno area. The main one is the **Fakultní Nemocnice,** Vihlavská 100 (☎547 791 111).

Post Office: Poštovská 3/5 (☎542 153 622). **Poste Restante** at corner entrance. Open M-F 7am-7pm, Sa 8am-noon. **Postal Code:** 601 00.

ACCOMMODATIONS

Brno's hotel scene is geared toward business suits, so it's no great surprise that one of the city's budget hotels was recently replaced by the "Moulin Rouge Erotic Night Club Disco." Though few and far between, budget options are available, especially in the summer. Student dormitories, transformed into hostels from July to September, are the best deal in town. During the low season, the local tourist office can arrange **private rooms** (from 500Kč).

Hotel Astorka, Novobranská 3 (☎542 510 370; astorka@jamu.cz). With your back to the train station, cross the tram tracks, turn right, and make an immediate left up a set of stairs. At the top, turn right on Novobranská and cross Orli. Centrally located, brand-new Astorka boasts clean, modern university-dorm-style rooms that come with a host of amenities. Reception on 3rd fl. Open July-Sept. Singles 520Kč; doubles 1040Kč; triples 1560Kč. Students 260/520/780Kč. AmEx/MC/V. ●

Pension U Leopolda, Jeneweinova 49 (☎545 233 036; fax 545 233 949). Take tram #12 or bus #A12 to the last stop, "Komárov." Take a left behind the *tábak* huts on Studnicni. At the end of Studnicni, turn right on Jeneweinova. Quite a trek from the center (15min. by public transport), this suburban pension offers small, beautifully furnished rooms with TV and private baths. Ground floor houses an intimate restaurant with a cozy fireplace. Check-out 11am. Singles 610Kč, with breakfast 690Kč; doubles 820/980Kč; triples 1100/1350Kč. ●

Travellers' Hostel Jánska, Jánska 22. (☎542 213 573; www.travellers.cz). Head up Masarykova from the train station and take a right on Jánska. Brand-new hostel located in the town center. While this installment of the Travellers' chain hostel is central and social, it is also lacking in comfort or personality. The building is a school during the rest of the year. The hostel offers rows of rusty metal beds with rock-hard mattresses. Breakfast included. Reception 24hr. Open July-Aug. 15-bed dorms 290Kč. MC/V. ●

FOOD

Street-side pizza joints and coffee bars abound. The fruit and vegetable **market** still thrives on Zelný trh. (Strawberries 19Kč per kg. Open M-F 9am-5pm.) **Tesco,** Dornych 4, behind the train station, carries groceries. (☎543 543 111. Store open daily 8am-10pm. Grocery section open M-F 6am-10pm.)

Caffetteria Top Shop, Jakubské nám. 4. From nám. Svobody, head up Rašínova and turn right on Jakubské. This charming cafe offers top-notch coffee drinks (27-61Kč). Revive yourself with a superb hot chocolate mixed with anything from orange syrup to Bailey's. Open M-F 9am-8pm, Sa 9am-noon. ❶

Dávné Časy, Starobrněská 20 (☎544 215 292), up Starobrněnská from Zelný trh. As the Czech inscription at the door reads, forget your problems and revisit the world of heroic knights and medieval feasts. Menu includes "Dishes from nations that have never known hunger." Mostly meat-based, but includes selections "with no meat (or just a little)." Excellent chicken with mustard sauce 115Kč. Salads 59-69Kč. Entrees 69-400Kč. Open daily 11am-11pm. AmEx/MC/V. ❸

Cafe and Cocktail Bar, Masarykova 8/10 (☎542 221 880). A hangout for Brno's jet-setters, this sleek, chic cafe serves up a touch of New York, along with some phenomenal breakfasts of omelettes and toasted baguette sandwiches (53-100Kč), ingenious pasta and fresh fish entrees (113-216Kč), and massive salads (90-147Kč). Cover 20Kč. Open M-Th 8am-10pm, F 8am-11pm, Sa 9am-11pm, Su 10am-8pm. MC/V. ❸

👁 SIGHTS

▨ PETER AND PAUL CATHEDRAL. Brno was allegedly saved from the Swedish siege of 1645 in one day. The attacking general promised to retreat if his army didn't capture the city by noon, so when the townsfolk learned of his claim, they rang the bells one hour early and the Swedes slunk away. The bells have been striking noon at 11am ever since. Although the Swedes burnt the cathedral (Biskupská katedrála sv. Petra a Pavla) as they retreated, some of it was left intact, and the remains of the earliest Romanesque church on Petrov are still visible in the current cathedral's crypt. *(On Petrov Hill. Climb Petrska from Zelný trh. Cathedral open M-Sa 8:15am-6:15pm. Su 7am-6pm. Chapel, tower, and crypt open M-Sa 11am-6pm, Su 1-6pm. Cathedral and chapel free. Tower 25Kč, students 20Kč. Crypt 25/10Kč.)*

▨ ŠPILBERK CASTLE (HRAD ŠPILBERK). Once home to Czech kings and a mighty Hapsburg fortress, Špilberk has had an illustrious past. After a brief stint as the city's fortress against the Swedes, the castle served as a prison for convicted criminals, and for Czech, Hungarian, Italian, and Polish revolutionaries during the 18th and 19th centuries. The gruesome torture methods employed here earned the castle a reputation for being the cruelest prison in Hapsburg Europe. During WWII, the Nazis kept their political and racial prisoners here. The corridors now contain extensive **galleries** detailing the prison's history and the art, architecture, and social history of Brno. For a taste of prison life, trek through the moat's tomb-like **encasements,** where the most dangerous criminals were imprisoned. The memorial to those who lost their lives here, in the final cell of the prison museum, is particularly moving. *(Take Zámečnická from nám. Svobody through Dominikánské nám. and go right on Panenská. Cross Husova and follow the path uphill. ☎542 123 611; muzeum.brno@spilberk.cz. Open May-Sept. Tu-Su 9am-6pm; Oct. and Apr. Tu-Su 9am-5pm; Nov.-Mar. W-Su 9am-5pm. Call ahead to reserve a tour in English. Full admittance to all exhibits 99Kč, students 45Kč. Castle tower 20/10Kč.)*

CAPUCHIN MONASTERY CRYPT (HROBKA KAPUCÍNSKÉHO KLÁŠTERA). If bones and bodies catch your fancy, you'll love this morbid resting place. The monks at this crypt developed an innovative burial method in which a series of air ducts allowed bodies to dry out naturally. As a result, the crypt preserved more than 100 18th-century monks and nobles. The displayed results now enlighten the living: the crypt opens with the Latin inscription, "Remember death!" and ends with the dead monks' dark reminder: "What you are, we were. What we are, you will be." *(Left of Masarykova from the train station.* ☎ *542 221 207. Open May-Sept. M-Sa 9am-noon and 2-4:30pm, Su 9am-noon. English brochures 40Kč, students 20Kč.)*

AROUND MENDEL SQUARE (MENDLOVO NÁMĚSTÍ). In the heart of Old Brno sits the beautiful Gothic **Basilica of the Assumption of the Virgin Mary** (Bazilika Nanebevzetí Panny Marie). Its intricate golden altar displays the 13th-century **Black Madonna,** the country's oldest wooden icon, which purportedly held off the Swedes in 1645. *(From Špilberk, walk downhill on Pelicova and take the stairs to Sladová. Go left on Úvoz to Mendlovo nám. Open Tu, Th-F, and Su 5:45-7:15pm.)* The Augustinian monastery next door was home to **Johann Gregor Mendel,** father of modern genetics. The newly renovated and expanded **Mendelianum,** Mendlovo nám. 1a, features slide shows, audio presentations, and exhibits documenting the his life and experiments. After watching the interactive **video** on how Mendel's pea plants led him to the theory of inherited genotypes, you can explore the garden that houses the foundation of his greenhouse and a recreated version of his pea garden. The barley grown is used by the brewery next door where, by tasting the beer, you fully appreciate Mendel's work. *(☎ 543 424 043; www.mendel-museum.org. Open May-Oct. Tu-Su 10am-6pm; Nov.-Apr. W-Su 10am-4pm. 80Kč. Abbey open for viewing at 10am; 60Kč. Tours of the monastery M-F 10am and 3pm, Sa-Su 10am and 6pm; 60Kč.)*

OLD TOWN HALL (STARÁ RADNICE). Brno's Old Town Hall facade is the subject of a range of legends. Its crooked Gothic portal supposedly took on its shape after the carver blew his commission on too much Moravian wine. As for the dismayed stone face looking out on Mecova from the back of the hall, rumor has it that it's the petrified head of a burgher, who met his doom there after siding with the Hussites in 1424. The most famous tale involves the stuffed "dragon" hanging from the ceiling in the passageway. Legend claims that the dragon perished after devouring an ox carcass that had been stuffed with quicklime. As thirst began to overwhelm him, he downed a whole river and his belly burst. Actually, the dragon is an Amazonian crocodile Archduke Matyáš gave Brno to garner favor among the burghers. *(Radnická 8, just off Zelný trh. Open daily Apr.-Oct. 9am-5pm; last entrance 4:30pm. 20Kč, students 10Kč.)*

🎭 🎟 ENTERTAINMENT AND NIGHTLIFE

The Old Town Hall hosts frequent summer **concerts;** buy tickets (100-600Kč) at the tourist office (p. 219). **Theater** and **opera** tickets available at Dvořákova 11. (☎ 542 321 285. Open M-F July-Aug. 8am-noon and 12:45-3pm; Sept.-June 8am-noon and 1-4:30pm.) **Cinemas** playing Western and Czech flicks abound (80-140Kč). **Palace Cinema,** Mecova 2, features American blockbusters and mainstream Czech films. (☎ 543 560 111; www.palacecinemas.cz. 145Kč, students 115Kč; M 99Kč.) **Lucerna,** Minská 19, shows British and American independent films, as well as Czech originals. (☎ 605 282 438 or 549 247 070. Showtimes 5-8:30pm.) Look for posters advertising **techno raves,** Brno's hottest summer entertainment. While it's surprisingly easier to find a beer hall than a wine cellar in the heart of wine-producing Moravia, there is an occasional *vinárna* (bottles 80-150Kč).

Divadelní hospoda Veselá husa (Merry Goose Theatrical Pub), Zelný trh 9 (☎ 542 211 630), just behind the theater. This pub's artsy crowd gathers after experimental performances in the attached Merry Goose Theater. Performances start between 7:30 and 8pm and last 1-3hr. Pilsner 23Kč. Open M-F 11am-1am, Sa-Su 3pm-1am.

Pivnice Minipivovar Pegas, Jakubská 4 (☎542 210 104). This modern microbrewery on the 1st fl. of Hotel Pegas has a young, loyal following that tosses back homemade brews. Pints 16Kč. Open M-Sa 9am-midnight, Su 10am-10pm. MC/V.

Mersey, Minská 15 (☎541 240 623; www.mersey.cz). Take tram #3 or 11 from Česká to Tábor and continue down Minská. This rock club-disco-pub hosts live bands and DJs playing funk, disco, and rock depending on the night. Easygoing atmosphere. Large crowds gather for theme events, like U2 and James Bond nights. Beer 25Kč. Internet access 30Kč per hr. Cover F-Sa 30Kč. Open Tu-W 8pm-2am, Th-Sa 8pm-4am.

OLOMOUC   ☎585

Today, Olomouc (OH-lo-mohts; pop. 103,372) is the echo of Prague before it was engulfed by hordes of tourists. The historic capital of Northern Moravia, Olomouc embodies the best aspects of the Czech Republic. By day, locals enjoy the Baroque architecture and cobblestone paths of the rebuilt town center. By night, students from the local university keep the clubs thumping until dawn.

▐ TRANSPORTATION

Trains: Jeremenkova 23 (☎785 490). To **Brno** (1½hr., 7-8 per day, 120Kč) and **Prague** (3½hr., 19 per day, 294Kč).

Buses: Rolsberská 66 (☎313 848). Info office open M-F 6am-6pm, Sa-Su 6am-2pm. To: **Brno** (1½hr., 10 per day, 75-85Kč) and **Prague** (4½hr., 3 per day, 310Kč).

Public Transportation: Buy tickets (6Kč) for the **trams** and **buses** at kiosks by the station and machines at each stop.

Taxis: Eurotaxi (☎603 449 541). Taxis congregate in front of the train station and at the intersection of Riegrova and Národních hridinů.

▮✳ ▐ ORIENTATION AND PRACTICAL INFORMATION

Olomouc's **Staré Město** (Old Town) forms a triangle, in the center of which is the enormous **Horní náměstí** (Upper Square). Behind the **radnice** (town hall), **Dolní nám.** (Lower Square) connects with Horní nám. **Masarykova třída** leads west from the train and bus stations to the town center, though not before changing its name to **1. máje** and then **Denišova.** Trams or buses marked "X" shuttle between the **train station** and the center (5 stops, 6Kč per ticket). Get off at Koruna, in front of the gigantic **Prior** department store, then follow **28. října** to Horní nám. Alternatively, trams #1-6 stop just outside the center. Get off at **nám. Hridinů** and follow **Riegrova** to the center. From the **bus station,** just beyond the train station, take the pedestrian passageway beneath Jeremenkova to reach trams #4 and 5, which run to the center.

Tourist Office: Horní nám. (☎513 385; www.olomoucko.cz), in the *radnice*. **Free maps** of the town center. Detailed city maps (49-59Kč). Books hotels, hostels, and private rooms. English spoken. Open daily Mar.-Nov. 9am-7pm; Dec.-Feb. 9am-5pm.

Budget Travel: CKM, Denišova 4 (☎222 148). Sells ISICs (250Kč) and train tickets. Open M-F 9am-5:30pm, Sa 9am-noon.

Currency Exchange: Komerční banka, Svobody 14 (☎550 91 11) and Denišova 47 (☎585 509 169), cashes most **traveler's checks** for 1% commission and gives MC **cash advances** for 2% commission; Denišova gives AmEx/MC cash advances for 2% commission. Svobody branch open M-F 8am-7pm.

Luggage Storage: At the train station. 15Kč per day per piece under 15kg, 30Kč per piece over 15kg. Open daily 1:45-6:15am, 6:30-10:30am, 11am-6:15pm, and 6:30pm-1am. Lockers 5Kč. Bus station lockers 5Kč.

English-Language Bookstore: Votobia, Riegrova 33 (☎685 223 99). A few shelves of English titles in the back of the store. Open M-F 8:30am-6pm, Sa 9am-noon.

Pharmacy: Lékárna, on the corner of Ostružnická and Horní nám., behind the *radnice*. Open M-F 7am-6pm, Sa 8am-noon.

Hospital: Fakultni Nemocnice, IP Pavlova 6 (☎851 111; fax 413 841), southwest of the center off Albertova.

Internet: Internet u Dominika, Slovenská 12 (☎777 181 857). Good connections and many terminals. 1Kč per min. Open M-F 9am-9pm, Sa-Su 10am-9pm.

Post Office: Horní nám. 27. Open M-F 8am-7pm, Sa-Su 8am-noon. **Postal Code:** 771 27.

ACCOMMODATIONS

The cheapest beds (from 230Kč) pop up in summer when **Palacký University dorms ❶** open to tourists; most are opposite the Botanical Gardens, on the other side of 17 Listopadu, a 15min. walk from the center. The tourist office has info on arranging these accommodations and **private rooms** (from 360Kč).

Poet's Corner Hostel, Sokolská 1 (☎777 570 730; www.hostelolomouc.com), near the center. From the train or bus station, take trams #4-7 to nám. Hridinů and walk 2 blocks continuing in the same direction to Sokolská. From Horní nám., walk down 28. října 2 blocks; go left on Sokolska. Run by 2 charming Australians, this apartment feels more like a home than a hostel. Laundry (100Kč) and bike rental (100Kč per day) available. Dorms Sept.-June 250Kč, July-Aug. 300Kč; doubles 800Kč; triples 1000Kč. ❶

Pension na Hradbách, Hrnčířská 3 (☎233 243; nahradback@quick.cz). From Horní nám., head down Školní, go straight along Purkrabská, and turn right on Hrnčířská. A small, homey pension on one of the quietest streets of the center. Call ahead. Singles with private bath and TV 600Kč; doubles 800Kč; triples 600-1200Kč. ❸

Penzion Best, Na Strelnici 48 (☎/fax 231 450). Take tram #1 or 4-7 to nám. Hridinů, then hop on bus #17, 18, or 22 to Na Strelnici. Continue in the same direction until the hotel appears on your right (5min.). Although a bit out of the way, Best is an excellent deal (as its name implies), as all rooms have bathrooms and TVs. Breakfast 40Kč. Singles 500Kč; doubles 750Kč. MC/V. ❷

FOOD

With cuisine from Czech to Chinese, Olomouc makes food easy to find. Numerous restaurants line both **Horní nám.** and **Dolní nám,** serving various types of fare for 50-150Kč. Grab groceries at **Supermarket Delvita,** 8. května 24, in the basement of Prior, at the corner of 28. října. (☎535 135. Open M-F 7am-8pm, Sa 7am-2pm.)

Čajovna Dřevená Panenka (Wooden Doll Teahouse), Hrnčířská 12. (☎233 858), across the street from Pension na Hradbách (see above). This labyrinthine, multi-story teahouse is a mecca for relaxation. Smoke a water pipe in a secluded enclave (75Kč), sip one of over 70 varieties of tea (35-65Kč), or enjoy freshly made couscous (45Kč), all in a peaceful, incense-filled atmosphere. "Secret" tea blend Yogi Yogi will open up new worlds for spiced-chai-lovers (50Kč). Open M-F 11am-11pm, Sa-Su 3-11pm. ❶

Hanácká Hospoda, Dolní nám. 38 (☎777 721 171). Always packed with locals. Serves up the very best of Czech food, like beer-braised duck with cabbage and dumplings (169Kč), in an atmosphere that exudes Moravian countryside comfort. English menu. Entrees 33-222Kč. Open daily 10am-midnight. AmEx/MC/V. ❷

Café 87, Denisova 47 (☎202 593). Owner Vera runs a remarkable cafe, with welcoming, English-speaking waitstaff, info about events around town, and Internet access in back (1Kč per min.). Relax with a cup of java (20Kč) and a slice of chocolate pie (25Kč) on a comfortable sofa. Quiches and sandwiches (25-40Kč) satisfy mid-afternoon hunger. Breakfast foods 23-58Kč. Open M-F 6:30am-10pm, Sa-Su 8am-10pm. ❶

Cafe Caesar, Horní nám. (☎685 229 287), in the *radnice*. Named after Caesar, the supposed founder of Olomouc, this Italian restaurant serves dishes that could have fed (and protected) his armies. Tourists and locals enjoy the garlicky pizzas (30 varieties; 25-110Kč) and plates of pasta (47-113Kč). Huge outdoor terrace good for people-watching. Entrees 52-169Kč. Open M-Sa 9am-1am, Su 9am-midnight. AmEx/MC/V. ❷

U Kejklire (The Juggler), Michalská 2 (☎543 590 799), behind the *radnice*. Elegant restaurant that serves hefty portions to satisfy the bloodthirsty and herbivorous alike. Salads 15-70Kč. Vegetarian options 27-83Kč. Steak 100-138Kč. Open M-Th 10am-9pm, F-Sa 10am-10pm, Su 11am-6pm. MC/V. ❸

🔵 SIGHTS

The massive 1378 **radnice** (town hall) and its spired clock tower dominate the town center; the tourist office arranges trips to the top. (Daily 11am, 3pm. 15Kč.) An amusing **astronomical clock** is set in the town hall's north side. In 1955, communist clockmakers replaced the mechanical saints with archetypes of "the people." Since then, the masses strike the hour with their hammers and sickles in show of socialist spirit. (Chimes daily at noon.) The 35m black-and-gold **Trinity Column** (Sloup Nejsvětější Trojice) soars higher than any other Baroque sculpture in the country. One of Europe's largest Baroque organs bellows each Sunday in the **Church of St. Maurice** (Chram sv. Mořice), 28. října. It also stars in Olomouc's **International Organ Festival** each September.

Returning to Horní nám., take Mahlerova to the intimate **Jan Sarkander Chapel** (Kaple sv. Jana Sarkandra), which, with its awesome frescoes, honors a Catholic priest tortured to death by Protestants in 1620 after he refused to divulge a confessor's secret. (Open daily 10am-noon and 1-5pm. Free.) On Mahlerova, turn left on Univerzitní, and then right on Denišova. The **Museum of National History and Arts** (Vlastivědné Muzeum), nám. Republiky 5, tells the history of the astrological clock and displays 16th- to 19th-century time pieces. There is a zoological exhibit on the first floor. (☎515 111; www.vmo.cz. Open Apr.-Sept. M-Tu and Su 9am-6pm; Oct.-Mar. M-W and Su 10am-5pm. 40Kč, students 20Kč.)

From nám. Republiky, continue away from the center on 1. máje and then climb Dómská, on the left, to reach Václavské nám. Let the spires of **St. Wenceslas Cathedral** (Metropolitní Kostel sv. Václava), reminiscent of Paris's Notre Dame, lead the way. The church interior is in excellent condition, having been reworked virtually every century since it was damaged by fire in 1265. Its delicate wall designs will impress even the most jaded travelers. The crypt exhibits the gold-encased skull of St. Pauline (Sv. Pavlína), Olomouc's protectress. (www.ado.cz/dom. Cathedral open W 9am-4pm, Tu and Th-Sa 9am-5pm, Su 11am-5pm. Free. Crypt open Tu and Th-Sa 9am-2pm, W 9am-4pm, Su 11am-5pm. 40Kč, students 20Kč. Donations requested.) Next door to the cathedral, the walls of the wondrous **Přemyslid Palace** (Přemyslovský palác) are covered in 15th- and 16th- century frescoes. (☎230 915. Open Apr.-Sept. Tu-Su 10am-6pm. 15Kč, students 5Kč; W free.) Continue away from the center on 1. máje and go right on Kosinova to reach the path that runs through **Bezrucovy sady,** the city park. Stroll through the forested paths and take a left past the statues. Go over the footbridge and along the tennis courts to reach the **Botanical Garden** across the stream. The highlight of the manicured grounds is the rosarium, which fills with blossoms in summer. (Bezrucovy sady open dawn-dusk. Free. Botanical gardens open Tu-Su Apr. 9:30am-4pm; May-Sept. 9:30am-6pm. 20Kč, students 15Kč.)

🎵 NIGHTLIFE

Exit Discoteque, Holická 8, is the Czech Republic's largest outdoor club and Olomouc's wildest. From Horní nám., walk to Dolní nám., then follow Kateřinská 400m to 17 Listopadu. Turn left, then take a right on Wittgensteinova; follow it across the bridge (200m). The club is on the right. The loud techno and spotlights emanating from the building draw clubbers like moths to a flame. Eight bars ensure that you'll never wait for a drink. The terraces are perfect for sipping a cocktail while watching youthful clubbers on the dance floor below. (☎230 573. Cover 50-60Kč. Open June-Sept. F-Sa 9pm-5am.) The popular **Depo No. 9,** nám. Republiky 1, pours *Staropramen* (20Kč) in three underground rooms with metallic decor and comfy seats. In the wee hours, the basement becomes Olomouc's most happening student dance club, with frequent live rock performances. (☎221 273. Occasional cover 50-100Kč. Open M-Th 10am-2am, F 10am-6am, Sa 7pm-6am, Su 7pm-midnight.) Closer to town is **Barumba,** Mlýnská 4, which churns out techno and beer. Follow Pavelčákova out of Horní nám.; go left on Mlýnská. (☎208 425. Beer 24Kč. Cover men 30-60Kč, women free. Open M-Th 7pm-3am, F-Sa 9pm-6am. MC/V.) If you're looking for a more low-key spot to have a drink or two, head next door to **The Crack,** an Irish pub set in the renovated cellar of the Staré Město brewery. (☎520 842 829. Open M-Th 11am-1am, F 11am-2am, Sa 4pm-2am, Su 4pm-1am.) For a unique experience, **Vinárna Letka,** Legionářská 6, an old Soviet airplane converted into a bar, is just the thing. The decor is tacky and the crowd touristy, but the opportunity to pretend the Cold War never ended is not to be missed. (Open M-Th 9pm-6am, F-Sa 9pm-7am.)

🏛 DAYTRIPS FROM OLOMOUC

KROMĚŘÍŽ

Buses from Olomouc (1¼hr., 12 per day, 37Kč). The center of town is very compact and spirals outward from Velké nám., the main square. From the stations, go left on Nádražni; left on Holínská, which leads over the river; right on Komenského nám.; and then left on Vodní, which leads to Velké nám. The cathedral is just off the main square. ☎573 502 011; www.azz.cz. Open July-Aug. Tu-Su 9am-6pm; Sept. and May-June Tu-Su 9am-5pm; Oct. and Apr. Sa-Su 9am-5pm. 80Kč, students 50Kč. 1½hr. tours in English 90/50Kč. Free English info with tours in Czech. Entrance to Gallery 50/25Kč. Halls and Gallery together 110/65Kč. Salá Terrena 20/10Kč. Tower 40/30Kč.

The tiny town of Kroměříž (KROHM-yer-sheesh) is dominated by the UNESCO-protected **Archbishop's Chateau** (Arcibiskupský zámek), which was founded in 1260 by Bishop Bruno of Schaumberk, leveled by the Swedish armies in the Thirty Years' War, and rebuilt from the ground up by Bishop Karel II of Lichtenstein-Kastelkorn. What he built as a Gothic castle was gradually transformed into the ornate Renaissance chateau that stands today, which served for years as the summer residence for the Bishops of Olomouc, as well as the home of the ill-fated Constitutional Congress of Austrian Nations of 1848-49. Among the chateau's multiple attractions, the main one is the tour of the Historical Halls, which leads through the chambers where the archbishops received and entertained tsars and kings, and where they judged feudal disputes, received fealty, and granted fiefdoms. Highlights include the enormous white-and-gold Assembly Hall where the Continental Congress was held, lined with chandeliers and mirrors; and the Feudal Hall where the bishops bestowed fiefdoms, the ceiling of which is covered in frescoes by Franz Maulbertsch, court painter to the empress Maria Theresa. Although it isn't in English, the tour of the Salá Terrena in the chateau's underground chambers and gardens is still worth it for the sights. In one room, trees reach their limbs up through the walls of rough-hewn rock and into the ceiling, framing a small grotto in the back. In another, tiny sculpted figures of miners work the stone walls of the chateau. The chateau also features a small art gallery whose main event is its original of Titian's "Apollo and Marsyas"; the canvas depicts Marsyas's punishment for daring to challenge the god to a contest on the panpipe, and then losing. The chateau's tower gives a view of the town and of any oncoming storms.

TELČ   ☎(0)66

The Italian aura of tiny Telč (TELCH; pop. 6000) stems from a 1546 trip made to Genoa, Italy by the town's ruler, **Zachariáš of Hradec.** He was so enamored of Renaissance style that he brought back a battalion of Italian artists and craftsmen to spruce up his humble Moravian castle and town. With a cobblestone footbridge and a square flanked by arcades of peach-painted gables, it is easy to see why UNESCO named the gingerbread village a World Heritage Monument.

The highlight of Telč's many attractions is its breathtaking **castle,** a monument from the town's glory days as a water fortress. Arguably the most magnificent castle in the country, the overwhelming stone building, complete with courtyard garden and lily pond, houses an amazingly well-kept interior. There are two options for viewing the castle—tour A and tour B, both 45min. Tour A goes through the Renaissance hallways, past tapestries and exotic hunting trophies, through the old chapel, and beneath extravagant ceilings. Tour B leads through the rooms decorated in the 18th and 19th centuries, untouched since the Czech state seized control of the castle in 1945. The free English information sheets are extremely helpful. (☎567 243 821, box office 567 243 943; www.zamek-telc.cz. Open Tu-Su May-Aug. 9am-noon and 1-5pm; Sept.-Oct. and Apr. 9am-noon and 1-4pm. 80Kč, students 40Kč. English tours: Tour A 140Kč; Tour B 140Kč.) In the courtyard, a **museum** displays examples of Telč's folklore. (Same hours as castle. 20Kč, students 15Kč.) The **gallery** is a memorial to artist **Jan Zrzavý** (1890-1977), who trained as a neo-Impressionist, dabbled in Cubism, and produced religious paintings. (Open Tu-F and Su 9am-noon and 1-4pm, Sa 9am-1pm. 30Kč, students 15Kč.) Beside the castle grounds stands the town's 14th-century **tower.** If you can bear the winding stairs, the climb to the top offers a stunning view of Telč. (☎604 985 3398. Open June-Aug. Tu-Sa 10-11:30am and 12:30-6pm, Su 1-6pm; Sept. and May Sa-Su 1-5pm. 20Kč, students 15Kč.) Those not fond of heights can stroll through the quiet **park** at the castle's edge, where the stone walls meet the river. (Open daily dawn-dusk. Free.)

While Telč has a curiously large amount of hostels and pensions, the central ones fill quickly in July and August, and there aren't many truly budget accommodations. **Campgrounds ❶** outside of town are available through the tourist office (see above; 80-100Kč), but the town's diminutive size means that you can get a **private room** with bath for 350Kč. Recently opened **Hostel Pantof ❶,** nám. Zachariáše Hradce 42, offers a few beds in an historic building. (☎776 887 466; www.pantof.com. 6-bed dorms 100Kč; double 400Kč.) **Privát U Šeniglů ❹,** nám. Zachariáše Hradce 11, offers clean, well-kept rooms with private baths, skylights, and kitschy decor for a decent price. (☎567 243 406. Doubles 300Kč.) **Šenk pod vež í ❷,** Palackého 116/11, serves cheap Czech food, from fried cheese to steak. A long stone terrace out back overlooks the town moat. (☎567 243 889. Salads 39-45Kč. Entrees 54-222Kč. Open daily 11am-10pm; bar open daily 8pm-5am.) The grocery store, **Horacké Potraviny,** is at nám. Zachariáše Hradce 65. (Open M-F 7am-6pm, Sa 7am-noon.)

The **bus station** (☎567 302 477), which provides the only viable means of intercity transport, is on Slavíčkova, a 5min. walk from the main square. Buses run to **Prague** (3hr., 7 per day, 100Kč) and **Brno** (2hr., 8 per day, 88Kč). **Taxis** line the main square (☎602 517 775). The town center forms a peninsula jutting into two conjoining rivers, with **nám. Zachariáše Hradce,** the oblong main square, in the middle. To reach it from the bus station, follow the walkway and turn right on Tyršova, then left on Masarykovo. Enter the square through the archway on the right. The **tourist office,** nám. Zachariáše Hradce 10, in the town hall, sells **maps** and has **Internet** and accommodations listings. (☎567 112 407; www.telc-etc.cz. Open M-F 8am-6pm, Sa-Su 10am-6pm.) Across the street, **Česká Spořitelna,** nám. Zachariáše Hradce 62, exchanges **traveler's checks** and has an **ATM.** (Open M and W-Th 9am-12:30pm and 1:30-5pm, Tu and F 9am-12:30pm.) There are two **pharmacies** on Masarykovoa. **Lékárna U sv Anny** is at Masarykova 65. (☎567 213 622; lektelc@volny.cz. Open M-F 7:15am-5pm, Sa 8:30-11am. MC/V.) **Lékárna Telč** is at Masarykova 66 (☎567 213 579. Open M-F 7:30am-5pm, Sa 8-11am. MC/V.) The **post office** is down the street at Tyršova 294. (☎567 243 212. **Western Union** and **Poste Restante.** Open M-F 8-11am and 1-6pm, Sa 8-10am.) **Postal Code:** 588 56.

ESTONIA (EESTI)

Happy to sever its Soviet bonds, Estonia has been quick to revive its historical and cultural ties to its Nordic neighbors, while Finnish tourism and investment help to revitalize the nation. The wealth that has accumulated in Tallinn, however, belies the poverty that still lurks outside of big cities, as well as the chagrin of the ethnically Russian minority over Estonia's European leanings. Still, having overcome successive centuries of domination by the Danes, Swedes, and Russians, Estonians are now proud to take their place as members of modern Europe.

 DISCOVER ESTONIA: SUGGESTED ITINERARIES

THREE DAYS If you're arriving in **Tallinn** (p. 237), spend a day exploring the streets and sights of the Old Town—don't miss the enthralling **Museum of Occupations.** Take another day going beyond the walls of the old city to see the **Maarjamäe** branch of the Estonian History Museum, before catching some afternoon rays at **Pirita Beach.** If you have a car, spend your 3rd day in the beautiful **Lahemaa Nature Preserve** (p. 246), or if you're traveling by bus, in the seaside town of **Haapsalu** (p. 250).

ONE WEEK Get out of Tallinn, seriously! Going beyond the capital city will be a welcome relief for your wallet. If arriving from the south, spend 2 days enjoying the unique sights and sounds of **Tartu** (p. 260) before moving west to **Pärnu** (p. 247), on the coast. After a day or so, head out to the island of **Saaremaa** (2 days; p. 251), where you can bike around and take in the unspoiled beauty of the region. Then catch a bus to **Tallinn** (2 days) where you can see the churches and towers of the historic Old Town.

FACTS AND FIGURES

Official Name: Republic of Estonia.
Capital: Tallinn (pop. 409,516).
Major Cities: Pärnu, Tartu.
Population: 1.4 million (65% Estonian, 28% Russian, 3% Belarusian, 4% other).

Land Area: 45,226 sq. km.
Time Zone: GMT + 2.
Languages: Estonian (official), Russian.
Religions: Evangelical Lutheran (65%), Russian and Estonian Orthodox (19%), Baptist (15%).

ESSENTIALS

WHEN TO GO

The best time to visit is in the late spring (Apr.-May) and summer (June to early Sept.), with highs of 30°C (86°F) in July and August. Winters can be cold, with limited daylight hours, but with an abundance of skiing and skating.

DOCUMENTS AND FORMALITIES

EMBASSIES AND CONSULATES. Embassies of other countries to Estonia are all in **Tallinn** (p. 237). Estonia's embassies and consulates include: **Australia,** 86 Louisa Rd., Birchgrove, Nsw 2041 (☎2 9810 7468; eestikon@ozemail.com.au); **Canada,** 260 Dalhousie St., Ste. 210, Ottowa, On K1N 7E4 (☎613-789-4222); www.estemb.ca);

ENTRANCE REQUIREMENTS
Passport: Required for all travelers.
Visa: Not required for citizens of EU countries, Australia, Canada, New Zealand, the US, and assorted other countries for stays under 90 days.
Letter of Invitation: Not required.
Inoculations: Recommended up-to-date on DTaP (diphtheria, tetanus, and pertussis), Hepatitis A, Hepatitis B, MMR (measles, mumps, and rubella), Polio booster, and Typhoid.
Work Permit: Required of all foreigners planning to work.
International Driving Permit: Required of all those planning to drive.

Finland, Itäinen Puistotie 10, 00140 Helsinki (☎622 0260; www.estemb.fi); **Sweden,** Tyrgatan 3/3a, 11427 Stockholm (☎8 5451 2280; www.estemb.se); **UK,** 16 Hyde Park Gate, London Sw7 5dg (☎020 7589 3428; www.estonia.gov.uk); **US,** 2131 Massachusetts Ave., NW, Washington, DC, 20008 (☎202-588-0101; www.estemb.org).

VISA AND ENTRY INFORMATION. Citizens of EU countries, Australia, Canada, New Zealand, the US, and some other countries can visit Estonia visa-free for up to 90 days in a six-month period. Visa **extensions** are not granted. For more info, consult **www.vm.ee/eng.** The easiest means of crossing the **border** is from Tallinn to Moscow, St. Petersburg, or Rīga. Visas are not granted at the border.

TOURIST SERVICES AND MONEY

Tourist offices, marked with a small white "i" on a green background, are present in most towns and sell **maps** and offer helpful advice. They keep extended hours during the summer months. The unit of currency is the **kroon (EEK),** divided into 100 **senti. Inflation** is around 3%. The best foreign currencies to bring to Estonia are the euro and US dollar. Many restaurants and shops accept **MasterCard** and **Visa,** and **ATMs** are available everywhere. Discounts are typically extended to student travelers with proper ID. **Tipping** is becoming more common; 10% is expected in restaurants. Expect to spend US$35-50 a day. Tallinn is painfully expensive

ESTONIA

compared to the rest of the country, including the islands. Accommodations, food, and transportation in the capital will cost US$40-45 per day, whereas in the rest of the country, US$30 will allow a fairly comfortable day of sightseeing, eating, and drinking to your heart's content.

ESTONIAN KROONI (EEK)		
	AUS$1 = 9.68EEK	10EEK = AUS$1.03
	CDN$1 = 10.54EEK	10EEK = CDN$0.95
	EUR€1 = 15.64EEK	10EEK = EUR€0.64
	NZ$1 = 8.94EEK	10EEK = NZ$1.12
	UK£1 = 23.04EEK	10EEK = UK£0.43
	US$1 = 12.85EEK	10EEK = US$0.78

HEALTH AND SAFETY

EMERGENCY **Police:** ☎ 110. **Ambulance:** ☎ 112. **Fire:** ☎ 112.

Medical services for foreigners are few and far between, and usually require cash payments. There are two kinds of **pharmacies** (both called "apteek"). Some only stock prescription medication, but most are well-equipped Scandinavian chains that stock just about everything else. Public **toilets** *(tasuline)*, marked by "N" or a triangle pointing up for women and "M" or a triangle pointing down for men, usually cost 3EEK and include a very limited supply of toilet paper. While Tallinn's tap water is generally safe to drink, **bottled water** is worth the extra money and is necessary in the rest of the country. The petty **crime** rate is low, though pickpocketing is common in Talllin's Old Town, especially along crowded Viru street. **Women** should not have a problem traveling alone, though it is wise to dress conservatively. **Minorities** in Estonia are rare; they receive stares but generally experience little discrimination. For English-speaking help in an emergency, contact your embassy. **Homosexuality** is generally treated with curiosity rather than suspicion, but same-sex displays of affection are typically kept private.

TRANSPORTATION

BY PLANE, TRAIN, AND BOAT. Several international airlines offer flights to Tallinn; try **SAS, AirBaltic**, or for flights from Europe, consider the budget airlines **easyJet** and **Fly Nordic**. If you're coming from another Baltic state or **Russia**, trains may be even cheaper than **ferries**, which also connect to **Finland, Sweden**, and **Germany**, but expect more red tape when crossing the border. There is a helicopter service from **Helsinki, FIN** to Tallinn. See **Tallinn Transportation**, p. 237, for more info.

BY BUS. Euroline buses are the cheapest method of reaching the Baltics, typically starting in Germany with stops along the way. Domestically, buses are much cheaper and more efficient than trains, though service can be infrequent between non-major cities. Though buses on the islands can be especially frustrating, it is possible to ride buses from the mainland to island towns (via ferry) for less than the price of a typical ferry ride. During the school year (Sept. to late June), students receive half-price bus tickets. Internationally, buses can be a painfully slow choice, as clearing the border may take hours.

BY CAR, TAXI, BIKE, AND THUMB. If crossing into Estonia by car, be sure to avoid the less-than-delightful routes through Kalingrad or Belarus. Although **road conditions** in Estonia are fair and steadily improving, the availability of **roadside**

assistance remains poor. For info concerning speed limits and license requirements, check out the **Estonian National Road Administration** (www.mnt.ee). **Taxis** (about 7EEK per km) are a safe means of transportation. Bicycling is great in Estonia, but be careful of aggressive motorists. Tallinn cycling maps can be found at www.tallinn.ee, listed under "Maps." Those who want to **hitchhike** should stretch out an open hand, but *Let's Go* does not recommend it.

KEEPING IN TOUCH

Though **Internet** cafes are not as common as you might expect, wireless Internet access is curiously rampant. If you have your own laptop, you can find free wireless connections throughout the country; check **www.wifi.ee** or look for places with the wifi.ee sign. Internet access usually costs 30-60EEK per hour. **Telephones,** which are very common at bus stations and shopping malls, require magnetic cards, available at any kiosk. Cards come in various denominations (50EEK min.). Pre-paid phone cards can get you rates of US$0.30 to US$0.50 per minute to phone the US. Otherwise, expect to pay US$1-4 per minute. International access codes include: **AT&T** (☎0 800 12 001), **Canada Direct** (☎0 800 12 011), and **MCI** (☎0 800 12 122). If you bring a GSM mobile phone, SIM cards offer a convenient and sometimes cheap way to keep in touch. An **airmail** letter costs 6.50EEK to Europe and the CIS, and 8EEK to the rest of the world. Postcards cost 6/7.50EEK. Mail can be received general delivery through **Poste Restante.** Address envelopes as follows: Neasa (First name) COLL (LAST NAME), POSTE RESTANTE, Narva mnt. 1 (post office address), 0001 (postal code) Tallinn (city), ESTONIA.

PHONE MAYHEM. The phone system in Estonia proves that the universe tends toward chaos. Tallinn numbers all begin with the number 6 and have 7 digits. Numbers in smaller towns, however, often have only 5 digits. Tallinn, unlike other Estonian cities, has no city code; to call Tallinn from outside Estonia on the digital system, dial Estonia's country code (372) and then the number. To call any city besides Tallinn from outside the country, dial the country code, the city code, and then the number. The 0 listed in parentheses before each city code need only be dialed when placing calls within Estonia.

ACCOMMODATIONS AND CAMPING

ESTONIA	❶	❷	❸	❹	❺
ACCOMMODATIONS	under 200EEK under €13 under US$16	201-400EEK €13-26 US$16-31	401-550EEK €26-35 US$32-43	551-600EEK €36-38 US$43-47	over 600EEK over €38 over US$47

Each tourist office has accommodations listings for its town and can often arrange a bed for visitors. There is little distinction between **hotels, hostels,** and **guesthouses;** some upscale hotels still have hall toilets and showers. The word *võõrastemaja* (guesthouse) in a place's name usually implies that it's less expensive. Many hotels provide laundry services for an extra charge. Some hostels are part of larger hotels, so be sure to ask for the cheaper rooms. **Homestays** are common and inexpensive. For info on HI hostels around Estonia, contact the **Estonian Youth Hostel Association,** Narva Mantee 16-25, 10121, Tallinn (☎372 6461 455; www.baltichostels.net). Camping is the best way to experience Estonia's islands and unique selection of fauna and flora, but doing so outside of designated areas is illegal and a threat to wildlife. Farm stays are growing popular, and provide a great peek into local life. For more info visit Rural Tourism, www.maaturism.ee, or search for a variety of accommodations at www.visitestonia.com.

FOOD AND DRINK

ESTONIA	❶	❷	❸	❹	❺
FOOD	under 50EEK under €3 under US$4	50-80EEK €3-5 US$4-6	81-100EEK €5-6 US$6-8	101-140EEK €6-9 US$9-11	over 140EEK over €9 over US$11

Most cheap Estonian food is fried and doused with **sour cream**. Local specialties include *schnitzel* (breaded, fried pork fillet), *seljanka* (meat stew), *pelmenid* (dumplings), and smoked fish. Bread is usually dark and dense; a loaf of *Hiiumaa leib* easily weighs a kilo. Pancakes with cheese curd and berries are a common, delicious dessert. The national beer *Saku* and the darker *Saku Tume* are acquired tastes; local beer, like Kuressaare's *Saaremaa*, is inconsistent. Värska, a brand of carbonated mineral water, is particularly salty. It is difficult to keep a vegetarian or kosher diet in Estonia. Buying your own groceries is probably the safest bet.

LIFE AND TIMES

HISTORY

THOR, BJÖRN, ET AL. Estonia has struggled for centuries to gain independence and retain its identity. Ninth-century AD **Vikings** were the first to impose themselves on the Finno-Ugric people who inhabited the area that is now Estonia. In 1219, King Valdemar II of **Denmark** conquered northern Estonia. Shortly thereafter, Livonia, now Estonia and Latvia, fell to German knights of the **Teutonic Order,** who purchased the rest of Estonia in 1346.

FOREIGN KINGS. German domination continued until the emergence of Russian **Tsar Ivan IV** (the Terrible), who, in the **Livonian War** of 1558-83, crushed many of the tiny feudal states that had developed in the region. In an attempt to oust Ivan, the defeated states searched for foreign assistance: northern Estonia capitulated to Sweden in 1629, while Livonia joined the Polish-Lithuanian Commonwealth. During the **Swedish Interlude** (1629-1710), **Tartu University** (p. 263) and a number of Estonian-language schools were established.

THE RUSSIANS INVADE. The 1721 **Peace of Nystad** concluded the Great Northern War, handing the Baltics to Peter the Great. Russian rule reinforced the power of the nobility, and serfs lost all rights until Estonian serfdom was finally abolished by **Tsar Alexander I** in 1819, 45 years earlier than in Russia. In 1881, reactionary **Tsar Alexander III** attempted to Russify Estonia, prompting a nationalistic backlash led by **Konstantin Päts,** who would later become president. The backlash peaked in a bid for independence during the Russian Revolution of 1905.

BETWEEN ESTONIA AND A HARD PLACE. At the start of **WWI,** Estonians were caught in a tough spot. Most of the Estonian-German population sympathized with Prussia, but had to fight in the Russian army. The **1917 Russian Revolution** spurred Estonian nationalism, but by the time the state declared **independence** in 1918 it was already under German occupation. After WWI, the country prospered until the **Depression** of the 1930s, which allowed extreme right-wing parties to gain public support. In 1934, President Päts proclaimed a state of emergency. Päts's tenure was cut short by the Soviets, who occupied Estonia in 1940 under the **Nazi-Soviet Non-Aggression Pact.** The Soviets deported Päts and arrested, deported, or killed many other Estonian leaders, as well as a significant portion of the Estonian population. **Hitler** reneged on the pact, annexing Estonia and stationing German troops there from 1941 to 1944. When the Red Army returned, thousands of Estonians fled and thousands more died trying to escape as Estonia became part of the **USSR.**

THE IRON CURTAIN DROPS. The 1950s saw extreme repression and Russification under **Soviet rule,** when internal purges removed the few native Estonians left in the ruling elite. It was not until *glasnost* and *perestroika* in the 1980s that Estonians won enough freedom to establish a political renaissance. In 1988, the **Popular Front** emerged in opposition to the Communist government, pushing a resolution on independence through the Estonian legislature. Nationalists won a legislative majority in the 1990 elections and successfully declared independence after the failed 1991 coup in the Soviet Union.

ESTONIA'S RISING STAR. The 1992 general election, Estonia's first after declaring independence, saw the rejection of the government of **Edgar Savisaar,** who had founded the Popular Front in the twilight of Soviet rule. Savisaar's regime was replaced by a coalition of parties committed to radical economic reform, a trend that has continued to the present. The government has managed to privatize most industries, lower trade barriers, and add a balanced budget amendment to its constitution. This success has made the country the darling of Western investors.

TODAY

Estonia is a **parliamentary democracy** with a much weaker presidency than most other post-Soviet states. After independence, relations with **Russia** grew troubled, when the Estonian government tried to deny citizenship to those unable to speak Estonian. However, in 1998, citizenship was automatically extended to the children of Russian speakers born in Estonia. **Prime Minister Andrus Ansip,** who was elected in April 2005, currently presides over the **Riigikogu** (Parliament). The ruling coalition consists of pro-business **Res Publica,** the centrist **Center Party,** and center-right **Reform Party.** Under the 2nd Estonian **President Arnold Rüütel,** elected in September 2001, the state made **NATO** and **EU** accession its top priorities. Estonia joined both organizations in spring 2004. In March 2005, the government of prime minister Juhan Parts, of Res Publica, collapsed, giving way to Andrus Ansip, of the Reform party, and his coalition government.

PEOPLE AND CULTURE

About 65% of Estonia's inhabitants are ethnically **Estonian.** The significant **Russian** minority comprises almost 30% of the population, and small **Ukrainian** (2.5%), **Belarusian** (1.5%), and **Finnish** (1%) minorities are also present. Estonia is a predominantly Christian country: most Estonians are members of the **Evangelical Lutheran** church, and the country has significant **Russian Orthodox** and **Estonian Orthodox** minorities. Estonian is a Finno-Ugric language, closely related to Finnish. Estonians speak the best English in the Baltic states; most young people know at least a few phrases. Many also know Finnish or Swedish, but German is more common among the older set and in the resort towns. Russian used to be mandatory, but Estonians in secluded areas are likely to have forgotten much of it since few Russians live there. For a phrasebook and glossary, see **Glossary: Estonian,** p. 772. Expect to be bought a drink if you talk with someone a while; repay the favor in kind. If you're invited to a meal in someone's home, bring a **gift** for the hostess (an odd number of flowers is customary). **Handshaking** is a form of greeting. **Shops** sometimes close for a break between noon and 3pm.

A MIDSUMMER NIGHT'S FREE PHONE CALLS

Are you a fan of ritual bonfires, hand-woven flower crowns, and free mobile phone calls? If so, look no further than the Baltic holiday celebrated every June 23-24; Midsummer's Eve, St. John's Day, or Joninfs—call it what you will—has ancient roots in pagan midsummer festivities. The holiday survived the Christian era through its convenient proximity to St. John's Day, with which it blended.

Traditionally, people gather near water to weave flowers, grasses, and herbs into crowns. Women wear the crowns as men-particularly those named "John"—build a ritual bonfire that is set on wheels and pushed into the nearest river. Each woman then takes off her wreath and floats it on the water, hoping that the path of her crown will indicate future marriage. Herbs collected between June 1 and Midsummer's Day are said to have curative powers, and are coveted for their rarity.

Today, you can expect most shops museums, banks, and government offices to be closed on June 24—and many will shut early on June 23. If the day falls close to a weekend, the holiday will be extended into a four-day break. And there are a few modern perks to the holiday, such as free mobile phone calls all night long. Find yourself a field and a good group of locals, and join the party.

THE ARTS

LITERATURE. The oldest book in Estonian is the **Wanradt-Koell Lutheran Catechism** (1535), but local literature didn't flower until the Estophile period (1750-1840) centuries later. The most notable publication of this period was **Anton Thor Helle's** 1739 translation of the Bible. Folklore provided the basis for **Friedrich Reinhold Kreutzwald's** *Kalevipoeg* (1857-61), an epic that became the rallying point of Estonian national rebirth in the Romantic period. Toward the end of the century, the neo-Romantic nationalist **Noor-Eesti** (Young Estonia) movement appeared, led by the poet **Gustav Suits** and the writer **Friedebert Tuglas. Anton Tammsaare's** *Truth and Justice* (*Tõde ja õigus;* 1926-33), is essential to the Estonian canon, and he has been praised as Estonia's foremost writer. The strictures of the official Soviet style of **Socialist Realism** sent many authors abroad or into temporary exile in Siberia, but under Khrushchev's thaw in the early 1960s, Modernism arose via the work of **Artur Alliksaar, Lydia Koidula,** and **Juhan Viidng.** Frequent Nobel nominee **Jaan Kross** managed to criticize the realities of Soviet life despite USSR censors in *The Tsar's Madman* (1978). In the same year, **Aimée Beekman** addressed plight of women in *The Possibility of Choice.* In the last decade, several Estonian writers have been nominated for the Nobel Prize. Among them are poet and essayist **Jaan Kapinski** and novelist **Emil Tode,** whose 1993 *Border State (Piiririik)* was internationally acclaimed as a great postmodern text. **Aarne Ruben** has attracted the public's attention with *The Volta Works Whistles Mournfully (Volta annab Kaeblikku vilet;* 2001). The most popular Estonian writer today is **Andrus Kivirähk,** best known for his humorous *Memoirs of Ivan Orav (Ivan Orava mälestused).*

MUSIC. Popular contemporary Estonian **composers** include **Arvo Pärt,** known for *Tabula rasa* (1977) and *St. James's Passion* (1992), pieces reminiscent of medieval compositions; **Veljo Tormis,** who revived the **runic,** an ancient chanting-style of choral singing; and **Alo Mattisen,** whose pop-rock songs became proindependence anthems. Conductors and musical groups from around the world are drawn to Pärnu, the so-called "summer capital" of Estonia.

FINE ARTS. The first Estonian art school was founded at **Tartu University** (p. 263) in 1803. The first nationally conscious Estonian art emerged at the close of the 19th century with painters **Johann Köler** and **Amandus Adamson** and sculptor **August Weizenberg.** The Neo-Impressionist paintings of **Konrad**

Mägi and the landscapes of **Nikolai Triik** moved increasingly toward abstraction at the end of the 19th century, while the later painting of the 1920s and 1930s was heavily influenced by European trends, including Cubism and the principles of the German *Bauhaus*.

HOLIDAYS AND FESTIVALS

Holidays: New Year's Day (Jan. 1); Independence Day (Feb. 24); Good Friday (Apr. 14, 2006; Apr. 6, 2007); Easter (Apr. 16, 2006; Apr. 8 2007); Labor Day (May 1); Pentecost (June 4, 2006; May 27, 2007); Victory Day (June 23); Jaanipäev (June 23-24); Restoration of Independence (Aug. 20); Christmas (Dec. 25); Boxing Day (Dec. 26).

Festivals: As of 2005, Jaanipäev is celebrated across the Baltic states every June 23-24. Tallinn's Beersummer (p. 245), held in early July, is the kind of celebration its name leads you to expect. The same city hosts the Dark Nights Film Festival in December, hosting student and animation subfestivals in addition to showcasing international films. Pärnu's mid-June Estonian Country Dance Festival culminates in a line dance the length of a city street. An updated list of Estonia's cultural events is at www.kultuuriinfo.ee.

ADDITIONAL RESOURCES

Baltic Revolution: Estonia, Latvia, Lithuania and the Path to Independence, by Anatol Lieven (1994). Provides a solid background in Baltic history.

Border State, by Emil Tode (1993). A look at tensions between East and West as played out in post-Communist Estonia.

Estonia: Independence and European Integration, by David Smith (2001). Examines Estonia's recent past and EU prospects.

The Tsar's Madman, by Jaan Kross (1978). A historical novel about a 19th-century Baltic nobleman. Arguably the best Estonian fiction available.

TALLINN

Crisp sea air gusts over the medieval buildings and spires of Tallinn (pop. 370,792), the self-proclaimed "Heart of Northern Europe." Unfortunately, invading tourists often give the cobblestone streets of the Old Town a theme-park feel. Visitors willing to venture beyond the compact center will be delighted by quirky cafes, lush parks, and the seaside promenade.

▐ TRANSPORTATION

INTERCITY TRANSPORTATION

Flights: Tallinn Airport, Lennujaama 2 (☎605 88 88, 24hr. info 605 88 87; www.tallinn-airport.ee). Bus #2 runs between the airport and the intersection of Gonsiori and Laikmaa, 300m southeast of the Old Town. Airlines include: **Estonian Air,** Lennujaama tee 1 (☎640 11 01; www.estonian-air.ee); **Finnair,** Roosikrantsi 2 (☎611 09 50; www.finnair.ee); **LOT,** Tallinn Airport (☎605 85 53; lot@lot.ee); **SAS,** Rävala pst. 2 (☎666 30 30; www.scandinavian.net). **Copterline,** Mere pst. 20, at the port side of the Linnahall arena (☎610 18 18; www.copterline.com) runs a **helicopter** service to **Helsinki, FIN** (18min., 1 per hr. 8:30am-9:30pm, €59-220). Open daily 9am-7pm.

Trains: Toompuiestee 35 (☎615 68 51; www.evr.ee). Book ahead for international routes, or buy your tickets upstairs 45min. before departure. Buy domestic tickets on the 1st fl. or on board. International ticket windows open daily 9am-10pm; domestic

ESTONIA

Tallinn

🏠 ACCOMMODATIONS
Poska Villa, **2**

🍴 FOOD
Eesti Maja, **3**

6am-10pm. To: **Pärnu** (3hr., 2 per day, 50EEK); **Tartu** (3-4hr., 4 per day, 80EEK); **Moscow, RUS** (14½hr., 1 per day, 515EEK); **St. Petersburg, RUS** (10hr., 1 per day on even days, 390EEK).

Buses: Lastekodu 46 (☎680 09 00), 1.5km southeast of Vanalinn. Trams #2 and 4 run between Hotel Viru and the station, "Bussijaam." Open daily 6:30am-11:30pm; ticket office 6:30am-9:15pm. International schedules www.eurolines.ee; domestic schedules www.bussireisid.ee. Buses run to: **Haapsalu** (1½-2½hr., 1-2 per hr., 45-65EEK); **Pärnu** (2½hr., 36 per day, 55-105EEK); **Tartu** (2½-3hr., 2-3 per hr., 65-85EEK); **Berlin, GER** (27hr., 1 per wk., 1360EEK); **Kaliningrad, RUS** (15hr., 1 per day, 300EEK); **Rīga, LAT** (5-6hr., 5 per day, 180-200EEK); **Vilnius, LIT** (10½hr., 2 per day, 340-400EEK); **St. Petersburg, RUS** (8-10½hr., 5 per day, 190-270EEK); **Moscow, RUS** (18½hr.; Tu, Th-F, Su; 500-900EEK). 10% ISIC discount.

Ferries: (☎631 85 50). At the end of Sadama. Boats, hydrofoils, and catamarans cross to **Helsinki, FIN. Eckerö Line,** Terminal B (☎631 86 06; www.eckeroline.ee). 3½hr.; 2 per day; 250EEK, students 150EEK. MC/V. **Viking,** Terminal A (☎666 39 66; www.vikingline.ee). 3hr.; 2 per day; M-Th and Su 235EEK, students 165EEK; F-Sa 315/250EEK. MC/V. **Nordic Jet Line,** Terminal C (☎613 70 00; www.njl.info). 1½hr., 7 per day, 330-610EEK. MC/V. **Silja Line,** Terminal D (☎611 66 61; www.silja.ee). 1½hr.; 7 per day; 360-705EEK, 50EEK student discount. MC/V. **Tallink,** Terminals A and D (☎640 98 08; www.tallink.ee). 3¼hr., 3 per day, 315-345EEK. Express ferries 1½hr.;

16 per day; 360-610EEK, ask for student discount. MC/V. **LindaLine Express,** Linnahall passenger terminal (☎699 93 33; www.lindaliini.ee). 1½hr., 370-430EEK.
Mainedd travel agency, Raekoja plats 18 (☎644 47 44; mainedd@datanet.nee). Books ferry tickets with no commission. Open M-F 9:30am-5:30pm. MC/V.

LOCAL TRANSPORTATION

Public Transportation: Buses, trams, minibuses, and **trolleys** run 6am-midnight. Buy tickets *(talong)* from kiosks (10EEK) or from drivers (15EEK). Booklets of 10 80EEK. Validate them in the metal boxes on board or face 600EEK fine.

Taxi: Price per km should be posted on your taxi window. Try to call ahead and order a car to avoid a "waiting fee." **Klubi Takso** (☎142 00). 5.50-7EEK per km, 35EEK min. **Kiisu Takso** (☎655 07 77). 5.50EEK per km. **Linnatakso** (☎644 24 42). Can provide taxis for disabled passengers. 7EEK per km.

Bike rental: CityBike, Narva mnt. 120b, inside Comfort Hotel Oru (☎511 18 19; www.citybike.ee). 35EEK for 1st hr., 30EEK per hr. thereafter; 200EEK per day. Rent for more than 3hr. for free delivery anywhere in town. Open Apr.-Oct. daily 10am-8pm.

◼ 🔽 ORIENTATION AND PRACTICAL INFORMATION

Even locals lose their way along the winding medieval streets of Tallinn's **Vanalinn** (Old Town), an egg-shaped maze ringed by five main streets: **Rannamäe tee, Mere pst., Pärnu mnt., Kaarli pst.,** and **Toompuies tee.** The best entrance to Vanalinn is through the 15th-century **Viru ärarad,** across from Hotel Viru, Tallinn's central landmark. **Viru,** the main thoroughfare, leads directly to **Raekoja plats** (Town Hall Square), the scenic center of the Old Town. It has two sections: **All-linn,** or Lower Town, and **Toompea,** a rocky, fortified hill. In the Old Town, **Pikk** and **Vene** run northeast of Raekoja plats. **Uus,** the first street on your right after entering the Old Town gates, runs north towards the ferry ports. South of Raekoja plats, a number of smaller streets run into each other and eventually cross **Muurivahe,** which borders the south and east edges of the Old Town.

TOURIST, FINANCIAL, AND LOCAL SERVICES

Tourist Office: Tourist Information Center (TIC), Kullassepa 4/Niguliste 2 (☎645 77 77; www.tourism.tallinn.ee). Sells city **maps** (45EEK) and the invaluable *Tallinn in Your Pocket* (35EEK), provides transportation schedules, and has a separate Estonian Tourism Information desk to help you plan trips around the country. Open July-Aug. M-F 9am-8pm, Sa-Su 10am-6pm; Sept. M-F 9am-6pm, Sa-Su 10am-5pm; Oct.-Apr. M-F 9am-5pm, Sa 10am-3pm; May-June M-F 9am-7pm, Sa-Su 10am-5pm. Branch at Sadama 25, in Ferry Terminal A (☎/fax 631 83 21). Open daily 8am-4:30pm.

Embassies: For a complete list, check www.vm.ee or consult *Tallinn in Your Pocket* (35EEK). **Canada,** Toom-kooli 13 (☎627 33 11; tallinn@canada.ee). Open M, W, F 9am-noon. **Russia,** Pikk 19 (☎646 41 75; www.estonia.mid.ru). Open M-F 9am-5pm. **UK,** Wismari 6 (☎667 47 00; www.britishembassy.ee). Open M-F 10am-noon and 2-4:30pm. **US,** Kentmanni 20 (☎668 81 00, emergencies 509 21 29; www.usemb.ee). Open M-F 9am-noon and 2-5pm.

Currency Exchange: Located throughout the city, though banks have better rates than hotels and private exchange bureaus. Try **Eesti Uhispank,** Pärnu mnt. 12. Open M-F 9am-6pm, Sa 10am-3pm. **ATMs** are located throughout the city.

American Express: Suur-Karja 15 (☎626 62 11; www.estravel.ee). Books hotels and tours, sells airline, ferry, and rail tickets, and provides visa services. Open June-Aug. M-F 9am-6pm, Sa 10am-5pm; Sept.-May M-F 9am-6pm, Sa 10am-3pm.

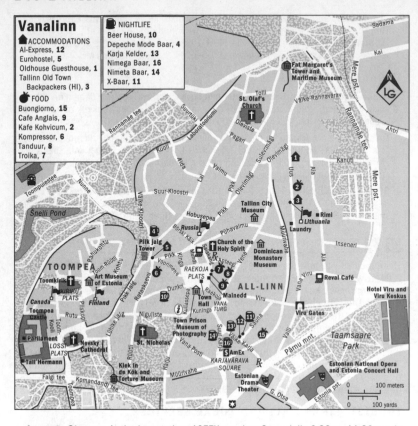

Vanalinn

🏠 ACCOMMODATIONS
Al-Express, **12**
Eurohostel, **5**
Oldhouse Guesthouse, **1**
Tallinn Old Town
Backpackers (HI), **3**

🍴 FOOD
Buongiorno, **15**
Cafe Anglais, **9**
Kafe Kohvicum, **2**
Kompressor, **6**
Tanduur, **8**
Troika, **7**

🍺 NIGHTLIFE
Beer House, **10**
Depeche Mode Baar, **4**
Karja Kelder, **13**
Nimega Baar, **16**
Nimeta Baar, **14**
X-Baar, **11**

Luggage Storage: At the bus station. 10EEK per day. Open daily 6:30am-11:30pm. At the train station. 15-30EEK per day. Open daily 8am-8pm.

English-Language Bookstore: Apollo Raamatumaja, Viru 23 (☎654 84 85; www.apollo.ee), stocks an impressive selection of guides, bestsellers, and classics. Open M-F 10am-8pm, Sa 10am-6pm, Su 11am-4pm. MC/V.

Laundromat: Kati Koduabi, Uus 9 (☎631 45 66). Look for the blue sign with washing symbols. 24hr. service 20EEK per kg. Open M-F 9am-6pm, Sa 10am-4pm. Cash only.

EMERGENCY AND COMMUNICATIONS

Pharmacy: Raeapteek, Raekoja plats 11 (☎631 48 30), has been in business since 1422 and features an adjoining **mini-museum.** Museum free. Open M-F 9am-7pm, Sa 9am-5pm. **Tallinna Linnaapteek,** Pärnu mnt. 10 (☎644 02 55). Open 24hr.

Medical Services: Tallinn Central Hospital, Ravi 18 (☎697 30 02, 24hr. info 620 70 15). **Tallinn First Aid Hotline** (☎697 11 45). The local emergency number is ☎112; operators speak English.

Internet: Metro, Viru valjak 4 (☎610 15 19), in the bus station below Viru keskus. Sells blocks of Internet time valid for 2 days and has the cheapest rates in town. 15EEK per 30min., 25EEK per hr., 35EEK per 2hr. Open daily 8am-11pm. **Central Library,** Estonia pst. 8, 2nd fl. (☎683 09 00). Free if you reserve in advance. Open M-F 11am-7pm, Sa 10am-5pm. **Kaubamaja,** Gonsiori 2 (☎667 31 00), on the 5th fl. of the department store. 35EEK per hr. Open daily 9am-9pm.

Post Office: Narva mnt. 1 (☎661 66 16), opposite Hotel Viru. **Poste Restante** in basement. Open M-F 7:30am-8pm, Sa 8am-6pm, Su 9am-3pm. **Postal Code:** 10101.

ACCOMMODATIONS

In summer, Tallinn's hostel situation is dire: landing a bed in the Old Town is expensive and difficult. If you haven't booked in advance, start knocking on doors early in the day to find a bed that someone else might have cancelled. **◙Rasastra,** Mere pst. 4, finds **private rooms** in central Tallinn and anywhere else in the Baltics. (☎661 62 91; www.bedbreakfast.ee. Open daily 9:30am-6pm. Breakfast 50EEK. Tallinn singles 275EEK; doubles 500EEK; triples 650EEK.)

◙Tallinn Old Town Backpackers (HI), Uus 14 (☎51 71 337; www.balticbackpackers.com). Just north of Tallinn's old city gates, this hostel offers a cozy, convenient place to stay—and the cheapest beds in the Old Town. With only 10 beds, it fills up quickly. Linens 25EEK. Internet 5EEK per 15min. Dorms 225EEK, members 200EEK. MC/V. ❷

◙Oldhouse Guesthouse, Uus 22 (☎641 14 64; www.oldhouse.ee). Oldhouse maintains 3 properties along Uus, including a cozy guesthouse with 6-bed dorms and a school that acts as a hostel during summer. Beds are clean and comfortable, and the 24hr. reception is always staffed by someone helpful and welcoming. Pianos available in the schoolhouse dorms. Shared bathrooms and kitchen. Breakfast included. 8-bed dorms 250EEK; 6-bed dorms 290EEK; singles 450-550EEK; doubles 650EEK; quads 1300EEK; luxury apartments 950-1900EEK. 10% ISIC discount. Cash only. ❸

Eurohostel, Nunne 2 (☎644 77 88; www.eurohostel.ee). From the TIC, walk up Niguliste, turn right on Rataskaevu, and continue to the brown wooden doors on the right on Nunne. Buzz to be let in, and go up to the 2nd fl. This modern hostel is not the quietest place, but does offer comfortable bunks in the thick of the Old Town. Whimsical baths. Fully equipped kitchen. 4- to 6-bed dorms 290EEK. Cash only. ❷

Al-Express, Sauna 1 (☎620 92 53; www.alhostel.com). At the corner of Sauna and Väike-Karja; enter the courtyard through the arch and turn left through the doorway, then follow the signs upstairs. Basic dorms with large windows overlook an Old Town courtyard. Shared shower and toilet, smiling receptionists, and a great location above a bar. Dorms 250EEK. Discount for Peace Corps volunteers. Cash only. ❷

Poska Villa, Poska 15 (☎601 36 01; www.hot.ee/poskavilla). From Vanalinn, follow Gonsiori; make a left on Laulupeo, which becomes Poska; it's the small green house. Charming B&B in a quiet residential neighborhood close to Kadriorg Park and Palace. Private baths. Breakfast included. Singles 650EEK; doubles 760-980EEK. MC/V. ❺

FOOD

International cuisine abounds in the Old Town, although at many of the restaurants in Raekoja plats, a meal will easily blow your budget. Terraces along Vene St. offer delicious meals at slightly more reasonable prices. A **Rimi** supermarket is at Aia 7. (☎644 38 55. Open daily 8am-10pm.) Well-stocked **Stockmann supermarket** is on the corner of Liivalaia and Tartu. (☎63 39 59. Open M-F 9am-10pm, Sa-Su 9am-9pm.) The **market,** Keldrimäe 9, is on the right as you take Lastekodu toward the bus station, and hawks a classically Eastern European assortment of excellent produce, shiny clothes, and ugly shoes. (Open M-Sa 7am-5pm, Su 7am-4pm.) **Kolmjalg,** Pikk 3, sells a decent selection of foods and is open 24hr.

▨ **Kompressor,** Rataskaevu 3 (☎646 42 10). Choose from incredible Estonian pancakes and giant portions of meat, fish, and veggie fillings (35-45EEK). If it's crowded, locals tend to share the large wooden tables with each other, so you might make some new friends, too. Open F-Sa noon-10pm, Su 11am-10pm. Cash only. ❶

▨ **Kafe Kohvicum,** Aia 13/Uus 16 (☎520 12 40). Look for an archway in the heavily graf-fitied wall on Aia; ring the bell if you're entering through Uus. To really get away from the hungry tourist hordes, relax for an afternoon in the Old Town's best-kept secret. Hidden in a courtyard, Kohvicum is an oasis of good coffee (20-30EEK), gelato (20EEK), and cakes (15-25EEK), served by charming baristas. Open daily 10am-11pm. Cash only. ❶

Eesti Maja, Lauteri 1 (☎645 52 82), at the corner with Rävala pst. This cellar kitchen serves traditional favorites like blood pudding (75EEK), sauerkraut stew (95EEK), and—for the adventurous diner with a strong stomach—*sült* (80EEK), an Estonian meat jelly of pig hooves, thighs, and beef. Entrees 45-165EEK. Open daily 11am-11pm. MC/V. ❷

Cafe Anglais, Raekoja plats 14 (☎644 21 60). Brilliant fresh sandwiches (75-80EEK) accompany views of Raekoja plats, from this spacious 2nd fl. art gallery and cafe. Spec-tacular salads 115EEK. Open daily 11am-11pm; kitchen closes 10pm. MC/V. ❷

Buongiorno, Müürivahe 17 (☎53 910 846). Signed footballs, murals of Venice, and photographs of Italians with spaghetti hanging from their mouths adorn the walls of this cellar. The pasta is perfection, and the menu will please vegetarians. The bruschetta (30EEK) delectable. An adorable resident dog is available for Lady and the Tramp moments. Open daily 10am-midnight. Entrees 75-135EEK. Cash only. ❷

Tanduur, Vene 7 (☎631 30 84). Spicy Indian fare with extensive vegetarian, lamb, and chicken menus. Sit on the terrace to enjoy your meal and people-watch along the cob-blestoned Vene. Entrees 115-225EEK. Open daily noon-11pm. MC/V. ❸

Troika, Raekoja plats 15 (☎627 62 45). Yes, the staff dress in silly poofy shirts, but this extravagant Russian restaurant dishes up true delicacies, including the always-hard-to-find stroganoff with bear meat (495EEK). The less adventurous can enjoy the outstand-ing pot roast (95EEK). Live music daily 7-10pm. Open daily 10am-11pm. MC/V. ❹

◔ SIGHTS

Tallinn's sights are concentrated in the Old Town, a well-preserved and well-restored bundle of cobblestone streets, medieval towers, and part of the original city wall. It's worth going beyond the walls to see the excellent Maarjamäe branch of the History Museum, the quiet expanse of Kadriorg Park, or the sands of Pirita Beach—and to sidestep the tourist stampedes that overwhelm the center.

LOWER TOWN (ALL-LINN). Tallinn's 14th-century **town hall** is the oldest in Europe, and contains several rooms decorated in classic medieval style. The hall features a **tower** with one of the world's tallest toilets (77m), built so that guards could relieve themselves without descending the winding, narrow steps. *(Raekoja plats. ☎645 79 00. Ask for booklet with English translations of captions. Open July-Aug. M-Sa 10am-4pm. 35EEK, students 20EEK. Tower open daily May 15-Aug. 31 11am-6pm. 25/15EEK.)* The other dominant feature of the All-linn skyline is the 123.7m tower of **St. Olaf's Church.** As you climb up, tread carefully to avoid the fate of the architect, who fell from the tower to his death. Also beware of lightning: a bolt struck the tower in 1820, knock-ing off nearly 20m and reducing it to its present height. The top offers a great view of the Old Town—so great that the KGB used it as an observation post. *(Lai 50. ☎641 22 41; www.oleviste.ee. Open daily Apr.-Oct. 10am-6pm. Church free. Tower 25EEK, students 10EEK. Services M and F 6:30pm; Su 10am, noon.)* On the south side of the Old Town is **St. Nicholas Church** (Niguliste Kirkko), Niguliste 3. The Soviets destroyed the original 13th-century Gothic building when they bombed Tallinn in 1944, but restored it years later so it could house part of the **Art Museum of Estonia** collection. Don't miss the 15th-century painting *Dance Macabre* by Bernt Notke, in the back right corner of the church. (☎631 43 27. *Open W-Su 10am-5pm; last entrance 4:30pm. 35EEK, students 20EEK. Organ concerts Sa-Su 4-4:30pm.*) The **Church of the Holy Spirit**, at the corner of Pikk and Pühavaimu, is notable for its intricate 17th-century exterior clock and its former minister, Jakob Koell, who wrote the first book in Estonian in 1525. (☎646 44 30. *Open May-Sept. M-Sa 10am-4pm; Oct.-Apr. M-Sa 10am-2pm. 10EEK, students 5EEK.*)

TOOMPEA. The **Castle Square** (Lossi plats), a cobblestoned hilltop shaded by trees, is home to the **Alexander Nevsky Cathedral**, named for the 13th-century Russian warrior who conquered much of Estonia. (*Open daily 8am-8pm. Services 9am, 6pm.*) **Toompea Castle**, the present seat of the Estonian **Parliament** (Riigikogu), also faces the square, but is closed to visitors. Directly behind it, a fluttering Estonian flag tops **Tall Hermann** (Pikk Hermann), Tallinn's tallest tower and most impressive medieval fortification. Follow Toom-Kooli north one block to get to the Lutheran Church of **Toomkirik**, Toom-Kooli 6, whose 13th-century spires tower over Toompea. As you walk in, you'll step over the tomb of the slatternly Johann Thume, who asked to be buried at the church's entrance, hoping that the steps of pious worshippers would wash away his carnal sins. (☎644 41 40. *Open Tu-Su 9am-5pm.*) To get to **Kiek in de Kök**, a 1483 tower, walk on Toompea away from Lossi plats and turn left on Komandandi tee. Its name, which means "peep in the kitchen," comes from the views it provides through the windows of neighboring houses. Inside the tower is a haunting **torture museum**. (☎644 66 86. *Open Mar.-Oct. Tu-Su 10:30am-6pm; Nov.-Feb. Tu-Su 11am-5pm. 15EEK, students 7EEK.*) Follow Toompea south just beyond the Old Town to reach **St. Charles's Church** (Kaarli Kirik), Toompuiestee 4, at the intersection with Kaarli pst. The highlight of the 19th-century limestone behemoth is Johann Köler's *Come to Me* mural, which the master painter finished in just 10 days. As you leave, look up to see the largest organ in Estonia. (☎611 91 00. *Open M-F 10am-2pm. Donations requested. Services Su 10am.*)

KADRIORG. Quiet paths, shady trees, and fountains adorn Kadriorg Park. Its jewel, ▨**Kadriorg Palace**, was designed by Niccolo Michetti, the architect of Peter-hof in St. Petersburg, as a summer palace for Tsar Peter the Great. (*Weizenbergi 37.* ☎606 64 00. *Open May-Sept. Tu-Su 10am-5pm; Oct.-Apr. W-Su 10am-5pm. 45EEK, students 35EEK.*) Its collection of 17th-century Dutch and Flemish art includes two works by Pieter Brueghel the Younger. The only Rembrandts in the Baltics are at the nearby **Mikkel Museum**; they include a 1621 self-portrait by the Dutch master. (*Weizenbergi 28.* ☎601 34 30; *www.ekm.ee. Open W-Su 11am-6pm. 15EEK, students 5EEK. Joint ticket with Kadriorg Palace 55/30EEK.*) Cross the flower garden to see the President's Palace, in a pink building. Admission is reserved for heads of state. Beyond the palace is the small cottage which houses the **Peter I (The Great) House Museum** (Peeter I Maja-muuseum). Peter stayed in this simple home before the Palace was completed, and today it houses many of his original furnishings, as well as an imprint of his extremely large hand. (*Mäekalda 2, near the New Building of the Art Museum of Estonia.* ☎601 31 36; *www.linnamuuseum.ee/peeter1maja. Open May 15-Sept. W-Su 10:30am-5:30pm. 10EEK, students 5EEK.*) To reach Kadriorg Park from the Old Town, follow Narva mnt. and veer right on Weizenbergi when it splits from Narva mnt. Trams #1 and 3 also run to Kadriorg. (*Flower garden open daily May-Aug. 9am-10pm; Sept.-Oct. 9am-9pm. Free.*) Behind the park is the Song Festival Grounds, where 20% of the country gathered in 1989 to sing the once-banned national anthem.

ROCCA-AL-MARE. This peninsula, 10km west of central Tallinn, includes a popular **Zoo** (Loomaaed), Paldiski mnt. 145, best-known for housing the endangered Bactrian red deer and wild yak. (*Take trolley #6 from Kaarli pst., at the edge of the Old Town, until the ZOO stop. The zoo is just across the street.* ☎694 33 00; *www.tallinnzoo.ee. Open daily 9am-9pm; ticket office closes 7pm. Elephant house open Tu-Sa 9am-8pm. 50EEK, students 25EEK.*) The peninsula's main attraction is the **Estonian Open Air**

Museum, a park with 68 buildings transplanted from the countryside, including the 1699 **Sutlepa Chapel.** *(Open Air Museum is a 15min. walk from the zoo: cross the shopping center parking lot and turn left on Vabaõhumuuseumi tee, which leads to the museum.* ☎ *654 91 00. Museum and chapel open May-Oct. daily 10am-6pm. Park and restaurant open daily May-Sept. 10am-8pm; Oct. 10am-4pm; Nov.-Apr. 10am-5pm. 28EEK, students 12EEK; last Tu of each month free. Tours in English Sa-Su noon. Bikes 35EEK per hr., 65EEK per 2hr.)*

⊞ MUSEUMS

▧ MUSEUM OF OCCUPATION AND OF THE FIGHT FOR FREEDOM. This eye-opening multimedia collection documents Estonia's time under Soviet and German rule, breaking the 20th century into seven distinct periods of development and decline. Artifacts, including telephone booths, household goods, a hairdresser's chair, and a piece of a spacecraft, accompany informative documentary videos dubbed in English. Soviet-era heroes have been removed to the basement, where massive memorials and sculptures sit next to the bathrooms. *(Toompea 8.* ☎ *6680 250; www.okupatsioon.ee. Open Tu-Sa 11am-6pm. 10EEK, students 5EEK.)*

ESTONIAN HISTORY MUSEUM (EESTI AJALOOMUUSEUM). Soviet archaeologists in the early 1950s tried to dispel the notion that Danes and Germans founded medieval Tallinn. Now, the museum's **Great Guild** branch restores Scandinavian warriors and Teutonic Knights to prominence. *(Pikk 17.* ☎ *641 16 30; www.eam.ee. Open M-Tu and Th-Su 10am-6pm. 10EEK, students 8EEK; last Sa of month free.)* Where it leaves off, the ▧ **Maarjamäe Loss** branch picks up. This restored palace east of the city documents modern Estonia, with jarring photos of Tallinn and Pärnu residents cheering the arrival of Nazi "liberators" in 1941. *(Pirita 56. From Kadriorg Park, follow Pirita along the bay 1km.* ☎ *601 45 99. Open W-Su 11am-6pm. 10EEK, students 8EEK; last Sa of month free.)*

TALLINN CITY MUSEUM (TALLINNA LINNAMUUSEUM). Exhibits on Tallinn characters, such as Old Thomas, the dutiful town watchman, and Johann von Uexkyll, the infamous serf-beating nobleman. *(Vene 17.* ☎ *644 65 53; www.linnamuuseum.ee. Open Mar.-Oct. M and W-Su 10:30am-5:30pm; Nov.-Feb. 11am-4:30pm. Museum 25EEK, students 10EEK. All captions in English and Estonian. Tours available in English.)*

EESTI KUNSTIMUUSEUM (ART MUSEUM OF ESTONIA). This gallery (Eesti Kunstimuuseum Ruutelkonna Hoonies) houses remarkable cityscapes of early 18th-century Tallinn and provocative sketches by Estonia's early 20th-century avant garde. Much of the collection will move to a new branch behind Kadriorg Palace, most likely by summer 2006. *(Kiriku plats 1.* ☎ *644 14 78; www.ekm.ee. Open W-Su 11am-6pm; last admission 5:30pm. 20EEK, students 5EEK.)*

TOWN PRISON MUSEUM OF PHOTOGRAPHY (RAEVANGLA-FOTOMUUSEUM). Take a peek inside this 14th-century jail to see Estonia's lengthy history of photography, which hit Tallinn just a year after Paris. Two "April Fool's Day" greeting cards are particularly quirky—combined photographs show the town gates flooded and a tower leaning off Toompea at a precarious angle. *(Raekoja plats 4/6, behind the town hall.* ☎ *644 87 67; www.linnamuuseum.ee. Open Mar.-Oct. M-Tu and Th-Su 10:30am-5pm; Nov.-Feb. M and Th-Su 11am-5pm. 10EEK, students 5EEK.)*

DOMINICAN MONASTERY MUSEUM (DOMINIIKLASTE KLOOSTRI MUUSEUM). To enter, you need to buy a copper coin (45EEK, students 30EEK), which you'll have to hammer into an amulet. Keep it, since it's a lifetime pass to this peaceful courtyard cloistered from the Old Town bustle. *(Vene 16.* ☎ *644 46 06; www.kloostri.ee. Open May 15-Sept. 23 daily 10am-6pm; in winter by appointment only.)*

ESTONIAN MARITIME MUSEUM (MEREMUUSEUM). A massive metal diving suit greets you at the entrance to this museum, which chronicles Estonia's relations with the vicious seas that surround the country. A refugee boat rowed from Hiiumaa to Sweden in 1944 is among the artifacts that illustrate the changing ways of sea transport throughout the centuries. *(Fat Margaret's Tower, Pikk 30. ☎ 641 14 08; www.meremuuseum.ee. Open W-Su 10am-6pm. 25EEK, students 10EEK.)*

🎵 🎆 ENTERTAINMENT AND FESTIVALS

Tallinn This Week, free at tourist offices, lists performances. The **Estonia Concert Hall** and the **Estonian National Opera** (Rahvusooper Estonia), both at Estonia pst. 4, hold performances of opera, ballet, musicals, and chamber music. (Concert hall ☎ 614 77 60; www.concert.ee. Box office open M-F noon-7pm, Sa noon-5pm, Su 1hr. before curtain. Tickets 30-150EEK. Opera ☎ 626 02 60; www.opera.ee. Box office open daily noon-7pm. Tickets 30-270EEK.) The **Forum Cinema** at Coca-Cola Plaza, Hobujaama 5, shows Hollywood films in English. (Tickets 50-80EEK during the day, 115EEK for evening and weekend shows.) There is a **beach** at Pirita (bus #1, 1a, 8, 34, or 38 from the post office). In early June, chefs from nearby countries face off during **Grillfest** (www.grillfest.ee). During **Old Town Days,** held the first weekend of June, the city hosts open-air concerts, fashion shows, singing, and skits. **Jaanipaev** (Midsummer's Day), June 23-24, is an pagan celebration featuring bonfires and barbecues. Celebrate the power of barley during **Beersummer** (www.ollesummer.ee), in early July. In late February, the **Student Jazz Festival** brings prodigies from all over northern Europe. In the midst of December, the international **Dark Nights Film Festival** (www.poff.ee) showcases cinematic talent.

🍺 WHERE THE STAG PARTIES DON'T GO

▒ Depeche Mode Baar, Nunne 4 (☎ 502 36 15). For those who just can't get enough Depeche Mode, the DM Baar is paradise. The red-and-black interior is outfitted with autographed posters, photographs, and album covers. A TV plays music videos and concert footage. Mixed drinks named after DM songs (35-60EEK) and cheap beer (35EEK per 0.5L) will convert even the non-fan. Open daily noon-4am. Cash only.

▒ Karja Kelder, Väike-Karja 1 (☎ 644 10 08). Look for the name above a doorway that leads to a warm, inviting cellar. Established in 1832 as a brewery, Karja Kelder claims to have the city's widest selection of beers, with over 40 on the menu. Beer 30EEK per 0.5L. Open July-Aug. M and Su 11am-midnight, Tu-Th 11am-1am, F-Sa 11am-3am; Sept.-June M-Th and Su 11am-2am, F-Sa 11am-4am. MC/V.

Beer House, Dunkri 5 (☎ 627 65 20). The only on-site microbrewery in Tallinn. Wander the 1st fl. to see the vats where the 2-week brewing process takes place, or head upstairs to the sauna disco. Live music F-Sa 10pm. House beer 30-40EEK per 0.5L. Open M-Th and Su 9am-midnight, F-Sa 9am-2am. MC/V.

Nimeta Baar (The Pub with No Name), Suur-Karja 4/6 (☎ 641 15 15). The place to meet jolly, rugby-loving expats. Beer 35EEK. Happy hour 6-7pm, 2-for-1 beers. Open M-Th and Su 11am-2am, F-Sa 11am-4am. MC/V.

Nimega Baar (The Pub with a Name), Suur-Karja 13 (☎ 620 92 99). With cushy couches and a big dance floor, Nimega is more upscale and has a more local crowd than its nameless twin. Beer 35EEK. Open M-Sa 11am-late, Su noon-2am. MC/V.

X-Baar, Sauna 1 (☎ 620 92 66). With a rainbow flag spray-painted outside, X has a relaxed atmosphere and a small dance floor. Largely gay male clientele, though straight women are known to stop by. Beer 35EEK. Open M-Th 2pm-1am, F-Sa 2pm-3am. MC/V.

COASTAL ESTONIA

East of Tallinn, vast Lahemaa National Park shelters pristine coastline, dense forests, and historic villages. To the west, exciting Pärnu and quiet Haapsalu offer beaches and mud baths and serve as a gateway to the Estonian islands.

LAHEMAA NATIONAL PARK

Founded in 1971, Lahemaa was the USSR's first national park. Today, it's one of Europe's largest, protecting numerous animals and over 838 unique plant species. **Palmse Manor** is among the best-restored estates in Lahemaa. The manor grounds include gardens, stables, a pond, and streams. The former servants' quarters now house an **Old Cars Museum.** (Kodanik Kirsi Erahobiklubi; ☎326 88 88. Manor open daily May-Sept. 10am-7pm; Oct.-Apr. 10am-3pm. 25EEK, students 15EEK. Car museum open daily May-Aug. 10am-7pm; Sept. 10am-5pm. 20/10EEK.) The stacked **famine stones,** 1km past the tourist office, were piled up by serfs picking rocks from the fields in preparation for plowing. Next to Lainela Puhkemajaad, the **Kásmús Maritime Museum,** Kásmús Merekööl 3, introduces visitors to the history of the surrounding fishing village. Ask the proprietor, Aarne Vaik, for a tour. (☎323 81 36. Open daily 9am-9pm. Free.) On the far side of the Puhkemajaad Neemetee, a path through the woods opens to a rocky beach where the **stone hill** is said to grant wishes to those who contribute a new rock to the pile. The fishing huts on the cape are part of an **open-air museum.** (Open 24hr.) As you continue around the cape and cross the river, white stripes on the trees mark a short trail through the forest and back to town. The harbor visible is **Vergi,** connected to the cape by a land bridge 2.5km farther along the road. In early July, every other year, the **Vihula Folklore Festival** summons storytellers from around the world. The biannual **Lahemaa Bagpipe Music Festival** draws bagpipers from across Lahemaa.

Near Palmse, the best bet is the **Ojaäärse Hostel ❶.** From Viitna, take the road to Palmse and turn right about 500m before the visitor center. (☎324 46 75. Singles 100EEK.) Situated a scenic 8km hike from Võsu in the village of Käsmu, **Lainela Puhkemajaad ❶,** toward the end of Neema, offers small, tidy rooms, a basketball court, tennis courts, and a sauna. (☎/fax 323 81 33. Singles 170EEK; doubles 340EEK. Campsites 40EEK per person.) In Viitna proper, the lakeside **campground ❶** is 400m past the bus stop, through the wooden arch on the right. Campsites and rooms in log cabins are available. (☎329 36 51. Campsites 20EEK per person. Doubles 180EEK.) In the wilds of Palmse Mõis, **Park Hotel Restaurant ❷** has fresh salads for 20EEK and *schnitzel* for 70EEK. (☎322 36 26. Open daily 11am-10pm.) The **tavern ❷** (☎325 86 81) in Viitna, opposite the bus stop, has dishes for 50-100EEK.

As Lahemaa is very large and public transportation is infrequent, your best bet for visiting is to rent a car in Tallinn. The most convenient base for exploring the park is **Palmse,** home to the **Lahemaa National Park Visitor Center,** which offers help in booking rooms and navigating the park. (☎329 55 55; info@lahemaa.ee. English spoken. Open daily May-Aug. 9am-7pm; Sept. 9am-5pm; Oct.-Apr. M-F 9am-5pm.) From Tallinn, take the **Rakvere bus** to **Viitna** (1hr.; 28 per day; 15-45EEK, ISIC discount). From there, catch a bus to Palmse Mõis or walk the 7km road. Call the visitor center for the bus schedule from Viitna to Palmse Mõis. As there are only four buses per week, visitors occasionally hitchhike from Viitna. *Let's Go* does not recommend hitchhiking. For direct access to the **coast** and the **Palmse Manor House,** inquire at the Tallinn station about buses to **Võsu** (3 per wk.). Rent **bikes** at the Park Hotel Restaurant (100EEK per day). **Postal Code:** 45202.

PÄRNU

In July and August, Estonians and cosmopolitan Europeans flock the beaches of Pärnu (PAER-noo; pop. 45,000), Estonia's summer capital. Music, theater, art, and film festivals throughout summer ensure that there's no shortage of fun to be had, whatever the weather. The city is also famous for its curative mud baths, which are good for rejuvenating tired muscles after a few late nights.

TRANSPORTATION. The **train station** is 3km east of the center, at Riia mnt. 116, near the corner of Riia and Raja; take bus #15 or 40 to Raeküla Rdtj (8EEK). **Trains** run to **Tallinn** (3hr.; 2 per day; 50EEK, ISIC discount). **Buses** are a better way to get to **Pärnu.** They run from the **bus station,** Ringi 3 (☎447 10 02, Eurolines 442 78 41; fax 444 17 55), to: **Haapsalu** (2½hr., 1-2 per day, 90EEK); **Kuressaare** (3¼hr., 4 per day, 140EEK); **Tallinn** (2hr., 42 per day, 55-80EEK); **Tartu** (2½hr., 21 per day, 70-100EEK); **Rīga, LAT** (3½hr., 6-8 per day, 110-150EEK). ISIC discounts are available for domestic fares. **Pärnu Takso** (☎443 92 20) and **E-Takso** (☎443 11 11) **taxis** both charge 7-8EEK per km. **City Bike** will deliver a bicycle to you anywhere in Pärnu. (☎56 60 80 90; www.citybike.ee. 120EEK per 12hr., 150EEK per day.)

ORIENTATION AND PRACTICAL INFORMATION. The **River Pärnu** neatly bisects the city. The town center stretches from **Tallinn Gate** to the bus station on **Ringi.** The main street is **Rüütli.** A short walk down **Nikolai** and **Supeluse** from the center of town leads to the **mud baths** and **Ranna pst.,** which runs along the **beach.** Be sure not to confuse the two streets **Aia** and **Aisa.** From the bus station, follow Ringi away from Pikk and hang a right on Rüütli to reach the **Tourist Info Center,** Rüütli 16, which offers **free maps,** bus timetables, and helpful advice. (☎447 30 00; www.parnu.ee. Open May 15-Sept. 15 M-F 9am-6pm, Sa 9am-4pm, Su 10am-3pm; Sept. 16-May 14 M-F 9am-5pm.) When it's closed, head to the 24hr. reception desk at **Best Western Hotell Pärnu,** Rüütli 44 (☎447 89 11; hotparnu@pergohotels.ee). Instead of turning right on Rüütli to the TIC, head left. The TIC and many hotels sell *Pärnu In Your Pocket* (25EEK). **Krediidipank** (☎447 3600), Rüütli 47, cashes **traveler's checks** for 1% commission or 25EEK. (Open M-F 9am-5pm, Sa 9am-2pm.) Rüütli is lined with 24hr. MC/V **ATMs. Cargobus,** along the bus station platforms, offers **luggage storage.** (6-25EEK per day per item, depending on size. Open M-F 8am-7:30pm, Sa 8am-1pm and 1:45-5pm, Su 9am-1pm and 1:45-5pm.) **Pärnu Hospital** is at Ristiku 1. (☎447 31 01; www.ph.ee.) **Keskraamatukogu (Central Library),** Akadeemia 3, a large, white building set back from the street, has 12 computers in a spacious reading room. Show your passport at the information desk to get a temporary pass. (☎445 57 07; www.pkr.ee. Free. Open M-F 10am-6pm, Sa 10am-5pm.) **Rüütli Internetipunkt,** Rüütli 25 (entrance through the courtyard in the yellow building), has 13 fast connections. (☎315 52. 25EEK per hr. Open M-F 10am-9pm, Sa-Su 10am-6pm.) At the west end of Rüütli, the **post office,** Akadeemia 7, has **Poste Restante** in the hall on the right. (☎447 11 11; www.prn.ee/post. Open M-F 8am-6pm, Sa 9am-3pm.) **Postal Code:** 80010.

ACCOMMODATIONS AND FOOD. Rooms at hotels and guesthouses fill quickly, so it's best to reserve as far in advance as possible. Booking even the day before can save you from being stranded upon arrival. **Tanni-Vakoma Majutusbüroo,** Hommiku 5, behind the bus station, rents **private rooms.** The office can be reached by phone year-round. (☎518 53 19; tanni@online.ee. Open May-Aug. M-F 10am-8pm, Sa 10am-3pm. From 200EEK.) To get to **Hostel Lõuna ❷,** Lõuna 2, from the bus station, walk down Ringi; turn right on Rüütli. Go 500m, then turn left on Akadeemia. It's at the end of the street on the left. Near the beach and the city center, Lõuna has comfortable rooms with clean shared baths and a large kitchen and common area. (☎443 09 43; www.hot.ee/hostellouna. Reception 24hr. Dorms 200EEK; doubles 500-800EEK; quads 1000EEK.) **Külalistemaja Delfine ④**, Supeluse 22, has cheery rooms with private baths, TVs, and phones. In the house next door, double rooms share a stylish bathroom and avocado-green kitchen. From the bus station, turn left on Ringi, left on Pühavaimu, and bear right onto Supeluse. (☎442 69 00; www.delfine.ee. Breakfast included. Reserve several months in advance. June 15-Aug. 15 singles 600EEK; doubles 890EEK; triples 1050EEK. Prices drop in low season. MC/V.) **Kalevi Pansionaat ②**, Ranna pst. 2, is literally steps from the beach. From the bus station, turn left on Ringi, left on Pühavaimu, and continue on Supeluse. Bear left at the fork and take a left onto Ranna pst. Kalevi is 350m down on the left. (☎442 57 99. Little English spoken. Basic, 2- to 3-bed dorms 250EEK; 4- to 5-bed family rooms with private bath 900EEK.)

An indoor **market** *(turg)* on the corner of Sepa and Karja sells everything from antiques to baked goods. (Open M-F 8am-6pm, Sa 8am-4pm, Su 9am-3pm.) **Georg ①**, Rüütli 43, is a cafeteria-style eatery packed with locals enjoying hot plates of fried fish and open sandwiches. (☎443 11 10. Sandwiches 6-8EEK. Open in summer M-F 7:30am-10pm, Sa-Su 9am-10pm; in winter M-F 7:30am-7:30pm, Sa-Su 9am-5pm.) **Kadri Kohvik ②**, Nikolai 12, around the corner from the TIC, serves filling dishes in a cafe environment. (☎444 53 34. Entrees 25-48EEK. Open M-F 7:30am-8pm, Sa-Su 9am-5pm.) **Trahter Postipoiss ③**, Vee 12, has authentic Russian cuisine. There is a buffet (95EEK) daily at 5pm. (☎446 48 64; www.restaurant.ee. Entrees 45-175EEK. Open M-Th and Su noon-midnight, F-Sa noon-2am. MC/V.)

⊙ SIGHTS. The 18th-century **Elizabeth's Church** (Eliisabeth Kirik), on Nikolai between Kuninga and Lõuna, was named after the Russian empress. J.H. Wulburn, the architect who planned its peacock-topped maroon spire, also designed the spire of St. Peter's Church in Rīga. Catherine the Great one-upped her predecessor with the Russian Orthodox **Catherine Church** (Ekateriina kirik), Vee 8, at the corner of Uus and Vee, a block north of Rüütli. (☎444 31 98. Open M-F 11am-6pm, Sa-Su 9am-6pm. Services Sa 8:30am, 6pm; Su 9am, 5pm.) The interior, which shimmers with icons, is even more astonishing than the imposing silver-and-green spires.

Take a stroll down **Kuninga,** named for King Gustav II of Sweden. On the east end, at the corner with Ringi, set in a pleasant public park, is the **statue of Lydia Koidula** (1843-1885), the Estonian poet who wrote the now-famous anthem, "My Fatherland is My Beloved." But it was in love that Koidula deserted her fatherland—marrying a German from Rīga and moving with him to Russia. At the opposite end of Kuninga stands the **Tallinn Gate,** a relic from the 17th-century days when walls surrounded the Swedish-controlled city. Stop by the ◪**Estonian Lithograph Center** (Eesti Litograafiakeskus), Kuninga 17, to see printmakers at work and check out the latest exhibition. The coolest postcards in the Baltics are for sale at the front desk (10EEK), and original artwork and printed t-shirts are also available. (☎55 604 631; www.hot.ee/litokeskus. Hours vary.)

A variety of sculpture, painting, and experimental work fills the **Museum of New Art,** Esplanaadi 10, also known as the **Chaplin Center** (in honor of the silent film star). Go around back to see an old Lenin statue sporting a new head with a glowing strobe light inside, and missing his right hand. (☎443 07 72; www.chaplin.ee. Open daily 9am-9pm. 15EEK, students 10EEK.) The white-sand **beach** has swings and trampolines, and a free waterslide (open June-Aug.). Women can bathe nude on the right side of the beach. **Mudravila** (☎442 5525; www.mudaravila.ee.), Ranna pst. 1, by the beach, offers mud bath treatments (head-to-toe 150EEK, localized therapy 100EEK). Add 60EEK for a medical examination beforehand.

NIGHTLIFE AND FESTIVALS. Head to the Swedish-owned **Veerev Olu** (The Rolling Beer), Uus 3a, in a courtyard behind the TIC, for live rock and folk Saturdays 9:30pm-1am. (☎534 03 149. Beer 20EEK per 0.5L. Entrees 17-35EEK. Open M-Sa 11am-1am, Su noon-1am.) You'll find live jazz (F 8 or 9pm) and "happy jazz" (vodka, pineapple juice and lemon soda; 40EEK) at **Jazz Cafe**, Ringi 11 (☎442 75 46; www.abijoon.ee). Try *Saku* (20EEK per 1L), Estonia's national brew, at **Tallinna Väravad**, Vana-Tallinna 1, atop the Tallinn Gate. If it's raining, you can sit inside the low-roofed tavern. (☎444 50 73. Open daily 11am-11pm.) Pärnu's most famous disco is **Sunset Club**, Ranna pst. 3. By the beach, this stylish club offers chill-out couches and a busy dance floor. (☎443 06 70. Cover M-Th and Su after midnight 50EEK, F-Sa 100EEK. Open in summer M-Th and Su 10pm-4am, F-Sa 10pm-6am.)

The **Estonian Country Dance Festival** takes place in mid-June at Sassi Horse Farm, near Pärnu. It ends in with a line dance that stretches the length of Rüütli (☎445 00 70; www.estonianlinedance.com). The longest day of the year, June 21, kicks off festival season with beachside celebrations. In late May and early June, song takes over the city for the **International Opera Museum Festival** (www.xxiso.ee). The **Pärnu David Oistrakh Festival**, from late June to early July, draws international musicians and conductors. Most concerts take place at the town hall and Elizabeth Church (☎446 65 40; www.oistfest.ee). The **International Film Festival**, in early July, has documentaries and anthropological films (☎443 07 72; www.chaplin.ee). In mid-July, the **Watergate Festival**, popular throughout Estonia, brings every watersport imaginable to Pärnu. (☎449 19 66; www.watergate.ee. 40-90EEK per day; 340EEK for entire festival, including admission to Sunset Club.)

DAYTRIP FROM PÄRNU: KIHNU ISLAND. The tiny rural island of **Kihnu** (pop. 540) offers a respite from the seaside antics of Pärnu. Still covered in dense woodland and ringed by deserted beaches, the island was first settled in 1518 and has since passed through Danish, Polish, Russian, and Swedish rule. Kihnu, where many women still wear folk dress and most men work in the fishing industry, offers a glimpse of traditional Estonian ways of life.

Although the island is small enough to see on foot, bicycling is the most enjoyable way to explore its trails and villages. It's easiest to bring a bicycle from the mainland, but you can arrange to pick one up at the ferry port from Kihnurand (☎446 99 24). The **tourist agency** organizes farmstays and camping on the island. When you arrive, turn right and follow the dirt paths through the forest to the beach, or continue inland from the ferry port along the main road. After 2km, you will reach an intersection and signpost. Continue ahead to reach the **post office** (open M-F noon-3pm) and **shop** (open M-F 9:30am-9pm, Sa-Su 9:30am-6pm). Turn left to see the **Kihnu Museum** (Kihnu Koduloomuuseum), housed in an old schoolhouse. Exhibits display photographs of island settlements from the mid-20th century, as well as artwork and artifacts relating to Kihnu history. (☎446 99 83. Open daily 10:30am-4pm. 15EEK, students 6EEK.) Across from the museum, a 16th-century church is locked behind an impressively elaborate iron-and-stone gate. Behind the church, hidden amongst the trees, is a graveyard of crosses, where the island's legendary hero, Kihnu Jõnn, is buried.

Ferries to the island run regularly during summer from Pärnu harbor, Kalda 2; follow Vee toward the river and turn left into the parking lot and harbor just before the bridge. (Ferries run May 16-Oct. 2 M and Th-Sa 9:15am, 6:15pm; Su 6:15pm. Ferries from Kihnu return to Pärnu M and Th-Sa 6:30am, 3:30pm; Su 3:30pm. 2½hr.; 70EEK, bikes 25EEK.) **Munalaid** (☎44 31 069), 50km from Pärnu, also runs ferries. (May 16-Oct. 2 M-Th 9am, 6pm; F 2, 6pm; Sa 9am; Su 3, 6pm. Ferries return from Kihnu M-F 7am, 4:15pm; Sa 7am; Su 2, 4:15pm. 50min.; 30EEK, bikes 10EEK.

HAAPSALU

Haapsalu (HAHP-sah-lu; pop. 12,000) is the gateway to the Estonian islands. Historically, its location was too strategic for its own good: the Soviets planted a military base there and cut the city off from the outside world. Today, it's a bright and lively seaside town, providing an invigorating getaway from the bustle of Tallinn.

🚆🚌 TRANSPORTATION AND PRACTICAL INFORMATION. The **bus station**, Raudtee 2, has a 216m long platform—and was once the train station. (☎473 47 91. Ticket office open daily 5am-1pm and 2-7pm.) Buses go to **Kärdla** (3hr., 3 per day, 80EEK), **Pärnu** (2-3hr., 2 per day, 75EEK), and **Tallinn** (1½-2hr., 24 per day, 40-65EEK). ISIC discounts are available. **Store luggage** with the people behind the ticket window (5-10EEK per day), but remember that they close for lunch. **Taxis** (☎473 35 00) charge 6EEK per kilometer. To reach the center from the bus station, walk down Jaama and turn left on Posti; you'll see a graveyard on your left. Rent **bikes** at **Rattad Vabatog**, Karja 22. (☎472 98 46. 100EEK per day. Open M-F 10am-6pm, Sa 10am-3pm.) At the **Tourist Information Center,** Posti 37, the friendly staff provide **maps** and city directories, and book rooms in Haapsalu and on the islands. (☎473 32 48; www.haapsalu.ee. English spoken. Open May 15-Sept. 15 M-F 9am-6pm, Sa-Su 10am-3pm; Sept. 16-May 14 M-F 9am-5pm. 20EEK fee.) A branch is outside the castle entrance. (Open daily 10am-6pm.) Free **Internet** is at the **Culture Center** (Kultuurikeskus), Posti 3. (Open M-F 10am-7pm, Sa 10am-3pm.) **Exchange currency** at **Hansapank**, Posti 41, which also has a 24hr. **ATM.** (☎472 02 00. Open M-F 9am-6pm, Sa 9am-2pm.) The **post office**, Nurme 2, is around the corner from the TIC. (☎472 04 00. Open M-F 7:30am-6pm, Sa 9am-3pm.) **Postal Code:** 50901.

🏠🍴 ACCOMMODATIONS AND FOOD. Ungru Majutus ❶, Ungru 3, boasts cozy private rooms. Cross the tracks behind the bus station and take a left on Kiltsi. Turn right on Ungru tee and continue 1.5km. (☎473 58 43; ungrukodu@hot.ee. Open May-Oct. Call in advance. Rooms 200EEK per person. Cash only.) Take Lahe toward Bergfeldt, then turn right on Wiedemanni to reach the **Sport Hostel ❶**, Wiedemanni 15, which offers spartan private rooms with shared baths and a common kitchen. (☎472 50 63 or 473 51 40; haapsalu@spordibaasid.ee. Reception M-F noon-8pm. Reserve ahead for weekends. Rooms 200EEK. Cash only.) **Endla Hostel ❶**, Endla 5, is conveniently located on a residential street between the bus station and the Old Town. From the traffic circle on Jaama, take a left on Jüriöö, which runs into Endla. Clean, basic doubles, triples, and quads share a common kitchen and bathrooms. (☎473 79 99. Reception daily 1-6pm.; call if arriving outside of those hours. Doubles 360EEK; triples 500EEK; quads 600EEK. Cash only.)

Overlooking the south wall of the castle, **Restoran Central ❹**, Karja 21, serves pork fillet with baked apple (89EEK), among other medieval dishes. (☎473 55 95; centraal@hot.ee. Entrees 35-140EEK. Open M-Th and Su noon-11pm, F-Sa noon-2am. MC/V.) **Pizza Grande ❷**, Karja 6, across from the castle, flips delectable pizzas (35-109EEK) and offers free delivery. (☎473 72 00. Open daily 11am-11pm.) **Lemmik**, Jaama 11, has an array of groceries and household goods. (Open daily 8am-10pm.)

🏛🎭 SIGHTS AND FESTIVALS. At the end of the bus station platform is the fantastic ■**Estonian Railway Museum,** which pays tribute to railway history with old conductor uniforms and equipment, photographs of Estonian train stations, and video footage of the last passenger voyage to Haapsalu's train station (Sept. 22, 1995). You can sit in the driver's seat of the vintage carriage on the tracks out back—but don't touch the controls! (☎473 45 74; www.jaam.ee. Open W-Su 10am-6pm. 15EEK, students 10EEK.) The well-preserved 13th-century **Episcopal Castle** (Piiskopilinnus) is in the center of town. Wander the castle courtyards free of charge; inside you'll find a tiny **museum** and the **Dome Church**. (☎473 70 76. Open May 15-Sept. 15 Tu-Su 10am-6pm. 15EEK, students 5EEK. In low season, call ☎473 5516 or email kk@haapsalu.ee to arrange a visit.) On the full moon of February and August, watch for the ghostly White Lady of Haapsalu, who was imprisoned in the castle. **White Lady Days** festivities in August include fencing tournaments and concerts. **Africa Beach**, northeast of the castle, features views of Haapsalu Bay. The best swimming is on the western edge of town at **Paralepa Beach**. Cross the train tracks and follow the signposts along the concrete path. You'll pass a skateboard park on your left; turn right at the fork to reach the lovely sand. Dance until sunrise at **Africa**, Tallinna mnt. 1/Posti 43, in the shopping center. Its restaurant is open daily 11am-midnight; the space next door is Haapsalu's best disco. (☎479 05 07. Cover 100EEK. Open F-Sa 10pm-4am.) The party starts early at **Gambrino,** Kalda 1, at the corner with Posti. (Happy hour noon-2pm. A. Le Coq 20-30EEK per 1L.)

Early August brings the **Augustibluus Blues Festival,** Estonia's only blues festival (☎56 489 01 66; www.haapsalu.ee/augustibluus). Since blues is a uniquely American musical form, the organizers of Augustibluus feature American cars at the same time in the **American Beauty Automobile Festival. The Only Girls in Jazz** festival brings female jazz musicians to Haapsalu, also early in August (☎50 977 95; www.kuursaal.ee). In mid-July, the **String Music Festival** (☎50 324 68) spotlights Pyotr Tchaikovsky, who spent a summer in Haapsalu in 1867. The TIC has free pamphlets describing summer festivities, including locations and ticket prices.

ESTONIAN ISLANDS

Many Estonians say the country's islands offer a glimpse of the way life used to be, with farms dotting their green and forested terrain. Afraid the more than 1500 islands would become an escape route out of the USSR, the Soviets isolated the region, shielding it from outside influence. Today, the islands remain naturally beautiful, and rural life is interspersed with just a few large towns. The coastal areas are a top holiday destination for vacationing foreigners and Estonians.

SAAREMAA

Meteorite craters, bubbling springs, rugged coasts, and formidable cliffs attest to the natural beauty of Saaremaa (SAH-reh-mah; pop. 38,760), Estonia's largest and most popular island. Come summer, Estonians from the mainland arrive in droves to party beachside and enjoy Saaremaa's pristine shores. The interior of the island is mostly farmland and green, dense woods. As distances are long and buses infrequent, the best way to see the entire island is to rent a car in Kuressaare. Ambitious travelers can take in all the major sights by bike; be sure to bring rain gear. Though you'll log 100-150km of cycling each day, Saaremaa's terrain is mostly flat.

KURESSAARE

Kuressaare (KOO-rehs-sah-re; pop. 15,820), on Saaremaa's southern coast, is the island's largest town. The local accent and folklore distinguish it from the mainland, although tourists seem to outnumber locals during the summer months.

▣ TRANSPORTATION. Buses run from **Tallinn** via **Haapsalu** (4-6hr., 9-11 per day, 100-160EEK) and from **Tartu** via **Pärnu** (6hr., 3-5 per day, 180-194EEK). **Flights** depart from **Tallinn** to **Kuressaare** (45min., 1-2 per day, 160-385EEK). See www.avies.ee for info. **Ferries** from the northern island of Hiiumaa depart from **Sõru** to **Triigi,** on Saaremaa. (Daily 7, 10am, 2, 6:30pm; F, Su also 9:30pm. 20EEK, students 10EEK, bikes 15EEK, cars 75EEK.) It's a 3km walk from Triigi

Estonian Islands

Tahkuna Lighthouse

Tahkuna
Lehtma

Hill of Crosses
Kärdla

Vormsi

Saxby
Hullo
Sviby

Haapsalu

Kõrgessaare
Reigi

Kalana
Köpu
Luidja
Hiiumaa

Suuremõisa
Rohuküla

Käina

Heltermaa

Baltic Sea

Orjaku
Kassari

Sääretirp

Väinameri

Sõru
Emmaste

Kassari Bay

Soela väin

Muhu

Tagaranna
Panga
Triigi
Koguva
Liiva

Leisi
Nautse
Kuivastu
Virtsu

Orissaare
Eemu Tuulik
Pädaste

Undva
Angla
Põide
Tornimäe

Mustjala
Saaremaa
Käo
Körkvere

Odalätsi
Springs
Pidula
Eikla

Kihelkonna
Karujärve
Lake
Aste
Kaali
Valjala

Viki
Kärla

Arandi
Köljala

Suurlaht
Lake

Karala
Kõrkküla
Mullutu
Lake
Kuressaare

Mändjala
Nasva

Järve
Tehumardi
Salme

Kaugatuma
Anseküla
Abruka

Gulf of Rīga

Jämaja
Ohessaare
Iide

Möntu

Sõrve Säär
TO VENTSPILS, LAT

0 10 kilometers
0 10 miles

to **Leisi,** where you can catch one of four buses daily to Kuressaare. You can also call the **bus station** (☎453 14 76) in advance to be picked up at the Triigi ferry terminal and taken south to Kuressaare. Ferries leave Triigi for Sõru (daily 8:30, 11:30am, 3:30, 8pm; F and Su also 11pm). The 2pm bus from Kuressaare heads north to catch the 3:30pm Triigi ferry, transporting passengers to Sõru. Ferries from Saaremaa head to the mainland, making the short trip from Kuivastu to Virtsu almost hourly during the summer. (30EEK, cars 45EEK, bikes 15EEK.) If you're headed back to **Tallinn,** book your bus ticket one day in advance. If you're traveling by car and headed east to the mainland, you must reserve a spot on the ferry in advance by contacting **AS Saaremaa Laevakompanii** (☎452 44 44; www.laevakompanii.ee); if you're traveling between the islands, contact the **Sõru booking office** (☎469 52 05; open daily 8am-1pm and 4-7pm). **Taxis** run from the town hall, the bus station, and Smuuli pst. (☎533 33. 6-

8EEK per km.) The cheapest **car rental** rates are at **Metra**, Aia 25, behind the hospital. (☎453 93 61; www.metra.ee. Open daily 8am-6pm. From 400EEK per day. MC/V.) Call at least one week in advance. Rent **bikes** from **Bivarix**, Tallinna 26. Call in advance, or show up early, as they sometimes sell out. Helmets (25EEK) are available upon request. (☎455 71 18; bivarix@bivarix.ee. 150EEK for the 1st day, 125EEK per day thereafter. Open M-F 10am-6pm, Sa 10am-2pm. MC/V.)

⬛🔃 ORIENTATION AND PRACTICAL INFORMATION. The town is centered on narrow **Raekoja pl.** (Town Hall Square). The **Tourist Information Center (TIC)**, Tallinna 2, inside the town hall, offers car rental advice, updated ferry and bus schedules, and **free maps**. Those planning to travel around the region should buy a detailed map (45 EEK) of Saaremaa. (☎453 31 20; www.visitestonia.com. Open May-Sept. 15 M-F 9am-7pm, Sa 9am-5pm, Su 10am-3pm; Sept. 16-Apr. M-F 9am-5pm.) The island's website, www.saaremaa.ee, is invaluable for information about transportation, accommodation, things to do, and a brief history of the region. **Eesti Ühispank**, Kauba 2, **exchanges currency**, cashes **traveler's checks,** and gives MC/V **cash advances.** (☎452 15 00; fax 452 15 33. Open M-Sa 9am-6pm, Su 9am-2pm.) In Kuressaare's center, 24hr. **ATMs** abound. **Store luggage** outside the bus station. (6-10EEK per day. Open M-F 7:15am-2pm and 2:30-8pm, Sa 7:15am-2pm and 2:30-6pm.) Free **Internet** is available at the **library,** Tallinna 8. Go upstairs and reserve a computer for a block of 1hr., or grab one of two terminals designated for 15min. use only. (Open July-Aug. M-F 11am-7pm; Sept.-June M-F 10am-7pm, Sa 10am-4pm.) The **post office,** Torni 1, is on the corner of Komandandi. (☎452 40 80. Open M-F 8am-6pm, Sa 8:30am-3pm.) **Postal Code:** 93801.

🔃🖸 ACCOMMODATIONS AND FOOD. The staff at the **TIC** make same-day bookings at local B&Bs free of charge. Family-run **🖾Transvaali 28 B&B ❷**, Transvaali 28, is a great deal. From the bus station, cross Pihtla tee and continue along Transvaali, a potholed but paved residential road, for three blocks. All three bright, cozy rooms (300EEK) include private bath, TV, and breakfast. (☎453 33 34; www.saaremaa.ee/transvaali28. Cash only.) From the station, follow Põhja past Tallinna, turn left on Hariduse, and turn right on Kingu to reach **SUG Hostel ❶**, Kingu 6. A dorm during the academic year, Sug offers clean, basic rooms with Internet, fitness facilities, and smelly bathrooms. (☎455 43 88. Open June-Aug. Singles 210-250EEK; doubles 150-175EEK; quads 120-145EEK. 15% discount M-W and Su. MC/V.) Follow Tallinna toward the TIC and turn right on Torni to reach **Arabella ❸**, Torni 12. The unadvertised economy rooms are virtually identical to the renovated rooms, and cost as much as 200EEK less. All rooms have phones, private bath, and breakfast included. (☎455 58 85; www.hot.ee/arabell. Economy rooms: singles 350EEK; doubles 590EEK; triples 790EEK. Discounts for 2-night stays. Rates drop 20% after Sept. 1.)

   🖾Pannkoogikohvik ❶, Kohtu 1, serves hearty "hot pots" (28-35EEK) of rice, pasta, or potatoes, mixed with your choice of meat, fish, or vegetables. Huge and delicious thin-crust pizzas with unique toppings (35-68EEK) are also available. (☎453 35 75. Open M-Th 8:15am-midnight, F-Sa 8:15am-2am, Su 9:15am-midnight. MC/V.) **🖾John Bull Pub ❷**, Lossipark 4, across the moat from the castle, may be the only place that serves *Saku* (30EEK per 0.5L) in a school bus. Sit outside for a spectacular view of the castle and grounds. (☎453 99 88. Open daily 11am-last customer.) **Öuemaja ❶**, Uus 20A, off Raekoja, dishes out generous portions of goulash, sauerkraut, and pancakes with minced meat. (☎453 34 23. Entrees 20-68EEK. Open M-W 10am-9pm, Th-Sa 10am-10pm, Su noon-7pm. Cash only.) **Vanalinna ❺**, Kauba 8, serves fish (99-130EEK) and steak with a number of different sauces. (☎/fax 553 09. Open daily noon-10pm. MC/V.) A small **market** is hidden among buildings between Kohtu and Torni, across from

ESTONIA

the TIC. Vegetables and homemade honey are sold at some tables, while handicrafts and knitted sweaters take up most of the space. (Open M-Sa 8am-3pm.) **Raekeskus,** Raekoja 10, just behind the TIC, is a huge shopping center with a supermarket. (Open daily 9am-10pm. MC/V.)

🄖 🎏 **SIGHTS AND FESTIVALS.** Follow Tallina and merge onto Lossi to reach the massive, 13th-century ⬛**Bishopric Castle** (Piiskopilinnus). Legend has it that when the Bishop of Saare-Lääne served as judge at the castle, convicts were thrown to a pack of hungry lions. You can hear the lions roar if you climb up the watchtower. The eclectic **Saaremaa Museum** inside the castle shows medieval weaponry, stuffed swans, and local contemporary art. At the end of the exhibits, don't miss the stairs that lead to the defense gallery, where the castle roof opens onto a spectacular view of the town and coast. (☎455 63 07. Open May-Aug. daily 10am-7pm, last admission 6pm; Sept.-Apr. W-Su 11am-6pm. Admission 30EEK, students 15EEK; with 2hr. audio tour in English, Estonian, Finnish, or Russian 60EEK.) For a complete medieval experience, test your **archery** skills outside. (Archery daily 10am-5pm. 4 arrows 15EEK, 15min. 60EEK.) Inside the 1670 **town hall** (*raekoja*), a gallery presents rotating exhibits of Estonian artwork, and the 2nd floor has a 17th-century ceiling painting. The biblical painting, whose creator remains anonymous, was discovered in an old house in Kuressaare after WWII. (☎443 32 66. Open Tu-F 10am-5pm, Sa 10am-3pm.) Kuressaare's most popular **beach** is directly behind the castle, complete with beach volleyball nets. On weekends in July, there's **live music** in the park around the castle. (Brass band Sa, orchestra Su. Shows 6pm.) In late July, **Õlletoober,** a beer festival, peps up Leisi, on the northern coast of Saaremaa, while an **Opera Festival** takes over Kuressaare. At the end of June and beginning of July is the **Saaremaa Waltz Festival,** which features Finnish-style dancing and a deluge of tourists from Helsinki.

WEST SAAREMAA

Follow Rte. 78 from Kuressaare 30km toward **Kihelkonna** to reach the **Mikhli Farm Museum,** where you can climb inside a working windmill, which spins only on very gusty days. If you're lucky, the blacksmith will teach you how to make horseshoes. (☎454 66 13. Open daily May-Sept. 10am-6pm. 15EEK, students 10EEK.) One kilometer down the road, hang a left at the signpost to reach the 13th-century **Kihelkonna Church.** Although there's a sign indicating that visitors can't enter the late 19th-century tower, an attendant may let you climb to the top as long as you pledge not to ring the bell. (☎45 46558. Open daily 10am-5pm.) Backtrack along Rte. 102, crossing Rte. 78, and continue 8km along a bumpy dirt path to reach **Pidula Fish Farm** (Pidula Veskitiigi Forellipüük) ❸, where the pond is swarming with trout. Cast a line, reel in your catch, and pay 100EEK per kilogram. They'll gut (extra 5EEK), salt (15EEK), and grill (40EEK) for you as well. You can also **rent your own island** ❷, in the center of the pond, where there's a one-room cabin. (☎45 46513; www.pidulakalakasvatus.ee. No running water. Reserve in advance. 350EEK per night.) It's another 7km to Rte. 101, where you'll hang a left toward **Mustjala.** The town **church,** 2km down the road, is a popular concert venue. Next door is a grocer, **Mustjala Kauplus.** (Open daily 9am-8pm. MC/V.) Just down the hill is a small art gallery and cafe, **Musta Jala Galerii.** Stop in for tea or coffee (15EEK) and home-baked pie (10EEK per slice). The road becomes unpaved; continue toward **Ninase** (6km), where a **windmill** decorated as a peasant greets you. Head straight to the fishing village of **Tagaranna,** which offers views of the **Panga cliffs** on your right. This infamous 16th-century child sacrifice site has been immortalized on the back of the 100EEK note. From Tagaranna, it's 40km back to Kuressaare.

SOUTHWEST SAAREMAA

Fifty kilometers from Kuressaare down the narrow **Sõrve Peninsula,** Southwest Saaremaa's southernmost tip affords glimpses of Latvia, 25km south across the Baltic. Riding out of Kuressaare, you'll pass a string of sandy **beaches** 8-12km out of town; you won't find a private place to bathe in the sun, however, as locals line the shores on summer weekends. At Tehumardi (17km from Kuressaare), a giant concrete sword and rows of **memorials** mark the location of a 1944 WWII battle. Your last chance to stock up on bottled water and snacks is 4km farther at **Salme Kauplus** (open daily 8am-10pm), which also has a 24hr. MC/V **ATM** outside. After another 15km, the road is paved only sporadically. Campsites are available throughout the peninsula. Ask at the TIC for more information before leaving Kuressaare.

MUHU

You can reach Muhu Island from the mainland via the **Virtsu-Kuivastu ferry** route (30min.; 10-12 per day; 35EEK, students 10EEK; cars 55-80EEK; bikes 15EEK); motorists should reserve a spot with the Kuressaare booking office in advance (☎452 44 44). **Buses** run frequently from **Kuressaare** to Muhu. There are no bike rental agencies on Muhu—you have to rent either on the mainland or on Saaremaa. It's an ambitious but manageable 55km ride from Kuressaare to Väikese Väine Tamm, the 1896 causeway that connects Saaremaa to Muhu. After you cross, watch for **Eeme Tuulik,** a windmill. (Open W-Su 10am-6pm. 5EEK, students 3EEK.) Buy ⬛**fresh bread** (23EEK) made from flour ground here. Past the windmill, go left toward Nautse; in 700m, you'll reach the Laasu **ostrich farm** (☎452 81 48; www.jaanalind.ee). Here you can buy a giant egg (300EEK), which can be cracked open only with a drill or a hatchet. About 1km down the dirt path, turn left on the paved road to **Koguva** (4km), a well-preserved 19th-century fishing village and open-air museum. (Open daily in summer 10am-7pm; in winter 10am-5pm.)

Vanatoa Tunsmitalu ❷ offers bright rooms in a stone longhouse with a shared bath/sauna. (Breakfast included. 275EEK per person; tent space with shower 40EEK.) The adjacent **restaurant ❹** (☎488 84) serves *solyanka* (40EEK), a thick Russian soup, and oven-baked eel in tartar sauce (180EEK). There's **bus** service (2 per day) here from Kuressaare and Kuivastu. It's 6km back to Rte. 10, where you'll turn left toward Liiva; on your right after 5km, you'll see the white-walled 13th-century **Muhu Katariina Church.** Portions of the early-Gothic church's 13th-century murals are still visible through the layers of whitewash with which they were covered during the Reformation. The trapezoidal tombstones are from the pagans who took refuge here when mainland Estonia was converted to Roman Catholicism. (Open daily 10am-6pm.) Next to the church, **Aki Kõrts ❶** offers tiny, windowless cabins, a shared bath, and a common kitchen. (☎459 81 04. Laundry 25EEK. Cabins: 2-person 250EEK, 4-person 500EEK. Tent space 50EEK.) Just down the road on your left, you'll find the well-stocked supermarket **Liiva Pood** (open daily 8am-10pm), with a 24hr. MC/V **ATM.** It's 65km back to Kuressaare; after 49km, you'll see a well-signed turn-off on the left to the Kaali meteorite **crater field** (Kaali meteoriidikraatrite rühm). The main crater, with a diameter of 110m, was created about 4000 years ago by a massive, 1000-ton meteor. A tranquil green pond now fills the impact mark. A **visitors' center** at the site houses a geological museum with rock core samples taken from all over the island, and showcases a piece of iron meteorite that fell in Russia on February 12, 1947. (☎459 11 84; www.kaali.kylastuskeskus.ee. Open May 1-Oct. 1 daily 9am-8pm.)

ESTONIA

HIIUMAA

By restricting access to the island of Hiiumaa (HEE-you-ma; pop. 11,497) for 50 years, the Soviets unwittingly preserved many rare plant and animal species, and the island's traditional way of life. Hiiumaa remains the most forested county in Estonia. While you travel around the island, try to imagine what might be lurking in the trees—locals still speak of the ghosts, giants, and devils of ancient legends.

More than two-thirds of all the plant species native to Estonia exist only on Hiiumaa. Due to this biodiversity, much of the island now belongs to the **West Estonian Islands Biosphere Reserve.** Hiking and camping are permitted and encouraged; just be sure to pick up info at the tourist office about off-limits regions. Motor vehicles are not allowed within 20m of the seashore, and campfires and smoking are prohibited in some areas due to dry conditions.

KÄRDLA

The Swedish settlers who stumbled across this sleepy spot on Hiiumaa's north coast named it "Kärrdal," meaning "lovely valley." Home to many more creeks and trees than houses, Kärdla (pop. 4118) is hardly an urban center, but remains the capital of the island and a popular stop for tourists.

☎❼ TRANSPORTATION AND PRACTICAL INFORMATION. Tiit Reisid, the tourist agency at Kärdla's **bus station,** Sadama 13, will help you navigate Hiiumaa's horrendous public transit system. (☎463 20 77; hiiumaa@tiitreisid.ee. Open M-F 7am-7pm; Sa-Su 7-9am, 11am-3pm, and 4-7pm.) From Kärla, **buses** run west to **Kõrgessaare** and **Kõpu** (2-3 per day; 15-30EEK) and south to **Käina** (3-4 per day, 14EEK). A **ferry** runs from Hiiumaa's southern town of **Sõru** to **Trilgi** on Saaremaa (1hr.; 20EEK, students 10EEK, bikes 15EEK, cars 70EEK). Bus fare to Kärdla from **Tallinn** (4½hr., 110EEK) includes a **ferry ticket** from Rohükla (on the mainland) to **Heltermaa,** Hiiumaa's easternmost port. For a **taxi,** call ☎463 14 47.

The island's **Tourist Information Center,** Hiiu 1, in **Keskväljak,** the main square, sells **maps** (5-40EEK) and the handy ⬛**Lighthouse Tour** guide (25EEK), available in English. (☎462 22 32; www.hiiumaa.ee. Open May-Sept. M-F 9am-6pm, Sa-Su 10am-3pm; Oct.-Apr. M-F 10am-4pm.) **Eesti Ühispank,** Keskväljak 7, **exchanges currency,** cashes **traveler's checks,** and has an **ATM.** (☎463 20 40. Open M-F 9am-4pm.) Rent **bikes** from **Nõmme Puhkemaja,** Nõmme 30. (☎463 13 38. 100EEK per day.) Arrive early or call the day before to reserve a bike at **Kerttu Sport,** Sadama 15, across the bridge past the bus station. (☎463 21 30; fax 463 20 76. 100EEK per day, 50EEK if returned before 6pm the day of rental. Open M-F 10am-6pm, Sa 10am-3pm.) The **pharmacy, Keskväljaku Apteek,** Põllu 1, is just off the main square. (☎463 21 37. Open M-F 9am-6pm, Sa 10am-2pm. MC/V.) Free **Internet** is available at the **cultural center,** Rookopli 18, but you must reserve in advance. (☎463 21 82. Open M-F noon-6pm, Su 10am-1pm.) The **post office,** Keskväljak 3, is on the main square. (☎463 20 13. Open M-F 8am-5:30pm, Sa 8:30am-1pm.) **Postal Code:** 92412.

☎❑ ACCOMMODATIONS AND FOOD. Eesti Posti Hostel ❷, Posti 13, 5min. from the town center and close to the beach, has comfortable private rooms, clean shared baths, a large kitchen, and a common room. Follow Sadama over the stream from the bus station and turn right on Posti. (☎533 118 60. Call ahead. Rooms May-Sept. 200EEK; Oct.-Apr. 150EEK. Cash only.) Every room at adorable **Padu Hotel ❸,** Heltermaa 22, has a balcony, private bath, TV, phone, and Internet. It's a short walk from Kärdla's main crossroads. Head toward Heltermaa and you'll see the hotel on the right. By bus, ask the driver to let you off at the Padu stop and backtrack 100m. (☎46 330 37; www.paduhotel.ee. Breakfast included. Reserve ahead. Singles 450EEK; doubles 650EEK; apartment with kitchen 750EEK, with sauna 900EEK. Prices drop 100EEK Sept.-Apr. MC/V.) The bubbly, English-speaking owner of **Nõmme Puhkemaja ❷**, Nõmme 30, offers one single (200EEK) and two doubles (400EEK) in a cozy cottage with a shared bath, kitchen, and common room. From the main crossroads, head toward Kõrgessaare for 300m, turn left on Metsa and right on Nõmme. (☎463 13 38; nommepm@hot.ee. Call ahead.)

If you're at the beach, try **Rannapaargu ❷**, Lubjaahja 3, a spacious dining room where you can enjoy drinks or full meals. (☎463 20 53. Entrees 35-90EEK. Open M-Sa noon-11pm, Su noon-9pm. MC/V.) **Arteesia Kohvik ❶**, Keskväljak 5, has generous portions of meat and seafood. (☎463 21 73. Entrees 30-65EEK. Open M-Th 9am-11pm, F-Sa 9am-midnight, Su 11am-10pm.) It's above the small grocer **Toidukauplus.** (Open daily 9am-11pm.) Toidukauplus and **Konsum**, Keskväljak 1 (open daily 9am-10pm; MC/V), stock the unskimmed Hiiumaa yogurt ▨**Anno** (7EEK per 500g).

◨ SIGHTS. Rannapark, at the end of Lubjaahju, is a shallow **beach** with walking trails and a 14-hole miniature golf course. (English descriptions. Open 10am-10pm. 10EEK, students 5EEK. Golf 20EEK.) Follow Rookopoli to the main crossroads to see a **memorial** to the Soviet soldiers who defeated the Germans in WWII. Nicknamed "Kivi Jüri" by the locals, it is jokingly called the last Russian soldier remaining on Hiiumaa. Turn left toward Heltermaa and, after 3km, bear left toward the airport to reach **Paluküla Church.** Continue along the road until you reach a triangular intersection; the church is in the trees on your right. Built in 1820, it was a landmark for sailors—and later target practice for Soviet soldiers. You'll see hundreds of rusty bullet shells scattered on the ground. What you can't see is that the church is built on the rim of a Paleozoic meteorite crater. The crater was discovered in the early 1970s; a signpost in the church yard describes the unique geology of the area and maps the various impact craters on Hiiumaa island.

▧ BIKING TO KÕPU. Heading west out of Kärdla toward Kõrgessaare, you encounter the spooky **Hill of Crosses** (Ristimägi) after about 6km. The crosses, which seem to emerge from the surrounding forest, commemorate the Hiiumaa Swedes who were deported to Ukraine by Catherine the Great in 1781. However, local folklore has it that the crosses are a result of two wedding parties who met on this spot but fought because the road was too narrow for both to pass. The bride of one couple and the groom of the other were killed in the squabble, but the families made the best of it and married the remaining bride and groom to each other. Among the crosses you will notice two millstones. This memorial, meant to commemorate the 210th anniversary of the deportation of the Swedes, was placed on August 20, 1991—the day that Estonia declared independence from the USSR.

About 2km past the Hill of Crosses, a right turn leads to the cast-iron **Tahkuna Lighthouse** (11km from the turn-off), built in Paris in 1874. The road is unpaved after 4km. The lighthouse consistently failed to warn ships about the coast's shallow waters, but no one seemed to mind, since salvaging loot and rescuing passengers was quite profitable. Before you reach the lighthouse, you'll see the **Tahkuna Defense Structures,** remnants of the gun pits and ammo bunkers built by locals and Soviet soldiers during WWII. Just past the lighthouse is the **Tahkuna Kivilaburint** (Tahkuna Labyrinth), built by the Hiiumaa Royal Association of Temperate Bee-Lovers in 1997. The association hoped to revive the tradition of labyrinth building and exploration, and here they recreated a copy of an old maze from the Kootsaare peninsula. Legend has it that mariners who landed on Hiiumaa because of bad weather would enter the labyrinth, and by the time they emerged, the weather would have improved enough to complete their voyage. Near the lighthouse is a **bell** memorializing the children lost in the 1994 sinking of the ocean liner *Estonia*.

On the way back to the main road, detour to the **Mihkli Farm Museum**, off the lighthouse road, on a plot of land that's been cultivated since 1564. The museum has been popular since 2001, when it hosted the television show *Farm*, in which contestants from all over the Baltics had to live in 200-year-old farm conditions. (☎463 20 91. Open May 15-Sept. 15 daily 10am-6pm. 10EEK, students 5EEK.)

Go back to the main road and turn right, heading toward Kõrgessaare. Down 7km, you'll see the red roof of **Reigi Church**, built between 1800 and 1802 by Count Ungern Sternberg in memory of his son, Gustav Dietrich Otto. The nobleman scolded his son for accruing massive gambling debts, leading Gustav to commit suicide soon after. Inside are a few impressive paintings and reliefs on otherwise spare white walls. After a few kilometers, turn right into Kõrgessaare, where you can take a break at excellent **Restoran Viinaköök ❸**, Sadama 2, in an old whiskey distillery. Lunch and dinner buffets (50-150EEK) feature hot meat and vegetarian dishes, as well as a fresh salad bar. Tea, coffee, bread, and biscuits are included. (☎469 33 37. Open daily noon-10pm. MC/V.) Continue 20km past Kõrgessaare to reach Western Hiiumaa's most impressive site, the 16th-century **Kõpu Lighthouse.** The ticket office houses a **cafe** with **Internet** access (15EEK per 30min.). It hosts **concerts** every Friday in July at 9pm (tickets 50-100EEK). Climb the lighthouse's narrow staircase to see how far you've come. (20EEK. Open daily 9am-10pm.)

KÄINA

Käina (pop. 2500), southwest of Suuremõisa, is Hiiumaa's 2nd-most populous area and an excellent base for exploring the island's southern tip. From the town, head toward the coast and the island of Kassari for a scenic and enjoyable daytrip.

▐▞ TRANSPORTATION AND PRACTICAL INFORMATION. Driving a car is by far the most reliable method of transport around the island. The main **bus stop** in town is located at Hiiu mnt. 11, next to the grocery store and a large map of the town. Infrequent buses (☎463 20 77; fax 463 20 65) run daily to **Haapsalu** and **Sõru** (M-F 7:25am and 1pm; Sa-Su 4:45pm), where a ferry connects to the port of Triigi, on **Saaremaa**. Local buses also go to **Kärdla** (25-30min., 3 per day, 14EEK). The morning bus from Käina (6:25am) makes a loop around **Kassari**. Rent **bikes** at **Rattad Vaba Aeg**, Hiiu mnt. 13, the yellow house next to the bus station. (☎56 491 372. 100EEK per day. Open M-F 10am-6pm, Sa 10am-3pm.) The **cultural center** has **tourist info** and free **Internet**. (☎463 62 31. Open M-F 10am-5pm, Sa 10am-2pm.) **Hansapank** is on the first floor. (Open M-F 9am-5pm.) A 24hr. **ATM** is outside.

▐▐ ACCOMMODATIONS AND FOOD. From Käina's center, head 2km toward Emmaste on Hiiu mnt. and hang a left toward Kassari. If arriving by bus, get off at the Luguse stop on the main road and follow the sign toward Kassari. After another 2km, you'll be at **Puulaiu Matkamaja ❶**, a certified Green Label accommodation, which has no adverse consequences for the surrounding environment. The friendly, English-speaking owner offers beautiful beachside cabins and tent space. (☎463 61 26 or 508 86 10. Breakfast 40EEK. Bikes 100EEK per day. Boats 20EEK per hr. Call ahead. Cabins 130-200EEK per person. Tent space 25EEK per person.) **Tondilossi öömaja ❶**, Hiiu mnt. 11, in Käina center, has small, wood paneled private rooms (250EEK) with a shared bath. (☎463 63 37; kylvi.rannu@mail.ee. Breakfast included.) The family-run **Tõidubaar ❶**, next door, serves the heartiest of hearty fare. (Entrees 25-38EEK. Open M-F 11:30am-6pm, Sa 10am-6pm.) Ask for a room with a balcony at luxurious **Hotell Liilia ❺**, Hiiu mnt. 22. Rooms have private bath. (☎463 61 46; www.hot.ee/liiliahotell. Breakfast included. By reservation only Nov.-Feb. May-Sept. singles 700EEK; doubles 800EEK; triples 1000EEK. In low season 500/600/1000EEK. MC/V.) The hotel's popular **restaurant Liilia ❸**, decorated with fishing nets and lanterns, offers plates such as beefsteak with juniper berries and gin sauce (130EEK), as well as a number of fish dishes. (☎463 61 46. Vegetarian options. Open daily 11am-11pm. MC/V.) The aptly named **Konsum**, Hiiu mnt. 9, is a well-stocked grocery store. (Open daily 9am-10pm. MC/V.)

◙ **SIGHTS.** Turn right on Hiiu mnt. toward the ▧**Rudulf Tobias House-Museum** (R. Tobiase Maja-Muuseum), Hiiu mnt. 33. The famous Estonian composer, who was born here in 1873, started writing music when he was six years old. Captions are in Estonian and Russian only, but the staff gives fabulously interesting tours in English. (☎463 6586. Open May 15-Sept. 15 daily 11am-5pm. 10EEK, students 5EEK. Call in advance during winter.) To pay for his son's piano—which you can play in the museum—Tobias's father worked to build the organ at **Käina Church** on the other side of town. A German fighter plane turned the house of worship to a smoldering ruin in WWII; reconstruction projects are underway. To get to the church, follow Hiiu through Käina past Lillia.

▧ **BIKING TO SUUREMÕISA AND KASSARI. Pühalepa Church,** in Suuremõisa, is the oldest on the island and contains the graves of the Baltic-German Count Ungern-Sternberg's family. The Count wanted to acquire the entire island, but his shipping business was cut short when he killed an employee and was banished to Siberia. From the church parking lot, take a right onto a gravel road to the mysterious **Contract Stones** (Põhilise leppe kivid). Some believe the stones were placed here in the 6th century to mark the grave of a Swedish king, while others think sailors stacked the boulders as a symbol of their devotion to God. From the stones, head back to the highway and take the next right onto an oak-lined alley. After about 200m is the **Suuremõisa Palace,** a beautiful 18th-century manor which was passed from generation to generation among the ruling families of the island. Call ahead for info about Night Tours, when you can visit the manor by candlelight to hear tales of ghosts that still haunt the halls. (☎469 43 91. Open July-Aug. M-F noon-6pm, Sa-Su 10am-3pm; Sept.-June M-F 8am-4pm. 10EEK, students 5EEK.)

The ride to **Kassari** (kah-SAH-ree; pop. 286), a tiny village on its own island southeast of Käina, passes through fantastic forest scenery. Roads from the east and the west feed into Kassari; a circular ride allows you to see all the sights. If you enter Kassari from the west, the **Hiiumaa Museum,** in the middle of the island, is about a 7km ride from the main turn-off to Kassari village. You'll see signs after you pass the village of Vetsi Tall. The exhibit chronicles the history and wildlife of the island and includes a huge reflective glass beacon from a lighthouse and a wooden desk from the time when the building was used as the island's school. (☎469 71 21. English captions. Open May 15-Sept. 15 daily 10am-5:30pm. 10EEK, students 5EEK.) Backtrack to the main road, head straight, and veer right at the signpost, following the road to the most beautiful of the island's sights, ▧**Sääretirp,** a 1.3m wide sandbar lined with strawberry and juniper bushes. Legend holds that this 3km peninsula is the remains of an ancient bridge between Hiiumaa and Saaremaa. Supposedly, a giant named Leiger built it so his brother could visit.

INLAND ESTONIA

All roads inland from Tallinn lead to Tartu, the intellectual, historic, and nationalistic heart of Estonia. However, smaller towns should not be overlooked. Visitors can immerse themselves in the mystical surroundings of Otepää or daytrip to Viljandi to see the huge lake and the medieval castle that once protected the town.

ESTONIA

TARTU

Tartu (pop. 110,000) bills itself as "the city of good thoughts," a fitting monicker for the intellectual capital of Estonia. It boasts a rich array of museums, a broad selection of performing arts events, and the top university in the country. Even as posh hotels and glittering casinos spring up in Tartu, it remains a down-to-earth college town, perfect for travelers on a budget.

▐ TRANSPORTATION

Trains: Vaksali 6 (☎615 68 51; www.edel.ee), at the intersection with Kuperjanovi, 1.5km from the city center. Although the station itself is closed, a few trains to **Tallinn** stop here (3hr., 3 per day, 75-80EEK). Buy your ticket from the conductor on board.

Buses: Intercity station (autobussijaam), Soola 2 (☎747 72 27), on the corner of Riia and Turu, 300m southeast of Raekoja plats along Vabaduse. Info office open daily 8am-8pm. To **Pärnu** (2½hr., 20 per day, 85-110EEK), **Tallinn** (2-3hr., 46 per day, 90-100EEK), and **Rīga, LAT** (5hr., 1 per day, 150EEK). 30-50% ISIC/ITIC discount on some routes. A complete bus schedule is available at ▩ **www.bussireisid.ee;** international connections schedule at **www.eurolines.ee.**

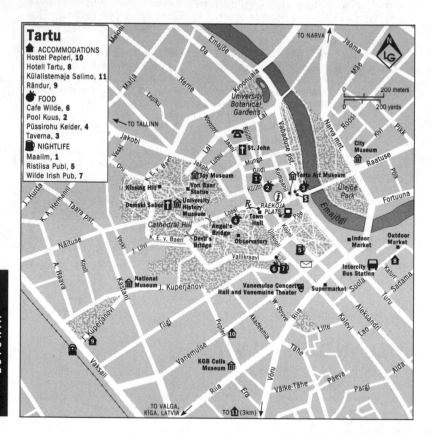

Tartu

🏠 **ACCOMMODATIONS**
Hostel Pepleri, **10**
Hotell Tartu, **8**
Külalistemaja Salimo, **11**
Rändur, **9**

🍴 **FOOD**
Cafe Wilde, **6**
Pool Kuus, **2**
Püssirohu Kelder, **4**
Taverna, **3**

🍸 **NIGHTLIFE**
Maailm, **1**
Ristiisa Pubi, **5**
Wilde Irish Pub, **7**

Public Transportation: Bus tickets 10EEK from kiosks, 12EEK on board. Buses #5 and 6 go from the train station to Raekoja plats and the bus station. Bus #4 travels up and down Võru. Buses #2 and 22 travel away from the river on Riia; #6, 7, and 21 head toward it; #3, 8, and 11 go both ways. Bus routes converge at the Kaubamaja on Riia.

Taxis: Tartu taksopark (☎730 02 00). 8EEK per km; 35EEK min. **Rivaal** (☎742 22 22). 10-15EEK base, 7EEK per km; 25-35EEK min. Ensure the meter is running.

Bike Rental: Sportex, Raekoja plats 11 (☎740 10 00), across from the TIC. 150EEK per day. Open M-F 10am-6pm, Sa 10am-4pm, Su 10am-3pm. MC/V.

⁊ PRACTICAL INFORMATION

Tourist Office: Raekoja plats 14 (☎442 111; www.tartu.ee). From the bus station, walk toward the glass high-rise and continue along the river. Cross Narva Mnt./Riia under the bridge, passing the park on your left. After another block, go left on Raekoja plats. From the train station, get there by following Kuperjanovi 2 blocks; turn left on Valikraavi and follow it as it curves right. When it ends at Kuuni, take a left and turn right on Raekoja plats. The office arranges guides, rental cars, and **private rooms** (180EEK; booking fee 15EEK, outside Tartu 25EEK). It also sells copies of *Tartu in Your Pocket* (25EEK), and offers a **free map** of Tartu and free **Internet** on 1 computer. Open June-Aug. M-F 9am-6pm, Sa 10am-5pm, Su 10am-3pm; Sept.-May M-F 9am-5pm, Sa 10am-3pm.

Currency Exchange: Hansapank, Raekoja plats 20 (☎740 07 40). Cashes AmEx and Thomas Cook **traveler's checks** and exchanges currencies, like most banks in the city. MC/V **cash advances.** 24hr. **ATM** outside. Open M-F 9am-5pm, Sa 10am-2pm.

American Express: Estravel, Vallikraavi 2 (☎440 300; www.estravel.ee). Open M-F 9am-6pm, Sa 10am-3pm.

Luggage Storage: Around the corner from the front door of the bus station. 6-20EEK per bag per day. Open daily 7:30am-9pm.

24hr. Pharmacy: Raekoja Apteek (☎433 528), around the side of the Town Hall building, facing Rüütli.

Internet: ZumZum, Küüni 2, below the ground-floor cafe. 8 quick connections for 25EEK per hr. Free Internet at the **Tourist Info Center** and the **Tartu Public Library** (Tartu Linnaraamatukoga); go upstairs to the 2nd fl., through the door on your left, and continue down the hallway until you see a door marked "Internet." 1st hr. free, 10EEK per hr. thereafter. Open M-F 9am-7pm, Sa 10am-4pm; summer hours may vary. If you have your own laptop, use free wireless connections in the town square, **Wilde Irish Pub** (p. 265), or anywhere with the **wifi.ee** sign.

Post Office: Vanemuise 7 (☎741 06 00; www.post.ee). Open M-F 8am-7pm, Sa 9am-4pm. **Postal Code:** 51003.

⁊ ACCOMMODATIONS

▨ **Hostel Pepleri,** Pepleri 14 (☎740 99 55; www.kyla.ee). From the bus station, walk down Vabaduse pst. toward town, take a left on Vanemuise, then turn left on Pepleri. These modern Tartu University dorms are more luxurious than many upmarket hotels, with private showers, kitchenettes, and cable TV. Towels and sheets provided. Laundry 30EEK; bring your own detergent. Singles 250EEK; doubles 400EEK. The university rents similar rooms across the Narva mnt. bridge. All can be booked online. MC/V. ❷

Hotell Tartu, Soola 3 (☎731 43 00; www.tartuhotell.ee), across the street from the intercity bus station. A blessing for late-night arrivals, this hotel provides Scandinavian-style rooms with private baths, phones, and TV. Breakfast included. Singles 696-

895EEK; doubles 995EEK; triples 1200EEK. 15% ISIC discount; 10% off online bookings. ❹ Space is always available in the **youth rooms**, with wooden bunk and single beds, where it's unlikely you'll have roommates. 3-bed rooms 300EEK. ❷

Rändur, Kuperjanovi 66 (☎742 71 90; randur66@hot.ee), opposite the train station. Quality varies: the shared-bath single (300EEK) and double (400EEK) on the 1st fl. are nicer than the identically priced rooms upstairs. All rooms have TVs. Doubles with private bath 500EEK. Cash only. ❸

Külalistemaja Salimo, Kopli 1 (☎736 18 50; salimo@khk.tartu.ee), 3km southeast of the bus station off Võru. Take bus #4 from Riia to Alasi. Cross Võru, and go left on Kopli. The rooms in this Soviet-style hostel are bright and spacious. Every 2 rooms share a bath. Free Internet for guests. Reception 24hr. Dorms 220EEK. Cash only. ❶

🍴 FOOD

Kaubamaja, a large **supermarket,** is at Riia 2, uphill from the bus station. (☎476 231. Open M-F 10am-8pm, Sa 10am-6pm, Su 10am-5pm. MC/V.) Near the river at the end of Soola, an **open-air market** sells fresh fruit and vegetables. (Open M-F 8am-5pm, Sa 8am-4pm, Su 8am-3pm). The indoor *turg* (market), on the corner of Vabaduse and Vanemuise, sells cheap fresh food, primarily meat and fish. (Open M-F 7:30am-5:30pm, Sa 7:30am-4pm, Su 7:30am-3pm.)

■ **Püssirohu Kelder** (Gunpowder Cellar), Lossi 28 (☎730 35 55), in the park behind the town hall. Look for the 2 cannons outside. Catherine the Great ordered the construction of this storehouse to fortify Tartu. Drink from tankards at massive wooden tables. Live music (Tu-Sa around 9pm) often ends in tabletop dancing. Beer 25EEK per 0.5L. Open M-Sa noon-2am, Su noon-midnight. MC/V. ❷

Pool Kuus (Half Past Five), Rüütli 1 (☎744 11 75), off Raekoja plats. Chalkboard boasts, "Est-Mex food here!" During happy hour (5:30-8:30pm), *Saku* is 25EEK per 1L. Don't be too excited if the wall clocks say the appointed hour has arrived—all are permanently set to 5:30pm. Entrees 30-75EEK. 10% ISIC discount. Open M-Tu and Su noon-4am, W-Sa noon-5:30am. MC/V. ❷

Taverna, Raekoja plats 20 (☎742 30 01). Large portions of meat, pasta, pizza, and vegetarian options. Vaguely upscale cellar setting. Entrees 39-79EEK. 7.5% ISIC discount. Open M-Th 11:30am-midnight, F-Sa 11:30am-1am, Su 1-11pm. MC/V. ❷

Cafe Wilde, Vallikraavi 4 (☎730 97 64). This is the place to linger with your coffee or tea (12EEK) and a good book—if you haven't brought one with you, check out the English titles at the Wilde Bookstore next door. Sit inside amid old printing presses, remnants of the building's previous life as a publishing house, or snag a table on the terrace. Hot sandwiches (25-35EEK), filled pancakes (25-35EEK), and desserts (25-40EEK) served. Open M-W and Su 9am-8pm, Th-Sa 9am-6pm. MC/V. ❶

👁 SIGHTS

TOWN HALL SQUARE (RAEKOJA PLATS). In front of the 1775 Dutch-style **town hall** stands a 1998 statue of students kissing in a fountain. Near the bridge, the ■**Tartu Art Museum** (Tartu Kunstimuuseum) hosts exhibits in a building that, like the student population, leans a little to the left. Until mid-2007, "Narratives of Art in Tartu" provides a comprehensive history of the city's vibrant art scene. Of particular note is the top floor, featuring Peeter Allik's massive canvas *State Secret to Cheat the People.* Every summer, check out new work by the graduating classes of the Tartu Art School, featured on the first floor. (*Raekoja plats 18.* ☎441 080. *Open W-Su 11am-6pm. 10EEK, students 5EEK; F free. Call ahead for a tour; 100EEK.*)

TARTU UNIVERSITY MAIN BUILDING (TARTU ÜLIKOO). In 1632, the Swedish King Gustavus Adolfus II established the first university in Estonia (Academia Gustaviana) on this spot. It became Tartu University when Estonia achieved independence in 1919. The **main building** of the university, featured on the back of the 2EEK banknote, includes an **assembly hall** *(aula)* that hosted concerts conducted by Liszt and Schumann. Today the magnificent blue-and-white room still holds concerts. The **student lock-up** *(kartser)* in the attic was used until 1892 to detain students for offenses like keeping library books late (2 days' confinement). Drawings and inscriptions by detainees still line the walls of the small room. Tartu was the only university in the Russian empire allowed to have fraternities after the Great Northern War, and it used the privilege well: in 1870, the **Estonian National Awakening** began here with the founding of the Estonian Student Association (Eesti Üliõpilaste Selts). The Association's members were so central to Estonia's struggle for independence that the Estonian flag bears the frat's colors: blue, black, and white. *(Ülikooli 18. With the town hall behind you, follow Ülikooli right. ☎375 384. Open M-F 11am-5pm. 10EEK, students 5EEK; student lock-up 5/4EEK.)*

CATHEDRAL HILL (TOOMEMÄGI). The hill's central site is the once-majestic 15th-century **Domski Sabor** (Dome Cathedral; a.k.a. **Cathedral of St. Peter and Paul**), which is now in ruins. Heed the sign: "Be cautious! The building is liable to fall down." An adjoining building houses the **Tartu University History Museum** (Museum Historicum Universitatis Tartuensis), featuring an array of intriguing displays, including old scientific instruments and artifacts from the museum's past. A museum ticket also grants access to the steep staircases of the Cathedral Towers—the view is worth the climb. *(Lossi 25. ☎375 674; www.ut.ee/ream. Some English captions. Open W-Su 11am-5pm. 20EEK, students 10EEK. Tours in English or German 120EEK.)* **Kissing Hill** (Musumägi), once part of a prison tower, is the site of an ancient pagan sacrificial stone—where Tartu University students burn their lecture notes at the end of every year. Each April, the university choirs compete on the two bridges that lead to the east hump of Toomemägi. Women crowd onto the wooden **Angel's Bridge** (Inglisild), while men stand on the concrete **Devil's Bridge** (Kuradisild). Cathedral Hill is also littered with **statues.** The seated figure of embryologist Karl Ernst von Baer might be recognizable from the 2EEK banknote. In keeping with tradition, biology students douse the sculpture with champagne each year.

OTHER SIGHTS. Don't miss the **Estonian National Museum** (Eesti Rahva Muuseum), which charts the evolution of Estonian culture from the Stone Age to the Soviet era, and features extensive collections of Estonian textiles and crafts. Among the USSR's stranger dictates: orders cracking down on the wearing of wedding rings and the cultivation of tomatoes and roses, which were considered "elements of the bourgeois past." *(Kuperjanovi 9. ☎742 13 11. Open W-Su 11am-6pm. Permanent exhibit 12EEK, students 8EEK; with admission to temporary display 20/14EEK; F free.)* Let your inner child loose at the **Tartu Toy Museum** (Tartu Mänguasjamuuseum). Rooms crammed with 19th-century dolls, stuffed animals, miniature cars, and an impressive model railway set would delight even a curmudgeon. Make a stop at the board game table, where you can learn to play a number of different games (instructions in English and Estonian) or take a break upstairs in the massive **play room.** *(Lutsu 8. ☎736 15 51, play room 736 15 54; www.mm.ee. Facing the town hall, turn right on Rüütli and hang a left on Lutsu. Open W-Su 11am-6pm; play room open W-Su 11am-4pm. 15EEK, students and children 10EEK. Play room 5EEK.)* The **KGB Cells Museum** (KGB Kongid muuseum) is housed in the Soviet spy agency's former South Estonian headquarters; prisoners in the tiny basement pens received just 200g of bread and a half-liter of cold soup once every three days. *(Riia 15b. ☎746 17 17; www.tartu.ee/linnamuuseum. Open Tu-Sa 11am-4pm. 5EEK, students 3EEK.)* The **Tartu City Museum** (Tartu Linnamuuseum) displays

THE LOCAL STORY

ESTONIANS GONE WILD

Combine the madcap antics of cooped-up university students with the wacky tendencies of Estonia—known for its mysterious folklore, meteorite craters, and inordinate love of Depeche Mode—and you've got yourself one of the weirdest collegiate environments in the world. For the students of Tartu University, fun-loving lunacy is a matter of tradition. There are a few "rules" to becoming a Tartu University student: you must fail at least one exam, live for a time in the dorms, and climb over the concrete arch that braces the bridge across from the Town Hall square. Some say sex in the library is another condition.

With these basics under your belt, move on to the festivities that culminate in April with Spring Days. Homemade rubber boats are raced down the Emajogi River, public pillow fights take place, and the university statue of Karl Ernst von Baer is doused with champagne. At the "Students' Market," the young and hopeful try to sell oddities such as dead birds, air, and ennui. The cleverest sale item wins a prize. At the end of each school year, students gather at the onetime pagan sacrificial stones on Toome Hill to burn all of their lecture notes, old papers, and exams. For all their goofiness, the students of Tartu have made a special mark on their nation: the Estonian flag is based on the black-white-and-blue tricolor flag of the Estonian Student Association, first flown at Tartu University in 1884.

the table on which the 1920 Peace Treaty of Tartu was signed with the USSR, granting Estonia independence. *(Narva mnt. 23. ☎461 911; www.tartu.ee/linnamuuseum. English captions. Open Tu-Su 11am-6pm. 20EEK, students 5EEK. Tours 120EEK.)* The ■**Tartu University Botanical Gardens** include a greenhouse with an impressive collection of cacti and other plants not indigenous to Estonia. Walk through the stone and dirt paths around the expansive outdoor gardens and you'll forget you're in a city. *(Lai 40. Open daily 7am-7pm. Greenhouse open daily 10am-5pm. Greenhouse 10EEK, students 5EEK.)*

🎵 📷 ENTERTAINMENT AND FESTIVALS

For listings of cultural events in Tartu, go to http://kultuuriaken.tartu.ee or check out *Tartu in Your Pocket* (25EEK). The Tourist Information Office provides a detailed pamphlet with listings for summer theatre, music, and art happenings in the city. The **Vanemuise Concert Hall** (Vanemuise Kontserdimaja), Vanemuise 6 (☎737 75 30; www.vkm.ee), has classical concerts. The 1870 theater **Vanemuine**, Vanemuise 6 (☎744 01 65; www.vanemuine.ee), holds theater performances and operas, including some in English. **Eesti Suve Teater** (Summer Theater; ☎742 74 71) hosts performances in July and August in and outside the medieval church on Cathedral Hill. The 2nd week of February brings the **Tartu Marathon,** which features a 63km cross-country ski race and non-competitive 31 and 16km group jaunts (☎742 16 44; tartumaraton@tartumaraton.ee). **Midsummer's Eve** festivities take over the city every June 23, when darkness falls for only about 4hr. A huge bonfire at the **Tartu Song Grounds** can be expected. Everyone makes a port call during the **Hanseatic Days** (www.tartu.ee/hansa) at the end of June, when the Middle Ages return with craft fairs and folk dancing in Raekoja plats.

🎇 NIGHTLIFE

Head up the wooden staircase to ■**Maailm,** Rüütli 12, and you'll feel like you've stepped into your crazy best friend's attic. With walls plastered in newspaper and magazine clippings, velvet armchairs and swings to sit on, and a menu as eclectic as the decor, this restaurant/bar shouldn't be missed. Food served before 10pm includes the baby octopus and vegetable roll (35EEK), but take heart—you can get one of Maailm's famous **ice cream shakes** (25EEK) at any hour. Try "Leonardo DiCaprio" (vanilla ice cream and strawberries) or "Coco Chanel" (vanilla ice cream, pineapple, ginger, coconut flakes). Beer is only 20EEK per half liter; but you still have to make it down the stairs at the end of the night. (☎742 90 99. Occasional special events. Open M-Sa noon-1am, Su noon-10pm. MC/V.) A bronze Oscar Wilde meets his Estonian counterpart Eduard Wilde (pronounced VIL-de) outside the ⊠Wilde Irish Pub, Vallikraavi 4. The pub serves Irish and Estonian dishes (49-170EEK) and a variety of brews, including Guinness (45EEK per 0.5L). A digital billboard registers every order of *Saku*. (☎730 97 64; www.wilde.ee. Vegetarian options. Tu karaoke, F-Sa live music 9pm. Open M-Tu and Su noon-midnight, W-Th noon-1am, F-Sa noon-3am. MC/V.) Ristiisa Pubi (Godfather Pub), Küüni 7, is down the street from Raekoja plats. Crowds mob the outdoor terrace on summer nights, but inside the brick building, you're part of the family. The mixed-drink list is as long as Al Capone's police record. (☎730 39 70; www.ristiisapubi.ee. Cuban cigars from 25EEK. 0.5L *Saku* 25EEK. Th 10pm live music. Open M-Tu and Su 11am-midnight, W-Th 11am-1am, F-Sa 11am-3am. MC/V.)

◪ DAYTRIP FROM TARTU

VILJANDI

Buses arrive from Tartu (1¼hr.; 20 per day; 35-50EEK; ISIC discount), and depart back no later than 8:30pm (check the schedule at the station or Tourist Info Center). The Tourist Info Center, Vabaduse plats 6, gives out free maps, provides pamphlets with a walking tour, and has free Internet. (☎304 42; viljandi@visitestonia.com. Open May 15-Sept. 15 M-F 9am-6pm, Sa-Su 10am-3pm; Sept. 16-May 14 M-F 10am-5pm, Sa 10am-2pm.) To get to the castle from the bus station, take a left on Tallinna and go through Vabaduse plats (the main square) toward the river. The road becomes Tasuja pst.; follow it to its end. The path just to your left leads to the castle. St. John's Church ☎330 00; viljandi.jaani@eelk.ee. Open daily May 15-Sept. 15 10am-5pm; Sept. 15-May 15 M-F noon-1pm. Free. Museum ☎433 3316; www.muuseum.viljandimaa.ee. Open W-Su 10am-5pm. 20EEK, students 15EEK.

The main sights of Viljandi can be seen in a couple of hours, while the town's beautiful lake is a place for peaceful repose, or a lengthy row-boat trip. The imposing Order's Castle (Ordulinnuse varemed), constructed by the Knights of the Sword in the 13th century, was once one of the largest in the Baltics, spanning three hilltops connected by bridges. Although the castle is now in ruins, the remainder offers a panorama of Viljandi Lake (Viljandi järv), the largest lake in the region, and provides the backdrop for a Folk Music Festival each summer. Around the back of the ruins is the red-and-white 1879 suspension footbridge *(rippsild)*, which leads to town. In the central castle park is the sparsely decorated 15th-century St. John's Church (Jaani kirik), Pikk 6. Its organ was shipped north to Poltsamaa when Soviet authorities converted the church into a granary in the mid-1950s. Its replacement is used for concerts each Saturday at 2pm. In the center of town, the Viljandi Museum, Kindval Laidoneri plats 10, sports a collection of stuffed lynx and wolves and the first-ever model of an Ericsson phone, dating from 1892. The 158-step staircase leading to the lake passes the statue of a runner; the names of past winners of hilly Viljandi's annual 15km foot race are engraved on the nearby pillars.

OTEPÄÄ

Otepää (pop. 4800), the highest town in Estonia (152m), becomes a mecca for cross-country skiers in winter. In summer, it's ideal for cyclists and hikers. Pühajärve (Holy Lake) is famous for being conducive to deep meditation, and was blessed by the Dalai Lama in 1991. Follow Pühajärve tee south from the town center and go left after 1km onto Mae to reach Otepää's Energy Column (Energiasammas), a 4m high wooden pole at a site selected by psychics for its positive vibes. Head back to Pühajärve tee and continue another 2.5km to reach Pühajärve, where you can enjoy the beach or rent boats and other water crafts.

Downhill skiers head to **Vaike-Munamae Skiing and Snowboarding Centre** (☎521 4040; www.munakas.ee), 4km from the center of town. At a height of 70m and with its longest run just 500m, it might be the best skiing in the flat-as-a-pancake Baltics. Take a **taxi** (about 25EEK from the bus station) to get there. (Ski rental M-F 250EEK per day, Sa-Su 70EEK per day. Snowboards 300/90EEK. Lift ticket 200/ 80EEK, free with rental. Open Oct.-Apr. M-F noon-8pm, Sa and holidays 10am-8pm, Su 10am-5pm.) **O'Boy Snowtubing Park** is off Valga mountain, just south of the center. (☎52 140 40; www.snowtubing.ee. Open late Oct. to late Apr. 250EEK per day; M-F 50EEK per hr., Sa-Su 100EEK per hr.) The **TIC** offers a free guide to the region's skiing opportunities. Karupesa Hotel is right by the **Tehvandi Olympic Center,** where Estonia's national ski-jumping team trains; they'll make way for amateurs. (☎766 9500; www.tehvandi.ee. Training session 50EEK per day, 200EEK per wk.) Beneath Karupesa, rent cross-country skis (150EEK per day) at **Fansport.** (☎050 77 537; www.fansport.ee. Bikes 200EEK per day. Reserve in advance.) **Club Tartu Marathon** (☎742 1644; www.tartumaraton.ee.) has the area's longest cross-country track (63km), which opens to tourists in the 2nd week of February. Rent **waterbikes, rowboats,** and **canoes** (70-90EEK per hr.) at the lake's **beach,** in a small hut near the pier. (☎765 52 19. Open in summer daily 10am-7pm.)

The TIC offers an extensive list of accommodations. Your best bet is **Hostel Allik ❶,** Parna 4, steps away from the center of town. From the TIC, turn left on Pühajärve tee and right on Parna. Enter from the backyard. It has bright, clean rooms with private baths. (☎501 4114; www.kite.ee/majutus. Breakfast 25EEK. Singles 200EEK; doubles 400EEK.) Farther down Pühajärve tee, turn left on Tamme to reach the **Tamme Guesthouse ❷,** Tamme 6. It has cramped, three-bed dorms and more comfortable doubles with private baths. (☎766 3474; www.hot.ee/tammekylalistemaja. Dorms 250EEK; singles 400EEK; doubles 600EEK.) Otepää's small number of restaurants, pubs, and nightclubs center on Lipuväljak and Pühajärve, within sight of the tourist office. Locals pack **Edgari Trahter ❶,** Lipuväljak 3, which serves up cheap sauerkraut, pancakes, fried fish, and meat. (Entrees 15-55EEK. Open M-Sa 9am-10pm, Su 10am-10pm.)

Buses run from **Tartu** (1hr.; 15 per day; 30EEK, with ISIC 25EEK). The last bus from Otepää to Tartu leaves at 7:10pm on weekends, but as late as 10pm on other days. The **tourist office,** Lipuväljak 13, next to the bus station, offers a small **guidebook** with **maps** (15EEK). The office has free guides to **hiking, biking,** and **cross-country skiing.** (☎766 12 00; otepaa@visitestonia.com. Open May 15-Sept. 15 M-F 9am-6pm, Sa-Su 10am-3pm; Sept. 16-May 14 M-F 9am-5pm, Sa 10am-3pm.) **Hansapank,** on Lipuväljak 3, **exchanges currency,** cashes Thomas Cook and AmEx **traveler's checks** for 1% commission, and has a 24hr. MC/V **ATM** outside. (Open M-F 9am-5pm.) The **post office** is at Lipuväljak 24. (☎767 9385; otepaapost@hot.ee. Open M-F 8am-6pm, Sa 8am-3pm.) **Postal Code:** 67405.

HUNGARY
(MAGYARORSZБG)

A country as singular as its language, Hungary is certainly more than its profusion of wine, goulash, and thermal spas. A must-see destination by any standard, hip and vibrant Budapest remains Hungary's ever-ascending social, economic, and political capital. But venture beyond the big-city rush and you'll be mesmerized by charming cobblestone towns and luscious wine valleys nestled in Hungary's northern hills, the cowboy plains in the south, the luxurious beach resorts in the east, and the generosity of the locals. Less eastern than it is central, Hungary can be more expensive than some of its neighbors, yet always feels like a steal.

DISCOVER HUNGARY: SUGGESTED ITINERARIES

THREE DAYS Three days is hardly enough for the action-packed city of **Budapest** (p. 276). Spend a day at the churches, labyrinths, and museums of **Castle Hill,** and an afternoon relaxing in the thermal waters of the **Széchényi Baths** before exploring the rest of the **City Park.** Get a lesson in Hungarian history on the **Parliament** tour before experiencing the country's more artistic side during an evening at the **Opera House.**

ONE WEEK After spending four days in the thriving capital, head up the Danube Bend by train or boat to experience the more rustic side of Hungary: in **Szentendre** (1 day; p. 297), cafes and cobblestoned streets welcome tourists, while farther down the river, **Visegrád's** citadel looms high above the town (1 day; p. 309). The next day, explore the boulevards of **Eger** (p. 299) and spend a day sampling the ample wines of the scenic **Valley of Beautiful Women** (p. 302).

BEST OF HUNGARY, THREE WEEKS Begin in the tiny northeastern town of **Tokaj,** renowned for its local wines (2 days; p. 306), before heading to **Eger** (2 days) and **Budapest** (4 days) to take in the sights and raging night life. After the Danube Bend towns of **Szentendre, Visegrád,** and **Esztergom** offer a change of pace from city life (4 days; p. 298), check out **Győr's** perfectly preserved architecture (1 day; p. 310). After Pannonhalma Abbey, head to **Lake Balaton** (p. 321). Hungary's summertime pride: spend two days lounging on the beach and touring Festetics Palace in **Keszthely** (p. 330), then hike in the vineyards of **Badacsony** (p. 327). Continue along the lake to **Balatonfüred** (1 day; p. 325) for more relaxation, tour the renowned Benedictine Abbey at the stunning **Tihany Peninsula** (1 day; p. 329), and then cross the lake to the party-town of **Siófok** (1 day; p. 321) before ending in **Pécs** (3 days; p. 334).

FACTS AND FIGURES

Official Name: Hungary.
Capital: Budapest.
Major Cities: Eger, Pécs, Siófok.
Population: 10,000,000. (92% Hungarian, 2% Roma, 6% other or unknown).

Land Area: 93,030 sq. km.
Time Zone: GMT + 1.
Language: Hungarian.
Religions: Roman Catholic (60%).

ESSENTIALS

WHEN TO GO

Spring is the best time, as flowers are in bloom throughout the countryside and the tourists haven't yet arrived. July through August is Hungary's high season, replete with crowds, booked hostels, and a summer swelter; consider going in May or June. Autumn is gorgeous, with mild, cooler weather through October. January and February can average freezing temperatures, and many museums and tourist spots shut down or reduce their hours during the winter months.

DOCUMENTS AND FORMALITIES

ENTRANCE REQUIREMENTS
Passport: Required for all travelers.
Visa: Not required for stays of under 90 days for citizens of Australia, Canada, Ireland, New Zealand, the UK, and the US.
Letter of Invitation: Not required for citizens of Australia, Canada, Ireland, New Zealand, the UK, and the US.
Inoculations: Recommended up-to-date on DTaP (diphtheria, tetanus, and pertussis), Hepatitis A, Hepatitis B, MMR (measles, mumps, and rubella), Polio booster, and Typhoid.
Work Permit: Required of all foreigners planning to work in Hungary.
Driving Permit: Required for all those planning to drive in Hungary.

EMBASSIES AND CONSULATES. Foreign embassies to Hungary are in Budapest (see p. 281). Hungary's embassies and consulates abroad include: **Australia,** 17 Beale Crescent, Deakin, ACT 2600 (☎6282 3226; www.hunconsydney.com); **Austria,** Bankgasse 4-6, A-1010 Vienna (☎42 94 30; kom@huembvie.at); **Canada,** 299 Waverley St., Ottawa, ON K2P 0V9 (☎613-230-2717; www.docuweb.ca/Hungary), Consulate 121 E. Bloor St., # 1115, Toronto, ON, M4W 3M5 (☎416-923-8981); **Ire-**

land, 2 Fitzwilliam Pl., Dublin 2 (☎661 2902; www.kum.hu/dublin); **New Zealand,** Consulate-General, 37 Abbott St., Wellington 6004 (☎973 7507; www.hungarian-consulate.co.nz); the **UK,** 35 Eaton Pl., London SW1X 8BY (☎020 7235 2664; www.huemblon.org.uk); the **US,** 3910 Shoemaker St. NW, Washington, D.C. 20008 (☎202-362-6730; www.hungaryemb.org), Consulate, 223 East 52nd St., New York, NY 10022 (☎212-838-4348; www.kum.hu/newyork/).

VISA AND ENTRY INFORMATION. Citizens of Australia, Canada, Ireland, New Zealand, the UK, and the US can visit Hungary without **visas** for up to 90 days, assuming they carry a passport which does not expire within six months of the trip's end and intend not to work. If you do need a visa, consult your embassy. There is no fee for crossing a Hungarian border. In general, border officials are efficient; plan on 30min. crossing time.

TOURIST SERVICES AND MONEY

TOURIST OFFICES. Tourinform has branches in most cities and is a useful first-stop **tourist service.** Tourinform doesn't make reservations but will find vacancies, especially in university dorms and private *panzió*. Agencies also stock maps and provide local information; employees generally speak English and German. Most **IBUSZ** offices throughout the country book **private rooms,** exchange money, and sell train tickets, but they are generally better at assisting in travel plans than at providing info. Pick up *Tourist Information: Hungary* and *Budapest in Your Pocket* and the monthly entertainment guide *Programme in Hungary* (all are free and in English). Local agencies may be staffed only by Hungarian- and German-speakers, but they are generally very helpful and offer unique local tips.

MONEY. The national currency is the **forint (Ft),** which is divided into 100 fillérs, which have almost entirely disappeared from circulation. Hungary has a **Value Added Tax (VAT)** rate of 25%. **Inflation** hovers around 5.3%, so expect price increases. Currency exchange machines are slow but offer good rates, and banks like **OTP Bank** and **Postabank** offer the best exchange rates for traveler's checks. Never change money on the street, and avoid extended-hour exchange offices, which have poor rates. Watch for scams: the maximum legal commission for cash-to-cash exchange is 1%. **ATMs** are common; major **credit cards** are accepted in some establishments. Standard business hours in Budapest are Monday to Thursday 9am-4pm, Friday 9am-1pm. Businesses generally close on holidays.

Expect to spend around 4500-5500Ft a day at a bare minimum, assuming accommodation in university dorms, often the cheapest option, transport, and food. For slightly less ascetic living, expect to spend roughly 5500-7000Ft for accommodations in hostels, food, sights, and transportation. Service is not usually included in bills and while tipping is not mandatory, it's generally appropriate to tip. Tipping bartenders is not customary, but waiters often expect tips from tourists. Don't bother bargaining with cabbies; make sure to set a price before getting in.

FORINTS (FT)		
AUS$1 = 150.13FT	1000FT = AUS$6.66	
CDN$1 = 163.86FT	1000FT = CDN$6.10	
EUR€1 = 243.21FT	1000FT = EUR€4.11	
NZ$1 = 138.83FT	1000FT = NZ$7.20	
UK£1 = 358.33FT	1000FT = UK£2.79	
US$1 = 199.74FT	1000FT = US$5.01	

HEALTH AND SAFETY

EMERGENCY	**Police:** ☎ 107. **Fire:** ☎ 105. **Ambulance:** ☎ 104 (in English 1 311 1666).

In Budapest, **medical assistance** is easily obtained. Embassies have lists of Anglophone doctors, and most hospitals have English-speaking doctors on staff. Outside Budapest, try to bring a Hungarian speaker to the hospital with you. **Tourist insurance** is valid—and necessary—for many medical services. **Tap water** is usually clean; the water in Tokaj is poorly purified. Buy **bottled water** at most food stores. Public bathrooms vary in cleanliness: pack soap, a towel, and 30Ft for the attendant. Carry **toilet paper,** as many hostels do not provide it and you get a single square in public restrooms. Gentlemen should look for *Férfi*, and ladies for *Nöi* signs. Many **pharmacies** (gyógyszertár) stock Western brands, tampons, and condoms. Most towns have pharmacies that list after-hours service availability.

Violent **crime** is low, but in Budapest and other large cities, foreign tourists are targets for petty thieves and pickpockets. Check prices before getting in taxis or ordering food or drinks. In an emergency, your embassy will likely be more helpful than the **police.** Lone **women,** the elderly, and families with children all travel in Hungary. **Minorities** are generally accepted, though dark-skinned travelers may encounter prejudice. Though Hungary is known for being open-minded, **GLBT** travelers may face serious discrimination, especially outside Budapest.

TRANSPORTATION

BY PLANE. Many international airlines arrive in Budapest. The cheapest options to Hungary are **Sky Europe** (www.skyeurope.com) and **WizzAir** (www.wizzair.com), two Eastern European budget airlines, as well as old dependables **Air Berlin** (www.airberlin.com) and **easyJet** (www.easyjet.com), all of which offer service from London or Paris to Budapest. The **national airline, Malév,** flies to Hungary from London, New York, and other major cities.

BY TRAIN. Most trains *(vonat)* pass through Budapest and are reliable and inexpensive. Several types of **Eurail passes** are valid in Hungary. Check schedules and fares at ▥www.elvira.hu. *Személyvonat* trains have many local stops and are excruciatingly slow; *gyorsvonat* trains, listed in red on schedules, move much faster for the same price. Large towns are connected by blue express lines; these air-conditioned InterCity trains are fastest. A *pótjegy* (seat reservation) is required on trains labeled "R," and violators face a hefty fine. A basic vocabulary will help you navigate: *érkezés* (arrival), *indulás* (departure), *vágány* (track), and *állomás* or *pályaudvar* (station, abbreviated *pu*). The *peron* (platform) is rarely indicated until the train approaches the station and will sometimes be announced in Hungarian; look closely out the window as you approach a station. Many stations are not marked; ask the conductor what time the train will arrive (if your Hungarian is a bit rusty, point at your watch and say the town's name).

BY BUS. Buses, which are cheap (though often slightly more expensive than trains) and clean but crowded, are best for travel between outer provincial centers. Purchase tickets on board, and arrive early for a seat. In larger cities, buy tickets at the kiosk, and they will be punched when you get on. There's a fine if you're caught without a ticket. A ferry runs down the Danube from Vienna and Bratislava to Budapest. For more info, contact **Utinform** (☎322 3600).

BY CAR. Taxi prices should not exceed the following: 6am-10pm base fare 200Ft, 240Ft per km, 60Ft per min. waiting; 10pm-6am 300/280/70Ft. Beware of taxi scams. Before getting in, check that the meter is working and ask how much the

ride will cost. Taxis ordered by phone charge less than those hailed on the street. To **drive** in Hungary, carry your **International Driving Permit** and your registration and insurance papers. Drinking and driving is illegal. For info on road conditions, call ☎322 7052 or 443 5651. Emergency phones are every two kilometers on Hungarian motorways. For 24hr. English assistance, contact the **Magyar Autóklub** (**MAK;** in Budapest ☎345 1800). Biking terrain varies. The northeast is topographically varied; the south is flat. Roads are usually well paved. Though it is common in Hungary, *Let's Go* does not recommend **hitchhiking.**

KEEPING IN TOUCH

PHONE CODES	**Country code: 36. International dialing prefix:** 00. From outside Hungary, dial int'l dialing prefix (see inside back cover) + 36 + city code + local number. Within Hungary, dial the national access code (06) + area code + local number, even when dialing inside the city.

EMAIL AND THE INTERNET. Internet is readily available in major cities. The Hungarian keyboard differs significantly from English-language keyboards. After logging on, click the "Hu" icon at the bottom right corner of the screen and switch the setting to "Angol" to shift to an English keyboard. Look for free Internet access at hostels. Most Internet cafes charge 150-300Ft per hour.

TELEPHONE. For **intercity calls,** wait for the tone and dial slowly; "06" goes before the phone code. **International calls** require red or blue phones. The blue phones tend to end calls after 3-9min. Phones often require *telefonkártya* (phone cards). The best ones for international calls are **Neophone,** available at the post office, and **Micronet,** available at Fotex stores. Calls to Australia, Canada, and Ireland cost 45-50Ft per min., to the US 35Ft per min., to the UK 39Ft per min. Make direct calls from Budapest's phone office. A 20Ft coin is required to start most calls. International access numbers include: **AT&T Direct** (☎06 800 01111); **Australia Direct** (☎06 800 06111); **BT Direct** (☎0800 89 0036); **Canada Direct** (☎06 800 01211); **MCI WorldPhone** (☎06 800 01411); **NZ Direct** (☎06 800 06411); and **Sprint** (☎06 800 01877).

Mobile phones are common in Hungary, and service can be purchased from Pannon GSM, T-Mobile, or Vodafone, which have shops in Budapest. Dialing a mobile from a public or private phone anywhere in Hungary is treated as a long distance call, requiring the entire 11-digit number.

MAIL. Hungarian mail is usually reliable; **airmail** *(légiposta)* takes one week to 10 days to the US and Europe. Mailing a letter costs about 36Ft domestically and 140-150Ft internationally. Those without permanent addresses can receive mail through **Poste Restante.** Use Global Priority mail, as it is reliable. Address envelopes: Amelia (First name) ATLAS (Last name), POSTE RESTANTE, Városház u. 18 (post office address), 1052 (postal code) Budapest (city), Hungary.

ACCOMMODATIONS AND CAMPING

HUNGARY	❶	❷	❸	❹	❺
ACCOMMODATIONS	under 2500Ft under €10 under $12	2500-4000Ft €10-16 $12-20	4000-7000Ft €16-28 $20-35	7000-12,000Ft €28-50 $35-60	over 12,000Ft over €50 over $60

Tourism is developing rapidly, and rising prices make **hostels** attractive. Hostels are usually large enough to accommodate summer crowds, and HI cards are often useful. Many hostels can be booked through Express (in Budapest ☎266 3277), a student travel agency, or through local tourist offices. From June to August, many

university dorms become hostels. These may be the cheapest options in smaller towns, as hostels are less common outside Budapest. Locations change annually; inquire at Tourinform and call ahead. **Guesthouses and pensions** *(panzió)* are more common than hotels in small towns. **Private rooms** booked through tourist agencies are sometimes a cheaper option. Singles are scarce, though some guesthouses have a singles rate for double rooms—it can be worth finding a roommate, as solo travelers must often pay for doubles. Check prices: agencies may try to rent you their most expensive rooms. Outside Budapest, the best offices are region-specific (e.g., Eger Tourist in Eger). They will often make advance reservations for your next stop. After staying a few nights, make arrangements directly with the owner to save your agency's 20-30% commission.

Over 300 **campgrounds** are sprinkled throughout Hungary. Most open from May to September and charge for unfilled spaces in their bungalows. For more information, consult *Camping Hungary*, a booklet available in most tourist offices, or contact Tourinform in Budapest (see **Tourist And Financial Services**, p. 281).

FOOD AND DRINK

HUNGARY	❶	❷	❸	❹	❺
FOOD	under 400Ft under €2 under $2	400-800Ft €2-4 $2-4	800-1300Ft €4-6 $4-7	1300-2800Ft €6-12 $7-14	over 2800Ft over €12 over $14

Hungarian food is more flavorful than many of its Eastern European culinary cohorts, with many spicy meat dishes. **Paprika**, Hungary's chief agricultural export, colors most dishes red. In Hungarian restaurants *(vendéglő* or *étterem)*, *halászlé*, a spicy fish stew, can make a traditional starter. Or, try *gyümölcsleves*, a cold fruit soup with whipped cream. The Hungarian national dish is *bográcsgulyás*, a soup of beef, onions, green pepper, tomatoes, potatoes, dumplings, and plenty of paprika. *Borjúpaprikás* is veal with paprika and potato-dumpling pasta. For **Vegetarians** there is tasty *rántott sajt* (fried cheese) and *gombapörkölt* (mushroom stew). Delicious Hungarian fruits and vegetables abound in summer. Vegetarians should also look for *salata* (salad) and *sajt* (cheese), as these will be the only options in many small-town restaurants. *Túrós rétes* is a chewy pastry filled with sweet cottage cheese, while *Somlói galuska* is a rich, rum-soaked sponge cake of chocolate, nuts, and cream. The Austrians stole the recipe for *rétes* and called it "strudel," but this concoction is as Hungarian as can be.

Hungary produces an array of fine wines (see **Wines of Tokaj**, p. 307). The northeastern towns of Eger and Tokaj produce famous red and white wines, respectively. *Sör* (Hungarian **beer**) ranges from first-rate to acceptable. Lighter beers include *Dreher Pils, Szalon Sör*, and licensed versions of *Steffl, Gold Fassl, Gösser*, and *Amstel*. Hungary also produces *pálinka*, which resembles brandy. Among the best-tasting are *barackpálinka* (like apricot schnapps) and *körtepálinka* (pear brandy). *Unicum*, advertised as the national drink, is an **herbal liqueur** that was used by the Hapsburgs to cure digestive ailments.

LIFE AND TIMES

HISTORY

THE MIGHTY MAGYARS. In the third century BC, **Celtic tribes** invaded what is now Hungary. They were followed by the **Romans,** who founded the provinces of Pannonia and Dacia, which they held until the fifth century AD. The **Mag-**

yars, Central Asian warriors, arrived in 896, one hundred years after Charlemagne conquered the previous residents, the Goths, Huns, and Turkish Avars. Led by **Prince Árpád,** the Magyars conquered the middle Danube. Árpád's descendant, **Stephen I,** became Hungary's first king on Christmas Day, 1000. Canonized as the nation's patron saint in 1083, Stephen is considered the founder of modern Hungary.

THOSE GOLDEN YEARS. As Hungary grew stronger, the nobles forced the king to sign the **Golden Bull** (1222), a charter that granted rights to the people and restricted monarchical power. Two decades later, a devastating Mongolian invasion swept through, killing over half a million people and effectively ending the Árpáds' reign. But as the 14th century progressed, Hungary entered a **Golden Age** of economic and military prowess. King **Matthias Corvinus** (1458-1490) reigned during Hungary's renaissance. As he kept conspiring nobles at bay, Corvinus consolidated the administration, supported education, and cultivated a huge library at Buda, though later rulers undid most of his reforms. A peasant rebellion in 1514 was unsuccessful, but its repercussions lingered for centuries. The Turks conquered the Hungarians at Mohács in 1526.

EMPIRE FALLS. Conflict between the Holy Roman Empire, Protestants, and Ottomans plagued Hungary for the next 150 years, until the Austrian **Hapsburgs** took over in the early 17th century. A movement for independence began in 1848, led by young poet **Sándor Petőfi** and lawyer **Lajos Kossuth.** The movement convinced the **Diet** (Parliament) to pass reforms known as the **March Laws.** Kossuth's newly-independent state resisted Austrian aggression for a year, but in 1849, Hapsburg Emperor Franz Josef I regained Budapest with the support of Russia's Tsar Nicholas I. Nonetheless, the revolution, coupled with Austria's defeat in a war with Prussia, led Austria to grant Hungary significant powers under the **Compromise of 1867.** Brokered by **Ferenc Deák,** the arrangement created the dual monarchy of the **Austro-Hungarian Empire. Magyarization,** a set of Hungarian nationalist policies, provoked opposition among restless Croats, Romanians, Serbs, and Slovaks. These divisions erupted in WWI and resulted in the permanent dissolution of the Austro-Hungarian Empire. After the war, Hungary lost two-thirds of its territory to the Allies in the 1920 **Treaty of Trianon.**

APOCALYPSE NOW. As the empire collapsed, a democratic revolution emerged in 1918, and gave way in less than six months to the communist **Hungarian Republic of Councils** under Bolshevik **Béla Kun.** Counter-revolutionary forces eventually took control and mercilessly punished those involved with the communist administration. Admiral **Miklós Horthy** settled in for 24 years of dictatorship just as brutal as that of Kun. A tentative alliance with Hitler in **WWII** led to Nazi occupation and the near-total destruction of Budapest during the two-month Soviet siege of 1945. Two-thirds of Hungary's **Jews,** whose pre-war population numbered close to one million, were murdered in the Holocaust. Nearly all survivors fled the country.

COME ON, RISE UP. In 1949 Hungary became a People's Republic under **Mátyás Rákosi.** Rákosi tied Hungary to the **USSR,** which used the country as a "workshop" for Soviet industry. Rákosi lost control in the violent **1956 Uprising,** in Budapest, during which **Imre Nagy** declared a neutral, non-Warsaw Pact government. Soviet troops crushed the revolt and executed Nagy and his supporters.

FIGHT FOR YOUR RIGHTS. Over the next three decades, Nagy's replacement, **János Kádár,** oversaw the partial opening of borders and a rising standard of living. Inflation halted progress in the 1980s, but democratic reformers in the Communist Party, seeking freedom and a proto-market economy, pushed Kádár aside in 1988. Hungary peacefully broke free of the Soviet orbit in 1989, and in 1990 power was transferred to the **Hungarian Democratic Forum** in the first free elections. As privatization began, slow progress, inflation, and unemployment eroded the Forum's popularity. Subsequent elections would see the Socialists return to power.

TODAY

Hungary has come a long way since communism. Its government is led by a **president** who serves a five-year term in a largely ceremonial role. Elected every four years, the powerful **National Assembly** elects the president, who appoints the **prime minister,** who in turn appoints the **cabinet ministers.** Four **parties** participate regularly in parliament: the Hungarian Democratic Forum, the Hungarian Civic Alliance, the Alliance of Free Democrats, and the Hungarian Socialist Party. In 1994, Hungary opened its borders to the West and recouped economic and social stability. Today, wage problems and inflation are of diminishing concern, and Hungary has managed to stem unemployment and stabilize GDP growth. The country is politically stable and entered the **European Union (EU)** on May 1, 2004. Though Hungary is ruled by a Socialist-Liberal coalition, the conservative opposition won the majority of Hungary's seats in the recent European parliamentary elections.

Since 2000, **Ferenc Mádl** has been president. In 2004, former Prime Minister **Péter Medgyessy,** sacked by his onetime Socialist allies for dismissals of cabinet members, was replaced by **Ferenc Gyurcsány,** the former sports minister.

PEOPLE AND CULTURE

DEMOGRAPHICS. Hungary's population is 90% **Magyar** (ethnic Hungarian), 4% **Roma,** 3% **German,** and 2% **Serb.** The country's major religion is **Roman Catholicism,** with a sizeable **Calvinist** minority and smaller **Lutheran** and **atheist** minorities.

CUSTOMS AND ETIQUETTE. Rounding up the bill as a tip is standard for everyone from waiters to hairdressers. Check the bill: gratuity may be included. Foreigners should tip 15%. When the waiter brings the bill, pay immediately. Hand your tip to your server. At meals, **toasts** are common and should be returned. *Egészségünkre* ("to our health") is a useful word. **Bargaining** over open-air-market goods and taxi fare is appropriate. **Clothing** is westernized—jeans and t-shirts are the norm. In cities, women often dress in tight or revealing attire. Religious sites may require covered knees and shoulders. **Smoking** seems to be the national pastime.

LANGUAGE. Hungarian, a Finno-Ugric language, is distantly related to Turkish, Estonian, and Finnish. After Hungarian and German, English is Hungary's third most commonly spoken language. Almost all young people know some English. *"Hello"* is often used as an informal greeting. Coincidentally, *"Szia!"* (sounds like "see ya!") is another greeting—friends will often cry, "Hello, see ya!" For a phrasebook and glossary, see **Glossary: Hungarian,** p. 773.

THE ARTS

LITERATURE. The writers who lived through the Revolution of 1848 greatly impacted the country's literature. The Populist **Sándor Petőfi** fueled nationalistic rhetoric that drove the revolution. **Ferenc Kazinczy** was an early promoter of national literature in the Hungarian language. **Mór Jókai's** nationalism and down-to-earth tone endeared him to 19th-century readers. Hungarian literature gained focus with the 1908 founding of the *Nyugat* (West) literary journal, and with the work of avant-garde poet and artist **Lajos Kassák,** whose subject matter was working-class life. **Attila József,** an influential poet, integrated politics and art when he merged Freudian thought with Marxism. After WWII, communists forced Hungarian writers to adopt Socialist Realism; the next generation developed individual styles more freely. In 2002, **Imre Kertész** won Hungary's first Nobel Prize in Literature for work drawing on his experiences as a teen in Nazi concentration camps. Less concerned with historical issues than with exploration of language, the work of **Péter Esterházy** marks a new movement in contemporary Hungarian literature.

MUSIC. Hungary has gained the most international acclaim for its **music**. The greatest piano virtuoso of his time, **Ferenc Liszt** (1811-1886) is the most prolific musician in Hungary's history. His contributions range from advancing piano composition technique to inventing the symphonic poem. Though Liszt spoke German, not Hungarian, his heritage shines through in his Hungarian Rhapsodies, 19 pieces based on Hungarian folk music. Similarly, **Béla Bartók** (1881-1945) was noted for his use of folk material to create music that expressed a strong sense of nationalism. His most famous works include string quartets and the *Concerto for Orchestra*. In recent years, **Roma** music has gained increasing popularity.

VISUAL AND PERFORMING ARTS. The growth of fine arts in Hungary was influenced by artistic evolution in the rest of Europe, yet Hungary managed to add its own character at each stage. Renaissance and medieval frescoes on buildings were the most widely practiced art forms, later giving birth to historical painting and portraiture. The 20th century saw **Lajos Kassák** and **László Moholy-Nagy** emerge as avant-garde painters, and **Miklós Jancsó** and **István Szabó** stand as pioneers in Hungarian **film**. In the architectural arena, organic influences are a recent source of inspiration. **Imre Makovecz's** pavilion at the Seville Expo won him international acclaim in 1992. Hungarian **folk dancing** is also a point of cultural and artistic pride. **Csárdás**, the national dance, includes a women's circle and men's boot-slapping dances. All begin with a slow section *(lassú)* and end in a fast section *(friss)*. Dancers don embroidered costumes and perform music in double time.

HOLIDAYS AND FESTIVALS

Holidays: New Year's Day (Jan. 1); National Day (Mar. 15); Easter Holiday (Apr. 16-17); Labor Day (May 1); Pentecost (June 4); Constitution Day (St. Stephen's Day, Aug. 20); Republic Day (Oct. 23); All Saints' Day (Nov. 1); Christmas (Dec. 25-26).

Festivals: Central Europe's largest rock festival, **Sziget Festival,** hits Budapest for a week in late July or early August, featuring rollicking crowds and international superstar acts. Eger's fabulous **World Festival of Wine Songs** celebration kicks off in late September, bringing together boisterous choruses and world-famous vintages.

ADDITIONAL RESOURCES

GENERAL HISTORY

A History of Hungary, ed. by Peter Sugar, Peter Hanak, and Tibor Frank (1994). More exhaustive than most books of its kind in its treatment of Hungarian history.

A History of Modern Hungary 1867-1994, by Jorg K. Hoensch (1996). Provides a brief summary of Hungarian history.

FICTION AND NONFICTION

Ballad of the Whiskey Robber, by Julian Rubinstein (2004). Whimsical memoir by Hungary's most famous hockey-player-turned-thief illuminates post-Communist Hungary.

The Bridge at Andau, by James Michener (1988). A gripping account of the doomed 1956 uprising against the Russians and the Hungarians' escape into Austria.

Embers, by Sándor Márai (1942). This recently rediscovered masterpiece depicts the reunion of two old men who were boyhood friends.

Fateless, by Imre Kertész (1975). Kertész's Nobel Prize-winning work based on his experiences as a 15-year-old in Auschwitz and Buchenwald.

The Melancholy of Rebirth: Essays from Post-Communist Central Europe 1989-1994, by György Konrád (1995). Humorous and depressing views of communism in Hungary.

Prague, by Arthur Phillips (2002). A lyrical novel about a group of American expats living in fin-de-siècle Budapest who long for the post-Soviet Elysium of the Czech capital.

BUDAPEST ☎(06)1

A vibrant mix of East and West, medieval and modern, Budapest (pop. 1.9 million) is one of the most exhilarating cities in Europe. While other parts of Hungary seem uninterested in adopting the hectic pace of contemporary Western life, Budapest has seized upon cosmopolitan chic with a vengeance—without giving up such old-time charms as thermal baths that bubble up from beneath the city. Unlike in toyland Prague, the sights of Budapest spread throughout the energetic city, giving it a life independent of the growing tourist crowds. Once two cities, Budapest was born in 1872 with the union of Buda and Pest, and became the Hapsburg Empire's number two city. Although the city was ravaged by WWII, proud Hungarians rebuilt it and restored its majesty. Through the same pride, Budapest weathered Soviet invasion and 40 years of communist rule. That spirit still resonates through the streets today as the city reassumes its place as a major European capital.

⊠ INTERCITY TRANSPORTATION

Flights: Ferihegy Airport, BUD (☎296 9696, departures 296 7000, arrivals 296 8000). **Malév** (Hungarian Airlines; reservations ☎235 3888). To the center, take **bus #93** (20min., every 15min. 4:55am-11:20pm, 150Ft), then take M3 to Kőbánya-Kispest (15min. to Deák tér, in downtown Budapest). To catch this bus, turn right from Terminal A or left from B and find the "BKV Plusz Reptér Busz" sign. Purchase tickets from the kiosk in Terminal B or the machines outside Terminal A. Alternatively, take the **Airport Minibus** (☎296 8555) to hotels or hostels. Service runs 24hr.; call 1 day in advance for flights leaving Budapest. One-way 2300Ft.

Trains: For a complete listing of Hungarian rail schedules, go to www.elvira.hu. (International ☎461 5500, domestic 461 5400.) The main stations—**Keleti pu., Nyugati pu.,** and **Déli pu.**—are also Metro stops. Train stations are favorite haunts of thieves and pickpockets, so be careful. Most international trains arrive at and depart from Keleti pu. To: **Berlin, GER** (12-15hr.; 2 per day; 35,852Ft, reservation 1500Ft); **Bucharest, ROM** (14hr., 5 per day, 20,986Ft); **Prague, CZR** (8hr., 4 per day, 13243Ft); **Vienna, AUT** (3hr.; 17 per day; 8148Ft, reservation 700Ft); **Warsaw, POL** (11hr.; 2 per day; 17,515Ft, reservation 2000Ft). The daily **Orient Express** stops on its way from **Paris, FRA** to **Istanbul, TUR.** Trains depart from Budapest to most major destinations in Hungary. Check www.elvira.hu for schedules and some prices or ask at the info booths in the stations. For **student discounts,** show your ISIC and tell the clerk "diák." On domestic trains an ISIC is technically invalid, but ask anyway.

International Ticket Office: Keleti pu. Open daily 8am-7pm; info desk 24hr. Nyugati pu. Open M-Sa 5am-9pm.

MÁV Hungarian Railways, VI, Andrássy út 35 (☎461 5500; www.mav.hu). Branch offices at all train stations. Sells domestic and international tickets. Check the website for prices. Ask about ISIC discounts. Open Apt.-Sept. M-F 9am-6pm, Oct.-Mar. M-F 9am-5pm.

Carlson Wagonlit Travel, V, Dorottya u. 3 (☎483 3384), off Vörösmarty tér. Open M-Th 9am-12:45pm and 1:30-5pm, F 9am-12:45pm and 1:30-3:30pm. AmEx/MC/V.

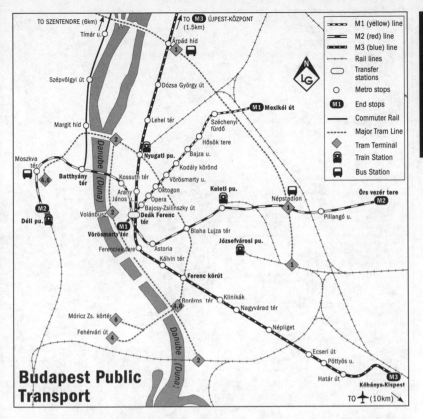

Budapest Public Transport

Buses: The most common and fastest mode of transport between towns in Hungary is by bus, but bring a cushion as seats can be hard. Bus schedules are at www.volanbusz.hu/english/index.php and www.volan.hu/new. Buses to international and some domestic destinations arrive at and depart from the **Népliget** station, X, Ulloi u. 131, near the Népliget metro station. (M3: Népliget. ☎382 0888. Ticket window open M-F 6am-9pm, Sa-Su 6am-4pm.) To: **Berlin, GER** (14½hr., 6 per wk., 16,900Ft); **Prague, CZR** (8hr., 6 per wk., 9900Ft); **Vienna, AUT** (3-3½hr., 4 per day, 5490Ft). Catch buses to and from destinations east of Budapest at the **Népstadion** station, XIV, Hungária krt. 46-48. (☎252 4498. Open M-F 6am-6pm, Sa-Su 6am-4pm.) M2: Népstadion. Buses to the Danube Bend and parts of the Northern Uplands depart outside **Árpád híd** metro station on the M3 line. (☎329 1450. Cashier open 6am-8pm.)

⚕ ORIENTATION

Buda and Pest are separated by the **Danube River** (Duna). The modern capital preserves the distinctive character of each. On the west side, **Buda's** tree-lined streets wind through the cobblestone **Castle District** on the way to the hilltop citadel. On the east side, grid-like avenues, shopping boulevards, and the Parliament spread over the commercial center of **Pest.** In contrast to Buda's backroads, Pest's lay-

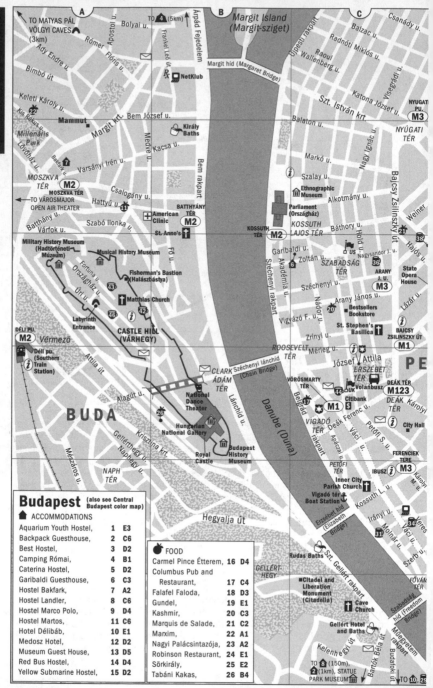

HUNGARY

TO MATYAS PÁL VÖLGYI CAVES (3km)

TO (5km)

Margit Island (Margit-sziget)

Margit híd (Margaret Bridge)

NetKlub

Király Baths

Mammut

Milenáris Park

MOSZKVA TÉR **M2**
MOSZKVA TÉR
TO VÁROSMAJOR OPEN AIR THEATER

American Clinic **M2**

BATTHYÁNY TÉR **M2**

St. Anne's

Military History Museum (Hadtörténeti Múzeum)

Musical History Museum

Fisherman's Bastion (Halászbástya)

Matthias Church

Labyrinth Entrance

CASTLE HILL (VÁRHEGY)

DÉLI PU. **M2** Vérmező

Déli pu. (Southern Train Station)

BUDA

National Dance Theater

Hungarian National Gallery

Royal Castle

Budapest History Museum

NAPH TÉR

Ethnographic Museum

Parliament (Országház)

KOSSUTH TÉR

KOSSUTH LAJOS TÉR **M2**

SZABADSÁG TÉR

US

State Opera House

ARANY J. U. **M3**

Bestsellers Bookstore

St. Stephen's Basilica

BAJCSY ZSILINSZKY **M1**

ROOSEVELT TÉR

CLARK ÁDÁM TÉR

Széchenyi lánchíd (Chain Bridge)

József Attila

ERZSÉBET TÉR

VÖRÖSMARTY TÉR

Volánbusz

DEÁK TÉR **M123**

Citibank

M1

DEÁK Károlyi TÉR

VIGADÓ TÉR

City Hall

Danube (Duna)

PETŐFI TÉR

FERENCIEK TERE **M3**

Inner City Parish Church

Vigadó tér Boat Station

Erzsébet híd (Elizabeth Bridge)

Hegyalja út

Rudas Baths

GELLÉRT-HEGY

■Citadel and Liberation Monument (Citadella)

Cave Church

Gellért Hotel and Baths

TO (150m), (1km), STATUE PARK MUSEUM

PE

NYUGATI PU. **M3**

NYUGATI TÉR

Budapest (also see Central Budapest color map)

🏠 ACCOMMODATIONS

Aquarium Youth Hostel,	1	E3
Backpack Guesthouse,	2	C6
Best Hostel,	3	D2
Camping Római,	4	B1
Caterina Hostel,	5	D2
Garibaldi Guesthouse,	6	C3
Hostel Bakfark,	7	A2
Hostel Landler,	8	C6
Hostel Marco Polo,	9	D4
Hostel Martos,	11	C6
Hotel Délibáb,	10	E1
Medosz Hotel,	12	D2
Museum Guest House,	13	D5
Red Bus Hostel,	14	D4
Yellow Submarine Hostel,	15	D2

🍴 FOOD

Carmel Pince Étterem,	16	D4
Columbus Pub and Restaurant,	17	C4
Falafel Faloda,	18	D3
Gundel,	19	E1
Kashmir,	20	C3
Marquis de Salade,	21	C2
Marxim,	22	A1
Nagyi Palácsintazója,	23	A2
Robinson Restaurant,	24	E1
Sörkirály,	25	E2
Tabáni Kakas,	26	B4

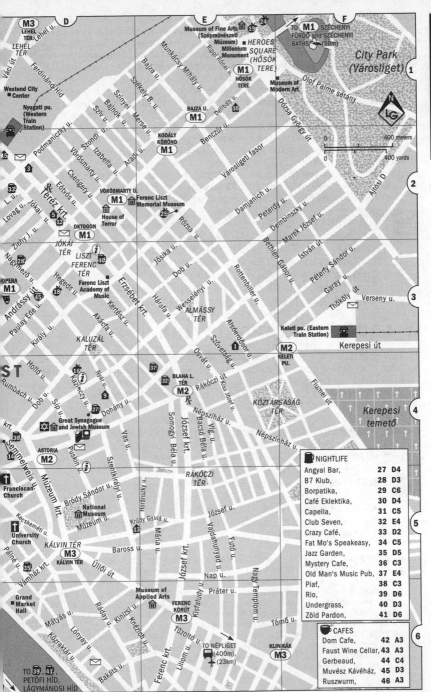

HUNGARY

NIGHTLIFE

Angyal Bar,	**27**	**D4**
B7 Klub,	**28**	**D3**
Borpatika,	**29**	**C6**
Café Eklektika,	**30**	**D4**
Capella,	**31**	**C5**
Club Seven,	**32**	**E4**
Crazy Café,	**33**	**D2**
Fat Mo's Speakeasy,	**34**	**C5**
Jazz Garden,	**35**	**D5**
Mystery Cafe,	**36**	**C3**
Old Man's Music Pub,	**37**	**E4**
Piaf,	**38**	**C3**
Rio,	**39**	**D6**
Undergrass,	**40**	**D3**
Zöld Pardon,	**41**	**D6**

CAFES

Dom Cafe,	**42**	**A3**
Faust Wine Cellar,	**43**	**A3**
Gerbeaud,	**44**	**C4**
Muvész Kávéház,	**45**	**D3**
Ruszwurm,	**46**	**A3**

out is easily navigable. Three main bridges tie Budapest together: **Széchényi lánchíd** connects **Roosevelt tér** to the **Várhegy** (Castle Hill) cable car. To the south, **Erzsébet híd** runs from near **Petőfi tér** to the St. Gellért monument at **Gellérthegy** (Gellért Hill). Farther along the **Danube**, **Szabadság híd** links **Fővám tér** to the south end of Gellérthegy. Finally, **Petőfi híd** and **Lágymányosi híd**, farther south, and **Margit híd**, to the north, also connect Buda with Pest. Budapest's tram and transportation hub is north of the Castle District at **Moszkva tér**, and the HÉV commuter railway, which heads north through **Óbuda** to **Szentendre**, starts at **Batthyány tér**, opposite Parliament, one Metro stop past the Danube in Buda. Budapest's **Metro** is the oldest in Continental Europe. Its three lines (orange M1, red M2, and blue M3) converge at **Deák tér**. Deák tér is at the center of Pest. Two blocks toward the river is **Vörösmarty tér**. The pedestrian shopping zone **Váci u.** is to the right, facing the statue of Mihály Vörösmarty. The zone ends at the central market, housed in a building with a multicolored tile roof. Addresses in Budapest begin with a Roman numeral representing one of the city's **23 districts**. Central Buda is I; central Pest is V. The middle two digits of postal codes indicate the district.

 BUS TICKETS. Hungarian buses, whether between cities or simply in local public transportation, are unfamiliar territory for the traveler. On intercity buses, tickets are purchased from the driver rather than in advance. It's first come, first serve, so people tend to jostle at the door to get a seat. On public transportation, tickets generally can be purchased in advance or from the driver. While it may seem easy just to jump on for the ride without paying, be careful: drivers often watch closely in the rearview mirror, and the fines can be steep.

⌐ LOCAL TRANSPORTATION

Commuter Trains: The **HÉV commuter railway** station is across the river from Parliament, 1 Metro stop past the Danube in Buda at Batthyány tér. Trains head to **Szentendre** (45min., every 15min. 5am-9pm, 430Ft). Purchase tickets at the station for transport beyond city limits or face a hefty fine. On the list of stops, those within city limits are in a different color. Békásmegyer is the last stop within city limits. For travel within the city, a simple transportation ticket or pass will work.

Public Transportation: Budapest's public transport is inexpensive, convenient, and easy to navigate. The **Metro** and **trams** run every few min. 4:30am-11:30pm, and **buses** are generally on time (schedules posted at stops). Many buses run 24hr.

 FINES. Riding ticketless means a 2000Ft fee if you can pay on the spot—much more if you need to pay by mail. Inspectors in red armbands prowl the **Deák tér** metro stop in particular, and are especially likely to stop tourists. They often wait at the top of escalators. Punch a new ticket when switching lines. Inspectors also issue fines for losing the cover sheet to the 10-ticket packet.

Budapest Public Transport (BKV; ☎80 406 686; www.bkv.hu) has info in Hungarian. Open M-F 7am-3pm. **Tickets** (160Ft, 10 tickets 1450Ft, 20 tickets 2600Ft; no transfers), sold in Metro stations, Trafik shops, and kiosks. Buses and trams use different tickets, both of which can also be purchased at machines at individual stops (160Ft, change only). Punch them in orange boxes at Metro gates and on buses and trams. A ticket is valid for a single trip on only 1 metro line; a *metrószakaszjegy* (115Ft) is valid for 3 Metro stops; a *metrószakaszállójegy* (260Ft) is valid for 5 Metro stops with transfer. Consider buying a **pass.** (Day pass 1275Ft, 3-day 2550Ft, 1-wk. 3000Ft, 2-wk. 3850Ft, 1-month 5700Ft. Unlimited public transportation and other perks available with the Budapest Card; see **Tourist and Financial Services,** below.) Monthly passes require a transport ID card (100Ft), so bring a photo. Budapest transport tickets are good on HÉV suburban trains within city limits. Otherwise, purchase separate HÉV tickets.

HUNGARY

Night Transportation: The Metro discontinues service around 11:30pm, but gates may lock at 10:30pm. All Metro stops post the times for the first and last trains by the tracks. Buses and trams stop running at 11pm. Buses with numbers ending in "É" run midnight-5am. Buses #7É and 78É follow the M2 route, #6É follows the 4/6 tram line, and bus #14É and 50É run the same route as M3.

Taxis: Because the transport system in Budapest is so efficient, there's rarely a need for a taxi. Beware of scams; check for a yellow license plate and a running meter. Before getting in, ask how much the ride costs. Prices should not exceed: 6am-10pm base fare 200Ft, 200Ft per km, 50Ft per min. waiting; 10pm-6am base fare 280Ft plus 280Ft per km, 70Ft per min. waiting. **Budataxi** (☎233 3333). 135Ft per km by phone, 200Ft per km on the street. To the airport: 3500Ft from Pest and 4000Ft from Buda. **Főtaxi** (☎222 2222). 140Ft per km by phone and 160Ft per km on the street. To the airport: 3500Ft from Pest and 4000Ft from Buda. **6x6 Taxi** (☎266 6666), **City Taxi** (☎211 1111), **Rádió Taxi** (☎377 7777), and **Tele 5 Taxi** (☎355 5555) are also reliable.

Car Rental: There are several reliable rental agencies. Cars from US$40-50 per day. Credit card required. Few agencies rent to those under 21. **Avis**, V, Szervita tér 8 (☎318 4859). Open M-Sa 7am-6pm, Su 8am-noon. **Budget**, I, Krisztina krt. 41-43 (☎214 0420). Open M-F 8am-8pm, Sa-Su 8am-6pm. **Hertz**, V, Apáczai Csere János u. 4 (☎266 4361). Open daily 7am-7pm.

⬛ PRACTICAL INFORMATION

TOURIST AND FINANCIAL SERVICES

Tourist Offices: Tourist offices, Metro stations, and travel agencies sell the **Budapest Card** (Budapest Kártya). It includes unlimited public transport, entrance to most museums, reduced rates on car rental and the airport minibus, and discounts at shops, baths, and restaurants. (2-day card 4900Ft, 3-day 5700Ft.) Pick up *Budapest in Your Pocket* (free), an up-to-date city guide.

Tourinform, V, Sütő u. 2 (☎438 8080), off Deák tér behind McDonald's. M1, 2, or 3: Deák tér. Open daily 8am-8pm. **Branch** at VI, Liszt tér 11 (☎322 4098), M1: Oktogon.

Vista Travel Center: Visitor's Center, Andrássy út 1 (☎429 9751; incoming@vista.hu). Arranges tours and accommodations. Go early to avoid crowds. Open M-F 9am-6:30pm, Sa 9am-2:30pm.

IBUSZ, V, Ferenciek tere 10 (☎485 2700). M3: Ferenciek tere. Books cheap tickets and sightseeing tours (3hr. tour 6400Ft, with Budapest Card 4350Ft); finds rooms (see **Accommodations,** p. 283); and **exchanges currency**. Open M-F 9am-5pm. Sa 9am-1pm for currency exchange only. **Western Union** available. AmEx/MC/V for some services. Branches are common around the city.

Embassies and Consulates:

Australia, XII, Királyhágó tér 8/9 (☎457 9777; www.australia.hu). M2: Déli pu., then bus #21 or tram #59 to Királyhágó tér. Open M-F 9am-noon.

Canada, XII, Ganz u. 12-14 (☎392 3360). Open M-Th 8:30-10:30am and 2-3:30pm.

Ireland, V, Szabadság tér 7 (☎302 9600), in Bank Center. M3: Arany János. Walk down Bank u. toward the river. Open M-F 9:30am-12:30pm and 2:30-4:30pm.

New Zealand, VI, Nagymezo u. 50 (☎302 2484). M3: Nyugati pu. Open M-F 11am-4pm by appointment only.

UK, V, Harmincad u. 6 (☎266 2888), near the intersection with Vörösmarty tér. M1: Vörösmarty tér. Open M-F 9:30am-12:30pm and 2:30-4:30pm.

US, V, Szabadság tér 12 (☎475 4464, after hours 475 4703; www.usembassy.hu). M2: Kossuth tér. Walk 2 blocks on Akadémia and turn on Zoltán. Open M-Th 1-4pm, F 9am-noon and 1-4pm.

Currency Exchange: Banks have the best rates. Avoid the steep premiums at the airport, train stations, and exchange shops. **Citibank,** V, Vörösmarty tér 4 (☎374 5000). M1: Vörösmarty tér. Provides MC/V **cash advances** and cashes **traveler's checks** for no commission. Open M-Th 9am-5pm, F 9am-4pm. **Budapest Bank,** V, Váci u. 1/3 (☎328 3155). M1: Vörösmarty tér. Offers credit card **cash advances** and cashes **traveler's**

HUNGARY

checks into US currency for 3.5% commission. Open M-F 8:30am-5pm, Sa 9am-2pm. Omnipresent **OTP** and **K&H** banks also have good rates. Limited **American Express** services, including cashing **traveler's checks**, are at V, Váci u. 10 (☎267 6262).

LOCAL SERVICES

Luggage storage: Keleti pu. Lockers across from international cashier 300Ft per day; large bags 600Ft per day. **Nyugati pu.**, in the waiting room near the ticket windows. 300Ft per day; large bags 600Ft. Open 24hr. **Déli pu.** 150Ft per 6hr., 300Ft per 24hr.; large bags 300/600Ft. Lockers 200Ft per day. Open daily 3:30am-11:30pm.

English-Language Bookstores: Libri Könyvpalota, VII, Rákóczi u. 12 (☎267 4843), M2: Astoria. The best choice. A multilevel bookstore, it has 1 fl. of up-to-date English titles. Open M-F 10am-7:30pm, Sa 10am-3pm. MC/V. **Bestsellers Livres**, V, Október 6 u. 11 (☎312 1295; www.bestsellers.hu), off Arany János u. M1, 2, or 3: Deák tér or M3: Arany János. Open M-F 9am-6:30pm, Sa 10am-5pm, Su 10am-4pm.

GLBT Hotline: GayGuide.net Budapest (☎0630 932 3334; www.budapest.gayguide.net). Posts an online guide and runs a hotline (daily 4-8pm) with info and reservations at GLBT-friendly lodgings. See also **GLBT Budapest,** p. 296

THE REAL VÁCI U. If you're hoping to do some shopping along Váci u., be careful: Budapest has two streets named Váci u. that are far apart from each other—one is in district XIII, while the shopping boulevard is in district V.

EMERGENCY AND COMMUNICATIONS

Tourist Police: V, Sütő u. 2 (☎438 8080). M1, 2, or 3: Deák tér. Inside the Tourinform office. Tourists can report stolen and lost items, and other police matters. Tourist Police often can't do much. Beware of people pretending to be Tourist Police who demand your passport. Open 24hr.

Pharmacies: II, Frankel Leó út 22 (☎212 4406). AmEx/MC/V. **VI**, Teréz krt. 41 (☎311 4439). Open M-F 8am-8pm, Sa 8am-2pm. **VII**, Rákóczi út 39 (☎314 3695). Open M-F 7:30am-9pm, Sa 7:30am-2pm; no after-hours service. **VIII**, Üllöi út 121 (☎215 3900). Look for a green-and-white *Apotheke, Gyógyszertár,* or *Pharmacie* sign in the window.

Medical Assistance: Ambulance (☎104). **Falck (SOS) KFT**, II, Kapy út 49/b (☎200 0100). Ambulance service US$120. **American Clinic**, I, Hattyú u. 14 (☎224 9090; www.americanclinics.com). Accepts walk-ins, but calling a day ahead is helpful. Open M 8:30am-7pm, Tu-W 10am-6pm, Th 11:30am-6pm, F 10am-6pm. You will be charged for physician's time plus tests. Direct insurance billing available. 24hr. emergency ☎224 9090. The US embassy also maintains a list of English-speaking doctors.

Telephones: Domestic operator and info ☎198; international operator 190, info 199. Most phones use **phone cards,** available at kiosks and Metro stations. 50-unit card 800Ft, 120-unit card 1800Ft.

Internet: Cyber cafes litter the city, but access can be expensive and long waits are common. Internet is available at many hostels, where it is usually cheaper than at cafes.

Ami Internet Coffee, V, Váci u. 40 (☎267 1644; www.amicoffee.hu). M3: Ferenciek tere. Lounge with drinks. 200Ft per 15min., 700Ft per hr. Open daily 9am-2am.

Libri Könyvpalota, VII, Rákóczi út 12 (☎267 4843; www.libri.hu). M2: Astoria. Inside English-language bookstore. 250Ft per 30min., 400Ft per hr. Open M-F 10am-7:30pm, Sa 10am-3pm.

NetKlub, II, Frankel Leó út 11 (☎212 3999; www.net-klub.hu). HÉV: Margit híd. On the Buda side. 290Ft per 30min., 500Ft per hr. Open M-F 10am-midnight, Sa-Su 2-10pm.

Post Office: V, Városház u. 18 (☎318 4811). **Poste Restante** (Postán Mar) in office around the right side of the building. Open M-F 8am-8pm, Sa 8am-2pm. Branches at Nyugati pu.; VI, Teréz krt. 105/107; Keleti pu.; VIII, Baross tér 11/c; and elsewhere. Open M-F 7am-8pm, Sa 8am-2pm. **Postal Code:** Depends on the district—postal codes are 1XX2, where XX is the district number (1052 for post office listed above).

ⓚ ACCOMMODATIONS

Tourists fill the city in July and August; phone first or store luggage while looking for a bed. If you book a room, call again the night before to confirm: hostels have been known to "misplace" reservations. Tourists arriving at Keleti pu. enter a feeding frenzy, as hostel solicitors jostle each other for guests. Don't be drawn in by promises of rides or discounts: some hostel-hawkers stretch the truth.

ACCOMMODATION AGENCIES

Private rooms ❷ (3000Ft-5000Ft; prices decrease with longer stays) are slightly more expensive than hostels, but offer what most hostels can't: peace, quiet, and private showers. Accommodation agencies are everywhere. For cheaper rooms, be there when the agency opens and be prepared to haggle. Before accepting a room, make sure the hostel is easily accessible by public transport. Bring cash. ▧**Best Hotel Service,** V, Sütö u. 2, in the courtyard, handles hotel, apartment, pension, and hostel reservations; car rentals; and city tours. (M1, 2, or 3: Deák tér. ☎318 4848. Rooms from 6000Ft. Open daily 8am-8pm.) **IBUSZ**, V, Ferenciek tere 10, books comparatively cheap rooms. (M3: Ferenciek tere. Doubles 5000-10,000Ft; triples 6500-12,000Ft. 1800Ft fee for stays of fewer than 4 nights.) IBUSZ also rents central Pest apartments with kitchen and bath. (1-bedroom flat from 8000Ft, 2-bedroom from 12,000Ft). Reserve by email or fax. (☎485 2700; accommodation@ibusz.hu. Open M-F 8:15am-5pm.) There's a branch at VIII, Keleti pu. (☎342 9572. Open M-F 8am-6pm.)

HOSTELS AND HOTELS

From wild hostels to hushed hotels, Budapest has accommodations to fit every preference. Some of the city's most exciting social centers, hostels are full of backpackers in summer and can be a great place to meet people. Many university dorms become hostels in summer. The **Hungarian Youth Hostels Association,** which operates from Keleti pu., runs many hostels. Their staff wear Hostelling International t-shirts and will—along with legions of competitors—accost you as you get off the train. Many provide free transport.

BUDA

▧ **Backpack Guesthouse**, XI, Takács Menyhért u. 33 (☎385 8946; www.backpackbudapest.hu), 12min. from central Pest. From Keleti pu., take bus #7 or 7a toward Buda. Get off at Tétényi u., then backtrack and turn left under the bridge. Take another left on Hamzsabégi út and continue to the 3rd right. With creatively themed rooms, a common room stocked with movies, and a slew of hammocks, this cozy neighborhood house will make you feel at home. Backyard gazebo is rented out at night. The 49E night bus runs here after trams stop. Laundry 1500Ft. Free Internet. Reception 24hr. Reserve ahead; confirm the night before. 7- to 11-bed dorms 2500Ft, 4- to 5-bed dorms 3000Ft; doubles 6600Ft; mattress in gazebo 1800Ft. Cash only. ❷

Hostel Martos, XI, Stoczek u. 5/7 (☎209 4883; reception@hotel.martos.bme.hu). From Keleti pu., take bus #7 to Móricz Zsigmond Körtér and go 300m toward the river on Bartók Béla út. Turn right on Bertalan Lajos and take the 3rd right on Stoczek u. Cheap, clean, student-run hostel with a kitchen on each floor. Martos expands in summer, but rooms are available year-round. A short walk to outdoor clubs along the river. Laundry 60Ft per hr., free to guests who stay a few days. Free Internet and satellite TV. Checkout 10am. Reserve a few days in advance. Singles 4000Ft; doubles 5000Ft, with shower 8000Ft; triples 7500Ft; apartments with bath 15,000Ft. Cash only. ❸

PEST

🏛 **Museum Guest House,** VIII, Mikszáth Kálmán tér 4, 1st fl. (☎318 9508; museumgh@freemail.c3.hu). M3: Kálvin tér. Take the left exit on Baross u.; at the fork, go left on Reviczky u. At the square, go to right corner and ring buzzer at gate #4. Convenient location, freshly painted rooms, and lofted beds that create a sense of privacy. English spoken. Kitchen, luggage storage, and free Internet. Laundry 1200Ft. Reception 24hr. Check-out 11am. Reserve ahead. Dorms 3200Ft. Cash only. ❷

🏛 **Caterina Hostel,** III, Teréz krt. 30, apt. #28, ring code: #48 (☎269 5990; www.caterinahostel.hu). M1: Oktogon. Or trams #4 or 6. Prime location in central Pest. Newly renovated and sunny, with spacious rooms. Fresh linens and in-room TVs. Transport to airport 1800Ft. English spoken. Laundry 1200Ft. Internet 100Ft per 15min. Reception 24hr. Check-out 10am. Lockout 10am-1pm. Reserve by fax or email. Dorms 2500-2800Ft; private room 6800Ft. Cash only. ❷

Red Bus Hostel, V, Semmelweis u. 14 (☎266 0136; www.redbusbudapest.hu). A fabulous value in downtown Pest. The Red Bus boasts new, clean, spacious dorms with yellow-and-orange walls; a large common room; and a kitchen. Simple breakfast included. Free luggage storage. Laundry 1200Ft. Internet 12Ft per min. Reception 24hr. Check-out 10am. Dorms 3000Ft; singles and doubles 7900Ft; triples 11,000Ft. V. ❷

Yellow Submarine Hostel, VI, Teréz krt. 56, 3rd fl. (☎331 9896; www.yellowsubmarinehostel.com), across from Nyugati pu. A great place to crash after a hard day's night. The Yellow Submarine is known as a party hostel: friends are easily made and rowdy crowds hang out in the common room. Large dorms with bunk beds and lockers. Doubles and triples in nearby apartments. Breakfast included for dorms. Laundry 1700 Ft. Internet 10Ft per min. Check-out 9am. Dorms 2900Ft; singles 7500Ft; doubles 9000Ft; triples and quads 3500Ft per person. 10% HI discount. MC/V. ❷

Aquarium Youth Hostel, VII, Alsóerdősor u. 12 (☎322 0502; aquarium@budapesthostels.com). Unmarked. Ring the buzzer with the hostel symbol on it. Close to Keleti pu., and near Metro, trams, and buses. Run by a hospitable staff, this small, fun-loving hostel is decorated with an underwater theme. Kitchen. Laundry 1200Ft. Free Internet. Reception 24hr. Dorms 3000Ft; doubles 8500Ft. Cash only. ❷

Best Hostel, VI, Podmaniczky u. 27, 1st fl. (☎332 4934; www.besthostel.hu). Take a left out of Nyugati pu.; it's the first street you come to. Ring bell #33 in the building on the corner. The name may be a tad ambitious, but this quiet hostel has large rooms with hardwood floors, a common room, and a kitchen. Lights-out in dorms 11pm. No smoking or drinking allowed. Breakfast included. Laundry 1000Ft. Internet 10Ft per min. Dorms 3000Ft; doubles 3600Ft; triples 4200Ft. 10% HI discount. Cash only. ❷

Hostel Marco Polo, VII, Nyár u. 6 (☎413 2555; www.marcopolohostel.com). M2: Astoria or Blaha Lujza tér. Has a luxury-hotel feel and more privacy than other hostels, as dorm bunk beds are in separate compartments blocked off by curtains. Courtyard patio and basement restaurant with bar. Laundry 600Ft. Internet 7Ft per min. Reception 24hr. Reserve ahead July-Aug. Dorms 5000Ft; singles 13,750Ft; doubles 18,900Ft; triples 21,000Ft; quads 26,000Ft. 10% HI and ISIC discount. Cash only. ❸

Medosz Hotel, VI, Jókai tér 9 (☎374 3001; info@medoszhotel.hu), a 5min. walk from Oktogon shopping center and the Opera House. Though the concrete facade may be foreboding, the rooms are clean and sunny. English-speaking staff arranges sightseeing tours. Breakfast included. Reserve ahead. Singles 11,000Ft; doubles 14,300Ft; triples 16,800Ft; apartments 17,500-20,000Ft. 10% student or HI discount. MC/V. ❸

Hotel Délibáb, VI, Délibáb u. 35 (☎342 9301; www.hoteldelibab.hu). M1: Hősök tere. This century-old neo-Renaissance building is in a quiet neighborhood just outside Heroes' Square. The rooms are less than exciting but provide a great base for exploring the museums and baths of the city's east end. Breakfast included. Laundry available. Singles 12,750-16,500Ft; doubles 14,750-19,000Ft; extra bed 3750Ft. MC/V. ❺

SUMMER HOSTELS, GUEST HOUSES, CAMPING

Many **university dorms** moonlight as hostels in July and August. Most are clustered around Móricz Zsigmond Körtér in District XI. All have kitchens, luggage storage, and common room TVs. For a home-away-from-home feel, stay in a **guest house** or **apartment.** Only a bit more expensive (about 1500Ft extra per person) than a hostel bed, guesthouses offer privacy, peace, and perks like private bathrooms and TV. Owners often allow guests to use the kitchen or laundry machine. Provided with keys, guests can come and go as they please. Budapest's nearest **campgrounds** are a bit out of the way, but can be peaceful and scenic alternatives to the city.

Hostel Bakfark, II, Bakfark u. 1/3 (☎413 2062). M2: Moszkva tér. Walk along Margit krt. and take 1st right after Mammut. Although across the river from the action, these dorms are among the most comfortable in town, with lofted beds. Students get a heavy discount, making this an unbeatable central Buda bargain. Check-out 10am. Open June 15-Aug. 28. Dorms 3300-3500Ft, students 2000Ft. 10% HI discount. Cash only. ❶

Garibaldi Guesthouse, V, Garibaldi u. 5 (☎302 3456; garibaldiguest@hotmail.com). M2: Kossuth tér. Head away from Parliament along Nádor u. and take 1st right on Garibaldi u. Welcoming and comfortable, and only a block from the Danube and the Parliament building. Spacious, beautiful rooms. Most have TVs, kitchenettes, and baths. Owner has rooms throughout the city, including some near Astoria. Dorms 3200-4000Ft; singles 6500-7000Ft; doubles 8000Ft; apartments 6000-10,000Ft per person. Prices decrease with longer stays, big groups, and low season dates. Cash only. ❷

Camping Római, III, Szentendrei út 189 (☎388 7167). M2: Batthyány tér, then take the HÉV to Római fürdő, cross the street, and go toward the river. The complex indulges guests with a grocery store, restaurants, a swimming pool, and a park. Bungalows are ranked by amenities. Complex is guarded. Kitchen and communal showers. Breakfast 880Ft. Laundry 800Ft. Tent space 990Ft per person. Tents 2100Ft per person, bungalows 1800-15000Ft. Electricity 600Ft. Tourist tax 3%. 10% HI discount. Cash only. ❶

Hostel Landler, XI, Bartók Béla út 17 (☎463 3621). Take bus #7 or 7A across the river to Gellért. Ample natural light bathes this antiquated building. Free transport from bus or train station. Laundry. Check-out 9am. Open July to early Sept. Singles about 7000Ft; triples about 13,000Ft; quads about 17,000Ft. 10% HI discount. Cash only. ❸

Zugligeti "Niche" Camping, XII, Zugligeti út 101 (☎/fax 200 8346; www.camping-niche.hu). Take bus #158 from above Moszkva tér to Laszállóhely, the last stop. Restaurant. Communal showers. 1200Ft per person, 800Ft per tent, 1200Ft per large tent, 900Ft per car, 2200Ft per caravan. Cash only. ❶

◘ HUNGARY?

For something cheap, explore the cafeterias beneath "Önkiszolgáló Étterem" signs (meals 300-500Ft) or seek out a neighborhood *kifőzés* (kiosk) or *vendéglő* (vendor). Corner markets stock the basics, and many have 24hr. windows. The king of them all, the █**Grand Market Hall,** IX, Várház körút 1/3 on Fövam tér, built in 1897, boasts 10,000 sq. m of stalls. You'll find produce, baked goods, meat, and every souvenir imaginable. (M3: Kálvin tér. ☎217 6067. Open M 6am-5pm, Tu-F 6am-6pm, Sa 6am-2pm.) Try **lángos,** Hungarian-style fried dough with cheese and

THE HIDDEN DEAL

THE SANDWICH OF DEATH

The descent into the Matyas Caves, situated in the depths of the Buda Hills, is met by overwhelming darkness and absolute silence. The air is so cold—hovering at a chilly 10°C—that you would be able to see your breath as clearly as a bellowing chimney—that is, if you could see.

What brings travelers so deep into the silent depths is the opportunity to partake in caving, the unforgettable experience of snaking through the underground labyrinthine caves. Yet what brings visitors to these particular caves is the "Sandwich of Death," the finale of the journey. Equipped only with a helmet and flashlight, spelunkers venture through the path that descends 220m to sea level and back up again, inching past heart-stopping 40m drops and squeezing through crevices barely large enough to fit your helmet. The climactic sandwich isn't quite as dangerous as it sounds—it's a 12m stomach-crawl through two slabs of limestone.

Caving is not for the claustrophobic. That said, the experience certainly isn't only for the rough-and-ready. Guides judge the skill level of their groups, and choose the difficulty of the path accordingly.

Follow directions to the Pál-Völgyi Caves (p. 290). Call ahead (☎28 49 69) to reserve a spot and check tour times. 2100Ft.

sour cream toppings. For ethnic restaurants, try the upper floors of **Mammut Plaza** (see **Entertainment,** p. 293), just outside the Moszkva tér Metro stop in Buda, or the **West End Plaza,** accessible from the Nyugati Metro stop in Pest.

■ **Columbus Pub and Restaurant,** V, Danube (☎266 9013), on the promenade near the Chain Bridge. If you haven't spent enough time with the beautiful Danube during your stay in Budapest, enjoy a meal on this moored ship. A great view of Castle Hill and the citadel go along with the fine selection of Hungarian food, beer, and drinks. Entrees 1300-3500Ft. Open daily 11am-midnight. AmEx/MC/V. ❹

■ **Nagyi Palácsintazója,** II, Hattyú u. 16 (☎201 5321). The perfect stop after a day of heavy sightseeing on Castle Hill or, better yet, after a night of even heavier drinking. This 24hr. joint dishes out both sweet (118-178Ft) and savory crepes (218-298Ft) piled high with cheese, fruit, chocolate sauce, or anything else you could possibly desire. Seats are squeezed in everywhere, even on the wall along the stairwell, in this tiny, mirror-covered restaurant. English menu. Cash only. ❶

Tabáni Kakas, I, Attila u. 27 (☎375 7165), behind Castle Hill. For the serious meat-eater. Pictures of Budapest line the otherwise bland interior; the real effort goes into the hearty, hearty fare. Fist-sized goose venison dumplings (1900Ft) will leave you floored. Hearty entrees 1500-2500Ft. English menu. Open daily noon-midnight. Cash only. ❹

Kashmir, V, Arany János u. 13 (☎354 1806). If you've had your fill of Hungarian knuckle dishes, this Indian restaurant offers a lighter alternative. Kashmiri specialties (saffron chicken, 1690Ft) and several vegetarian options (chana masala, 890Ft). Get comfortable on cushioned benches against dimly lit red walls, as Indian beats play softly in the background. For those who just can't get enough goulash, Hungarian dishes are also available. English menu. M-F 11am-11pm, Sa-Su 5-11pm. Cash only. ❹

Gundel, XIV, Allatkerti út 2 (☎468 4040). Hungary's most famous restaurant, Gundel has served its delicate cuisine to Queen Elizabeth II. There are 7-course meals (13,000-17,500Ft), but if you just want to say you've been here you should opt for a sandwich (400-600Ft) on the patio. Specialty is goose liver (6110Ft). Su brunch buffet 11:30am-3pm, 4900Ft. Open daily noon-4pm and 6:30pm-midnight. AmEx/MC/V. ❺

Marquis de Salade, VI, Hajós u. 43 (☎302 4086). At the corner of Bajcsy-Zsilinszky út, 2 blocks from the Metro. M3: Arany János. An elegant cellar restaurant with a huge menu of offerings from Azerbaijan and Russia, such as *jalancs dolma*, a vegetarian dish of savory veggies stuffed with rice. Portions are large and the appetizers can be as filling as an entree elsewhere. Entrees 1800-3500Ft. Open daily 11am-1am. Cash only. ❹

Robinson Mediterranean-Style Restaurant and Cafe, XIV, Városliget tó (☎422 0222), sits in a lake in the scenic City Park. The open-air dining area overlooks the castle and the lake. Robinson dishes up enchanting Mediterranean fare, albeit a bit slowly. Also serves local favorites like liver (2150Ft) and paprika veal (2600Ft). Vegetarian options available. Entrees 1800-5800Ft. Open daily noon-4pm and 6pm-midnight. MC/V. ❹

Sörkirály, VI, Király u. 112 (☎321 3177). M1: Oktogon. Hungarian classics at great value. The super-cheap "Beer Drinkers" menu offers a selection of sandwiches (vaguely named "Hungarian style" sandwich 350Ft), in addition to pasta and chicken dishes (*bakonyi* chicken 980Ft). A projector plays sports on the wall beneath the pale blue sky painted on the ceiling. Open daily 10am-midnight. Cash only. ❶

Carmel Pince Étterem, VII, Kazinczy út 31 (☎322 1834). M2: Astoria. In the old Jewish quarter near Dohány Synagogue. Serves generous portions of Jewish and Hungarian delicacies like matzah ball soup and heavy stews. Not kosher. Entrees 1000-3000Ft. Live *klezmer* 2nd Su of each month. Open daily noon-11pm. Cash only. ❸

Marxim, II, Kis Rókus u. 23 (☎316 0231; www.extra.hu/marxim). M2: Moszkva tér. Walk along Margit krt., then turn left after passing Mammut. Hip locals unite at this tongue-in-cheek, communist-themed pizzeria, painted with red stars and graffiti. Great pizzas (590-1290Ft) are named in ironic honor of gulags, Siberia, and "Papa Marx." No English menu. Open M-Th noon-1am, F-Sa noon-2am, Su 6pm-1am. Cash only. ❷

Falafel Faloda, VI, Paulay Ede u. 53 (☎351 1243; www.falafel.hu). M1: Opera. Cross Andrássy, continue on Nagymező, and go left on Paulay Ede. This is healthy fast food at its best: patrons choose their own falafel toppings, from tahini to fresh vegetables. Salads 550-650Ft. Falafel 600Ft. Open M-F 10am-8pm, Sa 10am-6pm. Cash only. ❷

◪ CAFES

The former haunts of writers, artists, and political dissidents, Budapest's cafes boast rich histories. The current expat and yuppie cafes of choice are at **Ferenc Liszt tér** (M1: Oktogon), and often prove pricier than cafes in other neighborhoods. Each cafe has a large summer patio—come early to grab a people-watching post.

▨ **Dom Cafe,** I, Szentháromság tér, behind the Castle Hill Church. If you're thirsty after climbing the hill, reward yourself with a coffee or beer (both from 360 Ft) at this cafe, which boasts amazing views of the Danube and Pest. Open daily 10am-10pm.

Gerbeaud, V, Vörösmarty tér 7 (☎429 9020; www.gerbeaud.hu). M1: Vörösmarty tér. Hungary's most famous cafe and dessert shop has served delicious, homemade layer cakes (620Ft) and ice cream (250Ft) since 1858, most recently to flocks of tourists. Large terrace sprawls over Vörösmarty tér. Open daily 9am-9pm. AmEx/MC/V.

Muvész Kávéház, VI, Andrássy út 29 (☎352 1337). M1: Opera. Across from the Opera. Before or after a show, stop in for cappuccino (330Ft) and a slice of sinfully good cake (350-480Ft) at the polished stone tables. Open daily 9am-11:45pm. Cash only.

Ruszwurm, I, Szentháromság u. 7 (☎375 5284), off the square on Várhegy in the Castle District. This tiny cafe has been causing salivation since 1827, when it began preparing desserts for the Hapsburgs. Pastries and rich cakes (170-460Ft) are made right behind the counter. Coffee and espresso from 300Ft. Open M-Sa 9am-8pm. Cash only.

Faust Wine Cellar, I, Hess András tér 1-3 (☎488 6873). Enter the Hilton on Castle Hill, head left, and descend into the 13th-century cellar. The patio is atop a high cliff overlooking the city. An overwhelming array of excellent Hungarian vintages served with cheese and salami. 300-4500Ft per glass. Open daily 4-11pm. Cash only.

HUNGARY

ⓖ SIGHTS

In 1896, on the verge of its Golden Age and its 1000th birthday, Budapest constructed many of its most prominent sights. These works included **Heroes' Square** (Hősök tere), **Liberty Bridge** (Szabadság híd), **Vajdahunyad Castle** (Vajdahunyad vár), and continental Europe's first **Metro**; they have since been damaged by time, war, and communist occupation. Budapest is easily explored on your own, but for a guided exploration, consider **Absolute Walking and Biking Tours.** The basic tour (3½hr.; 4000Ft, students 3500Ft) meets daily June through August at 9:30am and 1:30pm, on the steps of the yellow church in Deák tér. Low season tours, September through May, leave at 10:30am from Deák tér. Choose from among tours that focus on everything from communism to pubbing. (☎211 8861; www.absolutetours.com. Specialized tours 3½-5½hr. 4000-5000Ft.) **Boat tours** leave from Vigadó tér piers 6-7. **Danube Legend,** which runs in the evening, costs 4200Ft. **Duna Bella** is a daytime boat. (1hr. tour 2600Ft, 2hr. tour 3600Ft.)

BUDAPEST FOR POCKET CHANGE. The eager sightseer in Budapest is in luck, as many of the permanent collections in the city's museums are free. After dropping your bags at **Backpack Guesthouse** (p. 283), check out the Hungarian impressionists at the **National Gallery** (p. 293), where admission is free. Next, hike up the nearby **Citadel** (p. 289) for the best view in the city. Cross the bridge for cheap grub at **Grand Market Hall** (p. 285), then walk back to **St. Stephen's Basilica** (p. 290) for a glimpse of its grandeur.

BUDA

Older and less industrialized than Pest, Buda tumbles down from Castle and Gellért Hills on the east bank of the Danube and sprawls into Budapest's main residential areas. Rich in parks, lush hills, and islands, Buda abounds with beautiful views of the city and great opportunities to learn about its history.

CASTLE HILL (VÁRHEGY)

M1, 2, or 3: Deák tér; then take bus #16. Alternatively, M2: Moszkva tér; then walk uphill on Várfok u. Or take an elevator (650 Ft up, 550Ft to return). Bécsi kapu marks castle entrance.

CASTLE (VÁR). Towering above the Danube, the castle district has been razed and rebuilt three times over 800 years, most recently in 1945 after the Red Army destroyed most of it. Today, its winding, touristed streets are cluttered with art galleries, souvenir shops, and cafes that afford views of the city. The castle, first built in the 13th century, has recently undergone extensive restoration. Bombings during WWII unearthed artifacts from the original castle; they are now housed in the Budapest History Museum (Budapesti Történeti) in the Royal Palace (Budavári palota). For a description of Castle Hill museums, see p. 291.

MATTHIAS CHURCH (MÁTYÁS TEMPLOM). Rising from a multicolored roof, the oft-photographed Gothic tower of Matthias Church pierces the city sky. Inside, religious art and decorative patterns cover every inch of wall. When Ottoman armies seized Buda in 1541, the church was converted into a mosque. In 1688, the Hapsburgs defeated the Turks, sacked the city, and reconverted the building. Climb the staircase to reach the Museum of Ecclesiastical Art, which houses a replica of the St. Stephen's Crown of Hungary and provides a view of the church from above. (*I, Szentháromság tér 2. Open M-Sa 9am-5pm, Su 1-5pm. High mass daily 7, 8:30am, 6pm; Su and holidays also 10am and noon. Church and museum 600Ft, students 300Ft.*)

■ **CASTLE LABYRINTHS (BUDVÁRI LABIRINTUS).** The castle labyrinths extend 1200m underground, and were created naturally by thermal springs. Once home to prehistoric humans, the labyrinths were used more recently as bomb shelters and military barricades. The vastly dark and damp expanse has since been converted into a series of chambers that walks the line between museum and haunted house. Fantastical displays vary from cavern to cavern, with some holding statues and one memorable display centered on a fountain of red wine: you can taste it, if you don't mind the risk of spattering it on your clothes. For a creepier experience, go between 6 and 7:30pm, when they shut off the lights and hand out oil lamps. There's no minotaur in the center, but children under 14 and people with heart conditions are advised not to participate in the spooky experience. (*Úri u. 9.* ☎ *212 0207; www.labirintus.com. Open daily 9:30am-7:30pm. 1400Ft, students 1100Ft.*)

HUNGARY

OTHER SIGHTS IN BUDA

■ **GELLÉRT HILL (GELLÉRTHEGY).** In the 11th century, the Pope sent Bishop Gellért to the coronation of King Stephen, the first Christian ruler of Hungary, to convert the pagan Magyars to Christianity. Unconvinced, the Magyars revolted and hurled the bishop to his death from atop the hill that now bears his name. The Soviets closed off **St. Ivan's Cave Church** (Szikla Templom), on the south side of the hill, with a concrete wall in the 1960s, and the church did not reopen until 1990. (*Mass daily 11am, 5:30, 8pm. Additional Su mass at 9:30am.*) Atop Gellért Hill, the **Liberation Monument** (Szabadság Szobor), a bronze statue of a woman raising a palm branch, commemorates the liberation of Budapest after WWII. The adjoining **Citadel** was built as a symbol of Hapsburg power after the failed 1848 Revolution. Inside, you'll find unobstructed views of the city and an exhibit about the history of the hill. The view from the hilltop is fabulous at night, when the Danube and its bridges shimmer in black and gold. A short way from the Citadel, the **statue of St. Gellért,** complete with glistening waterfall, overlooks Erzsébet híd. Walk down the hill via the bus route and turn right at St. Gellért Étterem. At the base, **Gellért Hotel and Baths** is one of the city's major Turkish baths. (*XI. Tram #18 or 19, or bus #7, to Hotel Gellért. Follow Szabó Verjték u. to Jubileumi Park and continue on paths to the summit. Or, take bus #27, get off at Búsuló Juhász, and walk 5min. to the peak. Citadel 1200Ft.*)

MARGIT ISLAND (MARGIT-SZIGET). The garden pathways of Margit Island offer a refreshing break from the city heat. Off-limits to private cars, the shaded island park is named after King Béla IV's daughter, whom he vowed to rear as a nun if the nation survived the 1241 Mongol invasion. Though decimated, Hungary survived, and poor Margit was confined to the island convent. These days, however, nuns have been replaced by children ready to run you down with pedal cars. **Palatinus Strandfürdő**, on Borsodi Beach, has pools and waterslides. *(Open M-F 10am-6pm, Sa-Su 9am-7pm weather permitting. 1500Ft, children 1200Ft.)* You can rent **bikes** or **bike-trolleys**, cars that you pedal with your feet. (Bikes 400Ft per 30min. Bike-trolleys 1200Ft per 30min. Prices slightly lower at Margit híd, but selection is slimmer than at Bringóhintó, on the far side of the island.) **Golf carts** allow you to putter about (2500Ft per 30min.). **Szabadtéri Színpad** (☎340 4796), the theater at the island's center, hosts concerts. *(M3: Nyugati pu. Take tram #4 or 6 or the HÉV from Batthyány tér to Margit híd.)*

PÁL-VÖLGYI CAVES. Similar to the Aggtelek caves (p. 304) but smaller, these caverns introduce novices to the underground terrain. Descend the 40m ladder for a tour (1hr.) of the caves, which were formed by the thermal springs that now source the baths in the city. Wear warm clothing, as the caves are 10°C. For spelunking or a more challenging cave visit, see **The Sandwich of Death**, p. 286. *(Bus #86 from Batthyány tér to Kolosy tér; backtrack up the street and make the 1st right to get to the bus station. From there, catch bus #65 to the caves. ☎325 9505. Open Tu-Su 10am-4pm. Tours every hr. 750Ft, students 550Ft. Tour that also visits Szemlőhegy Cave 950/660Ft.)*

PEST

Though downtown Pest dates to medieval times, its feel is decidedly modern. Pest is Budapest's commercial and administrative center and holds many of the city's most interesting sights. Its streets, laid out on a grid in the 19th century, run past shops, cafes, restaurants, and Hungary's biggest corporations.

■ **PARLIAMENT (ORSZÁGHÁZ).** "The motherland does not have a house," Hungarian poet Mihály Vörösmarty lamented in 1846. In reponse to such national strivings, Budapest built a Parliament that looks more like a cathedral than a government building. It was modeled after the UK parliament, right down to the riverside location. Standing 96m tall, a number symbolizing the date of Hungary's millennial anniversary, architect Imre Steindl's design is the city's most dramatic architectural masterpiece. Upon construction, the neo-Gothic building required more electricity than the entire rest of the city for its massive 692-room structure. The gold-and-marble interior is stunningly ornate, and is now home to the **Hungarian crown jewels.** The informative tour leads past countless statues honoring the nation's past and through the glorious former chamber of the Upper House. *(M2: Kossuth tér. ☎441 4000. English tours M-F 10am, noon, 2, 2:30, 5, and 6pm; Sa-Su 10am. Min. 5 people. Ask the guard to let you in, and purchase tickets at gate X. Ticket office opens 8am. Entrance with mandatory tour 2300Ft, students 1150Ft; with EU passport free.)*

ST. STEPHEN'S BASILICA (SZ. ISTVÁN BAZILIKA). Although the city's largest church was seriously damaged in WWII, the red-and-green marble and gilded arches of its massive interior still attract tourists and worshippers. The 360° balcony of the Panorama Tower, Pest's highest vantage point, offers an amazing view. Don't miss **St. Stephen's mummified hand,** one of Hungary's most revered religious relics. A 100Ft offering in the box lights the hand for 2min. *(V. M1, 2, or 3: Deák tér. Church open May-Oct. M-Sa 9am-5pm; Nov.-Apr. M-Sa 10am-4pm. Mass M-Sa 7, 8am, 6pm; Su 8:30, 10am (High Mass), noon, 6pm. Free. See the relic Apr.-Aug. M-Sa 9am-5pm, Su 1-4pm; Oct.-Mar. M-Sa 9am-4pm, Su 1-4pm. 250Ft, students 200Ft. Tower open daily June-Aug. 9:30am-6pm; Sept.-Oct. 10am-5:30pm; Apr.-May 10am-4:30pm. 500Ft, students 400Ft.)*

GREAT SYNAGOGUE (ZSINAGÓGA). The largest synagogue in Europe and the second largest in the world, the 1859 Great Synagogue was designed to hold 3000 congregants. Its towering, arched ceiling weaves the Star of David into pink- and red-toned patterns, and two gigantic wrought-iron chandeliers hang overhead. Renovations begun in 1990 are nearly complete. Beside the synagogue is the last **ghetto** established in WWII. More than 80,000 Jews were imprisoned and 10,000 died in the final two months of the war. Today, the 2500 people whose bodies could be identified are buried here; the rest lie in a common grave in the Jewish Cemetery. In the garden sits the **Tree of Life,** an enormous metal tree honoring Holocaust victims. Each leaf bears the name of a Hungarian family whose members perished, and names can be added upon request. Next to it, four granite memorials honor Righteous Gentiles, non-Jews who aided Jewish victims during the Holocaust. The English-speaking guides give excellent tours. *(VII. M2: Astoria. At the corner of Dohány u. and Wesselényi u. Open May-Oct. M-Th 10am-5pm, F 10am-2pm, Su 10am-2pm; Nov.-Apr. M-Th 10am-3pm, F 10am-1pm, Su 10am-1pm. Services F 6pm. Admission often starts at 10:30am. Covered shoulders required. Tours M-Th 10:30am-3:30pm on the half-hour, F and Su 10:30, 11:30am, 12:30pm. Admission 1000Ft, students 400Ft; includes admission to the Jewish Museum, see p. 293. Tours 1900Ft, students 1600Ft.)*

ANDRÁSSY ÚT AND HEROES' SQUARE (HŐSÖK TERE). The elegant balconies and gated gardens of Hungary's grandest boulevard, laid out in 1872, echo the splendor of Budapest's Golden Age. The most vivid reminder of this era is the gilt-and-marble interior of the Neo-Renaissance **Hungarian State Opera House** (Magyar Állami Operaház), adorned with magnificent frescoes. *(Andrássy út 22. M1: Opera. ☎ 332 8197. 1hr. English tours daily 3, 4pm. 2000Ft, students 1000Ft. 20% off with Budapest Card. See Entertainment p. 293 for show info.)* The **House of Terror** (see p. 292), former home of both Nazi and Soviet police headquarters, lies on Andrássy út. The boulevard's most majestic stretch is near Heroes' Square, where the sweeping **Millennium Monument** (Millenniumi emlékmű) dominates the street. The structure, built for the city's millennial anniversary, commemorates prominent figures of Hungarian history. The seven horsemen at the base represent the Magyar tribes who settled the Carpathian Basin. Archangel Gabriel, atop the statue, offers the Hungarian crown to St. Stephen. On either side are the **Museum of Fine Arts** and the **Museum of Modern Art.** *(VI. Andrássy út runs along M1 from Bajcsy-Zsilnszky út to Hősök tere.)*

CITY PARK (VÁROSLIGET). The shaded paths of City Park are perfect for lazy strolls by the lake. Balloon vendors and hot dog stands herald a small **amusement park,** a permanent **circus,** and a **zoo. Vajdahunyad Castle** sits in the center. Created for the 1896 millennium celebration, the castle's facade is a quirky pastiche of Hungarian architecture through the ages. The only part open to visitors is the **Magyar Agricultural Museum** (Magyar Mezogazdasagi Múzeum), which has exhibits on rural life. *(Open Tu-Su 10am-5pm. 3000Ft, students 2000Ft.)* Outside the castle broods the hooded statue of Anonymous, King Béla IV's scribe and the country's first historian, who recorded everything about medieval Hungary but his own name. Across the castle moat lies the **Bridge of Love.** Legend holds that if sweethearts kiss below the bridge, they'll marry within three years. Those already married can kiss to secure eternal love. Be sure to take a dunk in the **Széchényi baths** (p. 294) before leaving. *(XIV. M1: Széchényi Fürdő. Zoo ☎ 343 3710. Open May-Aug. M-Th 9am-6:30pm, F-Su 9am-7pm; March and Oct. M-Th 9am-5pm, F-Su 9am–5:30pm; Apr. and Sept. M-Th 9am-5:30pm, F-Su 9am-6pm; Nov.-Jan. daily. 9am-4pm. 1300Ft, students 1000Ft. Park ☎ 363 8310. Open July-Aug. daily 10am-8pm; May-June M-F 11am-7pm, Sa-Su 10am-8pm. 300Ft.)*

🏛 MUSEUMS

The buildings that house Budapest's eclectic museums are a delight. Thoughtful patrons can find backroom gems that a see-the-sights plan would easily miss. Museums attract relatively little attention here—you'll have space to enjoy paintings and artifacts that would be mobbed in other capitals.

HUNGARY

⬛ MUSEUM OF FINE ARTS (SZÉPMŰVÉSZETI MÚZEUM). This magnificent building contains an roster of European painting's luminaries, from Giotto to Breugel to Monet. The museum also houses a precious stone collection, a pottery display, and many sculptures. The building itself is a work of art, resembling a dignified, worn temple from the outside, and opening onto a glorious marble atrium. *(XIV. Hősök tere. M1: Hősök tere. ☎469 7100, English 069 036 9300. Free English tours Tu-F 11am. Open Tu-Su 10am-5:30pm. Permanent collection free, temporary exhibits 800-100Ft.)*

⬛ LUDWIG MUSEUM (LUDVIG MÚZEUM). Newly relocated from the palace on Castle Hill to an industrial neighborhood on the outskirts of the city, the Ludwig Museum—LuMu, as it fancies itself—attests to Budapest's rising stature in the art world. The most recent incarnations of Hungarian painting and sculpture are here, in addition to a small collection of works by international favorites like Picasso and Warhol. The galleries are spare, with stark white walls; light flows through large windows overlooking the Danube. The museum inhabits the right wing of the Palace of Arts. *(IX. Komor Marcell u. 1. Take tram #4 or 6 to Boráros tér, then take the HÉV commuter rail one stop to Lágymányosi híd. The stop is right in front of the museum. ☎555 3444; www.ludwigmuseum.hu. Open Tu, F, Su 10am-6pm; W noon-6pm; Th noon-8pm; Sa 10am-8pm. Permanent collection free. Temporary exhibits 800Ft, students 400Ft.)*

NATIONAL MUSEUM (NEMZETI MÚZEUM). An exhaustive exhibition chronicles the history of Hungary, from the Neolithic Era through the 21st century. In one room, a cheery statue of Stalin reaches out to welcome visitors to rooms devoted to Soviet propaganda. Exhibits have English captions and historical maps, and there are several film displays. The building itself is palatial, with a columned facade, marble staircases, and a tremendous domed roof. *(VIII. Múzeum krt. 14/16. M3: Kálvin tér. ☎338 2122; www.mng.hu. Open Tu-Su 10am-6pm. 600Ft.)*

HOUSE OF TERROR (TERROR HÁZA). This museum is housed in the former headquarters of the Hungarian Nazi Party and, later, the Soviet secret police. The city's most high-tech museum, the House of Terror uses videos and an audioguide tour (1000Ft) to explain its strikingly realistic exhibits. For further explanation, pick up summaries, available in each of the rooms, of the horrific history of the German invasion and ensuing Communist regime. The basement, a series of actual torture chambers and prison cells, offers—and needs—little explanation. While this journey through trauma is difficult to confront, it provides important documentation of the country's past. *(VI. Andrássy út 60. M1: Vörösmarty u. ☎374 2600; www.terrorhaza.hu. Open Tu-F 10am-6pm, Sa-Su 10am-7:30pm. 1200Ft, students 600Ft.)*

STATUE PARK MUSEUM (SZOBORPARK MÚZEUM). Encircled by a brick wall so that locals can avoid seeing the faces of their oppressors, this darkly ironic park houses an imposing collection of Social Realist statues gathered from Budapest's parks and squares after the collapse of Soviet rule. There are no captions, but the indispensable English guidebook (1000Ft) explains the facts. *(XXII. On the corner of Balatoni út and Szabadkai út. Take express bus #7 from Keleti pu. to Étele tér, then take the Volán bus from terminal #2 bound for Diósd—15min., every 15 min.—and get off at the Szoborpark stop. ☎424 7500; www.szoborpark.hu. Open daily 10am-dusk. 600Ft, students 400Ft.)*

MUSEUM OF APPLIED ARTS (IPARMŰVÉSZETI MÚZEUM). This collection of handcrafted pieces—including ceramics, furniture, metalwork, and Tiffany glass—deserves careful examination. Excellent temporary exhibits highlight specific crafts, while videos show artists at work. Built for the 1896 millennium, the tiled art nouveau edifice is at least as intricate and important as the pieces within. Exhibits circle a central atrium where light pours through skylights. *(IX. Üllői út 33-37. M3: Ferenc krt. ☎456 5100. Open daily 10am-6pm. 1000Ft, students 500Ft. Tours, fewer than 6 people 2500Ft total; 6-25 people 200Ft each. English pamphlet 100Ft.)*

JEWISH MUSEUM (ZSIDÓ MÚZEUM). The small but beautiful Jewish Museum, beside the Synagogue, displays religious artifacts from the 18th and 19th century heyday of Jewish Budapest. A permanent exhibit commemorates the Holocaust victims of Hungary. The upper floor holds temporary exhibitions. The museum is the birthplace of Theodor Herzl (1860-1904), founder of the Zionist movement. Admission includes entrance to the Great Synagogue. *(VII. See p. 290 for directions. Open May-Oct. M-Th 10am-5pm, F 10am-1pm, Su 10am-2pm; Nov.-Apr. M-F 10am-3pm, F 10am-1pm, Su 10am-1pm. Tours M-Th 10:30am-3:30pm every 30min., F and Su 10:30, 11:30am, 12:30pm. Museum 600Ft, with ISIC 200Ft. Tours 1900Ft, students 1700Ft.)*

ROYAL PALACE. Leveled at the end of WWII, the rebuilt palace now houses several fine museums. You will not be able to traverse all of them in one day. *(I. Szent György tér 2. M1, 2, or 3: Deák tér, then take bus #16 across the Danube to the top of Castle Hill. ☎375 7533.)* **Wings B-D** hold the huge **Hungarian National Gallery** (Magyar Nemzeti Galéria), a definitive collection of the best in Hungarian fine arts. Organized chronologically from Medieval and Renaissance art to a spectacular 20th-century sculpture exhibit, its treasures include works by realist Mihály Munkácsy, medieval gold altarpieces, and a great many depictions of national tragedies. *(☎375 7533. Open Tu-Su 10am-6pm. English tour by appointment. Permanent collection free. Temporary exhibits 1500Ft, students 800Ft.)* **Wing E** houses the **Budapest History Museum** (Budapesti Történeti Múzeum), a collection of recently unearthed medieval artifacts, including weapons, tombstones, and glassware. *(☎375 7533. English captions. Open Mar.-Nov. M and W-Su 10am-6pm; Nov.-Mar. 10am-4pm. 900Ft, students 450Ft.)*

🎭 ENTERTAINMENT

Budapest's cultural life flourishes in a series of performance events. In August, Óbudai Island hosts the week-long **Sziget Festival,** an open-air rock festival that draws major European and American acts. *(☎372 0650; www.sziget.hu. Call for ticket prices.)* Hungary's largest cultural festival, the **Budapest Spring Festival** *(☎486 3311; late Mar.)* showcases Hungary's premier musicians and actors. The **Danube Festival** in late June celebrates the building of the Chain Bridge. Highlights include traditional Hungarian folk dancing, contemporary dance acts, fireworks. Racing enthusiasts zoom into the suburb of Mogyoró each August for the **Formula 1 Hungarian Grand Prix** *(☎317 2811; www.hungaroring.hu)*. Prices for most events are reasonable; check **Ticket Express Hungary,** Andrássy u. 18. *(☎312 0000; www.tex.hu)*. Free guides available at tourist offices and hotels detail everything from festivals to art showings. The "Style" section of the English-language *Budapest Sun* (www.budapestsun.com; 300Ft) has 10-day listings and film reviews, while the plucky web guide Pestiside (www.pestiside.hu) lists nightlife and cultural offerings. Movie theaters abound (Tickets 600-1200Ft). **Westend City Center,** next to Nyugati Pu. on the city's west end, is Budapest's biggest shopping mall, stocking everything from clothes to electronics. (M3: Nyugati Pu. ☎238 7777. Open daily 8am-11pm.) The five levels of **Mammut,** in central Buda, are packed with boutiques. (M2: Moszkva tér. 345 8020. Open M-Sa 10am-9pm, Su 10am-6pm.)

◪ **State Opera House** (Magyar Állami Operaház), VI, Andrássy út 22 (☎331 2550, box office 353 0170). M1: Opera. One of Europe's leading performance centers; hosts operettas, ballets, and orchestra concerts. While some shows sell out a year ahead, many have seats available the day of the performance. Tickets 800-8700Ft. Box office open M-Sa 11am-7pm, Su 4-7pm. Closes at 5pm on non-performance days.

National Dance Theater (Nemzeti Táncszínház), I, Szinház u. 1-3 (☎201 4407, box office 375 8649; www.nemzetitancszinhaz.hu), on Castle Hill. Hosts a variety of shows; Hungarian folklore shows are most popular. Most shows 7pm. Tickets 1200-4000Ft.

Millenáris Park, II, Lövőház u. 39 (☎438 5335, box office 438 5312; www.millenaris.hu). M2: Moszkva tér. This hidden park, which you have to enter through a building, has 3 indoor theaters, an outdoor theater, and an outdoor projection screen that broadcasts live sports. Occasional art shows take place, and the theaters host acts ranging from jazz performances to ballets to movie screenings. Call or visit the box office inside the theater for program listings. Tickets 400-1600Ft. Park open daily 6am-midnight.

⌐ BATHS

Hot water bubbles in underground springs just beneath the surface of Budapest. For nearly 2000 years, the city has been channeling this natural treasure into its distinctive thermal baths, which are a must for visitors. The medicinal baths, reputed to have healing powers, draw everyone from splash-happy children to curious tourists to elderly seekers of pain relief. Some baths have sections allocated for nude bathing, and most are separated by gender. Most are clean and enforce rules strictly. For more information, consult www.spasbudapest.com.

🞍 **Széchényi,** XIV, Állatkerti u. 11/14 (☎321 0310), in the center of City Park. M1: Széchényi fürdő. Statues and a fountain guard one of the biggest and most luxurious bath complexes in Europe. Play on floating chessboards in the outdoor pool. Massages, spas, and a variety of medical treatments are available among the 3 pools and 12 thermal baths. Open daily May-Sept. 6am-7pm; Oct.-Apr. M-F 6am-7pm, Sa-Su 6am-5pm. 2000Ft. 800Ft returned if you leave within 2hr., 500Ft within 3hr., and 200Ft within 4hr.; keep your original receipt. 15min. massage 2400Ft. Cash only.

Gellért, XI, Kelenhegyi út 4/6 (☎466 6166). Bus #7 or tram #47 or 49 to Hotel Gellért, at the base of Gellérthegy. Known as one of the most elegant baths in Budapest, Gellért boasts a rooftop sundeck, a wave pool, and a la carte spa options, including mud baths and massages (11,000Ft, reserve ahead). Baths and pools open May-Sept. daily 6am-7pm; Oct.-Apr. M-F 6am-7pm, Sa-Su 6am-5pm. Thermal bath and pool 3000Ft. Refunds based on time spent in the baths. 15min. massage 2400Ftt. MC/V.

Király, I, Fő u. 84 (☎202 3688). M2: Batthány tér. Basic baths in a building featuring Turkish architecture. Almost 500 years old, these baths have remained authentic and have no swimming pools. Bathing here is a truly relaxing experience. Women only M, W, F 7am-6pm; men only Tu, Th, Sa 9am-8pm; ticket office closes an hour earlier. 1100Ft. 15min. massage in private room 1900Ft, 30min. 2700Ft. Cash only.

Rudas, XI, Döbrentei tér 9 (☎356 1322). Take bus #7 to the 1st stop in Buda. On the river under a dome built by Turks 400 years ago, and renovated in 2005. Age hasn't altered the dome, the bathing chamber, or the thermal bath's men-only rule. The main swimming pool and 4 smaller ones allow women. Open May-Aug. M-F 6am-6pm; Sept.-Apr. M-F 6am-6pm, Sa-Su 6am-1pm. Baths 1000Ft. Pool 900Ft. Cash only.

▆ NIGHTLIFE

Budapest will never leave you bored. Whether you're looking to chill out in a mellow jazz club, down a beer at a local pub, or dance the night away along the Danube, you'll find it here. The scene ranges from lively all-night outdoor parties to thumping discos to elegant clubs. Despite throbbing crowds in the clubs and pubs, the streets themselves are surprisingly empty. The chic cafes in VI, **Ferencz Liszt tér** (M2: Oktogon), are the newest retreat for Budapest's youth. In summer, the scene moves to outdoor venues, the biggest of which are along the Danube, where great views and cheap drinks abound. Outdoor venues open from late April to mid-September. Ask Tourinform for entertainment guides.

NIGHTLIFE SCAM. Following reports of cafes and bars overcharging tourists by obscene amounts, the US embassy has advised against certain establishments in the Váci u. area. In one scam, a woman approaches a foreign man and asks him to buy her a drink. When the bill arrives, accompanied by imposing thugs, the price of the drink turns out to be astronomical. Check prices before ordering at places you don't know well, and try to keep cash and credit cards concealed. For a current list of establishments about which complaints have been filed, check the list at www.usembassy.hu/conseng/announcements.html#advisory. If you suspect you have been the victim of a scam, call the police. Keep receipts to complain formally at the Consumer Bureau.

CLUBS

Undergrass, VI, Ferencz Liszt tér 10 (☎322 0830). M1: Oktogon. Tram #4 or 6. The hottest club in Pest's trendiest area. Behind a barely noticeable bank vault door, the underground bar has little seating, but most patrons are happy to stand or to hit the dance floor. The soundproof door allows bar talk, while the disco spins funk and pop. Cover varies free-1000Ft. Open F-Sa 10pm-4am. Cash only.

B7 Klub, VI, Dessewffy u. 3 (☎633 6000; www.b7.hu). On the corner of Nagymező u. Hip-hop with a smattering of electronic plays to an international crowd under the disco lights at this up-and-coming club. A small, translucent dance floor hovers above the main one. Cover varies; usually free before midnight. Open M-Sa 5pm-5am. Cash only.

Piaf, VI, Nagymező u. 25 (☎312 3823). A much-loved after-hours spot. Guests are admitted into the red velvet lounge after knocking on an inconspicuous door and meeting the approval of the club's matron. Cover 800Ft; includes 1 beer. Open M-Th and Su 10pm-6am, F-Sa 10pm-7am; don't come before 1am. Cash only.

Jazz Garden, V, Veres Pálné u. 44a (☎266 7364). This joint has nightly live jazz, 3 dining rooms, and a full bar. Descend the stairs into the layered brick "garden" terrace, complete with lanterns, low-hanging vines, and a stage. The next room is more sophisticated and still has a good view of the center-stage piano. Beer 650Ft. Performances daily 9pm. Open M-F 3pm-5am, Sa-Su 5pm-5am. Cash only.

Club Seven, VII, Akácfa u. 7 (☎478 9030). M2: Blaha Lujza tér. Upscale, crowded local favorite plays funk, jazz, soul, or disco every night of the wk. Cover Sa-Su men 2000Ft, women free. Open M-F 3pm-5am, Sa-Su 5pm-5am. Casino open 10pm-5am. Cash only.

PUBS

Old Man's Music Pub, VII, Akácfa u. 13 (☎322 7645; www.oldmans.hu). M2: Blaha Lujza tér. Popular with locals, expats, and tourists, this eclectic institution features live blues and jazz every night at 11pm—check the schedule and arrive early, because it gets very crowded very quickly. Relax in the pub (open 3pm-3am) or hit the downstairs dance floor (11pm-late). Open M-Sa 3pm-4:30am. Cash only.

Fat Mo's Speakeasy, V, Nyári Pál u. 11 (☎267 3199). M3: Kálvin tér. "Spitting prohibited" in this bar, which celebrates 1920s speakeasies. Come for 14 varieties of draft beer (450-1000Ft) and stay for live jazz and blues (Su-Th 9-11pm). Th-Sa DJ after midnight. Open M-W noon-1am, Th-F noon-4am, Sa 6pm-4am, Su 6pm-2am. Cash only.

Crazy Café, VI, Jókai u. 30 (☎302 4003). M3: Nyugati pu. The place to start a long night of drinking. With 30 kinds of whiskey (shots 450-890Ft), 8 kinds of tequila (690Ft), and 17 kinds of vodka (590-690Ft), the scene at this vaguely jungle-themed basement bar has been known to get hot and rowdy. Live DJ. Karaoke M-Tu and Su. Open M-Th 4pm-1am, F-Su 11am-1am. Cash only.

STRIKE UP THE BAND

Whether you're sipping a coffee or downing a beer at one of Hungary's many cafes, chances are the soundtrack to your idyllic moment is supplied by a small band playing nearby. The music, however, is not typical touristy schmaltz, but the result of a rich, age-old musical tradition.

"Gypsy music," as this lively brand of street music is popularly know, has evolved dramatically over the years. The Roma, who migrated from North Central India many centuries ago, have been a presence in Hungary long enough that their music has become gradually intertwined with the Hungarian folk tradition. Originally sung *a capella,* Roma music is now usually set to fiddles, bass, and a string instrument played with two wooden hammers called the *cimbalom.*

The term "Gypsy music" is in fact an umbrella term for a variety of traditions. Many of the most common melodies have their roots in military recruiting songs from the 16th and 17th century Rákóczi rebellion, the major struggle against Hapsburg rule. Today, however, these songs are more likely to welcome visitors to Hungarian daily life. They also offer a reminder of the cultural contributions of the Roma population, a minority long oppressed, and still struggling, throughout Eastern Europe.

Borpatika (Wine Bar), XI, Bertalan L. út 26 (☎204 2644). Take tram #47 or 49 from Deák tér to Bertalan Lajos. This wine tavern is quiet, except during happy hour, when discounts lure boisterous student patrons. Open daily 8am-midnight. Cash only.

SUMMER VENUES

Zöld Pardon, XI, on the Buda side of Petőfi Bridge. If you're wondering where everyone has gone on seemingly quiet weeknights, wonder no more. In a club that easily holds 1000, 3 large screens project surreal graphic designs as well as a live feed of the goings-on on the giant dance floor; make yourself seen on camera. The music is hit-or-miss, but the chance to dance along the riverside is an undeniable hit. One of the many bars is elevated from the dance floor on a fake island. Snack bar satisfies late-night cravings. Beer 250-400Ft. Cover 100Ft. Open daily 9pm-6am. Cash only.

Rio, XI, on the Buda side of Petőfi Bridge. Budapest's young and raucous convene under the large white tents of Rio, the slicker sibling of Zöld Pardon, where students and scenesters groove to hip-hop and contemporary pop. Open daily 9pm-6am. Cash only.

GLBT BUDAPEST

An underground world for decades, GLBT Budapest is beginning to appear in the mainstream. Still, it's safer to be discreet. If you run into problems or are looking for info, contact the **gay hotline** (☎0630 932 33 34; budapest@gayguide.net), and take advantage of the knowledgeable staff. The website **www.budapest.gayguide.net** has up-to-date info on what's hot. **Na Végre** is a free monthly digest with English-language entertainment listings. It can be found at most of the establishments below, all of which are either gay or gay-friendly. **Omszki Lake** is a nude beach frequented by gay men. (Take the HÉV to Budakalász and walk 25min.)

Café Eklektika, V, Semmelweis u. 21 (☎266 2116). This centrally located, gay-friendly bar and cafe serves light meals and excellent wines. The jazz is as smooth as the interior, which has sleek leather chairs and a tiled marble floor. Dance classes with prize-winning instructors daily 6pm. Open M-F noon-1am, Sa-Su 5pm-1am. Cash only.

Capella, V, Belgrád rakpart 23 (☎318 6231; www.extra.hu/capellacafe). This very popular 3-level cafe along the Danube has reopened after renovations. Attracts a mixed gay, lesbian, and straight crowd. Open W-Su 10am-5am. Cash only.

Mystery Cafe, V, Nagysándor József u. 3 (☎312 1436; www.mysterybar.hu). M3: Arany János. A rainbow flag welcomes patrons to this cozy, laid-back bar, which attracts a primarily gay and lesbian clientele. Open M-F 4pm-4am, Sa-Su 6pm-4am.

Angyal (Angel) Bar, VII, Kazinczy u. 4. M2: Blaha L. tér. The 1st gay bar in Budapest, this huge 3-level disco, cafe, and bar is packed on weekends. F-Sa drag shows. Cover 1300Ft. Open F-Sa 10pm-5am. Cash only.

⊠ DAYTRIPS FROM BUDAPEST

⊠ SZENTENDRE ☎ (0)26

HÉV runs from Batthyány tér (45min., every 20min., 430Ft). Buses run from the station by Árpád híd Metro station (30min., every 20-40min., 303Ft). Boats (☎484 4000) leave from pier below Vigadó tér (1½hr.; 2 per day; 1400Ft). The train and bus stations are a 10min. walk from Fő tér, the main square. Descend stairs past the end of the HÉV tracks, go through the underpass, and head up Kossuth út. At fork in road, bear right on Dumtsa Jenő út. From ferry station, turn left on Czóbel sétány and left on Dunakorzó u.

To glimpse Hungary's rural past without straying far from Budapest, head to Szentendre (sehn-TEHN-dreh), where cobblestone streets and masterful art abound in a town known for its relaxing, pleasant pace. The streets are packed with tourists during summer, but the museums and art galleries remain uncramped. Start your visit by climbing **Church Hill** (Templomdomb), above the town center in Fő tér, to visit the 13th-century **Parish Church of St. John** (Plébánia-templom), one of the few intact medieval churches in Hungary, which boasts the best view in town. The sundial on the wall inside the church is one of the oldest in the country. (Open Tu-Su 10am-4pm. Services Su 7am. Free.)

The **Czóbel Museum,** Templom tér 1, left of the church, displays the work of Béla Czóbel, Hungary's foremost post-Impressionist painter, including his "Venus of Szentendre." Admission includes access to the adjoining exhibit of works by the Szentendre Artists' Colony. (☎312 721. English captions. Open Tu-Su 10am-6pm. 400Ft, students 200Ft.) Szentendre's most popular museum, the **Kovács Margit Museum,** Vastagh György út 1, exhibits whimsical ceramic sculptures by the 20th-century Budapest artist Margit Kovács. (☎310 244, ext. 114; fax 310 790. Open Mar. 16-Sept. M-Th 10am-5:30pm, F-Su 10am-7:30pm; Oct.-Mar. 15 daily 9am-5pm. 600Ft, students 300Ft.) The ⊠**National Wine Museum** (Nemzeti Bormúzuem), Bogdányi u. 10, is a cellar exhibit of wines from Hungary's eight wine-making regions. A wine tasting (1700Ft) includes 10 samples, Hungarian appetizers, and an English tour of the exhibition. (☎/fax 317 054. Open daily 10am-10pm. Exhibit 100Ft.) The edible exhibits of the ⊠**Szabó Marzipan Museum and Confectionery,** Dumtsa Jenő út 12, are made of **marzipan.** Watch the artists work; then look at more intricate creations, including scenes from fairy tales, historical figures, and a white chocolate life-size statue of Michael Jackson. Indulge your sweet tooth downstairs at the gift shop or the adjoining cafe. (☎311 931. Open daily May-Sept. 9am-7pm; Oct.-Apr. 10am-6pm. 350Ft.)

⊠**Nostalgia Cafe ❶,** Bogdányi u. 2, owned by opera singers, hosts occasional concerts in an outdoor courtyard. Try the "Special Nostalgia Coffee" (300Ft), made with orange liqueur, chocolate bits, and whipped cream. (☎311 660. Pastries and coffee from 300Ft. Open daily 10am-8pm.) The charming **Ilona Panzió ❸,** Rákóczi Ferenc út 11, rents rooms with private baths. (☎313 599. Breakfast included. Call ahead. Singles 4500Ft; doubles 6600Ft; triples 8000Ft.) **Pap-szigeti Camping ❷** is two kilometers north of the center along the main waterside road on its own island in the Danube, near a small but popular beach. (☎310 697; fax 313 777. Call ahead.

Open May-Oct. 15. Tent sites 2100Ft, 1-person tent 1900Ft. 2-person caravan 4200Ft; additional person 1000Ft. Pension doubles 5500Ft; triples 7500Ft. Motel doubles 4000Ft.) Get info and **maps** from **Tourinform,** Dumsta Jenő út 22. (☎317 966; www.szentendre.hu. Open Mar. 16-Nov. 2 M-F 9am-1pm and 1:30-4:30pm, Sa-Su 10am-1pm and 1:30-2pm; Nov. 3-Mar. 15 M-F 9:30am-1pm and 1:30-4:30pm.)

ESZTERGOM ☎(0)33

Trains run from Budapest (1½hr., 22 per day, 512Ft). Buses run from Szentendre (1½hr., 1 per hr., 476Ft) or Visegrád (45min., 1 per hr., 302Ft). Boats (☎484 4000) run from Budapest (4hr., 3 per day, 1200Ft); Szentendre (2¾hr., 2 per day, 980Ft); and Visegrád (1½hr., 2 per day, 700Ft). The train station is 15min. from town. Facing away from the station, go left on the main street. Follow the street around the bend and turn right at Kiss János Altábornagy út. From the bus station, walk up Simor János u. toward the market.

One thousand years of religious history have made Esztergom (ess-TAYR-gahm) a destination for pilgrims and tourists, who still flock to its winding streets. The birthplace of Saint-King Stephen and the site of the first Royal Court of Hungary, the town is also home to Hungary's largest cathedral. Named the **Basilica of Esztergom,** the Neoclassical cathedral was built on the site of an 11th-century cathedral and consecrated in 1856. The red-marble **Bakócz Chapel,** to the nave's left, is a Renaissance masterpiece, hundreds of years older than the cathedral itself. (English guidebook 100Ft. Open daily Mar.-Oct. 6:30am-6pm; Nov.-Dec. 7am-4pm. Chapel free.) The cathedral **treasury** houses icons, relics, and textiles spanning a millennium. A jewel-studded cross served as the **Coronation Oath Cross** (Koronázási Eskükereszt), on which Hungary's rulers pledged their oaths until 1916. (Open Mar.-Oct. Tu-Su 9am-4:30pm; Nov.-Dec. Tu-F 9am-4:30pm, Sa-Su 10am-3:30pm. 450Ft, students 220Ft.)

Ascend interminable staircases to the cathedral ⓢcupola (200Ft) for an incredible echo and the best view of the Danube Bend. On clear days, you can see the Slovak Low Tatras. The **crypt** below the cathedral holds the remains of Hungary's archbishops. (Open Tu-Su 9am-4:45pm. 100Ft.) The **museum** surrounding the cathedral was built atop the ruins of the **castle** where St. Stephen was born. An architecture-lover's boon, the museum exhibits fragments of the 10th-century castle. Peer through a glass floor onto an excavation site. (☎415 986. English captions. Open Tu-Su 10am-4:45pm. Free.) The **Maria Valeria Bridge** spans the Danube from Esztergom to Slovakia. Reopened in 2001, the bridge is now a major economic link between the two nations. **Csülök Csárda ❷,** Batthyány út 9, serves fine cuisine just below the basilica, adding creative variations to the usual repertoire of roasts and stews. Try the mushroom soup (790Ft) or the catfish fillet with garlic (1590Ft). (☎412 420. Vegetarian options available. Entrees 480-1800Ft. Open daily noon-10pm.) For info, visit **Grantours,** Széchényi tér 25, at the edge of Rákóczi tér, which also sells **maps.** (☎417 052; grantour@mail.holop.hu. Open July-Aug. M-F 8am-5pm, Sa 9am-noon; Sept.-June M-F 8am-4pm.)

SZÉKESFEHÉRVÁR ☎(0)22

Take the train from Budapest (1hr., 21 per day, 620Ft). To get to the center from the train station, walk down Deák Ferenc u. Turn left on Budai út and then right on Varkörút. Buses also run from Budapest (1hr., 4 per day, 752Ft). From the bus station (☎311 057), on Piac tér, veer left of terminal #2 and take a right on Liszt Ferenc u., which becomes Városház tér.

Géza, St. Stephen's father, established Székesfehérvár in AD 972, making it Hungary's oldest town. Today, those traveling from Budapest to Balaton stop in this friendly, unpretentious city to visit the extraordinary ⓢBory Castle (Bory-vár). Take bus #32 from the train station to Vágújhelyi u., walk downhill, and turn left on Bory tér. Not your typical Hungarian castle (partly because it remains intact), it was built over the course of nearly 40 summers, beginning in the 1920s. Architect and sculptor Jenő Bory constructed this mansion by hand in honor of his wife, his art, and his country's history. The beautiful palace resembles a fairy-tale castle: it is endowed with whimsical towers, terraced gardens, crooked paths, winding staircases, and stone chambers. Bory decorated every inch of his eccentric retreat and erected a chapel for his wife as the ultimate "monument to marital love." The small museum displays dozens of Bory's sculptures as well as paintings by the architect and his wife. Today his grandson and his family live in the castle and care for the museum. (☎305 570. Open daily 9am-5pm. 500Ft, students 250Ft.) Pick up a guidebook and **free maps** at **Tourinform**, Városház tér 1. (☎537 261. Open May 15-Sept. 15 daily 9am-7pm; Sept. 16-May 14 M-F 9am-4pm.) In the center, the **King St. Stephen Museum** (Szent István Király Múzeum), Fő u. 6, houses an archaeology exhibit that showcases Roman artifacts. (☎315 583. Open Apr. 29-Oct. Tu-Su 10am-4pm; Mar. 4-Apr. 28 Tu-Su 10am-2pm. 290Ft, students 130Ft.) The **Budenz House: Ybl Collection** (Budenz-ház: Ybl Gyűjtemény), Arany János út 12, includes exquisite 18th- to 20th-century Hungarian art and furniture. Learn more about Miklós Ybl, one of Budapest's preeminent architects and the designer of the State Opera House in Budapest, through the display of family portraits and medals on the second floor of the building. (☎313 027. Open Tu-Su 10am-4pm. 290Ft, students 130Ft.)

If you're spending the night in Székesfehérvár, check out the newly renovated **Szent Gellért Tanulmányi Ház ❹**, Mátyás Király krt 1, a 10min. walk from the city center. It offers rooms and cheaper dorms. (☎510 810; szentgellert@axelero.hu. Dorms 3700 for 1 person or 2300Ft per person for 2 or more people; singles 8800Ft; doubles 10,900Ft; triples 17,400Ft. Tax 300Ft. AmEx/MC/V.) **Match** supermarket, Palotai u. 1-3, inside Alba Shopping Plaza by the bus station, sells the basics. (Open M-Sa 7am-9pm, Su 8am-6pm.) Straddling Fő u., **Korzó Söröző ❷** serves Hungarian dishes like liver soup and goulash on one side, and beers and spirits on the other. (☎312 674. Entrees 800-3200Ft. Open daily 10am-midnight.)

NORTHERN HUNGARY

Hungary's northern upland is dominated by a series of low mountain ranges running northeast from the Danube Bend along the Slovak border. The mountain villages delight in local custom and opportunity to explore. The charming, historic towns of Eger and Tokaj are home to world-famous wineries, while Bükk and Aggtelek National Parks beckon hikers with scenic trails and stunning caves.

EGER ☎(06)36

Once marked by the Ottoman conquest of its castle in 1596, Eger (EGG-air; pop. 57,000) proves much more soothing these days, with its quiet square and pastel architecture. Although the town continues to pride itself on a rich history, hailing Captain István Dobó's victorious 1552 stand against the sieging Turks as a miracle, the region's real claim to fame is its legacy of homemade wines. The spirited cellars of the Valley of Beautiful Women lure eager travelers from Budapest with the promise of the strengthening powers of *Egri Bikavér* (Bull's Blood) wine, a blended red made with the indigenous, spicy Kadarka grape.

▗ TRANSPORTATION

Trains: Vasút u. (☎314 264). To: **Budapest** (2hr.; 21 per day, 4 direct; 1242Ft) and **Szeged** (4½hr., 12 per day, 3050Ft). Non-direct trains to **Budapest** via **Füzesabony.**

HUNGARY

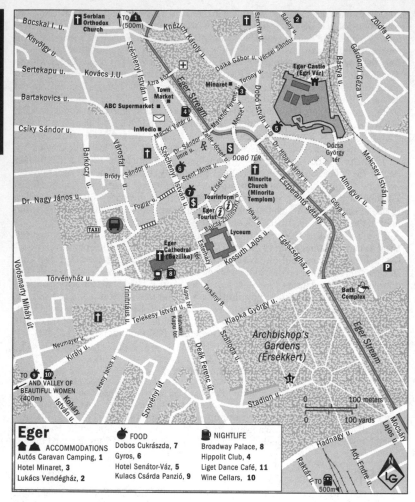

Eger

🔺🔺 ACCOMMODATIONS
Autós Caravan Camping, **1**
Hotel Minaret, **3**
Lukács Vendégház, **2**

🍎 FOOD
Dobos Cukrászda, **7**
Gyros, **6**
Hotel Senátor-Váz, **5**
Kulacs Csárda Panzió, **9**

🎵 NIGHTLIFE
Broadway Palace, **8**
Hippolit Club, **4**
Liget Dance Café, **11**
Wine Cellars, **10**

Buses: Barkóczy u. (☎517 777; www.agriavolan.hu). To: **Aggtelek** (3hr., daily 8:45am, 1330Ft); **Budapest** (2hr., 25-30 per day, 1360Ft); **Debrecen** (3hr., 10 per day, 1296Ft); **Szilvásvárad** (45min., 40 per day, 363Ft.)

Taxis: City Taxi (☎555 555).

✈ 🔲 ORIENTATION AND PRACTICAL INFORMATION

The **train station** lies on the outskirts of town. To walk to **Dobó tér,** the main square and town center, from the train station (15min.), head straight and take a right on **Deák Ferenc út,** a right on **Kossuth Lajos u.,** and a left on **Tokaj u.** To get to the center from the bus station, turn right on **Barkóczy u.** from terminal #10 and right again about two blocks down at **Bródy u.** Follow the stairs to the end of the street and turn right on **Széchényi u.**; a left down **Érsek u.** leads to Dobó tér. Most sights are within a 10min. walk of the square.

Tourist Office: Tourinform, Bajcsy-Zsilinszky u. 9 (☎517 715; www.ekft.hu/eger), has free maps. One computer with **Internet** (200Ft per 30min.). Open June-Sept. M-F 9am-7pm, Sa-Su 10am-6pm; Oct.-May M-F 9am-5pm, Sa 9am-1pm.

Bank: OTP, Széchényi u. 2 (☎310 866), at the corner of Érsek u., gives AmEx/MC/V **cash advances** and cashes **AmEx Traveler's Cheques** for no commission. An **ATM** (MC/V) stands outside. Open M 7:45am-6pm, Tu-Th 7:45am-5pm, F 7:45am-4pm; currency desk open M-Tu and Th 7:45am-2:45pm, W 7:45am-4:30pm, F 7:45am-noon.

Luggage Storage: Available at the bus station.

English-Language Bookstore: InMedio, next to the Széchényi u. post office, carries English-language periodicals. Open M-F 6am-6pm, Sa 6am-1pm, Su 6-11am.

Pharmacy: Rossmann (☎518 542), on the corner of Katona István Tér and Sándor Imre u., stocks international brands. Open M-F 8am-7pm, Sa 8am-1pm. AmEx/MC/V.

Hospital: Knézich Károly u. 1-3 (☎411 414). Open M-Th 7am-6pm, F 7am-4pm. Call for emergency service.

Internet: Broadway Palace, Pyrter 3 (☎517 221), has several computers in a secluded room of a bar beneath Eger Cathedral. Enter through the door labeled "cafe." 100Ft per 15min. The bar has a small dining area inside and a patio outside (see **Stayin' A-Lava,** p. 304). Open M-Sa noon-11pm, Su 3pm-11pm.

Post Office: Széchényi u. 22 (☎411 672). Open M-F 8am-8pm, Sa 8am-1pm. **Poste Restante** available. **Telephones** outside. **Postal Code:** 3300.

ACCOMMODATIONS

Accommodations are plentiful within Eger's central city. **Private rooms** ❷ (around 3000Ft) are a welcoming option. Look for *Zimmer frei* or *szoba eladó* signs outside the main square, particularly near the castle on Almagyar u. and Mekcsey István u. **Eger Tourist,** Bajcsy-Zsilinszky u. 9, arranges **private rooms**. (☎517 000; fax 510 270. Open M-F 9am-5pm. Rooms around 3000Ft.)

Lukács Vendégház, Bárány u. 10 (☎/fax 411 567), next to Eger Castle. With a private garden, outdoor seating, and spacious rooms, this family-run guesthouse provides comfort and privacy at a reasonable cost. Some rooms have fridges and microwaves. The area can be empty and dark at night. Singles 3500Ft; doubles 5000Ft. Cash only. ❷

Hotel Minaret, Knézich K. u. 4, (☎410 233; www.hotelminaret.hu), is centrally located. Named for the large minaret across the street, this pricier option offers simple rooms with satellite TV, a restaurant, a massage center, and a courtyard swimming pool that hosts grill parties in the summer. Singles 8400Ft; doubles 14,600Ft; triples 19,200Ft; quads 22,900Ft. Prices about 1000Ft lower Nov.-Mar. AmEx/MC/V. ❹

Autós Caravan Camping, Rákóczi u. 79 (☎/fax 410 558), 20min. north of the center by bus #5 or 11. Get off at the Shell station and follow the signs. Call ahead or reserve bungalows or camp space through Eger Tourist. Open Apr. 15-Oct. 15. Gates closed midnight-6am. 500Ft per person, 300Ft per tent. MC. ❶

FOOD

Piaccsarnok market runs along Katona I. tér, behind Széchényi u. Go right on Árva Köz; the market is on the right. (Open June-Sept. M-F 6am-6pm, Sa 6am-1pm, Su 6-10am; Oct.-May M-F 6am-5pm, Sa 6am-1pm, Su 6-10am.) **Hossó ABC** supermarket is across the street. (Open M-F 6am-7pm, Sa 6am-1pm, Su 6am-11am. MC/V.)

HUNGARY

■ **Kulacs Csárda Panzió** (☎/fax 311 375), in the Valley of Beautiful Women. Vines and ceramic dishes line the walls of this cavernous restaurant, which serves heaping portions of *goulash*, peasant sausage, and other Hungarian classics. Try the house specialty, boar stew, before walking down the street to the wine cellars. Live music. English menu available. Entrees 950-2000Ft. Open daily noon-11pm. AmEx/MC/V. ❸

Dobos Cukrászda, Széchényi u. 6. Offers a mouthwatering selection of decadent desserts (170-350Ft). Indulge your sweet tooth with a marzipan snail or rose (280Ft), ice cream (110Ft), or a creative sundae (760Ft). Open daily 9:30am-9pm. Cash only. ❶

Hotel Senátor-Váz Restaurant (☎320 466), just over the bridge, at the back of Dobó tér. Live music from the neighboring gazebo accompanies your meal of Hungarian originals like garlic soup and fried sheep cheese. If gloomy weather should drive you from the cobblestone patio, enjoy the airy white stucco and pink tablecloths of the interior instead. English menu. Entrees 900-2200Ft. Open daily 10am-10pm. MC/V. ❸

Gyros, Széchényi u. 10 (☎413 781). Serves gyros (450-950Ft) and roasts (850-1800Ft) on a basic outdoor patio surrounded by flower boxes. Seating also available inside. English menu. Vegetarian options. Open daily 9am-10pm. Cash only. ❷

⊙ SIGHTS

■ **VALLEY OF BEAUTIFUL WOMEN (SZÉPASSZONY-VÖLGY).** After exploring Eger's sights by day, spend the evening in the wine cellars of the Valley of Beautiful Women. (While the origins of the name are uncertain, the valley's charms are not.) Following WWII, low land prices allowed hundreds of wine cellars to sprout on this volcanic hillside. Most are little more than a tunnel and a few tables and benches, but each has its own personality: some are hushed while others burst with Hungarian and Roma singalongs. Subdued in the afternoon, the valley springs to life at night, when its 25 cellars open their doors to host both serious wine tasters and those who prefer to linger amidst the music and the revelers. The cellars are in a row, so it is easy to hop in and out to experience their different ambiences and sample their famous wines. Eger is Hungary's red wine capital: the most popular are *Bikavér* and the sweeter *Medok* or *Medina*. Sample the legendary **Bull's Blood** wine or the new **red wine mixed with Coke**—a favorite of the younger generation. After 10pm, some cellars become after-hours bars, with DJs or live music. For those who don't want to stumble back to town, *zimmer frei* signs and small hotels abound in the valley. (*Start out on Széchényi u. with Eger Cathedral on the right. Go right on Kossuth Lajos u. and continue until it dead ends into Vörösmarty u. Turn left and continue to Király u. Take a right and keep walking for several minutes directly to the valley. Some cellars open at 9am, but all remain quiet until nightfall. Closing times vary. Some open until midnight July-Aug. Most samples free, some 50Ft. 1L around 350Ft.*)

EGER CASTLE (EGRI VÁR). A pivotal military stronghold in the 1500s, Eger Castle gained fame when Dobó István, supposedly empowered by Bull's Blood Wine, led Hungarian troops to an unexpected victory against Ottoman invaders. Egri Vár's interior includes subterranean barracks, catacombs, a crypt, and a wine cellar. In the courtyard, hosts in medieval costume teach visitors to walk on stilts, sword fight, or play medieval games. The tower and the castle perimeter offer panoramic views of Eger. (*Open daily Apr.-Aug. 8am-8pm; Sept. 8am-7pm; Oct. and Mar. 8am-6pm; Nov.-Feb. 8am-5pm. Grounds ticket 200Ft, students 100Ft.*) Another ticket buys admission to the grounds and the castle's museums: the large **Dobó István Vármúzeum**, which displays armor and weaponry with English captions; a **gallery** with a surprisingly diverse collection of 16th- to 19th-century Hungarian paintings; and the **dungeon exhibition,** which features a small collection of torture equipment that will delight the sadist but frighten more innocent souls. (*Museums open Mar.-Oct. Tu-Su*

9am-6pm; ticket office closes at 4:20pm; Nov.-Feb. 9am-4pm. All 3 museums Tu-Su 500Ft, students 250Ft; M 250/120Ft.) A **wax museum** *(panoptikum)* displays sculptures of Captain Dobó and other Hungarian heroes. *(Open daily 9am-6pm. 350Ft, students 250Ft.)* The 400-year-old **wine cellars** are also open for tastings. *(Open daily 10am-7pm. Free admission; 200Ft per tasting.)* Sip warily, however: the bar is just beside the hands-on archery exhibit of longbows with real arrows. *(☎312 744; www.div.iif.hu. Underground passages open daily 9am-5pm. Tour guide required. English tour 600Ft.)*

LYCEUM. The ceiling fresco in the 20,000-volume **Diocesan Library** on the second floor of the Rococo Lyceum portrays the Council of Trent, the meeting that established the edicts of the Counter-Reformation. Built in the late 18th century, the Lyceum, now home to a teachers' college, also contains the equipment of astronomer Hell Miksa. Several flights up, the **Specula Observatory** displays Miksa's 18th-century telescopes and instruments. A marble line in the museum floor represents the meridian: at astronomical noon, the sun strikes it through a pinhole aperture in the southern wall. Two floors up, a 1776 **"camera obscura,"** constructed of a mirror and lenses inside a small darkroom, projects a stunning live picture of the surrounding town onto a table. Nicknamed the "eye of Eger," it justifies the 302-step hike to the top. *(At the corner of Kossuth Lajos u. and Eszterházy tér. Open Apr.-Sept. Tu-Su 9:30am-3:30pm; Oct.-Mar. Tu-F 9:30am-1pm, Sa-Su 9:30am-1:30pm. Library 500Ft, students 350Ft; museum and camera obscura 500Ft, students 350Ft. English captions.)*

EGER CATHEDRAL. The only Neoclassical building in Eger, the massive 1887 cathedral proclaims in bold letters atop its front columns, *"Venite adoremus dominum"* ("Come, let us adore Thee"). The soaring architecture, soft pastel hues, and stained-glass windows create an unusually bright feel for a Baroque interior. **Organ Concerts** (30min.) are held from May to mid-October. *(On Eszterházy tér just off Széchényi u. Concerts M-Sa 11:30am, Su 12:45pm. 500Ft. Church entrance free when concerts are not in progress.)*

OTHER SIGHTS. Once the Ottomans' northernmost possession in Hungary, the **Minaret,** Knézich K. u., was used to call Muslim villagers to prayer. While it appears to be simply a wide column, it actually contains a 97-step staircase. The climb might induce a touch of vertigo, but the view from the top rewards the effort. *(Open daily Apr.-Oct. 9:30am-6pm. 200Ft.)* Below the high-vault ceiling frescoes of the 1758 pink marble **Minorite Church** hang detailed sculptures and paintings of biblical scenes. *(In Dobó tér. ☎516 613. Open Apr.-Oct. Tu-Su 9am-6pm. Services Su 9am. Free.)* The 18th-century **Serbian Orthodox Church** *(Szerb Ortodox Templom)*, on Vitkovics u. at the center's northern end, drips with gilt decoration. Follow Széchényi u. from the center for roughly 10min. and enter at #55. Go up the stairs on the right, then up the stairs through the tunnel, and request admittance at the green fence behind the temple. *(Open daily 10am-4pm. 320Ft.)*

🎵 📷 ENTERTAINMENT AND NIGHTLIFE

While Eger's popular **bath complex** offers a desperately needed respite from the summer heat, the Turkish baths garnered fame for the supposedly curative effects of their thermal water. Fed by Artesian wells 3km away, the unique water is prescribed by local doctors as therapy for chronic diseases. The complex also includes swimming pools. From Dobó tér, take Jókai u. to Kossuth Lajos u. and continue on Egészségház u. Make a left on Klapka György u. and cross the stream. (☎311 585. Open May-Sept. M-F 6am-7pm, Sa-Su 8am-7pm; Oct.-Apr. daily 9am-7pm. Ticket window closes at 6pm. 900Ft, students 450Ft.) While Eger may seem quiet by day, the town livens up by evening. After drinking in the valley, check out one of the **underground discos** (see **Stayin' A-Lava,** p. 304).

THE HIDDEN DEAL

STAYIN' A-LAVA

A bustling town by day, Eger turns suspiciously quiet at night, with cafes closed and few people wandering the streets. Or at least so it seems. Underneath—quite literally—Eger continues to offer festive diversions in the form of clubs built into a series of lava tunnels.

Unknown to most visitors, an elaborate labyrinth lies below Eger, the carved remnants of a 120km bed of lava upon which the city was founded. Locals have converted three sections into nightclubs, invisible to the world above except for small, barely marked entrances.

One of the most popular (and cave-like) of these dens, **Broadway Palace**, on Pyrter 3, alongside Kossuth L. u, lies under the Eger Cathedral: Blaspheming youths dance the night away, wandering out just hours before the church above begins morning service. (Cover 500Ft. Open W-Sa, 10pm-6am.)

Another popular underground spot is **Liget Dance Cafe**, Erksekkert (☎427 754), under Excalibur Restaurant in the Archbishop's Gardens. (Cover 600Ft. Open F-Sa 10pm-6am. AmEx/MC/V.) Clearly marked by spotlights, the club draws a younger crowd to the neon lights of its central dance floor. **Hippolit Club and Restaurant**, Katona ter 2, is classier and more subdued. (☎411 031. Dancing starts around 11pm. Open M-Th noon-midnight, F-Sa noon-4am).

Eger hosts free music on **Small Dobó tér** nightly at 6pm. From late July to mid-August, the town celebrates its cultural heritage during the **Baroque Festival**. Nightly music and opera performances take place in and around the city. Buy tickets at the venue. An international folk dance festival, **Eger Vintage Days**, takes place in early September. Tourinform (see **Orientation and Practical Information**, p. 301) provides festival schedules.

◪ DAYTRIPS FROM EGER

▨ BARADLA CAVES.

A bus leaves Eger daily at 8:45am and arrives in Aggtelek at 11:25am. Returning bus leaves from the stop across the street at 3pm. Another bus leaves Miskolc at 9:15am, arrives in Aggtelek around 11am, and heads back from the same stop at 5pm. To get to the caves from the bus, cross the street and go down the path to the caves; the park entrance is on the right. (☎48 503 002. 1hr. Hungarian tours daily 10am, noon, 1, 3pm; in high season also 5pm. 1900Ft, students 1100Ft.) Tours of the main branch of the cave arranged by Tourinform. (☎48 503 000. 5hr.; 7km; 6000Ft, students 3600Ft. Call ahead.) Open daily Apr.-Sept. 8am-6pm; Oct.-Mar. 8am-4pm. If you choose to do the long hike, you will miss the return bus; plan to stay overnight.

Straddling the Slovak-Hungarian border, **Aggtelek National Park** is home to Hungary's fantastic Baradla Caves. Each year, over 200,000 visitors enter this forest of dripping stalactites, stalagmites, and imposing stone formations. A UNESCO World Heritage site, the limestone caves were formed 200 million years ago and span over 25km. Though the trip from Eger or Miskolc is long, the drive takes you through the region's lush hills before giving you a chance to explore the bizarre "drip-stone" of the cave. A chamber with perfect acoustics was converted into an auditorium, and tours take a dramatic pause here for a sound and light show. Concerts are given regularly (around 2000Ft; schedules available through Tourinform). Another chamber houses an Iron Age cemetery where 13 skeletons were found buried in sitting positions. Many weddings and other ceremonies take place in the caves. The numerous tours vary in length. There are 1hr. basic and Bat Branch tours (1900Ft, students 1100Ft), but cave-lovers might prefer the five-hour guided hike (6000Ft). The temperature is 10°C year-round, so be sure to bring a jacket. A scenic picnic spot up the stairs to the left of the ticket window overlooks the Slovakian countryside.

Baradla Hostel ❶, next to the park, is an excellent base from which to explore the caves and take hikes in the nearby region. (☎48 503 005. 1800Ft, students 1500Ft; cottage triples 4000Ft; quads 5300Ft; camping 1000Ft per adult, 700Ft per student, plus 1000Ft per site fee. Cash only.) Beside the ticket booth, **Barlang Vendéglo ❷**, offers a menu (in English) of reasonably priced Hungarian favorites on a pleasant outdoor terrace. (☎48 343 177. Entrees 750-2300Ft.)

SZILVÁSVÁRAD

Trains run from Eger (1hr., 7 per day, 326Ft). Buses are generally the most convenient transport; they go to Aggtelek (1¾hr., daily 9:20am, 744Ft) and Eger (45min., 1-2 per hr., 363Ft). The bus stops just outside the park entrance. The main street, Egri út, extends from the Szilvásvárad-Szalajkavölgy train station and bends sharply. Szalajka u. leads to the national park. Farther north, Egri út becomes Miskolci út. There's no tourist office, so get info and a basic map at the Eger Tourinform (p. 301) before heading out. The staff at Hegyi Camping provide a wealth of info about the area and sell maps. Hiking maps are posted throughout the park. Free maps of the mountains are available at the bike shop, on Szalajka u., just past the stop sign at the park entrance. (☎335 2695. Open M-W and Sa-Su 9am-6pm, Th-F 9am-1pm).

From leisurely biking in the Szalajka Valley to strenuous hikes through the mountains, Szilvásvárad's **Bükki National Park** offers a variety of outdoor opportunities. The arena on Szalajka u., just off the park entrance, hosts weekend **horseshows** (800Ft). You can learn to drive a carriage, brandish a whip, or ride a steed. In early July, the arena hosts the hugely popular **Lipicai Festival** (call Lipicai Stables or Hegyi Camping for info). The event draws carriage drivers from across the globe for a three-day competition. **Lipicai Stables,** the stud farm for Szilvásvárad's famed Lipizzaner breed and one of the few such sites in Europe, is at the heart of the town's horse tradition. In addition to the stables, the farm displays a historic carriage-barn and offers rides. For a glimpse of the famous horses, head away from the park on Egri út, turn left on Enyves u., and follow the signs to the farm. (☎355 155. Open daily 10am-noon and 2-4pm. 350Ft.)

Shaded walks through the **Bükk Mountains** and the **Szalajka Valley** are beautiful but not always tranquil—in May and June they swarm with school groups and picnicking families. The lazy trailside stream transforms into the most dramatic of the park's attractions at the **Fátyol Waterfall**. The journey takes 45min. at a leisurely pace along the green trail, or 15min. by the open-air train, which departs from the park entrance. (7 per day 9:25am-4:10pm. 220Ft, students 110Ft.) A 30min. hike past the waterfall on the green trail, **Stemberbarlang** is a cave that was once home to prehistoric humans. After the brook, the paved trail ends, though more adventurous hikers can explore the rugged terrain set off at sharp angles from the path. **Millennium Lookout Tower,** built in 2000, offers a spectacular view of the town and surrounding countryside. (Open W-Su 10am-9pm.) You can avoid the crowds by **renting a bike** (800Ft 1st hr., 200Ft per hr. thereafter), at Szalajka u., just past the stop sign at the park entrance. Pick up a tourist guide before hitting the trails. The shop can also arrange other outdoor activities (900Ft, children 800Ft) in the nearby trees at **Adventure Forest**. (☎380 443. Open Sa-Su 10am-7pm.)

While Szilvásvárad makes most sense as a daytrip from Eger, more avid hikers may want to spend the night. **Private rooms** are cheapest (from 2000Ft), but prices rise 1000-1500Ft during the Lipicai Festival; find rooms on either side of the park—look for *zimmer frei* signs outside the park entrance. After the booth on Szalajka u., a row of restaurants with indoor and patio seating includes **Csobogó Étterem ❷**, alongside a waterfall and miniature mill. (Entrees 600-2000Ft. Open daily noon-6pm.) For trail food, go to **Nagy ABC**, Egri út 6. (Open M-F 6am-6pm, Sa 6am-1pm, Su 8am-noon.) A small **bank** is to the left of the bus stop (☎354 105. Open M-F 8am-noon and 12:30-4pm.) and an **ATM** at Nagy ABC.

LILLAFÜRED

While a traveler can cover it in a day, Lillafüred may be more relaxing as an overnight getaway. From Eger, hop on a bus bound for Miskolc (1½hr., 2 per hr., 846Ft). When you get to Búza tér, the bus station, take bus #1, 1a, or 101 to Diósgyőr (160Ft). From the stop in Diósgyőr, catch bus #5 to Lillafüred and get off at Palotasszallo, the first stop after the lake. Together the buses in Miskolc take about 40min. For a trail map, inquire at hotels. For a rustic experience amid the forest and surrounding villages, try the scenic Forest Train (☎46 370 345, or see schedule at station; 340Ft) on your way back to Miskolc. The train takes slightly more than 30min. From last stop, cross the street and walk left 100m to the bus stop. Take bus #1, 1a, or 101, but not 101b, back to Búza tér.

Close to Eger and Miskolc, Lillafüred (pop. 481) is an ideal base from which to explore the Bükk Mountains and National Park. The mountains' elevated lookouts, varied rock surfaces, and winding cave system make for exciting **hikes,** which range 5-36km. **Rowboats** and **paddleboats** are available on Lake Hámori at **Neptun Rentals,** across from Hotel Palota, down a path off the main road. (250Ft per 30min. Pedal boats 300Ft.) The **Szent István Stalactite Cave,** smaller but similar to Aggtelek's Baradla Caves, has a 170m area where visitors can examine stalactites. The cave's unique climate, 10°C with 80% humidity, is alleged to cure respiratory ailments. (☎46 334 130. Open daily Apr. 15-Oct. 15 9am-5pm, last tour at 4pm; Oct. 16-Apr. 14 9am-4pm, last tour at 3pm.) The **Anna Cave** is at the bottom of the trail beneath Hotel Palota. The cave, which harbors calcium-covered plants, is adjacent to a waterfall and river and surrounded by hanging flower gardens. (☎46 334 130. Open daily Apr. 15-Oct. 15 9:30am-3:30pm, last tour 3pm. At both caves, tours start on the hr. and last 20-30min. 650Ft, students 450Ft.)

Lilla Panzió Motel ❸, Erzsébet sétány 7, provides simple rooms with quilted beds and an in-house restaurant. (☎379 299. English spoken. Breakfast included. Singles 4300Ft; doubles 9300Ft; quads 13,200Ft.) If traipsing through the outdoors gives you an appetite, stop by the **King Matthias Restaurant ❸,** tucked away in the basement of Hotel Palota. Matthias serves generous portions of wild game, fruit, and potatoes amidst a Renaissance ambience complete with carved walls, heavy wood tables, and stained glass. (☎331 411. Entrees 800-6000Ft. Open daily noon-11pm. Call ahead.) Several stands sell hot dogs, hamburgers, and other snacks.

TOKAJ   ☎(06)47

Called home to "the wine of kings and the king of wines" by French King Louis XIV, Tokaj (tohk-OY; pop. 5100) has enjoyed an illustrious reputation since the 12th century. While Eger is known for its reds, smaller Tokaj produces only white wines. If Tokaj gives the wine its name (*Tokaji Fehérbor*), the wine gives Tokaj its flavor: practically every other building is a wine cellar, and vineyards are visible in the lush hills above town. A popular base for hiking and canoeing, the town lies at the foot of the Kopasz mountains, bordered by the volcanic Zemplen hills to the north and the Tisza and Bodrog rivers to the south.

🖃🛉 TRANSPORTATION AND PRACTICAL INFORMATION. The **train station,** Baross G. u. 18 (☎352 020; www.elvira.hu), sends trains to: **Debrecen** (2hr., 8 per day, 838Ft) via **Nyíregyháza** and **Miskolc** (1hr., 10 per day, 700Ft). **Buses** from the train station serve local towns.

To get to the center of town, take a left from the train station entrance and follow the tracks, then turn left on **Bajcsy-Zsilinszky u.** Bear left as the road forks by Tokaj Hotel. Bajcsy-Zsilinszky u. becomes **Rákóczi u.** after the Tisza bridge, then **Bethlen Gábor u.** after **Kossuth tér. Tourinform,** Serház u. 1, on the right side of Rákóczi u. as you walk into town, arranges accommodations and can set you up with a horse, canoe, or rafting tour. (☎352 259; www.tokaj.hu. Open daily Apr. 15-Oct. 15 M 10:30am-6pm, Tu-Sa 9am-7pm, Su 10:30am-3:30pm; Oct. 16-Apr. 14 M-F 9am-4pm, Sa 10:30am-2:30pm.) **Exchange currency,** cash **traveler's checks,** and get MC/V **cash advances** at **OTP,** Rákóczi u. 35. (☎352 523. Open M noon-4pm, Tu-F 7:45am-1pm.) A MC/V **ATM** sits outside. **Paracelsus Pharmacy** (in a building labeled Gyógyszertár) is on Kossuth tér.; after hours, ring bell for emergencies. (☎352 052. Open M-F 8am-5pm, Sa-Su 8am-noon and 12:40-4pm.) There is a **medical center,** labeled "Szakorvosi Rendelő," on Bethlen G. u. 4, with doctors available daily 8am-7pm. An **ambulance service** (☎104) can take you to the nearest hospital in Miskolc. **Internet Club,** Bajcsy-Zsilinszky 34, provides **Internet.** (☎353 137. Open M-Sa noon-9pm.) There are **telephones** at the **post office,** Rákóczi u. 24. (☎353 647. Open M-F 8am-5pm, Sa 8am-noon.) **Postal Code:** 3910.

⌐⌐ ACCOMMODATIONS AND FOOD. You can check for rooms at **Tourinform,** but *zimmer frei* and *szoba kiadó* (rooms available) signs abound—your best bet is to walk along Rákóczi u. (Singles 2000-3000Ft; doubles 4000-6000Ft.) Don't be afraid to bargain, but beware: your host may talk you into sampling—and buying—expensive homemade wine. **Lux Panzió ❷,** Serház u. 14, provides sizeable rooms infused with light. Turn right on Vároháza-köz from Rákóczi u., just after OTP. Ask for the double with private bath—it's the same price as those that share baths. (☎352 145. Breakfast 700Ft. Reception 8am-10pm. Singles 3000Ft; doubles 5400Ft; triples 7500Ft. Tax 125Ft. Cash only.) The convenient **Makk Marci Panzió ❸,** Liget Köz 1, on the main street in the center, boasts a prime location just steps from some of the town's best wine cellars. (☎352 336; makkmarci@axelero.hu. Breakfast included. Reception 24hr. Singles 4800Ft; doubles 7500Ft; triples 10,640Ft; quads 12,300Ft. Tax 250Ft. AmEx/MC/V.) If you'd rather camp, cross the Tisza and take the second left to reach **Vizisport Centrum Youth Hostel ❶,** which provides a campground and bungalows with a river view. (☎352 645. First night 1400Ft, additional nights 1200Ft.) Keep going and you'll reach **Tiszavirág Camping ❶,** a peaceful campground with waterfront campsites and bungalows. (☎352 626. Camping 900Ft per person; bungalow 1500Ft per person.)

Enjoy Hungarian favorites in a dignified dining room with banquet-like tables, or outside in the garden, at **Toldi Fogadó ❷,** Hajdú Köz 2, at Rákóczi u. (☎353 403; www.toldifogado.hu. English menu available. Entrees 690-2000Ft. Open daily 11am-

ON THE MENU

WINES OF TOKAJ

Come to Tokaj and you'll know immediately that this town takes its wines seriously. Not only do vineyards loom above the main street, but nearly every door bears a sign proudly advertising its own variety of the local whites. In fact, 25-million-year-old fossils found in the area suggest it may even have been the origin of the grape.

Whereas dry wines are the specialty of Eger, Tokaj takes special pride in its sweet white wines and even has a unique system of measurement to determine its level of "puttonyos," or sweetness.

Furmint is a basic dry white wine, with a fruity, intensely aromatic character. The most common Tokaj wine, it complements seafood and poultry.

Harslevelu is made from a traditional thin-skinned grape. Served chilled, this dry, young, fresh wine particularly enhances a fish or shellfish entree. It can also be enjoyed as an aperitif.

Aszu grapes, which ripen more quickly than others, make the most famous of Tokaj's wines: a very sweet dessert wine.

Eszeneia, which means "essence," is a true delicacy, and is made from the first juices of Aszu grapes. It should be drunk alone or with a great cigar. The years 1972, '75, '83, '88, '93, and '99 are considered good vintages of wines from Tokaj. It's best to try wines in order from the driest to sweetest; when dry wines follow sweet wines, they taste unpleasantly bitter and acidic.

10pm. AmEx/DC/MC/V.) **Makk Marci Pizzeria Étterem ❷**, connected to Makk Marci Panzió (see above), serves homemade pizza with a variety of vegetable and meat toppings, all cooked under the cheese. (English menu. Pizzas 430-1800Ft. Spaghetti 440-580Ft. Open daily 8am-8pm. AmEx/DC/MC/V.) **Taverna ❷** is on Hősök tér, across the street from the Tisza bridge, burrowed into the hill. Its skinny rooms are modeled after local wine cellars. (☎352 346. Entrees 650-800Ft. Open daily 2pm-midnight. Cash only.) The **MaxiCoop** supermarket is on Kossuth tér. (Open M-F 6am-6pm, Sa 6am-1pm, Su 7-11am.) **ABC Coop,** on Rákóczi u., is a little more expensive but offers more vegetarian foods. (Open M-F 6:30am-6:30pm, Sa 6:30am-1pm, Su 7-11am.)

🎦 🗾 SIGHTS AND ENTERTAINMENT.

Signs reading *"Bor Pince"* herald **private wine cellars.** Owners are generally pleased to let visitors sample their wares (about 1000Ft for 5 or 6 0.1L samples). Ring the bell if a cellar is closed. Cellars on the main road are usually more touristy—on the side streets you'll find higher-quality wines and homier atmospheres. For an authentic wine-tasting experience, head to the 1.5km tunnel cellar of **🔲Rákóczi Pince,** Kossuth tér 15. Tastings take place in the 500-year-old, 10°C, underground hall, which has a small museum of wine-making implements, and where János Szapolyai was elected king of Hungary in 1526. Wine tastings and tours of the cellar and hall are arranged on the hour, but can be preempted by tour groups. Individual tours can be arranged at any time; English-speaking guides are available at no extra cost. (☎352 408; fax 352 741. Open 10am-7pm. 2100Ft for 1hr. tour and 6-glass tasting. Call ahead. AmEx/MC/V.) The 300-year-old **Tóth Family Cellar,** Óvár út 40, produces five exceptional whites, including a *puttonyos Aszú*. Take the street that begins opposite Tourinform on Rákóczi u. The door leads to a small cellar with dank, moldy walls and moisture dripping from the ceiling. (6-glass tasting 800Ft, 1L of *Tokaji 6 puttonyos* 4600Ft, 0.5L 3000F. Open daily 9am-7pm. See **Wines of Tokaj,** p. 307.) The young, family-run **Tokaji Hímesudvar Winery,** Bem u. 2, produces phenomenal *Aszú* wines—their 1993 *Tokaji 5 puttonyos* received national awards. The Várhelyi family happily guides you through the history of the region and the subtleties of Tokaj wines. Their 1999 *Aszú 6 puttonyos* is indescribably sweet. To get to the royal hunting lodge where the cellar is located, take the road to the left of the church in Kossuth tér and continue up the road roughly 50m. (☎352 416. Open daily 10am-9pm, in winter 10am-6pm. Tastings 2000Ft for 6 wines.)

If you've had enough to drink, venture to the low-key **Tokaj Museum,** down Bethlen Gábor u. past the square, built in 1790. The stairs inside are original, and the rooms are stuffed with a wide collection of artifacts representing Tokaj's rich history and culture. After viewing the collection of Catholic icons, visit the attic, which houses a large display of wine-making instruments. (☎352 636. Open Tu-Su 10am-4pm. 400Ft, students 200Ft.) From the museum, continue down Rákóczi u. until it meets Josef Attila u. and turn right. You'll come to the largest structure in Tokaj, the **synagogue,** which sits forlorn and boarded up. Once home to a thriving pre-war Jewish population, who were active members of the wine trade, the synagogue will likely be converted to a cinema or youth center.

Outdoor recreation in Tokaj is almost as popular as wine. The steep vineyard slopes make for challenging hikes, and the languid Tisza and Bodrog are often filled with paddleboats. **Vízisport Centrum** (☎352 645) rents bikes (1000Ft per day) and canoes (500Ft per person per day; 2-4 person canoes available) and arranges horseback riding (1800Ft per hr., 2500Ft with trainer; call 1 day ahead). **Spori Sport** also rents canoes. Take the first right after the Tisza bridge and follow the road 500m. (☎481 716; www.spori.sport.hu. 2-seater 900Ft per day, 4-seater 1600Ft per day.) The best place to canoe is the Bodrog River. Paddle upstream, and you will be rewarded with a pleasant ride back to town. Tourinform (see p. 301) gives advice about **hikes**. While the red and blue trails are easy to follow, the green is steep and poorly marked. **Halihó Sörkert ❶**, at the end of the block directly after *Toldi Fogadó*, a hamburger joint by day (5-10pm), is a hotspot at night where local youths sip drinks at outdoor picnic tables. Crowds begin to arrive around 8:30pm. (Open daily 6pm-midnight. Burgers 260-500Ft.) **Műhely Söröző**, Rákóczi u. 42, is an Irish pub that packs in students for an after-dinner round. (Beer 80-130Ft. Pool 60Ft per game. Open daily 2-10pm.)

VISEGRÁD   ☎(0)26

Once the seat of the royal court, Visegrád (VEE-sheh-grad) has literally turned to ruins. Turkish invaders destroyed the town in 1544, and it was only partly rebuilt when Germans resettled the region in the 18th century. Today, visitors wander the ruins of the royal palace and castle and view the excavation exhibits inside. Although the town is an easy daytrip from Budapest, its beautiful mountain trails and spectacular views of the Danube entice hikers and bicyclists to stay longer.

▐▀ TRANSPORTATION AND PRACTICAL INFORMATION. Buses depart from Budapest at Árpád híd, M3 (1½hr., 30 per day, 484Ft). There are four stops in Visegrád. Get off at the first stop for the citadel or the tower; stay on until the third stop to reach the town center. **Ferries** from the Budapest pier below Vigadó tér (3½hr.; 2 per day; 1090Ft) stop in front of the town center. **Buses** stop along **Harangvirag u.**, which runs parallel to the river. The town's main road, **Fő út**, is a pedestrian street behind Harangvirag u. **Visegrád Tours**, Rév út 15, across the street from the river at the third bus stop, provides accommodations info and hiking maps. (☎398 160; fax 397 597. Open daily Apr.-Oct. 8am-6pm; Nov.-Mar. M-F 10am-4pm.) There's an **ATM** at Fő út. 34, and a **post office** across the street (open M-F 8am-4pm).

▐▐ ACCOMMODATIONS AND FOOD. Visegrád's cheapest accommodations are **private rooms** outside the town center. Search for *Zimmer Frei* signs on the south side of Fő út and on Nagy Lajos út. **Mátyás Tanya ❹**, Fő út 47, has sunny rooms in a comfortable guesthouse. (☎398 309. Breakfast included. Reserve ahead. Doubles 9900Ft; triples 10,000-12,000Ft. Tax 300Ft.) The rooms at the comparatively posh **Hotel Visegrád ❹**, Rév út 15, boast balconies overlooking the castle and the Danube. (☎397 034; hotelvisegrad@visegradtours.hu. Breakfast included. Doubles 10,000Ft; triples 14,000Ft. Tax 300Ft.) On a sunny day, the grassy banks of the Danube provide a perfect picnic spot. Pick up supplies at **CBA Élelmiszer** supermarket, across from Visegrád Tours at the end of Rév út. (Open M 7am-6pm, Tu-F 7am-7pm, Sa 7am-3pm, Su 7am-1pm. AmEx/MC/V.) On weekends, **food stalls** lining Fő út sell *lángos* (150-300Ft), gyros (600-1000Ft), and a variety of fried foods. For something more substantial, head to **Don Vito Pizzeria ❷**, Fő út 83, where friendly waiters serve brick-oven pizza. (☎397 230. Pizza 300-1400Ft. Pasta 800-1100Ft. Live jazz Sa-Su 9pm. Open daily noon-midnight.) **Gulyás Csárda ❸**, Nagy Lajos út 4, prepares a variety of excellent Hungarian dishes; you'll smell the garlic cooking from the garden outside. (☎398 329. English menu. Entrees 1200-1700Ft. Open daily noon-10pm.)

▣▐ SIGHTS AND ENTERTAINMENT. The **citadel** is Visegrád's main attraction. This former Roman outpost is the highest vantage point for miles and provides a gorgeous, sweeping panorama of the Danube bend. Heading north on Fő út, go right on Salamontorony u. and follow the path, which turns into a dirt trail past the tower. The citadel has a **wax museum** where medieval torture techniques petrify wax victims. (Open Mar. 15-Oct. 15 daily 9:30am-5:30pm; Oct. 16-Mar. 14 Sa-Su 10am-5pm. 800Ft, students 350Ft.) Named for a king imprisoned here in the 13th century, the Romanesque **Solomon's Tower** (Alsóvár Salamon Torony), on the path to the citadel, gives a view of the medieval district. Inside, the **King Matthias Museum** displays artifacts from the palace ruins. (☎398 026. Open May-Oct. Tu-Su 9am-5pm; last admission 4:30pm. Free.) Considered mythical until archaeologists uncovered it in 1934, King Matthias's **Royal Palace** (Királyi Palota) sprawls above Fő út. The remains alone make for an interesting visit, but there is also an impressive reconstruction of the castle as it was in 1259. (☎398 026; fax 398 252. Limited English info. Open Tu-Su 9am-5pm; last admission 4:30pm. Free.) The second weekend of July, parades, jousting tournaments, concerts, and a market overtake the grounds for the **Visegrád Palace Games.** Contact the **Visegrád Cultural Center** (☎398 128; muvelodesihaz@visegrad.hu). **Nyári Bobpálya** hosts a popular, if frightening, toboggan slide. From the citadel, go left up Panorama út. (☎397 397. Open daily Apr.-Aug. 9am-6pm; Sept.-Oct. 10am-5pm; Nov.-Feb. 11am-4pm; Mar. 11am-5pm. M-F 320Ft, children 250Ft; Sa-Su 320/250Ft.) If you'd rather hike, pick up a **map** (400Ft) from Visegrád Tours or the Solomon's Tower ticket office. Visegrád Tours also **rents bikes** (1500Ft per day).

WESTERN TRANSDANUBIA

During the Cold War, authorities discouraged people from entering the pastoral region of Western Transdanubia, as they believed capitalist Austria and Tito's Yugoslavia were too close for comfort. Thus, a region that had always been a bit behind the times—electricity didn't arrive until 1950—fell even farther beyond modernity's reach, leaving much of the countryside unchanged. The rolling hills and stretches of farmland are perfect for leisurely strolls, bicycle rides, and hiking in summer, while holiday fairs light up town streets in winter.

GYŐR   ☎(0)96

The streets of Győr (DYUR; pop. 130,000) wind peacefully around the small city's abundant museums and 17th- and 18th-century architecture that seems to have defied the wear of time. With its thousand-year-old cathedral and the magisterial Archabbey of Pannonhalma nearby, Győr is a popular stopover for both religious pilgrims and tourists making their way from Budapest to Vienna. Though the city is quiet at night, by day visitors can join the large population of the Old Town in bringing the storybook beauty of these narrow streets to life.

▐▓ TRANSPORTATION AND PRACTICAL INFORMATION. The **train station,** Révai út 4-6 (domestic ☎311 613, international 523 366), is 3min. from the city center; as you exit the station, turn right. Turn left before the underpass and cross the street to pedestrian **Baross Gábor út.** Trains run to: **Budapest** (2½hr., 34 per day, 1338Ft); **Sopron** (1½hr., 10 per day, 838Ft); **Vienna, AUT** (2hr., 13 per day, 4488Ft). The **bus station,** Hunyadi út 9 (☎317 711), is connected to the train station at the end of the underpass. Buses run to **Budapest** (2½hr., 1 per hr., 1450Ft).
   Tourinform (☎311 771), Árpád út 32, provides accommodations info and **free maps.** (Open June-Aug. M-F 8am-8pm, Sa-Su 9am-6pm.) **IBUSZ** (☎311 700), Kazinczy út 3, has accommodations info. (Open M-F 8am-5pm, Sa 9am-1pm. AmEx/MC/V.) **OTP Bank,** Teleki L. út 51, at the corner of Bajcsy-Zsilinszky út, has good **exchange** rates. (MC/V **ATM** and currency exchange machine in the entrance. Open M 7:45am-6pm, Tu-Th 7:45am-5pm, F 7:45am-4pm.) The **Posta-**

bank desk in the post office cashes **AmEx Traveler's Cheques** for no commission. **Luggage storage** is at the train station. (300Ft per day. Open 3am-midnight.) A **pharmacy, Aranyhajó Patika** can be found at Jedlik Á. út 16. A sign in the window lists pharmacies with emergency hours. (☎328 881. Open M-F 7am-6pm, Sa 7am-2pm.) For **medical services**, go to Vasvári P. u. 2. (☎418 244. Open M-F 8am-5pm.) Aptly named **Different Internet Cafe & Club** (☎516 810), Liszt Ferenc út 20, is off a courtyard in a cellar decked with blue couches. The entrance is on Pálffy u. (250Ft per 30min. Open M-F 8am-9pm, Sa 2-9pm. Ring bell if door is shut.) The **post office** is at Bajcsy-Zsilinszky út 46. (☎314 324. **Poste Restante** available. Open M-F 8am-6pm.) **Postal Code:** 9021.

⌂♨ ACCOMMODATIONS AND FOOD. Accommodations may overflow in summer, so it's smart to make reservations before arriving. **Tourinform** (p. 310) can help you find a *panzió* or hotel room and will make reservations if you call ahead. They also keep a list of **campsites. IBUSZ** (see above) also arranges accommodations (rooms from 4200Ft). ▓**Katalin Kert ❹,** Sarkantyú köz 3, off Bécsi Kapu tér, is hidden in a quaint courtyard. Its huge, modern rooms include TVs and showers. A restaurant downstairs has live music most nights. (☎542 088; katalinkert@matavnet.hu. Breakfast included. Singles 7100Ft; doubles 9100Ft; triples 12,500Ft.) **Széchényi István Főiskola Egyetem ❷,** Hédevári út 3, is across the Moscow-Dune River. Follow Czuczor Gergely út, which runs parallel to Baross Gábor út, across the bridge. Hang a left on Káloczy tér and continue to the parking lot. The entrance is to the left, at K4; after 9pm, enter at K3. Modern buildings offer standard dorm rooms with private showers and shared hall baths. (☎503 400. Reception 24hr. Check-out 9am. Open July-Aug. Singles 3900Ft; doubles 3500Ft; triples 3000Ft.)

Kaiser's Szupermarket sprawls on the corner of Arany János út and Aradi út. (Open M 7:30am-7pm, Tu-F 6:30am-7pm, Sa 6:30am-3pm.) **Matróz Restaurant ❷** is at Dunakapu tér 3, off Jedlik Ányos. This local favorite fries up mouthwatering fish, turkey, and pork dishes in two cozy wooden rooms near the river, complete with folksy charm and dwarf-sized wooden chairs. (☎336 208. Entrees 440-1390Ft. Open M-Th and Su 9am-10pm, F-Sa 9am-11pm.) **Teátrum Étterem ❷,** Sch weidel út 7, couples an upscale location with medium-scale prices, boasting air-conditioning and a flower-dotted patio outside an old-fashioned building. (☎310 640. Entrees 990-1990Ft. Open daily noon-11pm.) Restaurant/pub **John Bull Pub ❸,** Aradi út 3, is a delicious respite from Hungarian food, with Italian options, lava-stone grilled meat, and salads (330-580Ft). Choose between tables on the street and a dim interior with a vague US Civil War theme. (☎618 320. 0.5L Guinness 800Ft. Entrees 1220-2850Ft. Open daily 10am-midnight. MC/V.)

◪ SIGHTS. Head uphill on Czuczor Gergely út, parallel to Baross Gábor u., and then take a left at Gutenberg tér to reach **Chapter Hill** (Káptalandomb), the oldest sector of Győr. Overlooking the junction of three rivers—the Danube, the Rába, and the Rábca—the hill is covered in monuments that call attention to Győr's rich history as a cultural crossroads. The striking 1731 **Ark of the Covenant statue** (Frigyláda Szobor) was bankrolled by taxes King Charles III levied on his impoverished mercenaries. The **Episcopal Cathedral** (Székesegyház), at the top of the hill, has been under frequent construction since 1030. Its exterior is now a medley of Romanesque, Gothic, and Neoclassical styles. Gilded cherubim perch above the heavenly frescoes that illuminate the Baroque interior. Seeking refuge from Oliver Cromwell's forces in the 1650s, a priest brought the miraculous **Weeping Madonna of Győr** to the Cathedral from Ireland. On St. Patrick's Day in 1697, the image reportedly wept blood and tears for the persecuted Irish Catholics. The painting is left of the main altar. The Hédeváry chapel, inside the cathedral, holds the **Herm of King St. Ladislas,** a medieval bust of one of Hungary's first saint-kings. It also contains the **tomb of Bishop Vilmas Apor,** a Győr martyr revered for his anti-Nazi and anti-communist stance. (Open M-Sa 8am-noon and 2-6pm, Su 8am-noon and 3-6pm. Free.) In the alley directly behind the cathedral, the **Diocesan Library and Treasury** (Egyházmegyei Kincstár), Káptalandomb 26, displays 14th-century gold and silver religious artifacts and an extensive collection of old books, including a display of some illuminated manuscripts. (☎311 153. English captions. Open Tu-Su 10am-4pm. 500Ft, students 350Ft.)

The ▓**Imre Patkó Collection** (Patkó Imre Gyűjtemény), Széchényi tér 4 (enter on Stelczera út), has two floors of expressionist and abstract works by modern Hungarian artists and one floor of 16th-century Asian and African works. The museum is housed in the **Iron Log House** (Vastuskós ház), a centuries-old former inn for traveling craftsmen. (☎310 588. English info available. Open Tu-Su 10am-6pm. Buy tickets in the Xántus János Museum next door. 400Ft, students 200Ft.) Down Kenyér Köz from Széchényi tér, the **Margit Kovács Museum** (Kovács Margit Gyűjtemény), Apáca út 1, displays the Győr artist's expressive ceramic sculptures and tiles. (☎326 739. Open Mar.-Oct. Tu-Su 10am-6pm; Nov.-Feb. Tu-Su 10am-5pm. 400Ft, students 200Ft.)

🔳🔳 **ENTERTAINMENT AND NIGHTLIFE.** In summer, locals delight in splashing in the water and basking in the sun. Across the river, thermal springs supply a large **water park** *(fürdő),* Cziráky tér 1. Sprawling over a beautiful complex at the crossing of two rivers, the park has a waterslide, two outdoor swimming pools, two thermal baths, and a spa. From Bécsi kapu tér, walk over the bridge to the island and take the first right on the other side. (Open daily 8am-8pm. 3hr. ticket 1300Ft, students 800Ft, full day ticket 1600Ft/1000Ft.) Győr spends most of June and July at **Győri Nyár,** a festival of concerts, drama, and the city's famous ballet. Schedules are at Tourinform (see **Practical Information,** p. 310); buy tickets at the box office on Baross Gábor út. or at the venue. The **Győr National Theater** (Nemzeti Színház), Czuczor Gergely u. 7, has a lineup of opera, rock, musicals, and plays; buy tickets at the box office. (☎314 800; fax 326 999. Theater open July 15-Aug. 22 M-F 9am-1pm and 2-6pm. Tickets 2000-3000Ft.) If you're looking to shop, head to **Skala Shopping Center,** above Kaiser's Szupermarket (see above).

Győr's energy tends to peter out at night, with the exception of the occasional bar or cafe. Sophisticates head to **The 20th Century,** Schweidel út 25, to sip cocktails outdoors. (Beer 195-400Ft. Mixed drinks 500-1250Ft. Open M-F 9am-midnight, Sa-Su 5pm-midnight.) **Komédiás Biergarten,** Czuczor Gergely u. 30, has a lively patio. (☎527 217. Beer 290-460Ft. Open M-Sa 11am-midnight.) For an after-hours drink, try **Patio Belvárosi Kávéház,** Baross Gábor út 12. Popular with locals for beer (400-450Ft), wine, and desserts (168-599Ft), it's perfect for a mellow evening set to piano music. (☎310 096. Open 24hr.)

🔳 **DAYTRIP FROM GYŐR: ARCHABBEY OF PANNONHALMA.** Visible from Győr on a clear day, the hilltop ▓**Archabbey of Pannonhalma** (Pannonhalmi Főapátság) has seen a millennium of destruction and rebuilding since the Benedictine order established it in 996. Now a UNESCO World Heritage site, it is home to some of the most valuable ecclesiastical treasures and diverse architecture in the world. About 50 monks live in the abbey, which houses a 13th-century basilica, an opulent 360,000-volume library, a small gallery of icons, and one of the finest boys' schools in Hungary. Its treasures include a 1055 deed founding the Benedictine abbey in Tihany, the oldest document with Hungarian writing, and a charter from 1001 establishing the Archabbey of Pannonhalma and bearing St. Stephen's signature. Unfortunately, these charters are in the archives, and only reproductions are on display. There is also a famous **mosaic** of the Madonna created from naturally bright stones. Though the large library, where students still work, is now wired with electric lights, one of its most interesting features is the natural lighting provided by a series of large windows and mirrors. Most of the aging books remain behind protective grates, but some hand-painted manuscripts and early scientific texts sit open in display cases. Although renovations in honor of the Pope's visit in 1996 left the abbey halls looking spiffy, Hungary's oldest graffiti is still visible: a soldier defending the hill against the Turks "was here" in 1578. You can hear **Gregorian chant** at the Sunday 10am mass and at frequent classical music concerts in the halls of the abbey. Required tours begin with a film on the monastic order at the recently built **TriCollis Tourist Office.** The office also arranges tours of the neighboring **winery**, which explain the process of wine-making and show off new, modern furnishings, concluding with a tasting in the cellar. For a bite to eat during your visit, stop in at **Szent Marton Étterem ❸**, opposite the tourist center, for the usual meaty Hungarian dishes (800-2300Ft), with a few healthful options, as well as local wine and a view of the abbey. *(Take the bus from platform #11; 35min., 1 per hr., 302Ft. Ask the driver if the bus is going to Pannonhalma vár. If so, get off at the huge gates. If not, the uphill walk from Pannonhalma takes 20min. From the bus stop, face the abbey, walk left, and turn right up the main road on the hill just after Borpince. The abbey can be visited only by guided tour. English tours Oct.-May Tu-Su 11:20am, 1:20pm; June-Sept. daily 11:20am, 1:20, 3:30pm. English tour 2000Ft, students 1200Ft. Winery tour including tasting 1200Ft. Tickets at TriCollis Tourist Office, Vár 1. ☎570 191; www.bences.hu. Leaving the abbey, take a left and head down the hill; the ticket office is on the right side. MC/V. Restaurant ☎470 793. Open daily 9am-5pm. AmEx/DC/MC/V.)*

SOPRON ☎(0)99

At first glance, Sopron (SHO-pron; pop. 54,000) appears to have drifted from its traditions and cultural history. Lined with brand-name boutiques and mouth-watering dessert shops, it exudes efficiency and industry. But the city's alleyways reveal the older town it hides. The winding cobblestone side streets of Inner Town are home to museums, monuments, churches, and fourth-century ruins from the Roman city Scarbantia. Many stop in Sopron en route to Vienna out of mere convenience, only to find themselves entranced by its charm.

[◨◪] TRANSPORTATION AND PRACTICAL INFORMATION. Trains run to: **Budapest** (3-4hr., 14 per day, 2656Ft); **Győr** (1½hr., 14 per day, 838Ft); **Szombathely** (1¼hr., 14 per day, 620Ft); **Vienna, AUT** (1-2hr., 1 per hr., 3000Ft). The **bus station,** Lackner Kristóf u. 9, sends buses to **Budapest** (4hr., 5 per day, 2500Ft) and **Győr** (2hr., 1 per hr., 1130Ft). **Belváros** (Inner Town), the historic center, is a 1km horseshoe bound by three main streets: **Ógabona tér, Várkerület u.,** and **Széchényi tér.** At the end farthest from the train station, museums and notable buildings line **Fő tér.** To get to the center from the **train station,** veer to the left following **Mátyás Király u.,** which leads to Széchényi tér and becomes Várkerület u. as it curves around the Inner Town. The **bus station** is 5min. from the center. Exit the station and turn right on **Lackner Kristóf u.;** turn left at Ógabona tér to reach Várkerület near Fő tér.

Tourinform, Liszt Ferenc u. 1, off Széchényi tér, has **free maps** and accommodations info. (☎338 892. Open M-F 9am-5pm, Sa-Su 9am-3pm.) **OTP,** Várkerület u. 96A, offers good **currency exchange** rates and cashes **traveler's checks.** There's a 24hr. MC/V **ATM** and a **currency exchange** machine outside. (Open M 7:45am-6pm, Tu-Th 7:45am-5pm, F 7:45am-4pm.) **Store luggage** at the train station. (150Ft per 6hr. 300Ft per day.) There are 5 **pharmacies:** Deák tér 35, Magyar út 6, Mátyás király út 23, and 2 on Várkerület u. A sign in the window of each lists emergency services. **Medical services** are at Győri u. 15 (☎312 120. Open M-F 9am-5pm.) **Cafe DataNet,** Balfi u. 1-3, has **Internet.** (☎523 070. Before 1pm 150Ft per 30min., 300Ft per 1hr.,

250Ft each additional hour; after 1pm 250/400/350Ft. Open M-F 7:30am-11pm, Sa-Su 9am-11pm.) The **post office** is at Széchényi tér 7/10, outside Belváros. **Telephones** are inside. (☎313 100. Open M-F 8am-7pm, Sa 8am-noon.) **Postal Code: 9400.**

⬛◨ ACCOMMODATIONS AND FOOD. Ciklámen Tourist, Ógabona tér 8, can set you up with a **private room.** (☎312 040. Singles from 4500Ft; doubles from 5600Ft. Open M-F 8am-4:30pm, Sa 8am-noon.) **Tourinform** (see **Orientation and Practical Information**) has a list of all the accommodations in the area and can check on room availability. ⬛**Ringhofer Vendégház ❸**, Balfi út 52, has large rooms with clean showers, TVs, and refrigerators, overseen by a wonderfully kind owner. From Széchényi tér, go down Várkerület u. Turn right on Ikva híd u. and right again on Balfi út. (☎325 022; ringhofer@freemail.hu. Breakfast 600Ft. Bike rental 1000Ft per day. Reception 24hr. Check-out 10am. Doubles 5000Ft; triples 8500Ft. Tax 300Ft. Cash only.) **Wieden Panzió ❸**, Sas tér 13, is just 5min. from the center. English-speaking staff offers advice on outdoor daytrips and even lends bikes for free. (☎523 222; www.wieden.hu. Breakfast included. Singles 5400-6600Ft; doubles 7900-9900Ft; triples 11,300-12,500Ft; 4-person apartments 12,500-15,900Ft. AmEx/MC/V.) **ETI Sopron Hallgatói Otthon ❶**, Damjanich u. 9, just 2 blocks from the bus station, is a standard university dorm that offers cheap beds in an unbeatable location near all the action. (☎314 339. Open July-Aug. Dorms 2000Ft. Cash only.)

Coffeehouses are more common than restaurants on the streets of Sopron, but a walk around the city's main loop yields a variety of tasty options. The large **Match** supermarket, at Várkerület u. 100/102, stocks groceries. (Open M-F 6:30am-7pm, Sa 6:30am-4pm. MC/V.) **Várkerület Restaurant ❷**, Várkerület u. 83, near Széchenyi tér, diversifies a traditional Hungarian menu with Asian wok items and the dumpling-heavy "Ilonka Granny's offerings" (dumplings with scrambled eggs and bacon, 700Ft). Efficient staff bring meaty entrees (680-1800Ft) and vegetarian dishes (690-1180Ft) to dining room and beer garden tables. (☎319 286. Open M-Sa 9am-1am, Su 11am-1am. AmEx/MC/V.) A hunting theme graces the pictures on the pink walls of the elegant underground restaurant **Graben ❷**, Várkerület u. 8. Located just outside Fő tér, Graben adds more meats to the Hungarian standards such as stewed stag. (☎340 256. Entrees 990-1800Ft. Open daily 8am-10pm. AmEx/DC/MC/V.) **Fórum Pizzéria ❷**, Szt. György út 3, in a quiet courtyard, provides a refreshing break from Hungarian fare. Choose from among 41 pizzas (650-1190Ft), 18 pastas (550-1100Ft), and a salad bar (350-480Ft). Dine in the candlelit dining room or on the summer terrace. (☎340 231. Open daily 11:30am-11pm. AmEx/DC/MC/V.)

◩◪ SIGHTS AND ENTERTAINMENT. Most of Sopron's sights are in the Inner City. You can purchase a ⬛**museum pass** (2000Ft, students 1000Ft) with access to nine of Sopron's museums, including all of those listed below. If you visit five, the pass pays for itself. Passes are available at the **Storno-Collection ticket office**, Fő tér 8. (☎311 327. Open Tu-Su 10am-6pm.) Built from the remains of a Roman town wall during Roman times, the ⬛**fire tower** (tuztorony), which a fire destroyed in 1676, stands rebuilt as the symbol of Sopron. During reconstruction, a balcony was added, from which guards could signal the position of fires with flags during the day and lanterns at night. Squeeze up the narrow spiral staircase to the balcony for a 360° view of the surrounding hills and the Inner City. Hungarian captions off the stairwell document the building of the tower. (Open Tu-Su Apr. and Sept.-Oct. 10am-6pm; May-Aug. 10am-8pm. 500Ft, students 250Ft.) Originally the site of an ancient Roman bath, the ⬛**Fabricius House,** Fő tér 6, boasts a well-organized **archaeological museum,** with artifacts of the area's inhabitants dating from the Bronze Age. Jewelry, urns, pottery, and tombstones are among its holdings. Thorough English captions provide a historical account of the region's settlements. The underground **Roman Lapidarium** (Római Kőtár) houses tombs and statues that date from Sopron's origins as the Roman colony of Scarbantia. Don't miss the museum showing regional 18th-century furniture, from inlaid writing tables to antique stoves. English info sheets are provided in each room. (Open Tu-Su 10am-6pm. Archaeological Museum and Lapidarium 500Ft, students 250Ft. Furniture exhibit 500/250Ft.) Built in the 13th century by a herder whose goats stumbled upon a cache of gold, the **Benedictine Church** (Bencés Templom) was the site of coronations for three monarchs. Since 1997, it has been under restoration to become a votive church to thank God for Hungary's liberation from communism. (Open daily 10am-5pm. Mass M-F 8am, Su 9:30am.) Just outside the church, the most prominent sight on Fő tér and one of Europe's first corkscrew column sculptures, the **Trinity Column** was built to commemorate the Great Plague of 1695-1701 and marks the center of the main square. The **Old Synagogue**, Kőzépkori Ó-zsinagőga, Új út 22, one of the few to survive the Holocaust, is now a museum depicting the daily life of the local Jewish community before it was expelled from Sopron in 1526. Built around 1300, it has a stone Torah ark, women's prayer room, and ritual bath well. An English info sheet is provided. (Open May-Oct. Tu-Su 10am-6pm. 400Ft, students 200Ft.)

Sopron is a good base for **outdoor** enthusiasts. Bike trails begin just north of the center, leading to **Lake Fertő-Hanság National Park** (a UNESCO World Heritage site), and Fertőd, 30km away (p. 315). Bike maps are free at Tourinform (see **Transportion and Practical Information,** p. 313), which also lists **bike** rental shops (rentals about 2000Ft per day). During the **Sopron Festival Weeks** (late June to mid-July), the town hosts opera, ballet, and concerts. Some are set in the **Fertőrákos Quarry,** 10km away, reachable by hourly buses from the terminal. (Quarry 300Ft, students 150Ft. Concerts 4000-8000Ft.) Fertőrákos also plays home to **watersports** on the lake, such as waterskiing and sailing. Buy tickets for all events from the **Festival Bureau,** Liszt Ferenc u. 1, on Széchényi tér, opposite the post office. (☎517 517. Open M-F 9am-5pm, Sa 9am-noon.) **Cinema City,** at Sopron Plaza, shows both Hungarian- and English-language films (490-950Ft).

Swing, Várkerület u. 15, a sophisticated, dimly lit piano bar, hosts mellow live music and has a well-supplied bar. The red curtains provide the perfect backdrop for the smooth melodies. (☎20 214 8029. Beer 450Ft. Open M-F and Su 5pm-midnight, Sa 5pm-2am.) **Cézár Pince,** Hátsókapu 2, is near Fő tér. You may never want to leave this classy bar, converted from a spacious 17th-century home. Sip a drink on the vine-draped patio, served by waitstaff in period garb. (☎311 337. Wine 650-950Ft. Open M-Sa 11am-midnight, Su 1-11pm.) Sopron youth pack **Goac Point,** Várkerület u. 22, so tight that it's hard to appreciate the eclectic decor, complete with painted waves, a sewing machine, and a *Gone With the Wind* poster. (☎524 018. Beer 250-380Ft. Open M-Th 6pm-1am, F-Sa 6pm-2am.)

▶ DAYTRIP FROM SOPRON

FERTŐD ☎(0)99

Buses leave from platform #11 in Sopron (45min., every 30-60min., 363Ft). Get off at the 3-way intersection in Fertőd. From the bus stop, walk in the direction the bus goes toward the castle. ☎537 640. Palace open Mar. 16-Sept. 30 Tu-Su 10am-6pm; Oct. 1-Mar. 15 F-Su 10am-4pm. Tours (1hr.) in summer 2 per hr.; low season variable; last tour 1hr. before closing. Call ahead to request a tour in English, or take an English info sheet along for a Hungarian tour. 1000Ft, students 600Ft. MC/V.

Twenty-seven kilometers east of Sopron, Fertőd (FER-tewd) is home to the magnificent **Eszterházy Palace,** Joseph Haydn 2. With its bright yellow Baroque facade and manicured gardens, the 126-room palace has been dubbed the "Hungarian Versailles." Prince Miklós Eszterházy ordered its construction in 1766 to host his Bacchic feasts and operas. A small exhibit inside recounts the life of **Joseph Haydn,** who lived here for almost 30 years as Eszterházy's composer. **Concerts** of his work are held in the castle's small concert hall, where Haydn himself conducted, during the semiannual **Haydn Festival,** in mid-July and during the first week of September. (Concerts 7pm. Reserve ahead. 5000-8000Ft.) On weekends throughout the year, less-expensive performances (2500Ft) are held. (Tickets ☎537 640. Open daily 10am-6pm.) **Gránátos Étterem ❸**, Joseph Haydn u. 1, just across the street, offers local dishes (950-1790Ft) and desserts. (☎370 944. Open daily 9am-10pm.)

Sarród, right next door to Fertőd, is part of **Fertő-Hanság National Park,** a UNESCO World Heritage site. Lake Fertő, in the park's center, is one of Europe's most diverse water habitats, while the surrounding swampland is home to over 200 species of birds. For preservation purposes, some parts of the park can be visited only with a certified guide, but bike and hiking trails are scattered throughout the park. Pick up a **map** from **Tourinform Fertőd,** Joseph Haydn 3, just behind the palace (☎557 620; www.ferto-hansag.hu; open Apr.-June Tu-F 10am-5pm, Sa 10am-4pm), or from **Park Information,** Sarród u. 4 (☎537 620). The trails begin 2km from the Palace; follow Sarród u., the street perpendicular to the bus stop. The paved bike path is popular. Bike rental info is available at the Park Information office.

SZOMBATHELY ☎(06)94

Beneath the cover of its modern storefronts and Baroque buildings, Szombathely (SOM-baht-hay; pop. 80,000), a major crossroads between Transdanubia and Austria, hides 2000-year-old ruins of Roman Savaria. Its lively cafes and festivals give it a contemporary feel, making it a relaxing stop for travelers crossing the border or for those hoping to hike in the beautiful Őrség National Park.

⌨ TRANSPORTATION AND PRACTICAL ORIENTATION. Trains (☎311 420) run to: **Budapest** (3¾hr., 12 per day, 2882Ft; InterCity 2¾hr., 3195Ft plus 400Ft reservation fee); **Győr** (2hr., 19 per day, 1010Ft; InterCity 1¼hr., 10 per day, 1641Ft plus 400Ft reservation fee); **Keszthely** (2½hr., 3 per day, 1475Ft); **Vienna, AUT** (4hr., 17 per day, 4394Ft). **Buses** (☎312 054; www.volanbusz.hu.) run to: **Budapest** (3½hr., 6 per day, 2360Ft); **Győr** (2½hr., 8 per day, 1100Ft); **Keszthely** (2½hr., 6 per day, 947Ft); **Sopron** (2hr., 5 per day, 989Ft).

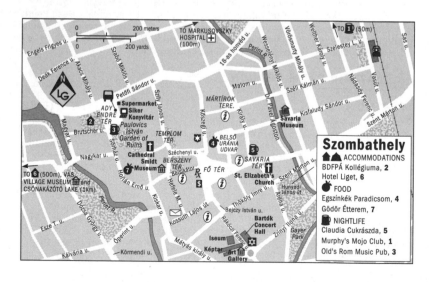

Szombathely

▲▲ ACCOMMODATIONS
BDFPÁ Kollégiuma, **2**
Hotel Liget, **6**

🍴 FOOD
Egszínkék Paradicsom, **4**
Gödör Étterem, **7**

🍸 NIGHTLIFE
Claudia Cukrászda, **5**
Murphy's Mojo Club, **1**
Old's Rom Music Pub, **3**

Szombathely is formed from several interconnected squares, the largest of which is **Fő tér**, home to the main **tourist offices**. From the train station, turn left and then right on **Széll Kálmán út**. Continue to **Mártirok tere**. Turn left on **Király u.**, which ends in **Savaria tér**. The **bus station** sits on the opposite side of the center; turn left on the street parallel to the station and follow it into town (5min.). Cross **Kiskar u.** and then head straight to the pedestrian **Belsikátor**, which ends in **Fő tér**.

Tourinform, Kossuth Lajos u., on the edge of Fő tér, has a helpful staff, who offer **free maps** and book rooms. (☎514 451. Open M-F 9am-5pm.) **Savaria Tourist ❶** provides info, books rooms, and gives out **free maps** at three locations: Király u. 1 (☎509 485), Mártirok tere 1 (☎511 435), and Berzsenyi tér 2 (☎511 446). All locations **exchange currency**. (Open M-F 8:30am-4:30pm, Sa 8am-noon.) **OTP Bank**, Fő tér 4, exchanges currency and has a MC/V **ATM** outside. (Open M 7:45am-6pm, Tu-Th 7:45am-5pm, F 7:45am-4pm.) A **pharmacy** is at Fő tér 9. (☎312 466. Open M-F 8am-6pm, Sa 8am-1pm. MC/V.) For **medical services**, go to **Markusovszky Hospital**, Markusovszky u. 3 (☎311 542). The best **Internet** rates are at **Szombathelyi Siker Könyvitár**, Ady tér 40, behind the bus station. (40Ft per 30min. Open M-F 9am-5pm.) The **post office**, Kossuth Lajos u. 18, has **Poste Restante**. (☎311 584. Open M-F 8am-6pm, Sa 8am-noon.) **Postal Code**: 9700.

▆▐▌ ACCOMMODATIONS AND FOOD. To book a **private room**, visit **IBUSZ**, Fő tér 44. (☎314 141; i090@ibusz.hu. Open M-F 8am-5pm, Sa 9am-1pm. Singles from 5000Ft; doubles from 5200Ft.) **Berzsenyi Dániel Főiskola Pável Ágoston Kollégiuma ❶**, Ady tér 3/A, books clean singles in two buildings near the bus station. (☎313 591. Check-out 9am. Singles 1600Ft.) **Hotel Liget ❸**, Szent István park 15, accessible by bus 2c or 2a from the train station, offers pleasant rooms in St. Stephen's Park, within easy reach of the city center and the Vas County Museum Village (see below). From the bus station, follow the directions for Vas Village but head to the left side of the park. (☎509 323; hliget@ax.hu. Reception 24hr. Singles 6990Ft; doubles 7900-8900Ft; triples 11,990-13,990Ft. MC/V.)

Most restaurants line Fő tér's pedestrian walkway. **Match** supermarkets are at Fő tér 17 (open M-F 7am-7:30pm, Sa 7am-4pm; MC/V) and behind the bus station (open M-F 6am-7pm, Sa 7am-3pm; MC/V). **▨Gödör Étterem ❸**, Hollán Ernő 10/12, dishes up Hungarian specialties in a brick cellar. (☎510 078. Entrees 690-2890Ft. Open M-Th 11am-11pm, F-Sa 11am-midnight, Su 11am-3pm.) **Égszínkék Paradicsom ❷** (Sky-blue Paradise), Belső Uránia udvar, serves up heavenly pasta (680-990Ft) by candlelight in its mural-covered dining room. Walk through the archway at Kőszegi u. 2, off Fő tér. (☎342 012. Open daily 11am-11pm.)

◑▐▌ SIGHTS AND ENTERTAINMENT. The outdoor **▨Vas County Museum Village** (Vasi Múzeum Falu) displays authentic 200-year-old farmhouses relocated from villages throughout the region, along with collections of pottery, kitchenware, and farming tools. A church and cemetery were recently added to the village, which sits alongside the lake and is home to many farm animals. From Ady tér, walk 10min. down Nagykar u., which becomes Gagarin u., cross Bartók Béla, the main street, then go up Árpád u. to the end. (English brochure 80Ft. Open Apr.-Nov. Tu-Su 9am-4:30pm. 500Ft, students 250Ft.) Szombathely is the proud site of Hungary's third-largest **cathedral**, built in 1797 in Baroque and Neoclassical styles. Red marble columns support a domed ceiling and gold-trimmed archways. The chapel to the right is the only portion of the original building that stands today. To the right of the cathedral, the **Paulovics István Garden of Ruins** (Paulovics Romkert), Templom tér 1, was once the center of the Roman colony of Savaria and now contains traces of 4th century buildings remaining from the town. From Fő tér, go left on Széchényi út, right on Szily János út, and straight to Templom tér. (☎313 369. English brochure 20Ft. Open Mar.-Dec. 15 Tu-Su 9am-5pm. 360Ft, students 180Ft.)

In the evening, laze on the banks of beautiful **Csókanázótó Lake** or rent a boat and paddle on its waters (500-1000Ft per hr.). Szombathely's active spirit has brought a range of new activities to the region, including golf, tennis, rock climbing, and the ever-popular paintball. The **Savaria Historical Carnival,** held in Fő tér at the end of August, brings the city's medieval history to life with historical reenactments and an open-air market. The **Bartók Seminar and Festival,** in the middle of July, attracts musicians and music-lovers from around the world. The two-week **Spring Festival** in March celebrates music and the performing arts. One of Hungary's most curious celebrations takes place on June 16th: **Bloomsday,** in honor of Leopold Bloom, the character from Irish author James Joyce's *Ulysses,* whose ancestors, the novel notes, had come from Szombathely.

Nightlife in Szombathely centers on **Fő tér.** The square hosts summer concerts and ice cream stands stay open late into the night. The younger set flocks to **Murphy's Mojo Club,** Semmelweis Ignác út 28. Enjoy beer (210-540Ft), Serbian food (420-1200Ft), and friendly conversation in a dining room filled with collector's items, from antique lamps to an entire old automobile. (☎315 891. English menu. Open daily 4:30pm-midnight.) Enjoy a gooey pastry (160-320Ft) at the cozy **Claudia Cukrászda,** Savaria tér 1. (☎313 375. Open M-Sa 9am-10pm, Su 2-10pm.) **Old's Rom Music Pub,** Ady tér, is a favorite among the dancing crowd. (Open M-Th and Su 9am-10pm, F-Sa 11am-2am. Cover 700Ft on Sa.)

⊠ DAYTRIP FROM SZOMBATHELY: ŐRSÉG NATIONAL PARK. Located near the Slovenian border, the Őrség National Park offers a healthy mixture of hiking and rural enlightenment. The trails reveal stunning views of the Slovenian and Hungarian hillsides, and the towns in the area, virtually unchanged over centuries, provide a glimpse into settlement life following the Hungarian conquest in the 10th and 11th centuries. You may want to stop in the village of **Szalafő,** 4km from **Őriszentpéter,** where the **Pityerszer Rural Museum** displays typical "encircled" cottages. (Open Tu-Su 10am-6pm.) **Magyarszombatfa,** 7km south of Őriszentpéter, is known for its ceramics. In nearby **Pankasz,** check out the famous wooden belfry, and the wooden headstones in the cemetery. Local buses run among the towns; check schedules posted on the bus stops. The park, popular for its variety of plants and animals, is home to 500 species of **butterflies**—more than anywhere else in Hungary—and **rare birds** like black storks and honey buzzards. For help locating wildlife, pick up an English guide from the park information building. If you have time, visit the **Árpádkori Műemlék Templom,** the small 12th-century church 500m from the park info building. Guarded by the statue of King Stephen I, Hungary's first Christian king, it was a fortress during Turkish invasions. (Mass Su 8:30am.)

Buy camping supplies in the building labeled **Iparcikkek,** in the center of Őriszentpéter. (☎548 015. Open M-F 7:30am-noon and 1-4:30pm, Sa 7:30am-noon.) **Keserűszer Camping ❶,** 2km to the right on the road in front of the Park Information Office, is a convenient base for wanderings on the trail. (700Ft per person.) (Entrance is Őriszentpéter. Take the bus from Ady tér in Szombathely, 1½-2hr., 8 per day, 520Ft) and turn right out of the bus station. From the center, take a right on Városszer u. and walk 1km to the park information building. Here you'll find maps (650Ft) as well as hiking and camping advice. (Open M-Th 8am-noon and 1-4:30pm, F 8am-2pm, Sa 10am-5pm. Before leaving Szombathely, ask at Tourinform for the free "Camping in Hungary" map.) An **ABC** supermarket, also in the center, provides granola bars for your hike. (Open M-F 6am-5pm, Sa 6am-1pm, Su 7-11am.) Before heading into the hills, fill up on fried Hungarian food at **Centrum Étterem ❷.** (Entrees 450-1200Ft. Open M-F 6am-10pm, Sa-Su 7am-10pm.)

KŐSZEG   ☎(06)94

At the foot of the Kőszeg mountains, the quiet town of Kőszeg charms visitors with beautiful churches, historical monuments, and country cottages. Just a mile from the Austrian border, the town was a defense against Austria's repeated attempts at expansion but became famous when, in 1536, it rejected the Turks and deflected their march on Vienna. The castle, which withstood the siege, serves as a reminder of this unlikely victory and enchants with views of the Austrian countryside.

TRANSPORTATION AND PRACTICAL INFORMATION. The **bus station**, Liszt Ferenc 16 (☎360 180), is a block from the town center. Buses to: **Szombathely** (30min., 8-10 per day, 302Ft) and **Sopron** (1¼hr, 10 per day, 790Ft). The **train station**, krt 2 (☎360 053), is 1km south of town. Trains to: **Szombathely** (30min., 15 per day, 170Ft). Várkör u. encircles the center of town. The two main squares, **Fő tér** and **Jurisics tér**, lie on the south end, while the **castle** *(vár)* sits in the north. To get to the center from the bus station, go right out of the station onto **Kossuth Lajos u.**, which leads to Fő tér. From the train station, follow **Rákóczi Ferenc ut** to get to Fő tér. **Tourinform**, upstairs at Jurisics tér 7, has **free maps** and helps find accommodations. (☎563 121. Open M-F 8am-4pm, Sa 9am-1pm; in winter closed Sa.) The **OTP bank**, Kossuth L. u. 8, has an **ATM** and a **currency exchange** machine. (Open M 7:45am-5pm, Tu-Th 7:45am-3pm, F 7:45am-12:30pm.) A **pharmacy** is at Kossuth L. u. 12. (☎563 078. Open M-F 8am-6pm, Sa 8am-2pm.) The **post office** is at Várkör u. 65. (☎360 094. Open M-F 8am-4pm, Sa 8am-noon.) **Postal Code:** 9732.

ACCOMMODATIONS AND FOOD. **Savaria Tourist**, Várkör u. 69, arranges **private rooms**. (☎563 048; koszeg@vivaosz.hu. Open M-F 8am-4pm, Sa 8am-noon. Singles from 4000Ft; doubles from 5500Ft.) Most restaurants in town have guest rooms upstairs, although the cheaper rooms generally lie off Várkör u. **Kóbor Macskához Pension ❸**, Várkör u. 100, offers clean rooms with views of the belltower of St. Imre Church. (☎362 273; www.hotels.hu/kobor. Breakfast 600Ft, free with singles. Reception 24hr. Singles and doubles 5300Ft; triples 6800Ft.) In the heart of town, **Hotel Arany Strucc ❸**, Várkör u. 124, provides luxurious, well-furnished rooms. Note that the bells of the nearby Church of Jesus' Heart toll once each quarter hour. (☎360 323; www.aranystucc.hu. Reception 24hr. Singles 5700Ft; doubles 8800-9800Ft; triples 12,000Ft.). You can set up camp at **Gyöngyvirág Camping ❶**, Bajcsy-Zsilinszky u. 6, on the shore of peaceful Gyöngyös River. (☎360 454. Breakfast 700Ft. 700Ft per person, 400Ft per tent, 400Ft per car. Cash only.) Pick up groceries at **Match** supermarket, Várkör u. 20 (Open M-F 6am-7pm, Sa 6am-4pm. MC/V.) **◙Pizzéria da Rocco ❷**, Várkör u. 55, bakes delicious pizzas in its wood oven. The castle is within view of the terraced patio; and if you prefer to eat indoors, you can relax to jazz under the arched roof of the dining room. (☎363 745. Salads 550-650Ft. Pizza 400-1350Ft. Open M-Sa noon-midnight, Su noon-10pm. Cash only.) Revert to the Middle Ages in the time-warped ambience of **Bécsikapu Étterem ❷**, Rajnis u. 5, where you can feast on game dishes fit for a king. (☎563 122. Entrees 690-1850Ft. Open daily 11am-10pm. Cash only.) The modern **Portré Restaurant ❸**, Fő tér 7, serves a variety of dishes. (☎465 722. Coffee 200-390Ft. Entrees 890-2190Ft. Open M-Sa 8am-10pm; Su 10am-8pm. Cash only.)

SIGHTS. The most imposing of Kőszeg's sights is **Jurisics Castle** (Vár), constructed in Gothic style during the late 13th century. It was at this castle that 4000 people fought the ultimately doomed Turkish siege of 1532. The last Turkish contingent left the outskirts of town at 11am on Aug. 30, 1532. The town church bells have since tolled daily at 11am as a reminder of the remarkable victory. The castle, now open to visitors, houses the **Jurisich Miklós Museum,** in memory of the man

HUNGARY

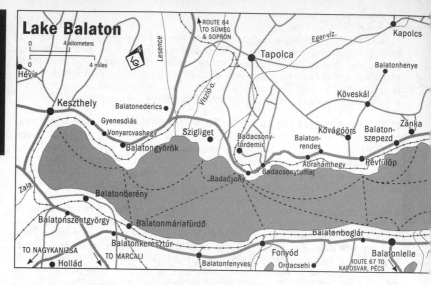

Lake Balaton

0 — 4 kilometers
0 — 4 miles

Hévíz
Keszthely
Lesence
Balatonederics
Gyenesdiás
Vonyarcvashegy
Balatongyörök
Szigliget
Viszló-o.
Badacsony-tördemic
ROUTE 84
TO SÜMEG
& SOPRON
Tapolca
Eger-víz.
Kapolcs
Balatonhenye
Köveskál
Balaton-rendes
Kövágóörs
Balaton-szepezd
Zánka
Abrahámhegy
Révfülöp
Badacsonytomaj
Badacsony
Zala
Balatonberény
Balatonszentgyörgy
Balatonmáriafürdő
Balatonkeresztúr
TO NAGYKANIZSA
Hollád
TO MARCALI
Balatonfenyves
Fonyód
Ordacsehi
Balatonboglár
Balatonlelle
ROUTE 67 TO
KAPOSVAR, PÉCS

who led the Hungarian forces. The museum displays artifacts from the blockade and other historical documents important to the town, but the most interesting part is the long hallway connecting the rooms, where you'll find paintings of the town during various stages of its history. The views from the **belltower,** just beside the museum, offer a glimpse of the city and nearby hills. (☎360 240. Castle open Tu-Su 10am-5pm. 120Ft, students 80Ft. Museum 460/230Ft.)

The 1894 **Church of Jesus' Heart** (Jézus Szíve Plébánia templom) dominates Fő tér. The colorfully patterned walls and columns complement the intricate stained glass windows behind the altar. (Open daily 9am-6pm. Mass Su 10am. Free.) Branching off Fő tér, Városház u. leads onto Jurisics tér, which is ringed by monuments. To enter the square, you'll pass under **Heroes' Gate** (Hősi kapu), built on the 400th anniversary of the Turkish blockade. A highlight of Jurisics tér is the patriotically striped **Town Hall** (Városház), Jurisics tér 8, which has served the town since the 15th century. The **Pharmacy Museum** (Apotéka), Jurisics tér 11, in an elegant, 18th-century pharmacy, houses instruments and medicine from old pharmacies in the region. Check out the special collection of medicinal herbs on the 2nd floor. (☎360 337. English info. Open Tu-Su 10am-5pm. 360Ft, students with ISIC 180Ft.) The highlight of **St. James Church** (Szent Jakab templom), in the center of the square, is the beautiful Gothic wooden Madonna sculpture near the altar. (Open daily 9am-6pm. Free.) The more modest **St. Henry's Church** next door has an equally dramatic Gothic altar. (Open daily 9am-6pm. Free.) The **synagogue ruins** stand on the corner of Várkör u. and Gyöngyös u. Though you can't go past the gates, the Hebrew inscription over the main entrance is worth a look.

🎵 🎰 **ENTERTAINMENT AND NIGHTLIFE.** Kőszeg is a quiet town, day and night. The serene **Chernel Kert** (Chernel Park) offers shaded walks at the base of the tree-covered Kőszeg mountains. You can also begin hikes from here—pick up maps and info at **Tourinform** (see p. 319). To get to the park, follow Várkör u. past Fő tér, keeping the Church of Jesus' Heart to your left. Go left on Hunyadi u. and continue to the end of the road. For something more upbeat, join the locals at **Ciao Amico,** Rákoczi Ferenc u. 13, where you can enjoy pizza (420-950Ft) and beer (220-750Ft) at the bar or try your luck in the adjoining casino and arcade. (☎349 952.

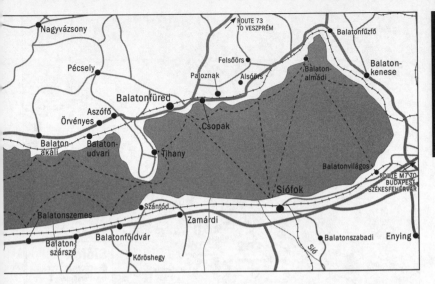

Bar, arcade, and casino open 24hr.; pizzeria daily noon-midnight.) In mid-June, the town's biggest festival, the **Ost-West Fesztival,** features open-air performances of folk music and dance in the town's main squares and the castle courtyard. For exact dates and tickets (2000Ft, students 1500Ft), contact Tourinform.

LAKE BALATON

Surrounded by the volcanic hills of Badacsony, the shaded parks of Balatonfüred, and the sandy beaches of Keszthely, Lake Balaton is one of Central Europe's most popular vacation spots. The lake became a playground for the European elite when the railroad linked the surrounding towns in the 1860s. Frequented by nature-lovers, history buffs, and partygoers, Balaton attracts the young and the old, the rich and the budget-conscious, with incomparable vistas, beautiful weather, and boisterous nightlife. Teeming with fish, the lake is the source of the region's distinct cuisine, which is complemented by wines from the nearby hills.

Storms roll over Lake Balaton in less than 15min., raising dangerous whitecaps on the usually placid lake. Yellow lights on top of tall buildings at Siófok's harbor give **weather warnings.** If the light flashes once per 2 seconds, stay within 500m of shore; 1 flash per second means swimmers must return to shore. Don't worry too much about storms spoiling your vacation; most last fewer than 30min.

SIÓFOK   ☎(06)84

There are more tourist offices per sq. km in Siófok (SHEE-o-foke, pop. 27,000) than in any other Hungarian city—its population more than quadruples in summer with vacationers. The lake provides ample excuse for the bikinis, beer, and bacchanalia that rule this summer capital. Students, families, elderly people, and everyone in between come to Siófok to take in the sun and party along the shore.

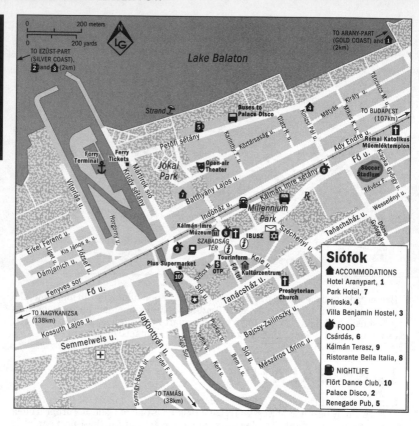

Siófok

🏠 ACCOMMODATIONS
Hotel Aranypart, 1
Park Hotel, 7
Piroska, 4
Villa Benjamin Hostel, 3

🍴 FOOD
Csárdás, 6
Kálmán Terasz, 9
Ristorante Bella Italia, 8

🎵 NIGHTLIFE
Flört Dance Club, 10
Palace Disco, 2
Renegade Pub, 5

📧 TRANSPORTATION

Trains: To: **Budapest** (2½hr.; 20 per day; 1142Ft, plus 480Ft reservation fee); **Keszthely** (3-5hr., 15 per day, 1920Ft); **Pécs** (4-8hr., 1 per day, 2226Ft). Siófok is a stop on the Budapest lines to: **Ljubljana, SLN; Split, CRO; Venice, ITA; Zagreb, CRO.**

Buses: To: **Budapest** (1½hr., 9 per day, 1320Ft) and **Pécs** (3hr., 4 per day, 2456Ft).

Ferries: The quickest way to north Balaton is the hourly **MAHART ferry**, 10min. from the train station in the Strand center. To: **Balatonfüred** (1hr.; 6-9 per day; 1020Ft, students 765Ft) and **Tihany** (1¼hr., 6-9 per day, 1020/765Ft).

🔢 ORIENTATION AND PRACTICAL INFORMATION

Siófok's excellent transport services to other parts of the lake make it an ideal base from which to explore the region. The **train** and **bus stations** straddle **Kálmán Imre sétány,** near the center of town. The main street, **Fő út,** runs parallel to the tracks in front of the station. **FA Canal** connects the lake to the Danube and divides the town. The eastern **Gold Coast** (Arany-part), to the right as you face the water, is home to older, larger hotels, while the **Silver Coast** (Ezüst-part), to the left, has newer and slightly cheaper accommodations. Each is a 20-30min. walk from the city center, which sits between them. The Silver Coast conveniently has its own train station, **Balatonszéplak felső.**

Tourist Offices: Tourinform (☎315 355; www.siofok.com), Fő út at Szabadság tér, in water tower opposite the train station. English-speaking staff find rooms and offer **free maps.** Open June 15-Sept. 15 M-F 8am-8pm, Sa-Su 9am-6pm; Sept. 16-June 14 M-F 9am-4pm. **IBUSZ**, Fő út 176, 2nd fl. (☎510 720). **Exchanges currency** for no commission and books **private rooms.** Open M-F 8am-6pm, Sa 9am-1pm. AmEx/MC/V.

Currency Exchange: OTP, Szabadság tér 10 (☎310 455). Exchanges currency for no commission and cashes **traveler's checks.** A MC/V **ATM** is outside. Open M 7:45am-6pm, Tu-Th 7:45am-5pm, F 7:45am-4pm.

Luggage Storage: Available at the train station. Small bags 150Ft per 6hr., 300Ft per 24hr. Large bags 600/300Ft.

Emergency: Police, Sió u. 14 (☎310 700). **Coast Guard:** ☎310 990.

Pharmacy: Régi Pharmacy, Fő út 202 (☎310 041). Posts lists of pharmacies open late other days. Extra 200Ft per item after hours. Open M-F 8am-7pm, Sa 8am-2pm; Th ring bell for after-hours service. AmEx/MC/V.

Internet: Net Game Pont, Fő út 45 (☎776 670). 200Ft per 15min., 300Ft per 30min. Open daily 10am-10pm.

Post Office: Fő út 186 (☎310 210). **Poste Restante** available; go upstairs and left. Open M-F 8am-7pm, Sa 8am-noon. **Telephones** and **ATM** outside. **Postal Code:** 8600.

⌐ ACCOMMODATIONS

Because Balaton is frequented by rich Western tourists, particularly Germans, sojourns in the lake country have become expensive. Expect prices to be higher than in Budapest. Several agencies offer **private rooms.** Your best bets are **Tourinform** (see above), which finds rooms and negotiates rates with hotels (doubles 6000-15,000Ft), and **IBUSZ** (doubles 6000Ft; tourist tax 150-300Ft per night; 30% surcharge for fewer than 4 nights). If you'd rather bargain on your own, knock on doors with *Panzió* and *Zimmer frei* signs on streets close to the water. Start hunting on **Erkel Ferenc u.**, on the far side of the canal, and on **Szent László u.**, to the left as you leave the train station. Campgrounds are surprisingly scarce, as high real estate prices mean that land often gets bought out by hotels. If you'd rather rough it than stay in a hostel, you're best off looking in neighboring towns.

▨ **Villa Benjamin Youth Hostel**, Siófoki u. 9 (☎350 704). Get off at the Balatonszéplak felső bus or train station, 1 stop after Siófok when coming from Budapest. Located on the Silver Coast. 25min. from Siófok center but next to the Palace Disco and near plenty of places to eat. Garden rooms, with a beach-bungalow feel, are simple but pleasant and have a closet, table, and sink. Kitchen. Picnic area. Garden singles 2500Ft, house singles 3000Ft; doubles 5000Ft; triples 7500Ft; 4- to 6-person apartments 14,000-21,000Ft; 8- to 10-person house 28,000-35,000Ft. 300Ft tax per night. ❷

Piroska, Petőfi sétány 14/a (☎314 251), just down the street from all the action on the main boardwalk. Simple, airy rooms with private baths in a big pink house with back balconies. Call ahead to reserve. Doubles 5000Ft; triples 7000Ft. Cash only. ❷

Park Hotel, Batthyány u. 7 (☎310 539; www.parkhotel.hu), near the main strand, 5min. from the center. Spacious rooms with high vaulted ceilings. All rooms have A/C, and many have cable TV and jacuzzis. Reception 24hr. Doubles July-Aug. 8000-15,000Ft; triples 12,000-18,000Ft; 4-person apartments 15,000-25,000Ft. MC/V. ❹

Hotel Aranypart, Beszédes J. sétány 82 (☎519 450; www.aranypart.hu). Take bus #2 from city center to the front of the hotel. On the Gold Coast beach. Views are beautiful. Spacious rooms with full baths. Restaurant, coffee shop, and safe in lobby. Sauna and tennis courts. Rooms have radio, TV, and freezer. Breakfast included. Singles 5900-13,000Ft; doubles 7600-14,750Ft. Extra bed 3750Ft. Tourist tax 310Ft. MC/V. ❸

🍴 FOOD

In the Lake region, many restaurants serve a combination of Hungarian and Italian food. Grab supplies for the beach at **Plus Supermarket,** Fő út 156-160. (Open M-F 7am-8pm, Sa 7am-3pm. MC/V.) For those staying on the Silver Coast, **CBA Supermarket** is open daily 7am-10pm. The strand kiosks offer snack foods, with *lángos* (200-300Ft), hamburgers (300Ft), and pizza (500Ft).

Kálmán Terasz, Kálmán Imre sétány 13 (☎310 651), at the far end of Kálmán Imre sétány on the corner of Fő tér. Offers a variety of fish dishes and other local foods, on a covered patio. The real treat is the decadent sundae (black forest cup with rum-soaked cherries; 990Ft). Entrees 520-1750Ft. Open daily 10am-10pm. Cash only. ❸

Ristorante Bella Italia, Szabadság tér 1 (☎310 826). The statue-flanked restaurant dishes out enticing entrees with speed and stellar service. Enjoy a cold glass of fresh squeezed orange juice (159Ft) on the roomy terrace. Pizza and pasta 630-1900Ft. Open daily 9am-midnight. Cash only. ❷

Csárdás, Fő út 105 (☎310 642). Proximity to the lake makes Csárdás's tasty local dishes ideal for an after-beach meal. Romantic candlelit terrace. Live gypsy music Th-Sa 6pm. Entrees 660-2500Ft. Open daily 11:30am-10pm. AmEx/MC/V. ❷

🎭 ENTERTAINMENT

Though Siófok's other daytime attractions are entertaining, none compare to the **strand,** a series of park-like lawns running to the shoreline. There are public and private sections; entrance to a private area costs around 200-400Ft, and with public spaces available, it seems unnecessary to pay. The largest private beach lies to the right of town as you face the water. (700Ft, children 350Ft. Open M-F 8am-3am.) Most sections of the beach rent an assortment of water vehicles, including **paddleboats** and **kayaks** (200-400Ft per hr.). The young often gather in the "party cafes" that line the streets, before heading out to beach parties.

For a taste of culture beyond the beach-bum variety, check out the nightly German and Hungarian operettas in the **Kultúrzentrum,** Fő tér 2. Tourinform (see **Tourist Offices,** p. 323) sells tickets (1200-5000Ft). In early July, the week-long **Golden Shell International Folklore Festival** (☎504 262) celebrates folk music and dancing. The **Kálmán Imre Múzeum,** Kálmán Imre sétány, next to the train station, displays the composer's piano and playbills. The second floor hosts art exhibitions. (Open Apr.-Oct. Tu-Su 9am-5pm; Nov.-Mar. Tu-Su 9am-4pm. 250Ft.) **Római Katolikus Műemléktemplom,** Fő út 57, holds organ concerts. (Sa 8pm; 900Ft, students 600Ft.)

🌙 NIGHTLIFE

At nightfall, excessive displays of skin, drunkenness, and debauchery move from Siófok's beaches to its bars. Nightclubs line the lakefront; many feature semi-nude dancers and sexy murals. Disco-lovers hop on **Discoschiff,** the disco boat. DJs, live pop, and ABBA keep the party alive. (☎310 050. Departs from the ferry dock daily July-Aug. at 9pm. Cover 1400Ft, under 19 1200Ft.)

■ **Renegade Pub,** Petőfi sétány 3 (www.renegade-pub.com), in the center of the strand. This bar and dance club is full by 11pm. Feast your eyes on the beautiful people dancing on tables to the latest Europop hits. If you aren't in the mood to be shoulder-to-shoulder, sit back with a drink. Enough beer (320-530Ft; 0.5L Carlsberg 750Ft) and liquor (500-700Ft) to float you home. Open daily June-Aug. 8pm-4am.

Palace Disco, Deák Ferenc sétány 2 (☎06 84 351 295; www.palace.hu), on the Silver Coast. You must purchase a ticket to the club or show a club stamp to ride the free buses that depart every hr. from behind the watch tower. Spotlights visible from town mark this open-air party complex—discos, bars, restaurants (pizza 800-950Ft), and an "erotic galerie" complete with dancers and surrounded by a well-lit courtyard with yet another dance floor. Beer from 600Ft. Mixed drinks 980-1750Ft. Cover 1500-2500Ft. Disco open daily May to mid-Sept. 10pm-5am. Pizzeria open daily 11am-5am.

Flört Dance Club, Sió u. 4 (☎333 303; www.flort.hu). Follow the spotlights to this 2-story hotspot in the center of town. Admire yourself—and the young crowd shaking it to house music—on the mirrored walls. Beer 650-850Ft. Cover 1500-3000Ft; Tourinform often has fliers for a 300Ft discount. Open daily mid-June to late Aug. 10pm-6am.

BALATONFÜRED ☎(06)87

Across the lake from Siófok, Balatonfüred (BAL-a-ton-FEWR-ed; pop. 13,500) is its quieter counterpart. Sandy beaches, a central park with volcanic springs, and a convenient location near Tihany and Badacsony make this friendly town the best way to experience the lake while avoiding Siófok's rowdiness and debauchery. Thanks to cheap yet central accommodations, it's easy to enjoy the bountiful outdoor activities and savor the fresh seafood that make Balaton famous.

▐ TRANSPORTATION

Trains: To: **Badacsony** (55min., 2 per hr., 326Ft); **Budapest** (2½hr., 1 per hr., 1336Ft); **Győr** (4hr., 20 per day, 1730Ft); **Keszthely** (2hr., 12 per day, 730Ft); and **Pécs** (4-8hr., 13 per day, 2376Ft).

Buses: Express buses *(gyorsjárat)* go to: **Budapest** (1½hr., 5 per day, 1320Ft) and **Keszthely** (1½hr., 9 per day, 846Ft).

Ferries: The quickest way to south Balaton is the hourly **MAHART ferry** (10min.), which leaves from the main pier. To: **Siófok** (1hr.; 6-9 per day; 1020Ft, students 765Ft); **Tihany** (15min., 6-9 per day, 720/540Ft).

▐ ▐ ORIENTATION AND PRACTICAL INFORMATION

The **train** and **bus stations** are next to each other, 10min. from the town center. To get to town, take a left on **Horváth Mihály u.,** then a right on **Jókai Mór u.,** and walk toward the lake. Jókai Mór u. runs perpendicular to the water from the upper part of town to the ferry dock. To the right of the ferry dock, **Záconyi Ferenc u.** is home to the tourist office, many restaurants, and the central market. To the left, **Tagore sétány** leads through the town park and to the main *strand* (beach). In **Gyógy tér,** above the park, you can fill your water bottle with sulfuric-smelling **volcanic spring water** under the **Well House Pavilion.** The **Tourinform** office, the bank, and a large supermarket line **Petőfi Sándor u.,** which runs through the center.

The **City Tourist Bureau,** left of the ferry dock on Záconyi Ferenc u., offers free info on accommodations and maps. (Open July-Aug. M-Sa 9am-9pm, Su 9am-2pm.) At **Tourinform,** Petőfi Sándor u. 68, the English-speaking staff suggest **private rooms** and supply **free maps** and info. (☎580 480; www.balatonfured.hu.)

Open July-Aug. M-F 9am-7pm, Sa 9am-6pm, Su 9am-1pm; Sept.-June M-F 9am-4pm.) **OTP**, Petőfi Sándor u. 8, **exchanges currency** for no commission and has **Western Union.** A MC/V **ATM** is outside. (☎581 070. Open M 7:45am-5pm, Tu-F 7:45am-4pm.) **Krisztina Pharmacy,** on Csokonal u., has 24hr. emergency service. (Open M-F 8am-6pm. AmEx/MC/V.) **Internet** is expensive; the cheapest is at **NETov@abb Eszpresszó,** Horváth M. u. 3, one street past Petőfi Sándor u. when walking up Jókai Mór u. (☎342 235. 12Ft per min.; min. 10min. Open M-F 8am-10pm, Sa-Su 10am-10pm.) The **post office** is on Zsigmond u. (Open M-F 8am-4pm.) The main post office, Kossuth L. u. 19, with the entrance off Ady Endre u., is 20min. from the beach. (Open M-F 8am-4pm, Sa 8am-noon.) **Postal Code:** 8230.

⌂ ACCOMMODATIONS

Accommodations in Balatonfüred are cheap, convenient, and comfortable. Almost every house on **Petőfi Sándor u.** offers **private rooms,** starting at about 5000Ft; look for *Zimmer frei* signs. The **City Tourist Bureau** and **Tourinform** can tell you where to look, but you're on your own when it comes to bargaining.

▨ **Sing-Sing,** Fürdő u. 32 (☎06 30 939 1156). Follow along the water to the right when facing the docks; turn right at the roundabout after 10min. Unlike the New York state prison of the same name, Sing-Sing offers simple dorm rooms close to the water and the shoreline action. Dorms July-Aug. 2000Ft; Sept.-Oct. and May-June 1000Ft. ❶

Ifjúsági Szálláshely-Jugendherberge-Youth Hostel, Hősök tere 1 (☎/fax 342 651). Accessible by bus or 25min. walk from town center. Bus #4 runs from the hostel to the main strand. One of the cheaper accommodations, with dorms, a common room, and free laundry. Dorms 2460Ft; 2 or more nights 1900Ft; 4 nights 1800Ft. Tax 300Ft. ❶

Hotel Aranyhíd, Aranyhíd sétány 2 (☎342 058), near the main strand. Though the exterior masks its luxury, this beachside hotel boasts large apartments with kitchenettes, baths, phones, TVs, and balconies. Ask for a room overlooking the water—it's the same price. July-Aug. singles 8500Ft; doubles 13,000Ft; triples 16,000Ft. Sept. and May-June 7000/10,500/13,000Ft. Oct. and Apr. 5700/8000/11,000Ft. Tax 314Ft. ❹

Camping Füred, Széchényi u. 24 (☎580 241), on the shore to the right of town when facing the water. At this luxurious campsite, bungalows are pricey but small tents are reasonable. 4-person bungalows 16,640-25,600Ft. Tents 1860Ft-3150Ft plus 650-1500Ft per person. Rates vary by season. MC/V. ❷

◖ FOOD

The local diet is based largely on seafood from the lake. Stock up on food, snacks, and beach supplies at the **Silbergold ABC** supermarket, on Tagore sétány. (Open daily 8am-8pm.) Restaurants and cafes line the beach promenade.

▨ **Halászkert Étterem,** Zákonyi u. 3 (☎581 050). Serves dozens of the region's famous fish dishes, including Balaton pike perch (1350Ft) and *halászlé* (700Ft), on a patio opposite the fishing docks. Entrees 480-1850Ft. Open daily 11am-10pm. Cash only. ❷

Borcsa Restaurant (☎580 070), next to the entrance to Esterházy Strand on Tagore sétány. Situated just off the harbor, Borcsa offers a range of fish and game dishes. The 2 terraces and beautiful dining room are filled with wicker furniture. Many vegetarian options. Entrees 980-2980Ft. Open daily 11am-11pm. AmEx/MC/V. ❸

Brázay Kert (☎321 633), at the entrance to Brázay Strand on Aranyhíd sétány. Offers a gypsy roast (890Ft). Satiate your desire for hamburgers (490Ft) and pizza (690Ft) at wood tables amid grassy woodlands with a small pond and bridge. Lounge on the private beach (280Ft, children 170Ft) behind the restaurant. Open daily 10am-10pm. ❷

🎵 🎧 ENTERTAINMENT AND NIGHTLIFE

Balatonfüred is a city visited mainly for its *strands* (beaches) and water sports. The most popular destination is the main beach, **Esterházy Strand**, on Tagore sétány. A walk through the park from the ferry dock reveals sandy beaches and many forms of entertainment for adults and kids: there is a a giant slide (100Ft per ride), a water castle (500Ft), paddleboats (1500Ft per hr.), kayaks (700Ft per hr.), a trampoline (250Ft per 5min.), and minigolf (400Ft per round). If you leave the park and return, you'll pay the entrance fee again, so bring everything you will need during your visit. (Beach ☎343 817. Open 8:30am-7pm. Admission 450Ft. Lockers 270Ft.) Should lazing about make you hungry, consider the countless restaurants and a mini **ABC** supermarket close to the beach. **Kisfaludy Strand**, on Aranyhíd sétány, is a quieter beach next door. Although it offers fewer water activities, its larger, less-shaded beach allows more room to swim and tan. (☎342 916. Open 8:30am-7pm. 305Ft, children 190Ft.) Also popular is **Oszi Go-Kart**, at the corner of Munkácsy Mihály u. and Kosztolányi Dezső u. (☎309 898 843. Open daily 10am-8pm. 5 rounds 1000Ft, 15 rounds 2000Ft.) **Bike rental** is at **Rent-a-Bike,** across from Esterházy Strand on Deák Ferenc u. (☎480 671. Open daily 9am-7pm. 350Ft per hr., 2400Ft per day, 12,000Ft per week.) There are **souvenir markets** on Jókai Mór u., off Petőfi Sándor u. (Open 9am-9pm.)

The tourist season kicks off with the **Sail Unfurling Ceremony** in mid-May. Sailing competitions abound throughout summer. The **Anna-ball,** in late July, is Balatonfüred's most famous event. The only ball held out of season in Hungary, it attracts both foreign and domestic guests. In early August, winemakers set up tents on Tagore sétány for **Balatonfüred Wine Weeks.** At night, folk-dancing ensembles perform; on the last day, there is a celebration complete with fireworks. Call Balatonfüred Tourinform (p. 323) for info and tickets.

While you won't find the same throngs of partygoers as in Siófok, the cafes and bars along the beach attract small crowds. **Borház**, on Blaha L. u., patronized by young and old both day and night, has slot machines. A dance floor opens on Saturday nights; mellower folk sit outside at beer-barrel tables. (Beer 220-690Ft. Wine 600-700Ft per L. Open 24hr.) On Saturday nights, **Átrium Music Club,** across the street at Blaha L. u. 7-9, throbs as local DJs spin and smoke machines puff. (☎343 229. Cover 800Ft. Open daily 10pm-5am.)

🎯 DAYTRIPS FROM BALATONFÜRED

BADACSONY ☎(06)87

Trains run from Balatonfüred (55min., 2 per hr., 326Ft). You can also get to Badacsony by bus from Keszthely (1hr., 12-14 per day, 363Ft).

Though four resort towns lie at the foot of the volcanic Badacsony Mountain (Badacsonyhegy), 🔲**Badacsony** and Badacsonytomaj (BAHD-uh-chohn TOH-mai) are the most popular and lie about two kilometers apart. The towns' main draw is the **wine cellars,** on the southern face of the hill, where you can sample a vintage or purchase it by the one-liter plastic jug (from 500Ft). Unlike those in Eger and Tokaj, the local wine cellars sit beside the vineyards on the hill. Each offers a different variety of the region's popular *Oraszrizling* and *Kéknyelü* (Blue Stalk) wines. For a free map and brochures about the cellars, head to **Tourinform Badacsony,** Park u. 6 (☎431 046). A steep walk uphill yields views of Balaton and the vineyards, but can take 20-30min. Alternatively, the Jeeps waiting in front of the post office take groups of up to six to the top of the hill for 3600Ft. The paved road ends at **Kisfaludy Ház ❸,** which serves Hungarian dishes and regional wines on a patio with a view of the lake. (☎431 016. Entrees 1090-2700Ft. Open daily 11am-10pm. Cash only.) Surrounded by vineyards, the cellar **Szent Orbán Borhány ❸**, Kisfaludy S. u. 5, serves Hungarian beef sirloin (2800Ft) and other game dishes. Their **wine tasting** (260-560Ft) is popular. (☎431 382. Entrees 1200-3500Ft. Open daily noon-10pm. MC/V.) Two less-pricey cellars sit on cobblestone Hegyalja u., which is part of the yellow-cross hiking trail. (Samples from 55Ft.)

If the wine samples haven't done you in, head farther uphill to one of Badacsony's pleasantly shaded—but challenging—hikes. Pick up a hiking map from Tourinform (450Ft). A short trek on the red trail leads to **Rose Rock** (Rózsa-kő), where legend has it that any couple who sits facing away from the water will marry within a year. An hour's hike farther up the rocky stairs brings you to **Kisfaludy Lookout Tower** (Kisfaludy kilátó), which offers a gorgeous view of Lake Balaton (free). Walk right when facing the Rose Rock, and follow the **Hegyeto trail**. The **stone gate** (kőkapu), a cliffside basalt formation, awaits farther along the trail. Although Badacsony's **beach** (open daily 9am-6pm; 250Ft, students 100Ft) is small and grassy, the lively **marketplace** around it creates a carnival atmosphere. **Egry Fogadó ❶**, Római út 1 in Badacsony-tomaj, rents cheap rooms. If you'd rather not walk the two kilometers from Badacsony, you can get off at the town train station. (☎471 057. Call ahead for July and Aug. weekends. June 20-Aug. 20 2000Ft; Aug. 20-Oct. 15 and Apr. 15-June 19 1700Ft. Cash only.)

VESZPRÉM

Buses (☎423 815) run from Balatonfüred (18 per day, 30min., 302Ft). Trains (☎329 999) also run into town (10 per day, 2½hr., 1094Ft). From the bus station (Jutasi u. 4) or train station (Jutasi u. 34), follow Jutasi u. and make a right on Budapest u. Take another right on Buhim u. and follow signs for the nearby entrance to Castle Hill.

Known as the "City of Queens," Veszprém has a regal air for a reason: it was part of the royal estate for centuries. Veszprém's romantic Castle District is known for preserved Baroque buildings and royal churches, cozy cafes along winding cobblestone roads, and hidden vistas with fantastic views of the valley below. The ◪**Fire Tower,** left of the **Hero's Gate** entrance, was once used as a watch tower. Its balcony now offers visitors a bird's-eye view of town. (Open daily 10am-6pm. 300Ft, students 200Ft.) Stylized paintings of Jesus, saints, and famous kings are displayed along the pastel walls of the **Piarist Church,** Vár u. 12. (Open daily Mar.-Aug. 10am-6pm; Sept.-Oct. 10am-5pm. Free.) Farther down Var u., 10th-century **St. Michael's Cathedral** is famous for its stained glass windows and royal artifacts, including a bone from the corpse of Gizella, Hungary's first queen. (Open daily Mar.-Aug. 10am-6pm.; Sept.-Oct. 10am-5pm. Mass Sa 7pm; Su 9 and 11:30am, 7pm. Free.) The current **Archbishop's Palace,** Vár u. 16, has been the seat of the Archbishop of Veszprém since 1993. Beautiful frescoes adorn the dining hall, where windows reveal a panoramic view of the valley. In an adjacent room, portraits of successive archbishops are displayed beside Herend stoves. (Open Mar.-Aug. Tu-Su 10am-6pm; Sept.-Oct. Tu-Su 10am-5pm. Groups only. Tours hourly. 500Ft, students 250Ft.) Across the street at Var. u. 35, the **Queen Gizella Museum** houses ecclesiastical relics such as a golden cloak that belonged to Bishop Albert Vetesi. (Open daily Mar.-Aug. 10am-6pm; Sept.-Oct. 10am-5pm. 300Ft, students 150Ft.) A short walk to the end of Var u. leads to a cliff with a glorious view of the valley. Statues of the first Hungarian royal couple, St. István I and Queen Gizella, look down on the town.

After seeing the sights, head down the hill to enjoy a variety of Italian dishes at **Elefant Étterem és Kávézo ❷**, Óváros tér 6, where colorful fish swim in the restaurant's tank. (☎334 1217. Salads 790-890Ft. Pizzas 850-890Ft. Pasta 920-1450Ft. Open M-Sa 9am-10pm, Su 10am-10pm. MC/V.) **Tourinform,** Vár u. 4, located under the entrance to Castle Hill, provides **free maps** and accommodations info.

TIHANY PENINSULA   ☎(06)87

A possible daytrip from Balatonfüred and a terrific destination for simple hikes, the beautiful Tihany (TEE-hahn-yuh) Peninsula is known as the pearl of Balaton. It is heavily touristed, but Tihany retains historical weight and outdoorsy charm, making this little gem seem more mature than its hard-partying peers.

▐▜ TRANSPORTATION AND PRACTICAL INFORMATION. Buses are the most convenient option, and run to **Balatonfüred** train station (15min., every 45min., 127Ft). The bus stops at Kossuth u., in front of the abbey. The **ferry** to **Balatonfüred** (15min.; 1 per hr.; 720Ft, students 540Ft) docks at the harbor down the hill, 2km away. You'll have to walk or take the bus into town if arriving by **train**—the station is at the edge of the peninsula.

The main road, **Kossuth u.**, spans the peninsula and runs through town, just below the abbey. There are five main bus stops on the peninsula. Get off at the first stop to hit the beach; otherwise, stay on until the bus stops in front of the abbey. The **red trail** runs beside the abbey stop; follow the red arrows. **Tourinform**, below the abbey, has **maps** of the town and of hiking trails. (☎438 804; tihany@tourinform.hu. Open June-Aug. M-F 9am-7pm, Sa-Su 9am-6pm; Sept. M-F 9am-5pm, Sa 9am-3pm; Apr. 16-May M-F 9am-4pm, Sa 9am-1pm; Oct.-Apr. 15 M-F 9am-3pm.) **Rent-a-bike** is at Kossuth u. 32. (2600Ft per day. Open daily 10am-6pm.) There's a **pharmacy** at Kossuth u. 10 (☎448 480; open M-F 8am-noon and 1-6pm, Sa 8am-noon) and an **ATM** up the hill at Kossuth u. 12. The **post office,** Kossuth u. 37, is adjacent to **Mini Market Élelmiszer,** which sells snacks and drinks. (Post office open M-F 8am-4pm. Market open daily 8am-8pm.) **Postal Code:** 8237.

▐▐ ACCOMMODATIONS AND FOOD. To find accommodations, head down **Kossuth u.,** then make a left on **Kiss u.** and a right on **Csokonai u.** This street consists of many houses that rent **private rooms,** marked by *Zimmer frei* signs. Most are reasonably priced (starting at 4000Ft) and have views of the valley and lake. **Kántas Pension ❸**, Csokonai u. 49, has good-sized doubles with balconies overlooking the valley. (☎448 072; kantaspension@axelero.hu. Breakfast included. Doubles 8700Ft. AmEx/MC/V.) Closer to the water, **Panorama Hotel ❺**, Lepke sor 9-11, offers luxurious doubles and triples across from the strand, near the base of the peninsula. (☎538 220; www.panoramaht.com. Breakfast included. Singles 13,210Ft; doubles 15,520Ft; triples 18,900-20,900Ft. Tax 300Ft. AmEx/MC/V.)

The food stalls around the beach and by the abbey will hold you over with fried fast food. If you'd rather sit down, try █Echo Restaurant ❸, Visszhang u. 23, along the green and red hiking trails. This beautiful restaurant serves typical Hungarian dishes atop a cliff overlooking Balaton. Ask for a spot on the roof for a great view of the lake. (☎448 460. Entrees 1200-2500Ft. Open daily Mar.-Nov. 10am-10pm. MC/V.) Farther down the road from Echo Hill, **Pál Csárda ❹** offers a variety of fish and poultry dishes, including *halászlé* soup (900Ft) and roasted trout (1700Ft), on a lovely vine-covered patio. The entrees are big enough to feed multiple people. (English menu. Entrees 1050-3000Ft. Open daily Mar.-June 10am-10pm. AmEx/MC/V.) Just outside the exit of the abbey museum, **Rege Kávézó ❷** dishes out delectable pastries while customers enjoy panoramic views of the lake. (☎448 280. Pastries 350-520Ft. Coffee 350-950Ft. Ice cream 450-1050Ft. Open daily 10am-8pm.)

◖▐ SIGHTS AND HIKING. The small but magnificent █Benedictine Abbey (Bencés Apátság) presides over the hillside. Its pastel frescoes, intricate Baroque altars, and views of the lake draw over a million visitors each year. On the ceiling, images of angels watch the tourist crowds from on high. The church's foundation letter, scripted in 1055, is the oldest written document in the Hungarian language.

A copy is on display inside the church, while the original is in the archives at the abbey in Pannonhalma (p. 312). The András I crypt (I. András kriptája) contains the remains of King András I, one of Hungary's earliest kings and the abbey's founder. To the right of the crypt, the **Tihany Museum**, an 18th-century former monastery, exhibits an odd combination of contemporary art, Roman archaeological finds, and monastic history, all on display in the subterranean lapidarium. (Abbey, crypt, and museum open daily Mar.-Oct. 9am-6pm. Mass M and Sa 7:30pm; Th 7:30am; Su 7:30, 10am, 7:30pm. Church, crypt, and museum together 500Ft, students 250Ft; Su free.) **Echo Hill** rises to the left of the church. On a calm day, if you (or one of the many schoolchildren inevitably visiting) stand on Echo Hill's stone pedestal and holler, the yell will echo off the church wall. Follow the promenade behind the church and descend to the **beach**, where you can rent paddleboats (1500Ft per hr.) and play beach volleyball and ping-pong beside the lake. (Open daily 9am-7pm. 380Ft, students 250Ft.) If you'd rather tan, walk along the shore toward the mainland, where you can rent beach chairs (400Ft per hr.).

With beautiful clearings, winding mountain paths, and steep inclines, Tihany was made for hikers. **Hiking** across the peninsula through hills, forests, farms, and marshes takes only an hour or two. For an even shorter hike, take the **red cross trail** around Belső-tó Lake and turn right on the **red line trail** on the opposite side. The path will take you to the summit of Kiserdő Tető (Top of Little Wood), from which you can see Belső-tó and Külső-tó, Tihany's other interior lake. The ⬛**green line trail**, covering the eastern slope of Óvár, snakes past Barátlakások (the Hermits' Place), where you can escape flocks of tourists and see cells and a chapel hollowed out of the rocks by 11th-century Greek Orthodox ascetics. Buy a **map** for 350Ft by the abbey before you start your hike, or pick up a free copy at Tourinform. If you'd rather stick to the paved roads, bikes are a great option for exploring the hillside.

KESZTHELY ☎(06)83

Sitting at the lake's west tip, Keszthely (KEST-hay) was once the toy-town of the powerful Festetics family. Though their palace continues to be the main attraction, the city that sprung up around the gates has a charm of its own. Street cafes and souvenir shops dot the promenade, while the beach draws a crowd with its waterslide and rows of food stands. In nearby Heviz, yet more swimmers relax in the healing waters of the thermal spring. Though the center of Keszthely has less of a resort feel than other Balaton towns, its streets are just as crowded.

⌨ TRANSPORTATION. The **train station** is on Kazinczy u. InterCity trains run to **Budapest** (3hr., 7 per day, 1926Ft plus 400Ft reservation fee), while slow trains *(személyvonat)* go to: **Balatonfüred** (2-3hr., 7 per day, 730Ft); **Pécs** (3-5hr., 10 per day, 1926Ft); **Siófok** (1½-2hr., 19 per day, 730Ft); **Szombathely** (3hr., 1 per day, 1338Ft). The **bus terminal** is next to the train station. Buses beat trains for local travel to **Balatonfüred** (1½hr., 9 per day, 846Ft) and **Pécs** (4hr., 5 per day, 1486Ft). Some buses leave from the terminal, while others use stops at either Fő tér or Georgikán u. Each departure is marked with an "F" or a "G" to indicate which stop it uses; check the schedule. April to September, **boats** run to **Badacsony** (1¾hr.; 1-4 per day; 1240Ft, students 930Ft) from the end of the dock near the beach.

◼ 🗺 ORIENTATION AND PRACTICAL INFORMATION. The main street, **Kossuth Lajos u.**, runs parallel to the shore a ways inland, from **Festetics Palace** (Festetics Kastély) to the center at **Fő tér**. To reach the main square from the train station, walk straight up **Mártirok u.** to its end at Kossuth Lajos u. and turn right to reach Fő tér (10min.). The main **beach** *(strand)* is to the right as you exit the stations. If coming from the pier, head straight and follow **Erzsébet kir. u.** to get to Fő tér.

HUNGARY

Tourinform, Kossuth Lajos u. 28, off Fő tér, distributes **free maps** and info and finds rooms. (☎/fax 314 144. Open July-Aug. M-F 9am-8pm, Sa-Su 9am-6pm; Oct.-June M-F 9am-5pm, Sa 9am-1pm.) **OTP Bank,** at the corner of Kossuth L. u. and Helikon u., **exchanges currency** and cashes **traveler's checks** for no commission. There's a 24hr. MC/V **ATM** and currency exchange machine outside. (Open M 7:45am-5pm, Tu-F 7:45am-4pm.) **Luggage storage** is at the train station. (150Ft per 6hr. Open 3:30am-11:30pm.) The **Ezüstsirály Patika pharmacy,** Sopron u. 2 in the hospital, posts a list of pharmacies with after-hours service. Walk through the palace gates on Kossuth L. u. and out the next set of gates; it's immediately on your left. (☎314 549. Open M-Th 7:30am-5pm, F 7:30am-7pm.) **Internet** is available at **Mikronet Internet Kávézó,** Nádor u. 13. Walking down Kossuth L. u. from the palace, take the first right. (☎314 009. 5Ft per min. Open daily 9am-9pm.) **Telephones** are outside the **post office,** Kossuth L. u. 48. (☎515 960. **Poste Restante** and **Western Union** available. Open M-F 8am-6pm, Sa 8am-noon.) **Postal Code:** 8360.

⌂⊡ ACCOMMODATIONS AND FOOD. Homes with *Zimmer frei* signs abound near the *strand,* off Fő tér on Erzsébet Királyné u. and near Castrum Camping on **Ady Endre** u. Head up Kossuth L. u. and turn right on Szalasztó u. before the palace entrance; Ady Endre is a few streets down on the right. Expect to pay 3000-4000Ft. To avoid finder's fees, try the folks at **Tourinform** (see above), who offer a few **private rooms** near the center from 3000Ft. ☒ **Kiss&-Máté Panzió ❸,** Katona J. u. 27, offers spacious rooms near the castle with TVs and fridges, plus a large common kitchen, free laundry, and access to a tennis court. (☎319 072. Single 5000Ft; doubles 6000Ft; triples 8000Ft; quads 10,000Ft.) Near the main market, **Szabó Lakás ❷,** Arany János 23, offers newly furnished rooms off a common room with a kitchen and cable TV, where the resident dogs tend to roam. (☎312 504; jutka.szabo@axelero.hu. Rooms 3000Ft.) **Castrum Camping ❶,** Móra F. u. 48, boasts large sites with full amenities: tennis courts, beach access, a restaurant, a swimming pool, and close proximity to the nightspots by the water. (☎312 120. 900Ft per person, 700Ft per child. July-Aug. 600Ft per tent, with electricity 750Ft; Sept.-June 480Ft per tent. Tax 250Ft.)

There has been a **fruit and flower market** on Piac tér since medieval times. At its center, the supermarket, **Match** sells everything you could need. (Open M-F 6:30am-6:30pm, Sa 6:20am-2pm. MC/V.) Most restaurants around Fő tér and on Kossuth L. u. are overpriced, but there are more reasonable options farther from the center. **Corso Restaurant ❸,** Erzsébet Királyné u. 23, closer to the *strand* in the Abbázia Club Hotel, draws on Balaton's fish stock for its concoctions. (☎312 596. Entrees 800-2800Ft. Pizza from 690Ft. Live music nightly from 6pm. Open M-Sa 7am-10pm. MC/V.) **Donatello ❷,** Balaton u. 1/A, serves pizza and pasta in a sun-drenched courtyard. Though named for the Teenage Mutant Ninja Turtle rather than the artist, the restaurant has great Italian cuisine. (☎315 989. Pasta 410-880Ft. Pizza 440-1080Ft. Open daily noon-11pm.) **Párizsi Udvar ❷,** Kastély u. 5, offers both Hungarian and Italian dishes ("pork cutlet a la countryman" 850Ft) in a casual setting en route to the palace. (☎311 202. Entrees 790-1800Ft. Open 11am-11pm. MC/V.) Stop by the cafe at the **Marcipán Muzeum,** Katona J. u. 19, for delectable pastries, hand-crafted candies, and a look at the marzipan model of the palace. (☎319 322. Open June-Aug. daily 10am-6pm; Sept.-Dec. and Mar.-May Tu-Su 10am-6pm. Museum 120Ft, children 80Ft. Cakes 400Ft.)

◙⊡ SIGHTS AND ENTERTAINMENT. Keszthely's pride is the ☒ **Helikon Palace Museum** (Helikon Kastélymúzeum) in the **Festetics Palace.** From Fő tér, follow Kossuth L. u. past Tourinform. Built by one of the most powerful Austro-Hungarian families of the 18th century, the storybook Baroque palace looks like a smaller version of Versailles, but without the crowds. Its fanciful architecture and lush gardens were once the backdrop for lavish literary events hosted by György Festetics (1755-1819); the name "Helikon" comes from Helicon Hill, the mythical Greek home of the nine muses. Of the 360 rooms, visitors may only enter those in the **central wing**, but if the mirrored halls and extravagantly furnished chambers aren't captivating enough, take a peak in the 90,000-volume, wood-paneled **Helikon Library**, just past the entrance, with its dramatic walls of books and hanging chandelier. The arms collection, with weapons spanning 1000 years, and the exhibit of the Festetics's elaborate porcelain pieces are also worth a look. To find out the details, rent an audioguide (500Ft) or pick up an English guidebook (700Ft). Sporadic English translations are available. The interesting "Trophies of Four Continents" exhibit, through a door in the back courtyard, features the exotic prizes of famous hunters. The **English park** around the museum provides photo-worthy panoramas for afternoon promenades around the gardens and woodland paths. (Open Sept.-May Tu-Su 10am-5pm; June Tu-Su 9am-5pm; July-Aug. daily 9am-6pm. 1300Ft, students 700Ft.) Popular chamber music **concerts** are held frequently in the mirrored ballroom; reserve tickets two weeks ahead by calling the ticket office. (☎312 192. 1000-5500Ft.) In summer, the palace holds individualized **candlelit tours** through the castle. (W and F-Sa 10pm. English tours upon request. Call the ticket office to reserve, or buy tickets at the door at 9pm. 2500Ft, reservation fee 500Ft.) The 1896 mint-green tower of the **Church of Our Lady** on Fő tér conceals the main structure, which dates from 1386 and is a shining example of Gothic architecture. Spectacular stained glass and 14th-century paintings adorn the dark sanctuary. (Open M-Sa 8am-7pm, Su 11am-7pm. Free.)

Keszthely boasts many sandy beaches, and families throng to the main *strand*. From the center, walk down Erzsébet u. as it curves right into Vörösmarty u. Cut through the park on the left and cross the train tracks on the other side. This arcade-lined strip along the shore offers volleyball nets, a giant slide, paddleboats, and kayaks. (Open daily 9:30am-7pm. 9:30am-4pm 440Ft, children 300Ft; 4-6:30pm 380/260Ft; after 6:30pm free.)

DAYTRIPS FROM KESZTHELY

HÉVÍZ ☎(06)83

Buses leave from Keszthely's Fő tér (15min., every 30min., 133Ft) and from Sümeg (55min., every 1-2hr., 363Ft). A visit to Hévíz can be combined with a trip to Sümeg.

Six kilometers outside Keszthely, Hévíz is home to the world's largest ◪**thermal lake.** Surrounded by trees, covered in gigantic lilies, and concealed by a slight mist, the sulfurous and slightly radioactive water is rumored to have miraculous healing powers. In summer, the water is naturally heated to a soothing 32-35°C (90-95°F), and it moves quickly: the spring that fills the enormous lake pumps so fast that the water is replaced every 28hr. To bathe in these legendary waters, head to the **Fin-de-Siècle bathhouse,** Dr. Schülhof Vilmos sétány 1, across from the bus station. Look for the sign that reads "Tó Fürdő." Unique because of its natural setting, the house sits on stilts above the center of the scenic lake. A personal specialist recommends treatment for persistent aches or pains. Massages and pedicures are also available. (☎501 700; fax 540 144. Open daily in summer 8:30am-5pm; in winter 9am-4pm. 900Ft for 3hr.; 1200Ft for 4hr.; 1400Ft for 5hr.; 1600Ft for the whole day. Tube rental 300Ft. Massages 2900-6800Ft.) Grab a snack at one of the cafeterias or cafes in the park or dine at **Grill Garten Restaurant ❸,** Kölesal u. 4, on the opposite side of the bus station from the bath, which serves delicious dishes on log tables. (☎540 425. English menu. Entrees 790-

2490Ft. Open daily 10am-11pm. Cash only.) If you plan to spend a few days cooling your heels in the hot healing waters, your best bet is a **private room** (3000Ft). Spa hotels have sky-high prices. *Zimmer frei* signs advertise all over town.

SÜMEG ☎(06)87

Buses run from Hévíz (45min., 1 per hr., 363Ft) and Keszthely (1hr., 1 per hr., 363Ft). From the station, cross Petőfi Sándor u. to Kossuth L. u., the main street. To reach the castle, take a right on Vak Bottyán u. off Kossuth L. u. Bear right at Szent István tér and continue up the street. Turn left onto Vároldal u. and walk until you see the path. From there, it's a 5min. walk to the castle. Easily combined with Hévíz as a daytrip.

Though only a little farther inland than its coast-hugging neighbors, Sümeg feels worlds away. This cobblestone town appeals more to families and school-children eager to get a glimpse of the medieval era than to the racy crowds that frequent most of Balaton's resorts. Trek up the stone path to visit the **castle** *(vár)*, one of Hungary's largest and best-preserved strongholds. Built as a defense against the Mongols, the 13th-century fortress also resisted the Turks, standing until the Hapsburg army burned it down in 1713. If the trek to the castle seems steep, ride up to the ticket counter in one of the Jeeps waiting at the bottom of the hill (350Ft). The atmosphere in the castle is kitschy, with magic shows, pony rides, archery ranges, and costumed characters performing with mandolin music. (☎352 737. Open daily May-Oct. 8am-8pm. 1500Ft, students 800Ft.) There's a **museum** inside, as well as the requisite **torture chamber,** but the wait may prove to be more torturous than the instruments themselves. As you leave the castle, stop at the tournament stadium at the bottom of the hill, where you can watch swordfighting, archery, and a horseshow, followed by a meal in an old-fashioned tavern. (Shows 6:30pm. 5000Ft, students 4000Ft; includes entrance to the castle and a meal at the restaurant.)

The **Church of the Ascension,** at the corner of Deák F. u. and Széchényi G. u., is a must-see. Follow Deák F. u. downhill from the intersection across from the OTP bank on Kossuth L. u. The church's mundane exterior conceals a frescoed marvel known to locals as the "Hungarian Sistine Chapel." While this comparison may be an exaggeration, Franz Anton Maulbertsch's 1757 Rococo master-piece covering the ceilings and walls of the church is highly impressive. Maulbertsch left his signature by painting himself—he's the one on the left side of the first fresco to the right as you enter the church. The platter of cheese he's holding is, curiously, a symbol of humility. (Open M-F 9am-noon and 1-6pm, Sa 10am-noon and 2-5pm, Su 2-5pm. Free.) **Ferences Templom,** on Szent István tér on the way up to the castle, is also a pleasant stop. Its frescoed ceiling, though not as famous, has vivid colors. (Open daily 7am-6pm. Free.) Across the street, **Scotti Udvarház ❷,** Szent István tér 1, serves pastas (650-990Ft) and pizzas (480-1400Ft) in a courtyard with ivy overhangings. Ask to try some water from the spring shooting up in the middle of the restaurant. (☎350 997. Open daily 10am-midnight.)

SOUTHERN TRANSDANUBIA

Framed by the Danube to the west, the Dráva to the south, and Lake Balaton to the north, Southern Transdanubia is known for its mild climate, rolling hills, and sun-flower fields. Once the southernmost portion of Roman Pannonia, the region abounds with historical memorials and palaces, weathered castles, and ancient burial grounds. The people of Southern Transdanubia are as diverse as the sights: the Bosnians, Croats, Germans, and Serbs who call the region home have added flavor to the food and culture west of the Danube.

PÉCS
☎ (06)72

Pécs (PAYCH; pop. 180,000), a vibrant city with a small-town feel, is the most popular destination in southern Hungary, as weekend busloads of tourists attest. The city has more than enough sights, museums, and festivals to keep visitors occupied. Nestled at the base of the Mecsek mountains, Pécs enjoys a warm climate and captivating architecture. Its monuments reveal a 2000-year-old legacy of Roman, Ottoman, and Hapsburg occupation, while the famous Zsolnay porcelain, produced in a factory just outside the city, adorns many of its buildings. Evenings bring out a more exuberant side of Pécs, as students pack local bars and clubs.

▛ TRANSPORTATION

Trains: Take bus #30, 32, or 33 from the center or walk 15min. from Széchényi tér down Jókai u. To: **Budapest** (2½hr., 16 per day, 2706Ft). 4 trains leave daily for the **Lake Balaton** towns; get tickets at the MÁV office in the station (☎215 003; www.elvira.hu; ☎212 734; open 5:30am-6:30pm) or at Jókai u. 4 (open M and F 9am-3:30pm, Tu-Th 9am-4:30pm).

Buses: ☎215 215; www.agria.hu. To **Budapest** (4½hr., 5 per day, 2540Ft), **Keszthely** (4hr., 6 per day, 1930Ft), **and Szeged** (4½hr., 7 per day, 2410Ft).

Public Transportation: Bus tickets cost 145Ft at kiosks and 155Ft on board.

Taxis: Volán and **Euro** are the reputable companies. Don't take other cabs, as they will likely scam you. Base 250Ft, 150Ft per km.

✦ ❔ ORIENTATION AND PRACTICAL INFORMATION

Conveniently, north and south correspond to uphill and downhill. Inconveniently, it seems as if you're always walking uphill. Tourists descend upon the historic **Belváros** (Inner City), a rectangle bounded by the ruins of the city walls. The center is **Széchényi tér,** where most tourist offices are located. Both the train and bus stations are south of the center, within walking distance. It takes less than 20min. to cross Belváros going downhill, but be wary of the steep incline.

Tourist Offices: Tourinform, Széchényi tér 9 (☎511 232; fax 213 315), offers free small **maps,** large maps for 520Ft, phone cards, and stamps. Open June 16-Sept. 15 M-F 8am-5:30pm, Sa-Su 9am-2pm; Sept. 15-Oct. 16 and May-June 15 M-F 8am-5:30pm, Sa 9am-2pm; Nov.-Apr. M-F 8am-4pm.

Currency Exchange: OTP Bank, Rákóczi út 44 (☎502 900). Cashes **traveler's checks** and **exchanges currency** for no commission. A 24hr. MC/V **ATM** is outside. Open M 7:45am-6pm, Tu-Th 7:45am-5pm, F 7:45am-4pm.

Pharmacy: Mozsonyi Gyógyszertár, Bajcsy-Zsilinszky u. 6 (☎315 604). Open M-F 7am-7pm, Sa 7am-2pm.

Internet: Matrix Internet Café, Király u. 15. (☎214 487). 5Ft per min. Open M-Sa 9am-11pm, Su 2-10pm. **Tourinform** (see above) also has Internet. 25Ft for up to 15min 100Ft per hr. Open M-F 9am-5pm.

Post Office: Jókai Mór u. 10 (☎506 000). 2nd fl. office has so many services there's an info desk to guide you. Open M-F 7am-7pm, Sa 8am-noon. **Postal Code:** 7621.

▙ ACCOMMODATIONS

Dorms are the cheapest option, and they're more comfortable in Pécs than in many other towns. **Private rooms** are a decent budget option, though they typically start around 3000Ft. Pécs's efficient bus system makes cheaper rooms outside town almost as convenient. Reserve ahead in summer and on weekends.

HUNGARY

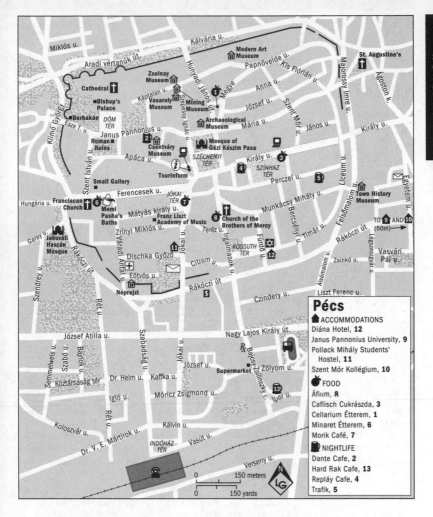

Pécs

⛺ ACCOMMODATIONS
Diána Hotel, 12
Janus Pannonius University, 9
Pollack Mihály Students'
  Hostel, 11
Szent Mór Kollégium, 10

🍴 FOOD
Áfium, 8
Caflisch Cukrászda, 3
Cellarium Étterem, 1
Minaret Étterem, 6
Morik Café, 7

🍸 NIGHTLIFE
Dante Cafe, 2
Hard Rak Cafe, 13
Repláy Cafe, 4
Trafik, 5

Pollack Mihály Students' Hostel, Jókai u. 8 (☎315 846). Ideally located in the center of town, this comfortable former university dorm has kitchen facilities and a lounge. Ring the unmarked door when you arrive. Call ahead. Dorms 2700Ft. ❷

Diána Hotel, Timár u. 4a (☎/fax 333 373), just off Kossuth tér in the center of town. This hotel offers luxurious rooms with hardwood floors and cable TV. Breakfast included. Singles 7700Ft; doubles 11,000Ft; 4-person apartments 13,000-17,000Ft. A/C 1000Ft extra. 10% credit card surcharge. MC/V. ❹

Szent Mór Kollégium, 48-as tér 4 (☎503 610). Take bus #21 from the main bus terminal to 48-as tér, or walk up the hill to Rákóczi út and turn right. This gorgeous old university wing houses spiffy rooms. Laundry by request. Reception 24hr. Check-out 10am. Curfew midnight. Ring the bell after 10pm. Open July-Aug. Triples 1700Ft. Cash only. ❶

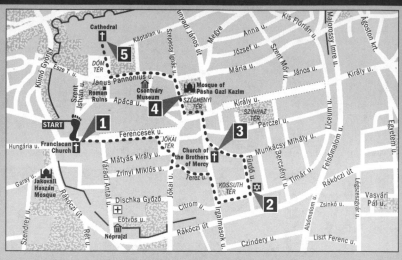

Like most cities and towns in Hungary, Pécs is dotted with religious monuments and architecture. But this small yet cosmopolitan city stands out for its diversity: the architecture here shows the mingling of many religious traditions within the city walls. Using these religious buildings as signposts not only offers a window onto the town's culture and history, but also leads you through the sunny squares and narrow pedestrian boulevards of Pécs.

START: Franciscan Church, at the corner of Ferencesek u. and Véradi A. u.

FINISH: Cathedral on Szent István tér

DISTANCE: 3/4 mi.

DURATION: 2hr.

WHEN TO GO: Early afternoon

1 FRANCISCAN CHURCH. Though the white Franciscan Church is not open to visitors, its tolling bells offer the perfect backdrop to begin your tour. The staid little church opens onto a Baroque interior and blends in perfectly among the quiet shop-lined Ferencesek u.

2 SYNAGOGUE. After looping down past the main square, you'll be rewarded with the worn yet dignified architecture of the synagogue. Although it is no longer used by worshippers, the synagogue opens to visitors for a few hours at mid-day, inviting them to take in the soaring arches and to learn about the Jewish history of Pécs from an English-language brochure.

3 CHURCH OF THE BROTHERS OF MERCY. On the way back towards Széchényi tér stands the Church of the Brothers of Mercy, looking out over the square. Its façade fuses multiple architectural styles, and inside you can examine the elaborate inlaid wooden altar.

4 MOSQUE OF PASHA GAZI KAZIM. Standing at the top of Széchényi tér, its bold green dome demanding attention, this architectural gem is the center of Pécs. This building's history traces the religious conflict that plagued the city for centuries: originally a church, it was rededicated as a mosque when Ottoman rule came to Pécs; when the Hapsburg Empire gained control of Pécs, the mosque reverted to its former identity as a church. Today, it has resumed its role as a parish church. Inside, verses from the Koran share the walls with portraits of the Christ child.

5 CATHEDRAL. Last but not least, up the hill to the left of the main square stands the magnificent Pécs Cathedral, its four spires piercing the sky. Inside, the walls are adorned with decorative flourishes and religious portraiture, including the recent addition of a depiction of the 12 apostles to the Southern front.

WALKING TOUR

Janus Pannonius University, Universitas u. 2 (☎311 966; fax 324 473). Take bus #21 from the main bus terminal to 48-as tér, or walk up the hill to Rákóczi út and turn right. The dorm is to the right, on the street behind McDonald's. Baths in suites. Reception 24hr. Check-out 9am. Call ahead. Open July-Sept. 3-bed dorms 2100Ft. Cash only. ❶

🔾 FOOD

Because of the town's steep incline, many of its restaurants, cafes, and bars lie underground in cellars. These vaults are attractions in themselves; most serve Hungarian dishes with an array of wines. Reservations are necessary at more popular restaurants on weekend nights, but a walk down **Király u., Apáca u.,** or **Ferencesek u.** yields a variety of tasty options. **Interspar,** Bajcsy-Zsilinszky u. 11, downstairs inside Árkád Shopping Mall, has a wide variety of food, a salad bar, a deli, and a bakery. (Open M-Th and Sa 7am-9pm, F 7am-10pm, Su 8am-7pm.)

🍴 **Cellarium Étterem,** Hunyadi u. 2 (☎314 453). Buried in a cellar at the bottom of a long stairway, this prison-themed restaurant will let you live out your fantasy of eating traditional Hungarian fare while being served by waiters in inmate costumes. The menu promises that the house champagne is "equal with a good foreplay on a table (instead of a bed)." Entrees 950-3200Ft. Live Hungarian music on weekends. AmEx/MC/V. ❸

🍴 **Áfium,** Irgalmasok u. 2 (☎511 434). Cellar restaurant packed with relics, from radios to sewing machines to antique photographs, features an Italian and Hungarian menu. Vegetarian options. Entrees 700-2800Ft. Open M-Sa 11am-1am, Su 11am-midnight. ❷

Minaret Étterem, Ferencesek u. 35 (☎311 338; www.minaretetterem.hu). This casual restaurant dishes out classic Hungarian recipes (gypsy roast; 1400Ft) in a lush, walled courtyard full of trees. The chiming of the bells from the Franciscan Church, which looms overhead, accompany your meal. Open daily noon-midnight. Cash only. ❹

Caflisch Cukrászda, Király u. 32 (☎310 391). Sink your sweet tooth into pastries (from 100Ft) and sundaes (300-650Ft) at one of the town's best cafes. Check out the Herend china espresso machine amid the antique chandeliers, marble cafe tables, and velvet-upholstered chairs. Open daily 10am-10pm. ❶

Morik Café, Jókai tér (☎415 233), allows you to pick your favorite coffee and have it specially brewed. The 2-dozen options include Costa Rican, Hawaiian, and Ugandan specialties. Enjoy your pick on the patio overlooking Jókai tér or enjoy the rich aroma inside the wooden shop. Coffee 230Ft. Open daily 9am-midnight. Cash only. ❶

👁 SIGHTS

MOSQUE OF GHAZI KASSIM PASHA (GÁZI KHASIM PASA DZSÁMIJA). Nicknamed the "Mosque Church," the green-domed building is a former Turkish mosque. Today, it serves as a Christian church, though it still retains some Turkish flavor. Verses from the Koran decorate the walls, and an ablution basin, where the faithful washed their feet before entering the mosque, now serves as a baptismal font. The largest Ottoman structure still standing in Hungary, the church intertwines Christian and Muslim traditions. (*Széchényi tér.* ☎321 976. *Open Apr. 16-Oct. 14 M-Sa 10am-4pm, Su 12:30-4pm; Oct. 15-Apr. 15 M-Sa 10am-noon. Mass Su 9:30, 10:30, and 11:30am. Admission free, but donations requested.*)

CATHEDRAL. Perched atop the Pécs hilltop, the fourth-century neo-Romanesque Cathedral and adjoining Bishop's Palace make the hill a perfect respite from the bustling city. Inside the cathedral, a small museum displays medieval stone carvings and intricate wall paintings, while the crypt that once housed the tomb of the first Bishop of Pécs is now a venue for music festivals. As you examine the painted ceiling and patterned columns, organ music reverberates through the vast cathedral. *(On Dóm tér. From Széchényi tér, walk left on Janus Pannonius u., take the 1st right, and then go left on Káptalan to Dóm tér. ☎ 513 030. Cathedral open M-F 9am-5pm, Sa 9am-2pm, Su 1-5pm. Mass M-Sa 6pm; Su 8, 9:30, and 11am; 6pm. 700Ft, students 350Ft.)*

SYNAGOGUE. The stunning 1869 synagogue has a painted ceiling and shelters an incredible replica of the Ark of the Covenant. Because the city's Jewish population now numbers a mere 140, however, services are no longer held here. The English pamphlet has detailed information on Jewish traditions and the devastating effect of WWII on the local Jewish community. *(On Kossuth tér. Walk downhill from Széchényi tér on Irgalmasok u. Open Mar.-Oct. M-F and Su 10-11:30am and noon-1pm. 300Ft, 200Ft.)*

ROMAN RUINS. Once a mass burial site for Roman Pécs (Sopianae), the fourth-century Christian mausoleum near the cathedral is the largest excavated burial ground in Hungary. Over 100 corpses have been uncovered from the area, and a chilling crypt with well-preserved Roman Christian paintings sits underneath the ruins. *(Across Janus Pannonius u. from the cathedral. Open Apr.-Oct. Tu-Su 10am-6pm; Nov.-Mar. 10am-4pm. 300Ft, students 150Ft. Cameras 400Ft.)*

🏛 MUSEUMS

█ ZSOLNAY MUSEUM. A family workshop has handcrafted the famously colorful and intricate Zsolnay porcelain since the 1800s. The porcelain adorns many central Pécs buildings: the Zsolnay Well, Széchényi tér 1, sports a rare Eosin glaze; the windows of County Hall, Jókai u. 10, are framed by detailed tiles; Vilmos Zsolnay's Shop, Király u. 1, has decorative tiles; and Pécs National Theater, Színáz tér, houses Zsolnay sculptures and reliefs. The museum itself showcases the Zsolnays' many wares, from delicate porcelain birdcages to iridescent glazed vases. *(Káptalan u. 2. Walk up Szepessy I. u. behind the Mosque Church and go left at Káptalan u. ☎ 324 822. Open Tu-Sa 10am-6pm, Su 10am-4pm. 700Ft, students 350Ft.)*

█ VASARELY MUSEUM. One of Hungary's most important 20th-century artists, Pécs native Viktor Vasarely (1908-97) is best known as the pioneer of Op-Art and geometric abstraction. The house in which he was born has been converted to a museum and now displays some of his most important paintings and sculptures, along with works by his contemporaries, among them Hans Arp, Frantisek Kupka, and François Morellet. *(Káptalan u. 3, next to the Zsolnay. ☎ 324 822, ext. 21. Open Apr.-Oct. Tu-Sa 10am-6pm, Su 10am-4pm. 500Ft, students 250Ft.)*

CSONTVÁRY MUSEUM. This museum displays the works of Tivadar Csontváry Kosztka (1853-1919), a local painter who won international acclaim. His mastery of luminous expressionism earned him the nickname "the Hungarian Van Gogh." The exhibit highlights Csontváry's interest in nature. *(Janus Pannonius u. 11. ☎ 310 544. Open Tu-Su 10am-6pm. 600Ft, students 300Ft.)*

MINING MUSEUM. The largest underground exhibit in Hungary, this labyrinth shares a courtyard with the Vasarely Museum. The museum (Mecseki Bányászati Múzeum), designed to show what mines were really like, explains—in Hungarian—the coal mining process that once drove Pécs's economy. The chilly tunnels are a refreshing refuge from the summer heat. *(Káptalan u. 3. ☎ 324 822. Open Apr.-Oct. Tu-Su 10am-6pm; Nov.-Mar. 10am-4pm. 400Ft, students 200Ft.)*

🌸 🎭 FESTIVALS AND NIGHTLIFE

The activities that fill the main square in summer range from theater performances to markets of handmade goods. September is the height of festival season in Pécs. Choir music and wine mingle at the mirthful █**Festival of Wine Songs** late in the month. For info, contact Pécsi Férfikar Alapitvány (☎/fax 211 606). Other festivals include the **Gastronomic Pleasures of the Pécs Region**, the **Pécs City Festival**, and the **Mediterranean Autumn Festival.** Pécs enjoys lively **nightlife** that ranges from mellow coffee shops to raging clubs. Hit the crowded, colorful bars near **Széchényi tér,** especially on the first two blocks of Király u. Clubs are located close to the train station and pack in a vivacious crowd.

■ **Dante Cafe,** Janus Pannonius u. 11 (☎210 361; www.cafedante.hu), in the Csontváry Museum building and the courtyard behind it. Originally founded to finance the Pécs literary magazine Szép Literaturari Ajándék, Dante now packs in artists and local youth. Live jazz on weekends plays in the outdoor courtyard in summers; a basement jazz club, **Alcafé,** opens in winter. Beer 350-420Ft. Open daily 10am-1am, later on weekends.

Trafik, Perczel M. u. 22 (☎212 672). A slick and spacious new bar on a quiet side street, Trafik will entice you to get comfortable on fabric-draped couches beneath a large TV screen. Drinks from 600Ft. Open M-Sa 4pm-1am.

Hard Rak Cafe, Ipar u. 7 (☎502 557), 10min. from the main town. Turn left at the corner of Bajcsy-Zsilinszky u. The name refers to the music and the walls built from boulders, not the American restaurant chain. Local teens swarm the entrance of this cavernous club, which boasts a fine lineup of drinks (shots from 400Ft) and live musical acts. Live rock in summer F-Sa nights. Cover Th-Sa 700Ft. Open M-Sa 7pm-6am.

Repláy Cafe, Király u. 4 (☎210 531). One of the liveliest cafes on Király u., Repláy is the perfect place to begin an evening on the town. Inside, the red brick walls evoke a villa, and the "Chill Out Bar" beckons guests to the downstairs lounge with a red, neon Buddha. Beer 500Ft. Mixed drinks from 1000Ft. Open daily 11am-midnight.

🖪 DAYTRIP FROM PÉCS

SZIGETVÁR   ☎(0)73

Buses run from Pécs (1hr., 26 per day, 274Ft). The bus station is very close to the town center. With the station behind you, follow the main road as it bears left toward the center. To reach the castle, turn left on József Attila u. at Kossuth tér and follow it until it opens into another square. Turn right on Vár u. and follow it to the castle entrance.

While the quiet town of **Szigetvár** (see-GHET-vahr) offers little on the surface, its historic castle is a major landmark and point of Hungarian pride. In 1566, **Zrinyí-Vár** marked the site of a Turkish siege in which Hungarian troops, led by Miklós Zrinyí, fended off the sultan's invasion for a month before finally sacrificing their lives as they stormed out of the fortress and into battle.

Today Szigetvár makes a pleasant daytrip from Pécs, as it is easy to fill a day strolling within the castle walls. (Open Tu-Su 9am-5pm. 400Ft, students 250Ft.) More a fortress than a castle, it offers ample space for exploration among park-like paths. You can walk the ramparts or cross a bridge over the empty moat. In one corner, a small **deer park** plays home to several rambunctious animals. The centerpiece of the castle is the **Vár-Múzeum,** which incorporates part of the old foundations. Its eclectic collection includes watercolors of Hungarian landscapes, stylized paintings of the 1566 battle, old-fashioned military equipment, and a wax model of the Turkish invaders. The brave can climb the dark and incredibly narrow winding wooden staircase of the lookout tower. (Free with castle entrance.)

Pick up supplies for a scenic picnic inside the castle walls at **ABC Coop,** at the end of VárVárda u., off József Attila u. on the way to the castle. (Open M-F 6am-6pm, Sa 6am-noon, Su 7-11am.) If you're looking for lunch, try **Sjeráj ❷,** on the corner of the road to the station. It serves creative dishes (turkey breast with pineapple; 1400Ft), along with classic Hungarian grub. (☎342 004. English menu. Open M-F and Su 11am-10pm, Sa 11am-midnight. Cash only.)

THE GREAT PLAIN (NAGYALFÖLD)

Romanticized in tales of cowboys and bandits, the grasslands of Nagyalföld stretch southeast of Budapest, covering almost half of Hungary. This tough region is home to arid Debrecen, fertile Szeged, and the vineyards of Kecskemét, which rise out of the flat soil like Nagyalföld's legendary mirages.

DEBRECEN   ☎(06)52

Protected by the mythical phoenix and dubbed the festival capital of Hungary, Debrecen (DEH-bre-tsen; pop. 210,000) has miraculously survived over 30 devastating fires. Fortunately, recent reconstructions have bestowed wide boulevards and lush parks upon the city; the largest, Nagyerdei Park, is called the "Great Forest." Today, the ultra-modern city, one of Hungary's largest, is filled with the active and outspoken: Debrecen is the historical center of Hungarian Protestantism and is famed for its Reformed College, one of the country's oldest and largest universities. The student population fills the streets by day and takes to the pubs by night.

▐ TRANSPORTATION

Trains: ☎316 777. Petőfi tér. To: **Budapest** (3hr., 13 per day, 2226Ft; InterCity 2½hr., 8 per day, 2192Ft); **Eger** (3hr., 6 per day, 1142Ft) via **Füzesabony; Miskolc** (2½-3hr., 5 per day, 1338Ft); **Szeged** (3½hr., 7 per day, 2536Ft) via **Cegléd.**

Buses: ☎413 999, at the intersection of Nyugati u. and Széchényi u. To: **Eger** (2½-3hr., 4 per day, 1690Ft); **Kecskemét** (5½hr., 1 per day, 2910Ft); **Miskolc** (2hr., 1-2 per hr., 1210Ft); **Szeged** (4-5½hr., 4 per day, 2910Ft); **Tokaj** (2hr., 2 per day, 1090Ft).

Public Transportation: The best way to get around. **Tram #1** runs from the train station through Kálvin tér, loops around the park past the university, and heads back to Kálvin tér. Ticket checks are frequent and fines are severe (2000-5000Ft); buy tickets (140Ft) or day passes (450Ft) from the newspaper shop inside the train station, or tickets (160Ft) from the driver. Prices change frequently. Once on board, validate your ticket in a red puncher. Get off at Városháza for tourist offices and most other necessities.

Taxis: City Taxi (☎555 555). **Főnix Taxi** (☎444 444).

◄ ▐ ORIENTATION AND PRACTICAL INFORMATION

Debrecen is a big city, but it has a small and easily navigable center 15min. from the train station. With your back to the station, head down **Petőfi tér,** which becomes **Piac u.,** a main street perpendicular to the station. Piac u. ends in **Kálvin tér,** where the huge, yellow **Nagytemplom** (Great Church) presides over the center. After Kálvin tér, Piac u. becomes Péterfia u., which runs north to **Nagyerdei Park** and **Kossuth Lajos University** (KLTE). Trams and buses run from the train station through Kálvin tér. to Nagyerdi Park; the info desk in the station offers schedules and prices. The **bus station** is 10min. from the center. From the station, go right on **Széchényi,** then left on Piac u., which opens onto Kálvin tér.

Tourist Office: Tourinform, Piac u. 20 (☎412 250; tourinform@ph.debrecen.hu), above Széchényi u., under the cream-colored building on the right side of Kálvin tér just after Kossuth u. **Free maps** and info on hostels, food, and daytrips. Open June 15-Sept. 15 M-F 8am-8pm, Sa-Su 10am-6pm; Sept. 16-June 14 M-F 9am-5pm.

Currency Exchange: Banks abound on Piac u. **OTP,** Piac u. 16 (☎522 610), **exchanges currency,** gives MC **cash advances,** accepts most **traveler's checks,** and has a 24hr. MC/V **ATM.** Open M 7:45am-5pm, Tu-F 7:45am-4pm.

Luggage Storage: Available at the train station. 120Ft per 6hr., large bags 240Ft; 240/
480Ft per day. After 10pm, luggage can be stored at the info desk, counter #9.

Pharmacy: Nap Patika, Hatvan u. 1 (☎413 115). Open M-F 8:30am-6pm, Sa 8am-
1pm. AmEx/MC/V. **Arany Egyszarvú,** Kossuth u. 8 (☎530 707). Open M-F 8:30am-
6pm. MC/V.

Medical Services: Emergency room (☎404 040), at **Főnix,** Lehel u. 22. English-speakers can call the free line ☎112.

Internet: DataNet Cafe, Kossuth u. 8 (☎536 724; www.datanetcafe.hu). 8Ft per min.
Open daily 8am-midnight.

Post Office: Hatvan u. 5-7 (☎412 111). Open M-F 7am-7pm, Sa 8am-1pm. **Postal
Code:** 4025.

ACCOMMODATIONS

IBUSZ, on Széchényi u. near Piac u., arranges centrally located **private rooms.** (☎415
5155; fax 410 756. Open M-F 9am-5pm, Sa 8am-1pm. Doubles 5000Ft; triples
7000Ft. AmEx/MC/V). The staff at **Tourinform** (see p. 340) can also arrange rooms.
In July and August, many **university dorms ❶** rent rooms (1300-2000Ft); ask at Tourinform, since many dorms book only groups. During the summer, this is the cheapest option; the rest of the year, most budget travelers stay in pensions. Reserve
rooms early during festival season.

Stop Panzió, Batthány u. 18 (☎420 301; www.stop.at.tf). From Kossuth u., turn right on
Batthány u. At the *Stop Panzió* sign, go down the left side of the building to the back to
find the entrance. Near the center. Bright, well-furnished rooms with TV and private bath
look out through lace curtains onto a courtyard. English spoken. Breakfast 900Ft.
Reception 24hr. Check-out 11am. Doubles 5900Ft; triples 7900Ft. Cash only. ❸

Kölcsey Kollégiuma, Blaháné u. 15 (☎502 780). From Kossuth u., go left on Újházi and
right on Blaháné. The rooms are tiny—doubles can barely fit 2 beds—and the baths are
shared, but the dorm is cheap and well located. Open June-Aug. Singles 1435Ft; doubles 2530Ft. Tax 400Ft. Cash only. ❶

Centrum Panzió, Péterfia u. 37/a (☎416 193). Comfortable and air-conditioned. Large,
well-decorated rooms in little houses with marble-floored private baths. Peaceful flower
garden with lounge chairs, swings, and a shower. Breakfast 1200Ft. Singles 6900Ft;
doubles 13,600Ft; apartments 12,190-19,090Ft. Tax 15%. Cash only. ❹

FOOD

The **Match Supermarket** at the Debrecen Plaza, Péterfia u. 18, is well stocked with
fresh fruits and vegetables. (Open M-F 7am-9pm, Sa 6am-9pm, Su 8am-8pm.)
Heliker, across from McDonald's, on Piac u., offers a smaller selection of snacks.
(Open M-F 6:30am-7:30pm, Sa 6:30am-2pm, Su 7-11am. MC/V.)

🍴 **Csokonai Söröző,** Kossuth u. 21 (☎410 802), in a posh, candle-lit cellar with brick
walls. The food proves as delectable as the pictures on the menu suggest. At the end of
your meal, enjoy a complimentary glass of Tokaj furmint as you try your luck at the dice
game—if you win, dinner is free. Entrees 580-1900Ft. Open daily noon-11pm. MC/V. ❷

Carpe Diem Tea & Cafe, Batthyány u. 8 (☎319 007). For an afternoon snack or a dosage of caffeine, this tea house is the best bet in town. The only thing more exotic than
the menu of international teas and coffees is the setting: red chiffon curtains conceal a
sideroom for hookah-smoking, and world beats play in the background. Teas 500-
800Ft. Open M-Th 9am-11pm, F-Sa 9am-midnight, Su 10am-10pm. Cash only. ❷

Pompeji Cafe-Ristorante, Batthyány u. 4, (☎220 760). An Italian restaurant with Hungarian flavor, Pompeji prides itself on ornate desserts and an ambience reminiscent of a Tuscan cafe. If you're up to the challenge, you can try out the spicy Vesuvian roast (870Ft) to see if it's as hot as the name promises. The bakery offers equally delectable treats to go (100-200Ft). Pizza 840Ft. Cash only. ❸

Aranybika Étterem, Piac u. 11-15 (☎533 408). To the left of the Aranybika Hotel, on the corner of Piac u. and Bajcsy-Zsilinszky u. Plush leather chairs, sleek wooden tables, and chandeliers make this brightly lit restaurant ideal for a relaxing meal. The diverse menu ranges from Italian pastas to richer Hungarian meat dishes. Large dining room and plentiful patio seating. English menu. Entrees 1000-2800Ft. Open M-Th and Su 10am-midnight, F-Sa 10am-2am. MC/V. ❷

👁 SIGHTS

REFORMÁTUS KOLLÉGIUM. Established in 1538 as a center for Protestant education, this building housed the government of Hungary twice, and today it is home to Calvinist schools and a museum that traces the history of the Reformation in Hungary. Its Reform origins are evident in its very architecture, with simple, arched hallways surrounding a central courtyard. The highlight, however, is the 650,000-volume library on the second floor. This impressive collection includes works dating as far back as the 16th century. *(Kálvin tér 16, behind the church. ☎414 744. Open Tu-Sa 9am-5pm, Su 9am-1pm. 300Ft, students 150Ft.)*

GREAT CHURCH. Hungary's largest Protestant church, built in 1836, looms over Kálvin tér. With a commanding yellow facade, white pillars, and twin spires, the Great Church (Nagytemplóm), is the city's emblem, appearing in almost every pamphlet and postcard. The bell tower offers a great view of Debrecen, but be forewarned: the narrow wooden stairs get steeper as you climb. Hear the huge organ every Friday at noon. *(☎412 694. Open Apr.-Oct. M-F 9am-4pm, Sa 9am-1pm, Su 10am-4pm; Nov.-Mar. M-F 10am-noon, Su 1-3pm. 200Ft, students 100Ft. Concerts 1hr. Free.)*

DÉRI MUSEUM. The Déri Museum displays a collection of cultural artifacts ranging from archaeological fossils to local tinware to Japanese lacquerware. Upstairs, awe-inspiring paintings by Hungarian artist **Mihály Munkácsy** depict Jesus's trial and crucifixion. You can spot the artist's self-portrait in *Ecce Homo*, next to the arch. Coming from Kossuth tér, steer left of the Great Church and turn left on to Múzeum u.; the museum is on the right, flanked by the sculpture garden. It can be recognized by the magisterial design of its domed roof. *(☎417 577. Open Apr.-Oct. Tu-Su 10am-6pm; Nov.-Mar. Tu-Su 10am-4pm. Museum 580Ft, students 290Ft; special exhibits 300Ft/150Ft. English guide 200Ft. No cameras.)*

🎵 🌿 ENTERTAINMENT AND FESTIVALS

Many of the city's students congregate in **Nagyerdei Park,** next to the university, where bars, tattoo salons, paddle boats, and tank-topped young men abound. (Paddleboats 900Ft per hr., rowboats 850Ft per hr.) There is also a **zoo** and an **amusement park** for children, both in the **Vidámpark** complex. (Info ☎514 100; fax 346 883. Zoo open M-F 9am-6pm. 300Ft, children 250Ft. Amusement park 200Ft; rides 100Ft each.) At the **municipal thermal bath,** you can soak in the steamy pools with elderly locals. (Thermal bath open daily 7am-8:30pm. 840Ft, children 660Ft. Sauna open daily Sept.-May 10am-10pm. 650Ft per 2hr. Swimming pool open M-F 7am-6:30pm. 350Ft, students 310Ft.) The air-conditioned theaters of **Cinema City,** Péterfia u. 18, on the second floor of Debrecen Plaza, offer refuge from the summer heat. (☎456 111. Movies in English. Last showing 10:45pm. 890-990Ft.)

The festival season officially runs from June to August. The end of June brings Hungarian bands to the **Vekeri-tó Rock Festival,** held at a park 10km from the city. Camp out, or take the free bus from Debrecen. In July of even-numbered years, the **Béla Bartók International Choral Competition** attracts choirs from around the world. Culminating the festival season is the popular **Flower Carnival** parade, in which floats are made entirely of flowers, held August 15-20. Starting the second week of September, well-known musicians and bands come to town for **Jazz Days.**

🎵 NIGHTLIFE

Debrecen is a city dominated by its students, where staid sightseeing plays second fiddle to the youthful energy radiating from the university. Locals prefer the bar scene to the club scene, so if it is frenetic dancing to techno-pop that you are seeking, you may have a hard time finding it.

El Tornado, Pallagi u. 2 (☎340 590), in Nagyerdei Park. This pub, with swinging doors, country music, and cowboy memorabilia, will transport you back to the Wild West. 0.5L *Borsodi* 250Ft. Open daily 6pm-4am.

Genius Bar-Cafe, in the center of town. Enter the Aranybika Hotel; it's in the left corner on the ground floor. A sophisticated alternative to the usual Western-themed bar. Dim lighting lends a romantic flair to the red, portrait-covered walls. Open M-Th and Su 10am-4am, F-Sa 10am-6am.

Yes Jazz Bár, Kálvin tér 4. Go right after the last building on the right side of Kálvin tér and enter through the Civis Étterem. The bar is at the upper end of the shopping area. Not the mellow jazz bar implied by its name, but rather a rock-and-roll hotspot for locals. Gösser 300Ft, Heineken 320Ft. Open M-F 3pm-4am, Sa-Su 5pm-4am.

Civis Gösser Söröző, Kálvin tér 8-12, across the way from Yes Jazz Bar. Quieter than its neighbor, this bar attracts an older crowd. A staircase winds upstairs to further seating above the bar. Open M-Sa 10am-midnight, Su 4pm-midnight.

SZEGED   ☎(06)62

The artistic capital of the Great Plain, Szeged (SEH-ged; pop. 166,000) has an easygoing charm that has prompted some to describe it as a Mediterranean town on the Tisza. After an 1879 flood practically wiped out the city, streets were laid out in orderly curves punctuated by large, stately squares. The result is the quiet, cosmopolitan atmosphere of a European seaside city. The colorful art nouveau buildings lining the sidestreets reflect Szeged's festival culture and vibrant social scene.

⬛ TRANSPORTATION

Trains: Szeged pu. (☎421 821; www.elvira.hu), on Indóház tér on the west bank of the Tisza. International ticket office on 2nd fl. Open daily 6am-5:45pm. To: **Budapest** (2½hr.; 11 per day; 2076Ft, students 675Ft); **Debrecen** (3-4hr.; 9 per day; 2526Ft, students 821Ft) via **Cegléd;** and **Kecskemét** (1¼hr., 11 per day, 838Ft).

Buses: (☎551 166), on Mars tér. From the station, cross the street at the lights and follow Mikszáth Kálmán u. toward the Tisza. This intersects Széchényi tér after becoming Károlyi u. To: **Budapest** (3½hr., 7 per day, 2170Ft); **Debrecen** (5¼hr., 3-6 per day, 2910Ft); **Eger** (5hr., 2 per day, 3020Ft); **Győr** (6hr., 2 per day, 3510Ft); **Kecskemét** (1¾hr., 9-10per day, 1090Ft); **Pécs** (4½hr., 7 per day, 2410Ft).

Public Transportation: Tram #1 connects the train station with Széchényi tér (4-5 stops). Otherwise, it's a 20min. walk. Tickets from kiosks 140Ft; from the driver 180Ft. Fine for riding without a ticket is a painful 2000Ft.

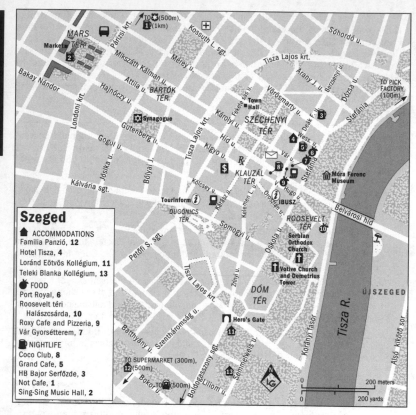

Szeged

🔺 ACCOMMODATIONS
Familia Panzió, **12**
Hotel Tisza, **4**
Loránd Eötvös Kollégium, **11**
Teleki Blanka Kollégium, **13**

🍴 FOOD
Port Royal, **6**
Roosevelt téri
  Halászcsárda, **10**
Roxy Cafe and Pizzeria, **9**
Vár Gyorsétterem, **7**

🍺 NIGHTLIFE
Coco Club, **8**
Grand Cafe, **5**
HB Bajor Serfőzde, **3**
Not Cafe, **1**
Sing-Sing Music Hall, **2**

Taxis: ☎ 444 444, 490 490, or 480 480. 200Ft base, 200Ft per km; students approximately 150Ft per km with no base fare. Taxis are more reliable here than in other cities, but it is still best to clarify the price before getting in.

■✳🛈 ORIENTATION AND PRACTICAL INFORMATION

Szeged is divided by the **Tisza River,** with the city center on the west bank and the parks and residences of **Újszeged** (New Szeged) on the east. The center forms a semicircle against the river, bounded by **Tisza Lajos krt.** and centered on **Széchényi tér,** the main square. Across **Híd u.** (Bridge St.) from Széchényi, shops and cafes line the pedestrian **Klauzál tér.** Large multilingual **maps** are sold in kiosks.

> **Tourist Office: Tourinform,** Dugonics tér 2 (☎ 488 690; szeged@tourinform.hu), in a courtyard on Somogyi u. Offers **free maps** and accommodations info. Open June-Sept. M-F 9am-6pm, Sa 9am-1pm; Oct.-May M-F 9am-5pm. **Branch** at Széchényi tér. Open daily June-Sept. 9am-9pm.

> **Currency Exchange: OTP,** Klauzál tér 5 (☎ 480 380). Cashes **traveler's checks** for no commission and gives MC/V **cash advances.** 24hr. currency exchange kiosk outside open M 7:45am-5pm, Tu-F 7:45am-4pm. **Budapest Bank Ltd.,** Klauzál tér 4 (☎ 485 585). Has **Western Union** and a 24hr. MC/V **ATM** outside. Open M-F 8am-5pm.

Luggage Storage: At the train station. 150-200Ft per bag. Open daily 4am-11pm.

Pharmacy: Kígyó Richter Referenciapatika, Klauzál tér 3 (☎547 174). Ring bell outside for after-hours service. Open M-Sa 7am-10pm, Su 7am-8pm. MC/V.

Medical Services: Kossuth Lajos sgt. 15/17 (☎474 374). From the Town Hall, walk across Széchényi tér, turn left on Vörösmarty u., and continue as it becomes Kossuth Lajos sgt. The medical center is at the intersection with Szilágyi u. Open M-F 5:30am-7:30pm, Sa 7:30am-7:30pm. Ring bell after hours.

Internet: Cyber Arena, Híd u. 1 (☎422 815). Internet and phones with cheap international rates. 6Ft per min; 840Ft for 8hr. midnight-8am. Open 24hr. **Matrix Internet Cafe,** Kárász u. 5 (☎423 830). Plays techno and trance under dim lights and pictures of Keanu Reeves. 6am-10pm 6Ft per min., 10pm-6am 3.60Ft per min. Open 24hr.

Post Office: Széchényi tér 1 (☎476 276), at intersection with Híd u. Open M-F 8am-7pm, Sa 8am-noon. **Western Union** available. **Postal Code:** 6720.

ACCOMMODATIONS

Tourinform (see **Orientation and Practical Information,** p. 344) has info on **pensions, hotels, hostels,** and **campsites.** (Singles 1100-9000Ft; doubles 3000-12,000Ft; triples 4600-14,500Ft; quads 4600-15,000Ft.) **IBUSZ,** Oroszlán u. 3, arranges **private rooms** in flats. (☎/fax 471 177. Open M-F 9am-6pm, Sa 9am-1pm. 3000-3500Ft; additional 30% charge for stays fewer than 4 nights.) **University dorms** are generally the cheapest option, but are only available in July and August.

Família Panzió, Szentháromság u. 71 (☎441 122; www.familiapanzio.hu), near the train station. This clean and comfortable family-run pension is a 15min. walk from the center; buses and trams run by regularly. Breakfast 800Ft. Singles with bath 6000Ft; doubles 6000-9000Ft; triples 9000-12,000Ft; quads 10,000-13,000Ft. Cash only. ❸

Hotel Tisza, Wesselényi 6 (☎478 278; www.tiszahotel.hu). In the historical center of town, this elegant 1886 hotel was once a haunt of the artistic elite: Bartók performed in its concert hall and Hungarian writers frequented its restaurant. Today, it offers spacious, intricately-designed rooms. Breakfast included. Reception 24hr. Singles 8900Ft, with baths 11,900 Ft; doubles 12,900/13,900Ft; triples 15,900Ft. MC/V. ❹

Loránd Eötvös Kollégium, Tisza Lajos krt. 103 (☎544 124; eotvos@petra.hos.u-szeged.hu). On your way out of town, the hostel is to the left of Hero's Gate. The entrance is hidden from the street, to the left of the restaurant. Cheap, centrally located dorms with mosquito-proof screens and clean bathrooms. Pleasant and well lit. Laundry service included. Call ahead. Open July-Aug. Singles 1000Ft; doubles 2100Ft. ❶

Teleki Blanka Kollégium, Semmelweis u. 5 (☎546 088). University dorm quads share clean bathrooms. Bring toilet paper, available at Rossmann on Klauzál tér. 2000Ft. ❶

FOOD

Not only is Szeged the paprika capital of Hungary, it is also home to the country's finest lunchmeats, courtesy of the local Pick Salami Factory. Don't miss the *halászlé* (spicy soup made with fresh Tisza fish). Keep in mind that it is taboo to order water with your soup, as it dilutes the paprika flavor; wine and beer are better matches anyway. The **CBA Supermarket,** Szentháromság u. 39, provides snacks. (Open M-Sa 6am-8pm, Su 7am-noon. MC/V.) The daily **open-air market,** with meat and fruits, is opposite the bus station.

■ **Roosevelt téri Halászcsárda,** Roosevelt tér 14 (☎424 111), next to the river. Aromatic waves of paprika wash over you as waiters carry out steaming vats of soup. Savor the famously spicy *szegedi halászlé* (1500Ft) or any of the *hallé* dishes (fish soup; 1100-1600Ft), heated with green paprika. View of Belvárosi híd. English menu. Entrees 610-2500Ft. Vegetarian options. Open daily 11am-11pm. MC/V. ❸

Port Royal, Stefánia 4 (☎547 988), to the right of the Móra Ferenc Museum. This ship-themed restaurant specializes in "lava rock grilling," a process in which gravy is steamed with meat. Live jazz almost every night; outdoor performances in summer. Great vegetarian options. Entrees 600-2450Ft. Open M-Th and Su 11am-midnight, F-Sa 11am-2am. Bar open M-Th and Su 11am-11pm; F-Sa 11am-midnight. AmEx/MC/V. ❸

Roxy Cafe and Pizzeria, Deák Ferenc u. 24 (☎423 496). Serves pizza (600-980Ft) and pasta (550-700Ft) to Szeged's hippest students in a cellar lined with retro movie posters. A perfect post-party, pre-hangover stop. Open M 10am-4pm, Tu-Th 10am-midnight, F-Sa 10am-2am, Su noon-midnight. Cash only. ❷

Vár Gyorsétterem, Vár u. 4. The speed and prices of fast food without the compromise in taste. A large, sit-down restaurant with an exhaustive menu, including spaghetti (550Ft), pizza (470-1350Ft), hamburgers (300Ft), and gyros (470-620Ft). Down a quick beer (190-330Ft) at the bar while you wait. Open M-Th 8am-midnight, F 8am-2am, Sa 11am-2am, Su 11am-10pm. Cash only. ❷

🄶 SIGHTS

◪ NEW SYNAGOGUE (ÚJ ZSINAGÓGA). Perhaps the most beautiful in Hungary, this 1903 synagogue is an awesome display of craftmanship and style, with Moorish altars and gardens, Romanesque columns, Gothic domes, and Baroque facades. The brilliant blue stained-glass cupola sheds light on the vestibule walls, which are lined with the names of the 3100 congregation members killed in Nazi death camps. Today's small Jewish community still worships here. *(Jósika u. 8. From Széchényi tér, walk away from the river on Híd u. past Bartók tér; turn left on Jósika. Synagogue is on the left. Open M-F and Su 10am-noon and 1-5pm. Closed to visitors on holy days, though worshippers are welcome at services. Men must wear hats. 250Ft, students 100Ft.)*

MÓRA FERENC MUSEUM. Exhibits in this eclectic riverside museum describe Szeged's history and its love-hate relationship with the Tisza River, which both fueled its growth and, in 1879, destroyed the city with a flood. Fascinating displays feature everything from archaeological digs to modern city plans. The permanent exhibit "They Called Themselves Avars" includes among its artifacts two corpses buried in a double grave. *(Roosevelt tér 1/3. ☎549 040. Open Tu-Su July-Sept. 10am-6pm; Oct.-June 10am-5pm. 400Ft, students with ISIC 200Ft.)*

VOTIVE CHURCH (FOGADALMI TEMPLOM). The dual clock towers of this unusual neo-Romanesque red-brick church pierce the skyline. The church houses a 9040-pipe organ that is used for occasional afternoon concerts. Inside you'll also find János Fadrusz's acclaimed sculptural masterpiece, "Christ on the Cross." The 12th-century **Demetrius Tower** (Dömötör torony) is all that remains of the original church that stood on this site. On the walls surrounding the church, in bright colors with gold trim, is the **National Pantheon,** which portrays Hungary's great political, literary, and artistic figures. *(Dóm tér. Open M-W and F-Sa 8am-5:30pm, Th noon-5:30pm, Su noon-5:30pm. Free guided tours daily 11am and 2pm; English tours available. Shoulders must be covered. 400Ft, students 250Ft; Su and after 5pm free. Tower open briefly M-F 11am and 3:30pm, Sa-Su 3:30pm. 600Ft, students 400Ft.)*

OTHER SIGHTS. The yellow **Town Hall,** reshingled with red-and-green tiles after the devastating 1879 flood, overlooks grassy Széchényi tér. The bridge joining the bright building to the drab former tax office next door was built so Emperor Franz Joseph wouldn't have to take the stairs. *(Széchényi tér 10.)* The 1778 **Serbian Orthodox Church** (Szerb templom) features impressive artwork. The iconostasis holds 80 paintings in interwoven gold frames, and reaches up to a ceiling covered by a starry fresco of God creating the Earth. *(Somogyi u. 3a.* ☎*325 278. Opened by request at the green door of the building opposite. 150Ft, students 100Ft.)* **Hero's Gate** (Hősök kapuja), actually a short tunnel, was erected in 1936 as a memorial to the soldiers who died in WWI. Two plaster soldiers guard the gate, while a mural of Jesus guiding soldiers during battle decorates the underside of the archway. *(Start at Dóm tér and head away from the center to reach the gate, in Aradi vértanúk tere.)*

🎵 ENTERTAINMENT

The **Szeged Open Air Festival,** from early July to late August, is Hungary's largest outdoor performance event. International troupes perform dances, operas, and musicals in the courtyard at Dugonics tér 2. Buy tickets (1500-12,000Ft) at Tourinform (see **Orientation and Practical Information,** p. 344) or Kelemen u. 7. (☎716 717; open M-F 10am-5pm). Other festivals fill the streets from spring to autumn. The mid-July **beer festival,** the **wine festival,** and the **jazz jamboree** are all popular. **Swimming pools** and **baths** line the **Partfürdő Strand;** from Szeged, cross the Belváros bridge and walk left along the river. Most pools and baths are open daily and charge 300-600Ft. Over the bridge from Szeged and to the left is a small **beach** and swimming area. **Bike paths** line the streets, and you can **kayak** on the Tisza River. To rent equipment, contact **Vízisporttelep** at Felső-Tisza part 4 (☎425 574).

🏙 NIGHTLIFE

For a city of moderate size, Szeged has a lot of cosmopolitan know-how. Many of the restaurants and cafes that line the streets convert into popular nightspots after dark, just as the city's bars and clubs are beginning to open their doors.

▓ Grand Cafe, Deák Ferenc u. 18, 3rd fl. (☎420 578), through an inconspicuous door. Start your night at this intimate cafe, which screens 3 art films each evening. Sip coffee or red wine (550Ft) as you watch a film, or relax to mellow jazz in the coffee shop. Films daily 5, 7, and 9pm. Open Sept.-July M-F 3pm-midnight, Sa-Su 5pm-midnight.

Coco Club, Híd u. 6 (☎552 882; www.cococlub.hu). What seems like a refined cafe upstairs opens up into a destination for clubbers down below. The suave red leather seating alongside the 2 extensive bars (mixed drinks from 890Ft) widens to a dance floor at the back. Cover 600Ft. Open M-F 7am-6am, Sa noon-6am.

Sing-Sing Music Hall (www.sing.hu), on Mars tér, C Pavilion, on the street to the left as you face the bus station. DJ turns popular beats for a ready-to-rave crowd of scantily clad local demons. 0.5L Amstel 500Ft. Cover around 500Ft. Open W-Sa 10pm-dawn.

Not Cafe, Római krt. u. 38 (☎696 109). An eclectic crowd frequents this popular brick-lined gay club, which often draws a mixed crowd. F-Sa go-go boys. Cover F-Sa 600Ft after 11pm. Cafe open daily 2-9pm. Disco open daily 9pm-late.

HB Bajor Serfőzde (Beer House), Deák Ferenc u. 4 (☎420 394), in the city center. A major sponsor of the annual beer festival, this no-nonsense pub has great snacks. Beer from 400Ft. Open M-Th 11:30am-11pm, F-Sa 11:30am-midnight, Su 11:30am-4pm.

HORTOBÁGY ☎(0)52

Europe's largest open pasture region, Hungary's central plain is home to some of the continent's most ancient species of cattle, birds, and fish. Much of the land is part of **Hortobágy National Park,** which is a UNESCO World Heritage site. A long-

A FESTIVAL A DAY

One of the joys of city-hopping in southern Hungary during the summer, I was surprised to find, is that the festival scene is almost always in full swing. On my first day back on the road after a two-week stint in Budapest, I was expecting a mellow evening far from the hectic pace of city life. But as I wandered the streets in the town of Kecskemét, I quickly discovered that it was anything but quiet—a raucous rock band had taken thte stage in the main square, cranking out power ballads to a packed crowd. Everybody in town seemed to be out to nod along to the music and to down ice cream from the stands set up throughout the park.

When I arrived in Pécs two days later, the festival scene only picked up. I stumbled on the Pécs Weeks of Art and Gastronomy, a festival celebrating regional crafts and cuisine. The street was lined with stalls cooking up meals on the spot. At one, the smell of some unidentifiable meat wafted up from a smoky skillet; at the next, a crew of old women crafted cylinders out of dough before baking them over an open flame and coating them in a sugar glaze. *Kurtos*, I learned as I happily tasted the wares, was the name of this sweet pastry.

At the end of this tempting row of makeshift wine cellars and candy shops, the street widened into a square beneath the cathedral, where a huge crowd was standing inspiration to Hungarian artists, the expanse sprawls over 72 sq. mi. of Hungary's central plain, making it the largest continuous natural grassland in Europe. Home to ancient indigenous animals like the Hungarian gray longhorn cattle, spiral-horned "Racka" sheep, and Nonius horses, the park is also a birdwatcher's paradise, as over 340 species of birds travel through each year.

Walks, hikes, and **cycling tours** are possible with admission. Most **trails** are clearly marked, and info boards are in a variety of languages. (Open daily Apr. 15-Oct. 15 9am-5pm; Oct. 15-Dec. 10am-4pm. 900Ft per day, students 300Ft per day. English guided tours 3300Ft.) For info, contact the Hortobágy or Debrecen Tourinform. In town, the famous **Nine-Hole Bridge** (*Kilene-lyuku hid*), an enduring symbol of the plain, crosses the River Tisza. Built in 1827 and named for its nine large arches, the white stone bridge connected Budapest to Debrecen and served as an important military and postal route. No longer a residence for weary travelers, the stucco **Hortobágy Csárda** (see below) was built in 1699, and, with its trademark windows, typifies plains architecture. The **Pasztormuzeum** across the street has a variety of traditional tools and costumes, most notably the heavy cloaks of the shepherds. (Open daily 9am-6pm. 250Ft, children 150Ft.)

Search for **private rooms** at Tourinform (see below). **Puszta Camping ❶,** behind Tourinform, offers spacious bungalows on the Puszta River. (☎369 300. Bungalows 1250Ft per person. Electricity 450Ft. Tax 250Ft.) **Hortobágy Fogadó ❸,** 1 Kossuth u., offers spare, though sizable, rooms with TV and private bath. (☎369 137. Singles 3500Ft; doubles 6000Ft; triples 9000Ft; quads 1200Ft.) If you're hungry, head downstairs to the simple but satisfying **Fogadó Étterem ❷** for some filling goulash soup (500 Ft). The terrace of the animal skull-lined **Hortobágy Csárda ❸,** Petőfi tér 2, across from Tourinform, looks out on the Nine-Hole Bridge. (☎369 144. Local dishes 700-2000Ft. Open daily mid-Feb. to Oct. 9am-9pm. MC/V.) Buy food at **ABC Coop,** Kossuth u. 6. (Open M-F 7am-6pm, Sa 7am-3pm, Su 7-11am.)

The **train station,** Kossuth u. 10, is five minutes from town. **Trains** run to: Debrecen (1hr., 10 per day, 404Ft); Eger (2hr., 2 per day, 698Ft); Füzesabony (1¼hr., 7 per day, 610Ft); Tsizafüred (45min., 1 per day, 395Ft). To reach the park, begin with your back to the station, follow **Kossuth u.** through town, and go right on Route 33 (45min.). Take the first right after crossing the Nine-Hole Bridge and follow the road until it ends. Turn right and continue ¾ mi. to the circular drive. The **ticket stand** and park entrance are on the left. **Tourinform,** Peófi tér 1, shares a building with

Pasztomuzeum, which sells **maps** (200Ft) and books rooms. (☎589 321. Open June 16-Sept. 15 M-F 8am-5pm, Sa-Su 9am-5pm; Sept. 16-June 15 M-F 8am-4pm.) The **post office,** Kossuth u. 2, has **currency exchange** and an **ATM;** there's a telephone outside. (☎369 001. Open M-F 8am-noon and 12:20-4pm.) The **pharmacy** across the street, **Fekete Gólya Gyógyszertár,** Kossuth u. 3, stocks a variety of products. (☎369 141. Open M-F 10am-noon and 12:20-4pm.)

KECSKEMÉT   ☎(06)76

Surrounded by vineyards, fruit groves, and dusty *puszta* (plains), Kecskemét (KETCH-keh-mate; pop. 110,000) lures tourists with a lush central square, famous *barackpálinka* (apricot brandy), and the musical genius of native composer Zoltán Kodály (1882-1967). While it resembles other large Hungarian towns, Kecskemét stands out for its many festivals and its proximity to Bugacpuszta, for which it serves as a convenient base.

⌐ ⌑ TRANSPORTATION AND PRACTICAL INFORMATION. The **train station** is on Kodály Zoltán tér, at the end of Rákóczi út. To: Budapest (2hr.; 15 per day; 946Ft, InterCity 1276Ft); Pécs (5hr., 13 per day, 2888Ft) via Kiskunfélegyháza; Szeged (1¼hr., 14 per day, 888Ft). **Buses** run from the **bus station,** just around the corner from the train station on Kodály Zoltán tér, to: Budapest (1hr., many per day, 1323Ft); Pécs (5hr., 3 per day, 1992Ft); Szeged (1¾hr., 12 per day, 1090Ft). The **Volán** bus terminal, for local routes, is a block from Kossuth tér; turn right from the terminal on Sík S. u. Timetables are posted at stops. Buses stop running around 10pm. Tickets are 132Ft from kiosks, 180Ft from drivers.

Most sights are within walking distance. The town surrounds a loosely connected string of squares. The largest, **Szabadság tér** (Liberty Square), is ringed by three squares, **Kossuth tér, Kálvin tér,** and **Széchényi tér.** To get to Szabadság from the train or bus station, go left, then continue to a right on Rákóczi út. Follow the street for 10min. **Tourinform,** Kossuth tér 1, has **free maps,** arranges accommodations, and provides events info. (Open July-Aug. M-F 9am-6pm, Sa-Su 9am-1pm; Sept.-June M-F 8am-5pm). **OTP,** Szabadság tér 1/a, at Arany János u., **exchanges currency** at good rates and cashes **traveler's checks** for no commission. (24hr. MC/V **ATM** outside. Open M 7:45am-5pm, Tu-F 7:45am-4pm.) The **pharmacy, Mátyás Király Gyógyszertár,** is at Szabadság tér 1. (Open M-F 7:30am-8pm, Sa 8am-4pm, Su 8am-2pm). For **Internet,** go to **DataNet,** Kossuth tér 6-7 in the shopping plaza. (5Ft per min. Open M-F 8am-10pm,

gathered listening to live music. The first night I heard a doo-wop-esque rock band in matching blue-striped suits. When I retuned the next evening, I caught the end of a performance by a drum quintent, playing complex rhythms on large plastic vats.

For me, festivals were the best way to get a taste (literally and figuratively) of local life. So head to southern Hungary in the summer—or anywhere besides Budapest at any time of year—and you'll never know what you might encounter.

Some of the many festivals that enliven the towns of rural Hungary throughout the year with music, dance, theater, film and folk culture include: the **Pécs Weeks of Art and Gastronomy** (late June-early July); the **Szeged Open Air Festival** (July-Aug.) and the **Thealter** alternative theater festival (end of July); the **Békéscsaba Sausage Festival** (Oct.), the **Gyula Castle Theatre Festival** (July-Aug.); the **Kecskemét Spring Festival** (Mar.), **Animation Film Festival** (late June), and the **International Kodaly Festival** (mid-July-Aug.); the **Szentendre Summer and Theater** festival (July-Aug.; the **Esztergom Castle Theatre Festival** (June-Aug.); and the **Hódmezővásárhely Saint George Day Shepherd Contest** (Sept.). For more information, consult www.artsfestivals.hu or www.hungarytourism.hu.

—*Amelia Atlas*

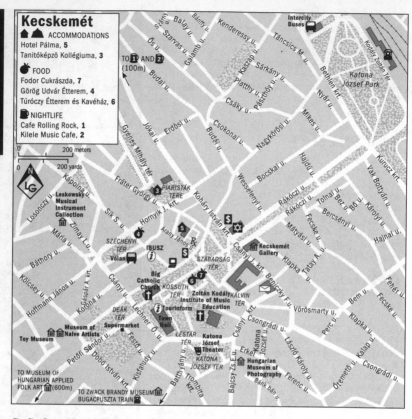

Sa-Su 9am-10pm.) The **post office** is at Kálvin tér 10/12. (Open M-F 8am-7pm, Sa 8am-1pm.) **Postal Code:** 6000.

█▐█ ACCOMMODATIONS AND FOOD. Dorm rooms and pensions are generally the best deals in town. **Hotel Pálma ❸,** Arany János u. 3, in the heart of the city, has rooms with full baths and beachy decor. (☎321 045. Singles 5000Ft, 1st-class 6500Ft; doubles 7000/8500Ft; triples 8000/9500Ft; quads 8600Ft.) **Tanítóképző Kollégiuma** (Teachers' College) ❶, Piaristák tere 4, five minutes from Kossuth tér, rents good-sized triples and quads on a per-person basis, but be prepared to brave curtainless showers. (☎486 977. Call 1-2 days ahead. 2000Ft, students 1600Ft.) Kecskemét is famous for its apricot *barackpálinka* (brandy), distilled from apricot. The **Coop Supermarket,** Deák tér 6, has a drugstore and cafe. (☎481 711. Market open M-F 6:30am-6:30pm, Sa 6:30am-noon.) ▓**Túróczy Étterem és Kaveház ❸,** Szabadság tér 2, serves Hungarian specialties in a plush, quiet atmosphere overlooking the main square. (☎509 175. Entrees 1250-4100Ft. Open M-Sa 8am-11pm, Su 8am-9pm. MC/V.) Try **Fodor Cukrászda ❶,** Szabadság tér 2, for dessert (100-450Ft) or ice cream. (Open M-F 9am-6:30pm, Sa-Su 9am-8:30pm). **Görög Udvár Étterem ❸,** Hornyik J. krt. 1, sells souvlaki, gyros, and veggie pitas in a Greek-style setting tucked into an outdoor courtyard. (☎426 513. Entrees 1000-2300Ft. Open daily 11am-11pm.)

◎ 🏛 SIGHTS AND MUSEUMS. The salmon-colored **Town Hall,** Kossuth tér 1, dominates the main square. (☎513 513. For a tour, register ahead at Tourinform. Tours M-Th 7:30am-4pm, F-Sa 7:30am-1:30pm. 300Ft.) Next door, the **Big Catholic Church,** the largest Baroque cathedral on the Great Plain, has marble columns and intricate ceiling frescoes. (Open daily 9am-noon and 3-6pm.) From the entrance on the right, climb the **tower** for a good view. (Open daily July-Aug. 10am-10pm; Sept.-June 10am-8pm. Groups only. 200Ft, students 100Ft.) At stalls in the square, vendors sell arts and souvenirs. The cupola-topped **Synagogue,** Rákóczi u. 2, is no longer used for worship, but boasts 15 fake Michelangelo sculptures and, strangely, a ground-floor bar. (☎487 611. Open M-F 10am-4pm.) At the **Leskowsky Musical Instrument Collection,** Zimay u. 6/a, Albert Leskowsky offers a one-hour concert and lesson with various musical instruments drawn from the large collection. (☎483 820. Call ahead. 500Ft, students 300Ft.)

At the ◪ **Zwack Fruit Brandy Distillery and Exhibition,** Matkói u. 2, over 15 tons of apricots are turned into *barackpálinka* each day. Tour the bottling lines where the famous brandy is prepared. (☎487-711. Open M-F to groups of 10 or more, Sa-Su to groups of 20 or more. Individuals can call ahead or join a F 1pm group. 1350Ft.) The **Hungarian Museum of Photography** (Magyar Fotográfiai Múzeum), Katona tér 12, displays a poignant collection of 19th-century photographic portraits and lithographs. (☎483 221; www.fotomuzeum.hu. Open W-Su 10am-4pm. 200Ft, students 100Ft.) The **Museum of Applied Folk Art** (Népi Iparmüvészet Múzeuma), Serfözö u. 19, has an extensive collection of costumes, furniture, ceramics, whips, and wood and bone carvings. Follow Petőfí Sándor u. from the center, turn left on Maria krt., and then left again on Serfözö u. (☎/fax 327 203. English guide 50Ft. Open Tu-Sa 10am-5pm. 200Ft, students 100Ft.) Once a boarding house with a casino and ballroom, the **Kecskemét Gallery** (Kecskeméti Képtár), Rákóczi u. 1, features works by local artists. The colorful building is an attraction in itself. (☎480 776. Open Tu-Su 10am-5pm. 300Ft, students 150Ft.)

🌿 🎭 FESTIVALS AND NIGHTLIFE. Festivals are held most weekends in Kecskemét. The **Kodaly Music Festival** remembers the famous composer through a series of concerts. March welcomes the **Kecskemét Spring Festival,** featuring music, theater, and literary readings. In late summer, regional food, music, and dance take over the town during the **Hírös Week Festival.** Shakespeare may lose something in translation, but the elegant stage at the **József Katona Theater** (Színház), Katona tér 5, lends grace to any script. (☎483 283; www.katonaj.hu. Box office open Sept.-June M-F 10am-7pm. Tickets from 1300Ft.) The city is generally quiet at night if there aren't performances in the main square, but **Cafe Rolling Rock,** Jókai u. 44, draws locals to its dance floor and bar. (☎506 190. Open W-Sa 6pm-1am.) An adult crowd relaxes to live jazz at the **Kilele Music Cafe,** Jókai u. 34. (☎418 813. Open M-F 5pm-1am, Sa 6pm-4am, Su 6pm-midnight.)

🔽 DAYTRIP FROM KECSKEMÉT: ◪BUGACPUSZTA. Cowboy legends abound on the Great Plain, and Bugacpuszta (BOO-gahtch-poo-stah) is the place to take in the traditions and culture of Hungary's "Wild Wild East." Don't be fooled by the appearance of the **cowboys,** who may look less than macho in their flowing white linen pants and feathered hats. These plainsmen ride without saddles: they stand up on horses galloping at full speed, and sometimes hold brimming pints of wine steadily in hand as they ride.

Bugacpuszta is the most touristed part of the **Kiskunság National Park** and the second largest *puszta* (plain) in Hungary. The 11am bus from Kecskemét is ideal, as it arrives in Bugac in time to visit the museum, see the stables, and grab a snack before the horse show. With admission, you can visit the **Shepherd's Museum,** which displays a teepee, musical instruments, and stuffed animals from the *puszta*. Then, head to the stables to see the pigs, sheep, and horses. Be sure to nab seats to the horseshow. The 30min. performance is action-packed: cowboys round up wild horses and crack their whips in synchronization. In an impressive trick, a cowboy stands with each foot on a different galloping horse and holds the reins of three others.

Take your time getting back to the entrance; the next bus won't come until 4pm. Once there, consider **Bugaci Karikás Csárda ❸,** Nagybugac 135, which serves a range of traditional Hungarian dishes and offers overnight stays in a luxurious *puszta* farmhouse. (☎575 112. Entrees 1000-2000Ft. Breakfast included. Doubles 9000Ft.) While Bugac tourism focuses on seeing horses, not riding them, there are a few opportunities to take the reins. **Táltos Reiterpension,** Nagybugac 135, offers **horseback riding** for 2000Ft per hour in the *puszta* or 1800Ft per hr. around their property. On the main road from the park, turn right and walk 150m. (☎372 633. Open daily 9am-5pm.)

Buses (45min., 3 per day, 423Ft) and trains (45min., 3 per day, 240Ft) depart from Kecskemét. The train leads to the village of Bugac, not the *puszta* 5km away. Get off the bus at the second-to-last stop, just after the bus turns left at the entrance to Bugacpuszta. From the stop, walk down the road (15-20min.) to the entrance. Take the carriage to the museum and stables (2200Ft), or continue down the path 15min. (1100Ft). Or, buy a package (4500Ft) including admission, carriage ride, and a full lunch at Bugaci Karikás Csárda. Horse show daily 1:15pm. Park open daily May-Oct. 10am-5pm.

LATVIA

The serenity and easy charm of Latvia belie centuries of suffering. The country has been conquered and reconquered so many times that the year 2004 was only the 35th year of Latvian independence—ever. These days, Latvia's vibrant capital, Rīga, is under siege by a new force: tourism. Cheap flights have brought so many Western visitors that the Rīga Old Town can feel like one big British bachelor party on summer weekends. You don't have to wander far from the beaten path, though, to discover the allure of Rīga's art nouveau elegance and student nightlife, the stunning seacoast, and the untamed beauty of Gaujas Valley National Park..

 DISCOVER LATVIA: SUGGESTED ITINERARIES

THREE DAYS Settle into **Rīga** (p. 359) to enjoy stunning **art nouveau** architecture, **cafe culture,** and the best **music and performing arts** scene in the Baltics. Daytrip to **Rundāle Palace** (p. 370).

ONE WEEK Begin your Latvian tour in seaside **Liēpaja** (2 days; p. 372). After three days in **Rīga,** head to **Cēsis** (2 days; p. 376) to enjoy **Cēsis Castle** and the wilds of **Gaujas Valley National Park.**

FACTS AND FIGURES

Official Name: Republic of Latvia.

Capital: Rīga.

Major Cities: Daugavpils, Rēzekne.

Population: 2,300,000. (58% Latvian, 30% Russian, 4% Belarussian, 3% Polish, 3% Ukrainian, 2% other.)

Land Area: 63,589 sq. km.

Time Zone: GMT + 2.

Language: Latvian.

Religions: Lutheran (55%), Roman Catholic (25%), Russian Orthodox (9%), Jewish (0.5%).

ESSENTIALS

WHEN TO GO

Latvia is wet year-round, with cold, snowy winters and short, rainy summers. Tourism peaks in July and August; if you'd prefer not to experience central Rīga in the company of throngs of British stag parties, late spring or early fall is the best time to visit. Much of the seacoast is delightfully untouristed even in summer.

DOCUMENTS AND FORMALITIES

EMBASSIES AND CONSULATES. Foreign embassies to Latvia are all in **Rīga** (p. 359). Latvia's embassies and consulates abroad include: **Australia,** 2 Mackennel St., East Ivanhoe, Victoria 3079, P.O. Box 23 Kew, VIC 3101 (☎9499 6920; fax 9499 7008); **Canada,** 350 Sparks St., Ste. 1200, Ottawa, ON K1R 7S8 (☎613-238-6014; embassy.canada@mfa.gov.lv); **Ireland,** "On a Clearday," Ballyedmonduff Rd., Kilternan, County Dublin, Ireland (☎1 295 41 82; fax 1 618 55 00); **UK,** 45 Nottingham Pl., London W1M 3FE (☎020 7312 0040; embassy@embassy-oflatvia.co.uk); **US,** 4325 17th St. NW, Washington, D.C. 20011 (☎202-726-8213; www.latvia-usa.org).

ENTRANCE REQUIREMENTS
Passport: Required for all travelers.
Visa: Not required for stays of under 90 days for citizens of Australia, Canada, Ireland, New Zealand, the UK, and the US.
Letter of Invitation: Not required for citizens of Australia, Canada, Ireland, New Zealand, the UK, and the US.
Inoculations: None required. Recommended up-to-date on DTaP (diphtheria, tetanus, and pertussis), Hepatitis A, Hepatitis B, MMR (measles, mumps, and rubella), Polio booster, and Typhoid.
Work Permit: Required of all foreigners planning to work in Latvia.
Driving Permit: Required for all those planning to drive in Latvia.

VISA AND ENTRY INFORMATION. Citizens of Australia, Canada, New Zealand, the UK, and the US do not need a visa for stays of up to 90 days. If you are staying longer, apply to the Department of Citizenship and Imigration for temporary residency. For special visas and residency permits, consult The Foreigners' Service Centre of the Citizenship & Migration Board, Alunàna 1, Riga, Latvia (☎721 9656; aad@pmlp.gov.lv). The best way to enter Latvia is by plane, train, or bus to Rīga.

TOURIST SERVICES AND MONEY

LATI (LS)		
AUS$1 = 0.43LS		1LS = AUS$2.31
CDN$1 = 0.47LS		1LS = CDN$2.13
EUR€1 = 0.70LS		1LS = EUR€1.43
NZ$1 = 0.40LS		1LS = NZ$2.51
UK£1 = 1.03LS		1LS = UK£0.97
US$1 = 0.57LS		1LS = US$1.76

Look for the green "i" marking official **tourist offices,** which are rather scarce. In Riga, employees of such establishments will speak fluent English, but elsewhere, they may not. Private tourist offices such as **Patricia** (see p. 363) are much more helpful. The Latvian currency unit is the **Lat (Ls),** which divides into 100 santîmi. **Inflation** averages around 2% per year. There are many MC/V **ATMs** in Rīga, and at least one or two in larger towns. Larger businesses, restaurants, and hotels accustomed to Westerners accept **MasterCard** and **Visa. Traveler's checks** are harder to use, but both AmEx and Thomas Cook checks can be converted in Rīga. It's often difficult to exchange non-Baltic currencies other than US dollars or euros.

HEALTH AND SAFETY

EMERGENCY	Police: ☎02. Ambulance: ☎03. Fire: ☎01.

Latvia was hotlisted by the World Health Organization for its periodic outbreaks of incurable varieties of tuberculosis, though none have been reported since 2000. As a precaution, drink **bottled water** (available at grocery stores and kiosks; it is often carbonated) or boil tap water before drinking. **Medical facilities** do not meet Western standards. **Pharmacies** carry tampons, condoms, and bandages. **Restrooms** are marked with an upward-pointing triangle for women, downward for men.

Foreigners in Rīga may be targets for petty theft and street assaults. **Pickpocketing** is a problem, especially in crowded areas such as markets and bus stations. At nights, beware of drunken crowds around bars and casinos. Both men and

women should avoid walking alone at night. If you feel threatened, say *"Ej prom"* (EY prawm), which means "go away"; *"Lasies prom"* (LAH-see-oos PRAWM) says it more offensively; and *"Lasies lupās"* (LAH-see-oos LAH-pahs; "go to the leaves"), is even ruder. You are more likely to find advice in English from your **consulate** than from the police. **Women** may be verbally hassled at any hour, especially if traveling alone, but usually such harassment is unaccompanied by physical action. After dark in Rīga, it is best to take a cab home. **Minorities** in Latvia are rare; they receive stares but generally experience little discrimination. **Homosexuality** is legal, but public displays of affection may result in violence. Women walk down the street holding hands, but this is strictly an indication of friendship and does not render Latvia gay-friendly. Safe options for GLBT travelers include **gay and lesbian clubs,** which advertise themselves freely in Rīga. Expect less tolerance outside the city. You can call the Latvian Gay and Lesbian Hotline at ☎ 959 2229.

TRANSPORTATION

Airlines **flying** to Latvia use the **Rīga** airport. **Air Baltic, SAS, Finnair, Lufthansa,** and others make the hop to Rīga from their hubs. **Trains** link Latvia to **Berlin, GER; Lviv, UKR; Moscow, RUS; Odessa, UKR; St. Petersburg, RUS; Tallinn, EST;** and **Vilnius, LIT. Trains** are cheap and efficient, but stations aren't well marked, so make sure to always have a map. The **commuter rail** system renders the entire country a suburb of Rīga. For daytrips from Rīga, you're best off taking the **electric train;** as a rule, a crowded train is more comfortable than a crowded bus. **Ferries** go to **Kiel** and **Lübeck, GER** and **Stockholm, SWE,** but are slow and expensive. Latvia's efficient long-distance **buses** reach **Berlin, GER; Kyiv, UKR; Moscow, RUS; Prague, CZR; Tallinn, EST; Vilnius, LIT;** and **Warsaw, POL.** Buses, usually adorned with the driver's collection of icons and stuffed animals, are quicker than trains for travel within Latvia. Beware of the standing-room-only long-distance jaunt. Road conditions in Latvia are improving after several years of deterioration. Urban and rural road conditions are generally fair. For more info, consult the **Latvian Road Administration** (www.lad.lv). **Taxis** are considered safe. Taxi stands in front of hotels charge higher rates. **Hitchhiking** is common, but drivers may ask for pay at least comparable to bus fare. *Let's Go* does not recommend hitchhiking.

KEEPING IN TOUCH

PHONE CODES	**Country code: 371. International dialing prefix:** 00. From outside Latvia, dial int'l dialing prefix (see inside back cover) + 371 + city code + local number. Within Latvia, dial city code + local number, even when dialing inside the city.

Internet is readily available in Rīga but rarer elsewhere and averages 0.5Ls per hour. Almost all **telephones** take **cards** (2, 3, or 5Ls denominations) from post offices, telephone offices, kiosks, and state stores. If a number is six digits, dial a 2 before it; if it's seven, you needn't dial anything before it. To call abroad from an analog phone, dial 1, then 00, then the country code. If it's digital, dial 00, then the country code. Phone offices and *Rīga in Your Pocket* have the latest info on changes to the phone system. **International calls** can be made from telephone offices or booths. International access codes include **AT&T Direct** (☎800 2288) and **MCI WorldPhone** (☎800 8888). Ask for *gaisa pastu* to send something by **airmail**. The standard rate for a letter to Europe is 0.30Ls, to anywhere else 0.40Ls; for a postcard 0.20/0.30Ls. **Mail** can be received through **Poste Restante**. Address envelopes: Neasa (First name) COLL (LAST NAME), POSTE RESTANTE, Stacijas laukums 1 (post office address), LV-1050 (postal code), Rīga (city), LATVIA.

ACCOMMODATIONS AND CAMPING

LATVIA	①	②	③	④	⑤
ACCOMMODATIONS	under 8Ls under €12 under US$14	8-14Ls €12-20 US$14-24	15-19Ls €22-27 US$26-33	20-24Ls €28-34 US$34-42	over 24Ls over €34 over US$42

There is one HI hostel in Rīga and a scattering of **hostels** around the beaches. Beware of large and raucous British stag parties' occupation of such hostels, especially on summer weekends. Contact the **Latvian Youth Hostel Association,** Aldaru 8, Rīga LV-1050 (☎921 8560; www.hostellinglatvia.com), for more info. **College dormitories** are often the cheapest option, but are open to travelers only in the summer. Rīga's array of **hotels** satisfies any budget. Most small towns outside the capital have at most one hotel in the budget range; expect to pay 3-15Ls per night. **Campgrounds** exist in the countryside, but camping beyond marked areas is illegal.

FOOD AND DRINK

LATVIA	①	②	③	④	⑤
FOOD	under 2Ls under €3 under US$4	2-3Ls €3-4 US$4-5	4-5Ls €6-7 US$7-9	6-7Ls €9-10 US$11-12	over 7Ls over €10 over US$12

Latvian food is heavy and starchy—and therefore delicious. Cities offer foreign, **kosher,** and **vegetarian** cuisine. Tasty specialties include *maizes zupa* (soup made from cornbread, currants, and cream), and the warming *Rīgas* (or *Melnais*) *balzams* (a black liquor). Dark rye bread is a staple. Try *speķa rauši*, a warm pastry, or *biezpienmaize*, bread with sweet curds. Dark-colored *kaņepju sviests* (hemp butter) is good but too diluted for "medicinal" purposes. A particularly good Latvian beer is *Porteris*, from the Aldaris brewery.

LIFE AND TIMES

HISTORY

INVASION. Like her Baltic sisters, Latvia has often struggled under the yoke of foreign rule. The Germans arrived in the late 12th century to convert the locals to Christianity. In 1237, the Teutonic Knights established the **Confederation of Livonia,** which ruled a territory that included present-day Latvia and Estonia for nearly 300 years. When Russian Tsar **Ivan IV** (the Terrible) invaded, the confederation collapsed, beginning the 25-year **Livonian War** (1558-83) and a half-century of partition.

SWEDISH INTERLUDE. The 1629 **Truce of Altmark** brought a long period of relative stability and freedom known as the **Swedish Interlude,** achieved by ceding control of eastern Livonia to the Poles and giving Rīga and the northern regions to Sweden. Sweden, however, was forced to grant the Livonian territories to **Peter the Great** under the 1721 Peace of Nystad, and with the 3rd partition of Poland in 1795 the entire country fell under Russian control. The Latvian peasantry, which became prosperous after the **abolition of serfdom** in 1861, continued to struggle for freedom from the Russian empire during the 19th century. **Nationalism** flared with particular strength during the Russian Revolution of 1905.

THE WAR YEARS. Reacting to the Bolshevik coup of November 1917, the **Latvian People's Council** proclaimed independence on November 18, 1918, establishing a government in Rīga led by **Kārlis Ulmanis.** The **Constitution of 1922** created a republic governed by a president and a unicameral parliament, but the large number of political parties in the legislature, or **Saeima,** kept the political situation unstable. Ulmanis encountered problems when German elements within Latvia became sympathetic to the Nazi party, and in 1934 he declared a state of emergency. Under the **Nazi-Soviet Nonaggression Pact,** Latvia fell under Soviet control in 1939. However, Germany reneged on the Pact and occupied Latvia in 1941, only to be driven back in 1945 by the Red Army, which annexed its smaller neighbor.

SUPREMELY SOVIET. Latvia entered the **Soviet Union** as one of its wealthiest and most industrialized regions. Under Soviet rule, the state was torn by radical economic restructuring, political repression, and the Russification of its national culture. Some 35,000 Latvians, including many members of the intelligentsia, were deported to Russia during the first year of the occupation, as immigrants poured in from the rest of the USSR. Foreigners soon dominated local politics, and within four decades ethnic Latvians accounted for only half the population.

FREE AT LAST. Under *glasnost* and *perestroika*, Latvians protested *en masse* against the Communist regime and created the **Popular Front** in 1988. Faced with competition, the Communists were trounced in the 1990 elections. On May 4, 1990, the new legislature declared independence, but Soviet intervention sparked violent clashes in Rīga in 1991. Following the failed Moscow coup in August, the Latvian legislature reasserted independence.

TODAY

HOW LATVIA IS RULED. A parliamentary democracy, Latvia has a unicameral **parliament,** the 100-seat Saeima (Supreme Council). The **president,** who appoints a **prime minister,** is elected by this body for a three-year term and is advised by a cabinet. Latvia, which is divided into 26 counties and seven municipalities, has over 20 political parties; most governments are formed by coalition.

ON THE MENU

THE SLEEPING WOLF

Order yourself a shot of Latvia's national liquor, *balsam,* for a refreshing, head-clearing experience. The strong black liquid, usually taken only in mixed drinks, is crafted from an 18th-century recipe with more than 24 ingredients. A combination of roots, berries, and flowers, the drink is aged in oak barrels, which help to foster its bittersweet taste. Black *balsam* is rumored to have cured the illnesses of Catherine the Great, but health benefits from large quantities are unlikely. Try a sip or take it in one of many mixed drinks, often with cola, lemon juice, or soda. Hot drinks prepared with the liquor are especially popular during cold, dark winter days. Bring home a bottle of the stuff and try these recipes:

Balsam Black Currant
1 measure Black Balsam
3 measures black currant juice
grenadine to taste

Innocent Balsam
1 measure Black Balsam
2 measures ice-cream
2 measures peach juice

Sleeping Wolf
1 measure Black Balsam
1 tablespoon honey
3 measures milk
1 yolk
Heat balsam, honey, and milk together. Add yolk and mix it up with a blender.

CURRENT EVENTS. Along with her two Baltic sisters, Latvia solidified her relationship with the West by becoming a member of the **European Union (EU)** and **NATO** in 2004. Latvian relations with both **Russia** and the large Russian minority at home remain thorny. Tensions have flared over a 2005 law requiring schools to conduct lessons mainly in Latvian, even for Russian-speaking children. Internal politics remain turbulent, with numerous parties, including the **For Fatherland and Freedom Party,** the **People's Party,** and the **Latvian Way Party,** jockeying for position in the Saeima. After Europe's first Green Party leader, **Indulis Emsis,** resigned in 2004 after losing a budget vote, **Aigars Kalvītis** became prime minister of a four-party center-right coalition government. Such rapid political turnovers, spurred in part by conflict over the pace of privatization of large government holdings in telecommunications and energy, have caused delays in economic reform. Current president **Vaira Vike-Freiberga,** the first woman to hold such a post in Eastern Europe, was elected in June 1999 and was re-elected in 2003.

PEOPLE AND CULTURE

Nearly 30% of the country's population is **Russian,** leaving a bare 57% ethnic Latvian majority. **Belarussians** constitute a sparse 4% portion, and **Poles** and **Ukrainians** combined make up an additional 5%. Latvia has one of the lowest birth rates in the world. A majority of ethnic Latvians are **Evangelical Lutherans.** Sizable **Roman Catholic** and **Russian Orthodox** minorities are also present. Heavily influenced by German, Russian, Estonian, and Swedish, **Latvian** is one of two languages (the other is Lithuanian) in the Baltic language group. Life, however, proceeds bilingually. **Russian** is acceptable and widespread in Rīga; it is still spoken in the countryside, but its popularity is waning. Many young Latvians study **English;** the older set knows some **German.** Restaurant customers should **tip** 5-10%. Expect to be bought a drink if you talk with someone for a while; repay the favor in kind. If you're invited to a meal in someone's home, bring a **gift** for the hostess (an odd number of flowers is customary). **Handshaking** is expected when meeting new people or greeting a friend. **Shops** sometimes close for a break between noon and 3pm.

THE ARTS

The mid-19th century brought a national awakening as the country asserted its literary independence in works such as *Lāčplēsis (Bearslayer),* **Andrējs Pumpurs's** 1888 national epic. Realism and social protest became important in the **New Movement** in the late 19th century. Writer **Jānis Rainis** used folk imagery to critique contemporary problems. **Aleksandrs Čaks** detailed everyday life and gave a haunting account of WWI. Many Latvian writers turned to psychological detail in the 20th century. **Anslavs Eglitis** reveled in intensifying human traits to the point of absurdity. Following WWII the Soviets imposed **Socialist Realism,** mandating that texts promote revolutionary ideals. **Jānis Medenis,** exiled to a Siberian labor camp, longed for a free Latvia in his poetry. **Mārtiņs Zīverts** is regarded as the best 20th-century Latvian dramatist. Using folk tradition in their late 19th-century works, **Jazeps Vitols** and **Andrejs Jurjans** became the country's first composers.

Contemporary painter **Miervaldis Polis** has begun to enjoy international acclaim for his hyper-realist art and is best known for *A Golden Man.* The **International Chamber Choir Festival,** held each September in Rīga, commemorates the choral appreciation and religious allusions of Latvian music. **Rīga** is the **art nouveau** capital of Europe, with blocks upon blocks of buildings designed in this style.

HOLIDAYS AND FESTIVALS

Holidays: New Year's Day (Jan. 1); Good Friday (Apr. 14, 2006; Apr. 6, 2007); Easter Holiday (Apr. 16, 2006; Apr. 8 2007); Labor Day (May 1); Ligo Day (June 23); St. John's Day (June 24); Independence Day (Nov. 18); Christmas (Dec. 25); Boxing Day (Dec. 26); New Year's Eve (Dec. 31).

Festivals: Midsummer's eve is celebrated across the Baltic states every June 23-24. An updated calendar of cultural events is available at http://latviatourism.lv.

ADDITIONAL RESOURCES

Baltic Revolution: Estonia, Latvia, Lithuania and the Path to Independence, by Anatol Lieven (1994). A solid background to 20th-century Baltic history.

Historical Dictionary of Latvia, by Andrejs Plakans (1997). A detailed survey of Latvia's history, and an analytical view of its present situation.

Latvia in Transition, by Juris Dreifelds (1996). An excellent look at the early years of Latvian independence.

The Testimony of Lives: Narrative and Memory in Post-Soviet Latvia, by Vieda Skultans (1998). Eloquently examines the recent difficulties experienced by Latvians.

Walking Since Daybreak: A Story of Eastern Europe, World War II, and the Heart of Our Century, by Modris Eksteins (2000). Latvian-born Eksteins' unconventional history takes a personal angle in its treatment of the region's plight before and after WWII.

RĪGA ☎ 8(2)

Rīga (pop. 756,000) is the unrivaled center of Latvia's cultural and economic life and offers a spectacular setting for tourism. The city's calendar is filled with music, theater, and opera festivals, while bright costumes and colors dominate the streets during holidays and celebrations. Founded in 1201 by the German Bishop Albert, Rīga is an architectural treasure: medieval church spires dominate the Old Town, while early 20th-century art nouveau masterpieces line the city's newer streets. The split Russian and Latvian population makes for an interesting mix of languages and cultures in the clubs and restaurants and on the streets.

 The phone code in Rīga is 2 for all 6-digit numbers; there is no phone code for 7-digit numbers. Dial ☎116 for a Latvian operator and 115 for an international operator. Still confused? Call ☎800 80 08 for info or 118, 722 22 22, or 777 07 77 for directory services.

⚔ INTERCITY TRANSPORTATION

Flights: Lidosta Rīga (Rīga Airport; ☎720 70 09; www.riga-airport.com), southwest of Vecrīga. The easiest way to get to the Old Town is to take a bus (30min., about every 15min., 0.20-0.25Ls) from 13-janvara iela, at the far right side of the airport parking lot. Bus #22 goes to the south edge of the Old Town, and #22a (express) stops by the Orthodox Cathedral. A taxi to Vecrīga is 6Ls. **Air Baltic** (☎720 77 77; www.airbaltic.com) flies cheaply to many European cities, not just Baltic capitals. **Finnair** (☎720 70 10; www.finnair.com) flies to **Helsinki, FIN. Lufthansa** (☎750 77 11; www.lufthansa.com) flies to **Frankfurt** and **Munich, GER.**

Trains: Centrālā Stacija (Central Station), Stacijas laukums (☎723 31 13), next to the bus station south of the Old Town; head toward the clock tower. International trains arrive at platform 2. Most *perons* (platforms) have 2 *cels* (tracks). Open daily 4:30am-midnight. The info center at the train station charges 0.10Ls per question, but a 2nd information center (marked with a yellow "i") is located near cash desk 15 and offers free help. Open daily 8am-1pm and 2-8pm. Tickets for domestic trains can be bought from counters 1-15, to the right of the main entrance to the station. If you have trouble deciphering your ticket, ask at information to find out which platform you need to sprint to. International train tickets are sold at counters 1-6 or counter 24 beside the pricey information desk. To: **Moscow, RUS** (18hr., 2 per day, 10.60Ls); **St. Petersburg, RUS** (14hr., 1 per day, 9Ls); **Vilnius, LIT** (8hr., 2 per day on odd-numbered days, 10-14Ls). **Baltic Express** also goes to **Berlin, GER** and **Warsaw, POL.**

Buses: Autoosta (Bus Station), Prāgas 1 (☎900 00 09; www.autoosta.lv). From the train station, face the Old Town and go left 100m, crossing under the train tracks. Across the canal from the central market. Open daily 5am-midnight. To: **Kaliningrad, RUS** (9-10hr., 2 per day, 11Ls); **Kaunas, LIT** (5-6hr., 2 per day, 8Ls); **Klaipėda, LIT** (6hr., 1 per day, 8Ls); **Minsk, BLR** (12hr., 1 per day, 12Ls); **Tallinn, EST** (4-6hr., 8 per day, 5.50Ls); **Tartu, EST** (4hr., 1 per day, 5Ls); **Vilnius, LIT** (5hr., 4-6 per day, 7Ls). **Ecolines** (☎721 45 12; www.ecolines.lv) books buses to **Moscow** (17hr., 2 per day) and **Prague, CZR** (25½hr.; 1 per wk.). Book other international destinations through **Eurolines** (☎721 40 80; www.eurolines.lv).

⚔ ORIENTATION

The streets of Rīga twist, turn, and remain chaotic in their names and numbers, disorienting even the most seasoned traveler. Be patient and allow yourself to get lost—you'll discover some splendid surprises—but keep a few landmarks in mind. The city is divided in half by **Brīvības iela,** which leads from the outskirts to the **Freedom Monument** in the center and continues through Vecrīga (Old Rīga) as **Kaļķu iela.** The **Daugava** river borders Old Rīga on the west, while the smaller canal separates Old from New Rīga on the east. To reach Vecrīga from the **train station,** turn left on Marijas iela, cross the street, and go right on one of the small streets beyond the canal. If all else fails, just head toward the towering spires. **K. Valdemāra iela** cuts through Vecrīga roughly parallel to Brīvības; from the river, it passes the National Theater on the left and the Art Museum on the right. The semi-circular **Elizabetes iela** surrounds Vecrīga and its adjoining parks. *Rīga In Your Pocket* (1.20Ls), available at kiosks and travel agencies, has **maps** and up-to-date listings. Similar *Rīga This Week* is free at most major hotels and some hostels.

⚔ LOCAL TRANSPORTATION

Trains: Suburban trains, running as far as the border with Estonia at **Valka/Valga,** leave from the smaller building of the train station. The Lugaži line includes **Cēsis** and **Sigulda.** Buy same-day tickets at counters 1-15 or advance tickets in the **booking office** next to the information center to the right of counter 15 (☎583 33 97). Open daily 8am-1pm and 2-8pm. Purchase tickets on board for a 0.30Ls surcharge.

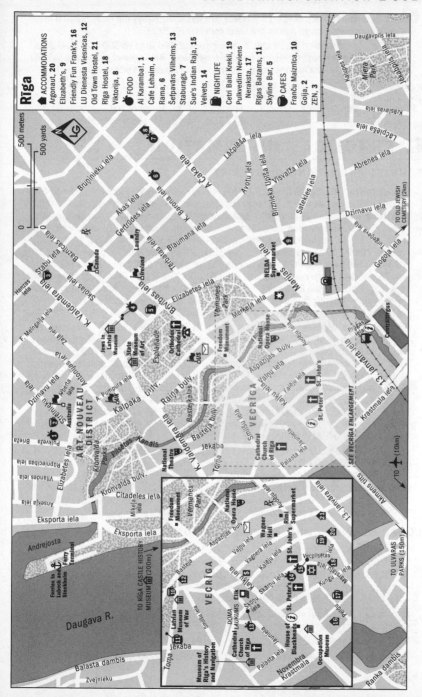

Rīga

ACCOMMODATIONS
Argonaut, 20
Elizabeth's, 9
Friendly Fun Frank's, 16
LU Dienesta Viesnicas, 12
Old Town Hostel, 21
Rīga Hostel, 18
Viktorija, 8

FOOD
Ai Karambai, 1
Cafe Lehaim, 4
Rama, 6
Šefpavārs Vilhelms, 13
Staburags, 7
Sue's Indian Raja, 15
Velvets, 14

NIGHTLIFE
Cetri Balti Krekli, 19
Pulkvedim Neviens
Neraksta, 17
Rīgas Balzams, 11
Skyline Bar, 5

CAFES
Franču Maiznica, 10
Goija, 2
ZEN, 3

LATVIA

Public Transportation: (www.ttp.lv.) **Buses, trams,** and **trolleys** run daily 5:30am-midnight. Buy tickets on board from the ticket collector (0.20Ls).

Taxis: Private taxis have a green light in the windshield. **Taxi Rīga** (☎800 10 10). 0.30Ls per km during the day; 0.40Ls per km midnight-6am. All licensed cabs have yellow license plates; be sure that the meter is turned on, or agree on a price before you leave.

Bike Rental: Gandrs, Kalnciema 28 (☎ 761 47 75; www.gandrs.lv). Take bus #22 or tram #4 or #5 from the Old Town to the intersection of Slokas and Kalnciema. From the tram stop, turn left on Kalnciema and continue 100m. Helmets and equipment available. 1Ls per hr., 5Ls per day. Open M-F 10am-7pm, Sa-Su 10am-5pm. MC/V.

🔏 PRACTICAL INFORMATION

TOURIST AND FINANCIAL SERVICES

Tourist Office: TIC, Rātslaukums 6 (☎703 43 77; www.rigatourism.com), next to the House of Blackheads and the Occupation Museum. Sells **maps** (from 1.20Ls), distributes **free maps,** and gives helpful advice in English, German, Latvian, and Russian. Open daily in high season 9am-7pm; in low season 10am-6pm. Branch, Prāgas 1 (☎722 05 55), at the intercity bus station. Open M-F 9am-7pm, Sa-Su 10am-7pm. (☎/fax 721 72 17. 1-day card 8Ls, 2-day 12Ls, 3-day 16Ls.) Branch, Smilsu 4 (☎722 46 64; www.latviatourism.lv). Provides helpful information and advice about the country. The office is less crowded than the main **TIC.** Open daily 9am-6pm. Most hotels and travel agencies sell the **Rīga Card,** which comes with a free copy of *Rīga in Your Pocket* and provides restaurant, museum, and transit discounts. However, unless you cram all of Rīga's museums into 1-2 days, the card is probably not worthwhile.

Embassies and Consulates: Australia, Alberta iela 13 (☎733 63 83; acr@latnet.lv). Open Tu 10am-noon, Th 3-5pm. **Canada,** Baznīcas 20/22. (☎781 39 45; riga@dfait-maeci.qc.ca). Open Tu and Th 10am-1pm. **Ireland,** Brīvibas iela 54. (☎702 52 59; fax 702 52 60). Entrance on Blaumana. Open M-Tu and Th-F 10am-noon. In an emergency, citizens can call or stop by M-Tu and Th-F 10am-6pm. **Russia,** Antonijas iela 2 (☎733 21 51; rusembas@delfi.lv), entrance on Kalpaka bul. Open M-F 8:30am-5:30pm. **UK,** Alunāna iela 5 (☎777 47 00; www.britain.lv). Open M-F 9:30am-noon. **US,** Raiņa bulv. 7 (☎703 62 00; www.usembassy.lv). Open M-Tu and Th 9-11:30am. US citizen services Tu-Th 2-4pm. In an emergency, citizens can stop by M and F 9-11:30am and 2-4pm or call an officer at ☎920 57 08.

Currency Exchange: At any kiosk labeled **"valutos maiņa." Unibanka,** Pils iela 23 and Valnu iela 11 (☎800 80 09; www.unibanka.lv). MC/V **cash advances** and cashes AmEx and Thomas Cook **traveler's checks** with no commission. Open M-F 9am-5pm. **Marika 24hr. currency exchange** desks are at Basteja bul. 14, Brīvibas 30 and at almost all of Rīga's casinos. **Latvia Tours,** Kaļķu iela 8 (☎708 50 01; www.latvia-tours.lv), has an AmEx representative. Open M-F 9am-7pm.

LOCAL SERVICES AND COMMUNICATIONS

Luggage Storage: At the bus station, near Eurolines office. 0.25Ls per 10kg bag for 1st hr., 0.20Ls per hr. thereafter. Open daily 6:30am-10:30pm. At the train station, under the stairs in front of the main exit. 1-1.5Ls per bag per day. Open 4:30am-midnight. At the airport, left of the exit. Arrange drop-off or retrieval using the red phone. 0.60Lt per day. Open M-Tu, Th, and Sa 4:30am-midnight; W, F, Su 5:30am-midnight.

English-Language Bookstore: Globuss, Vaļņu iela 26 (☎722 69 57). English-language classics, office supplies. Open M-F 9am-8pm, Sa 10am-7pm, Su 10am-5pm. MC/V.

GLBT Resources: Check out **www.gay.lv.**

Laundromat: Nivala, Akas iela 4 (☎728 13 46), between Ģertūdes iela and Lāčplēša iela. Self-service 3.40Ls per load. Open 24hr.

24hr. Pharmacy: Vecpilsetas Aptieka, Audeju 20 (☎721 33 40).

Telephones: A bank of public phones is located on **Brīvības,** next to the brown Laima clock. Phone booths are available throughout the city, particularly around the green space surrounding the river.

Internet: Internet cafes dot the Old Town. A centrally located option, **Elik,** Kaļķu iela 11 (☎722 70 79; www.elikkafe.lv). 47 computers, drinks, beer, and snacks. 0.50Ls per hr., 1Ls per 3hr., 3-4Ls per day. Open 24hr. Branch at Čaka iela 26 (☎728 45 06).

Post Office: Stacijas laukums 1 (☎701 88 04; www.riga.post.lv), near the train station. **Poste Restante** at window #9, or ask at any counter if window #9 is closed. Open M-F 7am-8pm, Sa 8am-6pm, Su 8am-4pm. Branches at Brīvības 19 (☎701 87 38; open M-F 7am-10pm, Sa-Su 8am-8pm) and Aspazijas bul. 24 (☎701 88 56; open M-F 8am-8pm, Sa 8am-6pm, Su 8am-4pm). **Postal Code:** LV-1050.

ACCOMMODATIONS

Lovers express their affection publicly along Rīga's streets in summer. You could tell them to get a room, but they probably can't find one. Though hostels have proliferated in Rīga, travelers should make reservations months in advance, especially in summer and on weekends. For a homestay (from 22Ls) or an apartment near the center (31-52Ls), try **Patricia,** Elizabetes iela 22. (☎728 48 68, 24hr. 721 0180; www.patriciahotel.com. Open M-F 9am-6pm, Sa-Su 11am-4pm.)

Rīga Hostel, Mārstaļu 12 (☎988 9915; www.riga-hostel.com). Head along Audēju toward the heart of the Old Town and turn left onto Mārstalu. Don't mind the "Foxy" strip club downstairs—the night bouncers are friendly. The cheapest beds in the Old Town yet maintains clean, well-decorated rooms and provides fresh sheets upon your arrival. Friendly English-speaking staff. Airport pickup or drop-off (24hr.) 4Ls. Free Internet and lockers. 4- to 12-bed dorms 6-17Ls; doubles 20Ls. Cash only. ❶

Argonaut, Kalēju 50 (☎614 7214; www.argonauthostel.com). Curiously, this hostel is also located above a strip club. Key-card door access to each room ensures security. The dorms are slightly crowded, and during summer you may share a bed with mosquitoes, but the staff is friendly and informative. Try an "Argonaut Adventure," such as bobsledding with the Latvian national team. Free Internet. 12-bed dorms from 8Ls; 8-bed dorms 10Ls; 4-bed dorms 12Ls. Prices vary by season and day of the week. MC/V. ❷

Elizabeth's, Elizabetes 101 (☎670 5476; info@youthhostel.lv). Go north on Marijas and turn left on Elizabetes; it's on the left. New wooden bunk beds and freshly painted rooms make for a soothing stay near the train station and the Old Town. Kitchen, common room, and free Internet. 14-bed dorm 8Ls, 8-bed 10Ls, 6-bed 12Ls. Cash only. ❷

Friendly Fun Frank's, Novembra krastmala 29 (☎599 06 12; www.franks.lv). From the bus and train stations, walk towards the river and go right on Novembra krastmala. Continue to the large peach building with a small koala beside the buzzer. This party hostel offers spacious dorms, a large common room, and nightly outings to pubs and clubs in Rīga. 1 free beer when you arrive. 12-bed dorms from 12Ls. Cash only. ❷

Old Town Hostel, Vaļņu iela 43 (☎722 34 06; www.rigaoldtownhostel.lv). Going toward the Old Town on K. Barona/Adeju, turn left on Valnu. With 4-12 backpackers per room, you'll get to know your fellow travelers very well. The pub downstairs helps the conversation flow freely. Kitchen, Internet, sauna (2Ls). English spoken. Lockers in rooms. Check-in noon. 12-person dorms from 10Ls, 8-person 12Ls, 4-person 14Ls. Prices vary by season, group size, and length of stay. MC/V. ❷

Viktorija, A. Čaka iela 55 (☎701 41 11; www.hotel-viktorija.lv). This 3-star hotel offers 1st-rate, renovated rooms with bathrooms and TVs. Breakfast included except in economy rooms. Unrenovated (and unadvertised) economy rooms have TVs, sinks, and

LATVIA

shared baths. If you want to save even more money, a 3rd wing of the hotel offers even cheaper rooms. Economy singles 8-12Ls, 3-star singles 30Ls; doubles 10-17/40Ls; economy triples 12-21Ls. AmEx/MC/V. ❷

LU Dienesta Viesnicas, Basteja bul. 10 (☎721 62 21; bastejahotel@inbox.lv). From bus station, cross under railroad tracks and take the pedestrian tunnel. Bear right on Aspazijas bul., which becomes Basteja bul. Enter through the Europcar Internet office. This dorm rents rooms June-Sept.; book months ahead. Ask for a student room, which has a shared bath but is larger, nicer, and cheaper than other rooms. Singles 10Ls, with bath 20Ls, student room 8Ls; doubles 16/30/12Ls; triples with bath 45Ls. ❷

🖸 FOOD

Rīga's diverse culinary offerings add flavor to the city's cosmopolitan atmosphere, particularly in the Old Town. Indian, Turkish, Spanish, Russian, and other international fare is widely available. For 24hr. food and liquor, try **Nelda,** Marijas 5. (☎722 93 55. Cash only.) The central supermarket **Rimi,** Audēju 16, stocks just about everything you could want. (☎701 80 20. Open daily 8am-10pm. MC/V.) Occupying five zeppelin hangars behind the bus station, **Centrālais Tirgus** (Central Market) is one of the largest markets in Europe. Fresh fruits and vegetables are sold in stalls outside of the main buildings. Bread, meat, and dairy are sold inside. Beware of pickpockets. (Open M and Su 8am-4pm, Tu-Sa 8am-5pm.)

🖾 **Rama,** Barona iela 56 (☎727 24 90), between Gertrudes and Stabu. Eat well for about 1Lt at this Hare Krishna cafeteria, which dishes out Indian vegetarian food. Main courses such as stewed vegetables or beet salad are sold by weight, while spicy samosas are sold individually (0.20Ls). Proceeds go to feed the poor. Open M-Sa 11am-7pm. ❶

🖾 **Šefpavārs Vilhelms,** Šķūņu iela 6. Look for the chef statue outside this pancake house that offers self-serve meat, potato, apple, banana, cheese, and plain pancakes. Slather on your fruit jam or sour cream, grab a glass of milk or yogurt, and you'll feed yourself for under 1Lt. Open M-Th 9am-10pm, F-Sa 10am-11pm, Su 10am-10pm. Cash only. ❶

Staburags, A. Čaka iela 55 (☎729 97 87). Follow A. Čaka iela away from Vecrīga. Servers in 19th-century serf costumes dish out portions fit for a tsar, including a number of seafood and potato dishes. Impressive interior features replicas of rural Latvian dwellings, complete with log tables, windmills, and miniature waterfalls. House beer 0.70Ls per 0.5L. Entrees 2-8Ls. Open daily noon-midnight. Cash only. ❷

Sue's Indian Raja, Vecpilsētas iela 3 (☎721 26 14). Serves Indian and Thai food in a dark basement in the Old Town. Try the chicken tikka (5Ls); don't forget the garlic *naan* (1.50Ls). Entrees 2-11Ls. Belly dancing most nights. Open daily noon-11pm. MC/V. ❸

Ai Karamba!, Pulkveža Brieža 2 (☎733 4672). Walk away from the train station and the center on Elizabetes iela, and turn right on Pulkveža Brieža; the diner is on the right. Complete with red walls, seats at the bar, and decorative license plates from Canada and the US, this diner offers a delicious all-day breakfast menu, including omelettes (1-3Ls), BLTs (1Ls), and lunch and dinner specials. Entrees 1.90-2.85Ls. MC/V. ❷

Cafe Lehaim, Skolas iela 6 (☎728 02 35), beneath the Jews in Latvia Museum. Popular among local Jews for its fish menu (entrees 0.65-3.70Ls), Rīga's only all-kosher restaurant provides a cozy basement dining area with wood tables and chairs. Fresh baked goods. Open M-Th and Su 10am-10pm, F 10am-sunset. ❷

Velvets, Skārņu iela 9 (☎721 50 75), just off Kaļķu iela in the Old Town. This stylish restaurant serves French-inspired cuisine, including beef tartare (3.80Ls) and a range of salads (2.35-2.95Ls). The shaded outdoor terrace is a good spot to sip coffee (1.20Ls). Entrees 3-11Ls. Open M-Th 10am-2am, F-Sa 10am-4am, Su 11am-2am. MC/V. ❸

⚑ CAFES

Summer in Rīga is all about being outside—breakfast, lunch, dinner, and drinks are enjoyed on the many terraces and beer gardens throughout town.

■ **Goija,** Strēlnieku iela 1a (☎ 703 3370), just off Elizabetes. Dark lighting, rich decor, and pillows galore make this teahouse a refuge from the bustling streets. Magnifying glasses show you the details of each tea available (from 1.20Ls), while free Internet is a bonus. Also has board games and books. Open M-Th and Su 11am-2am, F-Sa 11am-5am.

ZEN, Stabu iela 6 (☎ 731 65 21). Follow Brivibas east from the Old Town. Turn left on Stabu and walk for 1½ blocks. Slip off your shoes and relax among the pillows while your choice of tea is brewed—slowly—right before your eyes. The black tea (1.25Ls) promises to elongate your life. Water pipes 5-8Ls. Open daily 2pm-2am. MC/V.

Franču Maiznīca, Basteju bul. 8 (☎ 791 31 77). Arrive early in the morning for a hot, melt-in-your-mouth chocolate croissant (0.30Ls), or while away the afternoon hours with a coffee (0.60Ls) on the roof terrace. French and English magazines and newspapers augment the expat experience. Open M-Sa 7:30am-8:30pm, Su 10am-7pm.

◉ SIGHTS

VECRĪGA

The city's most famous landmarks are clustered in tiny Vecrīga (Old Town), a maze of crowded cobblestone streets mostly off-limits to automobiles. But Vecrīga hasn't kept capitalism out, as the golden arches at the eastern entrance attest. As you wander from place to place, don't forget to look up—Rīga's architecture is some of the most remarkable in Eastern Europe.

ST. PETER'S CHURCH (SV. PĒTERA BAZNĪCA). Built in 1209 by the Livs who accepted Christianity, the church is best known for its spire, which has fallen several times. In 1666, it toppled to the ground and crushed locals to death, and Germans shelled it on St. Peter's Day, June 29, 1941. The spire was rebuilt in 1973, and according to local lore, is haunted by the ghost of a soldier who guarded the church in the 18th century. *(Open Tu-Su in high season 10am-6pm; in low season 10am-5pm; staff sometimes shuts ticket office for lunch break 12:50-2:30pm. Exhibits 0.50Ls. Spire accessible via elevator; last elevator to the top 20min. before closing. 2Ls, students 1Ls.)*

CATHEDRAL CHURCH OF RĪGA (DOMA BAZNĪCA). This awe-inspiring house of worship is the largest church in the Baltics. When you enter, turn around and look up to see an impressive organ with over 6700

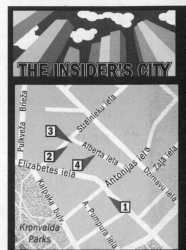

THE INSIDER'S CITY

ART NOUVEAU RĪGA

Look up while you wander the streets of Rīga to appreciate the city's remarkable architecture. About 40% of the downtown is built in the unique Art Nouveau style, with an international mix of influences. For a short tour of some of the most impressive buildings, take this walk:

1 From K. Valdemāra iela, turn left on Elizabetes iela to reach 10b, on your left. Admire the work from across the street.

2 Turn right on Strēlnieku to take in the blue-and-white masterpiece at 4b. The 1905 building is now the home of the Stockholm School of Economics.

3 Next door is the massive, cream-colored corner edifice at Alberta iela 13. Recently repaired, it has pronounced details and pointed turrets.

4 Turn on Alberta iela. Numbers 8, 6, 4, 2, and 2a, in various states of repair, showcase a colorful and impressive catalogue of Art Nouveau balconies and brickwork.

pipes. Wander the pews of the cathedral to see stonework and masonry from the original structure, or go outside and into the Cross-Vaulted Gallery, an outdoor museum in the castle's courtyard. On display are a Salaspilis stone head and a statue of Bishop Albert, the German missionary who founded Rīga in 1201. The original 1897 statue was moved to St. Petersburg during WWII and disappeared mysteriously. This 2001 replica commemorates Rīga's 800th anniversary. *(English captions. Gallery open May-Oct. Tu-F 11am-4pm, Sa 10am-2pm. 0.5Ls, students 0.3Ls. Separate payment for cathedral and gallery.)*

LATVIAN RIFLEMEN MONUMENT (LATVIEŠU STRĒLNIEKU LAUKUMS). Looming over the Museum of the Occupation, this granite monument is a controversial reminder of Latvia's Soviet past. The Socialist Realist statue depicts three soldiers guarding the square. The monument honors the team that served as Lenin's bodyguards during and after the Revolution; many locals would like to see it torn down.

HOUSE OF THE BLACKHEADS (MELNGALVJU NAMS). Originally erected in 1334, the building was purchased in 1687 by the Blackheads, a group of bachelor merchants. They adopted the quirky name to honor their patron saint, dark-skinned St. Maurice. Portraits and statues of Maurice can be found inside, and his symbol decorates the interior furniture. The intricate cream-pink 2nd-floor assembly hall, open to the public, is also used for official state functions. The building was severely damaged during WWII and demolished by the Soviets in 1948, but was rebuilt and completed in 2001. The basement houses a museum that displays artifacts from the original house. *(Rātslaukums 7, in the town square by the Occupation Museum. ☎704 43 00; melngalv@rcc.lv. Open Tu-Su May-Sept. 10am-5pm; Oct.-Apr. 11am-5pm. House and museum 1.50Ls, students 0.70Ls. Tours in English, French, German, or Russian; 5Ls.)*

RĪGA CASTLE. From the outside, the city's castle looks more like a stately home, watched by black-clad guards marching in unison at the gates. In 1487, locals destroyed the castle on the banks of the Daugava in a rebellion against the ruling Livonian Knights. The Livonians forced city dwellers to rebuild the structure in 1515. It has since been expanded, and served as the presidential residence of Karlis Ulmanis during the country's brief period of independence between the world wars. Inside the castle, the **History Museum of Latvia** is incomprehensible to those who can't read Latvian. *(Pils laukums 3, off Valdemāra iela. ☎722 30 04. Open W-Su 11am-5pm. Museum 0.70Ls, students 0.40Ls. Tours in English, German, and Russian; 5Ls.)*

POWDER TOWER (PULVERTORNIS). The German student fraternity Rubonia once held its debaucherous parties inside this 14th-century fortress, and nine cannonballs are still lodged in its walls (curiously enough on the side facing the city). No frat parties take place here anymore: the tower houses the **Latvian Museum of War** (Latvijas Kara Muzejs). A long history is jammed into four floors. Two sections are particularly captivating: the 2nd floor displays Latvia's post-WWI effort to win independence, and the 4th-floor exhibit details the fall of communism. Only these two sections have English captions. *(Smilšu iela 20. ☎722 81 47. Open W-Su May-Sept. 10am-6pm; Oct.-Apr. 10am-5pm. Museum 0.50Ls, students 0.25Ls. Tours in English; 3Ls.)*

NEW RĪGA

FREEDOM MONUMENT (BRĪVĪBAS PIEMINEKLIS). This beloved monument depicts Liberty raising her arms skyward as three gold stars appear to levitate above her fingertips. Dedicated in 1935, during Latvia's brief period of independence, the monument—affectionately known as Milda—survived the subsequent Russian occupation by masquerading as a Soviet symbol. Mighty Milda raises up the three main regions of Latvia (Kurzeme, Latgale, and Vidzeme), but the Soviets claimed it represented Mother Russia supporting the three Baltic states. Two steadfast guards protect her honor daily 9am-6pm; the changing of the guard occurs on the hour. *(At the corner of Raiņa bul. and Brīvības iela.)*

BASTEJKALNS. Rīga's central park, surrounded by the old city moat (Pīlsētas kanāls), houses ruins of the old city walls. Five red stone slabs around the canal commemorate January 20, 1991, when Soviet special forces stormed the Interior Ministry on Raiņa bul. At the northern end of Bastejkalns, on K. Valdemāra iela, is the **National Theater.** Latvia first declared independence here on November 18, 1918. Benches along the pathways and riverbanks are popular places to relax in summer. *(Kronvalda bul. 2. ☎ 732 27 59. Open daily 10am-7pm.)*

ESPLANADE. The park east of Bastejkals is home to Rīga's Byzantine **Orthodox Cathedral** (Pareizticīgo Katedrāle), built 1876-84. Soviets closed the church in 1961 and revamped it as a "house of atheism," containing a cafe, lecture hall, library, and planetarium. Restoration is underway, and the church is frequented by worshippers and tourists alike. *(Brīvības iela 23. ☎ 721 29 01; www.svet.lv. Open daily 7am-6pm. Services M-F 8am, 5pm; Sa 7, 9:30am, 5pm; Su 8, 10am, 5pm. Donations requested.)*

VICTORY PARK (UZVARAS PARKS). This expansive green space is marked with a stone Soviet war memorial depicting Victory and a slew of Comrades. At one point, Latvian extremists attempted to blow up the statue, but it remains standing today. Take tram #4 or 5 from Novembra krastmala to the 2nd stop over the Akmens Bridge, or walk over the bridge and continue straight for 600m.

JEWISH RĪGA

Jews were barred from Rīga until the 18th century. By 1935, the more than 40,000 Jews who lived in the city comprised about 10% of Rīga's total population. About 150 Jews remained at the end of WWII. Many returned during Soviet times, but thousands left after the fall of communism. Today, 10,000-15,000 Jews reside here.

JEWS IN LATVIA MUSEUM. Funded largely by non-Jewish German philanthropists, this museum contains photos and biographical information on Rīga's most famous Jewish residents, including intellectuals, teachers, musicians, and athletes. A sobering, black-painted room is filled with graphic photos of the Terror Against the Jews, beginning in 1941. Exhibits also tell the story of local Christians who sheltered Jews from Nazi persecution. *(Skolas 6, 3rd fl., at the intersection with Dzirnavu. ☎ 728 34 84; ebreji.latvija@apollo.lv. Open M-Th and Su noon-5pm. Donations requested.)*

OLD JEWISH CEMETERY. Before the graveyard was established in 1725, local Jews had to cart their dead all the way to Poland for burial. Much of the cemetery was destroyed by Nazi soldiers and Latvian Nazi-sympathizers on July 4, 1941. The Nazis later used it as a mass grave for the ghetto. The Soviets converted the site into a public **park.** A **monument** was erected here after the fall of communism. Most of the Hebrew inscriptions on the graves have worn away, but the large Star of David carved into granite is still surrounded with flowers and candles. *(2/4 Līksnas iela; tram #15 stops near the intersection of Ludzas and Līksnas.)*

BIĶERNIEKI FOREST. Erected in 2001 by the German War Graves Commission, this beautiful, powerful memorial commemorates the Jews who were murdered here between 1941 and 1944. A central altar is inscribed with Job's words, "O earth, do not cover my blood, and let there be no resting place for my cry." Around the altar, rocks jut out of the ground, representing the cities from which Jews were taken. *(Take tram #14 from Brīvības to "Keguma"; do not get off at "Bikernicku." Walk straight 1km and you will see a white gate leading to the memorial. The memorial extends into the woods on the left side of the road, 600m closer to the tram stop.)*

🏛 MUSEUMS

▨OCCUPATION MUSEUM (OKUPĀCIJAS MUZEJS). This compelling museum guides visitors through Latvia's tortured history under the Soviets, then the Nazis, and then the Soviets again. It takes at least an hour to make your way through the gripping displays; you might even find yourself going back another day. The exhibits include a recreation of gulag barracks and movies and photographs about the terror of the Checka, a Soviet squad of informants and tribunals, and the KGB. The museum offers a sobering account of Latvian Nazi sympathizers' role in the slaughter of the country's Jewish population. Collections of personal items from those shipped off to gulags are particularly poignant. *(Strēlnieku laukums 1, in the black building behind the Latvian Riflemen Monument. ☎721 27 15; www.occupationmuseum.lv. Open May-Sept. daily 11am-6pm; Oct.-Apr. Tu-Su 11am-5pm. Free; donations requested.)*

MUSEUM OF BARRICADES OF 1991. Vecrīga morphed into a medieval fortress in January 1991, when locals built makeshift walls to defend the city center from Red Army special forces. The barricades didn't stop the Soviets from firing on unarmed protesters. Although the tiny museum doesn't seem like much, it contains information about those killed during the resistance, as well as maps of Latvia and Rīga documenting the 10 days of events. Don't miss the 35min. English video with jarring footage taken by a Latvian TV crew during the gunfight. *(Kramu iela 3. Follow Jauniela from Doma laukums; knock on door #1 on the 2nd fl. ☎721 35 25; www.barikades.lv. Open M-F 10am-5pm, Sa 11am-5pm. Free; donations requested.)*

STATE MUSEUM OF ART (VALSTS MĀKSLAS MUZEJS). The building, which opened in 1905, is as interesting as the art within it. Don't let the magnificent salmon-and-green colored entrance overshadow the art. The museum showcases 18th- to 20th-century works by Latvian artists and a large collection of Russian art. Turn-of-the-century collages share space with ink-and-pencil sketches, while oil paintings dominate the rooms. Highlights include Nicholas Roerich's blue-hued Himalayan landscapes, on the first floor, and Karlis Padego's "Madonna with a Machine Gun" upstairs. *(Valdemāra iela 10a, near the Elizabetes iela intersection. ☎732 32 04; www.vmm.lv. Open Apr.-Oct. M, W, F-Su 11am-5pm, Th 11am-7pm; Oct.-Apr. M and W-Su 11am-5pm. 0.50Ls, students 0.40Ls. English audioguides 1Ls.)*

MUSEUM OF RĪGA'S HISTORY AND NAVIGATION (RIGAS VESTURES UN KUGNIECIBAS MUZEJS). A dazzling collection of 500,000 items fills this history museum established in 1773. The museum helped preserve Latvian culture when the country was a part of the USSR. Don't miss the giant statue of Latvia's patron saint, St. Christopher, on the top floor, and the lavish exhibit, "Rīga and its Citizens, 1918-1940." *(Palasta iela 4, next to Dome Cathedral. ☎721 13 58; http://vip.latnet.lv/museums/riga. Open W-Su May-Sept. 10am-5pm; Oct.-Apr. 11am-5pm. 1.20Ls, students 0.40Ls. Tours in English, German, and Russian; 3/2Ls.)*

OPEN-AIR ETHNOGRAPHIC MUSEUM (ETNOGRĀFISKAIS BRĪVDABAS MUZEJS). Nearly 100 18th- and 19th-century buildings from all over Latvia are gathered here, complete with artisans churning out traditional wares, from wooden spoons to pottery. *(Brīvības 440. Bus #1 from Merķela iela to "Brīvdabas Muzejs." ☎799 41 06. Open daily May-Oct. 10am-5pm. 1Ls, students 0.25Ls. Tours 8/5Ls; call ahead.)*

RĪGA MOTOR MUSEUM (RĪGAS MOTORMUZEJS). A wax figure of Stalin sits in the seat of his armored ZIS-1155 at this bizarre museum, which boasts a collection of the despot's automobiles. Particularly noteworthy is the 1966 Rolls Royce Silver Shadow that Brezhnev crashed in 1980; see the wax-figure bureaucrat gasping after denting his wheels. A treat for car-lovers and Soviet-philes. *(6 S. Eizensteina iela. Take tram #14 from Brīvības iela to Gailezers Hospital. Cross the street and follow Gailezera iela over the river 400m. Go right at the T-intersection. ☎709 71 70; rmm@apollo.lv. Some English captions. Open daily 10am-6pm. 1Ls, students 0.50Ls.)*

♫ ❀ ENTERTAINMENT AND FESTIVALS

Rīga offers the best array of music and performance art in the Baltics. Theaters close from mid-June through August, but the **Opera House** hosts summer events. The **Latvian National Opera** (☎707 37 77; www.opera.lv) performs in the Opera House, Aspazijas bul. 3. Richard Wagner once presided as director, and you can catch concerts for 2-30Ls. The **Latvian Symphony Orchestra** (☎722 48 50) has frequent concerts in the Great and Small Guilds off Filharmonija laukums. Smaller ensembles perform throughout the summer in **Wagner Hall** (Vāgnera zāle), Vāgnera iela 4 (☎721 08 17). The topnotch **Rīga Ballet** carries on the dance tradition of native star Mikhail Baryshnikov. The **ticket offices,** at Teātra 10/12 (☎722 57 47; open daily 10am-7pm) and Amatu iela 6 (☎721 37 98), on the first floor of the Great Guild, serve most local concerts. The fantastic and mostly free **Rigas Ritmi** is a street music festival early in July. Check out www.rigasritmi.lv for dates.

▟ NIGHTLIFE

Nightlife is centered on **Vecrīga,** where 24hr. casinos and *diskotekas* flourish. For a mellower evening, join Rīgans in their beer gardens.

Skyline Bar, Elizabetes iela 55, 26th fl. (☎777 22 22), in Reval Hotel Latvija. Arrive by 8pm for a coveted "Vecrīga seat" with a mind-blowing view of the Old Town. Modern decor, lively atmosphere and a well-stocked bar. Guinness and other foreign beers on tap (1-2.50Ls). Mixed drinks, including classics like White Russians (3.80Ls) and Sex on the Beach (2.95Ls). Salmon and caviar canapes 0.95-1.35Ls; other snacks 2-6Ls. Open M-Th and Su 3pm-2am, F-Sa 3pm-3am. MC/V.

Pulkvedim Neviens Neraksta, Peldu 26/28 (☎721 38 86; www.pulkvedim.lv), off Kungu iela. Wander into this dark, industrial bar for some of the friendliest bartenders and best DJs in town. The dance floor upstairs can get crowded—mostly with locals—but downstairs the bravely color-uncoordinated lounge plays salsa and chill-out mixes. Beer 1-2Ls. Cover Th-Sa 2-3Ls. Open M-Th noon-3am, F-Sa noon-5am, Su 4pm-1am. MC/V.

Cetri Balti Krekli (Four White Shirts), Vecpilsētas iela 12 (☎721 38 85; www.krekli.lv), off Kaleju and around the corner from Sue's Indian Raj. Hidden from the Old Town's crowds, this cellar club fills quickly with locals and visitors alike. Latvians come well dressed and ready to party. Live music F-Sa. No sneakers. Cover Tu-Th 1-2Ls; F-Sa 3-5Ls. Open M-F noon-5am, Sa 5pm-5am, Su 5pm-3am. MC/V.

Rīgas Balzams, Toṃa iela 4 (☎721 44 94), in the Old Town, 100m east of the Powder Tower, in a cellar of the long yellow building. In winter, sit inside the warm brick cellar to enjoy Latvia's potent national liquor in style. In summer, enjoy the terrace and choose from a range of mixed balsams to clear your head. Open M-Th and Su 11am-midnight, F-Sa 11am-1am. MC/V.

▐ DAYTRIPS FROM RĪGA

SALASPILS MEMORIAL

Electric trains run to Dārziṇi (20min., 14 per day, 0.22Ls). Do not take the train to "Salaspils." Last train back to Rīga is around 10pm. In the woods behind the Dārziṇi station house is a paved pathway. Turn right and continue 1km. Go left after the soccer field.

The Salaspils Memorial marks the remains of the Kurtenhof concentration camp, where an estimated 100,000 people were killed by the Nazis. As is the case at other Soviet-era Holocaust memorials, Communist officials omitted any references to religion and referred to the dead obliquely as "victims of the Fascist terror." A huge concrete wall marks where the camp entrance once stood. The inscription over the entrance reads, "Here the innocent walked the way of death. How many unfinished words, how many unlived years were cut short by a bullet." Go inside the massive concrete structure to walk a cold, somber pathway to a small display of woodcuts and a map of concentration camps in the area. Four sculptures—Motherhood, Solidarity, The Humiliated, and The Unbroken—watch over the Way of the Suffering, the circular path connecting barracks foundations.

RUNDĀLE PALACE

The palace is 10km west of Bauska. From Rīga, take the bus (1hr., about every 30min., 1.35Ls) to Bauska. (Ask for an express bus, or choose one from the schedule marked with an "E" after the departure time.) From there, take a bus (15min., 7-9 per day, 0.20Ls) or taxi (3Ls) to Rundāles. Buses are infrequent; check the schedule before you leave the station at Bauska. ☎621 97; www.rpm.apollo.lv. Gardens, palace, and exhibit open daily June-Aug. 10am-7pm; Sept. and May 10am-6pm; Nov.-Apr. 10am-5pm. 1.80Ls, students 1.20Ls. Other exhibits 0.10-0.50Ls.

The expansive Rundāle Palace long served as a countryside retreat for local nobility. A Russian empress, Anna Ioanova, built the palace as a gift to one of her advisers, Ernst Johann von Bühren, a Baltic German noble. The palace was designed by Italian architect Bartolomeo Rastrelli, who also designed St. Petersburg's Winter Palace, and required the work of 15,000 laborers and artisans. Construction began in 1730 but stalled after Anna's death in 1740. It was finished under Catherine the Great in 1767. Accordingly, images of Catherine's life adorn the majestic interior, allowing you to trace her growth—in power and in girth. Among the palace's 138 gilded rooms is the **Gold Room** (Selta Zāle), which contains the throne, murals, and soldiers' graffiti from 1812. The upstairs exhibit describes the palace's 1971-2002 restoration. Panels in each room date and name every piece of art, furniture, and porcelain. The magnificent **White Hall** shouldn't be missed. On your way out, spend some time wandering through the gardens, still a work in progress.

WESTERN LATVIA

JŪRMALA   ☎(8)77

The sandy resort of Jūrmala (YOUR-mala; sea shore; pop. 60,000) has been a holiday destination for decades. Composed of 14 small towns, the region is bordered by 32km of busy shore and calm, forested land. A short jaunt from Rīga, Jūrmala is popular for restorative spas and for its young, tanned, and toned beach bums.

> **THE REAL DEAL.** Jūrmala is known as Riga's playground, probably because the sandbox is crowded and dirty. Getting to and from the "Latvian Riviera" is a sticky, sweaty, and squishy train ride. The beach is littered with cigarette butts and crowded with oily, tanned people knocking soccer balls in your direction. For a real Latvian seaside experience, take a bus to the coast and walk along the beautiful white sands of Liepāja. You'll feel welcome and relaxed, and you won't be fighting dozens of British stag parties for space. —Neasa Coll

⚏ TRANSPORTATION AND PRACTICAL INFORMATION. A **commuter rail** (30min.; every 30min; 5am-11:30pm; 0.50Ls, 0.80Ls on board) runs from **Rīga.** Ride the Tukums-bound line to **Majori station** (☎583 03 15). **Public buses** (0.20Ls), **microbuses** (0.20-0.30Ls), and the same **commuter rail** connect Jurmala's towns. Rent a **bike** along the beach (1.50Ls per hr.) or at Juras iela 24. (☎911 90 91. 6Ls per day. Open daily 10am-7pm.) From the **train station** in **Majori,** follow the pedestrian boulevard Jomas iela east 100m to reach the **Tourism Information Center,** Jomas iela 42 (☎776 42 76; www.jurmala.lv). The English-speaking staff distributes **free maps** and brochures and sells guides. The free *Jurmala Visitor's Guide* offers extensive regional info, and excessive advertising. **Dubulti,** the town immediately to the west of Majori, has a **post office** at 16 Strelnieku pr. (☎776 24 30. Open M-F 8am-5pm, Sa 8am-4pm.) To the east of Majori lies **Dzintari.** Get there by following Jomas iela past the TIC and continuing for 1km. Along the way, you'll pass a **pharmacy, Majori Aptieka,** Jomas 41 (☎776 44 13; open daily 9am-8pm) and an **Internet** cafe, **Digitorklubs,** Jomas 62 (☎781 1411; open daily 10am-9pm). MC/V **ATMs** abound on Jomas iela. There is one outside **Hansabanka,** Jomas 37 (☎781 1482). For the 24hr. **currency exchange** at the eastern end of Jomas, head toward Jomas iela 62. In Dzintari, 24hr. currency exchange can be found at 92 Jomas iela. Turaidas 1.

▐▐ ACCOMMODATIONS AND FOOD. The **TIC** books reservations at local hotels and hostels from 6Ls per night. The TIC has no service charge and usually provides the best rates. **Hotel Majori ❺,** Jomas iela 29, across from the train station, has modestly sized rooms. All come with private baths and showers, TVs and fridges, and breakfast. The staff is friendly and speaks English. (☎776 13 80; www.majori.lv. Singles 33L; doubles 48L. MC/V.) **Elina ❺,** Lienes 43, has bright, clean doubles with private baths above a pleasant cafe. Heading east on Jomas, turn right on J. Prieskana iela; it's 200m down on the right. (☎776 16 65; www.elinahotel.lv. Doubles 25Ls. Cash only.) From the Dzintari rail station, walk 30m with the tracks to your left to reach **Dzintars ❹,** Edinburgas iela 15. It's on a noisy street but has good prices and friendly staff. (☎775 15 82; orthos@apollo.net. English spoken. Doubles May 15-Sept. 14 20-26Ls; Sept. 15-May 14 17-20Ls.)

Cafes line Jomas iela, particularly in summertime, when nearly every inch of open space in town becomes a beer garden. For spectacular seafood by the shore, head to ▒**Jurus Zakis ❷,** Vienibas 1 (☎775 3005), in Bulduri. Savor your meal at the restaurant's colorful outdoor picnic area. Follow Dzintari eastward from Jomas. After 2km, Dzintari becomes Bulduru. Continue to Vienibas and turn left. (Entrees 2.40-4Ls. Open daily noon-11pm. MC/V.) **Sue's Asia ❹,** Jomas 74 (☎775 59 00), has Indian, Thai, and Chinese cuisine. (Entrees 3-10Ls. Open M-Th noon-11pm, F-Su noon-late. MC/V.) After a filling Russian meal at **Slavu ❹,** Jomas 57 (☎776 14 01), head upstairs to the dance club, which has live DJs on some weekend evenings. (Entrees 4-12Ls. Restaurant open daily 11am-2am; nightclub 9pm-6am. MC/V.)

◎ SIGHTS. Jūrmala's main attraction is its beach. Powder-fine sand, warm waters, and festive boardwalks have drawn crowds since the late 19th century. A **statue of Lacplesis the Bear Slayer** protects the street across from the Majori train station. **Janis Pliekshans** (1865-1929), known by the pen name **Rainis,** was exiled by the tsar for participating in the 1905 Russian Revolution. The poet and playwright returned to Majori after Latvia gained independence, and from 1927 to 1929 lived in the two-story cottage at J. Plieksana iela 5-7. It's now the **Rainis and Aspazija Memorial Summer House** (☎776 4295), which contains Rainis and his wife Aspazija's personal library, sculptures, exquisite furniture, and original editions of their work. From the TIC, follow Jomas east 400m and turn left. (Open W-Su 10am-6pm; closed last F of each month. 0.5Ls, students 0.3Ls. Tour 0.2Ls.) Aspazija, whose real name was Elza Rozenberg (1865-1943), was a significant writer herself. After her husband's death, she lived at Meierovica prospekts 20 in Dubulti, now the **Aspazija House,** which includes a public library. The house is 1km west of the TIC. Follow Jomas away from Majori until it merges into Meierovica. (☎776 9445. Open M 2-7pm, Tu-Th and Sa 11am-4pm. 0.3Ls, students 0.1Ls.)

Take a left on Turaidas and head toward the beach to reach the **Dzintari Concert Hall,** Turaidas 1. (☎776 2086. Tickets 776 2005.) US and Soviet diplomats met here in 1986 for negotiations over the USSR's occupation of Latvia. The open-air stage hosts a stream of summertime performances, including **chamber music concerts** and an international youth **singing contest** in July. Posters across town advertise the monthly line-up of cultural events, which take place daily in high season.

LIEPĀJA

☎(8)34

The westernmost and 3rd-largest city in Latvia, Liepāja (lee-EP-ee-a; pop. 86,500) is an underappreciated coastal retreat. Bordered by sea, canals, and an estuary, the city maintains a calm, cool air, and offers a wealth of spectacular beaches. The northern suburb of Karosta, off-limits to civilians during most of its hundred-year history, is now a haven for artists and adventurous visitors.

☎☷ TRANSPORTATION AND PRACTICAL INFORMATION. Buses from **Rīga** (3-5hr., 8-10 per day, 4Ls) arrive at Liepāja Bus Station, Stacijas laukums. (☎342 75 52. Ticket window open daily 5am-9:30pm). Bus connections to **Ventspils** (2½hr., 2 per day, 2.40-3.15Ls) and **Klaipėda, LIT** (2hr., 4 per day, 2.10-3Ls) are also available. With your back to the bus station, walk down Rīgas iela, to your right, for about 1km, or take any tram (0.12Ls) along the way. Don't forget to validate your ticket on board after buying it from the driver. Cross the bridge to reach the city center. To the right, Jūras iela eventually becomes Kūrmājas prospekts and leads to the promenade and the beach. To the left of the bridge, along K. Zāles laukams, you'll find a **pharmacy, Centra Aptieka,** at #6 (☎342 35 95. Open M-F 7:30am-9pm, Sa 8:30am-8pm, Su 9am-6pm. MC/V.) Lielā iela continues from the bridge to the center of the Old Town. The **Lejaskurzemes Tourist Information Center (TIC),** Lielā iela 11, provides **free maps** and is well marked on your left, in the lobby of Hotel Līva. (☎348 08 08; www.liepaja.lv. Open daily May-Sept. 9am-7pm; Oct.-Apr. 9am-5pm) North of the bridge, in the New Town, Raiņa iela becomes O. Kalpaka iela, which runs parallel to the shore and eventually leads to Karosta tilts, the moveable bridge that must be crossed to reach **Karosta.** Atmodas bulvāris leads north through Karosta. Buses (0.20Ls), microbuses (0.25Ls), and trams (0.12Ls) make travel within the city quite easy between the hours of 6am and 11pm.

Just before the tourist office, **Latvia Tours** offers **AmEx** services. (☎342 71 73; www.latviatours.lv. Open M-F 8am-noon and 1-7pm). **Internet** can be found across the street at **Sapņu Sala,** Liela 12. (Enter around the corner. ☎348 53 33; www.sapnu-sala.lv. 0.50Ls per hr., ISIC discount. Open daily 9am-9pm). **Exchange money** or get MC/V **cash advances** at **Unibanka,** Brivības iela 4/6. (☎340 13 00. Open M-F 9am-5pm.) The **post office,** Pasta iela 4, has **Western Union** services. (Open M-F 7:30am-6:30pm, Sa 7:30am-4:30pm.) **Postal Code:** LV-3401.

☷☷ ACCOMMODATIONS AND FOOD. The **TIC** sells a useful guide (0.70Ls) to accommodations and attractions in the Liepāja region. If you're willing to stay outside the Old Town, head to **Brīze ❶,** O. Kalpaka 68/70, for spacious, clean rooms with hallway showers and toilets. Modern kitchens boast filtered drinking water, and the common area has a TV. The hotel is on the main bus route, and there is a small market behind the building. (☎344 15 66; www.brizehostel.lv. Singles 7Ls; triples 15Ls; quads 20Ls. Cash only.) Centrally located **Līva ❷,** 11 Lielā 11, is on the left after crossing the bridge to the Old Town. Economy rooms are small and can be stuffy in the heat, but have TVs, phones, and sinks. Hallway showers and toilets, though clean, can be far from your room. (☎342 01 02; www.liva.lv. Reserve ahead-for July-Aug. Economy singles 10Ls; doubles 15Ls. Singles 25Ls; doubles 45Ls; triples 36Ls; quads 44Ls. MC/V.) In **Karosta,** the **K@2 Hostel ❶,** Katedrāles 2, provides comfortable beds and delicious breakfast in an unusual setting. A gargantuan key opens the old, heavy front door to an eclectically decorated building, with a terrace and cafe out back. The dorm bunks are comfortable, the showers are hot, and the staff is fantastic. (Microbuses #1 and #3 run past the building, just off Atmodas bulv. ☎974 7962; www.karosta.lv/hostel. Breakfast included. Rooms 6Ls.)

Rock Cafe ❷, Stendera 18/20, offers food, drink, and Old Town people-watching all day long on an expansive terrace. Chow down on a range of entrees (0.90-3.45Ls), inluding a number of vegetarian dishes, or while away the hours with a few mugs of the local Līvu beer (0.60Ls per 0.50L). Stand warned: even customers must pay 0.10Ls to use the bathrooms. (☎348 15 55. Open daily 9am-4am. MC/V.) **Baltā bize ❷**, Kūrmājas prospekts 8/10, to the right after crossing the bridge, has whitewashed wooden furniture and country charm. The extensive menu offers such delicacies as chicken liver ragout in a pastry basket (1.45Ls) and cod filet seared in white wine for a mere 2.15Ls. (☎342 45 88. Open M-F 7:30am-midnight, Sa-Su 9am-midnight. MC/V.) Grab a seat at **Kiss Me ❶**, Lielā 13, inside the long window of the Kurzeme shopping center, to enjoy coffee (0.50Ls) and dessert (0.60-2Ls) while watching the crowds on the main thoroughfare. (☎342 54 64. Open daily 8am-10pm.) A large **RIMI hypermarket**, 8 K. Zāles laukams, is to the left of the bridge after crossing into the Old Town. (Open daily 8am-midnight.) **Peter's Market**, Kursu 5/7/9, just off Zivju, sells dairy and meat products inside, and fruit and vegetables in outdoor stalls. (Open M-Sa 8am-6pm, Su 8am-2pm.)

🖼 📣 **SIGHTS AND ENTERTAINMENT.** The **beach** at Liepāja is internationally recognized with a Blue Flag, indicating high water safety and cleanliness. The soft sandy shore is never too crowded, and a long pathway dotted with sculptures winds amongst the coastal trees. Turn right after you cross the bridge to the Old Town and continue to the beach. Alternatively, take the promenade along the harbor to the beachfront. **Karosta**, a naval port built by Tsar Alexander III from 1890-1904, was home to the first Baltic submarine fleet. During Soviet times, Liepāja's strategic importance kept it isolated, but today unique Karosta beckons tourists. You can reach the suburb on buses #1 and 3. When you're there, rent a bicycle from **K@2**, Ģenerāļa Dankera 1, to explore the streets. The helpful staff at the office provide maps and suggest routes. (☎979 82 24. 0.50Ls per hr.; tandem bicycle 1Ls per hr. Open daily 9am-5pm.) In Karosta, the massive **St. Nicholas Orthodox Cathedral**, Kateldrāles 7 (☎345 7634), shines above endless blocks of Soviet army housing. Though the cathedral has no internal support beams, extra strong walls keep it standing. **Karosta Prison**, Invalīdu 4 (☎636 94 70; www.karostascietums.lv) was built as a hospital in 1900, but used to hold prisoners from the Revolution of 1905. Since then, its history has been bloody. The last prisoner left in 1997, and today you can tour the prison (0.50Ls), participate in "Behind the Bars," a chilling experience during which you'll be taken into the prison and treated as an inmate (3Ls), or even spend the night incarcerated (see sidebar at right). Knowledgeable "prison wardens" brief you on the history of the prison and offer a chance to ask

THE BIG SPLURGE

HOSTILE HOSTEL

It's generally a good idea to avoid foreign prisons, but if you'd like to take home a very special souvenir—your own prison ID card, complete with mug shot—spend a night at Karosta Prison *(Karostas cietums)*. For the fair sum of 29Ls, you'll be given a set of black-and-white prison clothes, a bed of wooden planks with a bedroll, and a night of verbal abuse and regular cell checks.

The prison, located in the desolate naval port north of Liepāja, began incarcerating political prisoners in 1905. When the Soviets took over Karosta, they put the entire area on lockdown, even denying civilians any access to the seashore. Prisoners were killed in the courtyard where you and a group of fellow participants will be marched, yelled at, and made to do exercises in the summer sun. Men in uniform will interrogate you, criticize your form, and pull you aside for extra punishment if you give them any attitude. Inside the prison, you'll be sent to pitch-black cells and interrogation rooms, and eventually you'll be put to bed. Don't expect a restful night—ghosts are said to haunt the hallways. Breakfast, fittingly, is not included.

Book your night "Behind the Bars" at www.karostacietums.lv. Ask for English translators to participate with you. **Karosta Prison**, *4 Invalidu iela (☎636 94 70).*

questions after they've broken you in. Enjoy a walk along the 2km long **Northern Pier** to get some fresh air after you break out. For updates on events and happenings in Karosta, check out www.karosta.lv.

Back in the Old Town, **Holy Trinity Church**, Lielā 9, looks unassuming from the outside, but its bright white-and-gold interior is breathtaking. Built from 1742-1748, the church has an organ of over 7000 pipes, and hosts occasional concerts. (☎943 80 50. Open daily 10am-6pm. Church only 0.50Ls; church and spire 1Ls.) The **Liepāja Museum** (Liepājas muzejs), Kūrmājas prospekts 16/18, displays archaeological artifacts, traditional Latvian costumes and crafts, and 20th-century paintings. Don't miss the serene sculpture garden out back. (☎342 23 37. Open W-Su 10am-6pm. 0.50Ls, students 0.30Ls.) The small **Liepāja Under the Regimes of Occupation**, K. Ukstina 7/9, south of the market, provides a sobering account of the city's 20th-century history. Upstairs in the same building is an impressive collection of vintage Kodak cameras and photographic equipment. (☎342 02 74. No English captions. Open W-Th and Sa-Su 10am-6pm, F 11am-7pm. Free.)

Outside town, **Lake Pape Nature Park** offers a splendid setting for hiking, biking, and other outdoor activities. The World Wildlife Fund organizes guided excursions to see wildlife and the surrounding environment. (☎349 48 50; www.wwf.lv.) The park is virtually inaccessible without a car, but you can ask at Tourist Information for maps and suggested routes.

KULDĪGA   ☎8(33)

The town of Kuldīga (KOOL-di-ga; pop. 13,500), located in Western Latvia, maintains an authentic Old Town of red-tiled roofs and narrow streets. Many visitors come to the area to see Latvia's widest waterfall, **Ventas rumba**. You can wade in the flowing river and walk along the falls, or simply observe from the long red-brick bridge. The **Kuldīga District Museum**, 5 Pils iela, is housed in a building from the Paris World Fair. Roman numerals are still visible on some of the beams, which were numbered to aid with the rebuilding of the structure. Exhibitions include archaeological finds, as well as more-contemporary rotating displays. (☎335 01 29. Open Tu-Su 11am-5pm. 0.50Ls, students 0.30Ls.) The nearby **sculpture park**, on the site of the castle ruins, provides a shady vantage from which to watch the waterfall. The **Card Room**, 10 Smilšu iela, offers an eclectic collection of playing cards. (Open Tu-Sa 10am-4pm.) The **Sculpture Hall**, 19 Mucenieku iela, at the back of the building, is an interesting studio space. (Open Sa-Su 11am-4pm.) The very exciting **NEKAC** (Center for Non-Commercial Culture), Vijolīšu iela 24 (www.nekac.lv), often has shows and concerts on weekend evenings.

From the center, walk along Kalna iela to reach the **bridge** and the **waterfall**. Cross the bridge to stay at ▧**Ventas Rumba ❶**, Stendes iela, a hostel named for its proximity to the waterfall. Clean, renovated rooms and dorms are available in a house with a kitchen and dining area. (☎332 41 68. Dorms 5Ls; rooms 10Ls.) At the **Sport School ❶**, Kalna iela 6 (☎332 24 65), 2Ls gets you a bed in a shared room, with hallway baths. Near the waterfall, **Pīlādzītis ❶**, Stendes 2a, offers coffee (0.50Ls) and light snacks. (☎928 38 59. Open daily 9am-late.) A **Saulīte** grocery store is at the corner of Liepājas iela and Piltenes iela. (Open daily 8am-10pm.)

Buses from **Rīga** (3hr., 6 per day, 3Ls) arrive at the bus station, a short walk from town. Buses also run to **Liepāja** (2hr., 5 per day, 2Ls) and **Ventspils** (2hr., 5 per day, 2Ls). With your back to the station, turn right on Stacijas iela and left on Jelgaves iela. Bear to the right and turn left when you see an information sign. The **Tourist Information Center**, Baznīcas iela 5, provides **free maps**, accommodation listings, and info about outdoor activities. (☎332 22 59; tourinfo@kuldiga.lv. Open M-F 9am-5pm, Sa 10am-4pm, Su 10am-2pm.) Cash **traveler's checks** and **exchange currency** at **Hansabankas**, Liepājas iela 15. (Open M-F 9am-5pm.) An **ATM** is outside. Farther down the street is a **pharmacy**, Meness Aptieka. (☎332 24 73. Open M-Sa 8am-9pm, Su 10am-8pm.) Across the street, the **post office** is at Liepājas iela 34. (Open M-F 8am-6pm, Sa 8am-4pm.) **Postal Code:** LV-3301.

INLAND LATVIA

Latvia's longest river flows past the medieval castles of Cēsis and Sigulda. The lush Gauja Valley offers a wealth of opportunities for outdoor activities.

SIGULDA
☎(8)79

Situated in the Gaujas Valley National Park, Sigulda couldn't feel more removed from hectic Rīga. The Knights of the Sword, the Germanic crusaders who Christianized much of Latvia in the 13th century, made this their base. The town remains popular for its dramatic castle ruins and hiking and biking trails.

▐▓ TRANSPORTATION AND PRACTICAL INFORMATION. Trains from **Rīga** run on the Rīga-Lugaži commuter rail line (1hr., 9 per day, 0.71Ls). **Buses** from **Rīga** (1hr., 13 per day, 1Ls) go to the **bus station**, Raiņa iela 3. (☎721 06. Open daily 6am-8pm. Ticket office open M-Sa 8am-1:30pm and 2-5:30pm.) Buses to **Cēsis** may stop on the south edge of Sigulda along Highway A2; backtrack toward Rīga and turn right on Gāles to reach the center. The best way to explore Sigulda is by bicycle, but mind the erratic drivers who share the road. Choose from a variety of **bikes** at **Tridens**, Cēsu iela 15. Follow Raina from the bus station and turn left just before the tourist center onto Cēsu; continue past the green space, and the building will be on the left. (☎964 48 00. 1Ls per hr., 5Ls per day. Open daily 10am-8pm.)

From the **bus** and **train stations**, Raiņa iela runs 1km north to the **Gauja National Park Visitor Centre**, Baznicas 3, which has knowledgeable, English-speaking staff and **free maps** of Sigulda. They also sell essential maps (1.40Ls) of the park. (☎797 13 45; www.gnp.gov.lv. Open M 9am-5:30pm, Tu-Su 9am-7pm.) Follow Raina as it turns into Gauja iela, crosses the river, curves right and becomes Turaidas iela (P8). The **Turaidas Museum Reserve**, 3km after the bridge, is a 42-hectare site that includes a stone castle and endless forests. The reserve can be reached on bike or by bus #12 (1 per hr., 0.20Ls) from the station. A **cable car** (5min.; 2 per hr. 7:25am-6:25pm; M-F 1Ls, Sa-Su 1.50Ls) runs from the Sigulda side of Gaujas to Krimulda Castle. The **Sigulda Tourist Information Center**, K. Valdemāra iela 1a, is smaller and slightly less helpful than the GNP center. (☎713 35; www.sigulda.lv. Open M-F 9am-7pm, Sa 9am-4pm.) **Exchange money**, cash AmEx **traveler's checks**, and find **Western Union** services next door at **Latvijas Krajbanka**, K. Valdemāra iela 1a. (Open M-F 9am-5pm.) From Raiņa iela, turn right onto Ausekla iela; the bank is on the corner, two blocks down. A block closer to the bus station is a **pharmacy**, Pils iela 3. (☎797 09 10. Open M-F 7:30am-9:30pm, Sa 9am-8pm, Su 9am-6pm. MC/V.) For **Internet**, go around to the back of the pharmacy building, through the unmarked gray metal door, up one flight of stairs, and through the door labeled "Internet." (Open daily 10am-10pm.) Across the street is the **post office**, Pils iela 2. (☎797 21 77. **Telephones** outside. Open M-F 8am-7pm, Sa 8am-4pm.) **Postal Code:** LV-2150.

▐▐ ACCOMMODATIONS AND FOOD. The **GNP Visitors Centre** helps locate campsites and **private rooms;** if you're looking for the latter, they'll most likely send you to ▨**Viesu Nams Livonija ❷**, P. Brieža iela 55. Just 10min. from the bus and train stations, it offers pleasant rooms with baths and spacious shared-bath singles in a separate house in the lush back yard. From the bus station, head down Raiņa iela toward the train station, turn right on Ausekla iela, and cross the tracks at the pedestrian signs; continue down Gāles iela and hang a left on P. Brieza. (☎797 30 66; hotel.livonija@lis.lv. Kitchen, common room, and sauna. Breakfast 2Ls. Singles 14Ls, with shared bath 7Ls; doubles 16-20Ls.) **Hotel Sigulda ❺**, Pils iela 6, in the center of town near the bus station, is freshly renovated. (☎722 63; www.hotel-sigulda.lv. Breakfast included. Pool and sauna 2Ls per hr. In summer singles 36Ls in summer; doubles 44LS. In winter 24/30Ls. Reserve ahead. MC/V.)

⬛Pilsmuižas Restorāns ❹, Pils iela 16, serves generous portions of Latvian food. Try the pork chop with red bilberry jam (5.04Ls). The restaurant is in the 19th-century Pilseta Dome. (☎797 14 25. Entrees 3-12Ls. 10% service charge. Open daily noon-2am. MC/V.) **Trīs Draugi ❶** (Three Friends), Pils iela 9, is cafeteria-style, but the staff is friendly and the deep-fried fare, including fish and cheese, is tasty. (☎797 37 21. Entrees under 1L. Open daily 8am-10pm. MC/V.) It shares space with a **bar** that has Latvian beers on tap. (Beer 0.60Ls per 0.5L. Open daily 11am-2am.) A newer, brighter cafeteria is **Elvi ❶,** Vidus iela 1, which shares a building with a bowling alley and a supermarket of the same name. Hot dishes, soups, and salads are available by weight, and you can easily fill up on 1Ls worth of food. Follow Ausekla iela, keeping the train tracks to your left; the building is beside the large parking lot on your right. (☎797 35 39. Open daily 7am-11pm.) **Saulīte,** a large grocery store, is at Paegles iela 3. (☎797 14 63. Open daily 8am-10pm. MC/V.)

◐ ⬛ SIGHTS AND ENTERTAINMENT. From Sigulda, cross the river and follow **Turaidas** 1.5km until you reach the turn-off for **Gutman's Cave** (Gūtmaņa Ala), inscribed with coats of arms and scribblings dating from the 17th century. Farther down the path is **Turaida Castle** (Turaidas Pils). Inside, a **museum** chronicles the saga of Kaupo, chieftain of the Livs, a pagan group who maintained a castle here in the late 12th century. The wily Kaupo converted to Christianity in 1203 before plundering his tribe's fortress. (Info in English, German, and Russian. Tower open daily 9am-8pm. Museum open May-Oct. 10am-6pm; Nov.-Apr. 10am-5pm. Admission free with ticket from Turaidas Museum Reserve.) Left of the caves, climb 366 steps to a vigorous, forested hike that eventually leads to the scant ruins of 13th-century **Krimulda Castle** (Krimuldas Pilsdrupas). A cable car leads from the ruins back across the river to Sigulda. On the Sigulda side of the river, on a ridge behind GNP headquarters, is the 19th-century **Pilsetas Dome** (Castle Dome), the "new" castle-palace where the Russian Prince Kropotkin once lived. The immense ruins of the once glorious **Siguldas Castle** (Siguldas Pilsdrupas) are behind the palace. Constructed 1207-26, the castle was destroyed in the Great Northern War (1700-21) between Russia and Sweden. The castle forms the backdrop for the **Opera Festival** (☎727 79 00; www.lmuza.lv/sigulda) in late July.

⯅ OUTDOOR ACTIVITIES. The **Līgatne Nature Trail** (Ligatne dabas takas; round-trip from Sigulda 41km) takes visitors on a 5.5km loop past captive **bears, elk, deer,** and **hares.** The wooden pathway leads to viewing towers, where you can observe the wildlife without disturbing it. It is difficult to get to the trail without a car; you can take a local bus to Līgatne town and walk from there (about 6km); bring a good map of the area with you. To get to the trailhead, follow Auskeja/Darza iela east from the town and turn right toward Vildoga (9km) at the fork. At the Vildoga bus stop, head left and, after another 5km, hang a left on the main road. After 3km, make another left at the cafe. After another 2km, take a left at the signs for the trail. A **branch** of the **GNP Information Center** at the site will give you a **free map** of the trail. (Open M 9am-5:30pm, Tu-Su 9am-7pm. Entrance 1Ls; students 0.5Ls.)

An Olympic-sized **bobsled run** plummets from Sveices iela 13. You can take the plunge year-round; in summer, you'll be on wheels. (☎739 44; fax 790 16 67. Open Sa-Su noon-5pm. 3Ls.) To go **bungee jumping,** head to the cable car, sign a release, and battle gravity. (☎725 31; fax 722 53; www.lgk.lv. Open F-Su 6:30pm-last customer. F 17Ls, Sa-Su 20Ls.) Watching jumpers from the bridge is a popular activity on weekend evenings. Go left off Gaujas iela before you cross the river to reach **Makars Tourism Agency,** Peldu 1 (☎924 49 48; www.makars.lv), which rents **tents** (4-7Ls per day) and arranges **canoe** and **rafting trips** starting at 5Ls per hour.

CĒSIS
☎(8)41

Quiet Cēsis (TSEH-siss; pop. 17,500) is famous for sprawling medieval ruins and its local brew, Cēsu, sold in bottles all over the country. The country's 2nd-oldest city (after Rīga), it recently restored its landmark castle for its 800th anniversary in 2006. Keep an eye on www.cesis.lv for updates on the festivities, which include late-night concerts and events held in the beautiful castle park. Crusading Germans arrived to the area in 1209, and over the next three decades built the famous ▧Cēsis Castle, which hasn't fared so well over time. When Russia's **Ivan the Terrible** laid siege in 1577, its defenders chose to fill the cellars with gunpowder and blow themselves up rather than surrender. The castle was later rebuilt, but in 1703, an attack by **Peter the Great** left it in tatters. In the late 18th century, a Baltic German nobleman constructed a **new wing** as his personal estate; it now houses a **history museum** that displays archaeological artifacts. Museum admission includes access to the new castle's **tower**, with its impressive views of the Gauja Valley, and the old castle's recently reopened **ruins**. Put on a hard hat, grab a candle-lantern, and climb the narrow medieval staircases. Descend into the dank dungeon before emerging to enjoy the castle gardens. At the garden entrance, you will encounter a fallen Lenin statue sitting in a wooden coffin. (☎412 26 15. Open May 15-Sept. Tu-Su 10am-6pm; Nov.-May 14 W-Su 10am-5pm. Tours in English, German, Latvian or Russian; 15Ls.) Ivan also destroyed the nearby **Āraiši Castle**, which remains in ruins. The castle, on the near shore of Lake Āraiši, is part of the **Open-Air Archaeological Museum**. Steps away from the Āraiši castle is a reconstruction of a **Latgale settlement** that stood on the site from the 9th to 12th centuries. The Latgales were a short tribe—watch your head as you enter the huts. To the right is a small **Stone Age reed dwelling**, modeled after what archaeologists believe once stood here. The best way to Āraiši is by bike: head out of town on Piebalgas iela, take a right on P20 (in the direction of Rīga) and take a left when you see a sign post for the museum. Infrequent buses leave Cēsis for Drabeši, stopping at Āraiši. (☎419 7288. English captions. Open Apr. 15-Dec. daily 11am-5pm. 0.80Ls, students 0.40Ls.)

Cēsis is reached by infrequent **trains** from **Rīga** via **Sigulda** (1½-2hr.; 2 per day; about 1Ls, bikes 0.21Ls). **Buses** from **Rīga** (2hr., 1-2 per hr. 6am-9pm, 1.30Ls) are more convenient. Call ahead if you want to reserve a **bike** (5Ls per day) at **Cēsu Tourism Inventory**, Lencu iela 6 (☎942 32 70). It is a 2-3hr. ride to Sigulda each way. **Public transportation** consists of two **buses** (0.20Ls): bus #9 runs west to the Gauja River, while bus #11 runs east along **Jana Poruka iela** and down **Lapsu iela. Raunas iela** heads to the town center from the station and opens onto the main square, **Vienības laukums. Rīgas iela** and **Valnu iela** go downhill at the square's south end and meet at **Līvu laukums**, the original 13th-century heart of the town. **Lenču iela,** which leads from Vienības laukums, travels to Cēsis Castle (Cēsu Pils). The English-speaking staff at the **Tourist Information Center**, Pils laukums 1, across from the castle, arranges **private rooms** in the region or elsewhere in Latvia (1Ls) and has **free maps** and one computer with **Internet**. (☎412 18 15; www.cesis.lv. 1Ls per hr. Open May 15-Sept. 15 M-F 9am-6pm, Sa-Su 10am-5pm.) **Exchange currency** at **Unibanka**, Raunas iela 8, which cashes **traveler's checks** and gives MC/V **cash advances**. (☎220 31. Open M-F 9am-5pm.) There are 24hr. **ATMs** on Rigas iela. Ask the cashier at the **bus** and **train station** to **store luggage**. (☎412 27 62. Cash windows open 6am-8pm.) The **post office** is at Raunas iela 13, at the corner of Vienības laukums. (☎227 88. **Western Union**. Open M-F 7:30am-6pm, Sa 7:30am-4pm.) **Postal Code**: LV-4101.

Hotel Cēsis ❺, Vienības laukums 1, is luxurious, with huge beds and sparkling clean private baths. (☎412 0122; www.danlat-group.lv. English spoken. Breakfast included. Singles 30Ls; doubles 42Ls. Sept.-May 25% off. MC/V.) The hotel's lively **Cafe Popular ❶** serves superb Latvian food by the kilo. (☎412 23 92. Entrees 1-2Ls. Open M-Th and Su 11am-11pm, F-Sa 11am-midnight. MC/V.) **Putniņkrogs ❶**, Saules iela 23, isn't bad for 70s-style Soviet accommodations, with small beds and a lot of concrete. Cross the train tracks and follow Vaives iela away from town; turn right on Saules iela. (☎412 02 90. 5Ls per person.) **Madara '89,** Raunas 15, is a supermarket. (Open daily 8am-10pm.)

LITHUANIA
(LIETUVA)

Lithuania has always been an offbeat place. Once the last pagan holdout in Christian Europe, the tiny country continues to forge an eccentric path, from the breakaway artists' republic and Frank Zappa statue in its spectacular capital, Vilnius, to a magical countryside filled with drifting sand dunes, quirky folk art, and even a decaying Soviet missile base. More conventional treats include the wild beauty of the unspoiled coast and the Baroque architecture of Vilnius's Old Town. Lithuania became the first Baltic nation to declare independence from the USSR in 1990, gained EU membership in 2004, and continues to push ahead with optimism, growing more Western with every passing year but retaining its unique sensibilities.

 DISCOVER LITHUANIA: SUGGESTED ITINERARIES

THREE DAYS Head straight to the **Baltic Coast** to enjoy the stunning—and stunningly free of tourists—coastal sands of the **Drifting Dunes of Parnidis** (1 day; p. 415) and the bewitching folk art in the seaside forest of **Witches' Hill** (1 day; p. 415); then leave the **Curonian Spit** and head up the coast to the haunting **Soviet Missile Base** (p. 414).

ONE WEEK After three days on the **Baltic Coast,** go inland to the unique **Hill of Crosses** outside lively **Šiauliai** (1 day; p. 405). Continue to cosmopolitan **Vilnius** (3 days; p. 385), where you can explore the cobblestoned **Old Town,** wander offbeat **Užupis,** and take a daytrip to the ancient capital of Lithuania, **Trakai Castle** (p. 397).

FACTS AND FIGURES

Official Name: Republic of Lithuania.
Capital: Vilnius.
Major Cities: Kaunas, Klaipėda.
Population: 3,596,617. (83% Lithuanian, 7% Polish, 6% Russian, 4% other).

Land Area: 65,200 sq. km.
Time Zone: GMT + 2.
Language: Lithuanian.
Religion: Roman Catholic (79%).

ESSENTIALS

WHEN TO GO

Summer is brief but glorious in Lithuania, while winter is long and cold. Tourist season peaks in July and August, especially along the coast. A winter visit also has its charms, especially if you are headed for Vilnius or other major cities, but be aware that many establishments along the coast close in the low season.

DOCUMENTS AND FORMALITIES

EMBASSIES AND CONSULATES. Foreign embassies to Lithuania are in Vilnius (p. 385). Lithuanian embassies and high commissions abroad are: **Australia,** 40B Fiddens Wharf Rd., Killara, NSW, 2071 (☎02 9498 2571); **Canada,** 130 Albert St., Suite 204, Ottowa, Ontario, K1P 5G4 (☎613-567-5458; litemb@storm.ca); **Ireland,** 90

ENTRANCE REQUIREMENTS

Passport: Required for all travelers.

Visa: Not required for stays under 90 days for citizens of Australia, Canada, Ireland, New Zealand, the UK, and the US.

Letter of Invitation: Not required for citizens of Australia, Canada, Ireland, New Zealand, the UK, and the US.

Inoculations: Recommended up-to-date on DTaP (diphtheria, tetanus, and pertussis), Hepatitis A, Hepatitis B, MMR (measles, mumps, and rubella), Polio booster, and Typhoid.

Work Permit: Required of all foreigners planning to work in Lithuania.

Driving Permit: Required for all those planning to drive in Lithuania.

Merrion Rd. Ballsbridge, Dublin 4 (☎1 668 8292); **New Zealand,** 28 Heather St. Parnell, Auckland (☎ 9 379 66 39; saul@f1rst.co.nz); **UK,** 84 Gloucester Place, London W1U 6AU (☎020 7486 6401/2; http://lithuania.embassyhomepage.com); **US,** 2622 16th St., NW, Washington, DC 20009 (☎202-234-5860; info@ltembassyus.org).

VISA AND ENTRY INFORMATION. Citizens of Australia, Canada, New Zealand, the UK, and the US do not need a visa for stays of up to 90 days. "Special Visas" for temporary residence (€60; valid for up to 1 year), can be purchased from the

Migration Department of the Ministry of the Interior. Avoid crossing through Belarus to enter or exit Lithuania: not only do you need to obtain a visa (US$100) for Belarus in advance, but guards may hassle you at the border.

TOURIST SERVICES AND MONEY

LITAI (LT)		
	AUS$1 = 2.14LT	1LT = AUS$0.47
	CDN$1 = 2.32LT	1LT = CDN$0.43
	EUR€1 = 3.45LT	1LT = EUR€0.30
	NZ$1 = 1.97LT	1LT = NZ$0.51
	UK£1 = 5.08LT	1LT = UK£0.20
	US$1 = 2.81LT	1LT = US$0.36

Major cities have official **tourist offices. Litinterp** reserves accommodations and rents cars, usually without a surcharge. Kaunas, Klaipėda, Nida, Palanga, and Vilnius each have an edition of the *In Your Pocket* series, available at kiosks and some hotels. Employees at tourist stations often speak English.

The unit of **currency** is the **Lita** (pl. Litai; 1Lt=100 centas), which is fixed to the euro at €1 = 3.4528Lt. Prices are stable, with **inflation** at just under 1%. Exchange bureaus near the train station usually have poorer rates than banks. Most banks cash **traveler's checks** for 2-3% commission. Visa **cash advances** can usually be obtained with minimum hassle. **Vilniaus Bankas,** with outlets in major cities, accepts major credit cards and traveler's checks for a small commission. Most places catering to locals don't take credit cards. Additionally, some establishments that claim to take MasterCard or Visa may not actually be able to do so. **ATMs** are readily available in most cities, though few accept American Express.

HEALTH AND SAFETY

EMERGENCY	**Police: ☎ 112. Ambulance: ☎ 112. Fire: ☎ 112.**

Well-stocked **pharmacies** are common and carry most medical supplies, tampons, condoms, and toiletries. Drink bottled mineral water, and **boil tap water** for 10min. before drinking. A triangle pointing downward indicates men's **restrooms;** one pointing upward indicates women's restrooms. Many bathrooms are nothing but a hole in the ground; carry toilet paper. Lithuania's **crime rate** is generally low, though cab drivers will think nothing of ripping off a tourist. Vilnius is one of the safer capitals in Europe, although street crime does occur. Lithuanian **police** are helpful but understaffed; your best bet for assistance in English is your **consulate.**

Women traveling alone will be noticed but shouldn't encounter too much difficulty. Skirts, blouses, and heels are far more common than jeans, shorts, tank tops, or sneakers, though showing skin becomes more acceptable in the club scene. **Minorities** traveling to Lithuania may encounter unwanted attention or discrimination, though most is directed toward Roma (gypsies). Lithuania has made little effort to provide services or facilities for **disabled** travelers. **Homosexuality** is legal but not always tolerated. Lithuania has the most nightclubs, hotlines, and services for **GLBT** travelers to the Baltics (see **Vilnius: Practical Information,** p. 388).

TRANSPORTATION

Finnair, LOT, Lufthansa, SAS, and other **airlines** fly into Vilnius. **Trains** are more popular for international and long-distance travel. Two major lines cross Lithuania: one runs north-south from **Latvia** through **Šiauliai** and **Kaunas** to **Poland;** the other runs

MICROBUSING. White microbuses travel the main bus routes in most Lithuanian cities, and are faster and more frequent than city buses. Marked with the bus number and destination in the front window, the microbuses are usually 0.05Ls more expensive than regular transport, but you can hail them from anywhere along the side of the road by sticking out your hand, and be dropped off where you like—just ask the driver nicely, and in advance of your stop.

east-west from **Belarus** through **Vilnius** and Kaunas to **Kaliningrad,** branching out around Vilnius and **Klaipėda.** Domestic **buses** are faster, more common, and only a bit more expensive than trains, which are often crowded. Whenever possible, try to catch an **express bus** to your destination; such buses are normally marked with an asterisk or an "E" on the timetable. They are typically direct and can be up to twice as fast. Vilnius, Kaunas, and Klaipėda are easily reached by train or bus from **Estonia, Latvia, Poland,** and **Russia. Ferries** connect Klaipėda with **Arhus** and **Aabenra, DEN; Kiel** and **Mukran, GER;** and **Ahus** and **Karlshamn, SWE.** As of March 2002, all travelers planning to drive in Lithuania must purchase a **Liability Insurance Policy** at the Lithuanian border (79Lt for the 15-day min.). These policies may only be purchased with Litas, so make sure to convert some cash before reaching the border. **US** citizens may drive with an American driver's license for up to three months; all other motorists must have an **International Driving Permit.** Inexpensive **taxis** are in most cities. Agree on a price before getting in. **Hitchhiking** is common. Many drivers charge a fee comparable to local bus or train fares. Locals line up along major roads leaving large cities. *Let's Go* does not recommend hitchhiking.

KEEPING IN TOUCH

PHONE CODES	**Country code: 370. International dialing prefix: 00.** From outside Lithuania, dial int'l dialing prefix (see inside back cover) + 370 + city code + local number. Within Lithuania, dial 8 + city code + local number. Within cities, just dial the 6-digit number.

Internet is widely available in Lithuania, though rarely for free. Most well-located Internet cafes charge 3-6Lt per hour. There are two kinds of public **phones:** rectangular ones take magnetic strip cards, and rounded ones take chip cards. Phone cards (8-30Lt) are sold at phone offices and kiosks. Calls to Estonia and **Latvia** cost 1.65Lt per min.; Europe 5.80Lt; and the US 7.32Lt. International access numbers include: **AT&T Direct** (☎8 800 90028); **Canada Direct** (☎8 800 90004); **Sprint** (☎8 800 95877). **Airmail** *(oro pastu)* **letters** abroad cost 1.70Lt (postcards 1.20Lt) and take about one week to reach the US. **Poste Restante** is available in Vilnius but hard to find elsewhere. Address the envelope as follows: Neasa (First name) COLL (LAST NAME), POSTE RESTANTE, Laisves al. 102 (post office address), LT-3000 (postal code) Kaunas (city), LITHUANIA.

ACCOMMODATIONS AND CAMPING

LITHUANIA	❶	❷	❸	❹	❺
ACCOMMODATIONS	under 30Lt under €9 under US$11	31-80Lt €9-23 US$11-28	81-130Lt €24-38 US$29-46	131-180Lt €39-52 US$47-63	over 180Lt over €52 over US$63

Lithuania has many youth **hostels,** particularly in Vilnius and Klaipėda. HI membership is nominally required, but an LJNN guest card (10.50Lt at any of the hostels) will suffice. The head office is in Vilnius (see **Vilnius: Practical Information,** p. 386).

LITHUANIA

Their *Hostel Guide* has maps and info on bike and car rentals and hotel reservations. **Hotels** across the price spectrum abound in Vilnius and most major towns. **Litinterp**, with offices in Vilnius, Kaunas, and Klaipėda, assists in finding homestays or apartments for rent. **Camping** is restricted by law to marked campgrounds; the law is well enforced, particularly along the Curonian Spit.

FOOD AND DRINK

LITHUANIA	❶	❷	❸	❹	❺
FOOD	under 8Lt under €2 under US$3	8-17Lt €2-5 US$3-6	18-30Lt €6-9 US$7-11	31-40Lt €10-12 US$12-14	over 40Lt over €12 over US$14

Lithuanian cuisine is heavy and sometimes greasy. Keeping a **vegetarian** or **kosher** diet is difficult, but not impossible. Restaurants serve various types of *blynai* (pancakes) with *mėsa* (meat) or *varske* (cheese). *Cepelinai* are heavy, potato-dough missiles of meat, cheese, and mushrooms; *saltibarščiai* is a beet-and-cucumber soup prevalent in the east; *karbonadas* is breaded pork fillet; and *koldunai* are meat dumplings. Lithuanian **beer** flows freely. *Kalnapis* is popular in Vilnius and most of Lithuania, *Baltijos* reigns supreme around Klaipėda, and the award-winning *Utenos* is everywhere. Lithuanian **vodka** *(degtinė)* is also popular.

LIFE AND TIMES

HISTORY

PAGAN AND PROUD OF IT. The Baltic people settled in the region 2000 years before the Christian era. The **Žemaičiai** tribe occupied the western part of Lithuania, and the **Aukštaitiai** inhabited the east. Defiantly pagan Lithuania was the last country in Europe to accept Christianity. The Lithuanian tribes united briefly under Aukštaitiai leader **Mindaugas,** who accepted **Christianity** in 1251 and was named the country's first Grand Duke by Pope Innocent IV. Mindaugas was assassinated, likely by pagan princes, in 1263. In the 14th century, Lithuanian territory swelled as **Grand Duke Gediminas** consolidated power.

UNION. Jogaila, Gediminas's grandson, married the 12-year-old Polish Princess Jadwiga and became Wladisław II Jagiełło, King of Poland, in 1385. With this union, Jogaila introduced **Roman Catholicism** to Lithuania: the Aukštaitiai were baptized in 1387 and the Žemaičiai in 1413. Jogaila forged a bond between Lithuania and Poland that was to last 400 years and rival the power of Muscovy. Jogaila delegated control of Lithuania to his onetime rival **Vytautas Didysis** (the Great), most famous for his defeat of the Teutonic Knights at the 1410 Battle of Grunwald. Together, they expanded their empire until Vytautas's death in 1430, at which point Lithuanian territory included present-day Belarus and Ukraine, stretching from the Baltics to the Black Sea, from Vilnius to within 160km of Moscow. Lithuania solidified its ties to Poland with the 1569 **Union of Lublin,** which created the **Polish-Lithuanian Commonwealth,** heralding a period of prosperity and cultural development. Along with the alliance came further class division, as the nobility became steeped in Polish culture while the peasantry held on to the old customs.

DECLINE AND FALL. In the 18th century, the growing power of Russia and Prussia led to the three **Partitions of Poland** (p. 422), which ceded most of Lithuania to Russia. By 1815, Russia had complete control of the territory. Nationalist uprisings in Poland in 1830-31 and 1863 provoked intensified campaigns of **Russification** in Lithuania. German troops returned to Lithuania in 1915, 500 years after the defeat of the Teutonic knights. They left at the end of 1918. The Lithuanians next had to expel the Red Army in 1919. They then declared **independence,** but during the confusion Poland took **Vilnius**—the population of the city being predominantly Polish—and refused to release it. A dispute also arose with Germany over the port of **Klaipėda,** a predominantly German city that was Lithuania's only viable harbor on the Baltic. Germany won, claiming the city as their own.

STUCK IN THE MIDDLE AGAIN. Deprived of its capital and primary port, Lithuania did not remain independent for long. The country's parliamentary democracy collapsed in 1926 in a coup, as dictator **Antanas Smetona** banned opposition parties. Whatever autonomy remained disappeared with the 1939 **Nazi-Soviet Non-Aggression Pact,** which invited the Soviets to invade. In June 1941, the Soviets began to exile Lithuanians to remote regions of the USSR. Some 35,000 people were displaced. Nazi occupation caused even greater devastation, as Lithuania lost another 250,000 citizens, including most of its Jewish population.

POLITICAL FREE-FOR-ALL. The Soviets returned in 1944, opposed by Lithuanian guerrilla fighters—at their height 40,000 strong—into the early 1950s. It was not until the 1960s that **Antanas Sniečkus** managed to solidify Soviet rule. Even then, resistance persisted through the stagnation of the 1970s and 1980s, as the republic generated more *samizdat* ("self-made" dissident publications) per capita than any other region in the Soviet bloc. **Mikhail Gorbachev's** democratic reforms fell on dangerously fertile ground, and on March 1, 1990, Lithuania seceded from the USSR. Moscow retaliated, futilely attempting to disconnect the region's oil and gas resources. In what has come to be known as the "Lithuanian massacre," the Soviets launched an assault on Vilnius's radio and TV center, killing 14. In the wake of the failed Soviet *putsch* of August 1991, Lithuania finally achieved independence.

TODAY

Although still poor relative to the rest of Central Europe, Lithuania got off to an early start on economic reforms, and has been labeled by investors as one of Eastern Europe's economic "tigers." Having joined both the **EU** and **NATO** in the spring of 2004, Lithuania is attempting to break from its Russia-dominated past. Prime Minister **Algirdas Brazauskas,** elected to the position in 2001, is a former Communist. President **Rolandas Paksas,** who was elected in 2003, made history by being

IN RECENT NEWS

TRAFFICKING IN EXPLOITATION

Each month, dozens of young Lithuanian women are sold into slavery. Since the country joined the EU in 2004, the number of women sold into Western European brothels has been on the rise—drastically.

Young women are lured abroad with promises of legitimate work as nannies or waitresses, only to arrive in their destination country and find themselves sold into slavery. Often, trusted family friends are the perpetrators of the trade. When women manage to escape back to their homes in Lithuania, their stories of slavery abroad are often not believed. The stigma associated with prostitution weighs heavily upon victims of trafficking, and support for those who survive the ordeal is weak.

In the summer of 2005, Lithuania launched a three-year initiative to help victims of trafficking who have returned home. The program, Integration and Re-integration of Victims of Human Trafficking into Working Society, is meant to combat stereotypes and provide a brighter future for trafficking victims.

To find out more about the trafficking of women and children to and from Lithuania and neighboring countries, and the fight against the trade, visit the following websites:

www.thefuturegroup.org

http://gvnet.com/humantrafficking/Lithuania.htm

www.missing.lt

the first modern European head of state to be impeached. He was dismissed in April 2004. In a special election in June 2004, Lithuanians put former President **Valdas Adamkus** back in office.

PEOPLE AND CULTURE

The population of Lithuania is 80% **Lithuanian**, 9% **Russian**, and 7% **Polish**. The vast majority of Lithuanians are **Roman Catholic**. **Lithuanian** is one of only two Baltic languages (Latvian is the other). All "r"s are trilled. **Polish** is helpful in the south and **German** on the coast. **Russian** is understood in most places, although it is not as prominent as in Latvia. Most Lithuanians understand basic English phrases. If someone seems to sneeze at you, he might be saying *ačiu* (ah-choo; thank you). For a phrasebook and glossary, see **Glossary: Lithuanian**, p. 775. Reserve informal greetings for those you know personally. Say *"laba diena"* (good day) whenever you enter a shop. In polite company, you can never say *"prašau"* too many times (pra-sho; both "please" and "you're welcome"). Lithuanians usually **tip** 10%.

THE ARTS

The earliest Lithuanian writings were the *Chronicles of the Grand Duchy of Lithuania*, written in an East Slavic dialect. The first book in Lithuanian, a Lutheran catechism, was printed in 1547. The year 1706 saw the appearance of secular literature with the publication in Lithuanian of *Aesop's Fables*. A Lithuanian translation of the **New Testament** was published in 1701 and a Lithuanian Bible in 1727. After 1864, many writers violated the tsarist ban on publishing Lithuanian works in Latin letters (as opposed to Cyrillic), seeking to overthrow Russian political and Polish cultural control. Known for both dramatic and lyric poetry, **Jonas Mačiulis** (a.k.a. Maironis) launched modern Lithuanian poetry with his 1895 *Voices of Spring (Pavasario balsai)*. During the interwar period, ex-priest **Vincas Mykolaitis-Putinas** pioneered the modern Lithuanian novel with *In the Shadows of the Altars (Altorių sesėly)*. After WWII, Soviet rule gagged and shackled Lithuanian writers; however, the poetry of **Alfonsas Nyka-Niliunas** and the novels of **Marius Katiliskis** flouted propagandistic Soviet Socialist Realism. *Pre-Dawn Highways*, by **Bronius Radzevicius**, is considered the strongest work of the late Soviet period.

Both Lithuanian **music** and **painting** have been heavily influenced by traditional folk culture. Much of the visual arts' development has centered on the **Vilnius Drawing School,** founded in 1866; painter **Mikalojus Čiurlionis** was a major figure. Lithuanian-American independent filmmaker **Jonas Mekas** is best known for his 1976 film *Lost Lost Lost*—an account of his arrival in New York and his contact with New York counter-culture figures of the 50s, like Allen Ginsberg and Frank O'Hara.

HOLIDAYS AND FESTIVALS

Holidays: New Year's Day and Flag Day (Jan. 1); Independence Day (Feb. 16); Restoration of Independence (Mar. 11); Easter Holiday (Apr. 16, 2006; Apr. 8 2007); Labor Day (May 1); Statehood Day (July 6); Feast of the Assumption (Aug. 15); All Saints' Day (Nov. 1); Christmas (Dec. 25-6).

Festivals: Since the 19th century, regional craftsmen have gathered to display their wares each March in Vilnius at the Kaziukas Fair. In the fall, the capital also hosts the Vilnius Jazz Festival and the avante-garde theater festival, SIRENOS. Trakai Castle hosts classical music concerts in July and August during the Trakai Festival. During spring's Užgavėnės festival, citizens dress as animals or demons and burn an image of winter in effigy.

ADDITIONAL RESOURCES

GENERAL HISTORY

The Baltic Revolution: Estonia, Latvia, Lithuania and the Path to Independence, by Anatol Lieven (1993). Contrasts the Baltic states' respective histories.

The Jews of Lithuania, by Masha Greenbaum (1995). A must for anyone interested in Lithuania's rich Jewish history.

FICTION, NONFICTION, AND FILM

Bohin Manor, by Tadeusz Konwicki (1990). Set in Lithuania in the aftermath of the 1863 uprising in Poland, this dreamlike novel chronicles the inner turmoil of Soviet life.

The Issa Valley (1998) and **Native Realm** (1968), by Czesław Miłosz. In the former book, Poland's Nobel Laureate poet describes his childhood in the Vilnius of imperial Russia; the latter, his autobiography, reflects upon the history of his home city and all of Eastern Europe.

There Is No Ithaca: Idylls of Semeniskiai and Reminiscences, by Jonas Mekas (1996). A series of reflections from a Lithuanian who left the country to become an underground New York filmmaker.

Reminiscences of a Journey to Lithuania, directed by Jonas Mekas (1971-72). A film diary of Mekas's first trip to his country of birth after 25 years of exile.

VILNIUS ☎(8)5

Vilnius is rough around the edges. Just steps from the red tile roofs and color-drenched facades of the restored Old Town, beer cans lay scattered around decaying buildings and boarded-up apartment blocks are covered in graffiti. Many travelers consider this scruffiness part of the city's charm—it's certainly one reason that Vilnius remains so affordable for visitors. From the top of Gediminas' Hill, where an apparition convinced the Grand Duke Gediminas to build the city in 1323, you can take in the extraordinary breadth of the capital. Vilnius has suffered a series of foreign occupations: Russia, France, and Germany have all conquered the city, and WWII left it in shambles. On the other hand, this history has also lent Vilnius a more international feel than any other city in the Baltics.

⌐ TRANSPORTATION

Flights: Vilnius Airport (Vilniaus oro uostas), Rodūnės Kelias 2 (info ☎230 6666; www.vilnius-airport.lt), 5km south of town. Buy a bus ticket (0.80Lt) from the Lietuvos Spauda kiosk on your right as you exit the departure hall. Take Bus #1 to the Geležinkelio Stotis train station to reach the Old Town. Airlines include: **Air Baltic** (☎235 6000; www.airbaltic.com); **Austrian Airlines** (☎231 3137; www.austrianairlines.lt); **British Airways** (☎210 6311; www.ba.com); **Czech Airlines** (☎232 9292; www.czech-airlines.com); **Finnair** (☎261 9339; www.finnair.com); **Lithuanian Airlines** (☎233 6077; www.lal.lt); **LOT** (☎273 9020; www.lot.com); **Lufthansa** (☎230 6031; www.lufthansa.com); **SAS** (☎235 6000; www.scandinavian.net).

Trains: Geležinkelio Stotis, Geležinkelio 16 (☎233 0086, reservations 269 3722; www.litrail.lt). Domestic tickets are sold to the left and international to the right. Tickets for trains originating outside of Lithuania can be bought between 3hr. and 5min. before departure. Open daily 6-11am and noon-6pm. Most international trains pass through Belarus, which requires a Belarusian transit visa. To: **Berlin, GER** (22hr., 1 per day,

300Lt); **Kaliningrad, RUS** (7hr., 14 per day, 48Lt); **Minsk, BLR** (6hr., 2 per day, 19-50Lt); **Moscow, RUS** (17hr., 3 per day, 103Lt); **Rīga, LAT** (8hr., 1 per day, 80Lt); **St. Petersburg, RUS** (18hr., 3 per day, 91Lt); **Warsaw, POL** (8hr., 2 per day, 85Lt).

Buses: Autobusų Stotis, Sodų 22 (☎290 1661, reservations 216 2977; www.toks.lt), opposite the train station. Tickets for bus travel within Lithuania can be bought at the row of kiosks to the left of the information center. **Eurolines Baltic International (EBI**; ☎215 1377; www.eurolines.lt) offers routes to **Minsk, BLR** (5hr. 3 per day, 25Lt); **Rīga, LAT** (5hr., 4 per day, 40Lt); **St. Petersburg, RUS** (18hr., 4 per day, 45Lt); **Tallinn, EST** (9hr., 2 per day, 90Lt); **Warsaw, POL** (9-10hr., 3 per day, 97Lt); **Berlin** (17hr., 1 per day, 183Lt); and other points west. Buy tickets in EBI kiosks to the right of the main entrance to the bus station. English spoken at most EBI kiosks. Student discount with valid ISIC. Open daily 6am-10pm.

Public Transportation: Buses and **trolleys** link downtown with the train and bus stations and the suburbs. Most lines run daily 6am-midnight. Buy tickets for state-owned buses at any kiosk (0.80Lt) or from the driver (1Lt); some private buses require you to pay fare on board (0.70-1Lt). Be sure to punch your ticket in one of the red boxes on the state-owned buses to avoid a 20Lt fine—tickets are checked more often than you'd expect. Monthly passes are available for students (50Lt).

Taxis: Martino (☎240 0004, from a mobile 1422). Although slightly more expensive than other taxi companies, it is said to have the safest and most reliable service. Vilnius drivers are notorious for overcharging foreigners who hail cabs from the side of the street. If you're at a cafe or restaurant, ask your server to call for a cab, as the fare will likely be half the rate you would have paid if you tried to hail one yourself.

✚ ORIENTATION

The **train** and **bus stations** are located on opposite sides of **Geležinkelio.** With your back to the train station, turn and walk to your right, passing McDonald's on your left and continuing 300m until you reach the base of a hill with an overpass on your right; turn left onto Aušros Vartų, which leads through the **Aušros Vartai** (Gates of Dawn) into **Senamiestis** (Old Town). Aušros Vartų becomes Didžioji and then Pilies before reaching the base of **Gediminas' Hill.** Here, the Gediminas Tower of Higher Castle presides over **Arkikatedros Aikštė** (Cathedral Sq.) and the banks of the **Neris River.** Beyond Gediminas Hill to the east, the small **Vilnia River** winds north to the bigger Neris River. The commercial artery, **Gedimino,** leads west from the square in front of the Cathedral.

⑦ PRACTICAL INFORMATION

TOURIST AND FINANCIAL SERVICES

Tourist Offices: Tourist Information Center (TIC) maintains 3 branches with courteous and knowledgeable staffers who speak fluent English. All offer excellent **free maps** as well as train and bus schedules, international calling cards, and souvenirs. Bicycles for touring the Old Town are available at the Vilniaus location, for the unbeatable price of 1Lt per day. Main office at Vilniaus 22 (☎262 96 60; www.turizmas.vilnius.lt), 50m north of the Radvilai Palace. Branches at Didžioji 31 (☎262 6470), at the northeast corner of the Town Hall, and at Geležinkelio 16 (☎269 2091), in a kiosk inside the train station, to the left after passing through the main entrance. Open M-F 9am-6pm, Sa-Su 10am-4pm. **Kelvita Tourism Agency,** Geležinkelio 16 (☎210 6130; fax 210 6131), in a kiosk inside the train station at windows #29 & #30. German and English spoken. Turnaround is quick for visas to Russia. American visas priced 470Lt for 24hr. wait or 260Lt for 8-day wait. Citizens of other English-speaking countries pay roughly 20% less. Open M-F 8am-6pm, Sa 10am-4pm.

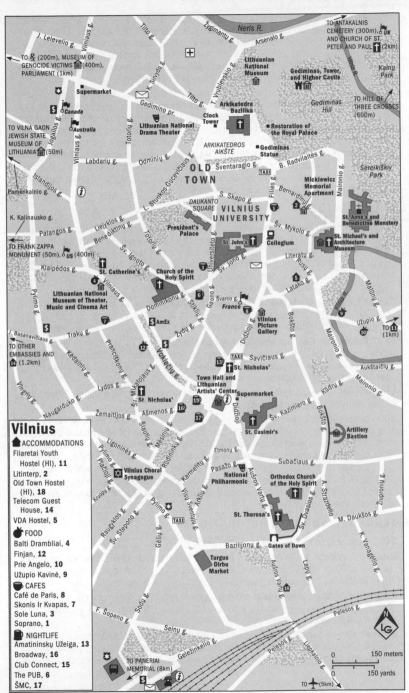

LITHUANIA

Vilnius

🏠 **ACCOMMODATIONS**
Filaretai Youth
    Hostel (HI), **11**
Litinterp, **2**
Old Town Hostel
    (HI), **18**
Telecom Guest
    House, **14**
VDA Hostel, **5**

🍎 **FOOD**
Balti Drambliai, **4**
Finjan, **12**
Prie Angelo, **10**
Užupio Kavinė, **9**

☕ **CAFES**
Café de Paris, **8**
Skonis Ir Kvapas, **7**
Sole Luna, **3**
Soprano, **1**

🎵 **NIGHTLIFE**
Amatininskų Užeiga, **13**
Broadway, **16**
Club Connect, **15**
The PUB, **6**
ŠMC, **17**

Embassies and Consulates: Australia, Vilniaus 23 (☎212 3369; australia@consulate.lt). Open Tu 10am-1pm, Th 2-5pm. **Canada,** Jogailos 4 (☎249 0950; vilnius@canada.lt). Visas M, W, F 9am-noon. Open daily 8:30am-5pm. **UK,** Antakalnio 2 (☎246 2900, emergency mobile 869 83 7097; www.britain.lt). Visas M-F 8:30am-11:30am. Open M-Th 8:30am-5pm, F 8:30am-4pm; **US,** Akmenų 6 (☎266 5500; www.usembassy.lt). Visas M-Th 8:30am-11:30am. Open M-F 8am-5:30pm.

Currency Exchange: Most currency kiosks exchange British pounds, euros, Latvian lats, Swedish crowns, Swiss francs, and US dollars. **Parex Bankas,** Geležinkelio 6 (☎233 0763), to the left with the train station at your back. Not the best rates, but changes several currencies that aren't accepted at many other banks. Open 24hr. **Vilniaus Bankas,** Vokiečių 9 (☎/fax 262 7869). Gives MC/V **cash advances** at no commission and cashes AmEx and Thomas Cook **traveler's checks.** Open M-F 8am-6pm. **Bankas Snoras** has good exchange rates, cashes traveler's checks, and gives Visa cash advances for a small commission. Look for blue-and-white kiosks throughout town. Open M-F 8am-7pm, Sa 9am-2pm. **ATMs** are ubiquitous.

LOCAL SERVICES

Luggage Storage: The storage center in the bus station near the main entrance charges 3Lt per bag per day. Open M-F 5:30am-9pm, Sa-Su 7am-9pm. A better option is the self-service, electronic facility beneath the train station. Take the stairs down from the ground fl. and turn right. Place your bag in an open locker, then insert 2Lt into the nearby machine. Save the receipt: you will need the PIN to retrieve your baggage. Rates start at 2Lt per 12hr., and are lower the longer you store your bag. Open 24hr.

English-Language Bookstore: J. Masiulio Knygynas, Pylimo 53, below the hill from the bus station (☎262 4528; prie-hales@masiulis.lt). Maintains a small section of English-language fiction, textbooks, and guidebooks. Open M-F 9am-6pm, Sa 9am-3pm.

GLBT Resources: Gay and Lesbian Information Line (☎233 3031; www.gay.lt). Info about organizations and events for gay and lesbian travelers. The **Lithuanian Gay and Lesbian Homepage** (www.gayline.lt) and **The Gay Club** (☎998 50 09; vgc@takas.lt) list gay and lesbian establishments in Lithuania.

Laundromat: Nearly all hostels and hotels in Vilnius offer full-service laundry, often even if you are not staying there (10-30Lt).

Bike Rental: Some hostels lend bikes to guests for free—ask a staff member. For touring the Old Town, rent a bicycle for just 1Lt per day from the **Tourist Information Center** at Vilniaus 22. Bicycle must be returned by 6pm. For more extensive trips, rent online from www.bicycle.lt, a website maintained by **Du Ratai** (Two Wheels), a branch of the Lithuanian Cyclists' Community. The very energetic Baltic cyclist can even rent in Lithuania and return the bicycle in Latvia or Estonia (or vice-versa). Rates start at €9 per day, and decrease to €6.50 per day for rentals of 15 days or more. Further discounts available for group or extended rentals.

EMERGENCY AND COMMUNICATIONS

24hr. Pharmacy: Gedimino Vaistinė, Gedimino pr. 27 (☎261 0135).

Medical Services: Baltic-American Medical and Surgical Clinic, Nemenčinės 54a (☎234 2020 or 698 526 55; www.bak.lt). Accepts major American, British, and other international insurance plans. Open daily 7am-11pm; doctors on call 24hr.

Telephones: Public **phone kiosks** are omnipresent in Vilnius. Except for emergency and toll-free lines, you must use a phone card, available from street vendors. See www.ntel.lt for more information.

Internet: Klubas Lux, Svitrigailos 5 (☎233 3788), just north of the intersection with A. Vivulsikio on the western edge of town, offers the best rates and fastest terminals. 2Lt per hr., 8Lt for all-night access 9pm-8am. Open 24hr. **Despina,** Pamėnkalnio 2 (☎268

5742; www.ic.lt). From Gedimino, turn left onto Jogailos and take the 2nd right, onto Paménkalnio, and go just beyond the park. 9am-noon and 8-10pm 3Lt per hr., noon-8pm 5Lt per hr. Metered rates, with a 1Lt min. 20% student discount. Open daily.

Post Office: Lietuvos Paštas, Gedimino 7 (☎261 6759; www.post.lt), west of Arkikatedros Aikštė (the Cathedral). **Poste Restante** at the window labeled "iki pareikalavimo"; 0.50Lt fee. Open M-F 7am-8pm, Sa 9am-4pm. **Postal Code:** LT-01001.

ACCOMMODATIONS

Litinterp, Bernardinų 7/2 (☎212 3850; www.litinterp.lt). This travel agency places guests in B&Bs in the Old Town or in its own beautiful, spacious rooms with spotless showers. English spoken. Breakfast included. Reception M-F 8:30am-5:30pm, Sa 9am-3pm. Reservations recommended. Singles 80Lt, with bath 100Lt; doubles 140-160Lt; triples 180-210Lt. 5% ISIC discount. MC/V. ❷

VDA Hostel, Latako 2 (☎212 0102; fax 210 5444). For most of the year, this Soviet-style concrete edifice offers both dorms for Lithuanian art students and low-cost private rooms for tourists. July 15-Sept. 20 the dorms are transformed into more accommodations. Rooms are equipped with desks, cupboards, and kettles. The free-flowing hot water is a backpacker's delight. Common area with kitchen and TV. 5-person dorms 18Lt; singles 43Lt; doubles 52-60Lt; triples 66-78Lt. Cash only. ❶

Telecom Guest House, A. Vivulskio 13a (☎264 4861; www.telecomguesthouse.lt). From the city center, follow Trakų, which turns into J. Basanavičiaus. Just before the green-domed church, turn left on Algirido, then right on A. Vivulskio; the guest house is located on a courtyard. New rooms with private bathrooms, TVs, minibars and A/C make the hard-to-find location well worth the search. English spoken. Hot and cold breakfast included. Singles 75Lt, with bath 220Lt; doubles 120/260Lt. MC/V. ❷

Old Town Hostel (HI), Aušros Vartų 20-15a (☎262 5357; www.balticbackpackers.com), in a courtyard 100m south of the Gates of Dawn. A great place to meet English-speaking travelers who stumble in from the clubs at 5am. Backpackers stuffed into mixed 8-person rooms complain about the lack of lockers, but the friendly staff make up for this shortcoming. Free coffee and Internet. Large, colorful communal kitchen and shared, and sometimes cold, showers. Linens extra. Reservations recommended. Dorms 34Lt, HI members 32Lt; 2- to 3-person apartments in central Vilnius 120-150Lt. MC/V. ❷

Filaretai Youth Hostel (HI), Filaretų 17 (☎215 4627; www.filaretaihostel.lt). Take #34 bus from the train station to "Filaretai," the 7th stop; on foot from downtown, go east on Užupio across the Vilnia River. Where road forks, bear left onto Krivių; at next fork, bear right onto Filaretų; hostel is in a courtyard on your right. The 1km hike from the Old Town is pleasant by day but dark at night. Rooms are large and windows keep the building bright during the day. Kitchen, laundry facilities, common room, free Internet, and bike rental. Luggage storage 3Lt. Linen 5Lt. Reserve ahead for June-Sept. and weekends. Dorms 24Lt; singles 68Lt; doubles 96Lt; triples 114Lt; quads 152Lt. Prices drop by 5Lt Oct.-Apr. 3Lt discount after 1st night. 4Lt fee for nonmembers. MC/V. ❷

FOOD

Vilnius's inexpensive restaurants dish out regional cuisine, though navigating untranslated menus can result in a surprise or two when your dishes arrive. Cafes offer delicious meals at almost any hour, but budget travelers might find supermarkets and picnic lunches more affordable. The several **Iki** supermarkets (www.iki.lt) on the outskirts of Vilnius stock local and Western brands. One convenient location is Sodu 22, opposite the bus station. (Open daily 8am-10pm.)

There are seven **Ikiukas** (literally "little Iki") minimarts inside the city, including branches at Uzupio 7, Pylmio 21, and A. Vivulskio 15. (Open daily 8am-11pm.) The centrally located **Rimi** supermarket, at Didžioji 28, is across the street from the Town Hall. For an authentic Lithuanian shopping experience, visit **Turgus Dirbu**, a sprawling indoor market at the corner of Pylmio and Bazilijonų. Inside the expansive building, rows of vendors offer freshly cut meat, homemade cheeses, fruits, vegetables, eggs, and baked goods. Walk south out of the Old Town through the Gates of Dawn; go right on Bazlijonu and continue for 250m. Look for locals selling flowers from baskets on the sidewalk. (Open Tu-Sa 7am-7pm, Su 7am-3pm.)

 Hop on a minibus (2Lt) outside the train station and head to Gariunai Market (Turgus Gariunv), about 8km from Vilnius. There, you can browse aisle upon endless aisle of food, tracksuits, shoes, scarves, power tools, wedding dresses, and almost anything else your heart desires. Your judgment of product quality will likely fall as the price does, so beware. Look for the minibus with "Gariunai" posted in the front window, usually parked directly across from the train station on Stoties. (Open Tu-Su 6-11am.)

■ **Balti Drambliai** (White Elephant), Vilniaus 41 (☎262 0875). Balti Drambliai is one of the few places in Vilnius that offers a decent range of options for vegetarians and vegans. Lanterns, seagulls, and flowers hang from a canopy in an outdoor courtyard with exposed brick walls, providing an ideal setting to enjoy dinner and drinks on long summer nights. Vegetable curry with spinach and paneer (8Lt) is flavorful, while the less adventurous might enjoy one of many vegetarian pizzas (from 5Lt). English menu. Live music many nights at 8pm. Open M-F 11am-midnight, Sa-Su 7pm-midnight. MC/V. ❶

Finjan, Vokiečių 18 (☎261 2104). With friendly Israeli servers, an Iranian chef, and seductive belly dancers (Th-Sa nights), recently renovated Finjan is one of the hottest spots in town. The hummus (8Lt) is spectacular, and spicy falafel is served in a steaming hot pita (7Lt). Vegetarians eat cheaply, and carnivores can devour mounds of meat like the mixed grill (37Lt). English menu. Open daily 11am-midnight. MC/V. ❸

Užupio Kavinė, Užupio 2 (☎212 2138). Offers a peaceful patio overlooking the Vilnia river and the opportunity to enjoy beer with breakfast. The extensive menu includes pages of salads (7-12Lt) and entrees (12-35Lt), including the "Ruins of Užupis," a pork-and-vegetable dish. English menu. Open daily 10am-11pm. MC/V. ❷

Prie Angelo, Užupio 9 (☎215 3790). Directly across from the Užupis Angel, this small restaurant serves up everything from delicate, thin-crust pizza (from 4Lt) to shared meat plates (65Lt). The charming decor and incredibly comfortable seats will only lengthen your stay. Bathrooms are perhaps the nicest in Vilnius. English menu. Entrees 9.50-22Lt. Open M-Th and Su 10am-11pm, F-Sa 10am-midnight. MC/V. ❷

◪ CAFES

■ **Sole Luna**, Universiteto 4 (☎212 0925). Step off the gray streets of Vilnius and into this vibrant Mediterranean-style cafe for a cup of Italian-crafted coffee (from 2.50Lt). With a spectacular courtyard beside the Presidential Palace, you can enjoy lunch (sandwiches 4Lt) or a glass of wine (from 3.50Lt) in the summer sun. English menu. Open M-W 10am-midnight, Th 10am-3am, F 10am-4am, Sa noon-4am, Su noon-11pm. MC/V.

Café de Paris, Didžioji 1 (☎261 1021; www.cafedeparis.lt). By day, homesick expats flow in from the adjacent French Embassy to enjoy authentic sweet or savory crepes (2.50-9Lt) and stylishly shabby decor. On W nights, live DJs rock the house, Café de Paris turns on the club lighting, and crowds pour out into the street. Open M-Tu 11am-10pm, W-Th 11am-2am, F 11am-3am, Sa noon-3am, Su noon-10pm. MC/V.

Skonis Ir Kvapas, Trakų 8 (☎212 2803). Tucked away in a quiet courtyard near the heart of the Old City, this charming cafe offers a fan-shaped menu of exotic teas (mug 5Lt, pot 7Lt). The name means "taste and smell," and, accordingly, servers will let you sniff your tea before ordering. English menu. Open daily 9:30am-11pm. MC/V.

Soprano, Pilies 3 (☎212 6042). At the end of the pedestrian thoroughfare, this cafe serves desserts to die for. The coffee is great, but it's the hazelnut or grapefruit gelato (2.50Lt cone, 3Lt bowl) that will keep you coming back for more. Flavors to please every ice-cream connoisseur. M-Th and Su 10am-11pm, F-Sa 10am-midnight. MC/V.

◙ SIGHTS

SENAMIESTIS AND BEYOND

▧ HIGHER CASTLE MUSEUM AND GEDIMINAS'
TOWER. Behind the cathedral (see below), a winding path leads to the top of the hill, from which visitors can enjoy awe-inspiring views of Vilnius. The hill has been crowned by a fortification since 200 BC, and is the present site of a majestic 15th-century Gothic structure. The **Higher Castle Museum** (Aukštutinės Pilies Muziejus) displays old maps and scale models of the castle, as well as turn-of-the-century photographs of the ruin. The main attraction, however, is an even more magnificent view of Senamiestis and Gedimino available from the top of **Gediminas' Tower.** *(Castle Hill, Arsenalo 5. ☎61 74 53. Open Mar.-Oct. daily 10am-7pm; Nov.-Feb. Tu-Su 11am-5pm. 4Lt, students 2Lt.)*

CATHEDRAL SQUARE (ARKIKATEDROS AIKŠTĖ). A shrine to the pagan god Perkūnas once stood upon the site of this Gothic cathedral. Years of renovations and a number of architects later, the cathedral has taken on a decidedly Neoclassical character. The remains of Casmir, Lithuania's patron saint, lie on the cathedral's southern side. The freestanding bell tower west of the cathedral dates to the 16th century, although the six bells inside were donated in 2002. Between the bell tower and the Cathedral, look for a small tile inscribed with the word "stebuklas" (miracle). This spot marks one end of the 1989 human chain that stretched from Vilnius to Tallinn, made up of about 2,000,000 Estonians, Latvians, and Lithuanians protesting Soviet rule. *(At the end of Pilies and Universiteto. ☎261 11 27. Open daily 7am-7pm.)* The **statue** of Grand Duke Gediminas, founder of Vilnius (see **History,** p. 382), was erected in 1996. To the east of the cathedral is the **Royal Palace,** which the city is hoping to rebuild in time for the 2009 millennial celebration of Lithuania's first mention in written records. *(Open daily 11am-6pm.)*

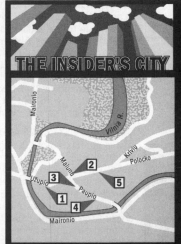

THE INSIDER'S CITY

REPUBLIC OF UŽUPIS

Cross over the Vilnia River to an eccentric neighborhood that declares itself an independent nation. Rising prices have driven many of the characters from this community of artists, but open studios and interesting landmarks make the winding streets of Užupis well worth a visit.

1 **Užupio Galerija** is filled with jewelry and metalwork by Lithuanian artists. You might catch someone working with goldsmithing tools. (Užupio 3.)

2 **Užupis Angel** was unveiled on April Fool's Day, 2002.

3 The **Constitution,** engraved in French, English, and Lithuanian, declares an offbeat list of rights for all people.

4 At the **Black Ceramics Workshop** you will find Eugenijus or his wife, Eglė, working at the potter's wheel. (Paupio 5.)

5 The **Kalvystės Amatų Galerija** is a working smithy where horseshoes, doorhandles, and traditional Lithuanian suncrosses are on display.

TOWN HALL SQUARE (ROTUŠĖS AIKŠTĖ). Located on Didžioji, Town Hall Square is an ancient marketplace dominated by the columns of the 18th-century **Town Hall**, now home to the **Lithuanian Artists' Center** (Lietuvos Menininkv Rumai), with exhibits of local work. When US President George W. Bush visited in 2002, he said that "anyone who would choose Lithuania as an enemy has also made an enemy of the United States of America." His words were immortalized in an engraving at the northeast corner of the hall. *(Didžioji 31.* ☎ *61 0619. Open M-F 9am-6pm.)* Lithuania's oldest church, the **Church of St. Nicholas** (Šv. Mikalojaus Bažnyčia), north of the Town Hall, was built in 1320 by German merchants while Lithuania was still a pagan nation. *(Didžioji 12.* ☎ *261 8559. Open daily 10am-6pm.)*

CHURCH OF ST. ANNE AND CHURCH OF ST. FRANCIS AND BERNARDINES. These churches, both dating to the 15th century, provide a beautiful architectural contrast. The Gothic exterior of St. Anne (Šv. Onos bažnyčia) may be the most frequently featured image on Vilnius postcards. Napoleon, arriving in the city triumphantly in the summer of 1812, supposedly said he wanted to carry the small church back to Paris in the palm of his hand. St. Francis and Bernardines (Bernardinų bažnyčia) housed the Vilnius Art Academy during Soviet times. It is worth a visit to see the faded paintings on the chipped plaster walls and the dull interior that maintains faint traces of past glory. *(Maironio 8, at the end of Bernardinų.)*

CHURCH OF ST. PETER AND PAUL (ŠV. APAŠTALŲ PETRO IR POVILO BAŽNYČIA). According to local lore, Italian stucco-workers built the incredibly ornate Baroque interior of this church in the late 17th century after the Grand Hetman of the Lithuanian armies, who commissioned the building, decided that Lithuanian sculptors were inferior. Note the chandelier, made from glass and brass beads and styled like a sailing ship. *(Antakalnio 1. Take tram #2, 3, or 4 from Senamiestis. Alternatively, head to the northeastern edge of the Old Town, where the Neris and Vilnia Rivers intersect, and follow T. Kosciuškos 2km until you reach the church.* ☎ *234 0229.)*

ANTAKALNIS CEMETERY (ANTAKALINO KAPINES). This stunning graveyard 3km outside the Old Town is a resting place for Lithuania's national heroes and artistic luminaries. Graves marked with folk-art crosses are mixed with large memorials to soldiers who died in WWI and WWII, as well as a sculpture commemorating the Lithuanians who died in clashes with the Soviet Army in 1991. Take the path to your left after entering to see a hill filled with rows of crosses marking Polish Legionnaire graves. *(Facing the Church of St. Peter and Paul, walk up Antakalnio, on your left, and continue 150m until the road forks. Bear right onto Sapiegos and continue 400m; at the archway, turn right onto Jūratės. Make the 1st left onto Kuosų, then the 1st right onto Kariu Kapu. Continue until you see a grassy hill with steps leading up to the cemetery.)*

HILL OF THREE CROSSES (TRJIŲ KRŽIŲ KALNAS). Here you'll find a view to rival that from Gediminas Hill, but in the company of fewer tourists and more Lithuanians, many of whom will be making out. From the northeast edge of the Old Town, cross the Arsenalo bridge and turn right up a winding road. Where the road diverges in front of an amphitheater, go right to reach the crosses and catch a breathtaking view of the area. Legend says that in the 13th century, pagans crucified Franciscan monks on the hill. Four centuries later, locals erected crosses to commemorate the martyrs; in 1950, Stalin dismantled the monuments. They were rebuilt in 1989 to both memorialize the martyred monks and pay homage to the Lithuanians who were deported to Siberia under the Soviet regime.

VILNIUS UNIVERSITY (VILNIAUS UNIVERSITETAS). This former Jesuit college dates to the late 16th century, when it figured prominently in the Counter-Reformation. Distinguished alums include 19th-century bard Adam Mickiewicz and Polish poet Czesław Miłosz, a Nobel Laureate in literature. *(3Lt, students 1Lt. Open M-Sa*

9am-6pm.) **St. John's Church** (Šv. Jonų bažnyčia), Šv. Jono 12, off Pilies, was a science museum under Soviet rule. *(Universiteto 3. ☎261 1795. Open M-Sa 10am-5pm.)* The 17th-century **Astronomical Observatory**, once rivaled in importance only by Greenwich and the Sorbonne, is opposite St. John's. With more than 5,000,000 volumes, the **university library** remains Lithuania's largest. The nearby **Church of the Holy Spirit** (Šv. Dvasios bažnyčia), a Baroque masterpiece, is the center of the Polish Catholic community of Vilnius. *(Dominikonų 8, near the intersection with Šv. Ignoto. ☎262 9595.)*

ST. CASIMIR'S CHURCH (ŠV. KAZIMIERO BAŽNYČIA). Named after the country's patron saint and topped with a golden crown to indicate Casimir's royal bloodline, this is the oldest Baroque church in Vilnius. Built by the Jesuits in 1604, the church has endured a painful history: Napoleon used it to store grain, tsarist authorities of the Russian Orthodox faith seized it from Catholics in 1841, invading Germans declared it a Lutheran house of worship in WWI, and the Soviets converted the church into a monument to atheism. The church returned to Catholic control in 1989. *(Didžioji 34. ☎222 1715. English info. Open M-Sa 4-6:30pm, Su 9am-1pm.)*

GATES OF DAWN (AUŠROS VARTAI). The Gates of Dawn, the only surviving portal of the city walls, have guarded the Old Town since the 16th century. The gates are a pilgrimage site for Eastern European Catholics, and it is common practice for locals to cross themselves before passing through, or to kneel and pray. After entering the Old Town, pass through a door to the right and climb the stairs; the gold-laced **portrait of the Virgin Mary** housed on the 2nd floor is said to have miraculous powers. When the chapel was built in 1671, the canvas reportedly healed a child who had fallen from a window. Karol Wojtyła sought to visit the Gates when he was archbishop of Kraków, but was blocked by Soviet authorities; he sent his skullcap instead, and—after being anointed as Pope John Paul II—finally visited Vilnius in 1993. *(Open daily 9am-6pm. Free.)* The highly decorated **St. Theresa's Church** (Šv. Teresės bažnyčia) was built between 1633 and 1652. The **Orthodox Church of the Holy Spirit** (Šv. Dvasios bažnyčia) is the seat of Lithuania's Russian Orthodox archbishop. It is the resting place of St. Antonius, Ivan, and Eustachius, martyred in 1347 by pagan militants. *(Aušros Vartų 10. ☎212 7765.)*

PARLIAMENT. In January 1991, the world watched as Lithuanians raised barricades to protect their parliament from the Soviet army. President Ladsbergis later said that all of the deputies expected to give their lives on the night of the Soviet invasion. West of the building, toward the river, a section of the barricade remains as a memorial. Crosses, flowers, and photographs honor those who perished at the TV Tower. An impromptu memorial remembers civilian victims of the ongoing conflict in Chechnya. *(Gedimino 53, just before the Neris River.)*

FRANK ZAPPA MONUMENT. Built by Konstantinas Bogdanas, a sculptor who once created busts of Lenin, this monument is reputed to be the only sculpture of Zappa anywhere in the world. Though the rock musician never visited Vilnius, his anti-authority message struck a chord among a population buckling under Soviet oppression. Today, he is immortalized through a bust of his head elevated on a 3m pole in a parking lot. Perhaps the most random monument in Eastern Europe, it was installed in 1995 after the Museum of Theater, Music, and Cinema Art (see **Museums,** p. 395) turned it away. *(Off Pylimo between Kalinausko 1 and 3.)*

TV TOWER (TELEVIZIJOS BOKŠTAS). Stretching to a height of 326.47m, the infamous tower is visible from the city center. This out-of-the-way monument will be an attraction only for those interested in Soviet history. Fourteen unarmed civilians were killed here on Jan. 13, 1991 as the Red Army tried to occupy the tower. Crosses and memorials surround the spot today, and the neighborhood's streets have been renamed in honor of the 14 victims. *(Sausio 13-Osios 10. Take tram #16 from* *in front of the train station, getting off about 30min. later at "Televizijos bokštas." Turn right upon exiting the tram and follow the concrete-and-dirt path through the grass and eventually to the tower on your left. ☎252 5333. Open daily 10am-10pm. 9Lt, children 6Lt.)*

JEWISH VILNIUS

Vilnius, known in Yiddish as "Vilna," was once called "Jerusalem of the North," and served as a center of Jewish learning and culture. It was a stronghold of the "Mitnagdim," the scholarly rabbis who resisted the Chasidic movement in the 18th century. Jews accounted for 100,000 of the city's 230,000 population at the outbreak of WWII. Only 6000 remained when the Red Army retook the city in 1944.

■ **VILNA GAON JEWISH STATE MUSEUM OF LITHUANIA.** Named for the 18th-century Talmudic scholar Elijah Ben Shlomo Zalman (known as the *gaon*, or genius), this three-site museum seeks to preserve Vilnius's Jewish heritage and commemorate those who lost their lives during the Holocaust. The **Green House** has a jarring exhibit on the elite Nazi Einsatzkommando's extermination of the city's Jews. The museum also provides an honest account of Lithuanian fighters' persecution of their Jewish neighbors on the eve of the German invasion, and a collection of photographs and maps that reveal the terror of life in the Jewish Ghetto. The last room includes a tribute to Chiune Sugihara, "the Japanese Schindler," a diplomat who helped 6000 Jews escape from Poland and Lithuania. *(Pamėnkalnio 12. Walk up a cobblestone drive on the south side of the street and look for a small sign or a green house. ☎262 0730; www.jmuseum.lt. English captions. Open M-Th 9am-5pm, F 9am-4pm. Donations requested.)* The **Tarbut Gymnasium** pays homage to the 550,000 Jews—many of Lithuanian descent—who fought for the US Army in WWII. The **Gallery of the Righteous** (Teisuoliu Galerija) honors Lithuanians who sheltered Jews during WWII, and documents the life of the great violin player, Jasha Cheifetz, who grew up and trained in Vilnius. *(Pylimo 4. ☎261 7917. English captions. Open M-Th 9am-5pm, F 9am-4pm; in summer also Su 10am-4pm.)* The **Tolerance Center** contains a permanent exhibition of fragments and artifacts from Vilnius's Great Synagogue, as well as paintings and drawings by Jewish Lithuanians. *(Naugarduko 10. ☎231 2356. Open M-Th 10am-5pm, F 10am-4pm, Su 10am-4pm; in winter M-F 11am-4pm. 4Lt, students 2Lt.)*

PANERIAI MEMORIAL (PANERIŲ MEMORIALAS). Hidden at the end of a desolate dirt road 8km southwest of the Old City, this quiet forest is where Nazis butchered 100,000 Lithuanians, including 70,000 Jews. The Gestapo found that the oil pits the Soviets had drilled made convenient mass graves. Scattered throughout Paneriai Forest, the pits are marked with large stone circles. Inscriptions at the memorial are in Hebrew, Lithuanian, and Russian. You can reach the memorial by rail (10min.); most trains bound for Trakai and Kaunas from Geležinkelio Stotis, Vilnius's main station, will make their first stop in Panerai. Inquire about tickets (0.90Lt) at the windows to the left of the central entrance of the station. *(From Panerai's small yellow station house, turn right on Agrastų, continuing for 2km until you reach the memorial. Return to Vilnius by train or catch a bus close to the station house that will be labeled "Stotis"—ask the bus driver to be sure you're headed to Vilnius.)* There is a museum with English captions, but if you find it closed, a large map on the door can act as a guide to the memorials. *(Agrastų 17. ☎260 2001. Open M and W-F 11am-5pm. Free.)*

VILNIUS CHORAL SYNAGOGUE (SINAGOGA). Vilnius was once home to more than 100 Jewish houses of worship, including the majestic Great Synagogue, which Napoleon likened to Notre Dame. The Vilnius Choral Synagogue, built in 1903, is the only Jewish holy site that was not destroyed in WWII. Recently, it has fallen on hard times, partially due to security concerns. The synagogue was closed in 2004. If you find it shuttered, head to Tarbut Gymnasium (see p. 394), which displays photographs of the synagogue's ornate interior. *(Pylimo 39.)*

CHABAD LUBAVITCH CENTER. This Jewish cultural center provides kosher meals (8Lt) for travelers; call or email well in advance. The only resident rabbi in Lithuania, American-born Sholom Ber Krinsky, coordinates community service and aids Jews visiting Vilnius with genealogical research. *(Šaltinių 12. ☎215 0387; www.jewish.lt. Open daily 9am-6pm.)*

🏛 MUSEUMS

▧ MUSEUM OF GENOCIDE VICTIMS (GENOCIDO AUKŲ MUZIEJUS). The horrors of the Soviet regime are highlighted at the former KGB headquarters, which also served as a Gestapo outpost during WWII. The basement remains as it was in 1991; its holding cells, isolation rooms, and torture chambers are open to the public. Prisoners who weren't shipped off to Siberia might have met their end in the execution cell, which provides a chilling glimpse into Soviet punishment methods. The upstairs exhibit documents Lithuanian resistance fighters and a 20th-century history of the city and country. *(Aukų 2a. Turn left after Gedimino 40, the building inscribed with names of KGB victims. ☎262 2449. English captions. Open Tu-Sa 10am-5pm, Su 10am-3pm. Museum 2Lt; W free. English audio tour 8Lt.)*

▧ LITHUANIAN NATIONAL MUSEUM OF THEATER, MUSIC, AND CINEMA ART (LIETUVOS TEATRO, MUZIKOS, IR KINO MUZIEJUS). Chronicling the esoteric history of Lithuanian performing arts over the past 200 years, this museum provides a unique glimpse into the country's cultural vibrancy. Impressive collections include musical instruments crafted in the Baltics, as well as exquisite costumes and shoes worn by famous Lithuanian thespians and dancers. Upstairs, particularly fascinating rooms are filled with movie cameras and gramophones. *(Vilniaus 41. ☎262 2406. English captions. Open Tu-F noon-6pm, Sa 11am-4pm. 4Lt, students 2Lt.)*

MUSEUM OF APPLIED ART (TAIKOMOSIOS DALIĖS MUZIEJUS). In spacious, dome-like rooms, this museum holds over 270 pieces of gold, silver, and jeweled religious objects. These treasures were hidden in the Cathedral walls on the eve of the Russian invasion in 1655 and were rediscovered in 1985. Photographs document the excavation of the artifacts, which will be on display until December 2007. The top floor features a collection of sacred art from the 17th through 20th centuries, including oak crosses, portable altars, and inscribed books. *(Arsenalo 3a, next to the National Museum. ☎212 1813; www.tdm.lt. Open Tu-Su 11am-6pm. 8Lt, students 4Lt.)*

LITHUANIAN NATIONAL MUSEUM (LIETUVOS NACIONALINIS MUZIEJUS). The permanent display details traditional Lithuanian life, with an emphasis on rural areas around the time of the emancipation of the serfs. Farming, fishing, and crafting tools are accompanied by early 20th-century photographs of rural Lithuanian life. *(Arsenalo 1, behind the Gedimino Tower. Enter Arsenalo 3 through the courtyard. ☎262 94 26; www.lnm.lt. English captions. Open W-Su 10am-6pm. 4Lt, students 2Lt.)*

MICKIEWICZ MEMORIAL APARTMENT (MICKEVIČIAUS MEMORIALINIS BUTAS). The Lithuanian-Polish poet Adam Mickiewicz (see **Poland: The Arts,** p. 424) lived in this apartment in 1822; his possessions, including desks, medals, and early editions of his books, remain. Although Mickiewicz wrote in Polish, Lithuanians cherish him for penning their national epic, *Pan Tadeusz.* The Baltic bard's words ring true to all the European nations whose authority over Vilnius proved ephemeral: "Litwo...Ile cię trzeba cenić, ten tylko się dowie, kto cię stracił (Lithuania...Only he who has lost you can know how much you are cherished)." *(Bernardinų 11. ☎279 1879. Open Tu-F 10am-5pm, Sa-Su 10am-2pm. English captions. 2Lt.)*

ARTILLERY BASTION (BASTEJA). Built for defense against the Swedish and Russian armies in the 17th century, this wall has been many things: an orphanage in the 19th century, a German ammunitions cache during WWII, and a post-war vegetable cellar. Watch your step as you make your way down into the damp corridors. *(Bokšto 20/18. ☎261 2149. Open Tu-Sa 10am-5pm, Su 10am-3pm.)*

VILNIUS PICTURE GALLERY (VILNIAUS PAVEIKSIŲ GALERIJA). Housed in the beautifully restored 17th-century Chodkevičiai Palace, this museum displays late 18th- and early 19th-century works, and drawings and sculptures by Lithuanian artists. *(Didžioji 4. ☎212 4258. Open Tu-Sa noon-6pm, Su noon-5pm. 5Lt, students 2.50Lt.)*

🎵 ENTERTAINMENT

Check *Vilnius in Your Pocket* or the Lithuanian-language morning paper *Lietuvos Rytas* for event listings, or pick up a free copy of *Exploring Vilnius*, distributed by hotels and **TIC** branches. TIC also has info on obtaining tickets. English-language movies are shown at **Lietuva Cinema,** Pylimo 17 (☎262 34 22), which has "seats for lovers" (2 seats not separated by an arm rest) and the biggest screen in Lithuania. Catch a flick at **Coca-Cola Plaza,** Savanoriu 7 (☎265 1625; www.forum-cinemas.lt). **Kino Centras Skalvija,** Goštauto 2/5 (☎268 5832), is the best independent film theater. *Lietuvos Rytas* and www.kinas.lt list locations and showtimes.

Lithuanian National Philharmonic (Lietuvos Naciolinė Filharmonija), Aušros Vartų 5 (☎266 5210; www.filharmonija.lt). Student pricing available during the regular season. Performances W-Sa 7pm, Su noon. Organizes the **Vilniaus Festivalis,** a month of concerts beginning in late May. Box office open Tu-Sa 10am-7pm, Su 10am-1pm. MC/V.

Opera and Ballet Theater (Operos ir Baleto Teatras), Vienuolio 1 (☎262 0727; www.opera.lt). Housed in a building of pure 70s Soviet concrete. Box office open Sept.-June M-F 10am-7pm, Sa 10am-6pm, Su 11am-3pm; closed in summer.

Lithuanian National Drama Theater (Lietuvos Nacionalinis Dramos Teatras), Gedimino 4 (☎262 9771; www.teatras.lt). Look for 3 muses carved in black stone. Most performances in Lithuanian, with occasional shows in English. Dance performances and an annual summer drama festival. Box office open Tu-Sa 10am-6pm.

🎭 NIGHTLIFE

The Vilnius bar and club circuit is vibrant and diverse, but also small. If you linger long in town, you'll begin to recognize names and faces. Keep an eye out in cafes for postcards advertising upcoming events and club nights throughout the city. Look to the **Lithuanian Gay and Lesbian Homepage** or the **Gay Club** (see **GLBT Resources,** p. 388) for the latest in Vilnius' gay nightlife scene.

Broadway (Brodvėjus), Mėsiniu 4 (☎210 7208), in the Old Town. Pub by day, club by night, Broadway is extraordinarily popular with local teens and is the place from which many backpackers stumble home in the early morning. Even the most die-hard patrons, however, complain of the crowded dance floor. Cover 10Lt; includes 2 drinks. No sneakers. Open M noon-3am, Tu noon-4am, W-Sa noon-5am, Su noon-2am. MC/V.

ŠMC, Vokiečių 2 (☎261 7097). Tucked behind the Contemporary Art Center, this bar gets crowded each evening with the hip and the interesting. Dance awkwardly to DJs on the outdoor patio, or chat with the affable bartenders as you drink inside (beer 5Lt). Open M-Th and Su 11am-midnight, F 11am-3am, Sa noon-1am. Cash only.

The PUB (Prie Universiteto Baras), Dominikonų 9 (☎261 8393; www.pub.lt). Frequented by students from the nearby Vilnius University, this late-night pub hangout is one of the only places in Lithuania with Guinness on tap (6Lt). The extensive drink menu includes 6 types of vodka—try the homemade stuff for 6Lt if you're feeling adventurous—and pub fare, including onion rings (4Lt). Open daily 11am-2am. MC/V.

Club Connect, Vokiečių 2 (☎212 2031; www.clubconnect.lt). Stylish night owls line up outside Club Connect, just waiting for the stainless steel door to open. When it does, glowing lights and thumping bass escape from the basement club. Cover varies, but is usually around 10Lt. Open W-Th 10pm-3am, F-Sa 10pm-5am. MC/V.

Amatininskų Užeiga, Didžioji 19, #2 (☎261 7968). The drinks aren't particularly cheap nor the scene particularly thrilling, but this bar remains lively even after the rest of town shuts down. A crowd of mixed ages and nationalities drinks itself silly on beer (5Lt per 0.5L). English menu. Open M-F 10am-5am, Sa-Su 11am-5am. Cash only.

◪ DAYTRIPS FROM VILNIUS

TRAKAI CASTLE
☎528

Buses run to Trakai, 28km west of Vilnius (40min., 1 per hr. 6:45am-9:30pm, 3Lt). Last bus back departs at 9.30pm. Check the bus schedule for changes. Bus station (☎900 016 61). Open daily 4am-midnight. The castle is 3km north of the bus station. Facing Lake Totoriskia, turn right from the bus station and follow Vytauto g. Within 100m, you will reach a map of the area. Continue along the street to reach the castle. The Tourist Information Center, Vytauto 69 (☎285 1934; www.trakai.lt), 1km from the bus station, offers free maps, bus schedules, and English-language guides. Open M 8:30am-noon and 12:45-4:15pm, Tu-F 8:30am-noon and 12:45-5:30pm, Sa 9am-noon and 12:45-3pm. Castle and museum open daily 10am-7pm. 8Lt, students with ISIC 4Lt. 1hr. tours in English 50Lt. English captions in most places. The best way to see Lake Galve is by paddleboat. Rental stands are just before the castle's footbridge; around 12Lt per hr.

Surrounded by tranquil waters, Trakai's red-brick **Insular Castle** served as home to the Teutonic Knights, who ruled Lithuania and Poland in the late medieval era. Following the defeat of the Teutonic Order at the Battle of Grunwald in 1410, Trakai became the capital of the Grand Duchy of Lithuania (see **History,** p. 382). In 1665, the Russians accomplished what the Germans could not, plundering the town and razing the castle. Perhaps out of guilt, the Soviets began restoring the castle in 1955. The original stone foundations are visible, but unfortunately the castle now looks like the 20th-century creation it is. Still, bus loads of tourists, young and old, flock to see the castle and grounds. Tickets are valid for both the 30m brick watchtower and the **City and Castle History Museum.** Actors dressed as knights sword fight in the courtyard during **Medieval Days** each June. Turn right before the drawbridge to try your hand at crossbow (1 arrow 1Lt), slingshot (10 stones 5Lt), or pistol (5 shots 1Lt). In July and August, the castle is a dramatic backdrop for concerts at the **Trakai Festival** (☎262 07 27; www.trakaifestival.lt).

Outside the castle, stop by the **Karaite Ethnographic Museum,** Karaimų 22. Trakai is home to a dwindling community of Karaites, a breakaway sect of Judaism which sprung up in the Byzantine Empire during the 8th century. In both Arabic and Hebrew, the word Kara means "to read or study the scriptures." In 1398, Vytautas the Great granted the Karaites religious freedom and brought a small group to Trakai to serve as his bodyguards. (☎225 5286. English captions. Open W-Sa 10am-6pm. 2Lt, students 1Lt.) North 50m is the **Kenesa,** Karaimų 30, a Karaite house of worship. (English pamphlet. Open Th-Sa 11am-6pm.) Try traditional Karaite fare at **Kybynlar ❷,** Karaimų 29, across from the museum. The house beer (3.50Lt per 0.5L) is especially good. (☎285 5179; kybynlar@takas.lt. MC/V.)

EUROPOS PARKAS

Take the #5 trolley (departs 3-10 times per hr.) from the train station to the 3rd stop after the Neris River. Then, at the adjacent bus stop (next to the kiosk) change to the #36 bus (leaves every 10-20min.) and continue to the last stop, which will drop you off about 3km away (30min. walk) from the park. There are also public transportation "minibuses" which run 4-7 times daily and leave from the same location as the #36 bus, but go directly to the park. Last minibus leaves the park M-F 5:50pm and Sa-Su 4:45pm, but be sure to check the bus schedule as times may change. Park includes a restaurant, post office, and gift shop. ☎237 7077; www.europosparkas.lt. Open daily 9am-sunset. Guided tours in English, Lithuanian, or Russian; 50Lt. Park 10Lt, students 8Lt.

In 1989, the French National Geographic Institute made a rather earth-shattering calculation: the geographical center of continental Europe does not lie in Budapest, Kraków, or even Prague. Rather, Europe's center is in a remote forest outside of Vilnius. In light of this discovery, **Gintaras Karosas**, a Lithuanian sculptor and artist, had the idea to build a sculpture park. By the time the USSR fell and Lithuania achieved its independence, Karosas's park had become a reality. His poignant sculpture, reminiscent of the equator line in Ecuador, or the Prime Meridian line in Greenwich, commemorates the center of Europe. The park gives the distance to all of Europe's capitals, and there are about 90 outdoor sculptures, created by artists from over 70 countries, spread across a forested area of 55 hectares. Particularly impressive are the **TV sculpture**—certified by the Guinness Book of World Records as the largest structure made from television sets—and a fallen statue of Lenin at the center of the park. There's also a wire-frame chair and a 6m pyramidal rock, and assorted other sculptural oddities.

INLAND LITHUANIA

Considered by many to be the bedrock of the nation, inland Lithuania is home to the country's 2nd capital, Kaunas, and the memorable Hill of Crosses, near Šiauliai. With a little bit more folk dancing, music, and home brew to go around, this region has a pace of life much more relaxed than that of Vilnius.

KAUNAS ☎37

Home to the 2005 Lithuanian Basketball Champions, Kaunas (KOW-nas; pop. 420,000) also boasts one of the longest pedestrian thoroughfares in Europe. The city offers both a glimpse into authentic Lithuanian culture and a curiously disproportionate number of shoe shops. From 1920 to 1939, Kaunas was the capital of independent Lithuania, while Vilnius languished under Polish rule. During those glorious decades, Kaunas became the center of the country's cultural and intellectual life; its wealth of museums and monuments is a testament to this history. Well-preserved Old Town architecture will charm any visitor, while green spaces and cobblestone streets provide plenty of space to relax in the summer sun.

▐ TRANSPORTATION

Trains: MK Čiurlionio 16 (☎29 22 60; www.litrail.lt), at the end of Vytauto, where it intersects with MK Čiurlionio. Open 24hr. To: **Vilnius** (1½-2hr., 13 per day, 11Lt), **Warsaw, POL** (7½hr., 1 per day, 86Lt), and **Kaliningrad, RUS** (2 per day, 4hr., 32Lt). Other connections include **Tallinn, EST** and **Rīga, LAT.** All international trains run through Vilnius.

Buses: Vytauto 24/26 (☎40 90 60, international reservations 32 22 22). Open daily 4:30am-10pm. To: **Klaipėda** (2½-4hr., 12 per day, 32-34Lt); **Palanga** (2½-6½hr., 7 per day, 34-36Lt); **Šiauliai** (2½-3½hr., 11 per day, 22-26Lt); **Vilnius** (1½hr., about every 30min., 14.50Lt). For bus schedules or advance tickets, visit **EuroLines,** Laisvės 36 (☎20 98 36; www.kautra.lt). Open M-F 9am-1pm and 2-6pm, Sa 9am-1pm.

Public Transportation: Bus and **tram** tickets are available from kiosks (0.90Lt) or from the driver (1Lt). Bus #7 runs parallel to Laisvės, never more than a block away from the main street. The best way to get around the city is by one of the **maršrutinis taksis vans** (1Lt, 2Lt at night) that zip along bus routes. Tell the driver where you want to get off.

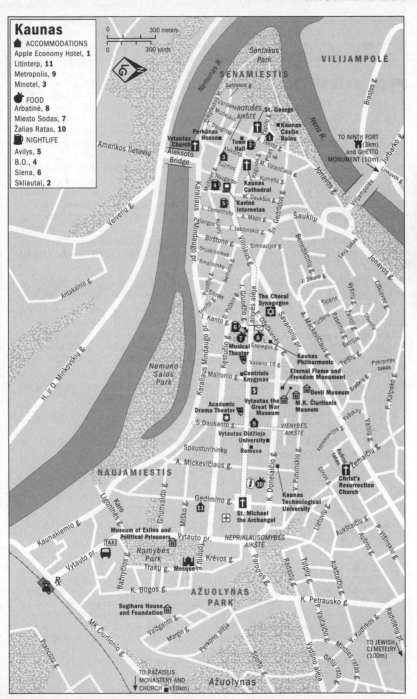

Kaunas

ACCOMMODATIONS
Apple Economy Hotel, **1**
Litinterp, **11**
Metropolis, **9**
Minotel, **3**

FOOD
Arbatinė, **8**
Miesto Sodas, **7**
Žalias Ratas, **10**

NIGHTLIFE
Avilys, **5**
B.O., **4**
Siena, **6**
Skliautai, **2**

LITHUANIA

0   300 meters
0   300 yards

VILIJAMPOLĖ

Santakos Park

Nemuno R.

SENAMIESTIS

Santakos g.

ROTUŠĖS AIKŠTĖ   St. George

Kaunas Castle Ruins

Perkūnas House

Vytautas Church

Aleksoto Bridge

Town Hall

Kaunas Cathedral

Kavinė Internetas

TO NINTH FORT (3km) and GHETTO MONUMENT (10m)

Neris R.

Amerikos lietuvių

Aukšto g.

Saukliu

The Choral Synagogue

Musical Theater

Kaunas Philharmonic

Centrinis Knygynas

Eternal Flame and Freedom Monument

Devil Museum

M.K. Čiurlionis Museum

Academic Drama Theater

Vytautas the Great War Museum

VIENYBĖS AIKŠTĖ

Vytautas Didžiojo University

Romuva

Christ's Resurrection Church

Kaunas Technological University

St. Michael the Archangel

Gedimino g.

Museum of Exiles and Political Prisoners

Ramybės Park

Mosque

NEPRIKLAUSOMYBĖS AIKŠTĖ

NAUJAMIESTIS

AŽUOLYNAS PARK

Sugihara House and Foundation

TO JEWISH CEMETERY (100m)

TO PAŽAISLIS MONASTERY AND CHURCH (10km)

Ažuolynas

Nemuno Salos Park

Taxis: Like everywhere in Lithuania, you will pay a much more reasonable fare if you call a taxi yourself (or have your waiter or hostel receptionist phone) than if you hail one at the side of the street. In Kaunas, expect to pay about 1Lt per km. **Einesa** (☎33 10 11). **Milvasa** (☎1400). **Zaibiškas Taksi** (☎33 30 00).

⬛🛈 ORIENTATION AND PRACTICAL INFORMATION

Kaunas stands at the confluence of the Nemunas and Neris rivers, with **Senamiestis** (Old Town) lying to the west of vibrant **Naujamiestis** (New Town). The train and bus stations are 300m apart, southeast of the city center, at the southern end of **Vytayo**. Follow this busy street north, past **Ramybes Park**, to meet the eastern end of **Laisvės**, the lengthy pedestrian boulevard that bisects the city center. Laisvės's most prominent feature, the **Church of St. Michael the Archangel**, visible throughout much of Kaunas, helps travelers across the city find their bearings. Laisvės forks about 2km west of the church. The right fork, heavily congested **Šv. Gertrūdos**, leads to the **Kaunas Castle** and **Santakos Park**, which overlook the **Neris River**. The left fork, narrow cobblestone **Vilniaus**—so named because it once ran all the way to Lithuania's largest city—now carries travelers through the Old Town to **Rotušės Square**, the site of Kaunas's oldest architectural gems. Take any street from the Old Town west to find yourself in the lush greenery of **Santakos Parkas**, a quiet peninsula bordered by the meeting rivers.

Tourist Office: Tourist Information Center (TIC), Laisvės 36 (☎32 34 36; http://visit.kaunas.lt), 1.5km from train station. Helpful English-speaking staff provides free maps of Kaunas and arranges excursions to nearby sights. Eurolines bus ticketing agency shares the office. Open M-F 9am-6pm, Sa-Su 9am-1pm and 2-6pm.

Currency Exchange: Look for *Valiutos Keitykla* signs on Laisvės and Vilniaus. **Hansabank,** Vilniaus 13 (☎85 268 44 44). Cashes AmEx and Thomas Cook **traveler's checks.** Open M-F 8am-6pm, Sa 9am-3pm. **Hotel Taioji Neris,** K. Donelaičio 27, has a **24hr. currency exchange. ATMs** are everywhere.

Luggage Storage: Electronic lockers on both ends of the main hall of the train station. Don't lose the PIN to your locker! Rates from 3Lt per 12hr. of storage.

English-Language Bookstore: Centrinis Knygynas, Laisvės 81 (☎22 95 72; fax 22 31 01), stocks classics and best-sellers. Open M-F 10am-7pm, Sa 10am-5pm.

GLBT Resources: Kaunas Organization for Sexual Equality (☎70 57 37; robe-jona@takas.lt). Info on gay clubs and events.

Telephones: To the right as you enter the post office. Open M-F 7am-7pm, Sa 7am-5pm. Also look for blue-and-red booths throughout the city.

Internet: Kavinė Internetas, Vilniaus 24 (☎40 74 27). Friendly, English-speaking staff and more than a dozen computers. 4Lt per hr. Open daily 10am-late.

Post Office: Laisvės 102 (☎40 13 68). **Poste Restante** at window #11; 0.50Lt per package. Open M-F 7am-7pm, Sa 7:30am-5pm. **Postal Code:** LT-3000.

🛏 ACCOMMODATIONS

Accommodations in Kaunas don't come cheap. The best option for the budget-conscious is to arrange a **private room** through ◼**Litinterp,** Gedimino 28. Most of Litinterp's rooms have excellent locations, either in Senamiestis or on Laisvės. (☎22 87 18, after-hours 20 53 12; www.litinterp.lt. Open M-F 8:30am-5:30pm, Sa 9:30am-3pm. Singles 80-120Lt; doubles 140-160Lt; triples 180-210Lt.) For those with cars, cheap accommodation can be found on the outskirts of the city. Ask at TIC for a list of motels, hotels, and guesthouses in the Kaunas area.

Apple Economy Hotel, M. Valanciaus 19 (☎32 14 04; www.applehotel.lt). Following Sv. Getrudos toward Kaunas Castle, turn left on M. Valanciaus. Hotel is in a courtyard on the right. True to the hotel's theme, the friendly, English-speaking staff provide apples at the front desk. Reserve ahead in summer. Singles and doubles 135-170Lt. MC/V. ❹

Metropolis, S. Daukanto 21 (☎20 59 92; www.takiojineris.com), just off Laisvės in the center of town. If the musty charm of former splendor is what you're looking for, then the mint-green enamel bathtubs, mismatched tile, and cigarette-smoke-scented rooms of this hotel will delight. The price is unbeatable in central Kaunas, and you can save 15Lt by foregoing the included breakfast. Soviet-era TV and bath in each room. Singles 70Lt, doubles 100Lt, triples 135Lt. Cash only. ❷

Minotel, Vl. Kuzmos 8 (☎20 37 59; www.minotel.lt). This quiet hotel in the heart of Senamiestis has cheerful new rooms with baths, minibars, phones, safes, and TVs. A remarkably good deal when contrasted with comparable but more expensive accommodations. Breakfast included. Reception daily 7am-10pm. Singles 200Lt; doubles 250-400Lt. 20% discount F-Su, 10% discount for stays of 3 or more days. Cash only. ❺

🍴 FOOD

Žalias Ratas, Laisvės 36b (☎20 00 71). Follow the narrow alley to the left of the TIC to reach this cozy, thatch-roofed cottage where the friendly staff dressed as Lithuanian peasants serves authentic regional cuisine (entrees 5-28Lt). The famous cold beet soup (3Lt) is only served before 3pm, so stop in for lunch. English menu. Live Lithuanian folk music F-Sa 8pm. Open daily 11am-midnight. MC/V. ❸

Miesto Sodas, Laisvės 93 (☎42 44 24). The eclectic menu at this popular restaurant includes a number of vegetarian options and takes an ambitious foray into East Asian cuisine. Watch out for surcharges (soy sauce 1Lt). Don't forget dessert: homemade ice cream (3.90Lt) and chocolate cake (5.90Lt) are deadly. Choose a seat on the expansive outdoor patio to enjoy nightly live music during the summer. Entrees 7-16Lt. Open M-W and Su 10am-11pm, Th-Sa 10am-midnight. MC/V. ❷

Arbatinė, Laisvės 100 (☎32 37 32). Look for the green-and-white striped canopy. This vegetarian and vegan cafe attracts locals with freshly baked pastries (1-2Lt). Sit inside the small but bright space at a white picnic table to enjoy a range of healthy entrees (5-6Lt). Open M-F 8:30am-8pm, Sa 10am-6pm. ❶

🔵 SIGHTS

Sights in Kaunas cluster around the two ends of Laisvės, the city's main pedestrian boulevard. St. Michael's Church and Unity Sq. lie at the eastern end, while Senamiestis and its cathedral, town hall, and smaller attractions are at the opposite end.

ST. MICHAEL THE ARCHANGEL CHURCH (Š. MYKOLO ARCHANGELO BAŽNYČIOJE). Originally built for the tsar's Russian Orthodox troops at the end of the 19th century, this breathtaking neo-Byzantine structure became a Catholic church in the 1990s. Its striking blue domes are visible throughout the city, but the exterior needs restoration. Outside, don't miss the detailed **Statue of Man** by Petras Mozuras. *(Nepriklausomybės aikštė 14, at the east end of Laisvės. ☎22 66 76. Open M-F 9am-3pm, Sa-Su 8:30am-2pm. Services M-F noon, Sa 10am, Su 10am and noon. Free.)*

UNITY SQUARE (VIENYBĖS AIKŠTĖ). On the south side of the square, Vytauto Didžiojo University and the older Kaunas Technological University draw a student population of more than 16,000. Across the street, in an outdoor shrine to Lithuanian statehood, busts of political and literary figures flank a corridor leading from the **Freedom Monument** (Laisvės paminklas) to an eternal flame commemorating those who died in the liberation struggle of 1918-20. These symbols of nationhood disappeared during Soviet occupation, but Lithuanians rebuilt the square when they gained independence. On a hill northeast of the square stands the enormous **Christ's Resurrection Church.** Construction began in 1932, but the structure languished for half a century due to the Soviet doctrine of atheism. In the Soviet era, the towering structure acted as a paper warehouse and a radio factory; it was consecrated by the Catholic Church at the end of 2004.

KAUNAS CATHEDRAL (KAUNO ARKIKATEDRA BAŽNYČIA). Lithuania's largest Gothic church—but with the floor plan of a basilica—Kaunas Cathedral is thought to have been built during the 1408-13 Christianization of Low Lithuania. The breathtaking interior reflects Renaissance and Baroque influences, although several damaging fires over the years have necessitated a series of repairs. Next to the altar, the neo-Gothic **Chapel of St. John the Baptist** holds the tomb of Maironis, the Kaunas priest whose poetry ignited Lithuania's 19th-century National Awakening (see p. 384). The remains of Bishop Motiejus Valančius, who printed books in Lithuanian in the 19th century, are also in the crypt. Tourists are not welcome in the chapel. *(Vilniaus 1, just before Rotušės Aikštė. ☎ 32 40 93. Open daily 7am-7pm. Free.)*

OLD TOWN SQUARE (ROTUŠĖS AIKŠTĖ). Just past the cathedral, the **town hall,** a stylistic melange constructed from 1542 to 1771, presides over Old Town Square. Today, it is used primarily for weddings. Behind and to the left of the town hall stands a **statue of Maironis.** His hand hides his clerical collar, a ploy that duped the atheist Soviets into allowing the city to erect a statue of a priest. On the south side of the square is the **St. Francis Church and Jesuit Monastery,** which has changed hands several times since construction began in 1666. The Catholic church was used as an ammunitions storehouse by Napoleon's army, converted into an Orthodox church in the mid-19th century, and employed as a sports hall under the Soviet regime. The Jesuits regained control in 1990. Follow Aleksoto toward the river to reach the 15th-century **Perkūnas House** (Perkū nas namas), built on the site of a temple to Perkūnas, pagan god of thunder. *(Open M-F 8am-5pm.)* At the end of the street is the Gothic **Vytautas Church** (Vytauto bažnyčia), also built in the early 1400s. According to legend, when Vytautas's army was defeated by the Tatars in 1398, the Lithuanian leader pledged to erect a church in the Virgin Mary's honor if his life was spared. *(☎ 20 38 54. Services Tu-Th 6pm; Su 10am, noon, 6pm.)*

NINTH FORT (IX FORTAS). The tsar's troops built this defensive installation in the late 19th century to protect Russia from an impending German invasion. Ironically, the fort eventually facilitated the mass murder of Jewish and other Lithuanians, Russians, and Europeans. During WWII the Nazis exterminated 50,000 people, including 30,000 Jews, in the surrounding fields. Begin your visit at the architecturally innovative **new museum,** which houses the ticket booth for both parts of the site and features an extensive display on the deportation of Lithuanians to Siberia during Stalin's rule. The journeys of Jews shipped en masse from France and Germany are also chronicled. Inside the fort, the **old museum** contains Cell no. 5, where tourists can see inscriptions carved by French Jews who were held there before being executed in May 1944. Past the fort, an enormous Soviet-era sculpture commemorates "the victims of fascism," as the Holocaust dead were called in Soviet jargon. To your right as you approach the sculpture, a series of commemorative plaques includes one placed there by the city of Munich, which reads, "in sorrow and shame, and appalled by the silence of the bystanders." *(Žemaičių Plentas 73. Most Telsai-bound buses from the main station stop in front of the fort;*

20 min., 1Lt. Return on the same bus, which stops every 20-30 min. on the highway in front of the new museum. ☎37 77 15. Open M and W-Su 10am-6pm. Each museum 2Lt, students 1Lt. Hire a guide to explore the tunnel connecting the prison with the barracks for 10Lt.)

JEWISH KAUNAS. Kovno, as the city is known in Yiddish, was home to 37,000 Jews on the eve of WWII. Most were slaughtered at the Ninth Fort during Hitler's occupation, and just 2500 Jews remained when the Soviets arrived in 1944. The Slobodka district, now known as Vilijampole, north of the Neris, traditionally served as home to the city's Jews. Little remains of the WWII ghetto except for a small **monument** to its former residents. To get there, cross the Jurbarko bridge and turn right at the end. At the first fork, bear left on Linkuvos and continue 50m to the intersection of Ariogalos and Krisciukaicio. The **Choral Synagogue** is renowned for its gold-trimmed *bimah* (altar). Inside are a memorial to Jewish soldiers who died fighting for Lithuanian independence between 1918 and 1920, and a memorial for the children killed at the Ninth Fort. Kaunas's remaining Jewish community cannot support a rabbi, but the synagogue is open daily for prayer. *(E. Ozeskienes 17. ☎20 68 80. Open M-F and Su 5:45-6:30pm, Sa 10am-noon.)* The **cemetery** (senosios Žydu kapinės), located 2km from the city center, was neglected after the near-total extermination of Kaunas's Jewish community during WWII and is now overgrown with vegetation. *(Go east down Parados, turn left on K. Petrausko and continue 750m, then turn right onto Radvilénų. The cemetery is 500m down, at the intersection with J. Basanaviciaus.)*

PAŽAISLIS MONASTERY AND CHURCH. This vibrant, fresco-filled, Baroque complex sits on the right bank of the Nemunas 10km east of central Kaunas. Originally designed by three Florentine masters in the 17th century, the church was a KGB-run "psychiatric hospital" before becoming a resort (not run by the KGB). The monastery was returned to the Catholic Church in 1990. The much-touted **Pažaislis Music Festival,** featuring classical music concerts, is held here from June to early August, and there are other **musical performances** year-round. Visit the website for up-to-date concert listings. *(Kauno juros 31. Take tram #5 from the train station to the end of the line; the church is 1km down the road past a small beach. ☎75 64 85; www.pazaislis.lt. Open Tu-Su 11am-6pm, but hours vary; call ahead. Free tour Tu-Su after 11am mass.)*

🏛 MUSEUMS

🏛 DEVIL MUSEUM (VELNIŲ MUZIEJUS). According to Lithuanian folklore, the devil was a guardian figure until the advent of Christianity, when he transformed into an evil creature whose hapless attempts to deceive humanity were doomed to fail. Painter Antanas Žmuidzinavičius (1876-1966) claimed that his longevity stemmed from his obsession with the devil. Over the course of his life, he amassed more than 2000 devil images. This odd-smelling but otherwise excellent museum preserves and expands his collection to include devils from all over the world. Most notable is "The Division of Lithuania," at the far left corner of the third floor gallery, which depicts a satanic Stalin chasing a horned Hitler across skull-covered Lithuania. *(V. Putvinskio 64. ☎22 15 87. Open Tu-Su 11am-5pm. 5Lt, students 2.50Lt.)*

🏛 MUSEUM OF EXILES AND POLITICAL PRISONERS (REZISTENCIJOS IR TREMTIES MUZIEJUS). This museum contains a collection of photographs and artifacts from the resistance to Soviet rule and has an exhibit on the daily life of Siberian exiles. The curator was an exile for 10 years, and gives tours in Lithuanian, German, and Russian. *(Vytauto 46, at the corner of Ramybės Park, a short walk from St. Michael's. ☎32 31 79. Open Tu-F 10am-4pm. Donations requested. English brochure free.)*

LITHUANIA

VYTAUTAS THE GREAT WAR MUSEUM (VYTAUTO DIDŽIOJO KARO MUZIEJUS).
Named after the 15th-century Lithuanian ruler, who conquered much of Eastern
Europe and built an empire, this museum houses all sorts of weapons and war
equipment, ranging from 17th-century armor to 19th-century cannons. Gun enthusiasts will be delighted with the oak-and-glass-encased pistols and rifles on the 2nd
floor. The museum also holds the airplane *Lituanica*, in which two Lithuanian-
Americans, Steponas Darius and Stasys Girėnas (both featured on the 10Lt banknote), attempted to fly nonstop from New York to Kaunas in 1933. They crashed
in present-day Poland but were lauded as heroes in Lithuania. *(Donelaičio 64, in Unity
Sq. behind 2 soccer-playing lions. ☎32 09 39. Open W-Su Mar. 15-Oct. 15 10am-6pm; Oct. 16-
Mar. 14 9am-5pm. 2Lt, students 1Lt.)*

M.K. ČIURLIONIS MUSEUM (M.K. ČIURLIONIS MUZIEJUS). The works of
painter and composer M.K. Čiurlionis (1875-1911) reflect Symbolist and Surrealist influences. His symphonies—both musical and visual—draw from Lithuanian folk art. This museum houses Ciurlionis's extensive portfolio of paintings,
in addition to temporary exhibits and permanent displays of Lithuanian folk art.
Lithuanian cross-making, a tradition that dates to pre-Christian times, is a particular focus of the museum. The carved poles and crosses that are used to
commemorate particular occasions—and still mark the Lithuanian countryside—are displayed along with beautiful black-and-white photographs of
crosses around the country. *(Putvinskio 55, in Unity Sq. ☎22 97 38. English captions. Open Tu-Su 11am-5pm. 5Lt, students 2.50Lt.)*

SUGIHARA HOUSE AND FOUNDATION. Chiune Sugihara, the so-called "Japanese Schindler," served as Tokyo's consul in Kaunas at the beginning of WWII. In
violation of government orders, Sugihara issued more than 6000 visas for Polish
and Lithuanian Jews to travel to Kobe, Japan in 1940. The museum at his former
home features powerful tributes from Jews who escaped death because of Sugihara's courage. *(Valzganto 30, at the eastern edge of Naujamiestis. From Vytauto, follow Toto-
riu east to a mosque. Turn right, then left on Putino. Climb the stairs with the green railing, then
turn right and walk 100m to the Japanese Studies Center. ☎33 28 81; sugihara@takas.lt. English
captions. Open May-Sept. M-F 10am-5pm, Sa-Su 11am-6pm; Oct.-Apr. M-F 11am-3pm. Free.)*

🎵 🎭 ENTERTAINMENT AND NIGHTLIFE

Although many theaters take a summer break, musical events will be announced
on posters plastered along Laisvės. The **Musical Theater** (Muzikinis Teatras),
Laisvės 91, performs operettas. (☎22 71 13. Box office open Tu-Su 10am-1pm and
3-6pm.) The **Academic Drama Theater** (Akademinis Dramos Teatras), Laisvės 71,
stages dances and plays in Lithuanian and Russian. (☎22 40 64; www.dramoste-
atras.lt. Box office open daily 10am-7pm.) The **Kaunas Philharmonic** (Kauno filharmonija), Sapiegos 5, has classical concerts. (☎22 25 58. Schedule posted at box
office. Box office open daily 2-6pm.) Cinemas with American films, usually in
English, can be found at www.cinema.lt. The large screen at **Romuva**, Laisvės 54
(☎32 42 12) is accompanied by huge, comfortable seats. Tickets average 10Lt,
although matinees are cheaper than evening shows. Kaunas nightlife is hidden
away in the cellars of clubs and pubs, and in the courtyards and side streets of the
Old Town. Walk along **Laisvės** and up **Vilniaus** and listen for thumping bass.

🍺 **Avilys,** Vilniaus 34 (☎20 34 76). This candlelit Old Town cellar serves Tibetan teas (4Lt),
and photos from the Dalai Lama's 2001 visit hang on the exposed brick walls. 2 excellent house microbrews on tap, including "Honey Beer" (4Lt per 0.33L), brewed on site.
You will leave enlightened by the pictoral representation of the brewing process on the
menu. Open M-Th 11am-midnight, F-Sa noon-2am, Su noon-midnight. MC/V.

B.O., Multines 9 (☎20 65 42). This vivacious Old Town bar overcomes its unfortunate name to attract a fun student crowd. The lengthy, bright bar serves crowds long into the night and will ensure a lively evening. Beer 4.50Lt per 0.5L. Live music Th 9pm. Open M-Th 10am-2am, F 10am-3am, Sa 3pm-3am, Su 3pm-2am. MC/V.

Siena (Wall), Laisvės 93 (☎42 44 24; www.siena.lt), beneath Miesto Sodas. The spacious main dance floor fills quickly, and the bar gets busy as DJs spin techno, while the 2nd room offers a more familiar Europop playlist to a younger dancing crowd. Open W 9pm-2am, Th-Sa 9pm-4am. MC/V.

Skliautai, Rotušės 26a (☎20 68 43). This cozy, smoke-filled tavern, located in a courtyard alongside the Old Town's central square, pays homage on its photo-lined walls to Kaunas's heyday as the capital of Lithuania. Locals and visitors will feel right at home at heavy wood tables on the outdoor patio. Cheap beer 3.50-5Lt per 0.5L. Live jazz W-Th 7pm. Open M-W and Su 10am-midnight, Th and Sa 10am-1am, F 10am-2am. MC/V.

⚡ DAYTRIP FROM KAUNAS

ŠIAULIAI AND HILL OF THE CROSSES

The most direct route to the Hill of the Crosses (Kryžių Kalna) is by bus. Routes that run from Kaunas or Vilnius to Rīga often let passengers off nearby; backtrack a few feet to the trailhead and turn left on the 2km paved path leading to the hill. An alternative route is to take a bus (3hr., 12 per day, 22.50Lt) to the bus station in the nearby town of Šiauliai (shoo-LAY), Tilžės 109 (☎52 50 58). Note that the last bus back to Kaunas is at 6:30pm. Luggage storage is available at the train station, a short walk across the green-railed overpass, and along Dubijos. (3Lt per bag per day. Open daily 8am-10pm.) To reach the Hill from the bus station, transfer to a Joniškis-bound bus, which stops at Domantai, at the trailhead to Kryžių Kalna (8 per day, last returning shuttle at 5:20pm). You can also reach the Hill by bike. The friendly staff at the Šiauliai Tourist Information Center (Šiauliu Turizmo Informacijos Centras), Vilniaus 213 (☎52 31 10; tic@siauliai.lt), rent bicycles (2-3Lt per hr.), provide free maps, and store luggage for free. To get to the TIC from the bus station, turn left on Tilžės and continue 300m to Vilniaus, then turn left and continue 50m. Once you have your bike, return to the intersection of Vilniaus and Tilžės and turn left; follow the road out of town 10km until you reach a brown sign marked "Kryžių Kalna." Turn right and continue 2km to the Hill of the Crosses. Note that although there is a designated bicycle path for most of the journey, these are busy roads, and TIC does not rent helmets.

The quiet city of Šiauliai, in northern Lithuania, is most prominently known as the gateway to the **Hill of the Crosses.** Tucked away in the countryside, 12km outside of town, the famous site attracts thousands of visitors each year, including throngs of Catholics who make the pilgrimage to the remote location on Easter. Former pope John Paul II visited in 1993, and postcards commemorating his visit are scattered among the numerous crosses, memorials, and relics planted on the hill. Some say the hill's history reaches back to the Middle Ages, when—according to legend— Lithuanians built a fort there to hold back the Teutonic Knights. Others speculate that the hill held significance for pagans or early Christians. In the 19th century, crosses dotted the hill as a memorial to those killed in the Lithuanian struggle for independence from tsarist rule. After the Soviet Union seized the country in WWII, Lithuanians planted crosses on the site to mourn loved ones who had been sent off to Siberian prison camps. Soviet authorities responded by burning the crosses, but Lithuanians persisted in replacing the symbols. Today, the hill is a dense forest of wooden crucifixes, where winding paths and wooden staircases lead visitors through the fascinating mix. Travelers can add to the collection by planting a cross of their own. Vendors sell wooden crosses in the parking lot.

The most popular attraction within the city of Šiauliai is the tall cathedral, known as the **Church of St. Peter and Paul** from 1625 until it became the seat of the local bishop in 1997 and was designated a cathedral. From the bus station, turn left on Tilžės and continue 400m. Once inside, notice the gunports that line the balcony level; they are vestiges of the church's use as a defensive installation. The TIC can provide a map of accommodations in the city. The conveniently located **Youth Hostel of Šiauliai College ❷**, Tilžės 159, is across from the cathedral. (☎41 523 764; administracija@siauliaukolegija.lt. Doubles 60Lt, 50Lt for just 1 person; triples 75Lt; suites 100Lt.) Wander along the pedestrian street Vilniaus to find a pub or cafe. The familiar but tasty menu at **Brodvejus ❷**, Vilniaus 146, offers pizza (5.80-30Lt) and Lithuanian pancakes (5.50-8Lt) to fill you up before a night of revelry. (☎41 50 04 12. Open M-Th 10am-11pm, F-Sa 10am-midnight, Su 11am-11pm.)

COASTAL LITHUANIA

Walk along Lithuania's luscious Baltic beaches and you'll see why Germany, Russia, and Latvia have all coveted these shores. Dance the night away in Palanga's glittering discos, shed your swimsuit and bathe on Smiltynė's bawdy beaches, and climb the sand dunes that extend from Nida to the Russian border. The coast is an extraordinarily tourist-friendly region in summer. Outside Klaipėda, which bustles year-round, winter traveling in these parts can be bleak.

KLAIPĖDA ☎(8)46

A port city, Klaipėda offers visitors a combination of historic architecture and lively beer halls. Famous as the birthplace of Lithuania's most popular beer, Švyturys, the brewery remains the pride and joy of the city. The shores of the Danė River offer a quiet place to sit and relax, although tourists arrive by the boatload during summer. Teutonic Knights and Prussian dukes kept Klaipėda in German hands from 1252 until 1919, except during brief periods of Swedish and Russian rule. The German language captions in Klaipėda museums reflect the continued popularity of the city with German visitors. France gained control of the city after WWI, but promptly surrendered it to newly independent Lithuania, which lost the city to invading Nazis in 1939.

▊ TRANSPORTATION

Trains: Geležinkelio stotis, Priestoties 1 (☎31 36 77). Station open daily 5:30am-11pm. *Kassa* (ticket booth) open daily 6am-6pm. To **Kaunas** (4hr., 1 per day, 29Lt) and **Vilnius** (5-6½hr., 3 per day, 33.80-46.20Lt).

Buses: Autobusų stotis, Butkų Juzės 9 (☎41 15 47, reservations 41 15 40). Station open daily 3:30am-midnight. To: **Kaunas** (3hr., 14 per day, 34Lt); **Palanga** (30-40min., 23 per day, 2.50-3Lt); **Šiauliai** (2½-3hr., 6 per day, 25Lt); **Vilnius** (4-5hr., 10-14 per day, 44Lt); **Kaliningrad, RUS** (4hr., 3 per day, 25Lt); **Rīga, LAT** (6hr., 2 per day, 40Lt).

Ferries: Old Castle Port Ferry Terminal, Žvejų 8 (☎31 42 17, info 31 11 17). Ferries to **Smiltynė** (7min.; every 30min. 5am-3am; 2Lt, students 1.50Lt, return trip 0.75Lt). Microbuses in Smiltynė connect to **Juodkrantė** (30min., 5Lt) and **Nida** (1hr., 7Lt). The **International Ferry Terminal** (☎39 50 50), is south of the city, and ships dock here from a number of countries, including **DEN, GER,** and **POL.** A taxi to town from the terminal costs about 10Lt. Or, you can catch the 8a microbus for 2Lt.

Public Transportation: City buses (0.80Lt, or 1Lt from the driver) and the wonderfully convenient **maršrutinis taksis** (route taxis; 6am-11pm 1.50Lt, 11pm-6am 2Lt) run all over town. #8 travels from the train station down H. Manto through Taikos.

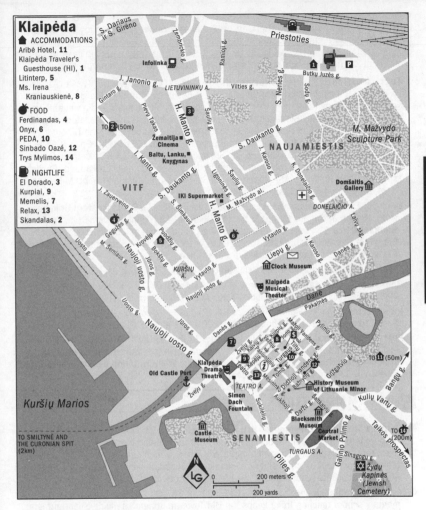

Klaipėda

🏠 **ACCOMMODATIONS**
Aribė Hotel, **11**
Klaipėda Traveler's
  Guesthouse (HI), **1**
Litinterp, **5**
Ms. Irena
  Kraniauskienė, **8**

🍴 **FOOD**
Ferdinandas, **4**
Onyx, **6**
PEDA, **10**
Sinbado Oazé, **12**
Trys Mylimos, **14**

🌙 **NIGHTLIFE**
El Dorado, **3**
Kurpiai, **9**
Memelis, **7**
Relax, **13**
Skandalas, **2**

LITHUANIA

Taxis: (☎006). The small size of the city makes walking convenient, and public transport covers most areas. Standard taxi fare 1.20Lt per km. The cabs of several **private companies** roam the streets and charge 1-1.50Lt per km. Try to have your waiter or hostel receptionist call ahead for a taxi, which will be cheaper than hailing one on the street.

🔆 🔽 ORIENTATION AND PRACTICAL INFORMATION

The **Danė River** divides the city into south **Senamiestis** (Old Town) and north **Naujamiestis** (New Town). **Kuršių Marios** (Curonian Lagoon) to the west cuts off **Smiltynė**, Klaipėda's **Kuršių Nerija** (Curonian Spit) quarter. **H. Manto,** the main artery, becomes **Tiltų** as it crosses the river into Senamiestis, and **Taikos** as it enters the more modern part of the city. All of mainland Klaipėda lies close to the **bus** and

train stations, which are separated by **Priestoties.** Facing away from the bus station, turn right on **Butkų Juzės** and then left on **S. Nėries.** Follow S. Nėries away from the train station to its end, then take a right on S. Daukanto to reach the heart of the city. As you exit the ferry at **Old Castle Port,** turn left on **Žvejų** with the river behind you. From Žvejų, make any right after crossing Pilies to reach Senamiestis.

Tourist Offices: Tourist Information Center (TIC), Turgaus 7 (☎41 21 86; www.klaipeda.lt). Follow H. Manto south as it becomes Tiltu; take the 6th right after crossing the Danė River; the office is on your right. Offers **free maps** and a valuable free **guidebook,** "Exploring Klaipėda." *In Your Pocket Klaipėda* (5Lt) includes information on Palanga and Nida. **Bicycles** are available for rent (30Lt per day), and the TIC organizes Švyturys **brewery tours** for groups (min. 5 people). **Internet** 2Lt per hr. Open M-F 9am-7pm, Sa-Su 10am-4pm. **Litinterp,** S. Šimkaus 21/4 (☎31 14 90; klaipeda@litinterp.lt). Arranges **private rooms** in Klaipėda, Nida, and Palanga. Call ahead. English spoken. Open June-Aug. M-F 9am-6pm, Sa-Su 10am-4pm; May and Sept. M-F 10am-6pm, Sa 10am-4pm; Oct.-Apr. M-F 9am-6pm.

Currency Exchange: Hansabankas, Taikos 22 (☎48 46 37). Offers **Western Union** services. Branch at Turgaus 6, next to the TIC. Open M-F 8am-6pm, Sa 9am-3pm. **Vilniaus Bankas,** Darzu 13 (☎31 09 25), cashes AmEx and Thomas Cook **traveler's checks.** Branch at Turgaus 15, near the Tourist Info Center. Open M-Th 8am-6pm, F 8am-5pm. **ATMs** and currency exchange kiosks are everywhere.

Luggage Storage: Lockers in the train station. 3Lt per 12hr. Open daily 5:30am-11pm.

Bookstore: Baltu, Lanku, Knygynas, Manto 21 (☎31 07 17). Inside the Mega Store Mall. English fiction and travel books. Open M-Sa 10am-8pm, Su 10am-6pm.

Internet: Infolinka, H. Manto 46 (☎ 21 04 42). Fast connections. 2Lt per hr. Open M-F 8am-11pm, Sa-Su 11am-11pm. Also at the **TIC** (see above). 2Lt per hr.

Post Office: Central Post Office, Liepų 16 (☎31 50 22; fax 31 50 45). Houses a 48-bell **carillon** (one of the largest musical instruments in the country), which rings Sa-Su at noon. **Poste Restante** at window #4. Also offers **Western Union** services. Open M-F 8am-7pm, Sa 9am-4pm. **Postal Code:** LT-5800.

ACCOMMODATIONS

Klaipėda Traveler's Guesthouse (HI), Butkų Juzės 7-4 (☎21 18 79; oldtown@takas.lt.), 50m from the bus station. Spacious dorms, hot showers, and friendly staff are a joy for the weary traveler. Make yourself a cup of tea, check your email for free, and chat with other backpackers. Owners organize excursions, including weekly trips to the nearby Soviet Missile Base. Laundry 12Lt. Bike rental 30Lt per day. Dorms 34Lt. Cash only. ❷

Ms. Irena Kraniauskienė, Kurpių 2-8 (☎67 31 71 88; jolita@klaipeda.lt). A retired elementary school teacher, Irena keeps her Old Town apartment sparkling-clean and lets travelers stay in her 2 spare rooms (60Lt). For an additional 10Lt, she'll stuff your belly full of *bliny* (pancakes). Be extra nice to her and she may offer you a home-cooked, Lithuanian-style lunch. Free coffee and tea. Irena speaks Russian and German, but her English-speaking daughter can also arrange bookings. Cash only. ❷

Litinterp, Puodžių 17 (☎41 06 44; klaipeda@litinterp.lt). Charming rooms with exposed beams and brickwork have been renovated to provide clean, spacious living, with breakfast delivery. Central location; most rooms overlook a small, quiet courtyard. Cheery red-and-white-tiled bathrooms. Reception M-F 8:30am-5:30pm, Sa 9am-3pm. In summer singles 80-100Lt; doubles 120-140Lt. In winter 70/120Lt. Cash only. ❸

Aribė Hotel, Bangų 17a (☎49 09 40; hotel@aribe.lt). Heading away from the Danė River on Tiltų, go left on Kulių Vartų and again on Bangų. Reserve 1 wk. ahead for this small hotel a short walk from the center. Bright, clean rooms have baths, Internet, phones, and TVs. Breakfast included. Singles 140Lt; doubles 180Lt; suite 260Lt. MC/V. ❹

FOOD

The **central market** is on Turgaus aikštė; follow Tiltų through Senamiestis and take a sharp right at the first rotary. Go inside the main building to find meat, or wander the surrounding stalls for fresh vegetables, fruit, and flowers. (Open daily 8am-6pm.) **Iki supermarket,** M. Mažvyado 7/11, is within walking distance of Senamiestis. (Open daily 8am-10pm.) The largest Iki in the Baltics is on Taikos.

Sinbado Oazé, Didzioji Vandeus 20 (☎21 17 86). Phenomenal falafel (8Lt) can be enjoyed while smoking a variety of hookahs in this basement den. Perhaps the most comfortable restaurant seating in town, with velvet couches and cushions lining the walls. English menu. Open M-Th and Su 11am-midnight, F-Sa 11am-2am. ❷

Trys Mylimos, Taikos 23 (☎41 14 79), 500m southeast of the Old Town. If you're particularly ravenous, head to this traditional beer hall, which dishes out gargantuan portions of deep-fried regional cuisine. Join the locals and wash down dishes such as veal liver with fried apples (8.50Lt) with a heavy mug of beer (4Lt per 0.5L). English menu. Entrees 6-16Lt. Live music F-Sa 8-11pm. Open daily 11am-midnight. MC/V. ❷

PEDA, Targaus 10 (☎41 07 10). Most art museums wouldn't dare let you bring food inside, but that's where this charming basement cafe and gallery is different. Admire the works of Lithuanian metal sculptor Vytautas Karčiauskas while sipping coffee (2Lt), or enjoy a delicious entree (10-16Lt) at an alcove table. Upstairs and around the corner, find the full gallery. Open M-Sa 10am-midnight. MC/V. ❷

Ferdinandas, Naujoji uosto 10 (☎31 36 84), at S. Daukanto. The Old Believers, a Russian Orthodox sect, came to Lithuania in 1650 to flee persecution. Leaders kept fastidious notes on their cuisine, and this cavernous restaurant recreates their recipes. Hearty Russian entrees (5-30Lt) include a variety of beef, pork, and poultry dishes. Try *kvas* (fermented bread drink; 2Lt) alone, or have it in your cold *okroshka* soup (5Lt). Beer from 3.50Lt per 0.5L. Open M-F 10am-midnight, Sa-Su noon-midnight. MC/V. ❸

Onyx, Manto 4 (☎41 19 95). Stylish young locals flock to this sleek New Town hangout, known for its extraordinarily generous portions and all-day breakfast menu (omelettes 5Lt). The corner location with large windows makes for perfect people-watching. English menu. Open M-F 8:30am-midnight, Sa 10am-midnight, Su 11am-midnight. ❷

 SIGHTS AND MUSEUMS

MAINLAND KLAIPĖDA

You could never guess that the lush, cheery **M. Mažvydas Sculpture Park** (M. Mažvydo Skulptūrų Parkas), between Liepų and S. Daukanto, was once the town's central burial ground. When Soviet authorities demolished the cemetery in 1977, townspeople saved some of intricately crafted crosses from the graves, which are now displayed at the **Blacksmith Museum** (Kalvystės muziejus), Saltkalviu 2. (☎41 05 26; www.mlimuziejus.lt. Open Tu-Sa 10am-5:30pm. 2Lt, students 1Lt.) Sculptures by Lithuanian artists and exhibits by international artists await you at the **P. Domšaitis Gallery** (P. Domšaicio paveikslų galerija), Liepų 33, across the park heading away from the bus station. The house features a magnificent sculpture courtyard, as well as a permanent exhibit of Lithuanian art from 1920-1940. (☎41 04 12. Most info in Lithuanian. Open Tu-Sa noon-6pm, Su noon-5pm. 4Lt, students 2Lt.) Exiting the gallery, continue right down Liepų to the **Clock Museum** (Laikrodžių Muziejus), Liepų 12. Its bizarre collection has every conceivable timekeeping device, from Chinese candle clocks to a modern watch-pen. The spacious back garden is decorated with stone sundials and zodiac symbols. It also hosts occasional classical concerts; call or stop by for a schedule. (☎41 04 17. English pamphlet in each room. Open Tu-Sa noon-5:30pm, Su noon-4:30pm. Museum 4Lt, students 2Lt.)

The 1857 **Klaipėda Drama Theater** (Klaipėdos Dramos Teatras), Teatro aikštė, on the other side of H. Manto, is famous as one of Wagner's favorite haunts and infamous as the site where Hitler proclaimed the town's incorporation into the Reich in 1939. (Tickets ☎31 44 53. Box office open Tu-Su 11am-2pm and 4-7pm.) In front, the **Simon Dach Fountain** spouts water over Klaipėda's symbol, a statue of Ännchen von Tharau. The original statue disappeared in WWII. Some say it was removed by the Nazis, who didn't want the statue's back to face Hitler during his speech. The copy standing today was erected by German expatriates in 1989. The **History Museum of Lithuania Minor** (Mažosios Lietuvos Istorijos Muziejus) features ancient relics and vivid photos of Klaipėda's more recent German past. (☎41 05 24. No English captions. Open W-Su 10am-6pm. 2Lt, students 1Lt; W free.) The **Klaipėda Castle Museum**, Pilies 4, beyond the port-authority building, features the remains of the 13th-century castle and documents an archaeological history of the area, including intricately detailed Gothic and Renaissance tiles. (☎31 33 23. Open Tu-Sa 10am-5pm. 4Lt, students 2Lt.) **Aukštoji**, near the history museum, is one of the best-preserved areas of Senamiestis, lined with the exposed-timber *Fachwerk* buildings for which prewar Klaipėda was famous. Past the central market, Aukstoji leads into **Sinagogu**, once the heart of Klaipėda's Jewish Quarter. On the eve of Hitler's invasion, Jews accounted for 17% of Klaipėda's population; today, just 300 remain. The historic **Jewish cemetery** is 150m from the market. Few gravestones or markers remain, but the park is peaceful. The gray and blue building next to the cemetery is home to the **Klaipėda Jewish Society**, Ziedu 3. (☎49 37 58. Open M-Sa 10am-3pm. Shabbat services Sa 10am.)

SMILTYNĖ

As you get off the ferry (see p. 406), make a right on Smiltynės and follow it along the lagoon 200m to the **Tourist Information Center (TIC)**, Smiltynės 11. (☎40 22 56; www.nerija.lt. Open M-F 8am-noon and 1-5pm, Sa 9am-4pm, Su 9am-2pm.) Buses from the ferry terminal (1Lt) carry passengers straight to the **Lithuanian Sea Museum** (see below), and horse-drawn buggies (parked to the right as you exit the ferry) charge 10Lt for the trek. The best way to see Smiltynė is to walk the 1km from the ferry terminal to the northern end of the Spit. Flanking the TIC on both sides is the three-house **Kuršių Nerija National Park Museum of Nature** (Kušrių Nerijos Nacionalinis Parkas Gamtos Muziejus), Smiltynės 9-12. The museum details the Spit's prominence as a site for tracking migratory birds. (Open June-Aug. Tu-Su 11am-6pm; Sept. and May Tu-Su 11am-5pm. 2Lt, students 1Lt, with ISIC free.) Just down the road, three ships sit on pillars as representatives of **Old Fishing Vessels** (Senieji Žvejybos Laivai). The nearby **Fishermen's Farmstead** (Ethnografinė Pajūrio Žvejo Sodyba), a reconstructed late 19th-century settlement, includes a boathouse, granary, smokeshed, and cattleshed. Close to the road is a traditional kornas boat, used for net fishing. (Open 24hr. Free.) Go to the end of Smiltynės for the main attraction, the **Lithuanian Sea Museum** (Lietuvos Jūrų Muziejus), Smiltynės 3. It is housed in an 1860s fortress that once guarded Klaipėda's bustling port. Seals and sea lions now frolic in the moat. Don't miss the highly amusing **sea lion show,** in which the feisty mammals shoot basketball hoops. (Shows 15min.; 11:15am, 1:15, 3:15pm. 3Lt). Dolphins leap, paint, and dance at the museum's **Dolphinarium.** (Shows 40min.; noon, 2 and 4pm. 12Lt, students 6Lt.) Watch where you sit: rows 1-6 get soaked. (☎49 07 54; www.juru.muziejus.lt. Open June-Aug. Tu-Su 10:30am-6:30pm; Sept. and May W-Su 10:30am-6:30pm; Oct.-Apr. Sa-Su 10:30am-5pm. 8Lt, students 4Lt.) If you're not wet yet, follow the forest paths 500m from the Fishermen's Village to the **beaches** along the Spit's western coast. To the left is a 1.5km long public bathing area. Straight ahead is the **women's beach** (clothing optional), and south is a **co-ed nude beach.** Lines separate the areas, but bathers in the latter section don't always respect the boundaries.

🎵 🎭 ENTERTAINMENT AND NIGHTLIFE

Klaipėda Musical Theater (Muzikinis teatras), Danės 19, hosts operas and other musical events. (☎39 74 02; www.muzikinis-teatras.lt. Season Oct.-May; brief series mid-Aug. Performances F 7pm, Sa-Su 6pm. Box office open Tu-Su 11am-2pm and 3-6pm.) **Žemaitija Cinema,** H. Manto 31, shows Hollywood films with Lithuanian subtitles. (☎31 40 90. 10Lt. MC/V.) The best barhopping is on **H. Manto.**

🎭 **Kurpiai,** Kurpių 1a (☎41 05 55; www.jazz.lt), in the middle of Senamiestis. This superb jazz club is a mix between a traditional tavern and a jazz museum, attracting groups from Lithuania and well beyond. Live music nightly, usually starting at 9:30pm. Beer 5Lt per 0.5L. Cover F-Sa 5-10Lt. Open M and Su noon-midnight, Tu-Sa noon-2am. MC/V.

Memelis, Žvejų 4 (☎40 30 40; www.memelis.lt), on the river across the street from the ferry port. It's a tough call between the 2 lines of "Memelio": Sviesusis (light beer) and Juodasis (dark beer) are brewed in 2 large vats behind the bar. Try them both (5Lt per 0.5L). Upstairs, talented DJs spin as young Klaipėdans dance and mix with expats. No cover. Open M and Su noon-midnight, Tu-Th noon-2am, F-Sa noon-3am. MC/V.

El Dorado, Lietuvininku 2 (☎41 20 59). Billed as an Italian-style bar, this place fashions a unique flavor of seaside funkiness. The bright peach-and-yellow walls will seem less abrasive under the late-night cover of dim lighting and smoke. Beer 3.50-4.50Lt per 0.5L. Open daily 8:30am-3am. MC/V.

Skandalas, I. Kanto 44 (☎41 15 85; www.skandalas.info). Statues of cowboys, Native Americans, and highway cops crowd this hopping New Town restaurant and bar. Well-prepared American food (entrees 14-29Lt) will cure any American traveler suffering a bout of homesickness. The french fries are spectacular (3Lt). Live bands F-Sa 9pm. Open M-Th noon-1am, F-Sa noon-2am, Su noon-midnight. MC/V.

Relax, Turgaus 1 (☎700 555 55). Floor-to-ceiling windows let you check out the scene before you sashay past the bouncers and head inside. Usually, you can count on a mix of pop/rock/dance music and a fun-but-small dance floor packed with locals and foreigners alike. Drinks from 5Lt. Open M-Th and Su 8am-3am, F-Sa 8am-6am.

PALANGA ☎(8)460

The day starts late in Palanga, and the night runs long. Spectacular sea and sand are the city's focus, and rightly so: kilometers of quiet, pristine beach are bordered by equally serene woods. In the late 17th century, Jan Sobieski, King of Poland and Grand Duke of Lithuania, invited English merchants to build a harbor along Palanga's shallow shores. Rampaging Swedes destroyed the merchants' efforts in 1701, but Palanga still warmly welcomes English-speakers to its beaches: almost all street signs and menus are translated, although the largest group of tourists still comes here from other parts of Lithuania.

📇 🚍 **TRANSPORTATION AND PRACTICAL INFORMATION.** Palanga is a short ride from **Klaipėda.** Buses depart from both cities every 30min. until 11:30pm (20min., 2.50Lt). The **bus station** (☎533 33) also sends buses to: **Kaunas** (3hr., 10 per day, 34Lt); **Klaipėda** (30min., every 30min., 2.50Lt); **Šiauliai** (2½-3hr., 7 per day, 20Lt); **Vilnius** (4hr., 11 per day, 47Lt); **Rīga, LAT** (5-6hr., 2 per day, 40Lt). Speedier **microbuses** also run to Klaipėda (20min., depart as they fill, 3Lt). During summer, **bike** rental kiosks line **J. Basanavičiaus, Vytauto,** and **Jūratės.** Pedestrian areas and paths through the woods and along the coast make for pleasant rides. (Helmets not available. Rates average 6Lt per hr. or 25-30Lt per day.)

LITHUANIA

The **bus station** and Tourist Information Center share the corner lot at the intersection of **Kretingos** with **Vytauto**, one of Palanga's main streets, which runs parallel to the beach. With your back to the bus station, turn left onto Vytauto and continue to reach **J. Basanavičiaus,** which eventually runs into the long **pier** that is a favorite spot to watch the sunset. The **Church of the Assumption,** facing the bus station, is a good point of reference near the center of town. The **tourist office,** Kretingos 1, adjacent to the bus station *kasa*, gives out **free maps** and books **private rooms** with no service charge. (☎488 11; palangaturinfo@is.lt. Open daily 9am-2pm and 3-6pm.) **Hansabankas,** Juratės 15/2, **exchanges currency,** cashes AmEx/MC/Thomas Cook **traveler's checks,** and gives MC **cash advances.** (☎412 12. **Western Union** inside. 24hr. **ATM** outside. Open M-Th 8am-4pm, F 8am-3:30pm.) Racks in the bus station, just to the right of the ticket counter, provide **luggage storage.** (1Lt per bag per day. Open daily 7am-1pm and 2-10pm.) **Internet** cafes line J. Basanavičiaus, including **Klubo Kaimynas,** along J. Basanavičiaus near intersection with S. Daukanto. (4Lt per hr. noon-midnight, 3Lt per hr. midnight-noon. Open 24hr.) The **post office,** Vytauto 53, has **Poste Restante** at window #1. **Western Union** services are also available. (☎488 71. Open M-F 9am-6:30pm, Sa 9am-4pm.) **Postal Code:** LT-00134.

🛏 ACCOMMODATIONS. Hotel prices rise considerably in the peak months of July and August. In the low season, you'll pay a pittance for luxurious digs near the beach. Arrange a **private room** (from 25Lt per night) through the TIC. **Palanga Welcome Host,** Vytauto 21, arranges rooms, many of which can be viewed online. The staff speaks limited English, but a catalog has English listings and pictures. Study it closely, and you'll find prices much lower than those printed in the agency's thinner pamphlet. (☎487 23; www.palangawelcomehost.lt. Doubles June €15-20; July €20-25; Aug. €25-30). **Mėguva ❷,** Valančiaus 1, just west of the Church of the Assumption, has charmless but clean rooms with private baths and TVs. The red brick building may look like a 1970s recreation center from outside, but the location, close to the bus station and the sights and sounds of Palanga's pedestrian area, is enviable. (☎488 39. June singles 50Lt; doubles 80Lt. July-Aug. 60/120Lt. Sept.-May 40/60Lt. Cash only.) **Ražė ❸,** Vytauto 74/2, not to be confused with the bar of the same name one block away, offers bright rooms with showers, refrigerator, and TV close to the city center. The swimming pool is a bonus for those unwilling to dip into the frigid Baltic. (☎482 65; palturas@is.lt. English spoken. June 1-19 singles 110Lt; doubles 120Lt; triples 150Lt. June 20-Aug. 21 150/160/190Lt. In low season 90/100/120Lt. Cash only.) Near the Botanical Gardens, **Eglė ❸,** Kestucio 15/Daukanto 31, offers sunny, clean rooms with TV, fridge, and private bath. (☎51 466; www.eglehotel.lt. English spoken. July singles 118Lt; doubles 160Lt; triples 190Lt. Aug. 100/160/190Lt. Sept.-June 70/85/110Lt. MC/V.) Follow Valanciaus from the church to get to **Alanga Hotel ❸,** S. Nėries 14. With a sun-drenched locale just off the main pedestrian street, Alanga offers modern baths and candies on your pillow. Colorful rooms feature TV, phone, and minibar; many have balconies. (☎492 15; www.alanga.lt. Reserve ahead. Doubles 120-160Lt. MC/V.)

🍽 FOOD. In true seaside-resort style, Palanga's streets are lined with vendors selling cotton candy, ice cream, popcorn, and Lithuanian snacks such as *čeburekai* (meat-filled pastries; around 3Lt). On **Vytauto** and **J. Basanavičiaus,** cafes and restaurants blare music across outdoor patios. There are several supermarkets in the center of town, including **Prekybos Centras,** J. Basanavičiaus 23. (Open daily 9am-2am.) A large **Maxima** supermarket is behind the bus station on Vytauto. (Open daily 8am-midnight.) The most popular **local beer** is HBH Vilkmerges, brewed just 7km from Palanga. The town is divided between adherents of the dark and light varieties. You'll find both on tap (3.50Lt per 0.5L) at **Dvitaktis ❷,** Vytauto 80, a thatch-roofed lean-to that also offers Lithuanian entrees. (Entrees 6-22Lt.

Open mid-day to midnight.) **Vila Aldona ❸**, J. Basanavičiaus 24, offers a delicious range of cuisine, including pastas (14.50Lt) and seafood dishes such as roasted trout (24Lt) and grilled salmon (22Lt), complemented by fresh vegetables. Be sure to sit outside among the flowers and fountain in the garden, or if it's a chilly evening, choose a table inside at the floor-to-ceiling windows. (☎403 13. English menu. Entrees 6-32Lt. MC/V.) **Senoji Dorė ❸**, J. Basanavičiaus 5, in a blue building surrounded with outdoor seating, is a typical Palangan restaurant serving Lithuanian cuisine amid nautical decorations. Red caviar pancakes (7Lt) and roast squid (26Lt) are among the many options. (☎534 55. Entrees 12-27Lt. Live music most nights 7pm-midnight. Open daily 10am-midnight.) **Monika ❷**, J. Basanavičiaus 12, has earned a name for itself as one of the most popular places on J. Basanavičiaus for its Lithuanian and Italian fare. Try the potato *bliny*, which make a good meal for just 6Lt. (☎525 60. Entrees 5-25Lt. Open daily 10am-midnight. MC/V.)

◪ SIGHTS. Palanga's pride and joy is the world's first **Amber Museum** (Gintaro muziejus), which showcases the fossilized resin known as "Baltic Gold." It hosts a collection of 15,000 "inclusions," pieces of amber with primeval flora and fauna trapped inside. Magnified display cases allow you to gaze at spiders, mosquitoes, and even a lizard trapped inside golden droplets of amber. (☎513 19. English captions in most rooms. Open June-Aug. Tu-Sa 10am-8pm, Su 10am-7pm; Sept.-May daily 11am-4:30pm; ticket office closes 1hr. earlier in summer, 30min. in winter. 5Lt, students 2.50Lt.) The museum is housed in the very grand 1897 palace of Count Tiškevičius. The surrounding estate grounds are now home to the **Palanga Botanical Gardens.** Through the main entrance to the gardens, on the corner of Vytauto and S. Dariaus ir S. Girėno, is one of the nation's most famous sculptures, **Eglė,** Queen of the Serpents. According to local lore, a serpent thrust himself on Eglė and forced her to marry him. When she did, he morphed into a charming prince. Eglė's brothers then slaughtered her husband, and in despair, she turned herself into a tree. Inside the garden, along a forest path behind the Amber Museum, stands **Birutė Hill.** In another legend of betrothal, Duke Kestutis kidnapped the virgin Birutė, made her his wife, and brought her to Trakai, where she gave birth to the famous Lithuanian warrior Vytautas. Archaeologists recently found the remains of a 14th-century pagan temple on the site; a 19th-century chapel stands atop the hill today. Less than 1km south of the Botanical Gardens, along tree-lined Vytauto, is a 1m high black marble marker pointing toward the **Holocaust Mass Graves** (Holokausto Auku Kapai). Follow the path into the woods, bear left at the fork, and continue 500m. A large grey stone, with worn words and a still-visible Star of David, marks the site. Palanga's Jewish community was among the first to be exterminated by the Nazi Einsatzgruppe A in June 1944.

Toward the center of town, you will find the **Dr. Jonas Šliūpas Memorial Gardens and House,** Vytauto 23a, set back from the street behind a yellow-and-green house. Sliupas, a physician, newspaper editor, and politician, spent much of his life in the US and played a leading role in the Union of Lithuanian Socialists in America in the early 20th century. The house is filled with his belongings, including his typewriter and letters, as well as exquisite furnishings and a photo album of 20th-century postcards of the region. (Captions in Lithuanian only, although a timeline and a brief history are in English. Open in high season daily noon-7pm; low season Tu-Su 11am-3pm. 2Lt.) A bit farther north on Vytauto, turn left on Kęstučio to reach the **Antanas Mončys House-Museum** (Antano Mončio Namai-Muziejus), a blue-and-white building at S. Daukanto 16. The sculptor left Lithuania in 1944 and didn't return for 45 years. As specified in Mončys's will, visitors may touch any of his abstract, mostly wooden works. (☎493 66. Open June-Aug. W-Su 2-9pm, Tu noon-5pm; Sept.-May Th-Su noon-5pm. 4Lt, students 2Lt, with ISIC 1.50Lt.)

LITHUANIA

📷📷 **ENTERTAINMENT AND NIGHTLIFE.** Summer visitors flock to the beach, the hallmark of any Palanga excursion. Beach volleyball and pickup games of soccer happen close to the pier. Walk just a bit north or south of the pier, however, and you'll find yourself all alone on the beautiful white sand. Palanga is also part amusement park, as the arcades and games lining the pedestrian streets attest. Play **minigolf** across from J. Basanavičiaus 42. Thrill-seekers can take a ride on the **bungee chair** (50Lt for 2 people) at J. Basanavičiaus 22. The **Summer Theater** (Vasaraos Estrada), at Vytauto 43, hosts **concerts** by the Lithuanian National Philharmonic and the Klaipėda Philharmonic, as well as visiting performers. (☎522 10. Box office open daily 3-9pm.) Cafes on **J. Basanavičiaus** and **Vytauto** feature live bands, many of which make a living covering Eurovision songs. **Kinoteatras Naglis,** Vytauto 82, shows Hollywood flicks (8Lt) with Lithuanian subtitles.

Palanga has no shortage of nightlife, as almost everyone here is on vacation and almost every restaurant morphs into a club at dusk. The night scene centers on J. Basanavičiaus, where dozens of street musicians battle for attention. **Arnėniski Šašlykai,** J. Basanavičiaus 27, is a restaurant by day and a club by night, featuring a popular house band. (Live music nightly 8pm-midnight. Open daily 11am-late.) Escape the crowds for an evening at **Kupeta,** S. Dariaus ir Gireno 13, just north of the Botanical Gardens. The bar makes good use of the large courtyard it shares with an art gallery, and hosts a steady stream of impressive local and international bands, including a number of funky jazz groups. (☎400 14; www.feliksas.lt. Occasional cover 5-10Lt. Open daily 9am-midnight.)

The **choir festival** opens at the end of May. The opening of the **summer season** takes place the first weekend of June, with theater, fireworks, and a giant feast to declare Palanga the summer capital of Lithuania. **Night Serenades,** evenings of classical music, are held every night during the first week of August at the Amber Museum and Botanical Gardens. On the first weekend of August, the **Palanga Cup,** a beach volleyball competition, draws crowds.

🔢 **DAYTRIP FROM KLAIPĖDA: SOVIET MISSILE BASE AT PLOKSTINE RESERVATION.** Tucked away in the forested Plokstine Reservation inside Zematijia National Park is one of the most remarkable sites in Lithuania: the remains of an underground ◾**Soviet missile base.** The large, gated field looks unremarkable on the surface, save for four concrete mounds, but the history of the base is striking. Attempting to keep pace with the US, which had begun to develop underground military installations, Soviet leader Nikita Krushchev ordered the construction of this site in September 1960. Lithuania was the ideal location for such a facility, as missiles fired here could have reached as far as Turkey and Spain. The base was put on high alert during the Czechoslovak revolution of 1968. During its working years, the base was home to thousands of soldiers, but the Soviets abandoned the site in 1978 after signing the SALT accords with the US. Locals looted the facility for scrap metal during the lean years of the 1980s; as a result, much of the site is falling apart, and only one of the four silos is open to tourists. As a visitor, you will walk through the underground maze and see the remnants of computer operating rooms, massive machinery and engines, and pump and plumbing systems necessary to cool the missile silos after firing. Crawl through a small door to peer down the 30m hole that once held warheads five times the strength of the atomic bomb dropped on Hiroshima. The structure is deteriorating so quickly that it may be too dangerous to enter within a few years.

The best route to the base is by organized excursion with the lovely **Jurga,** the owner of the Klaipėda Traveler's Guesthouse. Email or call in advance to arrange a trip. (3hr. including travel time and Jurga's English-language tour; usually on Tu, Th, or F afternoon; 120Lt per car, 4 people per car, 30Lt per person.) If you decide to go on your own, contact the **Zematija National Park Information Center** in advance to ensure that the base will be open and to organize a tour (20Lt) in English. (☎8448 49231; znp@plunge.omnitel.net. Open M-Sa 9am-noon and 1-5pm.) Go to Plungė from Klaipėda by **bus** (1hr., about 6 per day, 10Lt) or train (1hr., 2 per day, 6.40-8.30Lt). From there, board a **minibus** to the tiny town of Plateliai and ask the driver to let you off at Militarizmo Expozicija. You will be dropped off at a trail-head 5km from the site. Take the path and head left at the fork. (Tours daily June-Aug. every 2hr. 10am-6pm. Some guides speak only Lithuanian. 4Lt, students 2Lt.)

CURONIAN SPIT (NERINGA)

A product of the glaciers of the last Ice Age, the Curonian Spit is a great sandbar lined with majestic dunes and crisscrossed by lush forests. It is bordered by the Baltic Sea to the west and the beautifully calm Curonian Lagoon to the east. The Kuršių Nerija National Park preserves this pristine region. Outside of the major towns, Nida and Juodkrantė, endless kilometers of untouched waterfront are ripe for exploration. Rent a bike in Klaipėda, take the ferry to Smiltynė, and keep ped-aling until you're ready for a dip in the chilly Baltic.

WITCHES' HILL

Goblins, devils, and amused mortals frolic on ■Witches' Hill (Raganų Kalnas) in Juodkrantė. Set aside an hour to wander the worn trail through the dense, magical wood lined with 71 wooden sculptures in high Lithuanian folk-art style. Carved between 1979 and 1981, the artworks were crafted by artists who spent their sum-mers in Juodkrantė. To mingle with the gnomes, visitors can frolic on a seesaw, slide down a giant tongue, or climb into a saddle 2m off the ground. Don't miss the game of cards between the devil and a witch; they've left two seats free for you. Take a detour through the forest and head toward the sound of crashing water to find the **beach** on the Baltic side of the Spit. While Juodkrantė is always a site of mirth and ritual, Witches' Hill is especially popular on **Midsummer's Eve** and **St. John's Day** (June 23-24). **Buses** run hourly from 6am to 10pm along the Nida-Klaipėda (via Smiltynė) route and stop in the center of town; from the bus stop, walk south along L. Rėzos until you see a large wooden sign and a creature point-ing toward the start of the path. (30min., 5Lt to Nida. 15min., 3Lt to Smiltynė.)

NIDA   ☎(8)469

Settlers have lived in this section of the Curonian Spit since the late 14th century, but shifting dunes have buried their villages more than once. These days, 50,000 tourists bury tiny Nida (pop. 1550) each summer. Hike a couple of kilometers south from town, however, and you'll find yourself all alone in a dune-filled desert. Don't go too far, though: 4km south of Nida's center, a militarized border sepa-rates Lithuania from the Russian region of Kaliningrad. The stunning ■Drifting Dunes of Parnidis rise high above Nida, though they sink 30cm each year. Walk south along the beach or down forest paths to reach the peak of the tallest sand dune (52m), marked by the remains of an immense sundial. It was smashed by a hurricane in 1999, but its site offers awe-inspiring views of the dunes. On the far side of the dunes, the **Valley of Death** was used by Prussia—the Spit's former owner—as a prison camp for French soldiers in the early 1870s. The **wooden houses** clustered along Lotmiško, the narrow lane leading back to town, are classified as historical monuments; dozens more are buried under the sand. From the town center, go 500m north on Pamario to the Gothic-style 1888 **Nida Evangelical Luthe-ran Church** (Evangelikų liuteronų bažnyčioje), Pamario 43. Soviet authorities left it standing but looted the wooden pews to fuel a sauna. The handful of Nida's remaining Lutherans shares the house of worship with local Catholics, and concerts are held at the church during summer. (Open daily 10am-6pm.) Just 100m farther, the **Neringa Museum of History** (Neringos Istorijos Muziejus), Pamario 53, presents a thought-provoking exhibit on the Neringa fishing and craftwork. (☎511 62. Open June-Aug. M-Su 10am-6pm; Sept.-May Tu-Sa 10am-5pm. 2Lt, students 0.50Lt.) Bear right on Skruzdynės and climb the 3rd wooden staircase on the left to reach the renovated **Thomas Mann House** (Thomo Manno Namelis) at #17. The German Nobel laureate built this cottage in 1930. Mann, a vocal opponent of Hitler, immigrated to the US in 1936. (☎522 60. No English captions. Open June-Aug. daily 10am-6pm; Sept.-May Tu-Sa 10am-5pm. 2Lt, students 0.50Lt.) The **Thomas Mann Cultural Center** puts on classical concerts for the mid-July **Thomas Mann Festival,** which also includes art exhibits, films, and lecture series.

Hotel and guesthouse prices on the Curonian Spit rise during the summer season, but if you're willing to be away from the action at Nida, staying in Juodkrantė will save you some cash. The **TIC** arranges **private rooms** (40-50Lt) and is the best option for inexpensive accommodations. If you plan ahead, **Litinterp ❸** in Klaipėda offers pricier rooms. (See **Klaipėda: Orientation and Practical Information,** p. 408. Singles 90-120Lt; doubles 140-180Lt.) If you are in the market for a hotel, try **Jurates ❷**, Pamario 3, located in the center of town. Although the rooms don't directly overlook the water, they can be cheap during the low season. (☎526 18; juratenida@takas.lt. Singles 75-125Lt, doubles 105-175Lt.) To get to **Kempingas** (Camping) **❶**, Taikos 45a, walk beyond the path to Urbo Kalnas and continue until you see a road signposted on your left. Kempingas offers a taste of the outdoor experience, but with showers, flushing toilets, and an adjacent Chinese restaurant. (☎370 682 41150; www.kempingas.lt. Sleeping-bag rental 5Lt. Tent rental 10Lt. 15Lt per person, 10Lt per site.) Apartments are also available near the campsite. (Doubles 100-180Lt.) The regional specialty is *rūkyta žuvis* (smoked fish), served with bread. Stop by **Fischbrotchen ❶**, in a yellow hut next to the bus station, for a 5Lt herring sandwich. (Open daily 11am-8pm.) Nida's largest grocery store is **Kuršis**, Naglių 29, just north of the bus station. (Open daily 8am-10pm.) Its **cafe** serves a great breakfast for early risers. (Open daily 8am-midnight. MC/V.)

Buses run from the **bus station,** Naglių 18e (☎528 59), to **Klaipėda/Smiltynė** (45min., about 1 per hr., 7Lt), **Kaunas** (4½hr., 1 per day, 44Lt), and **Kaliningrad, RUS** (2½-4hr., 2 per day, 16.30Lt). Buses to Smiltynė leave Nida hourly from 6am to 10pm. **Bikes** are available for rent at many different points along the lagoon shore. (6Lt per hr., 25Lt per day.) From the water, **Taikos** runs inland. Perpendicular to it, **Naglių** eventually becomes **Pamario.** The **Tourist Information Center (TIC),** Taikos 4, opposite the station, arranges **private rooms** (5Lt fee) and has **free maps,** transport info, and slow but free **Internet.** (☎523 45; www.neringainfo.lt. English spoken. Open June-Aug. M-F 10am-8pm, Sa 10am-6pm, Su 10am-3pm; low season M-F 9am-1pm and 2-6pm, Sa 10am-3pm). **Hansabankas,** Taikos 5, **exchanges currency,** gives MC/V **cash advances,** cashes **traveler's checks,** and has **Western Union** services. (☎522 41. Open M-Th 8am-4pm, F 8am-3:30pm.) Buy phone cards at the **post office,** Taikos 13, farther up the road, past the police station on your left. (☎526 47. Open M-F 9am-noon and 1-5:30pm, Sa 9am-1pm.) **Postal Code:** LT-5872.

POLAND (POLSKA)

Poland is a big country where history casts a long shadow. Plains that stretch from the Tatras Mountains in the south to the Baltic Sea in the north have seen foreign invaders many times over, and the contrast between thoroughly Western cities like Wrocław and Eastern outposts like Białystok makes palpable the legacy of centuries of partition among competing empires. Ravaged by WWII and viciously suppressed by the USSR, Poland has finally been given freedom and self-rule, and its residents are not letting the opportunity slip by. Today's youthful, optimistic Poland is a haven for budget travelers. The rich cultural treasures of medieval Kraków and bustling Warsaw are complemented by wide Baltic beaches, rugged Tatras peaks, and tranquil Mazury lakes. All of it still comes cheap by Western standards, though prices are sure to rise now that Poland has joined the EU. Now is the time to explore this complex, intriguing country.

 DISCOVER POLAND: SUGGESTED ITINERARIES

THREE DAYS In **Kraków,** enjoy the stunning **Wawel Castle** (p. 452), the medieval grace of **Stare Miasto** (p. 453), and the bohemian nightlife of **Kazimierz** (p. 455). Take a day in the sobering **Auschwitz-Birkenau** death camp (p. 458).

ONE WEEK After three days in **Kraków,** head up to **Warsaw** (2 days), the capital city, where the new **Uprising Museum** (p. 440), the chaotic **Russian Market** (p. 439), and the edgy **nightlife** (p. 442) can't be missed; head north to wander the cosmopolitan streets and sights of **Gdańsk** (p. 500; 2 days) and soak up the sun on the beach of **Sopot** (p. 508).

BEST OF POLAND, THREE WEEKS Begin with five days in **Kraków,** including daytrips to **Auschwitz-Birkenau** and the **Wieliczka** salt mines (p. 458). Spend two days in lovely **Wrocław** (p. 476), then enjoy the mountain air of **Karpacz** (p. 481; 1 day). After stopping off for a night at the edgy bars and clubs of **Poznań** (p. 488) head east to dynamic **Warsaw** (4 days), then take a break in scenic, slow-paced **Toruń** (p. 493; 2 days). In **Gdańsk** (4 days), don't miss **Sopot** or **Malbork Castle** (p. 508). Spend your last two days in either eastern **Białowieża** (p. 514) or western **Międzyzdroje** p. 498), enjoying Poland's natural wonders.

FACTS AND FIGURES

Official Name: Republic of Poland.
Capital: Warsaw.
Major Cities: Katowice, Kraków, Lódź.
Population: 39,000,000.

Land Area: 312,000 sq. km.
Time Zone: GMT +1.
Language: Polish.
Religions: Roman Catholic (95%, 75% practicing).

ESSENTIALS

WHEN TO GO

Poland has warm summers and cold, snowy winters; summer weather can be capricious, and rain is frequent in July. Tourist season runs from late May to early September, except in mountain areas, which also have a winter high season (Dec.-

Poland Baltic Sea

Międzyzdroje · Kołobrzeg · Słupsk · Sopot · Gdynia · Hel · Gulf of Gdańsk · Kaliningrad · LITHUANIA · Kaunas
Woliński NP · Białograd · Koszalin · Gdańsk · Frombork · RUSSIA · Marijampole
Szczecin · POMORZE · Szczecinek · Malbork · Elbląg · Bartoszyce · Mamry · Ełk · Druskininkai · Hrodna
GER · Olsztyn · Mrągowo · Kętrzyn · Mazurian Lakes · BEL
Piła · Iława · MAZURY · Mikołajki
Gorzów Wlkp. · Krzyż Wlkp. · Bydgoszcz · Toruń · Nidzica
Kostrzyn · Warta · Vistula (Wisła) · Ciechanów · Ostrołęka · Łomża · Białystok
Kietz · Frankfurt Oder · Poznań · Gniezno · MAZOVIA · PODLASIE · Białowieski NP
Słubice · WIELKOPOLSKA · Płock · Warsaw · Bielsk Podlaski
Gubin · Zielona Góra · Odra · Leszno · Ostrów Wlkp. · Kalisz · L. Jeziorsko · Kutno · Żelazowa Wola · Wilanów · Łuków · Siedlce · Biała Podlaska · Brest
Głogów · Sieradz · Łódź · Wisła · Puławy
Jelenia Góra · Wrocław · Radom · Kazimierz Dolny · Lublin
Szklarska Poręba · Wałbrzych · ŚLĄSK · Częstochowa · Kielce · Majdanek · Chełm
Chojnik Castle · Karpacz · Opole · Olsztyn · Sandomierz · Zamość
Boboszów · SUDETY MTS. · Katowice · Pleskowa Skała · MAŁOPOLSKA
CZECH REPUBLIC · Auschwitz-Birkenau · Bielsko-Biała · Kraków · Wieliczka · Rzeszów · Łańcut · Przemyśl
Ostrava · Cieszyn · Szczyrk · Tarnów · Sanok · Lviv
CARPATHIAN MTS. · Spytkowice · Nowy Sącz · Krościenko
Zakopane · Szczawnica · Dunajec Gorge · UKRAINE
SLOVAK REPUBLIC

0 100 kilometers
0 100 miles

Mar.). Late spring and early autumn are pleasantly mild—though they too can be rainy—and late April, May, September, and early October are the best times to travel in Poland. Many attractions are closed from mid-autumn to mid-spring.

DOCUMENTS AND FORMALITIES

ENTRANCE REQUIREMENTS

Passport: Required for all travelers.

Visa: Not required for stays under 90 days for citizens of Australia, Canada, Ireland, New Zealand, the US, and the UK.

Letter of Invitation: Not required for most travelers.

Inoculations: Recommended up-to-date on DTaP (diphtheria, tetanus, and pertussis), Hepatitis A, Hepatitis B, MMR (measles, mumps, and rubella), Polio booster, and Typhoid.

Work Permit: Required for all foreigners planning to work in Poland.

Driving Permit: Required for all those planning to drive in Poland.

EMBASSIES AND CONSULATES. Foreign embassies to Poland are in Warsaw and Kraków. For Polish embassies and consulates at home, contact: **Australia,** 7 Turrana St., Yarralumla, Canberra, ACT 2600 (☎02 6273 1208; www.poland.org.au);

Canada, 443 Daly Ave., Ottawa, ON, K1N 6H3 (☎ 613-789-0468; www.polishembassy.ca); **Ireland,** 5 Ailesbury Rd., Ballbridge, Dublin 4 (☎ 01 283 0855; www.polishembassy.ie); **New Zealand,** 17 Upland Rd., Kelbum, Wellington (☎ 04 475 9453; polishembassy@xtra.co.nz); **UK,** 47 Portland Pl., London W1B 1JH (☎ 087 0774 2700; www.polishembassy.org.uk); **US,** 2640 16th St. NW, Washington, D.C., 20009 (☎ 202-234-3800; www.polandembassy.org).

VISA AND ENTRY INFORMATION. Citizens of Australia, Canada, New Zealand, the UK, and the US do not need a visa for stays of up to 90 days. Single-entry visas cost US$60, students US$45; multiple-entry visas cost US$100, students US$75; two-day transit visas are US$20, students US$15. Applications require a passport; two photos; and payment by money order, certified check, or cash. To extend your stay in Poland, apply in the city where you are staying or to the **Ministry of Internal Affairs,** Stefana Batorego 5, Warsaw 02-591 (☎ 621 02 51; fax 849 74 94).

TOURIST SERVICES AND MONEY

TOURIST OFFICES. City-specific **tourist offices** are the most helpful. Almost all provide free info in English and help arrange accommodations. Most have good **free maps** and sell more detailed ones. **Orbis,** the state-sponsored travel bureau, operates hotels in most cities and sells transportation tickets. **Almatur,** the student travel organization, offers ISICs, arranges dorm stays, and sells discounted transportation tickets. The state-sponsored PTTK and IT (Informacji Turystycznej) bureaus, in nearly every city, are helpful for basic traveling needs. Try **Polish Pages,** a free guide available at hotels and tourist agencies.

ZŁOTYCH (ZŁ)		
AUS$1 = 2.49ZŁ		1ZŁ = AUS$0.40
CDN$1 = 2.70ZŁ		1ZŁ = CDN$0.37
EUR€1 = 4.02ZŁ		1ZŁ = EUR€0.25
NZ$1 = 2.30ZŁ		1ZŁ = NZ$0.44
UK£1 = 5.92ZŁ		1ZŁ = UK£0.17
US$1 = 3.28ZŁ		1ZŁ = US$0.31

MONEY. The Polish currency is based on the złoty (plural: złotych; 1 złoty=100 groszy). Inflation is around 3%, so prices should be reasonably stable. *Kantory* (except those at the airport and train stations, which often attempt to scam tourists) offer better exchange rates than banks. Bank PKO SA and Bank Pekao have decent exchange rates; they cash traveler's checks and give cash advances. ATMs *(bankomaty)* are common, and are all in English; MasterCard and Visa are widely accepted at ATMs. Budget accommodations rarely accept credit cards, but some restaurants and upscale hotels do. Normal business hours in Poland are 8am-4pm.

HEALTH AND SAFETY

EMERGENCY	**Police:** ☎ 997. **Ambulance:** ☎ 998. **Fire:** ☎ 999.

Medical clinics in major cities have private, English-speaking doctors, but they may not be up to Western standards. Expect to pay 50zł per visit. Avoid state hospitals. In an emergency, go to your embassy. **Pharmacies** are well stocked, and some stay open 24hr. **Public restrooms** are marked with a triangle for men and a circle for women. They range from pristine to squalid and cost up to 2zł; soap, towels, and toilet paper may cost extra. **Tap water** is theoretically drinkable, but **bottled mineral water** will spare you from some unpleasant metals and chemicals.

Crime rates are low, but tourists are sometimes targeted. Watch for muggings and **pickpockets,** especially on trains and in lower-priced hostels. Cab drivers will invariably attempt to cheat those who do not speak Polish, and "friendly locals" looking to assist tourists are sometimes merely setting them up for scams. **Women** traveling alone should take usual precautions. Travelers of unfamiliar ethnicities may receive attention. Those with darker skin may encounter **discrimination,** as people labeled "gypsies" are generally considered dishonest and thieving. There may be lingering prejudice against Jews despite great efforts on the part of the government, and casual anti-Semitic comments are heard frequently. **Homosexuality** is not widely accepted; discretion is advised.

TRANSPORTATION

Warsaw's **Okęcie Airport** is modern. **LOT,** the national airline, flies to major cities, as do many discount airlines. It's usually better to take a **train** than a bus, as buses are slow and uncomfortable. For a **timetable,** see **www.pkp.pl.** *Odjazdy* (departures) are in yellow, *przyjazdy* (arrivals) in white. *InterCity* and *ekspresowy* (express) trains are listed in red with an "IC" or "Ex" in front of the train number. *Pośpieszny* (direct; in red) are almost as fast and a bit cheaper. Low-priced *osobowy* (in black) are the slowest and have no restrooms. If you see a boxed "R" on the schedule, ask the clerk for a *miejscówka* (reservation). Students and seniors buy *ulgowy* (half-price) tickets instead of *normalny* tickets. Beware: **foreign travelers are not eligible for discounts** on domestic buses and trains. **Eurail** is not valid in Poland. **Wasteels** tickets and **Eurotrain** passes, sold at Almatur and Orbis, get 40% off international train fares for those under 26. Buy tickets in advance or wait in long lines. Stations are not announced and can be poorly marked. Theft often occurs on overnight trains; **do not under any circumstances take night trains.** **PKS buses** are cheapest and fastest for short trips. There are *pośpieszny* (direct; in red) and *osobowy* (slow; in black). In the countryside, PKS markers (yellow steering wheels that look like upside-down Mercedes-Benz symbols) indicate stops. Buses have no luggage compartments. **Polski Express,** a private company, offers more luxurious service, but does not run to all cities. **Ferries** run throughout the Baltic area. For **taxis,** either arrange the price before getting in (in Polish, if possible) or be sure the driver turns on the meter. The going rate is 1.50-3zł per km. Arrange cabs by phone if possible. **Rental cars** are readily available in Warsaw and Kraków. Though legal, **hitchhiking** is rare and sometimes dangerous for foreigners. Hand-waving is the accepted sign. *Let's Go* does not recommend hitchhiking.

KEEPING IN TOUCH

PHONE CODES	**Country code: 48. International dialing prefix: 00.** From outside Poland, dial int'l dialing prefix (see inside back cover) + 48 + city code + local number. Within Poland, dial city code + local number, even when dialing inside the city.

Poland is **wired.** Most mid-sized towns have at least one Internet cafe, and larger cities have many. The cost ranges 2-6zł per hour. **Card telephones** are standard. Cards are sold at post offices, Telekomunikacja Polska (TP) offices, and kiosks. **Mail** is admirably efficient. Airmail *(lotnicza)* takes two to five days to Western Europe and seven to 10 days to Australia, New Zealand, and the US. Mail can be received via **Poste Restante.** Address the envelope as follows: Stephanie (First name) O'ROURKE (LAST NAME), POSTE RESTANTE, Długa 22/25 (post office address), 80-800 (postal code) Gdańsk (city), POLAND. Letters cost about 2.20zł. To pick up Poste Restante, show your passport.

ACCOMMODATIONS AND CAMPING

POLAND	❶	❷	❸	❹	❺
ACCOMMODATIONS	under 45zł under €11 under US$14	45-65zł €11-16 US$14-20	66-80zł €16-20 US$20-24	81-120zł €20-30 US$24-36	over 120zł over €30 over US$36

Hostels *(schroniska młodzieżowe)* abound and cost 15-60zł per night. They are often booked solid by tour groups; call at least a week ahead. **PTSM** is the national hostel organization. Dom Wycieczkowy and Dom Turystyczny hostels, which are geared toward adults, cost around 50zł. **University dorms** become budget housing in July and August; these are an especially good option in Kraków. The **Almatur** office in Warsaw arranges stays throughout Poland. **PTTK** runs **hotels** called Dom Turysty, which have multi-bed rooms and budget singles and doubles. These hotels generally cost 80-180zł. **Pensions** are often the best deal: the owner's service more than makes up for the small sacrifice in privacy. **Private rooms** *(wolne pokoje)* are available most places, but be careful what you agree to. **Homestays** can be a great way to meet locals; inquire at the tourist office. Private rooms should cost 20-60zł. Campsites average 10-15zł per person, 20zł with a car. They may rent **bungalows;** a bed costs 20-30zł. *Polska Mapa Campingów*, available at tourist offices, lists **campsites**. Almatur runs a number of sites in summer; ask them for a list. Camp only in campsites or risk a night in jail.

FOOD AND DRINK

POLAND	❶	❷	❸	❹	❺
FOOD	under 8zł under €2 under US$2	8-17zł €2-4 US$2-5	18-30zł €4-7 US$5-9	31-45zł €4-11 US$9-14	over 45zł over €11 over US$14

Polish cuisine blends French, Italian, and Slavic traditions. Meals begin with **soup,** usually *barszcz* (beet or rye), *chłodnik* (cold beets with buttermilk and eggs), *ogórkowa* (sour cucumbers), *kapuśniak* (cabbage), or *rosół* (chicken). **Main courses** include *gołąbki* (cabbage rolls with meat and rice), *kotlet schabowy* (pork cutlet), *naleśniki* (crepes filled with cheese or jam), and *pierogi* (dumplings). Finding **vegetarian** food is feasible if you stick to dumplings and crepes, but **kosher** eating is next to impossible. Most "Jewish" restaurants are not actually kosher. Poland offers a wealth of **beer, vodka, and spiced liquor.** *Żywiec* is the most popular beer. Even those who dislike beer will enjoy sweet ▓**piwo z sokiem,** beer with raspberry syrup. *Wyborowa, Żytnia,* and *Polonez* are popular *wódka* (vodka) brands, while *Belweder* (Belvedere) is a major alcoholic export. *Żubrówka* vodka comes with a blade of grass from Białowieża, where bison roam. It's often mixed with apple juice *(z sokem jabłkowym)*. *Miód* and *krupnik* (mead) are old-fashioned favorites; grandmas make *nalewka na porzeczce* (black currant vodka).

LIFE AND TIMES

HISTORY

THE NASCENT STATE. In AD 966, **Prince Mieszko I** accepted Christianity and united the tribes that had been occupying modern Poland since AD 800, but the union wasn't complete until his son, **Bolesław Chrobry** (the Brave), was crowned Poland's first king in 1025. The conglomeration of states was devastated by the Mongols in 1241, but recovered by the 14th century, when it became more prosperous—particularly under **King Kazimierz III Wielki** (Casimir III the Great)—and exhibited unprecedented religious and political tolerance. Subsequently Poland became a refuge for Jews expelled from Western Europe.

PROSPERITY. After Casimir III's death in 1370, Poland had great difficulty with the **Teutonic Knights,** who took East Prussia and cut off the Baltic Sea. To combat them, Polish nobles allied with Lithuania by marrying Casimir's only child, Princess Jadwiga, to the powerful Grand Duke of Lithuania, **Jogaila.** The duke was crowned King Władysław II Jagiełło of Poland. The new **Polish Commonwealth** lasted 187 years and defeated the Teutonic Order in 1410. Poland became a center of learning in 1394 with the establishment of Kraków's **Jagiellonian University.** In the 16th century, under King Zygmunt I Stary, the **Renaissance** reached Poland. The spirit of the age found fertile ground at Jagiellonian University, where Mikołaj Kopernik, an astronomer from Toruń known by his Latin name, **Copernicus,** developed the revolutionary heliocentric model of the solar system.

DELUGE. Poland and Lithuania drew even closer when the 1569 **Union of Lublin** established the **Polish-Lithuanian Commonwealth** with an elected king, a customs union, and a legislature, but with separate territories, laws, and armies. **King Zygmunt III Waza** moved the capital from Kraków to Warsaw. He and his successors embroiled the state in wars with Sweden, Turkey, and Muscovy throughout the 17th century. Poland only survived this devastating period, known as the **Deluge,** because of great military commanders like **Jan Zamoyski** and **Stanisław Żółkiewski.** During the wars, Poles persevered in the defense of **Częstochowa,** home of the revered Black Madonna icon, where a small force of monks and villagers threw off an invading Swedish army of 9000. Yet divisive nobles, separate Polish and Lithuanian administrations, and a weakened monarch hobbled the Polish state.

THE PARTITIONS. Fearing Russian influence, nationalist Poles formed the **Confederation of Bar** in opposition to the weak Polish king in 1768. The resulting civil war threw Poland into anarchy. While France and Turkey aided the confederates, Russia backed the monarchy. Fearful of losing its influence, Russia supported Prussian ruler Frederick the Great's schemes to shrink Polish lands. In the 1772 **First Partition of Poland,** Austria, Prussia, and Russia each claimed a sizable chunk.

In 1788, Polish noblemen called a meeting of the **Sejm** (Parliament); this "Great Sejm" produced a constitution calling for a parliamentary monarchy. Signed on May 3, 1791, the constitution was the second of its kind in the world. It established Catholicism as the national religion, set up a plan for political elections, and provided for a standing army. Nervous at the prospect of a newly powerful state, Russia and Prussia incited the **Second Partition of Poland** (1793). The government capitulated and many patriots fled abroad. The following year, **Tadeusz Kościuszko** led an uprising against Russian rule. He ended up in prison, and Poland was divided again in the **Third Partition** (1795). With this final partition, Poland ceased to exist for 123 years, during which Russia attempted to crush all traces of Polish nationalism and identity. Poland did not regain independence until 1918, when **Marshal Józef Piłsudski** pushed back the Red Army. A delegation led by **Roman Dmowski** worked **Polish statehood** into the Treaty of Versailles one year later.

WWII AND THE RISE OF COMMUNISM. The 1939 **Nazi-Soviet Non-Aggression Pact** rendered Poland's defense treaties obsolete. Nazi and Soviet forces then attacked simultaneously. Germany occupied the western two-thirds of the country, while the USSR got the rest. **Concentration camps** were erected throughout Poland, and over six million Poles, including three million Jews, were killed during **WWII.** In April 1943, a small group of Jews organized the **Warsaw Ghetto Uprising,** valiantly rebelling against the Nazis. Though the revolt was brutally put down, the uprising was one of the most remarkable acts of courage during the

Holocaust. Just as heroic, and just as doomed, was the 63-day-long **Warsaw Uprising,** in the wake of which the Nazis leveled the entire city of Warsaw. When Red tanks rolled in, they "liberated" the rubble of Warsaw and inaugurated 45 years of **communism.** The first years brought mass migrations and political crackdowns. The country grudgingly submitted, but **strikes** broke out in 1956, 1968, and 1970; all were violently quashed.

SOLIDARITY. In 1978 **Karol Wojtyła** became the first Polish pope, taking the name **John Paul II.** His visit to Poland the next year helped to unite Catholic Poles and was an impetus for the 1980 birth of **Solidarność** (Solidarity), the first independent workers' union in Eastern Europe. Led by **Lech Wałęsa,** an electrician from Gdańsk, Solidarity's anti-Communist activities resulted in the declaration of **martial law** in 1981. Wałęsa was jailed, and was released only after Solidarność was officially disbanded and outlawed by the government in 1982.

In 1989, Poland spearheaded the peaceful fall of Soviet authority in Eastern Europe. **Tadeusz Mazowiecki** was sworn in as Eastern Europe's first non-Communist premier in 40 years. In December 1990, Wałęsa became the first elected president of post-Communist Poland. The government opted to swallow the bitter pill of capitalism all in one gulp by eliminating subsidies, freezing wages, and devaluing the currency. This threw the economy into **recession** and produced widespread unemployment, but Poland has rebounded toward stability and prosperity.

ALEKSANDER ATTRACTS. In Poland's tightly contested 1995 presidential election, Wałęsa lost to **Aleksander Kwaśniewski.** A 1980s Communist, Kwaśniewski was elected on a platform of moderately paced privatization and stronger ties with the West. Following Kwaśniewski's election, however, the **Solidarity Electoral Action Party (AWS)** saw success in local elections, marked by the ascendance of **Jerzy Buzek** to the post of prime minister in 1997.

TODAY

The Solidarity-led coalition government fell in 2000, and Kwaśniewski was reelected in a landslide. A **NATO** member since 1999, Poland has improved its military and was a leading player in the war in Iraq. In 2003, Poland voted to accept its invitation to the **EU,** which it joined in May 2004. The same month, Kwaśniewski appointed **Marek Belka,** the former finance minister, to replace Leszek Miller as **prime minister.** In 2005, the country was cast into intense national mourning by the death of Pope John Paul II.

PEOPLE AND CULTURE

DEMOGRAPHICS. Homogenization that set in following WWII continues: 97% of today's population is ethnically Polish. Officially recognized ethnic minorities include Germans, Ukrainians, Lithuanians, Jews, and Belarusians.

RELIGION. Poland is one of the most **Catholic** countries in the world and the Church enjoys immense respect and political power. Polish Catholicism was bolstered in 1978 by the election of the Polish Pope John Paul II—and again in 2005 by his death. **Protestant** groups are generally confined to German-border areas. Only traces of the rich pre-war **Jewish** culture are still apparent.

LANGUAGE. Polish is a West Slavic language written in the Latin alphabet, and is closely related to **Czech** and **Slovak.** The language varies little across the country. The two exceptions are in the region of **Kaszuby,** where the distinctive Germanized dialect is sometimes classified as a separate language, and in **Karpaty,** where the highlander accent is thick. In western Poland and Mazury, **German** is the

OPPOSITE POLES

For decades, the Soviet yoke kept Poland yearning for liberation and a return to its largely Roman Catholic culture; now that same culture has left one of the country's largest minorities pining for social equality and a similar freedom. Gay rights have become an increasingly controversial topic around the country, especially in Warsaw, where a breakneck pace to modernize ushers in a wave of increasingly liberal thought. Yet for two years running, Warsaw's mayor, Lech Kaczyński, has banned the Gay Rights Parade on grounds that applications were incorrectly filed.

Nonetheless, gay rights groups chose to march forward. In June 2005, over 2500 attendees joined the parade despite the ban, holding signs that read "law and justice for all." Some political support emerged, as officials like Deputy Prime Minister Izabela Jaruga-Nowacha joined marchers.

Though police helped to stem violence during counter protests, the mayor's distaste for homosexuality is by no means rare in Poland: discrimination is rampant, and gays are prohibited from adopting children. Outcry from international gay activists has recently turned the rights issue into a diplomatic one. Poland is modernizing rapidly, and eager to endorse its EU membership, but how far will it go for European assimilation?

most common foreign language, although many Poles in big cities, especially children, speak **English.** Most can understand other Slavic languages if they're spoken slowly. The older generation may speak **Russian.** One more thing: the English word "no" means "yes" in Polish.

CUSTOMS AND ETIQUETTE. In restaurants, tell the server how much change you want and leave the rest as a **tip** (10-15%). In taxis, just leave the change. In any establishment, say *"dzień dobry"* (hello) as you enter, and *"do widzenia"* (goodbye) when you leave. Your waiter will often say *"smacznego"* when he serves you food; reply with *"dziękuję"* (thank you). But be careful: if you say *"dziękuję"* after receiving the bill, the waiter will assume you don't want change. When arriving as a guest, bring a female host an odd number of flowers. Smoking is often prohibited indoors. Always give up your seat to an elderly person, woman, or child.

THE ARTS

LITERATURE
Poland's medieval texts, mostly religious works, were written in Latin. Self-taught 16th-century author **Mikołaj Rej** was the first to write consistently in Polish and is the father of Polish literature. Loss of statehood in 1795 paved the way for **Romanticism,** which held the nation as an ideal. The great writers of this period—**Adam Mickiewicz, Juliusz Słowacki,** and **Zygmunt Krasiński**—depict Poland as a noble martyr. Mickiewicz's *Pan Tadeusz* is still considered the country's primary epic.

The early 20th-century **Młoda Polska** (Young Poland) movement was laden with pessimism. **Stanisław Wyspiański's** drama *Wesele* (The Wedding) addressed many problems that defined Poland in the era. In the years following WWII, many Polish writers published abroad. Nobel Laureate poet **Czesław Miłosz** penned *Zniewolony Umysł* (The Captive Mind), a commentary on Communist control of thought in the mid-1950s. In response to attempts to enforce **Socialist Realism,** the "thaw" brought an explosion of new work addressing life under communism. The **Generation of '68** ushered in a wave of works depicting life at an historical crossroads. In 1996, **Wisława Szymborska** became the second Polish writer in 16 years to receive the Nobel Prize. Numerous contemporary Polish poets, among them **Sławomir Mrożek, Adam Zagajewski,** and **Stanisław Barańczak,** have garnered praise at home and abroad. Journalist **Ryszard Kapuściński** and essayist **Adam Michnik** have also drawn critical acclaim.

MUSIC

Polish **music** is defined by the 19th-century work of **Frédéric Chopin** (Fryderyk Szopen), a master composer and the first of many acclaimed Polish instrumentalists (among them pianist **Artur Rubinstein**). Poland is a jazz hotbed. Performances occur regularly in Kraków (p. 457). Prominent contemporary composers include **Witold Lutosławski, Henryk Gorecki,** and **Krzysztof Penderecki.**

THE VISUAL ARTS

Poland's art history has often been rocky and diffuse, but Warsaw and Kraków both have lively contemporary art scenes. Galleries abound in the city centers, and the Kraków Academy of Fine Arts harbors some of Europe's finest young talents.

Polish **films** have consistently drawn recognition. **Andrzej Wajda** explored his country's conflicts in *Ashes & Diamonds* and *Man of Marble.* He received an honorary Oscar in 2000 for his work. Directors **Roman Polański** and **Krzysztof Kieślowski** have achieved international recognition, the latter for his trilogy *Three Colors: Red, White, and Blue.* The controversial Polański won the 2003 Oscar for Best Director for his film *The Pianist,* set in the Warsaw ghetto during WWII.

HOLIDAYS AND FESTIVALS

Holidays: New Year's Day (Jan. 1); Easter Holiday (Apr. 16, 2006; Apr. 8, 2007); May Day (May 1); Constitution Day (May 3); Corpus Christi (June 15, 2006; June 7, 2007); Assumption Day (Aug. 15); All Saints' Day (Nov. 1); Independence Day (Nov. 11); Christmas (Dec. 25-26).

Festivals: Festivals are tied to Catholic holidays, though folk tradition adds variety. Businesses close on holidays like **Corpus Christi** and **Assumption Day,** which are not as widely observed elsewhere.

ADDITIONAL RESOURCES

GENERAL HISTORY

Heart of Europe: A Short History of Poland, by Norman Davies (1986). An easy read that provides a good overview of Polish history.

The Polish Way: A Thousand Year History, by Adam Zamoyski (1993). Focuses on the quirks and intricacies of Poland's past.

FICTION AND NONFICTION

Pan Tadeusz, by Adam Mickiewicz (ed. 1992). A classic by one of the founding fathers of Polish literature.

Poems New and Collected, by Wisława Szymborska (ed. 2000). The haunting, human poetry that won Szymborska the 1996 Nobel Prize for Literature.

This Way for the Gas, Ladies and Gentlemen, by Tadeusz Borowski (1946). A gifted writer's firsthand account of daily life in Auschwitz.

The Captive Mind, by Czesław Miłosz (1953). Milosz's searing early critique of Soviet rule in Poland and a brave declaration of intellectual freedom.

Mila 18, by Leon Uris (1976). A gripping novel about the Warsaw Ghetto by the celebrated American author.

FILM

The Pianist, directed by Roman Polański (2002). The true story of pianist Władysław Szpilman's struggle to survive during the Nazi occupation of Warsaw.

POLAND

The Decalogue, directed by Krzysztof Kieślowski (1988-90). Commissioned by Polish television, this series of 10 short films explores the Ten Commandments in the context of post-Communist Poland.

WARSAW (WARSZAWA)   ☎(0)22

Construction cranes dominate the Warsaw skyline and the smell of wet concrete fills the air of the busy, youthful Polish capital. Massive rebuilding is nothing new for a city that raised itself from rubble at the end of World War II, when two-thirds of the population were killed and 83% of the city destroyed. Having weathered the further blow of a half-century of communist rule, Warsaw has now sprung to life as a dynamic center of business, politics, and culture. With Poland's recent accession into the European Union, the city is transforming its culture and landscape at an even faster clip. A proud survivor and an unabashed striver, resilient Warsaw is on the rise. Now is the time to visit this compelling and grossly underrated city.

✈ INTERCITY TRANSPORTATION

Flights: Port Lotniczy Warszawa-Okęcie ("Terminal 1"), Żwirki i Wigury (info desk ☎650 41 00, reservations 0 801 300 952). Take bus #175 to the city center (after 10:40pm, bus #611); buy tickets at the *Ruch* kiosk at the top of the escalator in the arrivals hall. (Open M-F 5:30am-10:30pm.) If you arrive past 10:30pm, you can buy tickets from your bus driver for a 3zł surcharge (students 1.50zł). The **IT** (Informacja Turystyczna) office is at the top of the escalator in the arrivals hall (see **Tourist Offices,** p. 430). Open M-F 8am-8pm. Airlines include: **Air France,** Nowy Świat 64 (☎584 99 00, open M-F 9am-4pm; at the airport ☎846 03 03, open M-Sa 5am-7pm, Su 7:30am-7pm); **American Airlines,** al. Ujazdowskie 20 (☎625 30 02; open M-F 9am-6pm); **British Airways,** Krucza 49, off al. Jerozolimskie (☎529 90 00, open M-F 9am-5pm; at the airport ☎650 45 20, open daily 6am-6pm); **Delta,** Królewska 11 (☎827 84 61; open M-F 9am-5pm); **KLM,** at the airport (☎863 70 00; www.klm.pl; open M-F 10:30am-4:30pm); **LOT,** al. Jerozolimskie 65/79 (☎22 95 72 from a mobile phone, 0 801 703 703 from a landline; www.lot.com; open M-F 9am-7pm, Sa 9am-3pm) in the Marriott; **Lufthansa,** Sienna 39 (☎338 13 00; www.lufthansa.pl; open M-F 9am-5pm); **Swiss International,** at the airport (☎650 45 25; open M-Sa 6am-8pm, Su 8am-8pm).

Trains: There are 3 major train stations, the most convenient is **Warszawa Centralna (Central Station),** al. Jerozolimskie 54 (☎94 36; www.pkp.pl). Most trains also stop at **Warszawa Zachodnia (Western Station),** Towarowa 1, and **Warszawa Wschodnia (Eastern Station),** Lubelska 1, in Praga. Warszawa Centralna has cafes, a 24hr. **pharmacy, ATMs, pay phones, luggage storage,** and a **post office.** On the main level, international counters are to the left and domestic are to the right. Write down where and when you want to go, along with *"Który peron?"* (Which platform?). Yellow signs list departures *(odjazdy);* white signs arrivals *(przyjazdy).* To: **Gdańsk** (4hr., 12 per day, 50-117zł); **Kraków** (2½-5hr., 15 per day, 80-105zł); **Łódź** (1½-2hr., 17 per day, 25-45zł); **Lublin** (2½hr., 17 per day, 25-92zł); **Poznań** (2½-3hr., 20 per day, 80-115zł); **Szczecin** (5½-6½hr., 4 per day, 80-125zł); **Toruń** (2½-5hr., 5 per day, 40-105zł); **Wrocław** (4½-6hr., 11 per day, 55-125zł); **Berlin, GER** (6hr., 4 per day, 160zł); **Budapest, HUN** (10-13hr., 2 per day, 280zł); **Prague, CZR** (9-12hr., 3 per day, 270-310zł); **St. Petersburg, RUS** (25-30hr., 1 per day, 300zł). Remember that many international trains originate outside Poland; for these trains you cannot make a reservation.

Buses: Both Polski Express and PKS buses run out of Warsaw.

Polski Express, al. Jana Pawła II (☎844 55 55), in a kiosk next to Warszawa Centralna. Faster than PKS. Kiosk open daily 6:30am-10pm. To: **Białystok** (4hr., 5 per day, 30zł); **Częstochowa** (5½hr., 2 per day, 46zł); **Gdańsk** (6hr., 2 per day, 65zł); **Kraków** (8hr., 2 per day, 62zł); **Łódź** (2½hr., 7 per day, 30zł); **Lublin** (3hr., 8 per day, 31zł); **Toruń** (4hr., 15 per day, 45zł).

PKS Warszawa Zachodnia, al. Jerozolimskie 144 (☎822 48 11, domestic info 94 33, international info 823 55 70; www.pks.warszawa.pl), same building as Warszawa Zachodnia train station. Cross to far side of al. Jerozolimskie and take bus #127, 130, 508, or E5 to the center. Open daily 6am-9:30pm. To: **Białystok** (4hr., 3 per day, 27zł); **Częstochowa** (4½hr., 12 per day, 30zł); **Gdańsk** (7hr., 14 per day, 50zł); **Kazimierz Dolny** (3½hr., 10 per day, 22zł); **Kraków** (6hr., 4 per day, 38zł); **Lublin** (3hr., 20 per day, 25zł); **Toruń** (4½hr., 11 per day, 35zł); **Wrocław** (9½hr., 3 per day, 43zł); **Kyiv, UKR** (14½hr., 1 per day, 155zł); **Vilnius, LIT** (9½hr., 3 per day, 115zł).

Centrum Podróży AURA, al. Jerozolimskie 144 (☎ 823 68 58; www.aura.pl), at the Zachodnia station left of the entrance. Many international options. Open M-F 9am-6pm, Sa 9am-2pm. Also at al. Jerozolimskie 54 (☎628 62 53), at Warszawa Centralna. International buses to: **Amsterdam, NED** (23hr., 2 per day, 300-320zł); **Geneva, SWI** (27hr., 2 per day, 370-400zł); **London, GBR** (27hr., 3 per day, 280-450zł); **Paris, FRA** (25hr., 1-3 per day, 300-470zł); **Prague, CZR** (11½hr.; 3 per wk.; 115zł); **Rome, ITA** (28hr., 1 per day, 350-400zł). A few buses leave from **Warszawa Station** on Zieleniecka, on the other side of the river. Take bus #101 or 509 or tram #7, 8, 12, or 25 from the center.

◪ ORIENTATION

The main part of Warsaw lies west of the **Wisła River**. Though the city is large, its grid layout and efficient public transportation make it easy to navigate and explore. The main east-west thoroughfare is **al. Jerozolimskie.** It is intersected by several north-south avenues, including **Marszałkowska,** a major tram route. **Warszawa Centralna,** the main train station, is at the intersection of al. Jerozolimskie and **al. Jana Pawła II.** The gargantuan **Pałac Kultury i Nauki** (Palace of Culture and Science) looms nearby, above **pl. Defilad** (Parade Square); its clock tower is visible throughout the center. The northern boundary of pl. Defilad is **Świętokrzyska,** another east-west thoroughfare. Intersecting al. Jerozolimskie east of the city center, the **Trakt Królewski** (Royal Way) takes different names as it runs north-south. Going north it first becomes **Nowy Świat** and then **Krakowskie Przedmieście** as it leads into **Stare Miasto** (Old Town). Going south, the road becomes **al. Ujazdowskie** as it runs past embassy row, palaces, and **Łazienki Park. Praga,** the part of the city on the east bank of the Wisła, is accessible by tram via **al. Jerozolimskie** and **al. Solidarności,** and the two most trafficked north-south thoroughfares are **Targowa,** near the zoo, and **Francuska,** south of al. Jerozolimskie.

▣ LOCAL TRANSPORTATION

Public Transportation: (from a mobile phone ☎ 720 8383, from a land line 0 300 300 130; www.ztm.waw.pl). Warsaw's public transit system is excellent. Day **trams** and **buses** 2.40zł, with ISIC 1.25zł; day pass 7.20/3.70zł; weekly pass 26/12zł. Punch the ticket in the yellow machines on board or face a 120zł fine. If you find that you're the only one validating your ticket, remember that many locals carry 90-day passes. Bus, tram, and subway lines share the same tickets, passes, and prices. It's wise to keep a supply of tickets because many corner stores and bright green *Ruch* booths that sell tickets are only open during the day; when drivers supply the tickets they charge a small commission. **Bus #175 goes from the airport** to Stare Miasto by way of Warszawa Centralna and Nowy Świat. Watch out for pickpockets. There are also 2 **sightseeing bus routes:** #180 (M-F) and #100 (Sa-Su). Purchase an all-day ticket and you can hop on and off the bus. Night buses are infamously difficult to figure out, but all start and end at **Warszawa Centralna** and run every 30min. 11:30pm-5:30am. If you need to use one, ask at a tourist bureau or accommodation. Warsaw's **Metro** has only 1 line; it is not particularly convenient for tourists. With the exception of limited night buses, urban transport runs daily 4:30am-midnight.

POLAND

Warsaw

Stare Miasto

Stare Miasto inset:
- Mickiewicz Literary Museum
- Warsaw Historical Museum
- St. John's Cathedral
- St. Zbawca
- Orbis
- Zamek Królewski (Royal Castle)
- RYNEK STAREGO MIASTA (OLD TOWN SQUARE)
- PLAC ZAMKOWY
- Pauline Church of the Holy Cross
- St. John of God
- Nowomiejska
- Podwale
- Szeroki Dunaj
- Wąski Dunaj
- Kanonia
- Celna
- Brzozowa
- Grodzka
- Krzywe Koło

Praga
- St. Mary Magdalene Cathedral
- St. Michael and St. Florian Cathedral
- Port Praski
- Jagiellońska
- Białostocka
- Targowa
- Sierakowskiego
- Kłopotowskiego
- Panieńska
- Jasińskiego
- Zamojskiego
- Okrzei
- Ratuszowa
- Wybrzeże Helskie

Ogród Zoologiczny
Praski Park
Wisła R.

Park Skaryszewski
al. Zieleniecka
Stadion Dziesięciolecia
Russian Market

most Śląsko-Dąbrowski
most Świętokrzyski
most Średnicowy
most Poniatowskiego

POWIŚLE
MARIENSZTAT

- Church of the Holy Sacrament
- Dominican Church of St. Jacob
- Church of the Visitation Nuns
- University of Warsaw
- Pałac Kazimierzowski
- Chopin Museum
- Almatur
- St. Anne's
- Holy Cross (Św. Krzyża)
- Maria Skłodowska-Curie Museum
- Zachęta Gallery
- Great Theater and Opera House
- Ogród Saski (Saxon Gardens)
- American Bookstore
- Nowy Świat
- Krakowskie Przedmieście

STARE MIASTO
- Royal Castle

NOWE MIASTO
- Ogród Krasińskich
- Rybaki
- Cmentarz Żydowski

SRÓDMIEŚCIE
- PL. PIŁSUDSKIEGO
- PL. DĄBROWSKIEGO
- PL. BANKOWY
- PL. ŻELAZNEJ BRAMY
- PL. GRZYBOWSKI
- National Philharmonic
- John Paul II Collection
- Nożyk Synagogue

TO WARSZAWA WSCHODNIA (200m)

TO CEMENTARZ ŻYDOWSKI (1km)
TO MUSEUM OF PAWIAK PRISON (1km)
UMSCHLAGPLATZ (1.5km)
Gen. W. Andersa

400 meters
400 yards

TO LG (150m)

POLAND

▲ ACCOMMODATIONS

Boutique B&B,	1 C4
Camping "123",	2 A5
Dom Przy Rynku,	3 B1
Hotel Mazowiecki,	4 B3
Nathan's Villa,	5 C5
Oki Doki,	6 B3
Schronisko Młodzieżowe "Agrykola",	7 E6
Szkolne Schronisko Młodzieżowe Nr. 2,	8 C4

● CAFES

Antykwariat Cafe,	9 B4
Coffee Karma,	10 C6
Pożegnanie z Afryką,	11 B1
Tea Art,	12 B2
Herbaciarnia,	13 C4
Wedel,	14 C4

● FOOD

Bar Vega,	15 A3
Cafe Stary Młynek,	16 D5
Gospoda Pod Kogutem,	17 B1
Między Nami,	18 C4
Pizza Marzano,	19 C3
Rendez-Vous,	20 F3
Warsaw Tortilla Factory,	21 B5

● NIGHTLIFE

Bar Lemon,	22 B4
Chimera,	23 E1
Cinnamon,	24 B3
Rasko,	25 A3
Enklawa,	26 B3
Ground Zero,	27 B5
Le Madame,	28 A1
Labo Music Bar,	29 B3
Piekarnia,	30 A3
Student Bar Complex,	31 D3
Underground Music Cafe,	32 B3

● SIGHTS

Chopin's Drawing Room,	33 C3
Copernicus Monument,	34 C3
Ghetto Wall,	35 F1
Little Insurgent Monument,	36 A4
Mermaid,	37 E1
Mickiewicz Monument,	38 F1
Monument of Ghetto Heroes,	39 C3
Monument to the Fallen and Murdered in the East,	40 A3
Pałac Radziwiłłów,	41 A1
Pałac Staszica,	42 B2
Palm Tree,	43 C3
Statue of Zygmunt III Waza,	44 C4
Tomb of the Unknown Soldier,	45 F2
Warsaw Insurgents' Monument,	46 B3
Warsaw Zoo,	47 B3
	48 C1

Solec
Wioślarska
Wilanowska
Okrąg
Solec
Ludna
Łazienkowska
Kuśnierskiego
Draganów
Kawaleri
Japan.
Czerniakowska
Koźmińska
Myśliwiecka
Szwoleżerów
Spała
Stała
Jackowska
Przemysłowa
Rozbrat
Szara
Fabryczna
Pałac Łazienkowski
Kruczkowskiego
Rozbrat
J. H. Wrońskiego
Myśliwiecka
Old Orangery
Pałac Lazienkowski
Czerniakowska
Park im. marsz. Śmigłego-Rydza
UJAZDÓW
Ogród Botaniczny (Botanical Gardens)
Łazienki Park
Książęca
al. Na Skarpie
Jazdów
Agrykola
Chopin Monument
TO BELWEDER (100m), POSIEK
MUSEUM (2km), WILANÓW (2km)
Center of Contemporary Art
Ujazdowski Castle
Prusa
F. Nulio
Frascati
Ludna
E. Plater
Bolesława
Wiejska
al. Ujazdowskie
al. Ujazdowskie
Bracka
Wiejska
Matejki
Lennona
PL. NA ROZDROŻU
al. Szucha
Military Museum
National Museum
PL. TRZECH KRZYŻY
Smolna
Foksal
Mysia
Bracka
Maszyńska
Sejm (Parliament) and Senat (Senate)
Canada
UK
CUS
Lituanialne
Lithuania
Bagatela
RONDO CHARLES DE GAULLE
Empik Megastore
Orbis
Domów Okrąszek
Czech Republic
F. Chopina
Koszykowa
Wilcza
Marszałkowska
Hoża
PL. KONSTYTUCJI
al. Róż
Natolińska
al. Wyzwolenia
Sempołowskiej
Oleandrów
Polna
MOKOTÓW
RONDO JAZDY POLSKIEJ
WARSAW UPRISING MUSEUM (1.5km)
RONDO ONZ
Świętokrzyska
Emilii Plater
Pawia
Sienna
Złota
Śliska
Śniadeckich
Jaworzyńska
Litewska
Marszałkowska
Krucza
Wilcza
Żurawia
Żulińska
STA
Australia
Żulińska
Hoża
Poznańska
Piękna
Lwowska
Rektorska
L. Waryńskiego
Polna
Park im. marsz. Józefa Piłsudskiego
TURKISH EMBASSY (800m)
al. Armii Ludowej
al. Niepodległości
Filtrowa
Lekarska
Nowowiejska
Warsaw Polytechnic University
Koszykowa
S. Nogakowskiego
PL. ZBAWICIELA
Marszałkowska
Marszałkowska
PL. DEFILAD
Pałac of Culture and Science
Sala Kongresowa
Warszawa Centralna Station
Marriott Hotel
Apteka Grabowskiego
Polski Express
TO WARSZAWA ZACHODNIA (2km), INTERNATIONAL AIRPORT (PORT LOTNICZY) (7.5km)
al. Jerozolimskie
Wojciecha Oczki
Chałubińskiego
Lindleya
Emilii Plater
Sosnowa
Chmielna
Złota
Śliska
Sienna
Pańska
Wiecha
Widok
Nowogrodzka
Św. Barbary
Wspólna
Poznańska
Simple Internet Cafe
R. DMOWSKIEGO
Świętokrzyska
Boduena
Szpitalna
Zgoda
Złota
Chmielna
Marszałkowska
Nowogrodzka

Taxis: Overcharging is a problem; ask a Polish speaker to arrange pickup and to confirm the price. The government sets cab fare at 2zł per km; with privately run cabs, stated prices may be lower but the risk of overcharging is greater. It helps to keep an eye on the meter. State-run: **ME.RC. Taxi** (☎677 77 77), **Wawa Taxi** (☎96 44). Privately run: **Euro Taxi** (☎96 62), **Halo Taxi** (☎96 23), **MPT Radio Taxi** (☎91 91).

Car Rental: Avis (☎630 73 16), at the Marriott. Open M-F 8am-8pm, Sa-Su 8am-4pm. Airport office (☎650 48 70). Open daily 7am-11pm. From 250zł per day. **Budget** (☎630 72 80), at the Marriott and the airport (☎650 40 52). From 293zł per day. Open daily 7am-7pm.

🔃 PRACTICAL INFORMATION

TOURIST AND FINANCIAL SERVICES

Tourist Offices: Informacji Turystyczna (IT), al. Jerozolimskie 54 (☎94 31; www.warsawtour.pl), inside Centralna train station. English-speaking staff is informative. Provides **maps** (some free, some 4zł) and arranges accommodations (no charge). Their free booklets list popular restaurants and special events. Open daily May-Sept. 8am-8pm; Oct.-Apr. 8am-6pm. **Branches:** al. Jerozolimskie 144. Open daily 9am-5pm. At the PKS bus station at Dworzec Zachodnia (Western Station). Open daily 9am-5pm. In the airport. Open daily May-Sept. 8am-8pm; Oct.-Apr. 8am-6pm.

Budget Travel: Almatur, Kopernika 23 (☎826 35 12). Offers discounted plane and bus tickets. ISIC 44zł. Open M-F 9am-7pm, Sa 10am-5pm. AmEx/MC/V. **Orbis,** Bracka 16 (☎827 38 57), entrance on al. Jerozolimskie. Sells plane, train, ferry, and international bus tickets. Open M-F 8am-6pm, Sa 9am-3pm. **Branch** at Świętokrzyska 23/25 (☎831 82 99; orbis.bis@pbp.com.pl). Open M-F 9am-6pm, Sa 10am-3pm. MC/V.

Embassies: Most are near al. Ujazdowskie. **Australia,** Nowogrodzka 11 (☎521 34 44; fax 627 35 00; ambasada@australia.pl). Open M-F 9am-1pm and 2-5pm. **Canada,** al. Matejki 1/5 (☎584 31 00; wsaw@international.gc.ca). Open M-F 8:30am-4:30pm. Open M-F 8am-4:30pm. **Ireland,** Mysia 5 (☎849 66 33; ambasada@irlandial.pl). Open M-F 9am-1pm and 2-5pm. **UK,** al. Róż (☎311 00 00). Open M-F 8:30am-12:30pm and 1:30-4:30pm. **US,** al. Ujazdowskie 29/31 (☎504 20 00). Open M-F 8:30am-5pm.

Currency Exchange: Except at tourist sights, *kantory* have the best rates for exchanging currency and traveler's checks. 24hr. **currency exchange** at Warszawa Centralna or at al. Jerozolimskie 61. Many 24hr. *kantory* offer worse rates at night. **Bank PKO SA,** pl. Bankowy 2 (☎521 84 40), in the blue glass skyscraper, or Grójecka 1/3 (☎59 88 28), in Hotel Sobieski, cashes AmEx/V **traveler's checks** for 1-2% commission and gives MC/V **cash advances.** All branches open M-F 8am-6pm, Sa 10am-2pm. 24hr. **ATMs,** called *bankomat,* accept Cirrus and Plus. **Branches** at many locations in major banks. Try **Bank Zachodni,** al. Jerozolimskie 91 (☎635 47 00). Open M-F 8am-6pm.

LOCAL SERVICES

Luggage Storage (Kasa Bagażowa): At Warszawa Centralna train station. 5zł per item per day, plus 2.25zł per 50zł of declared value if you want insurance. To sidestep the language barrier and retain more control over your bag, choose a locker. Open 24hr.

English-Language Bookstores: American Bookstore (Księgarnia Amerykańska), Nowy Świat 61 (☎827 48 52). Good but pricey selection of fiction, history, and maps. Open M-Sa 10am-7pm, Su 10am-6pm. AmEx/MC/V. **Empik Megastore,** Nowy Świat 15-17 (☎627 06 50). Great selection of maps. Open M-Sa 9am-10pm, Su 11am-5pm.

GLBT Resources: Lambda, (☎628 52 22; www.lambda.org.pl), in English and Polish. Open Tu-W 6-9pm and F 4-10pm. Other info can be found at the English-language site http://warsaw.gayguide.net. The GLBT scene in Warsaw is generally discrete and lacks widespread political support.

EMERGENCY AND COMMUNICATIONS

24hr. Pharmacy: Apteka Grabowskiego "21" (☎825 69 86), upstairs at Warszawa Centralna train station. AmEx/MC/V.

Medical Services: Centrum Medyczyne LIM, al. Jerozolimskie 65/79, 9th fl. (24hr. emergency line ☎458 70 00, 24hr. ambulance 430 30 30; www.cm-lim.com.pl), at the Marriott. English-speaking doctors. Open M-F 7am-9pm, Sa 8am-8pm, Su 9am-1pm. **Branch** at Domaniewski 41 (☎458 70 00). Open M-F 7am-9pm, Sa 8am-8pm. **Central Emergency Station,** Hoża 56 (☎999) has a 24hr. ambulance.

Telephones: Phones are at the post office, train station, and scattered throughout the city. All but a few accept only cards, available at the post office and many kiosks. Ask for a *karta telefoniczna*. Directory assistance ☎118 913.

Internet: ▧**Simple Internet Cafe,** Marszałkowska 99/101 (☎628 31 90), at the corner of al. Jerozolimskie, has English-speaking staff and good hourly rates. The largest and orangest Internet cafe in Warsaw. Open 24hr. Rates vary from 1zł per hr. late at night to 4zł per hr. midday. 24hr. Internet cafes line the bowels of Centralna train station.

Post Office: Main branch, Świętokrzyska 31/33 (☎827 00 52). Take a number at the entrance. For stamps and letters push "D"; packages "F." For **Poste Restante,** inquire at window #42. Open 24hr. *Kantor* open daily 7am-10pm. Most other branches open 8am-8pm. **Postal Code:** 00 001.

⌐ ACCOMMODATIONS

Warsaw accommodations are improving rapidly, but demand still overwhelms supply, so reserve in advance, especially on weekends. Conveniently located mid-range hotels are particularly hard to come by. IT can get you a **university dorm ❶** (25-30zł) room if you're traveling between July and September. They also maintain a list of accommodations, including **private rooms**.

HOSTELS

▧ **Oki Doki,** pl. Dąbrowskiego 3 (☎826 51 12; www.okidoki.pl). From the center, take any tram north on Marszałkowska to Świętokrzyska. Walk 1 block north on Marszałkowska and turn right on Rysia. Each room of this chic hostel was designed by a different Warsaw artist and has a unique geographical theme. Peruse the rotating photography exhibits in the halls. The friendly staff serve beer (5zł) and breakfast (10zł) in the dining room/in-house bar. Bike rental 35zł per day, 8zł per hr. Laundry 10zł. Free Internet. 24hr. reception. Check-in 3pm. Check-out 11am. Book ahead. May-Aug. dorms 45-60zł; singles 110zł; doubles 135zł, with baths 185zł. MC/V. ❷

▧ **Nathan's Villa,** Piękna 24/26 (☎0 509 358 487; www.nathansvilla.com). From the center, take any tram south on Marszałkowska to pl. Konstytucji. Go left on Piękna; the hostel is on the left. Nathan's matches a convenient location with unmatched facilities and services. Though guests have been known to pass out on the lawn of this relentlessly hard-partying hostel, the rooms gleam with bright colors and brand-new furniture. Just don't count on falling asleep early. Breakfast included. Laundry. Free Internet. Reception 24hr. Flexible check-out. Dorms 45-60zł; rooms 120-140zł. MC/V. ❷

Dom Przy Rynku, Rynek Nowego Miasta 4 (☎831 50 33; www.cityhostel.net). Take bus #175 from the center to Franciszkańska. Turn right on Franciszkańska, then take a right into the Rynek (main square); the hostel will be downhill on your left. In the summer this school for disadvantaged children makes money for supplies and furniture by converting into a hostel. Reception 24hr. Flexible lockout 10am-4pm. Open July to late Aug. daily; in low season F-Su. 2- to 4-bed dorms 40zł. Cash only. ❷

Szkolne Schronisko Młodzieżowe nr. 2, Smolna 30 (☎827 89 52), two blocks up Smolna from Nowy Świat. From the center, take any tram east on al. Jerozolimskie and get off at Rondo Charles de Gaulle. The small but well-kept rooms of this sunny hostel exude respectability, and the central location can't be beat. The several flights of stairs can be a bit daunting and the curfew and lockout are not conducive to partying, but the atmosphere is safe and friendly. Large kitchen. A/C. Free lockers. Reception 24hr. Lockout 10am-4pm. Curfew midnight. Dorms 36zl; singles 65zl. Cash only. ❶

Schronisko Młodzieżowe "Agrykola," Myśliwiecka 9 (☎622 91 10; www.hotelagrykola.pl), near Łazienki Park and Ujazdowski Castle. From Warszawa Centralna, take bus #151 or, from Marszałkowska, take bus #107, 420, or 520 to Rozbrat. From the bus stop, walk downstairs to the corner of Myśliwiecka and al. Armii Ludowej. Oddly located between Ujazdowski Castle and a major highway, this well-appointed hostel offers an escape from the ubiquitous bunk bed. Bath, TV, and free breakfast in the private rooms, but not in the hostel dorms. In-line skate rental for the track next door (6zł per hr.). Dorms 47zł; singles M-Th 240zł, F-Su 100zł; hotel doubles 320zł. MC/V. ❶

HOTELS AND CAMPING

Boutique Bed and Breakfast, Smolna 14/7 (☎829 48 01). From the center, take any tram east on al. Jerozolimskie to Rondo Charles de Gaulle. Smolna is a half block north on Nowy Świat. Enter through the unmarked double-doors, then the first door on your right, or dial 72 and someone will come down to you. With fresh flowers, blond wood, and homey touches, sophisticated Boutique B&B is like your rich aunt's apartment in the city. Rooms have independent entry from stairwell. Breakfast included. Shared kitchen, dining room, and office. Singles €45; doubles €60; suites €75. MC/V. ❺

Hotel Mazowiecki, Mazowiecka 10 (☎827 23 65; www.mazowiecki.com.pl), just north of Świętokrzyska between Marszałkowska and Nowy Świat. The curtains are faded and the mismatched rooms smell vaguely of smoke, but moderate prices and a location in the middle of the hottest nightlife in town recommend Mazowiecki. Breakfast included. Check-in 2pm. Check-out noon. Singles 150zł, with bath 198zł; doubles 200/248zł. Weekend discount 20%. AmEx/MC/V. ❺

Camping "123," Bitwy Warszawskiej 15/17 (☎822 91 21). From Warszawa Centralna, take bus #127, 130, 508, or 517 to Zachodnia bus station. Cross to the far side of al. Jerozolimskie and walk west on the pedestrian path to Bitwy Warszawskiej; turn left. The campground is on the right. Secluded by a buffer of trees, this tranquil campground is close to the center and provides reliable service but few amenities. Guarded 24hr. Open May-Sept. 10zł per person, 10zł per tent, 10zł per vehicle. Electricity 10zł. Spartan 4-person bungalows: singles 40zł; doubles 70zł; triples 100zł; quads 120zł. ❶

🍴 FOOD

The local street food of choice is the **kebab**, a pita stuffed with spicy meat, cabbage, and pickles (5-10zł). Excellent versions can be had at **Kebab Bar,** Nowy Świat 31, and **Kebab Tureck,** Marszałkowska 81. Food poisoning is a reality of the Warsaw kebab scene: be attentive to how clean all street food appears, and try to stick to stands that draw crowds of non-intoxicated locals. **Bakery stands** offer delicious treats: follow the smell of fresh baking to **Cukiernia** at Tamka 45. In spring and summer, farmers from the surrounding countryside sell **fresh produce** on Warsaw streets: the best produce is found in Praga. Grocery stores include **MarcPol** on pl. Defilad, and **Albert** at al. Jerozolimskie 56, facing Marszałkowska; both are open 24hr. **Domowy Okruszek,** Bracka 3, south of al. Jerozolimskie, sells ready-to-cook dishes like *naleśniki* (pancakes) and *pierogi* (dumplings) for 15-20zł per kilo. (☎628 70 77. Open M-Sa 10am-6pm, Su 10am-3pm.)

POLAND

▩ **Gospoda Pod Kogutem,** Freta 48 (☎635 82 82; www.gospodapodkogutem.pl). A rare find in touristy Stare Miasto: generous portions of delectable local food. Enjoy the barn-themed interior or sit outside on Freta. The place to try something shamelessly traditional, like *pierogi* with cabbage and mushroom (12zł) or *smalec*, surprisingly tasty fried bits of lard. Entrees 15-40zł. Open M noon-midnight, Tu-Su 11am-midnight. MC/V. ❷

Rendez-Vous, Francuska 24 (☎616 13 23), south of Praga's Russian Market, stands as evidence of the east bank's increasing offerings. In good weather, secluded sidewalk seating complements the blandly pleasant wine-themed interior. The sautéed vegetables with roasted feta cheese (14.50zł) is a standout on the eclectic contemporary menu, as are the desserts (8-16zł). Crowd is posh but casual, and prices are more modest than the decor suggests. English menu. Open daily 9am-9pm. MC/V. ❷

Bar Vega, al. Jana Pawła II 36c (☎652 27 54), near the former Ghetto. Secluded from the bustle of al. Jana Pawła II street vendors, Bar Vega serves a full vegetarian Indian meal for about the price of a coffee on Nowy Świat (small or big plate; 8-11zł). The inexplicably cheap cafeteria-style offerings allow you to sample a variety of *pakoras* and *koftas*. Instead of dessert, savor the knowledge that Bar Vega funds a nonprofit to feed Warsaw's homeless children. Open daily noon-8pm. Cash only. ❶

Cafe Stary Młynek, al. Ujazdowskie 6 (☎622 92 64), close to Ujazdowski Park. Located in the cellar of a renovated old mill, this restaurant combines traditional Polish cooking with spare yet comfortable, modern decor. Friendly waitstaff speak English, and with prices at 10-25zł, sampling a wide range of small dishes here is a great way to get to know Polish cuisine without having to endure a kitschy folk re-creation. Open M-F 10am-10pm, Sa noon-11pm, Su noon-9pm. AmEx/MC/V. ❷

Między Nami, Bracka 20 (☎828 54 17; www.miedzynamicafe.com). Packed in-crowd favorite serves a rotating menu of light pastas, traditional soups, and seasonal salads. A hotbed of photography and fashion, this cafe-club publishes its own in-house magazine. Friendly, attentive English-speaking staff. Homemade cake (8zł) is excellent. Entrees 15-25zł. Open M-Th 10am-10pm, F-Sa 10am-midnight, Su 4-11pm. MC/V. ❷

Warsaw Tortilla Factory, Wilcza 46 (☎621 86 22), enter from Poznańska. Drawing a boisterous crowd of expats and locals, this Tex-Mex local institution prides itself on having the best burrito—and arguably the spiciest food—in Poland. Stop by for the Hangover Brunch Special (25zł) Sa-Su noon-5pm, complete with a Bloody Mary "as spicy as you want it." Entrees 15-40zł. Open M-F noon-1am, Sa-Su noon-late. AmEx/MC/V. ❷

MILK IT FOR ALL IT'S WORTH

The milk bars of Warsaw are a dying breed. In the Soviet era, locals flocked to the subsidized cafeteria-style ibarsi out of pure necessity. Today, the *bar mleczny* is not only the cheapest traditional meal in town—it's a symbol of Poland's transformation. Milk bars, so named because of the dairy-heavy dishes they serve, still receive government subsidies, meaning it's cheaper to buy a plate of homestyle cooking here than to make one. Many of the patrons are homeless or elderly, but just as many are rushed students and young professionals looking for an inexpensive meal. The number of milk bars in Warsaw is between 10 and 20, and the withdrawal of government funds means this number will continue to dwindle. Patrons of the remaining bars rally around their unique social function, with websites such as www.barmyleczne.jawsieci.pl. Visit at least one of the following—and if you don't speak Polish, prepare to point:

Bar Uniwersytet, Krakowskie Przedmieście 20/22, resembles milk bars as they truly were. The camp-like interior and long lines set the tone for extremely traditional dishes. **PG Sandwicz**, *Nowy Świat 28, enjoys a steady stream of businessmen and street peddlers, and offers excellent desserts.* **Bar Kubus**, *Ordynacka 13, serves great soups and has a friendly staff.*

Pizza Marzano, Nowy Świat 42 (☎826 21 33). This trustworthy local chain cooks up a score of richly flavored pizzas (15-25zł) and savory appetizers. Artichoke-heart-and sun-dried-tomato pizza 18zł. Lazy, low-stress comfort food with a Nowy Świat sidewalk view. Open M-Th and Su 11am-11pm, F-Sa 11am-midnight. AmEx/MC/V. ❷

⊟ CAFES

Poland is more a tea than a coffee culture, but the cafes of the capital city offer excellent takes on both drinks, as well as exquisite hot chocolate.

▨ **Pożegnanie z Afryką (Out of Africa),** Freta 4/6 (☎602 356 287). This Polish chain of cafes brews consistently incredible coffee (8-15zł). Worth the wait for 1 of 4 tables in the candlelit interior. In warm weather, enjoy the Stare Miasto sidewalk seating and the iced coffee (8zł). Branches throughout the city. Open daily 10am-9pm. Cash only.

▨ **Antykwariat Cafe,** Żurawia 45 (☎629 99 29). Antykwariat ("Antiquarian") recalls an inviting old personal library with sloppily shelved books, an antique piano, and engravings of pre-war Warsaw. The cafe mesmerizes patrons with delicate cups of coffee (5-17zł) and tea (5zł) served with a wrapped chocolate. Also serves beer, wine, and desserts. Plush chairs and outdoor seating invite lingering. Open M-F 11am-11pm, Sa-Su 1-11pm. Cash only.

Wedel, Szpitalna 17 (☎827 29 16). The Emil Wedel house, built in 1893 for the Polish chocolate tycoon, was one of the few buildings to survive WWII, and its 1st fl. now houses an elegant dessert cafe. The stained-glass grandeur of this chocolate-themed cafe offers a rare glimpse of pre-war Warsaw. Miraculous hot chocolate (8zł). Enjoy rich mahogany, doilies, and the suspicion that you've traveled back in time. The adjacent **Wedel Chocolate** company store has a whimsical diorama of elves making chocolate. Open M-Sa 10am-10pm, Su noon-5pm. AmEx/MC/V.

Coffee Karma, pl. Zbawiciela 3/5 (☎875 87 09; www.coffee-karma.com). This student hangout has it all: great coffee (5-11zł), smoothies (9-12zł), and snacks (6-18zł); laid-back, English-speaking staff; and sidewalk seating with a view of impressive Zbawiciela Church. While you're in the area, check out the crepes (9.50-12zł) just around the corner at Bastylia (☎825 01 57) and the Soviet monumental art on nearby Marszałkowska. Open M-F 7:30am-10pm, Sa 9am-10pm, Su 10am-10pm. Cash only.

Tea Art, Bednarska 28/30 (☎826 24 16). Find refuge from the dreary Warsaw rain at this mellow cellar cafe just outside Stare Miasto, serving an encyclopedic selection of teas (small pot 10zł; large pot 18zł). Scrumptious desserts (6-12zł) include *szarlotka* (apple tart) and ginger cake. The fetching young staff is eager to speak English. Open daily 11am-10pm. AmEx/MC/V.

Herbaciarnia (The Tea Shop), Chmielna 17 (☎827 88 72). For the dedicated tea enthusiast, the Tea Shop offers dizzying rows of exotic blends that the staff will be happy to crack open for you. Read a book over a pot of green tea (12zł) or pause along the pedestrian street for a cup of a fruity mix (5zł). Ground fl. sells tea and accessories; upstairs is limited seating. Open M-F 11am-7pm, Su 11am-3pm. AmEx/MC/V.

◎ SIGHTS

At first glance, Warsaw offers two strains of architecture: impeccably restored historical facades and Soviet-era concrete blocks. However, from cutting-edge art installations in a rebuilt castle to the sobering stillness of the Jewish Cemetery, Warsaw holds out its most compelling sights to those who get to know the city better. The tourist bus routes #100 and 180 are convenient; they begin at pl. Zamkowy and run along pl. Teatralny, Marszałkowska, al. Ujazdowskie, Łazienki Park, and back up the Royal Way, then loop through Praga before returning to pl. Zamkowy.

STARE AND NOWE MIASTO

Warsaw's reconstruction shows its finest face in the cobblestone streets and colorful facades of Stare Miasto (Old Town), so well restored that it has been recognized as a UNESCO World Heritage site. The brick red Royal Castle anchors the neighborhood, and the reconstructed fortifications of the Barbican mark the old city walls. Just north, the Rynek (square) of Nowe Miasto (New Town) hosts summer music and dance performances. Both areas were rebuilt using large fragments of the original buildings. For many, the rubble from which they were made serves as a reminder of the Polish blood shed in the Warsaw Uprising, when nearly all of these buildings were destroyed. *(Take bus #175 or E3 from the center to Miodowa.)*

STATUE OF ZYGMUNT III WAZA. Built in 1644 by Władysław IV to honor his father, the king who moved the capital from Kraków to Warsaw, the statue stood for 300 years before it was destroyed in WWII. Rebuilt in 1949, Zygmunt and his cross again guard the entrance to Stare Miasto. *(Pl. Zamkowy in front of the Royal Castle.)*

ST. JOHN'S CATHEDRAL. Decimated in the 1944 Uprising, Warsaw's oldest church (Katedra Św. Jana) was rebuilt in the Vistulan Gothic style and features pure white walls trimmed with brick vaulting. Its **crypts** hold the dukes of Mazovia and such famous Poles as Nobel Laureate Henryk Sienkiewicz and Gabriel Narutowicz, the first president of independent Poland. A side altar contains the tomb of Cardinal Stefan Wyszyński, primate of Poland from 1948 to 1981. *(On Świętojańska and pl. Zamkowy. Open daily 10am-1pm and 3-5:30pm. Entrance to crypts 1zł.)*

OLD TOWN SQUARE. A stone plaque at the entrance commemorates the reconstruction of the square (Rynek Starego Miasta), finished in 1954. The square bustles with sidewalk cafes and souvenir peddlers, but the statue of the Warsaw **Mermaid** (Warszawa Syrenka) still marks the center. According to legend, a greedy merchant kidnapped the mermaid from the Wisła River, but local fishermen rescued her from captivity. In return, she swore to defend the city; she now protects Warsaw with her shield and raised sword. On the square's southeast side at #1/3, Dom Pod Bazyliszkiem immortalizes the Stare Miasto **Basilisk,** a reptile famous for its fatal breath and deadly stare. *(On Świętojańska.)*

NOWE MIASTO. The Barbican opens onto Freta, the edge of Nowe Miasto. The "New Town," established at the beginning of the 15th century, had its own separate town hall until 1791. Mostly destroyed during

THE LOCAL STORY

GREETINGS FROM JERUSALEM AVENUE

If you're craving the Caribbean, take a gander at the giant palm tree at the corner of Nowy Świat and Jerozolimskie. That's right, palm tree. It's no secret that Poland's climate does not readily give rise to such tropical flora, yet locals are quite accustomed to this 15m synthetic palm. Erected December 12, 2002, the palm tree is in fact a public work of art entitled "Greetings from Jerusalem Avenue."

So why a giant plastic palm in the middle of Warsaw? Joanna Rajkowska, the artist who designed and led the project, was inspired by both linguistic and cultural references. Situated on al. Jerozolimskie (Jerusalem Ave.), the palm tree is a way of transplanting a bit of "holy land" to Poland. The Polish language also includes the word "palma," meaning idiotic or silly to the point of being beyond comprehension, quite fitting for the sight of a palm tree in the rotary that connects two of Warsaw's biggest thoroughfares.

For a firsthand account of the building process, explanation of the initial artistic vision, and images of the design, you can visit the website maintained by Rajkowskala herself, www.palma.art.pl.

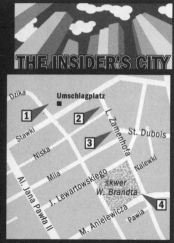

THE GHETTO UPRISING

The monuments that mark some of the most important sites of the heroic Warsaw Ghetto Uprising of 1943 are small and easily missed:

1 In 1942 and 1943, the Nazis gathered the Warsaw Ghetto Jews at the **Umschlagplatz** (Trans-Shipment Square) for transport to death camps. *(Corner of Dzika and Stawki.)*

2 A series of **black stone blocks** along Zamenhofa commemorates the leaders of the Ghetto Uprising.

3 At Mila 18, where a **command bunker** once housed the headquarters of ŻOB, the Jewish fighting organization, a small **monument** honors Mordechaj Anieliewicz and Arie Wilner, the ŻOB leaders who committed suicide when the Nazis discovered the bunker.

4 On Zamenhofa between Lewartskiego and Anielewicza, the **Monument to the Heroes of the Ghetto** is carved from stone originally intended for a Third Reich victory monument.

WWII, its 18th- and 19th-century buildings have enjoyed an expensive facelift. The great physicist and chemist **Maria Skłodowska-Curie**, winner of two Nobel prizes, was born at Freta 16 in 1867 (p. 442). Freta leads to New Town Square (Rynek Nowego Miasta), a smaller brother of the Old Town Square, and to the Baroque dome of the **Church of the Holy Sacrament**, founded in 1688 to commemorate King Jan III Sobieski's 1683 victory over the Turks. The ethereal white interior recalls past glories. *(www.sakramentki.opoka.org.pl. Open daily dawn-dusk. Free.)*

TRAKT KRÓLEWSKI

The 4km Trakt Królewski (Royal Way) begins on pl. Zamkowy at the entrance to Stare Miasto. From Krakowskie Przedmieście, Trakt Królewski becomes Nowy Świat (New World Street). The Royal Way, so named because it leads to Poland's former capital of Kraków, is lined with palaces, churches, and convents built when the royal family moved to Warsaw. The name New World Street dates to the mid-17th century, when a new settlement of working-class people was started here. It was not until the 18th century that the aristocracy started moving in and sprucing the place up with ornate manors and residences.

PL. ZAMKOWY. On the left as you leave pl. Zamkowy headed south, **St. Anne's Church** (Kościół św. Anny), with its striking gilded interior, dates from the 15th century but was rebuilt in the Baroque style. *(Open daily dawn-dusk.)*

CRAZY FOR CHOPIN. On your left, the **Pałac Radziwiłłów** was the site of Chopin's first public concert. The building, now the Polish presidential mansion (not open to the public), is guarded by four stone lions and at least as many military police. A block down the road and set back from the street behind a grove of trees, the **Church of the Visitation Nuns** (Kościół Wizytówek) once resounded with the romantic ivory-pounding of the mop-topped composer. *(Open daily dawn-1pm and 3pm-dusk.)*

HEART AND SOUL: HOLY CROSS CHURCH (KOŚCIÓŁ ŚW. KRZYŻA). Here you'll find Chopin's heart, literally. Although he died abroad at 39, his heart belongs to Poland and rests in an urn in the left nave. Nobel Prize-winning writer Władysław Reymont left his heart here, too. *(Krakowskie Przedmieście 3. Open daily dawn-dusk.)*

UNIVERSITY OF WARSAW. Continue down Krakowskie Przedmieście and the main entrance to the **University of Warsaw** (Uniwersytet Warszawski) will be on your left. Founded in 1816 on Enlightenment principles, the university was closed in 1831 by the

Russian tsar as punishment for its contribution to the November Uprising. Professors taught in private apartments during WWII bombings, lending the University the name "Flying University."

ŁAZIENKI PARK

The palaces and their park were built in the 18th century for Stanisław August Poniatowski, Poland's last king, but peacocks and schoolchildren rule the meandering paths. Rose bushes and benches ring the **Chopin Monument.** A nearby amphitheater hosts free **Chopin concerts** performed by acclaimed Polish and international musicians. (mid-May to Sept. Su noon and 4pm). The Neoclassical palace outbuildings host rotating exhibits of contemporary Polish art. The tranquil 1822 **Temple of Diana** (Świątynia Diany) perches above a wooded pond. *(Park borders al. Ujazdowskie and Trakt Królewski. Take bus #100 from Marszalkowska, #116, 180, or 195 from Nowy Świat, or #119 from the city center to Bagatela. Open daily dawn-dusk.)*

PAŁAC ŁAZIENKOWSKI. Farther into the park is the striking Neoclassical Pałac Łazienkowski, also called the **Palace on Water** (Pałac na Wodzie) or **Palace on the Isle** (Pałac na Wyspie). Surrounded by water, peacocks, and leafy boughs, this breathtaking building was the creation of King Stanisław August and his beloved architect Dominik Merlini. Displays of period furnishings and picture-window views of the park are concentrated in this small space. Be sure to pause before entering to put protective slippers over your shoes and check any bags (storage available to the left of the entry). The non-English-speaking staff will be sure to approach you if you forget to wear your slippers, or to remove them when you're about to leave. *(Open Tu-Su 8:30am-3:30pm. 12zł, students 9zł. Guided tour in English 66zł.)*

OTHER SIGHTS. Warsaw University's enchanting **Botanical Garden** (Ogród Botaniczny) welcomes visitors with a fragrant path lined by lilac trees. Student gardeners tend to this perpetual work-in-progress, which exhibits native and foreign plants. Highlights include the butterfly garden, alpine garden, and medicinal plants. The nearby Neoclassical **observatory** (Gmach Obserwatorium) was rebuilt in 1944 and shadows more exotic greenhouses. *(☎553 05 11. Open Apr.-Aug. M-F 9am-8pm, Sa-Su 10am-8pm; Sept. daily 10am-7pm; Oct. daily 10am-6pm. 4.50zł, students 2.50zł.)* **Belweder,** an 1818 palace just south of Łazienki, was built for the Russian tsar and was Józef Piłsudski's home. Now a residence for visiting heads of state, Belweder is closed to the public. Just north of Łazienki along al. Ujazdowskie is the **Ujazdowski Castle** (see **Museums,** p. 440), built in 1637 for King Zygmunt III Waza. Continue toward the center along al. Ujazdowskie and go right on Matejki to reach the **Sejm** (Parliament) and the **Senate building.** *(Both closed to the public.)*

THE FORMER WARSAW GHETTO

The term "ghetto" refers to the sealed Jewish district from 1939-45, and the modern Muranów (walled) neighborhood, north of the center, displays few vestiges of the nearly 400,000 Jews who comprised one-third of the city's pre-war population. During WWII the Ghetto shrank continually as its residents were deported to death camps, and parts of it, including the **Nożyk Synagogue,** were "re-Aryanized" long before the war's end. The Nazis razed the entire area after the 1943 Ghetto Uprising. Soviet-era concrete block housing now fills much of the former Ghetto. In the former Ghetto, absence, emptiness, and ruin tell the story for the silenced.

JEWISH CEMETERY. Perhaps the most haunting testament to the near-total annihilation of Jewish Warsaw is this final resting place of 250,000 Polish Jews. The 19th-century walled cemetery (Cmentarz Żydowski) lies in sad disrepair, as most of those buried here have no descendents to care for their graves. Notable figures buried here include Rabbi Szlomo Lipszyc (d. 1839), actress Ester Kamiń

POLAND

ska (d. 1925), and Ludwik Zamenhof (d. 1917), the creator of Esperanto. *(Okopowa 49/51, in the western corner of Muranów. From the center of town, follow al. Jana Pawła II north to Anielewicza and take a left. Or, take tram #22 from the center to Cm. Żydowski. ☎838 26 22; www.jewishcem.waw.pl. Open Apr.-Oct. M-Th 10am-5pm, F 9am-1pm, Su 11am-4pm; Nov.-Mar. closes at dusk. Closed Jewish holidays. 4zł.)* Nearby, the **Monument of Common Martyrdom of Jews and Poles,** Gibalskiego 2, marks the site of mass graves from WWII. *(Follow the street south of the cemetery to Gibalskiego, then turn left before the Nissenbaum building.)*

NOŻYK SYNAGOGUE. This restored synagogue is a living artifact of Warsaw's Jewish life. Used as a stable by the Nazis, it was the only synagogue to survive the war. The delicate white interior closely approximates the original decor. Today it serves as the spiritual home for 500 observant Jews who remain in Warsaw and also hosts meetings for Jewish student groups. There's a small kosher store in the basement. Men must wear traditional head-covering. *(Twarda 6. From the center, take any tram along al. Jana Pawła II to Rondo Onz. Turn right on Twarda and left at the Jewish Theater, Teatr Żydowski. ☎620 10 37. Open M-F and Su, Apr.-Oct. 10am-5pm; Nov.-Feb. 10am-3pm. Closed Jewish holidays. 5zł. Morning and evening prayer daily.)*

GHETTO WALL. Early in the occupation of Warsaw, the Nazis built a wall around the entire neighborhood, confining the Jews to the Ghetto until the entire area was liquidated in 1943 following the uprising. A small section of the original Ghetto wall still stands between two buildings on Sienna and Złota, west of al. Jana Pawła II. *(Enter at Sienna 55; the wall is on the left.)*

JANUSZ KORCZAK MEMORIAL. Physician and writer Janusz Korczak, revered by Jews and Christians alike, oversaw two orphanages in the years before WWII, one Catholic and one Jewish. When the Nazis ordered the liquidation of the Jewish orphanage, he chose to stay with the 200 children rather than escape to likely freedom. Korczak shepherded them to Umschplagplatz and died with them in Treblinka. Of his actions Korczak said, "You do not leave a sick child in the night, and you do not leave children at a time like this." The monument stands in front of the site of his Jewish orphanage. *(Jaktorowska 6, just west of Towarowa and south of al. Solidarności.)*

COMMERCIAL DISTRICT

PALACE OF CULTURE AND SCIENCE. Warsaw's commercial district (next to the train station, southwest of Stare Miasto) is dominated by the 70-story Stalinist Gothic Palace (Pałac Kultury i Nauki, PKiN), Poland's tallest structure. First named the Joseph Stalin Palace, the building has since been dubbed "The Wedding Cake" for its unattractive multi-tiered architecture. A 1955 "gift" from the Soviet Union, the Palace now houses offices, exhibition facilities, theaters, and the excellent Cafe Kulturalna. It hosts jazz and contemporary concerts as well as high-profile conventions and soirees. *(☎656 60 00. Open daily 9am-8pm. Observation deck on 33rd fl. 18zł, students 12zł; after 9pm 20zł.)* Social Realist statues surround its periphery. Below lies **pl. Defilad** (Parade Sq.), Europe's largest square. *(On Marszałkowska.)*

OTHER SIGHTS. Warsaw Insurgents' Square (pl. Powstańców Warszawy) is marked by a dark marble memorial barely elevated off the ground. On August 1, 1944, the insurgents of the Warsaw Uprising began their tragic battle against the Germans here. *(On Świętokrzyska, between Marszałkowska and Krakowskie Przedmieście.)* Interesting **neighborhood walks** include the daily **open-air market** on al. Jana Pawła II; the park- and gallery-dotted, hillside **Mariensztat** neighborhood (between Stare Miasto and the University of Warsaw); and the **shopping** along Chmielna and pedestrian Nowy Świat.

PRAGA

Cross the **Wisła River** to Warsaw's east bank and you will be rewarded with graceful parks, a gargantuan open-air market, and two of the most attractive churches in Warsaw. Often maligned as poorer and less safe than the rest of the city, Praga has become more fashionable in recent years, though many locals still recommend traveling there only in groups of three or more after dark. First settled in the seventh century and a suburb of Warsaw from the 16th century, Praga survived WWII relatively intact. During the Warsaw Uprising, the Red Army famously stopped its westward advance in Praga and stood by as the Germans and Poles battled across the river: some buildings were looted and bombed, but Praga escaped the utter annihilation that the rest of the city suffered.

■ **RUSSIAN MARKET.** Located in the **Stadion Dziesięciolecia,** Europe's largest open-air market kicks off every morning at dawn and winds down in the afternoon. The legendary Russian Market has great deals on everything from sunglasses and baked goods to t-shirts with subversive Polish phrases. Sketchier offerings include homemade vodka and counterfeit handbags; pirated DVDs have become scarce since Poland joined the EU. Many items won't have price tags, so bargain like the locals; you may find the nun next to you gets the best deal. Keep a low profile and beware of pickpockets. *(Take any tram from al. Jerozolimskie going east, and get off at the first stop over the river. The market is across the street on your left.)*

ST. MARY MAGDALENE CATHEDRAL. A sumptuous Russian Orthodox Church built in 1869. Bright frescoes and gold-framed icons adorn the walls, and the horizontal altar inspires awe in even the casual viewer. The telltale onion domes hint at the pre-Soviet Russian presence in Warsaw. *(Al. Solidarności 52. From Russian Market, take tram #2, 8, 12, or 25 to intersection of Targowa and al. Solidarności: church is across the street on the left. ☎ 619 84 67. Open M and Su 1-4pm, Tu-Sa 11am-3pm.)*

ST. MICHAEL AND ST. FLORIAN CATHEDRAL. With two tall spires above the entrance, high pointed arches, and a long nave, this 1972 reconstruction is less restrained than the churches of Stare Miasto. *(Floriańska 3, 1 block from St. Mary Magdalene. ☎ 619 09 60; www.katedra-floriana.wpraga.opoka.org.pl.)*

PRASKI PARK. Built on the ruins of Napoleonic fortifications, the park was completed in 1871 and spans 45 acres. The entrance to Praski Park contains the **Island of Bears,** or Bear Run, a concrete island on which bears have held sway since 1949. This tiny island is open to al. Solidarności and is a mini-zoo in its own right. The bears may appear harmless, but they have been known to maul intruders. *Let's Go* does not recommend feeding or wrestling the bears. *(Entrance on Floriańska, across the street from St. Michael and St. Florian Cathedral. Free.)*

WARSAW ZOO. Built in 1928, the zoo (Ogród Zoologiczny) originally bred many rare species, but the animals of Warsaw fared no better than the citizens, and the zoo was bombed during WWII. Surviving animals escaped, were eaten by desperate locals, or were sent to Germany. Heroic zoo director Jan Zabinski used the zoo to hide Jews throughout the war. Today souvenir stands and schoolchildren fill the zoo. Popular sections include the petting zoo, aquarium, cougars, monkeys, and reptiles. Make a game of guessing the animals, as you won't find any English captions. *(Ratuszowa 1/3. ☎ 619 40 41. Open daily 9am-4pm. 12zł, students 6zł.)*

SKARYSZEWSKI PARK. The most serene of Praga attractions contains sculptures by early 20th-century Polish artists and a lovely network of willow-lined ponds and streams. *(East of al. Zieleniecka. Free.)*

🏛 MUSEUMS

■ WARSAW UPRISING MUSEUM. This new museum has won praise as one of Poland's finest. Recorded testimonials, artifacts, letters, and interactive images of the tragic 1944 Uprising are arranged in themed rooms that include full-scale replica bunkers and ruins haunted by the sound of approaching bombs emanating from hidden speakers. No natural light filters through, completing the experience of this jagged and disorienting landscape. Wander through dark tunnels guarded by heavy rubber flaps to find the "red room," dedicated to the spread of Communism during WWII. Educational without being pedantic and somber without being heavy-handed, this powerful museum is sure to be a favorite for years to come. *(Grzybowska 79, enter on Przyokopowa. From the center, take tram #12, 20, or 22 to Grzybowska: the museum will be on your left. ☎ 539 79 01; www.1944.pl. Excellent English captions. Open W and F-Su 10am-6pm, Th 10am-8pm. 4zł, students 2zł; Su free. Cash only.)*

■ ROYAL CASTLE. In the Middle Ages, the castle (Zamek Królewski) was home to the Dukes of Mazovia. In the late 16th century, it replaced Kraków's Wawel as the official royal residence; later it became the presidential palace, and in September 1939 it was burned down and plundered by the Nazis. Following its destruction, many Varsovians risked their lives hiding the castle's priceless works. Some of the treasures were retrieved after WWII, but it took 40 years—and countless contributions from Poles, expats, and dignitaries worldwide, including former pope John Paul II—to restore this symbol of national pride. Although the loss of the original is grievous, consider that the castle now looks as new as it did to the royal family. There are two routes for viewing: Route Two is more impressive to the first-timer, with the magnificent gilded throne room, Marble Cabinet, and royal apartments, while Route One snakes through the parliament chambers and apartments. *(Pl. Zamkowy 4. ☎ 657 21 70; www.zamek-krolewski.art.pl. Tickets and guides at the kasa inside the courtyard. Open M and Su 11am-6pm, Tu-Sa 10am-6pm. 18zł, students 12zł. Highlights tour Su 11am-6pm free. Tour in English M-Sa, 70zł per group. MC/V.)*

■ CENTER OF CONTEMPORARY ART AT UJAZDOWSKI CASTLE. The center (Centrum Sztuki Współczesniej) is a hub of Polish avant-garde culture. *"Nowe jest stare"* (what is new is old) is etched on a museum wall; indeed, this reconstructed 17th-century castle speaks volumes to the interplay of modernity and tradition that infuses contemporary Polish art. The castle's winding cellars exhibit cutting-edge art installations, and a thought-provoking multimedia permanent exhibition features the work of 76 Polish and international artists. Don't miss the panoramic view of Łazienki Park or the exhibits in the Laboratorium outbuilding. Ujazdowski Castle also hosts modern dance and literary presentations, and is home to Kino-Lab, which screens art films, and the Artistic Kitchen, which serves up culinary innovation. *(Al. Ujazdowskie 6. Take the same buses as to Łazienki, but get off at pl. Na Rozdrożu; the museum is past the overpass. ☎ 628 12 713; www.csw.art.pl. Open Tu-Th and Sa-Su 11am-7pm, F 11am-9pm. 12zł, students 6zł. Cash only.)*

WILANÓW. Half an hour south of the city, this extraordinary residence is Warsaw's answer to Versailles. In 1677, King Jan III Sobieski bought the sleepy village of Milanowo and rebuilt the existing mansion as a palace. Inside are frescoed rooms, countless portraits, a detailed and delicate collection of European porcelain, and extravagant royal apartments. The exterior has undergone a massive reconstruction and should be complete in the summer of 2006. The French-influenced gardens feature an array of elegant topiary. *(Take bus #180 from Krakowskie Przedmieście or #516 or 519 from Marszalkowska south to Wilanów. From the bus stop, cross the highway and follow signs for the Pałac. ☎ 842 07 95. Open May 15-Sept. 15 M and W-Su 9:30am-4:30pm; Sept. 16-May 14 M and Th-Sa 9:30am-4pm, W 9:30am-6pm, Su*

9:30am-7pm. Last entrance 1½hr. before closing. 20zł, students 10zł. Th free. Tour in English 25zł; call ahead. Admission includes Polish-language tour, but it's better to let the English captions be your guide. Gardens open M and W-F 9:30am-dusk. 4.5zł, students 2.5zł. Cash only.)

POSTER MUSEUM. Polish artists have been producing stunning poster art for over a century, and the rotating exhibitions at this museum (Muzeum Plakatu), one of few in the world dedicated to this art form, are well worth the trip to Wilanów. The museum also hosts the International Poster Biennale in summers of even-numbered years. Phone ahead, since the museum closes between exhibitions. The museum store sells prints for 10-50zł. *(Stanisława Potockiego 10/16, by Pałac Wilanowski. ☎842 48 48. Open M noon-4pm, Tu-Su 10am-4pm. 8zł, students 5zł; M free.)*

WARSAW HISTORICAL MUSEUM. The tiny entrance belies the size of this massive museum (Muzeum Historyczne Miasta Warszawy), which fills an entire side of the Rynek. Clothing, utensils, and art complement reconstructed workshops, living quarters, and models of Warsaw to provide glimpses of daily life throughout the city's 700-year history. English captions are lacking. *(Rynek Starego Miasta 42. ☎635 16 25. Excellent English film about WWII-era Warsaw Tu-Sa noon. Open Tu and Th 11am-6pm, W and F 10am-3:30pm, Sa-Su 10:30am-4:30pm. 5zł, students 2.50zł; Su free. Cash only.)*

ZACHĘTA GALLERY. This state-funded gallery, housed in one of the few buildings left standing after WWII, is dedicated to controversial art. Displays feature photography, film, sculpture, and painting, and many rotating exhibits have works by 20th-century Polish photographers. The impressive building has played its own role in history: in 1922, Gabriel Narutowicz, first president of the Second Polish Republic, was assassinated in the exhibition hall. *(Pl. Malachowskiego 3. Buses #100 toward pl. Zamkowy and #160 toward Targowek from the center both stop at Zachęta. ☎827 58 54; www.zacheta.art.pl. Open Tu-Su 10am-8pm. 10zł, students 7zł; Tu free. Guided tour in Polish 40zł, in English 60zł; call 2 days in advance. Cash only.)*

NATIONAL MUSEUM. Poland's largest museum (Muzeum Narodowe) was looted by the Nazis in WWII but has since rebuilt an impressive collection of Polish art alongside a weaker collection of European art. Ruins of war come to life in history paintings, and the prolific Polish art community asserts its strength in the early 20th-century collection. Eclectic range of temporary exhibits, from Chinese traditional instruments to German Romantic paintings. *(Al. Jerozolimskie 3. ☎629 30 93, Tours in English 629 50 60; www.mnw.art.pl. Open Tu-W and F 10am-5pm, Th and Sa-Su 10am-6pm. Permanent exhibits 12zł, students 7zł; special exhibits 17zł, students 10zł. English audio tours 17zł, students 12zł; guided tour in English 50zł; call 1 wk. in advance. AmEx/MC/V.)*

MUSEUM OF PAWIAK PRISON. Built in the 1830s as a prison for common criminals, Pawiak (Muzeum Więzienia Pawiaka) later served as Gestapo headquarters. From 1939 to 1944, over 100,000 Poles, 10% of Warsaw's entire population, were imprisoned and tortured here. One room has been converted into a museum that exhibits photography and poetry as well as prisoners' possessions. The catacomblike hallways lead to preserved cells. A dead tree outside bears the names of some of the 30,000 prisoners killed at Pawiak during the war. *(Dzielna 24/26. ☎/fax 831 13 17. Open W 9am-5pm, Th and Sa 9am-4pm, F 10am-5pm, Su 10am-4pm. Donations requested.)*

FRÉDÉRIC CHOPIN MUSEUM. A small but fascinating collection of original letters, scores, paintings, and keepsakes, including the composer's last piano; his first published piece, the *Polonaise in G Minor* (penned at the ripe old age of seven); and his last composition, *Mazurka in F Minor*. A brief tour will interest those unacquainted with his music, and even casual visitors will be transfixed by the haunting bronze mold of his left hand. The museum (Muzeum Fryderyka Chopina) also hosts the International Chopin Festival, with concerts on selected days in July and August. *(Okólnik 1, in Ostrogski Castle. Enter from Tamka. ☎826 59 35. Open May-Sept. M, W, F 10am-5pm, Th noon-6pm, Sa-Su 10am-2pm; Oct.-Apr. M-W and F-Sa 10am-2pm, Th noon-6pm. 8zł, students 4zł. Audio tours 4zł. Concerts 30zł, students 15zł. Cash only.)*

MARIA SKŁODOWSKA-CURIE MUSEUM. Founded in 1967, on the 100th anniversary of the two-time Nobel Prize Laureate's birth, the exhibit (Muzeum Marii Skłodowskiej-Curie) chronicles Maria Skłodowska's life in Poland, immigration to France, and marriage to scientist Pierre Curie, with whom she discovered radium, polonium (named after Poland), and marital bliss. *(Freta 16, in Skłodowska's former house. ☎831 80 92. Open Tu-Sa 10am-4pm, Su 10am-2pm. 6zł, students 3zł.)*

JOHN PAUL II COLLECTION. This is not a museum about the late pope but a collection of paintings amassed by the Carroll-Porczynski family and donated to the city of Warsaw in honor of Poland's favorite son. Five themed rooms feature work by Dalí, Goya, Picasso, Rembrandt, Rubens, Titian, and Van Gogh. *(Pl. Bankowy 1, in the Old Stock Exchange building. Enter from Elektoralna. ☎620 27 25. Open Tu-Su May-Oct. 10am-5pm; Nov.-Apr. 10am-4pm. 11zł, students 5.50zł. Polish tour 1zł per person.)*

ADAM MICKIEWICZ MUSEUM OF LITERATURE. Old sketches, letters, books, a shrine room, and Mickiewicz's original inkpot offer evidence of Poland's dedication to national poets. A rotating exhibit of Polish art is found on the first floor. *(Rynek Starego Miasta 20. ☎831 40 61. Open M-Tu and F 10am-3pm, W-Th 11am-6pm, Su 11am-5pm. 5zł, students 4zł; Su free.)*

♫ ENTERTAINMENT

Warsaw boasts an array of live music, and free outdoor concerts abound in summer. Classical music performances are rarely sold out; standby tickets for major performances run as low as 10zł. Inquire at the **Warsaw Music Society** (Warszawskie Towarzystwo Muzyczne), Morskie Oko 2 (☎849 56 51). Take tram #4, 18, 19, 35, or 36 to Morskie Oko from Marszałkowska. The **Warsaw Chamber Opera** (Warszawska Opera Kameralna), al. Solidarności 76B (☎831 22 40), hosts a **Mozart Festival** in early summer. Łazienki Park has free Sunday concerts at the **Chopin Monument** (Pomnik Chopina; concerts mid-May to Sept. Su noon and 4pm). The **Opera Narodowa,** pl. Teatralny 1 (☎692 02 00) founded in 1778, hosts several operas each week, with standby tickets as low as 15zł. The first week of June brings the **International Festival of Sacred Music,** with performances at historic churches. **Jazz Klub Tygmont,** Mazowiecka 6/8 (☎828 34 09), hosts free jazz concerts. From July through September, the Old Market Square of Stare Miasto draws locals with nightly free jazz at 7pm. For tickets to rock concerts, call **Empik Megastore** (☎625 12 19).

Teatr Wielki, in the same building as **Opera Narodowa,** the main opera and ballet hall, has regular performances. (☎826 32 88; www.teatrwielki.pl. Tickets 10-100zł. AmEx/MC/V.) **Teatr Dramatyczny,** in the Pałac Kultury, has a stage for big productions and a studio theater playing more avant-garde works. (☎620 21 02; standby tickets 11-17zł.) **Teatr Żydowski** (pl. Grzybowski 12/16; ☎620 70 25), is a Jewish theater with shows mostly in Yiddish. **Kinoteka** (☎826 1961), in the Pałac Kultury, shows Hollywood blockbusters in a Stalinist setting. **Kino Lab,** al. Ujazdowskie 6 (☎628 12 71), features independent films.

▣ NIGHTLIFE

Warsaw's night scene is accessible, exuberant, and rapidly changing. New bars and clubs are emerging at fever pace, so check *Aktivist* or *Warsaw in Your Pocket* for the latest listings. Many locals arrive at bars as midnight approaches, and don't hit the clubs until the wee hours. While some gay clubs have become raucous places of interest for the "mixed" crowd, many more remain secluded and discreet. For info, call the gay and lesbian **hotline** (see **GLBT Organizations,** p. 430).

BARS

▨ **Chimera**, Podwale 29 (☎510 662 579). Near the corner of Freta, through the courtyard and downstairs. Chimera is an immensely popular student bar with curiously sinister decor and a resident cat prowling the secluded courtyard. Everything here is for sale, from the rusted tuba hanging from the ceiling to the chairs you sit on, meaning Chimera is constantly evolving. Far from pretentious, the University of Warsaw crowd here is lively and relaxed. Also serves lunch. Beer 6zł. Open M-F 3pm-late, Sa-Su 2pm-late. MC/V.

Labo Music Bar, Mazowiecka 11a (☎827 45 57; www.laboklub.pl). High-quality live music is of chief importance at Labo, where the 21+ age limit keeps the crowd's average age around 23. W night is "blakiz blak," serving up hip-hop and R&B, Th is always a jam session, and Labo hosts visiting DJs on F and Sa nights. At the Laboratory you can order 6 test-tube shots of hard liquor for 29zł. Open W-Sa 5pm-late. AmEx/MC/V.

Cinnamon, Piłsudskiego 1 (☎323 76 00), in the Metropolitan Building opposite the National Opera. A bar with attitude, Cinnamon is favored by the hottest locals and expats. The lunar-themed interior and pink accents complement suave and impeccably dressed staff who keep the martinis flowing all night long. Don't be surprised if you pop in for an elegant lunch and emerge at dawn the next day. Open daily 9am-late. MC/V.

Student Bar Complex, Dobra 33/35, at the corner of Dobra and Zajęcza. 3 popular student bars are grouped in this complex built from old storage houses and situated within a contained lot. **Duina** plays pop and 80s music to keep the bargoers singing. Next comes **Aurora,** a full-fledged dance floor that flashes lights through circular windows and chiefly plays house music. **Klub Czarny Lew** rounds out the group with an industrial atmosphere that plays on the utilitarian roots of this onetime warehouse. Open M-Tu and F-Su 7pm-4am, W-Th 5pm-2am. Cash only.

Rasko, Krochmalna 32A (☎890 02 99; www.rasko.pl). 1 block north of Grzybowska, turn left on Krochmalna; the bar is 2 blocks down on your right near a small sign and an unmarked door. Rasko is a discrete establishment that serves Warsaw's largely underground GLBT scene. Small, secluded, and artsy, Rasko's interior provides a welcome respite for an embattled community. Laid-back but cautious bouncer ensures your privacy. The close-knit and friendly staff will be happy to direct you to other GLBT establishments and organizations. Beer 7zł. Open daily 5pm-3am. Cash only.

NIGHTCLUBS

▨ **Piekarnia,** Młocińska 11 (☎636 49 79). Take the #22 tram to Rondo Babka and backtrack on Okopowa. Make a right on Powiązkowska, a right on Burakowa, and a right on Młocińska. The unmarked club will be down the road on your left. Boasting resident DJ Barry Ashworth, Piekarnia is proud to have been a pioneer as one of the first modern clubs in Poland. These days the so-hip-it-hurts scene really picks up around 4am. The selective bouncer, packed dance floor, and progressive house music make this a local institution. Cover F 20zł, Sa 25zł. Open F-Sa 10pm-late.

▨ **Le Madame,** Koźla 12. Tucked down a Stare Miasto side street is one of the edgiest clubs in Warsaw. The 1st floor looks like an artfully crumbling mansion and the basement is a warren of crooked furniture and secluded nooks. A hotbed of progressive politics, Le Madame hosts Green Party events, stages political theater, and screens independent films. Partygoers dance in the basement and lounge across low-slung beds on the ground level. GLBT friendly. Cover 10zł. Open daily 5pm-late. MC/V.

POLAND

Enklawa, Mazowiecka 12 (☎827 31 51). An elite crowd of expats, locals, students, and young professionals forks over hefty cover charges for a spot on the sexually charged dance floor. Hot but unintimidating, this place gets going by 11pm. Chat someone up in English and take in mainstream hip-hop and techno. Check out the plasma video screens in the bathrooms. Cover Th men 10zł, women 5zł; F-Sa before 11pm 20zł, after 11pm 30zł. Open M-Th and Su 9pm-3am, F-Sa 9pm-4am. AmEx/MC/V.

Ground Zero, Wspólna 62 (☎625 39 76), behind the church on Hoża. This former fallout shelter attracts a chic crowd intent on dancing all night. F and Sa feature Top 40 hits, while W and Th offer house and techno. Fills up past midnight. Cover F men 20zł; women 5zł before 11pm, 10zł after; Sa men 20zł; women 10zł before 11pm, 20zł after. Open F-Sa 9pm-late. For a slightly older, equally playful crowd, cross the church to **Amnesia** (☎424 66 65), run by the same owners. During the day, Amnesia also serves full meals. Cover 20zł. Open M-F noon-late. No sneakers at either club. MC/V.

Underground Music Cafe, Marszałkowska 126/134 (☎826 70 48; www.under.pl), behind the large McDonald's; walk down the steps. This 2-level dance club is a guaranteed weeknight party. Casual student crowd keeps the smoky dance floor packed until 4am. M-Tu and Su old-school house; W and Sa hip-hop; Th 70s and 80s. Beer 8.50zł. Cover W and F 10zł, students 5zł; Sa 20/10zł; Th 10zł; M-Tu and Su free.

Bar Lemon, Sienkiewicza 6 (☎829 55 44). On weekends, Lemon is a popular spot for the graceful of Warsaw to dance to house music spun by visiting DJs. The chic interior has clean lines and yellow accents, and the crowd schmoozes until the dancing picks up around midnight. Beer 7zł. Open daily 9pm-late. MC/V. Next door, **Cafe Lemon** serves contemporary meals 24hr.

▶ DAYTRIP FROM WARSAW

ŻELAZOWA WOLA

It's best to take the 9:45am PKS bus (1½-2hr.) that leaves from Zachodnia station. To reach Zachodnia from central Warsaw, take local bus #130, 517, 127, 508, or 523 east on al. Jerozilimiskie. From Zachodnia, take the bus (9.50zł) headed to Wyszogród. Żelazowa Wola (53km west of Warsaw) is a stop, so warn the driver that you're getting off here. Return buses run about once an hour, and you can buy a ticket to Zachodnia from the driver for about 5zł. The last return bus leaves at 4:30pm. Alternatively, trains leave from Warszawa Centralna (1hr., every 30min., 8.50zł) to Sochaczew. The #6 Sochaczew city bus heads to Żelazowa Wola (M-F every hr., Sa-Su every other hr.; 3zł). ☎46 863 33 00. Park and museum open May-Sept. Tu-Su 9:30am-5:30pm; Oct.-Apr. Tu-Su 9:30am-4pm. 12zł, students 6zł. Park only 4/2zł. English audio tour 20zł. MC/V.)

Escape from the sprawl of Warsaw to hear etudes and waltzes echo through the air of Żelazowa Wola. First-rate musicians perform Chopin's masterpieces in the parlor of the house where he was born, now a **museum.** Twice each Sunday, the enchanting gardens of Żelazowa Wola host **free Chopin concerts** (May-Sept. 11am, 3pm), and locals gather on garden benches to listen. Try to arrive early to snag a good seat. The gardens are well groomed near the museum, but charmingly overgrown as their paths ramble past ponds, a stream, and a black marble obelisk commemorating Chopin's birth. The museum features little more than rooms devoted to Chopin's parents, his birth certificate, and the cover page of his first published piece. The concerts, however, are well worth the visit. The schedule of performances is posted throughout Warsaw and at the Chopin Museum (p. 441). You can grab a bite at one of the snack bars across the street from the entrance, but you'll find that regulars pack lunches and eat in the garden.

MAŁOPOLSKA (LESSER POLAND)

Małopolska, strewn with gentle hills and medieval castle ruins, stretches from the Kraków-Częstochowa Uplands in the west to Lublin in the east. Kraków, which suffered minimal damage during WWII, remains Poland's cultural and social center. Lublin, with its many universities, is an intellectual hub. The surrounding area houses some of humanity's most beautiful and most horrific creations: the artistry of the Wieliczka salt caves and the serenity of the Pieskowa Skała castle contrast the remnants of the Auschwitz-Birkenau and Majdanek concentration camps.

KRAKÓW ☎ (0)12

Although Kraków (KRAH-koof; pop 758,000) only recently emerged as a trendy international hot spot, it has long been Poland's darling. The regal architecture, rich cafe culture, and palpable sense of history that now bewitch throngs of foreign visitors have drawn Polish kings, artists, and scholars for centuries. Kraków, unlike most Polish cities, emerged from WWII and years of socialist planning miraculously unscathed. The maze-like Old Town and the old Jewish quarter of Kazimierz hide scores of museums, galleries, cellar pubs, and clubs, with 130,000 students adding to the spirited nightlife. Still, the city's gloss and glamour can't completely hide the scars of the 20th century: the Auschwitz-Birkenau Nazi death camps that lie just 70km outside the city are a sobering reminder of the atrocities committed in the not-so-distant past.

▧ INTERCITY TRANSPORTATION

Flights: Balice Airport (John Paul II International Airport; Port Lotniczy im. Jana Pawła), Kapitana Medweckiego 1 (☎411 19 55; airport@lotnisko-balice.pl), 18km from the center. Connect to the main train station by bus #192 (40min.) or 208 (1hr.). A taxi to the center costs 50-60zł. Carriers include **British Airways, Central Wings, German Wings, LOT,** and **Sky Europe.** Open 24hr.

Trains: Kraków Główny, pl. Kolejowy 1 (☎624 54 39, info 624 15 35; www.pkp.pl). Ticket office open 24hr. Go to Kasa Krajowej for domestic trains and Kasa Międzynarodowej for international trains. To: **Gdańsk** ("Gdynia"; 7-10hr., 4 per day, 60-100zł); **Poznań** (6-8hr., 4 per day, 49-81zł); **Warsaw** (4½-5hr., 10 per day, 45-85zł); **Zakopane** (3-5hr., 4 per day, 19-56zł); **Bratislava, SLK** (8hr., 1 per day, 188zł); **Budapest, HUN** (11hr., 1 per day, 227zł); **Kyiv, UKR** (22hr., 21 per day, 230zł); **Odessa, UKR** (21hr., 1 per day, 240zł); **Prague, CZR** (9hr., 2 per day, 196zł); **Vienna, AUT** (8½hr., 2 per day, 223zł). *Let's Go* does not recommend traveling on night trains.

Buses: Cysterów 15 (☎300 300 120). Formerly on Worcella, the bus station has moved because of construction. Open daily 5am-11pm. To: **Bielsko-Biała** (2½-3½hr., 28 per day, 14zł); **Łódź** (6½hr., 5 per day, 40zł); **Warsaw** (6hr., 3 per day, 50zł); **Wrocław** (6½hr., 2 per day, 43zł); **Zakopane** (2hr., 33 per day, 11zł).

☀ ORIENTATION

The heart of the city is the huge **Rynek Główny** (Main Marketplace), in the center of **Stare Miasto** (Old Town). Stare Miasto is encircled by the **Planty** gardens and, a bit farther out, a broad ring road, which is confusingly divided into sections with different names: **Basztowa, Dunajewskiego, Podwale,** and **Westerplatte.** South of Rynek Główny looms the celebrated **Wawel Castle.** The **Wisła River**

POLAND

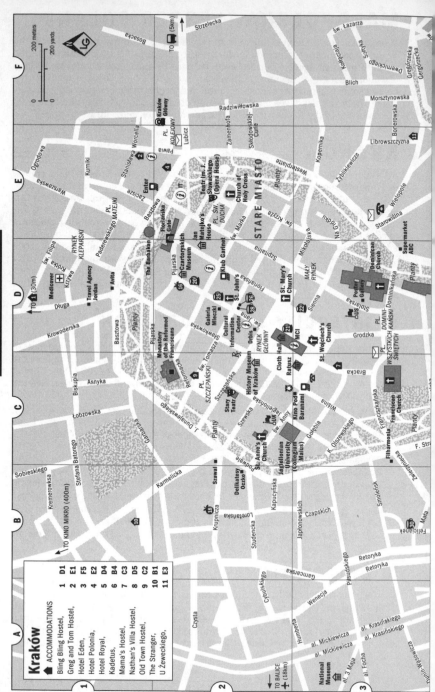

Kraków

▲ ACCOMMODATIONS

Bling Bling Hostel,	1	D1
Greg and Tom Hostel,	2	E1
Hotel Eden,	3	F5
Hotel Polonia,	4	E2
Hotel Royal,	5	D4
Kadetus,	6	B4
Mama's Hostel,	7	C3
Nathan's Villa Hostel,	8	D5
Old Town Hostel,	9	C2
The Stranger,	10	B1
U Żeweckiego,	11	E3

POLAND

CAFES
Camelot,	27 D2
Les Couleurs,	28 E5
Dym,	29 D2
Manggha,	30 B6
Massolit,	31 B3
Tribeca,	32 C6

New Jewish Cemetery
Siedleckiego
Mrozowa
Wrzesińska
Józefińska

Halicka
Starowiślna
Przmysłowa
Rzeszowska
Dajwór
Galicia Jewish Museum
Bartosza
Szeroka
Remuh Synagogue
Miodowa
Wąska
Lewkowa
Ciemna
Old Synagogue
Jakuba
Isaac Synagogue
Kupa
Izaaka
Brzozowa
Tempel Synagogue
Podbrzezie
Estery
Józefa
Izaaka
Meiselsa
Dielta
Dielta
Bogusławskiego
św. Sebastiana
św. Sebastiana
Salego
Gazowa
Bocheńska
Mostowa
Trynitarska
Bonifraterska
św. Wawrzyńca
KAZIMIERZ
PL. WOLNICA
Bożego Ciała
Krakowska
św. Katarzyny
Węgłowa
Augustiańska
Skałeczna
Piekarska
Skawińska
Wietora
Paulińska
Stradomska
św. Gertrudy
św. Andrew's Church
Planty
św. Agnieszki
St. Peter and Paul Church
Grodzka
św. Idziego
Orzeszkowej
Kościelna
Sukiennicza
ks. Kordeckiego
PL. ŚW. MARII MAGDELENY
Kanonicza
św. MARII MAGDELENY
Museum of the Archdiocese
Wawel Cathedral
Wawel Castle
Droga do Zamku
Bernardyńska
św. Stanisława
Podzamcze
Smocza
Szczepańskiego
Sebacka
bul. Inflancki
bul. Czerwieński
bul. Wołyński
most Grunwaldzki
Pl. Na Groblach
Pl. Na Groblach
Tartowska
Powiśle
Wisła
Mangha Museum
RONDO GRUNWALDZKIE
Killińskiego
bul. Poleski
Sandomierska
Konopnickiej
most Debnicki
Zamkowa
Zduńska
Konopnickiej
Powroźnicza
Barska
Wioślarska
Różana
Wasilewskiego
Konfederacka
Batuckiego
RYNEK DĘBNICKI
Tyniecka
Bałuckiego
Morawińskiego
Bielińskiego
Zagódž
Skwerowa
Syrokomli
Morawskiego
Włóczków
Kościuszki
bul. Rodła
Wyboda

NIGHTLIFE
Alchemia,	19 E5
Cień,	20 D2
Faust,	21 D2
Klub pod Jaszczurami,	22 D3
Propaganda,	23 E5
Prozak,	24 D4
Stalowe Magnolie,	25 D2

FOOD
Bagelmama,	12 E5
La Cuisine,	13 E5
Fabryka Pizzy,	14 E5
Momo,	15 E5
Pierogarnia,	16 D2
Restauracja Samoobsługowa "Polakowski",	17 F5
Vega Bar Restaurant,	18 B2

snakes past the castle and borders the old Jewish district of **Kazimierz**. The **train** station sits northeast of Stare Miasto. A large, well-marked (and well-kiosked) underpass cuts beneath the ring road and into the Planty gardens; from there a number of paths lead into the Rynek (10min.). Turn left from the train station to reach the underpass.

▣ LOCAL TRANSPORTATION

Public Transportation: Buy **bus** and **tram** tickets at Ruch kiosks (2.50zł) or from the driver (3zł) and punch them on board. Large backpacks need their own tickets. Night buses (after 11pm) 5zł. Day pass 10.40zł; 100zł fine if you or your bag are caught ticketless. Foreigners are fined frequently—be sure your ticket is in order. Student fare (1.35zł) for Poles only, though a good accent has been known to work.

Taxis: Reliable taxi companies include: **Barbakan Taxi** (☎96 61, toll-free 0800 400 400); **Euro Taxi** (☎96 64); **Radio Taxi** (☎919, toll-free 0800 500 919); **Wawel Taxi** (☎96 66). It is up to 30% cheaper to call a taxi than to hail one.

Bike Rental: Kraków is a bicycle-friendly city. **Retrobikes,** Bracka 4 (☎429 11 06; www.retrobikes.pl), near the Rynek. 20zł per 5hr., 35zł per day. Open daily 9am-midnight. MC/V. **Rentabike** (☎888 029 792; www.rentabike.pl). Will deliver a bike or scooter to anywhere in Kraków. Bikes 35zł per 5hr., 55zł per day; 400zł deposit. Scooters 70zł per 5hr., 130zł per day; 500zł deposit. Open 24hr.

▣ PRACTICAL INFORMATION

TOURIST AND FINANCIAL SERVICES

Tourist Office: City Tourist Information, Szpitalna 25 (☎432 01 10; www.krakow.pl/en). The official tourist office offers information, arranges accommodations and guided tours, and sells maps and guides (7-12zł). English spoken. Private tourist offices are scattered throughout town. **MCI,** Rynek Główny 1/3 (☎421 77 06; www.mcit.pl), in the main square. Sells maps and guides, including *Kraków in Your Pocket* (5zł), and the cultural guide *Karnet* (4zł; www.animatec.com/karnet/indexgb.php). Open May-Sept. M-F 9am-7pm, Sa 9am-1pm; Oct.-Apr. M-F 9am-5pm, Sa 9am-1pm.

Budget Travel: Orbis, Rynek Główny 41 (☎422 40 35; www.orbis.krakow.pl). Sells train tickets and arranges trips to Wieliczka and Auschwitz (each 120zł, both 238zł; up to 50% ISIC discount). Also cashes **traveler's checks** and **exchanges currency.** Open M-F 9am-7pm, Sa 9am-3pm. Other travel agencies abound in Stare Miasto.

Consulates: UK, św. Anny 9 (☎421 56 56; ukconsul@bci.krakow.pl). Open M-F 9am-4pm. **US,** Stolarska 9 (☎424 51 00; krakow.usconsulate.gov). Open M-F 8:30am-5pm.

Currency Exchange: *Kantory* (exchange kiosks) have widely varying rates. Avoid those around the train station and near Floriańska Gate. Also check rates carefully around Rynek Główny. **Bank PKO SA,** Rynek Główny 31 (☎422 60 22). Cashes **traveler's checks** for 1-2% commission (10zł min.) and gives MC/V **cash advances.** Open M-F 8am-6pm, Sa 9am-2pm. **ATMs,** found all over the city, offer the best rates.

Western Union: Bank BPH, Rynek Główny 47. Many other banks require those receiving money from abroad to change it into złotych at a bad rate. Open M-F 8am-6pm.

LOCAL SERVICES

Luggage Storage: At the train station. 1% of value per day plus 3.90zł for the 1st day and 2zł for each additional day. Lockers near the exit. Lockers also available at bus station. Small 4zł, large 8zł. Open 24hr.

POLAND

English-Language Bookstore: Massolit, Felicjanek 4 (☎432 41 50). Impressive selection of over 25,000 popular, classic, and academic English-language books. Cozy atmosphere. Open M-Th, Su 10am-8pm; F-Sa 10am-10pm. **Szawal,** Krupnicza 3 (☎0605 609 799), is somewhat more expensive. Open M-F 10am-7pm, Sa 10am-2pm.

Laundromat: Piastowska 47 (☎622 31 81), in the basement of **Hotel Piast.** Take tram #4, 13, or 14 to WKS Wawel and turn left on Piastowska. Wash 15zł, dry 15zł, detergent 3zł. Open Tu and Th 11am-4pm, Sa 11am-2pm. **Betty Clean,** Długa 17 (☎632 67 87), past the end of Sławkowska. More a drycleaner than a laundromat. Shirt 8.50zł, pants 12zł, nun's habit 25zł. Open M-F 8am-7:30pm, Sa 8am-2pm.

EMERGENCY AND COMMUNICATIONS

Pharmacy: Apteka Pod Żółtym Tygrysem, Szczepańska 1 (☎422 92 93), just off Rynek Główny. Posts a list of 24hr. pharmacies. Open M-F 8am-8pm, Sa 8am-3pm. MC/V.

Medical Services: Medicover, Krótka 1 (☎616 10 00). Ambulance services available. English spoken. Open M-F 8am-8pm, Sa 9am-2pm.

Telephones: At the post office and throughout the city. Buy phone cards at any kiosk or at **Telekomunikacja Polska,** Wielpole 2 (☎421 64 57). Open M-F 10am-6pm, Sa 10am-2pm. Some Internet cafes, such as **Internet Cafe,** Bracka 4 and Rynek Główny 23, offer very cheap (0.25zł per min. to US and UK) calls over the Internet, although the quality can be inconsistent.

Internet: You can't throw a rock in Stare Miasto without hitting an Internet cafe. **Internet Cafe,** Rynek Główny 23. 2zł per 30min., 3zł per hr. Open 24hr. **Enter Internet Cafe,** Basztowa 23 (☎429 42 25). 2zł per 30min., 3zł per hr. Open 8am-midnight. **Klub Garinet,** Floriańska 18 (☎423 22 33). 4zł per hr. Open daily 9am-midnight. **Telekomunikacja Polska** offers free Internet, but has standing room only.

Post Office: Westerplatte 20 (☎422 24 97). Poste Restante at counter #1. Open M-F 7:30am-8:30pm, Sa 8am-2pm, Su 9am-2pm. **Postal Code:** 31 075.

⌐ ACCOMMODATIONS

Kraków has a growing range of affordable hotels and conveniently located hostels, but travelers still outnumber beds during high season and prices have been rising lately. Call ahead for reservations. **Travel Agency Jordan,** Długa 9, arranges accommodations, including rooms above their office. (☎421 21 25; www.jordan.krakow.pl. Open M-F 8am-6pm, Sa 9am-2pm. Singles 65-100zł; doubles 130-160zł; triples 180-240zł. AmEx/MC/V.) Jordan also offers an SMS service: send an SMS to 7240 indicating your budget ("+" means 40-50zł, "++" 50-100zł, and "+++" 150-300zł) and they will respond with accommodations. Locals also rent rooms that vary in price and quality; watch for signs at the train station. It is advisable to see the room before agreeing to pay. **University dorms** open up in July and August.

All hostels listed have English-speaking staff, and all supply linens. Except where noted, storage and laundry facilities are provided, as well as free breakfast.

HOSTELS AND DORMITORIES

▨ **Nathan's Villa Hostel,** św. Agnieszki 1 (☎422 35 45; www.nathansvilla.com). From Kraków Główny, take tram #10 toward Wawel and get off at the 3rd stop. Kraków's most social hostel has expanded dramatically, with the addition of 4 new upstairs rooms and a fantastic new cellar bar with accompanying photo gallery. Friendly Nathan can often be found at reception, and a staff of amateur models leads guests on nightly pub- and club-crawls. Kitchen. Breakfast until 2pm. No linen. Wi-Fi. Reception 24hr. Dorms 50-60zł. MC/V, 3% surcharge. ❷

■ **Mama's Hostel,** Bracka 4 (☎429 59 40; www.mamashostel.com.pl). From the southern side of the Rynek, Mama's is a half block down Bracka on the left. The most centrally located hostel in Kraków, Mama's boasts 46 sturdy wooden beds, 4 bathrooms, and a beautiful kitchen—all in a 15th-century building with a small flower-lined balcony. Breakfast until 1pm. Reception 24hr. Flexible check-in and check-out. 10-bed dorms 50zł; 6-bed dorms 55zł. MC/V, 3% surcharge. ❷

The Stranger, Kochanowskiego 1 (☎634 25 16; www.thestrangerhostel.com). A social atmosphere and simple, clean dorms characterize this hostel. The common room is a playfully mismatched jumble of comfy couches, cushions, and chairs splayed out before a giant projection screen. The entertainment system is completed by an 8-speaker sound system, a wide selection of DVDs and—leapfrogging the competition—2 computers and free Wi-Fi. The friendly staff even does guests' laundry daily. Kitchen available. Reception 24hr. Dorms 55-60zł. Cash only. ❷

Bling Bling Hostel, Pędzichów 7 (☎634 05 32; www.blingbling.pl). From the train station, take the underpass to Basztowa and turn right on Długa. Bear right on Pędzichów. Warm staff, homey kitchen, and attention to detail give a familial feel. Sturdy wooden beds and sparkling bathrooms. Breakfast until 11am. No linens. 1 computer with free Internet. Reception 24hr. Flexible check-in and check-out. Dorms 55zł. MC/V. ❶

Greg and Tom Hostel, Pawia 12/15 (☎422 41 00; www.gregtomhostel.com). 2nd location on Warszawska 16/5. 30s from the train station, Greg and Tom is perfect for late-night arrivals. Look past the climb to the 4th fl. of a weary Soviet-era building: this small hostel is clean and attractive. Kitchen. Free Wi-Fi available in the salmon-pink common room. Reception 5:30am-10pm. Dorms 45zł; doubles 60zł. Cash only. ❷

Kadetus, Zwierzyniecka 25 (☎422 36 17; www.kadetus.com). Kadetus' dorms are simple in a zen sort of way. Rooms are bathed in pastel colors, and IKEA appears to have supplied all of the furniture. The kitchen is likewise shiny and modern. No linens. Internet available. Reception 24hr. 4- to 8-bed dorms 55zł; 2-bed dorms 60zł. Cash only. ❷

U Żeweckiego, Librowszczyzna 1 (☎429 55 96; www.zewecki.com). Dorms and private rooms with bright, multicolored bedspreads and modern bathrooms. Laundry 20zł. Reception 24hr. Dorms 40zł; private rooms 110-220zł. Cash only. ❸

Old Town Hostel, pl. Szczepański 6/5 (☎429 59 64; www.oldtownhostel.pl). Although located in a fairly ugly building, the hostel itself is pleasantly simple, cheap, and clean—if sparsely decorated and short on amenities. The location right near the center of Stare Miasto is also a draw. Small kitchen. No storage. Reception 24hr. Flexible check-in and check-out. 6- to 8-person dorms 45zł. Cash only. ❶

HOTELS

Hotel Polonia, Basztowa 25 (☎422 12 33; www.hotel-polonia.com.pl), across from the train station, 5min. from Rynek Główny. Features a Neoclassical exterior, modern rooms, and a great location. Quirky, see-through bathtubs in the suites. Breakfast 17zł, included for rooms with bath. Reception 24hr. Check-in 2pm. Check-out noon. Singles 89zł, with bath 295zł; doubles 109/345zł; triples 139/409zł; suites 509zł. MC/V. ❹

Hotel Eden, Ciemna 15 (☎430 65 65; www.hoteleden.pl). From Rynek Główny, follow Sienna, which becomes Starowiślna near Kazimierz. Bear right on Dajwór, then turn right onto Ciemna. In a restored 15th-century building, Eden offers the only *mikvah* (Jewish ritual bath) in Poland, kosher meals, and tours of Kazimierz. Rooms include baths, telephones, and satellite TVs. Kosher breakfast included. Internet. Wheelchair accessible. Singles 200zł; doubles 280zł; triples 370zł; suites 450zł. AmEx/MC/V. ❺

Hotel Royal, św Gertrudy 26-29 (☎421 58 49; www.royal.com.pl). From the train station, take tram #10 toward Łagiewniki and get off at Wawel. Nestled among the Planty gardens in Wawel's shadow, Royal is 2 conjoined hotels, with pricier, more elegant 2-

star rooms separated from 1-star rooms. Spotless rooms include phones and baths. Check-in 4pm. Check-out noon. 2-star singles 160-210zł, 1-star singles 180-190zł; doubles 280-295/250-260zł; triples 330zł; quads 440zł. AmEx/MC/V. ❺

◻ FOOD

While Warsaw turns its attention to international cuisine, Kraków remains solidly rooted in local culinary tradition. The restaurants and cafes on and around the **Rynek** satisfy both locals and the huge tourist population. **Grocery stores** surround the train station and dot the center. Two 24hr. grocery stores, **Delikatesy Oczko**, Podwale 4, and **Avita**, pl. Kleparski 5, off Bracka, are near the Rynek. **pl. Nowy**, in Kazimierz, boasts an **open-air market** with fresh fruits and vegetables. (M-F 6am-8pm, Sa 7am-1pm.) Alternatively, head to Rynek Kleparski, next to pl. Matejki, to find a food and **flea market**. (M-F 7am-8pm, Sa 7am-6pm, Su 7am-3pm.)

- 🍴 **Bagelmama,** Podbrzezie 2 (☎431 19 42), facing the Tempel Synagogue. Poland is the mother of the bagel; here the blessed foodstuff returns home in triumph. At this tiny bagel shop, an American-Polish couple, serve some of the best bagels east of New York with a variety of fresh spreads (2.50zł, 5-8zł with cream cheese or hummus). They also make the best burritos in Kraków (12-14zł). Open Tu-Su 10am-9pm. Cash only. ❶

- 🍴 **Pierogarnia,** Sławkowska 32 (☎422 74 95). By the counter in this miniscule dumpling outpost, a window reveals a cook rolling dough and shaping *pierogi*. Meals range from classic cheese-and-potato *ruskie* to the more daring groats-and-liver (7-8zł). Also serves excellent *gołąbki* (cabbage rolls; 8zł) and 8 fruit juices, including cherry and black currant (5zł). Remarkably fast service. *Pierogi* 7-10zł. Open daily 10am-9pm. Cash only. ❶

- **Vega Bar Restaurant,** Krupnicza 22 (☎430 08 46). Fresh flowers set the mood for munching on delightful, largely vegetarian cuisine (3-10zł). Faux-meat dishes like the cheese-and-soy *kotlety* (cutlet; 5zł) will please pining carnivores; the *fasola z grzybami* (beans with mushrooms, 7zł) is another great spin on a traditionally meat-based Polish favorite. 32 varieties of tea (2.50zł). Open daily 9am-9pm. MC/V. **Branch** at św. Gertrudy 7 (☎422 34 94). Open daily 9am-9pm. MC/V. ❶

- **Momo,** Dietla 49 (☎609 68 5775). This largely vegan Kazimierz outfit shuns microwaves, chemicals, and canned ingredients. The spare-yet-funky decor keeps up the theme of wholesome freshness, as do dishes such as spinach-and-tofu pancakes (6zł) and the eponymous Tibetan dumplings (10zł). Open daily 11am-8pm. Cash only. ❶

THE ORIGINAL

According to legend, a Jewish baker in Vienna concocted the first bagel in 1683 as a gift to Polish king Jan Sobieski to thank Sobieski for routing Turkish invaders. The bread (the story goes) was shaped like a stirrup "beugal' in honor of Sobieski's heroic horsemanship. The historical record, however, first spots the bagel in Kraków in 1610: community regulations decreed that bagels be given to pregnant women for easy childbirth, and to teething babies. Whatever the bagel's origins, it thrived in Poland, especially in the Kraków region. A 1915 chronicle of the Jewish neighborhood of Kazimierz recalls that the smell of freshly baked bagels often wafted through the streets, especially near the Tempel Synagogue, where a tiny shop called Pan Bejgul (Mr. Bagel) stood at the end of Podbrzezie Street.

In Kraków today, street vendors hawk the Polish descendent of the original bagel, a crisp ring of bread known as *obwarzanki*, for about a złoty. The smell of baking bagels, meanwhile, has returned to Podbrzezie St. **Bagelmama**, facing the Tempel Synagogue at Podbrzezie 2, opened in 2001. Run by an American expat chef, Navara, it is currently the only shop in Poland that sells fresh bagels as they have evolved among Polish Jewish immigrants to North America: soft and chewy, with cream cheese spreads.

Fabryka Pizzy, Józefa 34 (☎433 80 80). The wildly popular Kazimierz pizza place lives up to its hype. Excellent pizzas (12-20zł) and fabulous breadsticks and calzone (5-8zł). Open M-Th and Su 11am-11pm, F-Sa noon-midnight. MC/V. ❷

La Cuisine, Kupa 1 (☎429 60 18; www.lacuisine.pl). Small, chic, and full of brushed metal, La Cuisine is an iPod of a pastry shop. Crepes 4-12zł, with extras such as red pepper and egg at 1zł each. Naleśniki 4-12zł. Cakes 4-8zł. Open M-Th and Su noon-11pm, F-Sa 10am-2am. Cash only. ❷

Restauracja Samoobsługowa "Polakowski," Miodowa 39 (☎421 21 17). The menu, prices, and cafeteria service of a milk bar meet upscale ingredients and country decor. Sides 3-4zł. Soups 4-5zł. Entrees 6-11zł. Open daily 8am-10pm. AmEx/MC/V. ❷

⚑ CAFES

▓ **Dym** (Smoke), św. Tomasza 13 (☎429 66 61). A hub for sophisticated locals, Dym earns high praise for unbeatable coffee (4.50zł), though many prefer to enjoy the relaxed atmosphere over beer (5.50zł). The cheesecake (4zł) is divine. The watery, green-blue walls also sport art exhibitions. Open daily 10am-midnight. Cash only.

▓ **Massolit Books Café,** Felicjanek 4 (☎432 41 50). Fantastic wood-lined bookstore cafe with a fin de siecle atmosphere. At this tiny expat hangout, you can peruse your newest find at one of the 4 coveted tables while sipping coffee (4zł) or sampling a decadent dessert (banana cake; 7zł). Open mic night every 1st and 3rd Su, 7pm. Open M-Th and Su 10am-8pm, F-Sa 10am-10pm. MC/V.

Camelot, św. Tomasza 17 (☎421 01 23). The literati flock to Camelot, one of Stare Miasto's legends. The space is cluttered with paintings and photos, soothing jazz, and the occasional 17th-century document. Coffee 6-11zł. Breakfast 6-16zł. Sandwiches 3-6zł. Salads 19-21zł. Music, readings, or cabaret F 9pm, downstairs at Loch Camelot. English menu. Open daily 9am-midnight. Cash only.

Cafe Manggha, M. Konopnickiej 26 (☎267 27 03; www.manggha.krakow.pl), in the Center for Japanese Arts. Pricey, but the view and the green tea ice cream (11.50zł) are exquisite. Tea 6-7zł. One of the few places in Poland where you can trust the sushi (17-23zł). Sake 6-9zł. Other entrees 7-25zł. Open Tu-Su 10am-6pm. AmEx/MC/V.

Les Couleurs, Estery 10 (☎429 42 70). Begin your day at this Parisian cafe with buttery croissants (4zł), fresh-squeezed juice (9zł), and French newspapers. By afternoon the back patio fills with laid-back coffee drinkers (5zł), while Kazimierz regulars nurse beers at the bar (Żywiec; 6zł). Lively late at night. Open daily 7am-2am. Cash only. ❶

Tribeca, Rynek Główny 27 (☎695 602 727). Some of the best coffee on the Rynek. Black-clad waitstaff serves an impressive range of espressos and lattes (5-12zł) to patrons chatting throughout the bright, multicolored interior, and to people-watchers outside. Open daily 8am-10pm. AmEx/MC/V. ❶

◉ SIGHTS

WAWEL CASTLE AND CATHEDRAL

Entry is limited and only 10 tickets become available every 10min., so you may have to wait. It's advisable to buy tickets early in the morning because they often sell out, especially in summer. English info and tickets to all buildings except the cathedral at the main kasa. Tourist Service Office (BOT) ☎422 64 64; www.wawel.krakow.pl.

▓ **WAWEL CASTLE (ZAMEK WAWELSKI).** An extraordinary architectural work, the Wawel Castle and Cathedral complex—arguably the most impressive sight in Poland—lies at the heart of the country's history. Begun in the 10th century but remodeled in the 1500s, the castle contains 71 chambers and a magnificent sequence of 16th-century tapestries. Walk through the **Dziedziniec** (courtyard) and take in the beautiful architecture. The royal family's treasures can be seen in the **Komnaty** (State Rooms) while the **Apartamenty** (Royal Private Apartments) showcase the royal lifestyle. The Skarbiec (Treasury and Armory) features swords, spears, ostentatious armor, and ancient guns. The star of the collection is **Szczerbiec,** the coronation sword used from 1230 to 1734. The **Lost Wawel** exhibit traces Wawel Hill's evolution from the Stone Age, displaying archaeological fragments of ancient Wawel. You can also visit the **Oriental Collection** of Turkish military regalia, the spoils of Polish military victories, and Chinese and Japanese porcelain. *(Open Apr.-Oct. M 9:30am-noon; Tu, W, Sa 9:30am-3pm; Th-F 9:30am-4pm, Su 10am-3pm. Nov.-Mar. Tu-Sa 9:30am-3pm, Su 10am-3pm. Royal Private Apartments and Oriental Collection closed M. Wawel Castle 18zł, students 13zł; M free. Lost Wawel and Oriental Collection 6/4zł each. Royal Apartments and Treasury and Armory 14/8zł each.)*

WAWEL CATHEDRAL (KATEDRA WAWELSKA). On Wawel Hill, beside the castle, the magnificent Wawel Cathedral witnessed coronations of centuries of Polish kings and queens. As you enter, look for the miraculous **crucifix of St. Jadwiga.** Legend has it that the young Polish queen asked it whether she should marry King Władysław Jagiełło of Lithuania, who now rests here, and the crucifix spoke, advising her to marry. With the union of the couple came the unification of their respective countries in 1386. In 1997, Jadwiga was canonized by John Paul II, who had held mass in the cathedral when he was Archbishop of Kraków. Ascend the tower to **Sigismund's Bell** (Dzwon Zygmunta) for an unbeatable view of Kraków—in the company of half the schoolchildren in Poland. The bell, which weighs more than 11 tons, can supposedly be heard for up to 50km. Descend to the **Royal Tombs** through the Czartoryskich Chapel. The underground maze contains elaborately carved sarcophagi of royals and acclaimed military leaders, including heroic generals Tadeusz Kościuszko and Józef Piłsudski. The small **Cathedral Museum** (Muzeum Katedralne) boasts selections from the cathedral treasury, including exquisite textiles and a gold rose. *(Cathedral open M-Sa 9am-2:45pm, Su and holy days 12:15-2:45pm. Buy tickets at the kasa across from the entrance. 10zł, students 5zł. Cathedral Museum 5/2zł.)*

DRAGON'S DEN. Home to Kraków's erstwhile menace, the ◙**dragon's den** is in the southwest corner of the complex. According to legend, the dragon held the people of Kraków in terror, eating livestock and virgins, until a clever young shepherd set a fake sheep full of sulfur outside its cave. Upon devouring the trap, the reptile became so thirsty that it drank water from the Wisła until it burst. Enjoy the legendary cave, or skip the den altogether and walk down to the path that borders the castle walls to the real treat, a wonderfully ugly metal statue of the fire-breathing dragon. *(Open daily May-Oct. 10am-5pm. 3zł.)*

STARE MIASTO

At the center of Stare Miasto (Old Town) spreads **Rynek Główny,** the largest market square in Europe, and at the heart of the Rynek stands the **Sukiennice** (Cloth Hall). Surrounded by multicolored row houses and cafes, it's a convenient center for exploring the nearby sights. The Royal Road (Droga Królewska), traversed by medieval royals on the way to coronations in Wawel, starts at **St. Florian's Church** (Kościół św. Floriana), crosses pl. Matejki, passes the **Academy of Fine Arts** (Akademia Sztuk Pięknych), and crosses Basztowa to the **Barbakan.** The Gothic-style Barbakan, built in 1499, is the best preserved of the three such defensive fortifications surviving in Europe. *(Open daily 9am-6pm. 4zł, students 2.50zł.)* The royal road continues through **Floriańska Gate,** the old city entrance and the only remnant of the city's medieval walls. Inside Stare Miasto, the road runs down Floriańska, past the Rynek and along Grodzka, which ends with **Wawel** in sight. A **map** marking all the points can be found in front of Floriańska Gate.

WHAT DO YOU RECOMMEND?

You've scrambled through the castle ruins, the cemetery, and the museum, and now you're hungry. The only thing that stands between you and that hearty Polish dinner is a looming wall of gibberish known as the menu. The art of ordering can be incredibly important on the road, and I frequently find the best budget-friendly options, far from having English menus, write their daily offerings in Polish on posters or boards, leaving me famished, clutching my bag to my chest as I try to sound out the first of 30 choices. I've come to rely heavily on a phrase that brings me far more joy than any memorized plea for directions or train timetables: *co pan/pani poleca?* (pan for a man, pani for a woman—don't mess this up!), meaning, "what do you recommend?"

Cheerful or less rushed servers are more likely to put thought into recommendations instead of suggesting the most expensive item on the menu. On a few occasions, entire kitchen staffs gathered to argue over what to cook me. As a solo traveler, I found this display of hospitality encouraging, not to mention seriously delicious. I've had some weird meals (pizza with bananas, nutella, pineapples, and cheese...what?) and a number I wouldn't try a second time; but if variety is the spice of life, and "spice" a word I can't pronounce, then I'll defer for now to those who know best.

—*Stephanie O'Rourke*

ST. MARY'S CHURCH (KOŚCIÓŁ MARIACKI). Deep blues and golds accent the black marble columns of the church's interior. Look down from the exquisite, star-flecked ceiling and notice a 500-year-old wooden altar, carved by Wit Stwosz, which portrays the joy and suffering of St. Mary. This gorgeous artifact, the oldest Gothic altar in the world, barely survived WWII. Dismantled by the Nazis, it was discovered by Allied forces at the war's end and reassembled. Every hour, the blaring Hejnał trumpet calls from the taller of St. Mary's two towers and cuts off abruptly to recall the near-destruction of Kraków in 1241, when invading Tatars shot down the trumpeter as he attempted to warn the city. The two towers also stand as monuments to ancient sibling rivalry. According to legends, the larger Wieża Mariacka was the careful work of one brother. The architect of the smaller, less elaborate tower committed fratricide out of jealousy. Overwhelmed with guilt, he then mounted his own tower, publicly confessed to the murder, and stabbed himself with the same knife. The murder weapon is on display in the Cloth Hall. Both towers are now historic sites and visitors can ascend for a panorama. *(At the corner of the Rynek closest to the train station. Open daily 11:30am-6pm. Icon unveiled daily M-F 11:50am-6pm, Su and holidays 2-6pm. Covered shoulders and knees expected. No photography. Altar 4zł, students 2zł. Video camera 5zł. Wieża Mariacka open Tu, Th, Sa 9-11am and 2-6pm. 5zł. Smaller tower open daily 10am-1:15pm and 2-5pm. 5zł, students 2.50zł.)*

JAGIELLONIAN UNIVERSITY (UNIWERSYTET JAGIELLOŃSKI). Established in 1364, Kraków's Jagiellonian University is the third-oldest university in Europe. Among its celebrated alumni are astronomer **Mikołaj Kopernik (Copernicus)** and painter Jan Matejko. The picturesque Collegium Maius is the university's oldest building. The Collegium became a museum in 1964 and now boasts an extensive collection of historical scientific instruments. Highlights include the oldest known globe showing the Americas (look for them near Madagascar) and an 11th-century Arabian astrolabe. Call ahead to join or arrange a tour. *(Jagiellońska 15. ☎422 05 49. Open M-W and F 10am-3pm, Th 10am-6pm, Sa 10am-2pm. Guided visits only; tours begin every 20min. Tour in English daily 1pm. 12zł, students 6zł; Sa free.)*

CLOTH HALL (SUKIENNICE). In the Rynek, the yellow Cloth Hall remains as profit-oriented today as when medieval cloth merchants used it. The ground floor is lined with wooden stalls hawking crafts. Upstairs, the Cloth Hall Gallery houses 18th- and 19th-century sculptures and paintings. Of the many pastoral and military depictions, the most striking and famous are Jan Matejko's *Hołd Pruski*, Józef Chełmoński's *Four in Hand*, and Henryk Siemiradzki's *Nero's Torches*. During the academic year, students cruise the area between the Cloth Hall and St. Mary's and near the statue of Adam Mickiewicz, Poland's most celebrated poet. (☎422 11 66. *Open Tu and F-Sa 10am-7pm, W-Th 10am-4pm, Su 10am-3pm. 8zł, students 5zł; Th free.*)

CZARTORYSKICH MUSEUM. This branch of the National Museum displays **Leonardo da Vinci's** *Lady with an Ermine* and **Rembrandt's** *Landscape with a Merciful Samaritan*. Da Vinci's piece harbors several secrets: historians have debated whether the lady portrayed is Beatrice d'Este, the Duchess of Milan; or Cecilia Gallerani, the Duke of Milan's 16-year-old mistress. Also debatable are the painting's authenticity and where it spent its history prior to its 1800 purchase by Polish prince Adam Czartoryski. Read letters written by Copernicus, peer into a Turkish tent captured at the Battle of Vienna, or witness the national spirit of Jan Matejko's *Poland Enchained*. (św. Jana 19. ☎422 55 66. *Open Tu, Th 10am-4pm, W, F 11am-7pm, Sa-Su 10am-3pm; closed last Su of each month. 9zł; students 6zł; Th free.*)

OTHER SIGHTS. The main branch of the **National Museum** (Muzeum Narodowe) has permanent exhibits of armory and 20th-century art, and hosts acclaimed temporary exhibits. (*Al. 3 Maja 1. Take tram #15 to Cracovia.* ☎634 33 77; *www.muz-nar.krakow.pl. Open Tu, Th 9am-3:30pm, W, F 11am-6pm, Sa-Su 10am-3:30pm. Permanent exhibit 10zł, students 5zł. Temporary exhibits 6/3zł. MC/V.*) The **History Museum of Kraków** (Muzeum Historyczne Miasta Krakowa), another branch of the National Museum, displays ceiling frescoes and centuries-old documents from Kraków, including a 15th-century map of the city and religious and military artifacts. (*Rynek Główny 35.* ☎422 99 22. *Open daily 10am-5:30pm; closed 2nd Su of each month. 5zł, students 3.50zł; Sa free.*) The **Franciscan Church** (Kościół Franciscańska) is decorated with vibrant colors and Stanisław Wyspiański's amazing stained-glass window *God the Father*. (*Pl. Wszystkich Świętych 5.* ☎422 53 76. *Open daily until 7:30pm. Tours in English free; donations requested.*) The curving, wave-like design of Kraków's center for Japanese art, **Manggha,** complements the bends of the Wisła, which separates it from Wawel. The contemporary building houses a small gallery that juxtaposes traditional and modern Japanese arts, cloth, and armor. (*M. Konopnickiej 26.* ☎267 27 03; *www.manggha.krakow.pl. Open Tu-Su 10am-6pm; closed last Su of each month. 5zł, students 3zł.*) Both a store and gallery, **Galeria Autorska Andrzeja Mleczki** features satirical, funky, and fun drawings, offering a glimpse into Polish politics. (*Św. Jana 14. Open M-F 10am-7pm, Sa 10am-5pm. MC/V.*) For an even funkier experience, visit the **Poster Gallery** to view locally printed posters. (*Stolarska 8.* ☎421 26 40. *Open M-F 11am-6pm, Sa 11am-2pm. AmEx/MC/V.*)

KAZIMIERZ: THE OLD JEWISH QUARTER

Southeast of the Rynek and Wawel. The 15min. walk from the Rynek leads down Sienna past St. Mary's Church. Eventually, Sienna turns into Starowiślna. After 1km, turn right on Miodowa and take the 1st left onto Szeroka.

South of Stare Miasto is Kazimierz, Kraków's 600-year-old Jewish quarter. In 1495, King Jan Olbrecht moved Kraków's Jews there in order to remove them from the city proper. On the eve of WWII, 68,000 Jews lived in the Kraków area, most of them in Kazimierz. The occupying Nazis forced many of them out. The 15,000 remaining were resettled in the overcrowded Podgórze ghetto in 1941, and deported to death camps by March 1943. Only about 100 practicing Jews now live here, but Kazimierz, with its cafes and bars, is now both a favorite haunt of Kraków's artists and intellectuals and the center of a nascent resurgence of Central European Jewish culture. The **Jarden Bookstore**, the only Jewish bookstore in Poland, organizes guided **tours**, including a 2hr. tour of Kazimierz and the Płaszów death camp that traces the sites shown in the film *Schindler's List*. Płaszów, south of Kraków, was destroyed by the Nazis on their retreat and is now an overgrown field. *(Szeroka 2. ☎421 11 66; www.jarden.pl. Open M-F 9am-6pm, Sa-Su 10am-6pm. Kazimierz tour 35zł, 3 person min.; with ghetto 45zł. Schindler's List tour 65zł. Car tour of Auschwitz-Birkenau 110zł, private guide 130zł. 20% student discount. AmEx/MC/V.)*

■ **GALICIA JEWISH MUSEUM.** Galicia, a region that includes much of southern Poland, was once the heart of Eastern European Jewish culture. In this unconventional museum, photojournalist Chris Schwarz uses photographs of contemporary Poland to document the past and present of Jewish life in Galicia. Images of ruins, abandoned cemeteries, and surviving traces of Jewish culture pose difficult questions about the future of Judaism in Poland. A spare converted warehouse houses the museum, a cafe, and a bookstore. The non-profit organization also offers Yiddish language lessons and lectures on Judaism. *(Dajwór 18. ☎421 68 42; www.galicia-jewishmuseum.org. Open daily 10am-8pm. 7zł, students 5zł.)*

OLD SYNAGOGUE (STARA SYNAGOGA). Poland's oldest example of Jewish religious architecture, the Old Synagogue houses the **Kraków Jewish History and Culture Museum** (Dzieje i Kultura Żydów) depicting local Jewish history, tradition, and art. Historic religious objects and nostalgic pre-WWII photos are counterposed with WWII-era documents of segregation and deportation. *(Szeroka 24. ☎422 09 62; fax 431 05 45. Open Apr.-Oct. M 10am-2pm, Tu-Su 10am-5pm; Nov.-Mar. M 10am-2pm, W-Th, Sa-Su 9am-4pm, F 11am-6pm. 7zł, students 5zł. M free. Cameras 10zł.)*

REMUH SYNAGOGUE AND CEMETERY (SYNAGOGA I CMENTARZ REMUH). Rabbi Moses Isserles, a great scholar better known as the **Remuh**, founded this tiny synagogue in 1553 in honor of his wife, who had died in the plague of 1551-52. The Remuh, now buried under a tree to the left of the cemetery's entrance, is believed to have caused strong winds to rise up and cover the cemetery with sand, protecting it from 19th-century Austrian invaders. Many of the gravestones remained buried through WWII. Though the Nazis used the cemetery as a garbage dump, the sands protected it from the total destruction that was the fate of many Jewish graveyards. Much of the site has been painstakingly reconstructed. *(Szeroka 40. Open M-F, Su 9am-6pm. Services F at sundown and Sa morning. 6zł, students 3zł.)*

ISAAC'S SYNAGOGUE (SYNAGOGA IZAAKA). The main room of this gorgeous 17th-century Baroque synagogue shows two historical documentaries, while a smaller room features seven more, including *Ghetto Uprising*. Haunting photographs and movie stills are scattered throughout the synagogue. *(Kupa 18. ☎430 55 77; fax 602 144 262. Open M-F, Su 9am-7pm; closed Jewish holidays. 7zł, students 6zł.)*

CENTER FOR JEWISH CULTURE. The center organizes cultural events, arranges heritage tours, and aims to preserve Jewish culture in Kazimierz. Free exhibits are across from the info desk. Hosts occasional lectures and concerts. *(Meiselsa 17. ☎430 64 49; www.judaica.pl. Open M-F 10am-6pm, Sa-Su 10am-2pm.)*

OTHER SIGHTS. In 2000, restoration was completed on the ornate gold-trimmed and stained-glass interior of the **Tempel Synagogue** (Synagoga Tempel; Miodowa 24. Open M-F, Su 10am-6pm. 6zł, students 3zł.) The **New Jewish Cemetery** (Cmentarz Nowy), Miodowa 55, established in 1800, houses tombstones of many of 19th-century Kraków's prominent citizens and memorializes families killed in the Holocaust. *(Open M-F and Su 8am-4pm. Free. Head coverings required.)*

NOWA HUTA

To reach Nowa Huta from Kraków center, take tram #4 or 15 from the train station to the pl. Centralny stop. www.nh.pl. For a guided tour in an authentic East German Trabant, contact Crazy Guides, ☎888 68 68 71. Tour 99zł per person.

For a sharp contrast with both the tourist crowds and the prettiness of Wawel Hill, head to eerie **Nowa Huta** (New Steelworks), one of only two full-scale Soviet planned communities ever realized. Just 20min. by tram from Stare Miasto, Nowa Huta was fashioned by the Soviet Union beginning in 1949 in a bid to stir communist spirit and provide a proletariat counterweight to Catholic, intellectual Kraków. With broad streets, plentiful greenspace, and imposing Socialist Realist architecture, the town is a surreal and superb relic of the Soviet era. From the outset, the hyper-planned community backfired on its planners. The **Lenin Steelworks,** operating the biggest blast furnace in Europe in its heyday, showered industrial pollution on Kraków; the community's residents, meanwhile, launched a 20-year campaign to have a parish church built in Nowa Huta. By the 1980s, the 40,000 steelworkers of Nowa Huta were at the forefront of dissent against the Communist regime, frequently striking in protest of government policies. Today the irony of Nowa Huta continues: the central square has been renamed in honor of Ronald Reagan; layoffs at the now-renamed Sendzimir Steelworks have depressed the area's economy; and Nowa Huta has become a tourist attraction of sorts. Visitors can take in the modernist **Church of the Virgin Mary, Heart of Poland,** finally built in 1977, tour the Steelworks by appointment, and stroll along the streets where Andrzej Wajda set his seminal film about Communist Poland, *Man of Marble.*

🎵 🌺 ENTERTAINMENT AND FESTIVALS

The **Cultural Information Center,** św. Jana 2, sells the monthly guide *Karnet* (4zł) and directs visitors to box offices. (☎421 77 87. Open daily 10am-6pm.) The city jumps with jazz. Check out **U Muniaka,** Floriańska 3 (☎423 12 05; open daily 6:30pm-2am) and **Harris Piano Jazz Bar,** Rynek Główny 28 (☎421 57 41; shows 9pm-midnight; open daily 9am-3am). Or, take in the talent at **Indigo,** Floriańska 26 (☎429 17 43). Classical music-lovers will relish the **Sala Filharmonia** (Philharmonic Hall), Zwierzyniecka 1. (☎675 02 00 025; www.filharmonia.krakow.pl. Box office open Tu-F 2-8pm, Sa-Su 1hr. before performance; closed June 9-Sept. 20.) The **opera** performs at the **Słowacki Theater,** św. Ducha 1. (☎422 40 22. Box office open M-Sa 11am-2pm and 3-7pm, Su 2hr. before performance. Tickets 30-50zł, students 25-30zł.) The **Stary Teatr** (Old Theater) has a few stages that host films, plays, and exhibits. (☎422 40 40. Open Tu-Sa 10am-1pm and 5-7pm, Su 5-7pm. Tickets 30-60zł, students 20-35zł.) Enjoy a relaxing evening and catch a movie at **Kino Pod Baranami,** Rynek Główny 27. (☎423 07 68. Tickets M 9.90zł; Tu-Th 15zł, students 13zł; F-Su 16/14zł.) **Kino Mikro,** Lea 5, shows European films. (☎634 28 97. Open daily 30min. before 1st showing. M-F 10zł, Sa-Su 12zł.)

Notable festivals include the **International Short Film Festival** (late May), **Wianki** (the Floating of Wreaths on the Wisła; June), the **Festival of Jewish Culture** (early July), the **Street Theater Festival** (early July), and the **Jazz Festival** (late July).

🎤 NIGHTLIFE

Kraków in Your Pocket has up-to-date info on the hottest club and pub scenes, while the free monthly English-language *KrakOut* magazine has day-by-day listings of events. Most dance clubs are in Stare Miasto, while bohemian pubs and

cafes cluster in Kazimierz. For more info, see www.puby.krakow.pl. Be advised
that Kraków's night establishments have a high turnover rate. For tips on
Kraków's **gay nightlife,** see http://gayeuro.com/krakow.

▨ **Alchemia,** Estery 5 (☎292 09 70). Candles twinkle in the charmingly disheveled bar,
where patrons sip beer (Żywiec; 6zł) and linger until dawn. Frequented by students, artists, and young Brits, this quintessential Kazimierz bar masquerades by day as a smoky
cafe. Occasional live music and film screenings. Open M-Sa 11am-4am, Su 10am-4am.

▨ **Prozak,** Dominikańska 6 (☎429 11 28; www.prozak.pl). With more dance floors, bars,
and intimate nooks than you'll be able to count, Prozak is one of the top clubs in town.
Hipster students, porn star lookalikes, and many foreigners lounge beneath mood lighting and on low-slung couches. Pass on the pricey, undersized mixed drinks (12-22zł) for
pints of beer (7zł). No sneakers or sandals. Cover F-Sa 10zł. Open daily 4pm-2am.

Cień, św. Jana 15 (☎422 21 77). The underground vaults of the "Shadow" fill with
Kraków's beautiful people, who come here to see and be seen. Mostly house techno.
No sneakers or sandals. Open W-Th 7pm-3am, F-Sa 7pm-6am. Cash only.

Faust, Rynek Główny 6 (☎423 83 00). Sell your soul in this underground labyrinth,
where a raucous, friendly crowd sits at massive wooden tables and dances unabash-
edly to pop or techno hits. Occasional *klezmer* or metal nights. Beer 4-6zł. Disco W-Sa.
Cover F-Sa 5zł. Open M-Th and Su noon-1am, F-Sa noon-4am. Cash only.

Propaganda, Miodowa 20. Despite the candles and wobbly tables, Propaganda's take
on Kazimierz bohemia has a punk rock feel. Decor mixes posters of Stalin with guitars
of Polish rockers, some of whom have been known to tend bar here. One of the friendliest regulars is a large dog named Floyd. Open daily 2pm-late. Cash only.

Stalowe Magnolie, św. Jana 15 (☎422 60 84). Scarlet lights illuminate this decadent
jazz club and student hangout. Pass through the bar, then chat and chill out on the
comfy, king-sized beds in the lounge. Beer 6-10zł. Mixed drinks 14-25zł. Outstanding
live jazz Tu-Th; contemporary rock Sa-Su. Open daily 6pm-3am.

Klub pod Jaszczurami (Club under the Lizards), Rynek Główny 8 (☎292 22 02). A stu-
dents-only cafe by day and thumping club party by night. Familiar tunes fill the dark
dance floors as smoke wafts above tables of chatting 20-somethings. Beer 5.50zł.
Open M-Th and Su 10am-1am, F-Sa 10am-late.

▶ DAYTRIPS FROM KRAKÓW

AUSCHWITZ-BIRKENAU

*Tourist offices in Kraków organize trips that include transportation and guides. Buses (1½-
2hr., 5 per day, 10-15zł; get off at Muzeum Oświęcim) run to the town of Oświęcim from
Kraków's central bus station. The bus back to Kraków leaves from a different stop across
from the parking lot. Trains run from Kraków Płaszów (7-10zł). From outside the Oświęcim
train station, buses #2-5, 8-9, and 24-29 drop visitors off at the Muzeum Oświęcim stop.
Turn right as you exit the station, go 1 block, and turn left on Więźniów Oświęcimia; the
Auschwitz camp is 1.6km down the road.*

An estimated 1.5 million people—mostly Jews—were murdered, and thousands
more suffered unthinkable horrors, in the infamous Nazi death camps at **Auschwitz**
(Oświęcim) and **Birkenau** (Brzezinka). As the largest and most brutally efficient of
the camps, their names are synonymous with the Nazi death machine. In 1979, the
complexes were added to the UNESCO World Heritage List.

AUSCHWITZ I. In 1940, the Nazis built the first and smaller of two death camps
on the grounds of a Polish Army garrison. Originally consisting of 20 buildings,
the camp grew as prisoners were forced to build additional barracks. In 1942,

Auschwitz became the center of extermination of Jews, Roma, and other "inferior" peoples. The eerily tidy rows of red brick buildings seems almost peaceful until the bitter irony of the inscription on the camp's gate—*Arbeit Macht Frei* (Work Shall Set You Free)—sinks in. The chilling walk through the camp confronts visitors with an up-close look at the horrifying realities of the Holocaust. The barracks that once held Jews and political prisoners now showcase victims' ghostly remnants: suitcases, shoes, eyeglasses, and even hair provide a terrifyingly personal look at Nazi atrocities. The lynching post and gas chamber also remain on the grounds. At 11am and 1pm, the building at the entrance shows a 15min. English-language film (3.50zł) with footage recorded by the Soviet Army when it liberated the camp on January 27, 1945. Children under 14 are strongly advised not to visit. *(☎843 20 22. Open daily June-Aug. 8am-7pm; Sept. and May 8am-6pm; Oct. and Apr. 8am-5pm; Nov. and Mar. 8am-4pm; Dec.-Feb. 8am-3pm. Polish tour daily 11am, 1, 3pm. Tour in English daily 11:30am. Free. Tours 3½hr., 25zł; film and bus included. English guidebook 3zł.)*

AUSCHWITZ II-BIRKENAU. Auschwitz II-Birkenau was built when the massive influx of condemned prisoners being brought to Auschwitz motivated the Nazis to pursue a more "efficient" means of killing. Little is left now of the 300 barracks that spanned the 425-acre camp; the Nazis attempted to conceal their genocide by destroying the camp before it was liberated on January 27, 1945. The reconstructed railroad tracks beneath the original SS watchtower glide past the rows of selection barracks where individuals were chosen for work or death. The tracks end among piles of rubber, former gas chambers, and crematoria, the final stop for countless victims sent to the camps. Beyond the ruins, a memorial that pays tribute to those who died in the Auschwitz camps is a place for quiet reflection. Near the monument is a pond, still gray from the ashes deposited there more than half a century ago. *(Birkenau is 3km from Auschwitz I. Shuttle runs every hr. 11:30am-5:30pm, from the Auschwitz parking lot, 2zł. To walk to Birkenau, turn right from the parking lot, follow the path for about 1.5km, then turn left at the sign for the road, cross the bridge, and continue for about 1km. Open Apr. 15-Oct. 31 8am-dusk. Free.)*

 A PRISONER'S SACRIFICE. It is difficult to visit the concentration camps at Auschwitz and Birkenau without hearing the story of the priest Maksymilian Kolbe—prisoner 16670—who sacrificed his own life while imprisoned here. When another man was handed the brutal sentence of death by starvation, Kolbe willingly took the man's place and submitted himself to a torture even more ghastly than he and other prisoners were already enduring. Amazingly, he maintained his strength and staved off death for two weeks—but this triumph of will and faith was cut short by Nazi guards who, frustrated with his incredible endurance, executed him by lethal injection. After his death, Kolbe became a strong symbol of faith in the face of persecution. In 1971, he became the first Nazi victim to be proclaimed blessed by the Catholic Church, and in 1982, he was canonized by Pope John Paul II. Franciszek Gajowniczek, the man whom Kolbe replaced, survived through liberation and lived to the 50th anniversary of the end of WWII. He died in 1995. Visitors can see Kolbe's starvation cell (#18), located in Barrack II of Auschwitz I. A tribute to the priest lies inside.

AUSCHWITZ JEWISH CENTER AND SYNAGOGUE (CENTRUM ŻYDOWSKIE W OŚWIĘCIMIU). The center is next to the restored prewar synagogue. Exhibits focus on prewar Jewish life in the town. Oświęcim offers study and research opportunities, discussion groups, and video testimonials of Auschwitz survivors.

POLAND

The center also provides guidance for those interested in exploring their Jewish roots. Auschwitz guides are available for hire. *(Pl. Ks. Jana Skarbka 5. From the train station take bus #1, 3-6, 8, or 28 to the town center, get off at the stop after the bridge and backtrack, taking the 1st right and then a left to pl. Ks. Jana Skarbka. Alternatively, take a taxi for about 17zł. ☎844 70 02; www.ajcf.pl. English spoken. Open M–F, Su 8:30am-8pm.)*

WIELICZKA

Danilowicza 10. Many companies, including Orbis, organize trips to the mine. The cheapest way to go is to take one of the minibuses that leave from between the train and bus stations. (30min. "Lux-Bus" every 15min.; 2zł.) In Wieliczka, follow the old path of the tracks and then the "do kopalni" signs. ☎278 73 02; www.kopalnia.pl. Open daily Apr.-Oct. 7:30am-7:30pm; Nov.-Mar. 8am-4pm; closed holidays. Admission with guided tours only. Polish tours 35zł, students 20zł. Tours in English June and Sept. 8 per day, July and Aug. every 30min. 8:30am-6pm; 50zł, students under 25 40zł; Nov.-Feb. 20% off. Wheelchair accessible. MC/V.

Thirteen km southeast of Kraków and 100m below the tiny town of Wieliczka lies the 700-year-old ▓**Wieliczka Salt Mine.** Follow the footsteps of Goethe, one of the attraction's first tourists, and see how miners and artists transformed the salt deposits into a maze of chambers full of sculptures and carvings. Though salt has not been manually excavated here since July 1996, the mine still exports 20,000 tons of salt per year through natural processes. In 1978, UNESCO, citing the mine's beauty and its role in Polish history, declared it one of the 12 most priceless monuments in the world. Amazingly, the mine once provided a third of Poland's GDP, and with the sheer number of tourists in high season, it still contributes to the region's economy. The 2hr. tour meanders past spectacular underground lakes and sculptures of beloved Poles like Copernicus and the late pope John Paul II. The most impressive sight is **St. Kinga's Chapel,** with an altar, chandeliers, and religious relics, all carved from salt. At the end of the tour, take the lift 120m back to the surface or go to the **underground museum,** Muzeum Żup Krakowskich, which gives a more detailed history of the mines and features 14 additional chambers (1hr. tours 9zł, students 4.50zł; M free). Bring a sweater—the mine is chilly.

WADOWICE   ☎0(33)

Take one of 8 daily buses from Kraków PKS station (1½hr., 8zł). From Wadowice bus station, follow the paved path behind the ticket office through the park. Turn left on Sienkiewicza, then left on Mickiewicza, to reach pl. Jana Pawła II. Wojtyła House open May-Oct. Tu-Su 9am-1pm and 2-6pm; Nov.-Apr. Tu-Su 9am-noon and 1-4pm. Donations requested.

In the middle of rolling hills teeming with pheasants lies the birthplace of Poland's beloved Karol Wojtyła, former pope John Paul II. Since the pope's death, **Wadowice** has seen a deluge of tourists and pilgrims, and the tiny town is less than prepared for the influx of visitors. Accommodation and food options are limited, but the town offers a unique glimpse of Poland's adoration of its great modern hero, and will interest those who have followed the pope's long career.

The two primary sites of interest for visitors are the house where Wojtyła was born and raised, and the basilica where he was baptized and ordained. The **Wojtyła House** is a half block from the large pl. Jana Pawła II, at Kościelna 7. If you can brave the crowds, especially on weekends, you'll find a house with four small rooms, including the one where baby Karol was born May 18, 1920. The rooms are now filled with black-and-white photos and personal items that trace Wojtyła's early life and career. A few buildings over stands the large **Minor Basilica** (Bazylika Mniejsza), where the pope's baptismal font rests alongside the reputedly miraculous icon Our Lady of Perpetual Help (donations requested). Both items were blessed in a 1999 papal visit to Wadowice, and now attract reverent visitors.

You'll find most restaurants in pl. Jana Pawła II, but the real treat for travelers is the **cream cake** *(kremówka)* Wojtyła enjoyed as a child. During one of three visits to Wadowice, Pope John Paul II reminisced about his favorite dessert, and you can still find this pastry (2zł) at his favorite bakery, **Cukiernia Beskidzla,** Jagiellońska 23. (Open M-F 8am-5pm, Sa 8am-4pm, Su 10am-4pm.) Countless other bakeries off pl. Jana Pawła II also serve this extremely delicious local specialty.

LUBLIN   ☎ 0(81)

Much of the charm of Lublin (LOO-blin; pop. 400,000) derives from its authenticity. Unlike most Polish cities, Lublin escaped WWII largely unscathed: its medieval Old Town is no Disneyfied reconstruction like Warsaw's, but a slice of the romantically crumbling real thing. During the Communist era, Lublin was the stronghold of Polish Catholic resistance: its Katolicki Uniwersytet Lubelski was the country's only independent university, and the only church-run university in the Eastern Bloc. The presence of the church remains palpable, and today nuns and priests share Lublin's streets with an exuberant student population. The city houses five universities, and by night swarms of students infuse the city with youthful energy.

▐ TRANSPORTATION

Trains: Pl. Dworcowy 1 (☎ 94 36). To: **Częstochowa** (6hr., 4 per day, 37zł); **Gdańsk** (7hr., 3 per day, 49zł); **Kraków** (4hr., 3 per day, 43zł); **Poznań** (10hr., 4 per day, 48zł); **Toruń** (8hr., 3 per day, 47zł); **Warsaw** (3hr., 4 per day, 27zł); **Wrocław** (9½hr., 3 per day, 43zł); **Berlin, GER** (13hr., 1 per day, 153-226zł).

Buses: Tysiąclecia 4 (☎ 776 649, info 934). To: **Kraków** (6hr., 4 per day, 40zł); **Warsaw** (2¼hr., 43 per day, 26zł); **Wrocław** (8hr., 4 per day, 49zł). **Polski Express** (☎ 620 03 30; www.polskiexpress.pl) runs buses to: **Warsaw** (3hr., 8 per day, 34zł).

Public Transportation: Buy tickets for buses and trolleys at kiosks. 10min. ride 1.70zł, students 1zł; 30min. ride 1.90/1.40zł.

▇✚▐ ORIENTATION AND PRACTICAL INFORMATION

The city's main drag, **Krakowskie Przedmieście,** connects **Stare Miasto** (Old Town) in east Lublin to the **Katolicki Uniwersytet Lubelski** (KUL; Catholic University of Lublin) and **Uniwersytet Marii Curie-Skłodowskiej** (Marie Curie-Skłodowska University) in the west. It passes the urban oasis of the **Ogród Saski** (Saxon Garden) and becomes **al. Racławickie.** Take bus #5, 10, or 13 into town from the bus station. From the castle, **Zamkowa** runs toward Stare Miasto, becoming **Grodzka** and then **Bramowa** as it climbs. The street runs through the Rynek, emerges through **Brama Krakowska** (Kraków Gate), and intersects Krakowskie Przedmieście. From the train station, take trolley #150 or bus #13 to the city center.

Tourist Office: IT, Jezuicka 1/3 (☎ 532 44 12; itlublin@onet.pl), near the Kraków Gate. Sells **maps** (5zł) and has train and bus info. Open May-Aug. M-Sa 9am-6pm, Su 10am-3pm; Sept.-Apr. M-F 9am-5pm, Sa 10am-4pm, Su 10am-3pm. **Orbis,** Narutowicza 31/33 (☎ 532 22 56), books tours and transportation, provides travel insurance, and helps with visas. Open M-F 9am-6pm, Sa 9am-2pm. AmEx/MC/V.

Currency Exchange: Bank PKO S.A., Królewska 1 (☎ 532 10 16; fax 532 60 69) cashes **traveler's checks** for 1.5% commission and offers MC/V **cash advances.** Open M-F 8am-6pm, Sa 10am-2pm. **ATMs** are all over town.

English-Language Bookstore: Empik, Krakowskie Przedmieście 59 (☎/fax 534 32 86). Classics, contemporary favorites, CDs, and DVDs (25-40zł). Sells good maps and Metallica t-shirts. Open M-Sa 9:30am-8pm, Su 10:30am-6pm. AmEx/MC/V.

POLAND

POLAND

Lublin

ACCOMMODATIONS
Domu Rekolekcyjnym, **12**
PZMotel, **1**
Szkolne Schronisko
Młodzieżowe (HI), **2**

FOOD
Café Szeroka 28, **11**
Gaduka, **7**
Restauracja Ulice Miasta, **8**
Zadora, **9**

NIGHTLIFE
Hades, **6**
Irish Pub i Restauracja
U Szweca, **10**
Kino "Bajka," **3**
MC Klub, **4**
REJS, **5**

STARE MIASTO

ŚRÓDMIEŚCIE

Ogród Saski (Saxon Garden)

Cmentarz
Rzymsko-
katolicki

Lublin Castle and Museum
Holy Trinity Chapel
Park Podzamcze
Dworzec PKS
Gonet Internet Cafe
Dominican Church
Museum of Religious Art
Apothecary Museum
Grodzka Gate
Old Town Hall
Cathedral of St. John the Baptist and St. John the Evangelist
Historical Division of the Lublin Museum
Kraków Gate
Bernardine Church
New Town Hall
Church of the Holy Spirit
Tomb of the Unknown Soldier
Constitution of 3 May Monument
Obelisk
Teatr imienia Juliusza Osterwy
Empik
Enzo Internet
Katolicki Uniwersytet Lubelski
Orbis

TO (1km),
MAJDANEK (3km)

200 meters
200 yards

N
LG

Pharmacy: Apteka, Bramowa 2/8 (☎535 39 97). Window open 24hr. Store open daily 8am-8pm. AmEx/MC/V.

Hospital: Staszica 16 (☎532 39 35).

Telephones: Inside and outside the post office; inside bus and train stations. Purchase a phone card from the tellers inside the post office, or at most kiosks around town.

Internet: Gonet Internet Cafe, Grodzka 21 (☎532 81 18). 2zł per 30min., 3zł per hr. Open M-F and Su 10am-10pm, Sa 9am-10pm. **Enzo Internet,** Krakowskie Przedmieście 57/3 (☎534 75 25), upstairs. 2-4zł per hr. Open M-Sa 9am-10pm.

Post Office: Krakowskie Przedmieście 50 (☎/fax 532 20 71). Fax at window #3. **Poste Restante** at window #1. Open M-F 7am-9pm, Sa 7am-2pm. **Branch** at Grodzka 7. Open M-F 9am-4pm; June 15-Aug. also open Sa 10am-6pm. **Postal Code:** 20-950.

▐ ACCOMMODATIONS

▓ **Domu Rekolekcyjnym,** Podwale 15 (☎532 41 38). From the train station, take bus #1 to Lubartowska. Buzz the doorbell marked "director." Don't be surprised to see friendly nuns in full habit tending gardens and preparing breakfasts in this bright and inviting convent in the middle of Stare Miasto. Unusually comfortable pillows and excellent homemade jam. The nuns won't cramp your style, though unmarried co-eds can't share rooms. Breakfast 7zł. Flexible check-out. Quiet hours after 10pm. If arriving on Su, try to make arrangements in advance. Rooms usually 20-40zł. Cash only. ❶

Szkolne Schronisko Młodzieżowe, Długosza 6 (☎/fax 533 06 28), west of the center near the KUL. Standard dorm rooms offer few luxuries, and the exterior looks like a 1970s elementary school, but SSM remains a favorite of Polish university students, and is often full in summer. Guests gravitate to the front-lawn picnic tables and the comfortable lounge chairs of the TV lounge. Kitchen. Linen 6zł. Lockout 10am-5pm. Flexible curfew 10pm. 10-bed dorm 24zł, students 16zł; triples 84/69zł. Cash only. ❶

PZMotel, Prusa 8 (☎533 42 32; fax 747 84 93). From train station, take bus #1 to the bus station. The bright and well-kept interior is more than you might expect from a motel next to a gas station. In-house restaurant Fiesta on the ground floor. Squeaky-clean rooms with TVs. Breakfast included. Reception 24hr. Check-in 2pm. Check-out noon. Singles 120zł; doubles 160zł; 2-person apartment 350zł. MC/V. ❹

◖ FOOD

▓ **Café Szeroka 28,** Grodzka 21 (☎534 61 09; www.szeroka28.com), close to the Grodzka Gate. Named after the address where a charismatic leader of the Hasidic movement once lived, this homey restaurant and cafe hosts live *klezmer* music. Paying homage to Jewish history in Lublin, rooms display Jewish art and historic documents. After your meal, wander upstairs—follow the recordings of street sounds from before the war. Browse the "Book of the City," an original collection of pre-WWII testimonials and pictures. Entrees 15-45zł. Open M-Th and Su 1-10pm, F-Sa 1pm-late. MC/V. ❸

Gadułka, Narutowicza 32. Beneath a cloak of plastic garden furniture, hidden among travel agencies and shoe outlets, Gadułka has true cafe spirit. Brooding, razor-thin staff will finish their cigarettes before bringing you a silver tray of drinks and snacks. Excellent coffee and fruit tarts go for a third of the Krakoswkie Przedmieście rate (3zł), and massive cream puffs run a mere 2zł. Lublin students, not tourists, hang out here—so don't expect an English menu. Open M-Sa 9am-7pm, Su 10am-6pm. Cash only. ❶

Zadora, Rynek 8 (☎534 55 34). Squeeze through the rows of umbrellas to the end of the covered driveway. For those who love *naleśniki,* chocolate, or chocolate *naleśniki,* this hidden restaurant completes the experience with a chocolate-themed interior.

Smoked meats garnish Polish-style *naleśniki* (15zł), and the banana chocolate dessert (12zł) is lavishly dressed; if these don't appeal, have your own meal or dessert made to order (priced by topping). Open daily 11am-10pm. AmEx/MC/V. ❷

Restauracja Ulice Miasta, pl. Łokietka 3 (☎534 05 92; www.ulicemiasta.com.pl), in the shadow of the Historical Museum. Regional cuisine in Stare Miasto. Meat-heavy dishes such as "the gamekeepers' money bag" (cutlet with mushrooms; 23zł) and *forszmak* meat soup (9zł) dominate the menu. Open daily 10am-2am. AmEx/MC/V. ❸

◉ 🌿 SIGHTS AND FESTIVALS

The ochre facades of **Krakowskie Przedmieście** lead into medieval Stare Miasto. Pl. Litewski showcases an **obelisk** commemorating the 1569 union of Poland and Lithuania, a monument to Józef Piłsudski, a statue honoring the **Third of May Constitution** (Pomnik Konstytucji 3 Maja), and a **Tomb of the Unknown Soldier** (Płyta Grobu Nieznanego Żołnierza). The 1827 **New Town Hall** (Nowy Ratusz), the seat of Lublin's government, sits on pl. Łokietka, east of pl. Litewski. To the right begins Królewska, which runs down around the corner to the grand **Cathedral of St. John the Baptist and St. John the Evangelist** (Katedra Św. Jana Chrzciciele i Św. Jana Ewangelisty). Inside the church, a crypt holds open coffins of 18th-century religious figures, and near the building's exit hangs a full-size replica of the Shroud of Turin, a 2003 gift from the late pope John Paul II. (Open daily 10am-4pm. Crypt 4zł.) Krakowskie Przedmieście runs through pl. Łokietka to the fortified **Kraków Gate,** which houses the **Historical Division of the Lublin Museum** (Muzeum Historii Miasta Lublina), pl. Łokietka 3. Exhibits highlight town history during WWII and from 1585 to present. On the top floor of the display, windows offer views of the city. (With your back to pl. Łokietka, enter through the side door on the right. ☎532 60 01. Open W-Sa 9am-4pm, Su 9am-5pm. 3.50zł, students 2.50zł.)

Across the gate, Bramowa leads to the Rynek (market square) and the nearby Renaissance houses. For an unusual treat, stop in the **Apothecary Museum** (Muzeum Zakładu Historii Farmacji), Grodzka 5a, for a collection of medical artifacts seasoned with the smell of drying herbs. (☎747 64 16. Open Tu-F 11am-4pm. Free.) In the Rynek's center stands the 18th-century **Old Town Hall** (Stary Ratusz). A walk along Grodzka leads through the 15th-century **Grodzka Gate** to Zamkowa, which runs to **Lublin Castle** (Zamek Lubelski). Most of the structure was built in the 14th century by King Kazimierz Wielki. The castle retains a sinister air: during WWII, it functioned as a Gestapo jail and the region's Nazi headquarters. Inside, the permanent collection at the **Lublin Museum** (Muzeum Lubelskie) includes wood-carved folk art of the Lublin region, artifacts from nearby archaeological digs, and an exhausting collection of armaments and military paintings. Temporary exhibits showcase contemporary Polish art. The Lublin Museum houses the famed **Devil's Pawprint** (see sidebar, p. 465). The Russo-Byzantine frescoes in the attached **Holy Trinity Chapel** are truly stunning and the only ones of their kind in Poland. The panels, with gold figures depicting various biblical scenes against a midnight-blue background, were completed in 1418. (☎532 50 01, ext. 35. Museum open W-F 9am-4pm, Sa 10am-5pm, Su 9am-5pm. 6.50zł, students 4.50zł. Chapel open M-Sa 9am-3:30pm, Su 9am-4:30pm. 6.50zł, students 4.50zł. Devil's Paw and Tribunal Table 2zł. Polish tours of the museum and chapel 45zł each, 55zł combined.)

The ▓**Archdiocesan Museum of Sacred Art** (Muzeum Archidiecezjalne Sztuki Sakralnej) occupies the 17th-century **Trinitarska Tower** beside the cathedral. Medieval sacred music wafts through the rafters of this upward-winding museum as you climb past statues of saints, cherubs, and roosters. A side gallery halfway up the tower holds a 16th-century Madonna. Find your true reward 320 stairs later: a panoramic view of Lublin from the top of the tower. (☎444 74 50. Open Mar. 25-Nov. 15 daily 10am-5pm. 5zł, students 3zł.)

After dusk, the flickering votive candles of **Cmentarz Rzymskokatolicki,** Lublin's oldest cemetery, make for a stirring experience. Poles have a well-established Sunday tradition of visiting the graves of their deceased loved ones in addition to attending mass. Benches accompany most gravestones from the last 25 years, and a generous sprinkling of fresh flowers and offerings reveals just how frequently these sites enjoy visits. The mossy, sunken headstones of the older sections are engraved in Cyrillic. (Open daily dawn-dusk. Free.)

Festivals abound in Lublin. June brings a month-long festival called **Uncover Lublin: Lublin Days** (Odkryjmy Lublin: Dni Lublin). The city hosts musical performances and art exhibits. Schedules are available in English in the tourist office. For more info visit **Nowy Ratusz,** pl. Łokietka 1 (☎444 55 55; www.ym.lublin.pl), which displays event listings on a poster just inside the entrance.

▣ NIGHTLIFE

Lublin's ample nightlife concentrates in several distinct areas. Boisterous students fill spots clustered near **Radziszewskiego** and along less-traveled streets such as **Peowiaków,** while an older crowd keeps to the bars of **Grodzka** in Stare Miasto. The two scenes mingle on **Krakowskie Przedmieście.** Travelers can catch independent films and even the odd Hollywood blockbuster at **Kino "Bajka,"** Radziszewskiego 8. (☎533 88 72. 15zł, students 13zł.) The **Teatr Imienia Juliusza Osterwy,** Narutowicza 17, puts on classic shows. (☎ 532 42 44. Ticket window open Tu-Sa noon-7pm, Su 4-7pm. Most shows start at 7pm. 21-28zł, students 13-18zł.)

> **MC Klub,** MC Skłodowskiej 5 (☎743 65 16; www.mck-lub.pl), beneath the city philharmonium. If a night of drinking doesn't make your head spin, the winding staircases of MC Klub certainly will. Aiming to please the hordes of students who pack the place from wall to glow-in-the-dark wall on weekends, DJs spin mainstream dance music. Drinks 5-10zł. Cover Tu-Th and Su 5zł, F-Sa 10zł. Open Tu-Su 6pm-3am. Cash only.

> **Hades,** Peowiaków 12 (☎532 56 41; www.hades-lublin.pl), in the basement of the Centrum Kultury. One of the hottest nightspots in Lublin, Hades draws a stylish crowd to pub and club in crypt-like rooms and on a graffitied dance floor. The DJ spins techno, house, and

even Polish pop. Admission enters you in a nightly raffle for large bottles of vodka. Beer 5zł. Cover Th men 8zł, women 4zł; F men 10zł, women 8zł; Sa men 12zł, women 10zł. Open Th-Sa 7pm-late. AmEx/MC/V.

REJS, Krakowskie Przedmieście 55 (☎442 10 72), named after the Polish film of the same name. Art students fill the nooks of an intimate cellar. Also serves Greek food: the *gyro* (9zł) is popular. *Żywiec* 4.50zł. Open M-F 11am-midnight, Sa-Su noon-midnight.

Irish Pub i Restauracja U Szweca, Grodzka 18 (☎532 82 84). Still lively when the other Stare Miasto beer gardens are closing up for the night. The decor of this "Irish Pub" may not be very authentic, but its commitment to heavy drinking is. Conveniently, Lublin's best make-out spot is a brief stumble across the street. *Żywiec* 5zł. Beamish Stout 10zł. Open M-Th and Su noon-midnight, F-Sa noon-1am. MC/V.

▶ DAYTRIPS FROM LUBLIN

MAJDANEK

Take bus #28 from the train station, trolley #153 or 156 from al. Racławickie, or trolley #156 from Królewska. Or, walk the 4km from Lublin on Królewska, which becomes Wyszyńskiego, Zamojska, Fabryczna, and ultimately the Droga Męczenników Majdanka (Road of the Martyrs of Majdanek; 30min.). ☎744 26 48; www.majdanek.pl. Open Tu-Su May-Sept. 8am-6pm; Oct.-Nov. and Mar.-Apr. 8am-3pm. Free. Children under 14 not permitted. Tours in Polish 60zł; in English, German, and Russian 100zł per group. Detailed English guide (7zł) available at the ticket office; maps free.

During WWII, the Nazis used Lublin as their eastern base and built Europe's second-largest concentration camp in the suburb of Majdanek. About 235,000 died here. Many Warsaw Ghetto residents and Polish political prisoners were sent to Majdanek, which had the highest death rate of any concentration camp. Living conditions were extraordinarily harsh: fed bread made with sawdust, more prisoners died from malnutrition and starvation than from outright execution. **Majdanek State Museum** (Państwowe Muzeum Na Majdanku) was founded in 1944 after the Soviet liberation of Lublin. Since the Nazis didn't have time to destroy the camp in their retreat, the original structures stand untouched, including gas chambers, the crematorium, prisoners' barracks, watchtowers, guardhouses, and the electrified barbed-wire perimeter. On November 3, the camp holds a memorial service commemorating the day in 1943 when over 18,400 Jews were executed as part of a two-day plan to kill about 40,000 in operation "Erntefest" (Harvest Festival); it was the largest single mass execution of the Holocaust.

A visit to Majdanek begins in the visitors' center, where a 25min. documentary includes footage taken by the camp's liberators. (Last showing 2:30pm. 3zł. Available in English. Min. 5 people. If you have fewer than 5 people, you can pay the difference.) The guided tour is worthwhile, but a comprehensive "sightseeing path" also leads through the camp; walking through the camp takes a couple of hours. The path begins with the gas chambers; signs explain Nazi methods of experimentation and extermination. Guardhouses #43-45 contain historical exhibitions, including prisoners' clothes, instruments of torture, and samples of human hair and fabric. An astounding 730kg of prisoners' hair was exported to Germany and made into fabric. Exhibits of prisoners' artwork and poetry, confiscated religious articles, and photographs of prisoners and camp officials document daily life. Majdanek had the highest percentage of children of any concentration camp, and the collection of toys taken from the children's camp is a sobering sight. At the end of the main path, the intact crematorium ovens loom next to the concrete dome of the mausoleum, a giant open-air urn with a massive mound of ash and human bone. The chilling inscription reads, "Let our fate be a warning for you."

KAZIMIERZ DOLNY

Take the PKS bus from the Lublin bus station to Kazimierz Dolny (1½hr., 10 per day, 9.50zł). The last bus back to Lublin leaves Kazimierz around 7pm.

In summer, schoolchildren swarm Kazimierz Dolny's attractive Rynek to devour bread made in the shape of roosters, a local specialty. Tourists visit galleries and dine in garden-side restaurants. Of interest to the intrepid trekker, a network of hiking trails spreads into the surrounding hills and provides unparalleled views of the Wisła valley. Visit the **tourist office, PTTK,** Rynek 27, for info and **biking** and **trail maps. (☎**881 00 46; www.kazimierz-dolny.pl. Maps 5zł. Open May-Oct. 14 M-F 8am-5:30pm, Sa-Su 10am-5:30pm; Oct. 15-Apr. M-F 8am-4pm, Sa-Su 10am-2:30pm.) Uphill from the Rynek off Zamkowa, the ruined *zamek* (castle) and the restored *baszta* (watchtower) mark the start of two hiking routes (blue and red) and offer panoramas of the town and river. Both the castle and the tower were built by Kazimierz the Great in the 14th century, but the castle was destroyed by the Swedes in the 1700s. (Open May-Sept. daily 10am-5pm; Oct.-Apr. Tu-Su 10am-3pm. Admission to both 2.20zł, students 1.60zł.) To the right as you approach the castle on Zamkowa, the top of **Góra Krzyzowa** (Mountain of Crosses) is a scenic picnic spot. (Open daily 10am-5pm. 1zł.) Across from PTTK in the Rynek, **Parish Church** houses Poland's oldest organ, a wooden creation from 1620 that is still played on holidays. The **Jewish Cemetery,** destroyed when the Nazis paved the courtyard of their local headquarters with its tombstones, was reclaimed in 1984 when the powerful "Wailing Wall" *(Ściama Płaczu)* was fashioned from 600 of the original tombstones. A symbolic crack is designed into the wall. (2km from the Rynek. Walk southeast on Senatorska and turn right on Czerniawy. Free.)

The **folk music festival** that takes over Kazimierz in the last week of June is the largest such gathering in Poland. In mid-summer, Kazimierz hosts the **Lato Filmów film festival** (www.latofilmow.pl). Both the boat bars along the Wisła and the restaurants in town draw patrons with their views of the river. Situated next to a monastery and near this choice view, **Pod Wietrzną Górą ❷,** Krakowska 1, serves a winning asparagus soup (7zł), a sausage platter (15zł), and other traditional Polish cuisine. (☎881 06 40. Entrees 15-28zł. Open daily 9am-late. MC/V.) **Saloniku Restauracyjnym ❷,** Nadrzeczna 6, serves full meals, but mostly draws business with its layered cakes (6zł per piece) and famous bread roosters (5zł). The largest bakery in town, Saloniku is often packed. (☎881 06 43. Open daily 9am-10pm. Cash only.)

KARPATY (THE CARPATHIANS)

Once home to only the reclusive and culturally distinct Górale (Highlander*s*), the Carpathians now lure millions every year to superb hiking and skiing trails. Zakopane, the heart of the region, provides easy access to excellent trails.

ZAKOPANE ☎(0)18

Zakopane (zah-ko-PAH-neh; pop. 28,000) is set in a valley surrounded by jagged peaks and alpine meadows. This outdoor adventure mecca swells to over 100,000 during the high season (late June to Sept. and Dec.-Feb.), but retains mountain village charm with its log cabins, sweeping scenery, and native Highlander culture.

▐ TRANSPORTATION

Trains: Chramcówki 35 (☎201 45 04). To: **Częstochowa** (4hr., 3 per day, 24-30zł); **Kraków** (3-4hr., 19 per day, 18-20zł); **Poznań** (11hr., 3 per day, 50-55zł); **Warsaw** (8hr., 8 per day, 46-80zł).

Buses: Kościuszki 25 (☎201 46 03). To: **Bielsko-Biała** (3½hr., 5 per day, 16zł); **Kraków** (2-2½hr., 28 per day, 11zł); **Warsaw** (8½hr., 2 per day, 53zł). An **express bus** runs to **Kraków** (2hr., 10 per day, 11zł); buses leave from the "express" stop on Kościuszki, 50m toward Krupówki from the bus station.

Taxis: Interradio Taxi ☎96 21. **Radio Taxi** ☎919. **Zielone Taxi** ☎96 62.

Bike Rental: Villa Anna, Nowotarska 21 (☎201 28 20). Bikes 10zł per hr., 50zł per day. Cash only. **Rental Bikes and Scooters,** Piłsudskiego, just over the bridge. Bikes 10zł per hr., 50zł per day; scooters 35zł per hr., 135zł per day. AmEx/MC/V.

■ ◪ ORIENTATION AND PRACTICAL INFORMATION

The main drag in town is **Krupówki,** where you'll find most of the city's shopping, eating, and nighttime activity. The **bus station** is at the intersection of **Kościuszki** and **Jagiellońska** and faces the **train station**. The town center is 15min. down Kościuszki, which intersects Krupówki. The **Tatras** spread around Zakopane.

Tourist Offices: Centrum Informacji Turystycznej (CIT), Kościuszki 17 (☎201 22 11). Provides regional info on topics from dining to hiking. Sells **maps** (5-9zł) and **guides** (11-28zł), helps book accommodations, and books rafting trips on the Dunajec (70-80zł). Open daily July-Sept. 8am-8pm; Oct.-June 9am-6pm. **Tourist Agency Redykołka,** Kościeliska 1 (☎201 32 53; www.tatratours.pl). Arranges private rooms for 10% commission, runs tours (4hr., 320zł per group) around Zakopane, and organizes out-of-town excursions. Open M-F 9am-5pm, Sa 9am-1pm.

Currency Exchange: Bank PKO SA, Krupówki 71 (☎201 40 48), cashes **traveler's checks** for 1.5% commission (10zł min.) and gives AmEx/MC/V **cash advances.** Open M-F 8am-4pm, Sa 8am-2pm. **Bank BPH,** Krupówki 19 (☎132 13 21), offers **Western Union** services. **Kantory** and **ATMs** line Krupówki.

Luggage Storage: In a room at the train station. 4zł per day, plus 0.5zł per 50zł declared value. In lockers at the train station. Small 4zł per day, large 8zł per day. Open daily 7am-1pm and 1:30-9pm. At the bus station. 3zł per day. Open daily 8am-7pm.

Pharmacy: Apteka Zdrowie, Kościuszki 10 (☎201 38 30). Open M-Sa 8am-8pm, Sa 9am-8pm, Su 10am-6pm. AmEx/MC/V.

Medical Services: Ambulance ☎992. **Mountain Rescue Service,** Piłsudskiego 63a (☎206 34 44). **Samodzielny Publiczny Zakład Opieki Zdrowotnej** (Independent Public Enterprise of Healthcare), Kamieniec 10 (☎201 44 09).

Telephones: Telekomunikacja Polska, Zaruskiego 1. Phones outside. Open 24hr.

Internet: Widmo Internet Cafe, Gen. Galicy 8 (☎206 43 77). 3zł per 30min., 4.50zł per hr. Open M-F 7:30am-midnight, Sa-Su 9am-midnight. **Cafe Internet "Orion,"** Krupówki 30. 4zł per hr. Open daily 9am-midnight.

Post Office: Krupówki 20 (☎206 38 58). **Poste Restante** at *kasa* #5. Open M-F 7am-8pm, Sa 8am-2pm, Su 10am-noon. **Postal Code:** 34-500.

▟ ACCOMMODATIONS

Lodgings in Zakopane are not difficult to find, and reservations are generally unnecessary. While peak season (June-Sept. and Dec.-Feb.) sees an influx of tourists and a steep hike in prices, more **private rooms** (35-70zł) become available. Locals offering rooms swarm outside the bus and train stations. You can also easily find homes with rooms for rent (look for *noclegi* or *pokój* signs). Hikers and skiers also stay in *chaty* (mountainside cabins), but these fill quickly, so call two to three weeks ahead during high season.

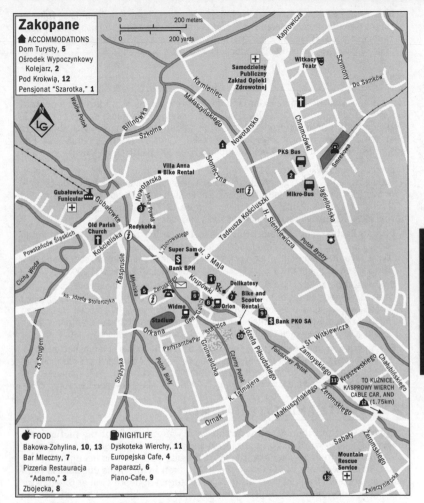

Zakopane

⛰ ACCOMMODATIONS
Dom Turysty, **5**
Ośrodek Wypoczynkowy
Kolejarz, **2**
Pod Krokwią, **12**
Pensjonat "Szarotka," **1**

0   200 meters
0   200 yards

Samodzielny
Publiczny
Zakład Opieki
Zdrowotnej

Witkacy
Teatr

Do Samków

PKS Bus

CIT ⓘ   Mikro-Bus

Villa Anna
■ Bike Rental

Gubałówka
Funicular

Old Parish
Church

Redykołka

Super Sam

Bank BPH

Delikatesy

Bike and
Scooter
Rental

Widmo   Orion

Stadium

Bank PKO SA

TO KUŹNICE,
KASPROWY WIERCH
CABLE CAR, AND
(1.75km)

Mountain
Rescue
Service

🍴 FOOD
Bakowa-Zohylina, **10, 13**
Bar Mleczny, **7**
Pizzeria Restauracja
"Adamo," **3**
Zbojecka, **8**

🍸 NIGHTLIFE
Dyskoteka Wierchy, **11**
Europejska Cafe, **4**
Paparazzi, **6**
Piano-Cafe, **9**

POLAND

▨ **Pensjonat "Szarotka,"** Notowarska 45G (☎201 36 18; www.szarotka.pl). This rugged, traditional Zakopane lodge has small, clean rooms and fresh new bathrooms. Only 10min. walk from the center. English spoken. Linen 5zł. Reserve ahead. 2- to 3- bed dorms with bath and 4- to 8-bed dorms with sink both 40zł. Cash only. ❷

Ośrodek Wypoczynkowy Kolejarz, Kościuszki 23 (☎201 54 68). Not an attractive building, but the prices can't be beat and the location, adjacent to the train and bus stations, is perfect for late-night arrivals or early morning departures. Thrill seekers will enjoy the retro elevator. Small 2- and 3-bed dorms. Check-in 2pm. Check-out noon. Dorms with sink 25zł, with bath 33zł. Cash only. ❶

Camping Pod Krokwią, Żeromskiego (☎201 22 56; www.mati.com.pl/camp), across from the ski jump in Kuźnice. Views of the Tatras, well-kept grounds, friendly staff, and proximity to the hiking trails are perfect for outdoors fanatics. Reception 24hr. Check-out noon. Open July-Aug. 7-10zł per tent; campers 20zł; rooms 35-40zł; 4- to 6-person apartments with kitchen and TV 140-200zł. MC/V. ❶

Dom Turysty PTTK, Zaruskiego 5 (☎206 32 07). Saggy mattresses and noisy hallways might mar your beauty sleep, but a central location makes this a good deal. Popular with tour groups. Check-in 2pm. Check-out noon. Dorms 22-35zł; singles with bath 55-70zł; doubles with sink 60-80zł, with bath 110-140zł. Cash only. ❷

🄵 FOOD

Restaurants run the gamut from familiar Western chains to traditional mountain eateries. Highlanders sell the local specialty, *oscypek* (smoked sheep cheese; 1-18zł), carved in delightful patterns. If your palate doesn't agree with the warm beer, try the local favorite, *herbata ceperska* (25mL vodka with 50mL tea). For groceries, check out **Super Sam,** Kościuszki 3. (☎200 19 10. Open 24hr.)

Zbojecka, Krupówki 28 (☎201 38 54). Eat by candlelight on rough-hewn wood tables, accompanied by live regional music. Waiters dress in traditional Highlander costume, making for an enjoyably kitschy experience. Fresh bread and homemade lard spread accompany meals. Partial English menu. Entrees 12-22zł. 2zł per person surcharge for live music. Open daily 10am-midnight. Cash only. ❸

Pizzeria Restauracja "Adamo," Nowotarska 10d (☎201 52 90). Serves both Polish dishes and pizza in a burly lodge seemingly carved from a single giant block of wood. *Danie dnia* (daily special; 11am-3pm; 14-17zł) includes soup, entree, coffee, and dessert. Pizza 8-22zł. Entrees 7-31zł. Open daily 11am-midnight. AmEx/MC/V. ❷

Bakowa-Zohylina, Piłsudskiego 28a (☎206 63 16). Serves traditional dishes like goulash (17zł) and the region's favorite fish, *pstrąg* (trout; 25zł). Animal pelts, an open hearth, and costumed waiters complete the mountain lodge spectacle. The garden offers a view of Krokiew Mountain. Additional locations on Strążyska and farther down Piłsudskiego. English menu. Entrees 15-28zł. Open daily noon-midnight. MC/V. ❹

Bar Mleczny, Weteranów Wojny 2 (☎206 62 57), off Krupówki. The unaffected atmosphere of this tiny milk bar matches its rustic cooking. For a true taste of Polish cuisine, try the *pierogi ruskie* (potato-and-cheese dumplings; 5zł) or the *omlet* (pancake with berries and whipped cream; 6zł). Entrees 3-7zł. Open daily 9am-7pm. Cash only. ❶

🄶🄹 SIGHTS AND ENTERTAINMENT

Zakopane is primarily a gateway to the Tatras Mountains, but the picturesque town itself is also worth visiting. Architect and artist **Jan Witkiewicz** designed seven of the houses along Kościeliska; the most famous of these was occupied by the writer **Stanisław Ignacy Witkiewicz** in the 1930s. Stop by the **Tytus Chałubiński Tatra Museum** (Muzeum Tatrzańskie), Krupówki 10, for an in-depth look at the geography and ecology of the Tatras. The museum displays traditional Highlander home interiors, antique objects, and regional costumes. (☎201 52 05. Limited English info. Open W-Sa 9am-5pm, Su 9am-3pm. 4.50zł, students 3.50zł. Su free.)

In the evening, the cafes of **Krupówki** fill with locals and tourists enjoying ice cream or chatting over tea. At **Piano-Cafe,** Krupówki 63, you can burrow into a corner couch or sit on a swing chair, which will certainly enhance the effect of your drinks. (Tea 3zł. 0.5L *Żywiec* 4.50zł. Open daily 3pm-midnight. Cash only.) Or, join the sharp young crowd at **Paparazzi,** Gen. Galicy 8, a popular pub where stylish black-and-white photos crowd the walls. (☎206 32 51. Open M-F 4pm-1am, Sa noon-2am. Cash only.) To experience Polish hits from the 60s, check out the retrochic **Europejska Cafe,** Krupówki 37, where a slightly older crowd unwinds over a frosty beer on weekdays and rocks out on weekends. (☎201 22 00. Beer 5zł. Desserts 4-6zł. Open daily 8am-11pm; later during high season. MC/V.) To dance to Europop with a younger crowd, try the **Dyskoteka Wierchy,** Małkoszyńskiego 1, on the corner of Krupówki. (18+. Cover 10zł. Open F-Sa 9am-3am. Cash only.)

Air-Taxi (☎060 228 75 28; fax 201 37 95) arranges **tandem paragliding;** jump from either **Nosal Mountain** (10-20min.; 150zł) or **Kasprowy Wierch** (30min.-3hr.; 300zł). Equally adventurous is the 60m bungee-jumping crane (next to **Gubałówka** funicular; 85zł per jump; open daily noon-7pm). At the entrance to Onbatówka, behind Nowotarska, step into a daily **open-air market** where locals sell tantalizing *oscypek* (sheep cheese). From mid- to late August, Zakopane resounds with the **International Festival of Highlander Folklore** (Międzynardowy Festival Folkloro ziem Górskich). Highland groups from around the world perform along Krupówki.

🔋 HIKING

Magnificent **Tatra National Park** (Tatrzański Park Narodowy; 5zł, students 2.50zł) is Zakopane's main attraction. Before heading out, consult a good map, such as the **Tatrzański Park Narodowy: Mapa Turystyczna** (7zł), and choose trails as gentle or as rigorous as you like. The best—and certainly the most popular—place to begin many of the challenging and scenic hikes is **Kuźnice.** Go uphill on **Krupówki** to Zamoyskiego; continue as it becomes Chałubińskiego and then Przewodników Tatrzańskich; the trailheads are 1 hr. from Zakopane center. You can also reach Kuźnice by *mikrobus* (2zł) from in front of the bus station. From Kuźnice, start one of the hikes listed below, or try the 1987m **Kasprowy Wierch cable car,** which leads to the amazing views atop Kasprowy Mountain, where you can wander over the border to the Slovak Republic. (Open July-Aug. 7am-7pm; June and Sept. 7:30am-6pm; Oct. 7:30am-3pm. Round-trip 29zł, students 19zł; up 19/14zł, down 15/10zł.) Alternatively, instead of going to Kuźnice, you can take the funicular to **Gubałówka** from Zakopane (1120m, located off Kościeliska. Open daily July-Aug. 8am-10pm; Apr.-June and Sept. 8:30am-7:20pm; Jan.-Mar. 7:30am-9pm; Oct.-Dec. 15 8:30am-6pm; Dec. 15-31 7:30am-10pm. Round-trip 14zł; up 8zł.)

📷**VALLEY OF THE FIVE POLISH TARNS.** Called the Dolina Pięciu Stawów Polskich, this hike is perfect if you have time for only one trail. It covers all the major highlights of the Tatras. An intense full-day hike takes you past five lakes between sharp peaks: Wielki (great), Czarny (black), Przedni (front), Zadni (rear), and Mały (small). Start this beautiful and rewarding hike at **Kuźnice** and follow the yellow trail through **Dolina Jaworzynka** (Jaworzynka Valley) until you reach the steep blue trail, which leads to **Hala Gasienicowa** (2½hr.) and the nearby mountain hut **Schronisko Murowaniec** (☎201 26 33; dorms 28-34zł). From the mountain shelter, the trail continues to **Czarny Staw,** a tranquil lake whose glassy surface reflects the tallest peaks of the Tatras. Continue on the blue trail to **Zawrat Peak,** where you'll have to use mountain chains and natural holds. Once you cross Zawrat, breathtaking views of the valley and its lakes await, along with **Schronisko Dolina Pięciu Stawów** (4hr.), where you can refuel or spend the night. (☎207 76 07. Linen 5zł. Beds 21-25zł.) Those ready to continue can take the blue trail (2hr.) to **Morskie Oko** and the popular 📷**PTTK Mountain Shelter,** which rests on its shores. (☎207 76 09. Linen 7zł. Beds with sheets 44zł; space on floor 34zł. Low season 34/24zł.) From here you can take a microbus down, hike down, or hike onward. A **shorter version** of the hike (4-6hr.) begins at **Palenica Białczań ska** (take bus from Zakopane station). Head toward Morskie Oko, as described above. The green trail breaks off to the right, leads past the crashing **Mickiewicza Waterfalls,** and ends on a small bridge near the Schronisko Dolina Pięciu Stawów, merging into the blue trail. Follow the blue trail to the majestic Morskie Oko.

SEA EYE (MORSKIE OKO). Glacial **Morskie Oko** Lake, surrounded by dramatic peaks, dazzles herds of tourists each summer. Take a bus from the PKS station to Palenica Białczańska (45min., 11 per day, 4zł) or take a private microbus from across the street (30min., 5zł). A 9km paved road leads to the lake, which is fabled to connect to the Baltic Sea. Alternatively, at Schronisko Dolina Roztoki (1¾hr. up road from Palenica Białczańska), take the green trail to the blue trail for an astounding view of Morskie Oko (1406m, 4hr.). From Morskie Oko, hike the red trail to reach the highest mountain lake, **Czarny Staw pod Rysami** (30min.).

GIEWONT. This popular trail traverses Giewont, a mountain whose silhouette resembles a man lying down. Local legend holds that the mountain is a sleeping prince who will awaken and defend the town of Zakopane if it is in danger. To remind tourists and locals of the Highlanders' Christian faith, a local priest, Kazimierz Kaszelewski, placed an enormous iron cross on the peak in 1901. The moderately difficult blue trail (7km, 3hr.) leads to the summit from **Kuźnice**. The path becomes much rockier toward **Hala Kondratowa**, where a variety of fast-food restaurants and local stalls awaits weary travelers. The trail wraps around the ridge of Giewont's peak and leads to the tricky final ascent; here, chains and footholds come to your aid. The summit offers a striking view of Zakopane and the icy peaks of the Tatras. From the peak, take the yellow trail to Kondracka Kopa to reach the **Red Peaks** (45min.), or return to Zakopane on the red trail to **Dolina Strążyska**. For a **shorter** and steeper **ascent,** take the red trail up from Dolina Strążyska (2-3hr.).

STRĄŻYSKA VALLEY (DOLINA STRĄŻYSKA). This trail from Zakopane is pleasant and easy to navigate. Walk down Koscieliska and head left on Kasprusie, which becomes Strążyska, to the entrance to the **Tatras National Park** (30-45min.). Follow the lush, forested path along streams until it ends at the dramatic **Siklawica waterfall.** Take the path to your right to **Mt. Sarnia Skala**. The peak offers unspoiled views of Zakopane and Mt. Giewont. The trail takes 4-5hr.

RED PEAKS (CZERWONE WIERCHY). This less rocky range is full of mild dips and ascents, during which the trail crisscrosses the Polish-Slovak border. Three of the **Red Peaks** that follow Kasprowy Wierch have trails that allow tired hikers to return to Zakopane, while the trail along the last peak, **Ciemniak,** continues to **Schronisko na Hali Ornak.** (3hr. ☎207 05 20. Beds 27-35zł. Cash only.) Take a right on the red trail at the top of Kasprowy Wierch. The trail passes through **Kościeliska Valley.** For a direct descent, follow the red trail to its end at **Kiry** (3hr.). The heights of the ridge are known as "Red Peaks" because native plants blossom throughout the area each autumn, coloring the rocks.

▶ DAYTRIP FROM ZAKOPANE

DUNAJEC GORGE

Take a microbus to Kąty (across from the bus station, 1-1½hr., 14zł). It is best to experience the rafting trip by scheduling an outing through a tourist agency. Many packages include trips to Dunajec Castle. Rafting tickets at Dunajec Gorge 40zł plus 4zł entrance fee. English tour guides usually available.

Both residents and tourists raft along the Dunajec in **Pieniński National Park** (☎262 97 21). The tranquil ride traces the steep peaks and rolling forests dividing Poland from Slovakia. To complement the scenery, guides sport traditional Highlander garb. Travelers shouldn't expect death-defying rafting—the smooth ride is virtually splashless. The waters afford unparalleled views of **Trzy Korony** (Three Crowns Peak) and **Dunajec Castle.** Unaccompanied rafting is not permitted. Visits to the 13th-century castle are best arranged through tourist agencies in Zakopane.

The end of the 2 hr. excursion deposits you in the town of Szczawnica. While Szczawnica is armed with souvenir stands and crowded bars, those seeking to savor the outdoors can rent bikes to tour the city or take leisurely rides near the river. **Rent bikes** at Pienińska 6, a left turn from the raft drop-off point. (☎262 12 46. 4zł per hr., 20zł per day. Open daily 7am-9pm.) Riding along the Polish riverside, you cross into Slovakia. Alternatively, walkers can follow the pathway that runs along the river for splendid views of the hills by the border. Those wishing to wander off the path can take the chair lift (9am-7.30pm, 10zł) and explore mountain paths with views of Szczawnica.

CZĘSTOCHOWA   ☎ (0)34

In 1382, a haggard traveler arrived in Częstochowa (chen-sto-HO-va) weary from her tribulations and scarred from a scuffle with Hussite thieves. The visitor, a Byzantine icon painting in the prime of her life at only 800 years old, found refuge atop the hill of Jasna Góra and entrusted herself to the care of the monks living there. Since she moved in, the city has been defined by little other than her presence; even the train station has a chapel. As the most sacred of Polish icons, she draws millions of Catholic pilgrims every year. The curious and the adoring flock to the city to catch a glimpse of her, the Black Madonna.

🖭🖪 **TRANSPORTATION AND PRACTICAL INFORMATION. Trains** run from **Częstochowa Główna,** Piłsudskiego 38 (☎366 47 89; fax 366 47 63) to: **Gdynia** (7¼-9½hr., 6 per day, 55zł); **Kraków** (2-2½hr., 6 per day, 17-28zł); **Łódź** (2hr., 8 per day, 31zł); **Poznań** (6hr., 3 per day, 42zł); **Warsaw** (3hr., 10 per day, 38zł); **Wrocław** (3-4hr., 5 per day, 32zł); and **Zakopane** (7hr., 3 per day, 40zł). **Buses** go from **PKS,** Wolności 45/49 (☎379 11 49), left on Wolności from the train station, to **Kraków** (3-3½hr., 18 per day, 20-25zł); **Łódź** (3hr., 12 per day, 20-29zł); **Lublin** (7hr., 4 per day, 50zł); **Warsaw** (3½-5hr., 11 per day, 30-35zł); **Wrocław** (4hr., 10 per day, 25-29zł); and **Zakopane** (5hr., 6 per day, 30-40zł). **Tram** and **bus** stops on al. Najświętszej Marii Panny (NMP) appear on bus schedules as Aleja I, II, and III. (Tickets 2zł per person and per backpack; students 1zł. Day pass 7zł, students 3.50zł.) Call **Auto Radio** (☎96 29) or **Carex** (☎96 26) for a **taxi.** (4zł base, 1.28zł per km.)

The **train** and **bus** stations lie across the post office parking lot from each other and are near the town center between al. Wolności and Piłsudskiego. **Al. NMP** links them to **Jasna Góra,** whose spire is visible throughout town. From either station, go right on Wolności to get to al. NMP. Go left to reach Jasna Góra. The **tourist office, MCI,** al. NMP 65, provides **free maps.** (☎368 22 50; www.czestochowa.um.pl. Open M-Sa 9am-5pm.) **Bank Pekao S.A.,** M. Kopernika 17/19, cashes **traveler's checks** for 1% commission (10zł min.), gives MC/V **cash advances,** and has a 24hr. **ATM** outside. (☎365 50 60. Open M-F 8am-6pm, Sa 10am-2pm.) **Punkt Medyczny Jasna Góra,** at the monastery, can provide medical assistance. (☎377 72 45. Open daily Apr.-Oct. 6am-7:30pm; Nov.-Mar. 8am-4pm.) Other services include: **ambulance** (☎999); **Apteka,** al. NMP 17 (☎368 27 70), in the Merkury building, a **24hr. pharmacy;** and the **post office,** Orzechowskiego 7, between the bus and train stations (☎324 29 59; **Poste Restante** at kasa 9; open M-F 7am-9pm, Sa 8am-8pm). **Postal Code:** 42-200.

🏠🗋 **ACCOMMODATIONS AND FOOD.** Reservations are recommended year-round, but are a must for May and August, when pilgrims descend en masse. Retreat houses are reliable, and smaller pensions can be found through the tourist office. Many pilgrims use as a home base the quiet, immaculate rooms at **Dom Pielgrzyma im. Jana Pawła II** (The Pilgrim's House) ❶, Wyszyńskiego 1. From the train or bus station, take any bus to the end of al. NMP and cross Jasna Góra. Dom Pielgrzyma is at the exact opposite side of the monastery from al. NMP, near the monastery gates. (☎377 75 64. Flexible check-in 3-10pm. Check-out 9am. Flexible curfew 10pm. Quiet hours 10pm-5:30am. Dorms 23zł; singles 70zł; doubles 100-120zł; triples 105-126zł. Cash only.) **Dom Rekolekcyjno-Formacyjny** ❶, Mąkoszy 1, is a brand-new retreat house with colorful, clean rooms. From the train or bus station, take bus #26 to the end of al. NMP and continue on W. Starucha for two blocks to the end of a short dirt road, Mąkoszy. (☎366 48 39. Dorms 20-40zł. Cash only.)

Częstochowa's restaurants and ice cream stands keep both pilgrims and locals well fed. Forget kebabs—the local street food of choice is french fries (*frytki*), which are best at the stands along **Piłsudskiego.** (0.50-0.75zł per 100g. Stands open roughly 8am-9pm.) The gigantic **Elea SuperMarket,** in the red building across from the bus station, is a good place to stock up on supplies. (Open M-F 8am-9pm, Sa 8am-8pm, Su 9am-4pm.) With a garden facing neo-Byzantine Biegańskiego Sq. and a cool stone interior, tranquil **Cafe Skrzynka ❷,** Dąbrowskiego 1, specializes in dessert and dinner crepes (6-18zł). Extensive coffee (5-10zł) and mixed drinks (9-16zł) highlight the menu. (☎324 30 98. Open daily 8am-10pm. Cash only.) **Chata ❷,** al. NMP 12c, overcomes its unfortunate location in a mini-mall to provides a good sampling of traditional dishes. The relatively inexpensive house specialties inexpensive and include a mushroom omelette (14zł) and pork shanks in beer and honey for a mere 15zł. (☎324 33 44. Entrees 5-30zł. Open daily 11am-midnight. AmEx/MC/V.) Attached to the Dom Pielgrzyma, **Restauracja and Bar Dom Pielgrzyma ❶,** Wyszyńskiego 1, is a devout variation on the milk bar that serves meaty *pierogi* and *kotlety* (3-6zł), beet and *flaki* soups (2-5zł), and non-alcoholic beverages (3-6zł) to pilgrims who don't mind the school gym ambience. (☎377 75 64. Open daily 7am-8pm.) **Pod Gruszką** (Under the Pear) ❶, al. NMP 37, serves warm drinks by day (3-4zł) in a tree-shaded courtyard, and by afternoon is a popular bar. (☎365 44 90. Free live jazz F 7pm. Open M-Th 10am-10pm, F-Sa 10am-midnight.)

 SIGHTS. The **Paulite Monastery** (Klasztor Paulinów), on top of **Jasna Góra** (Bright Mountain), is one of the world's largest pilgrimage sites. Erected in 1382, the monastery exterior, which resembles a Baroque fortress, belies its sanctity. Jasna Góra welcomes masses of pilgrims who come to see the reportedly miraculous **Black Madonna** (Czarna Madonna). The ornate 15th-century **Basilica** (Bazylika) houses the icon inside the small **Chapel of Our Lady** (Kaplica Matki Bożej). Countless crutches, medallions, and rosaries strung up on the chapel walls attest to the pilgrims' faith in the painting's healing powers, while several jewel-encrusted robes crafted by devotees decorate the Madonna herself. The icon is veiled and revealed several times per day, with solemn festivities. (Chapel open daily 5am-9:30pm. Icon revealed June-Aug. M-F 6am-noon and 1-9:15pm; Sa-Su and holidays 2-9:15pm. Sept.-May M-F 6am-noon, 3-7pm, and 9-9:15pm; Sa-Su and holidays 6am-1pm, 3-7pm, and 9-9:15pm. Free; donations requested.)

> ⬎ **A PILGRIM'S PRAYER.** Several of the rooms in the monastery are open only for prayer, not for sightseeing. Visitors to Jasna Góra who are not on pilgrimage should be mindful of the signs in seven languages posted at every entrance to the monastery: "This is a holy place; come here as a pilgrim."

The monastery also houses several small museums, all of which are free to the public (donations requested). The **Arsenal** documents Jasna Góra's embattled history with jewel-encrusted batons, medieval swords, and other military artifacts dating from the Middle Ages to WWII, as well as devotional items that include makeshift string rosaries crafted by concentration camp prisoners. (Open daily in high season 9am-5pm; in low season 9am-4pm.) The **Museum of the 600th Anniversary** (Muzeum 600-lecia), assembled in 1982 to commemorate the anniversary of the icon's arrival at Jasna Góra, highlights the work and history of the Paulite Fathers, and contains special displays for the late pope **John Paul II** and **Lech Wałęsa,** whose Nobel Prize rests here. The museum also protects the monastery's 1382 founding document. (Open daily 9am-5pm.) The **Skarbiec** contains art donated by kings, nobility, clergy, and pilgrims, and is often particularly crowded. (Open daily June-Aug. 9am-5pm; Sept.-May 9am-4pm.) The **Knight's Hall** (Sala Rycerska), features paintings of the major events of the monastery's turbulent history. Ascend the dizzying staircase of the *baszta* (tower) for excellent views. (Tower open daily Apr.-Nov. 8am-4pm. Suggested donation 2zł.) The largest crowds converge on the monastery on May 3 (Feast of Our Lady Queen of Poland), July 16 (Feast of Our Lady of Scapulars), August 15 (Feast of the Assumption), August 26 (Feast of Our Lady of Częstochowa), September 8 (Feast of the Birth of Our Lady), and September 12 (Feast of the Name Mary). The 12 daily masses include a Latin service (8am), and the monastery draws the largest crowd of worshippers on Sunday with an astounding 18 full services held in the chapel and the basilica.

⚡ DAYTRIP FROM CZĘSTOCHOWA

TRAIL OF EAGLES' NESTS (SZLAK ORLICH GNIAZD)
From Częstochowa, take bus #58 or 67 to Olsztyn-Rynek (40min.; 10 per day; 3zł, students 1.50zł) from Piłsudskiego, across from the Częstochowa train station. Castle tower open daily 8am-8pm. 2zł, students 1zł.

Crags of Jurassic limestone erupt from green hills along the narrow 100km strip of land known as the **Kraków-Częstochowa Uplands** (Jura Krakowska-Częstochowska). These breathtaking extensions were incorporated into the fortifications of 12th-century castles built in the area, whose perches high on the rocky cliffs alongside the nests of eagle owls earned them the name "eagles' nests." As artillery grew stronger, the defensive walls grew less effective, and the fortifications proved no match for the invading Swedes. By the end of the 17th century, the fortresses had badly deteriorated. Today, only a few, including Wawel Castle in Kraków, remain whole. The ruins of the rest lie along the uplands, waiting to be discovered.

The two biggest attractions on the trail, the **Olsztyn Castle** and the **Pieskowa Skała Castle,** are half-day trips from Częstochowa and Kraków, respectively. Constructed in the 12th and 13th centuries, the castle that currently stands in the pastoral town of Olsztyn has lost much of its former glory. In 1655, the Swedish army ransacked the complex and, a century later, the locals took bricks from the castle to rebuild the town church. The preserved sections are in the upper castle. Look for signs of the two famous castle ghosts: a young bride who got lost in the dungeon and Maćko Borkowic, who was starved to death in the circular tower for his rebellion against King Kazimierz the Great. The lack of formal paths surrounding the sprawling ruins and rock caves invites exploration. There are 20 **hiking trails** that run along the entire 100km: the full hike takes about seven days. The trail is a rewarding, if challenging, **bicycle route** with five variations. There are also two choice **equestrian trails.** Kraków and Częstochowa branches of **PTTK** provide maps. The trail, covering a broad range of terrain, is marked by red blazes with maps posted along the way. The route leads through 12 different castle ruins between Kraków and Częstochowa, and passes through several small towns that can provide food and accommodations.

ŚLĄSK (SILESIA)

Poles have long treasured Śląsk for the rough-hewn beauty of its limestone crags, pine forests, and medieval castles. The region's industrial lowlands bear scars from the uncontrolled Five-Year Plans of the Communist era, but the mountains remain pristine and lightly touristed, with hiking and biking trails fanning west into Karkonosze National Park and east into the Jura Uplands.

WROCŁAW

☎(0)71

Wrocław (VROTS-wahv), the capital of Lower Silesia (Dolny Śląsk), is a graceful city of Gothic spires and stone bridges, islands, and gardens. Breathtaking sights and vibrant nightlife make Wrocław one of the most alluring destinations in Eastern Europe. Beneath the tranquil main square, however, lie centuries of turmoil. Passed among competing powers for centuries, Wrocław gained infamy at the end of WWII as "Festung Breslau," one of the last Nazi holdouts on the retreat to Berlin. Today, investment has rejuvenated the city, which enjoys one of the fastest development rates in Poland and is gearing up for an onslaught of tourism.

⌐ TRANSPORTATION

Trains: Wrocław Główny, Piłsudskiego 105 (☎367 58 82). 24hr. **currency exchange** inside. International tickets at counter #20. MC/V. To: **Częstochowa** (4hr., 7 per day, 21-34zł); **Gdynia** (6½hr., 6 per day, 30-51zł); **Jelenia Góra** (3¼hr., 14 per day, 17-21zł); **Kołobrzeg** (6½hr., 3 per day, 28-48zł); **Kraków** (4½-5hr., 14 per day, 25-44zł); **Łódź** (6¼hr., 6 per day, 39zł); **Lublin** (8hr., 3 per day, 30-50zł); **Poznań** (3¼hr., 29 per day, 19-31zł); **Szczecin** (5½hr., 9 per day, 44zł); **Warsaw** (4¼hr., 12 per day, 27-42zł); **Berlin, GER** (6¼hr., 2 per day, 185zł); **Bratislava, SLK** (7½hr., 10:30pm, 240zł); **Dresden, GER** (4½hr., 4 per day, 120zł); **Prague, CZR** (5¼hr., 2 per day, 125zł).

Buses: Station at Sucha 1 (☎361 22 99), behind the trains. Open daily 5am-11pm. To: **Częstochowa** (4¼hr., 10 per day, 26zł); **Gdańsk** (8hr., 2 per day, 64zł); **Jelenia Góra** (2hr., 28 per day, 24zł); **Karpacz** (3hr., 4 per day, 23zł); **Kraków** (6hr., 7 per day, 37zł); **Łódź** (5hr., 5 per day, 33zł); **Lublin** (8hr., 24 per day, 49zł); **Poznań** (4hr., 5 per day, 26zł); **Warsaw** (6hr., 7 per day, 48zł).

Public Transportation: Most lines run 5am-midnight. **Tram** and **bus** tickets cost 2zł per person, 1zł per student, and 2zł per backpack. 1-day pass 6.60zł, students 3.30zł; 10-day pass 24/12zł. Express buses (marked by letters) 2.40zł. Night buses 3/1.50zł.

Taxis: ZTP (☎96 22) is reliable. From the train station to the Rynek costs around 15zł.

✳ 🛈 ORIENTATION AND PRACTICAL INFORMATION

Filled with bustling restaurants and shops, the **Rynek** (Market Square) is the heart of Wrocław. From the **train** and **bus stations,** turn left on **Piłsudskiego,** take a right on **Świdnicka,** and go past **pl. Kościuszki,** over the **Fosa Miejska** (City Moat), through the pedestrian underpass beneath Kazimierza Wielkiego, and into the Rynek.

Tourist Office: IT, Rynek 14 (☎344 31 11; www.dolnyslask.info.pl). **Maps** 6-16zł. Free Internet. Bike rental 10zł for 1st hr., 5zł thereafter, 50zł per day (11hr.); 400zł deposit. Open daily 9am-9pm. AmEx/MC/V. **Centrum Informacji Kulturalnej,** Rynek-Ratusz 24 (☎342 22 91; www.okis.pl). The cultural branch of the IT, specializing in info for events and festivals. Open M-F 10am-6pm, Sa 9am-2pm.

Currency Exchange: Bank Pekao SA, Oławska 2 (☎371 61 24). Cashes **traveler's checks** for 1.5% commission (10zł min.) and gives MC/V **cash advances.** Open M-F 8am-6pm, Sa 9am-2pm.

Western Union: Biuro Podróży, Kościuszki 27 (☎344 81 88). Open M-F 10am-6pm, Sa 10am-3pm.

Luggage Storage: Lockers in the train station 4-8zł per day. Also in the kiosk in the back of the bus station. 5.50zł per day plus 1zł per 50zł value. Open daily 6am-10pm.

English-Language Bookstore: Empik Megastore, Rynek 50 (☎343 39 72). Open M-Sa 9am-10pm, Su noon-8pm. MC/V.

Pharmacy: Apteka Podwójnym Złotym Orłem, Rynek 42/43 (☎343 44 28).

Hospital: Szpital Im. Babińskiego, pl. 1 Maja 8 (☎341 00 00).

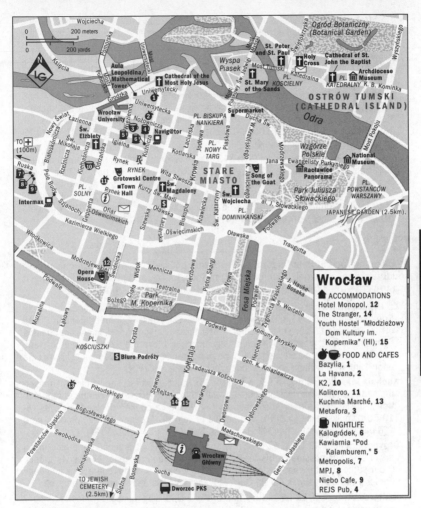

Wrocław

🏠 ACCOMMODATIONS
Hotel Monopol, 12
The Stranger, 14
Youth Hostel "Młodzieżowy
    Dom Kultury im.
    Kopernika" (HI), 15

🍴 FOOD AND CAFES
Bazylia, 1
La Havana, 2
K2, 10
Koliteroo, 11
Kuchnia Marché, 13
Metafora, 3

🍷 NIGHTLIFE
Kalogródek, 6
Kawiarnia "Pod
    Kalamburem," 5
Metropolis, 7
MPJ, 8
Niebo Cafe, 9
REJS Pub, 4

POLAND

Internet: Internet Klub Navig@tor Podziemia, Kuźnica 11/13 (☎343 70 69). 2zł per 30min., 3zł per hr. Open daily 9am-10pm. **Intermax,** Psie Budy 10/11 (☎794 05 73). 3zł per 30min., 5zł per hr. Open 24hr.

Post Office: Małachowskiego 1 (☎344 77 78), to the right of the train station. **Poste Restante** at window #22. **Telephones** inside and outside. Open M-F 6am-8pm, Sa-Su 9am-3pm. Branch at Rynek 28. Open M-F 6:30am-8:30pm. **Postal Code:** 50-900.

🏠 ACCOMMODATIONS

Rooms are plentiful in Wrocław, but reserve ahead for reasonable accommodations near the center of town. Check with the tourist office for info and to make reservations in **student dorms ❶,** a tram ride from the Rynek in pl. Grunwaldski, which rent rooms July through August (20-50zł).

▨ **The Stranger Hostel,** Kołłątaja 16/3 (☎634 25 16), opposite the train station, on the 3rd fl. behind an unmarked wooden doorway (ring buzzer #3). True to their motto "the stranger, the better," this new hostel is filled with quirky touches, from decorated glass toilet seats to a raised platform in the common room. Dorms are large and feature eclectic, comfortable stylings. Entertainment center, beautiful kitchen, free laundry, free Internet. Reception 24hr. No lockout or curfew. Dorms 50zł. AmEx/MC/V. ❷

Youth Hostel "Młodzieżowy Dom Kultury im. Kopernika" (HI), Kołłątaja 20 (☎343 88 56), opposite the train station. The lime-green walls of this institutional but cheerful hostel are plastered with student artwork. Kitchen and shared bathrooms. Sheets 7zł. Lockout 10am-5pm. Curfew 10pm. Call ahead. Dorms 22zł; doubles 58zł. Discount for stays over 1 night. Cash only. ❶

Hotel Monopol, Modrzejewskiej 2 (☎343 70 41; www.orbis.pl). From the train station, take tram "K" to Kazimierza Wielkiego. The glamor has faded from this Art Deco haven, but modern amenities like satellite TVs, telephones, and attentive service make the Monopol a good value. Price includes a princely breakfast buffet in the slightly creepy red-carpeted former ballroom. Check-in and check-out 2pm. Singles 120zł, with bath 180zł; doubles 160/260zł; triples with bath 310zł. AmEx/MC/V. ❹

◖ FOOD

Stock up on food at **Hala Targowa,** at the corner of Piaskowa and sw. Ducha, where you'll find a massive selection of fresh produce, meats, and pirated DVDs, housed in a towering 1908 building. (Open M-F 8am-6:30pm, Sa 9am-3pm.)

La Havana, Kuźnicza 12 (☎343 20 72). This tongue-in-cheek presentation of Cuban Communism is wildly popular with the locals. Enjoy tasty Cuban-influenced Polish dishes (entrees 10-20zł) in the company of a packed student crowd, images of Che and Castro, and fake plastic palm trees. Vegetarians will love the baked veggie omelette (10.50zł). Large tropical mixed drinks 12-18zł. Open M-Th and Su 11am-11:30pm, F-Sa noon-1am. Reservations recommended on weekends. MC/V. ❷

Kuchnia Marché, Świdnicka 53 (☎343 95 65). Value, freshness, and a tasteful market-themed interior make this spot popular with a hip, young crowd. At scattered food stations, the Marché offers fresh pastries (1-3zł), pasta cooked before your eyes (8-10.50zł), milkshakes (2.50zł), and salads (1.50-4zł). Accumulate stamps on a card and pay after you eat. Open M-F 9am-8pm; Sa-Su noon-8pm. MC/V. ❶

Bazylia, Kuźnicza 42 (☎375 20 65). Wrapped under the glass facade and chic metal decor of a businessman's bistro, Bazylia serves students cheap, homestyle meals. Order at the counter from the long list of milk bar classics—and prepare for a language barrier if you don't speak Polish. Open M-F 7am-7pm, Sa 8am-5pm. Cash only. ❶

Kaliteros, Rynek 20/21 (☎343 56 17). One of a surprising number of "Mediterranean" restaurants, Kaliteros impresses with colorful Etruscan-style frescoes and comfortable sidewalk seating on the Rynek. While Egyptian and Greek entrees (15-40zł) are not particularly authentic, the real draw is a seriously delicious dessert: fresh pudding with homemade fruit preserves (9zł). Open M-Th 11am-11pm, F-Su 11am-midnight. ❸

◎ SIGHTS

▨ **RACŁAWICE PANORAMA AND NATIONAL MUSEUM.** The 120m by 15m **Panorama** wraps viewers in the action of the 18th-century peasant insurrection against Russian occupation. This painting depicts the legendary victory of the underdog Poles led by Tadeusz Kościuszko (p. 422). It was damaged by a bomb in 1944 and hidden in a monastery for safekeeping. As it was considered politically imprudent for the Poles to glorify independence from Russia, the painting was displayed publicly only after the rise of Solidarity in the 1980s. The 30min. showings include audio narration; free headsets are available in eight languages. *(Purkyniego 11. Facing away from the town hall, bear left on Kuźnicza for 2 blocks and then right on Kotlarska, which becomes Purkyniego.* ☎344 23 44. *Open Tu-Su 9am-5pm; viewings every 30min. 9:30am-5pm. 20zł, students 15zł.)* The **National Museum** is in the massive ivy-clad building across the street and to the left. Permanent exhibits include provocative installations by 20th-century Polish artists Magdalena Abakanowicz and Józef Szajna, medieval statuary, and 18th- and 19th-century paintings. Check out the all-white atrium. *(Pl. Powstańców Warszawy 5.* ☎343 88 39. *Open W, F, Su 10am-4pm, Th 9am-4pm, Sa 10am-6pm. 15zł, students 10zł, Sa free.)*

OSTRÓW TUMSKI. Ostrów Tumski, the oldest part of Wrocław, occupies the islands and far shore of the Odra and was the site of the founding of the Wrocław bishopric in 1000. A thousand years later, the neighborhood remains largely devoted to archdiocesan buildings, and priests and nuns frequent its lovely and quiet streets. Biking and pedestrian paths connect the islands. A statue of St. Jadwiga, the patron saint of Silesia, guards **Most Piaskowy** (Sand Bridge), the oldest bridge in Wrocław. The sky-piercing spires of the 13th-century **Cathedral of St. John the Baptist** (Katedra Św. Jana Chrzciciela) dominate Ostrów Tumski's skyline. Inside, light filters through stained-glass windows, shrouding the Gothic interior with shadows. Climb the tower for a view of the surrounding churches. *(Open M-Sa 10am-5:30pm, Su 2-4pm. 4zł, students 3zł.)* Nearby, the Church of **St. Mary of the Sands** (Najświętszej Marii Panny) houses a 14th-century icon of Our Lady of Victory that medieval knights carried into battle. To the right of the nave is the incredible Chapel of the Blind, Deaf, and Dumb (Kaplica Nieśłyszących i Niewidomych), where the altar has been adorned with thousands of children's toys. Ask a nun to hit the switch, and try not to gape as the toy village comes to life. *(Open daily 10am-6pm. Daily services for the disabled. Donations requested.)* From Cathedral Sq., go north on Kapitulna to reach the enchanting **Botanical Garden** (Ogród Botaniczny). Sculptures of oversized acorns and pinecones are scattered throughout. Students from the nearby university study on benches and tables facing the stream that winds through the garden. *(Open daily 8am-6pm. 5zł, students 3zł.)*

WROCŁAW UNIVERSITY (UNIWERSYTET WROCŁAWSKI). This center of Wrocław's cultural life houses a number of architectural gems. **Aula Leopoldina,** an 18th-century frescoed lecture hall, is the most impressive and decadent. *(Pl. Uniwersytecka 1, on the 2nd fl.* ☎375 26 18. *Open M-Tu and Th-Su 10am-3pm. 4zł, students 2zł.)* Climb the **Mathematical Tower** for a sweeping

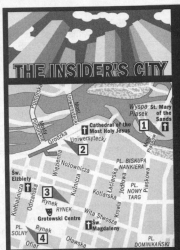

WROCŁAW NIGHTSIGHTS

While it rivals Kraków and Warsaw in cultural attractions and vibrant social life, Wrocław does so with a nonchalance that is particularly graceful in the evening. These sites show Wrocław's brightest moments after sunset:

1 To the right of the Most Piaskowy (Sand Bridge), behind St. Mary of the Sands, a small but well-manicured **park** boasts a view of the town's spires and waterways.

2 Sandwiched between the **Cathedral of the Most Holy Jesus** and Wrocław University, the marble-and-bronze **fountain,** Fontanna Szermierza, radiates light in a petite courtyard.

3 In the **Rynek,** the Zdrój **fountain** shimmers with rippled glass. Named for a former mayor, its name also means "spring" in old Polish.

4 An unexpected sight, the nearby **Plac Solny** bursts with **flowers** 24hr. These brightly lit stalls perfume the square at all hours.

view of the city. *(4zł, students 2zł.)* A ticket for the tower will also grant you access to **Longchamps Hall**, which displays the university's long history. The breathtaking 17th-century **Cathedral of the Most Holy Jesus** (Kościół Najświętszego im. Jezusa), built on the site of the Piast castle, retains much of its original interior. The colonialist, 18th-century sculptures on the vaults depict the Christianization of African, American, and Asian indigenous people. *(Open to tourists M-Sa 11am-3:30pm. 3zł, students 2zł.)*

AROUND THE RYNEK. The Rynek and its Gothic **Town Hall** (Ratusz) are the heart of the city. Inside the town hall, the **Museum of Urban Art** (Muzeum Sztuki Mieszczańskiej), displays both ancient and contemporary art in a medieval building whose decorations are equally engaging. Around the corner, you can enjoy the sights and sounds from a **horse-drawn carriage.** *(☎374 16 93. Open W-Sa 11am-5pm, Su 10am-6pm. Museum 12zł, students 8zł. Carriage 5-10zł.)*

JEWISH CEMETERY (CMENTARZ ŻYDOWSKI). That this Jewish Cemetery is one of the best-preserved in Poland is a sad comment on the state of Poland's Jewish sights. Among the faded and damaged headstones, the cemetery holds the remains of socialist Ferdinand Lasalle, the families of physicist Max Born and chemist Fritz Haber, and the wife of writer Thomas Mann. A walk around this shaded enclave reveals fragments of Jewish tombstones dating from the 13th century. *(Ślężna 37/39. From the stops along Kołłątaja and Piotra Skargi, take tram #9 and get off at Ślężna. ☎791 59 04. Free guided tours in Polish and English Su noon. Open Apr.-Oct. daily 9am-6pm. 5zł, students 3zł.)* The oldest Jewish tombstone in Poland, dated 1203 and discovered at the site of the now-vanished Wrocław Old Jewish Cemetery, is on display at the **Archaeology Museum** on Cieszyńskiego 9 *(☎347 16 96.)*

OTHER SIGHTS. The **Archdiocese Museum** (Muzeum Archidiecezjalne), pl. Katedralny 16, contains a grab bag of religious art and the earliest extant sentence written in the Polish language. *(☎327 11 78. Open Tu-Su 9am-3pm. Admission 4zl, students 3zl.)* The only of its kind in Poland, the **Japanese Garden** (Ogród Japoński) is a carefully trimmed and symmetrical version of paradise. *(Located 3km east of the Rynek. ☎347 51 40. Open daily 9am-9pm. Admission 3zl, students 1.50zl.)*

🎵🎭 ENTERTAINMENT AND NIGHTLIFE

For event info, pick up *City Magazine* or *Co jest grane?* (What's Going On?). Visit **Centrum Informacji Kulturalnej** (see **Orientation and Practical Information**) for info on Wrocław's experimental theater, which continues the work of local pioneer Jerzy Grotowski. The **Song of the Goat Theater** (Teatr Pieśń Kozła), Purkyniego 1 (☎342 71 10), and the **Grotowski Theater,** Rynek-Ratusz 27 (☎343 42 67), are two prominent outlets. An extremely popular festival, **Wrocław Non-Stop** (www.wroclawnonstop.pl) transforms the city in the last week of June and first week of July into a celebration of fine and performance arts. Free concerts, gallery openings, fireworks, and film screenings are among the more than 100 events at the festival.

Wrocław nightlife encompasses a wide range of options. The unquestioned center of student nightlife is **Ruska,** near the intersection with Nowy Świat, where a complex contains several clubs and bars that are filled every night of the week. A popular choice is the hip-hop dance floor and surrounding beer garden of **MPJ.** (☎344 34 65. Beer 5zł. Open daily 11am-late. Disco open 8pm. Cash only.) Next door, **Niebo Cafe** offers occasional free rock shows in a lovingly worn interior filled with plush velvet chairs. Patrons can play DJ with the alt-rock CD collection at the bar. (☎342 98 67. Beer 4.50zł. Open M-F 1pm-late, Sa-Su 5pm-late. Cash only.) The winding blacklit hallways of **Metropolis** are an intense dance spot for house and techno, with 80s and 90s pop in the basement. (☎343 13 73. Beer 6zł. Cover F 5zł; Sa men 10zł, women 5zł. Open daily 8pm-late. AmEx/MC/V.) At tiny **REJS Pub,** Kotlarska 32a, self-described "alternative" students and locals down cheap beer and enjoy the movie soundtracks playing. (☎509 796 771. Beer 4.50zł. Open M-Sa 9:30am-late, Su 11am-late. Cash only.) Hang with art students at **Kawiarnia "Pod Kalamburem,"** Kuźnicza 29a, in the university quarter. The art nouveau building includes a bar and cafe founded by the experimental theater group that used to occupy the building. Among many claims to fame, the biggest festival of avant-garde theater in Europe was hosted here in the 1970s and 80s, an impressive feat under the Communist yoke. (☎372 35 71, ext. 32. Beer and mixed drinks 3-15zł. Open M-Th 1pm-midnight, F-Sa 1pm-late, Su 4pm-midnight. Cash only.) In summer, join backpackers and carefree students next door on the multi-level patio of unpretentious **Kalogródek**, Kuźnicza 29b, for darts, foosball, and beer. (☎372 35 71. Open M-Th 10am-11pm, F-Sa 10am-late, Su 3-11pm.) Nestled in an unsuspecting alley, like many of Wrocław's best cafes, is the tiny **K2**, Kiełbaśnicza 2. In this farm-themed interior you'll find an encyclopedic array of teas, delicious homemade cakes, and a surfeit of charm. Try a fruit tea with preserves for 6.50zł. (☎372 34 15. Open daily 11am-11pm.) A more pensive option is **Metafora**, Więzienna 5b. The small but quality menu fortifies conversationalists who recline for hours on leather couches. (☎795 09 78. Coffee 5zł. Open daily noon-midnight. MC/V.)

KARPACZ   ☎(0)75

Visiting Poland without visiting Karpacz is like eating herring without vodka: you can do it, but it's inadvisable. Mountains cast long shadows over thickly forested valleys, and the beauty of the landscape is stunning, even within Karpacz itself. Trails and slopes lure visitors to the very brink of the Czech border year-round.

📳 **TRANSPORTATION AND PRACTICAL INFORMATION.** Most **buses** to Karpacz originate in, or at least pass through, **Jelenia Góra**. There is no bus station in town. Konstytucji 3 Maja is the main thoroughfare for buses—eight stops dot the way to **Karpacz Górny**, the top of town (45min., every 30-60min., 5.50-6zł). Catch any bus to ride among stops within Karpacz (1.50-3zł). The poorly marked stops are named for local landmarks. Buses to Jelenia Góra run to either the train station or the bus station. A scenic **bicycle path** also traverses the 28km from Jelenia Góra to Karpacz; maps are available at the Jelenia Góra tourist info office.

Karpacz is a vertical town: most of its restaurants and sights line a single road, **Konstytucji 3 Maja**, which meanders uphill. Poorly marked side streets provide steeply sloped shortcuts. Uphill from Biały Jar, a large circular bus stop with a restaurant and hotel (not to be confused with Biały Jar, the valley 1½hr. into the black trail), the road changes names to **Karkonoska**. Get off incoming buses at **Karpacz Bachus** and go downhill to the **tourist office**, 3 Maja 25, which is distinguished from the myriad private tourist offices by a large blue circle with "it" in white. Staff sell **maps** and reserve rooms. Ask about bicycling, skiing, rock climbing, horseback riding, and camping. (☎761 86 05; www.karpacz.pl. English spoken. Open M-Sa 9am-5pm, Su 9am-6pm.) A smaller tourist bureau just uphill from Karpacz Bachus, **Biuro Turystyczne Karpacz**, 3 Maja 52, **exchanges currency**. (☎761 85 53. Open July-Aug. M-F 9am-8pm, Sa 9am-6pm, Su 10am-4pm; Sept.-June M-F 9am-5pm, Sa 9am-2pm.) Hotel Orbis Skalny, Obrońców Pokoju 5, rents **bicycles**. (☎752 70 00. Open daily 7am-9pm. 10zł per 3hr., 18zł per 6hr., 25zł per 12hr.) **Szkoła Górska**, Na Śnieżkę 16, in **Schronisko Samotnia** (☎761 93 76), two hours into the blue trail, has rock climbing lessons, equipment, and excursions. Call ahead to make arrangements. **Bank Zachodni**, 3 Maja 43, cashes **traveler's checks** for a 30zł commission. It also has a Visa **ATM** and **Western Union** services. (☎/fax 753 81 20. Open M-F 9am-5pm.) There's a **K-Med pharmacy** at 3 Maja 33. (☎761 86 69. Open M-F 9am-7pm, Sa 9am-5pm, Su 9am-1pm.) The **post office** is at 3 Maja 23. (☎761 92 20; fax 761 95 85. Open M-F 8am-6pm, Sa 9:30am-3pm.) **Postal Code:** 58-540.

POLAND

⌐⌐ ACCOMMODATIONS AND FOOD. Reservations are not necessary. **Private pensions** (25-70zł) proliferate, especially on Kościelna just downhill from Karpacz Bachus. Unfortunately, some are open only part of the year—inquire at the tourist office. As a general rule, the better deals are farther uphill. **Hotel Karpacz ❸**, 3 Maja 11/13, has comfortably large rooms with TVs and baths, and a generous breakfast buffet. (☎ 761 97 28. Buffet 9-11am. Check-in noon-3pm. Check-out noon. Singles 70zł; doubles 120zł; triples 180zł. Prices fall 15zł in winter.) **D.W. Szczyt ❶**, Na Śnieżkę 6, is at the uphill end of town just a few steps from Świątynia Wang (p. 482). Take the bus to Karpacz Wang and head up the steep climb toward Świątynia Wang—the hike from the center of town (1hr.) is impossible with luggage. If the view doesn't leave you breathless, the great prices will—as will the 200m haul from the bus stop. Rooms are simple and worn, but the offbeat staff, tiny resident dog, and sweeping views make it a solid value. Call the tourist office to reserve. (☎ 761 93 60. Singles 25zł; doubles 50zł; triples 75zł; quads 100zł.) **Schronisko Samotnia ❶**, beside the stunning Mały Staw lake, a 2hr. hike along the blue trail from town, offers the most secluded accommodations in Karpacz. Though a physical challenge to reach, Samotnia is the newest and best-regarded hostel in Karpacz. There's a restaurant, ski rental, and a mountain rescue service. Call the tourist office to reserve. (Dorms 19-29zł; singles 31zł; doubles 58zł.)

Food in Karpacz is unpretentious and filling, an ideal conclusion to a long day of hiking or skiing. It can be difficult to tell the touristy from the extremely touristy, but there are great deals to be had. The grocery store **Delikatesy**, 3 Maja 29, has everything you need for a picnic in the mountains. (☎ 761 92 59. Open M-Sa 8:30am-9pm, Su 10am-6pm.) The small **open-air produce market,** in the alley beside 3 Maja 45, stocks some of the best food in town. It's marked by a "Warzywa Owoce" sign. (Open daily dawn-dusk.) Green-roofed **Karczma Śląska ❷**, Rybacka 1, just off 3 Maja, specializes in mouth-watering pork (8zł), great prices, and yard art. Pool tables (2zł per game) can be found at the restaurant's "Bar Oscar." (☎ 761 96 33. Open daily noon-10pm.) The seriously old-school **Zagroda Góralska ❶**, 3 Maja 46, offers meats, sauerkraut, and potatoes (3-6zł per serving) from massive grills on the counter; you may see a pig on a spit. The sturdy wood lean-to seems gimmicky, but the food is popular with locals. (Open daily 10am-late. Cash only.) The *pierogi* at **U Petiego ❶**, Parkowa 10, are so homemade that the chef's thumbprints are visible on the creases (7zł). For 13zł you can make one of the meaty entrees a full meal with fries and sauerkraut. (☎ 643 92 20. Open daily noon-10pm. Cash only.)

◨⚐ SIGHTS AND OUTDOOR ACTIVITIES. The uphill hike to **Wang Chapel** (Świątynia Wang), Śnieżki 8, takes hours from the center of town but is worth the effort. Follow 3 Maja and side streets marked by a blue blaze. Alternatively, take the bus to Karpacz Wang (10min.) and follow the signs. This Viking church was built in Norway at the turn of the 12th century. In the 1800s, it sorely needed a restoration that no one could afford, so Kaiser Friedrich Wilhelm III of Prussia sent it to Karpacz for the Lutheran community there to enjoy. Carved dragons, lions, and plants adorn the building. From the garden, look to the mountains for a glimpse of the peak, Śnieżka. (☎ 752 82 91. Open Apr. 15-Oct. 31 M-Sa 9am-6pm, Su 11:30am-6pm; Nov.-Apr. 14 closes 1hr. earlier. 4.50zł, students 3.50zł.)

Hikers aim for the crown of **Śnieżka** (Mt. Snow; 1602m), the highest peak in Poland. The border with the Czech Republic runs across the summit. Śnieżka and the trails lie within **Karkonosze National Park** (4zł, students 2zł; 3-day pass 8/4zł). All park trails lead to **Pod Śnieżka** (1394m), the last stop under the peak. Even during summer the peak averages 10°C—bring a sweater. To get there as quickly and painlessly as possible, take the Kopa chairlift, Olimpijska 4, off Turystyczna. Follow the black trail from Hotel Biały Jar until you see the lift on the left. From the top it's a rigorous 40min. hike to the peak. (☎ 761 92 84. Lift 20min. Runs daily June-Aug.

8:30am-5pm; Sept.-May 8am-4pm. Before 1pm 19zł, students 15zł; round-trip 23/19zł. After 1pm 16/11zł; round-trip 19/14zł.) There are several hiking routes up Śnieżka, all of which originate in Świątynia Wang or Biały Jar. The easiest route to Śnieżka is the **blue-blazed path** (3hr.) from Świątynia Wang. This trail is also suited to vigorous biking up to Spalona Strażnica. Follow the stone-paved road to **Polana** (1080m, 1hr.), then hike up to scenic **Mały Staw** (Small Lake; 1hr.). From there, it's 35min. to **Spalona Strażnica**, then 30min. to **Pod Śnieżka**. From Polana, endurance hikers should continue along the **yellow trail** (2½hr.) to another rock protrusion at **Słonecznik** (Sunflower; 35min.). This stretch, along a rocky stream bed, is a challenging, vertical haul not for the weak of ankle. Turning left here takes you to the red trail, which leads to **Pod Śnieżka** (1hr.). The scenic **red trail** (2½hr.) begins behind Hotel Biały Jar's parking lot. It travels along the Czech ridge to **Spalona Strażnica**, where it meets the yellow trail. Once you emerge above the tree line, it's a difficult hike up to **Pod Śnieżka**. The most physically challenging and least scenic of the trails, the **black trail** (2¼hr.) heads up from behind Hotel Biały Jar's parking lot. After splitting from the red trail (15min.), it shoots straight up the ski slopes in an exhausting trek to **Pod Śnieżka** (1½hr.), the top where it meets the red again for the final push (30min.).

From Pod Śnieżka, two trails lead to Śnieżka. The black **Zygzag** goes straight up the north side; look for the rubble path (20-30min.). The blue trail, **Jubilee Way,** winds around the peak (45min.). If incredible views of the Sudety aren't enough, climb to the **observatory** for the most expansive view. (Open daily June-Aug. 9am-5pm; Sept.-May 9am-3pm. 2zł, students 1zł.) Winter brings snow and skiers. Lift and equipment rental info is available at the tourist office and from **Kopa,** located in the Ski Complex Śnieżka, Turystyczna 4. (☎761 86 19; www.kopa.com.pl. Day pass 60zł, students 45zł. Ski rental 50zł, snowboard 45zł.) The longest lift is 2229m and leads to the Kopa peak. Back in town, be terrified by the alpine slide **CRIS Kolorawa,** Parkowa 10. (☎761 90 98; www.kolorowa.pl. 6zł per person per ride; 5 rides 20zł, 10 rides 35zł. Open daily 9am-8pm, weather permitting.)

WIELKOPOLSKA

The birthplace of the Polish nation, blessed with rich agricultural land and a strategic position between Berlin and Warsaw, has seen tanks roll across its green plains many times. In these quieter days, the westward-looking cities of Wielkopolska hum with commerce, while the countryside remains serene.

ŁÓDŹ   ☎(0)42

Łódź (WOODGE; pop. 813,000), Poland's second-largest city, is anything but a tourist town. Though most of the factories that once fueled Łódź have shut down, leading to the highest unemployment rate in Poland, their legacy remains in a thick layer of gray pollution on the city's buildings. Yet stop for a drink in one of Łódź's legendary bars, and you'll find that an offbeat music, film, and fashion scene thrives in what locals boast is American filmmaker David Lynch's favorite city. Beneath the soot and the graffiti, the ruins of industrial Łódź hide intriguing surprises and a charisma all their own.

⌐ TRANSPORTATION

Trains: There are 2 main train stations in town. **Łódź Fabryczna,** pl. B. Sałacińskiego 1 (☎664 54 67). To **Białystok** (4½hr., 1 per day, 42zł), **Kraków** (3¼hr., 3 per day, 41zł), and **Warsaw** (2hr., 17 per day, 28zł). **Łódź Kaliska,** al. Unii Lubelskiej 1 (☎41 02). To: **Częstochowa** (2hr., 4 per day, 33zł); **Gdańsk** (7½hr., 3 per day, 45zł); **Kraków** (3¼hr., 3 per day, 41zł); **Warsaw** (2hr., 3 per day, 28zł); **Wrocław** (3¾hr., 3 per day, 35zł).

POLAND

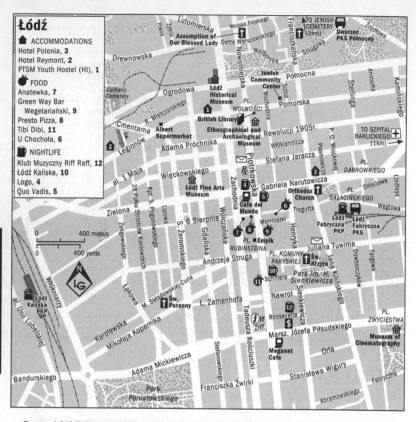

Łódź

🏠 **ACCOMMODATIONS**
Hotel Polonia, 3
Hotel Reymont, 2
PTSM Youth Hostel (HI), 1

🍴 **FOOD**
Anatewka, 7
Green Way Bar
  Wegetariański, 9
Presto Pizza, 8
Tibi Dibi, 11
U Chochoła, 6

🍷 **NIGHTLIFE**
Klub Muzyczny Riff Raff, 12
Łódź Kaliska, 10
Logo, 4
Quo Vadis, 5

Buses: Łódź Fabryczna PKS, pl. B. Sałacińskiego 1 (☎631 97 06), attached to the Fabryczna train station. To: **Częstochowa** (2¼hr., 16 per day, 20-28zł); **Kraków** (5hr., 10 per day, 34-49zł); **Warsaw** (2½hr., 6 per day, 12.50-36zł). **Polski Express** buses (☎620 03 30; www.polskiexpress.pl) also leave from here. **Biuro Turystyczne PKS,** pl. B. Sałacińskiego 1 (☎631 92 30; www.pks.lodz.pl). Provides international info. Open M-F 7am-5pm, Sa 9am-1pm.

Public Transportation: Trams and **buses** run throughout the city 4am-11pm. 10min. ticket 1.50zł, 30min. 2.20zł, 1hr. 3.40zł; students 0.75/1.10/1.65zł. Prices double at night. 1-day pass (8.80zł, students 4.40zł) and 7-day pass (35/17.50zł) available. A few late-night buses, designated by numbers over 100, run 11pm-4am.

◀▦ 🔢 ORIENTATION AND PRACTICAL INFORMATION

Piotrkowska is the 3km main thoroughfare. Its shop-lined pedestrian-only section stretches from **pl. Wolności** to **al. Marsz. Józefa Piłsudskiego** and is an attraction in its own right. From **Łódź Fabryczna,** cross under Jana Kilińskiego and head toward Łódźki Dom Kultury, a large building across the way. Continue on Traugutta to Piotrkowska. From **Łódź Kaliska,** cross under al. Włókniarzy via the tunnel; the second exit on the left leads to the tram stop. Take tram #12 or 14 toward Stoki and get off at Piotrkowska, or take tram #10 to Zielona.

Tourist Office: IT, al. Kościuszki 88 (☎638 59 55; cit@uml.lodz.pl). **Free maps,** brochures, and accommodations info. Open M-F 8:30am-6pm, Sa 9am-1pm.

Currency Exchange: Pekao SA, al. Piłsudskiego 12 (☎636 62 44). Cashes **traveler's checks** for 1.5% commission (10zł min.) and gives MC/V **cash advances.** Open M-F 8am-6pm, Sa 10am-2pm.

Luggage Storage: Locked rooms in Łódź Fabryczna and Łódź Kaliska. 4zł per item per day. Open daily 5am-10pm. Key lockers next to the ticket counter. 8zł per 24hr.; 4zł for small items. After 72hr. bags are removed and placed in storage room.

English-Language Bookstore: Empik, Piotrkowska 81 (☎631 19 98). Classic fiction, maps, and magazines. Open M-Sa 9am-9pm, Su 11am-7pm. MC/V.

Pharmacy: Apteka Pod Białym Orłem, Piotrkowska 46 (☎/fax 630 00 68). One of the oldest pharmacies in Łódź. Open M-F 8am-8pm, Sa 10am-3pm.

Medical Services: Szpital Barlickiego, Kopcińskiego 22 (☎677 69 50). English spoken. **Medicover,** al. Piłsudskiego 3 (☎639 66 66). 24hr. **emergency line** (☎96 77).

Internet: Łódź is wired; Internet cafes dot the alleys off Piotrkowska. **Meganet Caffe,** al. Piłsudskiego 3 (☎636 33 76; biuro@meganetcaffe.pl), on the 2nd floor of the Silver Screen complex. 0.90zł per 20min., 2.40zł per hr. Open daily 8am-midnight. **Cafe del Mundo,** Piotrkowska 53 (☎633 68 67), on the 2nd floor of a charmingly decrepit pink building. 1zł per 30min., 2zł per hr. Open M-Sa 9am-midnight, Su 9am-10pm.

Post Office: Tuwima 38 (☎633 94 52; fax 632 82 08). Take a ticket as you enter: "A/B" for stamps, "C" for international packages, "D" for fax services. **Telephones** are inside. **Poste Restante** at window #19. Post office open M-F 7am-8pm, Sa 8:30am-3:30pm. Poste Restante M-F 7am-6pm. **Postal Code:** 90-001.

ACCOMMODATIONS

IT maintains a list of **private rooms** and, in summer, rooms in **university dorms.** Beds in three-bed shared rooms begin at 25zł, while singles with bath run 45-65zł. Call from the train station, and they'll make arrangements.

PTSM Youth Hostel (HI), Legionów 27 (☎630 66 80; www.yhlodz.pl). Take tram #4 toward Helenówek from Fabryczna station to pl. Wolności; walk on Legionów past Zachodnia. The only hostel in town. Clean and cheery rooms, plenty of lounge space, and helpful staff. Free locked storage until 10pm. Reception 6am-11pm. Check-in 3pm. Check-out 10am. Flexible curfew 11pm. Dorms 30zł; 1 bathless single 45zł, singles with bath and TV 65zł; doubles with TV 80zł; triples with TV 120zł. MC/V. ❶

Hotel Reymont, Legionów 81 (☎633 80 23; www.hotelreymont.com), 4 blocks down from PTSM Youth Hostel. From pl. Wolności, take bus #43 along Legionów. Art Deco theme is grandly executed in the lobby but loses some steam in the small, colorful rooms. Each room has bath, phone, radio, cable TV, microwave, and refrigerator. Color-coordinated floors and access to a gym and free sauna. Breakfast included. Check-out 11am. Singles 160-198zł; doubles 210-258zł. 25% off Sa-Su. MC/V. ❺

Hotel Polonia, Narutowicza 38 (☎632 87 73). From Fabryczna, take tram #1, 4, or 5 to Narutowicza. The Hotel Polonia offers decent rooms a short walk from the station. Newer rooms have crisp linens and a muted color-scheme; cheaper singles have suffered some wear. Unless you're craving the sights and sounds of rattling trams, request a room that doesn't face the street. Check-in 2-10pm. Check-out noon. Singles 75zł, with bath 125-175zł; doubles with bath 140-270zł. 10% off Sa-Su. AmEx/MC/V. ❷

FOOD

Large servings and low prices mark the Łódź restaurant scene, and culinary diversity has recently begun to arrive. Vegetarian and healthier options are changing the ways of the sooty, hard-drinking city. The majority of restaurants are along **Piotrowska. Albert,** Legionów 16, is one of several grocery stores along Legionów. (☎633 48 36. Open M-Sa 7am-9pm, Su 9am-2pm.)

POLAND

■ **Anatewka,** 6 Sierpnia 2/4 (☎630 36 35). Meals start with complimentary matzah and a taste of wine at quietly elegant Anatewka, where Ashkenazi Jewish cuisine is served on lace tablecloths under 19th-century Yiddish etchings. Here's a chance for travelers to give the *pierogi* a break with delicate entrees such as chicken with honey and ginger (19zł). Entrees are stand-alone, so be sure to order a side dish for a full meal. Not kosher. Entrees 15-45zł. Open daily 11am-11pm. Call ahead F and Sa. Cash only. ❸

Green Way Bar Wegetariański, Piotrkowska 80 (☎632 08 52). Green Way pioneered vegetarian eating in Łódź and remains the city's leading outpost of all things green and tasty. Menu changes almost daily to include fresh seasonal produce. Berry and yogurt *koktajly* (1.50-3zł), rich coffee (3.50-4.50zł), and *naleśniki* with fruit (6.50zł) supplement a range of international options and veggie versions of traditional Polish favorites. Entrees 7.50zł. Open daily 10am-9pm. Cash only. ❷

Presto Pizza, Piotrkowska 67 (☎630 88 83), in the alley across from Hotel Grand. Alongside solid renditions of the old standbys, Presto cooks up a few culinary challenges for the adventurous, including "Per Bambi" with bananas, pineapple, raisins, and nutella (16zł). A *mała* (small) pizza is frightfully large. Pizzas 8-19zł. Open M-Sa 11am-midnight, Su 11am-11pm. MC/V. ❷

Tibi Dibi, Piotrkowska 107 (☎632 51 15), at the end of a well-marked alley. You won't find any industrial ovens at Tibi Dibi, where the kitchen looks much like your own and the food is homemade on a small scale. In addition to an a la carte menu, Tibi Dibi offers set Polish and Indian menus that change daily (12zł). Don't miss dessert. Open M-Th 9am-10pm, F-Sa 10am-11pm. Cash only. ❷

U Chochoła, Traugutta 3 (☎632 51 38), across the street from Hotel Savoy. Locals can't get enough of the heaping portions, waitstaff in folk costumes, and *Staropolski* (Old Polish) menu. Even the restroom adheres to the rustic theme. The pork loin with bone and cabbage (21zł) is a treat. Veggie options 8-13zł. 20-*pierogi* variety platter (20zł) is for serious eaters. Open M-Th and Su noon-11pm, F-Sa noon-midnight. AmEx/MC/V. ❸

◉ SIGHTS

JEWISH CEMETERY (CMENTARZ ŻYDOWSKI). Eerily beautiful, the sprawling Jewish cemetery, established in 1892, is the largest in Europe. There are more than 200,000 graves and 180,000 tombstones, some elaborately engraved although worn and overgrown. Instead of the flowers and memorial candles found in most Christian cemeteries, only cobwebbed stones mark visits here. Especially noteworthy is the colossal Poznański family crypt with its gold-mosaic ceiling. Near the entrance to the cemetery is a memorial to the Jews killed in the Łódź ghetto; signs lead the way to the **Ghetto Fields** (Pole Ghettowe), which are lined with the faintly marked graves of 43,527 Jews who died there. The cemetery is difficult to find and its gates are often locked during hours when it is supposedly open, so the best way to see it is to contact the helpful and English-speaking tourist information bureau ahead of time for assistance. *(Take tram #1 from Kilińskiego or #6 from Kościuszki or Zachodnia north to the last stop, 20min. away. Continue up the street; make a left onto Zmienna, a small stone road off Inflancka; and head to the small gate on your right. It is better to try this entrance than the main gate on Bracka, which is usually locked. ☎656 70 19. Open May-Sept. M-Th and Su 9am-5pm, F 9am-3pm; Oct.-Apr. M-F and Su 8am-3pm. Closed Jewish holidays. 4zł; free for those visiting the graves of relatives.)* In the center of town, the **Jewish Community Center** (Gmina Wyznaniowa Żydowska) has info on those buried in the cemetery. *(Pomorska 18. ☎633 51 56. English spoken. Open M-F 10am-2pm. Services daily.)*

POZNAŃSKI PALACE AND SCHEIBLER PALACE. Prewar Łódź, a hub of European industry, thrived at the intersection of Polish, Jewish, and German culture. In the late 19th century, factory magnates Izrael Poznański and Karol Scheibler competed fiercely for dominance of the city's lucrative textile industry. Striving to outdo one another, Jewish Poznański and German Scheibler each built lavish residences adja-

POLAND

cent to their factories. The intact interiors of the two palaces are now home to Łódź's most interesting museums: the Historical Museum occupies the Poznański Palace, and the Scheibler Palace holds the Museum of Cinematography. Today, the Poznański Palace is part of Manufaktura, the biggest urban revitalization project in Central Europe. Slated for completion by 2006, the reconstruction plans include state-of-the-art centers for art, fashion, and technology. *(See listings below for directions to and locations of palaces.)*

ŁÓDŹ HISTORICAL MUSEUM (MUZEUM HISTORII MIASTA ŁODZI).

Preserving the Poznański family home's Gilded Age splendor, this museum boasts an ornate neo-Baroque palace ballroom, gorgeously furnished rooms, and exhibits on Łódź's famous sons and daughters, including pianist Artur Rubinstein and writers Jerzy Kosiński and Władysław Reymont. Factory walls and workers' quarters are visible outside the palace. *(Ogrodowa 15. Take tram #4 toward Helenówek or #6 toward Strykowskar to intersection of Nowomiejska and Północna. Turn left on Północna, which becomes Ogrodowa. ☎654 00 82. Open Tu and Th 10am-4pm, W 2-6pm, F-Su 10am-2pm. 7zł, students 4zł; W free.)*

MUSEUM OF CINEMATOGRAPHY (MUZEUM KINOMATOGRAFII).

International film giants Krzysztof Kieślowski, Roman Polański, and Andrzej Wajda all got their start at Łódź's famous film school—the city, sometimes called "HollyŁódź," has its own "Avenue of the Stars" on Piotrkowska. Contributing to this tradition, the museum has acquired props and sets from recent Polish films and rebuilt them in and around the building. With neo-Baroque cherubs lolling on the ceilings and Venetian mosaics underfoot, the style of Scheibler Palace is best described as Industrial Magnate Eclectic. Museum highlights include a massive 1900 animation machine called the *fotoplastikon* and the animation sets on the second floor. The basement hosts rotating photography exhibits. *(Pl. Zwycięstwa 1, behind a park off Piłudskiego. ☎674 09 57; www.kinomuzeum.pl. Open Sept.-June Tu 9am-5pm, W and F-Su 9am-4pm, Th 11am-6pm; July-Aug. Tu-W and F-Su 10am-4pm. 4zł, students 3zł; Tu free.)*

🎵 🎭 ENTERTAINMENT AND NIGHTLIFE

As a hub of Polish film, Łódź hosts several annual film festivals. The most famous of these are the **International Festival of the Art of Cinematography** "Camerimage" (late Nov. to early Dec.) and the **International Film and Television School Festival** "Media School" (mid-Oct.). The **Dialogue of Four Cultures** (Festiwal Dialogu Czterech Kultur) in early September includes film, theater, and music presentations.

THE LOCAL STORY

ŁÓDŹ KALISKA

Chances are, most of the bars you know don't have manifestos. In Łódź, however, the line between a bar and an art movement can be blurry. Not just any drink-tank, Łódź Kaliska is named for the art group founded in Łódź in 1979 and has a seasoned cult following. If you're here on the weekend, you may run into some of Poland's most acclaimed actors and artists taking a flaming shot off their tilted bar. Łódź Kaliska, the group, was originally created as an anti-Communist art organization. Under martial law in the early 80s the group secretly produced an art magazine, *Tango*, and showed films in a hidden location.

Once a perennial object of criticism for both the political and the artistic establishment, today the group enjoys respect from scholars and bargoers alike. The walls and furniture of Łódź Kaliska—the bar—are adorned with some of the group's influential work, and the unusual toilets, along with the Bartender's Special Shot, are among the artistic touches tucked into this playful local institution. Spend a night here to understand why people drive all the way from Warsaw to drink at Kaliska—and why many locals consider this the best bar n Poland.

Łódź Kaliska, Piotrkowska 102 (☎630 69 55; www.lodzkaliska.pl). Disco F-Sa. Open M-Sa noon-3am, Su 4pm-3am.

Łódź prides itself on extraordinary nightlife. **Piotrkowska** turns into publand a little after 9pm, though plenty of drinking is already underway by mid-afternoon.

Łódź Kaliska, Piotrkowska 102 (☎630 69 55). This local legend—bar, club, and offbeat art space—has such a cult following that people drive from Warsaw to drink here for the night. Beer 7zł. Open M-Sa noon-3am, Su 4pm-3am (see sidebar, p. 487).

Quo Vadis, Piotrkowska 65 (☎632 19 19). Named for the Nobel Prize-winning 1896 novel by Henryk Sienkiewicz, Quo Vadis offers a Polish epic of a different sort: the house specialty drink is a towering 5L glass of beer (39zł). In summer, this sidewalk patio is a stronghold of the Łódź party scene. Open daily 10am-late. Cash only.

Logo Music Caffe, Piotrkowska 52 (☎630 77 88), upstairs through the ice cream shop. Like a younger, trendier version of Kaliska, Logo draws students and hipsters with a roster chock-full of artsy events, a fully stocked bar, and DJs who spin some of the best music in Łódź. Logo hosts fashion shows, screens independent animation, and exhibits work by local artists. The excellent espresso machine serves an Egyptian roast. Long lines for huge disco F-Sa. Coffee 6zł. Bottled beer 8zł. Open daily 3pm-late. Cash only.

Klub Muzyczny Riff Raff, Roosevelta 9 (☎637 58 89). Pub/club Riff Raff blends foosball, rock, and beer with flickering fluorescent lighting to create an atmosphere as appealingly gritty as Łódź itself. DJ and dancing every F and Sa after 8pm. 18+. Cover F-Sa 5-10zł. Open daily 6pm-late. Cash only.

POZNAŃ   ☎(0)61

Poznań (POZ-nayn; pop. 590,000) is a city of many faces. Influenced by the Prussians and the Germans, Poznań buzzes with economic efficiency, especially during its many international trade fairs. The romantic Stare Miasto (Old Town) swells with meandering tourists in summer, and a lively arts scene thrives just below the all-business surface. On the edges of Stare Miasto, a constant stream of construction speaks to the rapid changes that the cosmopolitan city is undergoing.

▐ TRANSPORTATION

Trains: Dworcowa 1 (☎866 12 12). *Kasa* 7 for international tickets. Open 24hr. To: **Częstochowa** (5hr., 3 per day, 48zł); **Gdynia** (4½hr., 7 per day, 44zł); **Gniezno** (1hr., 26 per day, 11zł); **Kołobrzeg** (4hr., 6 per day, 42zł); **Kraków** (5hr., 10 per day, 45-79zł); **Łódź** (5hr., 4 per day, 41zł); **Szczecin** (3hr., 19 per day, 36zł); **Toruń** (2½hr., 5 per day, 31zł); **Warsaw** (3hr., 23 per day, 47-92zł); **Wrocław** (2hr., 33 per day, 31-59zł); **Zakopane** (6hr., 3 per day, 55zł); **Berlin, GER** (3½hr., 7 per day, 92-125zł).

Buses: Towarowa 17 (☎833 15 11). Open 5:30am-10:30pm. To: **Gniezno** (1½hr., 54 per day, 10zł); **Jelenia Góra** (5½hr., 2 per day, 40zł); **Kraków** (9¾hr., 4 per day, 47zł); **Łódź** (4½hr., 7 per day, 34-38zł); **Malbork** (5½hr., 1 per day, 45zł); **Szczecin** (4¼hr., 5 per day, 33zł); **Warsaw** (4¼hr., 1 per day, 38zł); **Wrocław** (3½hr., 8 per day, 28zł).

Public Transportation: Tickets 1.20zł per 10min., 2.40zł per 30min. Students 0.65zł per 10min. Large luggage needs its own ticket. Prices double 11pm-4am. **Night buses** and **trams** distinguished by 3-digit route numbers.

Taxi: Radio Taxi (☎9191).

◣▐ ORIENTATION AND PRACTICAL INFORMATION

Poznań is a huge city, but almost everything you want can be found in **Stare Miasto.** The **train station,** Poznań Główny, is on **Dworcowa** at the edge of Stare Miasto. The **bus station** is on **Towarowa.** To get to the **Stary Rynek** (Old Market Square), exit the train station, climb the stairs, turn left on the bridge, and turn right on **Roosevelta.** After several blocks, turn right on **Św. Marcin.** Continue to **al. Marcinkowskiego,** go

Poznań

ACCOMMODATIONS
Hotel Lech, 3
Schronisko Młodzieżowe #3 (HI), 7
Przemysław, 6
Nasz Klub, 12

FOOD AND CAFES
Bar Mleczny Pod Kuchcikiem, 4
Cacao Republika, 9
Dramat, 10
Green Way Bar Wegetariański, 8

NIGHTLIFE
Czarna Owca, 5
Scena Pod Minogą, 2
W Starym Kinie, 1
Za Kulisami, 11

ENTERTAINMENT
Towarzystwo Muzyczne im. Henryka Wieniawskiego, 13

STARY RYNEK INSET

Szewska
Dominikańska
Wielka
Szewska
Siłusięska
Museum of Musical Instruments
Wodna
PL. KOLEGIACKI
Klasztorna
Żydowska
Mokra
Kramarska
Kozia
Wroniecka
Świętosławska
Old Town Hall
Gołębia
Wrocławska
Rynkowa
STARY RYNEK
CIT
Zamkowa
Franciszkańska
Góra Przemysława
Paderewskiego
BUS
Szkolna
Kozia
23 Lutego
Museum of Useful Art

MAIN MAP

Malta Lake
RONDO ŚRÓDKA
Majakowskiego
Podwale
ŚRÓDKA
Cathedral of St. Peter and St. Paul
Mieszka I
OSTRÓW TUMSKI
most Mieszka I
Church of the Virgin Mary
Panny Marii
Panny Marii
Warta
Szyperska
Pasłowa
Estkowskiego
Garbary
Szczecińska
Wielka
Park Cytadela
Poznań Garbary
Grochowe Łąki
Grobla
Małe Garbary
Stawna
Wielka
Wodna
Garbary
Mostowa
Muśnicheńgo
PL. BERNARDYŃSKI
Ku Cytadeli
STARE MIASTO
Dominikańska
Stawna
Szewska
Za Bramką
Park Chopina
Ne Podgórnej
Północna
Przepadek
Bóźnicza
WIELKOPOLSKI
Żydowska
Rynkowa
Kozia
Parish Church of the City of Poznań of St. Mary Magdalene
Podgórna
Zielona
Długa
PL. WIELKOPOLSKI
PL. Wolnica
SEE STARY RYNEK INSET
STARY RYNEK
Wrocławska
Szyna
Klika
PIASKI
Kurpiela
al. Niepodległości
Św. Wojciech
Działowa
National Museum
PL. Przemysłowa
Szymańskiego
Kościelna
Józefa
Mylna
Nowowiejskiego
23 Lutego
al. Marcinkowskiego
Empik Megastore
Krysiewicza
Strzelecka
Św. Marcin
Kórnicka
Ogrodowa
Półwiejska
Rybaki
Jackowa
PL. NIEPODLEGŁOŚCI
Dzierżyńska
Solna
Wrzeszcz
PL. RATAJSKIEGO
Piętroko
PL. WOLNOŚCI
Wysoka
Piekary
Kościuszki
Sporna
Spórna
Cicha
PL. 3 Maja
27 Grudnia
Omnibus Bookstore
Gwarna
Ratajczaka
ŚW. MARCIN
Taczaka
Kościuszki
Park Dąbrowskiego
Libelta
Nowowiejska
Kantaka
Garbaska
Taylora
Towarowa
Chopina
Palace of Culture
Św. Marcin
Monument to the 1956 uprising
al. Niepodległości
Park Marcinkowskiego
Przemysłowa
al. Wielkopolska
K. Pułaskiego
Fredry
Park Mickiewicza
Wieniawskiego
Statue of Adam Mickiewicz
PL. A. MICKIEWICZA
Powstańców
Towarowa
Kwiatowa
Dworzec PKS
Kómaroniec
Kościuszki
Zacisze
Krasińskiego
Dąbrowskiego
most Teatralny
Skośna
Dworcowa
Poznań Główny
most Dworcowy
Glob-Tour
Norwida
Poznańska
Jeżyce
Barżyńskiego
Niska
Roosevelta
F. Roosevelta
most Uniwersytecki
RONDO KAPONIERA
TO 6 (100m), 7 (1km)
Głob-Tour

POLAND

0 200 meters
0 200 yards

left, and turn right on **Pąderewskiego**. Alternatively, catch any **tram** going to the right along Św. Marcin from the end of Dworcowa. From Roosevelta, trams #5 and 8 run to Stare Miasto. Get off at Marcinkowskiego.

Tourist Offices: Centrum Informacji Turystycznej (CIT), Stary Rynek 59/60 (☎852 61 56; fax 855 33 79). Provides **free maps** and accommodation info, and arranges tours (220zł). Open June-Aug. M-F 9am-6pm, Sa 10am-4pm; Sept.-May M-F 9am-5pm, Sa 10am-2pm. **Glob-Tour**, Dworcowa 1 (☎/fax 866 06 67), in the train station. Offers tourist info, **maps** (6-8zł), and **currency exchange**. Open 24hr.

Currency Exchange: Bank Pekao S.A., Św. Marcin 52/56 (☎855 85 58), cashes **traveler's checks** for 1% commission. Open M-F 8am-6pm, Sa 10am-2pm. **Bank Zachodni**, Fredry 12 (☎853 04 16). Has **Western Union**. Open M-F 8am-6pm.

Luggage Storage: At the train station. 2zł plus 0.15% of declared value. Open 24hr. Lockers also available at the train and bus stations. Large bin 8zł, small 4zł.

English-Language Bookstore: Omnibus Bookstore, Św. Marcin 39 (☎853 61 82). Open M-F 10am-7pm, Sa 10am-4pm. AmEx/MC/V.

24hr. Pharmacy: Apteka Centralna, 23 Lutego 18 (☎852 26 25).

Hospital: Szpital Miejski, Szkolna 8/12 (☎999).

Internet: ■ **KLIK**, Szkolna 15 (☎609 276 072). Enter from Jaskółcza. Serving coffee (5zł), tea (4zł), and beer (7zł) in a chic interior, KLIK would draw patrons even without Internet. 5zł per hr., students 3.50zł per hr. Open daily 9am-late. **Pięterko**, Nowowiejskiego 7 (☎662 38 45). 2.50zł per hr. Open M-Sa 10am-midnight, Su noon-midnight.

Post Office: Kościuszki 77 (☎853 67 43; fax 869 74 08). For **Poste Restante**, go to windows #6 or 7 upstairs. Open M-F 7am-9pm, Sa 8am-6pm, Su 9am-5pm. **Branch** next to the train station open 24hr. **Postal Code:** 61-890.

■ ACCOMMODATIONS

During trade fairs, which occur all year except July-August and December, businesspeople fill the city. Some prices double. Finding a decently priced room is virtually impossible without calling ahead—and difficult even then. You can find the dates of all fairs online at www.mtp.com.pl. The helpful staff at ■**Przemysław ❶**, Głogowska 16, rent comfortable **private rooms** near the center. (☎866 35 60. Singles 42zł, during fairs 68zł; doubles 64/96zł. Open M-F 8am-6pm, Sa 10am-2pm; open 2hr. later during fairs; July-Aug. closed some Sa.)

Schronisko Młodzieżowe #3 (HI), Berwińskiego 2/3 (☎/fax 866 40 40). From train station, turn left on Roosevelta, which becomes Głogowska. Go right on Berwińskiego (3rd stoplight). Outside the center and short on frills, but has clean 2- to 10-bed rooms. Reception 5-9pm. Lockout 10am-5pm. Curfew 10pm. Dorms 24-30zł. Cash only. ❶

Nasz Klub, Woźna 10 (☎851 76 30; www.naszklub.pl). From the train station, take tram # 5 or 8 to Marcinkowskiego and cross the Rynek to Woźna; hotel is in a covered driveway on the left. A few short blocks from the Rynek, Nasz Klub offers tasteful and newly furnished rooms above a spacious, serene restaurant. A rare find in Stare Miasto. Rooms have baths, telephones, and TVs. Breakfast included. Check-in and check-out noon. Reception 24hr. Singles 120zł; doubles 180zł; triples 220zł. Cash only. ❹

Hotel Lech, św. Marcin 74 (☎853 01 51; www.hotel-lech.poznan.pl). With a history in hospitality that predates WWI, this lime-green hotel on busy św. Marcin has airy, modern rooms. Communications amenities cater to business travelers: all rooms have satellite TV, telephone, Internet, and baths. Breakfast buffet included. Singles 162zł, students with ISIC 72zł; doubles 244zł; triples 336zł; suites 254zł. During fairs singles 240-310zł; doubles 370-430zł; triples 480zł. Sa-Su 20% discount. MC/V. ❸

➊ FOOD

Along Wielka there are several **24hr. grocery stores.** In summer, enjoy the home-made treats and locally grown fruits of the **open-air market** in pl. Wielkopolski, off 23 Lutego. (Open M-Sa 7:30am-afternoon.)

▨ Bar Mleczny Pod Kuchcikiem, św. Marcin 75 (☎853 60 94). The traditional Polish food is so scrumptious that this milk bar earned the "Dobre bo Polskie" (Good because it's Polish) stamp of approval. Their sausages (4-6.50zł) and cucumber salads (4zł) stand out as favorites. Go early, as lunch food runs short with the onslaught of ravenous students. Entrees 3-5zł. Open M-F 8am-8pm, Sa 8am-5pm, Su 10am-5pm. Cash only. ➊

Dramat, Stary Rynek 41 (☎856 09 36). A rarity among the many overpriced, under-flavored Stary Rynek restaurants that coast on their prime location, Dramat serves good *naleśniki* at reasonable prices. If you find the multitude of sauces dizzying, ask your server for a recommendation. Beer 5.50-6.50zł. Breakfast 9.50zł. Main course *naleśniki* 6.50-9.50zł. Open daily 10am-midnight. Bar open 2pm-midnight. MC/V. ➊

Green Way Bar Wegetariański, Taczaka 2 (☎853 69 12). Branch at Zeylanda 3 (☎843 40 27). A rainbow of juice and smoothie pitchers lines the counter at this vegetarian favorite, where the servings are generous and the friendly staff make perfect *samosas* (7.50zł). Rotating menu of soy dishes, lasagnas, and hearty pastas and salads. Main dishes 5-9zł. Open M-F 11am-7pm, Sa noon-7pm, Su noon-5pm. Cash only. ➊

Cacao Republika, Zamkowa 7 (☎855 43 78). The steady whir of hot-chocolate mixers reveals the house specialty (5-8zł), sipped on wicker seats in the company of antiques. Romantic upstairs, where mixed drinks (7-13zł) flow freely, is strewn with plush red couches and low tables. Open M-Sa 10am-midnight, Su 10am-10pm. Cash only. ➊

➏ SIGHTS

Ostentatious 15th-century merchant houses, notable for their rainbow paint jobs, line the fountain-filled **Stary Rynek.** The houses surround the multicolored **Old Town Hall,** a triumph of Renaissance architecture. Every day at noon a crowd gathers outside the clock tower to watch two **mechanical billy goats** emerge from a door above the clock and butt heads a dozen times. According to legend, the cook hired to prepare a feast celebrating the clock's 1511 completion burnt the venison that was to be served to the governor. Frantic, the cook stole two goats to cook instead, but they exposed his ruse when they escaped to the clock tower and began fighting in front of the guests. The museum (Muzeum Historii) in the town hall recalls Wielkopolska's history since the 13th century, but the most captivating sights are the painted ceilings and 15th-century stone doorways. You can also find the 1913 version of the mechanical goats. (☎852 56 13. Open M-Tu 10am-4pm, W 11am-6pm, F 9am-4pm, Sa-Su 10am-3pm. 5.50zł, students 3.50zł; Sa free.) The vast **National Museum** (Muzeum Narodowe), Marcinkowskiego 9, contains a marvelous collection of 13th- to 19th-century Western European paintings and modern Polish art. (☎856 80 00; fax 851 58 98. Open Tu 10am-6pm, W 9am-5pm, Th and Su 10am-4pm, F-Sa 10am-5pm. 10zł, students 6zł; Sa free.) One of the National's daughter museums is the ▨**Museum of Musical Instruments** (Muzeum Instrumentów Muzycznych), Stary Rynek 45, which features antique and exotic instruments, as well as a piano that once belonged to Chopin. (☎852 08 57. Open Tu-Sa 11am-5pm, Su 11am-3pm. 5.50zł, students 3.50zł. Sa free.) Its sister museum, the **Museum of Useful Art,** Góra Przemysława 1, on the hill by Stary Rynek, exhibits 13th- to 18th-century swords. (☎852 20 35. Open Tu-W and F-Sa 10am-4pm, Su 10am-3pm. 3.50zł; students 2.20zł. Sa free.)

POLAND

One stop from the Old Town on trams #1, 4, 8, or 16 in **Ostrów Tumski** stands the **Cathedral of St. Peter and St. Paul** (Katedra Piotra i Pawła), the first cathedral in Poland. The original 10th-century church is said to have been the site of Poland's symbolic baptism, when Mieszko I, the first prince of the Piast dynasty, forsook paganism in 966. In its ornate ▓**Gold Chapel** (Kaplica Złota) lie the tombs of two Piast rulers: Prince Mieszko I and his oldest son, Bolesław the Brave, Poland's first king. (Cathedral open M-Sa 9am-6pm, Su 1:15-6:30pm. Gold Chapel 2zł.)

Within the striking rose-colored **Parish Church of the City of Poznań of St. Mary Magdalene,** at the end of Świętosławska off Stary Rynek, sculpted ceilings and columns spiral toward heaven. (Free concerts Sa 12:15pm.) **Pl. Mickiewicza** commemorates the 1956 clash over food prices between workers and government troops, which resulted in 76 deaths. Two stark crosses knotted together with steel cable are emblazoned with the dates of five additional Communist-era worker uprisings. A recording tells the story from a console in front of the monument. (In several languages, including English and Esperanto. Free.)

🎵 🌿 ENTERTAINMENT AND FESTIVALS

Poznań's music and theater scene is lively but fickle. The monthly *Poznański Informator Kulturalny, Sportowy i Turystyczny* (IKST) contains an English supplement on cultural events. (Sold at bookstores and some kiosks. 3.90zł.) The **Towarzystwo Muzyczne im. Henryka Wieniawskiego** (Music Society), Świętosławska 7, provides classical concert info. (☎852 26 42; fax 852 89 91. English spoken. Open M-F 9am-5pm. Ring the bell.) The huge **International Theater Festival** comes to Malta Lake in late June and early July. Other festivals include the **Jazz Festival** in early March, the **International Blues Festival** in late May and early June, and a **folk art festival** in July. For tickets and info on these and other cultural events, contact **Centrum Informacji Miejskiej,** Ratajczka 44, next to the Empik Megastore. (☎94 31. Open M-F 10am-7pm, Sa-Su 10am-5pm.) Poznań's many experimental artistic performances and film screenings are concentrated in venues along Nowowiejskiego. For current listings, check the free Mapa guide (www.czyli.info).

🍷 NIGHTLIFE

Bars and cafes—many of them inexplicably Wild West-themed—surround the Rynek, and dance clubs dot Stare Miasto. A more avant-garde scene thrives on **Nowowiejskiego,** where bars serve up attitude and drinks until morning.

▓ **W Starym Kinie,** Nowowiejskiego 8 (☎852 22 41; www.wstarymkinie.iq.pl). An antique film projector on the bar and a gregarious crowd welcome patrons to the magical "Old Cinema." Relax in old movie theater seats at the bar downstairs; head upstairs to take in one of the frequent film screenings, rock and jazz concerts, or innovative DJ sets. Beer 6.50zł. Tu movie night, W "Classic Vinyl," F Disko Inferno. 18+. Open M-Sa 10am-1am, Su 6pm-midnight. Cash only.

Czarna Owca (Black Sheep), Jaskółcza 13 (☎853 07 92; www.czarnaowca.pl). A Poznań institution. Wagon wheels festoon the sturdy bar upstairs, and a spirited crowd lounges on the leather couches downstairs. The dance floor hosts one of the most hedonistic parties in town. Beer 4.50-6zł. F house, garage, and hip-hop; Sa rock and pop. Open M-F 4pm-late, Sa 5:30pm-late. Cash only.

Za Kulisami (Behind the Curtains), Klasztorna 8 (☎853 23 97). With a slew of letters taped to the bar and a broken-in collection of wooden furniture, relaxed Za Kulisami is a favorite haunt of Poznań's young artists. Comedian regulars spice up the bar conversation, and blues and jazz patter lightly in the background. Beer 5zł, but a staggering 1.5L goes for a mere 15zł. Open daily 4pm-late. Cash only.

Scena Pod Minoga, Nowowiejskiego 8 (☎852 79 22). Neighboring W Starym Kinie is a tough act to follow, but exuberant Pod Minogą, a student dance favorite, holds its own. Rooms wind through 2 floors of a rambling house. Free live music upstairs M-Sa nights ranges from piano and bagpipes to old-fashioned jam sessions. You won't hear house or techno on this dance floor. The bartenders work all sorts of magic with grenadine. Beer 4-6zł. 18+. Open M-Sa 10am-late, Su 4pm-midnight. Cash only.

▓ DAYTRIP FROM POZNAŃ

LICHEŃ

From Poznań, take one of 9 daily buses to Konin (2hr., 19zł). From the intracity bus stop in the Konin bus station parking lot, hop on one of 8 daily mikrobusy to Licheń (25min., 4-5zł). Mikrobus stops at the main entrance, Klasztorna 4. To return to Konin, catch one of 30 daily PKS buses from the bus stop 100m from the main entrance (25min., 4-5zł). 12 daily buses run from Konin back to Poznań. ☎270 81 00; www.lichen.pl.

With the sprawling acreage of a theme park, the **Sanctuary of Licheń** is one of the world's most grandiose pilgrimage sites. Approximately one million pilgrims trek to Licheń annually to glimpse two of Poland's most stunning religious sights.

A petite masterpiece rests in the **Chapel of Saint Dorothy,** the brick church to the right at the end of the entrance drive. The image of the **Madonna Licheńska** revealed itself in an 1813 apparition to Tomasz Kłossowski, a Polish soldier wounded near Leipzig, Germany, while fighting for Napoleon. Kłossowski prayed to the Virgin Mary, begging to die on Polish soil, and she appeared before him clutching a white eagle. Kłossowski survived and sought her likeness, which he found in the tiny town of Lgota. In 1852, the icon was moved to Licheń, and when Nazis took over the church during WWII, the painting was hidden and escaped damage. Today, the stunningly beautiful icon is flanked by gold-fluted columns and red votive candles. Even the elderly take part in the physically uncomfortable ritual of circling the icon on their knees—to do otherwise would offend worshippers.

In contrast with the subtle beauty of the Madonna Licheńska, the colossal gold dome of the **Licheń Basilica** looms as Poland's largest temple, the seventh-largest in Europe. Begun in 1994 and completed in 1999, this massive structure impresses viewers with its sheer scale. Visitors can access the basilica only by way of the **Path of the Cross,** a flower-lined procession through the Stations of the Cross (10min., to the left at the end of the entrance drive). Heavy gilded columns line the marble-filled nave, whose solemnity is broken only by the warbling organ. The altar is an overwhelming sight, with marble detailing and the iridescent words *jestem który jestem.* The trimmed grounds boast enormous fountains, sculptures, and grottoes. The least expensive souvenirs lurk in the stands across the street from the main entrance. Food options are limited—fast food abounds in street stands outside the entrance, but bringing a bag lunch is a better option.

TORUŃ   ☎(0)56

Toruń (pop. 210,000; est. 1233), extols itself as the birthplace of Mikołaj Kopernik, a.k.a. Copernicus. Even before the local genius came to fame, the mercantile medieval city was known far and wide: it was called "beautiful red Toruń" for its impressive brick-and-stone structures. Today, parishioners pray in 500-year-old churches, and children scramble through the ruins of a Teutonic castle, while visitors stroll through the city's cobblestone streets and linger along the riverwalk.

POLAND

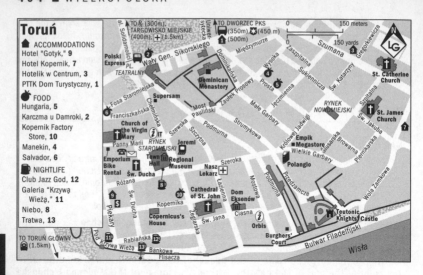

⌐ TRANSPORTATION

Trains: Toruń Główny, Kujawska 1 (☎94 36). International *kasa* sells Wasteels and InterRail. Open M-F 7am-5pm, Sa-Su 7am-2pm. To: **Gdańsk** (3¼hr., 7 per day, 36zł); **Gniezno** (1½hr., 5 per day, 23zł); **Łódź** (2¾hr., 4 per day, 32zł); **Poznań** (2¼hr., 5 per day, 31zł); **Szczecin** (4½hr., 1 per day, 44zł); and **Warsaw** (2¾hr., 6 per day, 37zł).

Buses: Dworzec PKS, Dąbrowskiego 26 (☎655 53 33). Open 4am-midnight. To: **Białystok** (8½hr., 1 per day, 52zł); **Gdańsk** (3½hr., 2 per day, 31zł); **Kołobrzeg** (7hr., 2 per day, 40zł); **Łódź** (3¼hr., 6 per day, 27zł); **Szczecin** (6½hr., 1 per day, 44zł); **Warsaw** (4hr., 9 per day, 29-36zł); and **Berlin, GER** (9½hr., 1 per day, 120zł). **Polski Express** (☎22 844 55 55) runs buses from the Ruch kiosk north of pl. Teatralny to: **Kołobrzeg** (6¾hr.; 1 per day; 44zł, students 27zł); **Łódź** (3hr., 2 per day, 29-31/21zł); **Szczecin** (5¼hr., 2 per day, 52/33zł); **Warsaw** (3½hr., 11 per day, 34-37/23zł).

Public Transportation: (☎655 52 00). **Bus** tickets 1.90zł at kiosks, 2.30zł from drivers. Prices rise annually. Luggage needs its own ticket.

Taxis: ☎91 91, wheelchair-accessible transport 91 96. To avoid being overcharged, make sure the driver uses a meter. 4.30zł base, 1.60zł per km.

Bike Rental: Emporium, Piekary 28 (☎657 61 08). Bikes 5zł per hr.; nonmonetary deposit accepted. Open M-F 10am-6pm, Sa-Su 10am-4pm. V.

◼✴◪ ORIENTATION AND PRACTICAL INFORMATION

The tourist office and most sights are in and around **Rynek Staromiejski** (Old Town Square). To get to the Rynek from the train station, take bus #22 or 27 across the **Wisła River** to **pl. Rapackiego.** Head through the park, with the river on your right, to find the square. On foot, take **Kujawska** left from the train station, turn right onto **al. Jana Pawła II,** and hike over the Wisła. Pl. Rapackiego is on the right, after **Kopernika.** From the bus station, walk through the park and take a left on **Uniwersytecka.** Continue along the street and turn right on **Wały Gen. Sikorskiego.** At **pl. Teatralny,** turn left onto **Chełmińska,** which leads to **Rynek Staromiejski. Szeroka** and **Królowej Jadwigi** run to **Rynek Nowomiejski** (New Town Square).

Tourist Offices: IT, Rynek Staromiejski 25 (☎621 09 31; www.it.torun.pl). Has some **free maps,** including map of bus and tram system, and sells others (5.50-7zł). Open May-Aug. M and Sa 9am-4pm, Tu-F 9am-6pm, Su 9am-1pm; Sept.-Apr. closed Su.

Currency Exchange: Bank PKO, Kopernika 38 (☎610 47 15). Gives Visa **cash advances.** Open M-F 8am-6pm. **ATMs** line Szeroka.

English-Language Bookstore: Polanglo, Wielkie Garbary 19 (☎/fax 621 12 22; www.polanglo.pl). A lot of English fiction. Open M-F 10am-6pm, Sa 10am-2pm. MC/V.

Pharmacy: Apteka Panaceum, Odrodzenia 1 (☎622 41 59), off al. Solidarności, is open fairly late. Open M-F 8am-10pm, Sa 8am-3pm, Su 10am-2pm. AmEx/MC/V.

Medical Services: Szpital Bielany, św. Józefa 53/59 (☎610 11 00). Take bus #11. **Nasz Lekarz** has registration at Szeroka 25 (☎622 61 89). Physicians' offices are around the corner at Szczytna 1. Open M-F 8am-8pm, Sa 8am-2pm.

Internet: Jeremi Internet Cafe, Rynek Staromiejski 33, 1st fl. (☎602 350 652; www.jeremi.pl). Ring the buzzer. 3zł per hr. Open 24hr.

Post Office: Rynek Staromiejski 15 (☎621 91 00). **Telephones** inside. **Poste Restante** at window #9 open M-F 8am-6pm. Open M-F 8am-8pm, Sa 8am-3pm. Branch at train station open M-Sa 6:30am-8:30pm. **Postal Code:** 87-100.

▐ ACCOMMODATIONS

There are a number of reasonably priced accommodations in the center, but vacancies fill fast, so call ahead. Inexpensive hotels are often the best-situated budget option, but deal-seekers can check the **IT** (see above) for far-flung rooms in university dorms in July and August. (Singles 45zł; doubles 60zł.)

▨ **Hotel Kopernik,** Wola Zamkowa 16 (☎652 25 73). From the Rynek, follow Szeroka, go right on św. Jakuba, and left on Wola Zamkowa. At the edge of Stare Miasto beside the Teutonic Knights' Castle, Kopernik has complimentary mineral water, fluffy towels, and satellite TV. Dorms are spacious and fresh-scrubbed but fill quickly with students. Sausage-happy breakfast buffet 11zł. Check-in and check-out 2pm. Dorms 25zł; singles 76zł, with bath 115zł; doubles 136/180zł. Rooms 25% less F-Su. AmEx/MC/V. ❸

Hotelik w Centrum, Szumana 2 (☎652 22 46). From Rynek Staromiejski, follow Szeroka, veer left on Królowej Jadwigi through Rynek Nowomiejski, and cross Szumana. An inexplicable bright-green paint job is overcome by like-new wood furnishings, floral bedspreads, and other comforts. Prices are competitive for the location on the periphery of Stare Miasto. Breakfast 10zł. Internet 2zł per hr. Check-in 2pm. Check-out noon. Singles 70zł, with bath 90zł; doubles 110-120zł; triples 170zł; quads 180zł. Cash only. ❸

PTTK Dom Turystyczny, Legionów 24 (☎/fax 622 38 55). Take bus #10 from the train station to Dekerta, then backtrack toward town on Legionów. Close to the bus station. Although this is a trek from town, the mirthful staff, tucked edges, and smoothed linens of Dom Turystyczny make the smoky dorms inviting. A favorite of Polish school groups, so be sure to book ahead. Check-in 2pm. Check-out noon. Dorms 27-37zł; singles 60zł; doubles 77zł; triples 96zł; quads 108zł; quints 135zł. Cash only. ❶

Hotel "Gotyk," Piekary 20 (☎658 40 00); gotyk@ic.torun.pl). The Gothic portal and burgundy walls may send you back a few centuries, but modern amenities will ease your return. The hotel staff escorts you to radiant rooms with carved bedsteads and Internet. Breakfast included. Reception 24hr. Check-in 2pm. Check-out noon. Singles 150-180zł; doubles 250-300zł; apartments 300-350zł. AmEx/MC/V. ❺

◖ FOOD

Toruń still offers its centuries-old treat: **gingerbread** *(pierniki)*. Toruń's tradition of ginger-cakes dates to the 14th century. The original cakes, tough and unsweetened, were considered a medicine rather than a snack. Toruń kept its gingerbread recipe a secret for centuries, and even today many gingerbread-makers guard their recipes closely. When selecting gingerbread, bear in mind that the intricately designed breads in the shapes of historical figures and buildings are made from the old recipes and are more decorative than edible. The smaller breads in simpler shapes are the soft, sweetened, modern form of gingerbread. **Supersam,** Chełmiska 22, is a 24hr. grocery store. **Targowisko Miejskie,** composed of an international bazaar and a farmer's market, offers an unusual collection of fruits, baked goods, and cheap clothing items. Two square blocks of bartering sprawl on Chełmińska and offer mild chaos and unparalleled bargains. (Open daily 8am-3pm.)

> **Kopernik Factory Store,** Żeglarska 25 (☎621 05 61), and Rynek Staromiejski 6 (☎622 88 32). Collect gingerbread likenesses of your favorite Polish kings, saints, and astronomers. Among the sweetened, modern gingerbread offerings, highlights include heart-shaped *katarzynki* and gingerbread-filled boxes in the shapes of Toruń's most beautiful buildings. Feel free to let the staff take some liberties with their selection. From 0.70zł for a small taste to 26zł for top-of-the-line historical figures. Sold by weight (about 12zł per kg) or pre-packaged. Open M-F 9am-7pm, Sa-Su 10am-2pm. MC/V. ❷

> **Manekin,** Wysoka 5 (☎652 28 85). Although somewhat confused in its country-western-mannequin-garden decor, Manekin sustains throngs of students on massive and delicious square *naleśniki* made to order. Sweet and savory are cooked up in endless varieties, but with gargantuan servings you'll be lucky to finish dinner, let along dive into dessert (*naleśniki;* 2-10zł). The curry chicken-and-cheese comes with all 3 of the best sauces (9.50zł). Open M-Th and Su 10am-10pm, F-Sa 10am-11pm. Cash only. ❶

> **Karczma u Damroki,** al. Solidarności 1 (☎622 36 60), in a Kashubian farmhouse in the Ethnographic Park. In medieval times, a *karczma* was an eatery for knights and peasants alike. Skirted by garden patios, Karczma u Damroki accurately recreates traditional dishes. The mushroom soup (6zł) and liver with apple and onion (15zł) are both popular, but the cult favorites are esoteric mixed drinks such as "Elvis Lives!!!" (10.50zł). Curiously translated English menu. Entrees 18-33zł. Open daily 10am-1am. MC/V. ❸

> **Hungaria,** Prosta 17 (☎622 41 89). In the company of a hefty disco ball and offbeat wall paintings, patrons dig into Hungarian specialties such as goulash (7.50zł) and potato pancakes (13zł). The wood benches are packed with locals for dinner, and many stop by just for a drink and a glimpse of French butlers and chubby prostitutes cavorting on the walls. Entrees 4-24zł. Open M-Sa 11am-10pm, Su 11am-9pm. Cash only. ❷

> **Salvador,** Franciszkańska 20 (☎501 50 51 94), in a flatiron building on the edge of Stare Miasto. Delivers tea (5-6zł per pot), coffee (cappuccino; 3.50zł), and alcohol to students and professors sprawled out on supple leather sofas in the company of an alarming number of Dali prints. Open daily 10am-midnight. Cash only. ❶

🗿 SIGHTS

An astounding number of attractions are packed into Toruń's ramparts, particularly in the 13th-century **Stare Miasto** (Old Town), built by the Teutonic Knights.

COPERNICUS'S HOUSE (DOM KOPERNIKA). The likely birthplace of astronomer Mikołaj Kopernik has been meticulously restored and showcases astronomical instruments, Kopernik family documents, and artifacts from some of the astronomer's lesser-known activities, such as improving the defenses of Olsztyn Castle and translating Greek poetry to Latin. A sound-and-light show centered on a miniature model of the city (c. 1550) plays every 30min. and features an excellent video about the town's early history. Choose from eight languages, including English. (*Kopernika 15/17.* ☎622 70 38, ext.13. Open W, F, Su 10am-4pm; Tu, Th, Sa noon-6pm. 10zł, students 6zł. Sound-and-light show 10/6zł. Both 18/11zł.)

TOWN HALL (RATUSZ). One of Europe's finest examples of burgher architecture, this 14th-century building dominates the Rynek Staromiejski. The building once contained the lively trading stalls of the 15th-century merchants who crowded Toruń daily with spices, foreign spirits, and fish. The hall also hosted clandestine meetings in which notable citizens organized their grievances against the Teutonic Order into a region-wide uprising. The Ratusz now contains the **Regional Museum** (Muzeum Okręgowe). Exhibits include a famous 16th-century portrait of Kopernik, artifacts from Toruń's numerous craft guilds, and a rich collection of 20th-century Polish art, in addition to early sacred art and stained glass. The neighboring tower provides a panorama of Toruń's most charming architecture. *(Rynek Staromiejski 1. ☎ 622 70 38. Museum open May-Aug. Tu-W and Sa noon-6pm, Th and Su 10am-4pm; Sept.-Apr. Tu-Su 10am-4pm. 10zł, students 6zł; Su free. Tower open May-Sept. Tu-Su 10am-6pm. 10/6zł.)* Outside, it's impossible to miss the statue of Kopernik watching over the city. Another local "hero," the Raftsman ringed by gold frogs, also flanks the Ratusz. Legend has it that his flute charmed animals, delivering the city from a pesky frog plague; he was rewarded with marriage to the mayor's daughter.

TEUTONIC STRUCTURES. The 13th-century **Teutonic Knights' Castle** survived two centuries before the burghers burned it to the ground in a 1454 revolt. The knights were originally called into the area to help defeat invading pagans, but soon established their own oppressive rule. The insurgent revolt against the castle set off a number of uprisings around the region, and hostilities continued for 20 years before Toruń was taken under the rule of the Polish king. The castle ruins house a booth where you can try your hand at archery (4zł). The 14th-century **toilet tower** served as indoor plumbing and as a kind of fecal defense, shooting more than just the cannons in the enemy's direction. *(Przedzamcze. ☎ 622 70 39. Open daily 9am-8pm. 1zł.)* The nearby **Burghers' Court,** at the end of Podmurna, was built in 1489 from bricks of the destroyed Teutonic castle and served as a medieval social and sporting center. Today, it hosts cultural events listed on the door and at the IT. Across town, to the right as you face the river, stands the **Krzywa Wieża** (Leaning Tower), built in 1271 by a knight as punishment for breaking the Order's rule of celibacy. The assumption was that the tower's "deviation" would remind the knight of his own. The less imaginative credit the shifting, sandy ground beneath. Either way, the 15m tower doesn't lean enough to scare away entrepreneurs, who have opened up a bar and a cafe inside. *(Krzywa Wieża 17.)*

CHURCHES. The **Cathedral of St. John the Baptist and St. John the Evangelist** (Bazylika Katedralna pw. Św. Janów) is the most impressive of the many Gothic churches in the region. Built between the 13th and 15th centuries, it mixes Gothic, Baroque, and Rococo elements. A 14th-century polychrome in the chancel depicts the cathedral's burgher patrons, Old Testament scenes, and the Last Judgment. In 1473, the baby Kopernik was baptized in the **baptismal font.** The tower holds Tuba Dei, the oldest bell in Poland. *(At the corner of Żeglarska and Św. Jana. Open Apr.-Oct. M-Sa 8:30am-5:30pm, Su 2-5:30pm. 2zł, students 1zł. Tower 6/4zł.)* The **Church of the Virgin Mary** (Kościół Św. Marii), with its slender stained-glass windows and patterned ceilings, is less ornate than many Polish churches and somewhat dusty. The chancel holds the mausoleum of Swedish queen Anna Wazówna. *(On Panny Marii. Open M-Sa around 8am-5pm. Recorded info 2zł.)* The undiscovered but beautiful **St. James Church** (Św. Jakuba) contains dramatically lit icons and is currently undergoing restorations which should render it an exceptional sight by 2006. Its treasure is the "Tree of Life" crucifix. *(Sw. Jakuba just off Rynek Nowomiejski. Open daily 10am-5pm.)*

🌸 🎭 FESTIVALS AND NIGHTLIFE

In May, Toruń hosts **Probaltica,** a celebration of chamber music and arts, and the "Kontakt" **International Theater Festival.** Eastern European folk musicians converge in early June for the **Folk Music Festival.** On June 20, the town celebrates the bi-annual **Gingerbread Day.** In June and July, during the **Music and Architecture Festival,** classical concerts are held in different historic buildings each weekend. July and August usher in the annual **Summer Street Theater** series, which stages weekly performances in July and August. Check **IT** for more info. Nightlife, especially at student bars and clubs, is lively.

🏛 **Niebo,** Rynek Staromiejski 1 (☎621 03 27). Niebo (heaven) may be an odd name for a subterranean cafe, but this Gothic cellar beneath the Ratusz proves itself worthy with celestial *szarlotka* (3zł) and summer outdoor seating. Run by a local singer-songwriter, Niebo hosts live jazz and cabaret. Open M-Th and Su noon-midnight, F-Sa noon-2am. Check out the folk art at the adjacent pub **Piwnica pod Aniołami** (Cellar Beneath the Angels; ☎658 54 82). Beer 4-5zł. Open M-F 10am-1am, Sa-Su 10am-4am. Cash only.

Club Jazz God, Rabiańska 17 (☎652 21 308; www.jazzgod.torun.com.pl). With free live jazz Su 10pm, this stone cellar pays homage to its name. The rest of the week, students fill its scattered seats for lively conversation and thunderous rock, reggae, and Polish pop. The party starts around 8:30pm. Open M-Th and Su 5pm-2am, F-Sa 5pm-4am.

Galeria "Krzywą Wieżą," Pod Krzywą Wieżą 1/3. On the 2nd fl. of the Leaning Tower, whose cramped and ancient interior doesn't have a single straight line. The toilets occupy a 14th-century women's prison. A must in summer for students and professors alike. A terrace precariously attached to the ramparts offers views across the Wisła. Beer 4.50-6zł. Open M-F 1pm-1am, Sa-Su 10am-2am.

Tratwa, Flisacza 7. The best of the bars alongside the Wisła, Tratwa occupies the former municipal gasworks, just outside the Monastery Gate. Foosball and darts offer a playful distraction, and exhibits feature artworks by bar regulars. Hemmed by lush vines, the patio hosts rock and reggae concerts and grills sausage and fish (10-15zł) on the open barbecue. Beer 5-6zł. Open M-Th and Su noon-2am, F-Sa noon-4am.

WOLIN ISLAND: MIĘDZYZDROJE ☎(0)91

On the Baltic Coast near the German border, Wolin Island cradles glacial lakes, sweeping sea bluffs, and a bison preserve. The largest of the island's resort towns, Międzyzdroje (myen-dzi-ZDROY-eh), lures visitors with a gorgeous stretch of coast and access to the hiking and cycling trails of pristine Woliński National Park. With a base in Międzyzdroje, intrepid visitors can explore the island's many hidden corners, from the scattered ruins of forts and churches to windswept marshes.

▊ TRANSPORTATION. Trains run to: **Kraków** (9¼hr., 2 per day, 52zł); **Poznań** (5hr., 5 per day, 42zł); **Świnoujście** (20min., 19 per day, 3.80zł); **Szczecin** (2hr., 18 per day, 26zł); **Warsaw** (7hr., 2 per day, 50zł); **Wrocław** (9½hr., 5 per day, 47zł). **Buses** run to: **Kołobrzeg** (3hr., 9 per day, 21zł); **Świnoujście** (20min., 44-65 per day, 3.60zł); **Szczecin** (2hr., 2 per day, 18zł); **Warsaw** (8hr., 1 per day, 36zł). Buses travel to points along the hiking trails, including the towns of **Kołczewo, Wolin,** and **Wisełka** (10-30min., 6:30am-8pm, 6zł).

▊ ▊ ORIENTATION AND PRACTICAL INFORMATION. To reach the center from the **train station,** walk downhill and go left on Norwida. The **PKS bus stop** is on Niepodległości in front of the Muzeum WPN, near the corner of Kolejowa. Pedestrian **pl. Neptuna,** at the intersection of Niepodległości and Kolejowa, harbors many restaurants and shops. Several blocks north, the beach promenade along Bohaterów Warzsawy and Promenada Gwiazd bustles with fried fish stands, cotton candy, and a new pier. **PTTK,** Kolejowa 2, sells **maps** (1-8zł) and provides info about the park and accommodations. Their map of the city and park (4.50zł) is useful for ventures in the

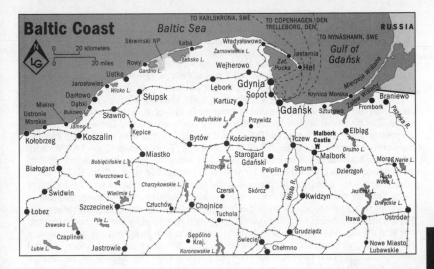

Baltic Coast

woods. (☎328 04 62. No English spoken. Open M-F 7am-4pm.) The *kantor* with the best **currency exchange** rates is at Niepodległości 2A. (Open M-F 9am-6pm, Sa 9am-3pm, Su 10am-1pm.) An **ATM** is outside the Polino Hotel at Zwycięstwa 1. **Luggage storage** is at the train station. (5zł per item per day. Open daily 7am-9:30pm.) A **pharmacy** is at Zwycięstwa 9. (☎328 00 90. Open M-F 8am-7pm.) Use the web at **Internet Cafe**, Norwida 17. (☎328 04 21. 4zł per hr. Open daily 10am-late.) The **post office** is at Gryfa Pomorskiego 7. (☎328 01 40. Open M-F 8am-8pm, Sa 8am-1pm.) **Postal Code: 72-500.**

⌐⌐ ACCOMMODATIONS AND FOOD. Watch for *wolne pokoje* (rooms available) signs, particularly along Gryfa Pomorskiego. Call ahead in July and August. Alternatively, talk to **PTTK**, Kolejowa 2, which arranges private rooms (32-35zł, 40-45zł with bath) and runs the tidy **PTTK Hotel Dom Turysty ❶**, in the same building as the office. Quirky rooms are variously outfitted with old radios and tropical-themed lanterns. (☎328 03 82. June-Aug. singles 30zł, with bath 55zł; doubles 60/110zł; triples 90/165zł. Sept.-May singles 25/40zł; doubles 50/80zł; triples 75/120zł. Cash only.) To get to **Camping Gromada ❶**, Bohaterów Warszawy 1, follow Kolejowa as it becomes Gryfa Pomorskiego. Take the right fork to Mickiewicza and turn left. A block from the beach, Gromada has aluminum cabins with small shaded rooms. (☎328 23 54. Complimentary beach towels. Reception 8am-10pm. Curfew 10pm. Campground open May-Sept. 1- to 4-person cabins with bath 30-59zł per person. Tents 9zł per person, students 7.50zł. Electricity 7.50zł. MC/V.)

Bistro Bar Pieróg ❶, Krasickiego 3, is a local favorite, with superb dumplings, soups to please the dedicated carnivore, and shark jaws decorating the walls. (☎328 04 23. Entrees 3-8zł. Open daily 9am-midnight; in low season 9am-9pm. Cash only.) The curious decor at **Dolce Vita ❷**, pl. Neptuna 2, involves bouquets of uncooked spaghetti. The eatery serves generous portions of tasty if unadventurous pizza and pasta adorned with mini EU flags. A pleasant terrace opens in summer. (☎328 17 70. Entrees 8-30zł. Open daily 10am-midnight. MC/V.) Cheery **Restauracja Cafeteria Centrum ❷**, pl. Neptuna 7/9, dishes up meaty *naleśniki* (9-12zł), superb coffee drinks (4-8zł), and daily Polish breakfasts including omelettes and grilled meats. (☎328 11 62. Open daily 10am-late. Cash only.) To grab some food on the run, head to the 24hr. convenience store **Sklep Smakasz**, Norwida 4. For **nightlife,** young locals go to beachfront **Klub Scena**, Bohaterów Warszawy 19, to the left of the entrance for the Wax Museum. Beware that most of the tables facing the dance floor are reserved for local VIPs, who may not take kindly to usurpers. (☎ 328 71 44. Beer 3zł. Cover F-Sa 10zł. Open daily 9pm-late.)

◪ **HIKING.** Although Międzyzdroje draws crowds as a prime beach resort, the true accolades belong to adjacent ◪**Woliński National Park,** whose wilds encompass much of Wyspa Wolin (Wolin Island) and shelter a dramatic stretch of coastline. The park is immaculately kept, with **hiking and bicycling trails** marked on trees and stones. The black and red trails begin at the end of **Promenada Gwiazd,** and the green at the end of **Leśna.** The blue trail begins on **Cmentarna** near the train station. These hikes are not very strenuous—don't expect Tatras trailblazing. Rent a **bike** at friendly **Willa 5,** Bohaterów Warszawy 16. (☎ 328 26 10. 5zł per hr. ID required. Open M-F 9:30am-8pm.) The **black trail,** the most demanding, immediately climbs the seaside cliffs to **Góra Kawcza** (61m), a lookout point with a breathtaking view of the Baltic. Look closely and you just might glimpse one of the park's famed eagles *(bieliki).* Just after Góra Kawcza, the trail hits a closed military area; backtrack a few steps and follow the trail into the woods. It eventually intersects the green trail and returns to Międzyzdroje. Lapping waves and secluded beach spots follow the **red trail,** a relaxed but visually sumptuous route which starts at the beach in Międzyzdroje and follows a 15km stretch of coastline beneath the cliffs. Just 2km from the pier, fishermen and pebbly coast replace the crowds. The trail passes under the highest of the Baltic's cliffs at **Góra Gosan** (93m), then turns back into the woods and passes the lakeside town of Wisełka, the Kikut lighthouse, and another scenic cliff at **Strażnica** (74m) before intersecting the green trail, where you can loop back around or continue off the island by way of Międzywodzie. Rent a bike to check out the **green trail,** which has an extensive set of **bike paths.** There are long stretches of less rewarding territory between the highlights, but the 15km route heads into the heavily forested heart of the park past glacial lakes. Just 1.2km from the trailhead is the popular **bison preserve** (rezerwat żubrów). (☎ 328 07 37. Open May-Sept. Tu-Su 10am-6pm; Nov.-Apr. Tu-Su 8am-4pm. 3zł, students 2zł.) The trail passes the villages of Warnowo (7km), Kołczewo (7km), and **Lake Czajcze.** The green trail ends where it hits the red trail, 3km past Kołczewo. The **blue trail** winds all the way from Międzyzdroje to Szczecin. At 74.5km, this trail is more conducive to bicycling than hiking. The tame stretch near Międzyzdroje heads south along the edge of Woliński Park, passing ruins, nature preserves, and lookout points, and leaves the island through the small town of Wolin.

TRI-CITY AREA (TRÓJMIASTO)

World-class beaches, a flurry of cultural life, and stunning Hanseatic architecture have made the portside Trójmiasto (pop. 465,000) Poland's summer playground of choice. The three cities on the Baltic make a study in contrasts: the restored splendor of old Gdańsk conceals a turbulent millennium of history. Sopot basks in beachfront glitz, while trade-rich Gdynia fuels the area's economy. Great public transportation makes it easy to find a bed in one city and explore the others.

GDAŃSK   ☎(0)58

At the mouth of the Wisła and Motława Rivers, Gdańsk (gh-DA-insk) has flourished for more than a millennium as a crossroads of art and commerce. The one-time Hanseatic trade city was treasured as the "gateway to the sea" during Poland's foreign occupation in the 18th and 19th centuries. Gdańsk has faced its challenges admirably—WWII left 90% of the ancient city center in ruins, yet today carefree tourists flock to the street opera, graceful brick buildings, and meandering waterways. The rise of Lech Wałęsa's Solidarity brought 16 months of hope to

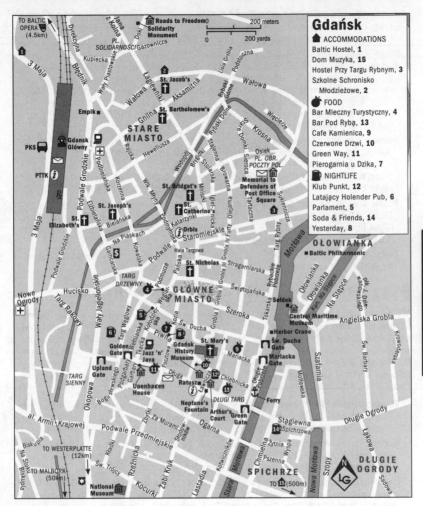

Gdańsk

🛏 ACCOMMODATIONS
Baltic Hostel, **1**
Dom Muzyka, **15**
Hostel Przy Targu Rybnym, **3**
Szkolne Schronisko
  Młodzieżowe, **2**

🍎 FOOD
Bar Mleczny Turystyczny, **4**
Bar Pod Rybą, **13**
Cafe Kamienica, **9**
Czerwone Drzwi, **10**
Green Way, **11**
Pierogarnia u Dzika, **7**

🍺 NIGHTLIFE
Klub Punkt, **12**
Latający Holender Pub, **6**
Parlament, **5**
Soda & Friends, **14**
Yesterday, **8**

POLAND

the now-famous shipyards and to all of the Eastern Bloc, gruesomely extinguished by martial law only to triumph again in 1989. Reconstructed and revitalized, with amber-filled beaches, cobblestone alleys, and sprawling construction sites, Gdańsk proves it has both beauty and brawn—as well as the Trójmiasto's heart.

▐ TRANSPORTATION

Trains: Gdańsk Główny, Podwale Grodzkie 1 (☎ 94 36). To: **Białystok** (7½hr., 3 per day, 50zł); **Częstochowa** (8hr., 5 per day, 53zł); **Kołobrzeg** (2¾hr., 8 per day, 41zł); **Kraków** (7hr., 13 per day, 58zł); **Łódź** (8hr., 6 per day, 46zł); **Lublin** (8hr., 3 per day, 51zł); **Malbork** (50min., 40 per day, 15-30zł); **Mikołajki** (5hr., 1 per day, 41zł); **Poznań** (4½hr., 7 per day, 42-73zł); **Szczecin** (5¾hr., 5 per day, 45zł); **Toruń** (3¼hr., 7 per day,

36zł); **Warsaw** (4hr., 22 per day, 46-79zł); **Wrocław** (6-7hr., 4 per day, 47-80zł). **SKM** (Fast City Trains; ☎628 57 78) run to **Gdynia** (35min.; 4zł, students 2zł) and **Sopot** (20min.; 2.80/1.40zł) every 10min. during the day and less frequently at night. Buy tickets downstairs. Punch your ticket in a *kasownik* machine before boarding.

Buses: 3 Maja 12 (☎302 15 32), behind the train station, connected by an underground passageway. To: **Białystok** (9hr., 2 per day, 51zł); **Częstochowa** (7½hr., 1 per day, 55zł); **Kołobrzeg** (6hr., 1 per day, 47zł); **Kraków** (10¾hr., 1 per day, 68zł); **Łódź** (8hr., 4 per day, 57zł); **Malbork** (1hr., 8 per day, 10-13zł); **Toruń** (2½hr., 2 per day, 31zł); **Warsaw** (5¾hr., 9 per day, 66zł); **Kaliningrad, RUS** (6-7hr., 2 per day, 28zł). Comfortable **Polski Express** buses run to **Warsaw** (4½hr., 2 per day, 45zł).

Ferries: Żegluga Gdańska (☎301 49 26; www.zegluga.gda.pl) runs ferries (May-Sept.) to domestic destinations, from Zielona Brama (The Green Gate). To: **Gdynia** (2hr.; 2 per day; 45zł, students 32zł); **Hel** (1½-3hr., 2 per day, 53/36zł); **Sopot** (1hr., 5 per day, 38/25zł); **Westerplatte** (50min., 9 per day, round-trip 39/20zł). **Polferries,** Przemysłowa 1 (☎343 02 12), in Gdańsk-Brzeźno. To **Nynäshamn, SWE** (19hr., 3 per wk., 250zł).

Public Transportation: Gdańsk has an extensive **bus** and **tram** system. Buses run 6am-10pm. 10min. 1.10zł; 30min. 2.20zł; 45min. 2.70zł; 1hr. 3.30zł; day pass 6.20zł. **Night buses,** designated by "n," run 10pm-6am. 3.30zł; night pass 5.50zł. Bags over 60cm tall or wide need their own tickets.

Taxis: To avoid paying inflated tourist rates for taxis, book a cab by phone or over the Internet at state-run **MPT** (☎96 33; www.artusmpt.gda.pl).

■ ⁊ ORIENTATION AND PRACTICAL INFORMATION

While Gdańsk sits on the Baltic Coast, its center is 5km inland. From the **Gdańsk Główny** train and bus stations, the center is just a few blocks southeast, bordered on the west by **Wały Jagiellońskie** and on the east by the **Motława River**. Take the underpass in front of the station, go right, and turn left on **Heweliusza**. Turn right on **Rajska** and follow the signs to **Główne Miasto** (Main Town), turning left on **Długa**, also called **Trakt Królewski** (Royal Way). Długa becomes **Długi Targ** as it widens near the Motława. Gdańsk has several suburbs, all north of Główne Miasto.

Tourist Offices: PTTK Gdańsk, Długa 45 (☎301 91 51; www.pttk-gdansk.com.pl), in Główne Miasto, has **free maps.** Tours available May-Sept., for groups of 3-10, 80zł per person. Open May-Sept. M-F 9am-5pm, Sa-Su 9am-3pm; Oct.-Apr. M-F 9am-6pm.

Budget Travel: Almatur, Długi Targ 11, 2nd fl. (☎301 24 03; www.almatur.gda.pl), in Główne Miasto. Sells **ISIC** (59zł), offers hostel info, and books international air and ferry tickets. Open M-F 10am-5pm, Sa 10am-2pm.

Currency Exchange: Bank Pekao SA, Garncarska 31 (☎801 365 365). **Cashes traveler's checks** for 1% commission and provides MC/V **cash advances** for no commission. Open M-F 8am-6pm, 1st and last Sa of each month 10am-2pm.

Luggage Storage: In the train station. Locked room downstairs (4zł plus 0.45zł per 50zł declared value, min. 6.25zł) or lockers upstairs (small 4zł, large 8zł). Lockers in bus station (small 4zł, large 8zł). Both open 24hr.

English-Language Bookstore: Empik, Podwale Grodzkie 8 (☎301 62 88, ext. 115). Sells maps and *Gdańsk in Your Pocket* (5zł). Open M-Sa 9am-9pm, Su 11am-8pm.

24hr. Pharmacy: Apteka Plus (☎763 10 74), at the train station. Ring bell at night.

Medical Services: Private doctors, Podbielańska 16 (☎301 51 68). Sign says "Lekarze Specjaliści." 50zł per visit. Open daily 7am-7pm. For **emergency care,** go to **Szpital Specjalistyczny im. M. Kopernika,** Nowe Ogrody 5 (☎302 30 31).

Internet: Jazz'n'Java, Tkacka 17/18 (☎305 36 16; www.cafe.jnj.pl), in the Old Town. 3zł per 30min., 5zł per hr. Open daily 10am-10pm. **Internet Cafe,** Podwale Grodzkie 10 (☎320 92 30), inside the movie theater across the street from the train station. 5zł per hr. Open M-Sa 9am-1am, Su 9:30am-1am.

Post Office: Długa 23/28 (☎301 88 53). **Exchanges currency** and has **fax** service. For **Poste Restante,** use the entrance on Pocztowa. **Telephones** inside. Open M-F 8am-8pm, Sa 9am-3pm. **Postal Code:** 80-801.

ACCOMMODATIONS

Gdańsk has limited accommodations; it's best to reserve ahead. In July or August you can stay in a **university dorm.** Consult **PTTK. Private rooms** (20-80zł) can be arranged through **PTTK** or **Grand-Tourist** (Biuro Podróży i Zakwaterowania), Podwale Grodzkie 8, connected to the train station via tunnel, near Empik. (☎301 26 34; www.grand-tourist.pl. Singles 50-60zł; doubles 80-100zł; apartments 180-280zł. Open daily July-Aug. 8am-8pm; Sept.-June M-Sa 10am-6pm. Cash only.)

▨ **Hostel Przy Targu Rybnym,** Grodzka 21 (☎301 56 27; www.gdanskhostel.com), off Targ Rybny, on the waterfront south of Podwale Staromiejskie and across from the *baszta* (tower). At Poland's wackiest hostel, guests enjoy a chummy common room where tango plays by morning and techno by afternoon. Hilariously bitchy staff. Free bowls of homemade pickles. Breakfast, coffee, and Internet all free. Bicycles and kayaks 20zł per day. Reception 24hr. Dorms 40zł; doubles 120-140zł; quads 250zł. Cash only. ❷

▨ **Baltic Hostel,** 3 Maja 25 (☎721 96 57; www.baltichostel.com), 3min. from the station. From train station, take the KFC underpass to bus station, then go right on 3 Maja and take the pedestrian path on the right. Inside an aging brick apartment building, the renovated Baltic has the best hostel rooms in Gdańsk. Bright colors, hardwood floors, and eclectic furnishings bustle with backpackers. Free breakfast, towels, laundry, Internet, and bike and kayak use. Reception 24hr. Dorms 35-40zł; doubles 50zł. Cash only. ❷

Szkolne Schronisko Młodzieżowe, Wałowa 21 (☎301 23 13). From the train station, follow Karmelicka from City Forum; go left on Rajska and right on Wałowa. Dorms feature new furnishings, and baths have enough showers and sinks to clean a small army. Full kitchen and common room set the facilities a cut above most HI hostels, but the living is as clean as the rooms: there's no smoking or drinking, and a midnight curfew. Reception 8am-10pm. Dorms 16-21zł; singles 25-30zł; doubles 50-60zł. Cash only. ❶

Dom Muzyka, Łąkowa 1/2 (☎300 92 60). From the train or bus station, take tram #8 or 13 to the Akademia Muzyczna stop. Dom Muzyka is on the corner of Łąkowa and Podwale Przedmiejskie, behind the gate of the yellow building. Just across the Motława from the Old Town, recently renovated Muzyka offers large, newly furnished, lyre-bedecked rooms that do their namesake pride. Rooms include TVs, phones, and modem connections, as well as a generous breakfast buffet. Singles 155-165zł; doubles 220-230zł; suites 345-350zł. MC/V. ❹

FOOD

For fresh produce, try **Hala Targowa,** on Pańska, in the shadow of Kościół św. Katarzyny, just off Podwale Staromiejskie. Row upon row of stands sell everything from raw meat and dried fruits to shoe soles. (Open M-F 9am-6pm, 1st and last Sa of each month 9am-3pm.) The supermarket, **Esta,** is nearby at Podwale Staromiejskie 109/112, in Targ Drzewny. (Open M-Sa 10am-10pm, Su noon-10pm.)

▨ **Cafe Kamienica,** Mariacka 37/39 (☎301 12 30), in St. Mary's shadow. Antique couches and an elegant stone patio promise languid meals, and Cafe Kamienica follows through with fresh, delicate entrees, such as salad with grilled chicken (14zł). Tea 4zł. Superb coffee drinks 6-11zł. Light entrees 7-26zł. Open daily June-Sept. 9am-midnight; Oct.-May 10am-10pm. AmEx/MC/V. ❷

Pierogarnia u Dzika (Wild Boar Pierogi Bar), Piwna 59/60 (☎305 26 76). Locals swear by these *pierogi* (12-18zł) stuffed with everything from caviar to strawberries. The rich offerings, especially the *pierogi farmerski* with chicken, nuts, and raisins (14zł), over-

RETURN OF THE BATTLE OF GRUNWALD

From under the smoke, you can make out the flash of swords and the cascade of arrows. Across the battlefield, a horn calls to the soldiers—or is that the soundtrack from a Hollywood battle epic? Well, it is the 21st century. Every year in mid-July, almost 100,000 Poles gather to reenact the famed 1410 Battle of Grunwald, to honor a famed Polish victory over the German Teutonic Knights. Walking the fine line between historical chaos and family barbeque, Grunwald on July 15 is perhaps the best sight in Poland. Camps of soldiers gather for the two weeks before the battle, carousing at night and honing their crafts by day. Daily Latin Mass and oratory competitions punctuate drinking and training. Local historical organizations often sponsor one or two soldiers and archers who train for several hours a week in preparation.

Upon arrival at the battlefield, be sure to change your złotych for medieval Talar (1 Talar=4 Złotych) at the numerous *kasy* in order to sample the abundant supply of sausages, lard, and, of course, beer. While waiting for the knights to suit up, you can try your hand at archery or peruse the stalls of homemade period goods. A small museum under the stone monument explains the battle sequence in great detail. (Open daily May-Sept. 9am-9pm. Entrance 6zł, students 3zł.) When

shadow the unadventurous decor. The 35-piece mixed platter (50zł) is terrific for large groups. Open daily 11am-11pm. MC/V. ❸

Bar Pod Rybą (Bar Under the Fish), Długi Targ 35/38/1 (☎305 13 07). With an unusual take on a Polish staple, serves huge baked potatoes with surprisingly addictive fillings (6-20zł) that run the gamut from chicken *shawarma* to chili (4-7.50zł). The Hungarian sausage topping is top-notch. Keep an eye out for the collection of antique coat-hangers. Open daily July-Aug. 11am-10pm; Sept.-June 11am-7pm. AmEx/MC/V. ❶

Green Way, Długa 11 (☎301 82 28). A small but thriving stronghold of vegetarianism in Gdańsk. With several varieties of organic quiche (3.50zł) and a wide selection of wraps (4.50-5zł), Green Way serves inexpensive, healthy food in a decor that is equally wholesome and colorful. Adventurous diners will enjoy their vitamin-rich beet juice (3.50zł). Open daily 10am-9pm. Cash only. ❶

Czerwone Drzwi (The Red Door), Piwna 52 (☎301 57 64). A telltale red door marks the entrance to the 19th-century burgher house, home to Gdańsk's most elegant cafe. High ceilings, velvet couches, and gold-frame mirrors match the graceful dishes, which fill Polish classics such as *pierogi* with unusual combinations like feta, saffron, and salmon (17zł). Despite high-class decor, The Red Door swings open to expats and weary travelers alike. Entrees 14-28zł. Open daily noon-11pm. AmEx/MC/V. ❷

Bar Mleczny Turystyczny, Szeroka 8/10 (☎301 60 13). If you can look past the plastic furniture and burnt-orange trays of this old-fashioned milk bar, you'll find truly delicious food for pocket change. *Gołąbki* (tasty stuffed cabbage, 4.20zł), are among the meaty specialties (3-6zł). Eat alongside deal-seeking workers and vacationing families. Open M-F 8am-6pm, Sa-Su 9am-4pm. Cash only. ❶

⊙ SIGHTS

▧ NATIONAL MUSEUM (MUZEUM NARODOWE).

Housed in the vaulted chambers of a former Franciscan monastery, this museum displays Flemish and Polish sacred art, with small collections of 18th- to 20th-century china and 18th-century Polish paintings. The jewel of the museum, Hans Memling's *Last Judgment* altar triptych, has a checkered history. In 1473, it was intercepted by Gdańsk pirates en route to England. The 20th century saw it ricochet between the Nazis and the Soviets before coming to rest in Gdańsk in 1956. If the massive triptych suits your fancy, don't miss Jacob van Swanenburgh's *Sybil and Aeneas in the Underworld,* similarly punctuated by fantastical creatures and damned nudes.

(Toruńska 1, off Podwale Przedmiejskie. ☎301 70 61; www.muzeum.narodowe.gda.pl. Open June to mid-Sept. Tu-F 9am-4pm, Sa-Su 10am-5pm; mid-Sept. to May Tu-Su 9am-4pm. 10zł, students 6zł; Sa free.)

▨ROADS TO FREEDOM (DROGI DO WOLNOŚCI). In the Gdańsk Shipyard where the Solidarity (Solidarność) movement was born, a powerful permanent exhibit documents the rise of the Eastern Bloc's first trade union. This moving multimedia journey begins with the early struggle against Soviet rule in the 1950s and chronicles the censorship, secret police, and propaganda that marked the era. Slides, films, and photographs trace the changing fortunes of Solidarity from the strikes of 1980 and the brutal period of martial law to the sweeping victory of 1989. *(Doki 1, in the Shipyard. ☎308 42 80. Open Tu-Su 10am-5pm. 6zl, students 4zl; W free.)*

DŁUGI TARG (LONG MARKET). The handsome main square, Długi Targ, is the heart of the painstakingly restored Główne Miasto. Gdańsk's characteristic row houses, adorned with dragon's head gutter spouts, line the surrounding cobblestones. The stone Upland Gate and the elegant blue-gray Golden Gate, emblazoned with gold-leaf moldings and the shields of Poland, Prussia, and Germany, mark the entrance to Długa. Ornate mechanical clocks and graceful sundials are a common sight. The 14th-century **Ratusz** (Town Hall), Długa 47, houses a branch of the **Gdańsk History Museum.** Baroque paintings adorn the ceiling of the museum's fantastic Red Chamber. Exhibits span Gdańsk's long history, from the first mention of the city to its reduction to rubble in WWII, with a large collection of amber art. Nearby, the 16th-century facade of **Arthur's Court** (Dwór Artusa), Długi Targ 43/44, now houses a 2nd branch of the History Museum, containing an elegant-but-quirky meeting hall with 3D paintings, suspended model ships, and a 16th-century stove. The palace faces **Neptune's Fountain,** where the sea god stands astride a giant shell. Closer to the city gates, the History Museum's 3rd branch, Rococo **Upenhagen House** (Dom Uphagena), Dluga 12, is an 18th-century merchant's home. Inside you'll find immaculately restored Rococo furnishings and a museum tracing the oft-forgotten history of mechanical clockmaking, which saw its "Golden Age" in Gdańsk from 1631-1775. *(Town Hall ☎301 48 71, Arthur's Court 301 43 59, Upenhagen House 301 23 71. Open June-Sept. M 10am-3pm, Tu-Sa 10am-6pm, Su 11am-6pm; Oct.-May Tu-Sa 10am-4pm, Su 11am-4pm. Each 8zł, students 4zł; combined ticket 15/7zł; W free.)*

the loudspeakers start to blare vaguely familiar full-orchestra Hollywood movie themes, join the crowds flocking to the battlefield, where a thousand knights kneel in prayer. An elaborately scripted and rehearsed exchange among cavalry, archers, and soldiers kicks off. The battle itself lasts about 50min., with emotional peaks and real wounds sustained. Although the advances and retreats have been planned, soldier-to-soldier combat is very real—mediators police the fields, making sure that soldiers lay down "dead" when they have suffered would-be fatal blows. As the battle draws to an end, everyone recommences drinking, eating, and shopping.

Getting to Grunwald might seem daunting, but is quite easy, as transport systems brace themselves for overflow. From Gdańsk or Warsaw, make connections in nearby Olsztyn. Buses leave the Olsztyn PKS station every 25-60min. from the 2nd bus stop for Olsztynek (50min., 3.70zł). From Olsztynek, PKS buses as well as private shuttle services ferry the crowds to the battlefield (25min., 3-5.10zł.) When the festivities come to an end, it is easy to find a ride directly back to Olsztyn from one of the PKS buses that line up in anticipation of the crowds to come (1½hr., 8.80zł).

CHURCHES. Massive Gothic **St. Mary's Church** (Kościół Mariacki) holds 25,000 red bricks. Don't miss the gigantic 1464 astronomical clock atop the church. Climb the 405 steps for a panoramic view of the city. *(Open June-Aug. M-Sa 9am-5:30pm, Su 1-5:30pm; low-season hours vary. 3zł, students 1.50zł.)* In the foreground on Wielkie Młyny, the 13th-century **St. Nicholas's Church** (Kościół św. Mikołaja) is the only church in Gdańsk not gutted during WWII. Behind it is the 12th-century **St. Catherine's Church** (Kościół św. Katarzyny), which preserves a cemetery dating from AD 997 and is the final resting place of astronomer **Jan Heweliusz.** Sixty-six steps above, the Baroque **Tower Clocks Museum** displays antique clocks and a 49-bell carillon that has rung on the hour since the 50th anniversary of the outbreak of WWII. Keep an ear out for carillon concerts every Friday at 11am. *(☎ 305 64 92. Museum open June-Sept. Tu-Su 10am-5pm. Cemetery 1zł. Museum 8zł, students 4zł; W free.)*

NAUTICAL SIGHTS. The **Central Maritime Museum** (Centralne Muzeum Morskie) spans both banks of the Motława, including a main museum, the medieval **Żuraw** (Harbor Crane), and the ship **Sołdek.** The crane, an oft-photographed symbol of the city, towers over the riverside promenade **Długie Pobrzeże.** An exhibit beside the crane displays traditional boats of Asia, Africa, and South America, while the main museum offers an exhaustive tour through the maritime Poland and Joseph Conrad's life at sea. *(To reach the Sołdek, take the shuttle boat or walk from the end of Długi Targ, cross 2 bridges, and bear left. ☎ 301 86 11. Open June-Aug. daily 10am-6pm; Sept.-May Tu-Su 9:30am-4pm. Crane 6zł, students 4zł. Museum 6/4zł. Sołdek 6/4zł. Shuttle boat round-trip 3/1.50zł. All museums and shuttle boat 14/8zł. English guide 20zł per group; call ahead.)*

MAIN TOWN. The flags of Solidarity fly at the **Solidarity Monument,** on pl. Solidarności, at the end of Wały Piastowskie. The **Memorial to the Defenders of Post Office Square** (Obrońców Poczty) recognizes the postal workers who bravely defended Gdańsk against the Germans in one of the first battles of WWII. On September 1, 1939, postal employees resisted the German army until the building was engulfed in flames. Those who survived the blaze were executed or sent to concentration camps. A museum inside the reconstructed post office documents the controversial establishment of a Polish postal service in occupied Gdańsk in 1920. An unexpected collection of modern art depicting Polish POWs and a world map with Poland at its center are exhibit highlights. *(From Podwale Staromiejskie, go north on Olejama and turn right at Urzad Pocztowy Gdańsk 1. ☎ 301 76 11. Open M and W-F 10am-4pm, Sa-Su 11am-4pm. 3zł, students 2zł. Captions in Polish only.)*

WESTERPLATTE. When Germany attacked Poland, the little island fort guarding the entrance to Gdańsk's harbor gained unfortunate distinction as the first target of WWII. Outnumbered 20 to one, the Polish troops held out for a week until a lack of food and munitions forced them to surrender. **Guardhouse #1** has been turned into a museum with a small exhibit recounting the fateful battle. *(☎ 343 69 72. Open May-Sept. daily 9am-7pm. 3zł, students 2zł. English booklet 6zł.)* The path beyond the exhibit passes the bunker ruins and the massive **Memorial to the Defenders of the Coast.** Follow the spiral path for a closer look at the monument and a glimpse of the shipyard and the sea. Below the monument the words "Nigdy Więcej Wojny" (Never More War) are inscribed. *(From the train station, take bus #106 or 606 south to the last stop. The bus stop is to the right of the station entrance in front of KFC. Żegluga Gdańska also runs a 50min. ferry; every hr. 10am-6pm; round-trip 34zł, students 18zł. ☎ 301 49 26. Board by the Green Gate, Zielona Brama, at the end of Długi Targ.)*

🎵 ENTERTAINMENT

Of the three cities that line this stretch of the Baltic, Gdańsk offers the most mainstream entertainment. The **Baltic Philharmonic,** Ołowianka 1 (☎305 20 40), performs free riverside concerts in summer. Opera-lovers can check out the **Baltic Opera** (Opera Bałtycka), al. Zwycięstwa 15 (☎341 46 42). Tickets to the Philharmonic and the Opera run 8-40zł. The **Church of the Blessed Virgin Mary** has organ concerts (20zł, students 10zł) every Friday at 8:15pm in July and August. Special summer events include a **Street Theater Festival** (mid-July), a **Shakespeare Festival** (Aug.), and the **International Organ Music Festival** (late June to late Aug.), at nearby Oliwa. For three weeks beginning the last week of July, the Old Town welcomes the immense **Dominican Fair,** a trading party begun in the 15th century when monks came to trade their handcrafts. Today you can buy homemade souvenirs, art, food, and jewelry.

NIGHTLIFE

When the sun sets, crowds turn to the party spots of Długi Targ. Gdańsk tends more toward pubs than clubs, and plays a sorry second to Sopot's nightlife, but a few worthy spots keep the local students supplied with music, art, and beer. *City* lists events in the Tri-City Area, and *Gdańsk in Your Pocket* offers updated club listings.

Klub Punkt, Chlebnicka 2 (☎302 18 11). At the intersection of Eastern Bloc debauchery and carnival haunted house, Klub Punkt stands apart from the tame crowd of Gdańsk bars. Drum-and-bass fans down vodka-and-tabasco shots (6zł) among plaster nudes beneath coffered ceilings. Often the last spot open in town. Open daily 4pm-late.

Latający Holender Pub, Wały Jagiellońskie 2/4 (☎802 03 63), near the end of Długa. A hot-air balloon appears to have crashed through the ceiling of this affable den of oddities, where an easygoing student crowd packs onto velvet couches beneath an array of flying machines. Drinks 4-22zł. Open daily noon-midnight.

Yesterday, Piwna 50/51 (☎301 39 24). Almost every surface of this popular student bar is painted with notables ranging from the Beatles to Mao, with a few bronze animal masks thrown in for good measure. Alternative rock gives way to pop and techno as dancing picks up around midnight in the cellar. Beer 6zł. Open daily 7pm-3am.

Parlament, św. Ducha 2 (☎302 13 65). This popular club entices a wild young crowd with a mile-long bar, a fog machine, and a maze of voyeuristic balconies overlooking the dance floor. Trailing glitter and resolve, the sleek crowd arrives in a flurry for hip-hop (F) and clubbing hits (Sa). Beer 5zł. 18+. Cover Th after 10pm 5zł; F-Sa 10zł, 5zł with ISIC. Open Tu-Sa 8pm-late. Dance floor open Th-Sa 10pm.

Soda and Friends, Chmielna 103/104 (☎346 38 61), across the 1st bridge at the end of Długi Targ, to the right. Hidden under a tame-looking restaurant, the basement of Soda and Friends is a pleasure palace outfitted with graffiti and porcelain theater masks. Known to host illustrious drag parties, the dance floor and neon bar fill with partygoers eager for hip-hop and hard liquor. Beer 6-9zł. Open daily 10am-late. MC/V.

DAYTRIP FROM GDAŃSK

MALBORK   ☎(0)55

Trains (40-60min.; 40 per day; 9.30zł, express 32zł) and buses (1hr., 8 per day, 9.40-13zł) run from Gdańsk to Malbork. From the station, turn right on Dworcowa, then left at the fork. Go around the corner to the roundabout and cross to the street across the way, Kościuszki. Follow it, then veer right on Piastowska, where signs for the castle appear. ☎647 08 00; www.zamek.malbork.com.pl. Castle open May-Sept. Tu-Su 9am-7pm; Oct.-Apr. Tu-Su 9am-3pm. Courtyards, terraces, and moats open May-Sept. Tu-Su 9am-8pm; Oct.-Apr. Tu-Su 9am-4pm. Kasa open 8:30am-7:30pm. Castle 30zł, students 17.50zł; 3hr. Polish tour included. English booklet 7zł. Tour in English 5zł. English-speaking guide 150zł. Grounds 6/4zł. Sound-and-light show May 15-Oct. 15 10pm; 10/5zł. AmEx/MC/V.

The largest brick castle in the world, ▓**Malbork** is a stunning feat of restoration and a rich lens onto the turbulent history of the surrounding region. The **Teutonic Knights** built Malbork as their headquarters in the 1300s. The Teutons first came to the region in 1230 at the request of Polish Duke Konrad Mazowiecki to assist the nation in its struggle against the Prussians. The Knights double-crossed the Poles, however, establishing their own state in 1309. In their heyday, the celibate order of warrior-monks marauded across the region, forcibly converting Lithuanians to Christianity and hunting bison in the forest surrounding Malbork. The knights' vows of poverty fell by the wayside, and while the Poles won several 15th-century battles against the order, it was the lavish lifestyle of the Teutonic Knights that lost them Malbork. In 1457, the Teutons had to turn over the castle to mercenary knights for outstanding debts, and the mercenaries promptly sold the castle to the Poles. It was under German control in WWII, when it housed a POW camp (Stalag XXB). Soviet bombing razed the castle at the war's end, but one of the world's largest works of reconstruction has since pieced the bricks of Malbork back together. The most beautiful rooms in the castle are the unfurnished **Grand Master's Chambers**, notable for columns in the shape of palm trees. The tour winds through the **High, Middle**, and **Low Castles** and visits the treasures of the **amber collection** and **weapons collection**. Keep an eye out for the **castle ghost**, Hans von Endorf, who has wandered Malbork's halls since he killed himself in 1330 out of guilt for the murder of his brother, the Grand Master. If you need to stay the night, consult IT or look for the ubiquitous signs advertising **private rooms** (20-60zł). An **IT tourist office** is outside the castle at Piastowska 15. (☎273 49 90. Open May-Sept. M 10am-6pm, Tu-F 9am-8pm, Sa 10am-6pm, Su 10am-4pm.)

SOPOT ☎(0)58

Poland's premier resort town, magnetic Sopot (pop. 50,000) draws throngs of visitors to its sandy beaches. Restaurants, shops, and street musicians dot the graceful pedestrian promenade, Bohaterów Monte Cassino, and the longest wooden pier in Europe rewards seaside amblers with spectacular Baltic views. Sopot's superb nightlife is renowned throughout Poland.

⌷ TRANSPORTATION. The **commuter rail (SKM)** connects Sopot to **Gdańsk** (20min.; 2.80zł, students 1.40zł) and **Gdynia** (15min.; 2.80/1.40zł) and runs 24hr. Trains leave from platform #1 every 10min. during the day and every 35-60min. at night. Stamp your ticket in the box or risk 50-100zł fines. **PKP trains** run to: **Białystok** (7¾hr., 3 per day, 49zł); **Kołobrzeg** (2hr., 3 per day, 39zł); **Kraków** (7hr., 9 per day, 58zł); **Lublin** (6hr., 2 per day, 51zł); **Łódź** (6hr., 5 per day, 48zł); **Malbork** (1hr., 29 per day, 18zł); **Poznań** (4½hr., 7 per day, 44zł); **Szczecin** (5hr., 4 per day, 46zł); **Toruń** (3½hr., 6 per day, 37zł); **Warsaw** (4¼hr., 14 per day, 47-81zł); **Wrocław** (6-7hr., 5 per day, 47-81zł); **Berlin, GER** (9¾hr., 1 per day, 264zł). **Ferries** (☎551 12 93) from the end of the pier go to: **Gdańsk** (1hr.; 2 per day; round-trip 53zł, students 36zł); **Gdynia** (35min., 2 per day, 39/22zł); **Hel** (1½hr., 7 per day, 55/38zł); **Westerplatte** (35min., 2 per day, 38/25zł). For a **taxi**, call the state-run **MPT** or order a taxi over the Internet through their website. (☎96 33; www.artusmpt.gda.pl. Base 5zł, 2zł per km.)

⁑⌷ ORIENTATION AND PRACTICAL INFORMATION. Dworcowa begins at the train station and heads left to the pedestrian **Bohaterów Monte Cassino**, which runs toward the *molo* (pier). Almost everything lies on or near Bohaterów Monte Cassino. The **tourist office IT**, Dworcowa 4, across from the train station, has **free maps** and brochures, sells **maps** (4-5zł) of the area, and arranges accommodations. (☎550 37 83; www.sopot.pl. Open daily June-Aug. 9am-8pm; Sept.-May 10am-6pm.) An **accommodations office** is in the same building. (☎551 26 17. Open June-Sept. 15. daily 10am-5pm; Sept. 16-May M-F 10am-3pm.) **PKO Bank Polski**, Monte Cassino 32/34, **exchanges currency**, gives MC/V **cash advances**, cashes **traveler's checks** for 1.5% commission (10zł min.), and has a MC/V **ATM**. (☎666 85 67. Open M-F 8am-7pm, Sa 9am-1pm.) A **24hr. pharmacy, Apteka pod Orłem**, is at Monte Cassino 37 (☎551 10 18). Head to **NetCave**, Pułaskiego 7a, for **Internet**. (3zł per 30min., 5zł per hr.; students 1/4zł. Open daily noon-10pm.) The **post office**, Kościuszki 2, has **telephones**. (☎551 17 84. Open M-F 8am-8pm, Sa 9am-3pm.) **Postal Code:** 81-701.

🏠🍴 ACCOMMODATIONS AND FOOD. Sopot is one of Poland's most popular and expensive resort towns, so reservations are a must in summer. Staying in Gdańsk will probably be cheaper. Consider renting a **private room**, which frequently requires a three-day stay; visit IT for help. (June-Aug. singles 46zł; doubles 78zł; triples 90zł; Sept.-May 39/62/90zł.) Beware of aggressive taxi drivers outside the IT offering **private rooms**—they operate illegally, and the quality of their rooms is dubious. **Hotel Wojskowy Dom Wypoczynkowy (WDW)** ❶, Kilińskiego 12, off Grunwaldzka, in the building marked "Meduza," offers the cheapest sea views in Sopot from its choice rooms. The pastel rooms, clustered in five vaguely themed buildings, have TVs and well-kept baths, and the premises include tennis courts. (☎551 06 85; www.wdw.sopot.pl. Breakfast included. Check-in 2pm. Check-out noon. Reserve at least 1 month ahead July-Aug. "Tourist Class" rooms without baths or breakfast 30zł; singles 120-175zł; doubles 220-260zł; triples 310-330zł; apartments 410zł. Oct.-May 10-15zł discount.) For travelers without the foresight to reserve a room months in advance, centrally located university dorms are a good option. **Universytet Gdański "Łajba"** ❶, Armii Krajowej 111 provides clean, spacious rooms with generous shared baths, and neighbors some of the most popular student bars. (☎550 91 64. Check-out 10am. Singles 46zł; doubles 64zł.) **"DS. 8"** ❶, 1 Maja 12, three blocks east of the train station, has similar rooms at similar prices. (☎550 91 91. Check-out 10am. Singles 42zł; doubles 84zł; triples 126zł; quads 168zł.) The nicest midrange beachside option is **Hotel Amber** ❸, Grunwaldzka 45, a small, modern hotel with bath, TV, and phone in each of its cheerfully colored rooms. (☎550 31 83. Breakfast included. Check-in and check-out 11am. Singles 260zł; doubles 320zł; triples 420zł.) Find camping at **Kemping nr. 19** ❶, Zamkowa Góra 25. Take the commuter rail (3min., every 10-20min., 1.25zł) to Sopot-Kamienny Potok, then go down the stairs, turn right, and cross the street. The site is behind the gas station on your left. Nr. 19 is a small, well-groomed, and friendly campground with clean bathrooms and a mid-sized playground. (☎550 04 45. Parking 7zł. Gates locked 10pm-7am. Open May-Sept. 10zł per person, 4-9zł per tent; 4-person bungalows 95-150zł.)

Monte Cassino is riddled with fashionable cafes and inexpensive food stands. A small 24hr. grocery, **Delikatesy**, Monte Cassino 62 (☎551 57 62), is steps away from the pier. For a more extensive selection, try **Elea SuperMarket,** Gen. Sikorskiego 8, at the base of Monte Cassino. (☎550 00 90. Open M-F 8am-9pm, Sa 8am-8pm, Su 9am-4pm. **Błękitny Pudel** ❷ (Blue Poodle) is at Monte Cassino 44. The garden of this quirky cafe is lovely in summer, while the interior, chock-full of tapestried chairs and antique curiosities, is as charismatic as the food. (☎551 16 72. *Pierogi* 18zł. Entrees 12-26zł. Open daily July-Aug. 10am-1am; Sept.-June noon-1am. Cash only.) *Naleśniki* are serious business at **Parasolka** ❶, Monte Cassino 31, where you can sample 50 different kinds of fillings (7-14zł), both traditional and innovative. The camembert with tomatoes and olives (12zł) is a veggie staple, best enjoyed in a garden complete with avant-garde fountain. (☎550 46 44. Entrees 7-18zł. Open daily 10am-10pm. Cash only.) Local institution **Przystań** ❶, al. Wojska Polskiego 11, along the beach, serves grilled and fried seafood under fishing nets and precariously hung dried blowfish. (☎550 02 41; www.barprzystan.pl. Fresh fish 4-7zł per 100g. *Hevelius* 5zł. Open daily 11am-11pm. Cash only.) **Pierogarnia "Szopa"** ❶, Powstańców Warszawy 1/3, just shy of the pier, has earned a reputation with locals for the best *pierogi* in town, bursting with pork, sweet cheese, or strawberries and yogurt. Local celebrities have signed the walls of the all-wood interior. (☎524 00 000. *Pierogi* 6.50-14zł. Open daily noon-midnight. Cash only.) **U Przyjaciół** ❷, Polna 55, 150m from the beach, offers rich but cheap traditional Polish food. Grilled cheeses with cranberries (12zł) and traditional pigs' knuckles (27zł) are house specialties, served among nostalgic bookcases beside a giant fireplace. (☎551 77 25; www.uprzyjaciol.pl. Entrees 8-27zł. Open daily noon-10pm. AmEx/MC/V.)

⚡ ENTERTAINMENT. Sopot's popularity stems from its vast white-sand **beach**, which offers endless recreation, from waterslides to outdoor theater. Stands along the beach rent equipment for watersports. The most popular sands lie at the end of Monte Cassino, where the 1827 wooden **pier,** Chopina 10, extends 512m into the sea. (☎551 00 02. M-F 2.50zł, Sa-Su 3.30zł.) Sopot, which is over 60% greenspace, also contains great **biking trails.** Buy a map from IT (4zł); all paths begin west of al. Niepodległości. Rent **bikes** at **Hotel Zhong Hua Hotel,** al. Wojska Polskiego 1, on the beach. (☎508 109 018. 8zł per 1hr., 20zł per 3hr., 30zł per 5hr., 40zł per 10hr. Open daily 9am-8pm. Cash only.) **Opera Leśna** (Forest Opera), Moniuszki 12, is an open-air theater with some of the best acoustics in Europe. Its rock and pop music festival, the **International Song Festival** (☎555 84 00) dominates the area in late August or early September. For tickets or info, call the theater or contact **IT Teatr Atelier,** Franciszka Mamuszki 2, stages independent theater on its beachside stage. (☎559 10 01. Show schedule at IT. Tickets 24-34zł.)

📸 NIGHTLIFE. Sopot is the Ibiza of the Eastern Bloc—in all of Poland, only Warsaw and Kraków can hold a candle to its nightlife. The beach town's legendary hedonism runs the gamut from exclusive discos to historic cafe-pubs. The flurry of cafes, pubs, and discos along Monte Cassino bears testament to Sopot's status as one of the hardest-partying towns in Poland. ▓**Soho clubogaleria,** Monte Cassino 61, brandishes art and attitude at every turn, playing jazz and alt-rock during the weeks and full-on house and techno on Fridays and Saturdays. Edgy, mildly disaffected students crowd the retro bar in the basement and the velvet couches upstairs. Exhibitions by local artists rotate bimonthly. (☎551 69 27. Beer 6.50zł. Open daily noon-5am.) Relive the Communist era's wackiest moments at ▓**Remanent,** al. Niepodległości 786/2, at the base of Monte Cassino. Soviet-standard vacuum cleaners and flags keep company with retro coffee-maker-fish-tanks and motorcycles in this cluttered bar just blocks from the university. On weekends, students flock for drinks served in mustard jars from an antique icebox. (☎888 333 444; www.saturator.net. Beer 5zł. Open daily 4pm-2am.) ▓**Józef K,** Kościuszki 4/1b, on the corner of Dworcowa and Kościuszki, is in the basement of a 19th-century apartment building. The copper-plated bar dispenses beer, wine, and mixed drinks at surreally good prices (4-11zł) in the midst of whitewashed wooden beams, stacks of books, and antique toys. (☎509 598 737. Open M-Sa 10am-late, Su 11am-midnight.) **Mandarynka,** Bema 6, off Monte Cassino, offers three floors of partying, each of which brings faster music and even faster drinking. The comfy cushions and large retro lamps of the ground floor are ideal for casual drinking and conversation, while the third floor's disco swells with dancing students on weekends. (☎550 45 63. Beer 6zł. Open M 1pm-late, Tu-Su noon-late.) **Papryka,** Grunwaldzka 11, lives up to its name with a spicy all-red interior outfitted in streamlined couches and offset by a few black antiques. Students and young entrepreneurs chat to folk and 80s remixes. (☎551 74 76. Open 3pm-late.) **Sfinks,** Powstańców Warszawy 18, not to be confused with the popular Polish restaurant chain of the same name, saw its heyday in 2003 as one of the country's hottest clubs. Today, vaguely Asian decor, strong liquors, and a lively crowd make a potent mix. In summer, monthly avant-garde theater and traveling DJs clinch Sfinks's position as a local favorite. (Cover F-Sa 15zł. Open daily 10pm-late. Disco open F-Sa 6pm-late.) **Galeria Kiński,** Kościuszki 10, to the right when coming from the station, is a smoky tribute to actor Klaus Kiński, born upstairs. Don't miss the scarlet-walled upstairs lounge or the stylish balcony. (☎551 17 56. Beer 5zł. Open daily 11am-3am.)

MAZURY

A train ride through the rolling hills of Mazury reveals an achingly beautiful landscape of pine groves, poppy fields, and glassy lakes. East of Pomorze, the region called the "land of a thousand lakes" actually cradles more than 4000 lakes. Small, quiet towns like Mikołajki greet visitors with waters to canoe, kayak, and sail.

MIKOŁAJKI (0)87

Serene little Mikołajki is a gateway to Poland's largest lake, Lake Śniardwy. In the center of town, a statue of a crowned fish leaps from a fountain, honoring Mikołajki's unlikely hero. Legend has it that the people of Mikołajki were bullied by a giant whitefish named Król Sielaw, who broke their nets and capsized boats until a fisherman caught him in a steel net. Król Sielaw said that if he were spared, Lake Mikołajskie would always be full of fish—and he kept his word. Today, the lakeside town boasts every amenity a traveler might seek, all in close proximity to the magnetic waters of the Mazury lakes.

▐▀▐ TRANSPORTATION AND PRACTICAL INFORMATION. Mikołajki is isolated from the rest of the country; make connections in Olsztyn. **Trains,** Kolejowa 1 (☎421 62 38), go to **Ełk** (1½hr., 2 per day, 16zł), **Olsztyn** (2¼hr., 3 per day, 13zł), and **Poznań** (7hr., 1 per day, 46zł). **Buses,** pl. Kościelny, go to **Lublin** (8¼hr., 1 per day, 68zł), **Olsztyn** (2hr., 7 per day, 16zł), and **Warsaw** (4-5hr., 6 per day, 58zł).

To reach the center from the train station, turn left on **Kolejowa** and then left on 3 Maja, which leads to **pl. Wolności,** the center of town. The **bus stop** is at the intersection of Kolejowa and 3 Maja, at the Protestant church. To get to the **lake,** take any right from pl. Wolności. **Al. Kasztanowa** and **al. Spacerowa,** pedestrian streets bordering the lake, bustle with restaurants and cafes. In the center, the **IT office,** pl. Wolności 3, provides visitors with **maps** (8zł) and info about accommodations and cultural events. (☎421 68 50; www.mikolajki.pl. Open June-Sept. daily 8am-8pm.) **Bank PKO BP,** pl. Wolności 7, cashes **traveler's checks** for 1.5% commission and provides MC/V **cash advances.** (☎421 69 36. Open M-Sa 9am-4pm, Su 10am-1pm.) A **pharmacy** is at 3 Maja 3. (☎421 63 16. Open M-F 8am-9pm, Sa 9am-6pm, Su 10am-4pm. MC/V.) Surf the **Internet** at **Piwnica Internetowa,** Szkolna 4d, off Kolejowa. (☎ 421 50 07. 3zł per 30min., 5zł per hr. Open daily 11am-9pm.) The **post office,** 3 Maja 8, has **telephones** outside. (Open May-Sept. M-F 8am-8pm, Sa 8am-2pm; Oct.-Apr. M-F 9am-5pm.) **Postal Code:** 11-730.

▐▐ ACCOMMODATIONS AND FOOD. Yellow signs point the way to **private rooms** and pensions. The best budget rooms are along Kajki. Decent lakeside accommodations run 40-50zł per person. **Pensjonat Mikołajki ❷,** Kajki 18, is a family-run business with stellar service and an amazing location on the banks of Lake Mikołajskie. From pl. Wolności, continue down 3 Maja until it turns into Kajki. Their generous breakfast will make *naleśniki*-lovers swoon. (☎421 64 37; www.pensjonatmikolajki.prv.pl. Kayak and bike rentals 8zł per hr., 30zł per day. Singles July-Aug. 70zł, with lake view 110zł; doubles 150/180zł. Low-season discount 25zł. Cash only.) Nearby **Noclegi ❶,** Kajki 8, offers inexpensive spic-and-span lakeside rooms. (☎421 63 62. Doubles and triples with bath 50zł per person. Cash only.) For local fish in a rustic garden sprinkled with plastic gnomes, head to open-air **Czarna Perła ❷** (Black Pearl), Okrężna 7a. Their specialty is *okonie na konie,* small and tasty Mazury lake fish (15zł). Fishing nets, pool tables, and foosball complete the vaguely pirate-themed experience. (Beer 4zł. Entrees 12-15zł. Open May-Sept. daily 11am-late. Cash only.) In a comfy green interior decorated with coconuts and modern art, **Pizza "Teja" ❶,** 3 Maja 18, dishes out pizzas, fries, and *zapiekanka* to patrons who've escaped the grip of the overpriced lakeside. (☎421 65 41. Pizza 8-12zł. Entrees 3-12zł. Open daily 8am-9pm. Cash only.) You can find fresh produce, not to mention the cheapest souvenirs in town, in the stalls behind Hotel Caligula, pl. Handlowy. (Open daily 9am-3pm.) **Tawerna pod Złamanym Pagajem,** Kowalska 3, boasts the best lake view in town from its terrace and hosts all-night house and techno dance parties in July and August. (☎421 60 40. Beer 4zł. Open daily 8am-late. Dance parties F and Sa 9pm-dawn.)

◙ ▨ **SIGHTS AND OUTDOOR ACTIVITIES.** Żeglarska Mazurska (☎421 61 02), on the shore on al. Żeglarska, offers excursions on Lake Śniardwy and round-trip ferry service to various Mazurian cities for 14-64zł. For lakeside adventure, **Wioska Żeglarska Mikołajki,** farther down the shore at Kowalska 3, above Tawerna Pod Złamanym Pagajem, rents yachts. Although law prevents anyone without a Polish sailing license from renting a sailing craft, you can charter a skippered boat. (☎421 60 40. Sailboats 20-30zł per hr., 150-300zł per day.) Rent **bicycles** in the 24hr. parking lot at Orzyszowa 2. (☎888 107 776. 4zł per hr., 30zł per day.) The **Kościół św. Trójcy** (Church of the Holy Trinity), one of the few Protestant churches in Poland, has a small museum. (☎421 62 93. Museum open daily 9am-5pm. Services Su 10:30am. Museum 4zł, students 3zł.)

BIAŁYSTOK ☎(0)85

Most tourists know Białystok only as a gateway to the outstanding national parks of Podlasie and take it in accordingly small doses. Much of the city is an unsightly jumble of Soviet-era concrete high-rises, with faint traces of a once-prosperous town at the crossroads of Polish, Russian, and Tartar cultures. While Poland's accession to the EU has ended Białystok's formerly roaring trade in used Kalashnikovs from Belarus and Ukraine, the town's atmosphere remains palpably eastern.

▐ TRANSPORTATION. The **train station,** Białystok Główny (☎94 36), is on Kolejowa 9. Trains run to: **Gdynia** (7¾hr., 3 per day, 49zł); **Kraków** (5hr., 1 per day, 50zł); **Łódź** (4½hr., 1 per day, 41zł); **Olsztyn** (6hr., 5 per day, 41zł); **Szczecin** (13¾hr., 2 per day, 64zł); **Warsaw** (2hr., 10 per day, 34-62zł). The **bus station** (☎94 16) is across the tracks from the train station on Bohaterów Monte Cassino 10. Buses run to: **Gdańsk** (9hr., 2 per day, 51zł); **Lublin** (6hr., 2 per day, 34zł); **Olsztyn** (4½hr., 5 per day, 35zł); **Warsaw** (3½hr., 5 per day, 25zł); **Wrocław** (12¾hr., 1 per day, 62zł); **Minsk, BLR** (8hr., 1 per day, 60zł). Comfortable **Polski Express** buses run to **Warsaw** (4hr., 4 per day, 28zł). **Local buses** cost 1-2zł. For a **taxi,** call ☎96 63.

▞ ▨ ORIENTATION AND PRACTICAL INFORMATION. The city center and most sights lie along a spine defined by **Lipowa.** To reach the center from the stations, catch city bus #2, 4, 10, or 21S from the far side of Bohaterów Monte Cassino. The **tourist office IT,** Sienkiewicza 3, inside Holiday Travel, sells **maps** (6-8zł) and has info about Białystok and the national parks. (☎653 79 50; www.city.bialystok.pl. Open M-F 9am-6pm, Sa 10am-2pm.) **PKO Bank Polski Oddział,** Rynek Kościuszki 16, **exchanges currency,** has a 24hr. **ATM,** cashes **traveler's checks** for 1.5% commission, and gives MC/V **cash advances.** (☎678 61 00. Open M-W and F 8am-7pm, Th 10am-5pm, Sa 8am-2pm.) **Luggage storage** is in the tunnel below the bus station. (3zł per day, 4zł per 2 days. Open daily 6am-5pm.) Lockers (4zł per small bag, 8zł per large bag) are in the train station. A **pharmacy** (☎653 79 49) is at Sienkiewicza 5. (Open M-F 8am-8pm, Sa 8am-3pm, Su 9am-2pm.) For **Internet,** head to **Cafe Piramida,** Grochowa 2, near Lipowa. (☎742 18 18; piramida.net@interia.pl. 3zł per 30min. Open M-F 8am-midnight, Sa-Su 9am-midnight.) The **post office,** Kolejowa 15, has **telephone** and **fax** services. For **Poste Restante,** go to window #4. (☎652 61 91. Open daily 6am-7pm.) **Postal Code:** 15-900.

▐ ▢ ACCOMMODATIONS AND FOOD. Białystok's few budget options rarely fill. **SSM "Podlasie" ❶** is at al. Piłsudskiego 7b. From the bus station, turn left on Bohaterów Monte Cassino and take a right on św. Rocha. Take the roundabout to al. Piłsudskiego, then follow the signs. Primary-color decor and curiously undersized tables and chairs give this friendly, impeccably clean hostel a nursery-school feel. The eager staff are a treasure trove of information about Podlasie, and the homey kitchen is a highlight. (☎652 42 50; www.ssm.bialystok.ids.pl. Linen 5zł. Dorms 25zł, under 26 21zł. With ISIC 23/19zł.) **Dom Turysty "Rubin" ❷** is at Warszawska 7. From the train station take city bus #2, 21, or 21S to Warszawska. In a yellow neo-Baroque building festooned with stone cherubs, the Rubin offers clean rooms with TVs. A small canteen sells drinks and snacks. (☎743 55 48; fax 743 62 71. Check-in 2pm. Check-out noon. Singles and doubles 70zł, with baths 120zł; triples 90/150zł.) **Hokus Pokus ❶**, Kilińskiego 12, takes pride in gale-force air conditioning that has the hanging lanterns swaying. A better reason to visit is the tasty range of "American" pizzas, salads, and sandwiches, not to mention the surprisingly pleasant decor of mirrors, faux fur, and metal. (☎741 63 48. Entrees 7-18zł. Open M-Sa 10am-11pm, Su noon-11pm. MC/V.) **Bar Podlasie ❶**, Rynek Kościuszki 15, buffered from the beer gardens by a small park, is the most popular lunch spot downtown, as 30-person lines attest. Serving traditional Polish dishes with rich sauces and thick soups, this spartan milk bar dishes out high-quality food at such low prices that diners happily partake of the Polish pastime of yore: queueing. (☎742 25 04. Entrees 3-7zł. Open daily 8am-8pm. MC/V.)

🌃🎭 **SIGHTS AND NIGHTLIFE.** From Lipowa, take a right on Sienkiewicza to get to the gardens of **Branicki Palace** (Pałac Branickich). A pretender to the Polish throne, Hetman Branicki, set out in the 18th century to build a palace that would compare to Versailles. Although Branicki fell short of his goal, the formal gardens and Baroque palace are an impressive feat of hubris. The best view of the garden is from the second-floor **Dzierżyński Balcony**, where Felix Dzierżyński proclaimed the Polish Soviet Republic in 1920. (Open daily Apr.-Sept. 6am-10pm; Oct.-Mar. 6am-6pm. Free.) The **Military Museum** (Muzeum Wojska), Kilińskiego 7, off Lipowa, displays artifacts from the city's embattled history, including the original declaration of the 1944 Białystok ghetto uprising and a series of silver eagles showing the evolution of Poland's national symbol. Military aficionados will love the 13th-century weaponry and jumble of WWII gear. (☎741 54 48. Open Tu-Su 9:30am-5pm. 5zł, students 3zł.) The large student population in Białystok makes for some decent nightlife, though more-sophisticated venues are hard to come by. You'll find most bars on **Lipowa** or tucked among its branching side streets. *Gazela Magazyn* has detailed info and is available free in most bars. Unmarked **Metro**, Białówny 9, has the telltale fluorescent lights and overgrown bouncers of the hottest disco in a small town. (☎732 41 54. Cover after 10pm 10zł. Open Th-Sa 6pm-late.) **Antidotum**, Akamemicka 26a, is a sign that things might be turning around for Białystok nightlife, with red walls, urban black-and-white photography, and a diverse playlist featuring both R&B and jazz leg-

GIVING BACK

THE FOREST PRIMEVAL

Ever wonder where exactly that degree in forestry was going to take you? The answer could be Poland. The Białowieża National Park takes on international volunteers each year to help with a wide range of conservation and research efforts, from investigating the region's amphibians to helping preserve the local bison, vole, and red deer population. Those who have studied biology or environmental protection at university are welcome to contact the park and local research institutions—both of which are in constant need of volunteers.

At 10,502 hectares, the Białowieża Primeval Forest is a natural wonder, and has long been treasured as such. The earliest recorded legislation to protect the land dates to 1538. Russian tsars were the last private owners, giving up the land in 1917. WWI brought German troops who hunted the wild bison. Just one month before Polish forces expelled the Germans from the forest in 1919, the Germans killed the last of the park's wild bison. Today the bison have been brought back to Europe's last primeval forest, and the park is an incredible ecological site.

Volunteers can expect to pay for accommodations and personal travel. Contact park authorities for info at Park Palacowy 11, 17-230 Białowieża. ☎85 681 23 06. You can also visit the multilingual website, www.bpn.com.pl.

ends. Although relatively new, it's already a hit with local students, who fill the secluded garden nightly. (☎744 70 06. Beer 5zł. Open daily noon-late.)

BIAŁOWIESKI NATIONAL PARK

Białowieża Primeval Forest (Puszcza Białowieska), Europe's last remaining primeval forest, is a sprawling natural treasury of centuries-old oak trees, European bison, and 12,000 species of fauna. Once the hunting ground of Polish kings, the park has been named a UNESCO World Heritage site and attracts visitors from around the world. Bordering Białowieża is the park's main attraction, the ◪**Strict Preserve** (Obszar Ochrony Ścisłej), where 300 bison roam freely. The last wild bison were killed in 1919, but captive-bred Lithuanian bison were introduced to the park in 1929 and have thrived since. Only **guided tours** can enter this section of the park. Although you will be lucky to see any large mammals, the well-guided tour winds deep into the preserve and will leave you with a sound understanding of the forest's complex ecology and biodiversity—dynamic guides will have humanities fans reconsidering the sciences. Consider buying repellent before the tour: the park has 23 species of mosquito. Just inside the park, the **Park Museum** (Muzeum Przyodniczo-Leśne) has exhibits on the park and an observatory tower, as well as a multimedia show on park history and local biology. The multimedia show is 40zł, and English-speakers with whom to split the price are few and far between; most opt for the Strict Preserve instead. (☎681 22 75. Open M-F 9am-4:30pm, Sa-Su 9am-5pm. 10zł, students 5zł.) To guarantee a view of the bison, head to the small **bison preserve** (Rezerwat Pokazowy Żubrów), 4km from the trailhead, where bison and other animals are kept in tighter quarters. It is accessible via the yellow trail (2hr.), which begins 2km from the PTTK office. (Open daily 8am-4pm. 6zł, students 3zł.) The yellow, red, green, and blue trails offer great biking and walking paths.

Most park visitors stay overnight in the town of Białowieża. Either IT in Białystok or PTTK in Białowieża can arrange accommodations. **Szkolne Schronisko Młodzieżowe ❶**, Waszkiewicza 6, across from the Orthodox church, is the most popular budget option in town, with both large and small comfortable dorm rooms and an informative staff who put PTTK to shame. Reserve ahead in summer. (☎681 25 60. 10- to 12-bed dorms 16zł; 3- to 4-bed 19zł; singles 25zł; doubles 50zł.) Ask PTTK about a stay in tranquil **eco-tourist rooms,** essentially **private rooms** arranged by local retired farmers, most of whom also rent bikes. Most eco-tourist rooms are along Waszkiewicza, the main road, and Tropinka, one block north. (Rooms 30-45zł.) After a day of hikes, enjoy decent *pierogi* at **Unikat ❸**, Waszkiewicza 39. (☎681 27 74. Entrees 20zł. Open daily 8am-10pm.)

Direct **buses** run from Białystok to **Bialowieża** (3hr., 2 per day, 16zł). The last return bus from Bialowieża is at 5:05pm. For quick access to the PTTK and hostel, get off at the main bus stop in front of the Orthodox church; for **private rooms**, wait and exit at the next stop. In the gateway of the park entrance, **PTTK**, Kolejowa 17, arranges guides for the Strict Preserve. From the Orthodox church, walk through the small park and turn left at the circle, taking the bridge between the two ponds. The price for the guide is 195zł, so it's a good idea to get there early and hang around until a few more English-speakers show up. (☎681 22 95; www.pttk.bialowieza.pl. **Maps** 10-12zł. Open daily 8am-4pm. AmEx/MC/V.) The only **ATM** in town is at the Best Western Hotel next to PTTK, Kolejowa 15.

ROMANIA
(ROMÂNIA)

Devastated by the lengthy reign of Nicolae Ceaușescu, modern Romania is in the midst of economic transition. This state of flux, combined with a reputation for poverty and crime, discourages foreign visitors. But travelers who dismiss Romania do themselves an injustice—it is a budget traveler's paradise, rich in history, rustic beauty, and hospitality. Romania's fascinating legacy draws visitors to Dracula's dark castle, and to the famous frescoes of the Bucovina monasteries. Meanwhile, new Romania is embodied by Bucharest, where visitors can explore the remnants of Ceaușescu's reign, and by the heavily touristed Black Sea Coast, where resorts entice throngs of vacationers..

DISCOVER ROMANIA: SUGGESTED ITINERARIES

THREE DAYS Head for **Transylvania** (p. 533), a budget traveler's dream, to relax in the Gothic hillside towns of **Sighișoara** (p. 536) and **Sinaia** (p. 532), hike in the spectacular, jagged **Făgăraș Mountains** (p. 540), and explore the wild ruins of **Râșnov** castle (p. 536).

ONE WEEK After 3 days in darkly intriguing **Transylvania,** head to medieval **Sibiu** for (1 day; p. 538) and stylish **Brașov** for another day (p. 533), before ending in **Bucharest** (2 days), the complex and enigmatic capital, home to imposing architecture and wild nightlife (p. 523).

FACTS AND FIGURES

Official Name: Romania.
Capital: Bucharest.
Major Cities: Constanța, Iași, Oradea.
Population: 22,400,000.

Land Area: 230,340 sq. km.
Time Zone: GMT + 2.
Language: Romanian.
Religions: Eastern Orthodox (87%).

ESSENTIALS

WHEN TO GO

Romania's varied climate makes it a year-round destination. The south has hot summers and mild winters, while winters are harsher and summers cooler in the north, especially in the mountains. Summer tourist season reaches an unpleasant pitch in July and August only along the Black Sea Coast; elsewhere, travelers will find a refreshing lack of crowds even in mid-summer; they should, however, remember that summer can be brutally hot in much of Romania.

DOCUMENTS AND FORMALITIES

EMBASSIES AND CONSULATES. Foreign embassies to Romania are in Bucharest. For Romanian embassies at home, contact: **Australia,** 4 Dalman Crescent, O'Malley, ACT 2606 (☎26 286 2343; www.roembau.org); **Canada,** 655 Rideau St., Ottawa, ON K1N 6A3 (☎613 789 4037; www.cyberus.ca/~romania); **Ireland,** 47

ENTRANCE REQUIREMENTS
Passport: Required for all travelers.
Visa: Not required for stays under 90 days for citizens of Canada, the UK, and the US. Citizens of Ireland may stay for only 30 days without a visa, and citizens of Australia and New Zealand require a visa for any length of stay.
Letter of Invitation: Not required for citizens of Australia, Canada, Ireland, New Zealand, the UK, and the US.
Inoculations: Recommended up-to-date on DTaP (diphtheria, tetanus, and pertussis), Hepatitis A, Hepatitis B, MMR (measles, mumps, and rubella), Polio booster, and Typhoid.
Work Permit: Required of all foreigners planning to work in Romania.
Driving Permit: Required for all those planning to drive in Romania.

Ailesbury Rd., Ballsbridge, Dublin 4 (☎01 269 2852; romemb@iol.ie); **UK,** 4 Palace Green, London W8 40D (☎0207 937 9666; www.roemb.co.uk); **US,** 1607 23rd St. NW, Washington, D.C. 20008 (☎202-332-4848; www.roembus.org).

VISA AND ENTRY INFORMATION. Romanian **visa** info changes frequently; check with your embassy or consulate for the most accurate and specific info. Citizens of Canada, the UK, and the US can visit Romania for up to 90 days without visas while citizens of Ireland may visit for up to 30 days without visas. Citizens of Australia and New Zealand need visas for any length of stay. In all cases, passports are required and must be valid for six months after the date of departure. Consult the Romanian embassy in your country of origin to apply for a visa. A visa application requires a passport, one application form per visa, a recent photograph, and the application fee. For Americans, a single entry visa costs US$35; multiple-entry US$70. Visas are not available at the border. Romanian embassies estimate a 30-day processing time for some visas. Apply early to allow the bureaucratic process to run its slow, frustrating course. **Visa extensions** and related services are available at police headquarters in large cities or at Bucharest's **passport office,** Str. Luigi Cazzavillan 11. Long lines are common at the border. Bags are rarely searched, but customs officials are strict about visa laws. Beware of tax scams.

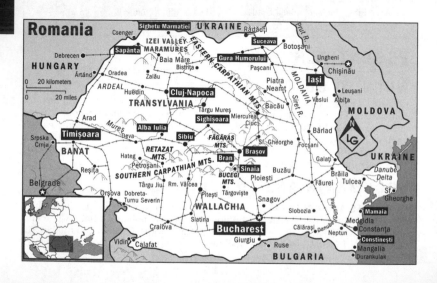

TOURIST SERVICES AND MONEY

Romania has limited resources for tourists, but the **National Tourist Office** is still useful. Check its website at www.romaniatourism.com. Most tourist offices are intended for Romanians, and much of the country has poor resources for foreign travelers. It can help to walk into the most expensive hotel in town and pretend to be important. The tourist offices of **Cluj-Napoca**, however, are a welcome relief.

The Romanian **currency** is the **leu**, plural lei (abbreviated **L**), which was revalued in 2005. Banknotes are issued in amounts of L1, L5, L10, and L50; coins come in amounts of 1, 5, 10, and 50 bani (singular ban). **Inflation** rates have dropped dramatically and now hover around 10%, though this statistic is liable to fluctuate. Romania has a **Value Added Tax (VAT) Rate** of 19%. **ATMs** generally accept MasterCard and sometimes Visa, and are the best way to get money. ATMs are found everywhere but the smallest towns, usually operate 24hr., and occasionally run out of cash. Many locals carry US dollars; **private exchange bureaus,** which often offer better exchange rates than **banks,** are everywhere and deal in common foreign currencies. However, few take **credit cards** or **traveler's checks.** Compare rates before exchanging money. Most banks will cash traveler's checks in US dollars, then exchange them for lei, with high fees. **American Express Travelers Cheques** are most useful. **Never change money on the street,** as it is illegal; those who attempt to do so are generally cheated or scammed.

LEI (L)		
AUS$1 = L2.20	L1 = AUS$0.45
CDN$1 = L2.40	L1 = CDN$0.42
EUR€1 = L3.56	L1 = EUR€0.28
NZ$1 = L2.03	L1 = NZ$0.49
UK£1 = L5.24	L1 = UK£0.19
US$1 = L2.92	L1 = US$0.34

HEALTH AND SAFETY

| EMERGENCY | Police: ☎955. Ambulance: ☎961. Fire: ☎981. |

If possible, avoid Romanian **hospitals,** as most are not up to Western standards. Pack a first-aid kit. Go to a private doctor for medical emergencies; your embassy can recommend a good one. Some **American medical clinics** in Bucharest have English-speaking doctors; pay in **cash.** *Farmacies* (pharmacies) stock basic medical supplies. *Antinevralgic* is for headaches, *aspirină* or *piramidon* for colds and the flu, and *saprosan* for diarrhea. *Prezervatives* (condoms), *tampoane* (tampons), and *şerveţele igienice* (sanitary napkins) are available at all drugstores and many kiosks. Most **public restrooms** lack soap, towels, and toilet paper, and many on trains and in stations smell rank. Attendants may charge L1-1.50 for a single square of toilet paper. Pick up a roll at a drug store and carry it with you. You can find relief at most restaurants, even if you're not a patron. Beware of **stray dogs,** common everywhere, including major cities, as they bite frequently and often carry **rabies.** Water in Romania is less contaminated than it once was. Still, avoid untreated **tap water** and do not use **ice cubes;** boil water before drinking it or drink imported **bottled water.** Beware of contaminated-water ice and vendor food.

Violent **crime** is not a major concern, but petty **crime** against tourists is common. Be especially careful on public transport and night trains. Beware of distracting children and con artists dressed as policemen who ask for your passport or wallet. If someone shows a badge and claims to be a plainclothes policeman, he may be lying and trying to scam you. When in doubt, ask the officer to escort you to the nearest police station. Pickpocketing, money exchange, and taxi scams are very prevalent. Many scammers speak good English and German, so don't be fooled. The **drinking age,** which is 18, is reportedly not strictly enforced. If you smoke marijuana, be prepared to spend the next seven years in a Romanian prison. Other **drug laws** are also strictly enforced. Solo **female travelers** shouldn't go out alone after dark and should say they are traveling with a male. Tank tops, shorts, and sneakers may attract attention. **Minorities,** and especially those with dark skin, may encounter unwanted attention or discrimination, as they may be taken for Roma (gypsies) and therefore considered untrustworthy. Practitioners of **religions** other than Orthodox Christianity may feel uncomfortable in the province of Moldavia. **Homosexuality** is now legal in Romania, but discrimination remains and public displays of affection are ill-advised. Most Romanians hold conservative attitudes toward sexuality, which may translate into harassment of **GLBT** travelers and often manifests itself in the form of anti-gay propaganda in major cities.

TRANSPORTATION

BY PLANE. Many **airlines** fly into Bucharest. **TAROM** (Romanian Airlines) recently updated its fleet; it flies directly from Bucharest to **New York** and major European and Middle Eastern cities. (☎21 201 4000; www.tarom.ro.) Though recently improved, Bucharest's **Otopeni International Airport** is not completely modern.

BY TRAIN. Trains are better than buses for **international** travel. To buy tickets to the national railway, go to the ▓CFR (Che-Fe-Re) office in larger towns. You must buy international tickets in advance. Train stations sell tickets 1hr. in advance. The English-language timetable *Mersul Trenurilor* (hardcopy L12; online at www.cfr.ro) is very useful. There are four types of trains: *InterCity* (indicated by an "IC" on timetables and at train stations); *rapid* (in green); *accelerat* (red); and *personal* (black). International trains (blue) are indicated with an "i." *InterCity* trains stop only at major cities. *Rapid* trains are the next fastest; *accelerat* trains start with "1" and are slower and dirtier. The sluggish and decrepit *personal* trains stop at every station. The difference between **first class** (*clasa întâi;* clah-sa untoy; 6 people per compartment) and **2nd class** (*clasa doua;* 8 people) is small, except on *personal* trains. In an **overnight train,** shell out for a *vagon de dormit* (sleeping carriage) and buy both compartment tickets if you don't want to share.

BY BUS. Traveling to Romania by **bus** is often cheaper than entering by plane or train. Tourist agencies may sell timetables and tickets, but buying tickets from the carrier saves commission and is often cheaper. Use the slow **local bus system** only when trains are unavailable. Local buses are cheap but are packed and poorly ventilated. They thus make perfect locations for pickpocketing and other forms of petty theft. Minibuses are a good option for short distances because they are often cheap, fast, and clean. Rates are posted inside.

BY FERRY, BIKE, FOOT, ETC. In the Danube Delta, boats are the best mode of transport. A ferry runs down the new European riverway from Rotterdam, NED to Constanța, and in the Black Sea between Istanbul, TUR and Constanța. Be wary of **taxis;** only use cars that post a company name, phone number, and rate per kilometer. Be sure the driver uses the meter. Your ride should cost no more than L6 per km plus a L7 flat fee. If you wish to drive a **car,** you must bring an **International Driving Permit;** make sure you are insured and have your registration papers. **MyBike** (www.mybike.ro) provides excellent info on **bicycling** in Romania.

BY THUMB. *Let's Go* does not recommend **hitchhiking.** Hitchhikers stand on the side of the road and put out their palm, as if waving. Drivers generally expect a **payment** similar to the price of a train or bus ticket for the distance traveled. In some places, hitchhiking is the only way to get around without a car.

KEEPING IN TOUCH

PHONE CODES	**Country code:** 40. **International dialing prefix:** 00. From outside Romania, dial int'l dialing prefix (see inside back cover) + 40 + city code + local number. Within Romania, dial city code + local number. For calls within a city, just use the local number, unless on a cell phone, in which case the city code is always required.

At the post office, request *par avion* for **airmail**, which takes two weeks for delivery. For postcards or letters, it costs L2.10 to mail within Europe and L3.10 for the rest of the world. **Mail** can be received through **Poste Restante**. However, you may run into problems picking up your package. Address envelopes as follows: Jordan (First name) HYLDEN (LAST NAME), Oficiul Postal nr. 1, (post office address) Bucharest-POSTE RESTANTE, Romania, 500057. Major cities have **UPS** and **Federal Express**. Most public phones are orange and accept **phone cards**. Buy phone cards at telephone offices, Metro stops, and some post offices and kiosks. Only buy cards sealed in plastic wrap. Rates run around L1.20 per min. to neighboring countries, L1.60 per min. to most of Europe, and L2 per min. to the US. Phones operate in English if you press "i." At an analog phone, dial ☎ 971 for international calls. You may need to make a phone call *prin comandă* (with the help of the operator) at the telephone office; this takes longer and costs more. There are **no toll-free calls** in Romania—you even need a phone card to call the police, an ambulance, or the operator. People with European cell phones can avoid roaming charges by buying a **SIM card** at **Connex, Dialog,** or **CosmoRom**. General info ☎ 931, operator ☎ 930. International access codes include: **AT&T Direct** (☎ 021 800 42 88); **Canada Direct** (☎ 021 800 50 00); **MCI WorldPhone** (☎ 021 800 18 00); and **Sprint** (☎ 021 800 08 770). **Internet** cafes are common in cities and cost L1.50-L3 per hr.

ACCOMMODATIONS AND CAMPING

ROMANIA	❶	❷	❸	❹	❺
ACCOMMODATIONS	under L40 under €11 under US13	L40-70 €11-19 US$13-24	L70-100 €19-28 US$24-38	L100-200 €28-55 US$38-67	over L200 over €55 over US$67

Many **hostels** are fairly pleasant, but few are accredited. Some have perks like free beer and breakfast. While some **hotels** charge foreigners 50-100% more, lodging is still inexpensive (US$7-20). Reservations are helpful in July and August, but you can usually get by without them. **Guesthouses** and **pensions** are simple and comfortable but rare. In summer, many towns rent low-priced rooms in **university dorms.** Consult the tourist office. **Private rooms** and **homestays** are a great option, but hosts rarely speak English. Rooms run US$7-12 in the countryside and US$15-20 in cities. Look at the room and fix a price before accepting. **Campgrounds** can be crowded and have frightening bathrooms. Still, **bungalows** are often full in summer; reserve far in advance. Hotels and hostels often provide the best info for tourists.

FOOD AND DRINK

ROMANIA	❶	❷	❸	❹	❺
FOOD	under L7 under €2 under US$2	L7-11 €2-3 US$2-4	L11-15 €3-4 US$4-5	L15-20 €4-5 US$5-7	over L20 over €5 over US7

A complete **Romanian meal** includes an appetizer, soup, fish, an entree, and dessert. Lunch includes **soup,** called *supă* or *ciorbă* (the former has noodles or dumplings, the latter is saltier and with vegetables), an entree (typically grilled meat), and dessert.

Soups can be very tasty; try *ciorbă de perişoare* (with vegetables and ground meatballs) or *supă cu găluşte* (with fluffy dumplings). **Pork** comes in several varieties; *muşchi* and *cotlet* are of the highest quality. Common entrees include *mici* (rolls of fried meat), *sarmale* (stuffed cabbage), and *mămăligă* (polenta). **Beef** and **lamb** are other common meats. *Clătite* (crepes), *papanaşi* (doughnuts with jam and sour cream), and *torts* (creamy cakes) are all fantastic. *Îngheţată* (ice cream) is cheap and good, while *mere în aluat* (doughnuts with apples) and sugary *gogoşi* (fried doughnuts) are delectable. In the west, you'll find as much **Hungarian food** as Romanian. Some restaurants charge by weight rather than by portion. It's difficult to predict how many grams you will receive. *Garnituri*, the extras that come with a meal, are usually charged separately. This means you're paying for everything, even a bit of butter or a dollop of mustard. Pork rules in Romania, so keeping **kosher** is difficult, but it's possible with planning. **Vegetarian** eating is feasible if you are willing to stick to foods that are not traditionally Romanian. Local **drinks** include *ţuică*, a brandy distilled from plums and apples, and *palincă*, a stronger version of *ţuică* that approaches 70% alcohol. A delicious liqueur called *vişnată* is made from wild cherries.

LIFE AND TIMES

HISTORY

GROWING PAINS. Dacian tribes inhabited ancient Romania, and trading cities flourished along the Black Sea Coast in the 7th century BC. The first Romanian state, **Wallachia,** was established in the south during the early AD 14th century. The 2nd, **Moldavia,** sprang up east of the Carpathians. The fledgling states constantly fought against the **Ottoman Turks,** who ruled Transylvania and other nearby lands. Moldavia's **Ştefan cel Mare** (Stephen the Great; 1457-1504) was most successful in warding off the attacks. During his 47-year rule, he built 42 monasteries and churches, one for each of his victories in battle. Successful resistance, however, died with Ştefan, and Moldavia and Wallachia became Turkish provinces.

TURMOIL. For the next 400 years, Austria-Hungary, Poland-Lithuania, Russia, and Turkey fought over the region. **Mihai Viteazul** (Michael the Brave) tried to unify Romanians to create an autonomous state in 1599, but Hungarian, Ottoman, and Polish attacks left the country decimated. Moldavia and Wallachia united in 1859. **King Carol I** reduced corruption, built railroads, and strengthened the army that won Romania its independence in 1877. After Austria-Hungary's defeat in **WWI,** independent Romania gained Bessarabia (now Moldova), Bucovina, and Transylvania. The population, which doubled with these annexations, was now more diverse, and ethnic tensions resulted. Under the 1941 **Nazi-Soviet Non-Aggression Pact,** Romania lost its new territory to the Axis powers. Hoping the Nazis would preserve an independent Romania, dictator **General Ion Antonescu** supported Germany in WWII. In 1944, **King Mihai** orchestrated a coup and surrendered to the Allies, but the bid for Western alliance was unsuccessful. The Soviets moved in and proclaimed the **Romanian People's Republic** in 1947.

THE EXECUTION WILL BE TELEVISED. The government violently suppressed opposition in the postwar era. Over 200,000 died in the **purges** of the 1950s, and farms were forced to collectivize. In 1965, **Nicolae Ceauşescu** took control of the Communist Party. He won praise for attempting to distance Romania from Moscow, but his ruthless domestic policies deprived his citizens of basic needs. By the late 1980s, Ceauşescu had turned Romania into a police state. When the dreaded **Securitate** (Secret Police) arrested dissident priest **Laszlo Tokes,** a violent protest erupted in **Timişoara,** and Romania was soon in a state of full-scale revolt. The 1989 **revolution** was as merciless as Ceauşescu himself. In December, clashes in Bucharest brought thousands of protesters to the streets. Ceauşescu was arrested, tried, and executed—on TV—all on Christmas Day. The enthusiasm following these days didn't last, as **Ion Iliescu's National Salvation Front,** composed largely of former communists, assumed power and won the 1990 elections. Iliescu made moderate reforms but received international criticism for using violence and terror tactics to repress student protests. Revolution, it seemed, had changed little.

TODAY

Romania is a constitutional democracy. The 1991 constitution stipulates an elected **president** who serves a four-year term and nominates a **prime minister.** Members of **Parliament** are elected to four-year terms. In November 1996, **Emil Constantinescu** succeeded Iliescu in the country's first democratic transfer of power. Constantinescu's **Romanian Democratic Coalition (RDC)** promised reforms but focused more on its internal disputes. Iliescu won back the presidency in 2000. Romania joined **NATO** in May 2004 and has subsequently amended its constitution and taken other steps toward a more open democracy. The country completed EU accession talks in 2004, but still must address rampant corruption in order to assume membership in 2007, as scheduled. In December 2004, **Traian Basescu** was elected president and **Calin Popescu Tariceanu** was elected prime minister.

PEOPLE AND CULTURE

DEMOGRAPHICS. Ethnic tensions trouble Romania, which is almost 90% ethnically **Romanian.** The 6% **Hungarian** minority, concentrated in Transylvania, and the 2.5% **Roma** minority both complain of discrimination. Most Romanians (87%) are **Eastern Orthodox;** most of the remainder are **Protestant** (6%) or **Catholic** (6%).

LANGUAGE. Romanian is a Romance language. Those familiar with French, Italian, Portuguese, or Spanish should be able to decipher many words. Romanian differs from other Romance tongues in its Slavic-influenced vocabulary. **German** and **Hungarian** are widely spoken in Transylvania. Throughout the country, **French** is a common 2nd language for the older generation, while **English** is common among the younger. Avoid **Russian,** which is often understood but disliked.

CUSTOMS AND ETIQUETTE. It is customary to give inexact change for purchase; restaurants usually round up to the nearest L1 or give candy instead of change. Locals generally don't **tip,** but foreigners are expected to tip 5-10% in restaurants. Hotel porters and helpful concierges are generally tipped modestly. Some tip **taxis,** but doing so is unnecessary. In all cases, tipping too much is inappropriate. **Bargain** over taxi fares and accommodations if there is no posted rate. Try for one third off in open-air markets.

TOP TEN LIST

ROMANIA TOP TEN

1 Best fairy-tale palace: the astounding Peleş Castle, complete with a retractable stained-glass roof (p. 532).

2 Best mountaintop experience: hiking in the cloud-topped Făgăraş Mountains (p. 540).

3 Best and worst moonshine brandy: palincă, which seems smooth at first but hits you like a 60% alcohol brick.

4 Best museum: the sobering Memorial Museum in Sighetu Marmaţiei, formerly a political prison (p. 549).

5 Best student nightlife: Cluj-Napoca, packed to the gills with students (p. 542).

6 Best cathedral: the otherworldly Metropolitan Cathedral in Timişoara (p. 547).

7 Best place to be pickpocketed: tie—the #41 bus from Constanţa to Mamaia, or anywhere in Bucharest (p. 523).

8 Worst use of space: the Parliamentary Palace in Bucharest, 2nd-largest building in the world, much of which stands empty (p. 529).

9 Best Lake of Fire: any of the terrifyingly imaginative Judgment Day murals on the painted monasteries of Bucovina (p. 553).

10 Best place possible for Dracula's hometown: the eerily medieval Sighişoara (p. 536).

Romanians take pride in their **hospitality.** Most will be eager to help and offer to show you around or invite you into their homes. Bring your hostess an odd number of flowers; even-numbered bouquets are only brought to graves. In rural areas, men should wear pants and closed-toed shoes, and women should wear dresses; for those over 30, these guidelines also apply in cities.

THE ARTS

While the Roman poet **Ovid** wrote his last works in exile near Constanţa, Romanian literature did not flourish until the **Văcărescu family** invigorated it in the late 1700s: grandfather **Ienăchiţă** wrote the first Romanian grammar, father **Alecu** wrote love poetry, and son **Iancu** is considered the master of Romanian poetry. **Grigore Alexandrescu's** 19th-century fables and satires are also famous. The next generation of writers ushered in a golden age of Romanian literature. From this generation, **Ion Creangă's** most important work, *Aminitiri din Copilărie* (Memories of My Childhood), depicts village life. **Mihai Eminescu** wrote in the **Romantic** style. In the 20th century, **Nicolae Iorga** set a new standard for poetry, drama, and history.

The end of WWII brought **Socialist Realism. Geo Bogza** and **Mihail Beniuc** were prominent adherents whose writings glorified the archetypal worker. Some sought freedom in other lands and languages—absurdist dramatist **Eugen Ionescu,** scholar of religion **Mircea Eliade,** writer **Elie Wiesel,** and father of Dada **Tristan Tzara** are the best known. Contemporary artists include composer **George Enescu** and painter **Nicolae Grigorescu,** who studied art in France before immortalizing the Romanian countryside. Famous **Constantin Brâncuşi** is considered one of the world's greatest Modernist sculptors; some of his best works stand outside in Târgu Jiu. These artists' work can be found in Bucharest's **National Art Museum.**

Folk music remains popular today, and fine craft traditions in glassware and decorated Easter eggs continue to thrive. Edgy, realist Romanian **cinema** is gaining recognition, especially through the popular **Film Festival Cottbus.** In music, opera singer **Angela Gheorghiu** and pianist **Radu Lupu** have won international fame.

HOLIDAYS AND FESTIVALS

Holidays: New Year's Holiday (Jan. 1-2); Epiphany (Jan. 6); Mărţişor (Mar. 1); Easter Holiday (Apr. 11-12); Labor Day (May 1); National Unity Day/Romania Day (Dec. 1); Christmas (Dec. 25-26).

Festivals: Romania Day (Dec. 1), commemorates the day in 1918 that Transylvania became a part of Romania. For *Mărţişor* (Mar. 1), locals wear *porte-boneurs* (good-luck charms) and give snow-drop flowers to friends and lovers.

ADDITIONAL RESOURCES

GENERAL HISTORY

Balkan Ghosts: A Journey Through History, by Robert Kaplan (1994). A deeply engaging travel narrative and an informative history on the chaotic region. Also see Kaplan's 2001 tome *Eastward to Tartary,* which examines similar themes on a broader scale.

Dracula, Prince of Many Faces: His Life and Times, by Radu R. Florescu (1990). Debunks cultural myths and tells the real story of Vlad Ţepeş (Vlad the Impaler).

FICTION, NONFICTION, AND FILM

Dracula, by Bram Stoker (1897). The horror novel that launched a national obsession.

Red Rats *(Şobolanii Roşii),* directed by Florin Codre (1991). Exposes Romanian disillusionment about the revolution of 1989.

Taste of Romania: Its Cookery and Glimpses of its History, Folklore, Art and Poetry, by Nicolae Klepper (1999). Primer on Romanian culture, with insight into the proclivity for larded pork.

Vampire Nation, by Thomas Sipos (2001). A novel connecting communism and vampirism in Romania.

BUCHAREST (BUCUREȘTI)   ☎(0)21

Once a fabled beauty on the Orient Express, Bucharest (pop. 1,929,615) is now infamous for its heavy-handed transformation under dictator Nicolae Ceaușescu. During his 25-year reign, Ceaușescu nearly ruined the city's splendor by replacing historic neighborhoods, grand boulevards, and Ottoman ruins with concrete blocks, wide highways, and communist monuments. Adults remember and probably participated in the 1989 revolution; all citizens have since endured a mix of communist nostalgia and break-neck capitalism, tempered by an unshakable vein of Christian Orthodoxy. Though Bucharest is no longer the "Little Paris" *(Micul Paris)* it once was, life here is as fascinating as it is frustrating.

⌐ TRANSPORTATION

Flights: Henri Coanda (Otopeni) Airport (☎204 10 00). Avoid taxis outside the terminal; the FlyTaxi company has exclusive rights to the space and charges several times the normal rate. Call a cab or buy a bus ticket (L4 per 2 trips) at the little kiosk in the corner. Bus #783 runs from the airport to Pța. Unirii (45min., 2-4 per hr.). It departs from the level beneath the international arrivals hall. Flying into Bucharest can be expensive; often, a better idea is to fly into Budapest or Zagreb and enter Romania via train or bus.

Trains: Gara de Nord (☎223 08 80, info 95 21). M1: Gara de Nord. To: **Brașov** (4hr., 16 per day, L24.70); **Cluj-Napoca** (10hr., 6 per day, L47.60); **Constanța** (3hr., 10 per day, L29.40); **Iași** (7hr., 5 per day, L46.70); **Sighișoara** (6hr., 9 per day, L35.20); **Timișoara** (9hr., 7 per day, L52.40); **Budapest, HUN** (14hr., 4 per day, L141.24); **Kraków, POL** (27hr., 1 per day, L286); **Prague, CZR** (36hr., 1 per day, L330); **Sofia, BUL** (13hr., 2 per day, L77). **CFR**, Str. Domnița Anastasia 10-14 (☎313 26 43; www.cfr.ro) books domestic and international tickets. Open M-F 7:30am-7:30pm, Sa 9am-1:30pm. **Wasteels** (☎222 78 44; www.wasteelstravel.ro), inside Gara de Nord, books international tickets. Open M-F 8am-7pm, Sa 8am-2pm.

Buses: There are 6 official bus stations in Bucharest; each serves a different sector of the city and sends buses to destinations in that sector's direction. Near the center, the **Filaret** station is at Cuțitul de Argint 2 (☎335 11 40). M2: Tineretului. Buses are the best way to reach **Athens, GCE,** and **Istanbul, TUR.** Multiple bus companies located near the train station sell tickets to most of Europe. **Toros,** Calea Griviței 134 (☎223 19 18), outside the station, sends 2 buses per day to Istanbul for L125. Open 24hr. Cash only. Next door at Calea Griviței 136-138, **Transcontinental** (☎202 90 30) sends 5 buses per week to Athens for €75. They also sell Eurolines bus tickets, which cover most of Western Europe. Open M-F 9am-7pm, Sa 9am-4pm. Cash only.

Microbuses: Comfortable, air-conditioned **Maxi-Taxi** leaves from outside Gara de Nord to domestic destinations for about half the price of trains.

Public Transportation: Buses, trolleys, and **trams** cost L1 and run daily 5:30am-11:30pm. Validate tickets by sliding them into the small boxes to avoid a L30 fine. The transportation system is invaluable, but figuring out how it works is a chore. **Express buses** take only magnetic cards (L4.40 per 2 trips). Tickets are sold at R.A.T.B. kiosks, often near bus stops. Pickpocketing is a problem during peak hours. The **Metro** offers reliable, less-crowded service. (L1.80 per 2 trips, L6 per 10.) Runs 5am-11:30pm.

Taxis: Many taxi drivers in Bucharest are dishonest; they will cheerfully charge you 10 times the regular fare, especially from airports, train stations, shopping centers, and hotels. Beware especially of private *(privat)* taxis. Normal rates should be around L1 base fee and L1 per km. The base fee is often posted; look for the "tarif," which should

ROMANIA

ROMANIA

Tei Lake

Floreasca Lake

Floreasca Park

Herăstrău Park

Circului Park

Dinamo Sports Complex

Kiseleff Park

N

400 meters
400 yards

TO OTOPENI AIRPORT (16km)

Tuzla
Maica
Domnului
Ionescu
Reînvierii
OBOR
Gypsy Market

Gh. Țițeica
Aromei
Opanez
B-dul Lacul Tei
B-dul Ghica-Tei
Vagonului
Ștefan cel Mare
Făinari
Alex Radovici
Ardeleni
Radu Armași
Toamnei
Viitorului
Episcopul Radu
Silvestru
Moșilor

Gh. Țițeica
C.F.R.
Judetului
Dr. Grozovici
Pîrgarilor
Ing. Iorceanu
Ion Ursu
Toamnei
Mihai Eminescu
Dacia
PIATA GEMENI
Str. Viitorului

Lopătarilor
Calafat
Turnul Eiffel
B-dul Ghica-Tei
Globus Circus
Aleea Circului
V. Lascăr
Domnița Ruxandra
Leonida
Ghiocei
PIATA GEMENI

Chopin
Mozart
Glinka
G. Rossini
Eugen Botez
Barbu Văcărescu
Dinu Vintilă
Tunari
Polonă
Aurel Vlaicu
Dacia
Ion Voicu
Aurel Vlaicu Park

Ceaikovski
J.S. Bach
Puccini
Calea Floreasca
Tudor Vianu
Ștefan cel Mare
STEFAN CEL MARE
Aurel Vlaicu
Polonă

Mircea Eliade
Str. av. N. Constantinescu
Puțul lui Zamfir
T. Iliescu
Calea Dorobanților
Emergency Hospital
Dinamo Stadium
Calea Dorobanților
Cădirea Bastiliei
PIATA LAHOVARI

Jean Monnet
Str. B-lat. Tolstoi
Mircea Eliade
Str. V. Radu Beller
PIATA DOROBANTILOR
Roma
Sofia
Ankara
Paris
Atena
Sevilla
Washington
Londra
Argentina
Tirana
Iancu de Hunedoara
Grigore Alexandrescu
Lascăr Catargiu
PIATA ROMANA
ROMANA
Canada
PIATA AMZEI
Biserica
G-ral. Magheru
Marshall Tourism

Pritvorul
Herăstrău
AVIATORILOR
Zambaccian Art Museum
Muzeul Zambaccian
Ing. Ermil Pangratti
At. Alexandru
Palatul Victoriei
PIATA VICTORIEI
Orlando
Gh. Manu
Iorga
Dacia
Victoriei
Art Collections Museum
Theodor

Bulevardul C. Prezan
PIATA CHARLES DE GAULLE
Bulevardul
Popa Savu
Ministry of Foreign Affairs
Aviatorilor
Geological Museum
Museum of the Romanian Peasant
Museum of Natural History
George Enescu Museum
Frumoasă
Sevastopol
Gr. Voievozilor

Alexandrina
Str. Uruguay
Str. Porumbaru
Gh. Bâtianu
Virgil Drăghiceanu
Șos Kiseleff
Dr. Felix
Dr. Sergiu
Veronica Micle
Dreapta
Ioan Cuza

Cantacuzino
Barbu Delavrancea
Petöfi Șandor
Arhitect Ion Mincu
Ady Endre
Scărlătescu
Dr. Titulescu
Str. Cernat
Gh. Polizu
Buzești
Calea Griviței
Popa Tatu

Village Museum
Arcul de Triumf
Mărăști
Mareșal A. Averescu
Ion Mihalache
Câmpeanu
Banu Maria
Nicolae
Alexandru Ioan Cuza
GARA DE NORD
Gara de Nord
Witing

Stadionul Tineretului
C. Sandu Aldea
A. Constantinescu
Ștefan Sănătescu
Ion Mihalache
Ion Neculce
Ion Mihalache
Gala Galaction
Turda
Lugoj
BASARAB
Gara Basarab
Dinicu Golescu
Orhideelor
Plevnei
Toros
Vespasian

Calea Griviței
Marinescu

ROMANIA

Bucharest

▲ ACCOMMODATIONS
Elvis' Villa, **12**
Funky Chicken Guesthouse, **9**
Hostel Casa (HI), **3**
Hotel Carpati, **14**
Villa 11, **5**
Villa Helga Youth Hostel (HI), **6**

● FOOD
Barka Saffron, **1**
Basilicvm, **2**
Burebista Vânătoresc, **11**
Cremcaffe, **15**
La Mama, **4, 7**

♪ NIGHTLIFE
Club A, **16**
Club Maxx, **8**
Deja-Vu, **10**
La Motor, **13**
Queen's Club, **18**
Twice, **17**

TO Australia
(100m)

TO FILARET (2km)

TO ⑧ (1km)

Prof. Dr. Gh. Marinescu

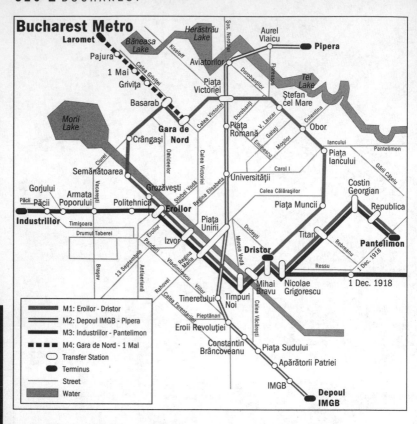

Bucharest Metro

Legend:
- M1: Eroilor - Dristor
- M2: Depoul IMGB - Pipera
- M3: Industriilor - Pantelimon
- M4: Gara de Nord - 1 Mai
- ○ Transfer Station
- ● Terminus
- Street
- Water

be around L1 per km. Only use taxis that have a company name, phone number, and rate posted. Make sure the driver uses the meter. Few drivers speak English, so carry a good map and directions to your hotel or hostel, written in Romanian. Reliable companies include **Meridien** (☎ 94 44), **ChrisTaxi** (☎ 94 61), and **Taxi2000** (☎ 94 94).

■✷⁊ ORIENTATION AND PRACTICAL INFORMATION

Bucharest's main street changes its name from **Şos. Kiseleff** to **Bd. Lascăr Catargiu** to **Bd. General Magheru** to **Bd. Nicolae Bălcescu** to **Bd. I.C. Brătianu** as it runs north-south through the city's four main squares: **Piaţa Victoriei, Piaţa Romană, Piaţa Universităţii**, and **Piaţa Unirii**. Another thoroughfare, running parallel, is **Calea Victoriei**, which crosses **Piaţa Revoluţiei**. The **Metro** M1 line forms a diamond that encloses the city center. The M3 passes horizontally along the bottom of this diamond, while M2 pierces it vertically, stopping at the main squares. To reach the center from Gara de Nord, take M1 to Pţa. Victoriei, then change to M2 in the direction of Depoul IMGB. Go one stop to Pţa. Romana, two stops to Pţa. Universităţii, or three stops to Pţa. Unirii. It's a 15min. walk between squares. **Maps** are sold throughout Bucharest. The "Bucharest 100%" map (L10) is detailed but unwieldy; the smaller Amco Press map (L10) is likely all you'll need. The ever-helpful *Bucharest In Your Pocket* (free) is available at hostels, museums, bookstores, and hotels.

Tourist Office: Tourist services in Bucharest are not as well developed as they are in many other Romanian cities. The information booth in the Gara de Nord is useful, but hotels and hostels are generally the best source of info.

Embassies and Consulates: Australia, Bd. Unirii 74, 5th fl. (☎320 98 02). M2: Pţa. Unirii, then bus #104, 123, or 124 to Lucian Blaga. Open M-Th 9am-1pm and 1:30-5:30pm, F 9am-2:30pm. **Canada,** Str. Nicolae Iorga 36 (☎307 50 00). M2: Pţa. Romană. Open M-Th 8:30am-5pm, F 8:30am-2pm. **Ireland,** Str. Vasile Lascăr 42-44, 6th fl. (☎212 21 81). M2: Pţa. Romană. Open M-F 10am-noon and 2-4pm. Citizens of **New Zealand** should contact the UK embassy. **UK,** Str. Jules Michelet 24 (☎201 72 79). M2: Pţa. Romana. Open M-Th 8:30am-1pm and 2-5pm, F 8:30am-1:30pm. **US,** Str. Nicolae Filipescu 26 (☎210 40 42, ext. 403; after hours 210 01 49). M2: Pţa. Universităţii. A block behind Hotel Intercontinental. Open M-Th 8am-5pm.

Currency Exchange: Exchange agencies and **ATMs** are everywhere. Stock up before heading to remote areas, but don't exchange more than you'll need—many won't buy *lei* back. Beware of exchange agencies charging commission; some take as much as 10%. Banks are usually a safe bet. **Banca Comercială Română** (☎312 61 85; www.bcr.com), in Pţa. Victoriei and Pţa. Universităţii, exchanges currency for no commission and AmEx **traveler's checks** for 1.5% commission. Open M-F 8:30am-5:30pm, Sa 8:30am-12:30pm. The Pţa. Universităţii location, at Bd. Regina Elisabeta 5, has both an **ATM** and a currency exchange machine, available 24hr. Changing money on the street is illegal and almost always a scam.

Luggage Storage: Gara de Nord. L3 per bag. L6 per large bag. Open 24hr.

English-Language Bookstore: Salingers, Calea 13 Septembrie 90 (☎403 35 34), in the Marriott. Open daily 10am-9pm.

GLBT Resources: Accept Romania, Str. Lirei 10 (☎252 16 37; www.accept-romania.ro). From the center, walk east on Bd. Carol I, which becomes Bd. Pache Protopopescu; turn left on Str. Horei. The helpful staff is a wealth of information.

Pharmacies: Sensiblu (☎ 0800 080 234) is a reputable chain. Branch, Bd. N. Balcescu 7. Open 24hr.

Medical Services: Spitalul de Urgenţă (Emergency Hospital), Calea Floreasca 8 (☎230 01 06). M1: Ştefan cel Mare. Open 24hr.

Telephones: Public pay phones are orange and take pre-paid phone cards, which come in L10 and L15 denominations, and can be bought at kiosks and convenience stores. These work for domestic calls and are a simple, if expensive, way to place international calls. You need a phone card to make any call, even to an emergency number. Place collect calls at **Romtelecom,** Calea Victoriei 35 (☎313 36 35,). M2: Pţa. Universităţii. It's the tallest building on the street. **Internet cafes** often have low overseas rates.

Internet: Internet cafes are everywhere. **Jazz Club,** Calea Victoriei 120 (☎312 48 41). M2: Pţa. Romană. 9am-11pm L3 per hr., 11pm-9am L1.50 per hr. Printing L0.50 per page. Open 24hr.

Post Office: Central Post Office, Str. Matei Millo 10 (☎315 87 93). M2: Pţa. Universităţii. From Bd. Regina Elisabeta, go north on Calea Victoriei and turn left on Str. Matei Millo. Like most branches, has **Poste Restante.** Open M, W, F 7am-3pm; Tu and Th noon-8pm. **Postal Code:** 014700.

⌐ ACCOMMODATIONS

Bucharest doesn't have many private rooms, and its hotels and hostels are more expensive than in other Romanian cities. The established hostels are fairly cheap, very international, and comfortable. Beware of people at Gara de Nord who claim to work for hostels—often they are con-artists and will scam you.

Elvis' Villa, Str. Avram Iancu 5 (☎312 16 53; www.elvisvilla.ro). M2: Pţa. Universităţii. From Gara de Nord, take trolley #85 to Calea Moşilor. Follow Bd. Carol I to Pţa. Pache Protopopescu, then go right on Str. Sf. Ştefan. At playground, take a left on Avram

Iancu. A newer hostel in a historic neighborhood, brightly painted Elvis' has A/C, fat mattresses, and an international clientele. Breakfast and laundry included. Internet L2 per 20min. Dorms €10. Cash only. ❶

Villa Helga Youth Hostel (HI), Str. Salcâcmilor 2 (☎610 22 14). M2: Pţa. Romană. Take bus #86, 79, or 133 2 stops from Pţa. Romană or 6 stops from Gara de Nord to Pţa. Gemeni. Go 1 block on Bd. Dacia, then right on Str. Viitorului. Romania's first hostel. Pleasant and homey, with comfortable beds, book exchange, kitchen, and friendly staff. Breakfast and laundry included. Internet L4 per hr. Check-out noon. Call ahead in summer. Dorms €10 per day, €60 per week; singles €14; doubles €12. Cash only. ❶

Funky Chicken Guesthouse, Str. General Berthelot 63 (☎312 14 25), from Gara de Nord, go right on Calea Griviţei, right on Str. Berzei, and left on Str. General Berthelot. Run by the owner of Villa Helga. Bucharest's newest, cheapest, and best-located hostel. Smallish kitchen. Thick mattresses and well-placed couches in bedrooms decorated with contemporary paintings. Laundry included. Dorms €8. Cash only. ❶

Hotel Carpati, Str. Matei Millo 6 (☎ 315 01 40; fax 312 18 57). M2: Universităţii. From Pţa. Universităţii, it's a short walk down Bd. Regina Elizabeta to Str. I. Brezoianu. Turn right; the hotel is at the 2nd corner. This fresh-smelling budget hotel boasts a central location, clean rooms, new furnishings, balconies, and a professional staff. Modest breakfast included. Call ahead to reserve. Singles €20-22; doubles €30-39. ❷

Hostel Casa (HI), Str. Lugoj 52 (☎260 04 08). M1 or M4: Gara de Nord or Basarab. From train station, turn left on Calea Griviţei; continue to Str. Lugoj. At this small, family-run hostel, everything is new and clean. Gara de Nord neighborhood is somewhat run-down. Breakfast and laundry included. 15min. Internet free. Dorms €12. Cash only. ❶

Villa 11, Str. Institut Medico Militar 11 (☎0722 495 900). M1 or M4: Gara de Nord. From the train station, take a right on Bd. Dinicu Golescu, then left on Str. Vespasian. This villa is a bit older, but you'll get a home-cooked breakfast every morning and a quiet respite from the sometimes-rowdy hostel scene. No lounge, TV room, kitchen, curfew, check-out, or safe storage for dorms. Dorms €9; singles €12.50. Cash only. ❶

🍴 FOOD

You'll find a wide range of restaurants in Bucharest, serving American, Chinese, French, Greek, Hungarian, Indian, Italian, and, of course, Romanian food. Fruit and vegetable stands are all over the city; a conveniently located **open-air market** at Pţa. Amzei, near Pţa. Romana, sells fruit, vegetables, meat, cheese, fish, bread, eggs, canned goods, and cooking supplies. (Open M-F 6am-9pm, Sa 6am-7pm, Su 6am-3pm.) **La Fourmi Supermarket,** in the basement of Unirea Shopping Center on Pţa. Unirii, is large. (Open M-F 8am-9:30pm, Sa 8:30am-9pm, Su 8am-4pm.)

🍲 **Burebista Vânătoresc,** Str. Batiştei 14 (☎211 89 29). M2: Pţa. Universităţii. Make a right off Bd. Nicolae Bălcescu. These people are serious about creating a traditional Romanian atmosphere: you'll be watched over by a stuffed bear and wild boar along with some medieval tapestries, and treated to music by a live folk band. Menu features tasty wild-game dishes, including, as it happens, bear and wild boar (L28 each). Full bar. Entrees L10-59. Open daily noon-midnight. MC/V. ❸

🍲 **Cremcaffe,** Str. T. Caragiu 3 (☎313 97 40). M2: Pţa. Universităţii, just off Bd. Regina Elisabeta and between the statues in Pţa. Universităţii. The gritty realities of Bucharest melt away in this elegant Italian coffeehouse, featuring delicious focaccia sandwiches (from L10) and coffee ("La Dolce Trieste," with smooth Belgian chocolate and ice cream; L13). On occasion, the relaxing background music gives way to mini-concerts on the house piano. Coffee/liqueur blends from L12. Ice cream from L8. Open M-F 7:30am-midnight, Sa-Su 9am-midnight. Cash only. ❷

La Mama, Str. Barbu Văcărescu 3 (☎212 40 86; www.lamama.ro). M1: Ştefan cel Mare. The menu isn't daring, but it isn't meant to be. Living up to its motto "like at mom's house," La Mama serves Romanian favorites for low prices in a down-to-earth atmosphere. Try the moussaka (meat-and-potato pie; L12.90). Branches, Str. Delea Veche 51 (☎320 52 13). M1: Pța. Muncii. Str. Episcopiei 9 (☎312 97 97). M2: Pța. Universității. Call ahead. Entrees L10-114. Beer and wine from L3.40. Vegetarian selection. Open daily 10am-2am. AmEx/MC/V. ❷

Barka Saffron (Saffron Boat), Str. Ștefan Sănătescu 1 (☎224 10 04), at the intersection with Bd. Ion Mihalache. M2: Aviatorilor. A hike from the center: consider calling a taxi. Delicious Indian and Thai cuisine in a relaxed, stylish atmosphere with a great bar. From the bar, try the strawberry daiquiri (L15). English menu. Vegetarian options. Entrees L11-26. Open daily noon-late. MC/V. ❷

Basilicvm, Str. Popa Savu 7 (☎222 67 79). M2: Aviatorilor. Serves praiseworthy Italian food amid white tablecloths, crisply folded napkins, and violin music. Lovely terrace and attentive service. The *saltimboca basilicvm* comes highly recommended (L26). Don't miss the weekend lunch special: everything 50% off. Beer from L5, large wine selection from L25. Entrees L14-65. Open daily 11am-1am. MC. ❹

◎ SIGHTS

▨ PARLIAMENTARY PALACE (PALATUL PARLAMENTULUI). With 16 levels and nearly 100,000 rooms totaling 365,000 sq. m, the Parliamentary Palace is the **world's 2nd-largest building,** after the Pentagon in Washington, D.C. Starting in 1984, 20,000 laborers and 700 architects worked around the clock to construct the so-called **House of the People** (Casa Poporuli); perhaps as much as 80% of Romania's GDP was consumed by the project during its construction. Built to the scale of Ceaușescu's ego, it is far too large to be fully used; today, many rooms sit empty. Intended to serve as home for Romania's Communist functionaries, the building now houses the **Parliament.** Extending eastward from the Parliamentary Palace is **Bd. Unirii,** a mammoth gray scar that was intentionally built 1m wider than Paris's Champs Elysées. Many of the apartment blocks on the west end sit nearly empty. *(M1 or 3: Izvor. M2: Unirii. Visitors' entrance is on the north side of the building. Open daily 10am-4pm. 40min. Tours in English L20, students L5.)*

HISTORIC NEIGHBORHOODS. In northern Bucharest, the peaceful, tree-lined side streets between Pța. Victoriei and Pța. Dorobanților (M2: Victoriei) are full of beautiful villas from pre-Ceaușescu Bucharest. What remains of Bucharest's **old center** lies near Str. Lipscani and Str. Gabroveni. The narrow, curving avenues, now pedestrian-only zones, contain the city's oldest church, **Biserica Curtea Veche** (Old Court Church), where Wallachian princes were crowned for centuries. The soot-stained frescoes, dating from the 16th century, are original. *(Free.)* Nearby are the ruins of **Palatul Voievoda,** a palace built in the 14th century and once inhabited by the notorious Impaler, Vlad Țepeș. *(☎314 03 75. Open daily 10am-5pm. L2.04, students L1.02).* During his aesthetic assault, Ceaușescu inexplicably spared **Dealul Mitropoliei,** the hill southwest of Pța. Unirii. Atop the hill is the small but old **Catedrala Mitropoliei,** with a very imaginative depiction of Judgment Day on its portico. Next door, the grand **Palatul Patriarhiei** (Patriarchal Palace), formerly commandeered by the Communist Parliament, is once again the **Romanian Orthodox Church** headquarters. *(M1, 2, or 3: Pța. Unirii. Up Aleea Dealul Mitropoliei. Not open to the public.)*

SIGHTS OF THE REVOLUTION. Crosses and plaques throughout the city commemorate the *eroii revoluției Române,* "heroes of the revolution," and the year 1989. The first shots of the Revolution were fired at **Piața Revoluției** on December 21, 1989. In the square are the **University Library,** the **National Art Museum,** and the **Senate Building** (former Communist Party Headquarters) where Ceaușescu delivered his final speech. Afterward, he fled the roof by helicopter, but didn't get very far. A white marble triangle with the inscription *Glorie martirilor noștri* (glory to our martyrs) commemorates the rioters who overthrew the dictator. *(M2: Pța. Universitatii. Turn right on Bd. Regina Elisabeta and then right on Calea Victoriei.)* **Piața Universității** overlooks

ROMANIA

ON THE MENU

ROMANIAN MOONSHINE

If you're tired of basic local plum brandy, commonly served in restaurants and touted as the major local drink, you may want to branch out and try the stronger version, *palincă*. This locally produced moonshine, widely available—but never in stores—is a triple-distilled version of tamer *tuica*. The alcohol content of *Palincă* varies wildly, but usually exceeds 60%.

You can find *palincă* at nearly any produce market, right along with all the other wholesome farm-fresh goods. It's commonly found in old plastic drinking water or soda bottles with the labels removed. It has a light-yellow color, and while it certainly has a powerful smell, it's perhaps less strong than one would expect for such a potent drink. Prices vary, but L11.50 per liter is usually fair.

As with any home-brew, a lot of caution is in order. Watch to see if a vendor's product is popular. If locals are safely drinking it, chances are you can too. Approach *palincă* with caution. It goes down easily, and can disorient those not accustomed to it quite rapidly. If you stay in a private home in Romania, especially in the countryside, you're more than likely to be offered a shot of the powerful pale brandy. If you accept, you'll be getting a real taste of the local culture—but don't taste too much of the local culture, or you might regret it in the morning.

memorials to victims of the revolution and the 1990 protests. Crosses line Bd. Nicolae Bălcescu—the **black cross** lies where the first victim died.

HERĂSTRĂU PARK. This immense park, north of downtown, surrounds a lake of the same name; its diversions include rowboat rentals (open M noon-8pm, Tu-Su 10am-8pm; L50,000 per hr.), ferry rides (L4, students L2), and a traveling-circus-style amusement park for children, open weekends. At the southern end of the park on Şos. Kiseleff, the **Arcul de Triumf** commemorates Romania's reunification in 1918 and honors those who died in WWI. Climb to the top for a view of the city. *(M2: Aviatorilor. Bus #131 or 331 from Pţa. Romana.)*

CIŞMIGIU PARK. One of Bucharest's oldest parks, Cişmigiu Park (Parcul Cişmigiu) is the peaceful, tree-filled eye of central Bucharest's storm of gray modernity. Stroll among carefully tended flower gardens, statues, cobblestone pathways, and fountains (rowboats L5 per hr.). This park is a focal point of the city's social life in summer. *(M2: Pţa. Universităţii. Bus #61 or 336. Open 24hr.)*

MUSEUMS

■ **VILLAGE MUSEUM (MUZEUL SATULUI).** This open-air museum, a replica 18th-to 19th-century village, contains nearly 100 houses, churches, mills, and even a sunflower-oil factory, all carted in from rural Romania. Festivals with musicians in traditional garb take place most weekends in spring and summer. The English brochure from the bookstore (L1) is an essential supplement. *(Şos. Kiseleff 28-30. M2: Aviatorilor. ☎ 222 90 68. Open M 9am-4pm, Tu-Su 9am-6pm. L5, students L2.50.)*

NATIONAL ART MUSEUM (MUZEUL NAŢIONAL DE ARTĂ AL ROMÂNIEI). This two-wing museum was built in the 1930s as a royal residence. The **European exhibit** presents an overview of European art history and boasts works by **El Greco, Monet, Rembrandt,** and **Renoir.** The highlight is the ■**Romanian section,** housing an extensive collection of medieval, modern, and contemporary art, including pieces by Romania's most famous painter, Nicolae Grigorescu, and sculptor, Constantin Brâncuşi. *(Calea Victoriei 49-53, in Pţa. Revolutiei. M2: Pţa. Universitatii. ☎ 315 51 93. English captions. Open W-Su in high season 11am-7pm; in low season 10am-6pm. L12, students L6.)*

MUSEUM OF THE ROMANIAN PEASANT (MUZEUL ŢĂRANULUI ROMÂN). This museum takes an ethnographic look at life from the perspective of Romanian peasants in the not-so-distant past. The windmill, waterwheel, and reconstructed peasant's cabin are the museum's most impressive pieces. Don't miss the small but fascinating collection of Communist memorabilia, tucked downstairs near the restrooms. On display is one of the few remaining publicly exhibited portraits of Nicolae Ceauşescu. Try to find a Romanian to explain the communism exhibit for you; there aren't any English captions. (Şos. Kiseleff 3. M2 or 3: Pţa. Victoriei or bus #300. ☎212 96 60. Open Tu-Su 10am-6pm. L6, students L2.)

🎵 🎧 ENTERTAINMENT AND NIGHTLIFE

Bucharest hosts numerous festivals and rock concerts every summer— Michael Jackson once greeted screaming fans here with "Hello, Budapest!" Check local guides, like the *Şapte Seri* or *B 24 FUN* booklets, for upcoming events. Fans of the classical arts will appreciate the **opera, symphony orchestra,** and **theater,** which are world class and dirt cheap; seasons run September to June. For all three, tickets can be purchased at the on-site box offices; a good rule of thumb is to stop by or phone five to six days before a performance. Soccer, or **football,** is Romania's favorite sport. The season is August to early June; major games are played at the **Dinamo** stadium (M1: Ştefan cel Mare). Bucharest has countless bars, pubs, and watering holes. The club scene, in particular, is one of the best in Romania. Check *Bucharest in Your Pocket.* Venues are concentrated in the old town center and in the student district by M1: Grozăveşti. Bring cab fare and directions to your hotel, written in Romanian, as public transit shuts down by midnight. Travel in groups and don't bring more money than you need. For info on **GLBT nightlife,** ask at **Accept Romania** (see **Orientation and Practical Information,** p. 527).

🎵 **Twice,** Str. Sfânta Vineri 4 (☎313 55 92). M2: Pţa. Universităţii. This large, multi-leveled club, long a popular Bucharest nightspot, boasts a top and bottom floor that pound away to different beats, while the chill outdoor terrace in-between sells pizza and provides a place to relax. Beer from L2. Cover men W L5; F-Sa L10. Open Tu-Su 9pm-5am.

La Motor/Lăptăria, Bd. Bălcescu 1-3 (☎315 85 08), on top of the National Theater. M2: Pţa. Universităţii. La motor, on the outdoor terrace between the 3rd and 4th fl., becomes indoor Lăptăria in winter. In summer, congregations of students chilling out on picnic tables sip beer (L3) from the cabana-style bar. Free open-air concerts or films in summer every night at 9:30pm. Open M-Th and Su noon-2am, F-Sa noon-4am.

Club A, Str. Blănari 14 (☎315 68 53; www.cluba.ro). M2: Pţa. Universităţii. Walk down Bd. Brătianu and take 3rd right by Kenvelo clothing store. A Bucharest institution since 1969, where a student crowd moshes to nightly rock bands while school's in session. Cheap drinks: beer from L1.40. Cover F-Sa: men L5, women L2. Open daily 11am-5am.

Club Maxx, Str. Independenţei 290 (☎223 00 39). M1: Grozăveşti. Giant room with 2 bars, house, and hip-hop, and raucous university students. Crowded all week. The thriving night scene here in the student quarter, with several bars and clubs to choose from, is an alternative to the city center. Beer from L5. Attached pizza parlor; pizza from L3.50. Cover F-Sa men L10, women L5; F students free. Open daily 10pm-5am.

Deja-Vu, Bd. N. Bălcescu 25 (☎311 23 22). M2: Pţa. Universităţii. Bring all the comrades to this faux-communist bar, decked out in propaganda and plenty of red paint. While there, toast Mother Russia with a flaming cocktail (L10-30). Open 9pm-5am daily.

Queen's Club, Str. Iuliu Barasch 12-14 (☎0722 642 891; www.queen-s-club.ro), near the Jewish Theater. M1 and M2: Unirii. Head up Calea Coposu and turn right on Iuliu Barasch. Inconspicuous entrance. This is both the most popular and the only GLBT nightspot in central Bucharest. Straight friends welcome; no membership card necessary. Beer from L5. Cover L20; includes one drink. Open F-Sa 11pm-5am.

WALLACHIA (ŢARA ROMÂNEASCĂ)

Known simply as "The Romanian Land," Wallachia is the heart of the country, the homeland of its royalty, and the seat of its capital. Along with Transylvania and Moldavia, it is one of Romania's three historical regions, a giant plain of sunflowers rolling from the Carpathians to the Black Sea.

SINAIA   ☎(0)244

The striking natural beauty of Sinaia (see-NI-ah), a small mountain town in the heart of the Carpathians, has long attracted attention. Romania's preeminent mountain resort, the town is full of luxury hotels and restaurants catering to the summer vacationers who flock here for excellent hiking, beautiful views, and a royal palace unmatched in southeastern Europe. The breathtaking ■Peleş Castle (Castelul Peleş) was once the home of Romania's first king, Carol I. A fantastic exterior of spires, colonnades, and Greco-Roman statuary is surpassed only by the interior, which emanates from the central **Hall of Honor.** Visitors enter through a red-carpeted marble staircase, paneled in carved walnut and topped by a retractable stained-glass skylight. Other rooms are themed; no expense was spared in creating opulent Florentine halls, Turkish lounges, and Moorish parlors. Look carefully in the king's library: one of the bookshelves is a secret passageway. Just down the road, ■Pelişor Castle (Castelul Pelişor) is modest only by comparison. It was built by King Carol I for his nephew and successor, Prince Ferdinand, and decorated in art nouveau style, with paintings by noted Romanian artists. Tours are available in English, and are included in the price of admission. Signs throughout town point toward the castles; both are a short walk up Str. Pelişului from the main road, Bd. Carol I. (☎310 918; www.peles.ro. In low season open W-Su 9am-5pm; in summer also Tu 11am-5pm. Peleş L10, students L5. Pelişor L8/3.)

The **Sinaia Monastery** (Mânăstirea Sinaia), at the intersection of Aleea Nifon and Aleea Carmen Silva, just off Str. Mânăstirii, was the area's first settlement when it was founded in 1695. It has since housed monks continually. There are two interior courtyards: one centers on a chapel dating to the monastery's founding, currently closed for renovations, and the other features a church in the Byzantine-Moldovan style. A small **museum** houses icons, religious artifacts, and the first Bible printed in Romanian. (☎314 917. Monastery open daily dawn-dusk. Free. Museum open July-Sept. M-Sa 9am-5pm. L3, students L1.50.)

Hiking and **skiing** opportunities abound in this mountain village; the trails are dotted with **cabanas** that offer beds and meals. **Cable cars** are the best way to get to the trails; **Telecabină,** the base station, is a short walk uphill, behind the Hotel New Montana. The first leg of the cable car runs to the Cota 1400 station (containing only a luxury hotel; no cabanas), and the 2nd to the Cota 2000 station; numbers indicate altitude. (☎311 939. Cars run Tu-F 8:30am-4pm, Sa-Su 8:30am-5pm. In summer, the last car can be as early as 3:45pm. L9 to Cota 1400; L18 to Cota 2000.) Several trails start from the Cota 2000 station, marked by posts with colored stripes. The **yellow-stripe trail** is a 5-6hr. hike past **Mt. Babele** (2200m) to **Mt. Omu** (2505m), the range's highest peak. **Cabana Omu,** the highest-altitude chalet in Romania, offers meals and inexpensive lodging year-round. Serious hikers can trek 6-8 hr. to **Bran Castle** (p. 536), but inexperienced hikers should always consult the tourist bureau first, before this or any other hike. **Salvamont,** the mountain-rescue organization, can be reached at ☎313 131.

Though it looks expensive, Sinaia does offer some budget options. Visitors are mobbed by locals offering **private rooms,** but it's wiser to peruse the tourist bureau's list of accommodations. Mountain **cabanas** have reasonably priced dorms, singles, and doubles; **Cabana Mioriţa ❶,** at Cota 2000, is equipped with a bar, restaurant, comfortable mattresses, and stunning views of mountain sunsets. (☎312 299. Reception 24hr. Dorms L30; private rooms L50. Cash only.)

Restaurant Bucegi ❷ serves dependable Romanian food, including such delicacies as grilled bear and wild boar (both L11). It's at Bd. Carol I 22, near Hotel New Montana. (☎313 902. English menu. Entrees L5.50-29. Cash only. Open daily 9am-10pm.) The open-air market offers **brânză în coaja de copac**, cheese with pine tree bark as the rind, found only in this region of Romania (L15 per kg). Sinaia nightlife is tame. The green leather sofas of candlelit **Old Nick's Pub**, at Bd. Carol I 8 next to Hotel Sinaia, are a nice place to kick back after a day of hiking and palace-gazing. (☎312 491. Open daily 9am-2am. Beer from L4. Cash only.)

Train destinations from Sinaia include: **Braşov** (1hr., 15 per day, L7.30); **Bucharest** (2hr., 15 per day, L1.57); **Cluj-Napoca** (5hr., 5 per day, L2.89). The **CFR** office, which sells tickets, is at the train station, down the hill from Bd. Carol I on Str. Gării. (☎542 080. Open M-F 9am-4pm.) Cheap, quick **buses** run from the train station to **Bucharest** and **Braşov** (every 30min. 7am-9pm, L6).

The helpful, English-speaking staff at the **tourist bureau**, on the main road at Bd. Carol I 47., has information about hiking, skiing, accommodations, restaurants, and nearly anything you could need. (☎315 656; www.infosinaia.ro. Open M-F 8:30am-4:30pm.) Most other necessities are also on Bd. Carol I, which runs along the base of the mountain; walk uphill from the train station and you can't miss it. **Banca Comercială Română**, Bd. Carol I 49, cashes **traveler's checks** for 1.5% commission and **exchanges currency**. (☎310 125. Open M-F 8:30am-5:30pm, Sa 8:30am-12:30pm.) An **ATM** is outside. **Farmacia Regală** is at Bd. Carol I 22. (☎311 029. Open daily 8am-9pm.) Several **supermarkets** line the street; an **open-air market** (Piaţa Centrala Sinaia) is on Pţa. Unirii, just off Bd. Carol I. (Open daily 9am-8pm.) The smoke-free **Internet Cafe** is in the shopping center on Bd. Carol I 41. (☎315 010. L2 per hr. Open daily 10am-midnight daily.) The **post office** is at Bd. Carol I 33, and has **Western Union**. (Open M-F 7am-8pm, Sa. 8am-1pm.) **Postal Code:** 106100.

TRANSYLVANIA (TRANSILVANIA)

Though the name evokes images of a dark, evil land of black magic and vampires, Transylvania, with a long history of Saxon settlement dating back to the 12th and 13th centuries, is a relatively Westernized region. Its green hills and mountains gently descend from the rugged Carpathians in the south to the Hungarian Plain in the northwest. The vampire legends do, however, take root in the region's remarkable architecture: Transylvanian buildings are tilted, jagged, and more sternly Gothic than anywhere else in Europe.

ARDEAL

Ardeal (Ar-DEE-al) is classic Transylvania: craggy mountains, peaked rooftops, and Gothic spires. Look for vestiges of medieval cities and plenty of vampiric lore. Much of the wilderness in this region remains untamed, making for excellent hiking in the Făgăraş Mountains.

BRAŞOV   ☎(0)268

The historic center of Braşov (BRAH-shohv; pop. 353,000) is a kaleidoscopic maze of 800-year-old buildings. Surrounded by the Carpathian mountains, Braşov's Old Town is dominated by the ancient Black Church and filled with pleasant squares, shops, and tree-lined boulevards, making it the perfect place for a nighttime stroll. The town is the natural base camp for excursions to Poiana Braşov's ski slopes, Bran Castle, and the ruins at Râsnov. Braşov is no secret, however—you'll undoubtedly run into other travelers.

⬛ TRANSPORTATION. Train destinations from Braşov include **Bucharest** (3-4hr., 20 per day, L258,000); **Cluj-Napoca** (5-6hr., 5 per day, L397,000); **Iaşi** (9-10hr., 1 per day, L310,000); **Sibiu** (4hr., 4 per day, L228,000). The **train station** (☎410 233) is along Bd. Gării, southwest of the Old Town. Buy tickets at **CFR**, Bd. 15 Noiembrie 43. (☎47 70 18. Open M-F 8am-7:30pm.) Braşov has two main **bus stations:** Autogară 1, next to the train station, is the main depot; Autogară 2, at Str. Avram Iancu 114, called "Gara Bartolomeu," runs **buses** to **Râşnov** and **Bran** (☎427 267). To get there, take bus #16 or 38 from the center of town, or #12 from Pţa Unirii. Buy tickets (L8,000 per ride) for **city buses** at "R.A.T." kiosks scattered throughout town.

⬛⬛ ORIENTATION AND PRACTICAL INFORMATION. The city is divided into the picturesque Old Town, wedged in a valley between two tall mountains, and the surrounding communist-era sprawl. The Old Town includes two districts. The old Saxon center, called **Kronstadt**, lies at the mouth of the valley and centers on **Piaţa Sfantului** and **Biserica Neagră** (Black Church). **Schei**, the old Romanian district, is farther up the valley and centered on the smaller **Piaţa Unirii.** To get to the Old Town from the **train station** or from **Autogară 1**, take bus #4 in the direction of Pţa. Unirii; watch for pickpockets. On foot, cross the street in front of the train station and head down **Bd. Victoriei.** Turn right on **Str. Mihai Kogălniceanu**, then bear right on **Bd. 15 Noiembrie**, which becomes **Bd. Eroilor. Str. Republicii** and **Str. Mureşenilor** branch off 1km apart, both converging on Pţa. Sfantului. Taxi fare from the train station to the Old Town should not exceed L5.

A good first stop is the **tourist information bureau,** housed in the yellow clock-tower building in Pţa. Sfatului. Helpful, multilingual staff offer **free maps,** English pamphlets, and information about accommodations, restaurants, and hiking. (☎419 078; www.brasovcity.ro. Open daily 9am-6pm.) **Maps** are sold at *librarie* (bookstores) along Str. Republicii; try **Libraria Ralu,** Str. Republicii 39, which sells maps for L9-12. (☎473 932. Open M-F 8:30am-8pm, Sa 9am-5pm, Su 11am-3pm. MC/V.) **Banca Comercială Română,** Pţa. Sfatului 14, cashes AmEx **traveler's checks** for 1.5% commission and **exchanges currency.** (☎47 71 09. Open M-F 8:30am-5pm, Sa 8:30am-12:30pm.) An **ATM** is in front of the bank; others line Str. Republicii. A **pharmacy, Aurofarm,** is at Str. Republicii 27. (☎14 35 60. Open daily 8am-midnight. V.) The **telephone office** is at Bd. Eroilor 23. (☎40 42 91. Open M-F 7am-9pm, Sa-Su 7am-8pm.) Find 24hr. **Internet** at the **Blue Club,** just off Str. M. Weiss, at Str. N. Balcescu 16. (7am-midnight L2 per hr., midnight-7am L1.50 per hr.) The **post office,** Nicolae Iorga 1, on Pţa. Revolutiei, provides **Western Union** services. (☎412 222. Open M-F 7am-8pm, Sa 8am-1pm.) **Postal Code:** 500000.

⬛⬛ ACCOMMODATIONS AND FOOD. The market for **private rooms** is booming. In high season, opportunists tourist-hunt in the train station. Look at the room and agree on a price (€15 is reasonable) before you accept. For a sure thing, head to ⬛**Kismet Dao Villa Hostel ❶**, Str. Democraţiei 2b, formerly known as Elvis's Villa Hostel. From Pţa. Unirii, walk up Str. Bâlea and turn right. Comfortable and well decorated, Kismet Dao has fabulous views of the surrounding hills. Free perks include breakfast, laundry, a drink per day (beer or soda), and 1hr. of Internet at a nearby cafe. (☎51 42 96. Dorms €10-11; doubles €25. MC/V.) For Romanian hospitality and spacious rooms, try ⬛**Eugene Junior ❶**, Str. Neagoe Basarab 1. From Bd. 15 Novembrie, turn on Str. Matei Basarab; it's an unobtrusive building at the intersection with Str. N. Basarab. (☎0722 54 25 81; ejrr68@yahoo.com. Call or email ahead, and Eugene will pick you up. Kitchen. Incredibly useful hand-drawn map free. Breakfast €2.50. Laundry €3. Rooms €12.50 per person, negotiable. Cash only.) At **Beke Guest House ❶**, Str. Cerbului 32, a kind Hungarian family rents out four smallish but clean and comfortable rooms on a quiet side street near the main square. Follow Str. Republicii to Pţa. Sfatului and go left on Str. Apollonia Hirscher, then turn right on Cerbului. (☎511 997. Rooms L50, negotiable. Cash only.)

Bella Muzica ❶, Str. G Barițiu 2, is across Pța. Sfatului from Str. Mureșenilor. Make your way through the music store and downstairs to a candlelit wine cellar. Bella offers an eclectic Romanian-Hungarian-Mexican menu, including the Romanian peasant dish "Maramuresan Bulz" (maize pudding with bacon and a fried egg; L9.80). Free chips and a free shot of *palincă* (Romanian plum moonshine) complete the meal. You can choose your own romantic music. (☎47 69 46. Entrees L70,000-385,000. Open daily noon-11pm. MC/V.) **Taverna ❸**, Str. Politechnicii 6, is also near the city center. From Pța. Sfatului, walk up Str. Republicii and go right. The menu features a long list of Romanian, Hungarian, and French dishes; the "Specialitate Brașoveană" is a blend of local meats for L1.89. (☎474 618. Entrees L1.09-L4.19. Dress nicely. Open daily noon-midnight. MC/V.)

⬛ SIGHTS. The area surrounding Pța. Sfatului is perfect for a stroll, as is Str. Republicii, the main pedestrian drag. Jagged and aging, Romania's largest Gothic cathedral looms above the square along Str. Gh. Barițiu. The **Black Church** (Biserica Neagră, or Schwartzen Kirche) earned its name in 1689 when it was charred by the Great Fire that destroyed most of Brașov. Inside is a renowned collection of 119 Anatolian carpets, compliments of 17th- and 18th-century German merchants, and an enormous 4000-pipe organ, the largest in southeastern Europe. (Open M-Sa 10am-5pm. L3, students L1.50. Organ concerts mid-June to mid-July Tu 6pm; mid-July to Aug. Tu, Th, Sa 6pm. Concerts L2.) The expansive view from the **summit of Mt. Tâmpa** shows the stark contrast between the spires and cobblestone of old Kronstadt and the concrete of new Brașov. Follow the red triangle markings to hike to the top (1½hr.), or take the *telecabina* (cable car). From Pța. Sfatului, walk down Apollonia Hirscher, go left on Str. Castelui, then right on Suișul Castelui, and head upstairs. (Car runs M noon-6pm; Tu-W and F 9:30am-6pm; Th 9:30am-5pm; Sa-Su 9:30am-7pm. L6.) Follow the blue stripe trail (15min.) to the peak.

Pța. Unirii is home to **St. Nicholas's Church** (Biserică Sfântu Nicolae), built in 1495 and filled to the brim with icons and colorful murals. **Romania's First School** (Prima Școală Românească), now a museum on church grounds, traces the history of Romanians in old Saxon Kronstadt and displays the first Romanian books printed in the Latin alphabet. (☎0720 024 717. Church open daily 8am-6pm. Liturgy 8am, vespers 6pm. Free. School open daily 9am-5pm. L3, students L2.) The **Brașov History Museum** (Muzeul de Istorie) is in the staid, clock-towered hall in the center of Pța. Sfatului containing items from Brașov's several centuries of existence. (☎472 350. Open Tu-Su 10am-6pm. L2.50, students L1.50.)

🎭🎬 ENTERTAINMENT AND NIGHTLIFE. Brașov's artistic offerings are rich and come cheaply. For the **opera** and **orchestra**, tickets are sold at the box office on Str. Republicii 4, the **Agencia Teatrală de Bilete.** (☎471 889. Open Tu-F 10am-5pm, Sa 10am-2pm. Opera tickets L6.30, students L3.15; orchestra tickets L8/4. Cash only.) The **Opera House** (Opera Brașov) is at Str. Biserica Române 51; the **Cercul Militar Brașov** hosts the orchestra at Str. Mureșenilor 29. For **theater** tickets, go to the **Teatrul Dramatic** at Pța. Teatrului 1, along Bd. Eriolor going away from the city center. (☎418 850. Box office open Tu-Su 9am-1pm and 4-7pm. Seats from L4. Cash only.) The end of summer brings both the **International Chamber Music Festival,** held the first week of September, and the **Golden Stag Festival** (Cerbul de Aur) held in Pța. Sfatului at the end of August, which showcases a wide variety of Romanian and international pop musicians. **Saloon,** Str. Mureșenilor 11, is a tourist favorite by day (decent pizza L1.36) and a hotspot by night, offering a selection of imported beers (from L4) and mixed drinks. Try "Sex in the Forest" (L10). On Friday and Saturday nights, the saloon opens its basement lounge, made up to give off a tough-guy vibe. (☎41 77 05. Open daily 9am-late.) **Opium,** Str. Republicii 2, bills itself as a "chill out cafe." They're serious about the opium den theme—strewn-about cushions, faux-Buddhist trappings, techno music, and dim candlelight create a trippy atmosphere. (☎050 575. Spiked coffee concoctions from L4.50. Beer from L3.50. Open daily 10am-midnight. No opium served.)

ROMANIA

BRAN CASTLE AND RÂŞNOV FORTRESS   ☎(0)268

Ever since Bram Stoker's novel identified **Bran Castle** with bloodthirsty **Count Dracula**, castle and legend have been linked in the popular imagination. But the history of this small turreted castle is more complicated than fables suggest. Residents of Bran built the castle in the 14th century to guard against Turkish invaders and to serve as a tollbooth along the trade route through Transylvania. In the early 15th century, the Hungarian king gave the castle to local ruler Mircea the Old, the grandfather of Vlad Ţepeş, or **Vlad the Impaler**—the historical model of the count-vampire. During his own reign, Vlad may have ruled from Bran Castle, but one of the only undisputed facts is that he was imprisoned here by the Hungarian king for two months in 1462. The restored castle commands a good view of both Bran and the surrounding countryside, and contains furnished rooms from the Middle Ages to the 20th century. Dozens of stands outside sell Dracula paraphernalia, from toy stakes to "blood wine," at what is very much a tourist attraction. (Castle and village open M noon-6pm, Tu-Su 9am-6pm. L10, students L5. English pamphlet L2.) From Braşov, take a **taxi** or **city bus** #5, 9, or 12 to Autogarb 2. From there, catch an intercity bus to **Bran** (45min., every 30-60min. 7am-11:30pm, L2.50.) Get off when you see the souvenir market or the "Cabana Bran Castle—500m" sign. Backtrack along the road; the castle is on the right amid souvenir shops.

On a windswept hill near **Râşnov** sits a ▨**ruined fortress** topped by an immense wooden crucifix. Much of the castle has been renovated recently, but work continues on the topmost portion, which shows every one of its nearly 800 years. Drop a coin down the spectacularly deep well (143m), dug by two Turkish prisoners, which enabled the fortress to withstand sieges throughout its centuries of use. The experience is less touristy than Bran, and the view from the top is breathtaking. (English captions. Open daily 9am-7pm. L8.50.) Most buses to Bran stop in **Râşnov** (25min.). From the bus stop, follow Str. Republicii past an open-air market. Go right and then left through an arch; if all else fails, keep watch for the archway. Travelers to Bran or Râşnov should stay in Braşov.

POIANA BRAŞOV   ☎(0)268

If Sinaia is Romania's longstanding summer alpine resort, Poiana Braşov (www.poiana-brasov.ro.) is its younger winter sibling. Nine ski slopes, picture-perfect mountain vistas, and four-star lodging attract an international crowd in winter, with a similar (although smaller) crowd during the summer. The summer scene revolves around hiking and bicycling on the many trails, playing tennis, and lounging about on the meadows. **Ski rental** starts at €6 per day, with daytime lift tickets from €10 and lessons from €10 per hour. **Equipment rental** is available at the base; nearly all staff are multilingual. The **Centru de Echitate** (Equestrian Center), down the road from the main resort area, rents **bicycles** (L8 per hr.), and offers **tennis** (L10 per hr.) and **horseback riding** (€10 per hr.). To avoid the throngs of luxury hotels, a budget traveler can book a room in cheaper Braşov or rent a two-floor **cabin** from the equestrian center. (☎262 161. Horse rental daily 8am-noon and 2-5pm. Kitchenettes, baths, and cable TV. 3-person cabins L150; 4-person cabins L300. Cash only.) Take Braşov **city bus** #20 (25min., 2-3 per hr. 7am-10pm, L2 from Livada Postei, at the western end of Bd. Eroilor). A **taxi** from town costs €6.

SIGHIŞOARA   ☎(0)265

Known as the Pearl of Transylvania and the birthplace of Vlad Ţepeş, the "real" Dracula, Sighişoara (see-ghee-SHWAH-rah; pop. 39,000), looks just like you'd imagine Dracula's hometown: cobblestone streets wind around Gothic spires, and a centuries-old Saxon clock tower houses an actual torture chamber. One of the best-preserved medieval citadels in Europe crowns the hillside town. No visit to Transylvania is complete without a nighttime stroll among the tombs of Sighişoara's enormous hilltop graveyard, which is enough to make even the most stout-hearted believe, just for a moment, in vampires.

🖃🖹 TRANSPORTATION AND PRACTICAL INFORMATION. Trains run to: **Alba Iulia** (2hr., 3 per day, L1.86); **Bucharest** (5hr., 6 per day, L3.71) via **Braşov** (2hr., 6 per day, L2.31); **Cluj-Napoca** (3½hr., 3 per day, L3); **Oradea** (6hr., 2 per day, L4.07). **Buses** leave for various locations, including **Târgu Mureş** (19 per day, L7) and **Sibiu** (4 per day, L7). The stations are next to each other on Str. Libertăţii; the train station is at Str. Libertăţii 51. To rent **bikes,** head to **Gia Hostel** on Str. Libertatii 41, near the train station. (☎ 772 486. L20 per day. Open daily 8am-late.)

It's hard to get lost in Sighişoara. It's a 5min. walk from the train or bus station to the center—turn right on Str. Libertăţii, then left on Str. Gării. Veer left at the cemetery, go right through the church courtyard, cross the pedestrian bridge over the river **Târana Mare,** and turn left on **Str. Morii.** A right at the fork leads to **Str. O. Goga,** the **citadel** *(cetatea),* the center of the modern town, and Str. Oberth; look for the statue of Romulus and Remus. If all else fails, aim for the highly visible clock tower. A left leads to the main street, **Str. 1 Decembrie 1918.**

Many hostels give out maps for free. You can buy one for L10 at **Librăria Hyperion,** Str. 1 Decembrie 1918 11. (Open M-F 8am-5pm, Sa 9am-3pm.) Most essential services line Str. 1 Decembrie 1918 and Str. Oberth, which run along the citadel. **BRD Bank,** Str. Oberth 20, has an **ATM** and **Western Union** services and **exchanges currency.** (☎ 771 617. Open M-F 8:30am-5:30pm.) The train station has **luggage storage.** (L3.50. Open 24hr.) The **Aescalop pharmacy** is at Str. Oberth 22. (☎ 779 913. Open M-F 8am-8pm, Sa 8am-1pm.) **Culture Cafe** in the citadel, attached to Burg Hostel, has **Internet.** (☎ 778 489. Open daily 7am-3am. L1.60 per hr.) The **telephone office** (☎ 777 701; open M-F 10am-6pm, Sa 10am-2pm) and the **post office** (☎ 774 110; open M-F 7am-8pm) are at Str. Oberth 16-17. **Postal Code:** 545400.

🖪🖸 ACCOMMODATIONS AND FOOD. Private rooms (US$8-12) are available in the Old Town. People offer them on the street or at the station. Check out the room and negotiate the price before agreeing to anything. The storied 🏠**Nathan's Villa Hostel ❶,** Str. Liber-tăţii 8, a right turn out of the train station, is Transylvania's leading party hostel. Ask the charis-matic American owner to make his famous punch, and watch out for the occasional pig roasted on a spit. (☎ 772 546. Breakfast and laundry included. Dorms L30; private rooms L74.) **Pensiune Chic ❶,** directly across from the train station at Str. Libertăţii 44, has clean,

THE LOCAL STORY

SON OF A...

Yes, Dracula did exist—sort of. He was not the ruler of Transylvania, but of Wallachia; he was not a count, but a *voivod* (a local governor or "prince"); and he was not a vampire. Still, the truth about Vlad Ţepeş (1431-1476) is enough to make anyone lock the lid to his coffin at night.

Dracula's story begins with his father, Vlad Basarab, who was nick-named 🐉Dragul (dragon) for his skill with arms. Dragul sent his son, Dra-gula (son of the dragon), to the Otto-man Empire as a hostage in 1442, at the tender age of 10. During his six years as a hostage, Vlad learned what was to become his preferred method of torture: impalement. Victims of impalement—which involved inserting a large wooden stake through the vic-tim's body without piercing the vital organs—usually begged for a swift death throughout the slow, agonizing process.

Vlad the Impaler earned his title during his reign as *voivod*. In addition to murderers, thieves, liars, and polit-ical rivals, he impaled the old, the destitute, and the crippled. His crown-ing achievement was in turning the Turks' gruesome practice against them. In 1462, the invading Turks turned tail at Wallachia's border, which had been decorated with 20,000 of their impaled countrymen. As his terror tactics became infa-mous, the son of the dragon was renamed the son of the devil, Vlad Dracula.

spacious rooms for reasonable prices, though the staff may not be able to tell you so in English. (☎ 775 901. Singles L45, doubles with bath L59.) In the Old Town proper, HI-affiliated **Burg Hostel ❶**, Str. Bastionului 6, in the square near the clock tower, has comfortable bunk beds. The bar/Internet cafe in the cellar is a popular hangout. (☎ 778 489. Breakfast L10. Laundry €1. Reception 7am-3am. Beds from L30.)

▧**Cafe Rustic ❶**, Str. 1 Decembrie 1918 5, serves Transylvanian dishes in a dark wood-and-brick-paneled dining room that is, indeed, rustic. Try the *goulash* (L9.85). The cafe turns into a bar at night. (Entrees L5-1.74. Open M-Th 9am-midnight, F-Su 9am-1am. Cash only.) In the Citadel, try **Casa Vlad Dracul ❷**, Str. Cositorarilor 5, under the big metal dragon sign. It really is Vlad's house—he was born here in 1431 and lived here until 1436. The medieval decor is fittingly spooky, and the traditional dishes are top-notch. (☎ 771 930. Entrees L10-40. Open daily 10am-midnight. Cash only.) **Grocery stores** line Str. 1 Decembrie 1918. An **open-air market** on Pța. Agroalimentară has a good selection of produce and cheeses; from the train station, follow Str. Libertății and cross the bridge. (Open daily dawn-dusk.)

◩ ※ SIGHTS AND FESTIVALS. The **Citadel,** built by the Saxons in 1191, is a truly fantastic medieval city-within-a-city. Enter through the **Clock Tower** *(Turnul cu Ceas)*, off Str. O. Goga. Climb to the top to see the clock's mechanism and painted figurines representing the days of the week. The deck above provides an expansive view of the area. Plaques state the exact direction and distance to major cities around the world. To the left as you leave the tower, the **Museum of Medieval Armory** (Colecția de Arme Medievale) displays weapons from all over the world and maintains a small exhibit on Vlad Țepeș. Underneath the clock tower, the **Torture Room** houses a tiny but gruesome collection of pain-inflicting instruments and shackles, as well as diagrams on how to use them. (English captions. Open M 10am-4:30pm, Tu-F 9am-6:30pm, Sa-Su 9am-4:30pm. Clock tower L4.03, students L2.55. Museum L2.55/1.53. Torture room L1.53.) Across the street at Str. Cositorarilor 13, the 13th-century Lutheran **Monastery Church** (Biserica Mănăstrii) was originally built by Dominican monks, who cleared out when the Reformation came to Transylvania. Turkish rugs donated by passing German merchants hang on the walls and the baptismal font dates to 1414. Organ concerts are held Friday afternoons. (☎ 771 195. English pamphlets. L2, students L1.) A left up Str. Școlii reveals the long, tunnel-enclosed 179-step **stairway**, built in 1642 to help children get to school. At the top is the Gothic **Church on the Hill** (Biserica din Deal), which dates to the 15th century. Its walls were once covered in medieval frescoes: many were destroyed by overzealous Reformers, but some have since been restored. A trip to the **crypt** (empty, thankfully) is always exciting. Don't miss the spooky hilltop graveyard. Remember your wooden stake. (Church open daily 10am-6pm. L2. No cameras.)

The 2nd weekend in July brings the **Medieval Festival** to Sighișoara. The **Folk Art Festival** arrives in late August.

SIBIU ☎(0)269

The one-time capital of Transylvania, well-preserved Sibiu (SEE-bee-oo; pop. 170,000) remains a town of medieval monuments and ornate architecture. Despite a colorful Old Town and proximity to some of the best hiking in the country, the unhurried town has been spared a tourist invasion. It is an idyllic base for exploring the nearby Făgăraș mountains. Much of the town is under renovation in preparation for its upcoming reign as European Cultural Capital in 2007.

▛ TRANSPORTATION. Train destinations include: **Brașov** (3½hr., 3 per day, L18.30); **Bucharest** (6hr., 3 per day, L29); **Cluj-Napoca** (4hr., 1 per day, L29); **Timișoara** (6hr., 3 per day, L29). **CFR,** Str. N. Bălcescu 6, past Hotel Împăratul Romanilor from Pța. Mare, sells tickets. (☎ 212 085. Open M-F 7:30am-7:30pm.) **Bus** destinations include: **Cluj-Napoca** (3½hr., 4 per day, L18) via **Alba Iulia** (1½hr., 4 per day, L10); **Bucharest** (5hr., 5 per day, L30); **Timișoara** (5½hr., 3 per day, L30). **Microbuses,** which stop at the bus station, are a cheap, fast option. They run to numerous destinations, including **Braşov** (3hr., 4 per day, L13) and **Sighişoara** (2½hr., 4 per day, L10). The bus station is beside the train station; incoming microbuses can drop off in Pţa. Unirii or elsewhere.

🖃🖪 ORIENTATION AND PRACTICAL INFORMATION. The train and bus station are at Pţa. 1 Decembrie 1918, about 2km east of the city center. Bus #5 runs to the center (L1.50 for 2 trips, buy tickets on board), and a taxi to the center will run about L4. From the station, turn left on **Str. General Magheru** to reach the center. At the small square with a statue of Nicolaus Olahus, either take the left fork or bear right on **Str. Avram Iancu.** Both routes lead to the main square of the Old Town, **Piaţa Mare.** To the right, through the tunnels, is **Piaţa Mică.** To reach **Piaţa Unirii,** the modern main square, proceed through Pţa. Mare and down **Str. Nicolae Bălcescu.**

🕮Librăria Friedrich Schiller, Pţa. Mare 7, sells city and hiking **maps** (L50,000-100,000) and has a **tourist office.** The owner is a wealth of information about Sibiu and the surrounding area, and will gladly answer questions about hiking, nearby villages, or anything else. Make this your first stop. (☎208 913. Open M-F 9am-5pm, Sa 10am-1pm. Call anytime and someone will pick up.) **IDM Exchange,** Pţa. Mică 8, cashes **traveler's checks** for no commission and **exchanges currency.** (☎214 369. Open M-F 9am-7pm, Sa 9am-2pm.) MC/V **ATMs** are on Str. Bălcescu, on Calea Dumăravii, and in Pţa. Unirii. **Farmacia Farmasib** is at Str. Bălcescu 53. (☎21 78 97. Open M-F 9am-7pm, Sa 9am-2pm. Open 24hr. for emergencies. MC/V.) The **telephone office** is at Str. Bălcescu 13. (☎204 110. Open M-F 10am-6pm, Sa 10am-2pm.) For **Internet,** try to find the **Hidden Internet Cafe** on Str. N. Bălcescu 51. (☎0 3691 101 039. Open 24hr. L1 per hr.) The **post office,** Str. Metropoliei 14, has **Western Union.** From Pţa. Mare, go down Str. S. Brukenthall and left on Str. Metropoliei. (☎232 222. Open M-F 7am-8pm, Sa 8am-1pm.) **Postal Code:** 550 450.

🛏🍴 ACCOMMODATIONS AND FOOD. Brand-new **Pensiuna Ela ❷,** is a bit of a walk from the city center, but well worth it for thick mattresses and beautifully decorated, spacious rooms with TVs and private baths. There's a kitchen available for cooking, and a quiet, peaceful backyard terrace—make yourself at home. From Pţa. Mare, proceed through the clock tower, across Pţa. Mica, and down a hill. Continue on Str. Ocnei, make a right on Str. Nová, and keep going. (☎215 197;www.hotel-ela.as.ro. Breakfast €4. Book ahead. Singles €20; doubles €25; triples €37. MC/V.) **Hotel Bulevard ❸,** Pţa. Unirii 10, offers rooms with TVs and private baths. The receptionists sell maps (L5-10) and speak good English. (☎210 158. Breakfast included. Singles €30, doubles €50. MC/V.) To reach hotel **Pensiune Leu ❶** (Lion), Str. Moş Ion Roată 6, walk along Str. S. Brukenthall from Pţa. Mare until it ends, and continue down the staircase on the right. Follow the road, looping back to Str. Moş Ion Roată. The hotel offers low prices, clean rooms, free laundry service, and hot showers. (☎218 392. Reception 24hr. Dorms L20; singles L50; doubles L80. Cash only.) For provisions, stop at **Supermarket Alcomsib,** next to the phone office on Str. Bălcescu 11. (Open M-F 7:30am-9pm, Sa 8am-9pm, Su 8am-2pm. MC.) To find the **open-air market,** in Pţa. Agroalimentara, walk north from the city center down Str. Turnului. It's on the river; if you cross a bridge, you've gone too far. You can buy meat, cheese, flowers, vegetables, fruit, fast food, and various trinkets. (Open dawn-dusk. Meat and dairy section open M-F 7am-8pm, Sa 7am-6pm, Su 7am-1:30pm.) For good, cheap Transylvanian food, walk north on Str. Turnului, pass the open-air market, cross the bridge, and veer left onto Str. Reconstructiei, which will turn into Str. Tudor Vladimescu, to get to **Kon-Tiki ❶,** Str. Tudor Vladimescu 10. Don't be fooled by the no-frills decor: the ridiculously good *ciorbă de burtă,* or Schweinefleischsuppe (pork soup; L4.50) is a local favorite. (☎220 350. Entrees L4.50-7. Open M-F 10am-10pm, Su noon-10pm. Cash only.) More convenient is **Crama Ileana ❶,** Pţa. Teatrului 2, downhill and to the left from Pţa. Unirii, off a side street called Str. Berariei. The food's as traditional as it gets, with a wide variety of authentic rural dishes (stuffed cabbage with smoked ribs; L7.50), in a setting that looks like an old peasant's cabin. (☎434 343. English menu. Entrees L6-15. Open daily noon-2am. Cash only.)

◙ ※ SIGHTS AND FESTIVALS. The town square boasts a number of historically and architecturally significant buildings, many under renovation, including a beautiful 14th-century Gothic cathedral, now a **Lutheran Church,** on Pţa. Huet 1. (☎211 203. English pamphlet. Open daily in summer 9am-8pm, in winter 10am-3pm. Free.) The main museum is **Muzeul Naţional Brukenthall,** Str. Metropoliei 2 and Pţa. Mare 7-9. The building on Str. Metropoliei houses a history museum, featuring various valuables from the House of Brukenthall, and the royal palace on Pţa. Mare displays a genuinely impressive art collection, including several notable Renaissance paintings, and furnished rooms which have been restored to their former royal glory. (History museum ☎218 143. Open Tu-Su 8:30am-4:30pm. L5, students L4. Art gallery ☎217 691. Open Tu-Su 9am-5pm. L6, students L3.) The biggest attraction lies just outside of town. The ▧**ASTRA Museum of Traditional Folk Civilization** (Muzeul Civilizatiei Populare Tradiţionale ASTRA), in a forest preserve south of the center, rivals Bucharest's Village Museum as one of the country's finest open-air exhibits. It's a 4km hike from Pţa. Unirii along Calea Dumbravii; your best bet is a taxi (about L4). At 96,000 sq. km, the museum occupies a fair bit of local forest and displays a large collection of buildings from across the country, such as mills, peasant farmsteads, and old plum brandy distillery. Try the 1.4m horn in the **instrument maker's residence.** The museum's charming 17th-century **Orthodox church** is covered inside with original paintings. Plan on at least 3hr. to see the whole thing. (☎242 599. English guidebooks L2. Open Tu-Su 10am-8pm. L8, students L4. Tours in English L30 per hr. Call ahead to reserve.) The **International Theater Festival,** in the first week of June, attracts groups from around the world. **Summer Fest** rages June 15 to September 15 near Pţa. Unirii, with free open-air concerts Thursday and Friday nights. The **Medieval Festival** arrives in late August.

◪ HIKING. The **Făgăraş Mountains** extend about 70km from the Olt Valley to the Piatra Craiului mountains, with a sharp ridge running east-west above the treeline. The tallest peaks, **Moldoveanu** and **Negoiu** (both slightly over 2500m), are snow-capped year-round. Wildflower meadows, cloud-shrouded summits, and superb views of Wallachian plains and Transylvanian hills have earned the Făgăraş renown among Romanian hikers. For food, shelter, and basic supplies, **cabanas** dot the area. Most are in the lowlands (500m), where facilities are more posh, or the middle uplands (1500m); few are above the treeline (2000m). Some offer sleeping sacks (L8-15); others have doubles with baths (L15-30).

Before hiking, stop by ▧**Librăria Friedrich Schiller** (see above), a goldmine of information about the numerous possible trails. There are two ways to get to the mountains: by car or by *personal* (slow) train. **Advantage Rent-A-Car** is at Str. N. Bălcescu 37; you'll need a valid driver's license and two years driving experience. (☎216 949. www.advantage-rentacar.ro. €24-30 per day.) Driving is only possible July to September: the main highway traversing the mountains is closed the rest of the year. The **train** route from Sibiu to Braşov stops in the villages of Avrig, Ucea, Arpaşu de Jos, Porumbaca de Jos, and Cârta, any of which makes a good base for hiking. Trains should take 1-3hr. For Mt. Negoiu, stop off at Avrig or Porumbaca de Jos; for Mt. Moldoveanu, try Ucea. Base camp Victoria, accessible by bus from Ucea (25min., 7 per day, L20,000), offers lodging. Trails of varying difficulty cross the mountains; if you aren't an experienced hiker, be sure to hire a guide.

One possible trip is a three-day, two-night excursion from Sibiu. Take a train to **Avrig,** 16km (4hr. hike) from **Cabana Poiana Neamţului** (☎0744 57 39 06), a road-accessible town at the foot of the mountains. Taxis are rare in Avrig, so many visitors traverse this stretch by hitchhiking, though *Let's Go* does not recommend it. You can also walk—follow the red cross markings from the train station. Continue up the mountains on the same trail (3hr.) as it separates from the road, and spend the night at **Cabana Bircaci ❶** (☎0744 85 81 40). Then, take the blue dot trail to glacial **Lake Avrig** (3hr.), and connect with the red stripe to the **Puha Saddle** (Şaua Puha). **Custura Sărății** (1hr. east of the Puha Saddle), the trail's most spectacular and difficult portion—a 2hr. path sometimes less than 30cm wide, with drops on either side—is only for experienced hikers. Stay the night at 1546m **Cabana Negolu ❶**, a 2hr. descent down the blue cross trail. Descend the blue triangle trail (1½hr.) and walk (4hr.), or catch a bus to **Porumbaco de Jos,** where trains return to Sibiu.

The most prized hike for serious hikers is across the entire Făgăraş ridge, which takes roughly seven days—10 for the less experienced—with a guide, going from west to east. The weather can be cold year-round. Bring a sleeping bag, head lamp, warm clothing, hiking boots, and plenty of iodine tablets to purify water. You can buy food at the *cabanas* along the way, but it's less expensive in the mountain villages. Call **SC Salişte-Bâlea SA** (☎21 17 03) in Sibiu to make reservations. In an emergency or for help planning a trip, contact the mountain-rescue organization **Salvamont,** Nicolae Balcescu 9 (☎21 64 77). Plan ahead, and try to consult with someone knowledgeable. The mountains' heavenly beauty make this a once-in-a-lifetime experience, well worth the preparation and time required.

ALBA IULIA   ☎(0)258

Alba Iulia (AHL-bah YOO-lee-ah; pop. 72,000) is a jewel set in the rolling hills of Transylvania, capped by an ancient citadel that many consider the spiritual center of Romania. Outside the city gates, on the magnificent Pţa. Tricolorului, the Great Assembly of Transylvania voted for union with Romania on December 1, 1918. Inside the walls, in a grand cathedral built for the occasion, King Ferdinand I was crowned the first king of all the Romanians. To this day, Alba Iulia retains a special place in the hearts of Romanians—and tourists from across Europe who come to see the town's citadel, museums, and cathedrals.

☐☑ TRANSPORTATION AND PRACTICAL INFORMATION. Most daily **trains** running in this area stop in Alba. Destinations include: **Bucharest** (6hr., 4 per day, L47); **Cluj-Napoca** (2hr., 5 per day, L15); **Sighişoara** (1¾hr., 4 per day, L19). **Buses** depart the station for numerous destinations; inquire within. To get from the train and bus stations to the citadel and the center, take city bus #3 or 4. Buy tickets on board (L0.80). **Taxis** line up outside the train station; ask to go to Str. Mihai Viteazul, which runs directly through the citadel (around L3). On foot, turn right from the train or bus station and walk north along Bd. Ferdinand I to the center; it's not very far. Turn left on Str. Mihai Viteazul to get to the citadel. You can't miss it: it's the giant hill with the brick walls and the gates.

In front of the Orthodox Cathedral, **Pţa. Tricolorului** leads to the intersection of Bd. Transilvania and Bd. 1 Decembrie, which are lined with shops that contain almost everything a traveler needs. **Librăria Mircea Eliade,** at the intersection of Bd. 1 Decembrie and Str. Closca, sells **maps.** (Open M-F 9am-8pm, Sa 9:30am-1pm.) **Internet** is at **VirusNet** on Bd. 1 Decembrie, near the intersection with Bd. Transilvania. There's a sign outside—open the unmarked door and go up the stairs. (☎401 023. M-Th L1.20 per hr., F-Su L1.60 per hr. Open daily 9am-1am.) The **pharmacy** is at Bd. Transilvania 11. (☎820 528. Open M-F 7:30am-midnight, Sa 8:30am-7pm, Su 8am-2pm.) **BCR,** Bd. Transilvania 25, has a 24hr. outdoor **currency exchange** machine and cashes AmEx **traveler's checks** for 1.5% commission. (☎834 522. Open M-F 8:30am-5pm, Sa 8:30am-12:30pm.) The **post office,** Bd. Transilvania 12, has **Western Union.** (Open M-F 7am-8pm, Sa 8am-1pm.) **Postal Code:** 510097.

☐☐ ACCOMMODATIONS AND FOOD. Pensiune Flamingo ❷, Str. Mihai Viteazul 6, is just to the right of citadel Gate #1. It has simple rooms, free-flowing hot water, and a small attached restaurant and bar. Enter through the bar if the front door is locked.

(☎816 354. Singles and doubles L60; with baths L100. Cash only.) Farther toward the center, Bd. Ferdinand becomes Str. Ardealului. **Hotel Transilvania** ❸, Pţa. Iuliu Manilu 22, is just off Str. Ardealului. Newly—albeit partially—renovated, Transilvania has an English-speaking concierge and rooms in better condition than Flamingo's, but it's more expensive and farther from the citadel. (☎812 052. Breakfast included. Old singles L97, doubles L130; renovated singles L142, doubles L190. Group discounts. MC/V.) Fresh **fruit and vegetable stands** cluster near the intersection of Bd. 1 Decembrie and Bd. Transilvania; look for signs that say "Legume Fructe." **Pizzeria Roberta** ❶, at Str. Tudor Vladimescu 4, next to the bank, serves the best pizza in town. The "Pizza Speciala" (L8.50) is a good choice for those who can't get enough meat. (☎823 592. Pizzas L3.50-9.50. Open daily 9am-11pm. Cash only.) A more Romanian choice, the **Restaurant Transilvania** ❶, is attached to the Hotel Transilvania at Pţa. Iuliu Manilu 22. The *sarmale* are luscious. (☎812 052. Entrees L5-11. Open daily 7am-11pm. MC/V.)

🔲 **SIGHTS AND ENTERTAINMENT.** To get to the star-shaped **citadel** *(cetatea)*, home to nearly all the town's sights, walk left from the train and bus stations along Str. Mihai Viteazul to Gate #1. (Open 24hr. Free.) Continue to Gate #2 to enter the inner citadel. Helpful orange-and-gray English signs, courtesy of the EU, mark the path. In the large square at the heart of the citadel, you'll see an imposing statue of **Mihai Viteazul** (Michael the Brave), who unified Romania in 1599-1601. Past the statue and to your right on Str. Mihai Viteazul 12-13, two grand old military buildings house museums: **Union Hall** (Sala Unirii) and the **National Union Museum** (Muzeul Naţional al Unirii). The National Union Museum traces the history of Romania from Dacian rule through Roman, Byzantine, medieval, and modern times, and showcases an excellent collection of Roman statuary. Vlad Ţepeş is included among the great men of Romanian history who crowd the murals on the walls of the Union Hall. It was here that Aurel Lazar ushered in Romanian unity in October 1918, by drafting the Transylvanian declaration of self-determination. (☎813 300. No English captions. Hall and museum open July-May Tu-Su 9am-4pm; June daily 9am-4pm. Hall and museum each L2.50; students L1.60. English brochure L1.20.) Beside the twin museums sit twin cathedrals, the **Catholic Cathedral** and the Orthodox **Reunification Cathedral.** Construction on the Catholic Cathedral began in the 13th century; its Gothic style reflects Western influences. Colonnades, a bell tower, and a sculpture-dotted courtyard skirt the Reunification Cathedral. Murals and plaques depicting the greatest hits of Romanian history adorn the interior. (Open daily 7am-11:30pm. Free.)

Kick back after a hard day of sightseeing at ▧ **Pub 13,** built into the citadel wall on Str. Mihai Viteazul between Gates #1 and #2. Look for the little bridge across the moat. An international crowd packs the dance floor, sidles up to the mile-long bar, and lounges on an outdoor terrace with an unparalleled view of the city. Beer from L1.90. Fish and chips (L12) are the stars on a winning menu of pub food. (☎839 555. Open daily noon-2am. Cash only.)

CLUJ-NAPOCA ☎(0)264

Cluj-Napoca (KLOOZH nah-POH-kah; pop. 400,000) is Transylvania's unofficial capital and undisputed student center. The beautiful but faded Old Town attests to both past glory and more recent hard times. Cluj-Napoca is a city on the move, filled with history and packed with life: twin cathedrals, graceful town squares, and some of Romania's best museums dominate the city by day, while at night the streets hum with students making their way to Cluj's numerous bars and clubs.

🚆 **TRANSPORTATION. International Airport Cluj-Napoca** (☎416 702) has flights to **Bucharest,** as well as regional flights to Austria, Germany, Hungary, and Italy. The best way to the airport from the center is by **taxi** (about L16.50). For train tickets,

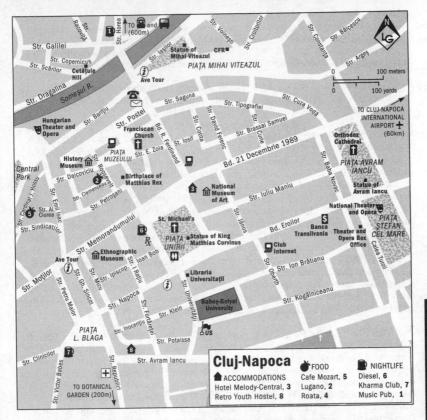

Cluj-Napoca

🍴FOOD
🍸NIGHTLIFE

🏠ACCOMMODATIONS
Hotel Melody-Central, **3**
Retro Youth Hostel, **8**

Cafe Mozart, **5**
Lugano, **2**
Roata, **4**

Diesel, **6**
Kharma Club, **7**
Music Pub, **1**

ROMANIA

CFR is at Pţa. Mihai Viteazul 11. (Domestic ☎423 001, international 534 009. Open M-F 9am-4pm.) **Trains** run to: **Bucharest** (8-13hr., 5 per day, L34.10) via **Braşov** (5-7hr., L27.90); **Oradea** (3hr., 5 per day, L18.30); **Sibiu** (4hr., 1 per day, L30); **Sighetu Marmatiei** (5-7hr., 1 per day, L23.50); **Timişoara** (6hr., 3 per day, L28); **Budapest, HUN** (6½-7hr.; 2 per day; L117, under 27 L93). **Local buses** and **trams** run 5am-10pm; buy tickets (L2.20 for 2 trips) at **RATUC** kiosks. (Open 5am-10pm.)

🛈🛈 ORIENTATION AND PRACTICAL INFORMATION. From the **train station**, walk right and cross the overpass to reach the intercity **bus station**, Str. Giordano Bruno 3. To get to the main square, **Pţa. Unirii**, from the train station, take city bus #9 (buses depart just across the street from the train station; buy a ticket at the RATUC kiosk), or walk down **Str. Horea**, which becomes **Bd. Regele Ferdinand**. Pţa. Unirii is on the right at its end. **Hotel Melody-Central**, Pţa. Unirii 29 (☎597 465), has a full-service **tourist bureau** that distributes the useful free pamphlet *Cluj-Napoca: What, Where, When.* The English-speaking staff are happy to book flights, arrange tours, and answer questions. **Banca Transilvania**, Bd. Eroilor 36, near Pţa. Avram Iancu, **exchanges currency**, cashes **traveler's checks** for no commission, and has **Western Union** services. (☎593 190. Open M-F 9am-6pm, Sa 9:30am-12:30pm.) MC/V **ATMs** line Bd. Ferdinand. **Farmacia Clematis** is at Pţa. Unirii 10. (☎191 363. Open daily 8am-10pm. MC/V.) In **medical emergencies**, dial ☎961 for ambulance service.

A **hospital, Spitalul Universitar C.F.R.**, is at Str. Republicii 16, near Pţa. L. Blaga. **Club Internet**, Str. Oberth 3, is just off Bd. Erialor. (8am-midnight L1 per hr., midnight-8am L0.50 per hr. Open 24hr.) The main **post office** is at Bd. Ferdinand 33. (Open M-F 7am-8pm, Sa 8am-1pm.) A 2nd post office, at Str. Aurel Vlaicu 3, has **Poste Restante.** (☎431 121. Open Tu and Th 8am-1pm.) **Postal Code:** 400110.

╓╔╝ ACCOMMODATIONS AND FOOD. █Retro Youth Hostel ❶, Str. Potaissa 13, is the place to stay in Cluj: bright and fresh-scrubbed with a helpful, English-speaking staff. (☎450 452; www.retro.ro. Breakfast L10. Laundry L10. Free Internet. Dorms L40. MC/V.) Central **Hotel Melody-Central ❸**, Pţa. Unirii 29, has a grand old hotel feel and a helpful tourist bureau in the elegant lobby. (☎597 465. www.hcm.ro. Breakfast included. Free Internet. Singles €37; doubles €43. MC/V.)

Cluj loves its desserts—**pastry shops** are everywhere. **█Cafe Mozart ❶**, Str. Cardinal J. Hossu 17, is a meticulously accurate old-Vienna coffeehouse, recreated down to the last detail. Costumed waitresses serve heavenly desserts and coffees; background music is by, of course, Mozart. (☎191 997. Coffee L3.50-6.40. Desserts L6. Open daily 9am-11pm. Cash only.) **Roata ❶**, Str. Alexandru Ciurea 6a, cleverly hidden off Str. Emil Isac, serves traditional Romanian dishes like *sarmale* (stuffed cabbage) in a shaded garden. The lack of an English menu may be inconvenient, but the food is authentic and the atmosphere is peaceful. (☎192 022. Entrees L12.50-22. Open M and Su 1pm-midnight, Tu-Sa noon-midnight. MC/V.) **Lugano ❷**, Str. Clemenceau 2, at the corner with Str. Roosevelt, boasts a wide variety of tasty Italian food, with a large drinks menu to match. Sit outside under the stars to sip wine, eat spaghetti, and avoid the grating elevator music inside. (☎594 593. Entrees L16-34. Restaurant open daily 11am-1am; bar 9pm-1am. MC/V.)

◙ SIGHTS. Begin at **Piaţa Unirii**, dominated by the Gothic **St. Michael's Church** (Biserica Sf. Mihail). The 80m steeple of this Catholic church sits atop some of the country's largest and most exquisite stained-glass windows. The church shares the square with an awesome yet controversial **statue** of Hungarian King Matthias Corvinus, pointedly surrounded by six large Romanian flags. To the left when facing the statue, **Bánffy Palace**, Pţa. Unirii 30, houses the **National Museum of Art** (Muzeul National de Arta Cluj), which specializes in Romanian paintings old and new. Don't miss the work of painter **Nicolae Grigorescu**, famous for his depictions of peasant life. (☎596 953. Open W-Su noon-7pm. L2, students L1.) Stroll down Bd. 21 Decembrie 1989 to Pţa. Avram Iancu, flanked on one side by the **Orthodox Cathedral** and on the other by the **National Theater and Opera.** Between the two looms a giant statue of **Avram Iancu**, revered for defending Romania from the Turks. The dazzling Cathedral is covered inside with otherworldly frescoes.

From Pţa. Avram Iancu, head back down to Bd. Regele Ferdinand, take a right, and then turn left onto Str. E. Zola to reach Pţa. Muzeului. There, the **History Museum** (Muzeul de Istorie), Str. Constantin Daicoviciu 2, traces Transylvanian history from the Bronze Age to the present, albeit without the benefit of English captions. Displays of medieval Transylvanian suits of armor and an ornately carved pulpit are highlights. (☎195 677. Open Tu-Su 10am-4pm. L2.04, students L1.02.) For a dazzling view of the city, head to **Cetăţuie Hill.** Walk up Bd. Regele Ferdinand, cross the bridge, turn left onto Str. Drăgălina, and climb the stairs on your right. Just across the river, the **Central Park** (Parcul Barnutiv) is a good place to picnic. To get there, walk up Bd. Regele Ferdinand from Pţa. Unirii and take a left on Str. Bariţiu along the riverbank. Bear right when Str. Bariţiu intersects Str. Emil Isac. The **Botanical Garden** (Grădina Botanică), Str. Republicii 42, counts a Japanese garden and exotic-plants greenhouse among its fragrant exhibits. (Open daily 9am-7pm; lily pad exhibit closes 6pm. L4. Map L1.)

◨▨ ENTERTAINMENT AND NIGHTLIFE. The **National Theater and Opera** (Teatrul Naţional şi Opera Română), in Pţa. Ştefan cel Mare, imitates the architecture of the Garnier Opera House of Paris. The box office is across the street. (☎ 595 363. Opera L10, students L3; theater L15/2.50. Box office open Tu-Su 11am-5pm. Theater and opera closed July-Sept. 15.)

For the latest on Cluj's nightlife, pick up the free *Şapte Seri* from hotels. **Music Pub,** Str. Horea 5, in an old wine cellar near the river, would be a good place to plot a revolution. Scuffed furniture and pounding music set the scene for punk-rockish students to shoot pool and drink cheap beer. (☎ 432 517. Live rock F-Sa 9 or 10pm. Open daily 4pm-3am. Cash only.) Clubbers might prefer **Diesel,** Pţa. Unirii 17, which has hosted some of Romania's most popular bands. Don't miss the cavernous rooms and nooks downstairs (☎ 439 043. Open daily 9pm-3am.) **Kharma Club,** Pţa. Lucian Blaga 1-3, is the place to be young and Romanian. The slick multi-level club spins intense house on weekends and offers a more relaxed scene during the week. (Beer L2. Open daily 9pm-4am. Cash only.)

BANAT

Romania's westernmost province, Banat was heavily influenced by its Austrian and Hungarian rulers. Lying squarely on the plains beyond the Carpathian mountains, it weathers hot, dry summers that contrast with the cooler temperatures of the surrounding mountains. Today, its population is more ethnically diverse than that of the rest of Romania, and its chicken *paprikash* is 2nd to none.

TIMIŞOARA   ☎(0)256

In 1989, 105 years after becoming the first European city with electric street lamps, Timişoara (tee-mee-SHWAH-rah; pop. 334,000) ignited the revolution that left Romanian communism in cinders. Romania's westernmost city, both geographically and politically, the city once dubbed Little Vienna is an elegant place of grand old boulevards, magnificent town squares, and peaceful riverside cafes.

◧▨ TRANSPORTATION AND PRACTICAL INFORMATION. To reach Timişoara by train, get off at **Timişoara Nord.** Buy tickets at CFR, Str. Măchieşor 3, just off Pţa. Victoriei. (☎ 22 05 34. Open M-F 8am-6pm.) **Trains** run to: **Alba Iulia** (4½hr., 2 per day, L22.50); **Braşov** (9hr., 1 per day, L31); **Bucharest** (8hr., 5 per day, L48.50); **Cluj-Napoca** (7hr., 4 per day, L26.50); **Oradea** (3½hr., 3 per day, L18); **Sibiu** (7hr., 1 per day, L25.50); **Budapest, HUN** (5hr.; 2 per day, L106; under 26, L84). The intercity **bus station** is across the river from the center, at Str. Vladimirescu and Str. Iancu Văcărescu. **Buses** depart regularly to numerous destinations.

The train station is less than 2km west of the city center. From the station, turn left down Bd. Regele Ferdinand. Alternatively, take city bus #11 or 14, heading to the center of town (L1.20; buy tickets at RATT kiosks). Get off when you see Pţa. Victoriei, the main square, with its multicolored cathedral. The old center is compact and circular, originally built within fortifications, which are now mostly gone.

You'll find nearly everything you need in the main square, Pţa. Victoriei. **Banc Post,** Bd. Mihai Eminescu, just off Pţa. Victoriei, has **Western Union** services, **exchanges currency,** and cashes **traveler's checks.** (Open M-F 8:30am-6pm, Sa 8am-noon.) **Librăria Mihai Eminescu,** Str. Macesilor 2, in Pţa. Victoriei, sells **maps.** (L1.20. Open M-F 9am-8pm, Sa 10am-1:30pm.) **Sensiblu pharmacy** is near Bd. Eminescu at Pţa. Victoriei 7. (☎ 201 217. Open daily 8am-10pm.) **Vlad Pharmacy** (☎ 201 889), Str. Lazar 8, near the hospital, is open 24hr. Seek **medical assistance** at **Spitalul Clinic Municipal,** Str. G. Dima 5 (☎ 433 612). In an emergency, dial ☎ 961 for an **ambulance** and 955 for **police.** The **telephone office** is at Str. Mihai Eminescu 2, past Banc Post. (Open M-F 10am-6pm, Sa 10am-2pm.) For **Internet,** try **Java Coffee House,** Str. Augustin Pacha 4, just below Pţa. Unirii, which doubles as a stylish cafe. (L3.30 per hr. Open 24hr.) The **post office,** Str. Craiului 1, is off Bd. Republicii and Pţa. Victoriei. (Open M-F 8am-7pm.) **Postal Code:** 300000.

ACCOMMODATIONS AND FOOD. Convenient **Hotel Nord ②,** Str. Gen. Ion Drăgălina 47, is one of the best values in town, with low-priced modern rooms that boast TVs, private baths, and fridges. It's the bright yellow-and-pink building across the street from the train station. (☎497 504. Breakfast included. Singles €18; doubles €28.) Centrally located **Hotel Cina Banatul ③,** Bd. Republicii 7, pampers guests with thick mattresses and plush carpets. All rooms have TVs, fridges, and private baths. (☎491 903. Breakfast included. Singles L100; doubles L140. Cash only.) The enormous **open-air market** on Pţa Timişoara 700, along Str. C. Brediceanu, hawks meat, cheese, fruit, vegetables, pots, pans, flowers, and almost everything else that your heart does or does not desire. (Open daily dawn-dusk.) Restaurants with outdoor seating line **Piaţa. Victoriei.** A standout is **Restaurant Lloyd ③,** on Pţa. Victoriei 2, overlooking the square. The daring can select frogs' legs or grilled shark from an English menu in the sumptuous paneled-and-mirrored interior. The drink menu is long and the view from the terrace is prime. (☎294 949. Entrees L11-80. Open 24 hr. AmEx/

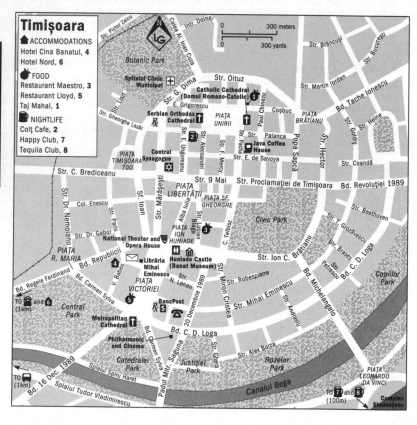

MC/V.) For the best Indian and Pakistani food this side of Bucharest, head to **Taj Mahal ❷**, Str. G. Coşbuc 1, at the corner of Pţa. Unirii. The tandoori specials (L17.50) are cheap and excellent. (☎437 845. Entrees L10-18. Open M-F noon-midnight, Sa-Su noon-8pm. Cash only.) **Restaurant Maestro ❸**, Str. Bolyai János 3, off Str. Lucian Blaga, boasts an ambitious menu of American, French, German, Hungarian, Italian, and Romanian dishes. Potentially disastrous as this may sound, the results are tasty. The terrace is elegant and the vaulted basement is a respite from the heat. (☎293 861. Entrees L10-65. Open daily 9am-late. Reservations recommended. Cash only.)

🎦 🎭 **SIGHTS AND ENTERTAINMENT.** Beautiful **Piaţa Victoriei** is flanked by the **National Theater and Opera** (Teatrul Naţional şi Opera Română) and the ▓**Metropolitan Cathedral** (Catedrala Mitropolitană). A fountain, flower garden, and statue of Romulus and Remus grace its regal center. Near the church, a modern sculpture commemorates the victims of the 1989 Revolution. The cathedral itself is a spectacular blend of Byzantine and Moldavian styles, capped by 13 green-and-gold spires. This Orthodox church, the largest in Romania, contains sculpted chandeliers, an awe-inspiring pure gold iconostasis, and the bones of St. Joseph of Partos, the patron saint of Banat. Go to nightly vespers for the full experience. Downstairs, the museum displays treasures like an illuminated sheepskin Bible. (Open daily 6:30am-8pm. Liturgy M-F 7:30am, Su 7 and 10am; vespers M-F and Su 6pm. Museum open W-Su 10am-3pm. L0.50, students L0.10.) The **Park of Roses** (Parcul Rozelor), along the riverbank, holds frequent free concerts. The unbelievably cheap shows at the **National Theater and Opera** are enhanced by the theater's stunning interior. (☎201 117. Box office open daily Sept. to mid-June 10am-1pm and 5-7pm. Theater L10 opera L5.)

 HIDDEN TREASURE. The Metropolitan Cathedral of Timişoara is a masterpiece of Eastern Orthodox architecture. Some of the real treasures, however, are cleverly hidden away in the basement. Open a small door on the right side of the front of the church—really, you're allowed in—then turn right and open an even smaller door. Go down the staircase to find a large collection of priceless artifacts, including the first Bible printed in Romanian and a golden Madonna and Child icon given to a Romanian princess by the Russian tsar. It's unbelievably cheap: 50 bani for adults, and 10 bani for students. Ask one of the priests to show you around, but don't ask what the names of the icons are. It's sacrilege to write them down, or even to speak them!

In the square to the right of Pţa. Victoriei, as you face the opera, the old **Huniade Castle** houses the **Banat Museum** (Muzeul Banatului), which traces Timişoara's history from ancient times through WWII. Check out the **sculpture garden.** (Open Tu-Su 10am-4:30pm. Two floors; L2 per floor, students L1.) The middle floor of the museum features ancient Roman and medieval Romanian curiosities, and the top floor is devoted to natural history, housing dinosaur fossils and a butterfly collection. The original antique electric **lamp posts** outside are the first in Europe. North of Victoriei, the increasingly gentrified Old Town stretches to **Piaţa Unirii**, where a fountain spouts water said to remedy stomach ailments. West of the square sits the **Serbian Orthodox Church;** the **Catholic Cathedral,** built in a *fin-de-siecle* revival style, presides over the eastern flank. The **Botanical Park,** northwest of Pţa. Unirii and near the hospital, is a good place to picnic. The elusive single entrance is on Str. G. Dima. (Open daily dawn-10pm. Free.)

At night, the place to be is the student district, **Complex Studenţesc.** From the main square, head down Bd. I.C. Brătianu, make a right on Bd. Michelangelo and cross the bridge. At Pţa. Leonardo da Vinci, turn onto Aleea F.C. Ripensia.

Veer left onto the busy Aleea Studenţilor, lined with fast-food joints, bars, and clubs. **Tequila Club,** A. Studenţilor 1, keeps the kids entertained with a video game room, poker tables, pool tables, dartboards, foosball, a bowling alley, and, of course, a bar. (☎292 618. Pool L15 per hr. Bowling L37 per hr. Beer L2.90. Open M-F 10am-4am, Sa-Su noon-4am. Cash only.) Next door, smoky **Happy Club,** A. Studenţilor 4, earns its name with a packed terrace and intense drinking and dancing. (☎295 299. Open 24hr. Cash only.) For those who don't want to trek to the student district, a hotspot in the center is slick **Colţ Cafe,** Str. Ungureanu 10, near Pţa. Unirii. From the plaza, follow Str. Lazar to the corner of Ungureanu. (☎229 385. Beer and shots from L4. Spiked coffee drinks from L4. Sandwiches L5. Open 24hr.)

MARAMUREŞ

Entering Maramureş (mah-rah-MOO-resh) is like stepping into a time capsule: life here proceeds the same as it did 50 or 100 years ago. The population is famous for its loyalty to traditional dress, especially during feasts and holidays, and takes pride in its ancient Dacian roots. Few visitors venture to the poorly connected region, but those who do are richly rewarded.

SIGHETU MARMAŢIEI ☎(0)262

Just across the Tisa River from Ukraine, well-preserved Sighetu Marmaţiei (pop. 46,000) is Maramureş's cultural center. Timeless beauty and tranquil isolation, as well as its status as Elie Wiesel's birthplace, make a trip to "Sighet" a must.

⊡⊠ TRANSPORTATION AND PRACTICAL INFORMATION: CFR is at Pţa. Libertăţii 25. (☎312 666. Open M-F 7am-5pm.) **Trains** run to: **Bucharest** (15hr., 1 per day, L45.20); **Cluj-Napoca** (6½hr., 2 per day, L23.50); **Sighişoara** (10hr., 1 per day, L51.50); **Timişoara** (13hr., 1 per day, L45.20). The **bus station** (☎311 512; ticket office open M-F 7am-7pm, Sa-Su 8am-2pm) is next to the train station; destinations include **Sapânţa** (40min., 4 per day, L4), **Oradea** (5hr., 1 per day, L28), and **Cluj-Napoca** (6hr., 4 per day, L20). **Minibuses** leave for **Budapest** from in front of the Hotel Tisa; inquire at the hotel desk and reserve in advance (8hr., daily 8pm, L75).

Head straight out of the train station and bear right down **Str. Iuliu Maniu.** At the T-intersection (about 1km), go left on **Str. 22 Decembrie 1989** to reach **Piaţa Libertăţii,** the main square. For info, especially about local village guesthouses, try the helpful, English-speaking staff at the tourist agency **⧓MTMM,** Piaţa Libertăţii 21, opposite Hotel Tisa in the main square. (☎31 25 52. Open M-F 10am-6pm.) **BCR,** Str. Iuliu Maniu 32, cashes AmEx **traveler's checks** at 0.5% commission (US$5 min.) and **exchanges currency;** an **ATM** is outside. Other banks are in the main square. (☎311 404. Open M-F 8:30am-5:30pm, Sa 8:30am-12:30pm.) **Farmacia Minerva** is at Pţa. Libertăţii 23. (☎31 19 77. Open M-F 8am-8pm, Sa 8am-3pm, Su 9am-1pm.) **Cafe Internet** is next to the Memorial Museum on Str. Corneliu Ceposu 5, off Str. Bogdan Vodă. (☎31 22 21. L1.50 per hr. Open daily 7am-4:30pm.) The **post office** is at Str. Bogdan Vodă 2, just off the main square, and has **Western Union** services and **Poste Restante.** (Open M-F 7am-8pm, Sa 8am-noon.) **Postal Code:** 435500.

⊓⊡ ACCOMMODATIONS AND FOOD. The best value is to stay in a **private villa** (€8-12), which you can rent from waiting proprietors at the train station. The charm of Maramureş is in its countryside; to properly take it in, ask the staff at **MTMM** (see above) to book a room in a village guesthouse (L25-50, no commission fee). **Hotel Tisa ❷,** Pţa. Libertăţii 21, was the grandest place in town in the good old days, but today is showing its age. Still, mid-sized rooms have comfortable (albeit small) beds, private baths, and high ceilings; some have balconies overlooking the main square. (☎311

610. Breakfast included. Singles L62; doubles L84. Cash only.) **Motel Buţi ❷**, on Str. Simion Bărnutiu 6 along Str. Corneliu Coposu, past the Memorial Museum, has midsized, newly furnished, clean rooms with private baths, cable TV, and fridges. (☎311 035. Breakfast included. Singles L82.50; doubles L95. Cash only.) The popular **Perla Sigheteana ❸**, Str. Avram Iancu 65a, offers comfortable doubles with TVs, private baths, and great views in a new building at the edge of town, on the way to Săpânţa. (☎31 06 13. Breakfast included. Call ahead. Doubles L150. MC/V.) The **open-air market**, one block up from the main square (turn off at the Farmacia Minerva) sells fresh fruits and vegetables. (Open daily dawn-dusk.) Affordable cafes and pizzerias surround the main square. The nicest place in town is ▨**Casa Iurca ❷**, on Str. Dragoş Vodă next to the Elie Wiesel house, where waiters in traditional dress serve food from an excellent Maramureşan menu. Try the roast ribs with sausages and horseradish for L19. (☎318 882. English menu. Entrees L6.50-21. Open daily 7:30am-10pm. MC/V.) For tasty Romanian food and a beautiful view, try **Restaurant Perla Sigheteană ❷**, inside the eponymous hotel. (☎31 06 13. Entrees L5-15. Open daily 7am-midnight.)

◙ **SIGHTS.** Sighet's ▨**Memorial Museum** (Muzeul Memorialui), Str. Copusu 4, south of the main square, is unique, sobering, and arguably the best museum in Romania. In the period after WWII, the building was the top-secret political prison of the Communist regime. The cells once imprisoned former leaders, famous intellectuals, and high-ranking Catholic clergy, and now contain different exhibits, from a re-creation of the prison's torture chamber to pictures, sculptures, and paintings of Nicolae Ceauşescu. (☎31 68 48. English captions. Open Apr.-Oct. daily 9:30am-6:30pm; Nov.-Mar. Tu-Su 9:30am-4:30pm. L4, students L2; includes tour in English.) **Casa Elie Wiesel**, the light-blue house on Str. Drogoş Vodă, one block up from Str. Traian, on the corner of Str. Tudor Vladimirescu, is the childhood residence of the 1986 Nobel Peace Prize winner, best known for his literary work *Night*. Wiesel, a Transylvanian Jew, spent WWII in concentration camps. The museum contains a Star of David-shaped monument in the courtyard, samples of Wiesel's writings, displays about the fate of the region's Jews, and a few rooms restored to their pre-WWII appearance. (Some English captions. Open Tu-Su 10am-6pm. L3, students L1.50.) The **Maramureş Museum** has two branches: an **ethnographic wing** (Muzeul Maramureşan), Str. Bogdan Voda 1, opposite the post office, notable for its collection of the fantastic, horned devil costumes used in the town Christmas drama (Dec. 25-26); and an **open-air village museum** (Muzeul Satului), 6km from the town center at the end of Bogdan Voda, filled with traditional Maramureşan buildings. Follow the signs from Str. Bogdan Voda just before the little bridge, or take a taxi (L7). Displays put the region in historical context. (English captions. Ethnographic wing and village open Tu-Su 10am-6pm. Each L3, students L1.50.)

SAPÂNTA

For an exuberant outlook on death, head to Sapânta, home of the world-famous ▨**Merry Cemetery** (Cimitirul Vesel). The cemetery, near the local church, is a sea of colorfully painted wooden grave markers that depict scenes from the life of the deceased and are engraved with witty poems—often in first person—using archaisms and slang. In 1935, local artisan Stan Ion Patras, drawing on rich traditions of folk art and woodworking, began carving these unique headstones; the tradition continues today. The crosses and markers have attracted worldwide attention and have been displayed in many foreign galleries. Despite its fame, this tiny village maintains a traditional lifestyle; its inhabitants sport straw hats, traditional dress, and head scarves. Sapânta is best visited as a **daytrip** from Sighet. (No English captions. Cemetery open daily dawn-dusk. L4.)

Buses run from **Sighet** train station (40min., 4 per day, L3-4). Many buses going elsewhere will stop in Sapânta; ask the driver. **Hitchhiking** from Str. Avram Iancu at the western edge of Sighet is very common and recommended by the MTMM travel agency (one-way L5), as a taxi costs significantly more (round-trip L40) and buses are scarce. *Let's Go* does not recommend hitchhiking. In Sapânta, take a left off the road from Sighet onto the only other paved road, and go up 200 yd.

IZA VALLEY

Those seeking a glimpse of Romanian country life should head to the **Iza Valley.** Here, horse carts outnumber automobiles, traditional dress is the norm, and ornately carved wooden gateposts and churches abound. Visitors soak up the mountain-town atmosphere along with the comfortable hospitality and authentic meals. The valley is defined by a series of small villages. At its mouth, 7km from Sighet, is **Vadu Iza,** the commercial hub. **Ieud,** another village, is home to the 1716 **Church of the Valley** (Biscerica de Lemn), on the main street, which is marked by its notably tall wooden steeple; it is a perfect example of wooden church architecture and is sometimes called the "cathedral in wood." The 1364 **Church on the Hill,** east along the dirt road that juts off north of the village council building, is the oldest of its kind. Cross the small river and ascend the hill; follow signs for the small museum (L1) near the church. The churches are often locked; ask around, and locals will find a key. At the east end of Maramureş, the old mining center of **Borsa** is a gateway to the Rodna mountains; a small ski area lies to the east. In the nearby Viseu river valley, the town of **Viseu de Sus** arranges rides daily at 8:30am on a restored cog railway. For info, inquire in Sighet. Food and lodgings are available at the many B&Bs in the villages for €10-20 per person. Book rooms through the **MTMM tourist agency** in Sighet (see p. 548) or look for signs and knock on doors.

Transportation within the Iza Valley is variable. **Buses,** which stop in front of the train station, run from **Sighet** to various villages within the valley. (30min.-2hr., in summer 6-8 per day, L4.) MTMM sells **maps** of the area for L7. Hitchhikers commonly stand in three places, depending on their destination: for the Vadu Iza and Baia Mare, in front of the Artima supermarket in Sighet, on Str. Bogdan Voda, a few blocks from the central square; for Sapânta, in front of Sighet's only hospital; for Borsa, on Str. Dragos Voda, at the crossroads with Str. Traian near a church. Buses also stop at each of these locations. Although the MTMM agency recommends hitchhiking as affordable and the best way to get around, *Let's Go* does not recommend hitchhiking. The best information on all towns described here can be obtained in Sighet.

MOLDAVIA (MOLDOVA)

Eastern Romania once included the entire Moldovan territory, but the Bessarabian section is now the independent Republic of Moldova. Romanian Moldavia, which extends from the Carpathians to the Prut River, is stark but relatively developed. Travelers from around the world come to see the many masterfully painted monasteries in the hills of Bucovina, the legacy of national hero Ştefan cel Mare.

IAŞI   ☎(0)232

Bustling Iaşi (YAHSH; pop. 340,000) is a city of fast-food joints and dance clubs. Yet the Moldavian capital is the most peaceful of Romania's big cities. Neoclassical homes and palaces that hosted late-19th-century intellectuals are remarkably well preserved and will delight any architecture connoisseur.

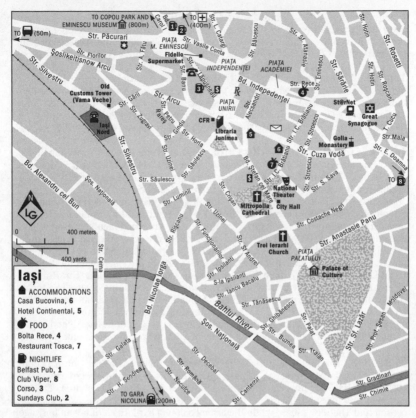

Iaşi

🏠 ACCOMMODATIONS
Casa Bucovina, **6**
Hotel Continental, **5**

🍴 FOOD
Bolta Rece, **4**
Restaurant Tosca, **7**

🎵 NIGHTLIFE
Belfast Pub, **1**
Club Viper, **8**
Corso, **3**
Sundays Club, **2**

ROMANIA

TRANSPORTATION. Trains run from the station, **Iaşi Nord**, on Str. Silvestru, to: **Braşov** (6hr., 1 per day, L34.10) via **Bucharest** (7½hr., 4 per day, L34.10); **Cluj-Napoca** (9hr., 4 per day, L34.10); **Constanţa** (8hr., 1 per day, L34.10); **Sighetu Marmaţiei** (13hr., 4 per day, L34.10) via **Salva; Suceava** (2hr., 4 per day, L17.20); **Timişoara** (17hr., 4 per day, L49.20). **CFR** is at Pţa. Unirii 9-11. (☎242 620. Open M-F 8am-8pm.) The **bus station**, Str. Moara de Foc 15 (☎214 720), behind the health club, sends buses to **Braşov** (8hr., 2 per day, L34) and **Suceava** (2hr., 12 per day, L17).

ORIENTATION AND PRACTICAL INFORMATION. Standing in the parking lot with the **train station** behind you, cross the street and walk up **Str. Gării** to the right of the **Vama Veche** (Old Customs Tower). Follow Str. Gării to the next major intersection, where the tram tracks curve right. These tracks follow **Str. Arcu**, which intersects with the main square, **Piaţa Unirii**, before changing its name to **Str. Cuza Vodă**. Here, **Str. Ştefan cel Mare** branches to the right. The center is also accessible by trams #3, 6, and 7 (L1), opposite the Vama Veche. **Banca Comercială Română**, Str. Ştefan cel Mare 8a, cashes AmEx **traveler's checks** for 1.5% commission. (☎21 17 38. Open M-F 8:30am-5:30pm, Sa 8am-12:30pm.) An **ATM** is outside; others can be found in and near the main square. **Luggage storage** is available at the train station. (L2.70 per small bag, L5.40 per large bag.) **Libraria Junimea**, Pţa. Unirii

4, sells **maps.** (☎41 27 12. Maps L9.80. Open M-F 8am-8pm, Sa 8am-4pm.) The **pharmacy, Sf. Paraschiva** (☎22 05 49), at the top of Pţa. Unirii near Bd. Independentei, has a 24hr. window. The urgent-care **hospital, "Spitalul Clinic de Urgentia,"** is near the university at Gen. Berthelot 6. (☎40 98 15. Open 24hr.) The **telephone** office, Str. Lăpuşneanu 14, is off the main square. (☎20 44 47. Open M-F 10am-6pm, Sa 10am-2pm.) For high-speed **Internet,** try **St@r Net,** Str. Sarariei 14. (☎27 61 71. L2.50 per hr. Open 24hr.) The Neoclassical **post office,** Str. Cuza Vodă 10, has **Poste Restante** at window #10 and **Western Union** services. (☎21 22 22. Open M-F 8am-7pm, Sa 8am-1pm.) To pick up packages from overseas, head to **Poste 13,** behind the telephone office on Str. Banu. (Open M-F 10am -5pm.) **Postal Code:** 700750.

⌐⌐ ACCOMMODATIONS AND FOOD. Casa Bucovina ❶, Str. Cuza Vodă 30-32, has clean, adequate rooms with TVs and sinks. (☎31 44 93. Singles L50; doubles with bath L80.) **Hotel Continental ❷,** Str. Cuza Vodă 4, has a convenient location and pleasant, recently renovated rooms with TVs, phones, and private baths. (☎21 18 46. Breakfast included. Singles L85; doubles L120.) Established in 1786, the rustic yet elegant **◼Bolta Rece ❶,** Str. Rece 10, has traditional food and music. The *tochitura moldoveanască* is typically Moldavian, with fried meats, sausages, and cornmeal pudding (L5.90). From Pţa. Unirii, take Str. Cuza Vodă past Hotel Continental; go left on Str. Brătianu. Go right at Bd. Independenţei and immediately left on Str. M. Eminescu, then left on Str. Rece. (☎21 22 55. No English menu. Entrees L3.60-L11.90. Open daily 10am-10pm. Cash only.) **Restaurant Tosca ❶,** Str. Brătianu 30, near the theater, has an array of tasty pizzas and international dishes in a theatrically upscale setting. (☎21 66 64. English menu. Pizzas L5.90-L9.30. Pasta L5.60-L9.30. Entrees L8.10-L15.60. Open daily noon-midnight. Cash only.) A grocery store, **Fidelio Supermarket,** is at Bd. Independenţei D1-D2, near the north end of Str. Lăpuşneanu 14, off the main square. (Open M-Sa 7am-9pm, Su 8am-6pm. MC/V.)

◉ SIGHTS. The massive, neo-Gothic **◼Palace of Culture** (Palatul Culturii) contains historical, technological, ethnographic, and art museums. It is marked by a **clock tower,** which plays the anthem of the 1859 founding of Romania. The **art museum** contains splendid 19th-century paintings by such masters as Nicolae Grigorescu and Theodor Aman, while the **history museum** explores Moldavian heritage from prehistory through WWI. The **technology museum** has an exhibit on music boxes and player pianos, and the **ethnography museum** displays artifacts of peasant life. (Open Tu-Su 10am-5pm. Each museum L1.50, students L1. Ticket for all L5/3.) The exterior of the gorgeous **Trei Ierarhi church,** on the right side of Str. Ştefan cel Mare as you walk toward the Palace of Culture, is covered in intricate carvings—the Moldavian, Romanian, and Turkish symbols date to 1637. Though invading Tatars melted the gold exterior in 1650, the interior retains its original sheen. (Open daily 9am-noon and 3-5:30pm. L1.) To get to **Copou Park,** Bd. Carol I, ride tram #1 or 13 from Pţa. Unirii or take a stroll from Pţa. Eminescu. Inside the beautifully tended park is the famous **Mihai Eminescu Linden,** the tree that shaded Romania's great poet as he worked. The small, adjacent **Eminescu Museum,** one of a dozen museums in Iaşi devoted to literary figures, exhibits dozens of portraits of the poet and some of his documents. (☎41 05 80. Open Tu-Su 10am-5pm. L1.)

◼ NIGHTLIFE. If you've never been to a bar in a flower garden beside a church, well, there's a first time for everything. **Corso,** Str. Lăpuşneanu 11, near the main square, distinguished by its unique location, is a great place to cool off after a hot day. (☎27 61 43. Beer from L3. Great milkshakes L5. Open 10am-1pm daily.) More traditional hangouts surround the **Casa de Cultura a Studenţilor,** near the university on Pţa. Eminescu, on the way to Copou park. The left side contains the **Belfast Pub,**

with a small, rustic interior and large, packed outdoor terrace. (☎25 20 48. Beer from L5. Open 24 hr.) To the right, **Sundays Club** advertises itself as the "no drugs" club "for normal people," which apparently means house, retro, and cheap beer but plenty of cushy brown leather sofas. (☎57 43 46. Beer from L3.50. Open M-Th and Su 6pm-3am, F-Sa 6pm-5am.) For a different sort of night out, relaxed **Club Viper** has bowling, an arcade, pool and air-hockey tables, and foosball. Don't expect to dance to any techno, though; there's no music. It's in the basement of the **Iulius Mall**, on Bd. Tudor Vladimirescu 2; a short taxi ride (L5) from the center. (☎20 86 59. Beer from L1.20. Pool L1.15. Bowling L24 per hr. Open 24hr.)

BUCOVINA MONASTERIES

Hidden in rural Romania, Bucovina's painted monasteries are a source of national pride. Built 500 years ago by Ştefan cel Mare—rumor has it that he built one after every victory over the Turks—the exquisite structures meld Moldavian and Byzantine architecture. They served as isolated outposts against Turkish and Tatar marauders, acquiring massive walls and towers over the years. After repression under communism, the churches are again active.

SUCEAVA   ☎(0)230

The capital of Moldavia under Ştefan cel Mare, Suceava (soo-CHYAH-vah) is the biggest town in monastery country and a good base for exploration. But it has more than just proximity to offer the monastery-seeker: you'll find Ştefan's citadel, and intriguing museums and historic churches around every corner.

⊏ TRANSPORTATION. **Gara Suceava Nord** is the main station, and sends **trains** to: **Braşov** (8hr., 1 per day, L34.10); **Bucharest** (6hr., 5 per day, L34.10); **Cluj-Napoca** (6hr., 4 per day, L27.90); **Gura Humorului** (1hr., 10 per day, L7.30); **Iaşi** (2hr., 8 per day, L17.20); **Sighetu Marmaţiei** (14hr., 4 per day, L27.90) via **Salva**. Buy tickets at **CFR**, Str. N. Bălcescu 4. (☎21 43 35. Open M-F 7:30am-7pm.) The **bus station** (☎52 43 40), at the intersection of Str. N. Bălcescu and Str. V. Alecsandri, sends buses to: **Bucharest** (8hr., 4 per day, L32); **Cluj-Napoca** (7hr., 1 per day, L31); **Constanţa** (9hr., 2 per day, L40); **Gura Humorului** (1hr., 12 per day, L4.50); **Iaşi** (3hr., 8 per day, L17).

◼▉ ORIENTATION AND PRACTICAL INFORMATION. From the train station, take any of the **Maxi taxis** (L1) waiting outside to reach the center, **Piaţa 22 Decembrie**. As you walk up the square, to your right runs Str. Nicolae Bălcescu. **Str. Stefan cel Mare** crosses in front of the concrete theater on the square. **Bilco Agenţia de Turism**, Str. N. Bălcescu 2, organizes car tours to the monasteries. (☎52 24 60. €40-50 per car. Private guides available. Open M-F 9:30am-5:30pm, Sa 9:30am-3:30pm. MC/V.) **Raiffeisen Bank**, Str. N. Bălescu 2, cashes AmEx **traveler's checks** for 1.25% commission, offers **Western Union** services, **exchanges currency**, and has a **24hr. ATM**. (☎52 25 06. Open M-F 8:30am-6:30pm.) **Librăria Lidana**, on Str. Stefan cel Mare behind the theater in the main square, sells **maps**. (☎37 73 24. Maps L11.90. Open M-F 9am-6pm, Sa 9am-3pm.) **Luggage storage** is at the train station. (L3.50 per day. Open 24hr.) **Farmacia Centrală** is at Str. N. Bălcescu 2b. (☎21 72 85. Open daily 7am-9pm.) High-speed **Internet** is in the nameless tower in Pţa. 22 Decembrie, Bd. Ana Ipătescu 7. (☎52 30 44. L2 per hr. CD burning, printing, and scanning available. Open daily 9am-10pm.) To get to the **post office**, Str. Dimitrie Onciul 1, turn right off Str. N. Bălescu after passing the Banc Post building. **Poste Restante** is available. (☎52 19 69. Open M-F 8am-7pm, Sa 8am-1pm.) **Postal Code:** 720290.

⬛⬛ ACCOMMODATIONS AND FOOD. Despite its remote location, budget travelers flock to the new ⬛**Class Hostel ❶**, Str. Aurel Vlaicu 195, for spacious rooms, comfortable beds, friendly atmosphere, and excellent cooking. The staff arranges car tours of the monasteries. From the train station, turn right along Aurel Vlaicu; it's a 1km walk. (☎78 23 28. Free maps. Breakfast included. Dinner €4. Vegetarian food available. Laundry €2.50. Dorms €13. MC/V.) **Villa Alice ❷**, Str. Simion Florea Marian 1b, left off Str. Nicolae Bălcescu in front of Cinema Modern (follow the signs), offers beautiful rooms with cable TV and fridges in a quiet neighborhood. (☎28 78 98. Breakfast L1-2. Singles L70; doubles L80-95. MC/V.) **Pensiuna Giardino ❷**, on Str. D. Ghereu (follow the signs in front of Cinema Modern), offers mid-sized, newly furnished rooms with cable TV, private baths, and fridges. (☎53 17 78. Breakfast included. Check-out noon. Singles L97.50; doubles L122. MC/V.) The freshest food in town is at the **open-air market**, Pţa. Agroalimentara on Str. Petru Rareş, off the pedestrian end of Str. Ştefan cel Mare. (Open daily dawn-dusk.) ⬛**Pub Chagall ❷**, on the corner of Str. N. Bălescu and Str. Ştefan cel Mare, serves excellent Romanian and international food in an atmospheric dark-wood-and-brick cellar. (No English menu. Large drink menu. Beer L3. Mixed drinks from L8.50. Entrees L5.40-15.60. Open M-Sa 10am-midnight, Su 11am-midnight. Cash only.) **Latino ❷**, Curtea Domnească 9, left of the pedestrian side of Str. Ştefan cel Mare, serves Italian food in a stylishly lit, finely appointed interior and on an outdoor terrace. Vegetarians might try the "Gnocchi vegetariana" for L11.50. (☎52 36 27. Pasta and pizza L9.50-15.50. Entrees L12.50-29.50. Open daily 9am-11pm. MC/V.) Around the corner on Str. Vasile Alecsandri, **Markiz ❷** offers good Middle Eastern dishes, like the "kebap condimentat" for L15. (☎52 02 19. Entrees L13-25. Open daily 7am-11pm. Cash only.)

⬛⬛ SIGHTS AND ENTERTAINMENT. The mammoth **statue** of Ştefan cel Mare is visible from Pţa. 22 Decembrie, across Bd. Ana Ipătescu, next to the ancient **Citadel of the Throne** (Cetatea de Scaun). The citadel was built in 1388 by Petru Muşat I, who moved Moldavia's capital to Suceava; it was refortified by his great-great-grandson, Ştefan cel Mare, and withstood the 1476 siege by Mehmet II, conqueror of Constantinople. The citadel is only a 10min. walk through the park in the valley. Although it was partially destroyed by the Turks, the ruins are still a great place for exploring. (Open daily in summer 8am-8pm; in winter 10am-5pm. L3, students L1.50.) The adjacent **Bucovina Village Museum** (Muzeul Satului Bucovinean) displays 18th- through 20th-century houses, churches, and workshops from the region. (Open Tu-Su 9am-6pm. L1.20, students L0.50.) **Mânăstirea Sf. Ioan cel Nou** (Monastery of St. John the New), completed in 1522 by Ştefan's son Bogdan III, holds beneath its colorful tile roof and bright frescoes the body of St. John, martyred in 1330 for refusing to join the Zoroastrian faith. In late June, his silver casket is opened and the faithful can kiss his bones. To get there, walk past the McDonald's on Str. Ana Ipătescu and take the first right on Str. Ion Vodă Viteazu. (Open daily 7am-8pm. Free. English pamphlet L3.50.) On the same street, walk in the opposite direction past the McDonald's and bus shelter in the other direction; turn left on the pathway to Str. Curtea Domnească, where you'll find **Biserica St. Dumitru** (St. Demeter Church), likewise covered with brilliantly colorful frescoes, these dating from 1535 and featuring a particularly vicious Hellmouth on the portico. (Open 8am-7pm daily. English pamphlet L2.)

Cinema Modern is at Str. Dragoş Vodă 1, down Str. N. Bălescu. (Films M-F 3 per day; Sa-Su 4 per day. Last show 7:30pm. L3.50-4.50.) Smack in the center of the main square in the basement of the Communist-era theater, a.k.a., "House of Culture," **Disco For You** cranks out thumping music and serves up cheap drinks to a packed young crowd—sort of a people's club, although you can bet the Soviets didn't have this in mind. (Beer from L3. Cover F-Sa L3. Open daily 10pm-late. Cash only.) The hottest game in town is the **Shock Club,** a two-level carnival of smoke machines and flashing lights centered on an enormous, crowded dance floor, surrounded by balconies and bars that seem to be more for dancing on than for drinking. It's a hike from the center and hard to walk to, so take a taxi (L3-5); any driver will know where it is. (Beer from L5. Open 10pm-late daily. Cash only.)

GURA HUMORULUI   ☎(0)230

Within walking distance of Humor and Voroneţ and close to the other monasteries, the sleepy town of Gura Humorului (GOO-rah hoo-MOHR-oo-loo-ee) is an ideal base from which to explore monastery country.

The English-speaking proprietors of ▨**Pensiunea Casa Ella ❶**, Str. Cetăţii 7, off Bd. Bucovina, make travelers feel at home with traditional cooked breakfasts and great big beds with fluffy pillows, and the rooms boast cable TV and balconies. To get there, keep walking past the park; it's down a side street to the left. (☎23 29 61. Breakfast L8. Singles L40, doubles L60. Cash only.) A step up in luxury is **Villa Fabian ❷**, Str. Câmpului 30, opposite Str. Voroneţ from Dispecerat de Cazare. Rooms are spacious and have TVs, large beds, and Narnia-quality wardrobes. Tea is served in a shady garden. (☎15 37 24. Breakfast included. Singles L50; doubles L100. Cash only.) Cheap and popular with the locals, **Nadianca ❶** serves traditional dishes near the park. Try the *ciorba rădoteană* (chicken soup; L5.30). From Pţa. Republicii, head down Bd. Bucovina and go right at Str. Parcului. Go right on Str. Mihai Eminescu and left on Str. Primăverii. Take the first right; the restaurant is on the left. (Entrees L4.50-9.50. Open daily 7am-11pm. Cash only.) On Bd. Bucovina, past the park from the main square, **Restaurant Lions ❷** offers an international menu, including pizza, in a royal-themed setting. (Beer from L2. Pizza L7-10. Entrees L10-26. Open daily 9am-11:30pm. MC/V.) If you have need of earthly pleasures after a day of monasteries, **VIP Dance Club**, Str. Sf. Gavril 12, left off Str. Mânăstirea Humorului from the main square, is the only option. (Open M 5pm-midnight, Tu-Th 10am-midnight, F 10am-2am, Sa noon-4am, Su noon-2am.)

Trains run from the station, **Gura Humorului Oras,** on Bd. Castanilor, to: **Bucharest** (6hr., 2 per day, L45.20); **Cluj-Napoca** (5hr., 4 per day, L25.60); **Iaşi** (3hr., 4 per day, L20.80); **Sighetu Marmatiei** (12hr., 4 per day, L25.60) via **Salva; Succava** (1hr., 6 per day, L3.20-5.80); **Timişoara** (14hr., 3 per day, L45.20). To reach the center from the train station, go straight down the tree-lined street to the main road, **Str. Ştefan cel Mare,** and make a right. The road crosses a river and runs into **Piaţa Republicii,** the main square. Get **tourist info** at ▨**Dispecerat de Cazare,** where Str. Câmpului ends at Str. Voroneţ. It's about 1km from the train station; follow signs to Voroneţ monastery. Turn left on Str. Ştefan cel Mare and left on Str. Câmpului. A friendly couple arranges car tours of local sights: monasteries, a pottery workshop, and a nearby salt mine with a tennis court and two chapels. If it's closed, ask at Villa Fabian across the street. (☎/fax 23 38 63. Tours €30-35 per car per day.) There is a 24hr. **ATM** at **Raiffeisen Bank,** Pţa. Republicii 16, which also offers **Western Union** services and cashes AmEx/MC **traveler's checks** for 0.5% commission. (☎23 13 65. Open M-F 8:30am-6:30pm.) Buy monastery **maps** at **Librăria Alexandria,** Bd. Bucovina 5. (☎23 50 97. Open M-F 7am-7pm, Sa 8am-5pm, Su 9am-2pm. MC/V.) The **pharmacy, Farmacia Delia,** is at Bd. Bucovina 4. (☎23 15 55. Open M-F 8am-9pm, Sa 8am-8pm, Su 8am-2pm. V.) For **Internet** or photocopies, try **Internet Cafe,** Bd. Bucovina 27. (☎235 349. Open daily 9am-9pm. L2 per hr.) The **post office** is at Str. Ştefan cel Mare 1, just before the bridge. (Open M-F 8am-7pm, Sa 8am-noon.) **Postal Code:** 725300.

MONASTERIES AND CONVENTS

Many visit Bucovina just for the painted monasteries, whose bucolic setting makes them both charming and hard to reach. Voroneţ and Humor are easily accessible by public transportation; getting to Moldoviţa and Putna is harder; reaching the others is incredibly difficult. Hitchhiking is possible, but *Let's Go* does not recommend it. Car tours entail hiring a driver, who may or may not speak English, to shuttle you around for a day. A car tour is by far the easiest way to see the monasteries. Tours cost €40-60 per car; arrange them in Gura Humorului or Suceava. Monasteries don't give tours, but some sell booklets (L7). It is considered respectful to wear long pants or skirts and to avoid tight-fitting clothing.

⁜VORONEŢ. In 1488, it took Ştefan cel Mare precisely three months, three weeks, and three days to erect Voroneţ. But it was Petru Rareş, his illegitimate son, who, in 1524, added the frescoes that have earned it the title "Sistine Chapel of the East." The rich **Voroneţ Blue** pigment, which changes shades depending on the humidity, still baffles art historians. Some believe the paint's secret ingredient to be finely crushed powder from the gemstone lapis lazuli, but many locals insist that divine intervention is the key ingredient. The west wall depicts the **Last Judgment** with a vivid clarity of composition that makes Voroneţ's version a masterpiece. The figures are arranged in five tiers and crossed by a river of fire from Hell—the damned wear the faces of Turks and Tatars. Restorations of the frescoes began in 2003. *(The monastery is accessible by bus from Gura Humorului; 15min., 3 per day M-F Sept. 15-June 15, L1. On foot, take Str. Ştefan cel Mare away from the center of town; following the signs, head left on Cartierul Voroneţ; the monastery is a scenic 5km down the road. A one-way cab should be L5-6. Open daily 7am-8pm. L4, students 2.)*

HUMOR. Founded in 1530 by landowner Teodor Bubuiog during the reign of Petru Rareş, Humor was one of the first monasteries painted in the Byzantine style. The exterior walls are covered in frescoes of Jesse's Tree, the Last Judgment, and the Siege of Constantinople. The paintings are notable for their marvelous pink hue. The secret room *(tainiţa)* was the first of its kind—it was filled with the monastery's valuables and paved over whenever invaders threatened. The tower, built in 1641, provides a tricky climb but a wonderful view. *(About 5km from Gura Humorului, this monastery is a painless walk or cab ride, L5-6, away. Facing the Best Western hotel at the center of town, go left on Str. Mânbstirea Humorului and follow signs. Shared vans, L1, ply the route occasionally. Open daily 7am-8pm. L4, students L2.)*

MOLDOVIŢA. Moldoviţa's frescoes are among the best-preserved in Romania. Though it was destroyed shortly after Alexandru cel Bun (Alexander the Good) constructed it in 1402-1410, the monastery was rebuilt in 1532-1537. The monastery, which combines Gothic and Moldovan architectural elements, is known for the painting of the monumental **Siege of Constantinople** that decorates its southern wall; in it, heroic Christians resist the inevitable onslaught of the Turks who took the city in 1452. The parallels to the Turkish rulers of Romania were intended; such depictions had an important dual meaning. Inside, the golden iconostasis is particularly ornate, and frescoes display an unusual degree of perspective and detail. The doorway to the church is incorporated into the portrayal of the Last Judgment—visitors enter ambiguously, between heaven and hell. The museum houses the throne of Prince Petru and remnants from Alexandru's original church. The small doors at the entrance were designed to keep out mounted enemies. *(From Gura Humorului, take a train to Vama; 20min., 9 per day, L3.90. Then to Vatra Moldovitei; 45min., 3 per day, L2.40. If you want to return the same day, take the earliest train out of Gura Humorului at about 6:40am. Open daily 7am-8pm. L4, students L2.)*

SUCEVIŢA. Suceviţa, the newest of the monasteries at 407 years young, looks like a fortress from the outside. During attacks, the population took refuge inside Suceviţa's incredibly thick walls. Its south wall presents the genealogy of Jesus, Moses receiving the 10 Commandments, and a procession that includes ancient

Greek philosophers. Plato, supposedly the first scholar to ponder the meaning of death, carries a casket atop his head. Unique among the Bucovina monasteries, the wall also depicts a 30-step ladder to heaven, with each step representing the virtues one must attain to acquire a heavenly crown. Those who slipped off the ladder are shown tumbling into hell. While most of the monastery is painted emerald green, the west wall remains incomplete—it is said that the artist fell to his death from a scaffold, and his ghost prevents completion. A museum displays a tapestry containing 10,000 pearls woven by the daughter of the monastery's builder. *(Sucevița lies 32km north of Moldovița. Public transportation is unavailable, but many car tours run out of Gura Humorului and Suceava. Hitchhiking from Moldovița is common, but Let's Go does not recommend it. Open daily 7am-8pm. L4, students L2.)*

PUTNA. Ștefan cel Mare's first creation and final resting place, the immaculately white 1469 Putna Monastery was not completely rebuilt until 1982. Only one of the original towers has survived the ravages of fires, earthquakes, and attacks. No original frescoes are left, but Putna's high-arching, blank white walls remain touchingly austere. Dozens of rosebushes provide a touch of color. The church contains the marble-canopied **tomb** of Ștefan cel Mare, and is thus one of the most revered churches in Romania. The king left Putna's location up to God; climbing a nearby hill, he shot an arrow into the air. A slice of the oak that it struck is on display at the museum. Take your first right in the direction of town from the monastery to climb **Dealul Crucii** (Hill of the Cross), Ștefan's shooting point, for a fantastic view. Two hills are marked with crosses—Ștefan's is the smaller one. *(Trains run from Suceava directly to Putna, 75km to the northwest; 2½hr., 4 per day, L5. The monastery is 1km from the train station. Turn right as you exit the platform and then left at the 1st intersection. Monastery open daily 6am-8pm. Free. Museum open daily 9am-8pm. L4, students L2.)*

AGAPIA. All of Agapia's paintings are by Nicolae Grigorescu, the 19th-century Neoclassical master on the shortlist of Romania's greatest artists. After winning a nationwide contest, he spent 1858-61 producing icons, canvases, and a famous altar screen for the 14th-century church. Grigorescu is best known for his scenes of peasant life, and Agapia is one of his only forays into religious art. Today, Agapia houses an Orthodox high school for girls. *(Trains run from Suceava, with a connection in Pascani, to Târgu Neamt, 9km from the monastery; 1½hr., 4 per day, L5.50. Try to take a morning train out—otherwise, the ride back to Suceava will entail a long midnight wait at Pascani. From the station at Targu Neamt, walk the 1km down Str. Cuza Voda to the bus station, which has buses to the monastery; 20min., 2-3 per day, L1.60. Monastery L3, students L1.)*

BLACK SEA COAST (DOBROGEA)

Controlled at different times by Greeks, Romans, and Ottoman Turks, the land between the Danube and the Black Sea has endured a turbulent history that has made it Romania's most ethnically diverse region. The stunning coastline stretches south, while the interior valleys hold Romania's best vineyards. Summer crowds pack the area and make prices steep. If you tire of resort crowds, take refuge in the delta to the north, where the Danube meets the Black Sea (see sidebar, p. 559). To get to the Black Sea towns by train or bus, you will have to pass through Constanța, the largest town on the coast, which is a useful transport hub but has little else to recommend it—it also lacks budget accommodations. The coast south of Constanța is lined with sandy beaches and 70s-style tourist resorts. **Mamaia** is closest to Constanța and remains perpetually overcrowded. **Costinești** is especially popular with young Romanians, and **Neptun** is one of several shoreline buildups of popular beaches and lots of hotels. On the whole, if you're looking for sunshine and an inexpensive beach holiday, the Black Sea fits the bill, but don't

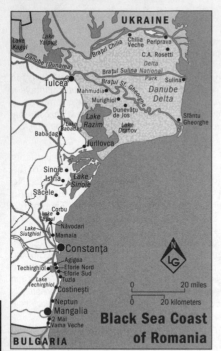

Black Sea Coast of Romania

have any illusions about escaping the tourist hordes. Resorts are open late June through early September and on May 1, which is a school holiday. Peak season hits July 1 to August 15, bringing heavy crowds and high prices. To be safe, call ahead for reservations, although you stand a good chance reserving on the spot as well.

MAMAIA

The all-purpose behemoth of Romanian resorts, crowded Mamaia is easily accessible for a quick beach holiday. Of all the Black Sea resorts, it sports the widest array of watersports, bars, and clubs, on a narrow spit of land running north and south.) If you can find an open spot, soak up rays on the **beach.** Check out **Aqua Magic,** a full-scale water park on the far south end, next to Hotel Perla. Visitors enjoy inner tubes, waterslides like the "Space Bowl" and the "Black Hole," and, of course, island bars. (Open daily 9am-7pm. L40, those under 1.5m tall L20.) The nightlife scene in Mamaia is a cross between a club and a county fair. **Disco No Limit,** at Bd. Al. Lăpușeanu 194, is one of many nighttime options, including carnival rides and plenty of junk food (☎338 137. Open daily 10pm-late). To reserve rooms, call the **Dispecerat de Cazare** office (☎55 55 55; 10-20% commission), or avoid the middleman and call a hotel directly. The blue-and-white **Hotel Saguna ❷,** toward the middle of the strip and near the reddish Hotel Piccadilly, offers small, basic rooms with shared bath. (☎83 19 56. Doubles L80; triples L110. Cash only.) Toward the northern end of the strip, there are several **campgrounds** and **bungalow colonies.** At the northern edge of Mamaia proper, **Tourist Camping ❷** rents bungalows for L75 per person and tent sites for L8 per person. (☎83 11 45. Reception 24hr. Cash only.) Farther north, past the end of Mamaia but not the end of the beach, **GPM Camping ❶** is less expensive, with roomy, clean bungalows. Follow the shoreline to the first campsite on the left past the **nude beach,** or skip the nudists by walking along the highway. (☎83 10 02. Reception 24hr. Bungalows L73.50 per 2 people, L110.25 per 3 people. Tents L10 per person. Cash only.) Produce stands, pastry kiosks, fast-food joints, and the occasional sit-down restaurant line the strip, but it's mostly a lot of carnival food; head to Constanța for better dining. To reach Mamaia from **Constanța,** take the #23E or #41 city bus. (20min. from train station; L1.20.)

COSTINEȘTI

Costinești (coh-stee-NEHSHT), crowded with boisterous young Romanians, offers loud fun at low prices. The main road, **Str. Tineretuiui,** runs parallel to much of the beach, but veers away towards the railroad tracks, where it turns into **Str. Principala.** Walk downhill from the main road to get to the beach; a paved walkway runs along it and past Costinești's artificial **lake,** where you can rent **boats** and hydrobikes. (Booth is on the lakeshore. L10 per hr.) One of the most popular **nightclubs** along the walkway is the outdoor **Disco Ring**, where Romanian youth dance to the latest hip-hop among smoke machines and strobe lights. (Beer L5. Cover L5. Open daily 9pm-late.) Along the walkway and past the lake, you'll find several hotels, including **DVG ❷**, which offers newly refurbished rooms near the sea with fridges, comfortable beds, cable TV, private bathrooms with hot showers, and balconies. The 24hr. reception is in the little glass room in the outdoor terrace restaurant. (☎73 42 00. Check-out noon. Doubles L100. MC/V.) **Hotel Azur ❸**, farther along the walkway, has simple, older rooms with private bathrooms. (☎73 40 14. Doubles L90; triples L135; 4-person apartments L160.) For less expensive accommodations, the **Mistral ❶** bungalow colony just off the walkway offers clean, small rooms with newish beds. The reception desk is on the side farthest from the Hotel Azur. (Rooms L40, with bath L60. Cash only.) Hot running water isn't a sure thing in Costineşti, so check with your place of accommodation. Cheap meals abound near the train station, on the main street, and on the terraces overlooking the coast. A swankier option is the traditional **Rustic Poieniţa ❶**, along the beach on Str. Marii, with plenty of outdoor seating. The *tigaie picanta* (L13) is a frying pan full of delicious pork, beef, chicken, and veggies. (☎73 40 21. No English menu. Entrees L8-24. Pizza L8-13. Cash only.) If you are arriving by **train**, get off at "Costineşti Tabără," head down Str. Tineretului, and take any right turn to get to the beach. Trains go to **Constanţa** (40min., 15 per day, L2.10) and **Neptun** (10min., 15 per day, L1.50). **Microbuses** stop at the shelter near the red post office on the main street. Check in Constanţa to be sure your bus is stopping in Costineşti. Return buses depart for **Constanţa** (30min., every 15min., L4.50).

NEPTUN

Along with Saturn, Jupiter, Venus, and Olimp, **Neptun** is one of a string of resort villages built one on top of the other on the shoreline. Its two freshwater lakes are ingeniously named Neptun I and Neptun II; they're sandwiched between the main road and the popular **beach**. The **nameless main street** runs north-south parallel to the beach, and is lined with restaurants, banks, pharmacies, hotels, clothing stores, ATMs, payphones, a post office/telephone office, and various other shops. Minibuses drop off here; just walk downhill to get to the beach. When you get there, you can straddle an oversized rubber banana (L10 per 5min.) for a motorboat-pulled joyride around the sea or rent **jetskis** (L70 per 10min. per 2 people) or

WHERE THE DANUBE ENDS

The mighty Danube stretches 1177 mi. through nine countries and four capitals, finally emptying into the Black Sea along the Romanian coast. Although the river winds itself near the homes of millions of Europeans, few venture to its end. Those who do, however, are rewarded by over 200 species of birds, 1150 species of plants, and some of the best fishing in Europe. The enormous delta, ranging over almost 2000 square miles, is a mass of marshes and islets, covered in reeds, water lilies, and animal life. It's off the beaten path—only about 15,000 people make their home in the entire area—but for nature lovers, it's well worth the trip.

To get there, take a train from Constanţa to Tulcea, the biggest city in the area. From there, several tour agencies offer boat rides into the delta; hotels also organize river expeditions. Ferries run downstream to tiny coastal towns like Sf. Gheorghe, a tiny fishing village on an island at the very tip of the southeastern branch, and Sulina, the only sizable town in the delta proper. Villages dot the area, most of them devoted to fishing or reed harvesting. The ancient traditions of the region's people, coupled with the unspoiled, rainforest-like landscape, make the Danube Delta unlike any other corner of Europe.

waterskis (L60 per 10min.); look for booths along the waterfront. Several tourist agencies in town act as room-reservation clearinghouses; look for *dispecerat de cazare* (room reservations). With commission rates up to 20% and plenty of hotels to choose from, you might be better off reserving a room yourself. Expect to pay around L90-120 per night. For a less expensive option, try **Camping Popas Zodiac ❶**, the cheapest place to spend the night and one of the coast's better campgrounds. Walk south on the main street to the intersection marked by large metal "Jupiter" and "Neptun" posts. (☎731 404. L10 per person, L3 per tent. Cash only.) ⊠**Restaurant Insula ❷**, on a deck overlooking Lake Neptun I, serves good seafood in a beautiful lakeside garden. It's toward the beach on the street marked by hotels Delta, Sulina, and Dobregea. (☎70 13 06. English menu. Entrees L15-60. Open daily 9am-11pm. MC/V.) **Club Why Not,** in the shopping center across the street from the Banca Comercială Română, attracts vacationers with house and pop music. (Beer L7. Cover L5. Open daily 10pm-late.) Across the street and a bit south, you'll find the Party at the retro-Soviet **Club Kremlin,** which looks appropriately like a giant red dungeon, replete with scarlet draperies, chains, and propaganda. (☎48 54 70. Beer L7. Cover L5. Open daily 10pm-late.) **Trains** go to **Constanța** (50min., 12 per day, L2.50) and **Costinești** (10min., 12 per day, L1.70). Buy tickets at the station or the **CFR** desk, in the Hotel Apollo. (Open M-Sa 7:30am-7:30pm, Su 8am-2pm.) To get to the station from the center, walk north on the main road, left when the road forks, and left again at the T-intersection. **Minibuses** are the preferred option for most travelers, although they offer no direct rides to Constanța. Switch buses in **Mangalia** (10min., every 15min., L2), for **Constanța** (30min., every 15min., L3).

ROMANIA

MOLDOVA

Once part of the Romanian province of Moldavia, Moldova gained independence in 1991 after enduring 45 years of Soviet rule. Today, Moldova is struggling to overcome poverty and instability, especially in the breakaway region of Transdniester.

ENTRANCE REQUIREMENTS
Passport: Required for all travelers.
Visa: Required for all travelers.
Letter of Invitation: Required of citizens of Australia and New Zealand.
Inoculations: Recommended up-to-date on DTaP (diphtheria, tetanus, and pertussis), Hepatitis A, Hepatitis B, MMR (measles, mumps, and rubella), Polio booster, and Typhoid.
Work Permit: Required for all foreigners planning to work.

ESSENTIALS

DOCUMENTS AND FORMALITIES

Moldova is updating its visa and entry laws; check with your embassy for the most up-to-date information. Citizens of Australia and New Zealand need both **visas** and **invitations** to travel in Moldova; citizens of Canada, the EU, and the US just need visas for travel of duration greater than three months. Single-entry visas cost US$85 (valid 1 month); multiple-entry travel visas US$95-165 (depending on length of stay); transit visas US$65 for single-entry, US$85 for double-entry. There is also a **processing fee.** Passports must be valid two months after departure from Moldova. Regular service takes seven business days; **rush service** costs extra, depending on the visa type. Costs are lower for those born in Moldova. To apply, submit an application, an invitation (if applicable), your passport, a photo, an envelope, and the fee by money order or company check to the appropriate Moldovan embassy or consulate. Invitations can be obtained from acquaintances in Moldova or from a private organization such as **MoldovaTUR**, which issues invitations after you book a hotel room. All foreigners in Moldova must **register** with the police within three days of arrival. Also **register your valuables** to avoid customs duties upon exit. Some international buses to and from Odessa pass through Moldova's unstable breakaway **Transdniester Republic**. You will pass through an additional passport control at the Transdniester/Moldovan border, where you will be given a slip of paper or passport stamp. The guards at the Transdniester/Ukrainian border demand to see this official Moldovan seal and will not let you pass without it.

TOURIST SERVICES AND MONEY

MoldovaTUR is the main tourist office. Its employees usually speak English. In general, though, there are few resources for tourists. Do not confuse **Moldovan lei** with the eponymous Romanian currency. Moldovan lei are fully convertible (1 leu = 100 bani). Current inflation is 8-10%, so prices will rise over the next year. **Bringing cash is necessary** since few places outside Chişinău take traveler's checks or give cash advances. **ATMs** are common in the capital. Normal business hours in Moldova are Monday to Friday 8am-5pm. Most businesses are closed on national holidays.

HEALTH AND SAFETY

EMERGENCY NUMBERS: Police: ☎902 **Fire:** ☎901 **Ambulance:** ☎903

Medical facilities exist, but they may not provide the standard of care that Westerners expect. In an emergency, contact your embassy, which can provide info about local medical facilities. If you decide to go to a hospital, you will be expected to pay with **cash**. Bring your own antibiotics, syringes, bandages, and the like. **Pharmacies** are generally equipped with Western products. The **water** is not safe to drink. Boil water for 10min. or drink imported bottled water. Beware of unclean food, especially from street vendors. **Cholera** and **diphtheria** are problems; talk with your doctor before going.

Streets are poorly lit at night; take a taxi from a reputable company if you're out at night. Manhole covers have been scavenged for scrap metal, so random holes litter the streets. This makes biking and driving unsafe. Do not walk after dark unless accompanied by a local. **Avoid traveling through the Transdniester region**, as violence and illegal activity are rampant; foreign embassies can do little to help travelers in this region. **Women** should dress conservatively. It is generally okay for women to travel alone in Moldova, but do not stay out after dark. Moldovans harbor **prejudice** against Roma (gypsies) and others with dark skin. Others of foreign **ethnicities** may receive suspicious looks, and **anti-Semitic** attitudes are prevalent. **Homophobia** persists. Discretion is strongly advised.

TRANSPORTATION

Chişinău International Airport (☎2 52 60 60, flight info 2 52 54 12). **Air Moldova** (☎2 52 55 02, reservations 2 52 50 02) is the national airline. **Trains** are extremely inefficient. The **Iaşi, ROM**-Chişinău train trip sometimes takes much more time in border controls and rail-gauge changing than in motion. If you do decide to take the train, opt for first class. **Buses** are crowded and old but provide a much cheaper and more comfortable way of getting in, out, and around.

Taxis in Moldova are generally overpriced and drivers will often charge more if they recognize you as a foreigner. If you do take a taxi, be sure to only ride in officially marked cars. **Rental cars,** though they do exist, are rare. **Gas** stations and repair facilities are relatively uncommon. If you are driving in Moldova, stop for fuel whenever you see a gas station. **Hitchhiking** is dangerous, and *Let's Go* strongly discourages this practice.

KEEPING IN TOUCH

Moldova's **country code** is ☎373. There are **no international access numbers** in Moldova; collect calls also remain impossible. Most local phones use Moldtelecom cards, available at the post office and from kiosks. For an **international operator,** dial ☎819. For domestic calls, use ☎813. **To call internationally,** dial 8, wait for the tone, then dial 10, the country code, and the number. Foreign calling cards do not call out of Moldova. **Internet access** is cheap and widely available in Chişinău.

ACCOMMODATIONS

There are no **hostels** in Moldova. **Homestays** are the cheapest option. You should have no problem finding quality **hotels** for under US$15. It is common to rent by the bed rather than by the room. Reservations are only needed in summer.

ROMANIA

MOSCOW AND ST. PETERSBURG

(МОСКВА И САНКТ-ПЕТЕРБУРГ)

Over a decade since the fall of the USSR, mammoth Russia still struggles to redefine itself. Between fierce, cosmopolitan Moscow and graceful, majestic St. Petersburg lies a gulf as wide as any in Europe—and a swath of provincial towns that seem frozen in time. Rich in history, mysterious, and inexpensive, with good public transportation and scores of breathtaking sights, Russia is in many ways an ideal destination for the adventurous budget traveler. While Communism's legacy endures through present-day bureaucratic headaches, the fragile situation in neighboring Chechnya raises tensions, and modernization rushes violently forward like so much oil, Russia remains the epitome of Eastern European grandeur. Opulent tsarist palaces, fossilized Soviet edifices, and a bounty of storied theaters and museums bear witness to one of the richest cultural heritages on Earth.

 DISCOVER MOSCOW AND ST. PETERSBURG: SUGGESTED ITINERARIES

BEST OF MOSCOW Once amid the stark grandeur of what remains of the Soviet Empire, queue up for the **Lenin Mausoleum** (p. 585) in the morning, then visit Russia's most recognizable landmark, colorful **St. Basil's Cathedral** (p. 585). Check out the minarets and armory inside the **Kremlin** (p. 583) and play secret spy on a private tour through the old **KGB Building** (p. 590). Don't miss the fantastic collections of Russian art held at the **State** and **New Tretyakov Galleries** (p. 589), or the shrines to literary success at museums dedicated to **Pushkin, Gorky, Tolstoy,** and **Mayakovsky** (p. 591).

BEST OF ST. PETERSBURG Begin with a stroll down **Nevskiy Prospekt** (p. 610), St. Petersburg's main drag, then stop for a moment of repose at the city's most famous Russian-style church, the **Church of Our Savior on Spilled Blood** (p. 611). Head next to the bell tower of **St. Isaac's Cathedral** (p. 609) for an incomparable view of the city. While in the area, visit that attic of aristocracy, the **Hermitage** (p. 607), where the riches of the ages are displayed in unthinkable abundance. Then wander through the labyrinthine canals for which St. Petersburg is nicknamed "the Venice of the North."

ESSENTIALS

WHEN TO GO

It may be wise to plan around the high season (June-Aug.). Autumn and spring (Sept.-Oct. and Apr.-May) are more appealing times to visit; the weather is still reasonable and flights are cheaper. If you intend to visit the large cities and linger indoors at museums and theaters, the bitter winter (Nov.-Mar.) is most economical. Keep in mind, however, that sights and accommodations often close or run reduced hours. Another factor to consider is hours of daylight—in St. Petersburg, summer light lasts almost to midnight, but in winter the sun may set at 3:45pm.

FACTS AND FIGURES

Official Name: Russian Federation.
Capital: Moscow.
Major Cities: Irkutsk, Novgorod, St. Petersburg.
Population: 143,421,000.

Land Area: 16,995,800 sq. km.
Time Zone: GMT + 3.
Language: Russian.
Religions: Russian Orthodox (72%).

DOCUMENTS AND FORMALITIES

ENTRANCE REQUIREMENTS

Passport: Required for all travelers.
Visa: Required for all travelers.
Letter of Invitation: Required for all travelers.
Inoculations: Recommended up-to-date on DTaP (diphtheria, tetanus, and pertussis), Hepatitis A, Hepatitis B, MMR (measles, mumps, and rubella), Polio booster, and Typhoid.
Work Permit: Required of all foreigners planning to work in Russia.
Driving Permit: Required for all those planning to drive in Russia.

EMBASSIES AND CONSULATES. Foreign embassies to Russia are in Moscow (p. 574). Russian embassies at home include: **Australia,** 78 Canberra Ave., Griffith, ACT 2603 (☎6 6295 9033; rusemb@dynamite.com.au); **Canada,** 285 Charlotte St., Ottawa, ON K1N 8L5 (☎613-235-4341; rusemb@magma.ca); **Ireland,** 186 Orwell Rd., Rathgar, Dublin 14 (russiane@indigo.ie); **New Zealand,** 57 Messines Rd., Karori, Wellington (☎64 4 476 6113, visa info 476 6742; eor@netlink.co.nz); **UK,** 13 Kensington Palace Gardens, London W8 4QX (☎44 171 229 3628, visa info 229 8027; dom.harhouse1@harhouse1.demon.co.uk); **US,** 2650 Wisconsin Ave. NW, Washington, D.C. 20007 (☎202-298-5700; www.russianembassy.org).

VISA AND ENTRY INFORMATION. Almost every visitor to Russia needs a **visa.** The standard tourist visa is valid for 30 days, while a business visa will allow a stay up to three months. Both come in single-entry and double-entry varieties. All applications for Russian visas require an **invitation** stating the traveler's itinerary and dates of travel. Hostels and hotels can often provide invitations for tourist visas. **Visa services** and **travel agencies** can also provide you with both types of invitations (US$30-80), and for a higher fee can get you an actual visa in a matter of days (from US$160). Some agencies may even be able to get you a visa overnight (up to US$700). For a list of agencies, see below. Students and employees may be able to obtain student visas from their school or host organization. Upon arrival, travelers are required to fill out an immigration card, part of which must be kept until departure from Russia, and to **register** their visa within three working days. Registration can be done at your hostel or hotel, or for a fee at a travel agency in-country. As a last resort, head to the central OVIR (ОВИР) office to register.

GETTING A VISA ON YOUR OWN. If you have an invitation from an authorized travel agency or Russian organization and want to get a visa on your own, apply for the visa in person or by mail at a Russian embassy or consulate. (Download an application form at www.ruscon.org.) Bring your original invitation; your passport; a completed application; three passport-sized photographs; a cover letter stating your name, itinerary, date of birth, and passport number; and a money order or certified check. (Prices vary by processing speed. Single-entry, 60-day visas US$100-300; double-entry visas add US$50, except on 6-day processing; multiple-entry US$100-450; prices change constantly, so check with the embassy).

Western Russia

TRAVEL AGENCIES. Travel agencies that advertise discounted tickets to Russia often are also able to provide invitations and visas to Russia. Helpful agencies include: **Host Families Association (HOFA),** 3 Linia 6, V.O., St. Petersburg, 199053, RUS (☎812 275 19 92; www.hofa.us; arranges homestays, meals, and transport; visa invitations for Russia, Ukraine, and Belarus; US$30-40); **Red Bear Tours/Russian Passport,** 401 St. Kilda Rd., Ste. 11, Melbourne 3004, AUS (☎9867 3888; www.travelcentre.com.au; provides invitations to Russia, sells rail tickets, and arranges tours); **VISAtoRUSSIA.com,** 309A Peters St. Atlanta, GA 30313, USA (☎404-837-0099; www.visatorussia.com; Russian visa invitations from US$30).

ENTERING RUSSIA. The best way to cross the **border** is to fly directly into Moscow or St. Petersburg. Another available option is to take a train or bus into one of the major cities. Expect long delays and red tape. Russian law dictates that all visitors must **register** their visas within three days of arrival (see p. 564). Many travelers skip this purgatory, but taking care of it will leave one less thing over which bribe-seeking authorities can hassle you—typical fines for visa non-registration run about US$150. While in Russia, carry your passport at all times.

TOURIST SERVICES AND MONEY

RUBLES (R)		
	AUS$1 = 21.50R	10R = AUS$0.47
	CDN$1 = 23.44R	10R = CDN$0.43
	EUR€1 = 34.79R	10R = EUR€0.29
	NZ$1 = 19.86R	10R = NZ$0.50
	UK£1 = 51.25R	10R = UK£0.20
	US$1 = 28.58R	10R = US$0.35

TOURIST OFFICES. There are two types of Russian tourist office—those that only arrange tours and those that offer general travel assistance. Offices of the former type are often unhelpful, but those of the latter are usually eager to assist, particularly with visa registration. While Western-style tourist offices are rare, big hotels often house tourist agencies with English-speaking staff. The most accurate maps are sold by street-kiosks. A great online resource is www.waytorussia.net.

 PAYING IN RUSSIA. Due to the fluctuating value of the Russian ruble, some establishments list their prices in US dollars. For this reason, some prices in this book may also appear in US$, but be prepared to pay in rubles.

MONEY. The Russian unit of currency is the **ruble,** which comes in denominations of 1, 5, 10, 50, and 100. One hundred **kopecks** make a ruble. Government regulations require that you show your passport when you exchange money. Find an **Obmen Valyuta** (Currency Exchange), hand over your currency—most will only exchange US dollars and euros—and receive your rubles. **Inflation** runs around 12%. **Do not exchange money on the street.** Banks offer the best combination of good rates and security. **ATMs** *(bankomat)* linked to all major networks can be found in most cities. Banks, large restaurants, and currency exchanges often accept major **credit cards,** especially Visa. Main branches of banks will usually accept **traveler's checks** and give **cash advances** on credit cards. It's wise to keep a small amount (US$20 or less) of dollars on hand. Most establishments don't accept torn, written-on, or crumpled bills, and Russians are wary of old US money; bring the new bills.

HEALTH AND SAFETY

EMERGENCY **Police: ☎02. Ambulance: ☎01. Fire: ☎03.**

In a **medical emergency,** either leave the country or go to the American Medical Centers in Moscow or St. Petersburg; these clinics have American doctors who speak English. Russian **bottled water** is often mineral water; you may prefer to boil or filter your own, or buy imported bottled water at a supermarket. Water is drinkable in much of Russia, but not in Moscow or St. Petersburg. Men's **toilets** are marked with an "M," women's with a "Ж." The 0.5-5R charge for public toilets generally gets you a hole in the ground and a piece of toilet paper. **Pharmacies** abound and offer a range of Western products; look for the "Аптека" (apteka) signs.

　　Crimes against foreigners are on the rise, particularly in Moscow and St. Petersburg. Although it is often tough to blend in, try not to flaunt your nationality. Seeming Russian may increase your chances of police attention, but keeps you safer among the citizenry. It is unwise to take pictures of anything military or to do anything that might attract the attention of a man in uniform—doing something suspicious provides an excuse to hassle you. Avoid interaction with the police unless an emergency necessitates it. Do not let officials go through your possessions; if they try to detain you, threaten to call your embassy (*"ya pozvonyu svoyu posolstvu."*)

The concept of **sexual harassment** hasn't yet reached Russia. Local men will try to pick up lone women and will get away with offensive language and actions. The routine starts with an innocent-sounding *"Devushka…"* (young lady); say *"Nyet"* (No) or simply walk away. Women in Russia generally wear skirts or dresses rather than pants. Those who do not speak Russian will also find themselves the target of unwanted attention. The authorities on the Metro will frequently stop and question dark-skinned individuals, who may also receive rude treatment in shops and restaurants. Outside of Moscow and St. Petersburg, where people are generally accepting, **homosexuality** is still largely taboo; it is best to remain discreet.

TRANSPORTATION

BY PLANE. Most major international carriers fly into Sheremetyevo-2 in Moscow or Pulkovo-2 Airport in St. Petersburg. **Aeroflot,** Frunzenskaya Naberezhnaya 4 (☎ 095 156 80 19; www.aeroflot.org) is the most popular domestic carrier. The majority of domestic routes are served by Soviet-model planes, many of which are in disrepair and have a poor safety record. From **London, ENG,** Aeroflot offers cheap flights into Russia. A number of European budget airlines land in **Tallin, EST** (easyJet; www.easyjet.com), **Riga, LAT** (Ryan Air; www.ryanair.com), or **Helsinki, FIN,** from which you can reach Russia by bus or train.

BY TRAIN AND BUS. In a perfect world, everyone would fly into St. Petersburg or Moscow, skipping customs officials who tear packs apart and demand bribes, and avoiding Belarus entirely. But it's not a perfect world, and you'll likely find yourself on an eastbound **train.** If that train is passing through **Belarus,** you will need a US$30 transit visa. If you wait until you reach the border, you'll likely pay more and risk a forced no-expense-paid weekend getaway in Minsk. **Domestically,** trains are generally the best option. Weekend or holiday trains between Petersburg and Moscow sometimes sell out a week in advance. The best class is *lyuks*, with two beds, while the 2nd-class *kupeyny* has four bunks. The next class down is *platskartny*, an open car with 52 shorter, harder bunks. Aim for places 1-33.

Women traveling alone can try to buy out a *lyuks* compartment or can travel *platskartny* with the regular folk and depend on the crowds to shame would-be harassers into silence. *Platskartny* is also a good idea on the theft-ridden St. Petersburg-Moscow line, as you are less likely to be targeted there. Try to board your train on time; changing your ticket carries a fee of up to 25% the ticket cost.

Buses, slightly less expensive than trains, are better for shorter distances. They are often crowded and overbooked; eject people who try to sit in your seat.

BY BOAT. Cruise ships stop in the main Russian ports: St. Petersburg, Murmansk, and Vladivostok. However, they usually allow travelers less than 48hr. in the city. In December 2002, a regular ferry route opened between Kaliningrad and St. Petersburg (1-2 per wk.). Kaliningrad ferries also operate to **Poland** and **Germany.** A river cruise runs between Moscow and St. Petersburg.

BY TAXI AND BY THUMB. Hailing a **taxi** is indistinguishable from **hitchhiking,** and should be treated with equal caution. Most drivers who stop will be private citizens trying to make a little extra cash (despite the recent restriction on this illegal activity). Those seeking a ride should stand off the curb and hold out a hand into the street, palm down; when a car stops, riders tell the driver the destination before getting in; he will either refuse altogether or ask *"Skolko?"* (How much?), leading to protracted negotiations. Non-Russian speakers will get ripped off unless they manage a firm agreement on the price—if the driver agrees without asking for a price, you must ask *"skolko?"* yourself (sign language works too). **Never get into a car that has more than one person in it.** *Let's Go* does not recommend hitchhiking.

KEEPING IN TOUCH

PHONE CODES	**Country code: 7. International dialing prefix: 00.** From outside Russia, dial int'l dialing prefix (see inside back cover) + 7 + city code + local number. Within Russia, dial 8 + city code + local number for intercity calls and 8 + local number within a city.

EMAIL AND THE INTERNET. Email is your best bet for keeping in touch while in Russia. Internet cafes have made quite a mark throughout St. Petersburg and Moscow, but aren't as popular outside these cities. When all else fails, check at the post office. Going rates for Internet access vary 35-70R per hour depending on location and time of day. Most Internet cafes are open 24hr.

 Mobile phones have become a popular accessory among Russians and a comforting safety blanket for visitors. Most new phones are compatible with Russian networks and cell phone shops are common, but service can be costly. On average, a minute costs US$.20, and unlike in much of Europe, users are charged for incoming calls. Major providers Megafon, BeeLine GSM, and MTS have stores throughout the cities, as do rental chains like Euroset and Svyaznoy.

TELEPHONES. Old **local** telephones in Moscow take special tokens, sold at Metro *kassy;* in St. Petersburg, they take Metro tokens. These old public phones are gradually becoming obsolete; the new ones take phonecards, which are sold at central telephone offices, Metro stations, and newspaper kiosks. When you are purchasing phonecards from a telephone office or Metro station, the attendant will often ask, "На улицу," (Na ulitsu; On the street?) to find out whether you want a card for the phones in the station/office or for outdoor public phones. Be careful: phone cards in Russia are very specific, and it is easy to purchase the wrong kind. Often, hostels and other such locations will attempt to sell you phone cards that work only in their establishments. For five-digit numbers, insert a "2" between the dialing code and the phone number. Make direct **international** calls from telephone offices in St. Petersburg and Moscow: calls to Europe run US$1-1.50 per minute, to the US and Australia about US$1.50-2. International access codes include: **AT&T** varies by region, see www.att.com for specific info; **Canada Direct** ☎810 800 110 1012; **MCI** ☎960 2222 in Moscow, ☎747 3322 elsewhere; **Sprint** ☎747 3324 in Moscow, outside Moscow add 8095 before this number.

MAIL. Mail service is more reliable leaving the country than coming in. Letters to the US arrive a week after mailing; letters to other destinations take two to three weeks. **Airmail** is *avia.* Send mail "заказное" (certified; 40R) to reduce the chance of it being lost. Letters to the US cost 16R; postcards 11R. **Poste Restante** is Pismo Do Vostrebovania. Address envelopes: HARPER (LAST NAME), Alexandra (First name), 103 009 (postal code), москва (city), Письмо До Востребования, RUSSIA.

ACCOMMODATIONS

RUSSIA	❶	❷	❸	❹	❺
ACCOMMODATIONS	under 400R under €11 under $14	400-700R €11-20 $14-25	700-1200R €20-34 $25-42	1201-2000R €34-57 $42-70	over 2000R over €57 over $70

The **hostel** scene in Russia is limited mostly to St. Petersburg and Moscow, often involves less-than-stellar service and facilities, and isn't the cheapest in Eastern Europe: US$18-25 per night is average. Still, the hostels that do exist are often English-speaking and amenity-filled. Reserve in advance. **Hotels** offer several classes of rooms. "Lux," usually two-room doubles with TV, phone, fridge, and bath, are the most expensive. "Polu-lux" rooms are singles or doubles with TV, phone, and bath. The lowest-priced rooms are *bez udobstv*, which means one room with a sink. Expect to pay 300-450R for a single in a budget hotel. As a rule, only cash is accepted as payment. In many hotels, **hot water**—sometimes all water—is only turned on for a few hours each day.

University dorms offer cheap rooms; some accept foreign students for about US$5-10 per night. The rooms are livable, but don't expect sparkling bathrooms or reliable hot water. Make arrangements through an educational institute from home. In the larger cities, **private rooms** and **apartments** can often be found for very reasonable prices (about 200R per night). Outside major train stations, there are usually women offering private rooms to rent—don't forget to bargain with them.

FOOD AND DRINK

RUSSIA	❶	❷	❸	❹	❺
FOOD	under 70R under €2 under $3	70-150R €2-4 $3-5	150-300R €4-9 $5-11	300-500R €9-14 $11-17	over 500R over €14 over $17

Russian cuisine is a medley of dishes both delectable and unpleasant; tasty *borscht* (beet soup) can come in the same meal as *salo* (pig fat). The largest meal of the day, *obed* (lunch), includes: *salat* (salad), usually cucumbers and tomatoes or beets and potatoes with mayonnaise or sour cream; *sup* (soup); and *kuritsa* (chicken) or *myaso* (meat), often called *kotlyety* (cutlets) or *bifshteaks* (beefsteaks). Other common foods include *shchi* (cabbage soup) and *blini* (potato pancakes). Ordering a number of *zakuski* (small appetizers) instead of a main dish can save money. Dessert includes *morozhenoye* (ice cream) or *tort* (cake) with *cofe* (coffee) or *chai* (tea), which Russians will drink at the slightest provocation. **Vegetarians** and **kosher** diners traveling in Russia will probably find it easiest to stick to the cuisine in large cities and to eat in foreign restaurants and pizzerias.

On the streets, you'll see a lot of *shashlyki* (barbequed meat on a stick) and *kvas*, a slightly alcoholic dark-brown drink. Beware of any meat products hawked by sidewalk vendors; they may be several days old. Kiosks often carry **alcohol;** imported cans of beer are safe (though warm), but be wary of Russian labels—you have no way of knowing what's really in the bottle. *Russky Standart* and *Flagman* are the best **vodkas;** the much-touted *Stolichnaya* is made mostly for export. Among local **beers,** *Baltika* (numbered 1-7 according to brew and alcohol content) is the most popular and arguably the best. *Baltika* 1 is the weakest (10.5%), *Baltika* 7 the strongest (14%). *Baltikas* 4 and 6 are dark; the rest are lagers.

ST. PETERSBURG

MOSCOW AND

LIFE AND TIMES

HISTORY

THE NOT-SO-GOLDEN AGE. The earliest recorded settlers of European Russia were the Scandinavian **Varangians,** or **Rus,** in the 9th century AD. In 862, several of these Slavic tribes chose as their leader **Ryurik,** who established Novgorod and Kyiv as centers of power, thus founding the Russian state. In 1223, Genghis Khan and the Mongol, or Tatar, **Golden Horde** invaded, significantly retarding the development of a Russian state. The Tatar reign, which lasted until 1480 and created the largest empire in the world, saw increasing contact between Russia and Western and Central Europe, and the emergence of **Muscovy** (today's Moscow) as a political and commercial center. Eventually the Mongol Khanate fell victim to civil war.

IVANS AND BORIS AND BOYARS, OH MY! Duke of Muscovy **Ivan III** (1462-1505) filled the void left by the departure of the Mongols and began a drive to unify all East Slavic lands—parts of present-day Belarus, Russia, and Ukraine—under his rule. His grandson **Ivan IV** (the Terrible) was the first to take the title "tsar." After Ivan's son Fyodor died childless in 1598, **Boris Godunov** became tsar until the **boyars** (nobles) deposed him. Instability followed until **Mikhail Romanov** ascended to the throne in 1613, ushering in the dynasty that ruled until the Bolshevik Revolution of 1917. Mikhail's grandson **Peter the Great,** whose reign began in 1682, created a **Westernized** elite, expanded Russia's borders to the Baltic Sea, and built European-style St. Petersburg. Thousands of workers died in the process, but Peter left Russia with a modernized military and administrative structure when he died in 1725.

FRENCH INVASION. After resisting the French during Napoleon's invasion in June 1812, Russian officers looked to the republican ideals of France in their **Decembrist coup** on December 14, 1825. Russia's loss to the West in the **Crimean War** (1853-1856) spurred reforms, including **emancipation of the serfs** in 1861. **Alexander II,** "The Great Emancipator," was assassinated by populists two decades later, hours before he was to introduce Russia's first constitution.

WAR AND PEACE. The famine, peasant unrest, terrorism, and strikes of the late 1800s culminated in the failed **1905 Revolution. Vladimir Ilyich Lenin,** leader of the Bolsheviks, led the coup of October 1917, which turned the nation Red. A **Civil War** followed the October Revolution, but the Communists won and the **Union of Soviet Socialist Republics (USSR)** was formed in 1922. After Lenin's death in 1924, **Josef Stalin** emerged triumphant from a period of infighting and proceeded to eliminate his rivals in a bloodthirsty reign that would kill as many as 20 million Russians and ethnic minorities. Stalin forced **collectivization** of Soviet farms and filled **Siberian gulags** (labor camps) with political prisoners.

MORE WAR. Stalin was able to find an ally only in **Adolf Hitler,** with whom he concluded the **Molotov-Ribbentrop Non-Aggression Pact** in August 1939. Later that year, the USSR helped Germany in its attack on Poland and subsequently occupied the Baltics. When the Nazi-Soviet alliance finally soured, Stalin brought the USSR into **WWII** unprepared, but Hitler's invasion was stymied by the long winter. The **Battle of Stalingrad,** in which 1.1 million Russian troops were killed, broke the German advance and turned the tide of the war. In 1945, the Soviets took **Berlin** and gained status as a postwar superpower. Feeling abandoned by the Allies, Stalin reneged on agreements made at the **Yalta Conference** and refused to allow free elections in the nations of Eastern Europe. The USSR left its army in Eastern Europe as far west as East Germany, and the **Iron Curtain** descended on the continent.

BEHIND THE CURTAIN. In 1949, the Soviet Union formed the **Council for Mutual Economic Assistance (COMECON),** which reduced the Eastern European nations to satellites of the Party's headquarters in Moscow. Under **Nikita Khrushchev,** who succeeded Stalin after his death in 1953, the 1955 **Warsaw Pact** drew Eastern Europe into a military alliance with the USSR to counterbalance the **North Atlantic Treaty Organization (NATO)** in the West. In the 1956 **"Secret Speech,"** Khrushchev denounced the terrors of the Stalinist period. He also inaugurated the space race with the US by launching **Sputnik,** the first space satellite, into orbit in 1957. A brief political and cultural "thaw" followed, lasting until 1964, when Khrushchev was ousted by **Leonid Brezhnev.** Over the coming decades, the Party elites aged and weakened, and the geriatric regime finally gave way to 56-year-old firebrand **Mikhail Gorbachev** in 1985. Gorbachev began an age of political and economic reform under **glasnost** (openness) and **perestroika** (rebuilding). Despite hopes of regaining superpower status, the country gradually turned into a bewildering hodgepodge of near-anarchy, economic crisis, and cynicism. Discontent with reforms, coupled with a failed right-wing coup in August 1991, led to Gorbachev's resignation and the **dissolution of the Soviet Union** on December 25, 1991.

THE PARTY'S OVER. Presiding over a freer but still-poor country, **Boris Yeltsin** instituted chaotic free-market reforms that resulted in widespread corruption and economic disparity. Any successful policies came crashing down in the financial crisis of August 1998, and **inflation** skyrocketed. In 1991, Russia banded together with many of the other former Soviet republics to create the **Commonwealth of Independent States (CIS),** but the largely symbolic organization has only begun to act as a common economic area. Only Belarus dreams of reunifying with Russia, and most of the former republics have drifted along their own trajectories.

TODAY

Yeltsin's resignation on January 1, 2000 marked the first-ever voluntary transfer of power by a Russian leader—Soviet leaders had maintained the tsarist tradition of either being forced from office or leaving in a casket. He passed on the presidency to his prime minister, ex-KGB official **Vladimir Putin,** who made economic growth a priority and helped stabilize the ruble. In March 2004, Putin appointed a new prime minister, **Mikhail Fradkov,** and won re-election with 71% of the vote. The road to democracy remains bumpy, however: Putin's domestic reform policies, which have included interference with the press and in corporations like the oil giant **Yukos,** sometimes smack of the old regime. So too does persistent corruption and bribery; in 2005, bribes were estimated to have reached US$316 billion per year, double the government's yearly revenue. Meanwhile, a series of attacks by rebels from neighboring **Chechnya,** including the horrific siege and massacre at a Beslan school in 2004, has prompted Russia to escalate its war on terrorism and provided a basis for continued cooperation with its old enemy, the United States. A rebel cease-fire declared in 2005 seems to have done little to calm high tensions.

PEOPLE AND CULTURE

DEMOGRAPHICS. The **atheist** program of the communists discouraged the open expression of religious faith. With the fall of the USSR, **Russian Orthodoxy,** headed by **Patriarch Aleksey II,** has emerged from hiding and is now winning converts. Despite the Patriarch's claim that the Orthodox Church does not seek state status, the Russian state has favored the Orthodox Church by making it difficult for other religious groups to own property or worship in public. Adherents to Orthodoxy in Russia are predominantly Slavic. Russia is home to over 85 ethnic groups. Most Tatar and Turkish groups in Russia, such as the **Turkmen** of the Caspian Sea region

TOP 10 TIPS FOR RUSSIA

1 Don't **smoke** while crossing a bridge; it's inexplicably punishable by fine.

2 Don't forget to give your seat on the **metro** to a woman (if you're a man), or an older woman, no matter who you are.

3 Don't **shake hands** through a doorway.

4 Don't drink the **tap water** in St. Petersburg.

5 Don't try to **hide items** from customs. They perform thorough check and are eager to punish.

6 Keep your **documents** with you at all times, and **register your passport** as soon as you arrive in a new town.

7 Ask people on the street for **help.** Most know some English, but almost everyone will try to help regardless.

8 **Haggle** for items at markets, but don't do so casually: bargaining is taken seriously and indicates your intent to buy.

9 It may be worth the hefty price to send packages via an international service. The Russian **postal service** is **unreliable.**

10 Expect customs to **confiscate** packages that might contain valuable works of Russian art. Additionally, all objects made before 1956 and those made from materials such as fur, gold, or silver are subject to **export controls** at airports.

and the **Tatars** around Kazan, are **Muslim; Asiatic Inuits** practice **animism** and Mongolian-speaking groups, such as the **Buryat,** are **Buddhist.**

LANGUAGE. Russian is an East Slavic language written in the Cyrillic alphabet. Once you get the hang of the Cyrillic alphabet, you can pronounce just about any Russian word, even if you sound like an idiot. Although **English** is increasingly common, come equipped with at least a few helpful Russian phrases. For a phrasebook and glossary, see **Glossary: Russian,** p. 779.

CUSTOMS AND ETIQUETTE. Bribery and corruption flow like vodka through Russia. While low-paid officials and police are largely respectful and honest, do not give them a reason to hassle you: carry your passport and visa at all times, obey the law, and follow their instructions. Be aware of transaction fees associated with being foreign, which are often legal. When boarding a bus, tram, or Metro car, forceful shoving is common. On **public transportation,** it's polite to give one's seat to elderly or pregnant women and women with children. Going through a row or aisle with your back to those you are passing is offensive. **Loud talking** and **whistling** in public is disrespectful, while the "ok" sign may viewed as a **vulgar gesture.**

Women should wear skirts and cover their heads when visiting Orthodox churches. Many locals say that criminals spot foreigners by their sloppy appearances. Russians wear blue jeans but never wear **shorts.** Russians draw strong distinctions among ethnic groups, and prejudice against minorities is common.

When at a dinner table put your wrists on the edge of the table. Keep the fork in your left hand and the knife in your right. If you are served **vodka** and do not wish to drink it, in order to avoid offending your hosts, invent a medical excuse or say you will have to drive later. In restaurants in St. Petersburg and Moscow, a 5-10% **tip** is becoming customary. Don't praise St. Petersburg while in Moscow or vice versa—there is a longstanding **rivalry** between the two cities.

THE ARTS

ARCHITECTURE, FINE ARTS, AND FILM. St. Basil's **Cathedral** epitomizes the splendor of Russian architecture. Since the demise of the Soviet Union, modern architecture has again begun to assume a more traditional Russian **folk** character. The period following the revolution saw the artists **Wassily Kandinsky,** Belarussian-born **Marc Chagall,** and neo-Primitivist **Natalya Goncharova** gaining international acclaim. Kandinsky, of Russian and Mongolian ancestry, is acknowledged as one of the pioneers of **Abstraction.** Soviet-period artists, confined by the strictures of **Socialist Realism**, were limited to painting canvases with such bland titles as "The Tractor Drivers' Supper." Among the filmmakers of the young Soviet Union was **Sergei Eisenstein**, who, along with his successor **Andrei Tarkovsky**, is considered one of the world's most influential filmmakers. Recent years have seen Russian films such as Sokurov's *Russian Ark* (2002) and Zvyagintsev's *The Return* (2003) find audiences in the West and collect awards at international competitions.

LITERATURE. Ever since Catherine the Great exiled **Alexander Radishchev**, whose *Journey from St. Petersburg to Moscow* documented the dehumanizing nature of serfdom, Russian literature and politics have been bound together. The country's most beloved literary figure, **Alexander Pushkin**, was a Decembrist sympathizer but ultimately chose aesthetics over politics. His novel in verse, *Eugene Onegin*, was a biting take on love and his own earlier Romanticism. The 1840s saw a turn, under the goading of **Vissarion Belinsky**, toward Realism. The **absurdist** works of **Nikolai Gogol** were read as masterful social comment in his own time: *Dead Souls* exposed the corruption of Russian society. **Fyodor Dostoevsky's** psychologically penetrating novels, such as *Crime and Punishment* and *The Brothers Karamazov*, remain classics in Russia and abroad. The same can be said for the sweeping epics of **Leo (Lev) Tolstoy**, who wrote *Anna Karenina* and *War and Peace*. **Realism's** last great voice belonged to **Anton Chekhov**, whose bleak domestic dramas and short stories distilled the power of his verbose predecessors.

At the beginning of the 20th century, with the influence of French symbolism drifting east, poetry entered its **Silver Age**, led by **Alexander Blok**. The metaphysical vagueness of the Symbolists was soon challenged, however, by other movements and poets: **Anna Akhmatova** became known for her haunting, melancholic love verses, while the **Futurists** embraced the furious onset of technology in their verse. In the 1920s the state mandated **Socialist Realism**, a coerced glorification of socialism. **Boris Pasternak** was internally exiled for his Civil War epic *Doctor Zhivago*. **Osip Mandelstam** composed many of his works in exile before dying in a Siberian *gulag*. The political "thaw" of the early 1960s allowed **Joseph Brodsky** to publish his verse and **Alexander Solzhenitsyn** to publish his novel *One Day in the Life of Ivan Denisovich*, detailing life in a labor camp. Premier Leonid Brezhnev, however, plunged the arts into an ice age from which Russia has yet to fully recover.

MUSIC. The early 20th century brought revolutionary ferment and artistic experimentation. This period saw the collaboration of composers **Igor Stravinsky** and **Sergei Diaghilev**, impresario of the Paris-based **Ballets Russes**. Despite repeated falls from official favor, **Dmitri Shostakovich** maintained his stylistic integrity, often satirizing the unwitting Soviet authorities in his famous symphonies. His contemporary **Sergei Prokofiev** enjoyed more approval from the government. Virtuoso pianist and composer **Sergei Rachmaninov** fused the traditional romanticism of the Western school with a unique Slavic lyricism. Russian music reached new audiences in 2002, when the controversial faux lesbian pop duo **t.A.T.u.** (or Тату) released an English version of their Russian debut album, selling 5 million copies worldwide.

HOLIDAYS AND FESTIVALS

Holidays: New Year's Holiday (Jan. 1-2); Orthodox Christmas (Jan. 7); Orthodox New Year (Jan. 14); Defenders of the Motherland Day (Feb. 23); Orthodox Easter Holiday (Apr. 23, 2006; Apr. 8, 2007); Labor Day (May 1); Victory Day (May 9); Independence Day (June Accord and Reconciliation Day (Nov. 7); Constitution Day (Dec. 12).

Festivals: The country that perfected the "workers' rally" may have lost Communism but it still knows how to Party. Midnight services, gift-giving, and elaborate candlelit folk celebrations mark Easter, Christmas, and the secular New Year, while national holidays are occasions for large parades through Moscow and Petersburg, often with military motifs.

Come Apr., St. Petersburg celebrates Music Spring, an international classical music festival, which has a twin in Moscow (Apr. through May), while in June, the city stays up late to celebrate the sunlight of White Nights (*Beliye Nochi*; mid-June to early July), with musical performances, concerts, and fireworks. Russian Winter Festival is celebrated in major cities from late Dec. to early Jan. with folklore exhibitions and vodka. *Maslyanitsa* (Butter Festival; end of Feb.) is a farewell to winter, occurring just before Lent, during which people eat pancakes covered in honey, caviar, fresh cream, and butter.

ADDITIONAL RESOURCES

GENERAL HISTORY

A People's Tragedy (1996) and **Natasha's Dance** (2003), by Orlando Figes. Two compelling overviews of Russian history, the first viewing the revolution through a political lens, the latter encompassing a much wider swath through an artistic lens.

The Russian Revolution, by Richard Pipes (1990). Remains the authoritative history of the revolutionary era by the foremost authority on Russian history.

FICTION AND NONFICTION

Casino Moscow, by Matthew Brzezinski (2002). A *Wall Street Journal* reporter's entertaining account of his days covering the reality of newly capitalist Russia.

A Day in the Life of Ivan Denisovich, by Aleksandr Solzhenitsyn (1963). A morally forceful account of life in the *gulag* under the Stalinist regime.

Kremlin Rising: Vladimir Putin's Russia and the End of Revolution, by Peter Baker and Susan Glasser (2005). A reporting couple's account of President Vladimir Putin's shift away from democracy toward what they describe as authoritarian rule.

Lenin's Tomb and **Resurrection,** both by David Remnick (1993 and 1997). The editor of the *New Yorker* chronicles the fall of the Soviet Union and post-Soviet life.

Peter the Great, by Peter Massie (1980). This magnificent, one-of-a-kind tome about Russia's "reforming tsar" and his world is a faster and more engrossing read than its 900+ pages of history might suggest.

MOSCOW (MOCKBA) ☎(8)095

Change happens quickly in Moscow (pop. 9,000,000). Western visitors may feel like they're balancing on a tightrope held tensely between the cosmopolitan and the underworld. When communism began to dissipate, it left behind dust, drab Soviet housing complexes, and countless statues of Lenin. Yet, on the 16th-century side streets, it's still possible to glimpse the same golden domes that Napoleon saw after reaching the city in 1812. Invading Europe's largest city today is a thrilling, intense experience, flashier and costlier than Petersburg, and undeniably rougher too. Despite the threat of street crime and terrorism, and the bribes demanded of foreigners, President Putin's emphasis on security has made Moscow safer for visitors than ever before. Slowly, Moscow is re-creating itself as one of the world's most urbane capitals and embracing innovation with the same sense of enterprise that helped it command and then survive history's most ambitious social experiment.

✈ INTERCITY TRANSPORTATION

Flights: International flights arrive at **Sheremetyevo-2** (Шереметьево-2; ☎956 46 66). Take the van under the "автолайн" sign in front of the station to M2: Rechnoy Vokzal (Речной Вокзал), or take bus #551 or 851 to M2: Rechnoy Vokzal or bus #517 to M8:

Planyornaya (Планёрная; 10R). Buses run 24hr., but the Metro stops running at 1am. Purchase bus tickets at the *kassa* (касса) at **Tsentralnyy Aerovokzal** (Центральный Аэровокзал; Central Airport Station), Leningradskiy pr. 37, corpus 6 (☎941 99 99), 2 stops on almost any tram or trolley from M2: Aeroport. **Taxis** to the center tend to be overpriced; bargain down to US$30. **Yellow Taxi** (☎940 88 88) has fixed prices. Cars outside the departures level charge US$15-20; agree on a price before getting in.

Air France, Koroviy Val 7 (Коровий Вал; ☎937 38 39; fax 937 38 38). M5: Dobryninskaya (Добрынинская). Open M-F 9am-6pm. Branch at Sheremetyevo-2, 2nd fl. (☎578 52 37). Open M-F 6:15am-4:15pm.

British Airways, 1-ya Tverskaya-Yamskaya 23 (1-я Тверская-Ямская; ☎363 25 25; www.britishair-ways.com). M2: Mayakovskaya (Маяковская). Open M-F 10am-7pm, Sa 10am-2pm.

Delta, 11 Gogolevskiy bul., 2nd fl. (Гоголевский; ☎937 90 90; www.delta.com). M1: Kropotkin-skaya (Кропоткинская). Open M-F 9am-6pm. Customer service by phone Sa 9am-1pm.

Finnair, Kropotkinskiy per. 7 (Кропоткинский; ☎933 00 56; www.finnair.com). M1 or 5: Park Kul-tury (Парк Культуры). Open M-F 9am-5pm. Branch at Sheremetyevo-2 (☎/fax 956 46 23).

Lufthansa, Olimpiyskiy pr. 18/1 (Олимпийский; ☎737 64 00; www.lufthansa.ru), in Hotel Renais-sance. M5 or 6: Prospekt Mira (Проспект Мира). Open M-F 9am-6pm, Sa 10am-3pm.

Trains: Moscow has 8 train stations arranged around the M5 (circle) line. Tickets for longer trips within Russia can be bought at the **Moskovskoye Zheleznodorozhnoye Agenstvo** (Московское Железнодорожное Агенство; Moscow Train Agency: ☎266 93 33; www.mza.ru), on the far side of Yaroslavskiy Vokzal from the Metro station. Tickets specify your name, seat, and station (вокзал; vokzal) of departure. Cyrillic schedules of trains, destinations, departure times, and station names are posted on both sides of the hall. *Kassa* open M-F 8am-7pm, Sa 8am-6pm, Su 8am-5pm. 24hr. service is avail-able at the stations. If you plan to take the **Trans-Siberian Railroad,** check out Travel-ler's Guest House, Hostel Sherstone, Hostel Tramp, or G&R Hostel Asia (see **Accommodations,** p. 581), who explain how the TSR works and arrange special tickets that allow you to skip the *kassa* and get on and off at all major cities along the way.

Belorusskiy Vokzal (Белорусский), pl. Tverskoi Zastavy 7 (☎251 60 93). To: **Berlin, GER** (27hr., 1 per day, 3500R); **Minsk, BLR** (10hr., 2-3 per day, 750R); **Prague, CZR** (35hr., 1 per day, 2860R); **Vilnius, LIT** (16hr., 1 per day, 1950R); **Warsaw, POL** (21hr., 2 per day, 2520R).

Kazanskiy Vokzal (Казанский), Komsomolskaya pl. 2 (Комсомольская; ☎264 65 56). M5: Komsomolskaya. Opposite Leningradskiy Vokzal. To **Kazan** (12hr., 2 per day, 600R).

Kievskiy Vokzal (Киевский), pl. Kievskogo Vokzala 2 (Киевского Вокзала; ☎240 04 15). M3, 5: Kievskaya (Киевская). To destinations in Ukraine, including **Kyiv** (14hr., 5 per day, 950R), **Lviv** (26hr., 1 per day, 1100R), and **Odessa** (25-28hr., 2-4 per day, 1100R).

Kurskiy Vokzal (Курский), Zemlyanoy Val 29/1 (Земляной Вал; ☎916 20 03). M3: Kurskaya (Курская). To **Sochi** (28hr., 1 per day, 1800R), **Sevastopol, UKR** (26hr., 1-2 per day, 1100R), and destinations in the **Caucasus.**

Leningradskiy Vokzal (Ленинградский), Komsomolskaya pl. 3 (☎262 91 43). M1 or 5: Komso-molskaya. To **St. Petersburg** (8hr., 10-15 per day, 700R), **Helsinki, FIN** (13hr., 1 per day, 2720R), and **Tallinn, EST** (14hr., 1 per day, 1550R).

Paveletskiy Vokzal (Павелецкий), Paveletskaya pl. 1 (Павелецкая; ☎235 68 07). M2: Pave-letskaya. Serves the **Crimea** and eastern **Ukraine.**

Rizhskiy Vokzal (Рижский), Prospekt Mira 79/3 (☎631 15 88). M6: Rizhskaya (Рижская). To **Rīga, LAT** (16hr., 2 per day, 2050R); and destinations in **Estonia.**

Yaroslavskiy Vokzal (Ярославский), Komsomolskaya pl. 5a (☎921 59 14). M1 or 5: Komsomol-skaya. The starting point for the legendary **Trans-Siberian Railroad.** To **Novosibirsk** (48hr., every other day, 1900R), **Siberia,** and the **Far East.**

✦ ORIENTATION

A series of concentric rings radiates from the **Kremlin** (Кремль; Kreml) and **Red Square** (Красная площадь; Krasnaya ploshchad). The outermost street, the **Mos-cow Ring** (Московское Кольцо; Moskovskoye Koltso), marks the city limits, but

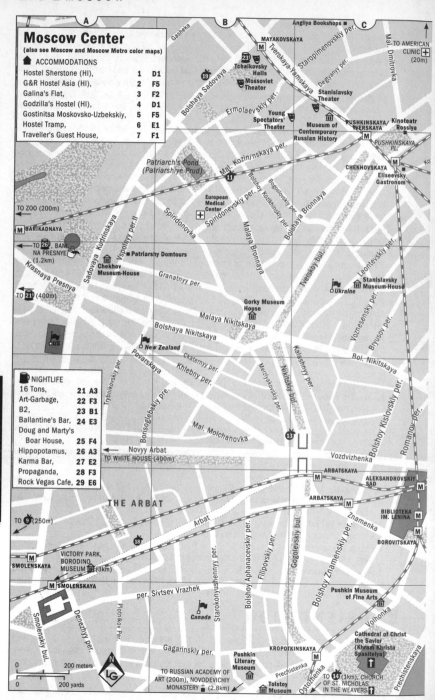

Moscow Center
(also see Moscow and Moscow Metro color maps)

♦ ACCOMMODATIONS

Hostel Sherstone (HI),	1	D1
G&R Hostel Asia (HI),	2	F5
Galina's Flat,	3	F2
Godzilla's Hostel (HI),	4	D1
Gostinitsa Moskovsko-Uzbekskiy,	5	F5
Hostel Tramp,	6	E1
Traveller's Guest House,	7	F1

🍺 NIGHTLIFE

16 Tons,	21	A3
Art-Garbage,	22	F3
B2,	23	B1
Ballantine's Bar,	24	E3
Doug and Marty's Boar House,	25	F4
Hippopotamus,	26	A3
Karma Bar,	27	E2
Propaganda,	28	F3
Rock Vegas Cafe,	29	E6

THE ARBAT

MOSCOW AND ST. PETERSBURG

Angliya Bookshops ■
MAYAKOVSKAYA
TO AMERICAN CLINIC (20m)
Tchaikovsky Halls
Tverskaya-Yamskaya
Staropimenovskiy per.
Degtyarny per.
Mal. Dmitrovka
Gasheka
Bolshaya Sadovaya
Mossoviet Theater
Stanislavsky Theater
Young Spectators' Theater
Ermolaevskiy per.
Museum of Contemporary Russian History
PUSHKINSKAYA/TVERSKAYA
Kinoteatr Rossiya
PUSHKINSKAYA PL.
Patriarch's Pond (Patriarshiye Prud)
Mal. Kozin/nskaya per.
Bolshoy Kozikhinskiy per.
Bogoslovskiy per.
CHEKHOVSKAYA
Eliseevsky Gastronom
Bolshaya Bronnaya
European Medical Center
Spiridonevskiy per.
Malaya Bronnaya
Tverskoy bul.
Leontevskiy per.
Stanislavsky Museum-House
TO ZOO (200m)
BARIKADNAYA
Spiridonovka
Vspolnyy per.I
Ukraine
Voznesenskiy per.
Bryusov per.
TO 26, BANI NA PRESNYE (1.2km)
Sadovaya Kudrinskaya
Patriarshy Domtours
Chekhov Museum-House
Granatnyy per.
Gorky Museum House
Malaya Nikitskaya
Bol. Nikitskaya
Krasnaya Presnya
TO 21 (400m)
US
New Zealand
Bolshaya Nikitskaya
Ckatemyy per.
Bolshoy Kislovskiy per.
Romanov per.
Povarskaya
Khlebny per.
Nikitsky bul.
Trubnikovskiy per.
Kalashnyy per.
Merzlyakovskiy per.
Borisoglebskiy pre.
Mal. Molchanovka
Novyy Arbat
TO WHITE HOUSE (400m)
Vozdvizhenka
ARBATSKAYA
ALEKSANDROVSKIY SAD
ARBATSKAYA
Znamenka
BIBLIOTEKA IM. LENINA
BOROVITSKAYA
TO 9 (250m)
Arbat
Bolshoy Aphanasevskiy per.
Filipovskiy per.
Gogolevskiy bul.
Bolshoy Znamenskiy per.
Pushkin Museum of Fine Arts
VICTORY PARK, BORODINO MUSEUM (3km)
SMOLENSKAYA
Volhonka
SMOLENSKAYA
per, Sivtsev Vrazhek
Starokonyushennyy per.
Canada
Bolshoy Znamenskiy per.
Cathedral of Christ the Savior (Khram Khrista Spasitelya)
Smolenskiy bul.
Denezhny per.
Plotnikov Per.
Gagarinskiy per.
Pushkin Literary Museum
KROPOTKINSKAYA
Prechistenka
Ostozhenka
Prechistenskaya
0 200 meters
0 200 yards
N
LG
TO RUSSIAN ACADEMY OF ART (200m), NOVODEVICHIY MONASTERY (2.8km)
Tolstoy Museum
TO 14 (1km), CHURCH OF ST. NICHOLAS IN THE WEAVERS

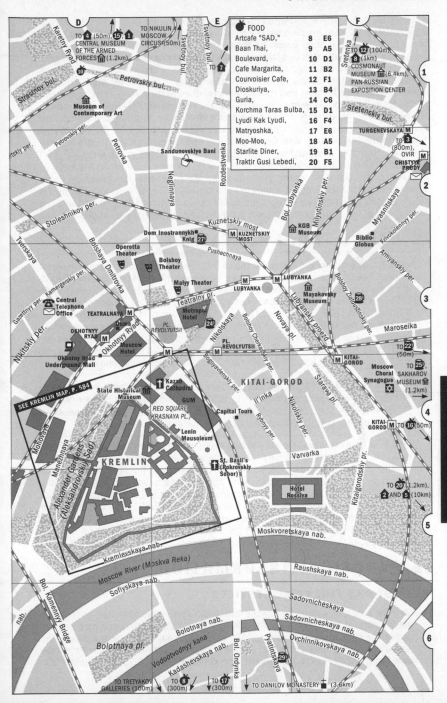

SEE KREMLIN MAP, P. 584

🍎 FOOD

Artcafe "SAD,"	8	E6
Baan Thai,	9	A5
Boulevard,	10	D1
Cafe Margarita,	11	B2
Courvoisier Cafe,	12	F1
Dioskuriya,	13	B4
Guria,	14	C6
Korchma Taras Bulba,	15	D1
Lyudi Kak Lyudi,	16	F4
Matryoshka,	17	E6
Moo-Moo,	18	A5
Starlite Diner,	19	B1
Traktir Gusi Lebedi,	20	F5

MOSCOW AND ST. PETERSBURG

Muscovites divide the world into two regions: the area that lies within the **Garden Ring** (Садовное Кольцо; Sadovnoe Koltso), and the area that doesn't. Most sights are within. The tree-lined **Boulevard Ring**, made up of 10 short, wide boulevards, makes an incomplete circle within the center. **Tverskaya** (Тверская), considered Moscow's main street, begins just north of Red Square and continues northwest along the green line of the Metro. The **Arbat** (Арбат) and **Novyy Arbat** (Новый Арбат), Moscow's hippest and most commercialized streets respectively, lie west of the Kremlin. **Zamoskvareche** (Замоскваречe) and **Krymskiy Val** (Крымский Вал), the neighborhoods directly across the **Moscow River** to the south of Red Square, are home to numerous pubs, museums, mansions, and monasteries. To the east of Red Square is the 9th-century **Kitai-Gorod** (Китай-Город) neighborhood, packed with towering churches and bustling thoroughfares. English and Cyrillic **maps** (35-60R) are sold at kiosks and bookstores all over. See this book's color insert for maps of the Metro and the city center. Note that the Metro station Izmailovskiy Park, located on line 3, has changed names to Partizanskaya (Партизанская). Be careful when crossing streets, as drivers are notoriously oblivious to pedestrians; for safety's sake, most intersections have an underpass (переход; perekhod).

⌐ LOCAL TRANSPORTATION

Public Transportation: The **Metro** (Метро) is fast, clean, and efficient—a masterpiece of urban planning. A station serving more than 1 line may have more than 1 name. The M5 is known as the circle line (кольцевая линия; koltsevaya liniya). Trains run daily 6am-1:30am; changes between stations close at 1am. Rush hours are 8-10am and 5-7pm. Buy fare cards (10R; 5 trips 45R, 10 trips 75R) from *kassy* in stations. Buy **bus** and **trolleybus** tickets (10R) at kiosks labeled "проездные билеты" (*proyyezdnye bilety*), and from the driver. Punch your ticket when you board or risk a 100R fine. Buses run 24hr. Monthly passes (единые билеты; *yedinyye bilety*), valid for bus, trolleybus, tram, and Metro are sold at Metro *kassy* after the 18th of the preceding month (500R).

> **METRO MADNESS.** Moscow's subway system can seem bewildering. *Let's Go* has tried to simplify navigation by artificially numbering each line; for correspondences, consult this guide's color map of the Moscow Metro. When speaking with Russians, however, use the color or name, and not the number.

Taxis: Most taxis do not use meters and tend to overcharge. **Yellow Taxis** charge 10R per km (15R after midnight). Hailing cars on the street is common in Moscow, and a cheaper option than a taxi. Moscovites hold an arm out horizontally (no thumb extended); when the driver stops, they tell him their destination and haggle over the price. Within the Garden Ring, a ride to almost anywhere is 100R; shorter trips cost around 50R. Be aware that even if you hail a car marked "taxi," you may still have to haggle, as many drivers use taxi markings simply to attract riders. If you're not fluent, be prepared to gesture. To be safe, never get into a taxi or car with more than 1 person already in it. *Let's Go* does not recommend hitchhiking.

⬛ PRACTICAL INFORMATION

TOURIST AND FINANCIAL SERVICES

Tours: The folks with loudspeakers on the north end of Red Square hawk Russian-language walking tours of the area (1hr., every 30min. 10am-12:30pm, 80R) and excellent bus tours of the city's main sights (1½hr., 150R). Translators are sometimes available for an extra charge. Many hostels also arrange tours. English-language tours include: **Patriarshy Dom Tours,** Vspolny per. 6 (Вспольньй; from the US ☎650 678 70 76, in Russia 095

795 09 27; http://russiatravel-pdtours.netfirms.com). M5 or 7: Barrikadnaya. Offers a wide selection of English language tours including a special behind-the-scenes tour of the former KGB headquarters (US$18). A schedule of their tours is available at various hotels and expat hangouts, including the Starlite diner. They also help with airline booking, Russian language classes, and visa support. Open M-F 9am-6pm and Sa 11am-5pm. **Capital Tours,** Ilyinka 4 (☎232 24 42; www.capitaltours.ru). M3: Ploschad Revolutsii. Offers 3hr. English-language bus tours of the city center; they cover everything from Cathedral of Christ the Savior to the Bolshoy Theater. Tours (US$20) daily 11am and 2:30pm. 3hr. tours (US$37) of the Kremlin and armory M-W and F-Su 10:30am and 3pm. MC/V.

Budget Travel: Student Travel Agency Russia (STAR), Baltiyskaya 9, 3rd fl. (Балтийская; ☎797 95 55; www.startravel.ru). M2: Sokol (Сокол). Discount plane tickets, ISICs, and worldwide hostel booking. Open M-F 10am-7pm, Sa 11am-4pm.

Embassies: Australia, Podkoloniy per. 10/2 (☎956 60 70). M6: Kitai Gorod (Китай Город). M3 or 5: Smolenskaya/Park Kultury (Смоленская/Парк Культуры). Open M-F 9:30am-12:30pm. **Canada,** Starokonyushennyy per. 23 (Староконюшенный; ☎105 60 00). M1: Kropotkinskaya or M4: Arbatskaya (Арбатская). Open M-F 8:30am-1pm and 2-5pm. **Ireland,** Grokholskiy per. 5 (Грохольский; ☎937 59 11). M5 or 6: Prospekt Mira. Open M-F 9:30am-1pm and 2:30-5:30pm. **New Zealand,** Povarskaya 44 (Поварская; ☎956 35 79). M7: Barikadnaya (Барикадная). Open M-F 9am-5:30pm. **UK,** Smolenskaya nab. 10 (Смоленская; ☎956 72 00; www.britemb.msk.ru). M3: Smolenskaya. Open M-F 9am-1pm and 2-5pm. **US,** Novinskiy 19/23 (Новинский; ☎728 50 00; www.usembassy.ru). M5: Krasnoprenenskaya (Краснопресненская). Open M-F 9am-6pm. **American Citizen Services** (☎728 55 77, after-hours 728 50 00) lists English-speaking establishments. Open M-F 9-10:30am and 2-4pm.

Currency Exchange: Banks are everywhere; check for ads in English-language newspapers. Typically only main branches change **traveler's checks** or issue **cash advances.** Almost all banks and hotels have **ATMs** that allow withdrawals in either US$ or rubles. Avoid machines protruding from buildings; they work erratically, and withdrawing cash on busy streets makes you a target for muggers. Indoor ATMs are invariably safer. Many ATMs do not take Visa; look for signs on the machines to know which cards they accept.

American Express: Usacheva 33 (☎933 84 00). M1: Sportivnaya. Use the exit at the front of the train, turn right, and then right again after the Global USA shop onto Usacheva. Open M-F 9am-6pm.

THE LOCAL STORY

FORM AND FUNCTION

With over 165 stations and almost 9 million passengers per day, the Moscow metro system is a tourist attraction in itself. Add the fact that many stations were designed by the Soviet Union's leading architects and artists, and you've got a virtual museum of Socialist Realist art available to anyone for the price of a metro ticket. Construction began on the first stations in 1931, executed by men and women drafted from all across the nation, soldiers from the Red Army, and more than 13,000 volunteers from the *Komsomol,* or Communist Youth League.

The yellow-and-gold **Komsomolskaya** station (M:1 and 5), named after the organization, was planned by Aleksey Shchusev, who won a prize at the New York World's Fair for its elaborate chandelier-accented design. Station art quickly developed a functional dimension. Some acted as state propaganda, like the red star formed by the station entrance to **Arbatskaya** (M:3). Similarly, **Ploshchad Revolutsii** (M:3) features two rows of bronze statues commemorating the role ordinary citizens played in establishing the Soviet State. Others were built deep underground to function as bomb shelters during war time. **Mayakaovskaya** (M:2), also a winner at the New York World's Fair, became the headquarters of the Anti-Aircraft Defense Forces in 1941.

Lost Cards: (☎956 08 29). The AmEx, Visa, MasterCard, Diner's Club, and JCB cards center can help cancel lost or stolen credit cards.

LOCAL SERVICES

English-Language Bookstores: Anglia British Bookshop, Vorotnikovskiy per. 6 (Воротниковский; ☎299 77 66; www.anglophile.ru). M2: Mayakovskaya. Large selection includes travel guides, phrasebooks, translated Russian literature, and English and American fiction. ISIC discount. Open M-F 10am-7pm, Sa 10am-6pm, Su 11am-5pm. AmEx/MC/V. **Biblio-Globus,** Miasnitskaya 6/3 (781 19 00; www.biblio-globus.ru). M7: Lubyanka. Additional locations around the city. English and German sections including classics, dictionaries, and fiction. Open M-F 9am-9pm, Sa-Su 10am-8pm.

English-Language Press: The *Moscow Tribune* and the more widely read *Moscow Times* (www.themoscowtimes.com) have foreign and national articles and weekend sections listing upcoming events, English-language movies, housing, and job opportunities. Moscow's infamous "alternative" paper, *The eXile* (www.exile.ru), is one of the funniest, most irreverent publications on earth, but is not for the easily shocked. Nightlife section is indispensably candid, though undeniably crude. *Where* magazine (www.whererussia.com), publishes monthly shopping, dining, and entertainment listings and has excellent maps, while weekly *Element* magazine has good club listings.

EMERGENCY AND COMMUNICATIONS

Emergencies: Police: ☎02. **Ambulance:** ☎03. **Fire:** ☎01. **Lost property:** Metro ☎222 20 85, other transport 298 32 41. **Lost documents:** ☎200 99 57. **Lost credit cards:** AmEx ☎755 90 01, other cards 956 48 06. **Int. Medical Clinic:** ☎280 71 71.

24hr. Pharmacies: Look for signs marked "круглосуточно" (*kruglosutochno;* always open). Locations include: Tverskaya 25 (☎299 24 59), M2: Tverskaya/Mayakovskaya; Zemlyanoi Val 25 (☎917 12 85), M5: Kurskaya; Kutozovskiy Prospekt 24 (Кутозовский; ☎249 19 37), M4: Kutuzovskaya (Кутузовская).

Medical Services:

American Medical Center (AMC), Grokholskiy per. 1 (☎933 77 00). M5 or 6: Prospekt Mira. Turn left out of the Metro onto Grokholskiy per. Walk-in medical care US$120 per visit. Open 24hr. AmEx/MC/V.

American Clinic, Grokholskiy per. 31 (☎937 57 57; http://americanclinic.ru). M5 or 6: Prospekt Mira. Same directions as for AMC. American board-certified doctors; family and internal medicine services. Consultations US$100. House calls US$150. Open 24hr. MC/V.

European Medical Clinic, Spiridoniyevskiy Per. 5/1 (☎933 65 55; www.emcmos.ru). Offers dental, gynecological, pediatric, and psychiatric care. Consultations US$120. Open 24hr.

Telephones: Moscow Central Telegraph (see **Post Offices,** below). Go to the 2nd hall with telephones to place international calls. Prepay at the counter or buy a prepaid phonecard. Collect calls and calling card calls not available. Calls to the US 9-20R per min., to Europe 12-35R per min. **Local calls** require phone cards, available at kiosks and some Metro stops. Dial ☎09 for directory assistance.

Internet: Timeonline (☎254 95 78), on the bottom level of the Okhotnyy Ryad (Охотный Ряд) mall, near Red Square. M1: Okhotnyy Ryad. At night, enter through the Metro underpass. 30-75R per hr. Open 24hr. **Cafemax** (☎787 68 58; www.cafemax.ru). Massive, modern Internet cafe has 3 locations, with English-speaking staff: Pyatnitskaya 25/1m (M2: Novokuznetskaya), Akademika Khokhlova 3 (M1: Universitet), and Novoslobodskaya 3 (M9: Novoslobodskaya). 70R per hr. Open 24hr.

Post Offices: Moscow Central Telegraph, Tverskaya ul. 7, uphill from the Kremlin. M1: Okhotnyy Ryad. Look for the globe and the digital clock. **International mail** at window #23. **Faxes** at #11-12. **Telegram** service available. Open M-F 8am-2pm and 3-8pm, Sa-Su 7am-2pm and 3-7pm. **Poste Restante** at window #24. Bring packages unwrapped; they will be wrapped and mailed for you. **Postal Code:** 103 009.

✏ ACCOMMODATIONS

Although the best deals are often found in Soviet standard-issue hotels, these tend to have receptionists with very limited English. Older women standing outside major rail stations often rent **private rooms** (сдаю комнату) or apartments (сдаю квартиру)—be sure to haggle.

🏨 **Godzilla's Hostel (HI),** Bolshoy Karetniy 6/5 (Большой Каретний; ☎299 42 23; www.godzillashostel.com). M9: Tsvetnoy Bulvar. Great location, 7min. from Pushkin Square and 20min. from the Kremlin. English spoken. Co-ed dorms unless you specify in advance. Reception 24hr. Check-out noon. Dorms US$25; doubles US$60. ❷

🏨 **Galina's Flat,** Chaplygina 8, 5th fl. #35 (Чаплыгина; ☎921 60 38; galinas.flat@mtu-net.ru). M1: Chistyye Prudy. Head down Chistoprudnyy bul., take a left on Bol. Kharitonevskiy per., then a right on Chaplygina. Go into the courtyard at #8, veer right, and enter the building with the "КВ35-36" sign. Superb location. Galina and her cats provide real hospitality. Airport transport US$30-35. Breakfast 60R. Reserve ahead. Dorms US$10; singles US$18; doubles US$25. ❷

Travellers Guest House (TGH), Bolshaya Pereslavskaya 50, 10th fl. (Болшая Переславская; ☎631 40 59; www.tgh.ru). M5 or 6: Prospekt Mira. Take the 2nd right across from Prospekt Mira 61, walk to the end of the *pereulok*, and go left on B. Pereyaslavskaya. Its popularity among English-speaking travelers reveals the dearth of quality budget accommodations in Moscow. Lax security and sometimes lackluster, if English-speaking, staff. Take advantage of their luggage storage and make sure your shared room is locked at night. Visa invitations (US$50, guests US$30). Kitchen access. Airport transport US$40. Breakfast included. Luggage storage 10R per bag. Laundry service 150R per 3kg. Internet 2R per min. Check-out 11am. Dorms 750R; singles 1450R; doubles 1750R, with bath 1900R. 30R HI discount. MC/V. ❹

Gostinitsa Moskovsko-Uzbekskiy, Zelenodolskaya 3/2 (Зеленодольская; ☎378 33 92 or 378 21 77; hotel@caravan.ru). M7: Ryazanskiy Prospekt (Рязанский). Exit the Metro near the back car of the outbound train. A "Гостиница" sign will be visible on top of the hotel to your left. A wide range of rooms; non-renovated ones are clean and ultra-cheap. 500R key deposit. Singles 750-1200R; doubles 1000-2000R. ❷

G&R Hostel Asia (HI), Zelenodolskaya 3/2 (Зеленодольская; ☎378 00 01; www.hostels.ru). M7: Ryazanskiy Prospekt. On the 5th fl. of the Gostinitsa Moskovsko-Uzbekskiy (see above). Clean rooms. Helpful staff. Visa invitations €25-35. Airport transport €30-35. Internet 2R per min. Reception daily 8am-midnight. Singles €25-40; doubles €40-55; triples €81. €1 HI discount. 10th day free. V. ❸

Hostel Sherstone (HI), Gostinichny proezd 8 (Гостиничны; ☎783 34 38; www.sherstone.ru). M9: Vladykino. Walk along the railway turning left from the Metro as far as the overpass, then take a left and go past a post office. Be careful at night. On the 3rd fl. of the Hotel Sherstone. Visa invitations €30. Breakfast included. Internet 2R per min. Reception (room 324) 8am-midnight. Dorms €17; singles €45; doubles €46. €1 HI discount. MC/V. ❷

Hostel Tramp, Selskohozyaistvennaya 17/2 (☎187 54 33; www.hostelling.ru). M6: Botanicheskiy Sad. From the Metro station, go left on Vilgelma Pika and walk to Gostinitsa Turist. The hostel is in Gostina building #7; reception is in room #524. Singles and doubles are clean and simple with private baths. Breakfast included. Singles US$49; doubles US$56. 10% off for HI or ISIC members. ❹

◖ FOOD

Restaurants range from the expensive to the outrageous. Those that serve local cuisine tend to be more affordable, and many higher-priced places now offer business lunch specials (бизнес ланч; typically noon-3pm; US$4-8). Russians dine in the late evening; avoid crowds by eating earlier. **Eliseevskiy Gastronom** (Елисеевский), Tverskaya 14, is Moscow's most famous supermarket. (☎209 07 60. Open M-Sa 8am-9pm, Su 10am-8pm.) For fresh produce, head to a **market**. Some of the best are by the **Turgenyevskaya** and **Kuznetsky Most** Metro stations. (Open daily 10am-8pm.) To find grocery stores, look for "продукти" (produkty) signs.

REGIONAL CUISINE AND CAFES

▨ **Lyudi Kak Lyudi** (Люди как Люди; "People like People"), Solyanskiy Tupik 1/4 (☎921 12 01). Enter from Solyanka. A favorite of young Russians. Business lunch is the cheapest in the city (soup, salad, and sandwich or *pierogi*; 110R). Smoothies 80R. Sandwiches 70R. Open M-Th 8am-11pm, F 8am-6am, Sa 11am-6am, Su 11am-10pm. ❶

▨ **Korchma Taras Bulba** (Корчма Тарас Бульба), Sadovaya-Samotechnaya 13 (☎200 00 56). M9: Tsvetnoy Bulvar. From the Metro, turn left and walk up Tsvetnoy bul. Any place with a 24hr. feedback hotline obviously takes service seriously. Delicious Ukrainian specialities. English menu. Entrees 140-400R. Open 24hr. MC/V. 12 locations. ❸

▨ **Cafe Margarita** (Кафе Маргарита), Malaya Bronnaya 28 (Малая Вронная; ☎299 65 34), at the intersection with Malyy Kozikhinskiy per. (Малый Козихинский). M2: Mayakovskaya. Go left on Bolshaya Sadovaya and left on Malaya Bronaya. Named for the 1930s novel, *The Master and Margarita*, this cozy, book-lined cafe capitalizes upon its proximity to author Mikhail Bulgakov's former apartment building a block away. Entrees 250-400R. Cover 100R during nights with music. Open daily 1pm-midnight. ❹

Matryoshka, (Матрёшка) Klimentovskiy per. 10 (☎953 94 00). Exit the Metro and restaurant is on nearby Klimentovskiy, off bul. Ordynka. Tasty, inexpensive Russian entrees from 150R. Open noon-midnight. Also at Triumfalnaya 1 (☎727 96 51). ❷

Guria (Гуриа), Komsomolskiy pr. 7/3 (Комсомольский; ☎246 03 78), opposite St. Nicholas of the Weavers. M1 or 5: Park Kultury. Walk behind 7/3 until you reach the restaurant; ask for the Georgian restaurant if you get lost (G-dye gruZINski restaRAN?) Tasty Georgian fare for some of the city's lowest prices; convenient to Gorky Park and the art galleries. Vegetarian options. Entrees 80-250R. Open daily noon-midnight. ❷

Courvoisier Cafe, Malaya Sukharevskaya pl. 8, bldg. 1 (Малая Сухаревкая; ☎924 82 42; www.courvoisier-cafe.ru). M6: Sukharevskaya. Rub elbows with the Moscow elite while enjoying tasty entrees (220-350R). Breakfast 5-11:30am. Open 24hr. MC/V. ❸

Artcafe "SAD" (Арткафе "САД"), Bul. Tolmachevskiy per. 3 (Толмачевский; ☎239 91 15), across from Krymskiy Val. M2, 6 or 8: Tretyakovskaya. Romantic atmosphere and great service, but English is rare. Entrees 150-360R. Open 10am-midnight. ❸

Moo-Moo (My-My), Koroviy Val 1 (☎237 29 00), M5 Dobryninskaya; and Arbat 45/42 (☎241 13 64), M4: Smolenskaya. Look for the chain's signature cow statue outside. Moo-moo's many locations offer cheap, tasty European and Russian home cooking, served cafeteria-style. Salads 40R. Pork cutlets 54R. Open daily 9am-11pm. ❶

Traktir Gusi Lebedi (Трактир Гуси Лебеди), Nikolayamskaya 28/60 (☎502 99 08). M5 or 7: Taganskaya. Walk down Zemlyanoy Val and go left on Nikolayamskaya. Modeled on a hunting lodge. Waitresses wear cartridge belts, but, as far as we know, they're not actually packing heat. Entrees 160-395R. Open daily 11am-midnight. MC/V. ❸

Dioskuriya, Merzlyakovskiy per. 2 (Мерзляковский; 290 69 08; www.dioskuriya.narod.ru). M4: Arbatskaya. Good Georgian eats close to the city center. Entrees 100-280R. Live Georgian music 7-11pm nightly. Open daily 11am-midnight. ❷

INTERNATIONAL CUISINE AND CAFES

Boulevard, Petrovka 30/7 (☎209 68 87). M2, 7 or 9: Pushkinskaya. Boasting French-inspired cuisine, Boulevard has survived by dint of its always high-quality food. Entrees from 590R; 10% off before 4pm. Open daily noon-midnight. AmEx/DC/MC/V. ❺

Baan Thai, Bolshaya Dorogomilovskaya 11 (☎240 05 97; www.baanthai.ru). M3, 4, or 5: Kievskaya. Pricey but authentic Thai cuisine. *Baa mee phad* (garlic noodle stir-fry) 180R. Open daily noon-midnight. AmEx/MC/V. ❹

Starlite Diner, Bolshaya Sadovaya 16 (☎290 96 38). M2: Mayakovskaya. Walk down Bolshaya Sadovaya toward the Mayakovskiy statue. American diner serves cheeseburgers with fries (210R) and delicious milkshakes (280R). Packed with expats on weekends. Free Wi-Fi. All-day breakfast. Entrees 350-599R. Open 24hr. AmEx/MC/V. ❸

◎ SIGHTS

Moscow's sights reflect the city's interrupted history: because St. Petersburg was the tsar's seat for 200 years, there are 16th-century churches and Soviet-era museums, but little in-between. Though Moscow has no grand palaces, and 80% of its pre-revolutionary splendor was demolished by the Soviet regime, the city's museums contain the very best of Russian art, and there is history around every corner.

THE KREMLIN

Enter through Borovitskaya gate tower in the southwest corner if you're going to the Armory; otherwise, enter between the kassy. Buy tickets at the kassa in Alexander Gardens. ☎202 37 76; www.kremlin.museum.ru. M1, 3, 4, or 9: Aleksandrovskiy Sad. Open M-W and F-Su 10am-5pm; kassy open 9:30am-4:30pm. Entrance to the Kremlin territory and all cathedrals 300R, students 150R. Ask for Cathedral Entrance. Audioguides 220R. English-speaking guides offer expensive tours; haggle away. Camera 50R. Buy separate tickets for the Armory. No large bags. Bag check (60R, camera 30R) is in the Alexander Gardens, under the arch (see map).

The Kremlin (Кремль; Kreml) is Moscow's historical center and the birthplace of much of Russian history and religion. It was here that Napoleon simmered while Moscow burned and here that the Congress of People's Deputies dissolved itself in 1991, breaking up the USSR. Much of the triangular complex is closed to tourists; the watchful police will blow whistles if you stray into a forbidden zone.

▌ARMORY MUSEUM AND DIAMOND FUND. The most beautiful treasures of the Russian state can be found in the Armory and Diamond Fund (Оружейная Палата и Выставка Алмазного Фонда; Oruzheynaya Palata i Vystavka Almaznogo Fonda). Room 2, on the 2nd floor, holds the legendary Fabergé Eggs and the royal silver. Room 6 holds pieces of the royal wardrobe. The thrones of Ivan the Terrible and Elizabeth stand imposingly next to the hats of Peter the Great and Vladimir Monomakh in Room 7. The **Diamond Fund** has still more glitter, including a 190-carat diamond given to Catherine the Great by Gregory Orlov, a "special friend." Among the emerald necklaces and ruby rings of the tsars are Soviet-era finds, including the world's largest chunks of **platinum.** *(To the left as you enter the Kremlin by the Armory entrance. ☎229 20 36. Open M-W and F-Su. Armory lets in groups for 1½hr. visits at 10am, noon, 2:30, 4:30pm. 350R, students 175R. Camera 50R. Diamond Fund lets in groups every 20min. 10am-1pm and 2-6pm. 350R, students 250R. Group size is limited; buy tickets early. Bags and cameras must be checked before entering Diamond Fund.)*

CATHEDRAL SQUARE. From the Armory, head to Cathedral Square, home of the most famous golden domes in Russia. The first church to the left, **Annunciation Cathedral** (Благовещунский Собор; Blagoveshchenskiy Sobor), guards the loveliest iconostasis in the country, with luminous icons by Andrei Rublyov and Theophanes the Greek. Originally only three-domed, the cathedral was enlarged and gilded by Ivan the Terrible. The 2nd entrance is also his; Ivan's seven marriages made him ineligible to enter the church; as penance, he was forced to stand on the porch during services. Across the way, the **Archangel Cathedral** (Архангельский Собор; Arkhangelskiy Sobor), with vivid icons, colorful fres-

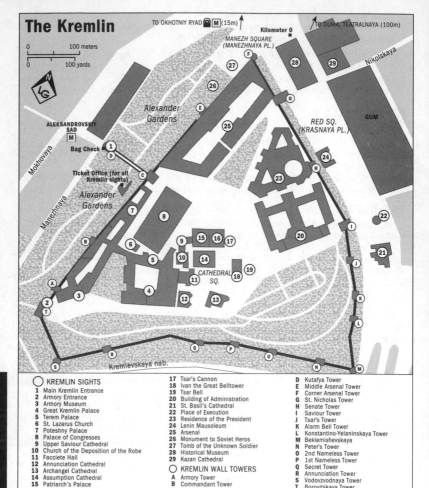

The Kremlin

TO OKHOTNIY RYAD 📷 Ⓜ (15m)

Kilometer 0

TO DUMA, TEATRALNAYA (100m)

MANEZH SQUARE (MANEZHNAYA PL.)

0 — 100 meters
0 — 100 yards

Alexander Gardens

ALEKSANDROVSKIY SAD Ⓜ

Bag Check

Ticket Office (for all Kremlin sights)

Alexander Gardens

Mokhovaya

Manezhnaya

Nikolskaya

RED SQ. (KRASNAYA PL.)

GUM

CATHEDRAL SQ.

Kremlevskaya nab.

○ KREMLIN SIGHTS
1 Main Kremlin Entrance
2 Armory Entrance
3 Armory Museum
4 Great Kremlin Palace
5 Terem Palace
6 St. Lazarus Church
7 Poteshny Palace
8 Palace of Congresses
9 Upper Saviour Cathedral
10 Church of the Deposition of the Robe
11 Facciete Hall
12 Annunciation Cathedral
13 Archangel Cathedral
14 Assumption Cathedral
15 Patriarch's Palace
16 Cathedral of the Twelve Apostles

17 Tsar's Cannon
18 Ivan the Great Belltower
19 Tsar Bell
20 Building of Administration
21 St. Basil's Cathedral
22 Place of Execution
23 Residence of the President
24 Lenin Mausoleum
25 Arsenal
26 Monument to Soviet Heros
27 Tomb of the Unknown Soldier
28 Historical Museum
29 Kazan Cathedral

○ KREMLIN WALL TOWERS
A Armory Tower
B Commandant Tower
C Trinity Tower

D Kutafya Tower
E Middle Arsenal Tower
F Corner Arsenal Tower
G St. Nicholas Tower
H Senate Tower
I Saviour Tower
J Tsar's Tower
K Alarm Bell Tower
L Konstantino-Yelaninskaya Tower
M Beklemishevskaya
N Peter's Tower
O 2nd Nameless Tower
P 1st Nameless Tower
Q Secret Tower
R Annunciation Tower
S Vodovzvodnaya Tower
T Borovitskaya Tower

coes, and metallic coffins, is the final resting place of many tsars who ruled before Peter the Great. Ivans III (the Great) and IV (the Terrible) rest beside the iconostasis; Mikhail Romanov is by the front right column. The center of Cathedral Square is **Assumption Cathedral** (Успенский Собор; Uspenskiy Sobor), one of the oldest religious buildings in Russia, dating from the 15th century. Napoleon used it as a stable in 1812. To the right of Uspenskiy Sobor stands **Ivan the Great Belltower** (Колокольная Ивана Великого; Kolokolnaya Ivana Velikogo), which holds exhibitions. The tower is visible over 30km away.

OTHER KREMLIN SIGHTS. Directly behind the bell tower is the **Tsar Bell** (Царь-колокол; Tsar-kolokol). The world's largest bell, it has never rung—an 11½-ton piece broke off after a 1737 fire. Behind Assumption Cathedral stands the **Patriarch's Palace** (Патриарший Дворец; Patriarshiy Dvorets), site of the **Museum of 17th-Century Russian Applied Art and Life** and the **Cathedral of the Twelve Apostles**

(Собор Двенадцати Апостолов; Sobor Dvenadtsati Apostolov). To the left of Assumption Cathedral and next to the Patriarch's Palace is the small **Church of the Deposition of the Robe.** The only other building inside the Kremlin that you can enter is the **Kremlin Palace of Congresses,** a square, white monster built by Khrushchev in 1961 for Communist Party Congresses. The giant bas-relief of Lenin that once dominated has been removed, and the space is used as a **theater** for the Kremlin Ballet Company and other performances.

RED SQUARE

Red Square (Красная Площадь; Krasnaya Ploshchad) has been the site of everything from a giant farmer's market to public hangings. On one side of the 700m long square is the **Kremlin;** on the other is **GUM,** once the world's largest purveyor of Soviet "consumer goods," now an upscale mall. **St. Basil's Cathedral,** the **State Historical Museum,** the **Lenin Mausoleum,** and **Kazan Cathedral** flank the square. You can buy a combined ticket (230R, students 115R) for St. Basil's Cathedral and the State Historical museum at either location.

ST. BASIL'S CATHEDRAL. There is nothing more symbolic of Moscow—or Russia—than the colorful onion domes of St. Basil's Cathedral (Собор Василия Блаженного; Sobor Vasiliya Blazhennogo). Commissioned by Ivan the Terrible to celebrate his 1552 victory over the Tatars in Kazan, it was completed in 1561. The cathedral bears the name of a holy fool, Vasily (Basil in English), who correctly predicted that Ivan would murder his own son. The labyrinthine interior, unusual for Orthodox churches, is filled with both decorative and religious frescoes. *(M3: Ploshchad Revolyutsii (Площадь Революции). Buy tickets from the kassa to the left of the entrance, then proceed upstairs. ☎ 298 33 04. Open daily 11am-6pm; kassa closes 5:30pm. 100R, students 50R. Services Su 10am. Tours 350R. Camera 100R, video 130R.)*

LENIN'S TOMB. Lenin's likeness can be seen in bronze all over the city, but here he appears eerily in the flesh. In the glory days, this squat red structure (Мфвзщлуй ВюИю Лунинф; Mavzoley V.I. Lenina) was guarded fiercely, and the wait to enter took hours. Today's line is still long and the guards are still stone-faced, but visitors now exude curiosity, not reverence. Entrance includes access to the **Kremlin wall,** where Stalin, Brezhnev, Andropov, Gagarin, and John Reed (founder of the American Communist Labor Party) are buried. During the hours that the mausoleum is open, access to Red Square is limited. The line to see Lenin forms between the Historical Museum and the Kremlin wall; arrive at least by noon to have a chance of making it through. *(Open Tu-Th and Sa-Su 10am-1pm. Free. No cameras or cell phones; check them at the bag check in the Alexander Gardens.)*

STATE DEPARTMENT STORE GUM. Built in the 19th century, GUM (Государствунный Унивурсальный Магазин (ГУМ); Gosudarstvennyy Universalnyy Magazin) was designed to hold 1000 stores. Its arched, wrought-iron and glass roofs resemble a Victorian train station. During Soviet rule, GUM's 1000 empty stores were a depressing sight. Today, it's depressing only to those who can't afford the designer goods (almost everyone). The renovated complex is an upscale arcade of boutiques and restaurants. *(M3: Ploshchad Revolyutsii. From the Metro, turn left, then left again at the gate to Red Square. ☎ 921 57 63. Open daily 10am-10pm.)*

STATE HISTORICAL MUSEUM. This comprehensive collection traces Russian history from the Neanderthals through Kyivan Rus to modern Russia. The museum (Государственный Исторический Музей; Gosudarstvennyy Istoricheskiy Muzey) provides printed info in English to help visitors make sense of its vastness. *(Krasnaya pl. 1/2. M1: Okhotnyy Ryad. Entrance by Red Square. ☎ 292 37 31; www.museums.ru/M296. Open M and W-Sa 10am-6pm, Su 11am-8pm; kassa closes 1hr. earlier; closed 1st M of month. 150R, students 75R. Camera 80R, video 100R.)*

KAZAN CATHEDRAL. The charming pink-and-green cathedral (Кфзфнский Сцбщз; Kazanskiy Sobor)was rebuilt and reopened for services after being demolished in 1936 to make way for the May 1 parades. *(M3: Ploshchad Revolyutsii. Opposite the State Historical Museum, just to the left of the main entrance to Red Square. Open daily 8am-8pm. Services M-Sa 9am, 5pm; Su 7am, 10am, 5pm. Free. No flash photography.)*

NORTH OF RED SQUARE

AREAS FOR WALKING. Just outside the main gate to Red Square is an elaborate gold circle marking **Kilometer 0,** the spot from which all distances from Moscow are measured. But don't be fooled by this tourist attraction—the real Kilometer 0 lies below the Lenin Mausoleum. Around the corner, the **Alexander Gardens** (Александровский Сад; Aleksandrovskiy Sad) are a respite from the urban bustle of central Moscow. At the north end of the gardens is the **Tomb of the Unknown Soldier** (Могила Неизвестного Солдата; Mogila Neizvestnogo Soldata), where an **eternal flame** burns in memory of the catastrophic losses suffered in WWII.

AREAS FOR SHOPPING. Bordering Red Square are two other major squares. On the west side is **Manezh Square** (Манежная Площадь; Manezhnaya Ploshchad), recently converted into a pedestrian area. The Manezh, which formerly served as the Kremlin stables and an exhibition hall, burned down in March 2004 and was rebuilt to look exactly the same. The famous **Moscow Hotel,** demolished in late 2004 and scheduled to be rebuilt within the next two years, separates Manezh Sq. from the older, smaller **Revolution Square** (Площадь Революции; Ploshchad Revolyutsii). The squares are connected in the north by **Okhotnyy Ryad** (Охотный Ряд; Hunters' Row), once a market for wild game. Now a ritzy underground mall, Okhotnyy Ryad is full of new trends and New Russians. Across Okhotnyy Ryad from the Moscow Hotel is the **Duma,** the lower house of Parliament; across from Revolution Sq. is **Theater Square** (Театральная Площадь; Teatralnaya Ploshchad), home of the **Bolshoy** and **Malyy Theaters** (see **Entertainment,** p. 592). Lined with posh hotels, chic stores, government buildings, and the homes of Moscow's richest, **Tverskaya** is the closest the city has to a main street.

RELIGIOUS SIGHTS

If the grime and bedlam get to you, escape to one of Moscow's houses of worship. Before the Revolution, the city had more than 1000 churches. Today, there are fewer than 100, though many are being restored. *(No shorts. Women should cover their heads and bare shoulders with scarves and wear long skirts.)*

CATHEDRAL OF CHRIST THE SAVIOR. Moscow's most controversial landmark is the enormous, gold-domed Cathedral of Christ the Savior (Храм Христа Спасителя; Khram Khrista Spasitelya). Stalin demolished Nicholas I's original cathedral on this site to make way for a huge Palace of the Soviets, but Khrushchev abandoned the project and built a heated pool instead. In 1995, after the pool's water vapors damaged works in the nearby Pushkin Museum, Mayor Yury Luzhkov and the Orthodox Church won a renewed battle for the site and built the US$250 million cathedral in five years. *(Volkhonka 15, between Volkhonka (Волхонка) and the Moscow River. M1: Kropotkinskaya. Open daily 10am-5pm. Free. No cameras or hats.)*

NOVODEVICHY MONASTERY AND CEMETERY. Moscow's most famous monastery (Новодевичий Монастырь; Novodevichiy Monastyr) is hard to miss thanks to its high brick walls, golden domes, and tourist buses. In the center, the **Smolensk Cathedral** (Смоленский Собор; Smolenskiy Sobor) shows off icons and frescoes. As you exit the gates, turn right and follow the exterior wall back around to the cemetery (кладбище; kladbishche), a pilgrimage site that holds the graves of such famous figures as Krushchev, Bulgakov, Chekhov, Shostakovich, and Stanislavsky. *(M1: Sportivnaya. Take the Metro exit that does not lead to the stadium, then turn right.* ☎ *246 56 07. Open M and W-Su 10am-5:15pm; kassa closes 4:45pm; closed 1st M of month. Cathedral closed on humid days. Cemetery open daily 9am-7pm; in low season 9am-6pm. Grounds 40R, students 20R. Cathedral and special exhibits each 150R, students 75R.)*

DANILOV MONASTERY. Founded in 1282, the monastery (Данилов Монастырь; Danilov Monastyr) has historically been as much a fortress as a house of worship. During the Stalinist Terror, the monks were all shot and the monastery fell into ruin. It has since been restored to its former glory and is now home to the Patriarch, head of the Russian Orthodox Church. The only thing missing from this perfect picture of ecclesiastical renewal are the bells. During the Revolution, they were sold to an American industrialist, who in turn donated them to Harvard University. Harvard has agreed to return them if the Orthodox Church will pay to move them and have a replica set built. The Church has agreed, and collection boxes for this purpose line the monastery walls. *(M9: Tulskaya (Тульская). Exit the metro near the last car on the outbound train. From the square, cut through the small park with the chapel, then follow the trolley tracks down Danilovsky val., in the direction away from the gray buildings and McDonalds.* ☎ *275 47 79. Open daily 8am-8pm. Services M-F 6, 7am, 5pm; Sa-Su 6:30, 9am, 5pm. Museum* ☎ *958 05 02. Open W, F, and Su 11am-1pm and 1:30-4pm.)*

MOSCOW CHORAL SYNAGOGUE. Constructed in the 1870s, the synagogue is a break from the city's ubiquitous onion domes. Though it remained open during Soviet rule, all but the bravest Jews were deterred by KGB agents who photographed anyone who entered. Today, more than 200,000 Jews live in Moscow. Services are increasingly well attended, but the occasional graffiti is a sad reminder that anti-Semitism in Russia is not dead. *(M6 or 7: Kitai-Gorod. Go north on Solyanskiy Proyezd (Солянский Проезд) and take the first left. A cafe in the courtyard serves kosher food. Open daily 8am-10pm. Services M-F 8:30am, 8pm; Sa-Su 9am, 9pm.)*

CHURCH OF ST. NICHOLAS IN THE WEAVERS. The red-brown and green trim gives St. Nicholas's (Церковь Николы в Хамовниках; Tserkov Nikoly v Khamovnikakh) the appearance of a giant Christmas ornament. It was founded by weavers in 1679, and its name is derived from its location in the former cloth-making district. The church is remarkable for being only slightly touristed and always filled with devout parishioners. Enter off Lva Tolstogo (Льва Толстого) for a view of the vivid interior. *(At the corner of Komsomolsky pr. M1 or 5: Park Kultury. Open daily 8am-8pm. Services M-Sa 8am, 5pm; Su 7, 10am, 5pm.)*

AREAS TO EXPLORE

■**MOSCOW METRO.** Most cities put their marble above ground and their cement below, but Moscow is not most cities. The Metro (Московское Метро) is worth a tour of its own. Each station is unique. Those inside the circle line have sculptures, stained glass, elaborate mosaics, and unusual chandeliers. See the Baroque elegance of **Komsomolskaya** (Космомолская), the stained glass of **Novoslobodskaya** (Новослободская), and the bronze statues of revolutionary archetypes from farmer to factory worker, of **Ploshchad Revolutsii** (Площадь Революции) all for the price of a Metro ticket. (See **Form and Function,** p. 579.)

■**PAN-RUSSIAN EXPOSITION CENTER.** The enormous center (Всероссийский Выставочный Центр; Vserossiyskiy Vystavochniy Tsentr) has changed a great deal since its conception. Formerly the Exhibition of Soviet Economic Achievements (VDNKh), this World's Fair-like park, filled with pavilions, has become a giant shopping mecca. Each of the buildings is filled with small shops with wares ranging from hand-crafted swords and Celtic music to aquariums, electric guitars, and computer equipment. If you can dream it up, they've probably got it. *(M6: VDNKh (ВДНХ). Exiting the Metro to "ВВЦ," go left down the kiosk-flanked pathway, and cross the street. Most shops open 10am-7pm.)*

THE ARBAT. Now a commercial pedestrian shopping arcade, the Arbat (Аръат) was once a showpiece of *glasnost* and a haven for political radicals, Hare Krishnas, and *metallisty* (heavy metal rockers). Old flavor lingers in the streets in the form of performers and guitar-playing teenagers, though today the Arbat is mostly populated by pricey souvenir stalls and shops. Intersecting but nearly parallel runs the bigger, newer, and uglier **Novyy Arbat**, lined with gray high-rises, foreign businesses, and massive stores. *(M3: Arbatskaya or Smolenskaya.)*

PUSHKIN SQUARE. Pushkin Square (ПушкинскаЯ Площадь; Pushkinskaya Ploshchad) has inherited the Arbat's penchant for political fervor. During the Cold War's thaw, dissidents came here to protest and voice their visions of a democratic Russia. Today, missionaries evangelize while unknown politicians hand out petitions. Follow Bolshaya Bronnaya downhill, turn right, and follow Malaya Bronnaya to Patriarch's Pond (Патриарший Пруд; Patriarshiy Prud). This area is popular with artsy students and domino-playing old men. *(M7: Pushkinskaya.)*

PARKS

VICTORY PARK. On the left past the **Triumphal Arch,** which celebrates the 1812 defeat of Napoleon, is Victory Park(Парк Победы; Park Pobedy), built as a monument to WWII. It includes the **Museum of the Great Patriotic War** (Музей Отечественной Войны; Muzey Otechestvennoy Voyny) and the **Church of St. George the Victorious** (Храм Георгия Победаносного; Khram Georgiya Pobedonosnova) which honors the 27,000,000 Russians who died in battle. *(M4: Kutuzovskaya.)*

KOLOMENSKOYE SUMMER RESIDENCE. The tsars' summer residence (Коломенское) sits on a wooded slope above the Moskva River. The centerpieces of the grounds are the cone-shaped, 16th-century **Assumption Cathedral** (Успенский Собор; Uspenskiy Sobor) and the seven blue-and-gold cupolas of the nearby **Church of Our Lady of Kazan** (Церковь Казанская Богоматери; Tserkov Kazanskoy Bogomateri). Noteworthy among the park's small museums is Peter the Great's 1702 **log cabin.** *(M2: Kolomenskaya. Follow the exit signs to "к музею Коломенское," turn right from the Metro, and walk down the tree-shaded path, through the small black gate, and 10min. uphill on the leftmost path. Museums open Tu-Su 10am-6pm. Grounds open daily Apr.-Oct. 7am-10pm; Nov.-Mar. 9am-9pm. Each museum 90R, students 45R. Grounds free.)*

IZMAILOVSKIY PARK. Your one-stop shop for souvenirs from Soviet kitsch to lacquer boxes, Izmailovsky Park (Измайловский Парк) and its colossal art market, **Vernisazh** (Вернисаж), are best visited on late Sunday afternoons, when vendors want to go home and are willing to make a deal. Compare prices and bargain hard, as the first set of nesting dolls (матрёшка; matryoshka) you see will not be the last. Beware of pickpockets amid the crowds. *(M3: Partisanskaya, formerly Izmaylovskiy Park. Go left and follow the crowd to what looks like a theme park. Open daily 8am-6pm.)*

GORKY PARK. Established in 1928, the park (Парк Горкого; Park Gorkogo) gained fame in the West through Martin Cruz Smith's novel (of the same name) and the film it inspired. In summer, out-of-towners and young Muscovites relax and ride the roller coaster at Moscow's main amusement park. In winter, paths are flooded to create a park-wide ice rink. Those seeking an American-style theme park will be disappointed, as ice-cream kiosks outnumber attractions. Still, the park's main draw is its rides, which include a giant ferris wheel, a mediocre roller coaster and an original Buran spacecraft. It's a fun place to mingle with delighted children, teenage couples, and a menagerie of "pet" (caged) animals. *(M1 or 5: Park*

Kultury or M5 or 6: Oktyabrskaya. From the Park Kultury stop, cross Krymskiy Most (Крымский Мост). From Oktyabrskaya, walk downhill on Krymskiy Val. Park is across from the complex housing the New Tretyakov Gallery. Open daily Apr.-Sept. 9am-10pm; Oct.-Mar. 10am-10pm. Admission 50R, students 20R. Most rides 80-160R. Ice rink open Nov.-Apr. M-F 40R; Sa-Su 50R.)

KRASNAYA PRESNYA AND ZOOPARK. One of the cleanest of the city's serene green areas, **Krasnaya Presnya** (КраснаЯ ПреснЯ и Зоопарк) attracts readers and small children with its scattered wooden playgrounds and quiet benches. *(M7: Ulitsa 1905 goda (Улица 1905 года). Exit to Krasnaya Presnya and cross it. The park is along 1905 goda.)* The action is livelier a few blocks down Krasnaya Presnya at the **Zoopark.** Going to the zoo used to be like watching calves raised for veal, until Mayor Luzhkov directed his energy and fundraising talents toward improving the animals' quality of life. *(Main entrance across from M7: Barrikadnaya. ☎ 255 53 75. Open Tu-Su 10am-8pm; kassa closes 7pm. 100R, students and children free.)*

🏛 MUSEUMS

Moscow's museum scene is by far the most patriotic part of the city. Government museums and small galleries alike proudly display Russian art, and dozens of historical and literary museums are devoted to the nation's past.

ART GALLERIES

▨ STATE TRETYAKOV GALLERY. A treasure chest of 18th- to early 20th-century Russian art, the Tretyakov Gallery (Государственная Третьяковская Галерея; Gosudarstvennaya Tretyakovskaya Galereya) also has a superb collection of icons, including works by Andrei Rublev and Theophanes the Greek. *(Lavrushinskiy per. 10. M8: Tretyakovskaya (Третьяковская). Turn left out of the Metro, left again, then take an immediate right on Bolshoy Tolmachevskiy per.; turn right after 2 blocks onto Lavrushinskiy per. Open Tu-Su 10am-7:30pm; kassa closes 6:30pm. 225R, students 130R.)*

▨ NEW TRETYAKOV GALLERY. Where the first Tretyakov chronologically leaves off, the new gallery (Новая Третьяковская Галерея; Novaya Tretyakovskaya Galereya) begins. The collection starts on the 3rd floor with early 20th-century art and moves through the neo-Primitivist, Futurist, Suprematist, Cubist, and Social Realist schools. The 2nd floor holds temporary exhibits that draw huge crowds; it's best to go on weekday mornings. Behind the gallery to the right lies a graveyard for Soviet statues. Once the main dumping ground for decapitated Lenins and Stalins, it now contains sculptures of Gandhi, Einstein, Niels Bohr, and Dzerzhinsky, the founder of the Soviet secret police. *(Krymskiy Val 10 (Крымский Вал). M5: Oktyabraskaya. Walk toward the big intersection at Kaluzhskaya pl. (Калужская) and turn right onto Krymskiy. Open Tu-Su 10am-7:30pm; kassa closes at 6:30pm. 225R, students 130R.)*

PUSHKIN MUSEUM OF FINE ARTS. Moscow's most important collection of non-Russian art, the Pushkin Museum (Музей Изобразительных Искусств им. А.С. Пушкина; Muzey Izobrazitelnykh Iskusstv im. A.S. Pushkina) houses major Renaissance, Egyptian, and classical works, as well as superb pieces by Van Gogh, Chagall, and Picasso. *(Volkhonka 12 (Волхонка). M1: Kropotkinskaya. Open Tu-Su 10am-7pm; kassa closes 6pm. 300R, students 150R.)* The smaller building to the right of the main entrance houses the **Pushkin Museum of Private Collections** (Музей Личныч Коллеций; Muzey Lichnych Kolletsiy), with art by Kandinsky, Rodchenko and Stepanov. *(Open Tu-Su 10am-7pm; kassa closes 6pm. 100R, students 50R.)*

MUSEUM OF CONTEMPORARY ART. Housed in the former Moscow English Club mansion, the gallery (Центральный Музей Современной Истории России; Tsentralnyy Muzey Sovremennoy Istorii Rossii) thoroughly covers Russian history from the late 19th century to the present. *(Tverskaya 21. M7: Pushkinskaya. A large red building across the street from Pushkin Sq. and 1 block down. ☎ 299 52 17; www.museum.ru/M388. Open Tu-Sa 10am-6pm, Su 10am-5pm; last admission 30min. before closing; closed last F of month. 150R. Tours in Russian 3500R per group, max. 25.)*

EXHIBITION HALL OF THE RUSSIAN ACADEMY OF ART. This 60-room gallery displays work from Moscow's elite art academy, including paintings, sculptures, mosaics, and costume designs. The paintings and sculptures of academy president Zurab Tsereteli, who created the monument to Peter the Great, occupy two floors. Don't miss his prolific work. *(Prechistenka 19 (Пречистенка). M1: Kropotkinskaya. From the Pushkin Literary Museum, go 2 blocks to the left. ☎ 201 41 50. Open Tu-Sa noon-8pm, Su noon-7pm; last admission 1hr. before closing. 150R; students 40R.)*

CENTRAL HOUSE OF ARTISTS. Part art museum, part gallery, and part gift shop, this house (Центральный Дом Художникаж; Tsentralnyy Dom Khudozhnika) attracts browsers and serious collectors alike with cutting-edge exhibits from young new names and opportunities to acquire older artists' work. *(Krymskiy Val 10. In the same building as the State Tretyakov Gallery. M1 or 5: Park Kultury, or M5: Okyabraskaya. ☎ 230 78 55. Open Tu-Su 11am-8pm; kassa closes 7pm. 50R, students 20R.)*

HISTORICAL MUSEUMS

KGB MUSEUM. Documenting the history and strategies of Russian secret intelligence from Ivan the Terrible to Putin, the KGB Museum (Музей КГБ; Muzey KGB) features guides with intriguing anecdotes and a chance to quiz a current agent from the FSB, one of the KGB's four successors. *(Bul. Lubyanka 12. M1: Lubyanka. Behind the concrete behemoth on the northeastern side of the square. By tour only. Patriarshy Dom Tours, p. 578, leads 2hr. group tours; US$18 per person.)*

CENTRAL MUSEUM OF THE ARMED FORCES. At the Armed Forces Museum (Центральный Музей Вооруженных Сил; Tsentralnyy Muzey Vooruzhennykh Sil) you can see collections of weapons, uniforms, and artwork dating back to the reign of Peter the Great. *(Sovetskoy Armii 2 (Советской Армии). M5: Novoslobodskaya. Walk along Seleznyovskaya (Селезнёвская) to the roundabout. Turn left after the theater and bear right at the fork. Open W-Su 10am-5pm. 30R, students 10R.)*

MUSEUM OF THE GREAT PATRIOTIC WAR. This impressive collection (Музей Отечественной Войны; Muzey Otechestvennoy Voyny) is one of Mayor Luzhkov's grandest completed projects, built to immortalize those who died fighting Germany in WWII. After the Hall of Memory and Sorrow (where 2.6 million pendants of bronze "weep" for 27 million Russian casualties), though, the emphasis shifts from death to glory. *(Pl. Pobedy. M3: Kutuzovskaya. Behind the tall black WWII monument obelisk in Victory Park. ☎ 142 38 75. Open Tu-Su 10am-7pm; kassa closes 6pm; closed last Th of month. 120R, students 70R. Camera 40R, video 55R.)* In the **Exposition of War Technology** (Экспозиция Военной Техники; Ekspozitsiya Voyennoy Tekhniki), a large display of aircraft, tanks, and weaponry sits outside the park, behind the museum. *(Open Tu-Su 10am-7pm. 40R, students 30R.)*

COSMONAUT MUSEUM. The tall, aesthetically challenged, and suggestive obelisk that stands atop the museum is the **Monument to Soviet Space Achievements.** Inside the museum (Ъузей Космонавтики; Muzey Kosmonavtiki) is a fascinating collection on Sputnik and life in space. The 15min. movie answers a burning question: yes, Russian cosmonauts do feast on freeze-dried *borshch*. *(Pr. Mira 111. M6: VDNKh. ☎ 683 79 14. Open Tu-Su 10am-6pm; closed last F of month. 30R, students 14R.)*

BATTLE OF BORODINO PANORAMA MUSEUM. The popular blue cylindrical museum (Музей Панорама Бородинкая Битва; Muzey Panorama Borodinkaya), guarded by an equestrian statue of General Kutuzov, features a 360° panorama of the bloody August 1812 battle against Napoleon at Borodino. *(Kutuzovsky pr. 38. M3: Kutuzovskaya. Walk 10min. down Kutuzovsky pr. toward the Triumphal Arch. It's on the far side of the street from the Metro entrance. Open M-Th and Sa-Su 10am-6pm; kassa closes 5:15pm and takes a break 2-2:30pm. 45R, students 20R. Call ahead ☎ 148 19 27 for tours in English; 300R.)*

ANDREI SAKHAROV MUSEUM. This diminutive two-story complex commemorates the Russian nuclear scientist and patron saint of anti-Soviet ideologues. Sakharov, a Nobel laureate, was placed under house arrest by the Soviet regime. The museum (Музей и Общественный Центр Имени Андрея Сахарова; Muzey i Obshchestvennyy Tsentr Imeni Andreya Sakharova) has exhibits on Stalinist purges, life in the gulag, and the pursuit of human rights. *(Zemlyanoy Val. 57, ctr. 6. M10: Chkalovskaya (Чкаловская). Go to the main street, turn left, and walk 1½ blocks. ☎ 923 44 01. Russian captions. Open Tu-Su 11am-7pm. Free.)*

HOUSES OF THE LITERARY AND FAMOUS

Russians take immense pride in their literary history, and preserve authors' houses in their original state, even down to half-full teacups on the mantelpiece. Each is guarded by a team of fiercely loyal *babushki* who often outnumber visitors to the museum in their trust. Plaques on buildings mark where writers, artists, and philosophers lived and worked. Be aware, however, that many of these sights are demonstrations of hero-worship rather than archives of interesting artifacts.

▨ MAYAKOVSKY MUSEUM. This four-story work of Futurist Art illustrates the biography of the Revolution's greatest poet. From 1919 to 1930, Mayakovsky lived—and by his own hand, died—in a communal apartment on the 4th floor. His room is preserved at the top of the building, and the rest of the museum (Музей им. В.В. Маяковского; Muzey im. V.V. Mayakovskogo), which includes an array of abstract art, was built around it as a poetic reminder. *(Lubyanskiy pr. 3/6 (Лубянский). M1: Lubyanka. Behind a bust of Mayakovsky on Myasnitskaya (Мясницкая). Open M-Tu and F-Su 10am-6pm, Th 1-9pm; closed last F of month. 60R.)*

▨ PUSHKIN LITERARY MUSEUM. Fifteen rooms in this beautiful, modern building (Литературный Музей Пушкина; Literaturnyy Muzey Pushkina) lead you through the key points in Pushkin's life and work, setting them in historical context. Portraits of the author of *Eugene Onegin*, along with the writer's personal posessions, will delight any Pushkin addict, or scare away the unconverted. *(Prechistenka 12/2 (Пречистенка). Entrance on Khrushchevskiy per. M1: Kropotkinskaya. Open Tu-Su 10am-6pm; kassa closes 5:30pm. 50R.)*

GORKY MUSEUM-HOUSE. Built by F. O. Shekhtel in 1900, the museum (Музей-дом Горкого; Muzey-dom Gorkogo) is worth visiting as much for its art nouveau architecture as for its exhibit of Maksim Gorky's possessions. *(Malaya Nikitskaya 6/2 (Малая Никитская). M3: Arbatskaya. Cross Novyy Arbat, turn right on Merelyakovskiy per. (Мереляковский пер.), and cross the small park. Open W-Su 10am-6pm; closed last Th of month. Free; donations encouraged.)*

TOLSTOY MUSEUM. This museum (Музей Толстого; Muzey Tolstogo), in the neighborhood of Tolstoy's first Moscow residence, displays original texts, paintings, and letters. *(Prechistenka 11 (Пречистенка). M1: Kropotkinskaya. Open Tu-Su 11am-6pm; kassa closes 5pm; closed last F of month. 100R, students 30R.)*

STANISLAVSKY MUSEUM-HOUSE. The venerated theater director held lessons and performances in his home, which is now a museum (Музей-дом Станиславского; Muzey-dom Stanislavskogo) that displays a collection of the costumes used in his theatrical productions, with captions in English. *(Leontyevsky per. 6. M7: Pushkinskaya. When facing the Kremlin on Tverskaya, turn right on Leontyevsky per.*

through the stone arch. Enter in back and ring the doorbell. ☎229 24 42. *Open Tu and F 2-7pm, Th and Sa-Su 11am-5pm; kassa closes 1hr. earlier; closed last Th of month. 7OR. Tours 600R. Concerts Sept.-June. Call* ☎299 11 92 *for more info.)*

LEO TOLSTOY ESTATE. The celebrated author lived here during the winters of 1882-1901. Each room has been laid out exactly as it would have been, with the original possessions of Tolstoy and his family. *(Lva Tolstogo 21. M1 or 5: Park Kultury. Exiting the Metro, walk down Komsomolsky pr. toward the colorful Church of St. Nicholas of the Weavers; turn right at the corner on Lva Tolstogo.* ☎246 94 44. *Exhibits in English. Open Tu-Sa 10am-5pm, winter 10am-3:30pm; closed last F of month. 150R, students 50R.)*

DOSTOEVSKY HOUSE-MUSEUM. This museum (Дом-Музей Достоевского; Dom-Muzey Dostoyevskogo) in Dostoevsky's childhood home displays some of the family's original furniture and photographs. The tour ends with the author's fountain pen. *(Dostoyevskogo 2. M5: Novoslobodskaya. From Seleznevskaya (Селезневская), take a left at the trolley tracks onto Dostoyevskiy per. and follow the tracks onto Dostoyevskogo; the museum is on the left.* ☎681 10 85. *Open May-Sept. W-F 2-8pm, Th and Sa-Su 11am-6pm; Oct.-Apr. W-F 2-6pm, Th and Sa-Su 11am-6pm; kassa closes 30min. earlier. Closed last day of each month. 30R, students 25R.)*

CHEKHOV HOUSE-MUSEUM. This museum (Музей-дом Чехова; Muzey-dom Chekhova) re-creates the literary atmosphere of the late 19th and early 20th century with pictures of Chekhov and friends and family, in addition to showcasing artifacts from Chekhov's career. *(Sadovaya-Kudrinskaya 6 (Садовая-Кудринская). M7: Barrikadnaya. From the Metro, turn left on Barrikadnaya, and a left on Sadovaya-Kudrinskaya.* ☎291 61 54. *Improbable English captions. Open Th and Sa-Su 2-9pm, W and F 11am-6pm; kassa closes 1hr. earlier; closed last day of month. 30R, students 25R.)*

🎵 ENTERTAINMENT

PERFORMING ARTS

From September through June Moscow boasts some of the world's best **theater, ballet,** and **opera,** as well as excellent **orchestras.** Most of the performance venues are in the northern part of the city center. If you buy **tickets** days in advance and don't demand front row center, you can attend quite cheaply (US$5). Beware, however, of steep markups for foreigners. Tickets can often be purchased from the Internet or from the *kassa* located inside each theater, which is usually open from noon until curtain. Kiosks around the city sell tickets and programs for the next two months. Be warned that many consider the acoustics of the Bolshoi's beautiful new 2nd theater a failure. During July and August, Russian companies are on tour, and the only folks playing in Moscow are touring productions from other cities, which, with the exception of those from St. Petersburg, tend to be of lesser quality. Check www.moscowtimes.ru for schedules.

Bolshoi Theater (Большой Театр), Teatralnaya pl. 1 (Театральная; ☎250 73 17; www.bolshoi.ru). M2: Teatralnaya. Home to the opera and world-renowned ballet company. Performances daily Sept.-June 7pm, with occasional afternoon performances. *Kassa* open daily 11am-3pm and 4-8pm. Tickets 250-3500R. MC/V. Main stage closed in summer 2005 and is set to undergo renovations until at least 2007.

Maly Theater (Малый Театр), Teatralnaya pl. 1/6 (☎923 26 21; www.maly.ru), just to the right of the Bolshoy. M2: Teatralnaya. Moscow's 1st dramatic theater, with an affiliate at Bolshaya Ordynka 69 (☎237 31 81). Performances daily Sept.-June 7pm. *Kassa* open daily noon-7pm, closes 1hr. earlier on non-performance days. Tickets 100-400R.

Moscow Operetta Theater, Bolshaya Dmitrovka 6 (Большая Дмитровка; ☎692 12 37; www.operetta.org.ru), left of the Bolshoy. Famous operettas staged year-round. Performances 1, 6pm. *Kassa* open daily 11am-7:30pm. Tickets 100-500R.

Tchaikovsky Concert Hall, 4/31 Triumfalnaya Ploshchad (☎299 36 81). M2: Mayakovskaya. Classical music performances by premier international musicians. *Kassa* open daily noon-3pm and 4-7pm. Tickets (150-1500R) go on sale 1-10 days in advance.

Old Moscow State Circus (Tsirk Nikulina), Tsvetnoy bul. 13 (Цветной Бульвар; ☎200 06 68). M9: Tsvetnoy Bulvar. Turn right and walk half a block; the circus is on the right. Animal acts in the 1st half and glittery acrobatics in the 2nd. Performances M and W-Su 7pm, Sa 2:30pm and occasionally 1pm. Buy tickets 2-3 days in advance. *Kassa* open M and W-Su 11am-2pm and 2-7pm, Tu 12:30-1:30pm. Tickets 100-450R.

BANYAS

Sandunovskiye Bani (Сандуновские Бани), Neglinnaya 14 (Неглинная; ☎925 46 31). M7: Kuznetsky Most. Enter on Zvonarskiy per. (Звонарский). Moscow's oldest *banya* features high ceilings, cavernous rooms, and classical statues. 2hr. sessions 500-700R, but worth every ruble. Private room 1000R. Open M and W-Su 8am-10pm.

Bani Na Presnye (Бани На Пресне), Stolyarnyy per. 7 (Столярный; ☎255 53 06). M7: 1905 Goda. Stolyarnyy per. is the 1st right on Presnenskiy Val (Пресненский Вал) from the Square. Modern, large, and reasonably priced *banya* gets crowded on weekends. More privacy for women than most. 2hr. sessions 600R. Open daily 8am-10pm.

🎭 NIGHTLIFE

Moscow's nightlife, the most Bacchanalian experience this side of the Volga, is varied, and often expensive. Steer clear of the drunken brawls common outside nightclubs. Some clubs enjoy flaunting their high cover charges and face-control policies, while some elite establishments even have club-cards, denying access to those passing through the city. Several more sedate venues draw bohemians and absinthe-seeking students with cheap prices. Check the *Moscow Times*'s Friday pull-out section, *Element*, or the *eXile*'s nightlife section (www.exile.ru) for excellent synopses of the week's events and up-to-date reviews of clubs. Those looking for something tamer can head to the English-language theaters **American Cinema,** 2 pl. Yevropy (☎941 87 47; M3: Kievskaya), inside the Radisson SAS Slavyanskaya Hotel, or **Dome Cinema,** Olympisky pr. 18/1 (☎931 98 73; M5 or 6: Prospekt Mira). **35MM,** Pokrovka 47/24 (M: Kurskaya), is Moscow's only independent movie theater, and shows films in their original languages with Russian subtitles.

 SAVE FACE. When navigating the hostile, exclusive world of Moscow nightlife, our researchers have found that there is only one proven technique to ensure that "face control" (bouncer) doesn't ruin the night before it even starts: become a wealthy, tall, blonde model with purely Russian style. More realistically, try to find friends in Moscow. If you find yourself in town without pals, roam the streets until a connected Muscovite takes pity and invites you to Propaganda. Otherwise, dress up, go early, and get ready to have your face controlled.

CLUBS

🎭 Propaganda (Пропаганда), Bolshoy Zlatoustinskiy per. 7 (Большой Златоустинский; ☎924 57 32). M6 or 7: Kitai Gorod. Exiting the Metro, walk down Maroseyka and take a left on Bolshoy Zlatoustinsky per. Get down to house music at this Moscow hotspot without feeling like you're in a meat market. Go early to eat (and avoid strict face control). Dancing after midnight. Th is the most popular night. Beer 70R. Sangria 120R per 0.5L. Cover Sa 100R. Open daily noon-6am.

Karma Bar, Pushechnaya 3 (☎924 56 33). M1 or 7: Kuznetzky Most. With your back to the Metro, walk through the arch on your left and turn right on Pushechnaya. Crowd-pleasing dance music emanates from this hip club. English spoken. Beer 100-140R per 0.33L. Vodka 80-150R. Mixed drinks 180R. Latin dance lessons 7-11pm. Su hip-hop. Cover F-Sa men 300R, women 200R. Bag check 50R. Open Th-Su 7pm-6am.

B2, Bolshaya Sadovaya 8 (☎209 99 09; www.b2club.ru). M5: Mayakovskaya. This multi-story complex truly has it all, and without the face control: a quiet beer garden, restaurant, sushi bar, karaoke, jazz club, billiard room, several dance floors, and ballroom dancing on weekends. Beer 60-160R. Concerts 200-500R. Open noon-6am.

Hippopotamus (Гиппопотам), Mantulinskaya 5/1 (Мантулинсая; ☎256 23 46). M7: 1905 Goda. Cross and continue down Tryokhgornyy Val (Трёхгорный Вал). After the park, go right on Shmitovskiy per. (Шмитовский), then take the 1st left onto 1905 Goda. Take the next right on Mantulinskaya; entrance is around back. The hip-hop, R&B, and soul reels in a diverse group of clubbers; weak face control means that everyone gets in. Beer US$2-3. Mixed drinks US$2-5. W Arabian night. Th Latin/rock night, with live band and "rock" dance lessons from 1am. Cover men 330R, women 264R. Open W-Su 10pm-6am.

Ballantine's Bar, Nikolskaya 17 (Никольская; ☎928 46 92). M3: Ploshchad Revolyutsii. Great dance music and a lively student crowd. Beer 55-165R. Live DJ Th-Sa 10pm. Cover F-Sa 100R. Open daily 11am-6am. AmEx/MC/V.

16 Tons, Presnenskiy Val 6 (☎253 53 00; www.16tons.ru). Chill with New Russians on weeknights and rock out to Russian electronic and alternative concerts on weekends. Cover F-Sa 150-200R. Open M-Th 11am-midnight; F-Su 24hr.

Art-Garbage, Starosadskiy per. 5 (☎928 87 45; www.art-garbage.ru). M6 or 7: Kitay Gorod. Art gallery, restaurant, and club, Art-Garbage is refreshingly more laid-back than many of the chic and trendy Moscow establishments. Better for drinking on the inviting patio than for dancing. Vodka tonic 90R. Cover F-Sa 150-300R. Open noon-6am.

EXPAT HANGOUTS

Doug and Marty's Boar House, Zemlyanoy Val 26 (☎917 01 50). M3: Kurskaya. Opposite the train station. Curiously emulating "American" culture, Doug and Marty's packs in a rowdy crowd every weekend. Beer 90-145R. Entrees 190-450R. Billiards 50R per game. Cover F-Sa men 150R, women 100R. Happy hour 6-9pm. 50% discount on food noon-8pm. Open daily 10pm-4am; patio open 8am-10pm. AmEx/MC/V.

Rock Vegas Cafe, Pyatnitskaya 29/8 (☎959 53 33), next to Pizza Hut. M2, 6 or 8: Tretyakovskaya. Expats and local students frequent jazz, blues, and rock concerts F-Sa. Beer 60-160R. Cover F-Sa men 150R, women 100R. Open daily noon-6am.

▶ DAYTRIP FROM MOSCOW

SERGIYEV POSAD (СЕРГИЕВ ПОСАД)

Take the Elektrichki (commuter rail) from Yaroslavskiy Vokzal (1½-2hr., every 20-50min., round-trip 128R). With Yaroslavskiy Vokzal on your left and the central train ticket office on the right, head to the line of green kassy straight ahead. Buy tickets to Sergiyev Posad at Kassa 8. For a round-trip ticket, ask for "Ser-gey-ev Po-sad too-DAH ee ah-BRAHT-nah." Departure times are listed outside the prigorodnaya kassa (ригородная касса; suburban cashier). Take the train heading toward Alexandrov. Alternatively, purchase a train ticket (64R) and return via the bus leaving from outside the Sergiyev Posad station (1-3hr., every 10min., 40R). Buses back to Moscow go to Yaroslavskiy Vokzal or VDNKh. To reach the churches, turn right from the train tracks toward the gold domes and follow the road to the city (10-15min.). Monastery open daily 9am-6pm. Free. Tours in English 560R per person for groups of 5 or fewer; larger groups 260R per person; ☎254 4 57 21. Otherwise, book excursions at the kassa to the right just inside the monastery gates. Map of the grounds 50R. Museums open W-Su 10am-5:30pm. 160R, students 80R. No photography inside cathedrals.

Russia's famous pilgrimage point, Sergiyev Posad (pop. 200,000), attracts believers to the several churches clustered around its main sight, **St. Sergius's Trinity Monastery** (Свято-Троицкая Сергиева Лавра; Svyato-Troitskaya Sergiyeva Lavra). During Soviet times, Sergiyev Posad was called Zagorsk, and many locals still use this name. After decades of state-propagated atheism, this stunning monastery, founded in the 1340s and one of the Russian Orthodox Church's four *lavras*, has again become a thriving religious center. The Patriarch of the Russian Orthodox Church, also known as the Metropolitan, resided here until 1988, when he moved to Moscow's Danilov Monastery (see **Religious Sights,** p. 587).

Each church is exquisite, but few moments match the serene calm of standing in **Trinity Cathedral** (Троицкий Собор; Troitskiy Sobor), surrounded in dim light by walls of gilded Andrei Rublyov icons. Nearby, the magnificently frescoed **refectory** (Трапезная; Trapeznaya) houses some of the most beautiful paintings in any church. The **Chapel-at-the-Well** (Надкладезная Часовня; Nadkladeznaya Chasovnya) has a miraculous history: allegedly, it was established after a spring with magical healing powers appeared here. *Babushki* still bring vessels to the well to carry the holy water home. Next door, in the center of the courtyard, the **Assumption Cathedral** (Успенский Собор; Uspenskiy Sobor), modeled after the cathedral in Moscow's Kremlin (see **Sights,** p. 583), proves itself as beautiful as any larger house of worship. On your left as you enter, the **grave of Boris Godunov** and his family (see **History,** p. 570) lies under the modest white tomb. The fortress wall at the far end of the monastery gives access to the 55m **Pilgrim's Tower** at the far wall of the monastery, from which you can see a panorama of the surrounding sights (20R).

ST. PETERSBURG ☎(8)812
(САНКТ-ПЕТЕРБУРГ)

St. Petersburg's splendid, wide boulevards and bright facades are exactly what Peter the Great envisioned when he turned a mosquito-infested swamp into his "window on the West." That window's curtains closed, however, when St. Petersburg (pop. 4,600,000) became the birthplace of the 1917 February Revolution, turning Russia into a Communist state and later changing the city's name to Leningrad. Recently, the city has rediscovered the artistic genius of former residents like Dostoevsky, Gogol, Tchaikovsky, and Stravinsky, whose legacies infuse the centuries-old buildings, streets, and canals of this remarkable city.

✈ INTERCITY TRANSPORTATION

Flights: The main airport, **Pulkovo** (Пулково), 18/4 Pilotov str. (www.pulkovo.ru) has 2 terminals: Pulkovo-1 (☎ 104 38 22) for domestic flights and Pulkovo-2 (☎ 104 34 44) for international flights. The airport is 17km south of the city. M2: Moskovskaya (Московская). From the Metro, take bus #39 for Pulkovo-1 (25min.) or bus #13 for Pulkovo-2 (20min.). Only small bills are accepted as bus fare (10R). Hostels can arrange a taxi (usually US$30-35), but taking a little initiative might save a good deal of money. Call a taxi service and request to be picked up (about 30min. wait), or learn the Russian name of your destination street or hotel and you should be able to negotiate a fare of around US$20 at the airport. **Taxi Millionnaya** (Такси Миллионная; ☎ 100 00 00) offers reliable, reasonably priced service and an English-speaking operator. Fare from the center to the airport (including booking and collection) is 500R (non-negotiated fare around US$17) and from the airport to the center 600R (US$20). Millionnaya also runs within the city center (see **Local Transportation,** p. 601).

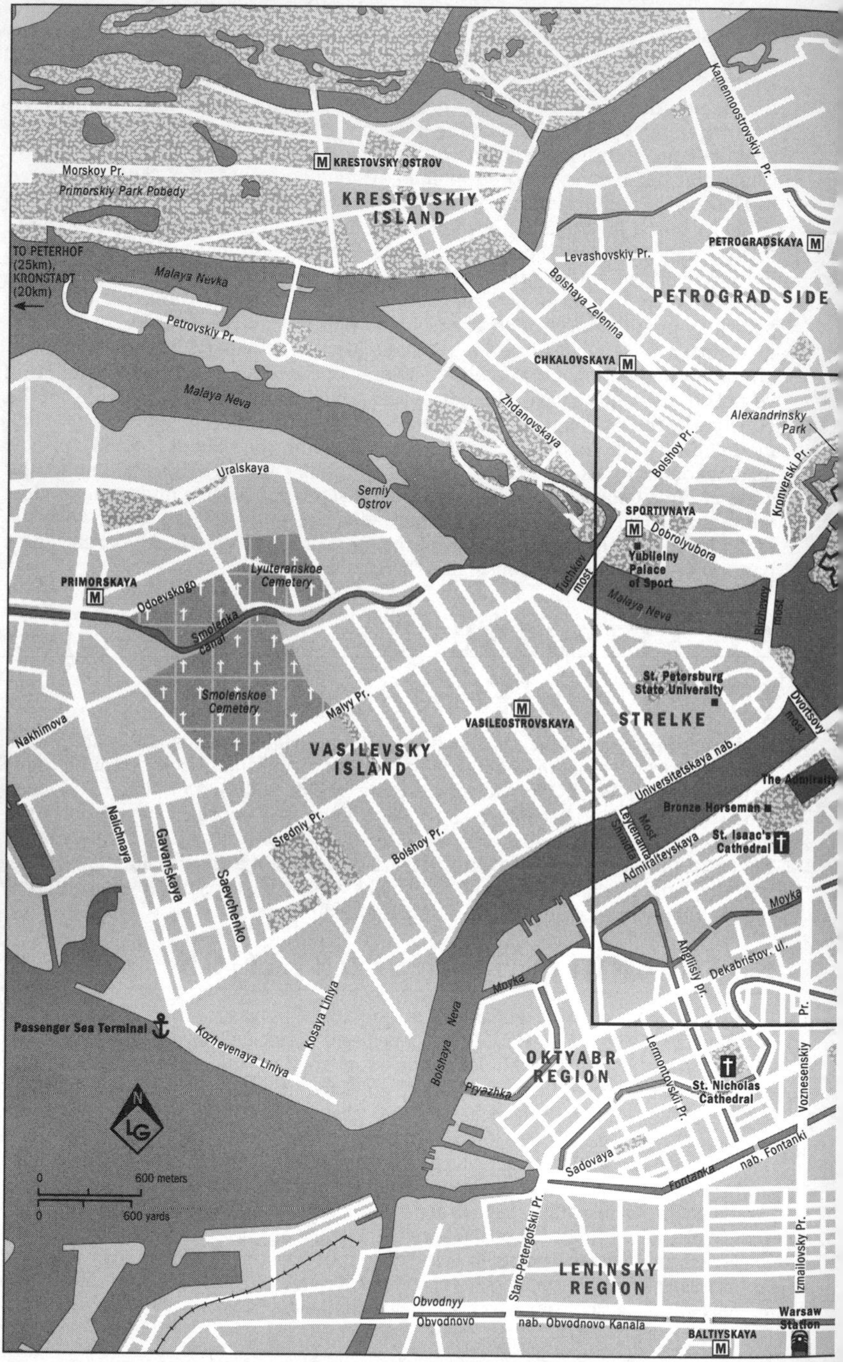

MOSCOW AND ST. PETERSBURG

St. Petersburg
(also see St. Petersburg color map)

NIGHTLIFE
Griboedov, 3
Moloko, 2
Triel, 1

Botanical Gardens

VYBORGSKAYA

VYBORG SIDE

Bolshoy Sampsonievskiy

Lesnoi Pr.

Pirogovskaya nab.

Arsenalnaya

Kondratevskii Pr.

Sverdlovskaya nab.

Neva

Rentgena

Botkinskaya

Lebedeva

Finlandskiy Vokzal

PLOSHCHAD LENINA

Pl. Lenina

Komsomola

nab. Arsenalnaya

Park Smolnovo

nab. smolnaya

GORKOVSKAYA

Museum of Russian Political History

Cruiser Aurora

Smolnyy Institute

Smolnyy Cathedral

PL. PROLETARSKKOY DIKTATURY

nab. Kronverkskaya

Fortress of Peter and Paul

Neva

Children's Gardens

Tavricheskii Palace

Shpalernaya

UK

Most Petra Velikogo

Chaykovskovo

Tavricheskiy Gardens

Furshtatskaya

CHERNYSHEVSKAYA

Suvorovskiy Pr.

Novgorodskay

Summer Gardens

Dvortsovaya nab.

Hermitage

nab. Canal Griboedov

Lliteyny Pr.

Degtyarnaya

SMOLNINSKII REGION

nab. Sinopskaya

Malookhtinskiy

Nevskiy Prospekt

Italyanskaya

NEVSKIY PROSPEKT

GOSTINYY DVOR

Vladimirskiy Pr.

5-ya Sovetskaya

Bakunina

Griboedova

Sadovaya ul.

Fontanka

PLOSHCHAD VOSSTANIYA

Nevskiy Prospekt

MAYAKOV-SKAYA

Moskovskiy Vokzal

Nevskiy Prospekt

PLOSHCHAD ALEKSANDRA NEVSKOGO

Most Aleksandra Nevskogo

SENNAYA PLOSHCHAD

SADOVAYA

DOSTOEVSKAYA

VLADIMIR-SKAYA

Mirgorodskaya

Obukhovskoy Oborony Pr.

Yusupovskiy Gardens

Reki

SEE CENTRAL ST. PETERSBURG MAP, P. 598

KUYBYSHEVSKI REGION

PIONERSKAYA PLOSHCHAD

LIGOVSKIY PROSPEKT

Kremenchugskaya ul.

Church of Annunciation

Aleksandr Nevskiy Monastery

Zagorodnyy pr.

PUSHKINSKAYA

Vitebsky Vokzal

Ligovskii Pr.

Chernyakhovskovo

TEKHNOLO-GICHESKII INSTITUTE

Moskovskiy Pr.

Serpukhovskaya ul.

Obvodnyy

Borova

Obvodnyy Canal

Canada

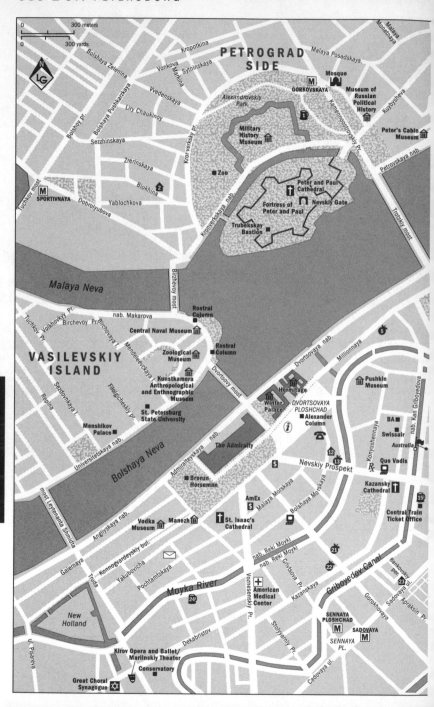

VYBORG SIDE

Bolshaya Nevka

PLOSHCHAD LENINA
M
Finlyandskiy Vokzal
ul. Komsomola
Pl. Lenina
Arsenalnaya nab.

Cruiser Aurora

Liteyniy most

Neva

nab. Kutuzova

Robespyera

Shpalernaya

Zakharevskaya

Chaikovskogo

Furshtatskaya
BUS
CHERNYSHEVSKAYA
M

Kirochnaya

Ryleeva

Pestelya

Gagarinskaya

Solyanoy Pr.

Mokhovaya

Pr. Chernishevskogo

Summer Gardens

Mars Field

Church of Our Savior on Spilled Blood

Russian Museum
Russian Ethnographic Museum
Tsirk
Inzhenernaya
Mussorgsky Theater
Shostakovich Philharmonic Hall
NEVSKIY PROSPEKT
M
Merchant's Yard
GOSTINYY DVOR
M
Statue of Catherine the Great
PL. OSTROVSKOVO
Aleksandrinsky Theater
Gostinyy Dvor

Sadovaya
Karavannaya
Italyanskaya
Kazanovaya

Mokhovaya
Liteyniy Pr.
Il. Belinskogo

Korolenko

Sheremetyev Palace
Anna Akhmatova Museum

Anglia

Chekova

Mayakovskovo

Nekrasova

Zhukovskovo

Ozernyy p.

Kovenskiy Pr.

24hr. Supermarket

Nevskiy Prospekt

Cafemax

MAYAKOVSKAYA
M

Stremyannaya

Vladimirskiy, pr.

Maly Theater

Theater and Music Museum

APRAKSIN DVOR.

Torgovy Pr.

nab. Reki Fontanka
nab. Reki Fontanka

DOSTOEVSKAYA
M

Kolokolnaya

Rubinshteyna

VLADIMIRSKAYA
M

Kuznechniy per.

Dostoevsky Museum

Covered Market

Lomonosova

Leshtukov Pr.

Berodinskaya

Zagorodny Pr.

Razyezzhay

Postoyskogo

Svechnoy per.

Fontanka

Marata

Pushkinskaya

Arctic and Antarctic Museum

PLOSHCHAD VOSSTANIYA
M

UPRISING SQUARE

Moskovskiy Vokzal
PLOSHCHAD VOSSTANIYA
M

Ligovskiy Pr.

Vosstaniya

Radishcheva

Vilenskiy pr.

Maltevskiy Rynok

Paradnaya

8-ya Sovetskaya
7-ya Sovetskaya
6-ya Sovetskaya
5-ya Sovetskaya
4-ya Sovetskaya
3-ya Sovetskaya
2-ya Sovetskaya
1-ya Sovetskaya

Suvorovskiy Pr.

Sindbad

TO 11 (20m)

TO 18 (50m)

Nevskiy Prospekt

Poltavskaya

Mirgorodskaya

TO VITEBSKIY VOKZAL (650m)

(1.5km)

Central St. Petersburg
(also see St. Petersburg color map)

ACCOMMODATIONS
Hostel "Zimmer Freie," **10**
International Youth Hostel (HI), **17**
Nord Hostel, **12**
Puppet Hostel (HI), **8**
Sleep Cheap, **6**
Traveller Hostel, **23**

FOOD
Al Shark, **7**
Cafe Zoom, **21**
Chaynaya Samovar, **22**
City Bar, **5**
Gin no Taki, **4**
Literaturnoye Kafe, **13**
Propaganda, **25**
Sakura, **14**
Traktir Shury Mury, **9**

NIGHTLIFE AND CAFES
CCCP, **19**
Che, **20**
Greshniki, **15**
JFC Jazz Club, **3**
Moloko, **16**
Ob'ekt, **24**
Par. spb, **1**
Red Club/Cadillac Club, **18**
Triel, **11**
Tunnel, **2**

THE LOCAL STORY

BRIDGE THE GAP

Inspired by his experiences in Holland, Peter designed a canal-crossed city to house his new Russian navy. In St. Petersburg's 300-year history, about 400 bridges have been built.

Between April and November, when the ice has melted, the bridges crossing the city's major waterways open to allow ships to pass. During White Nights (May-June), when St. Petersburg enjoys near-continuous daylight, the bridge raising is particularly fun to watch. Yet if you plan to party into the wee hours of the morning, be sure to keep these little over-passes in mind. Raised bridges have left many unfortunate tourists, residents, and literary characters on the wrong side of the river. Petersburg's bridges are raised during the following times:
Volodarskiy: 2-3:45am and 4:14-5:45am
Finlyandskiy: 2:30-5:10am
A. Nevskovo: 1:30-5:05am
Bolsheokhtinskiy: 2-5am
Lityenyy: 1:50-4:40am
Troitskiy: 1:50-4:50am
Dvortsovyy: 1:35-2:55am and 3:15-4:50am
Letyenanta Shmidta: 1:40-4:55am
Birzhevoy: 2:10-4:50am
Tuchkov: 2:10-3:05am and 3:35-4:45am
Sampsonievskiy: 2:10-2:45am and 3:20-4:25am
Grenaderskiy: 2:45-3:45am and 4:20-4:50am
Kantemirovskiy: 2:45-3:45am and 4:20-4:50am

Air France, Bolshaya Morskaya 35 (Большая Морская; ☎325 82 52). M3: Gostiniy Dvor. Open M-F 9:30am-5:30pm.

British Airways, Malaya Konyushennaya 1/3A, office 23B (Малая Конюшенная; ☎380 06 26). M2: Gostiniy Dvor. Open M-F 9am-5:30pm.

Delta, Bolshaya Morskaya 36 (☎311 58 20). M2: Nevskiy Prospekt. Open M-F 9am-5:30pm.

Finnair, Malaya Konyushennaya 1/3A, Office B33 (☎303 98 98). M2: Nevskiy Prospekt. Open M-F 9am-5pm.

Lufthansa, Nevskiy Prospekt 32, 3rd fl. (Невский; ☎320 10 00 or 320 10 03). M2: Nevskiy Prospekt. Open M-F 9am-5:30pm.

SAS, Nevskiy Prospekt 25 (☎326 26 00), in the Corinthia Nevskiy Palace Hotel. M2: Nevskiy Prospekt. Open M-F 9am-5pm.

Swissair, Nevskiy Prospekt 57 (☎325 32 50), in the Corinthia Nevskiy Palace Hotel. M2: Nevskiy Prospekt. Open M-F 9am-5pm.

Trains: Tsentralnye Zheleznodorozhny Kassy (Центральные Железнодорожные Кассы; Central Ticket Offices), Canal Griboyedova 24 (Грибоедова; ☎162 3344). Open M-Sa 8am-8pm, Su 8am-4pm. Buy tickets to Moscow from the *kassy* on the left side of the office. If you don't speak Russian, the aid of a travel agent or hotel staffer may be necessary to make a reservation. Ask your hostel receptionist to write down your preferred time, train, and destination in Russian and hand it to the person helping you. Many trains sell out a day in advance. Check your ticket for the station your train departs from; have your passport ready for inspection.

Baltiysky Vokzal (Балтиский Вокзал; Baltic station; ☎168 28 59). M1: Baltiyskaya. Serves a selection of Russian destinations.

Finlyandskiy Vokzal (Финляндский; Finland Station; ☎168 76 87). M1: Pl. Lenina (Ленина). To: **Helsinki, FIN** (6hr., 2 per day, 1375R).

Ladozhsky Vokzal (Ладожский; ☎055). M4: Ladozhskaya. Serves destinations in Russia and Finland.

Moskovskiy Vokzal (Московский; Moscow Station; ☎168 45 97). M1: Pl. Vosstaniya (Восстания). 24hr. luggage room; look for signs. From 40R. Remember which room you left it in, as there are several. Lockers available from 40R. To: Moscow (5-8hr., 12-15 per day, 300-1300R); Novgorod (3-4hr., 2 per day, 66R); Sevastopol, UKR (35hr., 2 per day, 754-1186R).

Vitebskiy Vokzal (Витебский; Vitebsk Station; ☎168 58 07). M1: Pushkinskaya (Пушкинская). To: **Kaliningrad** (26hr., 1 per day, 550-3300R); **Kyiv, UKR** (25hr., 2 every 2 days, 506-637R); **Odessa, UKR** (36hr., 1 per day, 654R); **Rīga, LAT** (13hr., 1 per day, 887R); **Tallinn, EST** (9hr., 1 per day, 350R); **Vilnius, LIT** (14hr., 1 every 2 days, 647R).

Buses: Nab. Obvodnogo Kanala 36 (Обводного Канала; ☎166 57 77). M4: Ligovsky pr. Take tram #19, 25, 44, or 49 or trolley #42 to the stop just across the canal. Facing the canal, turn right and walk 2 long blocks alongside it. The station will be on your right, behind the abandoned building. Surcharge for advance tickets. Open daily 6am-8pm. To: **Rīga, LAT** (12hr., daily at 7am and 8:30pm, 450R); **Tallinn, EST** (7hr., daily at 8am and 11pm, 280R). **Eurolines,** Nab. Obvodnogo Kanala 118 (Обводного Канала; ☎ 441 37 57), is located up the street and offers similar prices and destinations. (Open M-Sa 8am-8pm and Su 8am-6pm.)

■ ORIENTATION

St. Petersburg sits at the mouth of the **Neva River** (Нева) on 44 islands among 50 canals. The heart of the city lies on the mainland, between the south bank of the Neva and the **Fontanka River.** Many of St. Petersburg's major sights—including the Hermitage and the three main cathedrals—are on or near **Nevskiy Prospekt** (Невский Проспект), the city's main street, which extends from the **Admiralty** to the **Alexander Nevskiy Monastery** and the center's newer quarters, developed primarily in the late 19th century. In this area, east of the Fontanka, the **Smolnyy Institute** and most of the **train** and **bus stations** are found. **Moskovskiy Vokzal** on **Ploshchad Vosstaniya** (Восстания Площадь; Uprising Square) is midway down Nevskiy Prospekt, marking the change from what is oddly called Old Nevskiy (Старый Невский; Staryy Nevskiy) to the thoroughfare's more central section, simply called "Nevskiy." North of the center and across the Neva lies **Vasilevskiy Island** (Василевский Остров; Vasilevskiy Ostrov). Most of the island's sights, which are among St. Petersburg's oldest, sit on its eastern edge in the **Strelka** (Стрелка) neighborhood. Here the rectangular grid of streets recalls early plans for a network of canals on the island that was originally intended to be the base for Peter the Great's dream city, later moved to what is now known as Admiralteyskiy. The city's **Sea Terminal,** the ferry port, is at the island's southwestern edge on the Gulf of Finland. On the north side of the Neva, across from the **Winter Palace,** is the small **Petrograd Side** archipelago, which houses the Peter and Paul Fortress, quiet residential neighborhoods, and the wealthy **Kirov Island** trio. Outside the city center on the mainland are the southern suburbs and the northern **Vyborg Side** neighborhoods; both are vast expanses of tenements and factories with few sights for tourists.

The pipes and drainage system in St. Petersburg have not been changed since the city was founded. There is no effective water purification system, so exposure to *giardia* is very likely. Always boil tap water for at least 10min., dry your washed veggies, and drink bottled water. See **Essentials: Health,** p. 563.

▐ LOCAL TRANSPORTATION

Public Transportation: A **monthly transportation card** (360R) is good for unlimited public transportation for a given calendar month; purchase one at any Metro station.

The **Metro** (Метро), the deepest in the world, runs daily 5:45am-12:15am and is generally busy; avoid peak hours (8-9am and 5-6pm). A Metro **token** (жетон; zheton) costs 10R. Stock up, as lines are long and cutting is common. Multiple-journey tickets are valid for 7, 15, or 30 days.

Buses, trams, and **trolleys** (6R) run fairly frequently. Read the destination of each numbered line on the signs at the bus stop or check the list of stops posted on the outside of the bus. Trolleys #1, 5, and 22 run from Uprising Square to the bottom of Nevskiy pr., near the Hermitage. Buses, trams, and trolleys run 6am-midnight. Tickets (7R) should be purchased from the driver.

Marshrutki (маршрутки; private minibuses) are an option for Russian-speakers. They cost more than buses (7-20R) and are used more by commuters than by tourists, but move much more quickly through traffic and will stop on request (routes are displayed in the windows).

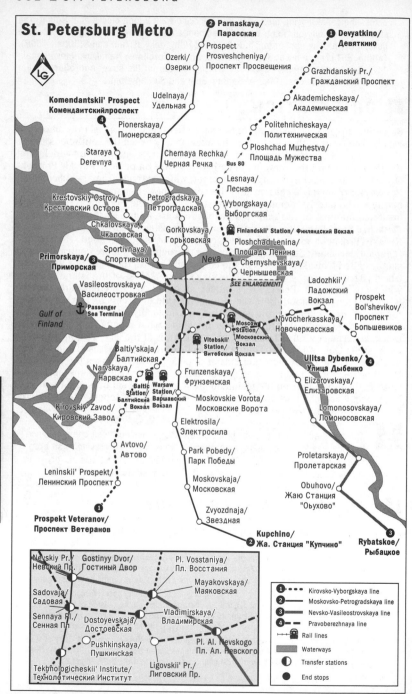

St. Petersburg Metro

② Parnaskaya/
Парасская

① Devyatkino/
Девяткино

Prospect
Prosveshcheniya/
Проспект Просвещения

Ozerki/
Озерки

Grazhdanskiy Pr./
Гражданский Проспект

Udelnaya/
Удельная

Akademicheskaya/
Академическая

**Komendantskii' Prospect
Комендаитскийлроспект**
④

Pionerskaya/
Пионерская

Politehnicheskaya/
Политехническая

Ploshchad Muzhestva/
Площадь Мужества

Staraya
Derevnya

Chernaya Rechka/
Черная Речка

Bus 80

Lesnaya/
Лесная

Krestovskiy Ostrov/
Крестовский Остров

Petrogradskaya/
Петроградская

Vyborgskaya/
Выборгская

Chkalovskaya/
Чкаловская

Gorkovskaya/
Горьковская

Finlandskii' Station/ Финляндский Вокзал

Primorskaya
③
Приморская

Sportivnaya/
Спортивная

Ploshchad Lenina/
Площадь Ленина

Chernyshevskaya/
Чернышевская

Neva

Vasileostrovskaya/
Василеостровская

SEE ENLARGEMENT

Ladozhkii'/
Ладожский
Вокзал

Prospekt
Bol'shevikov/
Проспект
Больщевиков

**Gulf of
Finland**

Passenger
Sea Terminal

Moscow
Station/
Московский
Вокзал

Novocherkasskaya/
Новочеркасская

Baltiy'skaya/
Балтийская

Vitebskii'
Station/
Витебский Вокзал

**Ulitsa Dybenko/
Улица Дыбенко**
④

Narvskaya/
Нарвская

Baltic
Station/
Балтийский
Вокзал

Warsaw
Station/
Варшавский
Вокзал

Frunzenskaya/
Фрунзенская

Elizarovskaya/
Елизаровская

Kirovskiy' Zavod/
Кировский Завод

Moskovskie Vorota/
Московские Ворота

Lomonosovskaya/
Ломоносовская

Elektrosila/
Электросила

Avtovo/
Автово

Park Pobedy/
Парк Победы

Proletarskaya/
Пролетарская

Leninskii' Prospekt/
Ленинский Проспект

Moskovskaya/
Московская

Obuhovo/
Жаю Станция
"Оьухово"

Zvyozdnaja/
Звёздная

**Prospekt Veteranov/
Проспект Ветеранов**
①

Kupchino/
② Жа. Станция "Купчино"

③
**Rybatskoe/
Рыбацкое**

Nevskiy Pr./
Невский Пр.

Gostinyy Dvor/
Гостиный Двор

Pl. Vosstaniya/
Пл. Восстания

Mayakovskaya/
Маяковская

Sadovaja/
Садовая

Sennaya Pl./
Сенная Пл

Dostoyevskaja/
Достоевская

Vladimirskaya/
Владимирская

Pushkinskaya/
Пушкинская

Pl. Al. Nevskogo
Пл. Ал. Невского

Tekhnologicheskii' Institute/
Технолотический Институт

Ligovskii' Pr./
Лиговский Пр.

① •••• Kirovsko-Vyborgskaya line
② —— Moskovsko-Petrogradskaya line
③ —— Nevsko-Vasileostrovskaya line
④ ■■■ Pravoberezhnaya line
⊢┿┿ Rail lines
Waterways
◐ Transfer stations
● End stops

Taxis: Both marked and private cabs operate in St. Petersburg. Marked cabs have a metered rate of 11R per km; add 35R if you call ahead (☎068). Instead of taking a taxi, many locals "catch a car": they flag down a car on the street, determine where it's going, agree on a price, and hop a ride. This practice is usually cheaper than taking marked cabs. *Let's Go* does not recommend hitchhiking. If you choose to flag down a car, keep in mind that it's a good idea to have some fluency in Russian and a degree of familiarity with the streets along your route. Never get in a car with more than 1 person in it.

>
> **BRIDGE OUT.** The bridges over the Neva go up at night to allow boats to pass. It's beautiful to watch, as long as you don't get caught on the wrong side. For more information, see **Bridge the Gap**, p. 600.

🔃 PRACTICAL INFORMATION

TOURIST AND FINANCIAL SERVICES

Tourist Office: City Tourist Information Center, Sadovaya 14/52 (Садовая; ☎310 82 62 or 310 28 22; www.ctic.spb.ru). M: Gostiniy Dvor. In addition to offering English-language advice and free brochures, the info center sells postcards and souvenir books. Open M-F 10am-7pm. There is also a smaller office, pl. Dvortsovaya 12, between the Hermitage and the Admiralty, which has fewer free pamphlets and no English-speakers, but more souvenirs. Open daily 10am-7pm. Also helpful are the free English-language publications *Where* and the *St. Petersburg Times* (www.sptimes.ru), which are available in hostel, hotels, and some restaurants.

Tours: Peter's Walking Tours, 3-ya Sovyetskaya 28 (3-я Советская; www.peterswalk.com), in the International Hostel. Offers a range of enjoyable, informative 3-6hr. English-language thematic excursions. Especially popular during White Nights is Peter's Big Night Out Tour, during which your guide takes you to the best party spots in town, then makes sure you get back in the morning. Tours, which cost 400-500R, can be booked online or in person, but those who simply turn up at the pre-arranged departure points are more than welcome. Pick up their widely available pamphlet for more info.

Budget Travel: Sindbad Travel (FIYTO), 3-ya Sovyetskaya 28 (☎332 20 20; www.sindbad.ru), in the International Hostel. Plane, train, and bus tickets. Student discounts on plane tickets. English spoken. Open M-F 9am-10pm, Sa-Su 10am-6pm. Branch, Universitetskaya nab. 11 (Университетская; ☎/fax 324 08 80). Open M-F 10am-6pm.

Consulates: In an emergency, citizens of **Ireland** and **New Zealand** can call the UK consulate. **Australia,** Italyanskaya 1 (☎/fax 325 73 33; www.australianembassy.ru). M2: Nevskiy Pr. Open M-F 9am-6pm. **Canada,** Malodetskoselskiy pr. 32/B (Малодетскосельский; ☎325 84 48; www.dfait-maeci.gc.ca/canadaeuropa/russia.) M2: Frunzenskaya. Open M-F 9am-1pm and 2-5pm. **UK,** Pl. Proletarskoy Diktatury 5 (Пролетарской Диктатуры; ☎320 32 00; www.britain.spb.ru). M1: Chernyshevskaya. Open M-F 9am-5pm. **US,** Furshtatskaya 15 (Фурштатская; ☎331 26 00, emergencies ☎331 28 88; www.stpetersburg-usconsulate.ru). M1: Chernyshevskaya. Open M-Tu, Th-F 2-5pm, W 10am-1pm. Phone inquiries M-Tu, Th-F 10am-1pm, W 3-5pm.

Currency Exchange: ATMs are omnipresent in the most cosmopolitan areas of the city. It's cheaper to take out rubles than other currencies, and many establishments accept only rubles. Many ATMs do not accept V. You can also get a **cash advance** at a bank. There are also currency exchange places every few blocks on Nevskiy Prospekt. Look for "обмен валюты" (obmen valyuti) signs everywhere, and don't forget your passport. Try the **Western Union,** on the corner of Nevskiy Prospekt across from the Admiralty. MC/V.

American Express: Malaya Morskaia 23 (☎329 60 60). Open M-F 9am-5pm.

Lost Cards: (☎095 956 08 29) Amex, Visa, MasterCard, Diner's Club, and JCB cards center in Moscow can help cancel lost or stolen credit cards.

English-Language Bookstore: Anglia British Bookshop (Англия), nab. Reki Fontanka 38 (Реки Фонтанки; ☎279 8284). Enter where the sign says Turgenev House; it's on the right. Stocks a variety of titles, including the Russian masters in translation. Open daily 10am-7pm. **Dom Knigi** (Дом Книги; House of Books), Nevskiy pr. 62 (☎314 58 88). Conveniently located Dom Knigi, one of the most famous bookstores in St. Petersburg, hosts a somewhat smaller branch of Anglia and sells a wealth of Russian books, as well as smaller selections of German and French literature. Open daily 9am-10pm. MC/V.

EMERGENCY AND COMMUNICATIONS

Be aware of rules about sitting, walking on, or otherwise harming the city's lawns and gardens, even if locals are doing it. You might have to do some quick-stepping to avoid fines. Police may merely take down the names of Russian offenders, but exact hefty fines from foreigners doing the same thing.

Police Services for foreigners: ☎278 30 14.

Pharmacy: Throughout the city center; look for "Аптека" signs accompanied by a green cross. **PetroFarm,** Nevskiy pr. 22 (☎314 54 01). Stocks Western medicines and toiletries. Open 24hr. Pharmacist daily 9am-10pm. MC/V.

Medical Services:

American Medical Clinic, nab. Reki Moyki 78, (Реки Мойки; ☎140 20 90 or 740 20 90; fax 310 46 64). M2/4: Sennaya Pl./Sadovaya. Follow per. Grivtsova across Griboyedov Canal and along to the Moyka river. English-speaking doctors provide comprehensive services, including house calls. Consultation US$50. Open 24hr. AmEx/MC/V.

British-American Family Clinic, Grafsky per. 7 (Графски; ☎327 60 30; fax 327 60 40), on the corner of Vladmirskiy pr. Expat staff offers primary care services. Consultation with a Western doctor €90, Russian doctor €60. 25% discount with ISIC on cash payment. Open 24hr.

Euromed Clinic, Suvorovsky pr. 60 (☎327 03 01; www.euromed.ru). M1: pl. Vosstaniya. 24hr. emergency and evaluation services, dental care, and billing services for major European and Asian insurance policies and credit cards. Consultation $100. 25% student discount with ISIC.

Internet: Straying from Nevskiy pr. yeilds far lower rates.

Quo Vadis, Nevskiy pr. 24 (☎311 80 11). Internet 80R per hr., with ISIC 70R. Long-distance calls to the US and Australia 19R per min.; to the UK 14R per min. Sells phones. Open 24hr. MC/V.

Cafemax, Nevskiy pr. 90-92 (☎273 66 55; spb@e-max.ru). M3/1; Mayakovskaya. Massive, modern Internet cafe. 70R per hr., students 60R; all night (11pm-7am) 120R. Open 24hr.

Internet (интернет), Bolshaya Morskaya 28 (☎717 66 97). Enter at the green Internet sign. 1R per min. on weekdays and 0.80R per min. on holidays. Open daily 10am-10pm. Cash only.

Post Office: Pochtamtskaya 9 (Почтамтская; ☎312 83 02). From Nevskiy pr., go west on Malaya Morskaya, which becomes Pochtamtskaya. **Currency exchange** and **telephone** service. International mail at windows #24-30. **Poste Restante** at windows #1 and 2. Open M-Sa 9am-7:45pm, Su 10am-5:45pm. **Postal Code:** 190 000.

⚐ ACCOMMODATIONS

Travelers can choose from a variety of **hostels** and **private apartments.** St. Petersburg hostels provide guests with linens and often a towel. In some cases, payment must be made in rubles. *The St. Petersburg Times,* an English-language newspaper, lists apartments for rent; find free copies at the City Tourist Information Center, the Russian Museum, or City Bar. Hostels will register your visa upon arrival and in most cases can provide you with the necessary invitation for a fee.

Nord Hostel, Bolshaya Morskaya 10 (☎571 03 42; www.nordhostel.com). M2: Nevskiy Prospekt. The most comfortable hostel in town boasts a central location and a friendly staff. Some rooms are small, and rooms are usually co-ed. Kitchen, TV lounge, and laundry available. Guests get free international calls, Internet use, and breakfast. Check-out 11am, with free luggage storage. Dorms Apr.-Jan. €24; Feb.-Mar. €18. Cash only. ❸

Sleep Cheap, Mokhovaya 18/32 (Моховая; ☎115 13 04; www.sleepcheap.spb.ru). M1: Chernyshevskaya. When you reach Mokhovaya 18, head into the courtyard; a sign indicates the hostel, on the right. Light pine floors and immaculate modern furnishings complement the many full-size dorm beds and private baths. The English-speaking staff is more than happy to help you book tickets. A/C. Airport and train transfer available. Breakfast included. Laundry 150R. Internet 86R per hr. Dorms 700R. Cash only. ❷

Hostel "Zimmer Freie," Liteyniy pr. 46 (Литейный; ☎273 08 67; www.zimmer.ru). Walk through the archway and bear left; enter at the sign "Fast Link." To check in, talk to the English-speaking manager, who sits in the front hall. Clean rooms, and sensational prices for the location. Showers, bathrooms, TV, refrigerator, kitchen, and free laundry. Fast Internet connection 50R per hr. Check-out noon. May 1-Sept. 30 dorms US$18; singles US$39. Oct. 1-Apr. 30 US$11/29. 5% discount with YIHA or ISIC. Cash only. ❶

International Youth Hostel (HI), 3-ya Sovetskaya 28 (3-я Советская; ☎329 80 18; www.ryh.ru). M1: Pl. Vosstaniya. Walk along Suvorovskiy pr. (Суворовский) for 3 blocks, then turn right on 3-ya Sovetskaya. Rooms offer large windows in a quiet neighborhood. TV and English movies in common room. Kitchen. English spoken. Breakfast included. Communal showers 8am-1am. Luggage storage. Laundry US$4 for 5kg. Internet 1R per min. Reception daily 8am-1am. Check-out 11am. 3- to 5-bed dorms US$23; doubles US$56. US$2 discount with HI, US$1 with ISIC. Cash only. ❷

St. Petersburg Traveller Hostel, Sadovaya 25 (☎310 04 12). Enter on Bankovskiy per. Professional hostel with modern decor and friendly staff, although most are unlikely to speak English. Security cameras and guard. Breakfast included in cafe with kitchen. Check-out 11am. Singles 1200R; doubles 1600R; triples 1950R. Cash only. ❹

Puppet Hostel (HI), Nekrasova 12. (Некрасова; ☎272 54 01; www.hostel-puppet.ru), on the 4th fl. M3: Mayakovskaya. Walk up Mayakovskogo (Маяковского); take the 2nd left on Nekrasova. Clean rooms. English spoken. Breakfast included. Reception 24hr. Check-out noon. Mar. 1-Nov. 1 dorms 672R; doubles 1664R. Nov. 1-Dec. 15 480/1216R. Dec. 15-Jan. 15 512/1344R. 32R discount with HI or ISIC. Cash only. ❷

◪ FOOD

Market vendors offer fresh produce, meat, bread, pastries, and honey. The biggest **markets** are the **covered market,** Kuznechnyy per. 3 (Кузнечный; open M-Sa 8am-8pm, Su 8am-7pm), just around the corner from M1: Vladimirskaya, and the **Maltsevskiy Rynok** (Мальцевский Рынок), Nekrasova 52, at the top of Ligovskiy pr. (Лиговский; M1: Pl. Vosstaniya. Open daily 9am-8pm.) **Parnas** (Парнас), Nevskiy pr. 56, stocks groceries, confections, liquors, and caviar. Buy sodas here instead of from vendors on the street; they're a third cheaper and twice as cold. (M2: Nevskiy Prospekt. Open M-F 10am-9pm, Sa-Su 11am-9pm.) The cheapest supermarkets in the city are **Dixie,** indicated by signs with orange lettering. **Nakhodka** (Находка), Nab. reky Fontanka 5 supermarkets are considered the best. There are **24hr. supermarkets** on side streets off Nevskiy pr. Look for the "24 Часа" (24 hours) signs.

Some of Russia's most unusual gastronomic offerings can be found in simple grocery stores or sold on street corners for only a few rubles. **Kvas (Квас)** is a non-alcoholic beverage made from bread especially popular in the Russian countryside. Vendors in the city often sell *kvas* from large barrels (10R). They tend to sell the beverage with water added, but it's still possible to distinguish the cider-like taste of the original *kvas*. **Kefir (Кефир)**, originally invented in the Caucasus area, is a sour milk beverage common in cities and other areas where pasteurization is possible. **Vegetarian** restaurants are often marked by a green cross above the door. However, so are pharmacies—just as nutritious but less tasty.

RUSSIAN RESTAURANTS

▨ **Cafe Zoom,** Gorokhovaya 22 (Гороховая; ☎972 18 05). With a sleek white-and-black decor and menus made from wooden card-catalogue trays, it's no wonder the city's artists and literati have swarmed to this hip eatery since it opened in 2004. Try the Chef's special (440R)—"some things show their true nature only upon closer inspection"—an opportunity for the chef to surprise his patrons. English spoken. Entrees 90-200R. Open daily 11am-midnight, 20% lunch discount until 4pm. Cash only. ❸

Literaturnoye Kafe (Литературное Кафе), 18 Nevskiy pr. (☎312 60 57). M2: Gostiniy Dvor. In its former incarnation as a confectioner's shop, this cafe boasted a clientele of luminaries from Dostoevsky to Pushkin, who came here the night before his fatal duel. It now caters to tourists with an excellent menu and reasonable prices. Live classical music during the day and Russian romances at night. English menu. *Bliny* with mushrooms 100R. Beef Stroganoff 250R. Cover 20R. Open daily 11am-11pm. Cash only. ❸

Lenin's Mating Call, Kazanskaya 34 (Казанская; ☎371 86 41). The bowl of condoms on the bar sets the tone for one of the most bizarre reactions to the demise of the Soviet system travelers are likely to find in former Leningrad. TVs juxtapose the wisdom of Russia's 1st socialist dictator with erotic scenes forbidden during Soviet times, while a low ceiling compels visitors to bow to the Lenin statues facing the entrance. Business lunch 160-260R. Usually no erotica until 9pm. Open daily 1pm-2am. AmEx/MC/V. ❹

Traktir Shury Mury (Трактир Шуры Муры), Belinskogo 8 (Белинского; ☎279 85 50). M2: Gostiniy Dvor or M1: Vladimirskaya. From Vladimirskaya, walk toward the Admiralty and take a right on nab. Reki Fontanka. At the next bridge, go right on Belinskogo. Russian and European cuisine served in a *dacha*-like setting by waitresses in traditional garb. English menu. Entrees 100-400R. Open 11am-6am. MC/V. ❷

Propaganda (Пропаганда), nab. Reki Fontanka 40 (Реки Фонтанка; ☎275 35 58). M2: Gostiniy Dvor. Walk toward pl. Vosstaniya on Nevskiy pr. Cross the Fontanka and turn left on nab. Reki Fontanka. American and Russian food in a Soviet-themed interior. Entrees 150-350R. English menu. Open daily noon-3am. Cash only, but ATM inside. ❸

Chaynaya Samovar (Чайная Самовар), Gorokhovaya 27 (☎314 39 45). M2: Sennaya Pl. Perhaps the best place in Petersburg to go for *bliny*. Branches of this popular chain can be found all over the city. English menu. Блины мяслом (bliny s myaslom; pancakes with butter) 16R. Entrees 12-67R. Open M-F 10am-9pm, Sa-Su 11am-9pm. ❶

INTERNATIONAL RESTAURANTS

Gin no Taki (Гин но Таки), Chernishevskogo 17 (Чернышевского; ☎272 09 58). M: Chernyshevskaya. Crowded with locals and favored by expats, this large Japanese restaurant combines an upscale atmosphere with some of the best prices and fastest service in the city. English menu. Fried dishes 70-270R. Open daily 11am-6pm. MC/V. ❸

City Bar, Millionnaya 10 (Миллионная; ☎314 10 37). Owned by Americans but staffed by locals, the City Bar is a popular expat hangout with standard American food. Breakfast 100-180R. Cheeseburgers 180-240R. *Amerikanskiy* business lunch 150R. Portions come in "regular" or "American-sized." Borrow English-language DVDs, videos, and books for free. Open daily noon-late; food served noon-11pm. AmEx/MC/V. ❸

Al Shark (Ал Шарк), Liteynyy pr. 43 (☎272 90 73). This shawarma chain has become a fixture on the St. Petersburg dining scene, serving a variety of Middle Eastern-inspired options. *Shvarma v pite* (spiced meat in pita) 53R. Arabic lunch, a healthy serving of rice, salad, potatoes, and meat of your choice 120R. Open 6am-midnight. ❶

Sakura (Сакура), nab. Griboedova 12 (Грибоедова; ☎315 94 74). Perfect for a quiet dinner in a traditional Japanese setting, right off Nevskiy Prospekt. Sushi—served by waitresses in geisha attire—starts at 80R for 2 pieces. Open noon-11pm. MC/V. ❸

⊙ SIGHTS

St. Petersburg is a city steeped in its past. Citizens speak of the time "before the Revolution" as though it were only a few years ago, and of dear old Peter and Catherine as if they were good friends. Signs such as the one at Nevskiy pr. 14 recall the harder times of WWII: "Citizens! During artillery bombardments this side of the street is more dangerous." The worst effects of those bombings were mitigated by Soviet-era reconstruction, and a more recent wave of projects restored the best sights in preparation for the city's 300th anniversary in 2003.

▩ THE HERMITAGE

Dvortsovaya nab. 34 (Дворцовая; ☎311 34 65; www.hermitagemuseum.ru). M2: Nevskiy Prospekt. Exiting the Metro, turn left and walk down Nevskiy pr. to its end at the Admiralty. Head right across Dvortsovaya pl. Individuals enter the courtyard through the gates on Palace Square. Allow at least 3hr. to see the museum. Open Tu-Sa 10:30am-6pm, Su 10:30am-5pm; kassa and upper floors close 1hr. earlier. All buildings 350R, students free. 1½hr. tours in English 120R. English audioguide 250R. Camera 100R, video 350R.

Originally a collection of 225 paintings bought by **Catherine the Great** in 1764, the **State Hermitage Museum** (Эрмитаж; Ermitazh), the world's largest art collection, rivals Paris's Louvre in architectural, historical, and artistic significance. The tsars lived with their collection in the Winter Palace and Hermitage until 1917, when both the palace and the collection were nationalized. Catherine II once wrote of the treasures, "The only ones to admire all this are the mice and me." Fortunately, since 1852 the five buildings have been open to all. Ask for an indispensable English audioguide at the info desk. The museum is organized chronologically by floor, starting with **prehistoric artifacts** in the Winter Palace and **Egyptian, Greek, and Roman art** on the ground floor of the Small and Great Hermitages. On the 2nd floors of the Hermitages are collections of 15th- to 19th-century **European art**. It is nearly impossible to absorb the museum's entire display in a day or even a week—a full tour would cover a distance of 24 mi. and would only reveal 5% of the museum's three-million-piece collection, most of which is in storage due to lack of space. Some of the collection's Russian artifacts are on display at the Russian museum. If you're running late, visit the upper floors first—they close earliest.

WINTER PALACE. Commissioned in 1762, the majestic architecture of the Winter Palace (Зимний Дворец; Zimniy Dvorets) reflects the extravagant Rococo tastes of Empress Elizabeth and the architect Rastrelli. Rooms 190-198 on the 2nd floor are the palace **state rooms.** The rest of the floor houses 15th- to 18th-century **French art** (Rooms 273-297) and 10th- to 20th-century **Russian art** (Rooms 151-187). The third floor exhibits **Impressionist, Post-Impressionist,** and **20th-century European art.** The famous **Malachite Hall** (Room 189) contains six tons of malachite columns, boxes, and urns, each painstakingly constructed from thousands of matched stones to give the illusion of having been carved from one massive rock.

OTHER BUILDINGS. By the end of the 1760s, the collection amassed by the Empress had become too large for the Winter Palace, and Catherine appointed Vallin de la Mothe to build the **Small Hermitage** (Малый Эрмитаж; Malyy Ermitazh), a retreat for herself and her lovers. The **Large Hermitage** (Большой Эрмитаж; Bolshoy Ermitazh) was completed in the 1780s and displays excellent **Italian** (Rooms 207-238) and **Dutch art** (Rooms 248-254). In Rooms 226-227, an exact copy of Raphael's *Loggia*, commissioned by Catherine the Great, covers the

THE HIDDEN DEAL

BLAST IN THE BANYA

The *banya* is the real Russian bathing experience—it has been a part of Slavic culture since long before there was a Russia to claim it as Russian. A modern *banya* is usually single-sex and involves several stages. During the first stage, you enter the *parilka* (парилка), a steam room that reaches temperatures upward of 70°C. The idea is to stay in the *parilka* as long as you can stand it, then cool down under a shower before going out into the open air. This is repeated several times in order to acclimate the body into cardiac workout, before a plunge into the icy cold pool (холодный бассейн) is added to the cycle. At this point, it is also customary to offer and receive a beating with a wet birch-tree switch —this actually feels like a pleasant massage.

Bring sandals and a sheet if you have them, or rent them upon arrival. Also bring shampoo and soap for a Western-style shower to wrap things up. Birch switches can be bought for 40-50R.

There is a public banya *at 11 Bolshoy Kazachiy per. (☎315 07 34). M1: Pushkinskaya. Enter the* banya *through the courtyard of Dom 11. Open M and W noon-10pm, Tu and F-Su 9am-10pm, Th (women's day) 10am-10pm. 50R. A private* banya *is at Gagarinskaya (☎272 96 82), in Dom 32. M1: Chernashevskaya. Call ahead to book for a group. Open 11am-2am. 450R per hr.*

walls just as in the Vatican. In 1851, Stasov, a famous imperial Russian architect, built the **New Hermitage** (Новый Эрмитаж; Novyy Ermitazh).

NEAR THE HERMITAGE

DVORTSOVAYA PLOSHCHAD. The windswept Palace Square (ДворцоваЯ Площадь) has witnessed many milestones in Russian history. Catherine was crowned here in 1762, and, years later, Nicholas II's guards fired into a crowd of peaceful demonstrators on Russia's "Bloody Sunday," precipitating the 1905 revolution. In October 1917, Lenin's Bolsheviks seized power from Kerensky's provisional government here during the storming of the Winter Palace. Today, the square is used for various goings-on, from concerts to political meetings. Palace Square's exquisite architecture is the work of Carlo Rossi, one of the last great Neoclassical architects in St. Petersburg. Overlooking it all is the angel at the top of the **Alexander Column** (Александрийская Колонна; Aleksandriyskaya Kolonna), which commemorates Russia's 1812 victory over Napoleon. At the base of the column are inscribed the words, "To Alexander I, from a grateful Russia." The 700-ton column took two years to cut from a cliff in Karelia; but when it arrived in St. Petersburg, it was raised in just 40min. by thousands of war veterans using a complex pulley system. At 47m, it is the largest freestanding monument in the world.

THE ADMIRALTY. The only way into the Admiralty (Фдмизфлтейство; Admiralteystvo) is to become an officer in the Russian Navy, but tourists can admire its impressive exterior and gleaming golden spire, visible throughout St. Petersburg. Construction of a naval force was Peter the Great's fondest dream, and the main inspiration for the fortress which would become Russia's new capital. To that end, the Admiralty began life as a fortified shipyard and was reincarnated by architect Andrey Zakharov in 1806 in homage to the successes of the Russian naval force. During WWII, the spire was painted black to hide it from German artillery bombers. Peter supposedly supervised the construction of St. Petersburg from the tower, one of the oldest buildings in the city. The gardens, initially designed as a firing range, now hold statues of important Russian literary figures. Inside, young Russian men live here for five-year stints, studying engineering in preparation for military careers. (*Admiralteyskaya Naberezhnaya 2. M2: Nevskiy Prospekt.*)

BRONZE HORSEMAN. This hulking statue of Peter the Great astride a rearing horse terrorized the protagonists in works by Alexander Pushkin and Andrey Bely by coming to life and chasing them through the streets. In reality, the statue hasn't moved from the site on which Catherine the Great had it set in 1782, and today it serves as a good-luck charm for newlyweds who take their photos in front of it. *(M2: Nevskiy Prospekt. On the river, in Decembrists' Square near St. Isaac's Cathedral.)*

VASILYEVSKIY ISLAND. Just across the bridge from the Hermitage, the Strelka (Стрелка; arrow or promontory) section of the city's biggest island (Ифсилувский Щстзцв; VasilYevskiy Ostrov) juts into the river, dividing it in two and providing a spectacular view of both sides. Peter the Great had intended to make the island home to his new capital's administration, but he abandoned these plans due to lack of a permanent bridge to the mainland. The former Stock Exchange (now the Naval Museum) dominates the square on the island's east end, and the ships' prows and anchors sticking out of the two red **Rostral Columns** proclaim the glory of Peter's modern navy. St. Petersburg State University and the Academy of Arts, as well as some of its most interesting museums (see **Museums,** p. 614), are housed on the embankment facing the Admiralty. *(Take bus #10 from Nevskiy pr.)*

◼ ST. ISAAC'S CATHEDRAL

Isaakievskaya pl. between Admiralteyskiy pr. and Malaya Morskaya. M2: Nevskiy Prospekt. Exit the Metro, turn left, and go almost to the end of Nevskiy pr. Turn left on Malaya Morskaya. Cathedral open in summer M-Tu and Th-Su 10am-8pm; in winter M-Tu and Th-Su 11am-7pm; kassa closes 1hr. earlier. 270R, students 150R. Camera 50R, video 100R. Colonade summer M-Tu and Th-Su 10am-7pm; winter Th-Tu 11am-3pm. 120R, students 70R. Cameras 25R, video 50R. Enter on the south side (from Malaya Morskaya). A kassa is in front. Colonnade often open at night during the summer M-Tu and Th-Su. 100R.

Intricately carved masterpieces of iconostasis find the home they deserve in the awesome **St. Isaac's Cathedral** (Исаакиевский Собор; Isaakiyevskiy Sobor), a 19th-century megalith built under the reign of Alexander I. On a sunny day, the 100kg of pure gold coating the dome can be seen for miles. The cost of this opulent cathedral was well over five times that of the Winter Palace, and 60 laborers died from mercury inhalation during the gilding process. Due in part to architect Auguste de Montferrand's lack of experience, construction took 40 years; the superstition that the Romanov dynasty would fall with the cathedral's completion didn't speed things up. The cathedral was completed in 1858 and is one of the world's largest cathedrals. Some of Russia's greatest artists worked on the 150 murals and mosaics inside. Although officially designated a museum in 1931, the cathedral still holds religious services on major holidays. The breathtaking 360° view of St. Petersburg is worth the 260-stair climb to the top of the **colonnade.**

 AN EYE FOR ICONOSTASIS. In a Russian Orthodox church or cathedral, iconostasis is the boundary screening off the sanctuary from the gaze of those in the main part of the church, often likened to a divide between Heaven and earth. Its construction is meticulously arranged with up to six tiers, each having unique significance within the religion.

FORTRESS OF PETER AND PAUL

M2: Gorkovskaya. Exiting the Metro, bear right on Kamennoostrovskiy pr. (Каменноостровский), the unmarked street in front of you. Follow it to the river and cross the wooden bridge to the island fortress. ☎238 07 61. Open M and W-Su 11am-6pm, Tu 11am-5pm; closed last Tu of month. Fortress free. Purchase a ticket for most sights (120R, students 60R) at the kassa in the "boathouse" in the middle of the fortress or in the smaller kassa to the right inside the main entrance. Tours in English 300R; call ahead.

THE HIDDEN DEAL

THE FORTRESS FOR FREE

The Peter and Paul Fortress offers many attractions that are well worth paying for, but some of the complex's best sights won't cost you a ruble:

At **Neva Gate,** also know as "Death Gateway," prisoners began their final journeys toward execution or exile. Neva flood levels are recorded on plaques beneath the arch. A few steps away, you can take in a stunning vista, including **Trotskiy Most,** a bridge constructed by Gustav Eiffel; the **Church of Spilled Blood;** the **Admirality; St. Isaac's;** the **Hermitage;** and the old **Court Theater.**

The bronze statue of **Peter the Great** by Kikhail Chemiakin spares none of the despotic leader's flaws, including his elongated, disproportionate body. The head is even modeled on a mask of the tsar's own face. Legend has it that rubbing his index finger will make your wishes come true. The seated monarch looks out over **Dancing Field,** which takes its name from the punishment soldiers convicted of petty crimes were forced to perform: "dancing" barefoot on a lawn of broken glass.

Finally, don't miss the cannon at Naryshkin Bastion, which booms mightily each day at noon. The tradition dates to 1873, with a hiatus between the revolution and 1957.

Across the river from the Hermitage, the walls and golden spire of the Fortress of Peter and Paul (Петроп-авловская Крепость; Petropavlovskaya Krepost) beckon. Construction of the fortress, supervised by Peter the Great himself, began on May 27, 1703; the date is now considered to mark the birthday of St. Petersburg. The fortress was originally intended as a defense against the Swedes, but was converted by Peter I into a prison for political dissidents. Inmates' graffiti is still legible on the citadel's stone walls. Arrive early to set your watch by the boom of the cannon that's fired from the spire of the cathedral every day at noon.

PETER AND PAUL CATHEDRAL. The main attraction within the fortress, the cathedral (Петропавловский Собор; Petropavlovskiy Sobor) glows with walls of rose and aquamarine marble. At 122.5m, it's the tallest building in the city. From the ceiling, cherubs keep watch over breathtaking Baroque iconostasis and the ornate coffins of Peter the Great and his successors. Before the main vault sits the recently restored **Chapel of St. Catherine the Martyr.** The bodies of Nicholas II and his family were entombed here on July 17, 1998, the 80th anniversary of their murder at the hands of the Bolsheviks. Mikhail Shemyakin's controversial bronze **statue** of Peter the Great sits outside. *(Open M-Sa 10am-7pm.)*

NEVSKIY GATE AND TRUBETSKOY BASTION. To the right of the statue, the **Nevskiy gate** (Невские Ворота; Nevskiye Vorota) was the site of numerous executions. The condemned awaited their fate in the fortress's southwest corner at the **Trubetskoy Bastion** (Труъецкой Бастион) prison, where Peter the Great tortured his first son, Aleksey. Dostoevsky, Gorky, and Trotsky spent time here as well.

PETER'S CABIN. Peter the Great supervised the construction of his city while living in this cabin (Домик Петра Первого; Domik Petra Pervogo), the oldest building in St. Petersburg, which is charmingly nicknamed the "Small House of Peter I." The museum contains many of his personal effects and describes his victories in the Northern War of 1700-1721. *(A small brick house along the river outside the Petrograd/east side of the fortress. Walk down Petroskaya until you reach a bronze gate with gold trim; the kassa is at the back. Open M 10am-5pm, W-Su 10am-6pm; kassa closes 1hr. before museum; closed last M of month. 150R, students 70R. Camera 100R.)*

ALONG NEVSKIY PROSPEKT

The easternmost boulevard of central St. Petersburg, Nevskiy Prospekt is the main thoroughfare. In accordance with Peter's vision, the wide avenue is epic, running 4.5km from the Neva in the west to the Alexander Nevskiy Monastery in the east.

■ **CHURCH OF OUR SAVIOR ON SPILLED BLOOD.** This church's colorful forest of elaborate "Russian style" domes was built from 1883 to 1907 over the site of Tsar Alexander II's 1881 assassination. Also known as the Church of Christ's Resurrection and the Church of the Bleeding Savior, the cathedral (Спас На Крови; Spas Na Krovi) has been beautifully renovated according to the original artists' designs after 40 years of Soviet neglect. Today it's been designated a State Memorial Museum. The interior walls are covered with 7000 sq. m of mosaics based mainly on the New Testament. The arrangement of mosaics follows the canons of Orthodox iconography; the southern wall shows events from the Nativity to the Baptism of Christ, while the northern wall displays miracles worked by Jesus. In the adjacent chapel is an exhibit on the life and death of reformist Alexander. Behind the church and to the left is an outdoor souvenir market popular with tourists. Wares are expensive, but prices are negotiable. *(2 Nab. Kanala Gibdoeva, 3 blocks off Nevskiy pr. up Canal Griboyedova from Dom Knigi. M2: Nevskiy Prospekt.* ☎ *315 16 36. Open Th-Tu in winter 11am-7pm; in summer 10am-8pm; kassa closes 1hr. earlier. Foreigners buy tickets inside. Church 270R, students 150R, under 7 free. Camera 50R, video 100R.)*

KAZANSKY CATHEDRAL. This colossal edifice (Казанский Собор; Kazanskiy Sobor) on the corner of Nevskiy pr. and the Griboyedov Canal was inspired by St. Peter's Basilica in Rome. Completed in 1811, the cathedral was originally created to house the icon Our Lady of Kazan, to whom the Russian general Mikhail Golenshokov Kutuzov prayed before his military campaign. After the Franco-Prussian conflict, Russian soldiers placed the keys of captured French cities and military emblems above Kutuzov's tomb in the cathedral, where they (and he) remain. Ironically, during the Communist era, the cathedral housed the Museum of Atheism. *(Kazanskaya pl. 2. M2: Nevskiy Prospekt.* ☎ *318 45 28; www.kazansky.ru. Open daily 8:30am-7:30pm. Services daily 10am, 6pm. Free. Tours daily 11:30am-5:30pm.)*

MERCHANTS' YARD. Built under Catherine the Great, this large yellow 18th-century complex (Гщстиный Двщз; Gostiniy Dvor) near the Metro is one of the oldest indoor shopping malls in the world. The two-floored ring of stores is like an open-air market—with vodka, electronics, pipes, and other miscellany—taken inside and made bourgeois. *(M3: Gostiniy Dvor. Open M-Sa 10am-10pm, Su 10am-9pm.)*

OSTROVSKOGO SQUARE. Ostrovskogo Square (Площадь Островского; Ploshchad Ostrovskogo) is home to a monument of Catherine the Great surrounded by the principal political and cultural figures of her reign: Potemkin, Marshall Suvorov, Princess Dashkova, and others. The oldest Russian theater, the Aleksandrinskiy (Александринский), built by the architect Rossi in 1828, is behind Catherine's monument. On Zodchevo Rossii (Зодчево России), behind the theater, is the **Vaganova School of Choreography,** whose graduates include Vatslav Nizhinskiy, Anna Pavlova, Rudolf Nureyev, and Mikhail Baryshnikov. *(M3: Gostiniy Dvor. Exit the Metro and head toward pl. Vosstaniya on Nevskiy pr. The square is on the right.)* To the right (with the **Aleksandrinskiy** at your back) is St. Petersburg's main public library, decorated with sculptures of ancient philosophers. Among the library's many treasures ranks one of Catherine's most monumental purchases, the library of Voltaire. *(Group tours of library US$10 per person; call ahead* ☎ *310 98 50. Foreigners can obtain a library card for free by taking their passport, visa, and 2 photographs to the library; card good through the duration of the visa. Library open July-Aug. M and W 1-9pm, Tu and Th-Su 9am-5pm; Sept.-June daily 9am-9pm.)* Also located on the plaza is a small **theater museum** featuring props, playbills, and some theatrical history. Spectacularly, the museum's small conservatory features a piano formerly owned and played by Tschaikovsky, used currently in small concerts and recitals held May through September. *(Ostrovskogo pl. 1, 3rd fl.* ☎ *571 21 95; www.museum.ru/M146. Russian captions. Open M and Th-Su 11am-6pm, W 1-7pm; closed last F of month. 50R, students 25R.)*

SHEREMETYEV PALACE. Constructed in the early 1700s as a residence for Peter the Great's marshal, Boris Sheremetyev, this restored palace (Дворец Шереметьевых; Dvorets Sheremetevykh) houses a music museum which contains a collection of 300 antique instruments, including the pianos of Rubenstein, Glinka, and Shostakovich and the violin of Antonio Stradivarius. The palace's mirrored hall hosts concerts on weekends, sometimes played with instruments from the museum's collection. During the summer, afternoon concerts from guest orchestras are held every week. *(Nab. Reki Fontanka 34. M3: Gostiniy Dvor. From the Metro, cross the Fontanka and turn left. The palace is about 2 blocks down on your right. ☎272 44 41; www.theatremuseum.ru. Russian captions. Open W-Su noon-6pm; closed last W of month. 150R, students 75R. Camera 50R, video 100R. Concerts Oct.-May F 6:30pm, Sa-Su 4pm; 10-100R.)*

UPRISING SQUARE. Some of the bloodiest confrontations of the February Revolution, including the Cossack attack on police, took place here (Площадь ВосстаниЯ; Ploshchad Vosstaniya). The obelisk, erected in 1985, replaced a statue of Tsar Alexander III that was removed in 1937. Across from the train station, the green Oktyabrskaya Hotel bears the words "Город-герой Ленинград" (Leningrad, the Hero-City), recalling the tremendous suffering during the German WWI siege. *(M1: Ploshchad Vosstaniya. Near Moskovskiy Vokzal.)*

ALEXANDER NEVSKIY MONASTERY

Pl. Aleksandra Nevskogo 1 (Александра Невского). M3 or 4: Pl. Aleksandra Nevskogo. The 18th-century Necropolis lies behind and to the left of the entrance archway. The Artists' Necropolis is behind and to the right. ☎274 04 09. Grounds open daily 6am-10pm; cathedral daily 6am-8pm; Annunciation Church Tu-W and F-Su 11am-5pm; both necropolises daily 10am-9pm; kassa closes 5pm. Services daily 5:45, 6, 6:20, 7, 10am, 5pm. Donations requested for upkeep of church and grounds. Admission to both necropolises 100R, students 50R. Camera 50R, video 100R. Museum of Sculpture 50R, students 25R. English map 7R.

A major pilgrimage destination, Alexander Nevskiy Monastery (Александро-невская Лавра; Aleksandro-Nevskaya Lavra) derives its name and importance from St. Alexander of Novgorod, a 13th-century Russian prince who defeated the Swedes and appeased the Mongol overlords without betraying his faith. His body was moved here by Peter the Great in 1724. In 1797, the monastery was promoted to *lavra*, a distinguished status bestowed on only four Russian Orthodox monasteries. A cobblestone path connects the cathedral and the two cemeteries.

TIKHVIN CEMETERY. Also known as the Artists' Necropolis (Некрапол Мастеров Искусств; Nekrapol Masterov Iskusstv), this cemetery (Тихвинское Кладбище; Tikhvinskoye Kladbishche) is the resting place of many famous Russians. Fyodor Dostoevsky could only afford to be buried here thanks to support from the Russian Orthodox Church. His grave, along the wall to the right, is always strewn with flowers. Mikhail Glinka, composer of the first Russian opera, and Mikhail Balakirev, who taught Nikolai Rimskiy-Korsakov, also rest here. Alexander Borodin's grave is graced with a gold mosaic of a composition sheet from his famous *String Quartet no. 1*. The magnificent tombs of Modest Mussorgsky, Anton Rubinstein, and Peter Tchaikovsky are next to Borodin's.

OTHER SIGHTS. Next to the Artists' Necropolis is the **18th-century necropolis,** St. Petersburg's oldest cemetery. Farther along the central path on the left is the **Church of the Annunciation** (Благовещенская Церков; Blagoveshchenskaya Tserkov), the original burial place of the Romanovs, who were moved to Peter and Paul Cathedral in 1998 (see p. 610). The church now houses the graves of military heroes, including **Suvorov** and minor members of the royal family. The **Holy Trinity Cathedral** (Свято-Тройтский Собор; Svyato-Troitskiy Sobor), at the end of the path, is a functioning church, teeming with priests and devout *babushki*.

SUMMER GARDENS AND PALACE

M2: Nevskiy Prospekt. Turn right on nab. Kanala Griboyedova (Канала Грибоедова), cross the Moyka, and turn right on Pestelya (Пестеля). The palace and gardens will be on your left. ☎314 03 74. Garden open daily May-Oct. 10am-9:30pm; Nov.-Apr. 10am-8pm. Free. Palace open Tu-Su 10am-5pm; kassa closes 4pm; closed last Tu of each month. Palace signs in English. 300R, students 150R; 3rd Th of month free. Camera and video 100R.

The Summer Gardens and Palace (Летний Сад и Дворец; Letniy Sad i Dvorets) are lovely places to rest and cool off. Both the northern and southern entrances lead to long, shady paths lined with replicas of classical Roman sculptures, crafted in the 1720s. In the northeastern corner of the Garden sits Peter's **Summer Palace,** which seems like more of a *dacha* (summer home) than a palace. The decor reflects Peter's diverse tastes: Spanish chairs, German clocks, and Japanese paintings fill the rooms. **Mars Field** (Марсого Поле; Marsogo Pole), named after military parades held here in the 19th century, extends to the **Summer Gardens,** now a memorial to the victims of the Revolution and the Civil War (1917-19). A round monument in the center holds an eternal flame.

SMOLNYY INSTITUTE AND CATHEDRAL

Pl. Rastrelli 3/1 (Растрелли). From M2: Nevskiy Prospekt, take trolley 5 or 7 or bus K147. Or, from the stop across Kirochnaya (Кирочная) from M1: Chernyshevskaya, take bus #46 or 136. Get off at the blue towers with gray domes (10-15min.). ☎271 76 32. Cathedral open M-W and Th-Su 11am-5pm; kassa closes 4pm; tower closes 4pm. 150R, students 75R. Camera 20R, video 50R. To see the Institute, call to make an appointment.

Once a prestigious school for aristocratic girls, the **Smolnyy Institute** (Смолный Институт) earned its place in history in 1917 when Trotsky and Lenin set up the headquarters of the **Bolshevik Central Committee** here and planned the Revolution from behind its yellow walls. In front of the institute stand busts of Engels, Marx, and Lenin, who lived here 1917-18. Next door, the blue-and-white **Smolnyy Cathedral** (Смолный Собор; Smolnyy Sobor), designed by Rastrelli, combines Baroque and Orthodox Russian styles. Climb to the top of the 68m bell tower and survey the city. Today, the Smolnyy Institute is the home of the city's government.

OCTOBER REGION

In the October Region (Октябрьский Район; Oktyabrskiy Raion), the Griboyedov Canal meanders through quiet neighborhoods.

ST. NICHOLAS CATHEDRAL. A striking blue-and-gold structure, St. Nicholas Cathedral (Никольский Собор; Nikolskiy Sobor) was constructed in 18th-century Baroque style. *(M4: Sadovaya. Cross the square, head down Sadovaya (Садовая), and fork right onto Rimskogo-Korsakogo (Римского-Корсакого). The cathedral across the canal. Enter through the gate on the right side. Lower church open daily 6:30am-7:30pm; upper church M-F 9:30am-noon, Sa 9:30am-noon and 6pm-vespers end. Services daily 7, 10am, 6pm.)*

YUSUPOVSKIY GARDENS. On the borders of the October Region, the Yusupovsky Gardens (Юсуповский Сад; Yusupovskiy Sad)—named after the prince who succeeded in killing Rasputin only after poisoning, shooting, and ultimately drowning him—provide a patch of green in the middle of the urban expanse. Locals come here to relax beside the pond. *(At the intersection of Sadovaya and Rimskogo-Korsakogo. M4: Sadovaya. Palace open 11am-6pm; last entrance 5pm.)*

THEATER SQUARE. The area (ТеатральнаЯ Площадь; Teatralnaya Ploshchad) between the Griboyedov and Kryukov (Крюков) Canals is dominated by two imposing turquoise buildings. The larger is the **Mariinskiy Theater,** home to the world-famous **Kirov Ballet and Opera.** Across the street stands the **Conservatory** (see **Entertainment,** p. 617), flanked by statues of composers Glinka and Rimsky-Korsakov. *(M2: Sennaya Ploshchad. From the western corner of Sennaya pl., follow the Griboyedov Canal left for 5-7min. until you reach the square.)*

MOSCOW AND ST. PETERSBURG

GREAT CHORAL SYNAGOGUE. Two blocks west of Theater Square lies Europe's 2nd-largest synagogue (Большая Хоралная Синагога; Bolshchaya Khoralnaya Sinagoga). Built in 1893 with the permission of Tsar Alexander II, its main dome covers a two-tiered worship space. Upon its completion, the city outlawed all other Jewish meeting houses, forcing St. Petersburg's 15,000 Jews to meet in a space intended for 2000. Though the Moorish exterior pays tribute to the architectural trends of the time, the interior is more traditional. The large synagogue holds services only on Shabbat (Saturday) and holidays. The small, adjacent synagogue holds regular services. A small cafe downstairs serves kosher food. *(Lermontovskiy (Лермонтовский) pr. 2. M4: Sadovaya. Turn right off Sadovaya, cross the canal onto Rimskogo-Korsakogo, continue to Lermontovskiy pr., and turn right. ☎259 68 59. Open daily 10am-7pm.)*

🏛 MUSEUMS

St. Petersburg's museums are famous worldwide, and with good reason. The city caters to all tastes: you'll be awed by the opulent extravagance of palatial residences and Soviet buildings. Exploring more specialized collections often yields greater understanding of the subject matter.

ART AND LITERATURE

🏛 RUSSIAN MUSEUM. Containing the world's largest collection of Russian art after Moscow's Tretyakov Gallery, this museum (Русский Музей; Russkiy Muzey) displays masterpieces, 12th- to 17th-century icons, 18th- to 19th-century paintings and sculpture, and Russian folk art, arranged chronologically. The museum's main building, the Mikhailovsky Palace, displays Russian art dating from the 14th to the early 20th century, while the stunning Marble Palace is home to exhibitions of Modern and Pop Art, in addition to being an architectural novelty itself—its facade uses 32 types of marble. The Stroganov Palace features a private collection of Russian icons, in addition to an exhibit of waxwork figures. A separate ticket is needed for the wax museum. *(Inzhenernaya 2. (Инженерная). M3: Gostiniy Dvor. In the yellow 1825 Mikhailov Palace (Михайловский Дворец; Mikhailovskiy Dvorets), behind the Pushkin monument. From the Metro, go down Mikhailovskaya past the Grand Hotel Europe. Enter through the basement in the courtyard's right corner; go downstairs and turn left. ☎595 42 48; www.rusmuseum.ru. Wheelchair accessible. English signs. Open M 10am-5pm, W-Su 10am-6pm; kassa closes 1hr. earlier. 270R, students 135R. No cameras.)*

ALEXANDER PUSHKIN APARTMENT MUSEUM. Visiting this former residence of Russia's most revered literary figure is a sort of pilgrimage for poetry-lovers. The museum (Музей Квартира Пушкина; Muzey Kvartira Pushkina) displays his personal effects and tells the tragic story of his last days. In the library where he died, all the furniture is original and the clock is stopped at the time of his death. *(Nab. Reki Moyki 12. M2: Nevskiy Prospekt. Walk toward the Admiralty; turn right on nab. Reki Moyki and follow the canal to the yellow building on the right. Enter through the courtyard; the kassa is on the left. Apartment ☎571 35 31, literary exhibition 314 00 07; www.museumpushkin.ru. Limited English info. Open M and W-Su 10:30am-6pm; kassa closes 5pm; closed last F of month. Apartment 60R, students 30R; literary exhibition 100/50R. MC/V for apartment entrance only.)*

DOSTOEVSKY HOUSE. While Fyodor Dostoevsky wrote some of *The Brothers Karamazov* and his diary in this house (Дом Достоевского; Dom Dostoyevskogo), he was surrounded—unlike most of his troubled characters—by a supportive wife and beloved children, two things he declared constituted 75% of a man's happiness in life. This museum exhibits the author's work while providing moving insight into the writer's domestic and literary existence. *Crime and Punishment* junkies should consider taking a themed Peter's Walking Tour (see

Practical Information, p. 603) devoted to the artist's literature. *(Kuznechnyy per. 5/ 2 (Кузнечный), on the corner of Dostoyevskogo (Достоевского), just past the market. M1: Vladimirskaya. ☎311 40 31. Open daily 11am-6pm; kassa closes 5pm. 90R, students 45R. English audioguide 70R.)*

HISTORY AND SCIENCE

KUNSTKAMERA ANTHROPOLOGICAL AND ETHNOGRAPHIC MUSEUM. This museum (Музей Антропологии и Этнографии—Кунсткамера; Muzey Antropologii i Etnografii—Kunstkamera) displays Peter the Great's grisly (and somewhat disordered) anatomical collection. *(Universitetskaya nab. 3, across the river from the Admiralty; enter on the left. ☎328 14 12. Open Tu-Su 11am-6pm; kassa, along the left side of building, closes 4:45pm; closed last Tu of month. 200R, students 100R.)*

ETHNOGRAPHIC MUSEUM. This museum (Музей Этнографии; Muzey Etnografii) exhibits the art, traditions, and cultures of Russia's 159 ethnic groups, spanning Ukraine and Belarus in the west and stretching across the Caucasus, Central Asia, and Siberia to the Pacific Ocean. An ambitious tableau on the wall depicts the ethnic makeup of old Russia. *(Inzhenernaya 4, bldg. 1. ☎219 17 10. Open Tu-Su 11am-6pm; kassa closes 5pm; closes 1hr. earlier on holidays. 200R, students 100R.)*

ST. PETERSBURG BOTANICAL GARDEN. In 1714, Peter I established the Drugstore garden, a plantation of rare flora and medicinal herbs, which became the Emperor's garden in 1823. The botanical garden (Санкт-Петербургский Ботанический Сад; Sankt-Peterbyrgskiy Botanichiskiy Sad) now houses about 6500 varieties of plants in over a hectare of greenhouses. *(Prof Popov 2. M: Petrogradskaya. Greenhouses open Th-Su 11am-4pm; park May 9th-Oct. 10am-9pm. 100R, students 50R.)*

ZOO. Founded in 1865, the zoo (ЗооПАРК; Zoopark) holds over 410 species. The zoo's mascot is the polar bear. Keep tickets until the end of your visit. *(Aleksandrovskiy park, 1. M2: Gorkovskaya. ☎232 82 60; www.spbzoo.ru. Open in summer 10am-9pm; in winter Tu-Su 10am-5pm; kassa closes 1hr. earlier. 120R, students 50R. Camera 30R.)*

ZOOLOGICAL MUSEUM. This museum (ЗоологиЧеский Музей; Zoologicheskiy Muzey) has 30,000 specimens of animals, fishes, and insects, including a fully preserved 40,000-year-old mammoth and a blue-whale skeleton. *(Universitetskaya nab. 1, next to the Kunstkamera Museum, across the bridge from the Admiralty. Bus #10. Open M-Th and Sa-Su 11am-6pm; kassa closes 4:45pm. 60R, students 20R; last Th of month free.)*

MUSEUM OF RUSSIAN POLITICAL HISTORY. Before the Bolsheviks set up shop here, this building housed Matilda Kshesinskaya, prima ballerina of the Mariinskiy Theater and Nicholas II's lover. Today, the museum (Музей Политической Истории России; Muzey Politicheskoy Istorii Rossii) includes a memorial to Lenin and a museum of general Russian political history. The east wing displays **Soviet propaganda,** as well as artifacts from WWII. *(Kuybysheva 2 (Куйбышева). M2: Gorkovskaya. Go down Kamennoostroskiy toward the mosque; turn left on Kuybysheva. ☎233 70 52. Open M-W and F-Su 10am-6pm. 150R, students 70R. Tours in English; 300R.)*

CENTRAL NAVAL MUSEUM. The old Stock Exchange building houses the boat that inspired Peter I to create the Russian navy. The museum inside (Центральный Военно-Морское Музей; Tsentralnyy Voyenno-Morskoy Muzey) displays submarines, weapons, artwork, and model ships chronicling the development of Russia's modern fleet. In one of the rooms devoted to the Cold War, a small golden ship model is on display, a gift from the Cuban commander in chief to his Russian equivalent; another displays Russia's first ballistic missile. The English-language tour (700R) is almost indispensable and heightens appreciation of the museum. *(Birzhevaya pl. 4 (Биржевая). Take bus #10 across the bridge to Vasilevskiy Island and get off at* *the 1st stop. Walk toward the Peter and Paul fortress; the museum is past the zoological museums, on the left. ☎328 25 02. English info. Open W-Su 11am-6pm; last entry 5:15pm; closed last Th of month. 300R, students 100R. Book tours 5 days ahead. Camera 20R, video 60R.)*

CRUISER AURORA. Deployed in the 1905 Russo-Japanese war, this ship (Аврора; Avrora) later played a critical role in the 1917 Revolution when it fired a blank by the Winter Palace, scaring Kerensky and his provisional government. Cannons and exhibits await on board. *(5min. past Peter's Cabin, on the Bolshaya Nevka River. ☎230 84 40. Open Tu-Th and Sa-Su 10:30am-4pm; last admission 3:30pm. Free.)*

MILITARY HISTORY MUSEUM. Military hardware from 15th-century armor to 20th-century tanks is showcased at this enormous museum (Центральный Военно-Исторический Музей; Tsentralniy Voenno-Istoricheskiy Muzey). Here's your chance to see genuine AK-47s and medium range missiles up close. On display are exhibits on all of the Russian wars in the 19th and 20th centuries. Those wanting only to view the weapons in the courtyard and visit the gift shop should purchase a ticket to the esplanade. *(Aleksandrovskiy Park 7 (Александровский Парк). M2: Gorkovskaya. Exit the Metro and walk toward the river, then bear right on Kronverskaya nab.; the museum is on the right. ☎232 02 96. Open W-Su 11am-6pm; kassa closes 1hr. earlier; closed last Th of month. Museum and esplanade 200R, students 100R; esplanade only 50/20R. Tours in English; 300R per person. Camera 100R, video 150R.)*

RUSSIAN VODKA MUSEUM. This museum (Музей Водки; Muzey Vodki) chronicles the history of Russia's favorite pastime in the space of two unexciting rooms. The quaint cafe in the back offers a hands-on vodka education. Indulge in the delectable three-shot tasting menu (US$15). Without an English guide or knowledge of Russian, it's best to skip the museum and head for the bar. *(Konnogvardeyskiy bul. 5 (Конногвардейский). Walk 1 block toward the river from the Manezh, turn left on Konnogvardeyskiy bul., and continue 1 block down on the right. ☎312 34 16. Open daily 11am-10pm. 25R; includes a shot at the bar. Call ahead for tours in English. Vodka shots 20-60R. MC/V.)*

ARCTIC AND ANTARCTIC MUSEUM. Science and history blend nicely in this museum (Музей Арктики и Антарктики; Muzey Arktiki i Antarktiki) devoted to the study of man's forays into the extreme conditions of the North and South poles. The museum displays ship models and nautical accoutrements such as a life-size seaplane, an explorer's hut, and archaeological remains from failed expeditions. In addition, detailed exhibits of polar species include a stuffed polar bear, sea duck, and polar wolf. *(Marata 24 (Марата). M1: Vladimirskaya. From the Metro, walk down Kuznechiy per. 2 blocks. On the corner of Kuznechnyy per. and Marata. ☎311 25 49; www.museum.ru/m132. Signs in Russian. Open W-Su 10am-6pm; kassa closes 5pm. Museum 100R, students 50R. Tours in English; 300R per person; call ahead. Video 150R.)*

🖫 SHOPPING

Countless souvenir shops line Nevskiy Prospekt with virtually identical goods. The **souvenir market** behind the Church of Our Savior on Spilled Blood offers variety, but also astronomical prices, which should always be negotiated. One particularly beautiful souvenir is the handcarved or painted **chess set** which folds out or opens to reveal its pieces, often modeled after the Russian army. Sets often cost as little as US$5, but can be sold for 10 times that. The most elaborate sets can cost over US$200 at nice stores, such as the ones in Gostiniy Dvor. The magnificent **Gostiniy Dvor** may have been the world's first indoor mall, and offers wares that reflect the Russian appreciation of European opulence. Other slightly less expensive clothing stores can be found along Nevskiy Prospekt. **Apraksin Dvor** (Апраксин Двор), near the city center, sells cheap to decent quality wares for half the price of nicer stores. Watch your pockets around Gostiniy and Apraksin yards.

❊ 🎵 FESTIVALS AND ENTERTAINMENT

Throughout June, when the evening sun barely touches the horizon, the city holds the famed **White Nights Festival.** In late June and early July, ballet and operas play at the theaters in celebration of White Nights. All year long, the former home of Tchaikovsky, Prokofiev, and Stravinsky lives up to its reputation as a mecca for the performing arts. It is fairly easy to get tickets to world-class performances for as little as 100R. *Yarus* (ярус) are the cheapest seats. The **theater season** ends in June and begins again in September. The **ticket office** is at Nevskiy pr. 42, near Gostiniy Dvor. (☎310 42 40. Schedule 20R.) The Friday issue of the *St. Petersburg Times* has comprehensive listings of entertainment and nightlife and indicates which performances are in English. If this is all too high-brow, head to the movies. Most films are dubbed in Russian, but it is increasingly common for movies to be shown in their original language. **Dom Kino,** Karavannaya 12 (Караванная), plays some movies in English. (M3: Gostiniy Dvor. ☎314 80 36. Tickets 30-100R.)

BALLET AND OPERA

Mariinskiy Teatr (Мариинский), also called **Kirov Teatr,** Teatralnaya pl. 1 (☎114 43 44, group bookings 314 17 44). M4: Sadovaya. Walk along Griboyedov Canal, then go right into the square. Bus #3, 22, or 27. This building premiered Tchaikovsky's *Nutcracker* and launched the careers of Pavlova and Baryshnikov. Performances 7pm, matinees Sept.-June 11:30am. *Kassa* open Tu-Su 11am-7pm. Tickets (160-4800R) on sale 20 days in advance. It is illegal but common for people to sell tickets at the entrance 15-30min. before shows. Discounts for foreign students at Russian universities. MC/V.

Mussorgsky Opera and Ballet Theater (Театр имени Муссоргского; Teatr imeni Mussorgskogo), also called the **Maly Theater,** pl. Iskusstv 1 (Искусств; ☎318 19 78). Hosts excellent performances of Russian ballet and opera. Bring your passport; documents are checked at the door. Open July-Aug. when the Mariinskiy is closed. Performances 7:30, 8pm; matinees noon. *Kassa* open M and W-Su 11am-3pm and 4-7pm, Tu 11am-3pm and 4-6pm. Tickets US$28-99.

Konservatoriya (Консерватория), Teatralnaya pl. 3 (☎117 85 74), across from Mariinskiy Teatr. M4: Sadovaya. Bus #3, 22, or 27. Ballets and operas performed by students of the elite St. Petersburg Academy. Performances 6:30pm, matinees noon. *Kassa* open daily 11am-7pm. Tickets 450R.

CLASSICAL MUSIC AND THEATER

Shostakovich Philharmonic Hall, Mikhailovskaya 2 (Михайловская; ☎314 10 58), across the square from the Russian Museum. M3: Gostiniy Dvor. Classical and modern performances by resident and visiting orchestras. During the summer, when the Philharmonic is on tour, other groups perform daily at 4 and 7pm. *Kassa* open daily noon-3pm and 4-7:30pm. Tickets 480-800R.

Akademicheskaya Kapella (Академическая Капелла), nab. Reki Moyki 20 (☎314 10 58), off Palace Square. M2: Nevskiy Prospekt. A venue for the Emperor Court Choir Capella, a professional choir that dates back to 1437 and was transferred from Moscow to St. Petersburg in 1703. Performances 7pm. *Kassa* open daily noon-3pm and 4-7pm.

Aleksandrinskiy Teatr (Александринский Театр), pl. Ostrovskogo 2 (Островского; ☎315 44 64). M3: Gostiniy Dvor. Turn right on Nevskiy pr., then right at the park with Catherine's statue. Ballet and theater shows of mostly Western classics like Hamlet and Cyrano de Bergerac. In summer, the theater features evening performances by St. Petersburg Ballet Company. *Kassa* open daily noon-6pm. Tickets 70-680R.

🔊 NIGHTLIFE

Pre-*glasnost*, there was only one Party-run club. These days, Petersburg is more than making up for lost time. Whether seeking a quiet drink, a rave, or a chance to show off designer duds, even the shyest will be tempted by the siren song of the city. Check the Friday issues of the *St. Petersburg Times* and *Pulse* for current events and special promotions. Note that the trendier clubs often exercise a door policy known as "face and dress control," so be sure to fix up and look sharp.

🎷 JFC Jazz Club, Shpalernaya 33 (Шпалерная; ☎272 98 50; www.jfc.sp.ru). M1: Chernyshevskaya. Go right on pr. Chernyshevskogo (Чернышевского), continue 4 blocks. Take a left on Shpalernaya and go into courtyard 33. The friendly club offers a wide variety of quality jazz in a relaxed atmosphere, and it holds occasional classical and folk concerts. Beer 50-400R. Hard liquor 40-150R. Live music 8-10pm. Cover 100-200R. Arrive early or call ahead for a table. Open daily 7-11pm.

Che, Poltavskaya 3 (Полтавская; ☎277 76 00). M1: Vosstaniya. Walk down Nevskiy pr. toward pl. Aleksandra Nevskogo 2-3 blocks, then make a right on Poltavskaya. Named for a fiery revolutionary, Che is a comfortable place to chill among the young, trendy, and well-to-do. Drinks 110-400R. Live music 10pm-2am. Open 24hr. AmEx/MC/V.

Ob'ekt, nab. Reki Moyki 82 (☎312 11 34). This basement bar and club is perfect for drinks after dinner or smoking a hookah with friends. Beer from 50R. Hosts frequent liquor-themed parties and has dancing at midnight. Open 24hr.

Griboedov (Грибоедов), Voronezhskaya 2A (Воронежская; ☎764 43 55). M4: Ligovskiy Prospekt. Go left exiting the underpass from the Metro. With your back to the station, go left at the intersection onto Konstantina Zaslonova (Константина Заслонова) and walk 2 blocks; take a left on Voronezhskaya. Look for a big mound. This laid-back but loud house and techno club also invites alternative acts. Beer and wine 30R. Vodka 20-50R. Live DJ daily midnight-6am. 18+. Cover 150R; 100R before 8pm with a voucher for 100R worth of drink. Open daily 6pm-6am.

Red Club/Cadillac Club, Poltavskaya 7 (☎277 13 66; www.clubred.ru). M1: Vosstaniya. Located in a former feed storage house behind Moscow Station. 2 stages attract top club bands, both local and international. Th-Su concerts at 8pm with DJs following at midnight. Cover 120-400R. Open Th-Su 7pm-6am.

Moloko (Молоко; Milk), Perekupnoy per. 12 (Перекупной; ☎274 94 67). Off Nevskiy pr., halfway between M1: Pl. Vosstaniya and M3/4: Pl. Aleksandra Nevskogo. Go toward Pl. A. Nevskogo, turn left off Nevskiy Prospekt on the unmarked street after the pharmacy and before Lomonosov Porcelain. Go 2 blocks and it's on the left. Catch the best Petersburg bands or mingle with the student crowd in a smoky but vivacious atmosphere. Beer 30R. Live music 8-11pm. Cover 100-200R. Open Tu-Su 7pm-midnight.

CCCP, Nevskiy Prospekt 54 (☎310 49 29). M: Nevskiy Prospekt. Though many of its patrons are almost too young to remember what its name stands for, this cafe exploits its Soviet theme for all that it's worth. Very popular among tourists and locals. Dancing F-Sa nights to house and techno music. Open daily 1pm-6am. AmEx/MC/V.

Par.spb, 5B Aleksandrovskiy Park (☎233 33 74; www.par.spb.ru). M2: Gorkovskaya. Exit the Metro and bear right, walk through the park in the direction of the Peter and Paul Fortress, and look for the red brick building. Popular with the cosmopolitan set, this hip spot spins house music and hosts a roster of international DJs. Be prepared for prolonged queuing while the door staff exercises its right to identify and privilege the beautiful people. Beer and vodka from 30R. Cover 100-500R. Open F-Su 11pm-late.

Tunnel, Blokhina 16 (Блохина; ☎233 40 15). M4: Sportivnaya or M2: Gorkovskaya. From Gorkoskaya, exit the Metro and bear left, walking along Kronverskiy pr. (Кронверский) in Alexandrinskiy Park toward Vasilevskiy Island. At Blokhina 16, turn at the unmarked street and head for the farthest bunker. Russia's pioneering techno club, located inside a camouflaged bomb shelter, offers cutting-edge jungle and house over an excellent sound system. Drinks 40R. Cover 150-300R. Open F-Sa midnight-6am.

 PRICEY DRINK. Though it's common to spot Russians of all ages sipping from beer bottles at any hour of the day, be aware that it's illegal to consume anything with more than 12% alcohol in public places, including vodka. Doing so can result in a 200-500R (US$7-15) fine.

GLBT NIGHTLIFE

Those interested in finding out more about the gay life of St. Petersburg should pick up a copy of *GAYP*, which lists gay services, from clubs to saunas. The website www.xsgay.com is another good resource.

Triel, 5-ya Sovetskaya ul, 45 (☎710 20 16). M1: Vosstaniya. Turn left on Suvorovsky pr., then right on 5-ya Sovetskaya. St. Pete's only lesbian club plays a mix of Russian pop. Drinks 50-100R. Women only except Th-F. Cover F men 200R; F-Sa women 100R. Open M-Tu 5pm-midnight, W 9pm-6am, F-Sa 10pm-6am; cafe Tu and Th 6pm-midnight.

Greshniki (Грешники; Sinners), nab. Kanala Griboyedova 28 (☎318 42 91; www.greshniki.ru), 2 blocks off Nevskiy pr., past Kazan Cathedral. M2: Nevskiy Prospekt. Rocker-dungeon-themed 4 fl. gay club, primarily for men. Plays disco, techno, and Europop. Drinks 40-250R. Drag shows W-Su 1, 2am. Male strip shows daily midnight-4am. 18+. Cover men 50-150R, women 300-500R. Open daily 10pm-6am.

SLOVAK REPUBLIC
(SLOVENSKÁ REPUBLIKA)

Known for high mountain peaks, a vibrant folk culture, and generous hospitality, the Slovak Republic appeals especially to hikers and lovers of rural life. The country enjoys the fastest-growing economy in the former Eastern Bloc, but is still struggling to reconcile its agricultural past with the industrialization imposed by the Soviets. An intriguing mix of conservative traditionalism and easygoing youthful spirit marks Slovak culture. From booming Bratislava to tiny villages in the famous Tatras Mountains, the Slovak Republic is gradually adapting to the modern world, but its people continue to celebrate their traditions and heritage.

 DISCOVER THE SLOVAK REPUBLIC: SUGGESTED ITINERARIES

THREE DAYS Devote your stay to a leisurely exploration of **Bratislava.** Make sure to check out **Primate's Palace** (no monkeys, unfortunately; p. 633). Also stop by the **UFO,** atop New Bridge, to see if there's a party going on (p. 632).

ONE WEEK From **Bratislava** (2 days), head to **Starý Smokovec** (5 days, p. 649) via **Poprad.** There you can mountain bike, hike, or ski the grand **High Tatras.** Leave time for a daytrip to **Štrbské Pleso** (p. 651), with its waterfalls and rigorous hikes.

FACTS AND FIGURES

Official Name: Slovak Republic.

Capital: Bratislava.

Major Cities: Bratislava, Košice.

Population: 5,400,000. (86% Slovak, 10% Hungarian, 2% Roma).

Land Area: 48,845 sq. km.

Time Zone: GMT + 2.

Language: Slovak.

Religions: Roman Catholic (69%), Protestant (11%), Greek Catholic (4%).

ESSENTIALS

WHEN TO GO

In the high season of July and August, it is advisable to book rooms in advance in the Tatras. Otherwise, it isn't hard to find a place to sleep. Slovakia is mostly mountainous, with plains to the south. The lowlands tend to be warmer; summers can be cool in the mountains, and winter brings good conditions for skiing.

DOCUMENTS AND FORMALITIES

EMBASSIES AND CONSULATES. Foreign embassies to the Slovak Republic are in Bratislava (p. 626). Slovak embassies at home include: **Australia,** 47 Culgoa Circuit, O'Malley, Canberra, ACT 2606 (☎2 6290 1516; www.slovakemb-aust.org); **Canada,** 50 Rideau Ter., Ottawa, ON K1M 2A1 (☎613 749 4442; www.ottawa.mfa.sk); **Ire-**

ENTRANCE REQUIREMENTS
Passport: Required for all travelers.
Visa: Not required for stays of under 90 days for citizens of Australia, Canada, New Zealand, and the US.
Letter of Invitation: Not required for citizens of Australia, Canada, Ireland, New Zealand, the UK, and the US.
Inoculations: Recommended up-to-date on DTaP (diphtheria, tetanus, and pertussis), Hepatitis A, Hepatitis B, MMR (measles, mumps, and rubella), Polio booster, and Typhoid.
Work Permit: Required for foreigners planning to work in the Slovak Republic.
Driving Permit: Required for all those planning to drive in the Slovak Republic.

land, 20 Clyde Rd., Ballsbridge, Dublin 4 (☎1 660 0012; fax 1 660 0014); **UK,** 25 Kensington Palace Gardens, London W8 4QY (☎20 7243 0803; www.slovakembassy.co.uk); **US,** 3523 International Ct. NW, Washington, D.C. 20008 (☎202 237 1054; www.slovakembassy-us.org).

VISA AND ENTRY INFORMATION. Citizens of Australia, Canada, Ireland, New Zealand, the UK, and the US can visit without a visa for up to 90 days. Those traveling to the Slovak Republic for business, employment, study, or specific program purposes must obtain a temporary residence permit. Contact your embassy for requirements and costs.

TOURIST SERVICES AND MONEY

The **Slovak Tourist Board** (☎48 413 61 46; www.sacr.sk) provides useful links for finding accommodations, enjoying the country's natural resources, and learning about its culture. Public tourist offices are marked by a green square containing a white "i." English is often spoken at tourist offices, which usually provide maps and information about transportation. Although the Slovak Republic is now a member state of the EU, the switchover to the euro has not yet taken place: the **Slovak koruna (Sk)** remains the main unit of currency. It is divided into 100 *halier*, issued in standard denominations of 50 *halier*. Bear in mind that smaller estab-

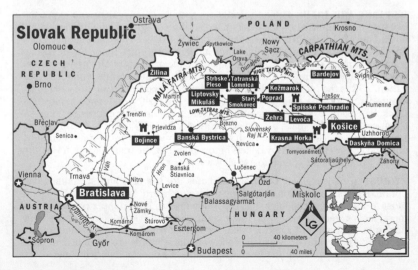

lishments may not be able to break 5000Sk bills. **Credit cards** are not accepted in many Slovak Establishments, but MasterCard and Visa are the most useful, followed by American Express. Inflation is currently around 8%, so expect price hikes. ATMs are plentiful and give the best exchange rates, but also tend to charge a flat service fee, so it is most economical to withdraw large amounts at a time. Banks **Slovenská-Sporiteľňa** and **Unibank** handle MC/V cash advances. Banks require you to present your passport for most transactions.

KORUNY (SK)		
AUS$1 = 23.85SK		10SK = AUS$0.42
CDN$1 = 26.01SK		10SK = CDN$0.38
EUR€1 = 38.60SK		10SK = EUR€0.25
NZ$1 = 22.04SK		10SK = NZ$0.45
UK£1 = 56.86SK		10SK = UK£0.18
US$1 = 31.70SK		10SK = US$0.32

HEALTH AND SAFETY

EMERGENCY	**Police:** ☎ 150. **Ambulance:** ☎ 155. **Fire:** ☎ 158.

In an emergency, dial ☎ 112 for English and German operators. **Tap water** varies in quality and appearance but is generally safe. If water comes out of the faucet cloudy, let it sit for 5min: air bubbles are probably to blame. *Drogerii* (drugstores) stock Western brands. Bandages are *obväz*, aspirin *aspirena*, tampons *tampony*, and condoms *kondómy*. **Petty crime** is common; be wary in crowded areas and secure passports and other valuables at all times. Accommodations for **disabled** travelers are rare. **Women** traveling alone will likely have few problems, but may encounter stares. Dress modestly and avoid walking or riding public transportation at night. **Minority** travelers with darker skin may encounter discrimination and should exercise caution at all times. **Homosexuality** is not accepted by all Slovaks; GLBT couples may experience stares or insults.

TRANSPORTATION

BY PLANE AND TRAIN. Flying to Bratislava may be inconvenient and expensive because many international carriers have no direct flights. Flying to **Vienna, AUT** and taking a bus or train is often much cheaper and doesn't take much longer. **East-Pass** is valid in the Slovak Republic, but Eurail is not. *InterCity* or *EuroCity* fast trains cost more. A boxed R on the timetable means a *miestenka* (reservation; 7Sk) is required. There is a fine for boarding an international train without a reservation. ŽSR is the national rail company. Master schedules *(cestovný poriadok)* are available for sale at information desks and are posted on boards in most stations. Reservations are recommended and often required for *expresný* (express) trains and first-class seats, but are not necessary for *rychlík* (fast), *spešný* (semi-fast), or *osobný* (local) trains. Both first and second class are relatively comfortable and considered safe. Buy tickets before boarding the train, except in very tiny towns. For up-to-date train info, check www.zsr.sk.

BY BUS. In hilly regions, **ČSAD** or **SAD buses** are the best and sometimes only option. Except for very long trips, buy tickets on board. You can probably ignore most footnotes on schedules, but the following are important: **x** (crossed hammers) means weekdays only; **a** is Saturday and Sunday; **b** is Monday through Saturday; **n** is Sunday; and **r** and **k** mean excluding holidays. *"Premava"* means including; *"nepremava"* is except; following those words are often lists of dates (day is listed before month). Check www.sad.sk for updated bus schedules.

BY BIKE. Rambling wilds and ruined castles inspire many great bike tours. Biking is very popular among the Slovaks, especially in the Tatras, the foothills of the western Slovak Republic, and Šariš. **VKÚ** publishes color bike maps (70-80Sk).

KEEPING IN TOUCH

PHONE CODES	**Country code:** 421. **International dialing prefix:** 00. From outside the Slovak Republic, dial int'l dialing prefix + 421 + city code + local number. Within the Slovak Republic, dial city code + local number for intercity calls and simply the local number for calls within a city.

Internet access is common in the Slovak Republic, even in smaller towns. **Internet** cafes usually offer cheap (1Sk per min.), fast access. Recent modernization of the Slovak **phone** system has required many businesses and individuals to switch phone numbers. The phone system is still somewhat unreliable; try multiple times if you don't get through. Some public phones allow international calls, while others do not. Both types of phones exist in each city, but there is no good way to distinguish them. **Card phones** are common and are usually much better than the coin-operated variety. Purchase cards (100-500Sk) at the post office. Be sure to buy the "Global Phone" card if you plan to make international calls. **Mail** service is efficient. Letters abroad take two to three weeks to arrive. Letters to **Europe** cost 11-14Sk; letters to the **US** cost 21Sk. Address envelopes for **Poste Restante** as follows: Piotr (First name) BRZEZINSKI (LAST NAME), POSTE RESTANTE, Horná 1 (post office address), 97400 (postal code) Banská Bystrica (city), SLOVAK REPUBLIC. Almost every post office *(pošta)* provides **express mail** services. To send a package abroad, go to a customs office *(colnice)*.

ACCOMMODATIONS AND CAMPING

SLOVAKIA	❶	❷	❸	❹	❺
ACCOMMODATIONS	under 250Sk under €6 under US$8	251-500Sk €6-13 US$8-16	501-800Sk €13-21 US$16-25	801-1000Sk €21-26 US$25-32	over 1000Sk over €26 over US$32

Beware of scams and overpricing. Foreigners are often charged up to twice as much as Slovaks for the same room. Finding cheap accommodations in Bratislava before student dorms open in July is very difficult. Without reservations, you may have a great deal of trouble in Slovenský Raj and the Tatras. In other regions, finding a bed is relatively easy if you call ahead. The tourist office, **SlovakoTourist,** and other tourist agencies can usually help. The Slovak Republic has few hostels, most of which are found in and around Bratislava. These usually provide towels and a bar of soap. **Juniorhotels (HI)** tend to be a bit nicer than hostels. **Hotel** prices are dramatically lower outside Bratislava and the Tatras, with budget hotels running 300-600Sk. **Pensions** *(penzióny)* are smaller and less expensive than hotels.

Campgrounds are common. They are located on the outskirts of most towns and usually rent bungalows to travelers without tents. Camping in national parks is illegal. In the mountains, *chaty* (mountain huts/cottages) range from plush quarters around 600Sk per night to friendly bunks with outhouses (about 200Sk).

FOOD AND DRINK

SLOVAKIA	❶	❷	❸	❹	❺
FOOD	under 120Sk under €3 under $4	120-190Sk €3-5 $4-6	190-270Sk €5-7 $6-9	270-330Sk €7-9 $9-11	over 330Sk over €9 over $11

The national dish, *bryndzové halušky* (small dumplings in sauce), is a godsend for **vegetarians** and those sticking to a **kosher** diet. Pork products, however, are central to many traditional meals. *Knedliky* (dumplings) or *zemiaky* (potatoes) frequently accompany entrees. Enjoy *kolačky* (pastry), baked with cheese, jam or poppy seeds, and honey, for dessert. White **wines** are produced northeast of Bratislava, while *Tokaj* wines (distinct from Hungarian *Tokaji Aszú*) are produced around Košice. Enjoy them at a *vináreň* (wine hall). *Pivo* (beer) is served at a *pivnica* or *piváreň* (tavern). The favorite Slovak beer is the slightly bitter *Spis*.

LIFE AND TIMES

HISTORY

EARLY CIVILIZATION. Archaeological evidence suggests that people first migrated to the Slovak region during the Early Paleolithic period, c. 270,000 BC. Various farming peoples came to populate the area, which benefitted during the Bronze Age from its natural wealth in copper ore. Romans began occupying small portions of the region in AD 6. In 174 Marcus Aurelius conquered more of the territory, creating the empire's farthest northern border; it was on the banks of a Slovak river that he wrote his philosophical treatise, *Meditations*. After the fall of the Roman Empire, the Slovak lands were brutally contested. The Slavs eventually won power, and a new state formed in 833 under Prince Mojmír of Moravia. Despite unification, the Slavs could not fend off the Franks and Germans. With the 907 triumph of the Magyars, the state was made part of the Hungarian Kingdom.

ESCAPING HUNGARY'S GRASP. The Tatar invasions of 1241-43 devastated the already weakened Hungarian Kingdom, which finally fell to the Ottomans in 1526. The Empire was divided and the Hapsburgs, a rising power in the region, gained control of Slovak lands. For the next 200 years, Slovakia was the front line in a continuous struggle between the Hapsburgs and the Turks. A Slovak nationalist movement emerged in the 18th century; however, Hungarian power continued to grow, thanks in part to the 1867 establishment of the **Austro-Hungarian Dual Monarchy**. The Hungarian government intensified its Magyarization policies, which only provoked the Slovak nationalist movement. On October 28, 1918, Slovakia, Bohemia, Moravia, and Ruthenia combined to form independent **Czechoslovakia**.

ENTER NAZIS. After Czechoslovakia was abandoned by Britain and France in the **Munich Agreement** of September 1938, the Slovaks clamored for autonomy. While Hitler occupied Prague, Slovakia declared independence in 1939 as a nationalist Christian state under the leadership of **Monsignor Jozef Tiso**. The Tiso government's decision to ally with Nazi Germany dealt a blow to the Slovaks, and over 70,000 Slovak Jews were sent to concentration camps. A partisan resistance emerged, culminating in August 1944 with the ill-fated two-month **Slovak National Uprising**.

THE AFTERMATH. After WWII, the Slovaks again became a part of democratic Czechoslovakia. In February 1948, as the coalition National Front government fell apart, the Communists seized control in a coup. Discontent simmered beneath the surface of Communist Czechoslovakia until the late 1960s, when Slovak **Alexander Dubček** steered the regime away from Moscow's grip. During the 1968 **Prague Spring**, Dubček expanded intellectual discussion in the censored society. Soviet tanks immediately rolled into Prague and reinstated totalitarian rule.

BREAKING UP IS HARD TO DO. The Communists remained in power until the 1989 **Velvet Revolution** (see p. 163), when Czech dissident **Václav Havel** was elected president; he introduced a pluralistic political system and market economy. Slovak nationalism emerged victorious with a **Declaration of Independence** on January 1, 1993. Coming out of the 1993 **Velvet Divorce** with only 25% of the industrial capacity of former Czechoslovakia, the Slovak Republic has had trouble adjusting to the post-Eastern Bloc world. Matters were worsened by **Vladimír Mečiar,** who has been thrice elected and removed as prime minister. During his tenure he violated the constitution and failed to reform the economy.

TODAY

Rudolf Schuster became president in May 1999. His election, along with the appointment of Prime Minister **Mikuláš Dzurinda,** brought much-needed economic changes. Reforms have attracted foreign investment, and the economy is in fairly good shape aside from high unemployment rates. In 2004, the World Bank declared that the Slovak Republic had the world's fastest-transforming economy. The same year, the country gained accession into both **NATO** and the **European Union (EU),** and **Ivan Gašparovič,** founder of the Movement for Democracy Party, was elected president. Racially motivated violence remains a problem in the Slovak Republic, and **minorities** face substantial discrimination.

PEOPLE AND CULTURE

Ethnic **Slovaks** comprise 86% of the population of the Slovak Republic, with a significant **Hungarian** minority accounting for another 11%. **Roma, Germans,** and various **Slavs** make up the remainder. After decades of state-enforced atheism, Slovakians are far more likely to have returned to religion than their Czech neighbors; the Czech Republic's reported rate of atheism (40%) is four times that of the Slovak Republic (10%). Around 60% of Slovakians are **Roman Catholic; Protestants** and members of **Orthodox** churches together make up an additional 13%. **Slovak** is a West Slavic language written in the Latin alphabet. It is closely enough related to the other languages in this group—**Czech** and **Polish**—that speakers of one will understand the others. Attempts to speak Slovak itself, however, will be appreciated. Older people will speak a little Polish. **English** is common among Bratislava's youth, but **German** is more useful outside the capital. **Russian** is occasionally understood but is sometimes unwelcome. The golden rules of speaking Slovak are to pronounce every letter and stress the first syllable. Accents over vowels lengthen them. For a phrasebook and glossary, see **Glossary: Slovak,** p. 781.

Tipping is common in restaurants, though the rules are ambiguous. Most people round up to a convenient number by refusing change when they pay. **Bargaining** is unacceptable—special offense is taken when foreigners attempt the practice. Most bus and train stations and some restaurants are **non-smoking,** though many Slovaks smoke. Social mores tend to be conservative; dress neatly and be polite.

THE ARTS

LITERATURE. Slovak remained indistinct from Czech until the end of the 18th century, when nationalist writers like Josef Ignác Bajza began to draw upon Slovak dialects. Anton Bernolák subsequently wrote a grammar and six-volume dictionary of the language. A fullblown **literary tradition** began after 19th-century linguist **Ľudovít Štúr's** "new" language, based on Central Slovak dialects, inspired a string of national poets. Foremost among these was **Andrej Sládkovič,** author of the Slovak national epic, *Marína* (1846). In the wake of WWI, Slovak nationalism and literature matured concurrently. Cosmopolitan influences appeared alongside Romanticism: **Emil Boleslav Lukáč** experimented with Symbolism while **Rudolf Fábry** championed Surrealism. Novelist **Janko Jesenský** satirized the interwar government in *The Democrats (Demokrati;* 1934-37). After WWII, the Slovak literati reacted to communist rule. **Ladislav Mňačko,** author of the novel *The Taste of Power (Ako chutí moc),* was an early and Stalin openly.

MUSIC. Slovak folk music uses instruments such as the flute-like *fujara* and Slovak bagpipes, called *gajdy.* Many folk songs relate the adventures of Juraj Jánošík, a Slovak bandit reminiscent of Robin Hood. Classical music is also popular, and famous composers like **Mikuláš Moyzes** and **Andrej Ocenáš** worked folk themes into their music in the early 20th century. Both the **Bratislava Philharmonic Orchestra** and the **Slovak Chamber Orchestra** enjoy international reputations.

FILM. The 1921 film *Jánosík* was one of the world's first full-length features. The **Czechoslovak New Wave** of the late 1960s was arguably the most important film movement to emerge from Eastern or Central Europe in the latter half of the 20th century. Ján Kadár, a Slovak involved in the movement, directed *The Shop on Main Street (Obchod na korze),* which won an Academy Award in 1965. Despite the current lack of both funding and facilities for filmmaking, Slovak directors **Martin Šulík** and **Štefan Semjan** are well known internationally.

HOLIDAYS AND FESTIVALS

Holidays: Origin of the Slovak Republic (Jan. 1); Epiphany (Jan. 6); Good Friday (Apr. 9); Easter Holiday (Apr. 11-12); May Day (May 1); Sts. Cyril and Methodius Day (July 5); Anniversary of Slovak National Uprising (Aug. 29); Constitution Day (Sept. 1); Our Lady of the 7 Sorrows (Sept. 15); All Saint's Day (Nov. 1); Day of Freedom and Democracy (Nov. 17); Christmas (Dec. 24-26).

Festivals: Banská Bystrica's **Festival of Ghosts and Spirits,** in late spring, is a celebration for the dead. Near Poprad, the **Vychodna Folk Festival** occurs in mid-summer.

ADDITIONAL RESOURCES

Czechoslovakia: The Short Goodbye, by Abby Innes (2001). An analysis of the causes and consequences of Czechoslovakia's division into the Czech and Slovak Republics.

A History of Slovakia: The Struggle for Survival, by Stanislav Kirschbaum (1996). This comprehensive history is well researched, though it gives controversial treatment to the decision of Josef Tifo to ally Slovakia with Hitler during WWII.

A History of Slovak Literature, by Peter Petro (1997). An exploration of the Slovak literary tradition with a keen eye to its political and cultural interactions.

The Shop on Main Street, directed by Jan Kadar (1965). An Academy Award-winning film about a Slovak man who befriends a Jewish woman during the Holocaust.

Verses, by Ivan Krasko (1912). Musical, melancholy verse by a pioneer of Slovak poetry.

BRATISLAVA ☎ (0)2

One of only two regions in Eastern Europe with living standards above the EU average, the booming Slovak capital surprises anyone willing take the time to discover it. A city that has come to terms with its turbulent past, modern Bratislava (pop. 500,000) manages to integrate old-world charm with chic modernity: villages, vineyards, and castles lace the outskirts, while the streets of the burgeoning downtown district are lined with shops, restaurants, and cafes.

Bratislava

🏠 **ACCOMMODATIONS**
Downtown Backpacker's
  Hostel, **4**
Družba, **23**
Orange Hostel, **19**
Patio Hostel, **7**
Pension Gremium, **18**
Slovenská Zdravotnicka
  Univerzita, **1**
Ubytovacie Zariadenie
  Zvárač, **2**
🍎 **FOOD**
1 Slovak, **5**
Bagetky, **20**
Chez David, **10**
Diétna Jadelen, **15**
El Diablo, **16**
London Café, **22**
Prašná Bašta and
  Café Kút, **9**
Vega Destination, **11**

🍺 **NIGHTLIFE**
Apollon Gay Club, **3**
Circus Barok, **25**
Elam Klub, **24**
Jazz Café, **17**
KGB, **6**
Klub Laverna, **14**
Medusa Cocktail
  Bar, **8**
☕ **CAFES**
Café Štúdio Music
  Club, **13**
Casa Dy, **12**
People's Lounge
  Café, **21**

TRANSPORTATION

Flights: M.R. Štefánik International Airport (☎48 57 11 11), 9km northeast of town. To reach the center, take bus #61 (1hr.) to the train station and then take tram #1 to Poštová on nám. SNP. Most airlines frequent the airport in Vienna, but the following carriers cross the Slovak border: **Austrian Airlines** (☎54 41 16 10; www.ava.com); **ČSA** (☎52 96 10 42; www.czech-airlines.com); **Delta** (☎52 92 09 40; www.delta.com); **LOT** (☎52 96 40 07; www.lot.com); **Lufthansa** (☎52 96 78 15; www.lufthansa.com). A few **budget airlines** service the city as well: **SkyEurope** (☎48 50 11 11; www.skyeurope.com); **easyJet** (www.easyjet.com) flies to **Luton, ENG.**

Trains: Bratislava Hlavná Stanica, at the end of Predstaničné nám., off Šancová. **Železnice Slovenskej republiky** posts schedules on its website (☎50 58 11 11; www.zsr.sk). To: **Banská Bystrica** (3-4½hr., 1 per day, 348Sk); **Košice** (5-6hr., 10 per day, 580Sk); **Poprad** (4¾hr., 2 per day, 420Sk); **Žilina** (2¾hr., 6 per day, 380Sk); **Prague, CZR** (4½-5½hr., 3 per day, 840Sk); **Warsaw, POL** (8hr., 1 per day, 1800Sk).

Buses: Mlynské nivy 31 (☎55 42 16 67, info 09 84 22 22 22). Bus 210 runs between the train and bus stations. Check your ticket for the bus number (č. aut.), as several depart from the same stand. **Eurolines** offers a 10% discount to those under 26. To:

Banská Bystrica (3-4½hr., 2 per hr., 290-450Sk); **Poprad** (6-7¾hr., 7-8 per day, 258Sk); **Žilina** (3-4hr., 11-15 per day, 300Sk); **Belgrade, SMN** (12hr., 1 per day, 1200Sk); **Berlin, GER** (12hr., 1 per day, 1200Sk); **Budapest, HUN** (4hr., 2 per day, 610Sk); **Prague, CZR** (4¾hr., 5 per day, 510Sk); **Vienna, AUT** (1½hr., 1 per hr., 380Sk); **Warsaw, POL** (13hr., 2 per day, 720Sk).

Hydrofoils: Lodná osobná doprava, Fajnorovo nábr. 2 (☎52 96 45 87; www.lod.sk), across from the **Slovak National Museum.** Hit the Danube in style. Open daily 8:30am-5:30pm. To: **Devín Castle** (20min., Tu-Su 2 per day, 140Sk); **Budapest, HUN** (4hr.; 1 per day; €69, students €59); **Vienna, AUT** (1¾hr., 2 per day, 550Sk).

Local Transportation: Tram and **bus** tickets (10min. 14Sk, 30min. 18Sk, 1hr. 22Sk) are sold at kiosks and at the orange *automaty* in bus stations. Use an *automat* only if its light is on. Stamp your ticket when you board; fine for riding ticketless is 1200Sk. Trams and buses run 4am-11pm. **Night buses,** marked with black-and-orange numbers in the 500s, run midnight-4am; 2 tickets required. Some kiosks and ticket machines sell **passes** (1-day 90Sk, 2-day 170Sk, 3-day 210Sk).

Taxis: BP (☎169 99); **FunTaxi** (☎167 77); **Profi Taxi** (☎162 22).

■✦🛈 ORIENTATION AND PRACTICAL INFORMATION

The **Dunaj** (Danube) runs east-west across Bratislava. Four bridges span the river; the main **Nový Most** (New Bridge) connects Bratislava's center, **Staromestská** (Old Town), in the north, to the commercial and entertainment district on the river's southern bank. **Bratislavský Hrad** (Bratislava Castle) towers on a hill to the west, while the city center sits between the river and **nám. Slovenského Národného Povstania** (nám. SNP; Slovak National Uprising Square). When arriving by train, make sure to get off at **Hlavná Stanica,** the central train station. To reach the center from the **train station,** take tram #2 to the 6th stop or walk downhill, take a right, then an immediate left, and walk down Stefanikova (15-20min). From the **bus station,** take trolley #202, or turn right on Mlynské nivy and walk to Dunajská, which leads to **Kamenné nám.** (Stone Square) and the center of town (15-20min).

TOURIST, FINANCIAL, AND LOCAL SERVICES

Tourist Office: Bratislavská Informačná Služba (BIS), Klobúčnicka 2 (☎161 86; www.bratislava.sk/bis). Books **private rooms** and hotels (800-3000Sk plus 50Sk fee); sells **maps** (free-80Sk) and a **pass** (75Sk) for 4 museums and zoo. Books **tours** (1000Sk per hr.; max. 19 people). Open June-Oct. 15 M-F 8:30am-7pm, Sa 9am-5pm, Su 9:30am-4pm; Oct. 16-May M-F 8am-6pm, Sa 9am-2pm. **Branch** in train station annex open M-F 8am-2pm and 2:30-7:30pm, Sa-Su 8:30am-2pm and 2:30-6pm.

Embassies: Citizens of **Australia** and **New Zealand** should contact the UK embassy in an emergency. **Canada,** Mostová 2 (☎59 20 40 31; ambassador resides in Prague). **Ireland,** Mostová 2 (☎59 30 96 11; mail@ireland-embassy.sk). Open M-F 9am-12:30pm. **UK,** Panská 16 (☎59 98 20 00; www.britishembassy.sk). Visa office open M-F 8:30-11am. **US,** Hviezdoslavovo nám. 5 (☎54 43 08 61, emergency 09 03 70 36 66; www.usembassy.sk). Open M-F 8am-4:30pm. Visa office open M-F 8-11:30am.

Currency Exchange: Ľudová Banka, nám. SNP 15 (☎54 41 89 84; www.luba.sk) cashes American Express **traveler's checks** for 1% commission and offers MC/V **cash advances.** Open M-F 8am-7pm. 24hr. MC/V **ATMs** are at the train station and throughout the center.

Luggage Storage: At bus station 25-35Sk. Open M-F 7am-noon, 12:30-7pm, 7:30-9pm; Sa-Su 7am-noon, 12:30-6pm. At train station 30-40Sk. Open daily 5:30am-midnight.

English-Language Bookstores: Eurobooks, Jesenského 5-9 (☎90 55 66 973; www.eurobooks.sk). Large selection of English-language literature and guidebooks. Open M-F 8:30am-6:30pm, Sa 9am-1pm. **Interpress Slovakia,** Sedlárska 2 (☎44 87

15 01; interpress@interpress.sk), on the corner with Ventúrska, has foreign magazines (110-400Sk) and newspapers (90-120Sk). Open M-F 7am-11pm, Sa 9am-11pm, Su 10am-10pm. MC/V (300Sk min.).

EMERGENCY AND COMMUNICATIONS

Pharmacy: Lekáreň Pod Manderlom, nám. SNP 20 (☎54 43 29 52). Open M-F 7:30am-7pm, Sa 8am-7pm, Su 9am-7pm. Ring bell after hours for emergency service.

Hospital: Milosrdni Braha, nám. SNP 10 (☎578 87 11), on the corner of Kolárska and Treskoňova.

Telephones: All over town. Purchase cards (local 80-120Sk, international 200-400Sk) at the post office and at kiosks.

Internet: There are Internet cafes all over central Bratislava, especially along Michalská and Obchodná. **Megainet,** Šancová 25. New PCs in a cafe. 1Sk per min. Open daily 9am-10pm. **Internet Centrum,** Michalská 2. 6-computer cafe with friendly staff. Tea 20-30Sk. M-F 2Sk per min., Sa-Su 1Sk per min. Open daily 9am-midnight. **Krist@n,** Michalská 10. 5 speedy computers and Wi-Fi. 1Sk per min. Open daily 11am-11pm.

Post Office: Nám. SNP 35 (☎59 39 33 30). Offers **fax** service. **Poste Restante** and phone cards at counters #5-6. Poste restante M-F 7am-8pm, Sa 7am-2pm. Open M-F 7am-8pm, Sa 7am-6pm, Su 9am-2pm. **Postal Code:** 81000 Bratislava 1.

ACCOMMODATIONS

The most affordable accommodations lie outside the city center. In mid-summer, **university dorms** open as hostels. Rooms are cheap and more central than at many hotels. **BIS** (see p. 628) has dorm prices and contacts, and books well-located **private rooms.** (Singles 800-2000Sk; doubles 1600-2500Sk. Booking fee 50Sk.)

HOSTELS AND DORMS

▨ Downtown Backpacker's Hostel (HI), Panenská 31 (☎546 411 91; www.backpackers.sk). Backpackers relax on worn sofas in this 19th-century building, enjoying the ambience of brick walls, a Lenin bust, and a common room bar (beer 35Sk). Comfortable rooms, a social atmosphere, and proximity to the Old Town make this one of Bratislava's most popular hostels—book ahead. Laundry 100Sk. Internet 2Sk per min. Some travelers report not being charged for either. Reception 24hr. Check-out noon. Dorms 600Sk, HI members 540Sk; doubles 800/720Sk. Tourist tax 30Sk. MC/V. ❸

Patio Hostel, Špitálska 35 (☎529 257 97; www.patiohostel.com). Clean and comfortable, with a lime-green common room lined by Warhol prints. Windows let in plenty of natural light—perhaps too much in the morning. Free Internet. Check-in 1pm. Check-out 10pm. 2- to 12-bed dorms 550-870Sk. MC/V. ❸

Orange Hostel, Dobrovičova 14 (☎902 84 29 00; www.hostelinbratislava.com). A quick walk from the main square. Cozy beds in dorms. Internet and laundry included. Reception 24hr. Check-out 10am. Open mid-July to late Aug. Dorms 550Sk. AmEx/MC/V. ❸

Slovenská Zdravotnicka Univerzita, Limbová 12 (☎59 37 01 00; www.szu.sk). From the train station, take bus #32 or electric cable bus #204 5 stops to Nemocnica Kramárel, then climb the steps to the right. This green tower is far from the center, but rooms are clean and comfy, and the doubles are a deal. New baths. Private fridges. Shared kitchen. Breakfast 35Sk. Reception 24hr. Check-out 11am. Singles 600Sk; doubles 700Sk; apartments 1000-1200Sk. Tourist tax 30Sk. Cash only. ❸

Ubytovacie Zariadenie Zvárač, Pionierska 17 (☎49 24 66 00; www.vuz.sk). Take tram #3 from the train station or #5 or 11 toward Raca-Komisárky to Pionierska. Backtrack to the intersection, then turn right. An university dorm that's open year-round. Inside the concrete-chic building, rooms are pleasant, with comfy beds. Shared baths, kitchen, and TV. Reception 24hr., ring bell after midnight. Check-in noon. Check-out 10am. Singles 550Sk, with bath 650Sk; doubles 1100/1300Sk. Tourist tax 30Sk. MC/V. ❸

HOTELS AND PENSIONS

Pension Gremium, Gorkého 11 (☎54 13 10 26; www.gremium.sk), off Hviezdoslavovo nám. Sparkling showers, English-speaking receptionists, a cafe, and an exceptional location make this a great find. Baths, fridges, phones, and TVs. Shared kitchen. Breakfast in the cafe downstairs €1.70-4. Check-in 2pm. Check-out 11am. Call ahead: the 5 rooms fill quickly. Singles 990Sk; doubles 1600Sk. AmEx/MC/V. ❹

Družba, Botanická 25 (☎65 42 00 65; www.hotel-druzba.sk). Take tram #1 from the train station toward Pri Kríži to Botanická Záhrada, cross the pedestrian overpass, and go to the farther of the 2 red-blue-and-green concrete blocks. Stick to the remarkably cheap dorms at this combination hotel/university dorm. Laundry 40Sk. Dorm reception 24hr. Hotel reception M-Th 7am-3:30pm, F 7am-1pm. July-Aug. 2- to 3-bed dorms 380Sk, students 190Sk. Hotel open year-round. Singles 730Sk; doubles 1280Sk. MC/V. ❷

◘ FOOD

Prices are substantially higher in Bratislava than elsewhere in Slovakia, but the capital is the only city with a wide range of international dining options. Head to **Tesco,** Kamenné nám. 1, for groceries. (Open M-F 8am-10pm, Sa 8am-8pm, Su 9am-8pm. MC/V.) Or, try the nearby indoor **fruit market** at Stará Trznícá, Kamenné nám. (Open M-F 7am-6pm, Sa 7am-1pm). For late-night grocery needs, check out **Potraviny Nonstop,** nám. 1. Mája 15. (Open 24hr. MC/V.)

TRADITIONAL FOOD

▨ **Prašná Bašta,** Zámočnícka 11 (☎54 43 49 57). Sit outside on the leafy terrace or head downstairs to sculptures and slick wooden decor. A 20-something crowd enjoys large portions of Slovak cuisine. Entrees 95-325Sk. Open daily 11am-11pm. MC/V. ❸

1 Slovak, Obchodná 62 (☎09 05 35 32 30). Join the student crowd at one of Bratislava's largest and cheapest Slovak restaurants. Each of the many wooden rooms has a different theme; the reconstructed country cottage is particularly cool. Lunch until 5pm. Lunch entrees 35-89Sk. Dinner entrees 79-179Sk. 10% discount for Patio hostel guests. Open M-Th 10am-midnight, F-Sa 10am-2am, Su noon-midnight. Cash only. ❷

Diétna Jadelen, Laurinská 8. A popular lunchtime destination. The long lines are just an opportunity to consider your choice fully before you reach the register. The terrific food is worth the wait. English menu. Entrees 55-85Sk. Open M-F 11am-3pm. Cash only. ❶

INTERNATIONAL

El Diablo, Sedlárska 8 (www.mexicana.cz). The hankering for Mexican food draws tourists in droves to this restaurant decorated with Wild West memorabilia. El Diablo is the best place in Bratislava to down tequila (25-75Sk) and delicious fajitas (167-300Sk). Huge portions. Entrees 180-400Sk. Open M-F 9am-3am, Sa-Su 11am-1am. MC/V. ❸

Vega Destination, Malý Trh 2 (☎57 52 69 94). It's worth the 10min. walk down Dunajská for Vega's modernist atmosphere and tasty mix of (mostly) vegetarian dishes. English menu. Entrees 115-280Sk. Open M-Sa 11am-11pm. AmEx/MC/V. ❸

Bagetky, Zelená 8. A small, simple, and relaxed sandwich bar, Bagetky is an ideal escape from the busy main streets and a great place to pick up something to go. Limited seating. Entrees 50-90Sk. Open M-Sa 9:30am-9pm, Su 1:30-9pm. Cash only. ❶

Chez David, Zámocká 13 (☎54 41 38 24). The only kosher restaurant in a quarter steeped in Jewish culture. Elegant decor and delectable dishes. Matzah ball soup 57Sk. Entrees 90-397Sk. Open M-Th and Su 11:30am-10pm, F 11:30am-3pm. MC/V. ❷

CAFES

Bratislava's burgeoning cafe culture is rapidly improving in quality and diversity, though cafes generally lack the bohemian ambience of their counterparts in other Central European capitals.

Café Kút, Zámočnícka 11 (☎54 43 49 57), connected to Prašná Bašta. Tucked behind an archway, this hidden cafe invites visitors to join locals on the comfortable wooden chairs and let the hours fly by. Occasional live reggae. Espresso 30-40Sk. Open M-F 8am-11pm, Sa-Su 4-11pm. Cash only.

Café Štúdio Music Club, Laurinská 11 (☎09 04 95 14 52). Vinyl LPs line the walls and parted curtains deck a small stage in this cafe. Even the rows of wooden seats look like they were taken straight from an early 20th-century theater. Weekly jazz. Espresso 36-48Sk. *Šaris* 27-45Sk. Pastries 20-30Sk. Open daily 11am-10pm. Cash only.

People's Lounge Café, Gorkého 1 (☎54 64 07 77), near the State Theatre. Ambient music and slick modern decor? The verdict is in: popular. Espresso 50-60Sk. Mixed drinks 120-250Sk. Open daily 10am-11pm. AmEx/MC/V.

Casa Dy, Klariská 7 (☎54 43 22 69). A simple, stylish haunt of Italian expats, bathed in Mediterranean yellows and reds. Espresso 44-55Sk. Panini 69-79Sk. Open M-F 8am-10pm, Sa-Su 10am-10pm; food served M-F 10am-noon and 1-7pm, Sa 9am-2pm.

London Café, Panská 17 (☎54 43 11 85). A taste of London in the heart of Bratislava. Run by the British Council, this cafe offers a light, daily rotating, 2-course British meal (99Sk). Also a small selection of salads (80-110Sk), and a wide range of day-old British papers. Open M-F 10am-6pm. Cash only.

◎ SIGHTS

DEVÍN CASTLE (HRAD DEVÍN). Perched on an imposing cliff 9km west of the center, the stunning castle ruins overlook the confluence of the mighty Danube and Morava rivers. Since 5000 BC, the hilltop settlement has changed hands many times and was repeatedly razed and rebuilt until Napoleonic armies blew it up for good in 1809. With the advent of communism, Devín became a symbol of totalitarianism: sharpshooters hid in the ruins with orders to open fire on anyone who tried to cross this stretch of the Iron Curtain—the barbed-wire fence beside the Morava. Today, visitors can walk along the paths, through the rocks and ruins. A **museum** details the castle's history. *(Bus #29 from Nový Most to the last stop. ☎65 73 01 05. English info. Open July-Aug. Tu-F 10am-5pm, Sa-Su 10am-6pm; May-June and Sept.-Oct. Tu-Su 10am-5pm; last admission 30min. before closing. Museum 70Sk, students 35Sk.)*

BRATISLAVA CASTLE (BRATISLAVSKÝ HRAD). Visible from the Danube banks, the four-towered castle is Bratislava's defining landmark. Ruined by a fire in 1811 and finished off by WWII bombings, the castle's current stark and boxy form is largely a communist-era restoration that doesn't quite capture its 18th-century glory. Its **Historical Museum** (Historické Muzeum) examines art history from clockmaking to interior design. The spectacular view from the **Crown Tower** (Korunná Veža) is a highlight of any visit. *(From underneath Nový Most, climb the stairs to Židovská, then turn left onto the "Castle Stairs" and climb up the steps to the hrad. Castle open daily Apr.-Sept. 9am-8pm; Oct.-Mar. 9am-6pm. Free. Museum ☎54 41 14 44; www.snm-hm.sk. Open Tu-Su 9am-5pm; last admission 4:15pm. 80Sk, students 40Sk. 1-1½hr. tour in English; 400Sk.)*

HVIEZDOSLAVOVO NÁMESTIE. With the feel of a central square, this restored promenade is graced by a sliver of a park and surrounded by stunning 19th-century edifices, including the **Philharmonic building.** Grab a bench, head to the popular restau-

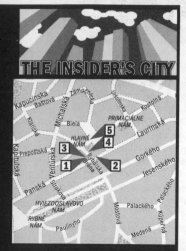

THE INSIDER'S CITY

STATUES OF BRATISLAVA

Bratislava's statues have attracted attention for their colorful subject matter. They are a highlight of the capital's downtown streets.

1 Cumil: While some say the bronze workman emerging from a sewer is resting, others believe he is looking up the skirts of women passing by.

2 Paparazzi: A photographer lurks at the corner of a restaurant that shares his name.

3 Schöne Naci (Handsome Ignatius): A local known for his jubilant smile, Ignatius serves as a poignant reminder of the personal tragedies experienced in WWII: his wife died in a concentration camp.

4 Napoleonic Soldier: Possibly weary from Waterloo, the soldier leans on a bench and looks at the fountain.

5 Roland Fountain: This 1572 fountain is Bratislava's oldest. The man isn't Roland, but Maximillian II, the first Hungarian emperor crowned in the city.

rants and cafes, or frolic in the beautiful and refreshing fountain. In the evenings, the square fills with tourists coming to watch ballets and operas at the 1886 **Slovak National Theater** (Slovenské Národné Divadlo; see below), by the square. (From Hlavné nám., follow Rybárska Brana until the road ends at Hviezdoslavovo nám.)

GRASALKOVICOV PALACE (GRASALKOVIČOV PALÁC). Guarded by two unyielding soldiers, the former Hungarian aristocratic residence now houses the offices of the Slovak president. Behind the palace, a peaceful park is a popular destination for lovers' strolls, family picnics, and friendly bocce games; it also hosts the occasional modern art display. Enter through the second gate in the back to avoid irking the presidential security staff. (Hodžovo nám. Gardens open daily May-Sept. 8am-10pm; Oct.-Nov. 10am-7pm; Dec.-Feb. 11am-6pm; Mar.-Apr. 10am-6pm.)

ST. MICHAEL'S TOWER (MICHALSKÁ VEŽA). The emerald-green St. Michael's Tower is the only gateway that survived the 1775 demolitions of the town's medieval fortifications, aimed at unifying suburbs with the inner city. Most visitors rush through the **Museum of Arms and Fortifications,** which exhibits a small display of weapons and army uniforms, to reach the real treat—the amazing view of the castle and surrounding Old Town. (On Michalská, near Hurbranovo nám. ☎54 43 03 44. English info. Open May-Sept. Tu-F 10am-5pm, Sa-Su 11am-6pm; Oct.-Apr. Tu-Su 9:30am-4:30pm; last admission 10min. before closing. 40Sk, students 20Sk.)

ST. MARTIN'S CATHEDRAL (DÓM. SV. MARTINA). When war with the Ottoman Empire forced the Hungarian kings to flee Budapest, this Gothic church became their coronation cathedral. Perched precariously atop the Cathedral's steeple, a golden replica of St. Stephen's crown reminds churchgoers of its glorious past. A highway now runs only a few feet from the Cathedral, which must undergo frequent repairs to combat automotive pollution. (Open M-F 10-11:30am and 2-4:30pm, Sa 10-11:30am, Su 2-4:30pm. 40Sk. Masses in Latin Su 9am.)

NEW BRIDGE (NOVÝ MOST). Built by the Communist government in 1972, Nový Most is one of the most unusual and prominent sights in Bratislava. Its space-age design was intended to balance the antiquated presence of Bratislava Castle. The bridge is suspended from two angular, concrete towers that are capped by what looks like a giant flying saucer. The UFO, as it is known, contains a viewing deck and a restaurant. (☎62 53 03 00; www.u-f-o.sk. Deck open daily 10am-10pm. 50Sk, free with restaurant reservations. Restaurant open M-F and Su 10am-1am, Sa 10am-10pm.)

𝄫 MUSEUMS

■ PRIMATE'S PALACE (PRIMACIÁLNÝ PALÁC). The pink Baroque palace on Primaciálne nám. houses the city magistrate and a small art gallery full of intricate 17th-century tapestries. There are a few eccentricities, too: you can stare nervously at the dog in Jana Fyta's *Polovnícke zátisie* painting as its eyes follow you around the room, or watch yourself reflect away to infinity in the **Hall of Mirrors** (Zrkadlová Sieň). Ponder any resulting existential crises in the impressive Chapel of St. Ladislaus, which is adorned with beautiful frescoes. *(Primaciálné nám. 1. Buy tickets on 2nd fl. Open Tu-Su 10am-5pm. 40Sk, students free. English pamphlets 40Sk.)*

■ DANUBIANA-MEULENSTEEN ART MUSEUM. Established in September 2000, the red, blue, and silver contemporary art museum is a piece of modern art in itself. Situated on a small peninsula near the Hungarian border, the museum is surrounded by a small park decorated with sculptures. The remote location prevents crowding, so you can admire cutting-edge exhibits at your leisure. *(Take bus #91, from beneath Nový Most to the last stop, Cunovo; 35min., 20Sk. Follow the signs 3.5km to the museum. Or, catch a bus from the main station toward Gabčikovo; 7-10 per day, 28Sk. Ask the driver to stop at the museum, about 35min. from Bratislava's main station. ☎ 090 360 55 05; www.danubiana.sk. Open daily May-Sept. 10am-8pm; Oct.-Apr. 10am-6pm.)*

OLD TOWN HALL (STARÁ RADNICA). The hall's **Town History Museum** has an impressive exhibit on Bratislava's political, commercial, and social development, displaying a range of artifacts from ancient pottery to medieval jewelry to 18th-century paintings. The rooms themselves are of considerable interest. The town council took responsibility oaths in the stark Gothic chapel. In the next room, frescoes adorn the walls of the pink, blue, and gold Court Hall. The "Feudal Justice" exhibit, in a subterranean dungeon, showcases relics of medieval trials, torture, and execution, including thumb screws and an executioner's hat. Climb the stairs to the tower for a view of the orange tile roofs of the Old Town. *(Hlavné nám. 1. From Primaciálne nám., head down Kostolná away from the tourist office. ☎ 59 20 51 30. Borrow an English guidebook. Open Tu-F 10am-5pm, Sa-Su 11am-6pm. Museum 50Sk, students 20Sk.)*

SLOVAK NATIONAL GALLERY (SLOVENSKÁ NÁRODNÁ GALÉRIA). Focused on Slovak art from the 15th to 18th century, the museum displays a fine collection of Gothic and Baroque sculptures, frescoes, and paintings. There is also a small Renaissance and Baroque collection of British, Italian, and Spanish art. Temporary exhibits tend toward modernism. *(Rázusovo nábr. 2. ☎ 54 43 45 87; www.sng.sk. Open Tu-Su 10am-5:30pm. 80Sk, students 40Sk. English tour guide 500Sk per hr.)*

MUSEUM OF JEWISH CULTURE (MÚZEUM ŽIDOVSKEJ KULTÚRY). Inside a former synagogue, this new museum chronicles the culture of Bratislava's dwindling Jewish population; **Schlossberg**, the Jewish quarter, was bulldozed in the 1970s in the name of "progress." *(Židovská 17. ☎ 54 41 85 07; www.slovak-jewish-heritage.org. Open M-F and Su 11am-5pm; last admission 4:30pm. 200Sk, students 50Sk.)*

🎜 ENTERTAINMENT

BIS carries the monthly *Kam v Bratislave*, which lists film, concert, and theater schedules, and in the summer the *Kultúrné Leto*, an all-inclusive arts calendar. The weekly English newspaper, *Slovak Spectator*, also has current events info. **Slovenské Národné Divadlo** (Slovak National Theater), Hviezdoslavovo nám. 1, puts on ballets and operas that draw crowds from afar. *(☎ 54 43 30 83; www.snd.sk. Box office open M-F 8am-5:30pm, Sa 9am-1pm. Closed July-Aug. 100-200Sk.)* The **Slov-**

enská **Filharmónia** (Slovak Philharmonic), Medená 3, has two to three perfor-mances per week in fall and winter. The **box office,** Palackého 2, is around the corner. (☎54 43 33 51; www.filharm.sk. Open M-Tu and Th-F 1-7pm, W 8am-2pm. 100-200Sk.) Posters everywhere announce concerts and festivals. The annual **Music Festival** (late Sept. to early Oct.), brings international performers to Brat-islava to play everything from pop to house. It is followed by the **Bratislava Jazz Days** festival. For **shopping,** try **AuPark** (cross Nový Most and go left).

■ NIGHTLIFE

By day, the Old Town bustles with tourists shopping and devouring *bryndza*. By night, it's filled with young people priming for a night out. Nightlife in Bratislava is relatively subdued, but there is no shortage of places to party. The GLBT scene is Slovakia's biggest, but is small by Western European standards. For info on **GLBT nightlife,** pick up a copy of *Atribut* at any kiosk.

Klub Laverna, Laurinská 19 (☎544 331 65; www.laverna.sk). Expect a floor packed with a young crowd at this dance-centric nightspot. A slide transports drunken clubbers from the upper level to the floor. Weekend cover 100Sk. Open daily 8pm-6am.

Medusa Cocktail Bar, Michalská 89, just after St. Michael's Tower. This happening cocktail bar defines chic. Posh decor and a huge selection of delicious, but expensive, drinks (130-240Sk). Open M-Th 11am-1am, Sa 11am-3am, Su 11am-midnight.

Krčma Gurmánov Bratislavy (KGB), Obchodná 52 (☎52 73 12 79). Stashed in a red-brick basement, KGB is where hip local students go to partake of rock music and beer (20-60Sk) beneath pictures of Lenin. Open M-Th 11am-1:30am, F 11am-3:30am, Sa 3:30pm-1:30am, Su 3:30-11pm. Kitchen closes 11:30pm.

Jazz Café, Ventúrska 5 (☎54 43 46 61; www.jazz-cafe.sk). Praiseworthy mixed drinks and live jazz draw tourists and local sophisticates. Beer 40Sk. Jazz Th-Sa 9pm-1am. Cafe open daily 10am-2am; club open M-F 2pm-2am, Sa-Su 11am-2am. MC/V.

Apollon Gay Club, Panenská 24 (☎54 41 93 43; www.apollon-gay-club.sk). Go through the archway and turn left. A crowd mostly of gay men lounge and chat at this laid-back pub—laid-back until the disco starts. Beer 45-60Sk. Dicso cover F-Sa 50-80Sk. Disco open W-Sa 10pm; pub M-Tu and Th 6pm-3am, W and F-Sa 6pm-5am, Su 6pm-1am.

Circus Barok, Razusovo Nábrezie (☎54 64 20 91). Popular club floating on the Danube. This boat is usually packed—if possible, make your way to the beach-bar top deck. Pop, hip-hop, or disco. Drinks 30-140Sk. Cover 50Sk. Open daily 3pm-3am.

Elam Klub, Staré Grunty 53 (☎65 42 63 04). Take bus #31 or 39 from nám. 1. Mája to the last stop. Go up the stairs and head left into the building. Good music and a lively atmosphere keep the university crowd dancing until dawn on the huge floor. Liveliest during the school year. Drinks 30-100Sk. Cover 39-100Sk. Open daily 9pm-6am.

CENTRAL SLOVAK REPUBLIC

It may be tempting to speed through the Central Slovak Republic on the way to the Tatras, but think twice. The area, rarely visited by tourists, has well-preserved folk traditions and endless opportunities to hike and bike.

BANSKÁ BYSTRICA   ☎(0)88

Banská Bystrica (BAHN-skah bis-TREE-tsah; pop. 84,280) has a perfect mix of cosmopolitan flair and rural scenery. The lively Old Town is packed with terraced cafes, shops, and folk-art boutiques, while the forested hills of the outskirts are an ideal playground for bikers and hikers.

⊑ TRANSPORTATION. The **train** and **bus stations** lie next to each other on c. K. Smrečine. **Trains** (☎436 14 73) run to **Bratislava** (3-4hr., 3 per day, 300Sk), **Košice** (4-5hr., 1 per day, 290Sk), and **Budapest, HUN** (5-7hr., 1 per day, 700Sk). **Buses** (☎422 22 22) go to: **Bratislava** (3½-4hr., 20-30 per day, 280-300Sk); **Košice** (4-5hr., 3-5 per day, 260Sk); **Liptovsky-Mikuláš** (2hr., 4 per day, 110Sk); **Prešov** (5hr., 5 per day, 260Sk); **Žilina** (2hr., 6-7 per day, 120Sk). For cabs, try **Fun Taxi** (☎167 77) or **BB Taxi** (☎411 57 57). Buy tickets for **local buses** from the driver (one-way 15Sk).

◪⁊ ORIENTATION AND PRACTICAL INFORMATION. The **Hron River** cradles the city's southeastern edge. The train and bus stations lie east of the square, and suburban neighborhoods sprawl in all directions. To reach the center, head out behind the bus station and cross **Cesta K. Smrečine** into the gardens. Take the pedestrian underpass beneath the highway and continue straight to **nám. Slobody.** Or, from the train station, head straight on 29 Augusta, turn left on Trieda SNP, then right onto **nám. Slobody.** From nám. Slobody, a left on Horná takes you through **nám. Š. Moyzesa** to **nám. SNP,** the town center (15min.). Alternatively, take a local bus to Narodna (5min., 15Sk) and walk uphill to **nám. SNP.**

Kultúrne a Informačné Stredisko (KIS), nám. SNP 14, between Horná and nám. SNP, has **maps** (20-100Sk) and accommodations info. The staff organizes city tours (1hr., 500Sk) and books **private rooms** for 300-500Sk. (☎415 22 72. Open M-F May 15-Sept. 15 9am-6pm, Sa 9am-1pm; Sept. 16-May 14 9am-5pm.) **Exchange currency** and cash **traveler's checks** for a 1% commission at **OTP Bank,** nám. SNP 15. (☎430 12 47. Open 8am-6pm, Sa 9am-1pm.) MC/V **ATMs** pervade the town; there is one outside the tourist office. **Luggage storage** is available at the train station. (20Sk, bicycles 30Sk, heavy bags 40Sk. Open daily 7am-7pm.) **Interpress Slovakia,** Dolná 19, sells newspapers (90-130Sk) and magazines (110-400Sk) in English. (☎412 30 75. Open M-F 7am-6pm, Sa 8am-1pm.) The **pharmacy, Lekáreň Nádej,** Dolná 5, posts a list of local pharmacies that remain open after it closes. (☎412 62 03. Open M-F 7:30am-5:30pm, Sa 8am-noon.) The hip underground bar **Level 12,** nám. SNP 12, offers **Internet.** (☎0484 15 41 77. 15Sk per 30min. Open M-Tu 1pm-midnight, W-Th 1pm-2am, F 1pm-3am, Sa 3pm-3am. MC/V.) Less stylish but cheaper Internet can be found at **Internet Centrum,** nám. SNP 3, through the arch. (☎475 65 97. 20Sk per hr. Save your password; it is valid for a week. Open M-F 9am-9pm, Sa-Su 1-9pm. Cash only.) There are phonecard-operated **phones** outside the **post office,** Horná 1. **Poste Restante** is upstairs at window #24. Packages are at window #1. (☎432 62 11. Open M-F 8am-7pm, Sa 8am-noon.) **Postal Code:** 97401.

⌂◖ ACCOMMODATIONS AND FOOD. KIS books **private rooms** (singles 300-350Sk; doubles 500-600Sk) for 25Sk and has info on hotels, hostels, and dorms. **Ubytovna Stavoprojekt ❸,** Robotnícka 6, offers pleasant, mid-range rooms in a great location 2min. from nám. SNP. Though it isn't the cheapest option, the prices are still decent. Follow directions to Horná, but turn left onto Robotícka just before the Prior. (☎414 29 29. Reception 24hr. Check-out noon. Singles 650Sk; doubles 900Sk. Cash only.) The popular **Študencké Domovy 4 ❶,** Trieda SNP 53, is near the center and stations. From the stations, head straight on 29 Augusta and turn right on Trieda SNP. The dorm is ahead on the left. Rooms are basic but rather pleasant. (☎471 15 16. Check-out noon. Open July-Aug. 2- to 3-bed rooms 200Sk, with ISIC 180Sk. Cash only.) **Hotel Milvar ❶,** Školská 9, rents small, spare rooms in a squat, gray, stained concrete hotel block. From nám. SNP, turn right through the arch to Horná Strieborná and follow the road as it angles left. Cross the river, go right on J.G. Tajovského to the fork, and turn right on Školská just before the highway underpass (20min.). The hotel is uphill on the left. Alternatively, hop on bus #3 or 34, which run to J.G. Tajovského. Be careful at night, as the street is poorly lit. (☎413 87 73. All rooms have private baths. Reception 24hr. Check-in 2pm. Check-out 10am. Rooms 220Sk. Tourist tax 10Sk. Cash only.)

In this landlocked country, locals and visitors alike can still find excellent seafood at **Restaurant Fishmen** ❸, Dolna 5. The IKEA-esque decor downstairs is spruced up by a fountain and an aquarium full of tropical fishes. Dishes range from basic *Pstruh Masle* (buttered trout; 95Sk) to *Zrolcie Platky* (shark slices in olive sauce; 165Sk) but also include Mexican, Italian, and Slovak foods. (☎412 51 05. Entrees 99-239Sk. Open M-Sa 10am-11pm, Su 11am-10pm. MC/V.) **Rictárova Pivnica** ❶, Lazovná 18 off nám. SNP, serves up traditional Slovak food; its *bryndza* is famed. (☎415 43 00. Entrees 50-140Sk. Open M-Sa 10am-10pm. Cash only.) At **Červený Rak** ❷, nám. SNP 13, the menu features something for everyone: pizza, salads, fish, pasta, and traditional Slovak dishes. It may be touristy, but you can enjoy watching the hustle and bustle of the main square as you sit under the canopy outside. (☎415 38 82; www.cervenyrak.sk. Entrees 89-219Sk. Open M-Th 10am-10:30pm, F 10am-midnight, Sa noon-11pm. Cash only.) Look for groceries at **Prior,** on the corner of Horná and c. K. Smrečine. (Open M-F 8am-7pm, Sa 8am-2pm. MC/V.) You can also head to **Billa Supermarket,** just across from the bus station. (Open M-Th and Su 8am-8pm, F 8am-9pm, Sa 7am-9pm. MC/V.) Get fresh veggies and fruits at the **open-air market** in front of the Prior building.

🗷 **SIGHTS.** Turn right out of the tourist office and take the immediate left onto Kapitulská to reach the 🗷**Museum of the Slovak National Uprising** (Múzeum Slovenského Národného Povstania), which chronicles the country's struggles during WWII. Banská Bystrica was home to the underground resistance after the Nazis breached the Slovak border on August 29, 1944. Stark photographs show the grim reality of the Nazi occupation, while exposition #34 depicts four men who escaped Auschwitz on April 7, 1944. (☎412 32 58; www.muzeumsnp.sk. Open Tu-Su May-Sept. 9am-6pm; Oct.-Apr. 9am-4pm. 60Sk, students 25Sk. 1hr. tours in English by request; 350Sk.) A cluster of the town's oldest buildings stands on nám. Š. Moyzesa. The restored **Pretórium,** now the **Štátna Galéria,** nám. Š. Moyzesa 25, hosts a new Slovak avant-garde exhibit every two months. (☎412 48 64. Open Tu-F 10am-5pm, Sa-Su 10am-4pm. 40Sk, students 10Sk. Free English pamphlet.) Behind the Galéria is the Romanesque **Church of the Virgin Mary** (Kostol Panny Márie). Breathtaking frescoes adorn the Baroque ceiling, but the real attraction is the Gothic altarpiece, by Master Pavol of Levoča, which is housed in the church's **Chapel of St. Barbora.** The church is open only for services (Su 7, 8:30, 11am, 4:30pm). Walk toward the square from the Galéria to find the **Museum of Central Slovakia** (Stredoslovenské Múzeum), nám. SNP 4. The small collection features a noteworthy furniture and folk-costume exhibit. (☎412 58 97. Open June 15-Sept. 15 M-F and Su 9am-noon and 1-5pm; Sept. 16-June 14 M-F and Su 8am-4pm. 30Sk, students 15Sk.) The restored 18th-century villa of local artist Dominik Skutecký (1848-1921), **Dom Skutecký,** Horná 55, now displays his work. A dogged Realist, Skutecký focused on folk scenes. Head left from the tourist office on Horná to reach the museum. (☎412 54 50. Open Tu-Su 10am-4pm. 40Sk, students 15Sk.)

🗷 **OUTDOOR ACTIVITIES.** Banská Bystrica offers ample outdoor adventures, including biking, horseback riding, and rafting. Visit the tourist office for current info or purchase the handy guide to Banská Bystrica and its environs. **Mr. Spedik-Jahn,** a travel agent in the village Tajov, arranges six-day **whitewater rafting** trips on the Hron River. (☎419 76 03. 3000Sk, including accommodation.) To get to Tajov, hop on a city bus from the station (20-25min., 15 per day, 25Sk). Popular hiking trails run from **Donovaly,** the ski area accessible by bus (40min., 50Sk). The trails, few in number, wind through tree-lined valleys and hills. Their tranquil beauty is hardly as dramatic as that of the Tatras, but a central Slovak location ensures their popularity. **Pegas Škola Paragliding,** Mistriky 230 (☎419 98 89), will teach you to fly for around 3500Sk. Call a week in advance. **Pony Farma-Suchý Urch,** Jazdiareň Uhlisko, offers horseback riding for all levels. (☎410 48 58. 240Sk per hr., 1200Sk per day. Lessons 250 per hr., 700Sk per 4hr.).

🎵 **NIGHTLIFE.** Banska's nightlife draws tourists and young locals to the Old Town each night. With walls cluttered by black and white photographs and an eclectic mix of knick-knacks, the 🔲**Irish Pub,** Horná 45, draws rebels of all ages to worn wooden chairs and tattered but comfortable couches. (☎0910 90 30 96. Pilsner 30Sk per 0.5L, Guinness 59Sk per 0.50L. Live rock Sa 8pm. Open M-F 11am-2am, Sa 2pm-2am.) Escape to 🔲**Jazz Club U Smadnedio Mnicha** (Jazz Club at the Thirsty Monk), Dolná 20, a popular local stop with a laid-back crowd. (Beer 17-59Sk. Live jazz most weekend evenings. Open M-F 10am-2am, Sa-Su 2pm-2am.) Another relaxing refuge is **Kapitol Pub,** Kapitulska 10, which has a lively courtyard and an underground cellar. (☎415 26 67. Beer 25-40Sk. Open M-Th 10am-2am, F 10am-4am, Sa noon-4am, Su 6pm-midnight.) Banská Bystrica's dance central, **Arcade,** nám. ŠMP 5, draws a slightly older crowd looking to let loose and get down. (☎430 26 00. Occasional cover 50Sk. Open M-Tu and Th 1pm-midnight, W and F 1pm-4am, Sa 6pm-4am.) If you're starved for hip-hop, join the kids at **Kaktus Bar,** Horná 12. (Beer 20-30Sk. Open daily 7pm-6am.) To escape the bar scene, watch a Hollywood film (sometimes dubbed into Slovak, but usually subtitled) at **Kino Korzo,** in Dome Kultúry on c. K. Smrečine. (☎415 24 66. Shows daily 6:30, 9pm. Open 30min. before show-time. M 70Sk, Tu-Su 25-85Sk.)

🏰 **DAYTRIP FROM BANSKÀ BYSTRICA: BOJNICE.** Many Slovak castles survive as only ruins or reconstructions, but 🔲**Bojnice Castle** remains a real-life fairy tale that revels in its splendor and opulence. Originally a 12th-century wooden fortress for a Benedictine monastery, the castle later became a royal residence. Guided tours through the post-Romantic, late-Gothic building traverse galleries, gardens, hunting rooms, and bedrooms before climbing a citadel, descending into a crypt, and leaving visitors breathless in the depths of a 26m underground natural **cave.** The most memorable stops are the intricate **Oriental Saloon,** which boasts magnificent 17th-century Turkish architecture; the **Music Room,** where cherubs stare down from the golden ceiling; and the **chapel,** where magnificent frescoes adorn the walls. Although you can take a Little Tour, the Grand Tour is worth the extra cash. (☎543 06 24; www.bojnicecastle.sk. Open May-Sept. Tu-Sa 9am-5pm, July-Aug. also M 9am-5pm; Oct.-Apr. Tu-Su 10am-3pm. Mandatory guided tour either 1¼hr. or 45min.; call ahead for tours in English, 10-person min.; 400Sk. Grand Tour 130Sk, students with ISIC 65Sk; Little Tour 80/40Sk. Night tours: July-Aug. F-Sa 9pm; otherwise call 3 days ahead to arrange; 200Sk, students 180Sk. Camera 50Sk, video 150Sk.) Ghost enthusiasts can attend the nightly tour, or visit the castle in early May for the **International Festival of Ghosts and Spirits** (180Sk, students 90Sk), when evening festivities include a candlelight ceremony for the Rising of the Dead. **Valentine's Day** brings a week of flirting and mistletoe (110Sk; 150Sk per couple, 90Sk per student couple). During the 2nd weekend in September, The **Knight's Days** festival features sword fighting and jousting. (110Sk, students 60Sk.). Various classical music concerts come to town in summer (30-80Sk).

Take the **bus** to **Prievidza** from **Banská Bystrica** (1-2hr., 7-8 per day, 115-120Sk). With the station to your right, walk to the stop on the right. Take bus #3 to the "Bojnice" stop and get off at the park next to a stretch of small shops (7min., 12Sk). Buses #15, 51, and 90 also go to Bojnice but don't stop next to the Castle.

MALÁ FATRA MOUNTAINS

The Malá Fatra range is an exhilarating medley of alpine meadows, steep ravines, and limestone peaks. The mountains boast hikes for adventurers of all abilities. You can visit for the day or stay overnight in one of the *chaty* (mountain huts).

ŽILINA ☎(0)41

Žilina (ZHI-li-na; pop. 87,000), the country's 3rd-largest city, is a convenient headquarters for exploring the nearby Malá Fatras. The picturesque setting and fountain-rich town square make it an inviting place for an extended, hiking-filled stay. **Hotel Slovan ❸**, A. Kmet'a 2, has small, well-furnished rooms with clean bathrooms and soft beds. The location is also great, just off nám. Andreja Hlinku. From the train station, go to the square, then turn right just past Tesco. Walk down Hurbanova; the hotel is on the right. (☎562 01 34. Reception 24hr. Check-out 10am. Singles 980Sk; doubles 1350Sk. Cash only.) Ten minutes south of the city center at Hlinská 1, **Domov Mládeže ❷** offers spartan-yet-clean university dorms year-round. Rooms are divided between Block III and V, set amid a field of indistinguishable concrete apartment blocks. Take bus #2, 4, 5, or 7 to the Hlinská stop, then cross the street and enter through the gate. Block III is the first on the left, and Block V is the 2nd on the right. Both dorms have kitchens, shared showers, and small 2- to 3-person rooms, but the Block III beds are bunked. (Block III ☎723 39 12, Block V 723 39 14. Reception 24hr. Check-out 10am. Dorms plus tourist tax 270Sk. Cash only.) While tourists eat in the square, locals prefer the calmer **Restaurácia a Vináreň na Bráne ❶**, Botová 10, which serves some of the town's finest Slovak food. With your back to the church in Mariánske nám., go to the far right corner and take the street to your right. (English menu. Lunch entrees 48-79Sk, dinner 79-120Sk. Open M-F 8:30am-10pm, Sa 9am-10pm. Cash only.) For simple, wholesome sandwiches (45-89Sk), visit the popular **Bageteria ❶**, Hlinkovo nám. 5. (Open M-Sa 7am-9pm, Su 9am-9pm. MC/V.) There is an enormous **Tesco** supermarket in nám. Andreja Hlinku. (Open M-F 8am-8pm, Sa 8am-4pm, Su 8am-1pm. MC/V.)

The **train station**, Hviezdoslava 7, is northeast of the center. (☎562 22 26. MC/V.) Trains run to: **Bratislava** (2-3hr., 18 per day, 270Sk); **Košice** (3¼hr., 11 per day, 316Sk); **Poprad** (2hr., 15 per day, 200Sk); **Budapest, HUN** (4¼-7hr., 2 per day, 1306Sk); **Prague, CZR** (7hr., 6 per day, 860Sk). The **bus station**, Jana Milca 23 (☎565 19 41), is on the corner of Hviezdoslava and 1 Mája. Buses run to: **Banská Bystrica** (2hr., 20 per day, 172Sk); **Bratislava** (3-4hr., 9-13 per day, 278Sk); **Liptovský Mikuláš** (1¾-2hr., 15 per day, 122Sk); **Prague, CZR** (6-7hr., 12 per day, 590Sk). For **local transportation**, buy train or bus tickets at kiosks or orange vending machines (12Sk).

The bus and train stations lie northeast of the center; budget accommodations are to the southwest. From the bus station, go left on **Hviezdoslava** to reach the train station. Take the underpass to **Narodná**, which runs into ■**nám. Andreja Hlinku,** the attractive New Town square where a church towers over a spacious, gardened plaza. Cross the square and take the stairs to the right of the church to **Farská,** which opens onto **Mariánske nám.,** the lively and touristy Old Town square. The tourist office **Selinan,** Jantárova 4, is on a street parallel to Farská, on the left. Buy hiking (VKU #110, 109Sk) or town (free-89Sk) **maps,** or ask about accommodations in Žilina or nearby Terhová, where many beautiful hikes start. (☎562 07 89; www.selinan.sk. Open M-F 8:30am-5pm.) **Exchange currency** and cash AmEx/MC/V **traveler's checks** for a 1% commission at **OTP Banka,** Sládkovičova 9. (☎562 09 40. Open M and W 8am-6pm; Tu, Th, and F 8am-5pm; Sa 8am-1pm.) **Luggage storage** is in the underpass in front of the train station. (30Sk per day. Open 24hr.) The pharmacy **Lekáreň na Bráne,** Bottova 7, posts the hours of nearby pharmacies that remain open late. (Open M-F 8:30am-noon and 12:30-5pm.) Public **telephones** are at the post office. Calling-card phones are at kiosks and at the post office. Try the slick ■**Internet Cafe,** Kálov 3, which also serves drinks. (8Sk per 15min.

Excellent mixed drinks 45-120Sk. Open M-Th 9am-10pm, F 9am-midnight, Sa-Su 10am-10pm.) The **post office**, Sládkovičova 14, has phone cards and **Poste Restante**. Facing the church in nám. A. Hlinku, go right and veer right with the street. (☎512 62 59. Poste Restante M-F 8am-noon and 12:30-6pm. Open M-F 8am-7pm, Sa 8-noon.)

HIKING IN THE MALÁ FATRAS

Hiking in the Malá Fatras is challenging; it is important to be prepared. Pack food and be ready for cold weather and fickle storms that can turn dirt roads into mud. Check conditions at the tourist office. **Emergency rescue** (☎569 52 32) is available, although pay phones are not found on most trails. Trail-markings are generally accurate but can be erratic. VKÚ **map** #110, sold at tourist agencies, is vital.

■ **MOUNT VEĽKÝ ROZSUTEC.** Though not the highest mountain in the range, **Veľký Rozsutec** (1609m) boasts some of the most exciting and challenging slopes. The **Štefanová** trail is possibly the best hike in the region, but the thrilling route is tricky and should not be attempted by amateurs. Take the Terchova-Vrátna bus from platform #10 in Žilina to Štefanová (1hr., every 1-2hr., 43-47Sk) and follow the yellow trail through lush woodland paths to **Sedlo Vrochpodžiar** (30min.). Take a right to start down the blue trail, where steep metal ladders, narrow bridges, and chains take you around, over, and occasionally through a slippery mass of tumbling waterfalls and rapids known as **Horne Diery** (Upper Hole). Continue on the blue trail to **Sedlo Medzirozsutce** (1½hr.). Take a right on the red trail to reach the **summit** (1¼hr.). To descend, follow the red trail to its intersection with the green trail near **Sedlo Medziholie** (1hr.). Turn right; the rocky green trail alternates between grass fields and towering pines, eventually returning to **Štefanová** (1¼hr.; total trip 5½hr.). For a less vigorous hike, follow the blue trail from Sedlo Medzirozsutce around the summit until it meets the green trail near Sedlo Medziholie (1hr.). A right here leads across a field to the green trail and back to Štefanová (1¼hr.).

MOUNT VEĽKÝ KRIVÁN. At 1709m, **Veľký Kriván** is the highest peak in the range. Take the bus from platform #10 in Žilina to **Terchová, Vrátna** (43Sk), and get off at Chata Vrátna. The taxing hike begins with the green trail, which heads straight up to **Snilovské Sedlo** (1¾hr.); from there, turn right on the red trail to reach the **summit** (1hr.). To save your strength, take the **Lanová Dráha Vrátna Chleb** chairlift to the red trail and enjoy a splended view of the tree-lined peaks on the way up. (☎569 56 42. Open June-Aug. daily 8:15am-7pm; Sept. 8:15am-4pm; Oct. and May Sa-Su 8:15am-4pm. 120Sk, round-trip 160Sk.) Turn left off the green trail to follow the red trail along 4km of beautiful vistas to **Poludňový Grúň** (1460m; 1½hr.). From Poludňový Grúň, turn left on the easier yellow trail to return to Chata Vrátna (1¼ hr.).

LOW TATRAS (NÍZKE TATRY)

Though not quite as impressive as the High Tatras, the slopes of the Low Tatras (Nízke Tatry) are still majestic, and benefit from being far less touristed. They and their peaceful valleys boast an extensive trail system as well as beautiful caves and streams. Hikers in these parts enjoy colorful promenades and unparalleled views after exerting themselves on arduous climbs.

LIPTOVSKÝ MIKULÁŠ   ☎(0)44

Liptovský Mikuláš (LIP-tohv-skee mee-koo-LASH; pop. 33,000) is a quiet hiking base town surrounded by magnificent mountains. On a rainy day, explore the charming square and cafes that crowd the center. Go down Stúrova and cross straight through nám. Osloboditeľov to reach a passage that leads to the **Galéria Petra Michala Bohúna**, Transovského 2. This gallery displays about 4500 works, ranging from 15- to 19th-century paintings to contemporary photography, video, and sculpture. (☎552 27 58. Open Tu-Su 10am-5pm. Combined ticket 60Sk, students 30Sk; each exposition hall 20/10Sk.) Housed in a former synagogue, **Múzeum Janka Kráľa**, nám. Osloboditeľov 31, offers a look at the city's past through historical artifacts, antique books, early photographs, and even a doll collection. (☎552 25 54; www.lmikulas.sk. Open June 16-Sept. 15 daily 10am-5pm; Sept. 15-June 16 M-F 9am-4pm, Sa 10am-5pm. Entrance every 30min. 40Sk, students 25Sk.)

Though **private rooms** fill quickly during the high seasons, hotels usually have a few vacancies. **Hotel Kriváň ❷**, Štúrova 5, opposite the tourist office, offers rooms that are small but centrally located. (☎552 24 14; fax 551 47 48. Reception 24hr., knock after midnight. Check-in 2pm. Check-out 10am. Singles 350Sk, with bath 450Sk; doubles 550/770Sk; quads with bath 1180Sk. Cash only.) **Hotel Garni ❶**, M. Népora 12, 25min. from the center, offers big rooms, comfy beds, and shared showers. From the train station, take bus #2, 7, 8, 9, 10 to 1. Mája, at the Maytex bus stop (10Sk). Backtrack and take the first left, then the first right. Inexplicably, most buses numbered 11 also go to the Maytex stop, but some do not. (☎562 56 59. Reception 24hr. Check-out noon. Singles 230Sk; doubles 460Sk. Cash only.) Restaurants are limited, though some are clustered along **nám. Osloboditel'ov.** The simple **Liptovská Izba Reštaurácia ❶**, nám. Osloboditel'ov 22, serves scrumptious local dishes in a pleasant, if austere, setting. (☎551 48 53. Entrees 55-115Sk. Open daily 10am-10pm. Cash only.) Stock up on supplies at **Coop Supermarket**, 1 Mája 54, in the Prior building on nám. Mieru. (Open M-F 7am-8pm, Sa 7am-7pm, Su 8am-5pm. MC/V.)

The **train station** (☎551 24 84) is at Štefánikova 2, with the **bus station** (☎551 81 21) just outside. Bus information can be found in the base of the small white tower (8am-3pm). **Trains** run to: **Bratislava** (4hr., 12 per day, 364Sk); **Košice** (2hr., 15 per day, 220Sk); **Poprad** (30min., 5 per day, 94Sk); **Žilina** (1hr., 7 per day, 138Sk); **Prague, CZR** (8½hr., 4 per day, 1128Sk). **Buses** run to: **Bratislava** (4½hr., 10 per day, 426Sk); **Košice** (3½hr., 3 per day, 262Sk); **Poprad** (1hr., 20 per day, 70-100Sk); **Žilina** (1½-2hr., 13-14 per day, 120Sk). To reach the center, turn left out of the train station on **Štefánikova**. Turn right onto **M.M. Hodžu**, which crosses **Štúrova** at the square **nám. Mieru.** Turn left to reach **nám. Osloboditeľov**, the main square. The friendly staff at **Informačné Centrum**, nám. Mieru 1, in the Dom Služieb complex, books **private rooms** (250-400Sk), **exchanges currency**, and sells hiking **maps**, including VKÚ maps (110-125Sk). Ask for the *Orava Litpov Horehronie*, a hiking and cycling map (145Sk). They also organize guided excursions (full-day; 1-3 people 1500Sk, 4-8 2000Sk, 8+ 2500Sk) in the Low Tatras. (☎552 24 18; www.lmikulas.sk. Open June 15-Sept. 15 M-F 8am-6pm, Sa 8am-noon, Su 11am-4pm; Sept. 16-Dec. 14 and Apr. 1-June 14 M-F 9am-6pm, Sa 8am-noon; Dec. 15-Mar. 31 M-F 9am-6pm, Sa 8am-noon.) **Exchange currency** for no commission and cash **traveler's checks** for 1% commission at **Slovenska-Sporiteľňa**, Štúrova 1 adjacent to nám. Osloboditeľov. (☎551 32 03. Open M-F 8am-5pm.) To use the **lockers** (5Sk) next to the window, write down the combination, drop in a coin, and lock the door. A **pharmacy** is at **Lekáreň Sabadilla**, nám. Mieru 1, in Dom Služieb. (☎552 13 18. Open M-F 8am-5pm. MC/V.) **Z@vináč Internet Bar**, nám. Osloboditeľov 21, has **Internet** (1Sk per min. **Telephones** outside. Open M-Sa 10am-11pm, Su 2-10pm). The **post office** is on M.M. Hodžu 3, near nám. Mieru. Phone cards are at window #2. **Poste Restante** is at window #7. (☎552 26 42. Open M-F 8am-6pm, Sa 8am-11pm.) **Postal Code: 03101.**

HIKING IN THE LOW TATRAS

MOUNT ĎUMBIER AND CHOPOK. To conquer Mt. Ďumbier (2043m), catch an early bus from platform #11 in Liptovský Mikuláš to **Liptovský Ján** (25-30min., every 1-2hr., 16-20Sk). The gentle blue trail winds along the calm Štiavnica River until it reaches the Svidovské Sedlo by Chata generála M. R. Štefánika (5hr.). For a strenuous hike, go right on the red trail (2hr. from Liptotvský Ján) and climb Sedlo Javorie (1½hr.). You'll pass two beautiful, oft-cloud-covered peaks, **Tanečnica** (1680m) and **Prašivá** (1667m). From here, head left on the yellow trail to summit Mt. Ďumbier (2½hr.). Continue on the red trail along the ridge past the intersection with the green trail to reach the range's 2nd-highest peak, **Chopok** (2024m), where your efforts will be rewarded with spectacular views of the surrounding mountains and green valleys. From Chopok, walk down the blue trail to the bus stop at **Otupné**, behind Hotel Grand (1¾hr.), or ride down on the **chairlift**. Chairlift box office in **Jasná** open 8:20am-3:40pm; follow the signs from Hotel Grand. (Chairlift every 30min. June-Sept. 8:30am-5pm, 130Sk.)

DEMÄNOVSKÁ JASKYŇA SLOBODY (DEMÄNOV CAVE OF LIBERTY). For a short hike, take the bus from platform #3 in Liptovský Mikuláš to Demänovská Dolina and get off at "Demänovská jaskyňa slobody" (20-35min., every hr. 6:25am-5pm, 20Sk) and walk to the cave on the blue trail toward Pusté Sedlo Machnate (1½hr.). Named for its role in WWII, this cave stored supplies for the Slovak Uprising. The 45min. tour of the two-million-year-old cave covers 1.5km and passes through underground chambers, lakes, and a waterfall, all carved out of rock long ago by water falling at a rate of one drop per day. The 2hr. tour includes another 2km of corridors. Bring a sweater. (☎559 16 73; www.ssj.sk. Open Tu-Su June-Aug. 9am-4pm, entrance every hr.; Sept.-Nov. 15 and Dec. 15-May 9:30am-2pm, entrance every 1½hr. 45min. tour 150Sk, students with ISIC 120Sk. 2hr. tour 300/240Sk.)

DEMÄNOVSKÁ ĽADOVÁ JASKYŇA (DEMÄNOV ICE CAVE). This ice cave rests midway between Liptovský Mikuláš and Jasná. Take the bus from Liptovský Mikuláš to Jasná, get off at "Kamenná chata" (20-30min., every hr., 20Sk), and follow the signs to the cave entrance (15min.). The cave was probably inhabited in the Stone Age, but the site first drew tourists after a set of large bear bones was mistaken for the remnants of a ▨dragon. The 25km cave contains a wall signed by some 18th-century visitors and a frozen waterfall that drapes over bleached stone. (☎554 81 70; www.ssj.sk. Open Tu-Su June-Aug. 9am-4pm, entrance every hr.; May and Sept. 9:30am-2pm, entrance every 1½hr. 140Sk, students 120Sk.)

SPIŠ

For centuries, Spiš was an autonomous province of Hungary. It was later absorbed into Czechoslovakia and, after the Velvet Divorce in 1993, into Slovakia. Its eastern flatlands are filled with quiet towns where time moves at about the same pace as farmers walking their cows. The medieval charm of Kežmarok, Levoča, and the sprawling ruins of Spišský Castle attract visitors and recall the region's rich past.

KEŽMAROK   ☎(0)52

The town of Kežmarok (KEZH-ma-rok; pop. 18,000) boasts colorful buildings, friendly locals, a storied history, and a vibrant atmosphere. From Hlavné nám., go down Hviezdoslavova to reach the ▨**Wooden Articulated Church** (Drevený Atikulárny Kostol). Built in 1717, the church is shaped like a Greek cross because of restrictions mandating that Protestants could build their churches only from wood, outside town walls, without solid foundations, and without towers or bells. Northern European Protestants sent money and craftsmen to help construct the church, and it was completed in a mere three months. The porthole-shaped windows still bear the marks of the Swedish sailors who helped build them. Adjacent to the Wooden Articulated Church is a light-green-and-red colossus, the ▨**New Evangelical Church** (Nový Evanjelický Kostol), which eclectically blends Byzantine, Middle Eastern, Renaissance, and Romanesque styles. (Both open daily June-Sept.

9am-noon and 2-5pm; Oct.-May Tu and F 10am-noon and 2-4pm. Buy tickets for both at the wooden church, 30Sk.) Down Hlavné nám. is the impressive **Kežmarok Castle**, Hradné nám. 42. Renaissance decor ornaments a stocky Gothic frame. The courtyard contains the foundations of a 13th-century Saxon church, while a Soviet-era tank sits in a park outside the walls. (☎452 26 18; www.muzeum.sk. Open Tu-F 9am-noon and 1-4:30pm, Sa-Su 9am-4pm. 1hr. tours every 30-60min. 60Sk, students 30Sk. English pamphlet 8Sk, guidebook 20-35Sk. Cash only.) During the 2nd weekend in July, the **European Folk Arts Festival** brings craftsmen from all over Europe to present their work in glass, gold, iron, wood, and wool.

The tourist office (see below) books **private rooms** (250Sk). **Pension Max ❹**, Starý trh 9, off Alexandra, is a family-run pension with spacious rooms, satellite TV, and a great location. If reception is empty, knock on the door in the entryway. (☎452 63 24; duchon@sinet.sk. English spoken. Reception 24hr. Check-out 10am. Singles and doubles 810Sk; triples 1030Sk; quads 1300Sk. Cash only.) Locals and tourists pack the popular **Cellar Classica Restaurant ❷**, Hviezdoslavova 2, to enjoy cheap drinks (20-45Sk) and tasty Italian food. (☎52 36 93. Entrees 79-159Sk. Open daily 11am-11pm. Cash only). There's a **grocery store** at Alexandra 35. (Open M-Sa 7am-10pm, Su 8am-10pm. Cash only.) Under the castle, the **Admiral Club** livens the quiet town by blasting pop and dance music. (Open M-Th 10pm-4am, F-Sa 9pm-6am.)

Trains (☎452 32 98) run to **Poprad** (25min., 14 per day, 20Sk) from the hilltop at the junction of Toporcerova and Michalská. **Buses** leave from under canopies behind the Lidl supermarket, to the right when exiting train station; destinations include **Banská Bystrica** (7-10 per day, 278Sk), **Levoča** (1hr., 6-8 per day, 40Sk), and **Poprad** (20-30min., every 10-40min., 23Sk). Buy bus tickets on board and train tickets at the station. To reach the center, take the pedestrian bridge to the left of the train station and follow **Alexandra** to **Hlavné nám.** The tourist office, **Kežmarská Informačná**, Hlavné nám. 46, in an alcove, offers tips, arranges **private rooms**, and sells **maps** for 80-125Sk. (☎52 452 40 47; www.kezmarok.net. Open M-F 8:30am-5pm, Sa 9am-2pm; also July-Aug. Su 9am-1pm.) **Slovenská Sporteľňa**, Baštová 28, **exchanges currency** (min. 30Sk) and cashes AmEx/MC/V **traveler's checks** (min. 20Sk) for a 1% commission. (☎452 30 41; www.slsp.sk. Open M and F 7:30am-4pm, W 7:30am-5pm, Tu and Th 7:30am-2pm.) A MC/V **ATM** is outside. The **post office,** Mučeníkov 2, where Hviezdoslavova becomes Mučeníkov, is past the hospital. (☎452 20 21. Open M-F 8am-noon and 1-7pm, Sa 8-10am.) **Postal Code:** 06001.

LEVOČA ☎(0)53

Levoča (LEH-vo-cha; pop. 14,000), the current administrative hub and former capital of Spiš, gained fame through the 16th-century "Law of Storage," which forced merchants to remain in town until they sold all their goods. The new wealth fostered a movement to form craft guilds led by Master Pavol, a renowned sculptor responsible for many of the detailed works that adorn Spiš's churches. With its rich artistic legacy, cobblestone-paved Old Town, and nearly intact medieval walls, Levoča is perfect for those seeking some quiet R&R. During the first weekend in July, the Festival of Marian Devotion attracts countless pilgrims.

◨◪ TRANSPORTATION AND PRACTICAL INFORMATION. The best way to reach Levoča is by bus. **Buses** run to: **Košice** (2½hr., 8 per day, 132Sk); **Poprad** (50min., 18 per day, 42Sk); **Prešov** (2hr., 5-9 per day, 58Sk); **Starý Smokovec** (1-1½hr.; M-F 4 per day, Sa-Su 1-3 per day; 55Sk). To reach the center, take a right out of the station, go straight through the intersection, and continue uphill as the road curves around a small park. Follow Nová up to the main square, nám. Majstra Pavla (15min.). To catch the infrequent local bus, turn left out of the train station and follow the road to the red-and-white **Zastavka** sign. The **tourist office,** nám. Majstra

Pavla 58, has **maps** of the city center (free-32Sk) and recommends **private rooms,** which start at 350Sk. (☎161 88; www.levoca.sk. Open May-Sept. M-Sa 9am-5pm, Su 10am-2pm; Oct.-Apr. M-F 9am-4:30pm.) **Slovenská Sporiteľňa,** nám. Majstra Pavla 56, gives MC/V **cash advances** and cashes AmEx/V **traveler's checks** (20Sk min.) for 1% commission. A MC/V **ATM** is outside. (☎451 01 21. Open M and F 8am-3:30pm, Tu and Th 8am-3pm, W 8am-4:30pm.) The **pharmacy, Lekáren K Hadovi,** nám. Majstra Pavla 13, posts the addresses and hours of other pharmacies. (☎451 24 56. Open M-F 7:30am-5pm, Sa 8am-noon.) At **Cafe,** nám. Majstra Pavla 38, you can buy an Internet pass that is valid for up to 15 days. (Weekdays 50Sk per hr., students 36Sk per hr.; weekends 30Sk per hr. Open daily 10am-10pm). The **post office** is at nám. Majstra Pavla 42. (☎451 24 89. **Poste Restante** at window #1. Open M-F 8am-noon and 1-5pm, Sa 8-10:30am.) **Postal Code:** 05401.

ЛЄ ACCOMMODATIONS AND FOOD. Though choices are limited, finding accommodations is usually not difficult. Book well in advance for the Festival of Marian Devotion; your best bet is to stay in Poprad and travel to Levoča. Those looking to spend the night can inquire at the tourist office (see above), where the English-speaking staff can help book lodging at **pensions** (350Sk-800Sk) and nearby **campsites.** The family-run ▧**Penzión Šuňavský ❷,** Nová 59, is in the Old Town and has an idyllic garden. Rooms are clean and comfortable. Follow the directions to the town center; the pension is on the left side of Nová. (☎451 45 26. Breakfast 100Sk. Laundry 100Sk. Call 2 days ahead in Aug. 3- to 4-person dorms with shared baths 400Sk. Spacious 2-person apartments 1400Sk. Tourist tax 15Sk.) The more luxurious **Penzión U Leva ❸,** nám. Majstra Pavla 24, is in the heart of the main square and offers elegant rooms with TV, kitchen-ettes, and access to a fitness center and sauna. The apartments are grand, complete with kitchens, satellite TVs, and large baths. Leva is worth the extra price for its location and quality. (☎450 23 11; www.uleva.szm.sk. Singles 700Sk; doubles 1150Sk. Apartments for 1 person 900Sk, for 2 people 1500Sk. Tourist tax 15Sk.) **U 3 Apoštolov ❷,** nám. Majstra Pavla 11, serves large portions of traditional and vegetarian dishes. Patrons can relax on a beautiful terrace or find refuge from the sun indoors. (☎450 23 11. Entrees 89-220Sk. Open M-Sa 8am-10pm, Su 10am-10pm. AmEx/MC/V.) Popular with locals for special occasions, **Restaurant Janusa ❶,** Kláštorská 22, specializes in *pierogi* (95-115Sk) and serves other traditional Slovak dishes. (☎451 45 92; www.slovakiaguide.sk. Entrees 70-138Sk. Open daily 10am-10pm. Sa-Su reservations only.) **Billa Supermarket,** next to the bus station, has a huge selection of food and drinks. (Open M-F 7am-9pm, Sa-Su 8am-8pm. MC/V.)

◪ SIGHTS. Levoča's star attraction is the 14th-century **St. Jacob's Church** (Chrám sv. Jakuba), home to the world's tallest Gothic altar (a staggering 18.62m), beautifully carved by Master Pavol between 1507 and 1517. Almost as dramatic as the altar are the frescoes on the left wall, depicting the seven heavenly virtues and the seven deadly sins. (☎090 752 16 73. Buy tickets across the street. Entrance every 30min.; Sept.-June every hr. after 1pm. Open July-Aug. M 11am-5pm, Tu-Sa 9am-1pm and 2-5pm, Su 1-5pm; Sept.-June Tu-Sa 9am-4pm. 50Sk, students 30Sk. Dress appropriately. Brief English-language informational tape 5Sk.)

Three branches of the **Spišské Museum** dot nám. Majstra Pavla. In addition to exhibits, the museums feature a worthwhile video about Levoča's history (20min., available in English). **Dom Majstra Pavla,** nám. Majstra Pavla 20 (☎451 34 96), details Pavol's life and work; displays include high-quality facsimiles of his greatest pieces. The most interesting branch is housed in the beautiful **Town Hall** *(radnica)* and provides a candid look at Levoča's past, displaying everything from regal chandeliers to basic torture instruments. Enter the museum through the stairs to the right of the town hall's main entrance. Next to the museum entrance stands the **Cage of Shame** (Klietka Hanby), in which accused "ladies of the night" were humiliated in the 16th century. The Spišské Museum's third branch (☎451 27 86), at #40, has a small collection of masterful portraits, ceramics, and statues. (www.snm.sk. All open daily May-Oct. 9am-5pm; Nov.-Apr. 8am-4pm. 40Sk, students 20Sk. 1 ticket per museum. English brochure 40Sk.) The neo-Gothic **Basilica of the Virgin Mary** (Bazilika Panny Marie), separated from Levoča by 3km of wheat fields but visible from town, towers forebodingly atop Mariánská hora.

SPIŠSKÉ PODHRADIE AND ŽEHRA

If you only visit one Slovak castle, make it ◼**Spišské Castle** (Spišský hrad) in Spišské Podhradie (SPISH-skay POD-hra-dyeh). The site has been home to forti-fied settlements for two millennia; the ruins crowning the hilltop today are rem-nants of a Hungarian castle that was abandoned in the 18th century. Long after a 1780 fire left the castle deserted, it was claimed as national property in 1945 and became a national treasure in 1961. The view of the surrounding villages from the castle is well worth the climb, and its free **museum** exhibits interesting war relics like musket balls, cannons, suits of armor, and grisly torture devices. In 1993, it was made a UNESCO World Heritage site. (☎454 13 36. Entrance with an English-speaking guide every 30min., min. 15 people. Open daily May-Oct. 9am-6pm. 160Sk, students 100Sk.) West of town stands the region's religious capital, **Spišské Kapitula.** Completely encircled by medieval walls, the 13th-century monastery con-tains a seminary, bishop's quarters, and **St. Martin's Cathedral** (Katedrála sv. Mar-tina). More impressive for its historical and cultural significance than for its aesthetics, the Cathedral weathered a sacking by invading Tatars in 1241 and a stint as a police academy under Soviet rule. It has since been returned to its origi-nal purpose and even hosted the Pope in 1995. Facing the bus station departure board, turn right, walk through the gardens, and cross the river. The winding road eventually leads to the Cathedral (15min.). Get tickets at the souvenir shop in the small bell tower, 50m from the church. (☎090 838 84 11; www.spiskap.sk. Tours every hr. on the hr. Open May-Sept. M-Sa 9am-4pm, Su 9-11am and 1pm-4pm; Oct.-Apr. M-Sa 9am-4:30pm, Su 11am and 1-3pm. 30Sk, students 20Sk. Knees and shoul-ders must be covered.) To escape the beer gardens and touristy restaurants, head along the road past the monastery for 10-15min. to **Spišský Salaš ❷**, Levočská cesta 11. This wooden cottage, serving traditional Slovak foods, is a local favorite. Enjoy great views of the surrounding countryside and the dubious English translations on the menu: dare you try the "Domestic Slaughter" (a lot of pork; 150Sk)? (☎454 12 02. Beer 30Sk. Entrees 69-250Sk. MC/V.)

A long, tranquil walk from the castle brings you to the ancient village of **Žehra,** home of the **Church of the Holy Spirit** (Kostol Svätého Ducha). Built in a late Romanesque/early Gothic style, it's not to be missed if you can manage the two hour trek to its doors. Though faded and in need of restoration, its UNESCO-pro-tected murals have made the church famous. The interior is decorated with remarkable frescoes painted in five stages during the 12th to 15th centuries and uncovered in the 1950s. From the castle entrance, descend to the closer parking lot and take the yellow trail—it is easily recognizable by its closely cut grass. Con-tinue past the limestone crags and bear left into the valley below. The church's brown, onion-domed tower is easy to spot. (Open M-F 9:30-11:30am with entrance every 30min. and 1-4pm with entrance every hr.; Su 2-4pm. 20Sk, students 10Sk.)

Buses come from **Levoča** (30min., 1 per hr., 22Sk), **Poprad** (1hr., 9 per day, 53 Sk), and **Prešov** (1½hr., 1 per hr. until 6pm, 57Sk). Many uphill paths lead to the castle (check the info map at the castle end of the main square). Or, turn left from the bus departure board and head through the tall grass to the main square. Turn left onto the bridge leading out of town, go immediately left then right up the steep narrow road that passes the cemetery. For an easier dirt path up to the castle, follow previous directions, but continue straight after the bridge and take the first road left.

SLOVENSKÝ RAJ NATIONAL PARK ☎(0)58

The peaks of Slovenský Raj National Park, southeast of the Low Tatras, don't match their neighbors in height, but they make up for it in pizazz. Here dazzling forests, dramatic waterfalls, and deep limestone ravines await hikers and lovers of the outdoors. The natural beauty of these mountains earns them their title: Slovenský Raj means Slovak Paradise. Few tourists have discovered the treasures here, however, and life moves slowly in the tiny mountain hamlets even as hikers and skiers speed through nearby trails.

TRANSPORTATION. Reaching the park is difficult. Nestled by the shores of Lake Palčmanská Maša, **Dedinky** (pop. 400) is the largest town on Slovenský Raj's southern border. Its sublime location makes it a favorite among hikers. Catch a train to **Spisska Nová Ves** (from Poprad: 30min., 7-10 per day, 22Sk) where buses head to Dedinky (1¼-1½hr., 8-9 per day, 71Sk). Alternatively, go straight from Poprad by catching the **bus** toward **Rožňava** (1hr., 4 per day, 65 Sk). The bus stops first at the Dobšinská ľadová jaskyňa where you can catch a train to **Dedinky** (25min., 7-8 per day, 15Sk), then at the village **Stratená**, and finally at a junction 2km south of Dedinky. From here, follow the yellow trail that branches off to the right about 150m from the bus stop. When you reach the road at the bottom, turn left, cross the dam, and walk left toward the visible lakeside town (25min.).

ORIENTATION AND PRACTICAL INFORMATION. The bus station is in the middle of Dedinky, while the train station is 15min. away, on the far side of the lake by the dam. The best trail guide is the **VKÚ map #4.** Pick up a copy at the Mlynky tourist office or Dedinky grocery store (125Sk). To find the **Sedačková Lanová Dráha tourist office,** head to **Mlynky,** a town neighboring Dedinky. From the train station, cross the dam, follow the road, and veer left as it descends to Mlynky. Signs point to **Penzión Salamander** at the bottom of the hill to the right (5-10min.). In Salamander's reception room, the tourist office staff sells VKÚ #4 (120Sk), has info on 200-400Sk **private rooms,** and rents **bikes** for 40Sk per hour. (☎449 35 45. Open daily 8am-10pm. AmEx/MC/V.) Bus and train schedules available at reception of Hotel Priehrada. Behind Hotel Priehrada, a **chairlift** runs to Chata Geravy. (☎058 798 12 12. 1 per hr. May-Aug M 9am-3pm, Tu-Su 9am-4pm; Sept-Oct. daily 9am-2pm and 2:45pm. 90Sk, round-trip 150Sk.) **Tókóly Tours,** 200m from Hotel Priehrada, rents **boats** and **bikes.** (☎905 592 30 11. Rowboats, paddleboats, canoes, or bikes 100Sk per hr. Open daily July-Aug. 9am-6pm; June 15-30 and Sept. 1-15 1-6pm.) There are **telephones** in the entryway of Hotel Priehrada (international calls require payment by coin). Dedinky's **post office** is behind the wooden tower near the bus stop. (☎058 798 11 34. **Poste Restante.** Open M-F 8-10am, 12:30-1:30pm, and 2-3pm.) **Postal Code:** 04973.

ACCOMMODATIONS AND FOOD. Book at least two weeks ahead in January, July, and August, or plan on getting a **private room** (200-350Sk). They rarely fill up, and furthermore they're often the cheapest and best options. Look for *privat, ubytowanie,* or *zimmer frei* signs. **Penzión Pastierňa ❷,** Dedinky 42, offers spacious rooms, furnished with unvarnished pine floors, beds, and tables, all with private baths. From the bus station, go uphill past the grocery store, and straight to the end of the street. (☎798 11 75. Reception daily 8:30am-9:30pm. Check-out 11am. 2- to 4-bed rooms 350Sk. Tourist tax 15Sk. Cash only.) **Hotel Priehrada ❷,**

Dedinky 107, rents older rooms with new, well-kept baths. It also runs a **camp-ground** by the lake. (☎ 798 12 12; fax 788 16 82. Reception 24hr. Strict check-in 2pm. Check-out 10am. Rooms 450Sk; extra bed 310Sk. Camping 40Sk per person, 40Sk per tent, 40Sk per car. Cash only.) Or, look for lodging in nearby **Mlynky.** From the Dedinky train stop, cross the dam and turn right. When the road splits, veer left toward Mlynky. **Turisticka Ubytovna NITA ❶**, Pakmanslá Maša 295 (50m behind Penzión Salamander), has simple but comfortable rooms and pleasant staff. (☎/fax 449 32 79. Shared baths. Check-in 2pm. Check-out 10am. Call ahead. 2- to 4-bed rooms 200Sk, with breakfast and dinner 320Sk. Cash only.)

Restaurants are few here and most hikers prefer to stock up on trail food before heading off. In Dedinky, the restaurant in **Penzión Pastierňa ❷** serves Slovak stan-dards, including fresh lake *pstruh* (trout; 135Sk), and vegetarian options. (Entrees 60-170Sk. Open daily 8am-10:30pm. Cash only.) Plan to eat in Dedinky if heading to the caves, where **Restaurant Ľadová Jaskyňa ❷** serves simple but overpriced food (entrees 79-290Sk). Or, stock up on *potraviny* (groceries) across from the bus sta-tion. (☎ 798 11 21. Open M-F 8am-noon and 2-6pm, Sa 7-11am. Cash only.)

🄶 **SIGHTS.** Discovered in 1870, the ▦**Dobšinská Ice Caves** (Dobšinská ľadová jaskyňa) contain over 110,000 cubic meters of beautifully held frozen water from as long ago as the last Ice Age. The caves hide awe-inspiring sights: hall after hall of frozen columns, gigantic ice walls, and hardened waterfalls. Dress in layers—the cave temperature hovers between -6°C and +0.5°C year-round. To get here from Dedinky, take the 10am **bus** from the Dedinky bus stop (20min., 20Sk) to the ice-cave parking lot; from there the blue trail leads up the steep forest incline to the cave, 15-20min. away. Or take one of seven daily **trains** (first 5:40am, last 6:40pm) toward **Červana Skala** for two stops. (15min., 11Sk.) Follow the road lead-ing from the station to the main road. Turn left, and then right after you pass the restaurant; the parking lot of Restaurant Ľadová Jaskyňa is up ahead. (☎ 788 14 70; www.ssj.sk. Open July-Aug 9am-4pm, entrance every hr.; May 15-June and Sept. 1-15 9:30am-2pm, entrance every 1½hr. by guided tour only; 40-person min. for tour in English. 150Sk, students with ISIC 120Sk.)

🄺 **HIKING.** Camping and fires are prohibited in all Slovak national parks except at registered campsites and some *chaty*. Tourists must stick to the clearly marked trails. Having a map is advisable, as cascade trails are one-way—you can go up, but not down. All cascade trails are closed from November to June except to those accompanied by certified guides. Guides can be hired from nearby resorts, *chaty*, and travel agencies (3000-4000Sk). **Biele vody** (White Waters; 45min.-1¾hr.) is a moderately difficult cascade hike up a series of rapids. Watch your footing on slip-pery and loose rocks, ladders, and bridges. From the parking lot to the right of Hotel Priehrada, take the red trail to **Mlynky** (25min.) and then join the relaxed blue cross-country ski trail around **Biele vody** (788m; 2-3hr.). Alternatively, from Mlynky take the moderately difficult blue trail up Chata Geravy (1027m; 1hr.). A memora-ble view of the surrounding peaks and forested hills rewards those who venture to the top, where **Chata Geravy** or a chairlift await the weary, while the green trail leads the energetic back down (50min.). **Veľký sokol** (Big Falcon; 6½hr.) is a demanding hike into the heart of Slovenský Raj and up its deepest gorge. Follow the road west from Stratená (1hr.) or east from the ice caves (with your back to the caves, take a right; 30min.). At the U-bend, follow the green trail until it meets the road (30min.) and then take the red path. After another 15min., cross the park-ing lot and take the yellow trail through the rocky **Veľký sokol** cascade, with magnif-icent views of the surrounding gorge, up to **Glacka Cesta** (971m; 2½hr.) From the top, a right on the red path returns to **Chata Geravy** (1hr.) and the chairlift or the green trail (50min.) down to **Dedinky.** An even more intense trek through Slovenský Raj, **Sokolia dolina** (Falcon Valley; 7hr.) mounts the highest of the park's waterfalls (70m). From Chata Geravy, take the red trail to the green trail and turn right (1¼hr.). After 20min., hang a right onto the yellow trail at **Pod Bykárkou.** Continue until you meet the green trail (1hr.) and head left toward Sokolia and Kamenná dolina. At **Sokolia dolina** (45min.) begin the arduous ascent up to the cascade (2hr.), where your efforts are rewarded with a dazzling view of the waterfall. When you reach the bottom, go left on the green trail to **Pod Bykárkou** (20min.) and retrace your steps back to Chata Geravy (1¾hr.). Or begin another tough ascent by turning right onto the green trail, taking it to the yellow trail, and then continuing on the yellow trail all the way to **Glac** (20-30min.). From there, make a left onto the blue path and head to **Malá Polana** (10min.). Make sure to then go right and follow the red trail to **Sokol** and **Diablova Polka** (1½hr.), not Geravy. When you reach the parking lot, head onto the yellow trail to Vemky Sokol (2-2½hr.; see above).

HIGH TATRAS (VYSOKÉ TATRY)

Spanning the border between the Slovakia and Poland, the High Tatras are the highest peaks in the Carpathian range and create mesmerizing valleys. Despite its popularity with hikers and tourists, the High Tatras region retains Slovak small-town charm, with affordable accommodations and welcoming locals. Starý Smokovec is a popular base for excursions and short hikes, but the most hardcore hikers seek shelter in mountain huts *(chaty)*. Many of the lower slopes on the Slovakian side of the High Tatras were devastated by a freak storm in the fall of 2004, and vast swaths of forest are now brown fields of broken pine trees. The upper regions, however, escaped largely unscathed.

POPRAD   ☎(0)52

Poprad (pop. 56,000) is one of the Slovakia's major tourist centers and transportation hubs. While Poprad provides amusement for a few hours, travelers may find it more pleasant to simply pass through en route to their final destination.

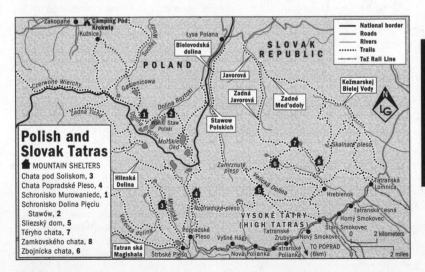

Polish and Slovak Tatras

🏠 MOUNTAIN SHELTERS

Chata pod Soliskom, 3
Chata Popradské Pleso, 4
Schronisko Murowaniedc, 1
Schronisko Dolina Pięciu
  Stawów, 2
Sliezský dom, 5
Téryho chata, 7
Zamkovského chata, 8
Zbojnícka chata, 6

National border
Roads
Rivers
Trails
Tež Rail Line

SLOVAK REPUBLIC

⌐ TRANSPORTATION. Trains run to **Bratislava** (4¾hr., 12 per day, 389Sk), **Košice** (1-2hr., 21 per day, 138Sk), and **Žilina** (2-3hr., 21 per day, 196Sk). The clean, efficient *Tatranská elektrická železnica* (TEŽ) runs between Poprad and the various **Tatran resorts** (10-60min., every 20min., up to 40Sk). The **bus station,** at the corner of Wolkerova and Alžbetina (☎776 25 55), sends buses to: **Banská Bystrica** (2½hr., 5 per day, 220Sk); **Bratislava** (7hr., 12 per day, 357Sk); **Kežmarok** (25 min., 20-25 per day, 23Sk); **Košice** (2½hr., 7 per day, 130Sk); **Žilina** (3hr., 13-14 per day, 173Sk); **Frankfurt, GER** (18hr., 2 per day, 2100Sk); **Prague, CZR** (11hr., 9 per day, 780Sk); and **Vienna, AUT** (8hr., 2 per day, 1000Sk). Call **Rádio Taxi** at ☎776 87 68.

▣❼ ORIENTATION AND PRACTICAL INFORMATION. To reach the center, exit right from the train station, turn left on **Alžbetina,** and follow it away from the **bus station.** Turn left again on **Hviezdoslavova,** then right on **Mnoheľova,** which leads to **nám. sv. Egídia.** To reach the old square from the train station, walk up Alžbetina, then turn left on **Štefánikova.** Continue about 2km and turn left on **Kežmarská.** Keep right as the road forks and head up into **Sobotské nám.** At **Popradská Informačná Agentúra (PIA),** nám. sv. Egídia 15, the English-speaking staff sells **maps,** offers info, and arranges accommodations. (☎772 13 94; www.poprad-online.sk. Open July-Aug. M-F 8am-6pm, Sa 9am-1pm; Su noon-3pm; Sept.-June M-F 9am-5pm, Sa 9am-noon. **Private rooms** 200Sk.) **VÚB,** Mnoheľova 9, cashes **traveler's checks** and **AmEx Traveler's Cheques** and provides **cash advances** for 1% commission. (☎713 11 11. Open M-W and F 8am-5pm.) Find 24hr. MC/V **ATMs** all over town. There's a **24hr. currency exchange** desk in the lobby of **Hotel Satel,** Mnoheľ'ova 5 (☎527 16 11; www.satel-slovakia.sk). **Store luggage** at the train station, opposite the ticket windows. (15Sk per bag, 30Sk per bag over 15kg.) **Internet** is at **Slovak Telecom,** nám. sv. Egídia 16 (free; open M-F 8am-5pm) and **T-Mobil,** nám. sv. Egídia 82 (upstairs; 20Sk per 30min.; open M-F 9am-6pm). **Postal Code:** 05801.

In winter, a guide is necessary for hiking in the Tatras. To hire one, check with the local tourist information office in your town. Snowfall is very high and avalanches are common. Dozens of hikers die each winter, often on "easy" trails. Even in summer, many hikes are extremely demanding and require experience. Before you begin, obtain a map and info about the trail. Updated information on trail and weather conditions is available at www.tanap.sk, but at the highest elevations, weather changes frequently and abruptly. Check with a mountain rescue team, a local outdoors store, or a tourist office before going anywhere without an escort. Always inform the receptionist at your hostel or hotel of your hiking route and the estimated time of your return.

∏❑ ACCOMMODATIONS AND FOOD. A student dorm during the school year, **Domov Mładeze ❶,** Karpatská 9, offers the cheapest rooms in town. Walk down Alžbetina from the train station and take the second right on Karpatská. (☎776 34 14. Reception daily 6am-10pm. Call ahead. Open July-Aug. 2- and 3-bed dorms 250Sk; singles with baths 300Sk. Cash only.) Affordable and right by the bus and train stations, **Hotel Europa ❷,** Wolkierowa 1, offers worn but comfortable rooms. All rooms have sinks; baths are shared. (☎772 18 97. Reception 24hr. Check-out 11am. Singles 350Sk; doubles 550Sk; triples 750Sk. Tourist tax 15Sk. Cash only.) A more luxurious accommodation option is the grand **Hotel Satel ❺,** Mnoheľova 5, which has friendly staff and large, comfortable rooms in a relaxing business-class atmosphere. (☎716 11 11. English spoken. Singles 1380Sk; doubles 1800Sk. AmEx/ MC/V.) Pizza places and traditional restaurants populate the center square. A particularly appetizing option is **Slovenska Restauracia ❶,** 1 Mája 7, which serves *bryndzove havlusky* (sheep cheese dumplings; 70Sk), and other traditional Slovak dishes. (☎772 28 70. English menu. Entrees 35-230Sk. Open daily 10am-11pm. AmEx/MC/V.) **Egídius ❷**, Mnoheľova 18, near the bus and train stations, specializes in *knedle* (dumplings with plums, 103Sk) served with hearty helpings of meat. (☎772 28 98. Entrees 40-300Sk. Open daily 9.30am-11:30pm. AmEx/MC/V. **Reduta ❷**, nám. sv. Egídia 44, serves decent, meaty international dishes in the center of town. (☎772 20 32. English menu. Entrees 60-225Sk. Open M-Sa 9am-10pm, Su 11am-10pm. Cash only.) Buy groceries at the **Billa Supermarket**, on the far side of the bus station parking lot. (Open M-Sa 7am-9pm, Su 8am-8pm. MC/V.)

STARÝ SMOKOVEC ☎(0)52

Starý Smokovec (STAH-ree SMOH-koh-vets), founded in the 17th century, is the High Tatras' oldest and most central base resort. Hiking paths originate at the town's summit and connect it with the mountains. While signposts with a dozen arrows and nameless streets may seem daunting, it's difficult to get lost—Starý Smokovec was developed with tourism in mind and is easy to navigate.

⌐ TRANSPORTATION. TEŽ **trains** go to **Poprad** (30min., 1 per hr., 20Sk), **Štrbské Pleso** (45min., every 30-50min., 30Sk), and **Tatranská Lomnica** (15min., every 25-40min., 15Sk). The **bus station** is 2min. away; follow the path right from the train station. **Buses** go to: **Bratislava** (6hr., 2 per day, 409Sk); **Košice** (3hr., 2-3 per day, 143Sk); **Levoča** (20-50min., 2-4 per day, 67Sk); **Poprad** (30min., every 30-60min., 41Sk). A **funicular** runs to **Hrebienok** (see p. 651). For **taxis**, call **Rigo** (☎442 25 25).

✱ ⁊ ORIENTATION AND PRACTICAL INFORMATION. Starý Smokovec's essential services are mostly along the main road that leads to **Horný Smokovec** to the east and **Nový Smokovec** to the west. To get to the center from the train station, walk uphill to the main road and turn left. Cross the road past the strip mall and head toward the white building, Dom Služieb, where signs point to hotels, restaurants, and services. The **hiking trails** are farther uphill.

The helpful staff of **Tatranská Informačná Kancelária (TIK)**, in Dom Služieb, provides weather and hiking info and **free town maps**; sells hiking guides and the crucial **VKÚ map #113** (110Sk); and points visitors to hotels, pensions, and **private rooms**. (☎442 34 40; www.zcrvt.szm.sk. Open July-Aug. daily 8am-6pm; Sept.-Dec. 26 and Jan. 12-June M-F 9am-noon and 12:30-4pm, Sa 9am-1pm; Dec. 27-Jan. 11 daily 8am-

DECIPHERING THE TRAILS

A splatter of red. A dash of green. A yellow line criss-crossing the page. Standing in the middle of nowhere, I scrutinized my map and despaired. This looked less like something that would lead me off the trail before nightfall than a work of abstract art. I kept walking. About 500m ahead, I gave a sigh of relief: there was a tiny green mark painted faintly on a tree. I studied the map again—at least I was going the right way.

Trail signals in the Tatras are not as easy as they seem. A yellow line signals a short path connecting major trails. Blue means long—and generally easier—trails that connect sights, like caves or lakes. Green marks connect larger trails but, unlike yellow, tend to lead to famous natural sights or historical attractions. A red mark means that the trail will be challenging and steep, with ledges and slippery slopes.

Keep your eyes peeled, as the marks are often sporadic. The standard trail mark shows the color (red, green, yellow, or blue), bordered by two white stripes. A colored arrow indicates that the trail forks or looks uncertain, and a colored square with the top corner missing means that you have reached a tourist attraction. A white square or circle with a colored square inside means that the trail has been completed.

There you go. Study up, and good luck!

—Calum Docherty

5pm. Private rooms 300-400Sk.) **Slovenská Sporiteľňa,** located in the commercial strip on the way to Dom Služieb, **exchanges currency,** cashes **traveler's checks,** gives MC/V **cash advances** for 1% commission (30Sk min.), and has a 24hr. MC/V **ATM** outside. (☎244 224 70; www.slsp.sk. Open M-F 8am-noon and 12:30-3:30pm.) A **pharmacy, Lekáreň U Zlatej Sovy,** is on the first floor of Dom Služieb. (☎442 21 65. Open M-F 8am-noon and 12:30-4:30pm, Sa 9am-noon.) **Internet** is available in the **Rogalo** restaurant to the left of the main entrance of Dom Služieb. (☎442 50 43. 1Sk per min. Open daily 9am-10pm.) The **post office** is the squat white building uphill to the left of the train station before the main road. **Poste Restante** is at the first window to the left. **Telephones** are located outside. (☎442 24 71. Open M-F 8am-1pm and 2-4pm, Sa 8-10am.) **Postal Code:** 06201.

⌗◨ ACCOMMODATIONS AND FOOD. Uphill from the train station on the way to Dom Služieb, an electronic **InfoPanel** lists current vacancies in the greater Smokovec area. The **TIK** (see above) lists available **private rooms** (300-400Sk). Although **Hotel Palace ❷** won't win any awards for its ambience or off-yellow exterior, its rooms are spacious and nicely furnished—especially those with baths. Overall, it's a great value. To get there, turn left out of the TEŽ station onto the main road, walk past the church, and head uphill past Penzión Gerlach; Palace will be on your right. (☎442 24 54. Breakfast 120Sk. Reception 24hr. Singles 300Sk, with bath 450-550Sk; doubles 600-700Sk. Cash only). To reach the family-run **Penzión Gerlach ❹,** follow the directions to Hotel Palace; Gerlach is on the right, just after the church. Central location and fabulously furnished rooms ensure comfort in style. (☎442 32 80; www.penziongerlach.sk. Breakfast included. Reception daily 10am-6pm. Call ahead in high season. Singles 800Sk; doubles 1000-1200Sk; triples 1500-1600Sk. Prices drop 200Sk in low season. Cash only.) Just behind Penzión Gerlach lies the equally pleasant **Villa Dr Szontagh ❺,** the angular roof and turret of which suggest a cottage married to a small fort. (☎421 44 33; szontagh@isternet.sk. Singles 1100Sk; doubles 1500Sk. Cash only.) **Hotel Smokovec ❺,** uphill from the train station, offers a swimming pool (50Sk per hr.), a weight room (50Sk per hr.), a sauna (350Sk per 1-2 people per 2hr), and beautiful rooms. (☎442 51 91; www.hotelsmokovec.sk. English spoken. Reception 24hr. Check-out 10am. Doubles 2380Sk; triples 3420Sk. In low season 1980/2820Sk. MC/V.) More budget options lie in the nearby hamlet of **Horný Smokovec,** two TEŽ stops away. **Hotel Poľana ❷** offers decent rooms at low prices. From the TEŽ stop, go left along the main road for roughly 10min. to find Poľana on your right. (☎443 22 18. Shared baths. Singles 380Sk; doubles 600Sk; triples 750Sk. Cash only.)

Most restaurants in the area are hard to distinguish, serving up typical Slovak dishes like *bryndza* (dumplings), or cabbage-and-sausage soup. For an excellent blend of Slovak and international cuisine, as well as fast and friendly service, try **Restaurant Tatra ❷,** just above the bus station. The *pastiersky syr* (fried cheese; 90Sk) is scrumptious. (Beer 20-40Sk. Entrees 90-230Sk. Open daily 11:30am-8pm. Cash only.) Popular with tourists and locals alike, **Restaurant Pizzeria La Montanara ❷** offers huge portions of traditional Italian food at appealing prices. From the train station, turn right and keep right for about 40m; the restaurant is behind a row of shops. (☎442 51 71. Entrees 90-210Sk. Open daily noon-9pm. MC/V.) Enjoy dining in **Restaurant Koliba ❸,** a spacious mountain cabin decorated with rough-hewn wooden tables, timber beams, wagons, and even a fake horse dangling from the ceiling. Exceptional quality makes up for the relative priciness. Try the *Tatranský čaj* (Tatran tea; 40Sk), which is spiked with pure grain alcohol. (☎442 22 04. Facing downhill, cross the parking lot to the right of the train station and then cross the tracks. Entrees 125-285Sk. Open daily 4pm-midnight. Cash only.) Hikers can stock up on supplies at the **Supermarket** in the strip mall just above the train station. (Open M-F 7:45am-5:45pm, Sa-Su noon-6pm. MC/V.) Another super-market, located in the shopping complex opposite the bus station, carries slightly cheaper items. (Open M-F 8am-6pm, Sa-Su 8am-12:30pm. MC/V.)

⚠️ OUTDOOR ACTIVITIES. T-ski, in the funicular station behind **Grand Hotel,** offers everything from ski classes to Dunajec river-rafting expeditions (690Sk), and rents sleds and snowboards. (☎442 32 65. Sleds 100Sk per day; skis 250-400Sk; snowboards 500Sk. Individual classes 600-900Sk per 2hr., groups 200-300Sk per person; guides from 500Sk per day. Open daily 9am-6pm. MC/V.) Thrifty travelers should bring food and drink for hikes or stays at *chaty.* **Tatrasport,** uphill from the bus lot, rents **mountain bikes.** (☎442 52 41; www.tatry.net/tatrasport. 200Sk per 5hr., 299Sk per day. Open daily 8am-6pm. MC/V.)

The **funicular** to **Hrebienok** (1285m) carries people to the crossroads of numerous hiking trails. (July 2-Sept. 4 ride up 90Sk, ride down 40Sk, round trip 110Sk. Sept. 5-July 1 80/30/90Sk. Open daily 8:30am-4pm). The six skiing trails vary in difficulty. Lengths range 100-530m. (Morning 440Sk, afternoon 540Sk, full day 690Sk). Hike the somewhat uninspiring first leg of the **green trail** behind **Hotel Grand** to reach Hrebienok (45min.). Another 20min. down the green trail lie the **Volopády studeného potoka** (Cold Stream Waterfalls); from here you can take the **yellow trail,** a subdued and tranquil route that meanders along the river to Tatranská Lesná (1¾hr.). The popular **red trail,** the **Tatranska Magistrála,** runs east-to-west along the Slovakian Tatras, through or above most of the resort towns. From Hrebienok, follow the red trail just past **Rainerova Chata** (20min.), then head right on the eastward **blue trail** to descend gradually through towering pines to Tatranská Lomnica (1¾hr.). Or, turn left and take the blue trail westward on an intense hike past **Zbojnícka Chata** (3hr.; ☎090 361 90 00; 330Sk) and up **Sedlo Prielom** (2290m, 1¼hr.), then turn onto the green trail (30min.) and ascend **Sliezsky dom** (1670m, 1½hr.). Alternatively, continue on the red trail to **Zamkovského Chata ❷** (☎442 26 36; 1475m, 20min., 380Sk) and then take the fairly relaxed green trail through the **Malá studená dolina** (Little Cold Valley) to **Téryho Chata ❷** (☎442 52 45; 2015m; 2hr.; 280Sk, with breakfast 390Sk) to a spectacular view of nearby Lomnický Štít. If you stick to the red trail, you will eventually reach **Skalnaté Pleso** and an awaiting *chata;* a cable car leads to great views atop Lomnický Štít (2½hr., p. 652).

Heading away from Rainerova Chata, the red trail eventually reaches **Sliezký dom ❸.** (1670m, 2hr. ☎442 52 61. Breakfast and dinner included. 675Sk.) Or, zig-zag farther down through the valley to reach the sharp ascent (3hr.) to **Chata Popradské Pleso ❸,** which sits on a calm, stunning lakefront. (☎449 27 65; www.horskyhotel.sk. 380-650Sk; in low season 320-550Sk.) Continue farther on the red trail for a pine-tree-lined descent to **Štrbské Pleso** (1355m, 1hr.). Weary hikers can hop off the wandering *magistrála* on one of the many trails that descend to the resort towns below. From **Sliezský dom,** the green trail leads to **Tatranská Polianka** (2hr.). Another hour down the red trail, the yellow branches off and descends to **Vyšné Hágy** (2hr.); both towns are on the TEŽ. A hard blue path branches from the *magistrála* 20min. west of Hrebienok to one of the highest peaks, **Slavkovský Štít.** (2452m, 8hr. round-trip from Hrebienok. Don't attempt without a full day and good weather.)

ŠTRBSKÉ PLESO

Hotels, ski jumps, and souvenir stands clutter placid **Štrbské Pleso** (SHTERB-skay PLEH-soh; Štrbské Lake), which offers some of the most cherished hikes and views in the Tatras. Peaceful trails expose Štrbské Pleso's natural beauty among awe-inspiring mountains. Take the TEŽ **train** (30min. from Starý Smokovec, 1-2 per hr., 20Sk). In summer (late May to Sept.) and winter (Dec.-Mar.), a lift carries visitors to **Chata pod Soliskom** (1840m), which overlooks the lake and the valleys that spread behind Štrbské Pleso. (☎449 22 21. 130Sk, round-trip 190Sk. Open daily 8:30am-4pm, last lift up 3:30pm.) To reach the lift, take the road from the train station and follow the signs or take the yellow trail.

Two magnificent day hikes loop out from Štrbské Pleso. Both can get cold, so bring layers as well as food and water. From the **Informačné Stredisko Tanapu** (Information Center; across from TEŽ station; open M-Sa 8-11:30am and noon-4pm; hours shorter in low season.) and the bus station, walk past the souvenir lot and head left at the junction. Continue uphill on the challenging **yellow trail** and along **Mlynická dolina** past several enchanting mountain lakes and the dramatic **Vodopády Skok** waterfalls. The path (6-7hr.) involves some strenuous ascents, mounting **Bystré Sedlo** (2314m) and **Veľké Solisko** (2412m). At the end of the yellow trail, turn left onto the red trail to complete the loop and return to Štrbské Pleso (30min.). The scenery justifies the effort.

The 2nd, even-more-difficult hike takes you to the top of **Rysy** (2499m), on the Polish-Slovak border; this is Poland's highest peak and the highest Tatra scalable without a guide. From Štrbské Pleso, follow the *magistrála* (red trail) and experience the awe-inspiring views and imposing grandeur of the Tatran peaks. The **green trail** branches off the *magistrála* and rolls by the **Hincov potok** (stream) to an intersection (45min.) where you can continue up on the **blue trail** or take a 2min. detour to **Chata Popradské Pleso** (see above). After 40min. on the blue trail, take the red branch to tackle Rysy (3-4hr. round-trip). Along the way, you can stop at **Chata pod Rysmi ❶** (2250m), where hot soups (40Sk) are available. (☎442 23 14. Rooms 250Sk). From the start of the red branch, backtracking along the blue then green trails to Štrbské Pleso should take 1½-2hr. Allow 8-9hr. for the round trip. This hike is for advanced hikers and should be attempted in good weather only. (☎524 46 76 76; www.tatry.sk.)

From the Chata Popradské Pleso, head south 30min. on the yellow trail to the **Symbolic Cemetery** (Symbolický cintorín; 1525m). Built between 1936 and 1940 by painter Otakar Štafl, the field of wooden crosses, metal plaques, and broken propeller blades serves as a memorial to the hikers who have died attempting the great Tatras. (Cemetery open July-Oct. daily dawn-dusk.) The trail ends at a paved blue path where the weary descend to reach the Popradské Pleso TEŽ stop (45min.). Those hardy souls looking to hike back to Štrbské Pleso will be rewarded with striking views from the steep descent. The *magistrála* continues from the *chata* for over 5hr. along scenic ridges to **Hrebienok**.

The stunning region is also popular among skiers of all abilities; the slopes of Štrbské Pleso boast excellent ridges and heavy snow. The six downhill trails range 80-2300m. (Morning 450Sk, afternoon 550Sk, full day 700Sk. Open Dec. 15-March 15.) Many other slopes are accessible from this region, including a fairly gentle ski from Chata Solisko on Predné Solisko, where a lift awaits. For a more challenging ride, take a cable car from the base and ski down a red trail.

Most people choose to stay in **Starý Smokovec** or **Tatranská Lomnica**, because there aren't many places available in Štrbské Pleso. However, those intent on staying out late on the trails can find a bed at **Hotel Toliar ❺**, on the first floor of the shopping center across from the train station. (☎478 10 11. Breakfast, swimming pool, and sauna included. Reception 24hr. Check-out 10am. 1 single 600Sk; doubles 1200-1400Sk; triples 1700Sk. MC/V.) A few **private rooms** are available; watch for *zimmer frei* signs (300-450Sk). Before starting a hike, stock up at the **grocery store** across from the train station. (Open daily 7am-7pm. MC/V.)

TATRANSKÁ LOMNICA

Though often dwarfed by the more lively and central Starý Smokovec, Tatranská Lomnica (TA-tran-ska LOM-nee-tsa) has a charming serenity. The town is little more than a scattering of buildings that dot the perimeter of a lush park. From Penzión Bělín (see below), take the road uphill and follow the signs to the

Kabinková Lanová Dráha lift (10min.), which rides up to the glacial lake of **Skalnaté Pleso**. (1751m. July 3-Sept. ride up 240Sk, ride down 190Sk, round-trip 380Sk; Sept. 2-July 2 200/160/320Sk. Open daily 8am-4:30pm; last ascent 4pm.). From the lake, a large gondola ascends to the summit of **Lomnický Štít** (2632m), the second highest in the Tatras. The gondola runs only once per hour, and tickets for the unparalleled view sell out fast, so buy them a few hours in advance at the base (June 28-Sept. 12 500Sk; Sept. 13-June 27 450Sk). From **Skalnaté Pleso** there is also a four-person chairlift to **Lomnické Sedlo**. (Open daily 9am-3:30pm, 160Sk). Alternatively, hike up to **Skalnaté Pleso** via the green trail (1½hr. up, 1¼hr. down). Much of the green trail runs through areas that were devastated by the 2004 storms.

In the winter, you can purchase a day ticket (550Sk) in **Skalnaté Pleso** to **ski** the excellent trails down to Tatranská Lomnica. On a clear day, the peak offers a staggering view of the mountains and valleys and makes for a fabulous picnic spot. At **Skalnaté Pleso**, the low-slung wooden *chata* (☎446 70 75; 250-300Sk) is a great spot to begin or end an adventure on the **Tatranská magistrála** (see below), although the hiking is generally better and the views more memorable from Starý Smokovec or Štrbské Pleso. The *magistrála* (red trail), heading from Skalnaté Pleso toward **Lomnická vyhliadka** (1524m, 50min.) and then to **Zamkovského Chata** (1¼hr.), is challenging, but remarkable mountaintop views reward your efforts (see **Hiking: Starý Smokovec**, p. 651). The **blue trail** leads to a gentler hike; follow it from the **InfoPanel**, located at the center of Tatranská Lomnica, to **Vodopády studeného potoka** (cold stream waterfalls; 1¾hr.), then take the yellow trail to Tatranská Lesná (1hr.) or double back along the blue trail (1¼hr.). The terrain here is flat enough to bike.

Many of the hotels and pensions in Tatranská Lomnica are cheaper than what you would find in Starý Smokovec, and you can also book **private rooms** from the tourist information office or look for *zimmer frei* signs. **Penzión Bělín ❷,** in the center of town, is cheap and comfortable. From the InfoPanel (see above), take the path across the street into the park. Take the first left and then a right onto the street ahead. Penzión Bělín is the large mustard-colored building to the right. (☎446 77 78; belin@tatry.sk. Reception daily 7am-9pm. Check-out 10am. July-Aug. 2- and 4-person rooms 280Sk. MC/V.) Dining options in town are severely limited. **Grill-Bar ❸,** above the train station, offers traditional Slovak meat dishes and, surprisingly, some vegetarian options. (English menu. Entrees 50-220Sk. Open M-Th and Su 10am-10pm, F-Sa 10am-midnight. Cash only). Stock up on snack food for the trails at **Supermarket Sintra,** just down the hill behind the train station. (Open M-F 7:45am-6pm, Sa 7:45am-1pm, Su 8am-1pm. MC/V.) To get to Tatranská Lomnica, take the TEŽ **train** (15min. from Poprad, 16 per day, 20 Sk). The bus station is 50m to the right, when facing the street from the train station. Uphill from the station, behind Uni Banka, get help from the attentive English-speaking staff at **Tatranská Informačná Kancelária.** (☎442 52 30; www.tatry.sk. Open July-Aug. M-F 8am-6pm, Sa-Su 9am-2pm; Sept.-June M and W-F 9am-3pm, Tu 10am-3pm, Sa 8am-1pm.) The **InfoPoint,** just outside the exit to the right of the train station, has a map of the town and a list of accommodations. The **Sports Shop,** in the town center, sells last-minute hiking supplies. They also rent bikes. (100Sk per hr., 400Sk per day. Open daily 7am-6pm. MC/V.) **Internet** is available at **Townson Travel,** in **Hotel Slalom** near the center of town. (Open M-F 9am-6pm, 2Sk per min.).

ŠARIŠ

More than just the home of Slovakia's most popular beer, Šariš is a region of natural wonder and cosmopolitan flair. Hidden away in the green hills of the eastern Slovak Republic, Šariš was long a buffer against Turkish invasions before spending the last century keeping mostly to itself. Šariš's cities tend to have lovely Old Towns surrounded by unattractive industrial sprawl.

KOŠICE ☎(0)55

Lying only 20km north of Hungary, Košice (KO-shih-tseh; pop. 236,000) is the Slovak Republic's 2nd-largest city. Košice is the place to visit if you want to see a typical Slovak Old Town without giving up the amenities and nightlife of a major city. Outside the Old Town, however, communist-era concrete blocks mar the area's otherwise beautiful landscape.

⌐ TRANSPORTATION

Trains: Predstaničné nám. (☎613 21 75). To: **Banská Bystrica** (3½-5hr., 292Sk); **Bratislava** (6hr., 13 per day, 550Sk); **Poprad** (1¼hr., 1 per day, 154Sk); **Prešov** (50min., 10 per day, 60Sk); **Rožňava** (1½hr., 12 per day, 88Sk); **Budapest, HUN** (5hr., 3 per day, 850Sk); **Kraków, POL** (6-7hr., 3 per day, 850-900Sk); **Prague, CZR** (10-11hr., 4 per day, 1200Sk).

Buses: (☎625 16 19), to the left of the train station. Destinations include: **Banská Bystrica** (4½hr., 1 per day, 260Sk); **Bardejov** (2-3hr., 12-20 per day, 110Sk); **Bratislava** (8hr., 12 per day, 500Sk); **Levoča** (3hr., 10 per day, 130Sk); **Poprad** (2½hr., 5 per day, 140); **Prešov** (50min., 30 per day, 47Sk); **Rožňava** (1¼hr., 37 per day, 100Sk); **Prague, CZR** (9hr., 3 per day, 1000Sk).

Public Transportation: Trams and **buses** cross the city and suburbs 5:30am-11pm. Night buses run every hr. midnight-3:50am. Tickets from kiosks and yellow boxes at bus stops (12Sk) or from driver (14Sk). Extra charge for large backpacks (6Sk). Punch ticket upon boarding. Fines for riding ticketless up to 1000Sk.

Taxis: Taxis wait on almost every corner. **Classic Taxi** (☎622 22 44), **CTC** (☎43 34 33), and **Radio Taxi** (☎163 33).

■✳☒ ORIENTATION AND PRACTICAL INFORMATION

To get to the heart of Košice's **Staré Mesto** (Old Town), exit the train station and follow the "Centrum" signs across the park. Walk down **Mlynská** to reach the main square, **Hlavná nám** (10min.).

Tourist Office: Informačna Centrum Mesta Košice, Hlavná 59 (☎625 88 88; www.kosice.sk/icmk). Provides helpful information on accommodations and cultural attractions. **Maps** free and 60-80Sk. Open M-F 9am-6pm, Sa 9am-1pm.

Currency Exchange: VÚB branches are everywhere; the one at Hlavná 8 (☎622 62 50) gives MC/V **cash advances** and cashes **traveler's checks** for 1% commission and a hefty 200Sk minimum. Also **exchanges currency,** but *kantory* along Hlavná generally give better rates. Open M-Tu and F 7:30am-5pm, W 8am-7pm, Th 8am-noon, Sa 9am-1pm. There are many 24hr. MC/V **ATMs** along Hlavná. **OTP Banka Slovenska,** Alžbetina 2 (☎681 12 67), cashes AmEx/V checks for 1%. Open M-F 8am-6pm.

Luggage Storage: At the train station. 25-35Sk per bag per day, 15-20Sk per additional bag. Open 6:30am-9pm. Small 24hr. lockers 5Sk.

English-Language Bookstore: Glossa, Hlavná 97 (☎623 36 76), through the arch and up the stairs. Small selection of English-language popular and classic literature (100-600Sk). Open M-F 9am-6pm, Sa 10am-1pm.

Pharmacy: Lekáreň Pri Dóme, Mlynská 1. Open M-F 7:30am-6:30pm, Sa 8am-noon. MC/V.

Telephones: Along Hlavná and outside the post office (see below).

Internet: At the central **tourist office** (see above), 10Sk per 20min. Or, try **Internet Centrum,** Hlavná 27 (www.kosez.sk). 0.58Sk per min., 30Sk per hr. Open daily 9am-10pm.

Post Office: Poštová 20 (☎617 14 01). **Poste Restante** at window #16. Open M-F 7am-7pm, Sa 8am-noon. **Postal Code:** 04001.

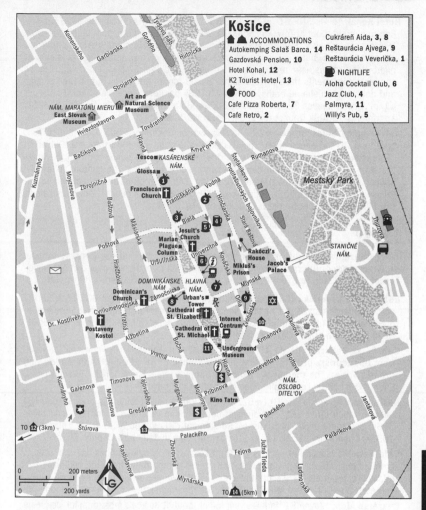

Košice

♠♠ ACCOMMODATIONS	Cukráreň Aida, **3, 8**
Autokemping Salaš Barca, **14**	Reštaurácia Ajvega, **9**
Gazdovská Pension, **10**	Reštaurácia Veverička, **1**
Hotel Kohal, **12**	
K2 Tourist Hotel, **13**	🍺 NIGHTLIFE
	Aloha Cocktail Club, **6**
🍴 FOOD	Jazz Club, **4**
Cafe Pizza Roberta, **7**	Palmyra, **11**
Cafe Retro, **2**	Willy's Pub, **5**

🏠 ACCOMMODATIONS

K2 Tourist Hotel, Štúrova 32 (☎625 59 48). Take tram #6 or bus #16, 21, or 30 from the train/bus station to the "Dom Umenia" stop, or follow Hlavná from the main square and turn right on Štúrova. A bargain within walking distance of the Old Town, this hostel provides simple and comfortable, albeit poorly lit, rooms. Shared showers lack curtains. Restaurant open M-Sa 10am-10pm, Su noon-10pm. Reception 24hr. Check-in and check-out noon. 3- to 4-bed dorms 350Sk. Tourist tax 20Sk. Cash only. ❷

Gazdovská Pension, Čajkovského 4, (☎625 01 43). The friendly staff at this central hostel helps visitors navigate the city. Clean, comfortable rooms with well-kept baths. Popular, so call ahead. Singles 800Sk; doubles 1000Sk. Tourist tax 20Sk. Cash only. ❸

Hotel Kohal, Trieda SNP 61 (☎/fax 642 55 72). Take tram #6 from the train/bus station to a roundabout at Toryská and Trieda SNP. Get off at the 5th stop, labeled as both "Ferrocentrum" and "Spoločenský Pavilón." Rooms in this hotel/hostel combo are cheap and clean, but it's a long walk back from the Old Town when the trams stop at night. Hotel rooms have radios, renovated baths, and TVs. Singles and doubles share showers; apartments have private baths. Hostel rooms are worn, bare-bones singles and doubles with shared baths. Laundry 10-70Sk per item. Reception 24hr. Check-out 11am. Hostel singles 325Sk; doubles 600Sk. Hotel singles 580Sk; doubles 1040Sk; apartments 1300Sk. Tourist tax 20Sk. AmEx/MC/V. ❷

Autokemping Salaš Barca (☎623 33 97; www.eurocampings.net). From the station, take tram #6 to Ferrocentrum/Spoločenský Pavilón and switch to tram #9. Get off at "Autokemping," cross the pedestrian bridge, go 20m up the ramp, and turn left down the stairs. Simple 2-bedroom bungalows with well-kept baths. Badminton, volleyball, soccer, and ping-pong available. Reception 24hr. Check-in and check-out noon. Reserve 3 days ahead. 70Sk per person, 60Sk per tent, 80Sk per car. 2-bed bungalows 600Sk; 3-bed 900Sk. Tourist tax 20Sk. AmEx/MC/V. ❶

◖ FOOD

With restaurants on rooftop terraces, under arches, and on the central square, Košice has more culinary variety than any Slovak city but Bratislava. Get groceries at **Tesco,** Hlavná 109. (☎670 48 10. Open M-F 8am-8pm, Sa-Su 8am-4:30pm. MC/V.)

Reštaurácia Veverička (Squirrel Restaurant), Hlavná 97 (☎622 33 60). Look for the pair of rodents carved out of dark wood. Enjoy a variety of local dishes on the sun-drenched patio (sadly, squirrel isn't on the menu). English menu. Entrees 68-250Sk. Open daily 9am-10pm. Cash only. ❷

Cafe Pizza Roberta, Hlavná 45 (☎0905 678 231). Delight in the spectacular views from this touristy pizzeria, located near the base of St. Elizabeth's Cathedral and Urban's Tower. The friendly waitstaff are happy to help decipher the Slovak menu. Entrees 59-155Sk. Open daily 10am-midnight. Cash only. ❶

Reštaurácia Ajvega, Orlia 10 (☎622 04 52). Vegetarians praise this organic-food restaurant, which offers veggie versions of both Mexican (enchiladas, tortillas, and tacos 89Sk) and traditional Slovak dishes. Some meat dishes. Soups 30-40Sk. Entrees 89-155Sk. Open M-Th and Su 11am-11pm, F-Sa 11am-midnight. Cash only. ❶

Cafe Retro, Kovácska 49 (☎728 77 01). Sketches of flying-machines line the walls, a gramophone sits on the windowsill, and model blimps hang from the ceiling in this relaxing cafe. Then there's the flatscreen TV showing sports. Somehow it all works. Espresso 25-40Sk. Open M-F 8am-10pm, Sa 2pm-midnight, Su 2-10pm. Cash only. ❷

Cukráreň Aida, Hlavná 81. Indulge your sweet tooth at Košice's most popular ice-cream parlor, which offers a wide range of flavors (6Sk per scoop) and sweets (15-80Sk). Espresso 18-24Sk. Open daily 8am-10pm. Cash only. 2nd location at Hlavná 44. ❶

◉ SIGHTS

CATHEDRAL OF ST. ELIZABETH (DOM SV. ALŽBETY). Dominating much of the Old Town, this gigantic cathedral practically spans the width of Hlavná. Begun in 1378 as a high-Gothic monument, the Cathedral has undergone repeated renovations. It is now a unique mixture of Western styles, from Baroque to Rococo. Inside, pay special attention to the impressive **altar,** complemented by majestic stained-glass windows on all sides. The church's North Tower offers a stunning view of the Old Town and a spectacular look at the intricate roof. (☎090 866 70 83. *Crypt open year-round M-F 9:30am-4:30pm. Tower open Apr.-Nov. M-F 9:30am-4:30pm. Admis-*

sion to exhibit 20Sk, students 15Sk. Cathedral tours 35/20Sk.) Nearby, a fountain dazzles crowds with musical water-dances to the likes of Simon and Garfunkel. The **Underground Museum** came to be after construction workers accidentally discovered the remains of underground fortifications in 1995. Two years of excavation revealed a series of archaeological wonders dating from the 13th to 15th centuries. *(At the start of Hlavná.* ☎ *625 83 93. Open Tu-Su 10am-6pm. 25Sk, students 15Sk. English pamphlet 10Sk.)*

EAST SLOVAK MUSEUM (VÝCHODOSLOVENSKÉ MÚZEUM). As you walk up, Hlavná, take a right at the **State Theater** onto Univerzitná to arrive at a branch of the East Slovak Museum, **Mikluš's Prison** (Miklušova väznica). Housed in the former city jail, the museum details life behind bars from the 17th to 19th century, exhibiting prisoner graffiti and torture instruments. Haunting descriptions of brutal deaths can be found in the photo collection in the reconstructed chambers—one woman, who killed her illegitimate baby, was thrown into her grave before a stake was driven into her heart. *(Hrnčiarska 7. English info. Open Tu-Sa 9am-5pm, Su 9am-1pm. Ticket office behind the gate at Hrnčiarska. Mandatory tours in Slovak every hr.; 40Sk, students 15Sk.)* At nám. Mieru Maratónu, in the ornate building closest to the runner's statue, stands the **archaeological branch** of the East Slovak Museum, which displays tools, bones, and black-and-white photos that detail the history of the Šariš region. The museum's best exhibit, in the vault downstairs, is a copper bowl filled with 2920 medieval gold *thaler* coins, discovered in 1935 while workers were laying foundations for new finance headquarters at Hlavná 68. *(Hviezdoslavova 2.* ☎ *622 05 71. Open Tu-Sa 9am-5pm, Su 9am-1pm. 40Sk, students 15Sk. English guide book 30Sk.)* Across the street, the **Art and Natural Science Museum,** is housed in a Baroque-inspired building. The large taxidermy exhibit could churn some stomachs but provides fascinating details about Carpathian fauna. Upstairs, exhibits chronicle art from the ancient Roman empire to the Middle Ages. *(Hviezdoslavova 3.* ☎ *622 01 81. Open Tu-Sa 9am-5pm, Su 9am-1pm. 40Sk, students 15Sk.)*

NIGHTLIFE

Jazz Club, Kováčska 39 (☎ 622 42 37). The stylish Jazz Club might not play much jazz, but it still deserves its popularity. Disco dominates Tu and Th-Sa, drawing in young cats looking to cut a rug. Other days, jazz and funk draw an older, sophisticated crowd; piano jazz fills the Su-M gap. Beer 25-35Sk. Concert/disco cover 30-50Sk. Open daily 4pm-2am, disco nights until 3am. Cash only.

Willy's Pub, Kováčska 49 (☎ 0903 243 130). Chill out at this underground bar before heading to the hopping Jazz Club across the street. An excellent choice for cheap pints. The jukebox (5Sk) is equipped with modern songs of all genres. Beer 15-35Sk. Open M-Th 10am-10pm, F 2pm-2am, Sa 4pm-midnight. Cash only.

Aloha Cocktail Club, Hlavná 69 (☎ 623 14 05). This Caribbean-themed club attracts a younger crowd with a loud mix of R&B, hip-hop, and pop. Party until dawn on the cavernous, sky-blue dance floor with the help of Aloha's exhaustive cocktail selection (60-140Sk). Open M-Th noon-midnight, F-Sa noon-2am, Su 3-11pm. Cash only.

Palmyra, Hlavná 24. Relaxed 20-somethings swing to the beats of salsa, reggae, and pop under a disco ball. If dancing isn't your thing, enjoy the pounding music from comfy booths. Beer 35-45Sk. Open 3pm-2am daily. Cash only.

DAYTRIPS FROM KOŠICE

JASKYŇA DOMICA

Take a bus to Plešivec (2hr., 7-10 per day, 160Sk) then catch the connecting bus (3Sk) to Jaskyňa Domica. Check the timetable across from the cave entrance for return buses. Be prepared to wait; it may be 1-2hr. between buses. The friendly, English-speaking TIC staff also have info about buses that make the trip to Plešivec and the caves. ☎ 788 20 10; www.domica.sk. Mandatory tours June-Aug. Tu-Su 9, 10:30am, 12:30, 2, 3, and 4pm; Sept.-Dec. and Feb.-May 9:30, 11am, 12:30, 2pm. 45min. tour (min. 4 people) 80Sk, students 60Sk. 1½hr. tour 110/90Sk.

Jaskyňa Domica is a challenge to reach, but the breathtaking caverns are worth the effort. Stalactites and stalagmites jut from three-million-year-old UNESCO-protected cave walls, creating complex patterns in the spacious chambers, the largest of which measures 48,000 cubic m. When underground water levels permit, the longer tour includes a boat ride covering 1.5km of the cave. The shorter tour covers a mere 780m of the grand expanse. Only 5km of the 23km cave lie on the Slovak side—the rest is accessible from Hungary. If you want to see more, travel 1km (10min. on foot, above ground) to the border and find the **Hungarian** entrance.

KRASNA HORKA CASTLE

Take the bus to Dobšiná and get off at "Krásnohorské Podhradie" (2hr., 90Sk). Check the timetable for return buses. Walk up the path to the castle. ☎ 732 47 69. Open May-Oct. M-F 8:30am-4:30pm. Mandatory 1hr. tours 9:30, 11am, 12:30, 2pm. 90Sk, students 45Sk.

The beautifully restored Krasna Horka Castle looms over the nearby picturesque village of Rožňava. One of Slovakia's most amazing castles, the imposing Krasna Horka was built in the Gothic style in the 14th century. Inside, the 1hr. tour takes you through 31 finely decorated rooms. Highlights include a former money counterfeiting shop and an eerie chapel where a mummified body, clad in black lace, lies in a glass sarcophagus with one arm raised. The creepiness continues downstairs, where torture instruments like clamps and a rack are displayed.

BARDEJOV ☎ (0)54

Although scenic Bardejov (bahr-day-YOW; pop. 38,000) is a favorite destination for Slovak newlyweds, life here hasn't always been a honeymoon. Having endured earthquakes, fires, and the occasional Turkish invasion, this former trade center underwent a complete reconstruction in 1986—a feat that earned it the UNESCO Heritage Gold Medal. Relaxing Bardejov attracts visitors who delight in the town's main attraction, its soothing baths.

⧉🚍 TRANSPORTATION AND PRACTICAL INFORMATION. Trains, Slovenská 18 (☎ 472 36 05) go to: **Košice** (1¾-2¼hr., 3 per day, 120Sk); **Prešov** (1¼hr., 5 per day, 65Sk); **Kraków, POL** (7hr., 2 per day, 950Sk). The best way to reach Bardejov is by **bus** (☎ 723 353). Buses head to: **Banská Bystrica** (4hr., M-F 5 per day, 300Sk); **Bratislava** (11hr., 4 per day, 560Sk); **Košice** (1¾hr., 5 per day, 106Sk); **Poprad** (2-2½hr., M-F 9 per day, 130Sk); **Prešov** (1hr.; M-F 10 per day, Sa-Su 4 per day; 58Sk); **Rožňava** (4hr., 3 per day, 176Sk). From the **train** and **bus station,** cross the parking lot, go to the left and turn right onto the cobblestone path just after the T-shaped intersection. Continue up the path past the ruined lower gate of **Staré Mesto** (Old Town), then turn right on **Paštová** to reach **Radničné nám.,** the main square. The **tourist office, Globtour Bratislava,** Radničné nám. 21, sells **maps** (40Sk) and provides useful info on accommodations and attractions. (☎/fax 472 62 73. Open May-Sept M-F 9am-5pm, Sa 9am-2pm; Oct.-April M-F 10am-4pm.) Get MC/V **cash advances** and **Western Union** services or cash AmEx/V **traveler's checks** (min. 200Sk) for 1% commission at **VÚB,** Kellerova 1. A 24hr. MC/V **ATM** stands outside. (☎ 472 26 71. Open M-W and F 8am-5pm, Th 8am-noon.) A **pharmacy, Lekáreň Sv. Egídia,** Radničné nám. 43, posts the addresses and hours of other pharmacies. (☎ 472 75 62. Open M-F 7:30am-5pm.) **Internet** is available at **Golem,** Radničné nám. 35. (25Sk per hr. Open

M-F 9am-11pm, Sa noon-midnight, Su 12:30-9:30pm.) The **post office,** Dlný rad 14, sells phone cards; **telephones** are outside. (☎472 40 62. Open M-F 7am-6pm, Sa 7:30-10:30am.) **Postal Code:** 08501.

🖪🗗 ACCOMMODATIONS AND FOOD. Accommodations are limited in Bardejov. Book rooms in advance June through September. More **private rooms** and **pensions** (200-300Sk) lie outside of town but are poorly connected. The tourist office can help book lodging. The Kaminsky family runs **🖫Penzión Semafór ❸,** Kellerova 13, and welcomes visitors with unmatched hospitality. Spacious rooms have TVs, private baths, and a shared kitchen. From the train station, cross the parking lot and exit straight on Nový sad. Walk 300m and turn right on Kellerova; the pension is ahead on the left. (☎474 44 33. Free tea or coffee. Breakfast 90Sk. Laundry 100Sk. Singles 700Sk; doubles 1000Sk; apartment with kitchens 1200Sk; extra bed 250Sk. Cash only.) **SOU Pod Vinbargom ❶,** with balconies, comfy beds, and well-kept baths, is a comfortable base near the train station. Turn left from the bus stop and follow the road as it curves. The hotel is on the left, past the supermarket. (☎472 40 10. Reception 24hr. Check-in noon. Check-out 10am. Call ahead. Singles 200Sk; doubles 350Sk; triples 500Sk; quads 575Sk.)

Though restaurants have besieged Radičné nám., few are more than snack bars and pubs. The classy and romantic **Roland ❷,** Radičné nám. 12, fuses Italian and Slovak flavors by day and takes on a pub-like atmosphere at night. Go through the arch and to the back to reach the patio, or sit amid the medieval decor in the cellar restaurant and pub. (☎472 92 20. Entrees 85-147Sk. Open M-F 10am-10pm, Sa-Su 11am-10pm. Cash only.) **Cafe Restaurant Hubert ❷,** Radničné nám. 6, serves beef, game meats, and fish. (☎474 26 03. English menu. Entrees 89-199Sk. Open M-Th 8am-11pm, F-Sa 8am-1am, Su 11am-11pm. AmEx/MC/V.) Locals satisfy their sweet tooth with ice cream (6Sk per scoop) and desserts (15-18Sk) at **Oaza ❶,** Radničné nám. 23. (☎474 64 70. Open daily 8:30am-10pm.) **Billa Supermarket,** next to the train station, offers a huge selection of groceries. (Open M-Sa 8am-9pm, Su 8am-8pm.)

🖸 SIGHTS. The waters of the **Bardejov Baths** (Bardejovské Kúpele) are rumored to have curative powers—powers so great the strong acidic taste doesn't deter the crowds who fill bottles here. Tsar Alexander I of Russia, Joseph II of Austria-Hungary, Napoleon, and Austrian Emperor Franz Josef's wives frequented the baths. For a dip in 28°C spring waters, head to the *kupalisko* (swimming pool) at the end of the park. (To reach the baths, which lie just outside the Bardejov city center, take bus #1, 6, 7 or 12 from the station to the end of the line; 20min., 9Sk. ☎477 44 21. Open May 10-Sept. 22 M-F 1-7pm, Sa-Su 9am-7pm. Tu-F 8am-noon patients with prescription only. M-F 50Sk, students 25Sk; Sa-Su 100/50Sk.) Or, drop into any of the hotels for various **spa treatments.** Near the baths, there is also the open-air **Museum of Folk Architecture,** which consists of 24 full-scale buildings taken from villages across Slovakia and reassembled here. Highlights include a rustic wooden church and a smith's workshop. (Open M-F 10am-5pm. 40Sk, students 20Sk.)

Back in town, the **Church of St. Egidius** (Kostol sv. Egídia), Radničné nám. 47, contains 11 Gothic wing altars crafted between 1450 and 1510 by Master Pavol. The largest of these, the detailed 15th-century **Nativity Altar,** was consecrated by St. Gilles, patron saint of the town and church. When examining the equally spectacular main altar, look up at the crucifixes for a painfully detailed depiction of Christ's death on the cross. (Open M-F 10am-4:30pm, Sa 10am-2:30pm, Su for services and visits 11:30am-2:30pm. 30Sk, students 20Sk. Tower 40/20Sk.) Head out from the end of the main square near Františkǎnov and turn right onto Mlynská to reach Bardejov's **Jewish quarter,** where there is a closed **synagogue** and a moving memorial plaque to the more than 7000 Jews from Bardejov who perished during the Holocaust. Twelve **bastions** mark the perimeter of the Old Town. Veterna ends at one of the remaining bastions, which served as a crossroads beacon and, later, as the local beheading stock. The **icon exhibit,** Radničné nám. 27, boasts a small collection of miniature religious figures and models of nearby wooden churches, striking for their detail. The collection's treasure is the gorgeous original **iconostasis** from the altar of a wooden church that stood in Zboy. (☎472 20 09. Open M-F 9am-noon, 12:30-4:30pm. 40Sk.) The **town hall** *(radnica),* Radničné nám. 48 (☎474 60 38), now serves as a **museum,** displaying historic trinkets. Among them is the key to the city, which the treacherous mayor's wife lent to her Turkish lover in 1697. The aptly named "Nature of Northeastern Slovakia" display, in the **Prirodopisne Museum,** Rhodýho 4, across from the entrance to the icon exhibit, will tickle the taxidermist in you, with finely detailed flora and fauna exhibits. Take note of the **Quail trees** at the uphill end, a gift from the US, brought by former Vice President Dan Quayle in 1991. (☎472 26 30. Both museums open May-Sept. 15 daily 8:30am-noon and 12:30-5pm; Oct.-Apr. Tu-Su 8am-noon and 12:30-4pm. 25Sk, students 10Sk.) The **Museum of Svidník,** Bardejovska 14, gives an overview of the WWII Battle for the Dukla Pass. The adjacent **battlefield** is hauntingly littered with abandoned tanks, artillery, and other vestiges of the brutal encounter. Don't stray from the dirt paths: some landmines remain in the field. A bus runs from Bardejov to Svidník (30min., 60Sk); a connecting bus runs to Dukla (20Sk). From behind the station, turn left and walk 10min. (☎054 742 13 98. Open Tu-F 8am-3:30pm, Sa-Su 10am-2pm. 35Sk; students, children, and soldiers 15Sk.)

🎵 **NIGHTLIFE.** Evenings in Bardejov are subdued. Nightlife is based around the beer gardens in the main square. Those determined to party late should head to **Morca Cafe,** Radničné nám. 37, where a mid-20s crowd chats under neon lights. (☎090 897 68 81. Open daily 7pm-4am.) The shamrock-lined **Irish Pub,** Radničné nám. 32, like many such Irish bars in Slovakia, is completely devoid of real Irish, but strangely popular and the only place in town to find Guinness. (☎090 597 18 34. Guinness 70Sk. Open M-Th 11am-11pm, F 11am-1pm, Sa 10am-1am, Su 1-11pm.)

SLOVENIA
(SLOVENIJA)

The first and most prosperous of Yugoslavia's breakaway republics, tiny Slovenia revels in a republicanism, peace, and independence largely unknown to its easterly neighbors. With a historically westward gaze, Slovenia's liberal politics and a high GDP helped it breeze into the European Union early on and further eroded its already weak affiliation with Eastern Europe. Fortunately, modernization has not adversely affected the tiny country's natural beauty and diversity: you can still go skiing, eat breakfast on an Alpine peak, explore a cave, bathe under the Mediterranean sun, and catch an opera, all in one day.

DISCOVER SLOVENIA: SUGGESTED ITINERARIES

THREE DAYS In eclectic **Ljubljana** the charming cafe culture and nightlife is worth at least a two day stay, followed by a tranquil digression in the fairytale alpine lake-town of **Bled** (1 day; p. 675)

ONE WEEK Spend a day each in **Ljubljana, Bled,** and its cousin **Bohinj** (p. 678). Train to **Piran** (2 days; p. 682), the mini-Venice, explore the spectacular **Škocjan Caves,** then revisit Ljubljana.

FACTS AND FIGURES

Official Name: Republic of Slovenia.
Capital: Ljubljana.
Major Cities: Celje, Kranj, Maribor.
Population: 2,012,000.

Land Area: 20,151 sq. km.
Time Zone: GMT + 1.
Language: Slovenian
Religion: Roman Catholic (58%).

ESSENTIALS

WHEN TO GO

In every way, July and August are the hot months in Slovenia; tourists flood the coast, and accommodation prices often rise. Wait until early autumn or spring to go, and you will be blessed with a dearth of crowds and great weather for hiking and exploring the countryside. Skiing is popular from December to March.

DOCUMENTS AND FORMALITIES

ENTRANCE REQUIREMENTS
Passport: Required for all travelers.
Visa: Not required for stays of under 90 days for citizens of Australia, Canada, Ireland, New Zealand, the UK, and the US.
Letter of Invitation: Not required.
Inoculations: Recommended up-to-date on DTaP (diphtheria, tetanus, and pertussis), Hepatitis A, Hepatitis B, MMR (measles, mumps, and rubella), Polio booster, and Typhoid.
Work Permit: Required of all foreigners planning to work in Slovenia.
International Driving Permit: Required of those planning to drive in Slovenia.

EMBASSIES AND CONSULATES. Foreign embassies to Slovenia are in Ljubljana. Embassies and consulates abroad include: **Austria,** Nibelungeng, 13, A-1010, Vienna (☎1 586 13 09; vdu@mzz-dkp.gov.si); **Australia,** Level 6, Advance Bank Center, 60 Marcus Clarke St., Canberra, ACT 2601 (☎2 6243 4830; vca@mzz-dkp.gov.si); **Canada,** 150 Metcalfe St. Ste. 2101, Ottawa, ON K2P 1P1 (☎613-565-5781; vot@mzz-dkp.gov.si); **Ireland,** Morrison Chambers, 2nd fl., 32 Nassau St., Dublin 2 (☎1 670 5240; vdb@mzz-dkp.gov.si); **New Zealand,** 201-221 Western Hutt Rd., Pmare, Lower Hutt (☎4 567 0027), mail to P.O. Box 30-247; **UK,** 10 Little College St. London SW1P 3SJ (☎020 7222 5400; vlo@mzz-dkp.gov.si); **US,** 1525 New Hampshire Ave., NW, Washington, D.C. 20036 (☎202-667-5363; www.embassy.org/slovenia).

VISA AND ENTRY INFORMATION. Citizens of Australia, Canada, Ireland, New Zealand, the UK, and the US do not need **visas** for stays of up to 90 days. Visas takes 4-7 business days to process: send your passport, a money order for the proper fee (5-day transit €10; 1-month single entry €25; 3-month single-entry €30; 3-month multiple-entry €35), two passport-size photos, a voucher from your travel agency or hotel reservations if available, and a self-addressed, stamped envelope. Visas are not available at the border, and there is no fee for crossing.

TOURIST SERVICES AND MONEY

There are **tourist offices** in most major cities and tourist destinations. Staffs generally speak English or German and, on the coast, perfect Italian. They can usually find accommodations for a small fee and generally give advice and maps for free. **Kompas** is the main tourist organization.

The Slovenian monetary unit is the tolar (plural: tolarjev; 1Sit=100 stotins), which comes in denominations of 20, 50, 100, 200, 500, and 1000. Inflation hovers around 2%. SKB Banka, Ljubljanska Banka and Gorenjska Banka are common banks. American Express Traveler's Cheques and Eurocheques are accepted in almost everywhere. Major credit cards are not consistently

TOLARJEV (SIT)	AUS$1 = 147.95SIT	100SIT = AUS$0.68
	CDN$1 = 161.37SIT	100SIT = CDN$0.62
	EUR€1 = 239.49SIT	100SIT = EUR€0.42
	NZ$1 = 136.71SIT	100SIT = NZ$0.73
	UK£1 = 352.70SIT	100SIT = UK£0.28
	US$1 = 196.65SIT	100SIT = US$0.51

accepted, but MC/V ATMs are all over. Normal business hours are Monday through Friday 8am-4pm; for banks and exchange offices Monday through Friday 7:30am-6pm, Saturday 7:30am-noon; for shops Monday through Friday 8am-7pm, Saturday 7:30am-1pm

HEALTH AND SAFETY

EMERGENCY	**Police: ☎ 112. Ambulance: ☎ 112. Fire: ☎ 112.**

Medical facilities are of high quality, and most have English-speaking doctors. UK citizens receive free medical care with a valid passport; other foreigners must pay cash. **Pharmacies** are stocked to Western standards; ask for *obliž* (band-aids), *tamponi* (tampons), and *vložki* (sanitary pads). **Tap water** is safe to drink. **Crime** is rare Slovenia. **Women** should, as always, exercise caution and avoid being out alone after dark. There are few **minorities** in Slovenia, but minority travelers won't encounter trouble, just curious glances. Navigating Slovenia with a **disability** can be difficult and requires patience and caution on slippery cobblestones. **Homosexuality** is legal, but may elicit unfriendly reactions outside urban areas.

TRANSPORTATION

Commercial **flights** arrive at **Ljubljana Airport**. Most major airlines offer connections to the national carrier **Adria Airways**. To save money, consider flying from **London, ENG** or **Berlin, GER** and jumping on an **EasyJet** (www.easyjet.com) to Ljubljana. Or, fly to **Vienna, AUT** or **Trieste, ITA** and take a train to Ljubljana, or a town along the border. A regular **ferry** service connects **Portorož** to **Venice, ITA** during the summer.

First and second class differ little on **trains**; save money and opt for the latter. Those under 26 get a 20% discount on most international fares. ISIC-holders should ask for the 30% *popust* (discount) off domestic tickets. Schedules often list trains by direction. *Prihodi vlakov* means arrivals; *odhodi vlakov* is departures; *dnevno* is daily. Usually more expensive than trains, **buses** may be the only option in the mountains. Buy tickets at stations or on board. Backpacks cost 220Sit extra.

Car rental agencies in Ljubljana offer reasonable rates, and Slovenia's roads are in good condition. Nearly every town has a **bike** rental office; renting one will generally cost you 2000-3000Sit per day. While those who partake in it insist upon its safety, **hitchhiking** is not recommended by *Let's Go*.

KEEPING IN TOUCH

PHONE CODES	**Country code: 386. International dialing prefix: 00.** From outside Slovenia, dial int'l dialing prefix (see inside back cover) + 386 + city code + local number. Within Slovenia, dial city code + local number for intercity calls and simply the local number for calls within a city.

SLOVENIA

Internet access is fast and common, and Internet cafes are common in major tourist destinations. Expect to pay 1000-1500Sit per hour. All phones take **phone cards,** sold at post offices, kiosks, and gas stations (750Sit per 50 impulses, which yields 1½min. to the US). Only **MCI WorldPhone** (☎ 080 88 08) has an international access number. Dial ☎ 115 for English-speaking operator-assisted collect calls. For the **international operator,** dial. Calling abroad is expensive (over US$6 per min. to the US). If you must, try the phones at the post office and pay when you're finished.

Airmail *(letalsko)* to the US, Australia, and New Zealand takes one to two weeks. US-bound letters and postcards cost 105Sit and 100Sit; to the UK 100/90Sit; to Australia and New Zealand 110/100Sit. To receive mail through **Poste Restante,** address envelopes as follows: Jenn (First name) KAN (LAST NAME), Poste Restante, Slovenska 32 (post office address), 1000 (postal code) Ljubljana (city), SLOVENIA.

ACCOMMODATIONS AND CAMPING

SLOVENIA	❶	❷	❸	❹	❺
ACCOMMODATIONS	under 3500Sit under €15 under US$18	3500-5000Sit €15-21 US$18-26	5000-6500Sit €21-27 US$26-33	6500-8000Sit €27-33 US$33-41	over 8000Sit over €33 overUS$41

All establishments charge a nightly **tourist tax. Youth hostels** and **student dormitories** are cheap (2500-3500Sit) and fun, but generally open only in summer (June 25-Aug. 30). **Hotels** fall into five categories (L, deluxe; A; B; C; and D) and are expensive. **Pensions** are the most common form of accommodation; usually they have private singles as well as inexpensive dorms. **Private rooms** are the only cheap option on the coast and at Lake Bohinj. Prices vary, but rarely exceed US$30. Inquire at the tourist office or look for *Zimmer frei* or *Sobe* signs. **Campgrounds** can be crowded, but are in excellent condition. Camp in designated areas to avoid fines.

FOOD AND DRINK

SLOVENIA	❶	❷	❸	❹	❺
FOOD	under 800Sit under €3 under US$4	800-1200Sit €3-5 US$4-6	1200-1800Sit €5-8 US$6-9	1800-2400Sit €8-10 US$9-12	over 2400Sit over €10 over US$12

For home-style cooking, try a *gostilna* or *gostišče* (country-style inn or restaurant). Traditional meals begin with *jota,* a soup with potatoes, beans and sauerkraut. Pork is the basis for many dishes, such as *Svinjska pečenka* (roast pork) or Karst ham. **Kosher** eating thus becomes very difficult within the confines of Slovenian cuisine, as does finding a **vegetarian** meal. Those with such dietary restrictions might consider eating pizza and bakery items. Slovenia's **winemaking** tradition dates from antiquity. Renski, Rizling, and Šipon are popular whites, while Cviček and Teran are favorite reds. Brewing is also centuries old; Laško and Union are good beers. For something stronger, try *žganje,* a fruit brandy, or Viljamovka, distilled by monks who know the secret of getting a whole pear inside the bottle.

LIFE AND TIMES

HISTORY

SLAVIC BEGINNINGS. The **Alpine Slavs,** predecessors of the Slovenes, migrated to the eastern Alps in the 6th century, absorbing the existing cultures. The emergence of a class of ennobled citizens with the right to vote yielded one of the first instances of democracy in the feudal Middle Ages. After initial resistance to German missionaries, the Slovenes converted to **Christianity** in the 9th century. Between 1278 and 1335, the territory fell to the **Austrian Hapsburgs,** whose influence would stifle Slovenian cultural consciousness for centuries to come. In the early 1800s, **Napoleon** temporarily displaced Austrian rule in the region, instituting some republican reforms and triggering the development of Slovenian **nationalism.**

PARTISANS AND PARTITIONS. After the collapse of Austria-Hungary following **World War I,** Slovenia agreed to join the newly formed **Kingdom of Serbs, Croats, and Slovenes** (renamed **Yugoslavia** in 1929). The new state was too weak, however, to withstand **Hitler's** forces during WWII. When Yugoslavia fell in 1941, Slovenia was partitioned among Germany, Italy, and Hungary. Slovenian resistance groups formed and united under the **Slovenian National Liberation Front,** which soon joined the Yugoslav Partisan Army of **Josip Brož Tito.**

WILD WESTERNIZATION. Following WWII, a unified state once again emerged, this time as the communist **Federal People's Republic of Yugoslavia,** with Slovenia as a republic. Tito liquidated Slovene politicians and leaders who failed to cooperate; tens of thousands of Slovene patriots were murdered at **Kočevje.** After a rift between Tito and Stalin in 1948, Yugoslavia followed its own brand of communism for half a century, slowly opening its doors to Western-style market reforms while retaining a political autocracy. The years following Tito's 1980 death saw a rise in Slovenian nationalism, and in 1990 Slovenia held the first democratic elections in Yugoslavia since before WWII. The new government adopted a Western-style constitution, and on June 25, 1991, Slovenia seceded from Yugoslavia. After a 10-day war with Yugoslavia that claimed the lives of 66 people, a peace treaty was brokered and independence was recognized by the European Community in 1992.

TODAY

Slovenia is a parliamentary democracy, consisting of an elected **president,** aided by a council of ministers, and a **prime minister.** The bicameral **legislature** *Skupscina Slovenije* (Slovenian Assembly), consisting of the 90-member *Drzavni Zbor* (State Chamber) and the 40-member, advisory *Drzavni Svet* (State Council), presides over 147 municipalities. In December 2002, long-time prime minister **Janez Drnovšek,** of the **Liberal Democratic Party,** took the presidency from **Milan Kučan,** who had been president since independence. Today's prime minister, **Janez Janša,** heads a center-right coalition government. Slovenia joined **NATO** and the **European Union (EU)** in 2004 and is scheduled to hold the EU presidency in the first half of 2008, by which time it plans to have adopted the euro as currency.

PEOPLE AND CULTURE

Over 88% of Slovenia's population is **Slovenian,** and most citizens are **Roman Catholic,** though a small number are **Protestants; Orthodox Christians, Muslims,** and **Jews. Hungarians** and **Italians** have the status of indigenous minorities under the Slovenian Constitution, which guarantees them seats in the National Assembly, but minorities from the former Yugoslavia have encountered a rougher integration. In 1991, about 18,000 Yugoslav citizens living in newly independent Slovenia were stricken from the population registry because they had not applied for citizenship. A 2004 referendum saw 95% of voters reject the decision of the Constitutional Court to restore resident status to the remaining 4000 country-less citizens, who are known as "the erased." Political leaders and non-governmental organizations have criticized the referendum, and the Ministry of the Interior has already issued thousands of decrees enacting the Court's decision. **Slovenian** is a South Slavic language written in the Latin alphabet. Most young Slovenes speak at least some **English,** but the older generations are more likely to understand **German** or **Italian**. The tourist industry is generally geared toward Germans, but most tourist office employees speak English. Some attempt at speaking Slovenian will be appreciated by locals. While not customary, a **tip** is sometimes included in the bill, which is considered rude to split. Generally, 10% is sufficient for good service. Cab drivers won't expect a tip but will be pleased if you round up the fare. Slovenes don't **bargain**, and attempts may cause offense. **Shorts** are rare in cities, but common in the countryside. **Jeans** are worn everywhere. When **hiking**, note that trails are marked with a white circle inside a red one. Hikers greet one another on the path. The ascending hiker should speak first: it is considered proper to show respect to those who have already summited.

THE ARTS

LITERATURE. Slovenian literature emerged as an important secular art form in the 19th century with the writings of the country's most beloved poet **France Prešeren** and the codification of the language by **Jernej Kopitar**. The surge in cultural activity during the first half of the century paralleled the period's nationalist interest and set the stage for the country's first political agenda. Throughout the later **Realist** Period (1848-1899), writers such as **Fran Levstik** focused on folkloric themes with a patriotic flavor; the first Slovenian novel, *The Tenth Brother (Deseti brat)*, by **Josip Jurčič**, was published in 1866. **Modernist** prose flowered with **Ivan Cankar's** 1904 *The Ward of Our Lady of Mercy (Hisa Marije pomocnice)*, while **Expressionist** poetry showed the social and spiritual tensions brought on by WWI through the works of **Tone Seliškar, Miran Jarc**, and **Anton Vodnik**. Soviet **Socialist Realism** crushed many of Slovak literature's avant-garde impulses. Postmodern literary trends emerged in the **Young Slovenian Prose** movement, which has its strongest representation in short prose pieces. Current internationally famed writers include poet **Tomaž Šalamun** and chic critic and philosopher **Slavoj Žižek**.

THE VISUAL AND MUSICAL ARTS. Coincident with the Modernist and Expressionist movements in Slovenian literature, architect **Jože Plečnik** was a major figure in the development of **Art Deco**. He transformed his otherwise baroque-leaning hometown, Ljubljana, into a cosmopolitan capital (p. 667). Musically, Slovenia experienced a politically minded **folk** revival after WWII. **Laibach**, an adventurous multimedia band, single-handedly ignited an explosion of punk rock.) The alternative music movement of the 1980s gave rise to a vigorous **contemporary art** scene, nurtured by the collagist art collectives **Irwin** and **NSK** (*Neue Slowenische Kunst*).

HOLIDAYS AND FESTIVALS

Holidays: New Year's Day (Jan. 1); Culture Day (*Prešeren* Day; Feb. 8); Easter Holiday (March 27-28); National Resistance Day (WWII; Apr. 27); Labor Day (May 1).

Festivals: Slovenia embraces its alternative artistic culture as much as its folk heritage, a fact evident in its lengthy festival calendar. Hitting Ljubljana in July and August, the International Summer Festival is the nation's most famous, featuring ballet, music, and theater. The Peasant's Wedding Day (*Kmecka ohcet*), a presentation of ancient wedding customs held in Bohinj at the end of July, and the Cows Ball (*Kravji Bal*) in mid-September, which celebrates the return of the cows to the valleys from higher pastures, are a couple of the country's many summertime folk exhibitions.

ADDITIONAL RESOURCES

Independent Slovenia: Origins, Movements, Prospects, edited by Jill Benderly (1996). Essays by economic theorists, Slovenia's foreign minister, and punk sociologists.

Slovenia and the Slovenes: A Small State and the New Europe, by James Gow and
Cathie Carmichael (2001). A critical assessment of the modern Slovenian experience
through examinations of Slovenian language, literature, culture, and geography.

LJUBLJANA ☎(0)1

Boasting a rich folkloric history, a mix of old-world Baroque and colorful art nouveau styles, and a spirited youth culture, Ljubljana (loob-LYAH-nah; pop. 266,000)
deserves to be treated as more than a stopover on the route to Budapest or Zagreb.
In fact, visitors find it hard to leave this bewitching town. Founded by Emperor
Augustus in 34 BC, long under Hapsburg rule, and revamped in the interwar years
by architect Jože Plečnik, Slovenia's compact riverside capital offers the romantic
delight and hip underground *élan* of Prague—without the cost or the crowds.

✈ INTERCITY TRANSPORTATION

Flights: Aerodrom Ljubljana-Brnik (☎206 10 00; www.lju-airport.si). **Info and Lost and
found:** Adria Airways (☎4 236 34 62), other airlines (☎4 206 19 81). **Adria Airways,**
Gosposvetska 6 (☎231 33 12; www.adriaairways.com), has an airport shuttle, *Avto-*

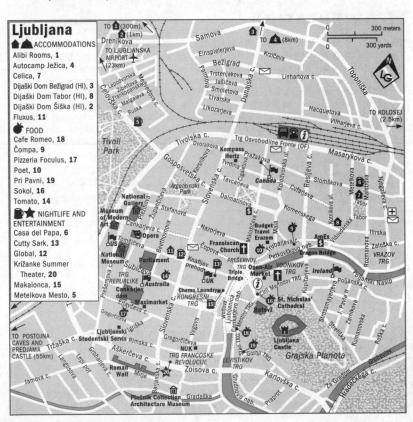

Ljubljana

▲▲ ACCOMMODATIONS
Alibi Rooms, 1
Autocamp Ježica, 4
Celica, 7
Dijaški Dom Bežigrad (HI), 3
Dijaški Dom Tabor (HI), 8
Dijaški Dom Šiška (HI), 2
Fluxus, 11

🍴 FOOD
Cafe Romeo, 18
Čompa, 9
Pizzeria Foculus, 17
Poet, 10
Pri Pavni, 19
Sokol, 16
Tomato, 14

🍸⭐ NIGHTLIFE AND
ENTERTAINMENT
Casa del Papa, 6
Cutty Sark, 13
Global, 12
Križanke Summer
Theater, 20
Makalonca, 15
Metelkova Mesto, 5

S
L
O
V
E
N
I
A

busni prevozi Markun (☎41 670 528), to and from the main bus terminal (30min., 8 per day, 1000Sit). The slower but cheaper local bus #28 runs from the main bus station (1hr.; M-F every hr. 6am-8pm, Sa-Su every hr. 6-9am and odd hr. until 7pm; 850Sit); **Austrian Airlines**, Gosposvetska 8 (☎239 19 00; www.aua-si.com); **Air France**, Igriška 5 (☎244 34 47; www.regional.fr); **British Air**, Trg Republike 3 (☎241 40 00; www.ba.com); **ČSA Czech Airlines**, info at airport (☎206 12 26; www.czechairlines.com); **easyJet**, at airport (☎4 206 16 77; www.easyJet.com); **JAT**, Slomškova 1 (☎231 43 40; www.jat.com); **Lufthansa**, Gosposvetska 6 (☎434 72 46; www.lufthansa.com); **Swissair**, Dunajska 156.

Trains: Trg OF 6 (☎291 33 32). To: **Bled** (1hr., 14 per day, 890Sit); **Koper** (2¼hr., 3 per day, 1660Sit); **Maribor** (1½hr., 3 per day, 1660Sit); **Belgrade, SMN** (9hr., 5 per day, 9000Sit); **Budapest, HUN** (9hr.; 3 per day; 14,836Sit); **Munich, GER** (7hr.; 3 per day; 15,200Sit); **Sarajevo, BOS** (11hr., 3 per day, 8315Sit) via **Zagreb, CRO** (2hr., 9 per day, 2700Sit); **Trieste, ITA** (3¾hr., 3 per day, 4110Sit); **Venice, ITA** (6hr., 3 per day, 7900Sit); **Vienna, AUT** (5-6hr., 3 per day, 12,800Sit).

Buses: Trg OF 4 (☎090 42 30; www.ap-ljubljana.si). To: **Bled** (1½hr., 14 per day, 1400Sit); **Koper** (2½hr., 13 per day, 2540Sit); **Maribor** (3hr., 10 per day, 2760Sit); **Rijeka, CRO** (2½hr., 21 per day, 3520Sit); **Sarajevo, BOS** (9¾hr., 1 per day, 9230Sit); **Skopje, MAC** (23hr., 2 per day, 10,650Sit); **Zagreb, CRO** (3hr., 2 per day, 3310Sit).

∎ ORIENTATION

The city center is easy to navigate by foot, and red bike paths line most streets. The curvy **Ljubljanica River** divides the city center, with the picturesque **Stare Miasto** (Old Town) on one bank and 19th- and 20th-century buildings on the other. About a half-mile from either bank, the historic area gives way to a concrete business district. The train and bus stations are next to each other on **Trg Osvobodilne Fronte** (Trg OF). To reach the center from the stations, turn right on Masarykova and left on Miklošičeva c.; continue to **Prešernov trg**, the main square. After crossing the **Tromostovje** (Triple Bridge), you'll see Stare Miasto at the base of Castle Hill. The tourist office is on the left at the corner of Stritarjeva and Adamič-Lundrovo nab.

⌐ LOCAL TRANSPORTATION

Buses: Most run until 10:30pm. Drop 300Sit in the box beside the driver or buy 190Sit tokens (*žetoni*) at post offices, kiosks, or the main bus terminal. Day passes (900Sit) sold at **Ljubljanski Potniški Promet**, Celovška c. 160 (☎582 24 26 or 205 60 45). Open M-F 6:45am-7pm, Sa 6:45am-1pm. Pick up a bus map at the **TIC**.

Taxis: ☎97 00 through 97 09. 150Sit base, 100Sit per km.

Car Rental: Avis Rent-a-Car, Cufarjeva 2, in Grand Hotel Union (☎430 80 10). **Budget Car Rental**, Miklošičeva 3 (☎421 73 40). **Kompas Hertz**, Trdinova 9 (☎434 01 47).

Bike Rental: Tir Bar, in the train station. Contact the bike rental company "Bajk Oglasevanje" (☎527 31 47). 200Sit per 2hr., 700Sit per day. Open daily 8am-8pm.

⍰ PRACTICAL INFORMATION

TOURIST AND FINANCIAL SERVICES

Tourist Office: Tourist Information Center (TIC), Stritarjeva 1 (☎306 12 15; 24hr. English info 090 939 881; www.ljubljana.si). Helpful staff speak excellent English. Also helps arrange accommodations. Pick up **free maps** and the useful, free *Ljubljana From*

SLOVENIA

A to Z. Open daily June-Sept. 8am-9pm; Oct.-May 8am-7pm. **Branch,** Trg OF 6 (☎/fax 433 94 75), at the train station. Open daily June-Sept. 8am-10pm; Oct.-May 10am-7pm. Box office in TIC open M-F 9am-6pm, Sa-Su 9am-1pm. AmEx/MC/V.

Budget Travel: Erazem, Trubarjeva c. 7 (☎433 10 76). Helpful, student-oriented staff. Open June-Aug. M-F 10am-5pm, Sa 10am-1pm; Sept.-May M-F noon-5pm. **Wasteels,** Trg OF 6 (☎/fax 611 339 281), on the train station platform. books discounted train tickets for students and those under 26. Open M-F 9:15am-5pm. AmEx/MC/V.

Embassies: Australia, Trg Republike 3 (☎425 42 52; fax 426 47 21). Open M-F 9am-1pm. **Canada,** Miklošičeva 19 (☎430 35 70; fax 430 35 77). Open M-F 9am-1pm. **Croatia,** Gruberjevo nab. 6 (☎425 62 20, consular department 425 72 87; hrvaske@siol.net). **Ireland,** Poljanski nasip 6 (☎300 89 70; fax 282 10 96). Open M-F 9am-noon. **UK,** Trg Republike 3 (☎200 39 10; fax 425 01 74). Open M-F 9am-noon. **US,** Prešernova 31 (☎200 55 00; fax 200 55 55). Open M-F 9am-noon and 2-4pm.

Currency Exchange: *Menjalnice* booths abound. **Ljubljanska banka** branches throughout town exchange currency for no commission and cash **traveler's checks** for a 1.5% commission. Open M-F 9am-noon and 2-7pm, Sa 9am-noon. **ATMs** are everywhere. Just look for the signs with a pink "b" and turquoise "a" and "Bančni Avtomat" or, occasionally just "Bankomat."

American Express: Trubarjeva 50 (☎438 08 50) Open M-F 8am-7pm.

LOCAL SERVICES AND COMMUNICATIONS

Luggage Storage: Lockers *(garderoba)* at train station. 500Sit per day. Open 24hr.

English-Language Bookstore: MK-Knjigarna Konzorcij, Slovenska 29 (☎252 40 57). The biggest English-language bookstore in town. Open M-F 9am-7:30pm, Sa 9am-1pm.

Laundromat: Tič (Student Campus), c. 27 Aprila 31, bldg. 9 (☎257 43 97). Self-service. Open M-F 8am-8pm, Sa 8am-2pm. **Chemo Express,** Wolfova 12 (☎251 44 04). 1200Sit per kg. Open daily 7am-6pm.

Medical Services: Bohoričeva Medical Center, Bohoričeva 4 (☎232 30 60). Open daily 5am-8pm. **Klinični Center,** Zaloška 2-7 (☎522 50 50). Take bus #2, 9, 10, 11, or 20 to the Bolnica stop. Open 24hr.

24hr. Pharmacy: Lekarna Miklošič, Miklošičeva 24 (☎231 45 58).

Telephones: Outside the post office and all over town. Buy phone cards at the post office and at newsstands (1700Sit).

Internet: Most hostels in Ljubljana offer free Internet. **Cyber Cafe Xplorer,** Petkovško nab. 23 (☎430 19 91; www.sisky.com), has fast connections. 530Sit per 30min., students 477Sit. 20% discount 10am-noon. Open M-F 10am-10pm, Sa-Su 2-10pm.

Post Office: Trg OF 5 (☎433 06 05). Open M-F 7am-midnight, Sa 7am-6pm, Su 9am-noon. **Poste Restante,** Slovenska 32 (☎426 46 68), at *izročitev pošiljk* (outgoing mail) counter. Open M-F 7am-8pm, Sa 7am-1pm. **Postal Code:** 1000.

◪ ACCOMMODATIONS

Finding a cheap bed in Ljubljana is easier in July and August, when university dorms open to travelers. **Hostelling International Slovenia** (**PZS;** ☎231 21 56) has info about hostels. The **TIC** (see p. 668) arranges **private rooms** (singles 4000-10,000Sit; doubles 7000-15,000Sit). There is a nightly 240Sit **tourist tax** at all establishments.

▨ **Celica,** Metelkova 8 (☎430 18 90; www.hostelcelica.com). With your back to the train station, go left down Masarykova, then right on Metelkova. Blue signs mark the way. Located in the bohemian neighborhood of **Metelkova Mesto,** near the center, this former prison is now an eclectic work of modern art—and the best budget option in town. Book yourself a comfortable cell and board amid the colorful work of a local artist. Room 116 is especially popular. Those seeking peace and quiet should look elsewhere, as parties and live music performances (see p. 674) occur frequently. Internet and breakfast included. Laundry 1200Sit. Reception 24hr. Reserve ahead. Dorms 3750-4950Sit; cells 4250-5250Sit. Cash-only deposit 2500Sit per person. MC/V. ❷

Dijaški Dom Šiška (HI), Aljazeva 32 (☎500 78 04; www.ddsiska.com). The entrance is past Kettejeva on the right side of the street, through the parking lot entrance. It's the last building on the left. The cheapest accommodation in Ljubljana is a 25min. walk from the train and bus stations. While old, the building is clean and quiet, and the rooms are nicer than the beige concrete entrance suggests. Shared baths. Breakfast €1. Check-in 6pm-midnight. Open June 1-Aug. 25. €14, students €11. Cash only. ❶

Autocamp Ježica, Dunajska 270 (☎568 39 13; ac.jezica@gpl.si). Take bus #6 or 8 to Ježica's wooded campgrounds. The peaceful atmosphere offers a respite for weary travelers. Offers both camping and spacious, impeccably clean rooms with TVs and showers. Reception 24hr. Flexible check-out 1pm. Reservations recommended. June 20-Aug. 20 camping 2160Sit per person; Aug. 21-June 19. 1680Sit. Electricity tax 480Sit. Bungalow singles 11,000Sit; doubles 15,000Sit. Tourist tax 162Sit. MC/V. ❶

Dijaški Dom Tabor (HI), Vidovdanska 7 (☎234 88 40; www2.arnes.si/~ssljddta4/), 1km from the bus and train stations. Fantastic location between stations and center. Turn left down Masarykova c. from stations, then right on Kotnikova. Walk almost to the end of the street. Tabor is on the left. Clean rooms with high ceilings and shared baths. Breakfast included. Laundry 1700Sit. Free Internet. Reception 24hr. Check-out 11am. Open June 25-Aug. 25. Dorms €10; rooms €18, students €16. HI discount 200Sit. ❶

Dijaški Dom Bežigrad (HI), Kardeljeva pl. 28 (☎534 00 61; dd.lj-bezigrad@guest.arnes.si). Take bus #6 (Črnuče) or #8 (Ježica) to Stadion. Cross the street, walk 1 block, and turn right on Dimiceva, then left at the sign on Mariborska. Clean, quiet, and comfortable. Free Wi-Fi. Open June 25-Aug. 25. Singles 4320Sit, with bath 4800Sit; doubles 3600/4080Sit; triples and quads 2880/3360Sit. Cash only. ❷

Fluxus, Tomšičeva 4 (☎251 57 60, www.fluxus-hostel.com). The hostel closest to the river and main square, Fluxus offers elegant decor. One bath for 15 beds. Kitchen. Free Internet. Reception 24 hr. Reserve ahead. 4900Sit; double 13,000Sit . Cash only. ❷

Alibi Rooms, Kolarjeva 30 (☎433 13 31; www.alibi.si). Take bus #14 or walk 25-min. from the town center. New, colorful hostel with friendly staff, in a quiet neighborhood. A Mercator store is conveniently located down the street. 3 baths for 50 beds. No common space, kitchen, or Internet. Dorms 4800Sit. Deposit 4800Sit. Cash only. ❷

◘ FOOD

The largest grocery store is in the basement of the **Maximarket,** Trg Republike 1. (Open M-Th 9am-8pm, F 9am-10pm, Sa 8am-3pm.) There is a large **open-air market** next to St. Nicholas's Cathedral. (Open June-Aug. M-Sa 6am-6pm; Sept.-May 6am-4pm.) Fast-food stands feature Slovenian favorites such as *burek*—fried dough filled with meat (*mesni*) or cheese (*sirov*), usually 400-500Sit.

▨ Cafe Romeo, Stari trg 6. Popular with local hipsters, this is one of the few places in town that serves food on Su. Riverside outdoor seating supplements a mod primary-color interior. Snack-oriented menu features sandwiches (Toast Grande 550Sit), nachos (800-1000Sit), and dessert crepes (650-890Sit). Open daily 10am-1am. Kitchen open M-Sa 11am-midnight, Su 11am-11pm. Cash only. ❷

Sokol, Ciril Metodov trg 18 (☎439 68 55), just off Prešernov trg. Take bus #2, 11, or 20 to Metodov. Sokol's pseudo-rustic environment features red brick walls and high wood tables. Slovenian Hause specialties include game goulash, served in a miniature kettle hung over a tea candle. Wine 200-9200Sit. Entrees 1290-3490Sit. Open M-Sa 7am-11pm, Su 10am-11pm. AmEx/MC/V. ❸

Čompa, Trubarjeva 4c. This cozy little restaurant serves light Slovenian cuisine, made to order. The meat is tender, and the vegetables and parmesan are fresh. It's a bit expensive and a bit slow, but worth both the wait and the splurge. Try the potato-and-goulash *čompa* cheese (1600Sit). Complimentary after-dinner drink is highly potent. Open M-Sa June-Aug. 11am-1am, Sept.-May 11am-11pm; Su noon-10pm. Cash only. ❸

Pri Pavni, Stari trg 21. Authentic Slovenian cuisine commended by the "Society for the Recognition of Sauteed Potato and Onions as an Independent Dish," according to a plaque. Dishes are heavy and flavorful. Try the "smoked meat with turnips and hard-boiled corn mush" (1500Sit) with a side of roasted potatoes (350Sit). Cash only. ❸

Pizzeria Foculus, Gregorčičeva 3. Pizza joint with outdoor seating in the university district; their pizza is flavorful; try the pepperoni, mushroom, and hot pepper (1420Sit)—a perfect match for local brew Laško (450Sit). Open M-F 10am-midnight, Sa-Su noon-midnight. AmEx/MC/V. ❷

Tomato, Šubičeva 1. (☎252 75 55). Slovenian fast food that predates (and tastes better than) McDonald's. Serves hot and cold sandwiches (390-820Sit, most 20% off after 4pm). Try a melted cheese and ham panini (360Sit). Vegetarian options 1050-1150Sit. Entrees 1150-1500Sit. Eat in or take out. Open M-F 7am-10pm, Sa 9am-4pm. ❷

Poet, Petkovško nab., next to the Triple Bridge. With courteous service and a view of the river, Poet has perfected the art of ice cream concoctions (700-1400Sit) and sandwich creation (550-750Sit). Open Apr. 15-Oct. 10 daily 9am-midnight. ❶

◙ SIGHTS

One way to see the sights is a 2hr. **walking tour,** in English and Slovenian, that departs from in front of the city hall (*rotovž*), Mestni trg 1. (July-Aug. M-F 10am and Su 11am; May-Sept. daily 10am; Oct.-Apr. F-Su 11am. 1500Sit, students 800Sit. Buy tickets at the tour or at TIC.) Ljubljana's open-air **market,** near the Dragon Bridge, opens at dawn (M-Sa). A crafts market lines the riverbank on summer Saturdays (June-Oct.), and on flea markets pop up along the river Su.

▧ **ST. NICHOLAS'S CATHEDRAL (STOLNICA SV. NIKOLAJA).** The dazzlingly ornate cathedral occupies the site of a 13th-century Romanesque church, but the current building dates from the 18th century. Aside from the 15th-century Gothic Pietà, little original artwork remains, yet nearly every inch is marvelous. The intricate bronze door, installed to honor the 1996 visit of former pope John Paul II, is especially impressive. *(On the Stare Miasto side of the river. Walk left to see gorgeous arcades designed by Jože Plečnik. Cathedral is to the right. Open daily 6am-noon and 3-7pm.)*

LJUBLJANA CASTLE (LJUBLJANSKI GRAD). While the castle's existence was first documented in 1144, most of the present buildings are 16th- and 17th-century renovations. In the past, the castle has served as a prison for high-profile captives such as Slovenia's most famous author, nationalist Ivan Cankar (see p. 666). Aside from the **Virtual Museum,** which presents a 3D version of Ljubljana's history (20min., every 30min., headphones available in multiple languages), the castle hosts exhibitions and performances throughout the year. It is also the only place in Ljubljana where couples can go for a common-law marriage. *(Take 1 of several paths up the hill: from Gornji trg along na Grad, or from Vodnikov trg following Študenska. Tower and Virtual Museum ☎ 232 99 94; www.festival-lj.si/virtualnimuzej. Open daily June-Sept. 10am-dusk; Oct.-May 10am-5pm. 790Sit, students 490Sit. Castle open daily May-Oct. 10am-9pm; Nov.-Apr. 10am-7pm. English tours 1100Sit, students 790Sit; 3 people min.)*

PREŠEREN SQUARE (PREŠERNOV TRG). Nestled between Miklošičeva c. and the gorgeous Triple Bridge, Prešernov trg is at the cultural heart of Ljubljana and is one of the city's liveliest spots. The statue of Slovenian poet France Prešeren (see

p. 666), whose namesake is the square, once caused local controversy for its inclusion of a nude likeness of Prešeren's muse. The enormous pink 17th-century **Franciscan church** (Frančiškanska cerkev) dominates the square and contains an altar designed by local master Francisco Robba. Don't miss the scale model of Ljubljana on the east side of the square. On warm nights, there are frequent live music performances. *(A short walk from City Hall, down Stritarjeva and across the Triple Bridge. Church open daily 6:45am-12:30pm and 3-8pm. Free.)*

◪DRAGON BRIDGE (ZMAJSKI MOST). The striking bronze dragons that flank each side of this 1901 art nouveau bridge have become the city's symbols, and a popular attraction for visitors. Amazingly, the bridge was designed not by the ubiquitous local architect Jože Plečnik but by the Dalmatian Jurij Zaninovič. The open-air market nearby is worth a visit, especially on Saturday mornings.

TRIPLE BRIDGE (TROMOSTOVJE). A motorway flanked by two footbridges, the Triple Bridge provides a majestic entrance to the Old Town. The current structure was created in the 1930s, when Plečnik modernized the old stone construction.

FRENCH REVOLUTION SQUARE (TRG FRANCOSKE REVOLUCIJE). Inhabited by the Teutonic Knights in the 13th century, this quiet square was named in 1793. The Plečnik-designed obelisk that crowns the square signifies the 1809-1814 Napoleonic occupation of Slovenia, which brought reforms unknown under Austro-Hungarian rule; it is considered the only monument in the world to an unknown soldier from another country. Today it is a university student hangout. The surrounding area of Križanke gained its present appearance between the World Wars, through restorations led by the masterful Plečnik. The highlight of the square is the beautiful stone **Križanke Summer Theater,** which hosts open-air music, dance, and theater performances from June to September. *(☎ 241 60 26. Tickets 2000-5000Sit. Box office open M-F 10am-1:30pm and 4-8pm, Sa 10am-1pm; also 1hr. before each performance.)*

OTHER SIGHTS. Walk down Zoisova past French Revolution Sq. and take a left on Barjanska c. to see the ruins of a **Roman wall** preserved from the previous settlement of Emona. Head back up Barjanska to reach **Slovenska c.,** Ljubljana's main artery, which hosts the best shopping. Behind the **Ursuline Church** on the left is Trg Republike, home to the **Parliament** and **Cankarjev dom,** the cultural center. **Kongresni trg,** on the other side of Slovenska c., is a shaded park just above **Ljubljana University** and has vibrant nightlife. One block below the University, the **Slovenian Academy of Arts and Sciences** (Slovenska Akademija Znanosti in Umetnosti; SAZU) is a former Baroque palace; the **National Library** (Narodna in Univerzitetna Knjiznica; NUK), another of Plečnik's creations, is across the street. It houses a copy of each book published in Slovenia. In front of **City Hall** (Rotovž) sits a **fountain** embellished with representations of three rivers—the Ljubljanica, the Sava, and the Krka.

🏛 MUSEUMS

Ljubljana is teeming with little galleries. Many of the museums are located close together, and an underpass to Tivoli Park is right in front of the Museum of Modern Art, making it easy to have a picnic before or after your cultural extravaganza.

◼ NATIONAL MUSEUM (NARODNI MUZEJ). Slovenia's oldest museum features well-laid-out exhibits on archaeology, culture, and local history from the prehistoric era to the present. It's full of surprises: as you enter, you'll see statues of eight women sliding down the banister. Impressive stone slabs date from the Roman era. Upstairs, the **Natural History Museum** features a wooly mammoth skeleton and animals realistic enough to make any taxidermist jealous. The museum also safeguards one of the oldest musical instruments in the world: a flute, made of bear bone 45,000 years ago, found in a Slovenian cave. *(Muzejska 1. ☎ 241 44 04. English information, including touchscreens in the Natural History Museum. Open Tu-W, F, Su 10am-6pm. Both museums 1000Sit, students 700Sit. 1 museum 700/500Sit. 1st Su of each month free.)*

MUSEUM OF MODERN ART (MODERNA GALERIJA LJUBLJANA). A simple, boxy exterior gives way to a fantastic, high-ceilinged space featuring provocative multimedia work, from paintings and sculpture to videos and projections. The permanent collection is of late 20th century Slovenian art; rotating exhibits display work by international artists. *(Cankarjeva 15, ☎ 241 68 00, www.mg-lj.si. Open Tu-Su 10am-6pm. 1000Sit, students 500 Sit. Free admission with Ljubljana Tourist card. AmEx/MC/V.)*

PLEČNIK COLLECTION ARCHITECTURE MUSEUM (PLEČNIKOVA ZBRIKA). This small museum chronicles the modest life and marvelous work of Jože Plečnik, Slovenia's premier architect, in a house built by the master himself. The informative guided tour leads through Plečnik's living and working quarters. Highlights include the artist's well-preserved studio, and mind-bogglingly intricate furniture that he crafted Plečnik's, as well as models of ambitious architectural projects that never came to fruition. *(Karunova 4. Walk toward the center on Slovenska; turn left on Zoisova, then right on Emonska. Cross the bridge and head behind the church. ☎ 280 16 00; fax 280 16 05. Open Tu-Th 10am-2pm and 4-6pm, Sa 10am-2pm. 1000Sit, students 500Sit. Mandatory 30min. tour available in English.)*

NATIONAL GALLERY (NARODNA GALERIJA). This handsome Austro-Hungarian building houses works by Slovenian and European painters and sculptors from the Romantic through Impressionist periods, as well as religious icons dating from 1270. The Realist and Modern Art pieces are a special treat. *(Prešernova 24. ☎ 241 54 34. Open Tu-Su 10am-6pm. 800Sit, students 600Sit; Sa afternoon free.)*

♫ ❀ ENTERTAINMENT AND FESTIVALS

Pick up a free *Where To?* events listing from the TIC (p. 668). **Cankarjev dom,** Prešernov trg 10 (☎ 241 17 64), hosts the **Slovenian Philharmonic.** (Performances Oct.-June. Box office in the basement of Maximarket. Open M-F 11am-1pm and 3-8pm, Sa 11am-1pm and 1hr. before performance. Tickets 2000-7000Sit.) The **Opera House,** Župančičeva 1, also houses the **ballet.** (☎ 241 17 64. Box office open M-F 1-5pm, Sa 11am-1pm, and 1hr. before each performance. Tickets 2000-9600Sit.) In December, the Old Town comes alive with church concerts, street fairs, and New Year's celebrations. **Tivoli Hall,** in Tivoli Park, hosts sports events and rock concerts. **Kolosej,** Šmartinska c. 152 (☎ 520 55 00; www.kolosej.si), shows English-language movies (1000Sit). Buses #2, 7, and 17 run from the center to the cinema.

The festival season kicks off with the **International Viticulture and Wine Fair** held at the **Fairgrounds** in April. Throughout June, the **Festival of Street Theater** (Ana Desetnica) transforms the city streets and squares into impromptu stages. In late June, the alternative arts scene hosts the international, avant-garde **Break 22 Festival;** meanwhile, the **International Jazz Festival** grooves in Cankarjev dom and Križanke in late June; inquire at TIC for a free schedule. The vaguely titled **International Summer Festival,** from mid-June to mid-September, is a conglomeration of music, opera, and theater performances held at Cankarjev dom and other local venues. The **Ljubljana International Film Festival** plays in early November. Don't miss **Križanke Summer Theater,** which hosts open-air music, dance, and theater June to September. *(☎ 241 60 26. Box office open M-F 10am-1:30pm and 4-8pm, Sa 10am-1pm, and 1hr. before performances. Tickets 2000-5000Sit.)*

🖪 NIGHTLIFE

Cafes and bars line the waterfront, **Trubarjeva, Stari trg,** and **Mestni trg.** For something more energetic, try Metelkova Mesto, especially on weekends after midnight.

🔯 **Makalonca,** Hribarjevo nab., just past the Triple Bridge. Hidden on a terrace below the waterfront's main drag, an arched stone door leads to this local favorite. This intimate cavern-bar has gorgeous views of the river and easygoing staff. Gay friendly. Sangria 400Sit. Mixed drinks 500-1000Sit. Open M-Sa 10pm-1am, Su 10am-3pm.

🔯 **Metelkova Mesto** (www.metelkova.org), the Metelkova block, from trg OF to the Ethnographic Museum. Formerly part of a military barracks, Metelkova was taken over by squatters in the early 90s when the city threatened to tear it down. Soon it became an artists' colony, with vivid grafitti covering its many bars and clubs, which are as many as 12. While there are gay and lesbian nights at only 2 of these clubs—Tiffany and Monokel, respectively—the whole scene is GLBT-friendly. Little is permanent at this self-proclaimed "autonomous cultural center," as ongoing attempts by the city to demolish the complex attest, but much of Metelkova's charm lies in its surprises. Hours vary.

🔯 **Global,** Tomsiceva 2 (☎426 90 20; www.global.si). The elevator is on the corner of Slovenska; look for the orange circle that says "Global." Take the glass elevator to the 6th fl. Considered the best dance club in Ljubljana, this rooftop hotspot draws the trendy with a 70s disco ambience, an extensive cocktail menu, and views of the castle. On weekends, the action gets going around midnight. Mixed drinks 900-1400Sit. Cover for men 1000Sit after 11pm. Bar open M-Sa 8am-9pm. Disco open Th-Sa 9pm-5am.

Casa del Papa, Celovška 54a (☎434 31 58). This island-themed bar on the outskirts of the center draws 20- and 30-somethings seeking a change from the packed waterfront nightlife. The decor pays homage to Hemingway, and the downstairs club throbs with Latin beats and sells Cuban cigars. Beer 280-550Sit per 0.25L. Mixed drinks 1000-1300Sit. Open M-Sa noon-midnight, Su noon-11pm.

Cutty Sark, Knafljev prehod 1 (☎425 14 77). From Prešernov trg, take 1st right into the arched entrance; Cutty Sark is on the left. Outside garden terrace and dimly lit interior make it both pub and outdoor cafe. Union 350Sit. Open M-Sa 9am-1am, Su 5pm-1am.

🖪 DAYTRIPS FROM LJUBLJANA

ŠKOCJANSKE CAVES   ☎(0)5

Škocjanske is an amazing system of UNESCO-protected **caverns** with limestone formations and a 120m gorge created by the Reca River. (☎057 63 28 40; www.gov.si/parkskj. Mandatory tours daily June-Sept. every hr. 10am-5pm; Oct.-May 10am, 1 and 3:30pm. 2500Sit, students 1800Sit.) **Trains** run from Ljubljana to Divača (1½hr., 10 per day, 1340Sit). Follow signs out of town, over the highway, through the village, and onto a narrow path across the woods to the ticket booth (40min.).

POSTOJNA CAVES (POSTOJNSKA JAMA)   ☎(0)5

Trains go to Postojna (1¼hr., 10 per day, 1250Sit), but the station is far from the caves. Buses are a better option; ask for a ticket to Postojna (1hr., about every 30min., 1320Sit). The caves are only a 20min. walk from the bus station. Walk uphill past the ivory-and-green-capped tower to the Tourist Information Center. Make a left at the square and continue; you'll see signs. ☎700 01 00; www.postojna-cave.com. Mandatory 1½hr. tours leave May-Sept. daily every hr. 10am-6pm; Oct. and April daily 10am, noon; Nov.-Mar. M-F 10am and noon, Sa-Su every hr. 10am-4pm. Adults 3590Sit, students 2690Sit.

You'll need to brave the crowds to reach one of Slovenia's greatest natural treasures, but the trip is well worth it. A gentle 2km walk will get you to the stalactites. Although its fame and the resultant flow of tourists have turned the caverns into a kind of amusement park ride, the crowds all but disappear against the array of multicolored rock formations inside the caves.

From the train station, an English tour is around the corner on the right. The tour, part on foot, part by train, covers only 20% of the two-million-year-old cave's 20km. Bring something warm, as the temperature in the cave is a constant 8°C, and a hat, unless you don't mind the occasional drip—the humidity is a constant 90%. Postcards of the caves are cheaper farther from the entrance.

PREDJAMA CASTLE

During the school year, buses go to Bukovje, 2km from the castle (15min.; M-F 7am, 12:35, 1:25, and 3:30pm; 380Sit). Alternatively, you can take a cab. From Postojna, taxis run to Predjama. (☎ 031 406 446, 5000-6000Sit.) Call ahead to arrange a visit to the cave below Predjama Castle. (☎ 756 82 60. Open May-Sept. daily 9am-7pm; Oct. and April daily 10am-5pm; Nov.-Mar. M-F 10am-3pm, Sa-Su 10am-5pm. 1100Sit, students 830Sit.) If you plan to visit both the caves and the castle as a single daytrip from Ljubljana, it may be cheaper and more convenient to rent a car (see p. 668).

Though challenging and costly to reach, **Predjama Castle** (Predjamski Grad), 9km from Postojna, is worth the hassle. Literally built into a 123m high cave on the side of a mountain, it is like nothing else in the world. This feat of natural architecture is actually of medieval inspiration, first constructed in the 12th century, and was renovated in the 16th century with Renaissance flair. Predjama's most famous inhabitant was Erasmus, a German knight who brazenly supported the Hungarian crown in its wars against the Austrian emperor Friedrich III. Friedrich III sent his entire army after the errant knight and besieged the castle with cannonballs for a year and a day, with nothing to show for it but gifts of cherries and roast bullock from Erasmus. Just as the besiegers were running low on supplies, Erasmus's servant turned the tides by betraying his master. After the servant alerted the Austrians that his master was in the outhouse, a single catapult round earned Friedrich his revenge on the rebel knight, who died in the least honorable of positions.

THE JULIAN ALPS (JULIJSKE ALPE)

Stretching across northwest Slovenia and high into the clouds, the Julian Alps are no less stunning than their Austrian or Swiss cousins. The serene wilderness around Lake Bohinj, the alpine peaks of Kranjska Gora, and the breathtaking beauty of Lake Bled and its enchanting island all lie within a short bus ride of one another. The Julian Alps are a pristine playground for all who relish the outdoors.

BLED ☎(0)4

Bled (pop. 11,000), perched on the shores of a gorgeous turquoise lake, and ringed by green alpine hills and snow-covered peaks, will make you wish it was never mentioned in a bestselling travel guide. More crowds show up each summer to swim, hike, paraglide, shop, or just enjoy the air. But its beauty is only slightly diminshed by popularity; little on Earth can compare with the crisp perfection of Slovenia's only island, and the small but stately castle at its serene center.

⌂☎ TRANSPORTATION AND PRACTICAL INFORMATION. Bled has no central train station; **trains to Ljubljana** (1hr., 15 per day, 1150Sit) depart from the Lesce-Bled station (☎ 294 41 54), 4km from town. To reach Bled from the station, take the frequent **commuter bus** (10min., 300Sit), which stops on Ljubljanska and at the bus station, c. Svobode 4 (☎578 04 20). **Buses** are a more convenient option and go to **Ljubljana** (1½hr., at least 1 per hr. 5am-9:30pm, 1400Sit) and **Bohinjsko Jezero** (35min., 1 per hr. 7:20am-8:20pm, 790Sit), **Kranjska Gora** (40min., 1 per hr., 1030Sit). A bus runs to **Vintgar Gorge**'s trailhead June 14-Sept. 30 (10am, 600Sit.)

The town spreads around **Lake Bled,** and most buildings cluster on the eastern shore. **Ljubljanska,** the main street, leads to the water, where it meets **c. Svobode,** which circles the lake. To get to the center, with your back to the bus station, turn right on **c. Svobode,** follow the road as it curves uphill and turns into Prešernova c., and turn right on Ljubljanska. From Ljubljanska, the **TIC,** c. Svobode 10, is on the right, toward the lake and past the Park Hotel. The staff give out **free maps** of Bled and sell hiking maps (1400-1750Sit) of the entire region. (☎574 11 22 or 574 15 55; www.bled.si. Open June-Sept. M-Sa 8am-7pm; Mar.-May 9am-7pm; Nov.-Feb. 9am-5pm.) **Gorenjska Banka,** c. Svobode 15, below the Park Hotel, has a MC **ATM.** (☎574 13 00. Open M-F 9am-11:30am and 2-5pm, Sa 8-11am.) **SKB Banka,** Ljubljanska c. 4, accepts all cards (☎574 22 61. Open M-F 8:30am-noon and 2-5pm.) **Zlatarog Pharmacy** is at Prešernova c. 36. (☎578 07 70. Open M-F 7am-7:30pm, Sa 7am-1pm.) **Internet** is available free to guests of most hotels and hostels and at the **library,** Ljubljanska c. 10. (☎575 16 00. 1000Sit per hr. 1 use per day. Passport or other ID required. Open M 8am-7pm, Tu-F 8am-2pm, Sa 8am-noon.) The **post office** is at Ljubljanska 10. (☎575 02 00. Open M-F 7am-7pm, Sa 7am-noon.) **Postal Code:** 4260.

⌐⌐ ACCOMMODATIONS AND FOOD. Agency Kompas, Ljubljanska 4, on the top floor of the shopping center, books **private rooms.** (☎572 75 00; www.kompas-bled.si. Open June-Oct. M-Sa 8am-8pm, Su 8am-noon and 4-7pm; Nov.-May M-Sa 8am-7pm, Su 8am-noon and 4-7pm; AmEx/MC/V.) **Globtour,** Ljubljanska 7, also arranges private rooms. (☎574 18 21; www.globtour-bled.com. Open M-Sa 8am-8pm, Su 9am-noon and 4-7pm. June-Sept. 15 and Dec. 21-Jan. 4 singles 4000-6000Sit; doubles 5500-8000Sit. Stays under 3 nights 30% more. Tourist tax 162Sit. AmEx/MC/V.) To find a room on your own, look for *sobe* signs, which are common outside the center of town. ▇**Bledec Youth Hostel (HI) ❷,** Grajska c. 17, up the street from the bus station, is a 10min. hike from Bled Castle. Facing away from the bus station, turn left and walk to the top of the hill, bearing left at the fork. Bledec has a cozy log-cabin feel, with dark wood, comfortable beds, and clean bathrooms. (☎574 52 50; bledec@mlino.si. Breakfast included. Laundry 2000Sit. Internet 500Sit per 30min. Reception 24hr. Check-out 10am. Reserve ahead. Open only in high season. Dorms 4560Sit, members 4080Sit. AmEx/MC/V.) **Camping Bled ❶,** Kidrieva 10c, in a beautiful valley on the west side of the lake, is about 2.5km from the bus station. From the station, follow c. Svobode downhill, turn left at the lake, and walk 25min. The campground has a store, a restaurant, and a beach. (☎575 20 00; www.camping.bled.si. Laundry 1000Sit. Internet 1800Sit per hr. Reception 24hr. Check-out 3pm. 1625-2400Sit per person. Electricity 710Sit. Tourist tax 121Sit.)

If days of hostel-made sandwiches have left you feeling extravagant, try **Okarina ❹,** Riklijiva 9, just uphill from the bus station, which specializes in Indian-inspired and vegetarian dishes. Colorful carpets on the wall, Bollywood paraphernalia, and a round open-air courtyard complement the tasty food. The chicken masala (*masala mesna;* 2400Sit) with the *parata* (790Sit) should not be missed. (☎574 14 58. Entrees 2400-3400Sit. Open M-F 6pm-midnight, Sa-Su noon-midnight.) Excellent service and huge portions of high-quality food distinguish **Gostilna pri Planincu ❷,** Grajska c. 8, diagonally across the street from the bus station. (☎574 16 13. Crepes 600-800Sit. Pizza 1100-2500Sit. Open daily 9am-11pm.) Popular with the locals, **Slaščičarna Šmon ❶,** Grajska c. 3, between Okarina and the bus station, offers good coffee (230Sit) and seductive desserts (130-550Sit). Their torte arsenal (350-400Sit) includes *grmada,* a chocolate biscuit with vanilla cream, nuts, raisins, and rum. (☎574 22 80. Sandwiches 280Sit. Pizza 300Sit. Open daily 7:30am-10pm.) Most of the restaurants in Bled are touristy and overpriced. Your best bet is to pick up supplies at **Mercator,** Ljubljanska c. 13, in the shopping center and find a good picnic spot. (Open M-Sa 7am-8pm, Su 8am-noon.)

◙ **SIGHTS.** **Bled Castle** (Blejski grad) is nice, but the view from it is even nicer. Built in 1004, Slovenia's oldest citadel rises 100m above the lake, framing the perfect angle on the island in the lake. The official path to the castle is on Grajska c., but there are several pleasant hikes through the forest. One runs uphill from **St. Martin's Church** (Cerkev sv. Martin), on Kidričeva c. near the lake. Another route begins behind the swimming area; follow blazes marked with a "1" uphill. The shortest path is a 10min. hike from behind the parking lot of Bledec Hostel.

Inside the castle wall, the entrance to the castle is through the souvenir shop. Turn left at the top of the stairs, go to the end of the red carpet, and make sure to look out the window. Castle tickets include admission to the compelling **History Museum,** on the ground floor, stocked with furniture, weapons, and Roman coins. Poke your head into the small printing studio opposite the museum to watch an artist in traditional dress produce medieval, Gutenberg-style prints. Videos in English depict the history of the glacier-formed lake, the castle, and Bled. There are touchscreens in the castle for interactive, detailed info. (☎578 05 25. Open daily May-Oct. 8am-8pm; Nov.-Apr. 8am-5pm. 1200Sit, students 1100Sit. MC.)

The centerpiece, wooded Bled Island (Blejski Otok), is home to the **Church of the Assumption** (Cerkev Marijinega Vnebovzetja). Ring the bell in the church to make a wish. There are several ways to reach the island. The supervised swimming area below the castle rents row boats, as does **Janez Palak,** Koritenska 27. (☎578 05 28. 3-seaters 2400Sit for 1st hr., 1200Sit per additional hr.; 5-seaters 2880/1440Sit. 1000Sit deposit.) You can also cross the lake on gondola-style *plentas,* stationed at the **Rowing Center** and in **Mlino** under Hotel Park. (Round-trip 1½hr., 20min. each way, with 30min. on the island; 2400Sit per person.) In summer, swimming to the island is permitted; the closest starting point is the west side of the lake, next to the camping grounds. Or, you can dive in from the **Castle Swimming Grounds** (Grajsko Kopališoe) under Bled Castle. (Day ticket 1200Sit, students 800Sit; afternoon 900/700Sit.) In summer, the water averages 21-24°C; in winter, the lake becomes an ice-skating rink. (Open Dec.-Feb. daily 7am-7pm. Lockers 720Sit.)

◪◩ **ENTERTAINMENT AND NIGHTLIFE.** The tourist office distributes a free brochure listing local events. The 2nd weekend in July draws together orchestral musicians for **Bled Days** (www.festivalbled.com), which features concerts, arts and crafts, and fireworks on the lake. The folk music extravaganza **Okarina Ethno Music Festival** (☎574 14 58) is held each August. Other annual events include a rowing regatta in late June, an international music festival in the first two weeks of July, and Merry December events. Bled's nightlife is low-key. Pass up the disco at the shopping center and the casinos and check out **Devil,** c. Svobode 15, under the Park Hotel. With brick walls, red-and-yellow vaulted arches, and wrought iron chairs, it feels delectably dark and medieval. The wooden deck overlooks the lake. (Mixed drinks 450-1000Sit. Wine 200-750Sit. Ice cream 150Sit. Open daily 9am-4am. Cash only.) Backpackers mingle with locals on the rustic patio of **The Pub,** c. Svobode 8a. (☎574 22 17. *Union* 400Sit per 0.3L. Open daily 7pm-1am.)

▨ **OUTDOOR ACTIVITIES.** The **Kompas** agency, in the shopping center, rents **bikes** (700Sit per hr., 1500Sit per ½-day, 2200Sit per day), **skis** (3000Sit per day, parabolic skis 4000Sit per day), **snowboards** (4000Sit per day), and **sleds** (3000Sit per day); and offers whitewater rafting trips. (☎572 75 00; www.kompas-bled.si. Rafting 5500 Sit per day. Open 8am-7pm, Su 8am-noon and 4-7pm. AmEx/MC/V.) Many hiking paths snake from the lake into the hills, each marked with a name and trail number. The tourist office sells detailed trail maps (1400-1750Sit). **Promontana Outdoor Agency**, Ljubljanska 1, located across the street from Kompas and the shopping center, rents **bikes** and offers an assortment of guided outdoor excursions around Bled and Triglav National Park, ranging from the tame to the extreme. (☎578 06 60; www.sigov.si/trip. Hiking 4800-8400Sit; climbing 4800-24,000Sit; spelunking 2160Sit; rafting 4800Sit, paragliding 13,200-16,800Sit. Bikes 700Sit per hr., 1500Sit per ½-day, 2200Sit per day. Open M-Sa 8am-4pm.)

Traced by the waterfalls and rapids of the Radovna River, nearby **Vintgar Gorge** (Soteska Vintgar) offers one of the best hikes in the area. Walk the 4km instead of taking the bus to the trailhead, and you'll pass charming small towns and open fields. Bring some food: a picnic bench tucked neatly into a nook lies halfway along the hike. The 1.6km gorge carves through the rocks of the nearby **Triglav National Park** (Triglavski Narodni Park). The park info office is at Kidričeva c. 2. (☎574 11 88; fax 574 35 68. 600Sit, students 500Sit) To get there, go over the hill on Grajska c., away from the town center, and right at the bottom of the hill. Turn left after 100m and follow signs for Vintgar. Alternatively, hop on one of the frequent buses to Podhom (10min., M-Sa 10 per day, 280Sit) and follow the 1.5km route. From mid-June through September, **Alpetour** (☎532 04 40) runs a bus to the trailhead (15min., 10am; one-way 600Sit , round-trip 1080).

LAKE BOHINJ (BOHINJSKO JEZERO) ☎(0)4

Bohinjsko Jezero (BOH-heen-skoh YEH-zeh-roh), 26km southwest of Lake Bled, may surpass even its neighbor in natural beauty. The lake is larger, and the surrounding mountains rise right out of the water. Protected by the borders of Triglav National Park, this glacial lake is one of the best spots for alpine adventures. Some travel here for the water sports, but most come to scale the local summits.

📞🛈 TRANSPORTATION AND PRACTICAL INFORMATION. Trains do not run to or from the three villages around Lake Bohinj, but you can catch a bus to **Bohinjska Bistrica,** the largest town in the area, 6km from the lake, and take a train from there to **Ljubljana** (2½hr., 8 per day, 1250Sit) via Jesenice. **Buses,** the more convenient option, run from Hotel Zlatorog in Ukanc to Ribčev Laz (10min., 1 per hr., 300Sit) and from Ribčev Laz to: **Bled** (35min., 11-16 per day, 790Sit); **Bohinjska Bistrica** (15min., 1 per hr., 380Sit); **Ljubljana** (2hr., 1 per hr., 1950Sit). Buses going to **Bohinjsko Jezero** (Lake Bohinj) stop at Hotel Jezero in Ribčev Laz or at Hotel Zlatorog in Ukanc.

The town nearest the lake is **Bohinjska Bistrica,** 6km east, but **Ribčev Laz,** where the bus drops you off, should have everything you need. The lake is surrounded by two other villages, Stara Fužina and Ukanc. The **tourist bureau,** Ribčev Laz 48, provides maps and transportation info; issues fishing permits; books private rooms, which are cheaper than in Bled; and arranges guided excursions. (☎574 60 10; www.bohinj.si. Open July-Aug. M-Sa 8am-8pm, Su 8am-7pm; Sept.-June M-Sa 8am-6pm, Su 9am-3pm.) The nearest bank, **Gorenjska Banka,** Trg Svobode 2B, in

HAPPY END. The town of Ukanc ("the end") was so named by locals who once considered it the limit of the natural world. Ironically, it marks the beginning of gorgeous Bohinjska Bistrica.

Bohinjska Bistrica, **exchanges currency** for no commission and cashes **traveler's checks.** (☎572 16 10. Open July-Aug. M-F 8am-6pm, Sa 8-11am; Sept.-June M-F 9-11:30am and 2-5pm, Sa 8-11am.) The closest **pharmacy** is in Bohinjska Bistrica, at

Triglavska 15. (☎572 16 30. Open M-F 8am-7:30pm, Sa 8am-1pm.) **Internet** is at **Pansion Rožic,** Ribčev Laz 42, just up the street from the TIC. (☎572 33 95. 20Sit per min.) The **post office** in Ribčev Laz, Ribčev Laz 47, has a MC/V **ATM** outside. (Open July-Aug. M-F 8am-7pm, Sa 8am-noon; Sept.-June M-F 8-9:30am, 10-10:30am, and 4-6pm, Sa 8am-noon.) **Postal Code:** 4265.

⌐⌐ ACCOMMODATIONS AND FOOD. The tourist bureau arranges **private rooms** and other accommodations in all three villages year-round. (Breakfast €4. Rooms €8.50-12.25. Tourist tax €1.) **AutoCamp Zlatorog ❶,** Ukanc 2, is on the lake's west side, near the Savica Waterfall and many trailheads. The complex, run by Alpinum Tourist Agency, has sports facilities, showers, baths, and a restaurant. Take a bus to Hotel Zlatorog in Ukranc and then backtrack 300m. (☎572 34 82; fax 572 34 46. Reception July-Aug. 24hr.; Sept.-May daily 8am-noon and 4-8pm. Check-out noon. July-Aug. 1800-2300Sit per day; Sept. and May-June 1300-1700Sit. Tourist tax 121Sit. Cash only.) On the way, check out the Mt. Vogel **gondola** (10min.; 2 per hr. 7am-7pm; one-way 1400Sit, round-trip 2000Sit) that takes you 1535m up to a view of the mountains and lake. **Camping Danica ❶,** Bohinjska Bistrica 4264, is just outside town in a quiet area below the mountains. Get off the bus in Bohinjska Bistrica and backtrack about 75m; the site is on the right. Tennis courts, a restaurant, and showers compensate for a lack of shade. (☎572 10 55; www.bohinj.si/camping-danica. Camping July 18-Aug. 21 1850Sit; Aug. 22-Sept. 4 and June 13-July 17 1600Sit; Sept. 5-30 and May-June 12 1300Sit. Electricity 500Sit. 10% off stays longer than 1 week. Tourist tax 121Sit. AmEx/MC/V.)

On the shores of Bohinj, **Gostišče Kramar ❶,** Stara Fužina 3, has a view of the lake. The menu is limited to pizza (200-1200Sit), hot dogs, and other fast food (350-900Sit). From Ribčev Laz, walk over the stone bridge and follow the first path on the left through the woods for 7min. (☎572 36 97. *Union* 400Sit per 0.5L. Open M-Th and Su 11am-midnight, F-Sa 11am-1am.) **Restavracija Center ❸,** Ribčev Laz 50, also has pizzas (1100-1450Sit) and a fairly good "tourist menu" (1400-1600Sit), which always features a seafood or vegetarian option. (☎572 31 70. Open daily 8am-11pm.) **Mercator Supermarket,** Ribčev Laz 49, by the tourist office, has groceries. (☎572 95 34. Open M-F 7am-8pm, Sa 7am-8pm, Su 7am-5pm.)

⌐ OUTDOOR ACTIVITIES. The shores of Bohinj are a gateway to a range of outdoor adventures. Good **hiking maps** are available at the tourist office (1700Sit). The most popular destination is the somewhat overrated **Savica Waterfall** (Slap Savica), which cascades into the Sava Bohinjka River. Take the local bus from **Ribčev Laz** toward "Bohinj-Zlatorog" and get off at Hotel Zlatorog (15min., 1 per hr. 8am-7pm, 290Sit). Follow the signs uphill to Savica Waterfall for 1hr. to the trailhead, Dom Savica, where visitors must pay 400Sit before heading up to the waterfall (20min. upstairs from the trailhead). In July and August, a bus runs to the trailhead from Ribčev Laz (20min., 4 per day 9am-6pm, 380Sit). If you forego the bus, turn left at the lake in Ribčev Laz and follow the road along the lake past **Ukanc** (1½hr.).

If the hiking spirit compels you to continue past the waterfall, follow the signs up the mountain toward **Black Lake** (Črno Jezero) at the base of the Julian Alps' highest peaks (1½hr.). The hiking is extremely steep; avoid going alone. Facing the small lake's shore, a trail to the right (Dol Pod Stadorjem) leads to **Mt. Viševnik,** a grassy hillside that overlooks the small peaks. Facing the valley below, veer left and follow the signs and trailblazes to reach **Pršivec** (1½hr.; 1761m). Return the way you came or follow the trail east for a quicker and easier return (1hr.) along the ridge through Vogar. When you hit the highway at the base, turn right and proceed via **Stara Fužina** and Ribčev Laz (2½hr.). **Alpinsport,** Ribčev Laz 53, rents **mountain bikes, kayaks,** and **canoes** and organizes **mountaineering** guides and **canyoning** trips in nearby gorges. (☎572 34 86; www.alpinsport.si. Bikes 950Sit per hr., 2100Sit per 3hr., 3200Sit per day; kayaks 950/2200/3400Sit; canoes 1100/2700/4900Sit. Open daily July-Aug. 9am-7pm; Sept.-June 10am-5pm.) In winter, Bohinj becomes an enormous **ski** resort with five main ski centers: **Soriška Planina, Kobla, Senožeta, Pokljuka,** and **Vogel.** The season runs from late December to mid-April, depending on weather conditions. Vogel, the most popular area, is a hot destination for intermediate and expert skiers. (Morning or afternoon lift pass 3450Sit. Day pass 5000Sit. Ski rental with boots €16, snowboard and boots €18, poles €3, helmet €4.) Nearby Kobla offers gentler slopes for beginners. During winter, **Alpinsport** rents skis and snowboards and holds group and private ski lessons. (Skis and ski boot set rental 3910Sit per day. Private ski lessons 5200Sit per hr. Snowboard set 4140Sit per day.) For more info, contact **Vogel,** Ukanc 6 (☎574 60 60; vogel@bohinj.si), or **Kobla,** c. na Ravne 7 (☎574 71 00; kobla@siol.net). For more info on outdoor activities, check out **www.bohinj.si.**

KRANJSKA GORA ☎(0)4

The village of **Kranjska Gora** (KRAN-ska GOR-ah; pop. 1500) mixes a quaint town center with a serious outdoors scene. Skiiers come for Slovenia's best trails. Even less experienced adventurers will appreciate scenic cycling and hiking in the Kara-vanke ridge to the north. Beyond this, the town is suburbia and *sobes.* For a fairly short hike, take trail #3 (40min., 2.2km) or more difficult #4 (1½hr., 3.5km) to the relatively tame incline **Podkoren,** 3km from Kranjska Gora, known for its folk architecture. From there, you can pick up trail #12 toward **Rateče,** a small village 7km from Kranjska Gora that sits below **Pec** (1510m), a peak on the border with Austria and Italy. One of the best hikes runs through the **Planica Valley** to **Tamar Valley.** From town, take trail #9 to Planica (2hr., 5km), where you'll see impressive ski runs and enjoy an amazing view of the **Mojstrovka, Travnik, Šita,** and **Jalovec Mountains.** Jalovec peak is considered the most beautiful mountain in Slovenia and is the symbol of the Alpine Association. Continue on the trail past the ski ramps for 45min. to reach the mountain hut **Tamar,** from which Jalovec can be seen.

The nearest **train station** is in Jesenice (24km). **Buses** run to and from: **Bled-Lesce** (40min., 2 direct to Bled M-F, at 9:15am and 1:10pm; from Lesce: 38-40 past the hr., every hr. from 6:38am-6:40pm plus 11:40 on Sa; 1030Sit); **Jesenice** (15min.; M-F 25 per day, Sa 12 per day, Su 8 per day; 700Sit); **Ljubljana** (2¼hr.; 6 per day M-F, 5 Sa; 2150Sit). **Sport Point,** Borovška c. 93A, rents **bikes** (800-900Sit per hr., 2400-3000Sit per day), **rollerblades** (300/1500Sit), **trikkes** (like scooters with 3 wheels; 300/1500Sit), and two apartments upstairs (12,000-16,800Sit; prices vary by season). (☎588 48 83. Open daily 7am-8pm; shop open daily 8am-8pm. AmEx/MC/V.) **Agencija Julijana,** Borovška 93, next to the Prišavik Hotel, arranges **hiking** and **skiing** excursions, and also leads **raft, bike, sled,** and **toboggan** trips. (☎588 13 25; www.sednjek.si. Bike rentals 700Sit per hr., 1500Sit per ½-day, 2000Sit per day. Rafting trips 7200Sit. Open daily 8am-noon and 3-8pm.) Your best budget option is a **private room**—there are plenty available in town, marked by *sobe* signs. The **tourist office,** on Tičarjeva, arranges rooms for no additional fee and has a comprehensive price list of all hotels and pensions in the city. (*Sobes* Aug. 1-26 €13-17; Jun. 18-Jul. 30 and Aug. 27-Sept. 17 €11-15; Sept. 17-Dec. 3 and Mar. 31-June 17 €10-14. Tax €1 per day.) Though pricier than most HI establishments, **HI Pension and Youth Hostel Borka** ❸, Borovška 71, is one of the best options in town. (☎587 91 00. Breakfast included. 2- to 4-bed suites with bath 6000Sit per person.) The traditionally clad servers at **Gostilna pri Martinu** ❸, Borovška 61, deliver huge portions of Slovenian fare like goulash and polenta for 800-2200Sit. (☎582 03 00. Vegetarian plates 1000-1200Sit. Open daily 10am-11pm.)

ISTRIA

Slovenia claims only 40km of the Adriatic coast, but its remarkable stretch of green bays and vineyards has a palpable Italian flavor. Reminiscent of the French Riviera or Dalmatian Coast, Slovenian Istria is the site of bustling coastal villages.

PORTOROŽ ☎ (0)5

The "Port of Roses" (pohrt-oh-ROHZH; pop. 9,000) is Slovenian Istria's giant resort town. Streams of visitors have washed away the distinctly Slovenian flavor retained by neighboring coastal towns, but the grassy beach, seaside restaurants, and deep blue tide of Portorož remain unblemished.

⊏ TRANSPORTATION. Buses go to **Koper** (30min., every 20min. 5am-10:30pm, 700Sit) and **Ljubljana** (2¾hr., 4-8 per day, 2950Sit). A **minibus** runs from Lucija through Portorož and on to **Piran** (every 15min. 5:30am-midnight, 200-240Sit). A **catamaran** speeds to **Venice, ITA** (2½hr.; Apr.-Nov. 2-4 per week; June-Aug. 15,800Sit, Sept.-May 14,700. Buy tickets at any tourist agency). **Atlas Express,** Obala 55, has **AmEx travel services** and rents **bikes** and **scooters.** (☎674 88 21; Bikes 1900Sit per 2hr., 2900Sit per 6hr., 4300Sit per day. Scooters 4600/8100/9200Sit. Open July-Sept. M-F 9am-8pm, Sa 9am-7pm, Su 10am-1pm and 6-8pm; Oct.-June M-Sa 8am-7pm.) **Maestral,** Obala 123, rents **boats.** (☎677 92 80; www.maestral.si. July-Aug. 24,000Sit per 4hr., 43,200Sit per day; Sept. and June 21,600/36,000Sit.)

⬛🖪 ORIENTATION AND PRACTICAL INFORMATION. Most streets start at **Obala,** the waterfront boulevard. If you arrive by bus, you'll see the tourist office, Obala 16, right across the street (☎674 02 31; www.portoroz.si. Open July-Aug. daily 9am-1:30pm and 3-9pm; Sept.-June M-Tu and Th-Su 10am-5pm, W 10am-3pm.) Commission-free **exchange offices** line Obala, and a 24hr. MC/V **ATM** is at Obala 32, by Banka Koper. A **pharmacy, Lekarna Potorož,** is at Obala 41. Walk down Obala in the direction of Piran, turn right into the Hotel Palace Courtyard, and follow the sign. (☎674 86 70. Open M-F 8am-8pm, Sa 8am-1pm, Su 9am-1pm. AmEx/V.) **Telephones** line Obala and are inside and outside the post office. **Internet** is available at **Pub Planet,** Obala 14, next door to restaurant Paco. (250Sit per 15min. Open daily 9am-2am.) The **post office,** Stari cesti 1, off Obala past the old Palace Hotel, beside the pharmacy, cashes **traveler's checks** for 2% commission and has **Poste Restante.** (☎674 60 40. Open M-F 8am-7pm, Sa 8am-noon.) **Postal Code: 6322.**

🖬🖸 ACCOMMODATIONS AND FOOD. Maona Portorož, Obala 14b, arranges **private rooms.** (☎674 03 63; www.maona.si. July-Aug. doubles 7900Sit; triples 10,200Sit; Sept.-June 6200/8600Sit.) **Tourist Service Portorož,** Postajališka 2, right next to the bus station, is another reliable option. (☎674 03 60. Open M-Sa 9am-9pm, Su 10am-5pm. Singles €12-20; doubles €19-30; triples €26-40. Registration 500Sit. Tourist tax 126-154Sit.) **Kamp Lucija ❶,** Seča 204, just beyond the Marina Portorož, is a mid-sized seaside campground with showers and toilets; a restaurant and supermarket are nearby. Hop on a minibus from any point along Obala and ride it away from Piran to the stop "Lucija." Continue walking away from Piran and turn right at the sign on c. Solinarjev. Follow the street as it curves left into Seča. (☎690 60 00; camp@metropolgroup.si. Reception daily 6am-10pm. Guarded 24hr. Camping July-Aug. 2200-2800Sit; Sept. and May-June 1700-2000Sit. Electricity 500Sit. Tourist tax 81Sit.) ⬛**News Cafe ❷,** Obala 4f, serves everything from all-day breakfast (omelettes 590-1040Sit) to pasta, fajitas, salads, and burgers. By night, it is one of the best bars in town. You can kick back to live music and enjoy wild mixed drinks (570-1390Sit) or beer (290-780Sit). The tastefully decadent,

1920s-style interior makes it a local favorite. (☎674 10 04. Entrees 990-2000Sit; bring a doggie bag. Open daily 8am-2am.) Beachside **Paco 2 ❸**, Obala 18a, delights patrons with excellent food at reasonable prices. Choose from pizza (1000-1600Sit), Slovenian entrees, and seafood (1400-3800Sit) under the shade of the thatched roof. (☎674 10 20. Open daily 9am-12:30am.) **Supermarket Mercator,** on Obala 8 between Piran and Portorož (open M-F 7am-8pm, Sa 7am-6pm, Su 8am-noon), or Obala 53 next to the bus station in Portorož, is a more wallet-friendly option for beachside picnics. (Open M-Sa 7am-8pm, Su 8-11am.)

🖸🖪 **ENTERTAINMENT AND NIGHTLIFE.** For some fun in the sun, head to the manmade sand **beach.** (Open 8am-8pm. Entrance 8am-1pm 600Sit; 1-5pm 500Sit; 5-8pm free. Lockers 700Sit, 1100Sit deposit.) When night falls, Obala's main stretch melds into one mammoth beach party. Local favorite **The Club,** at Hotel Belvedere in nearby Izola, is one of the hottest nightclubs in Istria. Take the intercity bus from the station in the direction of Koper (15min., every 20min., 360Sit). Stay until closing to catch an early bus back to Portorož; otherwise a taxi is the only way home. (☎153 93 11. Beer 400Sit. Open daily 11pm-6am.) Also in Izola, the nightclub **Ambaceda Gavioli,** is internationally famous for its wild parties. The club is not open regularly, so keep your eyes out for flyers advertising an event, or inquire at the tourist office for info. In February, Portorož hosts the **Pust,** a carnival that attracts visitors from all along the coast with its crazy costumes and performances. Portorož also participates in events based in its neighbor Piran, such as the theater-oriented Primorska Summer Festival in July.

PIRAN ☎(0)5

In contrast to its resort-filled neighbor Portorož, the small fishing village Piran retains an undeniable old-world charm and a distinctly Venetian feel. Dubbed "the pearl of Istria," Piran cradles beautiful churches, crumbling medieval architecture, and a lighthouse that is a beacon for ships on their way along the Istrian coast.

🗐🖬 **TRANSPORTATION AND PRACTICAL INFORMATION.** Buses go to **Ljubljana** (2¾hr., 4-8 per day, 2670Sit). A **minibus** runs the length of Obala, from Lucija through Portorož and on to Piran (every 15min. 5:30am-midnight, 240Sit). Alternatively, a 25min. walk takes you from Piran to Portorož; facing the sea, head left.

The streets of Piran radiate from two main squares. **Tartinijev trg,** named for the native violinist and composer Giuseppe Tartini, is the city's commercial heart and home to its shops and services. From the bus stop, face the sea, turn right, and continue 5min. The square is on the right. Following Verdijeva from Tartinijev trg leads to the quieter **Trg 1 Maya.** The center of medieval Piran, the square serves as an open-air stage for theater and dance performances during the Primorska Summer Festival. The **tourist office,** Tartinijev trg 2, in the far left corner of the square (with your back to the water, facing the square), offers **free maps** and bus schedule info. (☎673 02 20. Open daily 9am-1pm and 3-9pm.) **Banka Koper,** Tartinijev trg 12, on the opposite corner of the square, **exchanges currency** for no commission, gives MC **cash advances,** and has a 24hr. **ATM** outside. (☎673 32 00. Open M-F 8:30am-noon and 3-5pm, Sa 8:30am-noon.) The **pharmacy, Obalne Lekarne Koper,** is at Tartinijev trg 4. (☎611 00 00. Open M-F 7:30am-8pm, Sa 7:30am-1pm, Su 8am-noon. AmEx/MC/V). **Internet** (240Sit per hr., free for guests) is available at **Youth Hostel Val** (see below) or for free at the **library,** Mestna Knjiznica Piran, Tartinijev trg 1. (30min. limit. Open M-F 10am-6pm, Sa 8am-1pm.) There is one **telephone** right in front of the tourist office. The **post office,** Leninova 1, between the bus station and the main square, **exchanges currency,** cashes **traveler's checks,** and gives MC **cash advances.** (☎673 26 88. Open M-F 8am-7pm, Sa 8am-noon.) **Postal Code:** 6330.

⌐❍ ACCOMMODATIONS AND FOOD. Accommodations tend to be pricey. The staff at **Maona Travel Agency,** Cankarjevo nabrezje 7, on the waterfront before Tartinijev trg, find **private rooms.** (☎673 45 20; www.maona.si. Open daily 8am-7pm. Singles 4300-5500Sit; doubles 6900-8000Sit.) More like a pension than a hostel, ◪**Youth Hostel Val ❸,** Gregorčičeva 38a, has spotless rooms. From the bus station, follow the waterfront past Tartinijev trg as it curves around and away from the harbor. Look for the sign three blocks up on the right. (☎673 25 55; www.hostel-val.com. Book early. Breakfast and Internet included. Reception daily 8am-10pm. May 15-Sept. 15 5760Sit per person; Sept. 16-May 14 4800Sit per person. 240/480Sit HI discount. 480Sit additional for stays of fewer than 2 nights in high season.)

Many similar waterfront cafes are on the shoreline **Prešernovo nab. Tri Vdove ❹,** Prešer ovo nab. 4, stands out for delicious seafood, meat, and pasta dishes. The squid stuffed with ham and cheese (1800Sit) is particularly good. (☎673 02 90. Entrees 1300-3600Sit. Open daily 11am-midnight. AmEx/MC/V.) **Riva Pizzeria ❸,** Gregorčičeva 43, is at the end of the strand. Don't let the name fool you—they sell seafood, too. Try the linguini with salmon for 1300Sit. (☎673 22 25. Open daily 9am-midnight. AmEx/MC/V.) A cheaper and less elegant option is the local favorite **Gostiše Pirat ❸,** Župančičeva 26, between Tartinijev trg and the bus station. (☎673 14 81. Entrees 900-1800Sit. Open M-Sa 10am-10pm, Su noon-10pm.) There is an open-air **produce market** behind the tourist office at Zelenjavni trg. (Open daily 7am-6pm.) A small but well-stocked **Mercator supermarket,** Levstikova 5, stands one block behind. (Open M-F 7am-8pm, Sa 7am-1pm, Su 8-11am. AmEx/MC/V.)

◫❒ SIGHTS AND ENTERTAINMENT. The sea is Piran's primary attraction. Discover the secrets of Piran's seaside past at the ◪**Maritime Museum** (Pomorski Muzej), just off Tartinijev trg on Cankarjevo nab. The three-story building has exhibits on marine archaeology and seamanship, and a collection of ship replicas. (☎671 00 40; muzej@pommuz-pi.si. English captions. Open Tu-Su 9am-noon and 3-6pm. 600Sit, students 500Sit.) A short walk uphill from Tartinijev trg leads to the Gothic **Church of St. George** (Crkva sv. Jurja) and the nearby **St. George's Tower,** constructed in 1608, which commands a spectacular view of Piran and the Adriatic. (Church and tower open daily 10am-10pm. Church free. Tower 150Sit.) From the tower, head uphill and continue parallel to the shoreline to reach the old **city walls.** Along with supporting Slovenia's sole national marine preserve and Piran's economy, the coastal waters offer **scuba diving** opportunities. **Sub-net,** Prešernovo nab. 24, gives certification classes and guided dives. (☎673 22 18; www.sub-net.si. 1 to 3hr. dive plus equipment 6000-8400Sit, beginners 9600Sit. Equipment and use of showers 3000Sit. Open M-F 10am-4pm, Sa 9am-7pm. Cash only.) Meet the ocean critters at the **aquarium,** Kidričeva 4, on the opposite side of the marina. (☎673 25 72. Open daily 10am-noon and 2-7pm. 600Sit, students 500Sit.)

Piran lacks sand beaches, but paved swimming and sunning areas line the peninsula. Best of all, unlike in neighboring Portorož, they are free. Nightlife in Piran tends to be relaxed. Perched above the old city stage, the beautiful terrace cafe **Teater,** Kidričevo na., a large yellow building on the corner, is a perfect place to relax under the sunset. (Mixed drinks 600-1000Sit. *Lasko* 800 Sit. Open daily 8am-1am. Cash only.) **Da Noi,** Prešernovo nab. 1, draws a laid-back crowd with nightly drink specials. (Sangria 450Sit. *Laško* 480Sit per 0.5L. Open M-F and Su 9am-midnight, F 9am-2am.) If you're tired of tourists and looking for something mellow, go down the strand and around the peninsula. **Punta Bar,** Prešernovo na. 24, located next to Sub-net Diving Center, is a simple "beach bar" on the water. (Open daily 9am-midnight. Cash only.) In June, a classic car rally rolls through town, while July brings a regatta of classic boats, as well as the **Primoska Summer Festival,** which features outdoor plays, ballets, and concerts. Inquire at the tourist office for event schedules. In September, the cultural life of the city peaks with the **International Painting Reunion Ex tempore.** Some of Europe's most promising young painters set up shop on the city's streets and squares.

ŠTAJERSKA

Štajerska's green hills and rolling farmland lie in sharp contrast to the alpine peaks to the west. To Slovenes, the name evokes vineyards, natural springs, and delicious cuisine. The region preserves a strong local character and doesn't hesitate to welcome visitors with open arms and maybe even a bottle of wine.

MARIBOR ☎(0)2

Surrounded by the wine-growing Piramida Hill, the slow Drava River, and the adventuresome ski haven of Pohorje, Maribor (MAHR-ee-bohr; pop. 106,000) possesses a youthful vibrance which belies its deep history. Although 2nd in size to Ljubljana, this 700-year-old university town exudes a charmingly provincial feel.

⌑ TRANSPORTATION. From the **train station,** Partizanska c. 50 (info ☎292 21 00, tickets 292 21 64), trains run to **Ljubljana** (1½hr., 12 per day, 1710-2895Sit) and **Ptuj** (1hr., 9 per day, 620Sit). The **bus station,** Mlinska 1 (☎090 72 30), sends buses to **Ljubljana** (2½-3hr., 10 per day, 2760Sit) and **Ptuj** (50min., 6 per day, 790Sit).

◪⌘ ORIENTATION AND PRACTICAL INFORMATION. The majority of Maribor's sights lie in the city center, on the north shore of the **Drava River,** which invites exploration by foot. From the train station, turn left and follow Partizanska past the large Franciscan **Church of St. Mary** to **Grajski trg,** where you'll see the **Florian Column.** Turn left down **Vetrinska,** follow it past the shopping complex on the right, and turn right on **Koroška cesta** to reach **Glavni trg.** From the main bus station, turn right on Mlinska, follow it to Partizanska, and take a left. **Maribor Tourist Information Center "Matic,"** Partizanska c. 47, just across from the train station, is stocked with **maps** and brochures and can book **private rooms.** (☎234 66 11; www.maribor-tourism.si. 2hr. city tours 15,000Sit. Open M-F 9am-6pm, Sa 9am-1pm.) **Nova KBM,** ul. Vita Kraigherja 4, **exchanges currency** for no commission, and **traveler's checks** for 1.5% commission, and has **Western Union** and **American Express** services. (☎062 229 229. Open M-F 8-11:30am and 2-5pm.) A **24hr.** **ATM** is at **A-Banka,** Glavni trg 18, perpendicular to Gosposka ul. A 24hr. **pharmacy, Lekarna Glavni trg,** is at Glavni trg 20. Use the side window for night service. You can find a **hospital** at Ljubljanska ul. 5 (☎321 10 00). For free **Internet,** head to **Kibla Multimedia Center,** ul. Kneza Koclja 9. It also has a lively bar and modern art gallery, and stocks the free English-language newspaper *Slovenian Times.* Enter Narodni Dom and go through the large art space on the left. (☎229 40 12; www.kibla.org. Open M-F 9am-10pm, Sa 4-10pm; closed July 15-Aug. 15.) In the summer months, similarly named **Kibla Multimedia,** Glavni trg, next to Benetton, has fast connections. (150Sit per 30min., 200Sit per hr.) **Telephones** are located near both **post offices,** Partizanska c. 1 (open M-F 8am-7pm, Sa 8am-noon) and Partizanska c. 54 (open M-F 8am-7pm, Sa 8am-1pm). Both have **currency exchange. Postal Code:** 2000.

⌗⌕ ACCOMMODATIONS AND FOOD. "Matic" (see **Orientation and Practical Information**) can arrange **private rooms** (singles 3500-9000Sit; doubles 7000-12,000Sit). **HI Dijaški Dom 26 Junij ❷,** Železnikova 12, is a 15min. walk from the center. From the local bus station in front of the train station, take bus #3 (Brezje) to the "Pokopališče" stop. Cross the street and walk a few paces to the right, then take the first left and follow the road as it curves. Past the Mercator supermarket, you'll see a building with "12" painted on the side. Tidy rooms and quiet environs make it the best deal in town. (☎480 17 10. Free Internet. Check-in 7-10am and 7-11pm. Open June 25-Aug. 25. Singles 3500Sit; doubles 6000Sit. 20% HI discount.) If you're willing to pay a bit more to be in the center, **Uni Hostel ❸**, Grajski trg 3a, inside the Orel Hotel, has simple singles with private bathrooms. (☎250 67 00; www.teremb.si. 5800Sit, HI members 4800Sit. AmEx/MC/V.) **Toti Rotovž ❸**, Glavni trg 14, has savory set meals (1600Sit) and a variety of international dishes, from local specialties to Thai satay. (☎228 76 50. Entrees 700-3400Sit. Open M-Th 8am-midnight, F-Sa 8am-2am. AmEx/MC/V.) A favorite among locals and one of the only restaurants in town open on Sundays, **Ancora ❸**, Juriciceva 7, offers large portions of delicious seafood, pastas, and brick-oven pizzas. (☎250 20 35. Pizza 590-1360Sit. Seafood 1030-1650Sit. Open M-Th 9am-midnight, F-Sa 9am-1am, Su 10:30am-10:30pm.) **TAKO'S ❸**, Mesarski prehod 3, in a small alley off Glavni trg, serves the freshest salads in town, along with excellent Mexican food. (☎320 38 63. Entrees 900-2600Sit. Open M-W 11am-midnight, Th-Sa 11am-2am, Su noon-5pm.) For groceries in the center, head to **Mercator**, Partizanska 7 (open M-F 7am-7pm, Sa 7am-1pm) or Mlinska 1, near the bus station (open daily 6am-midnight; both AmEx/DC/MC/V). An **Interspar**, Pobreska 18, can be found in the **Europark** shopping mall on the river. (Open M-F 9am-9pm, Sa 8am-9pm, Su 9am-3pm. MC/V.)

◪ SIGHTS. Maribor's historical neighborhood, **Lent**, runs along the Drava River and is flanked by three old, small towers: **Sodni stolp** (Law Court Tower), built in 1310; **Vodni stolp** (Water Tower); and **Židovski stolp** (Jewish Tower), home to a small art gallery with surrealistic modern pieces (open M-F 10am-7pm, Sa 10am-1pm). Cross Koroška c. from Glavni trg and take the stairs next to Stari Most down to the river. Face the water and go left to reach Vodni stolp, which used to be the city's major wine cellar. Just up from Vodni stolp is Židovski trg. The **synagogue** dates from the 14th century. (Open M-F 7:30am-2:30pm. Free.) Facing the river down Dravška ul. **Stara Trta**, a 400-year-old hanging vine still produces a red wine called Žametna Črnina (Black Velvet), which is only distributed in small bottles as gifts for special visitors to Maribor. Glavni trg centers on the elaborate **Plague Memorial**, built in 1743 to commemorate the 1679 epidemic. Up from Grajski trg on ul. Heroja Tomšiča 5, the **Maribor National Liberation Museum** (Muzej Narodne Osvoboditve Maribor) commemorates the city's struggle against Nazi occupation during WWII and contains an exhibit on the Allied bombing of the city. (☎221 16 71. Open M-F 8am-6pm, Sa 9am-noon. 300Sit, students 200Sit.) To sample some of the Štajerska region's best wines, head to **Vinag**, Trg Svobode 3, a wine cellar with a very knowledgeable staff. (☎220 81 13; www.vinag.si. Open M-F 7:30am-7pm, Sa 8am-1pm. Call ahead for cellar tours. AmEx/MC/V.)

◪ ◪ NIGHTLIFE AND FESTIVALS. Most nightlife is concentrated in the old **Lent** neighborhood, where lively cafes line the waterfront. **Bongo's Latin Club**, next door to TAKOS (see **Accommodations and Food**), puts a little fire into the evening with music, salsa, and a lot of tequila. (Sangria 400Sit. Mixed drinks 400-1000Sit. Open F-Sa 11am-2am.) Cuban-themed **Cantente**, Pariške Komune 37, pours the best mixed drinks in town in a red-lit underground cafe. (☎331 29 89; www.cantante.net. Mixed drinks 550-1250Sit. Open M-Th 7am-midnight, F 7am-2am, Sa 9am-2am, Su noon-midnight.) Hang out with the university crowd at **Štuk**, Gosposvetska c. 83, Maribor's most popular disco. (☎228 56 30; www.gaudeamus.si/stuk. *Union* 300Sit. Open M-Tu 8am-2am, W-F 8am-4am, Sa 4:30pm-4am, Su 4:30pm-midnight. Closed mid-July to mid-Aug.) **Kolosej** cinema, on the river at Blagana, shows English-language Hollywood films. (☎230 14 40; www.kolosej.si. 900Sit.) From late June to early July, Maribor's historical waterfront neighborhood explodes in the **Lent Festival**. Theater, dance, and outdoor jazz and folk concerts take place virtually nonstop for 17 days. (Info and tickets ☎229 40 00.) The mid-September **International Chamber Music Festival** features classical concerts in Narodni Dom Maribor, ul. Kneza Koclja 9. (Info ☎229 40 07; www.nd-mb.si.)

MARIBORSKO POHORJE

Just a 20min. bus and stunning cable-car ride from the center of Maribor, the Pohorje hills are an outdoor adventurer's haven. Lively year-round, the steep mountains host intense skiing during the winter, and their numerous trails and footpaths make for excellent biking and trekking during the warmer months. Whether you're passing through on a short hike or enjoying a full ski weekend, Pohorje is a peaceful respite from the urban bustle of Maribor. **Bolfenk,** Pohorje's gateway to the wilderness, centers on picturesque stucco **Bolfenk Church.** To take full advantage of the footpaths that criss-cross the mountains, pick up a **free trail map** at the church. For a short but scenic **hike** (2.5km), turn right out of the Bolfenk Church and follow the gravel road as it forks up the hill. The trail winds around to the **lookout tower** Razelinski stolp, which provides a panoramic view of the Štajerska valley, before leading to the mysterious black waters of the **waterfall** Slap Skalca. In summer, you can also explore the hills by **horseback** (2200Sit per hr.), **bicycle** (550-1400Sit per hr.), or **summer toboggan** (1500Sit per hr.), a contraption that resembles a skateboard with a seat on it. All are available at kiosks directly below the gondola terminal at Hotel Bellevue. From December to March, Pohorje boasts some of Štajerska's most popular **skiing.** The best slopes are just above Bolfenk, accessible by **chairlift** from the village center. For information, contact Sportni Center Pohorje, Mladinska ul. 29. (☎220 88 25. Daily pass 4500Sit; skis 1800-3000Sit per day; snowboards 4000Sit per day.) The Bolfenk Church houses the area's only **museum,** which features exhibits on the history of Pohorje and a small archaeological collection. (☎603 42 11; www.pohorje.org. Open May-June W-F 10:30am-3:30pm, Sa-Su 9:30am-4:30pm; July-Aug. W-Su 9:30am-5:30pm. Free.)

To reach Pohorje, take local bus #6 from the main station outside the train station in Maribor to the last stop, Vzpenjača. A **free bus map** is available at the Maribor tourist office. From the terminus, a **gondola** runs up the mountain to Pohorje. (Gondola open daily 8am-10pm. Round-trip 1500Sit, students 1200Sit.) Because food and accommodations in Pohorje are extremely limited and other tourist services are virtually nonexistent, the most comfortable and economical way to experience the hills is to commute from Maribor, where restaurants, rooms, and bars abound. If proximity to the slopes is your top priority, choose among a small number of **private apartments** (from 4000Sit per person) on the hill.

PTUJ

From its beginnings as the Roman town of Poetovio, Ptuj's (puh-TOO-ee; pop. 19,000) rich winemaking tradition has kept it thriving through the centuries. To reach the beautiful ■**Ptuj Castle,** head up the hill from Slovenski trg along Grajska. The current fortress dates from 1549, but settlers have occupied its hillsides since 3000 BC. The exquisite structure is one of the best preserved in Slovenia and contains an impressive collection of Gothic and Baroque art, musical instruments, and festive **Kurent** (carnival spirit) costumes. (☎748 03 60. Open May-June 15 M-F 9am-6pm; July-Aug. M-F 9am-6pm, Sa-Su 9am-8pm; Oct. 16-April M-F 9am-5pm. 700Sit, students 400Sit. Guide 200/150Sit.) Down the hill, on the opposite side of the castle, is the 13th-century **Dominican Monastery,**

Muzejski trg 1, which holds prehistoric and Roman finds from the Ptuj area. (☎ 748 03 60. Open Apr. 15-Dec. 1 M-F 10am-5pm. 700Sit, students 400Sit.) Ptuj's most famous celebration is **Kurent Carnival,** which takes place in late winter, from Candlemas to Ash Wednesday. Dancing along the streets, the Kurents don sheepskins and headpieces to chase away the evil spirits of winter and beckon spring. ◪**Gostilna Amadeus ❷,** Prešernova 36, across from the library, offers traditional Slovenian entrees. The *štruklji* (dumplings with cheese filling; 700-800Sit) are phenomenal. (☎ 771 70 51. Entrees 700-2200Sit. Open M-Th noon-10pm, F-Sa noon-11pm, Su noon-4pm. AmEx/MC/V.)

Reach Ptuj from Maribor by **bus** (50min., 12 per day, 790Sit). The heart of Ptuj is **Slovenski trg.** To get there from the bus station, turn right into the Mercator shopping complex, go straight through the parking lot, and turn left on Trstenjakova. Turn right on Ulica h. Lacka, which opens into the main square, Mesti Trg. Continue straight to Slovenski trg. The **tourist office,** Slovenski trg 3, offers free **maps** of town. (☎ 779 60 11. Open M-F 8am-6pm, Sa 8am-noon and 3-6pm, Su 10am-1pm.)

UKRAINE (УКРАЇНА)

In late 2004, Ukraine's Orange Revolution won international fame for the country. New President Viktor Yushchenko and his administration have since enacted important reforms, like firing the notoriously corrupt traffic police en masse. From a tourist's perspective, Ukraine is changing fast, and for the better. However, plenty of work remains to be done, and Ukraine can be frustrating to navigate. Don't be surprised if a desk clerk and a website provide two different prices for a room, and don't expect anyone outside Kyiv to speak much English. For those who look past such inconveniences, however, Ukraine will prove to be a beautiful, diverse, and culturally rich treasure.

DISCOVER UKRAINE: SUGGESTED ITINERARIES

THREE DAYS Stick to **Kyiv** (p. 697), the epicenter of the Orange Revolution. Check out **Independence Square,** stop by **Shevchenko Park** to enjoy authentic Ukrainian cuisine at **O'Panas** (p. 704), and contemplate your mortality among the mummified monks of the **Kyiv-Cave Monastery** (p. 707).

ONE WEEK After three days in **Kyiv,** take a 9-10hr. train to **Lviv** (3 days; p. 726), the cultural capital of Ukraine. Don't miss the magnificent wooden church at the **Open-Air Museum of Folk Architecture and Rural Life** (p. 732), and make sure to experience high culture for cheap at the **Theater of Opera and Ballet.**

BEST OF UKRAINE, THREE WEEKS Begin with five days in **Kyiv,** spend another four in **Lviv,** then head to **Yaremche** (3 days; p. 737) to revel in the sweet Carpathian air and hike **Mt. Hoverla,** the tallest point in Ukraine. Next hit **Odessa** (4 days; p. 710), where you should visit the **Catacombs** that hid Ukrainian partisans during WWII (p. 714). Spend the rest of your time by the **Black Sea** in **Crimea,** heading first to **Sevastopol** (2 days; p. 723). If you get tired of the beach, visit the ruins at **Chersonesus** (p. 726). Finish in **Yalta** (3 days; p. 718), making sure to sample the stores at nearby **Massandra Winery** (p. 722). Expect a full day of travel between each leg.

ESSENTIALS

WHEN TO GO

Ukraine is a huge country with a diverse climate. Things heat up from June to August in Odessa and Crimea, which are just barely subtropical. It is best to reserve in advance at these times. Kyiv enjoys a moderate climate, while the more mountainous west remains cool even in summer. Winter tourism is popular in the Carpathians, but spring and summer are probably the best times to visit the country. Book accommodations early around the May 1 holiday.

DOCUMENTS AND FORMALITIES

EMBASSIES AND CONSULATES. Foreign embassies to Ukraine are in Kyiv (p. 697). For Ukrainian embassies and consulates at home, contact: **Australia,** Level 12, St. George Centre, 60 Marcus Clarke St., Canberra ACT 2601 (☎02 6230 5789; www.ukremb.info); **Canada,** 310 Somerset St., Ottawa, ON, K2P 0J9 (☎613-230-

FACTS AND FIGURES

Official Name: Ukraine.

Capital: Kyiv.

Major Cities: Lviv, Odessa, Sevastopol, Simferopol, Yalta.

Population: 47,430,000.

Land Area: 603,700 sq. km.

Time Zone: GMT + 2.

Language: Ukrainian.

Religions: Ukrainian Orthodox (29%), Orthodox (16%), Ukrainian Greek Catholic (6%), other (48%).

ENTRANCE REQUIREMENTS

Passport: Required for all travelers.

Visa: Not required for citizens of Canada or EU countries, nor US citizens returning to Ukraine, but mandatory for all other citizens of the US and for citizens of Australia, and New Zealand.

Letter of Invitation: Required for citizens of Australia and New Zealand.

Inoculations: Recommended up-to-date on DTaP (diphtheria, tetanus, and pertussis), Hepatitis A, Hepatitis B, MMR (measles, mumps, and rubella), Polio booster, and Typhoid.

Work Permit: Required of all foreigners planning to work in Ukraine.

Driving Permit: Required for all those planning to drive in Ukraine.

2400; www.infoukes.com/ukremb); **UK,** 60 Holland Park, London W11 3SJ (☎020 7727 6312, consular/visas ☎020 7243 8923; www.ukremb.org.uk); **US,** 3350 M St., NW, Washington, D.C. 20007 (☎202-333-0606; www.ukraineinfo.us).

VISA AND ENTRY INFORMATION. Ukraine's visa requirements changed rapidly in 2005 and are likely to continue to do so as the new government works to encourage tourism. As of August 2005, a **visa** is no longer required of US citizens revisiting Ukraine after an absence of less than six months. Visas are no longer required of Canadian citizens or citzens of the EU. All visas are valid for 90 days, and all visa-free regimes are applicable for stays of up to 90 days.

Single-entry visas cost US$100, double-entry US$110, multiple-entry US$165. Three business-day rush service costs US$200, double-entry US$220; multiple-entry US$330; there is no next-day service. Transit visas cost an additional US$10, or US$20 for rush service. The visa fee is waived for children under 16 years of age and American students with proper documents. Submit a completed visa application, your passport, one passport-size photo, and payment by money order. US citizens can find applications and plenty of useful information at www.ukraineinfo.us. Citizens of Australia and New Zealand require a letter of invitation, but citizens of Canada, the EU, and the US do not. Perplexingly, an invitation is required even when a "letter of invitation" is not; such invitations are available on request from info@hihostels.com.ua. Make sure to allow plenty of time for processing and to fill out the application thoroughly: some consulates will simply return an application to you if it contains any problems. Wherever the application asks for a name, supply an address and telephone number as well. You can extend your visa in Ukraine, at the OVYR office in Kyiv.

When proceeding through **customs** you will be required to declare all cash, traveler's checks, and jewelry regardless of value. Check with your country's Ukrainian embassy for more restrictions. **Do not lose the paper given to you when entering the country to supplement your visas.** The **Office of Visas and Registration** (ОВИР; OVYR)—in Kyiv at bul. Tarasa Shevchenka 34, or at police stations in smaller cities—extends visas. Make sure to carry your passport and visa at all times.

TOURIST SERVICES AND MONEY

Lviv's tourist office is extremely helpful, but is unfortunately the only official tourist office in Ukraine. There is no state-run tourist office. The remains of the Soviet giant **Intourist** have offices in hotels, but staff usually don't speak English. They're used to dealing with groups, to whom they sell "excursion" packages to nearby sights. Local travel agencies can be helpful, but staff rarely speak English and will be delighted to lighten your wallet. The Ukrainian unit of currency is the **hryvnya** (hv). *Obmin Valyut* (Обмшн Валют) kiosks in most cities offer the best rates for **currency exchange.** **Traveler's checks** can be changed into dollars for small commissions in many cities. **ATMs** are everywhere. Most banks will give Mastercard and Visa **cash advances** for a high commission. The lobbies of fancier hotels usually exchange US dollars at lousy rates. **Private money changers** lurk near kiosks, ready with brilliant schemes for scamming you. **Exchanging money with them is illegal.**

HRYVNY (HV)	AUS$1 = 3.79HV	1HV = AUS$0.26
	CDN$1 = 4.10HV	1HV = CDN$0.24
	EUR€1 = 6.10HV	1HV = EUR€0.16
	NZ$1 = 3.47HV	1HV = NZ$0.29
	UK£1 = 8.99HV	1HV = UK£0.11
	US$1 = 4.96HV	1HV = US$0.20

HEALTH AND SAFETY

EMERGENCY **Police: ☎02. Ambulance: ☎03. Fire: ☎01.**

Hospital facilities in Ukraine are limited and do not meet American or Western European standards. Patients may be required to supply their own medical supplies (e.g., bandages). You are required to have medical insurance to receive health care, but be prepared to front the bill yourself. When in doubt, get to your embassy, and they will find you adequate care or fly you out of the country; medical evacuations to Western Europe cost US$25,000 and upwards of US$50,000 to the US. **Boil all water** or learn to love brushing your teeth with soda water. Peel or wash **fruits and vegetables** from open markets. Meat purchased at public markets should be checked carefully and cooked thoroughly; refrigeration is infrequent and insects run rampant. Avoid the tasty-looking hunks of meat for sale out of buckets on the Kyiv metro. Embassy officials declare that Chernobyl-related **radiation** poses minimal risk to short-term travelers. Public restrooms range from disgusting to frightening. **Pay toilets** (платні; platni) are cleaner and might provide toilet paper, but bring your own anyway. **Pharmacies** (Аптеки; Apteky) are quite common and carry basic Western products. Aspirin is the only painkiller on hand, but plenty of cold remedies and bandages are available. Anything more complicated should be brought from home. Sanitary napkins (гігіенчні пакети; hihienchni pakety), condoms (презервативи; prezervativy), and tampons (прокладки, prokladky; or in Russian, тампон, pronounced "tampon" with a long "o") are sometimes sold at kiosks. While Ukraine is politically stable, it is poor. Pickpocketing and wallet scams are the most common **crimes;** instances of armed robbery and assault have been reported. Do not accept drinks from strangers, as this could result in your being drugged and robbed. Credit-card and ATM fraud are endemic; it is wiser not to use credit or ATM cards while in Ukraine. Be careful when crossing the street—drivers do not stop for pedestrians. It's wise to **register** with your embassy once you get to Ukraine.

Women traveling alone will be addressed by men on the street, in restaurants, and pretty much anywhere they go, but usually will be safe beyond that. Ukrainian women rarely go to restaurants alone, so expect to feel conspicuous if you do. Women may request to ride in female-only compartments during long train rides, though most do not. Although non-Caucasians may experience **discrimination,** the biggest problems stem from the militia, which frequently stops people whom it suspects to be non-Slavic. **Disabled** travelers may encounter some difficulty, as few locations are wheelchair accessible. **Homosexuality** is not yet accepted in Ukraine; discretion is advised.

TRANSPORTATION

BY PLANE. Ukraine is an expensive place to fly to, and few budget airlines run out of the country. Ground transportation tends to be safer and more pleasant, but can take a long time to traverse the great distances between cities. If you need to get somewhere quickly, there are several options. Air Ukraine flies to Kyiv, Lviv, and Odessa from many European capitals. Aerosvit, Air France, ČSA, Delta, Lufthansa, LOT, Malév, and SAS fly to Kyiv.

BY TRAIN. Trains run frequently and are the best way to travel. They usually run overnight and are timed to arrive in the morning. While *Let's Go* discourages the use of night trains, Ukraine's system is generally safe. When coming from a nonex-Soviet country, expect a two-hour stop at the border. When purchasing train tickets, you must present a passport, driver's license, or student ID. Once on board, you must present both your ticket and ID to the *konduktor*. On most Ukrainian trains, there are three classes: плацкарт, or *platskart*, where you'll be crammed in with *babushki* and baskets of strawberries; купе, or *kupe*, a clean, more private, four-person compartment; and first class, referred to as CB, or *SV*, which is twice as roomy and expensive as *kupe*. Unless you're determined to live like a local, pay the extra two dollars for *kupe*. The *kasa* will sell you a *kupe* seat unless you say otherwise. Except in larger cities, where platform numbers are posted on the electronic board, the only way to figure out which platform your train leaves from is by listening to the distorted announcement. In large cities, trains arrive well before they are scheduled to depart, so you'll have a few min. to show your ticket to cashiers or fellow passengers and ask "plaht-FORM-ah?"

BY BUS. Buses cost about the same as trains, but are often much shabbier. For long distances, the train is usually more comfortable. One exception is AutoLux (АвтоЛюкс), which runs buses with A/C, snacks, and movies. Bus schedules are generally reliable, but low demand sometimes causes cancellations. Buy tickets at the *kasa* (ticket office); if they're sold out, try going directly to the driver, who might just magically find a seat and pocket the money. Navigating the bus system can be tough for those who do not speak Ukrainian or Russian.

BY TAXI AND BY THUMB. Taxi drivers love to rip off foreigners, so negotiate the price beforehand. In major urban areas road conditions are fair; in rural areas roads are poor and are not well lit. *Let's Go* does not recommend hitchhiking. Few Ukrainians hitchhike, but those who do hold a sign with their desired destination or just wave an outstretched hand.

KEEPING IN TOUCH

PHONE CODES	**Country code:** 380. **International dialing prefix:** 00. From outside Ukraine, dial int'l dialing prefix (see inside back cover) + 380 + city code + local number. Within Ukraine, dial 8 + city code + number. Within a single city, simply dial the local number.

Internet cafes can be found in every major city and typically charge 3-7hv per hour of use. **Telephones** are stumbling toward modernity. The easiest way to make international call is with **Utel**. Buy a Utel phonecard (sold at most Utel phone locations) and dial the number of your international operator (counted as a local call; see the inside back cover). International access codes include: **AT&T Direct** (☎8 100 11); **Canada Direct** (☎8 100 17); and **MCI WorldPhone** (☎8 100 13). Alternatively, call at the central telephone office—estimate how long your call will take, pay at the counter, and they'll direct you to a booth. Calling can be expensive, but you can purchase a 30min. international calling card for 15hv. Local calls from gray payphones generally cost 10-30hv. For an English-speaking operator, dial ☎8192. **Mail** is cheap and reliable, taking about 8-10 days to reach North America. Sending a letter internationally costs 3.34hv. Mail can be received through **Poste Restante** (до запитання; do zapytannya). Address envelopes as follows: Jason (First name) CAMPBELL (LAST NAME), до запитання Хрещатик 22 (post office address), 01 001 (postal code) Київ (city), UKRAINE.

ACCOMMODATIONS AND CAMPING

UKRAINE	❶	❷	❸	❹	❺
ACCOMMODATIONS	under 55hv under €9 under US$11	55-105hv €9-17 US$11-21	106-266hv €18-45 US$22-54	267-480hv €46-79 US$55-96	over 480hv over €79 over US$96

Not all **hotels** accept foreigners, and those that do often charge them many times more than Ukrainians. Though room prices in Kyiv are astronomical, singles run anywhere from 50-90hv in the rest of the country. Youth **hostels** are practically non-existent in Ukraine, though a few can be found in Lviv, Kyiv, and Yalta; budget accommodations are usually in unrenovated Soviet-era buildings. More expensive lodgings aren't necessarily nicer. In some hotels women lodging alone may be mistaken for prostitutes. Standard hotel rooms include TVs, phones, and refrigerators. You will be given a *vizitka* (hotel card) to show to the hall monitor *(dezhurnaya)* to get a key; return it upon leaving. **Hot water** is rare—ask before checking in. **Private rooms** are the best bargain and run 20-50hv. They can be arranged through overseas agencies or bargained for at the train station. Most cities have a **camping** facilites—usually a remote spot with trailers. Camping outside designated areas is illegal, and enforcement is merciless.

FOOD AND DRINK

UKRAINE	❶	❷	❸	❹	❺
FOOD	under 11hv under €2 under US$2	11-27hv €2-4 US$2-5	28-54hv €5-10 US$6-12	55-105hv €11-17 US$13-21	over 105hv over €17 over US$21

New, fancy restaurants accommodate tourists and the few Ukrainians who can afford these restaurants, while *stolovayas* (cafeterias), dying bastions of the Soviet Union, serve cheap, hot food. Pierogi-like dumplings called *vavenyky* are ubiquitous and delicious. **Vegetarians** beware: meat has a tendency to show up in so-called "vegetarian" dishes. Finding **kosher** foods can be daunting, but it helps to eat non-meat items. Fruits and veggies are sold at **markets;** bring your own bag. **State food stores** are classified by content: *hastronom* (packaged goods); *moloko* (milk products); *ovochi-frukty* (fruits and vegetables); *myaso* (meat); *khlib* (bread); *kolbasy* (sausage); and *ryba* (fish). Throughout the country, *Kvas* is a popular, nonalcoholic fermented-bread drink. Grocery stores are often simply labeled *mahazyn* (store).

LIFE AND TIMES

HISTORY

PREHISTORY AND KYIVAN RUS. The ancestors of modern Ukrainians, known as **Slavs,** established the first Kyiv settlement by the 7th century AD. Recorded Ukrainian history begins with the Kyivan Rus dynasty, founded by **Oleh of Novgorod** in 882. Oleh and the Rus elite were Scandanavian Varangians who were quickly assimilated into the local Slavic culture. The empire eventually stretched as far north as modern St. Petersburg, reaching its greatest size under **Prince Volodymyr the Great.** In 988, Volodymyr converted to Christianity; the new religion ushered in a written language and various forms of Byzantine culture. Volodymyr's son **Yaroslav** produced the Slavic world's first codified laws and promoted the arts.

SHIFTING BORDERS. Genghis Khan invaded Ukraine in the 1230s; his grandson Batu sacked Kyiv in 1240. By the mid-14th century, Ukraine proper was divided among the **Mongols,** the **Grand Duchy of Lithuania,** and the **Kingdom of Poland.** Mongolian rule was to persist as late as 1783 in Crimea. Most of Ukraine soon came directly under Polish rule, and the Polish and Ukrainian nobles forced the Ukrainian peasantry into serfdom. The **1596 Union of Brest-Litovsk** folded Orthodox Ukrainians into the Catholic flock while allowing them to retain traditional liturgy. A fruitless attempt to diffuse growing tension between members of Orthodox and Catholic churches, the agreement ultimately led to violence.

THE COSSACKS. In the 15th century, escaped serfs and outcasts gathered on Ukraine's southern frontier. Known as Cossacks (after a Turkish word for "freemen"), they formed a democratic, fiercely militaristic society. Poland valued the Cossacks for the protection they offered from Tatars, Turks, and Muscovites, but considered them a threat during peace time. Such suspicions were well founded: a rebellion led by Cossack commander **Bohdan Khmelnytsky** in 1648 escalated into a full-blown war with Poland. Khmelnytsky's forces were initially successful, but after subsequent defeat, Khmelnytsky entered into a dissatisfying alliance with Muscovy. Following a disintegration of Cossack organization known as "The Ruin," the Ukraine of 1667 again found itself divided among foreign powers. Russia won everything east of the Dnipr, including Kyiv and Odessa, while the west went to Poland. The east maintained Cossack autonomy for about a century. By 1775, Catherine II had abolished what little power the Cossacks had left.

RUSSIA RUSHES IN. With the decline of Polish power, Western Ukraine fell under the authority of Hapsburg Austria in 1772; Russia absorbed the rest of Ukraine by 1795. Jews were restricted to the territory that Poland had formerly controlled. Numerous pogroms, beginning in 1781, worsened the oppression of Jews. Reacting against harsh conditions instituted by the government of Tsar Alexander II, which included bans that affected teaching and publishing, a national movement sprung up in the 1840s. Its major figure was the poet-painter **Taras Shevchenko,** who sought to revitalize the Ukrainian language and establish a democratic state. For his efforts, Shevchenko was arrested and exiled to Central Asia. Conditions improved with the 1905 revolution in Russia: the ban on publishing was dropped, and Ukrainians briefly enjoyed some representation in the Duma.

CLAIMING UKRAINE. Caught between two warring nations, Ukraine suffered heavy casualities in WWI. Ukraine declared its independence in 1918, but the **Bolsheviks** set up a rival government in Kharkiv and seized complete power during the Civil War (1918-20). Chaos ensued as one group after another assumed control of Kyiv. Following the war, Ukraine again lay divided: Poland, Czechoslovakia, and Romania each laid claims to western territory, while the eastern area was reorganized as the Ukrainian Soviet Socialist Republic. With the rise of Joseph Stalin came the beginning of a long series of tragedies. The new dictator deported nearly 100,000 Ukrainian families to Siberia and Kazakhstan, engineered a 1932-33 famine that claimed millions of lives, and attempted to eradicate Ukrainian culture. Ukrainians outside of the Soviet Union fared better but still chafed at their lack of autonomy; thus many welcomed the Nazis as liberators. When the brutality of the Nazi regime became apparent, partisan cells sprung up in western and northern Ukraine. The country suffered enormous destruction during the war; millions of lives and as much as 40% of national wealth were lost.

BACK TO THE USSR. The last years of Stalin's regime brought another devastating famine and further Russification. Matters improved under **Nikita Khrushchev,** but attacks on Ukrainian culture intensified during the 1970s. In 1986, the worst nuclear accident in history struck **Chernobyl,** close to Kyiv. Nationalist movements grew during the reign of **Mikhail Gorbachev,** and in a 1991 referendum, more than 90% of voters chose to declare independence from the Soviet Union.

TODAY

The new government struggled to escape economic problems and corruption. Public outcry arose during President **Leonid Kuchma's** second term, amidst widespread allegations that he was behind the 2001 murder of journalist Grigory Gongadze. In November 2004, **Viktor Yanukovich,** the presidential candidate endorsed by Kuchma and Russian President Vladmir Putin, was declared the winner in a rigged election. Protests erupted across the country, and the Supreme Court mandated an unprecedented additional runoff between Yanukovich and his opponent, reform candidate **Viktor Yushchenko.** Yushchenko soundly won the second round, effectively pulling off a nonviolent "Orange Revolution," named for the color that Yushchenko had chosen to represent his campaign. Yushchenko is currently the president of Ukraine, and he named the stylish **Yulia Tymoshenko** as prime minister.

PEOPLE AND CULTURE

DEMOGRAPHICS. A 78% majority of the population of Ukraine is ethnically **Ukrainian; 17%** is **Russian.** Russians are heavily concentrated in the east and south. No one religious group dominates the area, though various **Orthodox** churches incorporate 38% of the population. In western Ukraine, the **Roman Catholic** church predominates.

LANGUAGE. Traveling in Ukraine is much easier if you know some **Ukrainian** or **Russian.** Ukrainian is an East Slavic language written in the Cyrillic alphabet. In Kyiv, Odessa, and Crimea, Russian is more commonly spoken than Ukrainian (although all official signs are in Ukrainian). If you're trying to get by with Russian in western Ukraine, you may run into some difficulty: everyone understands Russian, but some people will answer in Ukrainian out of habit or nationalist sentiment. Try to preface what you say with "I'm sorry, I don't speak Ukrainian." This simple gesture can make a big difference. *Let's Go* provides city names in Ukrainian for Kyiv and western Ukraine, while Russian names are used for Crimea and Odessa. Street names follow a similar convention.

CUSTOMS AND ETIQUETTE. A rudimentary knowledge of a few customs can make or break a trip to Ukraine. Several **gestures** that are considered positive in other cultures have a different meaning in Ukraine. The "OK" sign, with the thumb and forefinger touching each other and forming a circle, can be considered crude. The same goes for a shaken fist and a pointed index finger. At the Ukrainian dinner table, hands are usually kept on the table. **Tipping** in restaurants is minimal; never more than 10%. When taking a taxi, bargain the price down and do not give a tip. When on trains, give up seats to the elderly and women with children. In churches, men should wear long pants, and women should cover their heads and shoulders.

GIVING BACK

PLAY THERAPY

Ukrainian orphanages are notoriously underfunded and understaffed. Kids spend much of their time idle, stuck inside undecorated concrete buildings. The situation is even worse for those who ost their mothers to AIDS or were abandoned by mothers who were at risk of HIV/AIDS. These children not only must overcome the stigma of being orphaned, but also must deal with the stigmas associated with HIV/AIDS.

Marianna Peipon, an American expat, works with Ukraine Medical Outreach to recruit volunteers and engage some ofthese orphans in "play therapy." "We feed 'em, hold'em, and just do the things the overworked staff is often not able to do," explains Marianna.

Ukraine Medical Outreach, which started its work in Kyiv in 2001, primarily provides medical services and education, but in 2003, Marianna came across 7 AIDS orphans in a hospital—their orphanage was, and still is, under renovation—and has been visiting them ever since. Today, the number of AIDS orphans at the hospital has increased to 24 and there is an even greater need for volunteers to devote a few hours to helping with "play therapy," and to provide attention to these orphaned kids.

If you're interested in lending a hand, contact Marianna Peipon of Ukraine Medical Outreach at www.ukrainemedicaloutreach.org or by phone at ☎ 8 066 746 3550.

THE ARTS

LITERATURE. National literature first flowered in the 19th century. **Taras Shevchenko,** Ukraine's most revered literary figure, emerged from the Romantic movement of this era to ignite nationalist fervor with his poetry. A period of realism gave rise to the work of **Ivano Franko,** who wrote drama, poetry, and short stories. The early 20th century saw an outburst of artistic activity. Major literary movements overtook one another rapidly: the Modernism of **Lesya Ukrainka** gave way to Realism in prose and Symbolism in verse. Another new movement, Futurism, inspired one of Ukraine's greatest poets, **Mykola Bazhan.** Mikhail Bulkagov, author of the famous satire, *The Master and Margarita,* hailed from Kyiv.

MUSIC. In addition to a history of church **choral music,** Ukraine boasts a rich **folkloric tradition.** Historical songs called *dumy* are sung a capella or feature folk instruments like the *bandura,* similar to a lute, and the *tsymbaly,* a hammered dulcimer. In classical music, Ukraine's most notable pianist is **Sviatoslav Richter** (1915-1997). In 2004, **Ruslana Lyzhichko** won the Eurovision song contest by infusing pop music with folk techniques from the Hutsul people of the Carpathian mountains. As a result, the pan-European contest was held in Kyiv in 2005. (This is one reason for the government's suspension of visa requirements for EU citizens.)

FINE ARTS. Byzantine art had a great influence on early Ukrainian art; mosaics, frescoes, domed buildings, illuminated manuscripts, and above all, iconic paintings mark the centuries between the advent of Christianity and the introduction of more Western forms in the 17th century. Taras Shevchenko's paintings typify the realist trend of the 19th century. Following experimentation wtih avant garde forms during Ukraine's brief independence in the early 20th century, Socialist Realism dominated the Soviet years. Some artists, like photographer **Boris Mikhailov,** managed to subtly critique Soviet oppression.

A delightful folk art form is the Ukrainian easter egg, called **pysanky.** The eggs are painstakingly decorated with beeswax and multiple treatments of dyes; they often feature intricate geometric patterns, and styles differ according to region.

HOLIDAYS AND FESTIVALS

Holidays: New Year's Day (Jan. 1); Orthodox Christmas (Jan. 7); Orthodox New Year (Jan. 14); International Women's Day (Mar. 8); Easter (May 1); Labor Day (May 1-2); Victory Day (May 9); Holy Trinity Day (June 19); Constitution Day (June 28); Independence Day (Aug. 24).

Festivals: One of the most widely celebrated festivals is the **Donetsk Jazz Festival,** usually held in March. The conclusion of the 20th century brought the **Chervona Ruta Festival,** which occurs in different Ukrainian cities each year, celebrating both modern Ukrainian pop and traditional music. The **Molodist Kyiv International Film Festival,** held in the last week of October, sets the stage for student films and film debuts.

ADDITIONAL RESOURCES

Borderland: A Journey Through the History of Ukraine, by Anna Reid (2000). Provides a general overview of Ukrainian history.

Everything Is Illuminated, by Jonathan Safran Foer (2002). The innovative, best-selling novel about a young Jewish man who travels to Ukraine in an attempt to find the young woman who saved his grandfather during the Holocaust.

Execution by Hunger: The Hidden Holocaust, by Miron Dolot (1987). A riveting memoir of Stalin's forced collectivization of agriculture.

Journey to Chernobyl: Encounters in a Radioactive Zone, by Glenn Cheney (1995). A depiction of Ukraine's most recent national tragedy.

KYIV (КИЇВ)

☎(80)44

The Kyivan Rus empire was born here, and the city has stood as a social and economic center for more than a millennium. No stranger to foreign control, Kyiv weathered a 20th century that saw it razed by the Nazi army only to be rebuilt with extravagant Stalinist pomp by the Soviets. Since Ukraine gained its independence from the USSR in 1991, Kyiv has reemerged as a proud capital and recently gained international acclaim for being the epicenter of the Orange Revolution. The streets buzz with optimistic energy, even as the cost of living rises and the new government struggles to institute promised reforms.

◼ INTERCITY TRANSPORTATION

Flights: Boryspil International Airport (Бориспіль; ☎490 47 77), 30km southeast of the capital. **Polit** (Політ; ☎296 73 67), just to the right of the main entrance, sends buses to Ploscha Peremohi and the train station. Buy tickets on board (every 30-60min., 20hv). A taxi to the center costs 70-100hv. Negotiate with drivers near the Polit bus stop: those stationed outside customs will take you for a ride.

Trains: Kyiv-Pasazhyrskyy (Київ-Пасажирський), Vokzalna pl. (☎005 or 465 48 95). MR: Vokzalna (Вокзальна). Purchase tickets for domestic trains in the main hall. For international tickets, go to window #40 or 41 in the newest section of the train station, across the tracks. For the *elektrychka* commuter rail (електричка), go to the *Prymiskyy Vokzal* (Приміский Вокзал; Suburban Station) next to the Metro station. A passport is required for the purchase of any train ticket. Information (довідка; dovidka) windows are located in each section of the train station; some stay open 24hr. There is an **Advance Ticket Office** next to Hotel Express at Shevchenka 38. Train tickets can also be purchased at the central bus station at window #9. Trains to: **Lviv** (10hr., 5-6 per day, 50hv); **Odessa** (11hr., 4-5 per day, 60hv); **Sevastopol** (20hr., 2 per day, 54hv); **Bratislava, SLK** (18hr., 1 per day, 440hv); **Budapest, HUN** (24hr., 1 per day, 550hv); **Moscow, RUS** (15-17hr., 12-15 per day, 150hv); **Prague, CZR** (35hr., 1 per day, 540hv); **Warsaw, POL** (17hr., 2 per day, 350hv).

Buses: Tsentralnyy Avtovokzal (Центральний Автовокзал), Moskovska pl. 3 (Московська; ☎525 57 74 or 527 99 86), 10min. from MB: Libidska. Window #10 sells international tickets. To: **Lviv** (10hr., 4 per day, 53hv) and **Odessa** (8-10hr., 8 per day, 55-60hv); **Moscow, RUS** (20hr., 2 per day, 96-115hv), and **Prague, CZR** (28hr.; 1 per day Tu, Th-F, and Su; 420hv). **Avtolyuks** (Автолюкс; ☎451 86 28; www.autolux.ua), left of the main entrance, provides more comfortable domestic buses at a slightly higher price. To **Lviv** (8hr., 2 per day, 63hv) and **Odessa** (10hr., 4 per day, 70hv). Smaller bus stations are located throughout the city:

Dachna (Дачна), pr. Peremohy 142 (Перемоги; ☎424 15 03).

Darnitsya (Дарниця), pr. Haharyna 1 (Гагарина; ☎559 46 18).

Pivdenna (Південна), pr. Akademika Hlushkova 3 (Академіка Глушкова; ☎257 40 04).

Podil (Поділ), Nizhniy Val 15a (Нижній Вал; ☎417 32 15).

Polissya (Полісся), pl. Shevchenka (Шевченка; ☎430 35 54).

Vydubychi (Видубичі), Haberezhno-Pecherska 10 (Набережно Печерска; ☎524 21 82).

◼ ORIENTATION

Most of Kyiv's attractions and services lie on the west bank of the **Dniper River** (Дніпро; Dnipro). The **train station**, at MR: Vokzalna (Вокзальна) on the western edge of the city center, is three Metro stops from **Khreshchatyk** (Хрещатик), Kyiv's main avenue. Khreshchatyk runs from **Bessarabska Ploshcha** (Бессарабська Площа) to **European Square** (Європейська Площа; Evropeyska Ploshcha) through **Independence Square**

UKRAINE

Mezhyhirsk

PODI[L]

Kostyantynivska vul.

Lukianivska vul.

Lukianivska vul.

Solyana

Olehivska

Olehivska vul.

Hlybochytska vul.

vul. Nyzhniy Val

vul. Verkhniy Val

Vozdvyzhens'ka vul.

St. Andrew's Church

Mikhail Bulgakov's House

Andriyivsky

Petryvska vul.

Kosohirny prov.

Kududravskyy uzviz

Smyrnova-Lastochkina

Kozhumyatska

Bekhterevskyy

Kudriavska vul.

Kudryavska vul.

Nesterivskyy

Kiyanivskyy

National Museum of Ukrainian History

Desiatynny prov.

vul. Mykoly Pymonenka

Bekhterevskyy pr.

US

Velyka Zhitomirska vul.

UPPER CITY

TO 3, AMERICAN MEDICAL CENTER

vul. Artema

Observatorna vul.

LVIVSKA PLOSHCHA

Strileltska vul.

SOFIYIRSKYY PLOSHCHA

St. Sofia's Monastery

Heorhiivskyy prov.

Canada

vul. Yuriya Kotsyubinskoho

vul. Yaroslaviv Val

vul. Reytarska

Central Indoor Market

Chekhovsky prov.

Pavlivska vul.

Hoholivska vul.

vul. Vorovskoho

British Airways

Volodymyrska vul.

TO BABYN YAR

Turhenyevska vul.

vul. Chapayeva

5

vul. Lysenko

6

Dnytrivska vul.

vul. Olesya Honchara

vul. Ivana Franka

ZOLOTI VOROTA

Shevchenka Opera and Ballet

TO 8, UKRANIAN NATIONAL AIRLINES

Circus

Lufthansa

US

Prosp. Peremohy

PLOSHCHA PEREMOHY

vul. Mykhayla Kotsyubinskoho

KLM, LOT, and ČSA Airlines

vul. Khmelnytskoho Bohdana

Aeroflot

Advanced Ticket Sales (Kassy)

11

Volodymyrskyy Cathedral

bul. Tarasa Shevchenka

Shevchenko Museum

Starovokzalna vul.

12

UNIVERSYTET

Delta Airlines

15

Russian Art Museum

Australia

vul. Kominternu

Botanical Gardens

Taras Shevchenko University

Tereshchenkivska

VOKZALNA

vul. Saksahanskoho

Monument to Taras Shevchenko

Khanenko Museum

VOKZALNA PLOSHCHA

vul. Lva Tolstoho

Vul. Lva Tolstoho

vul. Pankivska

PLOSHCHA LVA TOLSTOHO

TO ZHULYANY AIRPORT (12km), RUSSIAN EMBASSY

Tarasivska vul.

TO YANA (100m)

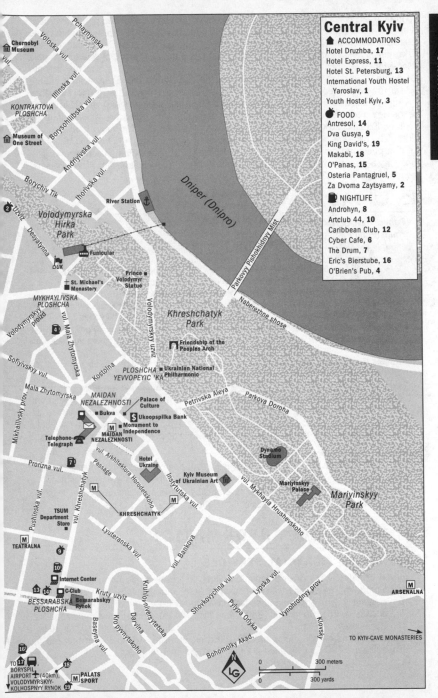

Central Kyiv

ACCOMMODATIONS
Hotel Druzhba, **17**
Hotel Express, **11**
Hotel St. Petersburg, **13**
International Youth Hostel
  Yaroslav, **1**
Youth Hostel Kyiv, **3**

FOOD
Antresol, **14**
Dva Gusya, **9**
King David's, **19**
Makabi, **18**
O'Panas, **15**
Osteria Pantagruel, **5**
Za Dvoma Zaytsyamy, **2**

NIGHTLIFE
Androhyn, **8**
Artclub 44, **10**
Caribbean Club, **12**
Cyber Cafe, **6**
The Drum, **7**
Eric's Bierstube, **16**
O'Brien's Pub, **4**

Chernobyl Museum
Pchaynynska vul.
Voloska vul.
Illinska vul.
Borysohlilbska vul.
KONTRAKTOVA PLOSHCHA
Museum of One Street
Andriyivska vul.
Ihorivska vul.
Borychiv Tik
Uzviz
Desatynna
Volodymyrska Hirka Park
River Station
Dniper (Dnipro)
Funicular
DUK
Prince Volodymyr Statue
St. Michael's Monastery
Volodymyrsky uzviz
MYKHAYLIVSKA PLOSHCHA
Mykhaylivskyy proizd
vul. Mala Zhytomyrska
Volodymyrskyy proizd
Khreshchatyk Park
Friendship of the Peoples Arch
Parkovy Pishokhidnvy Mist
Naberezhne shose
Sofiyivskyy vul.
Kostolna
Mala Zhytomyrska
PLOSHCHA YEVVOPEYIC 'KA
Ukrainian National Philharmonic
MAIDAN NEZALEZHNOSTI
Palace of Culture
Petrivska Aleya
Parkova Doroha
Mikhailivsky prov.
Bukva
Ukoopspilka Bank
Monument to Independence
MAIDAN NEZALEZHNOSTI
Telephone-Telegraph
Prorizna vul.
vul. Arkhitektora Horodetskoho
Passage
Hotel Ukraine
Kyiv Museum of Ukrainian Art
Dynamo Stadium
vul. Mykhayla Hrushevskoho
Mariyinskyy Palace
Mariyinskyy Park
Pushkinska vul.
vul. Khreshchatyk
Instytutska vul.
KHRESHCHATYK
TSUM Department Store
Lyuteranska vul.
vul. Bankova
TEATRALNA
Internet Center
C-Club
BESSARABSKA PLOSHCHA
Bessarabskyy Rynok
Kruty uzviz
Kruhloviuniversytetska
Darvina
Shovkovychna vul.
Pylpa Oriyka
Lypska vul.
Vynohrodnyy prov.
Klovsky
ARSENALNA
TO KYIV-CAVE MONASTERIES
Baseyna vul.
Kropyvnytskoho
Bohomolky Akad.
TO BORYSPIL AIRPORT (40km), VOLODYMYRSKYY-KOLHOSPNYY RYNOK
PALATS SPORT
0   300 meters
0   300 yards

(Майдан Незалежності; Maidan Nezalezhnosti), the city's social and patriotic center. Three blocks uphill from Khreshchatyk is **Volodymyrska** (Володимирська), which runs past the **Ukrainian National Opera** (Національна Опера України; Natsionalna Opera Ukrayiny), **Zoloti Vorota** (Золоті Ворота; the city's ancient gate), and the **St. Sophia Monastery.** The area surrounding the square, known as the **Upper City,** was the first site of ancient settlement in Kyiv. At the end of Volodymyrska, **St. Andrew's Church** (Андріївська Церква; Andriyivska Tserkva) sits atop winding **Andrew's Rise** (Андріївський Узвіз; Andriyivskyy Uzviz), Kyiv's famous historical street. This in turn leads down to the monument-filled **Podil** (Поділ) district. Along the west bank of the Dniper, **Khreshchatyk Park** covers the slope that runs from the city center to the water's edge. The **Kyiv-Cave Monastery** (Киево-Печерська Лавра; Kyivo-Pecherska Lavra), full of churches and museums, is a 10min. walk from MR: Arsenalna (Арсенальна). The territory across the river, around MR: Livoberezhna (Лівобережна; left bank), became a part of Kyiv in 1927 and is now a major residential area.

⌐ LOCAL TRANSPORTATION

Public Transportation: Most public transport runs 6am-midnight, but some buses and *marshrutki* run later.

Metro: 3 intersecting lines—blue (MB), green (MG), and red (MR)—cover the city center, but stops are far apart and the Metro does not reach most residential areas. Purchase tokens (ЖИТОН; zhyton, 0.50hv) at the window (каса; kasa), or from the machines, which accept only 1hv or 2hv notes. "Перехід" (perekhid) indicates a walkway to another station; "вихід у місто" (vykhid u misto) an exit onto the street; and "вхід" (vkhid) an entrance to the Metro.

Buses (автобуси; avtobusy): Stop at each station. Buy tickets (0.50hv) at kiosks or from conductors on board. Punch your ticket on board to avoid the 10hv fine for riding ticketless.

Marshrutki (маршрутки; marshrutky): Numbered vans follow bus routes, usually pulling over just behind corresponding bus stops. *Marshrutki* tickets cost 1hv-1.50hv and are purchased on board; request stops from the drivers.

Trolleys (Тролейбуси; troleybusy): May have different routes than identically-numbered buses; it's best purchase a route map.

Taxis: ☎058. Taxis (Таксі; taksi) are everywhere. Always negotiate the price before getting in. Write down your destination if you don't know the name in Ukrainian or Russian. A ride within the city center should be 10hv or less. Owners of **private cars** often act as taxi drivers. Locals hold an arm down at a 45° angle to hail a ride. It is unwise to get in a car with more than 1 person already in it. *Let's Go* does not recommend hitchhiking.

GETTING A LIFT IN KYIV. To hail a taxi, open the passenger door and tell the driver your destination and a price; the driver will either invite you in or scowl and drive off. Locals often stop several cabs before agreeing on a price. Avoid taking taxis from directly outside nightclubs, as prices tend to be inflated.

🛈 PRACTICAL INFORMATION

TOURIST AND FINANCIAL SERVICES

Tourist Offices: Kyiv lacks official tourist services. Representatives of various agencies at the airport offer vouchers, excursion packages, hotel arrangements, and other services. Travel agencies also organize tours. **Carlson Wagonlit Travel,** Ivana Franka 33/34, 2nd fl. (☎238 61 56). Open daily 9am-9pm. **Yana Travel Group,** Saksahanskoho 42 (Саксаганського; ☎246 62 13; www.yana.kiev.ua). Open M-F 10am-7pm, Sa 10am-5pm. Students should check out **STI Ukraine,** Priorizna 18/1 #6, on the 2nd fl. (Пріорізна; ☎490 59 60). Open M-F 9am-9pm, Sa-Su 10am-4pm.

UKRAINE

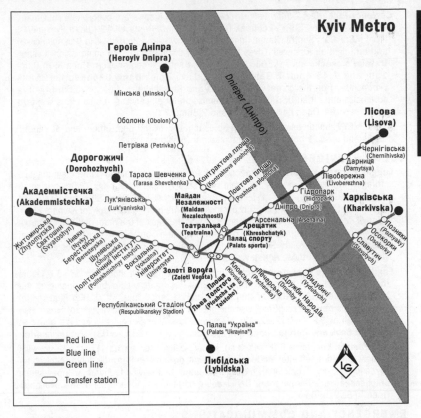

Kyiv Metro

Героїв Дніпра
(Heroyiv Dnipra)

Мінська (Minska)

Оболонь (Obolon)

Петрівка (Petrivka)

Дніпро (Дніпро)

Лісова
(Lisova)

Чернігівська
(Chernihivska)

Дарниця
(Darnytsya)

Лівобережна
(Livoberezhna)

Гідропарк
(Hidropark)

Дніпро (Dnipro)

Харківська
(Kharkivska)

Дорогожичі
(Dorohozhychi)

Тараса Шевченка
(Tarasa Shevchenka)

Контрактова площа
(Kontraktova ploshcha)

Поштова площа
(Poshtova ploshcha)

Академмістечка
(Akademmistechka)

Лук'янівська
(Luk'yanivska)

Майдан
Незалежності
(Maidan
Nezalezhnosti)

Театральна
(Teatralna)

Хрещатик
(Khreshchatyk)

Арсенальна (Arsenalna)

Познякі
(Poznyaky)

Осокорки
(Osokorky)

Славутич
(Slavutych)

Палац спорту
(Palats sportu)

Житомирська
(Zhytomyrska)

Святошин
(Svyatoshyn)

Нивки
(Nyvky)

Берестейська
(Beresteyska)

Шулявська
(Shulyavska)

Політехнічний Інститут
(Politekhnichny Insytut)

Вокзальна
(Vokzalna)

Університет
(Universytet)

Золоті Ворота
(Zoloti Vorota)

Площа
Льва Толстого
(Ploshcha Lva
Tolstoho)

Кловська
(Klovska)

Печерська
(Pecherska)

Дружби Народів
(Druzhby Narodiv)

Видубичі
(Vydubychi)

Республіканський Стадіон
(Respublikanskyy Stadion)

Палац "Україна"
(Palats "Ukrayina")

Либідська
(Lybidska)

━━━ Red line
─── Blue line
━━━ Green line
⬭ Transfer station

N
LG

General Information: The website **www.uazone.net** is an excellent resource for information on Kyiv and all of Ukraine. The **Kyiv Business Directory** (20hv), available in many *Soyuzpechaty* (Союзпечать) and press kiosks (пресса; pressa), lists useful information about dining, shopping, and travel in English and Ukrainian. Several of the major hotels sell **foreign-language newspapers.**

Embassies: Australia, Kominternu 18/137 (Комінтерну; ☎/fax 235 75 86). Open M-Th 10am-1pm. **Canada,** Yaroslaviv Val. 31 (Ярославів; ☎270 71 44; fax 270 65 98). Open M-F 8:30am-1pm and 2-5pm. **Russia,** Povitroflotskyy pr. 27 (Повітрофлотський; ☎244 09 63). Open M-Tu and Th 9am-1:30pm and 3-5pm, W 10am-1:30pm, F 10am-1:30pm and 3-4pm. **Visa section** at Kutuzova 8 (Кутузова; ☎284 68 17). Open M-Th 9am-1pm and 3-6pm, F 9am-1pm and 3-5pm. **UK,** Desyatynna 9 (Десятинна; ☎490 36 60; fax 490 36 62). Consular section at Hlybochytska 4 (Глибочицька; ☎494 34 00; fax 494 34 18). Open M-Th 9am-1pm and 2-5:30pm, F 9am-1pm and 2-4pm. **US,** Yu. Kotsyubynskoho 10 (Ю. Коцюбинського; ☎490 40 00; www.usembassy.kiev.ua). Consular section at Pymonenka 6 (Пимоненка; ☎490 44 22; fax 486 33 93 and 484 42 56). From the corner of Maidan Nezalezhnosti and Sofievska (Софіевска), take trolley #16 or 18 for 4 stops. Continue on Artema (Артема) until it curves to the right, then take the 1st right, Pymonenka. Open M-F 8:30am-12:30pm.

Currency Exchange: *Obmin valyut* (обмін валют) windows are everywhere, but many take only US$ and EUR€. **Lehbank** (Легбанк), Shota Rustaveli 12 (Шота Руставелі). From MG: Palats Sportu (Палац Спорту), go northwest on Rohnidynska (Рогнідинська) and turn right on Rustaveli. Gives MC/V **cash advances** for 2.5% commission. Cashes **traveler's checks** for a 0.30hv fee per check and 2% commission. Open M-Th 9am-1pm and 1:45-4pm, F 9am-1pm and 1:45-3pm. **Bank Ukoopspilka** (Банк Укоопспілка) on the corner of Instytutska and Khreshchatyk. Charges 3.5% (4% if in currencies other than USD or euros) commission for all services. It also offers **Western Union** services. Open daily 9am-1pm and 2-8pm.

ATMs: MC/V machines are all along Khreshchatyk, at the post office, and at various banks and upscale hotels. Look for bankomat (банкомат) signs.

LOCAL SERVICES

Luggage Storage: At the train station. Look for *kamery skhovu* (камери схову; luggage storage), downstairs outside the main entrance. 7hv per large bag, 3.50hv per small bag. Open daily 8am-noon, 1-7:30pm, 8pm-midnight, 1-7:30am. Storage lockers just to the left of the luggage room. 5hv per locker. At the bus station, look for *Kamera Zberihannya Rechey* (Камера Зберігання Речей), at the back of the main hall. 5hv per large bag, 4hv per small bag. Open daily 6-11am, 11:30am-5pm, 5:30-10:30pm. **Hotel Rus,** Hospitalna 4, MG: Palats Sportu, has free luggage storage; they sometimes even provide the service for those not staying at the hotel. Open 24hr.

English-Language Bookstores: Bukva (Буква), Maidan Nezalezhnosti (☎585 11 41), in the Globus mall by the food court. Sells English-language guidebooks, including the indispensable *Touring Kiev* (72hv). Open daily 10am-11pm. MC/V. For English-language maps of Kyiv (10-35hv), visit the nearby **Karty Atlas** (Карти Атлас) kiosk, also in the mall at 1-Я. (☎537 22 76). Many expats exchange English-language books at **Baboon Book and Coffee Shop,** B. Khmelnitskoho 39 (☎234 15 03). MR: Universytet.

Laundromats: Komiterna 8 (Комітерна). MR: Vokzalna (Вокзальна). Exit the Metro, walk straight, then turn left after McDonald's and walk downhill. In Budynok Pobutu Stolychnyy (Будинок Побуту Столичний), off Victory Square. Self-service laundromat (прачечная; prachechnaya). 29hv per load. Dry cleaning (хімчистка; khimchystka) also available. Open Tu-Sa 9am-6pm.

EMERGENCY AND COMMUNICATIONS

24hr. Pharmacy: Aptechnyy Kiosk (Аптечний Кіоск), at the train station in the corridor that crosses over the tracks.

Medical Services: Ambulance: ☎03. **American Medical Center,** Berdycherska 1 (Бердичерска; ☎490 76 00; www.amcenters.com). English-speaking doctors; will take patients without documents or insurance. Open 24hr. MC/V. Similarly, no documents are required at the **Center of European Medicine,** Shovkovychna 18-a, #2 (Шовкєвична; ☎253 82 19; sokrnta@ln.ua). Appointment recommended. Open Sept.-June M-F 8am-8pm, and sometimes Sa 9am-1pm; July M-F 9am-6pm.

Telephones: English operator ☎81 92. **Telephone-Telegraph** (Телефон-Телеграф; telefon-telehraf) around the corner of the post office (enter on Khreshchatyk). Open daily 8am-10:30pm. Buy cards for **public telephones** (таксофон; taksofon) at any post office. Less widespread than *taksofon,* **Utel phones** are in the post office, train station, hotels, and nice restaurants. Buy Utel cards at the post office and upscale hotels.

Internet: Internet Center, Khreshchatyk 48, 2nd fl. (☎230 04 99). Also has an international calling center. Internet 10hv per hr. Open 24hr. The main **post office** (see below) houses 2 Internet cafes. Each 12hv per hr. The cafe to the right of the main hall is open M-Sa 9am-9pm and Su 9am-7pm. The other, through the door to the right of the Maidan Nezalezhnosti entrance, is open 24hr. **C-Club,** Byesarabskaye pl. 1 (Бесарабскае; ☎247 56 47), in the underground mall between Byesarabsky market and the Lenin statue. Over 100 computers. 3hv per hr. Open 24hr.

Post Office: Khreshchatyk 22 (☎278 11 67). No English spoken. **Poste Restante** at counters #28 and 30. For packages, enter on Maidan Nezalezhnosti. Copy, fax, and photo services available. Open M-Sa 8am-9pm, Su 9am-7pm. **Postal Code:** 01 001.

ACCOMMODATIONS

Hotels in Kyiv are expensive. It's worth looking into short-term apartment rentals, which are listed in the *Kyiv Post* (www.kyivpost.com); bear in mind that these also tend to be pricey, since they are geared toward expats. People at the train station offer **private rooms** (from US$5), but quality is inconsistent. Check out rooms before agreeing to pay. The telephone service **Ocean-9** (Океан; ☎443 61 67) helps find budget lodgings. Tell them your price and preferred location, and they'll reserve you a room for free. (Open M-F 9am-5pm, Sa 9am-1pm.) The best budget options are Kyiv's few **hostels**, or apartments on the left bank near the metro. Mark Kushelman, a Ukrainian who speaks perfect English, can assist in arranging apartments (☎259 59 95).

International Youth Hostel Yaroslav (Ярослав), Yaroslavska 10 (Ярославська; ☎417 31 89). MB: Kontraktova Ploshcha (Контрактова Площа). Take the exit nearest to the front of the train. Follow the underground walkway on the left to its end and exit straight ahead. Turn right on Konstyantynivska (Константинівська), then left on Yaroslavska. The courtyard surrounding the hostel is on the left. Located in Kyiv's historic Podil district, this is one of the few youth hostels in Ukraine with a Western European feel. Friendly staff and good rates attract backpackers from all over the globe. Refrigerator and baths are communal. Ring bell for 24hr. service. 3- to 4-bed dorms 114-132hv. ❸

Youth Hostel Kyiv, Artema 52-A (Артема), building #2 (Корпус; korpus), 9th fl. (☎482 28 17). MG: Luk'yanivska (Лук'янівська). From the Metro, walk 15min. to the right on Artema, or take trolley #18 to the Poltavska (Полтавська) stop. From the stop, follow Pymonenka (Пимоненка) 1 block to the US consulate. The hostel is behind the consulate in a 9-story building. Look for the hostel sign on the entrance to building #2. The facilities are well kept, and some staffers speak English. Dorm rooms have baths, fridges, and TVs. 2- to 3-bed dorms 110hv. Cash Only. ❸

Hotel Express (Експрес), bul. Shevchenka 38/40 (☎239 89 95; www.expresskiev.com.ua), up Kominternu (Комінтерну) from the train station or MR: Universytet (Університет). Clean rooms with fridges, telephones, toilets, and TVs. Rooms without showers are deals. Train tickets next door. Internet 4hv per 30min. Singles 144-160hv, with shower 270-300hv; doubles 225-250/387-430hv. Cash Only. ❸

Hotel St. Petersburg (Санкт-Петербург), bul. T. Shevchenka 4 (☎279 73 64; s-peter@i.kiev.ua). MR: Teatralnaya (Театральная). The hotel has an ideal location, just up the street from Bessarabska Square. Be sure to reserve at least a month in advance. Many rooms share bathrooms, and the hotel has no hot water June-Aug. Singles 148-343hv; doubles 162-480hv; triples 90-270hv. MC/V. ❸

Hotel Druzhba, bul. Druzhby Narodiv 5 (Дружби Народів; ☎528 34 06; fax 528 33 87). From MB: Lybidska (Либідська), take a left on bul. Druzhby Narodiv and walk 200m; hotel is on the left. Clean, spacious rooms with baths, fridges, phones, and TVs. Singles 210hv, with A/C 225hv; doubles 225/270hv. Cash only. ❸

FOOD

Kyiv has a large selection of restaurants and **markets**, as well as an army of **street vendors** who sell cheap snacks. Cafes in the city center tend to cost more than similar establishments in outlying areas. For complete Kyiv restaurant listings, check out *What's On* magazine (www.whatson-kiev.com). High-quality produce can be found at the open-air **Bessarabskyy Rynok** (Ђессарабський Ринок), at the intersection of Khreshchatyk and bul. Shevchenka. (Open 24hr.) For more urban grocery shopping, head to **Furshet** (Фуршет), Yaroslavska 57. (Open 24hr.)

▨ **Antresol (Антресоль),** bul. Shevchenka 2 (☎235 83 47). MR: Teatralna. Just up the street from Bessarabska Sq. on the right, before Hotel St. Petersburg. Downstairs are a hip bookstore (some English selections) and a colorful cafe. The restaurant upstairs serves European cuisine. English menu. Salads 27-44hv. Business lunch 25hv. Entrees 37-75hv. Live piano Tu and Th 8-10pm. Open daily 9am-last customer. Cash Only. ❸

▨ **O'Panas** (О'Панас; ☎235 21 32), Tereshchenkivska 10 (Терещенківська), in the Taras Shevchenko Park. Beautifully decorated restaurant with a 19th-century, rural Ukrainian theme serves outstanding meals and tea (9-17hv). Try "Odarka's Dream" a salad of ham, pineapple, eggs, cheese, and mayo (21hv). A booth outside sells pancakes (2-4hv) in summer. English menu. Entrees 28-98hv. Open daily 10am-2am. MC/V. ❸

Za Dvoma Zaytsyamy (За Двома Зайцями; Two birds in the bush), Andriyivskyy Uzviz 34 (☎279 79 72). Located near the top of the Uzviz, Za Dvoma Zaytsyamy is surrounded by galleries and artists peddling their wares on the streets. Named after the famous 1961 Ukrainian film. 19th-century dishes are served in a classically elegant dining room. Vegetarian menu. Entrees 35-120hv. Open daily 11am-11pm. MC/V. ❹

King David's, Esplanadna 24 (Еспланадна; ☎235 74 36). MG: Palats Sportu. Outside the Metro, face away from the sports complex: King David's is a 1min. walk away. Pictures of Jerusalem decorate one of Ukraine's only kosher restaurants, which draws patrons from across the globe. The excellent salads and bread that accompany meals make the prices seem more reasonable. Great service. English menu. Breakfast 35hv. Business lunch 55hv. Entrees 40-110hv. Open M-Th and Su 10am-11pm, F 10am-8:30pm. Cash only. ❹

Osteria Pantagruel, Lysenko 1 (☎278 81 42). MG: Zoloti Vorota. The Italian chef prepares an array of pasta, fish, and meat entrees (43-195hv). Open daily 11am-11pm. Also open for breakfast M-F 7-11am. MC/V. ❹ In summer, stop by the Pantagruel-affiliated **Osteria Pantagruel Cafe,** just down the street on the fountained terrace, next to the Golden Gates. Similar, slightly less expensive options. Open daily 10am-11pm. ❸

Makabi, Shota Rustaveli 15 (Шота Руставелі; ☎235 94 37), 1 block from King David's. MG: Palats Sportu. Walk up Rohnidynska (Рогнідинська) from King David's and turn left on Rustaveli. Provides kosher fast food. English menu. Entrees 10-20hv. Open M-Th and Su 8:30am-11pm, F 8:15am-5pm. Cash only. ❷

Dva Gusya (Два Гуся), Khreshchatyk 42 (☎279 76 83), upstairs in the Gastronom. The hall on the left is a cafe serving omelettes and other light food (entrees 3-9hv); the larger hall on the right serves Ukrainian dishes in a cafeteria setting. Go through the line pointing out what you want. Quick and cheap. Entrees 3-12hv. 7% discount with ISIC. Cafe open daily 8am-10pm. Cafeteria open daily 10am-10pm. Cash only. ❷

◎ SIGHTS

Kyiv bursts at the seams with museums and parks. First-time visitors usually devote a few days to wandering Khreshchatyk and Volodymyrska, enjoying the city's sights and historic buildings. More seasoned travelers spend time exploring the many hidden avenues and monasteries that make the ancient city so charming. No matter where you look, you're sure to find something interesting.

CENTRAL KYIV

INDEPENDENCE SQUARE (МАЙДАН НЕЗАЛЕЖНОСТІ; MAIDAN NEZALEZHNOSTI).

Independence Square, often called simply "Maidan," is considered the official center of Kyiv and has been renamed and redesigned many times over the past century. Most recently, it hosted a massive tent city that persevered through bitterly cold weather during the Orange Revolution protests of 2004. The Monument to Independence, a 12m bronze statue of a woman atop a 50m column, was built in 2001 to commemorate the 10th anniversary of Ukraine's independence. Speeches and concerts are held here on national holidays. *(MB: Maidan Nezalezhnosti.)*

KHRESHCHATYK STREET (ХРЕЩАТИК). Kyiv centers on this broad commercial avenue. The houses along Khreshchatyk were destroyed during the Nazi occupation in 1941. After liberation, war criminals were publicly hanged on the street, which was eventually rebuilt in the Soviet style. People come here now to stroll and relax. Students often play guitar on the sidewalks of Khreshchatyk in the evenings, and the street is closed to traffic on weekends and holidays. An archway leads to the **Passage** (Пасаж; pasazh), one of Kyiv's most fashionable areas, home to high-priced cafes and bars. *(MR: Khreshchatyk.)*

TARAS SHEVCHENKO BOULEVARD (ТАРАСА ШЕВЧЕНКА; TARASA SHEVCHENKA). Named for the poet who revitalized the Ukrainian language in the mid-19th century (see p. 696), this boulevard is home to bright-red **Taras Shevchenko University,** which still promotes progressive ideas 165 years after its founding. Farther down the street, the interior of the **Volodymyrskyy Cathedral** is decked with Art nouveau saints and seraphim. *(Cathedral across from the botanical garden at the intersection with Leontovycha (Леонтовича). MR: Universytet. Open daily 9am-8pm.)*

KHRESHCHATYK PARK
Khreshchatyk continues up to Evropeyska pl. (Европейська; European) and meets Volodymyrska uzviz, which runs along Kyiv's Khreshchatyk Park. Within the park are the **Friendship of the Peoples Arch** and several smaller monuments. The bronze arch, known locally as the "Yoke," was built to honor the 1654 Russian-Ukrainian Pereyaslav Union. Spanning sculptures of the diplomatic proceedings, and of a Russian and a Ukrainian worker, it provides a romantic view of the Dniper. Farther on lies baroque **Mariyinsky Palace,** which is today used for formal state receptions. It was originally built for Tsarina Elizabeth's visit to Kyiv in 1755. (From European Sq., walk up Hrushevskoho. The palace is on your left, about 500m after the entrance to Dynamo Stadium.)

ST. SOFIA AND ENVIRONS
Take trolley #16 from Maidan Nezalezhnosti or get off at MG: Zoloti Vorota.

ST. SOFIA MONASTERY COMPLEX. The monastery, established in the 11th century, served as the religious and cultural center of Kyivan Rus. The

SEEING ORANGE

On November 21, 2004, a seemingly routine runoff election was held between two candidates for president: Prime Minister Viktor Yanukovich, favored by the departing current regime, and reform candidate Viktor Yushchenko. The next day, Yushchenko's camp contested the official count, which pronounced Yanukovich the winner. Hundreds gathered in Kyiv's Independence Square to protest the election results. The square was awash in orange: protestors wore orange and stuck orange ribbons on subway cars, monuments, anywhere a ribbon would stay. People poured into Kyiv from across Ukraine, and a tent city quickly went up. It was reported that police were stopping most traffic from entering the city, so taxi drivers began to shuttle people from the outskirts to metro stations free of charge. Independence Square became the center of the Orange Revolution, protesting not only the election results, but also the perceived corruption of the status quo. Babushki delivered home-cooked meals to protesters in the square and debated presidential politics with neighbors. As the ranks of protestors in Kyiv continued to swell, the departing regime conceded to an unprecedented third round of voting. Yushchenko won. A bloodless revolution had taken place, and the world watched to see how Ukraine would live up to its new dedication to democracy.

site became a national reserve in 1934, and includes a history museum and an architecture museum. The **St. Sofia Cathedral** is notable for its golden domes and its magnificent 260 sq. m of mosaics; some additional mosaics, along with drawings and design plans, are on display in the **architecture museum.** The St. Sofia **bell tower,** located above the entrance gate, is 76m tall and dates to the late 17th century. A **statue of Bohdan Khmelnytsky** (see **History,** p. 693) stands near the entrance. *(Volodymyrska 24.* ☎ *278 26 20. Monastery grounds open daily 8:30am-8pm. 1hv. Museums open M-Tu and Th-Su 10am-6pm, W 10am-5pm. Ticket kiosk on the left past the main gate. Ticket for both museums 11hv, students 4hv. Special exhibits 3hv. 45min. 10-person tours in English 40hv.)*

ST. MICHAEL'S MONASTERY (МИХАЙЛІВСЬКИЙ ЗОЛОТОВЕРХИЙ МОНАСТИР; MYHAYLIVSKYY ZOLOTOVERKHYY MONASTYR). This 11th-century monastery was destroyed in 1934 to make way for a government square, the plans for which never materialized. Instead, a sports center occupied the site for over 60 years. Before the monastery was razed, some of the original mosaics and frescoes were moved to St. Sofia, where they are still displayed. The current blue-and-gold-domed monastery was reconstructed in the 1990s. *(At the top of Mykhaylivska pl. Open daily 9am-9pm. Free.)* A **museum** in the bell tower leads to the chamber of the bells. The bells ring every 15min., and the carillon plays every hour during the day. *(*☎*278 70 68. English captions. Open Tu-Su 10am-6pm; ticket office closes 5pm. 6hv.)* Tryokhsvyatytelska (Трйохсвятительська) runs alongside the monastery and past a series of smaller churches on its way to the **Volodymyrska Hirka Park** (Володимирська Гірка Парк), which features folk sculptures in a number of tiny pavilions.

GOLDEN GATE (ЗОЛОТІ ВОРОТА; ZOLOTI VOROTA). This wood-and-stone gate has marked the entrance to the city for more than a millennium. According to legend, the gate's strength saved Kyiv from the Tatars during the reign of Yaroslav the Wise (see **History,** p. 693), whose statue stands nearby. Inside, a museum devoted to the gate is closed for restoration. *(300m down Volodymyrska from St. Sofia.)*

ANDREW'S RISE AND THE PODIL DISTRICT

ANDREW'S RISE (ANDRIYIVSKYY UZVIZ). Andrew's Rise is Kyiv's most touristed area. The steep, winding cobblestone street is lined with historic buildings, souvenir vendors, and cafes. From Mykhailivska Sq., walk down Desyatynna to get to the top of Andriyivskyy Uzviz. There you'll see **St. Andrew's Church** (Андріївська Церква), conceived by Empress Elizabeth Petrovna in the 18th century and designed by her favorite architect, Italian Bartolomeo Rastrelli. The church was renovated in the 1970s according to Rastrelli's original plans. *(*☎*278 58 61. Open M-W and Su 10am-6pm, Tu 10am-5pm; ticket office closes 4:30pm. 2-5pm 4hv, students 1hv; before 2pm free. Tours in English 40hv; call ahead. Church is open for services M-Tu and Th-Su 5-7:30pm.)* Down Andriyivskyy Uzviz 100m, steep wooden stairs lead to a great view of **Podil,** Kyiv's oldest district. Farther down are writer **Mikhail Bulgakov's house** (Andriyivskyy uzviz 13) and the **Museum of One Street.** Andriyivskyy Rise ends at **Kontraktova Sq.** (Контрактова пл.), the center of Podil.

BABYN YAR (БАБИН ЯР). The monument at Babyn Yar marks the mass grave of the first Ukrainian victims of the Holocaust. More than 33,000 people were murdered at this ravine on September 29 and 30, 1941. Although plaques state that 100,000 Kyivans eventually died here, current estimates double that figure. Many of the victims—most of them Jews—were buried alive. Above the grass-covered pit, a statue shows the victims falling to their deaths. *(MG: Dorohozhychi (Дорогожичі). Babyn Yar is actually outside Podil, at the intersection of Oleny Telihy (Олени Теліги) and Melnykova (Мельникова) in the park near the TV tower.)*

KYIV-CAVE MONASTERY

Kyiv's oldest and most revered holy site, the Kyiv-Cave Monastery (Києво-Печерська Лавра; Kyivo-Pecherska Lavra) merits a full day. First mentioned in chronicles in 1051, the ▓**monastery** can be viewed in two parts: the churches, bell tower, and museums are all atop a hill, while the caves are below. Admission to the monastery includes access to the grounds and churches, but the museums and caves cost extra. *(Take the Metro to MR: Arsenalna (Арсенальна). Turn left as you exit the Metro, and walk 10min. down Sichnevoho Povstannya (Січневого Повстання), or take trolley #38. Alternatively, take bus #24 from Bessarabskyy market or along Khreshchatyk.* ☎ *290 30 71. Buy tickets at the white kiosks beside main entrance. Open daily May-Aug. 9am-7pm, cashier until 6pm; Sept.-Apr. 9:30am-6pm, cashier until 5pm. Monastery 10hv, students 5hv. Tours in English for up to 10 people 160hv; students 80hv.)*

UPPER GROUNDS. Most of the monastery's sights are located on the top of the hill and accessed from the main entrance. The 12th-century **Holy Trinity Gate** Church (Троїцка надбрамна церква; Troyitska Nadbramna Tserkva) contains some beautiful frescoes, a 600kg censer, and the ruins of an ancient church. Step into the operating **Refectory Church,** home to one of the largest and most decorated domes in the complex. The exhibits inside have English captions. The 18th-century **Great Lavra Bell Tower** (Велика Лаврська Дзвінниця; Velyka Lavrska Dzvinnytsya), currently undergoing renovations, offers fantastic views of the river and the golden domes. The **Museum of Historical Treasures of Ukraine** (Музей Історичних Коштовностей України; Muzey Istorychnykh Koshtovnostey Ukrayiny) displays precious stones and metals. *(Open Tu-Su 10am-5:45pm. Cashier closes at 4:45pm.)* The incongruous **Micro-Miniature Exhibit** contains amazingly small books, chess sets, and other oddities. *(Open daily 10am-1:30pm and 2:30-6pm; closes in heavy rain or snow, and last Tu of the month. 5hv, students 3hv.)*

▓ **CAVES.** Monks once lived here in isolation, receiving nothing but food from the outside world. When they died, they were mummified and wrapped in cloth, sometimes with one or both hands left exposed. Without a guided tour you may view only a 15m section of the caves. All visitors must buy a candle (1hv) and carry it with them through the caves. The tours have a religious tone. Women must wear headscarves (available at the monastery), and long skirts or pants; men must wear long pants and remove their hats. *(*☎ *254 33 90. Open daily May-Sept. 9am-5:30pm; Oct.-Apr. 9am-4:30pm. 50min. tours in Russian every 15min.; 8hv, students 6hv. Tours in English; 1 person 60hv, 3 people 80hv, 5 people 120hv.)*

🏛 MUSEUMS

▓ **STATE MUSEUM OF FOLK ARCHITECTURE AND LIFE OF UKRAINE (ДЕРЖАВИЙ МУЗЕЙ НАРОДНОЇ АРХІТЕКТУРИ ТА ПОБУТУ УКРАЇНИ; DERZHAVHYY MUZEY NARODNOYI ARKHITEKTURY TA POBUTU UKRAYINY).** Over 100 huts and wooden churches representing seven cultural regions of Ukraine cover the grounds of this open-air museum. Traditional folk performances occur throughout the year. *(Outside Kyiv in the Pirohiv village. MB: Libidska. Take trolley #11 outside the Metro station to the last stop, 30min., which is the park entrance; cross under the road and walk against traffic about 30m to the park entrance. A sign reads "Музей." 10min. walk to museum. Or, take marshrutka #156 from outside MB: Respublykanskyy Stadion (Республіканський Стадіон) to its last stop—the museum entrance. Both trolley #11 and marshrutka #156 return to Kyiv.* ☎ *526 24 16. Open daily 10am-6pm. 10hv, students 5hv. 1½hr. tours in English 120hv.)*

▓ **MUSEUM OF ONE STREET (МУЗЕЙ ОДНІЄЇ ВУЛИЦІ; MUZEY ODNIYEYI VULYTSI).** This small museum at the bottom of Andriyivskyy Uzviz recounts the famous street's colorful history with photos and old documents. *(Andriyivskyy uzviz 2b.* ☎ *425 03 98; mus1str@ua.fm. Open Tu-Su noon-6pm. 5hv. 45min. tours in English 50hv.)*

CHERNOBYL MUSEUM (ЧЕРНОБИЛЬ УКРАЇНСЬКИЙ НАЦІОНАЛЬНИЙ МУЗЕЙ; CHERNOBYL UKRAYINSKYY NATSIONALNYY MUZEY). In April of 1986, a nuclear reactor exploded in the town of Chernobyl, north of Kyiv near the border with Belarus. The museum describes the day of the tragedy, its long-term effects, and the reaction of government and power plant officials. *(Provulok Khoryva 1 (Провулок Хорива). MB: Kontraktova. At the lower end of Andriyivskyy uzviz. ☎417 54 22. Open M-Sa 10am-6pm; closed last M of each month. 5hv, students with ISIC 1hv. Tours in English 40hv.)*

NATIONAL MUSEUM OF UKRAINIAN HISTORY (НАЦІОНАЛЬНИЙ МУЗЕЙ ІСТОРІЇ УКРАЇНИ; NATSIONALNYY MUZEY ISTORIYI UKRAYINY). This museum glorifies Ukraine's ancient past and its most recent achievements. *(Volodymyrska 2, up the stairway at the crossroad with Andriyivskyy uzviz. ☎278 29 24. Open M-Tu and Th-Su 10am-5:30pm; cashier closes at 4:45pm. 6hv, additional exhibits 1.20hv each.)*

THE KYIV MUSEUM OF RUSSIAN ART (КИЇВСЬКИЙ МУЗЕЙ РОСІЙСЬКОГО МИСТЕЦТВА; KYYIVSKYY MUZEY ROSIYSKOHO MYSTETSVA). A lavish interior and works by Russian greats like Shishkin and Repin attract visitors to this museum. *(Tereschenkivksa 9, near the Tarasa Shevchenka Park. MR: Teatralna. ☎234 62 18. Open M 11am-6pm, Tu and F-Su 10am-6pm; cashier closes 5pm; closed last day of each month. 6hv, students 3hv. Short English booklet 6hv, English brochure 1.80hv.)*

TARAS SHEVCHENKO MUSEUM. This museum, dedicated to the exiled poet and artist, contains a huge collection of sketches, paintings, and prints. It's housed in a 19th-century mansion which looks like it's straight out of a Russian novel. *(Bul. Tarasa Shevchenka 12. MR: Universytet. ☎224 25 56. Open Tu-Su 10am-5pm; closed last F of each month. 3hv, students 1hv. Tours in English 60hv.)*

🎵 🎭 ENTERTAINMENT AND FESTIVALS

The last Sunday of May brings **Kyiv Days,** when drama, folklore, jazz, and rock performances are staged all over the city. If you're in town between late spring and fall, don't miss **Dynamo Kyiv,** one of Europe's top soccer teams. (Ticket office in front of the stadium. Tickets 2-30hv.) Hot summer days are perfect for a boat ride down the Dniper or a trip to **Hydropark** (Гідропарк), which is an **amusement park** and **beach** on an island along the left bank of the Dniper (MR: Hidropark). The beach has showers, toilets, and changing booths. The **National Philharmonic,** Volodymyrsky uzviz 2, holds regular concerts. (☎278 16 97. Ticket office (Kaca; kasa) open Tu-Su noon-3pm and 4-7pm.) **Shevchenko Opera and Ballet Theater,** Volodymyrska 50, puts on several shows each week. (MR: Teatralna. ☎279 11 69. Shows at noon and 7pm. Ticket office open M 3-7pm, Tu-Su 11am-2pm and 3-7:30pm.)

🎵 NIGHTLIFE

Kyiv's nightlife scene has developed considerably in the past decade, with a lot of new bars and discos, many of them owned and run by expats. Check out *What's On* (www.whatson-kiev.com), *Kyiv Weekly,* or the *Kyiv Post* (www.kyiv-post.com), for the latest hotspots in town.

BARS AND CLUBS

🎵 **Artclub 44,** Khreshchatyk pr. 44 (☎279 41 37), in the basement. Walk into the courtyard; it's through an unmarked brown door on the left. Kyiv's most popular jazz club provides excellent live music daily 10pm-midnight. Cover Th-Sa 10-50hv. Beer 6-22hv. Wine 3-16hv. Open daily 10am-2am. Cash Only.

Eric's Bierstube, Chervonoarmiyiska 20 (Червоноармійська; ☎235 94 72). From MB: pl. Lva Tolstoho (Льва Толстого), walk 10m towards Khreshchatyk on Chervonoarmiyiska. At #20, a small sign reads, *Кафе бар* (cafe bar) with an arrow pointing into an alley. Eric's is through the alley on the right. This longstanding staple draws a crowd of regulars with reasonable prices and a comfortable atmosphere. Wash down a late-night "peasant's breakfast" (fried potatoes with bacon and eggs; 19hv) with a "meter" of beer (5 glasses 35hv; you might want to enlist the help of friends). Beer 5-22hv. Entrees 19-48hv. Live music M nights. Open daily 8am-2am. Cash Only.

Caribbean Club, Kominternu 4 (☎244 42 90). Salsa rules the dance floor; the DJ sits in a red car with a Rio plate. Beer 6-26hv, mixed drinks 26-46hv. Dance lessons M, W, Su 6:30pm; 20hv. Cover Th-Su men 50hv, women 30hv. Open daily 6pm-6am. Cash Only.

The Drum, Prorizna 4a (Прорізна; ☎279 23 55). Up the street from MR: Khreshchatyk. Owned by a local musician, this pub primarily draws expats and locals. Try the flaming sausages (28hv). English menu. Business lunch M-F 11am-3pm, 24-28hv. Entrees 16-38hv. Beer 6-17hv. Wine 4-14hv. Open daily 11am-midnight. Cash Only.

O'Brien's Pub, Mykhaylivska 17a (Михайлівська; ☎229 15 84). Kyiv's original Irish pub is a great place to catch sporting events. Offers satellite TV, darts, billiards, and typical pub grub like fish and chips (69hv). Live music 9pm-midnight. Happy hour 5-7pm. Beer 5.50-28hv. Open daily 8am-2am. AmEx/MC/V. Cash Only.

GLBT CLUBS

Although homosexuality is not widely accepted in Ukraine, Kyiv's GLBT scene continues to grow. Clubs tend to favor gay men: they make up the numbers, the drag shows are geared toward them, and "VIP" back rooms cater to them. In summer, the gay scene centers on the **Hydropark;** follow the mob to **Youth Beach** (Молодіжний Пляж; Molodizhnyy Plyazh). Buy a 1hv boat ride to the opposite beach, where the crowd welcomes people of all orientations.

Androhyn (Андрогин), a.k.a. Rostok (Росток), or the Big Boys Club (BBC), Harmatna 26/2 (Гарматна; ☎453 06 13; MR: Shulyavska—Шулявська). Arguably the most popular of the few gay clubs in town. Drag shows start at 2am. Reservations recommended F-Sa. Cover F-Sa 40hv, club cardholders 25hv. Open Tu-Su 7pm-6am.

Cyber Cafe (Сибер Кафе), Prorizna 21 (Прорізна). MG: Zoloty Vorota toward Khreshchatyk. For a less intense atmosphere and cheaper prices, try this small club, housed in what used to be an Internet cafe. Disco daily 10pm-6am, drag shows F-Sa 2am. Cover F-Sa 20hv; M-Th and Su 10hv. Open daily 11am-6am.

◪ DAYTRIP FROM KYIV

CHERNIHIV (ЧЕРНІГІВ) ☎(80)46

The best way to get to Chernihiv is from MR: Lisova (Лісова). Exit to the right and take a marshrutka (1½hr., 13hv). Alternatively, take a bus from the same place, but expect the trip to take an extra 30-60min. The main bus station in Kyiv also runs buses to Chernihiv (3hr., 6 per day, 15-18hv. Only 5 per day return to Kyiv). Pick up marshrutki back to Kyiv from Chernihiv at 90 pr. Peremohy (Перемоги), near Hotel Ukrayina (Україна) and one block off pr. Miru. Electrichki run daily to Chernihiv from Kyiv (3hr., 2 per day, 6.45hv).

 To make calls from outside Chernihiv, dial 22 before five-digit local numbers and 2 before six-digit local numbers.

Situated near the borders with Russia and Belarus, Chernihiv contains churches and monuments dating from the Kyivan Rus empire. Today the city is still noticeably struggling from the collapse of the Soviet Union, but those who look past the crumbling sidewalks will find a beautiful place with a fascinating history. At the start of Prospekt Myru (Миру), the 18th-century **St. Catherine's Church** has been converted into a small **museum** (Музей Народого Декоративного Мистецтва Чернігівщини; Muzey Narodoho Dekoratyvnoho Mystetsva Chernihivshchyny) displaying a collection of gorgeous regional embroidery. (☎432 36. Open M-Tu and F-Su 9am-4:30pm. 1.50hv.) Across the street, the **Cathedral of the Savior and Transfiguration** (Спасо-Преображенський Собор; Spaso-Preobrazhenskyy Sobor) dates from 1036. To the left of the cathedral, the 12th-century **Cathedral of Boris and Gleb** (Борисо-Глібський Собор; Boriso-Hlibskyy Sobor) houses archaeological artifacts found on the grounds. Continuing left, the 16th-century **Collegium** (Колегіум; Colehium) building displays religious artifacts with English captions. (☎744 63. Open daily 9am-5pm. 2hv. English booklet about Chernihiv 10hv.) The **Chernihiv History Museum,** which contains a copy of the 1581 Osfroh Bible, is located to the right and behind the Cathedral of the Savior of Transfiguration. (☎731 67. Open M-W and F 10am-6pm, Sa-Su 9am-5pm. 2.50hv. Brochure with some English 5hv.)

To get to the **Yeletsky Convent** (Собор Єлецького Монастиря; Sobor Yeletskoho Monastyrya) and its imposing 12th-century Dormition Cathedral, cross back over Pr. Miru past the area in front of St. Catherine's and catch trolley #8 just after the corner on the road's right side. Take the trolley one stop to the foot of the hill leading to the convent. The next stop down the road brings you to the 17th-century **Monastery of the Holy Trinity,** Tolstogo 92E (Толстого). For a nice view of town, ascend the steps of the monastery's bell tower (2hv, students 1hv).

Backtracking toward town, cross the park to the right to reach the 12th-century **Church of St. Elijah,** beside which loom the enigmatic **Antoniyevy Caves** (Антонієви Печри; Antoniyevi Pechry). Inside, 318m of labyrinthine paths lead into the **Church of St. Theodosis,** past burial chambers full of red-lit bones. According to legend, these are the remains of monks killed during the Mongol invasion in 1239. (☎462 21. Open M-Th and Sa-Su 9am-4:30pm, F 9am-3:30pm. 3hv, students 1.50hv.)

Options for accommodations and food in Chernihiv are very limited, but you can find everything you need at the central **Hradetsky Hotel ❷** (Градецький), Miru 68. Rates are reasonable, and there are almost always rooms available. (☎450 25 or 16 74 22. Singles 87-132hv; doubles 136-156hv.) Small, cheap dishes are available at Hradetsky's **restaurant ❶,** next to the hotel. (Entrees 3-15hv. Open daily 11am-midnight.) A small cafe and a grocery store ❷ are at Pyatnitska 15 (П'Ятницька) on the corner of pr. Peremohi (Перемоги), a block off pr. Miru. (☎17 67 81. English menu. Entrees 8-18hv. Open daily 9am-11pm. MC/V.)

ODESSA (ОДЕССА)   ☎(80)482

Since its 1794 founding by Catherine the Great, Odessa (pop. 1,100,000) has been blessed with a bustling culture but also cursed by pollution and corruption. Still, its abundance of Soviet apartment buildings, abandoned mines, and rusty industrial ruins gives this shipping port an eerily appealing aura, refined by its museums and the elaborate 19th-century Opera and Ballet Theatre. Odessa has served as a backdrop for writers from Alexander Pushkin to local boy Isaac Babel, who wrote about Odessa's Jewish mafia in his *Odessa Tales. Let's Go* uses the Russian spelling of the city's name, as most Odessans speak Russian.

⌸ TRANSPORTATION

Flights: Ovidiopolskaya Doroga (Овидиопольская Дорога; ☎006 or 21 35 49), southwest of the center. *Marshrutka* #129 runs from the airport to the train station; #101 goes to the city center (Grecheskaya).

ODESSA FOR POCKET CHANGE. It's easy to get snared by the tacky, overpriced cafes along Deribasovskaya, or by hotels that provide TVs but lack hot water and decent service. To be at one with thrift, rent an apartment (preferably one with is own water heater) from a woman at the train station (p. 713). The beaches we list all have free areas where you can catch your rays, and museums near the center al cost under 10hv (US$2). You can grab dinner from the **Provoz market** (p. 713), and then catch a ballet or opera for 10hv. If you're strolling down the boardwalk at **Arkadiya** (p. 716), buy your drink for 2.50hv from a stand rather than paying 15hv or more inside the clubs.

Trains: Zheleznodorozhniy Vokzal (Железнодорожный Вокзал), pl. Privokzalnaya 2 (Привокзальная; ☎005). International and advance tickets must be purchased at the **service center;** after going through the main entrance, enter the hall on the right, then go left and through the doors to the back room. Expect a long wait. To: **Kyiv** (10hr., 4 per day, 57hv); **Lviv** (12hr., 2-4 per day, 53hv), **Simferopol** (12hr., 1 per day, 45hv); **Moscow, RUS** (25hr., 2-4 per day, 215hv); **Warsaw, POL** (24hr., even days, 374hv).

Buses: Avtovokzal (Автовокзал), Kolontayevskaya 58 (Колонтаевская; ☎004). From the train station, cross the road behind McDonald's and take tram #5 to the last stop. From there, walk down 1 block. To: **Kyiv** (8-10hr., 8 per day, 63hv); **Sevastopol**

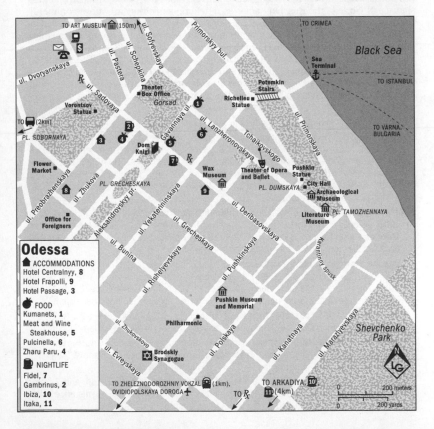

Odessa

🏠 ACCOMMODATIONS
Hotel Centralnyy, **8**
Hotel Frapolli, **9**
Hotel Passage, **3**

🍴 FOOD
Kumanets, **1**
Meat and Wine
  Steakhouse, **5**
Pulcinella, **6**
Zharu Paru, **4**

🍸 NIGHTLIFE
Fidel, **7**
Gambrinus, **2**
Ibiza, **10**
Itaka, **11**

(13½hr., 1 per day, 66hv); **Simferopol** (12hr., 1 per day, 56hv); **Yalta** (11½-15hr., 2 per day, 60hv); **Rostov-na-Donu, RUS** (18hr., 2 per day, 140hv). Buy international tickets on the 2nd fl. (☎732 66 67). Open daily 8am-12:30pm and 1:30-4pm.

Ferries: Morskoy Vokzal (Морской Вокзал), Primorskaya 6 (Приморская; ☎729 38 03). To: **Sevastopol** (19hr., 1-2 per wk. May-Sept., 400hv); **Varna, BUL** (9hr., 2 per wk., 400hv); **Istanbul, TUR** (30-36hr., 2 per wk., 400-500hv). Open daily 9am-6pm.

Public Transportation: Trams and **trolley** run almost everywhere 7am-midnight. Buy your ticket (0.50hv) from the badge-wearing *konduktor*. On **buses,** pay as you exit (0.60hv). When entering **marshrutki** (1-1.50hv), look for a sticker that says "оплата при входе" (obplata pri vkhode; payment at entry) or "оплата при выходе" (obplata pri vikhodc; payment at exit). If payment is at entry, it's common to sit down first, then pass money to the driver; your change will make its way back to you.

Taxis: ☎070, 345, 077. Yellow taxis are expensive. Check the price before you ride, and have the driver write it down. Don't pay more than 15hv from pl. Grecheskaya to the train station. When returning from Arcadia at night, try to bargain down to 20hv.

◆ ⁊ ORIENTATION AND PRACTICAL INFORMATION

Odessa's center is bounded by the **train station** to the south and the **port** to the north. Almost all streets have been recently renamed and labeled in both Ukrainian and Russian; *Let's Go* lists the Russian names as a default, since they are more commonly used. Numbering of streets begins at the sea and increases as you head inland. **Deribasovskaya** (Дерибасовская) is the main pedestrian thoroughfare. The main transport hub is right off **pl. Grecheskaya** (Греческая); from the McDonald's opposite the train station, take trolley #1 or any of several *marshrutki* to get there. The tree-lined promenade of **Primorskiy bul.** (Приморский) is separated from the sea terminal by the famous **Potemkin Stairs.** Odessa's **beaches** stretch for miles starting east of the center. **Arkadiya,** the beachside strip home to all the summer nightlife, is southeast of the city center; take *marshrutka* #195 from Preobrazhenskaya.

Tourist Offices: FGT Travel (a.k.a. Fagot; Фагот) Deribasovskaya 13 (☎37 52 01 or 35 68 01; www.odessapassage.com), on the 2nd fl. of Hotel Frapolli. Provides info about accommodations and runs a variety of excursions, including city tours and catacomb tours (each 2½hr., 63hv per person), and wine-tasting tours (100-140hv). Open daily 8:30am-8pm. **Office for Foreigners** (Канцелярия для иностранцев; Kantselyariya dlya inostrantsev), Bunina 37, 2nd fl. (☎28 28 22, 28 28 46). Visa assistance. Open Tu-Th 10am-12:30pm and 2-4:30pm.

Currency Exchange: An *obmen valyut* (обмен валют) is on every corner. Rates vary, so check several. **Bank Aval** (Аваль), Sadovaya 9 (Садовая; www.avalbank.com) cashes **traveler's checks** for 2% commission, gives **cash advances** for 2% commission, and provides **Western Union** services. Open M-F 9am-5pm.

Luggage Storage: Kamera Zberihannya (Камера Зберігання), outside the train station, 50m down far right track on the right-hand side. 4hv per bag, 5hv per large bag. Open 24hr. Downstairs in the bus station. 2hv per bag. Open daily 5am-midnight. Downstairs in the sea terminal. 1.50hv per bag per day, 3hv per night. Open daily 8am-6pm.

English-Language Bookstore: Dom Knigi (Дом Книги), Deribasovskaya 27 (☎22 34 73). Good city maps (6-8hv) and a few books in English. Open daily 10am-7pm.

Pharmacy: Apteka Help (Аптека Хелп), Admiralskiy Prospekt 37 (Адмнральский Проспект; ☎22 71 27). Apteka Gayevskogo (Аптека Гаевского), Sadova 21 (☎22 24 08). MC/V. 24hr. pharmacies (☎27 41 65) in the train station.

Telephones: At the post office, to the left. Pay in advance. Open 8am-1pm and 2-5pm. Also at the sea terminal, to the left of the entrance, are 4 phones for long distance calls. Rates are better 8-11pm and on the weekends. Open daily 8am-11pm.

Internet: Tech-21, Sadovaya 5 (☎728 64 79), opposite the post office. 3hv per hr. Open 24hr. **VIP Bar,** Preobrazhenskaya 34 (☎715 50 09; vipbar_odessa81@mail.ru), in the back of Hotel Passage's lobby. 3 computers with fast connections. Has a phone center with cheap international calls. 7hv per hr.

Post Office: Sadovaya 10 (☎726 74 93). Mail letters abroad at window #19. Open M-Sa 8am-2pm and 3-8pm, Su 8am-2pm and 3-6pm. **Fax** service at #22 (☎726 64 17). Open daily 8am-1pm and 1:45-5pm. **Photocopies** at window #21. Open M-Sa 8am-8pm, Su 8am-6pm. **Postal Code:** 65 001.

ACCOMMODATIONS

Comfort doesn't come cheap in Odessa, especially during summer, when only the best hotels have hot water. The city's run-down **budget hotels** are found in the center. **Private rooms** are cheap but not always safe, and most are far from the center. Train station hawkers hold signs reading "Сдаю комнату" (Sdayu komnatu; I'm renting a room). Ask "Skolko?" (Сколько; how much). The asking price is usually 75-100hv; bargain down, and don't pay until you see the room. Apartments are also available from women at the train station, but cost 100hv or more.

Hotel Passage (Пассаж), Preobrazhenskaya 34 (☎22 48 49, 728 55 00; fax 22 41 50), near the corner of Deribasovskaya. The best budget option, though the building has seen grander days. The rooms differ, so look before checking in. Reservations, when accepted, add 50% to the price of the 1st night; it's best to just show up at noon. Luggage storage 3hv. Singles 55hv, with bath 95-295hv; doubles 85/125-295hv. ❶

Hotel Centralnyy (Центральний), Preobrazhenskaya 40 (☎726 84 06; fax 726 86 89), 1 block from Hotel Passage. Pricier than other options, but breakfast is included. No hot water in summer. Singles 60hv, with bath 110hv; doubles 92/197hv. ❷

Hotel Frapolli, Deribasovskaya 13 (☎35 68 01; frapolli@te.net.ua), next to Mick O'Neill's Pub. Perfect location. Summer in Odessa is the time and place to consider splurging on a room; despite being "economy class," these rooms have private baths with A/C, hot water year-round, Internet, mini-bar, and TV. Breakfast included. Reservations recommended. Singles 316-827hv; doubles 474-985hv. MC/V. ❹

FOOD

The streets of central Odessa are lined with cafes and restaurants, most of which are expensive. For the budget traveler, Odessa is *shawarma* (шаурма) town: **Top Sandwich** and similar competitors have locations throughout town, especially along Deribasovskaya. **Privoz** (Привоз), Privoznaya (Привозная), to the right of the train station, sells food. (Open daily 6am-6pm.)

Zharu Paru (Жару Пару), Grechevskaya 45 (Гречевская; ☎22 44 30), just down from Hotel Passage. This cafeteria serves up excellent Ukrainian dishes and is a favorite among locals, especially students. For the prices, it can't be beat. Soups 2hv. Salads 2hv. Entrees 5-6hv. Open daily 8am-10pm. Cash only. ❶

Pulcinella, Lanzheronovskaya 17 (Ланжероновская; ☎777 30 10), between Gavannaya and Yekaterinskaya. This beautiful pizzeria serves excellent brick-oven Italian and Ukrainian dishes in a charming dining room with Mediterranean decor. English menu. Entrees 20-95hv. Pizza 16-29hv, group-size 100hv. Open daily 11am-11pm. MC/V. ❷

Kumanets (Куманець), Gavanna 7 (Гаванна; ☎37 69 46). A good place to try traditional Ukrainian dishes. The decor has a country theme, and servers wear folk outfits. Beware that "vegetable" dishes often contain meat. Try the *golubtsy* (голубци; stuffed cabbage rolls; 18hv) and a glass of *Kvas* (Квас; 5hv). English menu. 11 kinds of *varenyky* (варенки; dumplings) 14-19hv. Red or green *borshch* (борщ) 15hv. Fish and meat dishes 14-78hv. Open 11am-midnight. Cash only. ❷

Meat and Wine Steakhouse, Deribasovskaya 20 (☎34 87 82). The dining room of this classy steakhouse looks out on the main thoroughfare. International wine list. English menu. Salad bar with a variety of prepared salads to choose from 18hv. Steaks 38-68hv. English spoken. Open daily 9am-midnight. MC/V. ❹

👁 SIGHTS

◼CATACOMBS. When Catherine the Great decided to build Odessa, the limestone used for its construction was mined from below, leaving the longest catacombs in the world. During WWII, Odessa's partisans hid in these dark, intertwining tunnels, surfacing only for raids against the Nazis. The accessible portion of the labyrinths lies under the village of Neribaiskoye, where the city has set up an outstanding subterranean **museum.** You can enter the catacombs (legally) through one entrance only and you must have a guide. At the recreated resistance camp, rocks covered with original partisan's graffiti have been transported to the recreated resistance camp. One declares "Blood for blood; death for death." *(30min. by car from Odessa. Many tour agencies provide rides and tours. FGT offers 2hr. tours in English; 150hv per guide plus 315hv transportation. Dress warmly.)*

411TH BATTALION MONUMENT. Far from the busy commercial center lies one of Odessa's more entertaining monuments. Typical armaments of the Soviet forces are spread throughout a large park, where swarms of kids clamber over tanks and torpedoes. There is a small museum by the battleship. The cliffs along the rocky coast are a short walk from behind the bus stop to the left. *(From the train station, take marshrutka #127 30-40min. to the last stop; daily 6am-10pm. Walk straight and take a right at the concrete "411." Museum ☎44 45 27. Open M-Th and Sa-Su 10am-6pm. 1hv.)*

PUSHKINSKAYA STREET (РУШКИНСКАЯ). This street is named for the Russian poet who, during his exile, lived at #13, which was then a hotel. The building is now a museum dedicated to Pushkin and his time here. At #15, on the corner of Bunina (Бунина), is the **Philharmonic building** (Филармония; Filarmoniya), built between 1894 and 1899. A block farther down is the **Brodskiy Synagogue** (Синагога Бродського), which was once the center of Odessa's Jewish community.

SHEVCHENKO PARK. This large park separates the city center from the sea. At the entrance is a **monument** to the poet Taras Shevchenko (p. 696). Within are the ruins of **Khadzhibey Fortress** and monuments to the dead of the Great Patriotic War and the Afghanistan War. An eternal flame commemorates an unknown soldier.

DERIBASOVSKAYA STREET (ДЕРИБАСОВСКАЯ). Odessa's most popular street is filled with cafes, vendors, and performers. Don't be surprised by all the snakes, monkeys, and exotic lizards—some residents make a living by photographing tourists with their odd pets. On the east end of the street is the **Gorsad** (Горсад), where artists sell jewelry, landscape paintings, and *matryoshka* dolls.

PRIMORSKIY BOULEVARD (ПРИМОРСКИЙ). Primorskiy's shaded promenade is home to some of Odessa's finest buildings. The **statue of Alexander Pushkin** turns its back to the City Hall, which refused to help fund its construction. On either side of the hall are Odessa's two symbols: **Fortuna,** goddess of fate; and **Mercury,** god of trade. From Primorskiy, descend the **Potemkin Stairs** (Потомкинская Лестница; Potomkinskaya Lestnitsa) to reach Primorskaya and the Sea Terminal.

🏛 MUSEUMS

◼WAX MUSEUM. This small, private museum (Музей Восковых Скульптур; Muzey Voskovykh Skulptur) displays wax figures of the city's most famous inhabitants, from José De Ribas, the Spanish conqueror who won the city from the

Tatars, to Russian poet Pushkin. *(Rishelyevskaya 4. ☎ 22 34 36. English placards. Open daily 9:00am-10pm. 11hv, students 5hv. Even for students, the adult ticket is a good deal—it includes a photo and 7hv credit at the museum's bar.)*

ART MUSEUM (ХУДОЖНИЙ МУЗЕЙ; KHUDOZHNIY MUZEY). A great collection of 19th-century art, including works by Kandinsky, Ayvazovski, and Levitskyy, is displayed in a former palace. One of the rooms, containing golden religious icons, requires an additional ticket. The most exciting part of the museum is the grotto underneath. It is rumored that the underground passageways leading from the palace have been used to conduuct secret trysts. Entrance is permitted only with a guide. *(Sofiyevskaya 5a (Софиевская). ☎ 23 82 72, tours 23 84 62. Open M and W-Su 10:30am-6pm; ticket office closes 5pm; closed last F of each month. Museum, icon room, and grotto each 2hv; students 0.50hv.)*

PUSHKIN MUSEUM AND MEMORIAL. This building was Pushkin's residence during his exile from St. Petersburg from 1823 to 1824. The fascinating museum (Литературно-мемориальный Музей Пушкина; Literaturno-memorialnyy Muzey Pushkina) displays his manuscripts and possessions, as well as portraits of his family. *(Pushkinskaya 13. Enter through the courtyard. ☎ 25 10 34; tours 22 74 53. Open Tu-Su 10am-5pm; last admission 4:30pm. 3.50hv, students 1.50hv. Tours in Russian 15hv, students 10hv; tours in French 29hv. Tours in English; call ahead.)*

LITERATURE MUSEUM (ЛИТЕРАТУРНЫЙ МУЗЕЙ; LITERATURNIY MUZEY). In the beautiful, 19th-century summer residence of a prince, this museum provides a fascinating look at the city's intellectual and cultural heritage, with emphasis on writers Pushkin and Gogol. The collection includes the famous letter from the Odessan mayor to the tsar, requesting that Pushkin be expelled "for his own development," because he "is getting the notion into his head that he's a great writer." *(Lanzheronovskaya 2. ☎ 22 00 02. Open Tu-Su 10am-5pm. 3.50hv per period, students 1.50hv. 10.50hv for all 3, students 4.50hv. Sculpture courtyard 3hv. Tour in English of all periods, 75hv.)*

ARCHAEOLOGICAL MUSEUM. The museum (Археологический Музей; Arkheologicheskiy muzey) displays ancient Greek and Roman artifacts found in the Black Sea region and contains Ukraine's only Egyptian collection. *(Lanzheronovskaya 4. ☎ 22 01 71 or 22 63 02. Open Tu-Su 10am-5pm. 5hv; students, children, and seniors 2hv. Call ahead to arrange a tour in English, 10hv per person.)*

🏖 BEACHES

Arkadiya (Аркадия), the city's largest and most popular beach, is the last stop on tram #5, which stops next to the McDonald's at the train station; *marshrutka* #195 also runs to the beach. The shoreline from Shevchenko Park up to Arkadiya is great for an early-morning jog. **Zolotoy Bereg** (Золотой Берег; Golden Shore) is farther from town, but boasts the most impressive beach. Take tram #18 or *marshrutka* #215 or 223 (runs May-Aug.) to the end. Tram #18 also goes to **Riviera** (Ривиера) and **Kurortniy** (Курортный). Trams #17 and #18 head to **Chaika** (Чайка). Tram #5 stops at **Otrada** (Отрада) where you can avoid the numerous steep steps to the beach by riding the funicular (6hv). To get to **Lanzheron** (Ланжерон), the beach closest to central Odessa, cross Shevchenko Park or take *marshrutka* #253, 233, or 2MT. Some beaches are free, but others charge up to 15hv admission and offer beach chairs, umbrellas, and waiter service.

🎭 ENTERTAINMENT

Buy tickets for all shows in town at the **theater box office,** Preobrazhenskaya 28. Same-day tickets are available until 2pm. *(☎ 22 02 45. Open daily 10am-5pm.)*

Theater of Opera and Ballet (Театр Оперы и Балета; Teatr Opery i Baleta), pr. Chaikovskogo 1 (Чайковского; ☎29 13 29), at the end of Rishelyevskaya. Famous, recently renovated 19th-century theater hosts performances Tu-Su 6:30pm. Tickets 10-50hv; check with the box office for the schedule. Open Tu-Su 10am-6pm.

Odessa Russian Drama Theater, Grecheskaya 48 (☎24 07 06). Several performances each week. Schedule is posted outside entrance. Shows start at 7pm. Tickets 5-20hv; 10hv tickets are the best value. Box office open daily noon-3pm and 4-7pm.

Philharmonic (Филармония; filarmoniya), Bunina 15 (☎25 69 03, 21 78 95; www.odessaphilharmonic.org), on the corner of Pushkinskaya. The orchestra has won international acclaim for its concerts conducted by American Hobart Earle. Tickets 3-20hv. Box office open daily 10am-6pm on performance days.

■ NIGHTLIFE

From May to September, almost all the nightlife is at the beach clubs of **Arkadiya.** To get there, take tram #5 or *marshrutka* #195. A taxi back to the city center is about 25hv. The glitziest Arkadiya club is **Ibiza,** complete with fashion shows and professional dancers. Call three days ahead to reserve a table near the dance floor. (☎777 02 05. Th-Sa live music or other performances, 40-50hv. Cover M-W and Su 20hv. Open daily noon-6am.) Not far from Ibiza, and less pretentious, is local favorite **Itaka,** which features live performances and a large dance floor. (☎34 91 88. Cover 35hv. Open daily 10pm-6am.) Farther down the strip, student-oriented **Pago** blasts lots of Russian pop. (☎715 38 30. Only women W 9pm-midnight. Cover M-Th and Su 15hv; students M-Th 10hv; F-Sa 25hv. Open daily 9pm-6am.) For house, trance, and big-name DJs from Moscow and London, check out **Stereo.** (☎37 42 37. Cover M-Th and Su 20-30hv; F-Sa 30-40hv. Open daily 10pm-6am.)

If you want to stay in town, start your night listening to folk music at **Gambrinus** (Гамбринус), Deribasovskaya 31, at the corner of Zhukova. (Жуковаж. ☎26 36 57. Beer 3-36hv. Live folk music M and Th-Su 6-10pm. Tu-W live modern music. Open daily 10am-midnight.) **Fidel** (Фидел), Deribasovskaya 23, at the corner of Aleksandrovsky pr., is also known as "Havana Club." Live music most nights counteracts tacky decor like fake palm trees. Avoid the bland, inauthentic Cuban food. (☎22 71 16. Beer 15-30hv. Entrees 25-100hv. F-Sa band 11:30pm-2:30am. No shorts allowed. Open M-Th and Su 10am-2am, F-Sa 10am-5am. MC/V.)

CRIMEA (КРЫМ)

An important trading thoroughfare on the Black Sea Coast, the Crimean peninsula has a 2500-year history of Greek, Turkish, Mongol, and Russian rule. Though bequeathed to Ukraine in 1991, it remains Russian at heart—Crimeans are Russian-speaking, call Ukrainian currency "rubles," and feel closer to Moscow than Kyiv. In summer, hordes of vacationers mean scarce hotel rooms and high prices. It is best to visit in September, when the crowds have left but the sea is still warm.

PHONE CALLS. Crimea is an autonomous republic within Ukraine, and its phone system mirrors the political situation. Dialing from one Crimean town to another requires special Crimean area codes; the area codes listed in *Let's Go* for each Crimean town work only when calling from outside the peninsula. The intra-Crimean area codes (all preceded by 8) are: Simferopol 22, Bakhchisaray 254, Feodosiya 262, Kerch 261, Yalta 24, Sevastopol 0692.

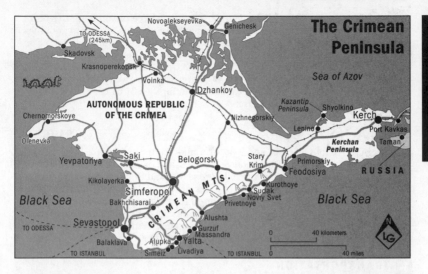

The Crimean Peninsula

Sea of Azov

TO ODESSA (245km)

Skadovsk

Novoalekseyevka

Genichesk

Krasnoperekopsk

Voinka

Dzhankoy

Chernomorskoye

AUTONOMOUS REPUBLIC OF THE CRIMEA

Nizhnegorskiy

Kazantip Peninsula

Shyolkino

Kerch

Port Kavkas

Olenevka

Lenino

Kerchan Peninsula

Taman

Yevpatoriya

Saki

Belogorsk

Stary Krim

Primorskiy

Feodosiya

RUSSIA

Kikolayerka

Simferopol

Bakhchisarai

CRIMEAN MTS.

Kurothoye

Sudak

Novyi Svet

Privetnoye

Black Sea

Sevastopol

TO ODESSA

Balaklava

Alupka

Simeiz

Yalta

Livadiya

TO ISTANBUL

Alushta

Gurzuf

Massandra

Black Sea

0   40 kilometers

0   40 miles

TO ISTANBUL

UKRAINE

SIMFEROPOL (СІМФЕРОПОЛЬ) ☎(80)652

Simferopol is the capital of the Autonomous Republic of Crimea and the transport hub of the peninsula. Most pass through en route to more pleasant coastal destinations. The **train station** (вокзал; vokzal) at Vokzalnaya pl. (Вокзальная; ☎005), sends trains to: **Kyiv** (19hr., 3 per day, 75hv); **Lviv** (27 hr., 1 per day, 75hv); **Odessa** (12hr., 1 per day, 45hv); **St. Petersburg, RUS** (31hr., 1 per day, 307hv). The **information desk** charges 1hv per question. Tickets for the **elektrichka** (Елекчрика; commuter rail) are sold behind the main station at the window marked "пригородный кассы" (prigorodniy kassy). These head to **Sevastopol** (2-2½hr., 7 per day, 3.10hv) via **Bakhchisarai** (1hr., 2.26hv). **Buses** and **marshrutki** vans to various Crimean destinations leave from the square next to the McDonald's. Buses (☎25 25 60) run to: **Feodosiya** (2hr., 2 per hour, 15hv); **Sevastopol** (2hr., 3-4 per hr., 11-14hv); **Yalta** (2hr., 4-5 per hr., 11-16hv). The 2-3 hr. **trolley** #52 ride to Yalta, the longest trolley bus route in the world, costs 10hv. Buses to more distant destinations leave from the central station, across town at Kiyevskaya 4. Take trolley #6, which leaves across the street from the train station to get there. Destinations include: **Kyiv** (14½hr., 3 per day, 69-100hv); **Odessa** (12hr., 4 per day, 55-86hv); **Rostov-na-Donu, RUS** (13½hr., 2 per day, 107hv). *Marshrutki* are usually faster than buses but typically charge 5-20hv more than a standard bus.

 Currency exchange offices are everywhere, but look beyond the train and bus stations for the best rates. **ATMs** are at the post office and train station, and along Pushkina. **Store luggage** at the train station in the building next to track #1, through the door marked with "камера хранения" (kamera khraneniya; guarded 3-4hv, lockers 4hv). There is a **24hr. pharmacy** in the same building complex as Hotel Ukraina, Rozy Luksemburg 7 (☎54 56 82. MC/V). There's also a **24hr. medical center** (медпункт; medpunkt; ☎24 21 03) at the train station, to the right of the luggage storage room. *Babushki* peddle **private rooms ❶** at the train station and the next-door trolley station; most are offering rooms in Yalta or other coastal towns. If you need to stay overnight, try **Hotel Moskva ❷**, (Гостиница Москва; Gostinitsa Moskva) Kievskaya 2, in the city center. (☎23 72 25, 23 75 20; fax 23 97 95. Singles 90-190hv; doubles 165-330hv.) A nicer place to stay is the newly renovated **Hotel**

Ukraina ❸ (Украина), Rozy Luksemburg 7. All rooms have private baths. (☎55 12 44, 51 01 65; fax 27 84 95; jscukrcomp@crimea.com. Singles 207-285hv; doubles 350-510hv. Reservations add 50% of the room price to the 1st night's stay.) The ▨Istanbul Restaurant and Cafe, Gorikoho 5 (Горикого) is visited primarily by Simferopol's Turkish community. (☎52 78 62. Entrees 12-18hv, baklava 6hv. Open 8am-10pm). The cafe **Vinogradnaya Loza** ❶ (Виноградная Лоза), Pushkina 4, has large seafood salads as well as typical Ukrainian fare. (☎51 54 65. Salads 9-11hv. Entrees 5-15hv. Open daily 8am-11pm.)

YALTA (ЯЛТА)   ☎(8)0654

Though inaccessible by train and a bit of a hike from Simferopol, Yalta is well worth visiting for its striking mountains, beaches, and palaces. It is also the site of the 1945 conference at which Churchill, Roosevelt, and Stalin decided the fate of postwar Europe. Over the years the city has drawn such famous inhabitants as Tsar Nicholas II, writers Anton Chekhov and Lesya Ukrainka, and composer Sergei Rachmaninov. Today, it primarily hosts the flashiest and wealthiest Russia and Ukraine have to offer. Nonetheless, budget travelers can find treasures of a different sort by looking past overpriced hotels and nightclubs.

▐ TRANSPORTATION

Trains: Yalta is **not accessible by train** but has an Advance Booking office, Ignatenko 14 (☎32 43 47), where you can get tickets to depart from **Sevastopol** or **Simferopol.** Purchase tickets in advance (3 wk. min. in summer). From pl. Lenina, walk up Ignatenko and look for the "Железнодорожные Кассы" sign. Open daily 8am-8pm.

Buses: On Moskovskaya (☎34 20 92). To: **Bakhchisarai** (3hr., 4 per day, 15-20hv); **Feodosiya** (5hr., 2 per day, 28hv); **Kerch** (7hr., 1 per day, 52hv); **Kyiv** (17½hr., 2 per day, 110-150hv); **Odessa** (14½hr., 2 per day, 70-100hv); **Sevastopol** (2hr., 2-3 per hr. 7am-9pm, 15hv); **Simferopol** (2hr., 2-6 per hr., 16hv). **Intourist, LTD.** arranges bus trips to Kyiv during summer.

Ferries: Buy tickets at the waterfront past the Gastronom, the store below the clock (☎32 42 74). To: **Alupka** (1¼hr., July-Aug. 15 per day, 13-20hv) via **Livadiya** (15min., 5-7hv) and **Lastochkino Gnezdo** (45min., 10hv). Ferry tickets to **Istanbul, TUR** from **Sevastopol** (33hr.; 600hv) are available in the main hall of the sea terminal on the left hand side at the window marked Предприятие Морское (predpryyatye morskoye), Ruzvelta 5 (Рузвельта; ☎23 03 02). Open daily noon-3pm.

Public Transportation: Buses and **trolleys** run throughout the city (0.50-0.75hv). Trolley #1 covers most of the central area; it travels from the bus station to pl. Sovetskaya. From the stop "Kinoteatr Spartak," bus #8 goes to Polyana Skazok and Chekhov's house; bus #24 goes from Chekhov's house to Polyana Skazok. Private **marshrutki** depart from the square at the corner of Moskovskaya and Karla Marksa. They run the same routes as buses, are faster, and make fewer stops, but cost 0.50-5hv more.

▣ ⚐ ORIENTATION AND PRACTICAL INFORMATION

Yalta's main drag is the pedestrian **nab. Lenina** (Ленина), which runs along the Black Sea waterfront (naberezhnaya; Набережная) from **pl. Lenina.** From the **bus** and **trolley stations,** take trolley #1 toward the center. It runs down Moskovskaya (Московская) past the circus and market to **pl. Sovetskaya** (Советская), where Moskovskaya converges with **Kievskaya** (Киевская). You can get off there and walk two blocks to **pl. Lenina.** There, nab. Lenina begins to the right, while a left

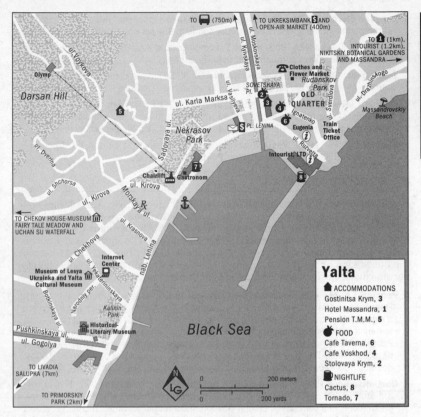

Yalta

🏠 ACCOMMODATIONS
Gostinitsa Krym, **3**
Hotel Massandra, **1**
Pension T.M.M., **5**

🍴 FOOD
Cafe Taverna, **6**
Cafe Voskhod, **4**
Stolovaya Krym, **2**

🎵 NIGHTLIFE
Cactus, **8**
Tornado, **7**

turn leads to the **Old Quarter.** At the other end of nab. Lenina, both pedestrian **Push-kinskaya** (Пушкинская) and parallel **Gogolya** (Гоголя) run inland to **Kinoteatr Spartak.** Trolley #1 and many *marshrutki* stop there.

Tourist Offices: Eugenia Travel, Ruzvelta 10 (☎27 18 29; www.eugeniatours.com.ua). English-speaking office helps arrange apartment rental and provides tours and info. Open M-F 9am-6pm. **Intourist, LTD.,** Ruzvelta 5 (☎32 76 04; intour@yalta.crimea.ua), across from Eugenia Travel, beside the sea terminal. Books hotel rooms, arranges tours, offers visa support, provides interpreters, and runs luxury buses to Kyiv in the summer. Open M-F 10am-5pm. **Intourist,** Drazhinskogo 50 (☎27 01 32; fax 35 30 93), in Hotel Yalta, uphill from Hotel Massandra. Books flights and organizes excursions with English-speaking guides. Open daily 8am-7pm. MC/V.

Currency Exchange: Exchange booths and banks are everywhere, but offer the worst rates in the country. It's better to exchange money before arriving in Yalta. **Ukreksim-bank,** Moskovskaya 31a (☎32 79 35), to the left of the Tsirk (Цирк; Circus) stop. Cashes **traveler's checks** for 2% commission. Open M-Th 9am-1pm and 2-3pm, F 9am-1pm. **Avalbank** (☎32 03 35), in the central post office (see below). Offers **Western Union** services, gives MC/V **cash advances** for 2.5% commission, and cashes **traveler's checks** for 2% commission. Open daily 9am-1pm and 2-6pm.

ATMs: At the bus station, the post office (see below) and along nab. Lenina.

UKRAINE

Luggage Storage: At the bus station. Look for "Камера-Хранения" (Kamera-Khraneniya) at the bottom of the stairs, in back of the building. 3hv per day. Open daily 8am-7pm.

Pharmacy: Apteka #26, Botkinskaya 1 (Боткинская; ☎32 30 42). From nab. Lenina, walk up Pushkinskaya and turn right. Open 8am-8pm.

Telephones: Ukrtelecom, Moskovskaya 9 (☎32 43 02), down the alley, across from the market. Internet 3hv per hr. Open 24hr. **Fax** available 9am-5pm.

Internet: Internet Center, Yekaterininskaya 3 (☎32 30 72). From nab. Lenina, go up Yekaterininskaya, descend steps marked with a sign to the right, and cross courtyard. Slower connections than Ukrtelecom, but less crowded. 4.50hv per hr. Open 24hr.

Post Office: Pl. Lenina. **Poste Restante** (Востребования) at window #4. Open M-F 8am-7pm, Sa 8am-6pm, Su 9am-4pm. **Postal Code:** 98 600.

ACCOMMODATIONS

If you plan to stay in a hotel in Yalta during July or August, reserve in advance and be prepared to pay a hefty price. Without a reservation, you may have to negotiate with bus station middlemen for **private rooms** ❸ (25-50hv per person) or contact Eugenia Travel for **apartment rentals** (150hv per person). Those who speak Russian or like playing charades can go straight to the *babushki* hawking rooms behind the bus station or along Drazhinskovo (25-50hv). During other seasons, hotels become much cheaper, and availability is not a problem.

Pension T.M.M., Lesi Ukrayinki 16 (☎/fax 23 09 50; kag@lu16.firmatmm.com.ua). From the bus station, take trolley #1 to Sadovaya (Садовая). Backtrack a few steps to a sign pointing toward the pension, uphill to the left. Take the 1st left going uphill, then turn right at the end of the road. The entrance is in an unmarked black fence on the left. Peaceful, stately mansion with views of the sea and its own courtyard. The airy rooms have balconies, TVs, and private showers. Includes 3 meals per day. Singles 160hv; doubles 300-415hv. Rooms cost 25hv less without meals; see the manager. ❸

Gostinitsa Krym (Крым), Moskovskaya 1/6 (☎27 17 10, reservations 27 17 03). The 3rd stop on trolley #1 from the bus station, between pl. Lenina and pl. Sovetskaya. Clean rooms in a convenient, central location. Intermittent hot water. The budget rooms have shared bath; shared toilets lack seats. Singles 30-210hv; doubles 40-310hv. ❶

Hotel Massandra (Массандра), Drazhinskovo 46 (Дражинсково; ☎27 24 27; fax 27 24 01). Near the beach and 20min. from the town center. Go up Drazhinskovo and left at Avalon Cafe (Авалон) or take *marshrutka* #34 up the hill. Expensive but worth the price, since you get comfy rooms with private baths, TVs, and fridges. Doubles June-Oct. 300-600hv; Nov.-May 150-350hv. ❹

FOOD

Most of the cafes and restaurants on and near nab. Lenina are expensive, especially in the summer. Soviet-style **cafeterias** (столовая; stolovaya) in the city center offer a cheap, quick alternative (10-20hv), though they are often crowded at lunch and have few selections at dinner. **Gastronom** (Гастроном), the grocery store at nab. Lenina 15, sells cheap, fresh bread. The **open-air market,** opposite the circus, has a large selection of fruits and vegetables. To get there, take trolley #1, or walk up Moskovskaya. (Open daily 8am-7pm.)

Read menus carefully: some places sneak in large surcharges for service and live music or list very expensive wines with names similar to cheaper counterparts.

UKRAINE

Cafe Voskhod (Восход), Ignatenko 2 (Игнатенко; ☎23 39 43), near pl. Sovetskaya. Turkish dishes, plus some Russian and European. Try the sudak fish (19hv), or meat dishes (18-21hv), grilled in the dining room. English menu doesn't list all entrees. Entrees 18-45hv. Open June-Sept. 24hr.; Oct.-May daily 8am-midnight. Cash only. ❷

Stolovaya Krym (Столовая), Moskovskaya 1/6, next to Gostinitsa Krym. One of Yalta's best self-service cafeterias, serving classic Russian lunch food. The *solyanka* (meat soup; 5hv) is phenomenal. Entrees 4-8hv. Open daily 9am-9pm. Cash only. ❶

Cafe Taverna (Таверна), Ruzvelta 3, near pl. Lenina. Were it not for a rusty watch tower, dilapidated shed, and "crazy bus" amusement ride, Taverna would have a great view of the harbor. Unlike the view, however, the food is top-notch. Typical Ukrainian fare, served up delicious-style. Entrees 9-22hv. Open daily noon-midnight. Cash Only. ❷

👁 🏛 SIGHTS AND MUSEUMS

Most of Yalta's impressive sights are outside town. The most efficient way to see the main attractions is to divide them into three days: one day for the museums and beaches in town; one day for Massandra and the Nikitskiy Botanical Garden, and one day for Livadiya, Swallow's Nest, and Alupka. Absolute must-see sights are the Chekhov House-Museum and the Livadiya and Massandra palaces.

▓ ANTON CHEKHOV HOUSE-MUSEUM. The Russian writer Anton Chekhov (see p. 573) lived in Yalta for the final five years of his life. In 1899, he built a house (known as the "white dacha") on the hill. Nearly two decades after his 1904 death from tuberculosis, his sister established the property as a museum (Дом Музей А. П. Чехова; Dom Muzey A. P. Chekhova). A modern building displays photos, letters, and manuscripts, as well as the desk at which Chekhov wrote *Three Sisters, The Cherry Orchard,* and *Lady with a Lapdog.* Chekhov's **garden** represents "eternal spring"—at any time of year, some plants remain in bloom. The house retains its original furnishings. *(Kirova 112. From the center, take marshrutka #8 from Kinoteatr Spartak at the end of Pushkinskaya. Alternatively, take trolley #1 to Pionerskaya (Пионерская), cross the street, turn left, then turn right onto per. Krayniy (Крайний). Go up the steps and turn left on Kirova (Кирова); #112 is on the left. ☎39 49 47. Open June-Sept. Tu-Su 10am-5:15pm; Oct.-May W-Su 10am-4pm; closed last day of each month. 15hv, students 7hv. English booklet 12hv, English brochure 4hv.)*

OTHER SIGHTS. For a great view of the city, take the **chairlift** (канатная дорога; kanatnaya doroga) up to **Olymp**, a hilltop mock-Greek temple. The lift starts just up from nab. Lenina, to the right of the Gastronom. *(☎32 81 62. Open daily June-Sept. 10am-8pm; Oct.-May 10am-4pm. 12hv, students 6hv.)* The **Museum of Lesya Ukrainka,** Yekaterinskaya 8, honors the famous Ukrainian writer, who lived here briefly in 1897, and pays tribute to the Ukrainian cultural heritage of Crimea. *(☎32 55 25. Open June-Aug. Tu-Su 11am-7pm; Sept.-May W-Su 10am-5pm. 3hv, students 2hv. Tours in English 10hv; call ahead.)* The **Yalta Cultural Museum,** in the same building, highlights aspects of local life from the 19th and 20th centuries. The entrance is to the left as you enter. *(Open Sept.-May Tu-Su 11am-6pm. 2hv.)* From June to August, special exhibits take over the Cultural Museum's space. *(☎32 16 34. Open daily June-Aug. 11am-6:30pm. 3hv, students 2hv.)* The young-at-heart will enjoy the **Fairy Tale Meadow** (Поляна Сказок; Polyana Skazok), dotted with sculptures of Snow White and characters from Russian and Ukrainian fairy tales. *(Take bus #24 from Kinoteatr Spartak. ☎39 64 02. Open daily July-Sept. 8am-8pm; Oct.-June 9am-5pm. 10hv, children 5hv.)*

🎵 📻 ENTERTAINMENT AND NIGHTLIFE

Yalta's many **beaches** stretch from both sides of the harbor. (Entrance to most city beaches 2hv, commercial beaches 2-5hv.) Many are crowded and lack sand. There are amusement park rides on nab. Lenina (10-12hv). **Organ concerts** are held in the Roman Catholic church, Pushkinskaya 25. (☎23 00 65. July-Sept. M-Su 8pm; Oct. and May-June M-Sa 7:30pm, Su 5pm. Buy tickets on-site.) Enjoy free music and dancing on pl. Lenina in front of the Lenin monument, or walk down **nab. Lenina** to **Primorsky beach,** where there are a number of affordable outdoor bars (beer 2-3hv). Popular nightclub **Tornado,** nab. Lenina 11, up the stairs through the arch and to the left, features house music, nightly laser shows, and lively clientele. (☎32 20 36. Beer 8hv. Cover 50-100hv. Open June-Sept. daily 10pm-5am; Oct.-Nov. Th-Sa 10pm-5am; Dec.-May F-Sa 10pm-5am.) **Cactus** (Кактус), Ruzvelta 7, above the Sea Terminal, has Tex-Mex food, disco music, theme nights, billiards, and a sea view. (☎32 16 14 and 32 36 59. Beer 5-20hv. Entrees 46-140hv. Cover after 10pm M-F and Su 30hv; Sa 50hv. Open daily 11am-5am.)

🎏 DAYTRIPS FROM YALTA

LIVADIYA (ЛІВАДІЯ). The ■ **Great Livadiya Palace,** built in 1911 as a summer residence for Tsar Nicholas II, is famous for hosting the **Yalta Conference** at the end of WWII. At this historic meeting, Winston Churchill, Franklin Roosevelt, and Josef Stalin negotiated post-war claims. On the first floor is the **White Hall,** where the talks took place. The round table at which the three leaders sat is just outside the hall. The **billiard room,** where the final agreement was signed, looks out onto the **Italian courtyard,** where the famous photo of the "Big Three" was taken. The 2nd floor of the palace houses the **Nicholas II Museum,** which displays the imperial family's living quarters, photographs, and possessions. *(Take bus or marshrutki #11 or 45 from the bus station or from "Kinoteatr Spartak." Bus #13 (1hv) also leaves from "Spartak." Ferries (15min., 1-2 per hr., 5-7hv) stop at the dock; from there, hike 150m up the hill. Alternatively, a 1hr. hike along the beach from Yalta will get you to Livadiya. Palace ☎31 55 81. Open May-Nov. M-Tu and Th-Su 10am-5pm; Dec.-Apr. Tu and Th-Su 10am-5pm. 15hv. English booklet 10hv.)*

MASSANDRA (МАССАНДРА). Overlooking Massandra from atop the hill, the elegant ■ **Massandra Palace** has a past that traces many major historical developments in Crimea. In the mid-1800s, the house of the former military Governor Count Mikhail Vorontsov was located here. After the house was wrecked by a storm in 1881, Vorontsov's son commissioned a French architect to build a palace on the site. Work was left unfinished when the son died, but construction resumed in 1892 when Tsar Alexander III hired a Russian architect to complete the structure in a Baroque style. The building served as the tsars' palace until 1920, and later became a base for the Crimean cadet corps, a tuberculosis sanatorium, a German officers' hospital, a Soviet hospital, Stalin's summer residence, and a favorite vacation spot for Soviet officials. The palace was opened to the public as a museum in 1992. The first floor contains particularly impressive dining and billiard rooms. Founded in 1894, the ■**Massandra Winery** holds in its cellars one of the largest wine collections in the world—about one million, including a rare 1775 "Jerez de la Frontera" vintage. Much of the collection was hidden under floorboards during WWI, and thousands of bottles were shipped abroad during WWII; thanks to this foresight, much of the collection escaped the German pillagers. Guided tours and tastings are available, and there's a store inside. *(To get to Massandra Palace, take trolley #2 or 3, or marshrutka #2 from Yalta, cross the street, and take the road uphill until you see the "Дворец" sign and arrow on the* street pointing to a forest path on the left. The path is poorly marked—when in doubt head up and left. ☎32 17 28. Open July-Aug. Tu-Su 9am-6pm; Sept.-Oct. and May-June Tu-Su 9am-5pm, Nov.-Apr. W-Su 9am-4pm. 15hv, students 7hv. English booklet 12hv. Massandra Winery is at Vinodela Egorova 9 (Винодела Егорова). From Yalta, take marshrutka #40 from the downtown station, by the clothing market, to Vinzavod (Винзавод). ☎23 26 62. 1hr. tours daily every 2hr. starting at 11am; last tour May-Oct. 7pm, Nov.-Apr. 5pm. Tours 40hv, with cellar admission 80hv; tasting without tour 25hv.)

NIKITSKIY BOTANICAL GARDEN (НИКИТСКИЙ САД; NIKITSKIY SAD).

Founded in 1812, the Nikitskiy Botanical Garden has over 15,000 species of native and foreign flora, including 1000 varieties of roses and many kinds of trees from around the world. Russian tour groups flood the grounds in summer. A walking path runs between the upper and lower entrances to the garden; follow the blue signs if you're going up, or the green signs if you're going down. Below the lower entrance is a ◼**cactus orangerie**, with a greenhouse and a garden. A stand in the garden sells cacti—pretty, but hard to pack. (From Yalta, take bus #34 or trolley #2 past Massandra. Ask the driver to let you off at "Nikitskiy Sad." ☎33 55 28. Open daily June-Aug. 8am-8pm; Sept.-May 9am-4pm. 7hv, students 3.50hv. Cactus orangerie 3/1hv.)

ALUPKA (АЛУПКА). The village of Alupka is the site of the **Vorontsov Palace** (Воронцовский Дворец; Vorontsovskiy Dvorets), built for Count Vorontsov during the first half of the 19th century. The palace has the grandeur and elegance of its English architects' native castles; Winston Churchill remarked that he felt at home when staying here during the Yalta Conference. The interior includes a majestic entrance hall, a large dining room with a balcony for musicians, and an indoor winter garden with a fountain and rare plants. Portraits and English landscapes decorate the walls. The palace **gardens** extend down toward the sea. The Lion Staircase, with three pairs of lions in different poses, provides a favorite photo op. For a view of the area, go to the nearby village of Miskhor and take the **cable car** (канатная дорога; kanatnaya doroga) 1234m up to the top of **Ay-Petri Mountain** (Ай-Петри). To get there from the palace, exit to the left and walk one kilometer through the park up the coast. From the top of Ay-Petri, you can take a *marshrutka* to Yalta. On the coast between Yalta and Alupka is Swallow's Nest (Ласточкино Гнездо; Lastochkino Gnezdo), a castle on a cliff. Built for a German businessman in 1912, it is now a popular symbol of the Crimea and is one of the peninsula's most-photographed sites. There is an Italian restaurant inside the castle. The ferry between Yalta and Alupka stops at the dock below the palace. You climb up to it, but the building is overrated. Stay on the ferry, snap a picture, and go on to Alupka. (In summer, take a ferry (1¼hr., 15 per day, 20hv) or marshrutka #27 (every 20-60min., 3hv) from Yalta, or the ferry from Livadiya (9hv). Palace ☎72 22 81 or 72 29 51. Open July-Aug. daily 8am-7:30pm; Sept.-Nov. 15 and Apr.-June daily 9am-5pm; Nov. 16-Mar. Tu-Su 9am-4pm. 15hv, students and children 7hv. To avoid waiting hours in line in July and Aug., show up before 10am or after 6pm. Miskhor (Мисхор) cable car ☎72 28 94. Runs every 10min. daily May-Sept. 9am-6pm; Oct.-Apr. 10am-5pm. 16hv.)

SEVASTOPOL (СЕВАСТОПОЛЬ)   ☎(80)692

Sevastopol (pop. 400,000) first gained international attention in the Crimean War (1854-55). In WWII, it was named one of the Soviet "Hero Cities" for its tragic losses. Sevastopol is not part of the Autonomous Republic of the Crimea and is governed directly by Kyiv. Both Russia and Ukraine use the city as a naval base. Some tourists come here to visit the historical museums and the naval port, while others relax on the beach and take boat rides in Sevastopol's many bays.

☐ TRANSPORTATION

Trains: Privokzalnaya pl. 3 (Привокзальная; ☎54 30 77, 48 79 26). Purchase tickets for non-Crimean destinations several weeks in advance for travel during July and Aug. Advance ticket office across the street from the bus station (open M-F 7am-6pm; Sa-Su, holidays, and the last day of the month 7:30am-5pm). To: **Kyiv** (18hr., 2 per day, 60hv); **Moscow, RUS** (24hr., 2 per day, 235hv); **St. Petersburg, RUS** (35hr., 1 per day, 317hv). All Crimean *elektrichki* (commuter rail) connect through **Simferopol** (2-2½hr., 7 per day, 3.10hv). Tickets are sold to the right of the train station. All trolleys at the train station go to the center; #17 and 20 run to the very start of Bolshaya Morskaya; all others head to pl. Lazaryova (0.40hv). For a **taxi**, call ☎050.

Buses: Pl. Revyakina 2 (Ревякина; ☎48 81 99). Open daily 6am-9pm. Luggage fee 1-6hv. To: **Alupka** (3hr., 3 per day, 12-14hv); **Bakhchisarai** (1hr., 2 per hr. 7am-8pm, 6-7hv); **Feodosiya** (4½hr., 2 per day, 23-35hv); **Kerch** (7½hr., 2 per day, 35-52hv); **Odessa** (13½hr., 1 per day, 44-73hv); **Simferopol** (2hr., 2 per hr. 6am-9pm, 11-14hv); **Yalta** (2hr., 1-3 per hr., 12-16hv); **Krasnodar, RUS** (15hr., 1 per day, 92hv); **Rostov-na-Donu, RUS** (16hr., 1 per day, 84hv).

Ferries: Leave from Artilleriyskaya Bay behind Gostinitsa Sevastopol and from Grafskaya Pristan (Графская Пристань) for the **north shore** (Северная Сторона; Severnaya Storona), landing near pl. Zakharova (Захарова; 20min., 1 per hr., 1.25hv). Take the ferry from Artilleriyskaya to **Radiogorka** (10-15min., 1 per hr., 1.50hv).

Public Transportation: Less crowded **marshrutki** (1hv) run the same routes as **buses** (0.60hv). *Marshrutki* leave from pl. Zakharova to popular Uchkuyuvka Beach (Учкуювка). **Trolleys** (0.40hv; pay on board) are efficient and convenient. #12 runs up Bolshaya Morskaya. #7 and 9 circle the center, stopping at the train station. #5 goes up Admirala Oktyabrskova to the west of the peninsula.

■✴▮ ORIENTATION AND PRACTICAL INFORMATION

The town center is on a peninsula below the Sevastopol harbor. **Pl. Lazaryova** (Лазарёва), up the street from Gostinitsa Sevastopol (p. 725), is a good starting point for exploring the city center. **Generala Petrova** (Генерала Петрова) delves inland, while **pr. Nakhimova** (Нахимова) curves from here along the peninsula, where it meets **Lenina** (Ленина) at pl. Nakhimova. Lenina runs parallel to the sea until **pl. Ushakova** (Ушакова). **Bolshaya Morskaya** (Болшая Морская) runs back to pl. Lazaryova. Vendors sell **maps** along nab. Kornilova and Primorskiy bul.

Tourist Offices: Kiosks along Primorskiy bul. offer city tours (50-80hv). Those near pl. Nakhimove advertise boat tours of the harbor (30min., 20hv). **Sanmarin** (Санмарин; ☎45 57 10; tour@sunmarine.biz), in Gostinitsa Sevastopol. Provides walking tours of the city (80-85hv) and other excursions. Open M-Sa 9am-7pm.

Currency Exchange: Exchange booths are everywhere. **Oshchadbank** (Ощадбанк; ☎54 12 16), at Bolshaya Morskaya 41. Cashes AmEx/Thomas Cooke **traveler's checks** and gives MC/V **cash advances,** all for 1.5% commission. **Western Union** services are available here and at the post office. Open M-F 8am-1pm and 2-6pm, Sa 8am-4pm.

Luggage Storage: Lockers in bus station. 2hv per 24hr. Open daily 6am-7pm. Guarded luggage storage in the train station, to the far right of the *elektrichka* ticket office. 3-4hv until 8pm the next day. Open daily 8am-1pm and 2-6pm.

Pharmacy: (Аптека; Apteka), Bolshaya Morskaya 48 (☎54 30 26 or 55 41 75). English "pharmacy" sign. Large selection. Open 24hr.; closed 2nd W of each month. MC/V.

Telephones: (☎55 02 66), to the left of the post office. Open 24hr.

Internet: Absolutnaya Realnost (Абсолутняа Реалность; ☎54 40 79), on Bolshaya Morskaya on the 2nd fl. of Kinoteatr Pobeda (Кинотеатр Победа). 5hv per hr. Open 24hr. **Soyuz** (Союз), pr. Nakhimova 4 (☎45 59 90), in the Pioneer's House (Дом Пионира) basement, down stairs and to right through the metal fence. 6hv per hr. Open 24hr. **Alpha Club** (☎55 93 09), on the first floor of Hotel Krym. 6hv per hr. Open 24hr.

Post Office: Bolshaya Morskaya 21. **Western Union.** Open June-Aug. M-F 8am-7pm, Sa-Su 8am-6pm; Sept.-May M-F 8am-6pm, Sa-Su 8am-5pm. **Postal Code:** 99 011.

ACCOMMODATIONS AND FOOD

Private rooms and short-term **apartments** are inexpensive and easy to arrange in summer. A desk at the entrance of the bus station sets up accommodations for a 25hv fee. Rooms fill quickly in July and August; the safest option is to reserve well in advance. At **Gostinitsa Sevastopol ❷**, pr. Nakhimova 8, elegant pre-Soviet architecture meets bland Soviet interior design. The central location is ideal, just five stops from the bus station on trolley #1, 3, 7, or 9. Many rooms have sea views, and the lobby is downright grand. (☎46 64 00; fax 46 64 09. Hot showers 2.50hv. Singles 40-265hv; doubles 66-266hv; triples 87-339hv. MC/V.) **Gostinitsa Krym ❷** (Крым), Shestaya Bastionnaya 46 (Бастионная), is up Admirala Okty-abrskova from Bolshaya Morskaya, near pl. Vosstavshikh (Восставших). To get there, take trolley #5, 6, or 10; or, hop on any 100-numbered *marshrutka* from the train or bus station. All rooms have balconies and private baths; most have sea views. (☎46 90 00 or 55 51 51. Breakfast included. Hot water 7-9am and 7-9pm. Singles 132hv; doubles 204hv.) The **central market** is downhill from pl. Laz-aryova at the intersection of Partizanskaya (Партизанская) and Odesskaya (Одесская; open Tu-Su 8am-8pm). A local favorite is ▧**Traktir ❷** (Трактир), Bolshaya Morskaya 8. Waitresses in sailor uniforms serve excellent Ukrainian food and drinks, including wonderful *solyanka* (meat soup; small 11hv, large 18hv) and *kulebyaka* (pie with meat and cabbage; 7hv). The outdoor terrace is pleasant in summer. (☎54 47 60. English menu. Entrees 15-45hv. Open daily 10am-11pm.) **Cafe Zdorovye ❶** (Здоровье; Health), Partizanskaya 5, is at the end of the road leading off to the left from the front of the central market. Although Zdorovye serves "health food," sour cream still makes it into almost every dish. (☎55 05 07. Open M-F 9am-5pm, Sa 9am-3pm. Chicken cutlets with soy 2.20hv. *Piroshki* (пирошки) with soy filling 0.50hv.)

SIGHTS AND ENTERTAINMENT

▧**PANORAMA DEFENSE OF SEVASTOPOL 1854-1855.** One of the most impres-sive sights in Ukraine, the panorama (Панорама Оборона Севастопола; Pan-orama Oborona Sevastopola) was built in 1905 to commemorate the heroic defense of the city during the Crimean War against Britain and France. Though destroyed during WWII, it was recreated by a team of Moscow artists and reopened in 1954. The display artfully blends a painted backdrop with a realis-tic 3D foreground. The 360° canvas is 14m high and 115m in circumference. English captions are posted in the lower viewing area. *(Enter the park at pl. Usha-kova and continue to the end of Istoricheskiy bul. (Исторический). It's the round build-ing, opposite the fountain. ☎49 97 38. Open July-Sept. daily 9:30am-6pm; Oct.-Apr. Tu-Su 9:30am-6pm; May-June daily 9:30am-5pm; ticket office closes 30min. earlier. 15hv, students 8hv. Tours in English 20hv.)*

RUINS AT CHERSONESUS. The austere, beautiful ruins at Chersonesus (Херсонес; Khersones) are 2500 years old. They include an ancient amphitheater, acres of overgrown foundation, and the remains of several basilicas. In the middle stands the modern **St. Vladimir's Cathedral** (Владимирский Собор; Vladimirskiy Sobor), built in the late 19th century and reconstructed in 2001. *(Take minibus #22, labeled "Херсонес"; 0.75hv. ☎ 24 13 01. Open daily June-Aug. 8am-8pm; Sept.-May 9am-5pm. 7hv, students 5hv. Tour in English 16hv. Tour in Russian 10/6hv.)*

MUSEUM OF THE BLACK SEA FLEET. This museum (Музей Чёрноморского Флота; Muzey Chyornomorskogo Flota) tells the military history of the Black Sea with documents, models, and original weapons. The lower floor displays maps and items recovered from ships. The upper floor has Soviet flags and decorated uniforms. *(☎ 54 22 89 or 54 03 92. Russian captions only. Open W-Su 10am-6pm; closed last F of each month. 7hv, students 4hv. Tours in English 12hv, min. 10 people.)*

OTHER SIGHTS. Impressive monuments to Sevastopol's naval heroes decorate the streets and the harbor. In the bay near pl. Nakhimova is a **monument** to sunken ships: during the Crimean War, the Black Sea Fleet sunk many of its own ships to prevent the enemy from entering the bay. The **obelisk** that marks Sevastopol as a Soviet Hero City is visible from nab. Kornilova; the nearby **Monument to the Black Sea Submariners** can also be seen from there. **Park Pobediy** (Парк Победий) at **Omega Beach** (Пляж Омега; Plyazh Omega) is constantly packed during summer; its bars and discos thump until dawn. *(Take trolley #10 to the Plyazh Omega stop.)*

WESTERN UKRAINE

Proud residents of Western Ukraine will tell you that their region is "the most Ukrainian" part of the country. It has stubbornly maintained its unique identity. During WWII, some Western Ukrainians fought against both the Nazis and the Soviets, aiming instead for independence. Since the fall of the USSR, the western region has earned a reputation as the core of Ukrainian nationalism. Lviv is the cultural center, with a large proportion of the country's historic monuments, while the beautiful Carpathian Mountains are home to traditional peasant communities.

LVIV (ЛЬВІВ)   ☎(80)32[2]

While Kyiv is the political and economic capital of Ukraine, many consider Lviv (pop. 830,000) to be the cultural and patriotic center of the country. The city was at the crossroads of international trade during medieval times and experienced Austrian and Polish rule before the rise of the Soviet Union. Unlike Kyiv, Lviv was not destroyed during WWII, so its historic sights were spared. In contrast to tourist-heavy Prague and Kraków, Lviv feels lived-in rather than on display. The modern city, which stretches far beyond the historic center, is bustling, chock full of cafes, and close to the beautiful Carpathian mountains.

All phone numbers in Lviv that used to begin with "9" now have a "2" added in front when dialed locally. But when dialed from a different area code, the number remains the same as before, as the "2" added in front for local calls is actually the last digit of the area code. For example, a phone number that used to be 90 00 00 is now dialed 290 00 00 from within Lviv, but is still dialed 80 32 290 00 00 from elsewhere. Numbers that do not begin with 9, like 70 00 00, remain as before, and are still dialed 80 322 70 00 00 from elsewhere.

⎕ TRANSPORTATION

Flights: Lviv Airport, Lyubinska (Любінська; ☎ 69 21 12). **Traident** (Траидент), Kopernyka 18 (Коперника; ☎/fax 297 14 93 or 297 13 32), books tickets for major airlines. **Tourist Agency Mandry** (Мандри), Rynok 44 (Ринок; ☎ 297 56 46, fax 297 16 61; www.mandry-travel.lviv.ua, books flights, provides help with other travel arrangements, and plans excursions (3hr. min., US$35). Open M-F 10am-6pm, Sa 10am-2pm.

Trains: Pl. Vokzalna (Вокзальна; ☎ 26 11 76, info 005). Buy tickets at Hnatyuka 20 (Гнатюка; ☎ 35 25 79 or 39 00 53), marked by the "каси" (kasy) sign. Open M-Sa 8am-2pm and 3-8pm, Su 8am-2pm and 3-6pm. Bring your passport. You may have to go to the train station for same-day tickets. Info about trains 2hv. To: **Kyiv** (9hr., 9 per day, 55hv); **Odessa** (12hr., 2 per day, 51hv); **Simferopol** (26hr.; 1-2 per day; 69hv); **Bratislava, SLK** (22hr., 1 per day, 360hv); **Budapest, HUN** (13hr., 1 per day, 420hv); **Kraków, POL** (8hr., every other day, 220hv); **Moscow, RUS** (25hr., 3 per day, 210hv); **Prague, CZR** (24hr., 1 per day, 400hv); **Warsaw, POL** (14hr., 1 per day, 230hv).

Buses: Main station, Stryyska 189 (Стрийська; ☎ 294 98 17). From pl. Halytzka (Галицька) take bus #5 or *marshrutka* #71. To: **Kraków, POL** (8-9hr., 1 per day, 98hv); **Przemyśl, POL** (4hr., 7 per day, 32hv); **Warsaw, POL** (10hr., 3 per day, 109hv). Lviv also has three **regional stations.** The one at Khmelnytskoho 225 (Хмельницького; ☎ 52 04 89) can be reached by tram #4 from Shevchenka (Шевченка).

Public Transportation: Maps, available at the English-language bookstore (see **Orientation and Practical Information**), show lines for **trams, trolleys,** and **buses.** Buy tickets (0.50hv for trams and trolleys, 0.60hv for buses, and 1hv for *marshrutki*) on board from the conductor. If none are present, simply pass your money to the driver once seated. 10hv fine for riding ticketless. In the Old Town, pl. Halytska is a hub for buses.

Taxis: ☎ 39 34 34 or 298 19 95. Agree on the price before you get in. 7-20hv.

◪ ◪ ORIENTATION AND PRACTICAL INFORMATION

The center of town is **pl. Rynok** (Ринок), the old market square. Around it, a grid of streets forms the **Old Town,** where most of the sights are located. Toward the train station, broad **pr. Svobody** (Свободи) runs from the **Opera House** to **pl. Mitskevycha** (Міцкевича), the Old Town's center of commerce. **Pr. Shevchenko** (Шевченко) extends to the right of pl. Mitskevycha. Trams #1 and 9, and *marshrutka* #68 run from the main train station to the Old Town's center; tram #6 runs to the north end of pr. Svobody, behind the Opera. Tram #9 goes from the Old Town to the station.

▨ Tourist Office: Lviv Tourist Information Center, Pyidvalna 3 (Підвальна; ☎ 297 57 51 or 297 57 67; www.tourism.lviv.ua). Enter the building and turn right; it's the door at the end of the hall. Some staff speak English, and all are eager to welcome tourists and provide information. A few brochures are free, but most cost 2-11hv. **Maps** also 2-11 hv. City tour 50hv per hr. Open M-F 10am-6pm except for a 1hr. lunch break, which occurs between 1 and 3pm. For personal, English tours of Lviv and its environs, contact Roman Harbuzyuk (☎ 067 670 24 31; www.ukraine-tour.narod.ru).

Currency Exchange: Western Union services (M-F 9am-1pm and 1:30-6:30pm, Sa 9am-1pm) available at the **post office's** window #10, on the 2nd fl. In the same building at window #12, **Availabank** cashes **traveler's checks** (3% commission) and gives MC/V **cash advances.** (☎ 93 46 77. Open M-F 9:30am-1pm and 2-6pm, Sa 10am-2pm.) Storefronts along pr. Svobody and throughout town **exchange currency.** Look for the Обмін Валут (Obmin Valut) signs. **ATMs** show Банкомат (bankomat) signs.

Luggage Storage: At the train station. 6hv. Open 24hr.

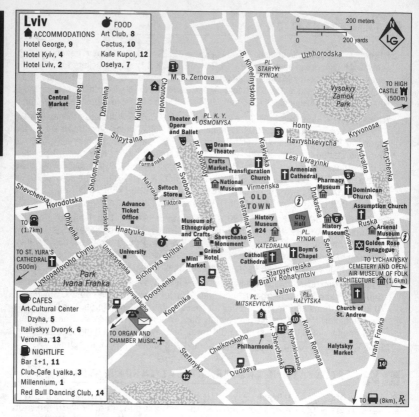

Lviv

🏠 ACCOMMODATIONS
Hotel George, **9**
Hotel Kyiv, **4**
Hotel Lviv, **2**

🍎 FOOD
Art Club, **8**
Cactus, **10**
Kafe Kupol, **12**
Oselya, **7**

☕ CAFES
Art-Cultural Center
Dzyha, **5**
Italiyskyy Dvoryk, **6**
Veronika, **13**

🎵 NIGHTLIFE
Bar 1+1, **11**
Club-Cafe Lyalka, **3**
Millennium, **1**
Red Bull Dancing Club, **14**

English-Language Bookstores: Budynok Knihi (Будинок Книгі), Pl. Mitskevycha 8 (☎74 41 64). Go here for city **guidebooks** (15hv) and **maps** (6hv). Open June-July M-F 10am-7pm, Sa 10am-4pm; Aug.-May M-F 10am-6pm, Sa 10am-3pm. **Knihy Ksiazky**, Pl. Mitskevycha 8 (☎72 27 29), next door to Budinok Knihi. Wide selection of English-language literature. English-language books 15-60hv, **guidebooks** 10hv, **maps** 7hv.

24hr. Pharmacy: Добра Аптека (Dobra Apteka), Tyktora 3 (Тиктора; ☎72 50 48). **Apteka #28** (Аптека), Zelena 33 (Зелена; ☎75 37 63).

Emergency: Ambulance ☎03. **City-wide information:** ☎09.

Telephones: Telecommunication Service Center, Doroshenka 39 (Дорошенка; ☎72 90 12), around the corner from the post office. Local pay phones in boothless area near entrance. Farther down are phone booths for long-distance calls, which must be paid for in advance. To place a long distance call, visit the cashier window in the boothed area that is nearest the local phones. State the city being called and number of min. to be on the line. Prices vary by destination. Local telephone cards for pay phones available at the same window. 6hv for 90min. Open daily 7am-11pm.

Internet: Internet Club, Dudaeva 12 (Дудаева; ☎72 27 38). Walk into the alley; the door is on the right. Fast Internet on 25 computers. 4hv per hr.; 10hv for midnight-8am; 15min. minimum. Printing. Open 24hr. **Chorna Medeya** (Чорна Медея), Doroshenka

50 (☎298 72 75). 4hv per hr. in the main room, 6hv per hr. in the VIP room, which has computers with CD-RW capability. All night (11pm-8am) 12hv main room, 16hv VIP; ½-night (11pm-3am or 3-8am) 8hv main room, 12hv VIP. Open 24hr.

Post Office: Slovatskoho 1 (Словатского; ☎74 40 62), 1 block on right from Park Ivana Franka. **Poste Restante** at window #3, 2nd fl. To collect packages, take claim slip to 1st fl. window #3. ID required to pick up packages. Open M-F 8am-8pm, Sa 8am-4pm; lower fl. open same hours and Su 9am-3pm. **Postal Code:** 79 000.

◤ ACCOMMODATIONS

Budget accommodations in Lviv are limited and generally unpleasant. Women at the train station, or occasionally near hotel entrances, hawk apartments and **private rooms** (25hv). Before agreeing on anything, be sure to check the place out: there are many dilapidated buildings in the city center. It is typical for hot water to shut off twice daily, 6-9am and 6-9pm. Some places lack it altogether.

Hotel Lviv (Готель Львів), Chornovola 7 (Чорновола; ☎79 22 70 or 79 22 72; fax 72 86 51), down the street from the Opera off the end of pr. Svobody. Despite its ugly concrete exterior and dreary Soviet-style lobby, many foreign backpackers gravitate toward this clean hotel. The rooms without baths are a good deal. Singles without bath 55hv, with bath 100hv; doubles 90hv/140hv; triples without bath 105hv; quads 140hv/260hv. The disco downstairs is loud; upper floors are best. Daytime luggage storage for departing guests 5hv; ask the staff on your floor. Utel phone in the lobby for international calls; reception staff sells cards (15-48hv). Cash only. ❶

Hotel George (Готель Жорж), pl. Mitskevycha 1 (☎74 21 82; www.georgehotel.com.ua). In the square where pr. Svobody meets pr. Shevchenko. The architecture combines Austro-Hungarian aesthetics with Soviet functionality: a columned lobby and ornate staircase contrast a plain reception area, casino, and bar. Renovated rooms with bath are pricey, but budget rooms are reasonable. All but budget rooms have cable TV including BBC World. Breakfast included. Free safe-deposit box and luggage lockers (2hv per piece) both with 24hr. service. Laundry 2.50-6hv per g, depending on the type of garment. Singles US$28-86; doubles US$33-91. MC/V. ❸

Hotel Kyiv (Готель Київ), Horodotska 15 (Городоцка; ☎72 85 71). Entrance on Furmanska (Фурманська), near the corner of Horodotska. From the train station, take *marshrutka* #66 and ask to be let off at the hotel. A bargain for groups of 3-4, if you don't mind that the building is over a century old. All singles have baths and are more comfortable than other options, which are dorm-like. Singles 75-78hv; doubles 50hv, with bath 90hv; triples 60/105hv; quads without bath 80hv. Cash only. ❶

◖ FOOD

The main market is **Tsentralnyy Rynok** (Центральний Ринок; Central Market), also called **Krakivskyy Rynok** (Краківський Ринок; Kraków Market) by locals. (Open M-Sa 9am-6pm.) A 24hr. **Mini Market,** Doroshenka 6 (☎72 35 44), is a block from the Grand Hotel. Lviv is famous for its **Svitoch** (Світоч) confectionery; Svitoch stores are scattered throughout town. The main store is at pr. Svobody and Tyktora. (☎72 76 84. Candy bars 3-4.50hv. Open M-F 9am-9pm, Sa 9am-8pm, Su 11am-6pm. MC/V.) For a cheap lunch, stop by one of the hot dog stands on pr. Svobody. (Hot dog with cabbage, corn, ketchup, mayonnaise, mustard 2.80hv).

Oselya (Оселя), Hnatyuka 11 (Гнатюка; ☎72 16 01). With its background of folk music, embroidered shirts strung on a clothesline, and wicker baskets of Ukrainian Easter eggs, Oselya flirts with tackiness in its homage to traditional, rural life. Nevertheless, it's worth visiting for the authentic Ukrainian cuisine. Start with the vegetarian *borshch* (борщ; 8.96hv), then try *kremzlyky po-hutsulsky* (кремзлики по-гутсулський; potato pancakes and pork with mushrooms served in a clay pot; 25.96hv). Soups 8.68-14.17hv. Cold appetizers 7-26hv. Entrees 7.72-84.42hv, most 15-24hv. Vegetarian entrees 10.20-24.62hv. Live folk music Sa-Su 7pm. Open daily 11am-11pm. MC/V. ❷

Kafe Kupol (Кафе Купол), Chaykovskoho 37 (вул Чайковского; ☎74 42 54; kupollviv@ukr.net). From Hotel George walk down pr. Shevchenka to McDonald's and turn right onto Chaykovskoho. Continue to a hill and climb ½ a block; Kupol is on the left. Located in the former home of the Polish poet Wanda Monne, Kupol fittingly specializes in Polish cuisine. Free tours on request. Dine on the patio or in the 1920s-style dining room. Entrees 13.15-46.50hv. Open daily 11am-11pm. MC/V. ❷

Art Club (Арт Клуб), pl. Pidkovy 1 (Підвоки; ☎72 88 91), off pr. Svobody behind the Shevchenko monument. A favorite among Lviv's few backpackers, although locals dominate the scene. A large patio, complete with comfy wicker chairs, affords views of several sights, including a monument to Cossak Ivan Pidkova. Traditional Ukrainian cuisine. English menu. Beer 2-7hv. Breakfast 4.80-7.70hv. Entrees 11.10-32.40hv. MC/V. ❷

Cactus (Кактус), O. Nyzhankivskoho 18 (О. Нижанківського; ☎74 50 61). Abstract paintings clash with the desert ranch motif set up by decorations like cacti and a wooden fence. The creative menu, however, fits the offbeat mood perfectly. Breakfast daily 7am-noon. Omelettes 10.50hv; potatoes with minced meat and sauce 10.50hv. The 3-course business lunch is a good deal (soup, salad, and an entree; M-F noon-3pm; 22hv). English menu. Entrees 16.50-150hv. Open M-Th and Su 7am-11pm, F-Sa 7am-2am. MC/V. ❷

■ CAFES

▦ **Art-Cultural Center Dzyha** (культурно-мистецький центр Дзига), Virmenska 35 (Вірменська; ☎75 21 01). Inside a free art gallery, this small cafe boasts unique coffee concoctions with a touch of artistic pretense. Rev your engine with a flaming coffee (3.50-5.20hv), or unwind with a unique cocktail, like vodka with honey and Carpathian herbs (3hv). Desserts include a bizarre "lard in chocolate" dish (4.50hv). English menu. Vegetarian options 4.20-14.35hv. Open daily 10am-10pm.

▦ **Veronika** (Вероніка), pr. Shevchenko 21 (☎297 81 28). Famous for its delicious cakes (4.50-7hv per slice), pastries (2-3hv), and truffles (2.30hv). A menu is available in English, but most people choose from the display case. Outdoor tables in summer. The iced coffee (7.50-18hv) is particularly good. Claustrophobes might want to avoid the smoky European restaurant downstairs. Hot appetizers range from pastries (15.50hv) to foie gras with Bordeaux sauce (86hv). Try the sweet Odessa sparkling wine (28hv) with dessert. Soups 22.50-68.20hv. Entrees 8.50-98hv. Open daily 10am-11pm. V.

Italiyskyy Dvoryk (Італійський Дворик), pl. Rynok 6, in the courtyard of the building that houses the History Museum. Walk through the museum entrance past the security guard and cashier to reach this beautiful courtyard and cafe. Once owned by a wealthy 16th-century merchant, the building is now one of Lviv's most pleasant spots for coffee (2.50-4.50hv) or tea (2-3hv). Classical musicians accompany patrons' sipping Sa-Su, starting around 5 or 6pm. In winter, the cafe moves to a room inside the building. Open M-F 10am-8pm, Sa-Su 10am-7pm.

◉ SIGHTS

The Old Town is full of churches, squares, and old buildings that show the influence of Aremenians, Austrians, Greeks, Hungarians, Italians, Jews, and Poles, among others. Most of the sights and museums are located in or near pl. Rynok. The best time to visit churches is 5-7pm, when the doors are open for services.

PLOSHCHA RYNOK (ПЛОЩА РИНОК). This historic market square lies in the heart of the city, surrounded by richly decorated merchants' homes dating from the 16th to 18th centuries. The ratusha (ратуша; town hall) is a 19th-century addition. For a wonderful view of the Old Town, climb the wooden staircase of the ▓tower in the middle of the square. *(Ticket office is downstairs, to the left of the main entrance. ☎297 57 73. Open Tu-F 10am-5pm, Sa-Su 11am-7pm. 10hv, children 2.50hv.)*

ARMENIAN CATHEDRAL (ВІРМЕНСЬКИЙ КАФЕДРАЛЬНИЙ). Solemn music adds to the spiritual atmosphere at this cathedral, built in the 14th century by Lviv's Armenian community. To the left, in the painting "Burial of St. Odelone," Death holds melting candles to indicate how much longer individuals will live; one man seems slightly worried about the size of his. Near the altar, Judas appears as a shadow in a representation of the Last Supper. A mosaic above the altar is illuminated by the magnificent light that pours into the dome. Be sure to visit the courtyard where the cathedral keeps its medieval Armenian inscriptions, and where the cemetery allots each family only one gravestone. *(Virmenska 7-9. Open M-F 9am-5pm.)*

GOLDEN ROSE SYNAGOGUE. For centuries, Lviv was an important center of Jewish culture. Little remains of this synagogue, which was built in the late 16th century and destroyed by the Nazis in 1942. A sign in English is posted to the left of the remains of the synagogue's back wall. *(Walk up Staroyevreiska—Староєврєіск, or Old Jewish Road; the synagogue is on the left before the Arsenal Museum. Call the tourist office to arrange a guided tour (50hv per hr.) of the city's Jewish heritage sites.)*

BOYM'S CHAPEL (КАПЛИЦЯ БОЇМІВ; KAPLYTSYA BOYIMIV). This small chapel was commissioned in the early 17th century by Gregory Boym, a rich Hungarian merchant and one-time mayor of Lviv. Legend has it that Boym built the chapel after he discovered his wife's infidelity; perhaps this is why the intricate sculptures covering the walls stare down at visitors with accusatory expressions. *(Pl. Katedralna 1. ☎74 40 47 or 75 22 77. Open daily 11am-5pm; Nov.-Apr. call ahead. 2hv.)*

OTHER OLD TOWN SIGHTS. The massive **Assumption Church** (Успенська Церква; Uspenska Tserkva) lies just up Pidvalna (Підвальна); enter through the archway. Next to the church, **Kornyakt's Tower** (Башта Корнякта; Bashta Kornyakta) hangs its bell 60m above ground. The Baroque **Dominican Church** (Домініканський Костел; Dominikanskyy Kostel) is on pl. Muzeyna (Музейна); look for the elliptical

TRAVEL AT A STANDSTILL

"Are you the last in line?" someone asked while I was attempting to purchase a train ticket. What a ridiculous question, I thought to myself, of course I am! Though the line was rather mangled and chaotic, I was clearly at the end of it. "Yes, I'm last," I replied. She asked me to save her spot as she jumped into another line. A couple of minutes later someone barged right in front of me: his spot had also been saved. A few others filled in at various places in the line as a nearby ticket window went on a "technical break." These frequent lapses in service occur at set times throughout the day, on schedules specific to each window. I started to feel like I was in a Kafka novel and that this line would never end.

Lines for train tickets reflect the Soviet era, when supplies and services were not contingent on market forces. Ukrainians consequently are experts at negotiating multiple lines. They know technical break schedules, and learn to gauge line length and how many spots might be on hold. They have developed incredible levels of patience.

Finally, an hour after I took my place in line, I reached the ticket window just in time for the clerk to slam it shut and shout, "Pererva!" (break).

—Jason Campbell

dome. The **Church of the Transfiguration** (Преображенська Церква; Preobrazhenska Tserkva), Krakivska 21 (Краківська), is packed with beautiful side altars and icons. The Church's underground passageways run throughout the city, but getting into them requires a researcher's permit. **St. Andrew's Church** at pl. Soborna demonstrates how Greek Catholics blend Orthodoxy and Catholicism.

HIGH CASTLE HILL (ВИСОКИЙ ЗАМОК; VYSOKYY ZAMOK). For a great workout and an even better view of the city, climb up High Castle Hill, the former site of the Galician king's palace. A Ukrainian flag and a cross, the two most potent symbols of religious, nationalist Lviv, sit high atop the hill. *(Follow Krivonosa (Кривоноса-вул) from its intersection with Hotny and Halytskoho. Go until you pass #39, then take a left down the dirt road and wind your way up around the hill counter-clockwise.)*

LICHAKIVSKY CEMETERY (ЛИЧАКІВСЬКИЙ ЦВИНТАР; LYCHAKIVSKYY TSVYNTAR). Enter through the main gate of the cemetery and follow the path to the right to visit the graves of famous Ukrainian artists. On the left, a hammer-armed Stakhanovite decorates the eternal bed of Ivan Franko (Іван Франко), poet, socialist activist, and celebrated national hero. *(Take tram #4 or 7 from the beginning of Lichakivşka (Личаківська), and get off at the 1st stop after the sharp right turn. ☎ 75 54 15. Open daily 9am-6pm. 3hv. Tours in English 40hv. Call 2 days in advance.)*

IVAN FRANKO PARK (ПАРК ІМ. ІВАНА ФРАНКА; PARK IM. IVANA FRANKA). Walk uphill through Ivan Franko Park past amorous young couples and old men playing cards to Lystopadovoho (it's on the right side of the park). Continue up Lystopadovoho and **St. Yura's Cathedral** (Собор св. Юра; Sobor sv. Yura) is on the right. While the grounds are under construction, the Cathedral and its elaborate altar can still be viewed. *(Open daily 7am-1pm and 3-8pm.)* Toward the train off Horodotska is **St. Elizabeth's Cathedral.** Constructed by Poles who settled in Lviv, it appears run-down at first glance—but the interior has been fully refurbished and is full of activity. *(From pr. Svobody, head down Hnatyuka, then take a left on Sichovykh Striltsiv (Січових Стрільців) to the park, which faces the columned facade of Lviv University.)*

🏛 MUSEUMS

■ OPEN-AIR MUSEUM OF FOLK ARCHITECTURE AND RURAL LIFE. This outdoor museum (Музей Народної Архітектури та Побуту у Львові; Muzey Narodnoi Arkhitektury ta Pobutu u Lvovi) at Shevchenkivskyy Hai (Шевченківський Гай) features a collection of Ukrainian buildings made entirely out of wood (скансен; skansen). Don't miss the 18th-century wooden church. *(From Doroshenka, take tram #2 or 7 to Mechnykova. Cross the street and follow Krupyarska all the way up the hill, bearing right at the top. Tours ☎ 71 23 60. Open Tu-Su 10am-6pm. 1.50hv, children 0.75hv. English map with museum description 2hv.)*

■ PHARMACY MUSEUM (АПТЕКА-МУЗЕЙ; APTEKA-MUZEY). This fascinating museum, located in one of Lviv's old pharmacies, details the history of the pharmaceutical business. There are vials of chemicals, Lviv's earliest written prescriptions, and an old wine bar in the basement. Make sure to check out the spooky alchemist's room and the "iron wine." A modern pharmacy is located in the front of the building. *(Drukarska 2. ☎ 72 00 41. Open M-F 9am-7pm, Sa-Su 10am-5pm. 3hv.)*

HISTORY MUSEUM (ІСТОРИЧНИЙ МУЗЕЙ; ISTORYCHNYY MUZEY). A complex of three museums on pl. Rynok. The main building, at #6, was the 17th-century home of Polish King Jan III Sobieski. It was here that the "eternal peace" of 1686 was signed. The agreement split Ukraine in two—the western half went to the Polish empire and the eastern to the Russian empire. The museum at #4 recounts the horrors of WWII and Soviet occupation. The museum at #24 traces the history of the region from Kyivan Rus to annexation by the Polish empire in 1686. *(Pl. Rynok #4, 6, and 24. ☎ 72 06 71. Open M-Tu and Th-Su 10am-5pm. Tours in English 10-15hv, when guides are available. Each museum 3hv, except for museum at #24, which is 2hv.)*

NATIONAL MUSEUM (НАЦІОНАЛЬНИЙ МУЗЕЙ). This museum holds the world's most important collection of Ukrainian icons, most of which were created by village amateur artists. They are unusual in that they are painted in the Orthodox style but depict Catholic subjects. *(Pr. Svobody 20. ☎ 74 22 82 or 74 22 18; fax 75 92 93. Open M-Th and Sa-Su 10am-6pm. 4hv, children 1.50hv. Tours in English 25hv.)*

ARSENAL MUSEUM (МУЗЕЙ АРСЕНАЛ; MUZEY ARSENAL). Housed in a stone fortress that used to produce weapons, this museum has a neatly presented collection of cannons, swords, daggers, guns and armor gathered from over 30 countries. Artifacts date from the 11th to the 20th centuries. *(Pidvalna 5. ☎ 72 19 01. Open M-Tu and Th-Su 10am-5pm. 3hv; students, children, and seniors 1.50hv.)* At Salon Arsenal (Салон Арсенал), in front of the museum, you can get your picture taken with a variety of weapons and armor (10-15hv). *(Open M-F 11am-6pm, Sa-Su 11am-5pm.)*

🎭 ENTERTAINMENT

After lunch, pr. Svobody fills with colorful characters singing tunes to accordion accompaniment. On summer evenings, the sounds of light jazz from sidewalk cafes permeate the avenue, elderly men play chess near the Shevchenko monument, and couples stroll the walkway leading to the Opera House. Purchase tickets for the opera and other performances at the box offices (театральни касси; teatralny kassy), pr. Svobody 37. (Open M-Sa 10am-1pm and 2-5pm.) During Lviv City Days (☎97 59 13), held in early May, concerts, theater performances, and competitions are held at venues throughout the city. Easter is celebrated at the **Open-Air Museum of Folk Architecture** with folk and religious traditions and games for children. In September of even-numbered years, the **Golden Lion Theater Festival** takes to the streets with free performances by local and international troupes.

Theater of Opera and Ballet (Театр Опери Та Балету; Teatr Opery Ta Baletu), pr. Svobody 1 (☎ 72 88 60). Many of the world's foremost artists have graced the stage of this beautiful theater, which still hosts several performances per week. It's a safe bet that the schedule posted in front of entrance will feature a Tchaikovsky production. Ticket office open daily 11am-7pm, but often closed on days without shows. Shows 10-75hv.

Philharmonic (Філармонія; Filarmoniya), Chaykovskoho 7 (☎72 10 42), the next block down on Shevchenka from Hotel George. The Philharmonic puts on classical music performances by renowned guest performers. Ticket office open daily Sept.-May 11am-2pm and 3-6pm. 5-30hv, children's show 2hv.

Organ and Chamber Music (Будинок органної і камерної музики; Budynok ophannoi i kamernoi muzyky), s. Bandery 10 (Бандери). Take tram #2 or 9 down S. Bandery to the Lviv Polytechnic stop. Concerts Sa-Su 5pm. Tickets at the door 1hv.

🍸 NIGHTLIFE

Club-Cafe Lyalka (Клуб-Кафе Лялька), Halytskoho 1 (Галицького; ☎298 08 09), below Puppet Theater (Театр Лялок; Teatr Lyalok), in the basement. A young crowd fills this lively club, where locals jam to disco and live performances. The energetic dancers, packed floor, and decorative art installations contrast starkly with the building's sterile, concrete exterior and poorly lit surroundings; call ahead for schedule, and keep your wits about you. Cheap food (2-20hv) and drinks (wine 3-6hv; beer 3-10hv). English menu. Cover free-25hv. Open daily 1pm-7am or until last guest. Cash only.

Millennium (Міленіум), Chornovola 2 (☎40 35 91). From Hotel Lviv, cross Chornovola and take a left; Millenium is a few blocks farther. A classic Eastern European dance club well worth a visit. Elaborate light effects play across the warehouse-like room, while a large movie screen shows silent cartoons. Surrounding the dance floor is plenty of comfortable seating where groups take vodka shots (bottle 30hv) chased with Coca-Cola (6hv). Beer 5hv. Cover 30hv. Open Tu-Su 9pm-4am. Cash only.

Bar 1+1, pr. Shevchenka 11 (Шевченка; ☎74 37 47), downstairs. A cozy bar decorated with stone and stained glass. Heineken 6hv. Entrees 10-25hv. Open 24hr. Cash only.

Red Bull Dancing Club (Ред Бул), Ivana Franka 15 (☎296 51 51). Red bikes and trucks decorate the walls of Red Bull. Young patrons dance the night away in the basement, while a DJ spins hard-core and rave music that keeps pace with the strobe lights. Beer 3-14hv. Cover 10-20hv with a 20-40hv min. order, depending on night and gender. Open Su-Th 11am-11pm, F-Sa 11am-3am. Dancing Th-Su 9pm-3am. Cash only.

UZHHOROD (УЖГОРОД) ☎(80)312[2]

Charming Uzhhorod (pop. 125,000) is tucked at the foot of the Carpathian Mountains along the banks of the Uzh River, only one kilometer from the Slovak Republic and 21km from Hungary. Uzhhorod's proximity to these borders yields a diverse, multilingual populace, but it also facilitates a different kind of exchange: the area has a reputation for attracting smugglers. During peaceful evenings, residents stroll along the river and central pedestrian thoroughfare or lounge at cafes, sipping beer or Italian espresso. The calm town is best used as a base for trips into the nearby mountains; agencies in town arrange excursions.

When calling Uzhhorod from outside the city, the area code you should dial depends on the number. For 6-digit phone numbers, use the area code 80 312. For 5-digit numbers, use the area code 80 3122.

⎘ TRANSPORTATION. The **train station**, Stantsiyna 9 (Станційна; ☎6 92 962) sends trains to **Lviv** (7hr., 2 per day, 35hv), and **Kyiv** (18hr., 2 per day, 55hv). Trains to **Hungary** and the **Slovak Republic**, including **Bratislava** (5½hr., 1 per day, 180hv), leave from the border hub of **Chop**; to get there, take a **marshrutka** (30min., every 15-30min., 4hv) from behind the bus station. Buy train tickets at the **advance ticket office**, Lva Tolstoho 33. (Льва Толстого; ☎3 23 33. Open M-Sa 8am-1pm and 2-7pm, Su and holidays 8am-noon and 1-3pm.) The **bus station**, Stantsiyna 2 (☎3 21 27), sends buses and *marshrutki* via **Mukachevo** (1hr., 2-4 per hr., 4hv) to **Budapest, HUN; Košice, SLK;** and **Prague, CZR. City buses** and *marshrutki* within the city cost 0.65-1hv. **Taxis** cost 5-8hv for rides within the city.

◪◪ ORIENTATION AND PRACTICAL INFORMATION. The **Uzh River** runs east-west through Uzhhorod, dividing the town roughly in half. The Old Town, which includes the castle and the museum, lies on the north side, while the bus and train stations are close together on the south side. To get to the center from the train or bus stations, follow **pr. Svobody** (Свободи) to Shvabska (Швабска). Take a right on Shvabska and follow it until it ends at pl. Shandora Petefi (Шандора Петефі). Cross the street and follow the path to the left through the square and down one block to a small road on the right. The road, still pl. Petefi, connects to a walking bridge. Cross the bridge to get to the center. Taxis (10hv) and *marshrutki* (to pl. Koryatovycha; Корятовуча) also go to the center. For tourist information and brochures, visit the **Regional Office for Tourism and Resorts**, pl. Narodna 4 (Народна), on the sixth floor in room 612 or 610. The friendly staff has info about Uzhhorod and excursions in the Transcarpathian Region. The office runs the English-language website **www.transcarpathia.org**, which lists festivals, news, and events, and offers printable maps of the region. (☎61 28 39 or 61 28 17; turizm@uzhgorod.ukrsat.ua. Open M-F 8am-1pm and 2-5pm.)

Eximbank (Ексимбанк), in Hotel Uzhhorod, cashes **traveler's checks** for 1.5% commission. (☎67 48 06. Open M-F 8:30am-noon and 1-4:30pm, Sa 8:30-11:30am.) A second branch, pl. Petefi 19, provides the same services. (☎61 22 62. Open M-Th 9am–12:45pm and 2-4pm, F 9am-12:45pm and 2-3pm.) The lobby of Hotel Zakarpattya (see below) has an **ATM** and offers **currency exchange** and **Western Union** services. (☎61 23 57. Open 24hr.) **Store luggage** at the train station or at Hotel Zakarpattya (4hv per day). You can find **24hr. pharmacies** at pr. Svobody 40, near Hotel Zakarpattya (☎2 56 02); at pl. Koryatovycha 14/16 in the center (☎3 07 82); and at Korzo 6 (Корзо), also in the center (☎3 41 89). The **telephone** office, **Ukrtelekom** (Укртелеком), is located near the post office at Nab. Nezalezhnosti 6 (Незалежності; ☎61 11 50; open daily 8am-8pm). **Utel** phones can be found inside Hotels Zakarpattya and Uzhhorod. **Internet** is available at **X-net Internet Club** (Х-нет Інтернетклуб), Volotsina 26 (Волоціна) in the center of town. (2.50hv per hr. Open 24hr.) **Planeta I-Net** (Планета І-Нет); at Nab. Nezalezhnosti 1, offers slower access. (2hv per hr. Open 24hr.) The **post office** is at pl. Poshtova 3 (Поштова; ☎3 40 90; open M-F 7am-7pm, Sa 7am-6pm, Su 8am-1pm). **Postal Code:** 88 000.

ⲅⲎ ACCOMMODATIONS AND FOOD. The most pleasant place to stay is **Hotel Atlant ❸** (Атлант), pl. Koryatovycha 27, in the Old Town. Except for the one single (105hv), all rooms have private baths. In order to keep the mosquitoes from the nearby river away, the hotel staff provides Raid; unwrap the block of Raid, insert it into the colored bulb, and plug it into an outlet. Don't let this put you off, though. The building is modern and the great location makes Atlant worth a visit. (☎61 40 95 or 61 49 88; www.hotel-atlant.com. Reservations recommended. Rooms 105-310hv. MC/V.) Two hotels vie for second place. Both offer rooms with views of the far-off mountains. Although more affordable, **Hotel Zakarpattya ❷** (Закарпаття), at the intersection of pl. Kyryla and Mefodiya 5 (Кирила, Мефодія), has limited hot water (usually 6-10am and 9pm-midnight). The rotary phone and orange carpeting make the building look older than it is. Check out the metal map of the USSR at the far left end of the lobby. (☎67 25 72 or 69 71 05; untur-zak@yandex.ru. Singles 80-100hv, with breakfast 92-112hv; doubles 122-142/134-154hv. Cash only.) **Hotel Uzhhorod ❸**, pl. Bohdana Khmelnytskoho 2 (Богдана Хмельницького), though still under renovation, provides more comforts, including a fridge in each room and constant hot water. These amenities, however, come at a price. (☎3 50 60; hotel@email.uz.ua. Singles 119-239hv; doubles 189-279hv.)

There is a large **market** on pl. Koryatovycha, near Hotel Atlant. The indoor hall of this classic bazaar has bread, vegetables, and meat; the space out back has drinks and non-edible items. (Open M 7am-3pm, Tu-Sa 7am-8pm, Su 7am-2pm; shorter hours in the fall and winter.) A string of cafe-bars with outdoor seating lines the river, near the pedestrian bridge. Cheap beer (2-7hv), a chuck wagon, and multiple expats support the claim that ▓**Cactus ❷** (Кактус), Korzo 7, provides a "Real Old West Atmosphere." However, a Euro-dance soundtrack and locals give Cactus a unique ambience. The English menu offers such diverse options as "Georgian fried pork" (19hv), "Transylvanian dishes" (19hv), "American BBQ" (12hv), and "sun-dried Redneck" (12hv), a dish of ham, cheese, tongue, and meat. (☎61 22 95. Wine 3-20hv. Entrees 5-40hv. Live music downstairs Th-Su 8-10pm. Open daily 11am-midnight. Cash only) **Delizia Pizza ❷** (Делізія), near the walking bridge on pl. Petefi, draws a young, energetic crowd to the southern banks of the Uzh river. (☎61 29 11. English menu. Pizzas 5-25hv. Omlettes 8-10hv. Open daily 9am-11pm. Cash only. Branch on pr. Svobody, a block down to the left from Hotel Zakarpattya. Cash only.) The **Atlant restaurant ❷**, on the first floor of Hotel Atlant, features friendly service and dishes like "Transcarpathian twisted meat with stuffing," a tantalizing meal of pork stuffed with cheese and mushrooms. (☎61 40 95. English menu. Entrees 5-18hv. Open daily 8am-11pm. Cash only.)

⑥ 🎵 SIGHTS AND ENTERTAINMENT. Uzhhorod's three main attractions are all conveniently clustered just east of the city center. Take Kapitulna (Капітульна) to its end, away from the intersection with Voloshyna (Волошина). Near the top of the hill is the 1644 twin-spired **Catholic Cathedral.** Continue on Kapitulna to number 33, the site of the town's **castle** (замок; zamok), which dates to the Middle Ages, though its current facade was built in the 16th century. Inside is a quaint museum that showcases local musical instruments, including two-meter mountain longhorns. (☎3 44 42. Open Tu-Su 9am-5pm. 4hv. Tours 20hv.) Next door, at Kapitulna 33a, the open-air ▨**Transcarpathian Museum of Folk Architecture and Daily Life** (Закарпатський Музей Народної Архітектури та Побуту; Zakarpatskyy Muzey Narodnoyi Arkhitektury ta Pobutu) displays examples of houses from the region, with textiles and pottery inside. The museum features the 1777 **St. Michael's Church,** a nail-less, wooden basilica. (☎3 73 92. Open M and W-Su 9am-5pm. 3hv, children 1hv. Tours 20hv, children 10hv.) **English info booklets** (8-10hv) are available at the entrances of the three sites.

Of the town's clubs, ▨**Kashtan** (Каштан), Koshitskaya 22 (Кошіцкая), is the most popular. International DJs spin hip-hop, trance, and R&B. (Beer 4-6hv. Wine 4hv. Cover 30hv. Open F 10pm-3am, Sa 10pm-4am, Su 10pm-2am.)

The Transcarpathian region is full of religious, musical, and cultural **festivals** held throughout the year, including January's **Dark Wine Festival,** May's **Blacksmith Festival,** June's **Sheep-pasturing Festival,** and September's **Local Sheep Cheese Festival** (бринзи; brynzy). The festivals take place in Uzhhorod and in smaller towns in the mountains. Exact dates are released about a month in advance; check at the tourist office or log onto their website, www.transcarpathia.org.

🏞 OUTDOOR ACTIVITIES. Boussole Voyage (Бусоль Вояж; busol voyazh), Vysoka 8 (Висока), runs tours to the **Valley of the Narcissus,** the **Salt Lake,** and various local **castles.** (☎61 66 47 or 61 99 47. English spoken.) **Zakarpatturyst** (Закарпаттурист), Koshytska 30 (Кошицька), in Turbaza Svitanok, runs 12 resorts throughout the region. They also organize hiking and sightseeing tours. (☎3 43 17. Open M-F 8am-noon and 1-5pm.) **Turkul** (Туркул) organizes active tours, including **hiking** and **mountain biking.** (☎3 41 75; www.turkul.com. Contact at least 2 wks. in advance.) **Blues** (Блуз; bluz), pr. Svobody 55/63, organizes tours. (☎61 61 16. English spoken.) **Kameliya-Tour** (Камелія-Тур; ☎5 07 26) has **horseback riding** and opportunities to visit **traditional peasant villages.**

For a short **daytrip** from Uzhhorod, visit the **Serednye Castle** (Середнє), 12km from town near Kamyanitsya (Камяніця) village. Take *marshrutka* #115 from pl. Koryatovycha in the center of Uzhhorod, where Fedyntsya (Фединця) meets pl. Koryatovycha, and ask the driver to let you off near the castle. Catch the same *marshrutka* on the other side of the street to get back to town (daily 6am-9pm). Cross the bridge and walk up the trail, which quickly turns into a road (20min.). The castle, built during medieval times, was the site of numerous battles in the 16th and 17th centuries, and underwent several transformations before a Transylvanian prince destroyed it in 1644. It was restored in the 1970s and is now a popular tourist attraction. Litter somewhat mars the experience of the ruins, but the view of the Uzh Valley makes up for it. The castle is also the site of an **archaeological excavation** that started in the 1990s and offers volunteer opportunities from May to September. (Contact Olexander Dzembas, head of the ecological-archaeological expedition "Castle of Transcarpathia," Vysoka 8. ☎3 41 45 or 3 25 69; centour@mail.uzhgorod.ua. Russian and/or Ukrainian language skills recommended.)

YAREMCHE (ЯРЕМЧЕ) ☎(80)3434

A small resort town in the Carpathians, Yaremche provides easy access to mountain biking, hiking, and downhill skiing. Nearby, Mt. Hoverla (Говерла) rises to 2061m, making it Ukraine's highest peak. Three smaller towns lie between Yaremche and Hoverla: Mykulychyn (Микуличин), Tatariv (Татарів), and Vorokhta (Ворохта), which is closest to the mountain.

🖃🛈 TRANSPORTATION AND PRACTICAL INFORMATION. The **train station**, Svobody 268 (☎2 23 56), in the center of town, sends trains to **Ivano-Frankivsk** (2 per day) and **Lviv** (11hr., 1 per day, 30hv). The station keeps unconventional hours. (Open daily 8am-noon, 4:30-6:30pm, 9-11pm, and 2-6am.) The **bus station** is just down the street from the train station, on Svobody next door to #23. It's the lot with a half dozen *marshutki* by the gas station. (☎2 23 17. Open daily 6am-9:30pm.) Buses go to: **Ivano-Frankivsk** (1½hr., 8 per day, 7hv); **Kyiv** (12hr., 1 per day, 74hv); **Lviv** (6½hr., 2 per day, 22hv); and **Vorokhta** (1hr., numerous, 5hv).

Yaremche is a small town spread out in a big space. Its center is dominated by the post office and train station. Hotels and cottages dot the main corridor, Svobody (Свободи), from the northern end of Yaremche down to the town of Vorokhta. Tourist agency **Zori Karpat** (Зорі Карпат), Svobody 246, organizes hiking tours (150hv) and trips to Hoverala (320hv), as well as mushroom-picking expeditions (a favorite Ukrainian pastime). The agency also rents mountain bikes and arranges horseback riding. The director does not speak English, but is more than willing to work through language barriers. (☎2 11 82. Open daily 8am-8pm.) The local government **tourist office**, Khotkevicha 6 (Хоткевіча), offers information (mostly in Ukrainian and Russian) regarding hotels and sights. (☎2 26 06; www.yaremche.if.ua. Open M-Th 8am-noon and 1-5pm, F 8am-noon and 1-4pm).

An **Obmin Valut** (Обмін Валут) **currency exchange** is available in Yaremche's souvenir market, Svobody 81. **Ukrsotsbank** (Укрсоцбанк), Svobody 266, has a **Western Union** office. (Open M-F 8:45am-1pm and 2-5pm, Sa 10am-2pm.) A 24hr. **ATM** is near the main entrance of the train station, just before the steps. There is a 24hr. **pharmacy** (Apteka) at Dovbusha 5 (Довбуша), and a **mini-market** at Svobody 236. The train station has a local pay **telephone**. Make international calls at the **Ukrtelekom** (Укртелеком) service center, Halytskoho 45 (Галуцького), in Vorokhta. (Open M-F 9am-1pm and 2-8pm.) The Yaremche **post office** is at Svobody 307 (☎2 24 31), in the center. Vorokhta's **post office** is at Halytskoho 45. (Open M-F 9am-2pm and 3-5pm, Sa 9am-4pm). **Postal Codes:** 78 500 (Yaremche); 78595 (Vorokhta).

🖃🗘 ACCOMMODATIONS AND FOOD. Most accommodations are built in the tradition of local ethnic Hutsuls, and Soviet-style concrete complexes are rare. Having invested in saunas and hot tubs, many hotels charge a premium—even though they charge a separate fee for these amenities. Prices everywhere double or triple during the popular winter season (Dec.-Mar.).

The best deal is to rent a beautiful, riverside ▨**private cottage ❷**, Svobody 332a. From the Yaremche bus station, take a *marshrutka* toward Mykulychyn, Tatariv, or Vorokhta, and ask the driver to let you off at the address. Or, call ahead and arrange to be picked up at the train station for 5-10hv. (☎3 12 37. 2- to 4-person rooms 80hv; 4- to 8-person cottage with full kitchen and sauna 400hv; single floor that accommodates 2-6 people 250hv. Cash only.) **Yaroslava ❸** (Ярослава), Svobody 233, near the center, has 10 rooms available in Hutsul-style cottages where river sounds soothe guests to sleep. (☎2 27 44. Sauna 10-20hv. 2- to 4-person rooms with full kitchen 150hv. Cash only.) Conveniently close to Mt. Hoverla and a ski resort, **Ruslana ❸** (Руслана), s.m.t Vorokhta, offers six cottages with international themes (e.g., Cossak, Hutsul, Turkish). The director speaks English and

UKRAINE

French. The best deal is to rent half a cabin during the low season. (☎4 15 42 or 4 16 99; www.carpathiantours.com. Mountain bikes 25hv. Hiking guides 50hv. Minibus to ski resort Bukovela, (Буковела), or to Hoverla; 8-10 people 120hv. Rides from Ivano-Frankivsk; rates negotiable. July-Aug. 400-800hv. Dec. 15-Feb. 900-1600hv; Apr.-June 15 and Sept.-Dec. 15 1 fl., 2 people 265hv; 3 people 350hv; 4 people 400hv; whole cabin 800hv. Cash only.) Those traveling alone may prefer **Ukraina ❷** (Україна), Halytskoho 68. This dorm-like concrete building feels a little out of place among the wooden cabins that surround it in the center of Vorokhta, but its low rates make up for the lack of aesthetics. (☎4 13 74; fax 4 10 30. Rooms Apr.-Dec. 65hv; Jan.-Mar. 100hv. Cash only.)

Many hotels have restaurants attached, and cottages often include breakfast and dinner; independent restaurants are scarce. **Lsha ❶** (Лша), Svobody 81 (☎2 22 34), has great shish kebabs (16hv) and is near the souvenir market. **Hoverla Restaurant ❷**, Halytskoho 14, in the center of Vorokhta, serves *varenyky* (5hv), *borshcht* (4hv), and other typical Ukrainian cuisine. (Open daily 10am-midnight. Cash only.)

GATEWAY CITIES

EUROS (€)		
AUS$1 = EUR€0.62	1EUR€ = AUS$1.62
CDN$1 = EUR€0.68	1EUR€ = CDN$1.47
NZ$1 = EUR€0.57	1EUR€ = NZ€1.75
UK£1 = EUR€1.48	1EUR€ = UK£0.67
US$1 = EUR€0.82	1EUR€ = US$1.22

Getting to Eastern European cities like Warsaw, Kyiv, and Budapest has never been easier and cheaper; often, it involves traveling through more-central cities first. With their world-class museums and monuments, nonstop cafe and club culture, and irrisistable budget options, Berlin and Munich, Germany; Vienna, Austria; and Venice, Italy are some of the best gateways to the east. As much as they ease the west-east transition, these vibrant cities are hardly easy to leave.

GATEWAY CITIES	❶	❷	❸	❹	❺
ACCOMMODATIONS	under €15	€15-25	€26-35	€36-55	over €55
FOOD	under €5	€5-10	€11-18	€19-23	over €23

BERLIN

Dizzying, electric, and dynamic, this city of 3.5 million is always in flux, due as much to its ambitious, ongoing construction projects as to its increasingly diverse population. Yet while Berlin surges ahead as one of the continent's most vibrant and trend-setting cities, memories of the past century—in particular, the Nazi regime and the DDR—remain etched into residents' daily life. Psychological division between East and West Germany (the problem known as "Mauer im Kopf," or "wall in the head") is still felt more acutely here than anywhere else in the country.

⌐ TRANSPORTATION

Flights: Berlin has 3 airports (☎0180 500 01 86). **Flughafen Tegel** is western Berlin's main international airport. Follow signs at Tegel to get to buses. To get to Tegel, take express bus X9 from Bahnhof Zoo, bus #109 from U7: Jakob-Kaiser-Pl., bus #128 from U6: Kurt-Schumacher-Pl., or bus TXL from U2: Potsdamer Pl. **Flughafen Schönefeld** services intercontinental flights and travel to Eastern Europe, and the Middle and Far East. Take S9 or the 45 to Flughafen Berlin Schönefeld or take the Schönefeld Express, which runs every 30min. through most major Bahn stations, including Bahnhof Zoo, Ostbahnhof, Alexanderpl., and Friedrichstr. **Flughafen Tempelhof,** Berlin's smallest airport, has flights to European destinations. Take U6 to Pl. der Luftbrücke.

Trains: Scheduled to open in time for the World Cup in May of 2006, **Lehrter Stadtbahnhof** will be Europe's biggest train station. For now, trains to and from Berlin stop at **Zoologischer Garten** (a.k.a. **Bahnhof Zoo**) in the west and at **Ostbahnhof** in the east. (☎0180 599 66 33; www.bahn.de.) Trains run every hr. to **Cologne** (4¼hr., €89), **Frankfurt** (4hr., €95), and **Hamburg** (1½-2½hr., €45-55). Direct trains run at least every 2hr. to **Dresden** (2¼hr., €30), **Leipzig** (2hr., €31), and **Munich** (6½-7hr., €92). Times and prices for international connections change frequently; check at computers located in stations. Reserving as much as 3 wks. in advance can save up to 50% on

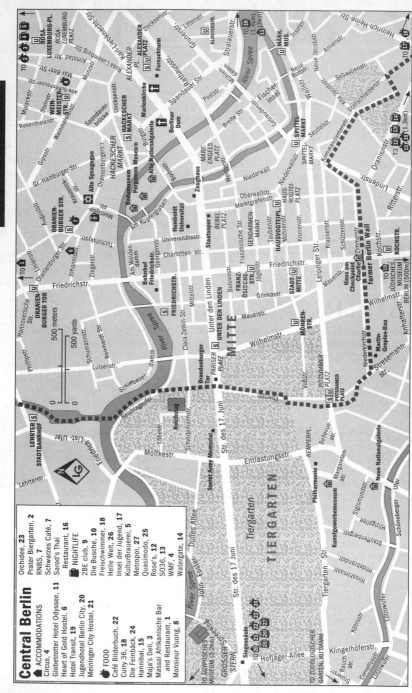

Central Berlin

⚑ ACCOMMODATIONS

Circus, **4**
Globetrotter Hotel Odyssee, **11**
Heart of Gold Hostel, **6**
Hotel Transit, **19**
Jugendhotel Berlin City, **20**
Meininger City Hostel, **21**
Orchide, **23**
Prater Biergarten, **2**
RNBS, **7**
Schwarzes Café, **7**
Sarod's Thai
Restaurant, **16**

🍴 FOOD

Café Bilderbuch, **22**
Curry 36, **18**
Die Feinbäck, **24**
Hannibal, **15**
Maja's Deli, **3**
Massai Afrikanische Bar
and Restaurant, **1**
Monsieur Vuong, **8**

🎵 NIGHTLIFE

2BE club, **9**
Die Busche, **10**
Freischwimmer, **18**
Heile Welt, **26**
Insel der Jugend, **17**
KulturBrauerei, **5**
Metropol, **27**
Quasimodo, **25**
Rose's, **12**
SO36, **13**
WMF, **4**
Watergate, **14**

listed prices. Destinations include: **Amsterdam, NED** (6½hr.); **Brussels, BLG** (7½hr.); **Budapest, HUN** (12hr.); **Copenhagen, DEN** (7½hr.); **Kraków, POL** (8½-11hr.); **Moscow, RUS** (27-33hr.); **Paris, FRA** (9hr.); **Prague, CZR** (5hr.); **Rome, ITA** (17½-21hr.); **Stockholm, SWE** (13-16hr.); **Vienna, AUT** (9½hr.); **Warsaw, POL** (6hr.); **Zurich, SWI** (8½hr.). **Euraide** counters sell tickets and have English-language information.

Buses: ZOB (☎301 03 80), by the *Funkturm* near Kaiserdamm, in the central bus station. U2 to Kaiserdamm or S4, 45, or 46 to Witzleben. Open M-F 6am-7:30pm, Sa-Su 6am-noon. Check *Zitty* (€2.30) or *Tip* (€2.50) for deals on long-distance buses, which are slower, but cheaper, than trains. **Gullivers**, Hardenbergpl. 14 (☎0800 48 55 48 37; www.gullivers.de), is at the far end of the parking lot in Bahnhof Zoo. To **Paris** (14hr., €59) and **Vienna** (10½hr., €49). Open daily 9am-2:30pm and 3-7pm. AmEx/MC/V.

Public Transportation: Berlin's extensive **bus, Straßenbahn** (streetcar), **U-Bahn** (subway), and **S-Bahn** (surface rail) systems can take you anywhere. Berlin is divided into 3 transit zones. **Zone A** encompasses central Berlin, including Flughafen Tempelhof, while **Zones B** and **C** contain increasingly outlying areas. **AB tickets** are the best deal, and allow for the purchase of extension tickets for Zone C. A one-way ticket *(Einzelfahrausweis)* is good for 2hr. after validation. (Zones AB €2, BC €2.25, ABC €2.60.) Since single tickets can become pricey, it often makes sense to buy a pass. A **Tageskarte** (AB €5.60, ABC €6) is good until 3am the next day; the **WelcomeCard** (sold at tourist offices; €22) remains valid for 72hr. and discounts sights in addition; the **7-Tage-Karte** (AB €24.30, ABC €30) remains valid for 7 days; and the **Umweltkarte Standard** (AB €64, ABC €79.50) is valid for 1 calendar month.

Night Transport: U- and S-Bahn lines shut down 1-4am on weeknights (with final runs around 12:15am), but **night buses** (with numbers preceded by the letter N) run every 20-30min.; pick up the *Nachtliniennetz* map at a *Fahrscheine und Mehr* office.

Taxis: ☎26 10 26, 21 02 02, or 690 22. Call at least 15min. in advance.

Car Rental: Most companies have counters at all 3 airports and at Bahnhof Zoo, Ostbahnhof, and Friedrichstr. **Hertz** (☎261 1053; open M-F 7am-8pm, Sa 8am-4pm, Su 9am-1pm) and **Avis** (☎230 9370; open M-F 7am-7pm, Sa 9am-2pm) also have counters in the EuropaCenter, Budapester Str. 39.

Bike Rental: Pedal Power, Kreuzberg, Großbeerenstr. 53 (☎78 99 19 39). €10 per day. Open M-F 10am-6pm, Sa 11am-2pm. Bikes can also be rented at some hostels.

✈ 🛈 ORIENTATION AND PRACTICAL INFORMATION

Berlin covers an area eight times the size of Paris. Its main landmarks include the **Spree River**, which flows through the city from west to east, and the narrower **Landwehrkanal** that flows into it from the south, and the vast central park, the **Tiergarten**, stretching between the waterways. Grand, tree-lined **Strasse des 17. Juni** runs east-west through the Tiergarten, ending triumphantly at the **Brandenburger Tor** in the east. The street next becomes **Unter den Linden**, which beelines through most of Berlin's imperial architecture. Near the gate is the **Reichstag**. Several blocks south, **Potsdamer Platz** bustles beneath the glittering Sony Center and the headquarters of the Deutsche Bahn. **Charlottenburg** and **Schöneberg**, in former West Berlin, have become the city's commercial heart. Also in the former West, despite its geographical location in the east, **Kreuzberg** is a bastion of counter-culture. **Mitte, Prenzlauer Berg,** and **Friedrichshain,** in the former East, host much of the city's chaotic nightlife. Berlin's streets change names often; well-indexed maps are invaluable.

PHONE CODES	**Country code:** ☎49. **Berlin city code:** ☎030 within Germany, 30 abroad. **International dialing code:** ☎00.

TOURIST AND FINANCIAL SERVICES

Tourist Offices: EurAide, in Bahnhof Zoo's Reisezentrum. Sells rail tickets, **maps,** phone cards, and walking-tour tickets; also recommends hostels. Open May-Sept. daily 9am-1:30pm and 2:30-6pm; Oct.-Dec. and Feb.-Apr. M-F 9am-1:30pm and 2:30-5pm.

City Tours: A city tour lets you take in all of the major sights in just a few hours. ▓**Terry Brewer's Best of Berlin** (www.brewersberlin.com) features guides who are legendary for their vast knowledge of the city and engaging personalities. 8hr. tours (€12) leave daily 10:30am from Friedrichstr. Station in front of the Australian Ice Cream, and 11am from the Neue Synagoge on Oranienburger Str., near the intersection with Tucholskystr. (S1, 2, or 25 to Oranienburger Str.). **New Berlin Tours** (☎0179 973 0397; www.newberlin-tours.com) offers free walking and biking tours of the city; be sure to bring some cash to tip the guides. 3½hr. walking tours leave daily 10:30am and 12:30pm from Zoologischer Garten in front of Dunkin' Donuts; they also pick up visitors at 11am and 1pm at Brandenburger Tor in front of the Starbucks (S1, 2, or 25 to Unter den Linden).

Embassies and Consulates: Australia, Mitte, Wallstr. 76-79 (☎880 08 80; www.australian-embassy.de). U2 to Märkisches Museum. Open M-F 8:30am-5pm, F closes 4:15pm. **Canada,** Mitte, Leipziger Pl. 17 (☎20 31 20; www.canada.de). U2 or S1 to Potsdamer Pl. Open M-F 8:30am-12:30pm and 1:30-5pm. **Ireland,** Mitte, Friedrichstr. 200 (☎22 07 20; www.botschaft-irland.de). U2 or 6 to Stadtmitte. Open M-F 9:30am-12:30pm and 2:30-4:45pm. **New Zealand,** Mitte, Friedrichstr. 60 (☎20 62 10; www.nzembassy.com). U2 or 6 to Stadtmitte. Open M-F 9am-1pm and 2-5:30pm, F closes 4:30pm. **UK,** Mitte, Wilhelmstr. 70-71 (☎20 45 70; www.britischebotschaft.de). S1-3, 5, 7, 9, 25, or 75, or U6 to Friedrichstr. Open M-F 9am-4:30pm. **US,** Clayallee 170 (☎832 9233; www.usembassy.de). U1 to Oskar-Helene-Heim. Open M-F 8:30am-noon. Phone advice M-F 2-4pm; after-hours emergency advice ☎830 50.

Currency Exchange: The best rates are usually found at exchange offices with *Wechsel-stube* signs at most major train stations and large squares. **ReiseBank,** at Bahnhof Zoo (☎881 71 17; open daily 7:30am-10pm) and Ostbahnhof (☎296 43 93; open M-F 7am-10pm, Sa 8am-8pm, Su 8am-noon and 12:30-4pm) has higher rates.

American Express: Main Office, Charlottenburg, Bayreuther Str. 37-38 (☎21 47 62 92). U1, 2, or 15 to Wittenbergpl. Cashes AmEx Travelers Cheques for no commission. Long lines F-Sa. Open M-F 9am-7pm, Sa 10am-1pm. Another branch in Mitte at Friedrichstr. 172 (☎20 17 400). U6 to Französische Str. Same services and hours.

LOCAL SERVICES

Luggage Storage: At all stations. Bahnhof Zoo rates start at €0.50 per day. If lockers are full, try luggage deposit (€2 per piece per day). Open daily 6:15am-10:30pm.

Bookstores: Marga Schöler Bücherstube, Charlottenburg, Knesebeckstr. 33, between Savignypl. and the Ku'damm. S3 to Savignypl. Contemporary reading material in English. Open M-W 9:30am-7pm, Th-F 9:30am-8pm, Sa 9:30am-4pm.

GLBT Resources: Lesbenberatung, Kulmer Str. 20 (☎217 2253), offers counseling for lesbians. Open M-Tu and Th 4-7pm, F 2-5pm. **Schwulenberatung,** Charlottenburg, Mommsenstr. 45 (☎194 46), has similar services for gay men. Open M-F 9am-8pm.

EMERGENCY AND COMMUNICATIONS

Emergency: Police: ☎110. **Ambulance** and **Fire:** ☎112.

Crisis Lines: Helpline International (☎44 01 06 07) is Berlin's emergency phone service for English-speaking foreigners. Open daily 2-6pm. **American Hotline** (☎0177 814 15 10) is a crisis and referral service. **Berliner Behindertenverband,** Jägerstr. 63d (☎204 3847), has advice for the disabled. Open M-F 8am-4pm. **Frauenkrisentelefon** (☎614 2242) is a women's crisis line. Open M-Tu and Th 10am-noon, Th also 7-9pm; F 7-9pm.

Pharmacies: Pharmacies *(Apotheken)* are everywhere. **Europa-Apotheke,** Tauentzienstr. 9-12 (☎261 4142), is conveniently located near Bahnhof Zoo. Open M-F 6am-8pm, Sa 9am-4pm. **Schlecker** drug stores can be found throughout the city.

Medical Services: The American and British embassies list English-speaking doctors. **Emergency doctor:** ☎31 00 31. **Emergency dentist:** ☎89 00 43 33. Both 24hr.

Internet Access: Netlounge, Mitte, Auguststr. 89 (☎24 34 25 97). U-Bahn to Oranienburger Str. €1.50 per hr. Open noon-midnight. Wireless Internet free anywhere in the **Sony Center** (p. 745).

Post Offices: City-wide general service hotline ☎018 02 33 33 (www.deutschepost.de). **Postamt Charlottenburg,** Joachimstaler Str. 7, near Bahnhof Zoo; look for Postbank sign. Open M-Sa 9am-8pm. **Postal Code:** 10623. **Postamt Mitte,** Georgenstr. 17. Open M-F 6am-10pm, Sa-Su 8am-10pm. **Postal Code:** 10117.

↟ ACCOMMODATIONS

Longer stays are most conveniently booked through one of Berlin's many **Mitwohnzentrale,** which can arrange house-sitting gigs or sublets (from €250 per month). **Home Company Mitwohnzentrale,** Joachimstaler Str. 17, has a useful placement website. (☎194 45; www.homecompany.de. U9 or 15 to Kurfürstendamm. Open M-Th 9am-6pm, F 9am-5pm, Sa 11am-2pm. MC/V.)

▧ **Circus,** Weinbergsweg 1a (☎2839 1433). U8 to Rosenthaler Pl. Clean and modern. Wheelchair accessible. Reception and bar 24hr. Dorms €15-18; singles €32, with shower €45; doubles €48/60; triples €60; apartments with kitchen and balcony €75. Also at Rosa-Luxemburg-Str. 39-41. U2 to Rosa-Luxemburg-Pl. Low season discount. ❷

▧ **Meininger City Hostel,** Meininger Str. 10 (in Germany ☎0800 634 6464, from abroad 666 36 100; www.meininger-hostels.de). U4 or bus #146 to Rathaus Schöneberg. Walk toward the Rathaus tower on Freiherr-vom-Stein-Str., turn left onto Martin-Luther-Str. and right on Meininger Str. This well-run hostel, complete with bar and beer garden, is the best value in town. Internet €3 per hr. Reception 24hr. Dorms €12.50; 4- to 5-bed dorms €21; singles €33; doubles €46. 10% *Let's Go* discount on 1st night stay. Cash only. ❶

Meininger City Hostel, Hallesches Ufer 30 (in Germany ☎0800 634 64 64, from abroad ☎666 36 100; www.meininger-hostels.de). Located between Hallesches Tor (U6 or U1) and Möckernbruke (U1 or U7). This location of the popular hostel chain features a bar, big-screen TV, and a comfortable roof terrace. All rooms with bath and TV. Breakfast included. Reception 24hr. Dorms €13.50; 4- to 5-bed dorms €25; singles €49; doubles €66. 10% *Let's Go* discount on 1st night stay. Cash only. ❶

Hotel Transit, Hagelberger Str. 53-54 (☎789 0470; www.hotel-transit.de). U6 or 7; bus #119, 219, or 140; or night bus N4, 6, 19, or 76 to Mehringdamm. Hip hostel with attention to detail. Helpful brochures and maps fill the lounge. All rooms with bath. Breakfast included. Reception 24hr. Check-in 2pm. Check-out noon. Dorms €19; singles €59; doubles €69; triples €90; quads €120. AmEx/MC/V. ❷

Globetrotter Hostel Odyssee, Grünberger Str. 23 (☎29 00 00 81; www.globetrotterhostel.de). U1 or 15 to Warschauer Str. or U5 to Frankfurter Tor. Gothic statues and candlelit tables greet you as you enter, but rooms are modern and spotless. Bar open until dawn. Breakfast €3. Linen deposit €3. Internet €3 per hr. Reception 24hr. Check-in 4pm. Check-out noon. Reserve ahead. Dorms €13; doubles €45-52; triples €57; quads €68. Low season discount. MC/V. ❶

Heart of Gold Hostel, Johannisstr. 11 (☎29 00 33 00; www.heartofgold-hostel.de). S1, 2, or 25 to Oranienburger Str. or U6 to Oranienburger Tor. Designed as a tribute to *The Hitchhiker's Guide to the Galaxy.* Breakfast €3. Internet €3 per hr. Reception and bar 24hr. Dorms €17-21; singles €24-28; doubles with shower €48-56. ❷

Jugendhotel Berlincity, Crellestr. 22 (☎78 70 21 30; www.jugendhotel-berlin.de). U7 to Kleistpark. Fancy lounge and helpful staff make this small hotel fill up quickly; book ahead. Breakfast included. Cheaper prices for extended stays. Singles €38, with bath €55; doubles €60/79; triples €84/99; quads €108/118. AmEx/MC/V. ❸

◘ FOOD

Indian, Italian, Thai, and Turkish cuisine provide an array of tasty options on top of local fare. A cherished culinary tradition is breakfast, which street-side cafes extend well into the afternoon; Germans love to wake up late over a *milchkaffee* (a bowl of coffee with foamed milk). Quick bites are handily supplied by vendors of *currywurst* or *bratwurst*, but more often by the 24hr. Turkish *imbiß* stands.

▨ **Schwarzes Café,** Kantstr. 148 (☎313 8038). S3, 5, 7, 9, or 75 to Savignypl. This popular Bohemian cafe boasts candlelit tables and a 24hr. breakfast menu. The ground-floor bathrooms must be seen to be believed. Open 24hr. except Tu 3-10am. Cash only. ❸

▨ **Massai Afrikanische Bar and Restaurant,** Bart Lychener Str. 12 (☎48 62 55 95; www.massai-berlin.de). U2 to Eberswalder Str. African art and carved wooden chairs complement savory entrees (€8-10) and 15 delicious vegetarian options (€7-9). Banana beer €3.30. Open daily noon-2am. Cash only. ❸

▨ **Prater Biergarten,** Katanienallee 7-9 (☎448 5688; www.pratergarten.de). U2 to Eberswalder Str. Sit with locals under giant chestnut trees at picnic tables at Berlin's oldest beer garden. Outdoor theater and big-screen TV for watching sports. Bratwurst €2. Beer €2.20-3.10. Open in good weather daily Apr.-Sept. noon-late. Cash only. ❶

Monsieur Vuong, Alte Schönhauser Allee 46 (☎30 87 26 43). U2 to Rosa-Luxemburg-Pl. Serves from a limited but delicious menu of Vietnamese food. Outdoor seating available. All entrees €6.40. Open M-Sa noon-midnight, Su 2pm-midnight. ❷

RNBS, Oranienburger Str. 27 (www.rnbs.de). This tiny cafe serves healthful, Asian-themed fast food. Meatball with scallions and fresh herbs €1.90. Noodles with sesame tofu, scallions, sprouts, and fresh herbs €3. Open daily noon-midnight. Cash only. ❶

Orchidee, Stuttgarter Pl. 13 (☎31 99 74 67; www.restaurantorchidee.de). *Won ton, pho,* and *maki* all under one roof; the Vietnamese food especially stands out. During the 11am-5pm lunch special, get half-price sushi or a free appetizer with any €5-11 entree. Open M-Sa 11am-midnight, Su 3pm-midnight. Cash only. ❸

Café Bilderbuch, Akazienstr. 28 (☎78 70 60 57; www.cafe-bilderbuch.de). U7 to Eisenacher Str. Relax in a dramatic Venetian library or sit in the airy courtyard. Customers can choose what CDs to play. Known for their daily breakfasts named after fairy tales (€7-8). Open M-Th 9am-1am, F-Sa 9am-2am, Su 10am-1am. ❸

Die Feinbäck, Vorbergstr. 2 (☎81 49 42 40; www.feinbaeck.de). U7 to Kleistpark or Eisenacher Str. Swabian cuisine as unassuming as the restaurant's tasteful interior. Unbeatable *spätzle* (noodles; €6.50) and weekday lunch special (€4.90; M-F 10am-5pm). Open daily noon-midnight. Cash only. ❷

Hannibal, (☎61 15 16) on the corner of Wiener Str. and Skalitzerstr. U1, 12, or 15, or night bus N29 to Görlitzer Bahnhof. Excels in massive burgers (€6) and blueberry pancakes (€4.50). Open M-Th 8am-3am, F-Sa 8am-4am, Su 9am-3am. AmEx/MC/V. ❷

Sarod's Thai Restaurant, Friesenstr. 22 (☎69 50 73 33). U7 to Gneisenaustr. Enjoy the €5 all-you-can-eat lunch on weekdays noon-4pm. Open M-F noon-11:30pm, Sa-Su 2-11:30pm. Cash only. ❷

Curry 36, Mehringdamm 36. U6 or 7 to Mehringdamm. Berlin's best curry sausages and burgers (€1-4). Open M-F 9am-4am, Sa-Su 10am-4am. Cash only. ❶

Maja's Deli, Pappelallee 11 (☎48 49 48 51). U2 to Eberswalder Str. Escape from smoke-filled eateries to this cozy vegan cafe. The homemade organic lasagna (€4) is a particular stand-out. Fruit shakes €2.80. Open M-F noon-6pm. Cash only. ❶

👁 SIGHTS

Most of central Berlin's major sights lie along the route of **bus #100,** which runs every 5min. from Bahnhof Zoo to Prenzlauer Berg. It passes by the **Siegessäule, Brandenburger Tor,** other sights along **Unter der Linden,** the **Berliner Dom,** and **Alexanderplatz.** Remnants of the **Berlin Wall** still survive in a few places: in **Potsdamer Platz;** near the **Haus Am Checkpoint Charlie;** in Prenzlauer Berg, next to the sobering **Documentation Center;** and at the memorable **East Side Gallery** in Friedrichshain.

▧ BRANDENBURGER TOR. Built as a tribute to peace in the 18th century, this gate at the end of Unter der Linden later came to symbolize the city's division: facing the Berlin Wall, it became a barricaded gateway to nowhere. Visitors can reflect in the **Room of Silence** at the northern end of the gate.

▧ THE REICHSTAG. Today home to the *Bundestag,* Germany's governing body, the Reichstag was central to one of the most critical moments in history. When it mysteriously burned down in 1933, Adolf Hitler declared a state of emergency and seized power. Today, a modern glass dome offers visitors 360° views of the city as they climb the spiral staircase inside. Go before early or late to avoid long lines. (☎ *22 73 21 52. Open daily 8am-midnight. Last entrance 10pm. Free.)*

▧ EAST SIDE GALLERY. The longest remaining portion of the wall, this 1.3km stretch of cement slabs and asbestos also serves as the world's largest open-air art gallery, unsupervised and open at all hours. The murals are not remnants of Cold War street art, but efforts of an international group of artists who gathered here in 1989 to celebrate the end of the city's division. They returned to repaint their work in 2000, but many of the new paintings are being rapidly eclipsed by graffiti. *(Along Mühlenstr. Take U1 or 15, or S3, 5, 6, 7, 9, or 75 to Warschauer Str.)*

FORSCHUNGS- UND GEDENKSTÄTTE NORMANNENSTRAßE. The Lichtenberg suburb harbors the most feared building of the DDR regime: the headquarters of the **secret police** (*Staatssicherheit,* or *Stasi*). During the Cold War, the *Stasi* kept dossiers on six million East Germans. An exhibit displays a collection of tiny microphones and cameras used by the *Stasi* and a bizarre shrine filled with busts of Lenin. *(Ruschestr. 103, Haus #1. U5 to Magdalenenstr. Walk up Ruschestr. from the exit and turn right on Normannenstr.; it's in the office complex. ☎ 553 6854; www.stasimuseum.de. All exhibits in German. Open Tu-F 11am-6pm, Sa-Su 2-6pm. €3.50, students €2.50.)*

POTSDAMER PLATZ. First designed to allow the rapid mobilization of troops under Friedrich Wilhelm I, Postdamer Pl. is Berlin's commercial center and during the 1990s, formed the city's largest construction site. Today, its ambitious architecture never fails to impress visitors. The central complex includes the towering central office of the Deutsche Bahn, Berlin's Film Museum, and the glitzy **▧Sony Center,** where travelers can watch a movie, enjoy free wireless Internet, or window-shop. *(U2, or S1, 2, or 25 to Potsdamer Pl.)*

BERLINER DOM. Berlin's most recognizable landmark, this multi-domed cathedral, built during the reign of Kaiser Wilhelm II, suffered damage in a 1944 air raid and only recently emerged from two decades of restoration. Search out the glorious view of Berlin from the tower. *(Open M-Sa 9am-8pm, Su noon-8pm. Closed for services daily 6:30-7:30pm. Organ recitals W-F 3pm. Ticket office open M-Sa 10am-8pm, Su noon-8pm. Admission to Dom, crypt, tower, and galleries €5, students €3. Buy tickets to frequent summer concerts in the church or call ☎ 20 26 91 36.)*

🏛 MUSEUMS

Berlin's superb art collections span over 170 museums. *Berlin Programm* (€1.60) lists museums and galleries. **Staatliche Museen zu Berlin (SMB)** runs over 20 museums throughout the city. All museums sell single admission tickets (€6, students €3) and the three-day card (*Drei-Tage-Karte;* €12, students €6). Admission is free the first Sunday of every month and Thursdays after 6pm. Unless otherwise noted, all SMB museums are open Tuesday through Sunday 10am-6pm, Thursday until 10pm. All offer free English-language audio tours. Current renovations mean that the **Bodemuseum** won't reopen until 2006, the **Neues Museum** until 2008. *(S3, 5, 7, 9 or 75 to Hackescher Markt or bus #100 to Lustgarten. ☎ 20 90 55 55.)*

SMB MUSEUMS

▨ **PERGAMONMUSEUM.** One of the world's great ancient history museums, this the Pergamon is named after the Turkish city from which the enormous **Altar of Zeus** (180 BC) was taken. Collections include enormous artifacts from the ancient Near East, including the colossal blue **Ishtar Gate of Babylon** (575 BC) and the Roman **Market Gate of Miletus.** Be sure to get the headsets for your choice of free audio tours. *(Bodestr. 1-3. ☎ 20 90 55 77. Last entry 30min. before closing.)*

▨ **GEMÄLDEGALERIE.** One of Germany's best-known museums, the Gemäldegalerie beautifully displays nearly 3000 masterpieces by Italian, German, Dutch, and Flemish masters from the 13th to 18th centuries, including works by Botticelli, Dürer, Raphael, Rembrandt, Titian, and Vermeer. *(Stauffenbergstr. 40. ☎ 266 29 51.)*

HAMBURGER BAHNHOF/MUSEUM FÜR GEGENWART. North of the Tiergarten, Berlin's foremost modern art collection occupies a full 10,000 sq. m. of this former train station. Its artist roster includes Beuys, Kiefer, and Warhol. With few space constraints, the museum also hosts outrageous sculptures and temporary exhibits. *(Invalidenstr. 50-51. U6 to Zinnowitzer Str. or S3, 5, 7, 9, or 75 to Lehrter Stadtbahnhof. ☎ 39 78 34 11; www.hamburgerbahnhof.de. Open Tu-F 10am-6pm, Sa 11am-8pm, Su 11am-6pm. Tours Su 4pm. €8, students €4; Th 2-6pm free.)*

ÄGYPTISCHES MUSEUM. This stern Neoclassical building displays a wide variety of ancient Egyptian art complemented by dramatic lighting. The most famous work in the collection is the limestone bust of **Queen Nefertiti** (1340 BC), but the sarcophagi and mummified cats will also draw the adventurer out in every traveler. *(Schloßstr. 70. ☎ 34 35 73 11. Open daily 10am-6pm. Th 2-6pm free.)*

NON-SMB MUSEUMS

▨ **HAUS AM CHECKPOINT CHARLIE.** A strange mix of eastern sincerity and glossy western salesmanship, Checkpoint Charlie documents the history of the Berlin Wall and the dramatic escapes that once centered around its wire-and-concrete barrier. Skip the audio tour—there are plenty of English-language captions. *(Friedrichstr. 43-45. U6 to Kochstr. ☎ 253 7250; www.mauer-museum.com. Open daily 9am-10pm. German films every 2hr. from 9:30am. €9.50, students €5.50.)*

JÜDISCHES MUSEUM BERLIN. Daniel Libeskind designed this enlightening and jarring museum so that no facing walls run parallel; most jagged hallways end in windows overlooking "the void." Wander through the labyrinthine Garden of Exile or shut yourself in the Holocaust Tower, a room virtually devoid of light and sound. *(Lindenstr. 9-14. U6 to Kochstr. or U1, 6, or 15 to Hallesches Tor. ☎ 25 99 33 00. Open daily 10am-8pm, M until 10pm; Last entry 1hr. before closing. €5, students €2.50.)*

🎵 ENTERTAINMENT

Berlin hosts myriad exhibitions, concerts, plays, and dance performances. Box offices often offer student discounts of up to 50% on tickets bought at the *Abendkasse* (evening counter; generally open 1hr. before shows). **KaDeWe** has a city-wide ticket counter. *(☎ 217 7754. Open M-F 10am-8pm, Sa 10am-4pm.)* Many venues close from mid-July to late August. Spring for *Zitty* (€2.30) or *Tip* (€2.50), which contain listings for film, theater, concerts, and clubs. Find the best theater in town at **Deutsches Theater,** Mitte, Schumannstr. 13a (☎28 44 12 25; www.deutsches-theater.berlin.net) and the **Berliner Ensemble,** Mitte, Bertolt-Brecht-Pl. 1 (☎28 40 81 55; www.berliner-ensemble.de). Check www.berlin.de for more info.

■ **Berliner Philharmonisches Orchester,** Mitte, Herbert Von Karajanstr. 1 (☎25 48 81 32; www.berlin-philharmonic.com). Take S1, 2, or 25, or U2 to Potsdamer Pl., and walk up Potsdamer Str. The *Berliner Philharmoniker,* housed in an acoustically perfect concert hall, is one of the world's finest orchestras—and one of its greatest steals, with tickets available for as little as €7. Tickets are hard to come by, however; either check 1hr. before concert time or write at least 8 weeks in advance. Box office open M-F 3-6pm, Sa-Su 11am-2pm. Standing room tickets from €7, seats from €15.

Deutsche Oper Berlin, Charlottenburg, Bismarckstr. 35 (tickets ☎343 84 01; www.deutscheoperberlin.de). U2 to Deutsche Oper. Berlin's youngest but best opera features newly commissioned works as well as German and Italian classics. No performances July-Aug. Box office open M-Sa 11am until 1hr. before performances, Su 10am-2pm. Doors opens 1hr. before performances. Tickets €10-112. 25% student discounts.

▣ NIGHTLIFE

Berlin's largest bar scene sprawls down pricey, packed **Oranienburger Straße** in Mitte. Prices fall only slightly around **Kollwitzplatz** and **Kastanianallee** in Prenzlauer Berg, but areas around **Schönhauser Allee** and **Danziger Straße,** such as the **"LSD" zone** (named for Lychener Str., Schliemannstr., and Dunckerstr.) still harbor an edgy alternative scene. Gay and lesbian nightlife centers on **Nollendorfplatz,** in the West. Between 1 and 4am, take advantage of the **night buses** and **U-Bahn** 9 and 12, which run all night on Friday and Saturday. Info about bands and dance venues can be found in the pamphlets *Tip* (€2.50) and *Zitty* (€2.30), available at newsstands, or in *030* (free), distributed in hostels, cafes, and bars.

■ **SO36,** Oranienstr. 190 (☎61 40 13 06; www.SO36.de). U1, 12, or 15 to Görlitzer Bahnhof or night bus N29 to Heinrichpl. Berlin's best mixed club. A massive dance floor packs in a friendly crowd for techno, hip-hop, and ska; music is often played live. Gay night last Sa of each month. Cover €4-8, concerts €7-18. Open daily 11pm-late.

■ **Freischwimmer,** vor dem Schlesischen Tor 2 (☎61 07 43 09; www.freischwimmer-berlin.de). U1 or 15 to Schlesisches Tor or night bus N65 to Heckmannufer. Relax by the water amidst roses, chill inside on a comfy sofa, or lounge in a beach chair on their floating dock. M summer poetry readings on the dock. €8.20 Su brunch 11am-4pm; reserve ahead. Open M-F noon-midnight, Sa-Su 11am-midnight.

WMF, Karl-Marx-Allee 34. U5 to Schillingstr. Moves often; check www.wmfclub.de for location. In a former cabaret, its 2 dance floors fill with electro-loungers Th and Sa. Gay night Su. Beer €3. Cover €8-12. Open Th and Sa 11pm-late, Su 10pm-late.

Insel der Jugend (Island of Youth), Alt-Treptow 6 (☎20 91 49 90; www.insel-berlin.net). S4, 6, 8, or 9 to Treptower Park, then bus #265 or N65 to Rathaus Treptow. Located on an island in the Spree River, the club is a winding 3-story tower crammed with gyrating bodies, multiple bars, riverside couches, and an open-air movie theater. Depending on the night, the top 2 floors spin reggae, hip-hop, ska, or house—sometimes all at once—while a techno scene dominates the basement. Open Th-Sa €4-6. Open W 7:30pm-late, F-Sa 10pm-late. Movies (€6) play in the summer M-Tu and Th-Su and start between 8:30 and 9:30pm. Cafe open daily in summer 2pm-late; in low season Th 2-7pm, Sa-Su 2pm-late.

2BE Club, Ziegelstr. 23 (☎89 06 84 10; www.2be-club.de). U6 to Oranienburger Tor. Reggae and hip-hop in a huge space that includes 2 dance floors and a tented courtyard with palm trees. Cover €7.50-8; women free until midnight. Open F-Sa 11pm-late.

Quasimodo, Kantstr. 12a (www.quasimodo.de). U2 or 12, or S3, 5, 7, 9, or 75 to Zoologischer Garten. Beneath a huge cafe, this cozy venue showcases soul, R&B, and jazz. Cover €5-24. Concert tickets available from 5pm at the cafe upstairs or through the Kant-Kasse ticket service (☎313 45 54). Open M-F 5pm-late, Sa-Su 2pm-late. Concerts start 11pm. Call or check the website for schedules.

Metropol, Nollendorfpl. 5 (☎21 73 68 11). U1, 2, 4, or 15, or night buses N5, 19, 26, 48, 52, or 75 to Nollendorfpl. Don't meet a friend here without specifying on which floor. **Tanz Tempel,** the main venue of Metropol, pumps out 650,000 watts of light and 35,800 watts of sound onto its giant dance floor. Also check out the **West-Side Club** and **Love Lounge.** Drinks €2.50-4. Cover €5-10. Music and hours vary.

Watergate, Falckensteinstr. 49 (☎61 28 03 95; www.water-gate.de). U1 to Schlesisches Tor. Overlooking the river, this club is one of the hottest night attractions in town. Beer €3. Cover €10. Terrace open daily 8pm-late.

KulturBrauerei, Knaackstr. 97 (www.kulturbrauerei.de). U2 to Eberswalder Str. An enormous party space in an old East German brewery, housing the popular clubs **Soda** (www.soda-berlin.de) and **Kesselhaus** (www.kesselhaus-berlin.de), a Russian theater, upscale cafes, and an art school. Dance floors and stages abound. Music includes disco, hardcore, reggae, techno, and *Ostrock*. Cover and hours vary between venues.

GLBT NIGHTLIFE

Berlin is one of the most gay-friendly cities in Europe. *Siegessäule*, *Sergej*, and *Gay-yellowpages* have entertainment listings for gays and lesbians.

▨ **Heile Welt,** Schöneberg, Motzstr. 5 (☎21 91 75 07). U1, 2, 4, or 15 to Nollendorfpl. Clientele pack this bar and spill out into the street. 2 sitting rooms in the back offer quieter ambience for conversation. Mostly male crowd during "prime time," mixed in the early evening and latest hours of the night. Open daily 6pm-4am.

▨ **Rose's,** Kreuzberg, Oranienstr. 187 (☎615 6570). U1 or U8 to Kottbusser Tor or U1 to Görlitzer Bahnhof. Marked only by a sign over the door that reads "Bar." A friendly, mixed clientele packs this glowing, glittery, and claustrophobic party spot at all hours. Daiquiris €3.50. Open daily 10pm-6am.

Die Busche, Friedrichshain, Mühlenstr. 12 (www.diebusche.de). U1, 12, or 15, or S3, 5-7, 9, or 75 to Warschauer Str. East Berlin's most famous disco in the DDR days, Die Busche is still a color-saturated haven for dancers, spinning an incongruous rotation of techno, Top 40, and German *Schlager* to a mixed crowd. Cover €3.50-6. Open W and Su from 10pm-5am, F-Sa 10pm-6am.

VIENNA (WIEN)   ☎01

Vienna (pop. 1,500,000) was transformed by war, marriage, and Hapsburg maneuvering from a Roman camp along the Danube into the political linchpin of the continent. Beethoven, Mahler, Mozart, and Schönberg have made Vienna an everlasting arbiter of high culture—yet Vienna, as always, keeps to the beat of the younger generation. On any given afternoon, cafes turn the sidewalks into a sea of umbrellas, and on warm summer nights, bars and clubs pulse with experimental techno and indie rock until dawn.

▐ TRANSPORTATION

Flights: The **Wien-Schwechat Flughafen** (VIE; ☎700 70), 18km from the city center, is home to **Austrian Airlines** (☎517 89; www.aua.com). The cheapest way to reach the city is S7 Flughafen/Wolfsthal, which stops at **Wien Mitte** (30min., every 20-30min.

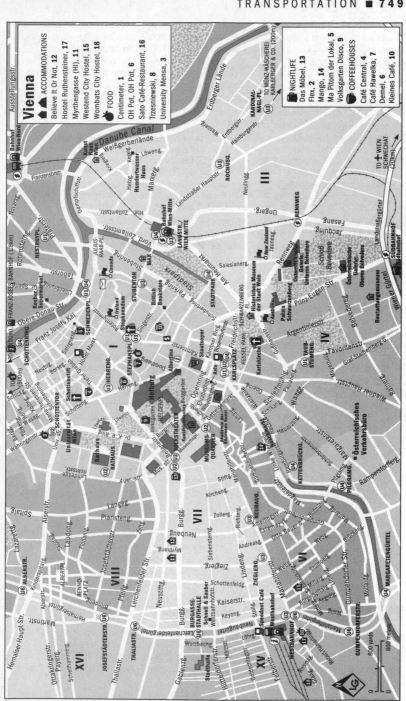

Vienna

▲ ACCOMMODATIONS
Believe It Or Not, **12**
Hostel Ruthensteiner, **17**
Myrthengasse (HI), **11**
Westend City Hostel, **15**
Wombats City Hostel, **18**

♦ FOOD
Centimeter, **1**
OH Pot, OH Pot, **6**
Sato Café-Restaurant, **16**
Trzesniewski, **8**
University Mensa, **3**

■ NIGHTLIFE
Das Möbel, **13**
Flex, **2**
Mango, **14**
Ma Pitom der Lokal, **5**
Volksgarten Disco, **9**

♦ COFFEEHOUSES
Café Central, **4**
Café Hawelka, **7**
Demel, **6**
Kleines Café, **10**

5am-10pm, €3). The Vienna Airport Lines **shuttle** (☎65 17 17; english.viennaairport.com/bus.html) takes 25min. to reach Südbahnhof and 40min. to Westbahnhof (every 30min. 6:05am-12:05am; €6, round-trip €11). The **City Airport Train** (CAT; ☎25 250; www.cityairporttrain.com) takes only 16min. to reach **Wien Mitte** (every 30min. 6:05am-11:35pm) but is expensive (€9, round-trip €16; €1 discount when bought from ticket machine, further discounts when bought online; Eurail not valid).

Trains: Vienna has 2 main train stations with international connections. Call ☎05 17 17 (24hr.) or check www.oebb.at for general train information. Ticket counters and machines generally take AmEx/DC/MC/V.

Westbahnhof, XV, Mariahilferstr. 132. Info counter open daily 7:30am-9pm. To: **Amsterdam** (12hr., 10 per day, €111); **Berlin** (11hr., every 2hr., €80); **Budapest** (3hr., 10 per day, €36); **Hamburg** (9hr., every 2hr., €80); **Innsbruck** (5-6hr., every 1½hr., €49); **Munich** (5hr., 1 per hr., €68); **Paris** (14hr., 1 per hr. 7am-4pm, €110); **Salzburg** (3hr., 1 per hr., €37); **Zurich** (9hr., 8 per day, €165).

Südbahnhof, X, Wiener Gürtel 1a. Trains generally go south and east. Info counter open daily 7am-8pm. To: **Graz** (2½hr., every 2hr., €32); **Kraków** (7-11hr., 5 per day, €48); **Prague** (4hr., 9-10 per day, €43); **Rome** (14hr., every 2hr., €100); **Venice** (9-10hr., 4 per day, €70).

Buses: Buses in Austria are rarely cheaper than trains; compare prices before buying a ticket. **City bus terminals** at Wien Mitte/Landstr., Hütteldorf, Heiligenstadt, Floridsdorf, Kagran, Erdberg, and Reumannpl. **BundesBuses** run from these stations; tickets sold on board. Many international bus lines also have agencies in the stations. For info, call BundesBus (☎711 01; 7am-10pm).

Public Transportation: The **subway** (U-Bahn), **tram** (Straßenbahn), **elevated train** (S-Bahn), and **bus** lines operate on a 1-ticket system, so you can transfer between types of transportation without having to buy a new ticket. Buy tickets on board or at a machine, counter, or tobacco shop. (General info ☎790 91 00.) A **single fare** (€2 on board, €1.50 in advance) lets you travel to any destination in the city and switch from bus to U-Bahn to tram to S-Bahn, as long as your travel is uninterrupted. Other ticket options include a **1-day pass** (€5), **3-day rover ticket** (€12), **7-day pass** (€12.50; valid M 9am to the next M 9am), and an **8-day pass** (€24; valid any 8 days, not necessarily consecutive; valid also for several people traveling together). The **Vienna Card** (€16.90) offers free travel for 72hr. as well as discounts at sights and events. Regular trams and subway cars don't run midnight-5am. **Night buses** run every 30min. along most routes; "N" signs designate night bus stops. Single-fare €1.50; day passes not valid. A night bus schedule is available in U-Bahn stations.

Taxis: ☎313 00, 401 00, 601 60, or 814 00. Stands are at Westbahnhof, Südbahnhof, Karlspl. in the city center, and by the Bermuda Dreieck for late-night revelers. Accredited taxis have yellow-and-black signs on the roof. €2.50 base, €0.20 per additional 0.2km; slightly more expensive holidays and 11pm-6am.

Car Rental: Avis, I, Opernring 3-5 (☎587 62 41 or 700 327 00). Open M-F 7am-6pm, Sa 8am-2pm, Su 8am-1pm. **Hertz** (☎70 07 32 661), at the airport. Open M-F 8am-11pm, Sa 8am-8pm, Su 7am-11pm.

Bike Rental: Pedal Power, II, Ausstellungsstr. 3 (☎729 72 34). €5 per hr., students €4; €17/14 per 4 hr.; €27/24 per day. They run bike tours (€19-23) daily May-Sept. Vienna Card discounts. Open Apr.-Oct. daily 8am-7pm. Pick up *Vienna By Bike* at the tourist office. Hostels are also a cheap and convenient option for less serious bikers. **Hostel Ruthensteiner** (p. 752) rents bikes for €12 per day.

■↘ ORIENTATION AND PRACTICAL INFORMATION

Vienna is divided into 23 **districts** *(Bezirke)*. The first is **Innenstadt** (city center), defined by the **Ringstraße** (ring road) on three sides and the Danube Canal on the fourth. At the center of the Innenstadt lies **Stephansplatz** and the heart of the pedestrian district. Many of Vienna's major attractions are in District I and immediately around the Ringstr. Districts II-IX spread out from the city center following the clockwise traffic of the Ring. The remaining districts expand from yet another ring road, the **Gürtel** (Belt). Like the Ring, this major thoroughfare has numerous segments, including Margaretengürtel, Währingergürtel, and Neubaugürtel. Street signs indicate the district number in Roman or Arabic numerals before the street and number, as does *Let's Go*.

PHONE CODES	**Country code: ☎43. Vienna city code: ☎01** within Austria, ☎011 43 1 abroad. **International dialing prefix: 00**

Main Tourist Office: I, Albertinapl. (☎211 140). Follow Operng. up 1 block from the Opera House. The staff books rooms for a €2 fee and gives out **free city maps,** the pamphlet *Youth Scene,* and brochures on events and festivals. Open daily 9am-7pm.

Embassies and Consulates: Australia, IV, Mattiellistr. 2-3 (☎506 74). Open M-F 8:30am-4:30pm. **Canada,** I, Laurenzerberg 2 (☎531 38 30 00). **Ireland,** I, Rotenturmstr. 16-18, 3rd fl. (☎71 54 24 6). Open M-F 9:30-11am and 1:30-4pm. **New Zealand,** Salesianer-gasse 15 (☎318 85 05). **UK,** III, Jauresg. 10 (☎716 13 51 51). Open M-F 2-4pm. **US,** IX, Parkring 12 (☎313 390). Open M-F 8-11:30am.

Currency Exchange: ATMs are your best bet. Nearly all accept Cirrus, MC, and V. **Banks** and **airport exchanges** use the same official rates. Most open M-W and F 8am-12:30pm and 1:30-3pm, Th 8am-12:30pm and 1:30-5:30pm. **Train station** exchanges offer long hours (daily 7am-10pm at the Westbahnhof) and a €6 min. fee for the 1st 3 checks (€300 max.). Stay away from the 24hr. bill-exchange machines in Innenstadt, as they generally charge outrageous prices.

American Express Travel Agency: I, Kärntnerstr. 21-23 (☎515 40), near Stephanspl. Cashes AmEx and Thomas Cook checks (€7 min. commission for up to €250, €12 for €251-500) and sells event tickets. Open M-F 9am-5:30pm, Sa 9am-noon.

Luggage Storage: Lockers available at all trains stations. €2 per 24hr.

Bookstores: The **British Bookshop,** I, Weihburgg. 24 (☎512 19 45), has an extensive travel section. Open M-F 9:30am-6:30pm, Sa 9:30am-5pm. AmEx/DC/MC/V.

GLBT Resources: Pick up the *Vienna Gay Guide* (www.gayguide.at), *Extra Connect, Bussi,* or the tourism bureau's *Queer Guide* from any tourist office or gay bar, cafe, or club. ▧**Rosa Lila Tip,** VI, Linke Wienzeile 102 (lesbians ☎586 5150, gays 585 4343; lesbenberatung@villa.at), is a knowledgeable resource and social center for homosexual Viennese and visitors alike. Friendly staff speaks English. Take the U4 to Pilgrimg. and look for the pink house. Open M, W, F 5-8pm.

Emergency: Police: ☎133. **Ambulance:** ☎144. **Fire:** ☎122. **Emergency care:** ☎141.

Crisis Hotlines: All have English speakers. **Rape Crisis Hotline:** ☎523 22 22. Line staffed M and Th 1-6pm, Tu and F 10am-3pm. **24hr. immediate help for women:** ☎717 19.

24hr. Pharmacy Hotline: ☎15 50. Consulates have lists of English-speaking doctors, or call **Wolfgang Molnar** ☎330 34 68.

Hospital: Allgemeines Krankenhaus, IX, Währinger Gürtel 18-20 (☎404 00 19 64).

Internet Access: Speednet Cafe, Europapl. 1 (☎892 56 66), in Westbahnhof. €3.30 per 30min., €5.80 per hr. Open M-Sa 7am-midnight, Su 8am-midnight. AmEx/MC/V. **bigNET.internet.cafe** (☎533 29 39), I, Kärntnerstr. 61 or I, Hoher Markt 8-9. €3.70 per 30min. Open daily 9am-11pm.

Post Office: Hauptpostamt (☎0577 677 1010), I, Fleischmarkt 19. Open 24hr. Branches throughout the city and at the train stations; look for the yellow signs with the trumpet logo. **Postal Codes:** A-1010 (1st district); A-1020 (2nd district); A-1030 (3rd district); continues to A-1230 (23rd district).

ACCOMMODATIONS

Hunting for cheap rooms in Vienna during high season (June-Sept.) can be unpleasant; call for reservations at least five days in advance. Otherwise, plan on calling between 6 and 9am to put your name down for a reservation. If full, ask to be put on a waiting list. The summer crunch for budget rooms is slightly alleviated in July, when university dorms convert into makeshift hostels.

Hostel Ruthensteiner, XV, Robert-Hamerlingg. 24 (☎893 4202; www.hostelruthensteiner.com). Exit Westbahnhof, turn right onto Mariahilferstr., and continue until Haidmannsg. Turn left, then right on Robert-Hamerlingg. Knowledgeable staff, spotless rooms, a secluded courtyard, and kitchenettes. 4-night max. stay. Reception 24hr. 32-bed summer dorm €12; 4- to 10-bed dorms €13-15; singles €26; doubles €44; quads €60. AmEx/MC/V; €0.40 per day surcharge. ●

Wombats City Hostel, XV, Grang. 6 (☎897 2336). Exit Westbahnhof, turn right on Mariahilferstr., right on Rosinag., and left on Grang. Despite its proximity to train tracks, this wildly colorful hostel compensates with an in-house pub, English-language movie nights, and guided tours. Bike rental €12 per day, €3 per hr. All rooms with bath. Dorms €18; singles €24; doubles €48. Breakfast €3.50. Cash only. ●

Westend City Hostel, VI, Fügerg. 3 (☎597 67 29), near Westbahnhof. Exit on Äussere Mariahilferstr., cross the large intersection, go right on Mullerg. and left on Fügerg. A rose-filled courtyard and plain dorms with bath provide a respite after the train station chaos. Breakfast included. Internet €2 per 20min. Reception 24hr. Check-out 10am. Lockout 10am-2pm. Dorms €17-20; singles €43-58; doubles €52-68. Cash only. ●

Myrthengasse (HI), VII, Myrtheng. 7. Take U6 to Burgg./Stadthalle, then bus #48A (dir.: Ring) to Neubaug. Backtrack on Burgg. 1 block and take the 1st right on Myrtheng. Or take U3 to Neubaug. Also runs the nearby **Neustiftgasse (HI),** VII, Neustiftg. 85 (☎523 63 16). These simple hostels are a 20min. walk from Innenstadt. Breakfast included. Locks €4. Internet €2.60 per 18min. Reception for both at Myrthengasse 24hr. 5-night max. stay. Dorms €19.50-21.50. €3.50 HI discount. AmEx/MC/V. ●

Believe It Or Not, VII, Myrtheng. 10, Apt. #14 (☎526 46 58). A converted apartment with kitchen. 2-night min. stay. Reception daily 8:15am-12:30pm. Lockout 10am-noon. Ages 18-30. Tightly packed 12-bed dorm €13.50; roomier 4-bed dorm €15.50. ●

FOOD

The neighborhood north of the university, where Universitätsstr. and Währingerstr. meet (U2: Schottentor), is a budget-friendly area, as is **Burggasse** in District VI and the area surrounding the Rechte and Linke Wienzeile near Naschmarkt (U4: Kettenbrückeg.). The **Naschmarkt** itself boasts the city's biggest market of fresh (if pricey) produce, and its many eateries make for cheap and quick meals. (Produce stands open M-F 6am-6:30pm, Sa 6am-2pm.) Supermarket chains include **Zielpunkt, Billa,** and **Spar.** Also available is the **kosher** supermarket, II, Hollandstr. 10. (☎216 96 75. Open M-Th 8:30am-6:30pm, F 8am-3pm, Su 10am-noon.)

Trzesniewski, I, Dorotheerg. 1 (☎512 32 91), 3 blocks down the Graben from Stephansdom. Once Kafka's favorite place to eat, this stand-up establishment has been serving open-faced mini-sandwiches (€0.80) for over 100 years. Toppings include salmon, onion, paprika, and egg. Open M-F 8:30am-7:30pm, Sa 9am-5pm. Cash only. ●

OH Pot, OH Pot, IX, Währingerstr. 22 (☎513 42 59). U2: Schottentor. This adorable restaurant serves filling "pots," stew-like veggie or meat concoctions with influences from Ethiopia to Bolivia (€8.20). Lunch special offers any pot, soup or salad, and dessert for €6.20. Open daily 11am-midnight. AmEx/DC/MC/V. ●

Centimeter, IX, Liechtensteinstr. 42 (☎319 84 04). Tram D to Bauernfeldpl. This chain offers huge portions of greasy Austrian fare (€4.50-6.50) and an unbelievable selection of beers (€3-4 per L). Cold and warm sandwiches for €0.15 per cm. Open M-F 10am-midnight, Sa-Su 11am-midnight. AmEx/MC/V. ❶

Sato Café-Restaurant, XV, Mariahilferstr. 151 (☎897 54 97). U3 or U6: Westbahnhof. Near the Ruthensteiner and Wombats hostels. Free baskets of fluffy, sesame-studded Turkish bread accompany the scrumptious Turkish food. Vegetarian options. Delicious breakfast omelettes €3-4. Entrees €5-9. Open daily 8am-midnight. Cash only. ❶

University Mensa, IX, Universitätsstr. 7, on the 7th fl. of the university building. U2: Schottentor. A fantastic conveyor-belt ▓**elevator** takes you to the 6th fl. cafeteria. Meat or veggie entree plus salad or dessert for €4. Adjoining snack bar offers more choices (€4-5) and a self-serve salad bar. Snack bar open M-F July-Aug. 8am-3pm; Sept.-June 8am-6pm. Open Sept.-June M-F 11am-2pm. Cash only. ❶

▐ CAFES

▓ **Kleines Café,** I, Franziskanerpl. 3. Turn off Kärntnerstr. onto Weihburg. and follow it to the Franziskanerkirche. Escape from the busy pedestrian streets with a *mélange* (expresso with hot milk; €2.90) and conversation on a couch in the relaxed interior or by the fountain in the square. Sandwiches €2.80-4. Open daily 10am-2am. Cash only. ❶

▓ **Café Central,** I, Herreng. 14 (☎533 37 6246), at Strauchg. inside Palais Ferstel. With green-gold arches and live music, this luxurious coffeehouse deserves its status as mecca of the cafe world. Open M-Sa 8am-10pm, Su 10am-6pm. AmEx/DC/MC/V.

Café Hawelka, I, Dorotheerg. 6 (☎512 82 30), off Graben. Josephine and Leopold Hawelka put this legendary cafe on the map in 1939. Today, customers enjoy a mean *buchteln* (cake with plum marmalade; €3) amid sofas scattered along the walls and old-fashioned lamps. Open M and W-Sa 8am-2am, Su 4pm-2am. Cash only.

Demel, I, Kohlmarkt 14 (☎535 17 17). 5min. from the Stephansdom, down Graben. The most lavish *konditorei*, or confectioner, Demel once served its creations to the imperial court. The chocolate is made fresh every morning, and the desserts are legendary. *Mélange* €3.80. Tortes €4. Open daily 10am-7pm. AmEx/MC/V.

◉ SIGHTS

To wander on your own, grab the brochure *Vienna from A to Z* (€4 with Vienna Card) from the tourist office. There are 50 themed walking tours in the brochure *Walks in Vienna* (free at the tourist office).

STEPHANSDOM, GRABEN, AND PETERSPLATZ. In the heart of the city, the massive **Stephansdom** is one of Vienna's most treasured symbols. For a view of the old city, take the elevator up the North Tower or climb the 343 steps of the South Tower. Downstairs, skeletons of plague victims fill the **catacombs**. From Stephanspl., follow Graben for *Jugendstil* architecture, including the **Ankerhaus** (#10), the red-marble **Grabenhof,** and the underground public toilet complex designed by Adolf Loos. Graben leads to Peterspl. and the 1663 **Pestsaüle** (Plague Column), built to celebrate the passing of the Black Death. *(U1 or 3: Stephanspl. Stephansdom ☎515 52 3526. North Tower open daily July-Aug. 8:30am-6:30pm; Sept.-Oct. and Apr.-June 8:30am-5:30pm; Nov.-Mar. 8:30am-5pm. South Tower open daily 9am-5:30pm. Catacombs tours M-Sa every 30min. 10-11:30am and 1:30-4:30pm, Su and holidays 1:30-4:30pm. South Tower €3. North Tower and catacombs €4.)*

HOFBURG. The sprawling palace, begun in 1275 and not complete until 1918, was the winter residence of the Hapsburgs. On the left of the courtyard called **In der Berg** is the **Schweizerhof,** the inner courtyard of the **Alte Burg** (Old Fortress), which sits on the same site as the original 13th-century palace. The **Weltliche und Geistliche Schatzkammer** contains the Hapsburg jewels and Napoleon's cradle; the legendary Lipizzaner stallions train nearby at the **Spanische Reitschule** (Spanish Riding School). The double-headed golden eagle on the roof of the Neue Berg, the youngest wing of the palace, symbolizes the double empire of Austria-Hungary. Today, it houses Austria's largest library, the **Österreichische Nationalbibliothek.** High Mass is still held in 14th-century **Augustinerkirche** (St. Augustine's Church) on Josefspl. The Hapsburgs left their hearts here—in storage in the **Herzgrüftel.** *(Tram #1 or 2 to Heldenpl., or enter from Michaelerpl. Prices differ by wing; some free.)*

SCHLOß SCHÖNBRUNN. The **Imperial Tour** of Empress Maria Theresa's hunting lodge-turned-palace passes through the **Great Gallery,** where the Congress of Vienna met, and the dazzling **Hall of Mirrors,** where Mozart played. As impressive as the palace itself, the classical **gardens** behind the palace contain a **labyrinth** and a profusion of manicured greenery, flowers, statuettes, and Empress Elizabeth's favorite **Gloriette** across the lake. *(Schönbrunnerstr. 47. U4: Schönbrunn. Apartments open daily July-Aug. 8:30am-6pm; Sept.-Oct. and Apr.-June 8:30am-5pm; Nov.-Mar. 8:30am-4:30pm. English audio tours available. Gardens open daily 6am-dusk. Imperial Tour €8.90, students €7.90. Grand Tour €11.50/10.20. Labyrinth €2.60/€2.20. Gloriette €2/1.50. Gardens free.)*

ZENTRALFRIEDHOF. The Viennese like to describe the Central Cemetery as half the size of Geneva but twice as lively. **Tor I** (Gate 1) leads to the old **Jewish Cemetery.** Many of the headstones are cracked and neglected because the families of most of the dead have left Austria. Behind **Tor II** (Gate 2) are Beethoven, Strauss, and an honorary monument to Mozart, whose true resting place is an unmarked pauper's grave in the **Cemetery of St. Mark,** III, Leberstr. 6-8. **Tor III** (Gate 3) leads to the Protestant section and the new Jewish Cemetery. *(XI, Simmeringer Hauptstr. 234. Tram #71 from Schwarzenbergpl. or tram #72 from Schlachthausg. ☎ 760 410. Open daily May-Aug. 7am-7pm; Sept.-Oct. and Mar.-Apr. 7am-6pm; Nov.-Feb. 8am-5pm. Free.)*

🏛 MUSEUMS

All museums run by the city are free Friday before noon (except public holidays).

▨ ÖSTERREICHISCHE GALERIE (AUSTRIAN GALLERY). Home to *The Kiss* and other works by Klimt, the **Oberes Belvedere** supplements its magnificent permanent collection of 19th- and 20th-century art with rotating exhibits. The **Unteres Belvedere** contains the Austrian Museum of Baroque Art and the Austrian Museum of Medieval Art. *(Oberes Belvedere, III, Prinz-Eugen-Str. 27, in the Schloß Belvedere behind Schwarzenbergpl. Walk up from the Südbahnhof, or take tram D to Schloß Belvedere. Unteres Belvedere, III, Rennweg 6. Tram #71 to Unteres Belvedere. ☎ 795 570. Both Belvederes open Tu-Su 10am-6pm. €7.50, students €5.)*

▨ KUNST HAUS WIEN. Artist-environmentalist Friedenreich Hundertwasser built this museum without straight lines—even the floor bends. Besides the comprehensive Hundertwasser exhibit, Kunst Haus also hosts contemporary art. *(III, Untere Weißgerberstr. 13. U1 or 4 to Schwedenpl., then tram N to Hetzg. ☎ 712 04 91; www.kunsthauswien.com. Open daily 10am-7pm. Each exhibit €9, students €7, M €4.50, except holidays.)*

HAUS DER MUSIK. Science meets music in this über-interactive museum. Experience the physics of sound, learn about famous Viennese composers, and entertain yourself with a fascinating invention called the Brain Opera. *(I, Seilerstatte 30, near the opera house. ☎ 516 480. Open daily 10am-10pm. €10, students €8.50.)*

KUNSTHISTORISCHES MUSEUM (MUSEUM OF FINE ARTS). One of the world's largest art collections features Venetian and Flemish paintings, Classical art, and an Egyptian burial chamber. The **Ephesos Museum** exhibits findings from excavations in Turkey, the **Hofjagd- und Rustkammer** is the second-largest collection of arms in the world, and the **Sammlung alter Musikinstrumente** includes Beethoven's harpsichord and Mozart's piano. *(U2: Museumsquartier. Across from the Burgring and Heldenpl. on Maria Theresia's right.* ☎525 2441. *Open Tu-W and F-Su 10am-6pm, Th 10am-9pm. €10, students €7.50. English audio tour €2.)*

MUSEUMSQUARTIER. At 60 sq. km, it's one of the 10 biggest art districts in the world. Central Europe's largest collection of modern art, the **Museum Moderner Kunst (MUMOK)**, highlights a range of modern and contemporary movements in a building made from basalt lava. The **Leopold Museum** has the world's largest Schiele collection, plus works by Egger-Lienz, Gerstl, Klimt, and Kokoschka. Themed exhibits of contemporary artists fill **Kunsthalle Wien**. *(U2: Museumsquartier. MUMOK open Tu-Su 10am-6pm, Th 10am-9pm. €8, students €6.50. Leopold open M, W, Tu-W and F-Su 10am-7pm, Th 10am-9pm. €9, students €5.50. Kunsthalle open M-W and F-Su 10am-7pm, Th 10am-10pm. Kunsthalle 1 €7.50, students €6. Kunsthalle 2 €6/4.50; both €10.50/8.50. M students €2. "Art" combination ticket admits visitors to all 3 museums; €21.50. "Duo" ticket admits to Leopold and MUMOK; €16, students €11.)*

🎵 ENTERTAINMENT

All but a few of classical music's marquee names lived, composed, and performed in Vienna. Cheap seats for the visitor abound, but none of the venues listed below has performances in July or August. The **Bundestheaterkasse**, I, Hanuschg. 3, sells tickets for the Staatsoper, the Volksoper, and the Burgtheater. (☎514 44 78 80. Open M-F 8am-6pm, Sa-Su 9am-noon; Sa during Advent 9am-5pm.)

Staatsoper, I, Opernring 2 (☎514 44 22 50; www.wiener-staatsoper.at). Vienna's premier opera performs nearly every night Sept.-June. No shorts. Box office in the foyer open 9am until 1hr. before curtain, Sa 9am-noon; 1st Sa of each month and during Advent 9am-5pm. Seats €5-254. 500 standing-room tickets go on sale 80min. before every show (1 per person; €2-3.50); arrive 2hr. before curtain.

Vienna Philharmonic Orchestra (Wiener Philharmoniker; www.wienerphilharmoniker.at) plays in the **Musikverein**, Austria's premiere concert hall. Visit the box office (Bösendorferstr. 12) well in advance, even if you only want standing-room tickets.

Vienna Boys' Choir (Wiener Sängerknaben; reservations ☎533 99 27) sings during mass every Su at 9:15am (mid-Sept. to late June) in the Hofburgkapelle (U3: Herreng.). Despite rumors to the contrary, standing room is free; arrive before 8am.

🍸 NIGHTLIFE

Take U1 or 4 to Schwedenpl., which will drop you within blocks of the **Bermuda Dreieck** (Bermuda Triangle), an area packed with crowded clubs. If you make it out, head down **Rotenturmstraße** toward Stephansdom or walk around the areas bounded by the synagogue and Ruprechtskirche. Slightly outside the Ring, the streets off **Burggasse** and **Stiftgasse** in District VII and the **university quarter** in Districts XIII and IX have outdoor courtyards and hip bars. Viennese nightlife starts late, often after 11pm. For listings, pick up the indispensable *Falter* (€2).

🏠 **Das Möbel** (☎524 9497; www.das-moebel.net), VII, Burgg. 10. U2 or 3: Volkstheater. An artsy crowd chats and reads amid metal couches and Swiss-army tables, all created by designers and available for sale. Don't leave without seeing the bathroom. Internet free for first 15min. Open daily 10am-1am. Cash only. MC/V accepted for furniture.

Ma Pitom der Lokal, I, Seitenstetteng. 5 (☎535 43 13). A cavernous, arched space draws together a diverse crowd to chat over cheap drinks and price-skewing pub grub. Happy hour 5-7pm, beer €1.60. Open M-Th and Su 5pm-3am, F-Sa 5pm-4am.

Volksgarten Disco, I, Volksgarten (☎ 532 42 41; www.volksgarten.at). U2: Volkstheater. One of the trendier clubs in town. M tango with all levels welcome. Th alternative and house; F hip-hop; Sa house. Cover €5-10. Open M 8pm-2am, Th 8pm-4am, F 11pm-6am, Sa June-Aug. 9pm-6am; Sept.-May 11pm-6am. MC/V; €70 min.

Flex, I, Donaulände (☎ 533 75 25; www.flex.at), near the Schottenring U-Bahn station (U2 or U4) at Maria-Theresien-Str. By the river. DJs start spinning techno, reggae, house at 11pm. Beer €4. Cover before 3:30am €2-8. Open daily 8pm-4am.

Mango, VI, Laimgrubeng. 3 (☎ 587 44 48). U2: Museumsquartier. Walk down Getriedmarkt toward the city center, turn right on Gumpendorferstr. and left on Laimgrubeng. With walls as golden as its namesake, Mango draws gay men with pop music and a casual atmosphere. Open daily 9pm-4am. AmEx/MC/V.

VENICE (VENEZIA)

There is a mystical, defeated quality to Venice's (pop. 274,000) decadence. Lavish palaces stand proudly on a steadily sinking network of wood, treading in the clouded waters of age-old canals. The maze of knotted streets leads to a treasury of Renaissance art, housed in scores of palaces, churches, and museums that are themselves architectural delights. The city that once earned the name *La Serenissima* (most serene) is now saturated with visitors, as Venice struggles to retain its authenticity in a climate where 70% of economic growth comes from tourism.

▐ TRANSPORTATION

The **train station** is on the northwest edge of the city; be sure to get off at **Santa Lucia,** not at Mestre on the mainland. Buses and boats arrive at **Piazzale Roma,** just across the Canal Grande from the train station. To get from either station to **Piazza San Marco** or the **Ponte di Rialto** (Rialto Bridge), take *vaporetto* #82 or follow the signs for a 40min. walk—from the train station, exit left on Lista di Spagna.

Flights: Aeroporto Marco Polo (VCE; ☎ 260 92 60; www.veniceairport.it), 10km north of the city. Take the **ATVO shuttlebus** (☎ 042 138 36 72) from the airport to P. Roma (30min., every hr., €3).

Trains: Stazione Santa Lucia, northwest corner of the city. Open daily 3:45am-12:30am. **Information office** (☎ 89 20 21) to the left as you exit the platforms. Open daily 7am-9pm. To: **Bologna** (2hr., 27 per day, €8); **Florence** (3hr., 9 per day, €19); **Milan** (3hr., 24 per day, €23); **Rome** (4½hr., 7 per day, €35).

Buses: ACTV (☎ 24 24; www.hellovenezia.it), in P. Roma. Local buses and boats. **ACTV long-distance carrier** runs buses to **Padua** (1½hr., 2 per hr., €4).

Public Transportation: The **Canal Grande** can be crossed on foot only at the Scalzi, Rialto, and Accademia *ponti* (bridges). **Vaporetti** (water buses) provide 24hr. service around the city, with reduced service midnight-5am. Single-ride €3.50, €5 for the Canal Grande. 24hr. *biglietto turistico* pass €10.50, 3-day €22 (€13 with Rolling Venice Card). Validate them before boarding to avoid a fine.

▣ ORIENTATION

Venice is composed of 118 bodies of land in a lagoon and is connected to the mainland by a thin causeway. To orient yourself, locate the following landmarks on a map: **Ponte di Rialto** (the bridge in the center), **Piazza San Marco** (central south), **Ponte Accademia** (the bridge in the southwest), **Ferrovia** (the train station, in the northwest), and **Piazzale Roma** (directly south of the station). The **Canal Grande**

Central Venice

▲ ACCOMMODATIONS
Albergo San Samuele, 7
Alloggi Gerotto Calderan, 2
Foresteria Valdese, 5
Hotel Bernardi-Semenzato, 4

● FOOD
Ae Oche, 1
Le Bistrot de Venise, 6
Cantinone Gia Schiavi, 9
Gelateria Nico, 10

★ NIGHTLIFE
Piccolo Mondo, 8
Paradiso Perduto, 3

V Vaporetto Stops

0   100 yards
0   100 meters

TO ⑤ (150m)

CAMPO DI S. MARIA FORMOSA
S. MARIA FORMOSA
Querini Stampalia
C. delle Rasse
Bridge of Sighs
Basilica di San Marco
Campanile
PIAZZA SAN MARCO
Torre dell'Orologio
Museo Civico Correr and Biblioteca Marciana
Museo Archeologico
C. dell'Ascensione
Frezzeria
La Zecca
Giardini Reali
SAN MARCO GIARDINETTI
MARCO VALLERESE
San Lio
TO ④ (200m)
S. Bartolomeo
Libreria Studium
San Zulian
S. Lio
CAMPO S. LIO
S. MARIA della Fava
S. Salvatore
RIALTO
S. Maria del Giglio
Teatro Goldoni
CAMPO S. LUCA
S. Luca
CAMPO MANIN
La Scala Del Bovolo
San Fantin
Teatro La Fenice
S. Moise
S. d. 13 Martiri
Servizio Gioventù
AmEx
Palazzo Fini
Bacino di San Marco
SALUTE
SANTA MARIA DEL GIGLIO
S. Maria d. Giglio
CAMPO S. MARIA ZOBENIGO
CAMPO S. MAURIZIO
Ca' Grande
SAN SILVESTRO
Palazzo Grimani
Palazzo Grimani di San Luca
CAMPO DI SAN SILVESTRO
SAN ANGELO
Palazzo Corner Spinelli
CAMPO SAN ANGELO
Palazzo Pesaro
CAMPIELLO NOVO
Teatro Rossini
Chiesa d. Teatro
CAMPO S. BENEDETTO
Palazzo degli Avvocati
San Stefano
CAMPO SAN STEFANO
CAMPO SAN VIDAL
Palazzo Pisani
Palazzo Cavalli
ACCADEMIA
Ponte dell'Accademia
CAMPO DI CARITÀ
Gallerie dell'Accademia
TO ⑩ (200m)
CAMPO DEI FRARI
S. Maria Gloriosa dei Frari
TO ② (300m)
TO ③ (500m)
TO (800m)
CAMPO SAN POLO
Sal Polo
Casa del Goldoni
SAN TOMÀ
CAMPO S. TOMÀ
Ca' Foscari
SAN SAMUELE
CA' REZZONICO
Ca' Rezzonico (Museo de Settecento Veneziano)
Canal Grande
CTS

Canal Grande

N
LG

winds through the city, creating six *sestieri* (sections): **Cannaregio** is in the north and includes the train station, Jewish ghetto, and Cà d'Oro; **Castello** extends east toward the Arsenale; **Dorsoduro**, across the bridge from S. Marco, stretches the length of Canale della Giudecca and up to Campo S. Pantalon; **Santa Croce** lies west of S. Polo, across the Canal Grande from the train station; **San Marco** fills in the area between the Ponte di Rialto and Ponte Accademia; and **San Polo** runs north from Chiesa S. Maria dei Frari to the Ponte di Rialto.

🛈 PRACTICAL INFORMATION

PHONE CODES	Country code: ☎39. **Venice city code:** ☎041. The city code must always be dialed, even when calling from within the city. All 10-digit numbers below are mobile phones and do not require a city code. **International dialing prefix:** 00

Tourist Office: APT, Cal. della Ascensione, S. Marco 71/F (☎529 87 40; www.doge.it), directly opposite the basilica. Open daily 9am-3:30pm. Avoid the eternally mobbed branch at the train station. The **Rolling Venice Card** offers discounts on transportation and at over 200 restaurants, cafes, hotels, museums, and shops for ages 14-29. APT provides a list of participating vendors. Cards cost €3 and are valid for 1 year from date of purchase.

Currency Exchange: Exchange offices charge high prices for service. Use banks whenever possible and inquire about fees beforehand. The streets around S. Marco and S. Polo are full of **banks** and **ATMs.**

Emergency: ☎113 or 112. **Ambulance:** ☎118. **Fire:** ☎115.

Carabinieri (tourist police): Campo S. Zaccaria, Castello 4693/A (☎27 41 11). **Questura,** Fta. S. Lorenzo, Castello 5056 (☎270 55 11). Contact the Questura if you have a serious complaint about your hotel.

Pharmacy: Farmacia Italo-Inglese, Cal. della Mandola, S. Marco 3717 (☎522 48 37). Follow C. Cortesia out of Campo Manin. Open Apr.-Nov. M-F 9am-1:30pm and 2:30-7:30pm, Sa 9am-12:45pm; Dec.-Mar. M-F 9am-12:30pm and 3:45-7:30pm, Sa 9am-12:45pm. MC/V. There are no 24hr. pharmacies in Venice; late-night and weekend pharmacies rotate—check the list posted in the window of any pharmacy.

Hospital: Ospedale Civile, Campo S. S. Giovanni e Paolo, Castello (☎529 41 11).

Internet Access: ▧ **Casanova,** Lista di Spagna, Cannaregio 158/A (☎275 01 99). Hip bar with Internet access on high-speed computers. €7 per hr., students €4. Open daily 9am-11:30pm. AmEx/MC/V; €10 min. purchase.

Post Office: Poste Venezia Centrale, Salizzada Fontego dei Tedeschi, S. Marco 5554 (☎271 71 11), off Campo S. Bartolomeo. Open M-Sa 8:30am-6:30pm. **Postal Codes:** 30121 (Cannaregio); 30122 (Castello); 30123 (Dorsoduro); 30135 (S. Croce); 30124 (S. Marco); 30125 (S. Polo).

⌂ ACCOMMODATIONS

The **VeneziaSi** finds rooms with same-day availability, but they will not be cheap. If you're looking for a miracle, try religious institutions, which often offer rooms in the summer for €25-70. Options include: **Casa Murialdo,** Fond. Madonna dell'Orto, Cannaregio, 3512 (☎71 99 33); **Patronato Salesiano Leone XIII,** Cal. S. Domenico, Castello, 1281 (☎240 36 11); **Domus Cavanis,** Dorsoduro 896 (☎528 73 74), near the Ponte Accademia.

▧ **Alloggi Gerotto Calderan,** Campo S. Geremia 283 (☎71 55 62; www.casagerottocalderan.com). Half hostel, half hotel, all good. Location makes it the best deal in Venice. Check-in 2pm. Check-out 10am. Curfew 12:30am. Reserve at least 15 days ahead. Dorms €21; singles €36, with bath €41; doubles €60/93; triples €84/93. 10% Rolling Venice discount; lower prices for extended stays. Cash only. ❷

■ **Foresteria Valdese,** Castello 5170 (☎528 67 97). From Campo S. Maria Formosa, take Cal. Lunga S. Maria Formosa; it's over the 1st bridge. A crumbling but grand 18th-century guesthouse run by Venice's largest Protestant church. 2min. from major sights. Lockout 10am-1pm. Reservations for groups only. Dorms €21-22; doubles with TV €58, with bath and TV €75; quads with bath and TV €106. Rooms larger than singles require 2-night min. stay. €1 Rolling Venice discount. MC/V. ❷

Hotel Bernardi-Semenzato, Cal. dell'Oca, Cannaregio 4366 (☎522 72 57; www.hotelbernardi.com). From V: Cà d'Oro, turn right on Str. Nuova, left on Cal. del Duca, then right on Cal. dell'Oca. Spacious, airy rooms with great views. Singles with shared bath €30; doubles €45-60, with bath €60-90; triples €78-90; quads €85-118. 10% Rolling Venice discount on larger rooms. AmEx/MC/V. ❸

Albergo San Samuele, Salizzada S. Samuele, S. Marco 3358 (☎522 80 45; www.albergosansamuele.it). Follow Cal. delle Botteghe from Campo S. Stefano and turn left on Salizzada S. Samuele. This centrally located, quirky treasure boasts a mix of antique and retro furniture. Reception until midnight. Reserve 1-2 months ahead. Singles €26-45; doubles €50-100, with bath €60-105; triples €135. Cash only. ❸

FOOD

Beware the overpriced restaurants that line the canals around San Marco. With few exceptions, the best restaurants lie along less traveled alleyways.

■ **Cantinone Gia Schiavi,** Fond. Meraviglie, Dorsoduro 992 (☎523 00 34). From the Frari, follow signs for Ponte Accademia. Just before Ponte Meraviglie, turn right toward the church of S. Trovaso. Cross the 1st bridge. Friendly owner serves chilled wine along a broad marble bar, including a delicate strawberry wine that goes for €8.50 a bottle. Enjoy a glass (€0.80-3) at the bar with some flavorful *cicchetti* (from €1). Bottles from €3.50. Open M-Sa 8am-8pm. Cash only. ❶

■ **Le Bistrot de Venise,** Cal. dei Fabbri, S. Marco 4685 (☎523 66 51; www.bistrotdevenise.com). From P. S. Marco, head through 2nd Sottoportego dei Dai under the awning. Follow road around and over a bridge; turn right. Scrumptious Venetian pasta dishes listed with century of origin served under an outdoor awning or in the art-adorned dining room. *Primi* from €15. *Secondi* from €24. Service 12%. Open daily noon-1am. 10% Rolling Venice discount. MC/V. ❺

Gelateria Nico, Fond. Zattere, Dorsoduro 922 (☎522 52 93). Near V: Zattere, with a great view of the Giudecca Canal. For a guilty pleasure, try the Venetian ■ **gianduiotto de passeggio** (a brick of dense chocolate-hazelnut ice cream dropped into a cup of dense whipped cream; €2.50). Gelato €1, 2 scoops €1.50, 3 scoops €2, more if eaten at tables. Open M-W and F-Su 6:45am-11pm. Cash only. ❶

Ae Oche, Santa Croce 1552A/B (☎524 11 61). From Campo S. Giacomo, take Cal. del Trentor. 60s American advertisements painted onto the unfinished wooden walls make strange bedfellows with the cartoonish duck logo everywhere, but the overall effect is charming, if a bit strange. *Primi* €5.50-7. *Secondi* €7.50-12.50. Cover €1.40. Open daily noon-3pm and 7pm-midnight. Service 12%. MC/V. ❷

SIGHTS

■ **BASILICA DI SAN MARCO.** Venice's crown jewel graces **Piazza San Marco** with symmetrical arches and incomparable mosaic portals. The city's largest tourist attraction, the **Basilica di San Marco** also has the longest lines. Visit in the early morning for the shortest wait or in late afternoon for the best natural light. Begun in the 9th century to house the remains of St. Mark, the interior now sparkles with mosaics from the 13th-century Byzantine and 16th-century Renaissance periods. Behind the altar, the **Pala D'Oro** relief frames a parade of saints in thick, gem-encrusted gold. Farther back, the tomb of St. Mark rests within the altar, adorned with a single gold-stemmed rose. To the right rests the **Tesoro** (treasury), containing gold and relics from the Fourth Crusade. Steep stairs in the atrium lead to the **Galleria della Basilica,** which provides an eye-level view of the tiny golden tiles that compose the basilica's vast ceiling mosaics, an intimate view of the original bronze **Cavalli di San Marco** (Horses of St. Mark), and a balcony overlooking the *piazza.* *(Basilica open M-Sa 9:30am-5pm, Su 2-4pm. Modest dress required. Pala D'Oro open M-Sa 9:45am-5pm. Treasury open M-Sa 9:45am-5pm. Galleria open M-F 9:45am-4:15pm, Sa-Su 9:45am-4:45pm. Basilica free. Pala D'Oro €1.50. Treasury €2. Galleria €3.)*

■**PALAZZO DUCALE (DOGE'S PALACE).** Once the home of Venice's *doge* (mayor), the Palazzo Ducale museum now contains spectacular artwork. Climb the elaborate **Scala d'Oro** (Golden Staircase) to the **Sala delle Quatro Porte** (Room of the Four Doors), where the ceiling is covered in pictorial biblical judgements, and the **Sala dell'Anticollegio** (Antechamber of the Senate) is decorated with mythological tales related to events in Venetian history. More doors lead through the courtrooms of the much-feared Council of Ten, the even-more-feared Council of Three, and the **Sala del Maggior Consiglio** (Great Council Room), dominated by Tintoretto's *Paradise,* the largest oil painting in the world. Near the end, thick stone lattices line the **Ponte dei Sospiri** (Bridge of Sighs), continuing into the prisons. Casanova was condemned by the Ten to walk across this bridge, which gets its name from the mournful groans of prisoners descending into the damp cells. *(☎520 90 70. Open daily Apr.-Oct. 9am-7pm; Nov.-Apr. 9am-5pm. €11, students €5.50.)*

THE GRAND CANAL. The Grand Canal is Venice's "main street." Over 3km long and nearly 50m wide, it loops through the city and passes under three bridges: the **Ponte Scalzi, Rialto,** and **Accademia.** The candy-cane posts used for mooring boats on the canal are called "bricole;" they are painted with the family colors of the adjoining *palazzo. (For great facade views, ride vaporetto #82, 4, or the slower #1 from the train station to P. S. Marco. The facades are flood-lit at night, producing dazzling reflections.)*

RIVOALTUS LEGATORIA. Step into the book-lined **Rivoaltus** on any given day and hear Wanda Scarpa shouting greetings from the attic, where she has been sewing leatherbound, antique-style ■**journals** for an international cadre of customers and faithful locals for more than three decades. The floor-to-ceiling shelves of the shop overflow with the products of Wanda's efforts. *(Ponte di Rialto 11. Basic notebooks €18-31. Photo albums €31-78. Open daily 10am-7:30pm.)*

COLLEZIONE PEGGY GUGGENHEIM. Guggenheim's Palazzo Venier dei Leoni displays some of the finest works of modern masters. The Marini sculpture *Angel in the City,* in front of the *palazzo,* was designed with a detachable penis so that Ms. Guggenheim could make emergency alterations to avoid offending her more prudish guests. *(Fond. Venier dei Leoni, Dorsoduro 710. V: Accademia. Turn left and follow the yellow signs. Open M and Th-Su 10am-6pm. €8, ISIC or Rolling Venice €5.)*

🎵 💺 ENTERTAINMENT AND NIGHTLIFE

Admire Venetian houses and *palazzi* via their original canal pathways. Rides are most romantic about 50min. before sunset and most affordable if shared by six people. The rate that a gondolier quotes is negotiable, and the most price-flexible gondoliers are those standing by themselves rather than those in groups at the "taxi-stands" throughout the city. The "official" price starts at €73 per 50min., with a maximum of six people; prices rise at night. The weekly *A Guest in Venice,* free at hotels and tourist offices or online at www.unospitedivenezia.it, lists current festivals, concerts, and gallery exhibits.

Venetian student nightlife—what exists of it—is concentrated around **Campo Santa Margherita**, in Dorsoduro, while the areas around the **Lista di Spagna**, in Cannaregio, are more touristy.

■ **Paradiso Perduto**, Fond. della Misericordia, Cannaregio 2540 (☎099 45 40). From Str. Nuova, cross Campo S. Fosca, cross the bridge, and continue in the same direction, crossing 2 more bridges. Dreadlocked students flood this unassuming bar, where wait-staff dole out large portions of *cicchetti* (mixed plate; €19). F nights live jazz. Open M-Sa 9:30am-3pm and 7pm-2am.

Piccolo Mondo, Accademia, Dorsoduro 1056/A (☎520 03 71). Facing away from the canal toward the Accademia, turn right and follow the street around. Disco, hip-hop, and vodka with Red Bull (€10) keep a full house at this small but popular disco. 40 years in operation make it the most reliable bet for a night on the town. Framed collages of the wide-ranging clientele include notables like Michael Jordan and Prince Albert of Monaco. Ring bell to enter. Drinks from €7. Cover varies, free with *Let's Go*. Open nightly 10pm-4am. AmEx/MC/V.

MUNICH (MÜNCHEN)

The capital and cultural center of Bavaria, Munich (pop. 1.3 million) is a sprawling, liberal metropolis where world-class museums, handsome parks and architecture, and a cosmopolitan population create a city of astonishing vitality. *Müncheners* party zealously during *Fasching*, or Mardi Gras (Feb. 24-28, 2006), shop with abandon during the Christ Child Market (Dec. 1-23, 2006), and chug unfathomable quantities of beer during the legendary Oktoberfest (Sept. 16-Oct. 1, 2006).

⌐ TRANSPORTATION

Flights: Flughafen München (☎97 52 13 13). S1 and S8 run between the airport and the Hauptbahnhof and Marienpl. (40min., every 20min. 3:57am-12:57am, €8 or 8 strips on the Streifenkarte); buy a *Gesamtz Tageskarte* (€9) that covers all zones. The Lufthansa Airport Bus makes the same trip (40min., every 20min., €9.50).

Trains: Munich's **Hauptbahnhof** (☎118 61) is the transportation hub of southern Germany, with connections to: **Amsterdam** (7-9hr., 15 per day); **Berlin** (6½hr., 2 per hr.); **Cologne** (6hr., 2-4 per hr.); **Frankfurt** (4½hr., 2 per hr.); **Füssen** (2hr., every hr. 6am-9pm); **Hamburg** (6hr., 1-2 per hr.); **Paris, FRA** (8-10hr., 9 per day); **Prague, CZR** (6-7hr., 7 per day); **Rome, ITA** (11hr., 7-8 per day); **Salzburg, AUS** (2hr., 2 per hr.); **Vienna, AUT** (5hr., every hr.); **Zürich, SWI** (4½-5½hr., 14 per day). Purchase **Bayern-Ticket** (single €19, 2-5 people €26) for unlimited train transit in Bavaria and parts of Austria on weekdays 9am-3am, and on weekends midnight-3am. **EurAide**, in the station, provides free train info in English and sells train tickets. **Reisezentrum** info counters at train station open daily 7am-9:30pm.

Ride-Share: Mitfahr-Zentrale, Lämmerstr. 6 (☎194 40). Arranges intercity transportation with drivers going the same way. Around €30. Open M-Sa 8am-8pm. AmEx/MC/V.

Public Transportation: MVV (☎41 42 43 44), operates the U-Bahn (subway) M-Th, Su 5am-12:30am and F-Sa 5am-2am. S-Bahn trains run from 4am until 2 or 3am. Night buses and trams serve Munich's dedicated clubbers (route number prefixed by "N"). Eurail, InterRail, and German railpasses are valid on the S-Bahn (S) but *not* on the U-Bahn (U), streetcars, or buses.

Tickets: Buy tickets at the blue vending machines and validate them in the blue boxes marked with an "E" before entering the platform. If you jump the fare *(Schwarzfahren)*, you risk a €40 fine.

Prices: Single-ride tickets €2.20 (valid 3hr.). **Short-trip** *(Kurzstrecke)* tickets €1.10 (1hr. or 2 stops on the U- or S-Bahn, 4 stops on a streetcar or bus). A **10-strip ticket** *(Streifenkarte)* costs €10 and can be used by more than 1 person. Cancel 2 strips per person for a normal ride, or 1

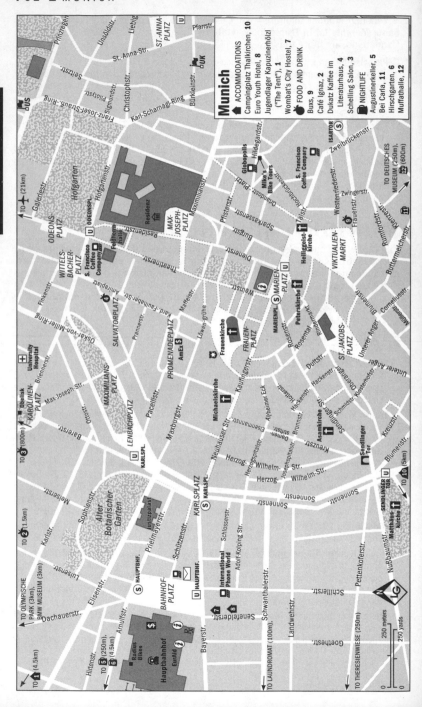

Munich

▲ ACCOMMODATIONS
Campingplatz Thalkirchen, **10**
Euro Youth Hotel, **8**
Jugendlager Kapuzinerhölzl
("The Tent"), **1**
Wombat's City Hostel, **7**

● FOOD AND DRINK
Buxs, **9**
Café Ignaz, **2**
Dukatz Kaffee im
Literaturhaus, **4**
Schelling Salon, **3**

▦ NIGHTLIFE
Augustinerkeller, **5**
Bei Carla, **11**
Hirschgarten, **6**
Muffathalle, **12**

strip for a short trip; for rides beyond the city center, cancel 2 strips per zone. A **single day ticket** *(Single-Tageskarte)* is valid until 6am the next day (€4.50). At €11, the **3-day pass** is a great deal. The **Munich Welcome Card**, available at the tourist office (p. 763), also has transportation discounts. The **XXL Ticket** gives day-long transit on all transport in Munich and surroundings (€6 single; €10.50 for up to 5 people).

Taxis: Taxi-München-Zentrale (☎216 10 or 194 10) has stands in front of the train station and every 5-10 blocks in the city center. Women may request a female driver.

Bike Rental: Mike's Bike Tours, in Discover Bavaria, 10 Bräuhausstr. (☎25 54 39 87); with your back to the Hofbräuhaus, take a left on Bräuhausstr. and a right onto Hochbrückenstr. All-day bike rental €12, overnight €18. Half off with a tour (p. 763). Open M and F-Sa 8:35am-9:15pm, Su and Tu-Th 10am-1pm and 3-9pm. To return your bike after hours, call ☎0172 722 0435.

ORIENTATION AND PRACTICAL INFORMATION

Downtown Munich is split into quadrants by thoroughfares running east-west and north-south. These intersect at Munich's central square, **Marienplatz,** and link the traffic rings at Karlsplatz (called Stachus by locals) in the west, Isartorplatz in the east, Odeonsplatz in the north, and Sendlinger Tor in the south. In the east beyond the Isartor, the Isar River flows north-south. The **Hauptbahnhof** is just beyond Karlspl. to the west of the ring. The **university** is to the north amid the budget restaurants of the **Schwabing** district; to the east of Schwabing is the **English Garden,** to the west, the **Olympiapark.** South of downtown is the **Glockenbachviertel,** filled with night hot spots and many gay bars. A seedy area with hotels and sex shops surrounds the Hauptbahnhof. Oktoberfest takes place on the large and open **Theresienwiese,** southeast of the train station on the U4 and 5 lines. The most comprehensive list of services, events, and museums can be found in the English monthly *Munich Found* (€3), available at newsstands.

PHONE CODES	**Country code:** ☎49. **Munich city code:** ☎089 **International dialing prefix:** 00.

Tourist Offices: Main office (☎23 39 65 55), on the front side of the train station, next to the SB-Markt on Bahnhofpl. Books rooms for free with a 10-15% deposit, sells English-language city maps (€0.30), and sells the **Munich Welcome Card** for discounts and passes to transportation and sights (1-day €6.50, 3-day €16). Open M-Sa 9am-8pm, Su 10am-6pm. ■ **EurAide** (☎59 38 89), room #3 along track 11 of the Hauptbahnhof, near the Bayerstr. exit. Books train tickets for free, explains public transportation, sells maps (€1), and books English-language city tours. Pick up the free brochure *Inside Track.* Daily except June M-Sa 7:45am-noon and 1-6pm; Aug.-Sept. 8am-12:30pm and 2-5pm; Oct. 7:45am-12:45pm and 2-4pm; Nov.-Apr. 8am-noon and 1-4pm; May 7:45am-12:30pm and 2-4:30pm. Su, closed.

Tours: ■ **Mike's Bike Tours,** 10 Bräuhausstr. (☎25 54 39 88; www.mikesbiketours.com). If you only have 1 day in Munich, take this tour. Starting from the Altes Rathaus on Marienpl., the 4hr., 6.5km city tour includes a *Biergarten* break. Tours leave daily June-July 11:30am and 4pm. Look for coupons at youth hostels. €24.

Consulates: Canada, Tal 29 (☎219 95 70). Open M-Th 9am-noon and 2-5pm, F 9am-noon. **Ireland,** Dennigerstr. 15 (☎20 80 59 90). Open M-F 9am-noon. **UK,** Bürkleinstr. 10, 4th fl. (☎21 10 90). Open M-F 8:45-11:30am and 1-3:15pm. **US,** Königinstr. 5 (☎288 80). Open M-F 8-11am.

Currency Exchange: ReiseBank (☎551 08 13; www.reisebank.de), at the front of the train station on Bahnhofpl. Slightly cheaper than other banks. Open daily 7am-10pm.

GLBT Resources: Gay services information (☎260 3056), hotline open 7-10pm. **Lesbian information** (☎725 4272). Phones staffed M and W 2:30-5pm, Tu 10:30am-1pm. The reception desk of **Hotel Deutsche Eiche,** Reichenbachstr. 13, can provide information 24hr. (☎231 1660; www.deutsche-eiche.com.)

Emergency: Police: ☎110. **Ambulance** and **Fire:** ☎112. **Medical service:** ☎192 22.

Pharmacy: Bahnhofpl. 2 (☎59 81 19), on the corner outside the train station. Open M-F 8am-6:30pm, Sa 8am-2pm.

Internet Access: Just around the corner from Mike's Bike Tours (see **Bike Rental,** p. 763), **Glopolis** charges €2.50 for unlimited Internet time. Open M and F-Sa 8:35am-9:15pm, Su and Tu-Th 10am-1pm and 3-9pm.

Post Office: Bahnhofpl. In the yellow building opposite the main train station exit. Open M-F 7:30am-8pm, Sa 9am-4pm. **Postal Code:** 80335.

ACCOMMODATIONS AND CAMPING

During mid-summer and Oktoberfest, rooms are hard to find and prices jump 10-15%. In summer, book a few weeks in advance or to start calling before noon.

▓ **Euro Youth Hotel,** Senefelderstr. 5 (☎59 90 88 11). From the Hauptbahnhof, make a left on Bayerstr. and a right on Senefelderstr. Informed staff, cheerful rooms, and a busy bar make this the best hostel in Munich. Breakfast €3.90, included in private rooms. Free lockers. Wash €2.80, dry €1.30. Internet €3 per hr. Key deposit €20. Reception 24hr. 22-bed dorms €19.50; 3- to 5-bed dorms €22; 3-bed dorms with shower €25; singles €42; doubles €54, with private shower €70; triples with bath €84. MC/V. ❷

▓ **Jugendlager Kapuzinerhölzl ("The Tent"),** In den Kirschen 30 (☎141 43 00). Streetcar #17 from the Hauptbahnhof (dir.: Amalienburgstr.) to Botanischer Garten (15min.). Make a right at Franz-Schrank-Str., follow the signs, and turn left at In den Kirschen. 250 spaces with a big tent on a wooden floor. Evening campfires. Free English-language city tours. Reception 24hr. Check-in 4:30pm. Open June-Aug. Foam pad, blankets, shower, and breakfast €8.50. Actual beds €11. Camping €11. Cash only. ❶

Wombat's City Hostel, Senefelderstr. 1 (☎599 89 18 0). The first in a row of 3 hostels on Senefelderstr. Hang in the inner greenhouse courtyard and enjoy free board games and weekly English-language movie nights. Bright, colorful rooms, all with bath. Breakfast €4. Reception 24hr. Dorms €19-22; singles €49; doubles €62. Cash only. ❷

Campingplatz Thalkirchen, Zentralländstr. 49 (☎723 17 07; www.camping.muenchen.de). U1 or 2 to Sendlinger Tor, then U3 to Thalkirchen, and change to bus #135 (every 30min.); Campingpl. is the 3rd stop (8min.). 550 sites on the lush banks of the Isar. TV lounge, convenience store, and cafe. Electricity €1.80. Showers €1. Wash €4, dry €0.50. Reception 7am-11pm. 14-day max. stay. Open mid-Mar. to Oct. Tent sites €12.50, extra person €4.50. Tent rental €3-4. Cash only. ❶

 REMINDER. HI-affiliated hostels in Bavaria generally do not admit guests over age 26, except families or groups of adults with young children.

FOOD

Off **Ludwigstraße,** the university district supplies students with inexpensive, filling meals. Many reasonably priced restaurants and cafes cluster on **Schellingstraße, Amalienstraße,** and **Türkenstraße** (U3 or 6 to Universität). Munich is also the place where someone first connected the "beer" concept to the "garden" concept to create the **beer garden.** Now they're all over the city.

▓ **Dukatz Kaffee im Literaturhaus,** Salvatorpl. 1 (☎291 9600). This sunny, open-air cafe is Munich's unofficial literary hub. Gourmet food from €4 complements creative drinks (€5-8.50). Book discussions and readings are frequent and often free; for more information call ☎29 19 34 27. Open M-Sa 10am-1am. Cash only. ❷

Café Ignaz, Georgenstr. 67 (☎271 6093). U2 to Josephspl. Crepes, pasta, stir-fry, and more at this vegetarian bakery and cafe. Entrees (€5-9) include dessert. Get main dishes to go for €4. Breakfast (€5-7), lunch (€6), and weekend brunch (€8) buffets. M-F 3-6pm entrees €6. Open M and W-Su 8am-11pm, Tu 11am-1pm. Cash only. ❷

Schelling Salon, Schellingstr. 54 (☎272 07 88). Bavarian *knödel* and billiard balls since 1872. Rack up at the tables where Lenin, Rilke, and Hitler once played (€7 per hr.). Traditional German entrees include *weißwurst* with mustard (€3.20) and *beuscherl*, or pig's lung, with *knödel* (€4) for the adventurous. Breakfast €3-5. English menu. Open M and Th-Su 10am-1am. Cash only. ❶

buxs, Frauenstr. 9 (☎291 9550), on the southern edge of the Viktualienmarkt. A delicious variety of fresh, unique salads, as well as hot foods, soups, and desserts. Sit on the terrace or in the modern, upscale cafe. Everything (excluding drinks) €2 per 100g. Open M-F 11am-6:45pm, Sa 11am-3pm. Cash only. ❸

⊙ 🏛 SIGHTS AND MUSEUMS

The *Münchner Volkshochschule* (☎48 00 62 29) gives tours of many museum exhibits for €6. Purchase a **day pass** to all of Munich's state-owned museums at the tourist office and at many larger museums (€15). All state-owned museums are discounted on Sunday.

■**RESIDENZ.** Down the pedestrian zone from Odeonspl., the ornate rooms of the Residenz (palace) celebrate the wealth left behind by the Wittelsbach dynasty. The **Schatzkammer** (treasury) contains crowns, swords, china, precious stones, and ivory. The **Residenzmuseum** comprises the Wittelsbach apartments and State Rooms, a vast collection of European porcelain, and a 17th-century court chapel. *(Max-Joseph-pl. 3. U3-6 to Odeonspl. ☎29 06 71. Open Apr. to mid-Oct. M-W and F-Su 9am-6pm, 9am-8pm; mid-Oct. to Mar. M-W and F-Su 10am-4pm. Last admission 30min. before closing. Schatzkammer and Residenzmuseum each €6, students €5. Combination ticket €9/8.)*

■**DEUTSCHES MUSEUM.** Even if you don't know (or care) how engines power a Boeing 747, the Deutsches Museum's more than 50 departments on science and technology will still keep you entertained and educated. *(Museuminsel 1. S1-8 to Isartor or streetcar #18 to Deutsches Museum. ☎217 91; www.deutsches-museum.de. Open daily 9am-5pm. Tour in English daily 1:15pm. €7.50, students €3.)*

■**PINAKOTHEKE DER MODERNE.** Designed by *Münchener* Stephan Braunfels, the beautiful Pinakothek is four museums in one. Subgalleries display architecture, design, drawings, and paintings by a wide range of artists from Picasso to the latest contemporary works. *(Barerstr. 40. U2 to Königspl. ☎2380 5360. Open Tu-W and Sa-Su 10am-5pm, Th-F 10am-8pm. €9, students €5; Su €1.)* Commissioned in 1826 by King Ludwig I, the **Alte Pinakothek** houses Munich's most precious art, including works by da Vinci, Rembrandt, and Rubens. *(Barerstr. 27. ☎2380 5216. Open Tu 10am-8pm, W-Su 10am-5pm. €5, students €3.50. Su €1.)* Next door, the **Neue Pinakothek** exhibits artists of the 19th and 20th centuries, including Cézanne, Manet, and van Gogh. *(Barerstr. 29. ☎2380 5195. Open M and Th-Su 10am-5pm, W 10am-8pm. €9, students €5; Su €1. Combination ticket for the Alte and Neue Pinakotheke €8/5. Day pass to all 3 €12/7.)*

■**MARIENPLATZ.** The **Mariensäule,** an ornate 1683 monument to the Virgin Mary, commemorates the city's survival of the Thirty Years' War. At the **Neues Rathaus,** the **Glockenspiel** pleases tourists with a display of jousting knights and dancing coopers. At 9pm, a mechanical watchman marches out and the Guardian Angel escorts the *Münchner Kindl* (Munich Child) to bed. Be wary when passing through Marienpl.: with all the tourists looking upward, pickpockets have a field day. *(Daily at 11am, noon, 3pm; in summer also 5pm.)*

PETERSKIRCHE AND FRAUENKIRCHE. The 12th-century Peterskirche is the city's oldest parish church. Scale over 300 steps for a spectacular view of Munich. *(Open M-Sa 9am-7pm, Su 10am-7pm; last admission 6:30pm. Tower €1.50, students €1.)* Take Kaufingerstr. one block toward the Hauptbahnhof to the onion-domed towers of the 15th-century Frauenkirche—one of Munich's most notable landmarks. *(1 Frauenpl. Tower open daily Apr.-Oct. 10am-5pm. €3, students €1.50, under 6 free.)*

ZAM: ZENTRUM FÜR AUSSERGEWÖHNLICHE MUSEEN. Munich's Center for Unusual Museums corrals such treasures as the Peddle-Car Museum, the Museum of Easter Rabbits, and the Chamberpot Museum. *(Westenriederstr. 41. S1-8 or streetcar #17 or 18 to Isartor. ☎290 41 21. Open daily 10am-6pm. €4, students €3.)*

🎵 🎭 ENTERTAINMENT AND NIGHTLIFE

Monatsprogramm (€1.50) and *Munich Found* (€3) list schedules for Munich's stages, museums, and festivals. In July, a great **opera festival** arrives at the ▨**Bayerische Staatsoper** (Bavarian National Opera), Max-Joseph-pl. 2. (Tickets ☎21 85 01; www.bayerische.staatsoper.de.) Afterwards, while unwinding at a cafe or beer garden, asking for "*Ein Bier, bitte*" will order a *Maß* (liter; €4-6). Specify for only a *halb-Maß* (half-liter; €3-4) or a *Pils* (0.3L; €2-3).

▨ **Hirschgarten,** Hirschgarten 1 (☎17 25 91). Streetcar #17 (dir.: Amalienburgstr.) to Romanpl., near Schloß Nymphenburg. Seating 9000, Europe's largest beer garden should rather be called a beer park. Vast expanses of grass, trees, and giant chess pieces promise something for everyone. Entrees €2-8 in food stands, €5-17 in the restaurant. *Maß* €5.50. Open daily 10am-midnight; last drink 11:30pm; kitchen closes 10pm. Su brunch starts 11am. MC/V.

▨ **Muffathalle,** Zellstr. 4 (☎45 87 50 10; www.muffatwerk.de), in Haidhausen. S1-8 to Rosenheimerpl. and walk toward the river on Rosenheimer Str. for 2 blocks, or take streetcar #18 to Deutsches Museum. A former power plant, Muffathalle now generates techno, rock, hip-hop, jazz, dance, and spoken word performances from local and international artists every night. Cover usually €5-20, depending on venue. Beer garden open May-Sept. Muffathalle open daily 7 or 8pm, Su-Th until 2-3am and F-Sa as late as 5-6am.

Bei Carla, Buttermelcherstr. 9 (☎22 79 01). S1-8 to Isartor. Walk south on Zweibrückenstr., then turn right on Rumfordstr., left on Klenzestr., and left again onto Buttermelcherstr. A friendly lesbian cafe and bar. Open M-Sa 4pm-1am, Su 6pm-1am.

Augustinerkeller, Arnulfstr. 52 (☎59 43 93), at Zirkus-Krone-Str. S1-8 to Hackerbrücke. Many view Augustinerkeller, est. 1824, as the finest beer garden in town for its lush grounds, century-old chestnut trees, and sharp Augustiner beer (*Maß;* €6.40). Open daily 10am-1am; Kitchen open daily 10:30am-10pm.

GLOSSARY

PHONETIC TRANSCRIPTION

	PRONOUNCE		PRONOUNCE		PRONOUNCE
a	Battle of Stalingrad	f	Former USSR	oy	Oy
ai	Iron Curtain	g	glasnost (soft)	p	Poland
ah	Prague	h	have	r	revolution
au	orange	ih	betw. indie and evil	rr	rascal (rolled, with the tip of the tongue)
aw	like saw, but shorter	iy	ski	t	tank
ay	Romania (short)	j	Joseph, edge	th	theft
b	Bosnia	k	Kremlin	s	Serbia
ch	China	kh	fricative, Ger. *Bach*	ts	Let's Go
d	dictatorship	l	Lenin	sh	dictatorship
dz	comrades	m	Macedonia	uh	Russia
e	lend	n	Non-Aggression Pact	v	Volga
ee	Eastern Europe	oh	Croatia	w	workers of the world
eh	Estonia	oe	rounded, Fr. *sœur*	y	Yalta
ehr	aerial (rolled, with the tip of the tongue)	oo	Budapest	z	Communism
ey	vey!	ow	wow (with rounded lips)	zh	mirage

BULGARIAN (БЪЛГАРСКИ)

ENGLISH	BULGARIAN	PRONOUNCE
Hello	Добър ден	DOH-bir dehn
Yes/no	Да/Не	dah/neh
Please/you're welcome	Моля	MO-lyah
Thank you	Благодаря	blahg-oh-dahr-YAH
Goodbye	Добиждане	doh-VEEZH-dah-neh
Good morning	Добро утро	doh-BROH OO-troh
Good evening	Добър Вечер	DOH-buhr VEH-cher
Good night	Лека Нощ	LEH-kah nohsht
Sorry/excuse me	Извинете	iz-vi-NEH-teh
Help!	Помощ!	POH-mohsht
Where is...	Къде е...	kuh-DEH eh
...the bathroom?	...тоалетната?	toh-ah-LYEHT-nah-tah
... the nearest phone booth?	...най-близкия телефон?	nai-bleez-kee-yah teh-leh-FOHN
...the center of town?	...центъра на града?	TSEHNT-ur-a nah grahd-AH
How much does this cost?	Колко Струва?	KOHL-koh STROO-vah
When?	Кога?	koh-GAH
Do you speak English?	Говорите ли Английски?	goh-VOH-ree-teh lee ahn-GLEEY-skee
I don't understand.	Не разбирам.	neh rahz-BEE-rahm

GLOSSARY

ENGLISH	BULGARIAN	PRONOUNCE
I don't speak Bulgarian.	Не говоря по-български.	neh gah-var-YA po-buhl-GAHR-skee
Please write it down.	Може лида ми го запишете.	MOH-zhe LEE-dah mee goh za-pee-SHEE-teh
Do you have a vacancy?	Имате ли свободна стая?	ee-MAH-te lee svoh-BOHD-nah STAH-ya
I'd like a room.	Искам стая.	EES-kahm STAH-yah
I'd like to order...	Искам да поръчам...	EES-kahm dah por-RUH-cham
I don't eat...	Не ям...	neh yahm...
I'm allergic.	Имам алергия.	EE-mahm ah-LEHR-gee-yah
I'd like to pay	Искам да платя.	EES-kahm dah plah-TYAH
I want a ticket to...	Искам билет да...	EES-kahm bee-LEHT dah
Go away.	Махнете се.	makh-NEH-teh seh
Cheers!	Наздаве!	nahz-DRAHV-eh
I love you.	Ас те обичам.	ahs tey OHB-ee-chahm

ENGLISH	BULGARIAN	PRONOUNCE	ENGLISH	BULGARIAN	PRONOUNCE
one	едно	ehd-NOH	six	шест	shehst
two	две	dveh	seven	седем	SEH-dehm
three	три	tree	eight	осем	O-sehm
four	четири	CHEH-tee-ree	nine	девет	DEH-veht
five	пет	peht	ten	десет	DEH-seht
single room	единична	ye-din-EECH-nah	one-way	отиване	o-TEE-vahn-eh
double room	двойна	dvoy-NAH	round-trip	отиване и Връщане	oh-TEE-vahn-eh ee VRUH-shtah-neh
reservation	резевация	re-zer-VAH-tsee-yah	ticket	билет	bee-LEHT
departure	заминаващи	zaminavashti	train	влак	vlahk
arrival	пристигащи	pristigashti	bus	автобус	ahv-toh-BOOS
airport	летище	LEHT-ee-shteh	bank	банка	BAHN-kah
train station	гара	gahrah	police	полиция	poh-LEE-tsee-yah
bus station	автогарата	AHV-toh-gah-rah-tah	exchange	обменно бюро	OHB-mehn-noh byoo-ROH
luggage	багаж	bah-GAHZH	passport	паспорт	pahs-POHRT
breakfast	закуска	za-KOO-ska	market	пазар	pah-ZAHR
lunch	обяд	oh-BYAHD	grocery	бакалия	bah-kah-LEE-yah
dinner	вечеря	veh-cher-YAH	meat	месо	meh-SO
menu	меню	mehn-YOO	coffee	кафе	kah-FEH
bread	хляб	hlyahb	milk	мляко	MLYAH-koh
vegetables	зеленчуци	ZEH-lehn-choot-zee	beer	бира	BEE-rah
left	ляво	LYAH-voh	toilet	тоалетна	toh-ah-LEHT-nah
right	дясно	DYAHS-noh	square	площад	PLOH-shad
straight ahead	на право	nah PRAH-voh	post office	поща	POH-shtah
doctor	лекарят	LEH-kahr-yaht	stamp	марка	MAHR-kah

ENGLISH	BULGARIAN	PRONOUNCE
hospital	болнитцата	BOHL-neets-ah-ta

ENGLISH	BULGARIAN	PRONOUNCE
airmail	въздушна поща	vuhz-DOOSH-nah POH-shtah

CROATIAN (HRVATSKI)

ENGLISH	CROATIAN	PRONOUNCE
Hello/hi	Zdravo/bog	ZDRAH-vo/bohg
Yes/no	Da/ne	Dah/Neh
Please/you're welcome	Molim	MOH-leem
Thank you	Hvala lijepa/hvala	HVAH-la lee-ye-pah/hvah-lah
Goodbye	Bog	Bog
Good morning	Dobro jutro	DOH-broh YOO-tro
Good evening	Dobro večer	DOH-broh VEH-chehr
Good night	Laku noć	LAH-koo nohch
Sorry/excuse me	Oprostite	oh-PROH-stee-teh
Help!	U pomoć!	OO pohmohch
Where is...?	Gdje je...?	gdye yeh
...the bathroom?	...zahod?	ZAH-hod
...the nearest telephone booth?	...nalazi najbliža telefonska govornica?	NAH-lah-zee nai-BLEE-zhah teh-leh-FOHN-skah goh-vohr-NEE-tsah
...the center of town?	...centar grada?	TSEHN-tahr GRAH-dah
How much does this cost?	Koliko to košta?	KOH-lee-koh toh KOH-shtah
When?	Kada?	KAH-dah
Do you speak English?	Govorite li engleski?	GO-vohr-ee-teh lee ehn-GLEH-skee
I don't understand.	Ne razumijem.	neh rah-ZOO-mee-yehm
I don't speak Croatian.	Ne govorim hrvatski.	neh goh-VOH-reem KHR-va-tskee
Please write it down.	Molim, napišajte mi to.	MOH-leem, nah-PEE-shee-teh mee to
Do you have a vacancy?	Imate li slobodnih soba?	EE-mah-teh lee SLOH-boh-dneh SOH-bah?
I'd like a room.	Želio bih sobu.	ZHEL-ee-oh beeh SOH-boo
I'd like some...	Želio bih ...	ZHEL-ee-oh beeh
I don't eat...	Ne jedem...	neh YEH-dem
I'm allergic.	Imam alergiju.	EE-mam ah-lehr-GEE-yoo
Have you got any vegetarian dishes?	Imate li vegetarijanska jela?	EE-mah-teh lee veh-geh-tah-REE-YAN-skah YEH-lah
Check, please.	Račun, molim.	ra-CHOON MOH-leem
I want a ticket to...	Htio bih kartu za...	HTEE-oh beeh KAHR-too zah...
Go away.	Bježi	BYEH-zhee
Cheers!	Živjeli!	ZHIV-yehl-ee
I love you.	Volim te.	VOH-leem teh.

ENGLISH	CROATIAN	PRONOUNCE
one	jedan	YEHD-ahn
two	dva	dvah
three	tri	tree
four	četiri	CHEH-tee-ree

ENGLISH	CROATIAN	PRONOUNCE
six	šest	shehsht
seven	sedam	SEH-dahm
eight	osam	OH-sahm
nine	devet	DEH-veht

ENGLISH	CROATIAN	PRONOUNCE	ENGLISH	CROATIAN	PRONOUNCE
five	pet	peht	ten	deset	DEH-seht
single room	jedno-krevetnu sobu	yehd-noh-KREH-veht-noo SOH-boo	one-way	u jednom smjeru	oo YEH-dnohm smee-YEH-roo
double room	dvokrevetnu sobu	dvoh-KREH-veht-noo SOH-boo	round-trip	povratna karta	POHV-raht-nah KAHR-tah
reservation	rezervacija	reh-zehr-VAH-tsee-yah	ticket	kartu	KAHR-too
departure	odlazak	OHD-lahz-ahk	train	vlak	VLAHK
arrival	polazak	POH-lahz-ahk	bus	autobus	OW-toh-bus
Monday	ponedeljak	POH-neh-djehl-ahk	airport	zračna luka	ZRAH-chnah loo-kah
Tuesday	utorak	OO-toh-rahk	train (bus) station	(autobusni) kolodvor	(OW-toh-boos-nee) KOH-loh-dvohr
Wednesday	srijeda	SREE-yehdah	luggage	prtljaga	PEHRT-lyah-gah
Thursday	četvrtak	CHEHT-vehr-tahk	bank	banka	BAHN-kah
Friday	petak	PEH-tahk	police	policija	poh-LEE-tsee-yah
Saturday	subota	SOO-boh-tah	doctor	liječnik	lee-YECH-neek
Sunday	nedjelja	NEH-dyehl-yah	hospital	bolnica	BOHL-neet-sa
today	danas	DAH-nahs	exchange	mjenjačnica	myehn-YAHCH-nee-tsah
tomorrow	sutra	SOO-trah	passport	putovnica	POO-toh-vnee-tsah
day	dan	dahn	market/ grocery	trgovina	TER-goh-vee-nah
week	tjedna	TYEHD-nah	breakfast	doručak	doh-ROO-chahk
morning	ujutro	oo-YOO-troh	lunch	ručak	ROO-chahk
afternoon	popodne	poh-POH-dneh	dinner	večera	VEH-cheh-rah
evening	večer	VEH-chehr	menu	karta	KAR-tah
hot	vruće	VROO-cheh	bread	kruh	krooh
cold	hladno	HLAHD-noh	vegetables	povrće	POH-vehr-chay
left	lijevo	lee-YEH-voh	meat	meso	meh-so
right	desno	DEHS-noh	coffee	kava	KAH-vah
straight-ahead	pravo	PRA-vo	milk	mlijeko	mlee-YEH-koh
toilet	W.C.	vay-tsay	beer	pivo	PEE-voh
stamp	markica	MAHR-kee-tsah	post office	pošta	POSH-tah
square	trg	terg	airmail	zrakoplovom	ZRAH-koh-ploh-vohm

CZECH (ČESKY)

ENGLISH	CZECH	PRONOUNCE
Hello	Dobrý den *(formal)*	DOH-bree dehn
Yes/no	Ano/ne	AH-noh/neh
Please/you're welcome	Prosím	PROH-seem
Thank you	Děkuji	DYEH-koo-yee
Goodbye	Nashedanou	NAS-kleh-dah-noh
Good morning	Dobré ráno	DOH-breh RAH-noh

ENGLISH	CZECH	PRONOUNCE
Good evening	Dobrý večer	DOH-breh VEH-chehr
Good night	Dobrou noc	DOH-broh NOHTS
Sorry/excuse me	Promiňte	PROH-meen-teh
Help!	Pomoc!	POH-mots
Where is...?	Kde je...?	gdeh yeh
...the bathroom?	...kúpelňa?	KOO-pehl-nyah
...the nearest telephone booth?	...nejbližší telefonní budka?	NEY-bleezh-shnee TEH-leh-foh-nee BOOT-kah
...the center of town?	...centrum města?	TSEN-troom MYEHST-steh
How much does this cost?	Kolik to stojí?	KOH-leek STOH-yee
When?	Kdy?	gdee
Do you speak English?	Mluvíte anglicky?	MLOO-veet-eh ahng-GLEET-skee
I don't understand.	Nerozumím.	NEH-rohz-oo-meem
I don't speak Czech.	Nemluvím Česky.	NEH-mloo-veem CHESS-kee
Please write it down.	Mohl byste to napsat?	MO-huhl BI-ste to NAP-sat
Do you have a vacancy?	Máte volný pokoj?	MAH-teh VOL-nee POH-koy
I'd like a room.	Prosím pokoj.	proh-SEEM PO-koy
I'd like to order...	Prosím...	proh-SEEM
I don't eat...	Nejím maso.	NEH-yeem MAH-soh
I'm allergic	Jsem alergický	ysehm AH-lehr-gits-kee
Check, please.	Paragon, prosím.	PAH-rah-gohn proh-SEEM
I want a ticket to...	Chtěl bych jízdenku do ...	khytel bikh YEEZ-den-koo DOH
How long does the trip take?	Jak dlouho ta cesta trva?	yahk DLOH-ho tah TSE-stah TER-vah
Go away.	Prosím odejděte.	pro-SEEM ODEY-dyeh-teh
Cheers!	Na zdraví!	nah ZDRAH-vee
I love you.	Miluji tě.	MEE-loo-yee tyeh

ENGLISH	CZECH	PRONOUNCE
one	jedna	YEHD-na
two	dvě	dvye
three	tři	trzhee
four	čtyři	CHTEER-zhee
five	pět	pyet
single room	jednolůžkový pokoj	YEHD-noh-loozh-koh-vee POH-koy
double room	dvoulůžkový pokoj	DVOH-loozh-ko-vee POH-koy
reservation	rezervace	REH-zehr-vah-tseh
departure	odjezd	OHD-yehzd
arrival	příjezd	PREE-yehzd
one-way	jedním směrem	YED-neem SMNYE-rem
round-trip	zpáteční	SPAH-tehch-nyee
Monday	pondělí	POHN-dyeh-lee

ENGLISH	CZECH	PRONOUNCE
six	šest	shest
seven	sedm	SEH-doom
eight	osm	OH-suhm
nine	devět	DE-vyet
ten	deset	DE-set
ticket	lístek	LEES-tehk
train	vlak	vlahk
bus	autobus	OW-toh-boos
airport	letiště	LEH-teesh-tyeh
station	nádraží	NAH-drah-zhee
bus station	autobusové nádraže	OW-toh-boo-sohv-eh NAH-drazh-eh
luggage	zavadla	ZAH-vahd-lah
bank	banka	BAHN-kah

GLOSSARY

ENGLISH	CZECH	PRONOUNCE
Tuesday	úterý	OO-teh-ree
Wednesday	středa	STRZHEH-dah
Thursday	čtvrtek	CHTVER-tehk
Friday	pátek	PAH-tehk
Saturday	sobota	SOH-boh-tah
Sunday	neděle	NEH-dyeh-leh
today	dnes	dnehs
tomorrow	zítra	ZEE-trah
day	den	dehn
week	týden	tee-dehn
morning	ráno	RAH-noh
afternoon	odpoledne	OHD-pohl-ehd-neh
evening	večer	VEH-chehr
hot	teplý	TEHP-leeh
cold	studený	STOO-deh-nee
left	vlevo	VLEH-voh
right	vpravo	VPRAH-voh
straight ahead	přímo	PRZHEE-moh
toilet	W.C.	VEE-TSEE
square	náměstí	NAH-myeh-stee

ENGLISH	CZECH	PRONOUNCE
police	policie	POH-leets-ee-yeh
doctor	doktor	DOHK-tohr
hospital	nemocnice	NEH-mo-tsnyi-tseh
exchange	směnárna	smyeh-NAHR-nah
passport	cestovní pas	TSEH-stohv-nee pahs
market	trh	terh
grocery	potraviny	POH-trah-vee-nee
breakfast	snídaně	SNEE-dahn-yeh
lunch	oběd	OHB-yehd
dinner	večeře	VEH-cher-zheh
menu	listek	LEES-tehk
bread	chléb	khlep
vegetables	zelenina	ZEH-leh-nee-nah
meat	maso	MAH-soh
coffee	káva	KAH-vah
milk	mléko	MLEH-koh
beer	pivo	PEE-voh
post office	pošta	POSH-tah
stamp	známka	ZNAHM-kah
airmail	letecky	LEH-tehts-kee

ESTONIAN (ESTI KEEL)

There are many dipthongs (double vowels) in Estonian. Note that the first vowel of the dipthong is always pronounced short.

ENGLISH	ESTONIAN	PRONOUNCE
Hello	Tere	TEH-reh
Yes/no	Jaa/ei	yah/ay
Please	Palun	PAH-loon
Thank you	Tänan	TAH-nahn
Goodbye	Head aega	heh-ahd AI-gah
Sorry/Excuse me	Vabandage	vah-bahn-DAHG-eh
Help!	Appi!	AHP-pee
ticket	pilet	PEE-leht
train/bus	rong/buss	rohng/boos
toilet	tualett	twah-LEHT
doctor	arst	arzt

ENGLISH	ESTONIAN	PRONOUNCE
one	üks	ooks
two	kaks	kahks
three	kolm	kohlm
four	neli	NEH-lee
five	viis	vees
six	kuus	koos
seven	seitse	SAYT-seh
eight	kaheksa	KAH-hek-sah
nine	üheksa	OO-hek-sah
ten	kümme	KOO-me
hospital	haigla	hai-glah

ENGLISH	ESTONIAN	PRONOUNCE
Where is...?	Kus on...?	koos ohn
How much does this cost?	Kui palju?	kwee PAHL-yoo
Do you speak English?	Kas te räägite inglise keelt?	kahs teh RA-A-GEE-teh EEN-GLEE-seh kehlt

ENGLISH	ESTONIAN	PRONOUNCE
Go away!	Jätke mind rahule!	YAT-keh meend RA-hule
Cheers!	Proosit!	PROH-seet

HUNGARIAN (MAGYAR)

Stress falls on the first syllable of each word in Hungarian. After consonants, especially *g*, *l*, or *n*, the *y* is not pronounced but serves to soften the letter it follows.

ENGLISH	HUNGARIAN	PRONOUNCE
Hello	Szervusz (pol.)/Szia (inf.)/Hello	SAYHR-voose/See-ya/Hello
Yes/no	Igen/nem	EE-gehn/nehm
Please	Kérem	KAY-rehm
Thank you	Köszönöm	KUH-suh-nuhm
Goodbye	Viszontlátásra	VEE-sohnt-laht-ah-shrah
Good morning	Jó reggelt	YAW RAHg-gailt
Good evening	Jó estét	YAW EHSH-teht
Good night	Jó éjszakát	YAW AY-sah-kaht
Sorry/excuse me	Elnézést	EHL-nay-zaysht
Where is...?	Hol van...?	haul vahn
...the bathroom?	...a W.C.?	ah VAY-tsay
...the nearest telephone booth?	...a legközelebbi telefonfülke?	ah LEHG-kawz-ehl-ehb-ee teh-leh-FAWN-FOOHL-keh
...the center of town?	...a városkőzpont?	ah VAH-rosh-kohz-pohnt
How much does this cost?	Mennyibe kerül?	MEHN-yee-beh KEH-rool
When?	Mikor?	MEE-kohr
Do you speak English?	Beszél angolul?	BESS-ayl AHN-gawl-ool
I don't understand.	Nem értem.	nem AYR-tem
I don't speak Hungarian.	Nem tudok (jól) magyarul.	nehm TOO-dawk (yawl) MAW-jyah-rool
Please write it down.	Kérem, írja fel.	KAY-rem, EER-yuh fel
Do you have a vacancy?	Van üres szoba?	vahn oo-REHSH SAH-bah
I'd like a room.	Szeretnék egy szobát.	seh-reht-naik ehj SAW-baht
I'd like to order...	...kérek.	KAY-rehk
I don't eat...	Nem eszem...	nem eh-sem
I'm allergic.	Allergia's vagyok.	ah-lehr-ghee-ahsh vah-jawk
I'm a vegetarian.	Vegetarianus vagyok.	vej-et-ar-ee-an-ush vad-jawk
Check, please.	A számlát, kérem.	uh SAHM-lot KAY-rehm
I want a ticket.	Szeretnékegy jegyet.	sehr-eht-nayk-ehj yehj-at
Go away.	Távozzék.	TAH-vawz-zayk
Cheers!	Egészségedre!	ehg-eh-SHEHG-eh-dreh
I love you.	Szeretleu.	sehr-EHT-lyuh

ENGLISH	HUNGARIAN	PRONOUNCE
one	egy	ehj
two	kettő	KEHT-tuh
three	három	HAH-rohm
four	négy	naydj
five	öt	uht
single room	egyágyas	EHD-ahd-awsh

ENGLISH	HUNGARIAN	PRONOUNCE
six	hat	hawt
seven	hét	hayt
eight	nyolc	nyawltz
nine	kilenc	KEE-lehntz
ten	tíz	teehz
one-way	csak oda	chohk AW-doh

ENGLISH	HUNGARIAN	PRONOUNCE	ENGLISH	HUNGARIAN	PRONOUNCE
double room	kétágyas szoba	keht-AHGAHS soh-bah	round-trip	oda-vissza	AW-doh-VEES-soh
reservation	helyfoglalás	HEY-fohg-lah-DASH	ticket	jegyet	YEHD-eht
departure	indulás	IN-dool-ahsh	train	vonat	VAW-noht
arrival	érkezés	ayr-keh-zaysh	bus	autóbusz	AU-OO-toh-boos
Monday	hétfő	hayte-phuuh	airport	repülőtér	rep-oo-loo-TAYR
Tuesday	kedd	kehd	train station	pályaudvar	pah-yoh-OOT-vahr
Wednesday	szerda	SEHR-dah	bus station	buszmegálló	boos-mehg-AH-loh
Thursday	csütörtök	choo-ter-tek	luggage	csomag	CHOH-mahg
Friday	péntek	payne-tek	bank	bank	bohnk
Saturday	szombat	SAWM-baht	police	rendőrség	REHN-doer-shayg
Sunday	vasárnap	VAHSH-ahr-nahp	doctor	kórház	KAWR-haaz
today	ma	mah	hospital	orvos	AWR-vahsh
tomorrow	holnap	HAWL-nahp	exchange	pénzaváltó	pehn-zah-VAHL-toh
day	nap	nahp	passport	az útlevelemet	ahz oot-leh-veh-leh-meht
week	hét	hayht	market	piac	PEE-ohts
morning	reggel	REHG-gehl	grocery	élelmiszerbolt	AY-lehl-meh-sehr-bawlt
afternoon	délután	deh-lu-taan	breakfast	reggeli	REHG-gehl-ee
evening	este	EHS-te	lunch	ebéd	EHB-ayd
hot	meleg	MEE-lehg	dinner	vacsora	VAWCH-oh-rah
cold	hideg	HEE-dehg	vegetables	zöldségek	ZUHLD-seh-gehk
left	bal	bohl	meat	húst	hoosht
right	jobb	yawb	coffee	kávé	KAA-vay
straight ahead	egyenesen	EHDJ-ehn-ehs-hen	milk	tej	tay
toilet	W.C.	VAY-tsay	beer	sör	shurr
square	tér	tehr	stamp	bélyeg	BAY-yeg
post office	posta	PAWSH-tah	airmail	légiposta	LAY-ghee-PAWSH-tah

LATVIAN (LATIVSKA)

ENGLISH	LATVIAN	PRONOUNCE	ENGLISH	LATVIAN	PRONOUNCE
Hello	Labdien	LAHB-deean	Sorry/excuse me	Atvainojiet	AHT-vain-wa-eeat
Yes/no	Jā/nē	yah/ney	Help!	Palīga!	PAH-lee-gah
Please/ you're welcome	Lūdzu	LOOD-zoo	ticket	biļete	BEE-leh-teh
Thank you	Paldies	PAHL-dee-ahs	train/bus	vilciens/autobuss	VEEL-tsee-ehns/AU-to-boos
Goodbye	Uz redzēšanos	ooz REH-dzeh-shan-was	toilet	tualete	TWA-leh-teh

ENGLISH	LATVIAN	PRONOUNCE	ENGLISH	LATVIAN	PRONOUNCE
doctor	ārsts	AHRsts	hospital	slimnīca	SLIM-nee-tsuh
one	viens	vee-ahnss	six	seši	SEH-shee
two	divi	DIH-vih	seven	septini	SEHP-tih-nyih
three	trīs	treess	eight	astoņi	AHS-toh-nyih
four	četri	CHEH-trih	nine	devini	DEH-vih-nyih
five	pieci	PYET-sih	ten	desmit	DES-miht

ENGLISH	LATVIAN	PRONOUNCE
Where is...?	Kur ir...?	koohr ihr
How much does this cost?	Cik maksā?	tsikh MAHK-sah
Do you speak English?	Vasi jūs runājat Angliski?	vai yoohss ROO-nai-yat AHN-glee-skee

LITHUANIAN (LIETUVIŠKAI)

ENGLISH	LITHUANIAN	PRONOUNCE	ENGLISH	LITHUANIAN	PRONOUNCE
Hello	Labas	LAH-bahss	Goodbye	Viso gero	VEE-soh GEH-roh
Yes/no	Taip/ne	tayp/neh	Sorry/excuse me	Atsiprašau	aht-sih-prah-SHAU
Please	Prašau	prah-SHAU	Help!	Gelbėkite!	GYEHL-behk-ite
Thank you	Ačiū	AH-chyoo	ticket	bilietas	BEE-lee-tahs
doctor	gydytojas	GEE-dee-toh-yas	hospital	ligoninė	LI-gon-een-eh
one	vienas	VYEH-nahss	five	penki	pehn-KIH
two	du	doo	six	šeši	sheh-SHIH
three	trys	treese	seven	septyni	sehp-tee-NIH
four	keturi	keh-tuh-RIH	eight	aštuoni	ahsh-too-oh-NIH
nine	devyni	deh-vee-NIH	ten	dešimt	DASH-imt

ENGLISH	LITHUANIAN	PRONOUNCE
Where is...?	Kur yra...?	Koor ee-RAH
How much does this cost?	Kiek kainuoja?	kee-yehk kai-NOO-OH-yah
Do you speak English?	Ar Jūs kalbate angliškai?	ahr yoos KAHL-bah-teh AHNG-leesh-kai

POLISH (POLSKI)

ENGLISH	POLISH	PRONOUNCE
Hello	Cześć	cheshch
Yes/no	Tak/nie	tahk/nyeh
Please/you're welcome	Proszę	PROH-sheh
Thank you	Dziękuję	jehn-KOO-yeh
Goodbye	Do widzenia	doh veed-ZEHN-yah
Good evening	Dobry wieczór	doh-brih VYEH-choor
Good night	Dobranoc	doh-BRAH-nohts
Good morning	Dzień dobry	jehn DOH-brih
Sorry/excuse me	Przepraszam	psheh-PRAH-shahm
Help!	Pomocy!	poh-MOH-tsih!
Where is...?	Gdzie jest...?	GJEH yehst
...the bathroom?	...łazienka?	wahzh-EHN-ka

ENGLISH	POLISH	PRONOUNCE
...the nearest telephone booth?	...najbliziej budka telefoniczna?	nai-BLEEZH-ay BOOT-kah teh-leh-foh-NEE-chnah
...the center of town?	...centrum miasta?	tsehn-troom MYAH-stah
How much does this cost?	Ile to kosztuje?	EE-leh toh kohsh-TOO-yeh
When?	Kiedy?	KYEH-dih
Do you (male/female) speak English?	Czy pan(i) mówi po angielsku?	chih pahn(-ee) MOO-vee poh ahn-GYEHL-skoo
I don't understand.	Nie rozumiem.	nyeh roh-ZOOM-yehm
I don't speak Polish.	Nie mowię po polsku.	nyeh MOO-vyeh poh POHL-skoo
Please write it down.	Proszę napisać.	PROH-sheh nah-PEE-sahch
Do you have a vacancy?	Czy są jakieś wolne pokoje?	chih SAWN yah-kyehsh VOHL-neh poh-KOY-eh
I (male/female) would like a room.	Chciał(a)bym pokój.	kh-CHOW-(ah)-bihm POH-kooy
I'd like to order...	Chciałbym zamówić...	kh-CHOW-bihm za-MOOV-eech
I don't eat...	Nie jadam...	nyeh JAH-dahm
I'm allergic.	Mam uczulenie.	MAHM oo-choo-LEHN-yeh
Check, please.	Proszę rachunek	PROH-sheh rah-HOON-ehk
I want a ticket to...	Poproszę bilet do...	poh-PROH-sheh BEE-leht do
Go away.	Spadaj.	SPAHD-ai
Cheers!	Stolat/na zdrowie!	STOH-laht/nah ZDROH-wyeh
I love you.	Kocham cię.	koh-HAHM cheh
Good morning	Dzień dobry	jehn DOH-brih

ENGLISH	POLISH	PRONOUNCE
one	jeden	YEH-den
two	dwa	dvah
three	trzy	tshih
four	cztery	ch-TEH-rih
five	pięć	pyainch
breakfast	śniadanie	shnyah-DAHN-yeh
lunch	obiad	OH-byahd
dinner	kolacja	koh-LAH-tsyah
bus	autobus	ow-TOH-booss
airport	lotnisko	loht-NEE-skoh
train station	dworzec	DVOH-zhehts
bus station	dworzec autobusowy	DVOH-zhehts ow-toh-boo-SOH-vih
luggage	bagaż	BAH-gahzh
bank	bank	bahnk
police	policja	poh-LEETS-yah
doctor	lekarz	LEH-kahsh
exchange	kantor	KAHN-tohr
passport	paszport	PAHSH-pohrt
market	rynek	RIH-nehk
grocery	sklep spożywczy	sklehp spoh-ZHIV-chih

ENGLISH	POLISH	PRONOUNCE
six	sześć	sheshch
seven	siedem	SHEH-dehm
eight	osiem	OH-shehm
nine	dziewięć	JYEH-vyainch
ten	dziesięć	JYEH-shainch
menu	menu	MEH-noo
bread	chleb	khlehp
vegetables	jarzyny	yah-ZHIH-nih
meat	mięso	MYEN-soh
coffee	kawa	KAH-vah
milk	mleko	MLEH-koh
beer	piwo	PEE-voh
toilet	toaleta	toh-ah-LEH-tah
hospital	szpital	SHPEE-tahl
square	rynek	RIH-nehk
post office	poczta	POHCH-tah
stamps	znaczki	ZNAHCH-kee
airmail	lotniczą	loht-NEE-chawm
hot	gorący	goh-ROHN-tsih
cold	zimny	ZHIH-mnih

ENGLISH	POLISH	PRONOUNCE	ENGLISH	POLISH	PRONOUNCE
Monday	poniedziałek	poh-nyeh-JOW-ehk	right	prawo	PRAH-voh
Tuesday	wtorek	FTOH-rehk	left	lewo	LEH-voh
Wednesday	środa	SHROH-dah	straight ahead	prosto	PROH-stoh
Thursday	czwartek	CHVAHR-tehk	single room	jednoosobowy	YEHD-noh-oh-soh-BOH-vih
Friday	piątek	PYOHN-tehk	double room	dwuosobowy	DVOO-oh-soh-BOH-vih
Saturday	sobota	soh-BOH-tah	reservation	miejscówka	myay-STSOOF-ka
Sunday	niedziela	nyeh-DZEH-lah	departure	odjazd	OHD-yahzd
today	dzisiaj	JEE-shai	arrival	przyjazd	PSHIH-yahzd
tomorrow	jutro	YOO-troh	one-way	w jedną stronę	VYEHD-nowm STROH-neh
day	dzień	JAYN	round-trip	tam i z powrotem	tahm ee spoh-VROH-tehm
week	tydzień	TIH-jayn	ticket	bilet	BEE-leht
morning	rano	RAH-noh	train	pociąg	POH-chaung
afternoon	popołudnie	poh-poh-WOOD-nyeh	bus	autobus	au-TOH-boos
evening	wieczór	VYEH-choor			

ROMANIAN (ROMÂNA)

ENGLISH	ROMANIAN	PRONOUNCE
Hello	Bună ziua	BOO-nuh zee wah
Yes/no	Da/nu	dah/noo
Please/you're welcome	Vă rog/cu plăcere	vuh rohg/coo pluh-CHEH-reh
Thank you	Mulțumesc	mool-tsoo-MEHSK
Goodbye	La revedere	lah reh-veh-DEH-reh
Good morning	Bună dimineața	BOO-nuh dee-mee-NYAH-tsah
Good evening	Bună seara	BOO-nuh seh-AH-rah
Good night	Noapte bună	NWAHP-teh BOO-nuh
Sorry/excuse me	Îmi pare rău/Scuzați-mă	ih PAH-reh ruh-oo/skoo-ZAH-tih muh
Help!	Ajutor!	AH-zhoot-ohr
Where is...?	Unde e...?	OON-deh YEH
...the bathroom?	...toaleta?	toh-ah-LEH-ta
...the nearest telephone booth?	...un telefon prin apropiere?	oon teh-leh-FOHN preen ah-proh-PYEH-reh
...the center of town?	...centrul orașului?	CHEHN-trool oh-RAHSH-oo-loo-ee
How much does this cost?	Cât costă?	kyt KOH-stuh
When?	Cînd?	kynd
Do you speak English?	Vorbiți englezește?	vohr-BEETS ehng-leh-ZEHSH-teh
I don't understand.	Nu înțeleg.	noo-ihn-TZEH-lehg
I don't speak Romanian.	Nu vorbesc Românește.	noo vohr-BEHSK roh-myn-EHSH-teh
Please write it down.	Vă rog să scrieți.	vuh rog suh SCREE-ehts
Do you have a vacancy?	Aveți camere libere?	a-VETS KUH-mer-eh LEE-ber-e

ENGLISH	ROMANIAN	PRONOUNCE
I'd like a room.	Aş vrea o cameră.	ahsh vreh-AH oh KAH-mehr-ahr
I'd like to order...	Aş vrea nişte...	ahsh vreh-AH NEESH-teh
I have an allergy.	Eu am o alergie.	eu ahm o ah-ler-jee-yeh
I don't eat...	Eu nu mănînc...	eu nu mă-nînk
Check, please.	Nota, vă rog.	NO-tah VUH rohg
I want a ticket to...	Vreau un bilet pentru...	vrah-oo oon bee-LEHT PEHN-troo
Go away.	Du-te.	doo-TEH
Cheers!	Noroc!	noh-ROHK
I love you.	Te iubesc.	TEH YOO-behsk

ENGLISH	ROMANIAN	PRONOUNCE	ENGLISH	ROMANIAN	PRONOUNCE
one	unu	OO-noo	six	şase	SHAH-seh
two	doi	doy	seven	şapte	SHAHP-teh
three	trei	tray	eight	opt	ohpt
four	patru	PAH-tru	nine	nouă	NOH-uh
five	cinci	CHEEN-ch	ten	zece	ZEH-cheh
single room	cu un pat	koo oon paht	one-way	dus	doos
double room	o cameră dublă	oh KAH-meh-rah DOO-blah	round-trip	dus-întors	doos-ihn-TOHRS
reservation	rezervarea	reh-zehr-VAHR-eh-ay	ticket	bilet	bee-LEHT
departures	plecări	pleh-CUHR	train	trenul	TREH-nuhl
arrivals	sosiri	soh-SEER	bus	autobuz	AU-toh-booz
Monday	luni	loon	airport	aeroportul	air-oh-POHR-tool
Tuesday	marţi	mahrts	station	gară	GAH-ruh
Wednesday	miercuri	MEER-kuhr	luggage	bagajul	bah-GAHZH-ool
Thursday	joi	zhoy	bus station	autogară	AU-toh-gah-rah
Friday	vineri	VEE-nehr	bank	banca	BAHN-cah
Saturday	sâmbătă	SIHM-buh-tuh	police	poliţia	poh-LEE-tsee-ah
Sunday	duminică	duh-MEE-nee-kuh	doctor	doctor	DOK-tor
today	azi	az	hospital	spitalul	spi-tah-lul
tomorrow	mâine	MUH-yih-neh	exchange	un birou de de schimb	oon bee-RO deh skeemb
day	zi	ZEE	passport	paşaport	pah-shah-POHRT
week	săptămână	septa-mOOnch	grocery	o alimentară	a-lee-men-TA-ra
morning	dimineaţa	dee-mee-NYAH-tsah	breakfast	micul dejun	MEEK-uhl DEH-zhoon
afternoon	după-amiază	DOO-pah-MYAH-zuh	lunch	prânz	prunz
evening	seara	seh-AH-rah	dinner	cină	CHEE-nuh
hot	cald	kahld	menu	mehn-EE-oo	men-EE-oo
cold	rece	REH-cheh	bread	pâine	PUH-yih-nay
left	stânga	STYN-gah	vegetables	legume	LEH-goom-eh
right	dreapta	drahp-TAH	meat	carne	CAHR-neh
straight-ahead	drept înaink	drehpt i-nah-in-ke	coffee	cafea	kah-FEH-AH

ENGLISH	ROMANIAN	PRONOUNCE	ENGLISH	ROMANIAN	PRONOUNCE
toilet	toaleta	toh-AHL-eh-tah	milk	lapte	LAHP-teh
square	piața	pee-AHTZ	beer	bere	BEH-reh
post office	poșta	POH-shta	stamps	timbru	TEEM-broo
market	piața	pi-AH-tsa	airmail	avion	ahv-ee-OHN

RUSSIAN (РУССКИЙ)

Voiced consonants are pronounced voiceless at the end of a word. **Ь** makes the previous consonant soft, adding a sound similar to the *y* in *yet*. **Ъ** may be used to indicate separations of syllables when pronouncing syllables on either side.

ENGLISH	RUSSIAN	PRONOUNCE
Hello	Здравствуйте	ZDRAHV-zvuht-yeh
Yes/no	Да/нет	dah/nyeht
Please/you're welcome	Пожалуйста	spa-ZHAHL-oo-stah
Thank you	Спасибо	spa-SEE-bah
Goodbye	До свидания	da svee-DAHN-ya
Good morning	Доброе утро	DOH-breh OO-trah
Good evening	Добрый вечер	DOH-bryy VEH-chehr
Good night	Спокойной ночи	spa-KOY-noy NOHCH-ee
Sorry/excuse me	Извините	ihz-vi-NEET-yeh
Help!	Помогите!	pah-mah-GEE-tyeh
Where is...?	Где...?	gdyeh
...the bathroom?	...туалет?	TOO-ah-lyet
...the nearest telephone booth?	...ближайший телефон-автомат?	blee-ZHAI-shiy teh-leh-FOHN-ahf-tah-MAHT
...the center of town?	...центр города?	TSEHN-tehr GOHR-rah-dah
How much does this cost?	Сколько это стоит?	SKOHL-kah EH-tah STOH-eet
When?	Когда?	kahg-DAH
Do you speak English?	Вы говорите по-английски?	vy gah-vah-REE-tyeh pah ahn-GLEE-skee
I don't understand.	Я не понимаю.	yah neh pah-nee-MAH-yoo
I don't speak Russian.	Я не говорю по-русски.	yah neh gah-vah-RYOO pah ROO-skee
Please write it down.	Напишите пожалуйста.	nah-pee-SHEET-yeh pah-ZHAHL-uy-stah
Do you have a vacancy?	У вас есть свободный номер?	oo vahs yehst svah-BOHD-neey NOH-mehr
I'd like a room.	Я бы хотел(а) номер.	yah bui khah-TYEHL(ah) NOH-mehr
I'd like to order...	Я хотел(а) бы...	ya khah-TYEHL(a) bih
I don't eat meat	Я не ем мясо	Yah nyeh yem mee-AH-sah
I have an allergy	У меня алергия	oo mehn-YAH all-ehr-gee-yah
Check, please.	Счёт, пожалуйста.	SHYOHT pah-ZHAHL-oo-stah
I want a ticket to...	Один билет до...	ah-DEEN bee-LYEHT dah
Go away.	Уходите.	oo-khah-DEE-tyeh
Cheers!	Ваше здоровье!	vahsh-yeh zdah-ROH-vyeh
I love you.	Я люблю тебя.	yah lyoob-LYOO teh-BYAH

ENGLISH	RUSSIAN	PRONOUNCE	ENGLISH	RUSSIAN	PRONOUNCE
one	один	ah-DEEN	six	шесть	shest

ENGLISH	RUSSIAN	PRONOUNCE
two	два	dvah
three	три	tree
four	четыре	chih-TIH-rih
five	пять	pyaht
single room	одноместный номер	ahd-nah-MYEHS-nee NOH-myehr
double room	двухместный номер	dvookh-MYEHS-nee NOH-myehr
reservation	предваритель-ный заказ	prehd-vah-REE-tyehl-nee zah-KAHZ
departure	отъезд	aht-YEHZD
arrival	приезд	pree-YEHZD
Monday	понедельник	pah-nyeh-DYEHL-neek
Tuesday	вторник	FTOHR-neek
Wednesday	среда	sryeh-DAH
Thursday	четверг	chyeht-VYEHRK
Friday	пятница	PYAHT-neet-sah
Saturday	суббота	soo-BOT-tah
Sunday	воскресенье	vahs-kryeh-SYEH-nye
today	сегодня	see-VOHD-nya
tomorrow	завтра	ZAHF-trah
day	день	dyehn
week	неделя	nyeh-DYEHL-yah
morning	утром	OO-trahm
afternoon	днём	dnyohm
evening	вечером	VYEH-chehr-ahm
hot	жаркий	ZHAHR-keey
cold	холодный	khah-LOHD-nee
left	налево	nah-LYEH-vah
right	направо	nah-PRAH-vah
straight ahead	прямо	PRYHA-moh
toilet	туалет	too-ah-LYET
square	площадь	PLOH-shahd'
post office	почта	POHCH-tah
airmail	авиа	AH-vee-ah

ENGLISH	RUSSIAN	PRONOUNCE
seven	семь	syehm
eight	восемь	VOH-syehm
nine	девять	DYEHV-eet
ten	десять	DYEHS-eet
one-way	в один конец	v ah-DEEN kah-NYEHTS
round-trip	туда и обратно	too-DAH ee ah-BRAHT-nah
ticket	билет	beel-YEHT
train	поезд	POH-yehzd
bus	автобус	af-TOH-boos
airport	аэропорт	ah-eh-roh-POHRT
station	вокзал	VOHK-zahl
luggage	багаж	bah-GAHZH
bus station	автовокзал	ahf-toh-VAHK-zahl
bank	банк	bahnk
police	милиция	mee-LEE-tsee-yah
doctor	доктор	DOHK-tohr
hospital	больница	BOHL-nee-tsa
exchange	обмен валюты	ahb-MYEHN vahl-YOO-ty
passport	паспорт	PAHS-pahrt
market	рынок	RIYN-nahk
grocery	гастроном	gah-stra-NOHM
breakfast	завтрак	ZAHF-trahk
lunch	обед	ah-BYEHD
dinner	ужин	OO-zheen
menu	меню	mehn-YOO
bread	хлеб	khlyehp
vegetables	овощи	OH-vah-shee
meat	мясо	mee-AH-sah
coffee	кофе	KOH-fyeh
milk	молоко	mah-lah-KOH
beer	пиво	PEE-vah
stamp	марка	MAHR-kah

SLOVAKIAN (SLOVENSKY)

ENGLISH	SLOVAKIAN	PRONOUNCE
Hello	Dobrý deò	dau-BREE deh-AU
Yes/no	Áno/Nie	AH-nau/ni-ye
Please.	Prosím Vás.	prau-SEEM vas
Thank you.	Ïakujem.	jah-KOO-yehm

ENGLISH	SLOVAKIAN	PRONOUNCE
You're welcome.	Nemáte za èo.	nem-AHT-eh tsa AY-au
Goodbye.	Dovidenia.	doh-veed-EHN-yah
Good morning.	Dobré ráno.	doh-breh RHA-nau
Good day.	Dobrý deò.	doh-bree den
Good evening.	Dobrý večer.	doh-bree veh-CHEHR
Good night.	Dobrú noc.	doh-broo naukh
Sorry/excuse me...	Prepáète...	pre-PAH-eh-te
Help!	Pomoc!	po-MAUTS
Go away!	Choď preč!	khauhd PRECH
When?	Kedy?	KEDH-ih
Where is...?	(Prosím Vás) kde je...?	(pro-SEEM vahs) kdeh yeh
...the bathroom?	...W.C.?	vay-TSAY
...the nearest telephone booth?	...najbližšia telefónna búdka?	nab-lee-ZHEE-ah tel-eh-FOH-na BUHD-kah
...the center of town?	...centrum mesta do?	TSEN-truhm MEHS-ta dau
I would like a ticket to...	Prosím si lístok do...	pro-SEEM sih LEES-tauk dau
round-trip/one-way trip	spiatoèný/jednosmerný	spih-uh-toh-AY-NEE yed-naus-mehr-NEE
How much does this cost?	Koľko to stojí?	kaull-kau tau STOH-yee
Do you speak English?	Hovoríte anglický?	hau-vau-REE-teh ahn-glih-kee
I don't understand.	Nerozumiem.	neh-rau-ZOO-mee-ehm
I don't speak Slovak.	Neviem po slovensky.	neh-viee-ehm poh slo-VEN-skee
Please write it down.	Mohli by ste to napísať?	MOH-lih bih steh tau nap-EE-SAHT
Do you have a vacancy?	Máte voľnú izbu?	MAH-teh VOLL-noo ihz-boo
I'd like a single/double room.	Chcel(a) by som jednotku / dvojku.	kh-sehl (ah) bih sohm yed-NAUT-koo / DVOY-koo
I'd like to order...	Rád(a) by som si objednal...	RAHD (-ah) bih saum sih aub-YED-nal
Do you have any vegetarian options?	Mate vegetariánske jedlá?	MAH-teh vehg-eht-uhr-ih-AHN-skih YED-luh (note hard g)
Check, please.	Účet prosím.	uh-CHEHT pro-SEEM
Cheers!	Na zdravie!	nah ZDRAHV-ee
I love you	Milujem Ta	mih-LOO-yem TAH

SLOVENIAN (SLOVENSKO)

ENGLISH	SLOVENIAN	PRONOUNCE	ENGLISH	SLOVENIAN	PRONOUNCE
Hello	Dober dan	DOH-behr dahn	Sorry/excuse me	Oprostite	oh proh-STEE-teh
Yes/no	Ja/ne	yah/nay	Help!	Na pomoč!	nah POH-mohch
Please	Prosim	proh-SEEM	ticket	karta	KAHR-tah
Thank you	Hvala	HVAHL-ah	bus	avtobus	au-TOH-boos
Goodbye	Nasvidenje	nah-SVEE-dehn-yay	toilet	Toaleta	toh-ah-LEH-tah
doctor	zdravnika	zdrav-NEE-kah	hospital	bolnišnica	bohl-NIHSH-nihtsa
one	eden/eno	EH-dehn/EH-noh	six	šest	sheyst
two	dva	dvah	seven	sedem	SEH-dehm

ENGLISH	SLOVENIAN	PRONOUNCE	ENGLISH	SLOVENIAN	PRONOUNCE
three	tri	tree	eight	osem	OH-sehm
four	štiri	SHTIHR-ee	nine	devet	DEH-veht
five	pet	peyt	ten	deset	DEH-seht

ENGLISH	SLOVENIAN	PRONOUNCE
Where is...?	Kje...?	kyay
How much does this cost?	Koliko to stane?	KOH-lee-koh toh STAH-nay
Do you speak English?	Ali govorite angleski?	AH-lee goh-VOHR-ee-tay AHNG-lehsh-kee
I don't eat meat.	Ne jem mesa.	neh yehm MEH-sa
Cheers!	Na zdravje!	nah zh-DRAHV-yay
I love you.	Ljubim te.	LYOO-bihm tay

UKRAINIAN (УКРАЇНСЬКА)

ENGLISH	UKRAINIAN	PRONOUNCE
Good day	добрий день	DOH-bree den
Good morning	доброго ранку	DOH-broh-hoh RAHN-koo
Good evening	добрий вечір	DO-bree VECH-eer
Goodbye	до побачення	DO po-BACH-ehn-yah
Yes/no	так/ні	tahk / nee
Please/you're welcome	прошу	PROH-shoo
Please/you're welcome (Kyiv and East)	будь ласка	bood-LAS-kah
Thank you	дякую	DYAH-koo-yoo
Sorry/excuse me	вибачте	Vih-bach-te
Help!	допомогайте!	doh-poh-moh-HAI-te
Where is...?	де...?	de
...the bathroom?	...ванна?	VAHN-nah
...a telephone?	...телефон?	te-le-fon
...the center of town?	...центр міста?	TSEN-trr MEES-tah
How much does this cost?	скільки коштує?	SKEEL-kih KOHSH-too-ye
When?	коли?	koh-LIH
Do you speak English?	чи ви говорите по-англійському?	chih vih hoh-VOHR-ih-te poh-ahn-HLIYS-koh-moo
I don't understand.	я не розумію.	ya ne roh-zoo-MEE-yoo
I don't speak Ukrainian.	я не говорю по-українському.	ya ne hov-OHR-yoo poh-oo-krah-YEENS-koh-moo
Speak slower, please.	прошу, говріть повільно.	PROH-shoo hoh-vohr-EET poh-VEEL-noh
Please write it down.	прошу пишіть це.	PROH-shoo PIH-sheet tse
I'd like a room.	прошу, я хочу кімнату.	PROH-shoo yah KHO-choo keem-NAHT-oo
I want a ticket to...	я хочу квиток...	ya KHO-choo kvih-TOHK
Go away.	геть.	het
Cheers!	за здоров'я!	zah zdohr-OH-vya
I love you.	я кохаю тебе.	ya ko-KHAH-yoo TE-be

ENGLISH	UKRAINIAN	PRONOUNCE	ENGLISH	UKRAINIAN	PRONOUNCE
one	один	OHD-ihn	six	щось	shchohs
two	два	dvah	seven	сім	seem

ENGLISH	UKRAINIAN	PRONOUNCE	ENGLISH	UKRAINIAN	PRONOUNCE
three	три	trih	eight	вісім	VEE-seem
four	чотири	choh-TIHR-ee	nine	девять	DEV-yat
five	п'ять	p'yat	ten	десять	DES-yat
single bed	односпальне ліжко	ohd-NOHS-pahl-ne LEEZH-koh	departure	відправлення	veed-PRAH-vlehn-yah
double room	двоспальне ліжко	dvos-PAHL-ne LEEZH-koh	arrival	прибуття	pree-boot-YAH
reservation	попередне замовлення	poh-per-ED-neh zam-OV-len-nya	round-trip	поїздка в обидва кінці	po-YEEZD-kah v ob-IHD-vah KEEN-tsee
Monday	Понеділок	poh-ne-DEE-lohk	ticket	квиток	KVY-tohk
Tuesday	Вівторок	VEEV-tohr-ohk	train	поїзд	poh-YEEZD
Wednesday	Середа	ser-e-DAH	bank	банк	bahnk
Thursday	Четвер	CHET-ver	police	поліція	po-LEET-see-ya
Friday	П'ятниця	PYAT-nih-tsyah	passport	паспорт	PAS-pohrt
Saturday	Субота	soo-BOHT-ah	market	ринок	RIH-nohk
Sunday	Неділя	ne-DEEHL-ya	breakfast	сніданок	snee-DAH-nohk
today	сьогодні	soh-HOHD-nee	lunch	другий сніданок	DRU-hiy sni-DAHN-ohk
tomorrow	завтра	ZAHV-trah	dinner	вечерять	vech-ER-yat
day	день	den	menu	меню	MEN-yoo
week	тиждень	TIZH-den	bread	хліб	khleeb
morning	ранок	RAHN-ohk	vegetables	овочі	OH-voh-chee
afternoon	після полудня	PEES-la poh-LOOD-nya	coffee	кофе	KOF-e
evening	вечір	VECH-eer	milk	молоко	moh-loh-KOH
left	ліворуч	LIV-or-ooch	beer	пиво	PIH-voh
right	праворуч	PRAH-vohr-ooch	toilet	туалет	too-ah-LET
bus	автобус	AV-toh-boos	post office	пошта	POHSH-tah
bus station	автобусний вокзал	av-toh-BOOS-niy vokh-ZAHL	stamp	поштова марка	posh-TOHV-ah MAR-kah
airport	аеропорт	AY-RO-pohrt	airmail	авіапошта	ah-vee-ah-POSH-tah
luggage	бараж	ba-HAHZH	doctor	лікар	LEE-kar
train station	вокзал	vog-ZAL	hospital	лікарня	li-KAR-nya

INDEX

ABOUT LET'S GO

NOT YOUR PARENTS' TRAVEL GUIDE

At Let's Go, we see every trip as the chance of a lifetime. If your dream is to grab a machete and forge through the jungles of Brazil, we can take you there. If you'd rather bask in the Riviera sun at a beachside cafe, we'll set you a table. We write for readers who know that there's more to travel than sharing double deckers with tourists and who believe that travel can change both themselves and the world—whether they plan to spend six days in London or six months in Latin America. We'll show you just how far your money can go, and prove that the greatest limitation on your adventures is not your wallet, but your imagination.

BEYOND THE TOURIST EXPERIENCE

To help you gain a deeper connection with the places you travel, our fearless researchers scour the globe to give you the heads-up on both world-renowned and off-the-beaten-track attractions, sights, and destinations. They engage with the local culture, only to emerge with the freshest insights on everything from local festivals to regional cuisine. We've also opened our pages to respected writers and scholars to hear their takes on the countries and regions we cover, and asked travelers who have worked, studied, or volunteered abroad to contribute first-person accounts of their experiences. In addition, we increased our coverage of responsible travel and expanded each guide's Beyond Tourism chapter to share more ideas about how to give back while on the road.

FORTY-SIX YEARS OF WISDOM

Let's Go got its start in 1960, when a group of creative and well-traveled students compiled their experience and advice into a 20-page mimeographed pamphlet, which they gave to travelers on charter flights to Europe. Four and a half decades later, we've expanded to cover six continents and all kinds of travel—while retaining our founders' adventurous attitude toward the world. Laced with witty prose and total candor, our guides are still researched and written entirely by students on shoestring budgets, experienced travelers who know that train strikes, stolen luggage, food poisoning, and marriage proposals are all part of a day's work.

THE LET'S GO COMMUNITY

More than just a travel guide company, Let's Go is a community. Our small staff comes together because of our shared passion for travel and our desire to help other travelers see the world the way it was meant to be seen. We love it when our readers become part of the Let's Go community as well—when you travel, drop us a postcard (67 Mt. Auburn St., Cambridge, MA 02138, USA), send us an e-mail (feedback@letsgo.com), or post on our forum (http://www.letsgo.com/connect/forum) to tell us about your adventures and discoveries.

For more information, visit us online: www.letsgo.com.

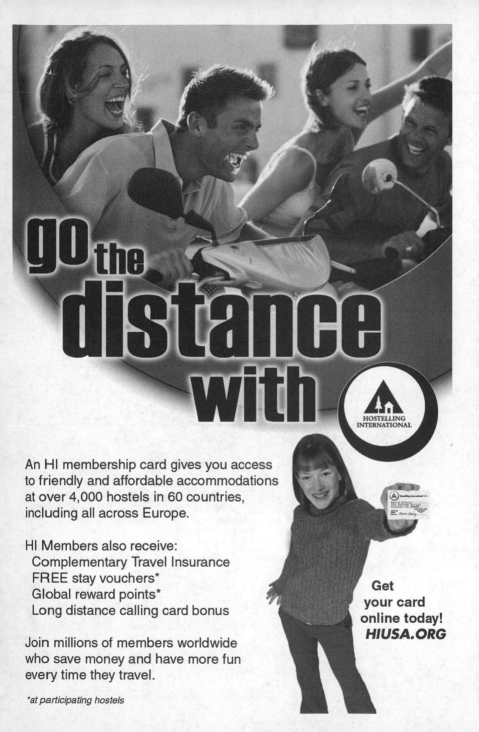

MAP INDEX

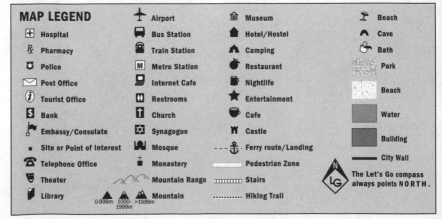

MAP LEGEND

- ✈ Airport
- 🏛 Museum
- 🛇 Beach
- ✚ Hospital
- Bus Station
- Hotel/Hostel
- Λ Cave
- ℞ Pharmacy
- Train Station
- Camping
- Bath
- Police
- M Metro Station
- Restaurant
- Park
- Post Office
- Internet Cafe
- Nightlife
- Beach
- (i) Tourist Office
- Restrooms
- ★ Entertainment
- Bank
- Church
- Cafe
- Water
- Embassy/Consulate
- Synagogue
- Castle
- Building
- Site or Point of Interest
- Mosque
- Ferry route/Landing
- City Wall
- Telephone Office
- Monastery
- Pedestrian Zone
- Theater
- Mountain Range
- Stairs
- The Let's Go compass always points NORTH.
- Library
- 0-999m 1000-1999m >1999m Mountain
- Hiking Trail